AMERICAN SERMONS

AMERICAN SERMONS

THE PILGRIMS TO
MARTIN LUTHER KING JR.

THE LIBRARY OF AMERICA

Some of the material in this volume is reprinted by
permission of the holders of copyright and publication rights.
Acknowledgments can be found in the Note on the Texts.

The paper used in this publication meets the
minimum requirements of the American National Standard for
Information Sciences—Permanence of Paper for Printed
Library Materials, ANSI z39.48—1984.

Distributed to the trade in the United States
by Penguin Putnam Inc.
and in Canada by Penguin Books Canada Ltd.

Library of Congress Catalog Number: 98-34295
For cataloging information, see end of Notes.
ISBN 1–883011–65–5

Second Printing
The Library of America—108

Manufactured in the United States of America

American Sermons:
The Pilgrims to Martin Luther King Jr.
is published with support from

LILLY ENDOWMENT, INC.

This volume will be kept in print
by the Endowment's gift to
the Guardians of American Letters Fund,
established by The Library of America
to ensure that every volume in the series
will be permanently available.

Contents

THE TWENTIETH CENTURY

ROBERT CUSHMAN

A Sermon Preached at Plimmoth in New-England December 9. 1621.

In an assemblie of his Majesties faithfull Subjects, there inhabiting.

Wherein is shewed the danger of selfe-love, and the sweetnesse of true Friendship. Together with a Preface, shewing the state of the Country, and Condition of the Savages.

ROM. 12. 10.
Be affectioned to love one another with brotherly love.

Written in the yeare 1621.

———

To His Loving Friends, the Adventurers for New-England; Together with all Well-Willers, and Well-Wishers Thereunto, Grace and Peace, &c.

NEW ENGLAND, so call'd, not onely (to avoyd novelties) because Captaine *Smith* hath so entituled it in his Description, but because of the resemblance that is in it, of England the native soile of English-men; It being much what the same for heate and colde in Summer and Winter, it being Champion ground, but not high mountaines, somwhat like the soile in *Kent* and *Essex*; full of Dales, and meddow ground, full of ryvers and sweete springs, as England is. But principally, so farre as we can yet find, it is an Iland, and neere about the quantitie of England, being cut off from the maine land of *America*, as England is from the maine of *Europe*, by a great arme of the Sea, which entreth in fortie degrees, and runneth up North west and by West, and goeth out either into the South Sea, or else into the Bay of *Canado*. The certaintie whereof, and secrets of which, we have not yet so found as that as eye-witnesses we can make narration thereof, but if

I

God give time and meanes, we shall erelong, discover both
the extent of that River, together with the secrets thereof; and
also try what territories, habitations, or commodities, may be
found, either in it, or about it.

It pertaineth not to my purpose to speake any thing, either
in prayse, or disprayse of the country, so it is by Gods providence, that a few of us are there planted to our content, and
have with great charge and difficultie attained quiet and com-
petent dwellings there. And thus much I will say for the satisfaction of such as have any thought of going thither to
inhabit; That for men which have a large heart, & looke after
great riches, ease, pleasure, dainties, and jollitie in this world
(except they will live by other mens sweat, or have great
riches) I would not advise them to come there, for as yet the
country will afford no such matters. But if there be any, who
are content to lay out their estates, spend their time, labours,
and endevours, for the benefit of them that shall come after,
and in desire to further the Gospell among those poore
Heathens, quietly contenting themselves with such hardship
and difficulties, as by Gods providence shall fall upon them,
being yet yong, and in their strength, such men I would advise and encourage to goe, for their ends cannot faile them.

And if it should please God to punish his people in the
Christian countries of *Europe*, (for their coldnesse, carnality,
wanton abuse of the Gospel, contention, &c.) either by
Turkish slavery, or by Popish tyrannie, which God forbid, yet
if the time be come, or shall come (as who knoweth) when
Sathan shall be let loose, to cast out his flouds against them,
here is a way opened for such as have wings to flie into this
Wildernesse; and as by the dispersion of the Jewish Church
thorow persecution, the Lord brought in the fulnesse of the
Gentiles, so who knoweth, whether now by tyrannie, and affliction, which he suffereth to come upon them, he will not
by little and little chafe them, even amongst the Heathens,
that so a light may rise up in the darke, and the kingdome of
heaven be taken from them which now have it, and given to
a people that shall bring forth the fruit of it. This I leave to
the judgement of the godly wise, being neither Prophet nor
sonne of a prophet, but considering Gods dealing of olde,
and seeing the name of Christian to be very great, but the

true nature thereof almost quite lost in all degrees & sects, I cannot thinke but that there is some judgement not farre off, and that God will shortly, even of stones, rayse up children unto *Abraham*.

And who so rightly considereth, what manner of entrance, abiding, and proceedings, we have had amongst these poore Heathens since we came hither, will easily thinke, that God hath some great worke to doe towards them.

They were wont to be the most cruellest and trecherousest people in all these parts, even like Lyons, but to us they have beene like Lambes, so kinde, so submissive, and trustie, as a man may truely say many Christians are not so kinde, nor sincere.

They are very much wasted of late, by reason of a great mortalitie that fell amongst them three yeares since, which together with their owne civill dissensions and blouddie warres, hath so wasted them, as I thinke the twentith person is scarce left alive, and those that are left, have their courage much abated, and their countenance is defected, and they seeme as a people affrighted. And though when we came first into the countrie, we were few, and many of us were sicke, and many dyed by reason of the colde and wet, it being the depth of winter, and we having no houses, nor shelter, yet when there was not sixe able persons amongst us, and that they came daily to us by hundreths, with their *Sachems*, or *Kings*, and might in one houre have made a dispatch of us yet such a feare was upon them, as that they never offred us the least injury in word or deede. And by reason of one *Tisquanto*, that lives amongst us, that can speake English, we have daily commerce with their *Kings* & can know what is done or intended towards us amongst the Savages; Also we can acquaint them with our courses and purposes, both humane and religious. And the greatest Commander of the countrie call'd *Massasoit*, commeth often to visite us, though hee live fiftie myles from us, and often sends us presents, he having with many other of their governours promised, yea, subscribed obedience to our Soveraigne Lord King JAMES, and for his cause to spend both strength and life. And we for our parts, thorow Gods grace, have with that equitie, justice, and compassion carried our selves towards them, as that they have received much favour,

helpe, and ayde from us, but never the least injury, or wrong
by us. Wee found the place where we live emptie, the people
being all dead & gone away, and none living neere by 8. or

10. myles; and though in the time of some hardship wee found (travelling abroad) some 8.
Bushels of Corne hid up in a Cave, and knew no
owners of it, yet afterward hearing of the owners
of it, we gave them (in their estimation) double the value of
it. Our care also hath beene to maintaine peace amongst
them, and have alwayes set our selves against such of them as
used any rebellion, or trecherie against their governours, and
not onely threatned such, but in some sort payd them their
due deserts; and when any of them are in want, as often they
are in the Winter, when their corne is done, wee supply them
to our power, and have them in our houses eating and drinking, and warming themselves, which thing (though it be
something a trouble to us) yet because they should see and
take knowledge of our labours, orders, and diligence, both for
this life and a better, we are content to beare it, and we find
in many of them, especially, of the younger sort, such a
tractable disposition, both to Religion and humanitie, as that
if we had meanes to apparell them, & wholly to retaine them
with us (as their desire is) they would doubtlesse in time
prove serviceable to God and man, and if ever God send us
meanes we will bring up hundreths of their children, both to
labour and learning.

They offer us to dwell where we will.

But leaving to speake of them till a further occasion be offered; If any shall marvell at the publishing of this Treatise in
England, seeing there is no want of good bookes, but rather
want of men to use good bookes, let them know, that the
especiall end is, that wee may keepe those motives in memory
for our selves, & those that shall come after, to be a remedie
against selfe-love the bane of all societies. And that also we
might testifie to our Christian Country-men, who judge di-
versly of us, that though we be in a Heathen Country, yet the
grace of Christ is not quenched in us, but we still hold, and
teach the same points of faith, mortification, and sanctification, which we have heard and learned in a most simple and
large maner in our owne country. If any shall thinke it too
rude and unlearned for this curious age, let them know, that

to paint out the Gospell in plaine and flat English, amongst a company of plaine English-men (as we are) is the best and most profitablest teaching; and we will study plainnesse, not curiositie, neither in things humaine, nor heavenly. If any error, or unsoundnesse be in it, (as who knoweth) impute it to that frayle man which endited it, which professeth to know nothing as he ought to know it. I have not set downe my name, partly because I seeke no name, and principally, because I would have nothing esteemed by names, for I see a number of evils to arise thorow names, when the persons are either famous, or infamous, and God and man is often injured; if any good or profit arise to thee in the receiving of it, give God the prayse, and esteeme me as a sonne of *Adam*, subject to all such frailties as other men are.

And you my loving Friends the Adventurers to this plantation; as your care hath beene, first to settle religion here, before either profit, or popularitie, so I pray you, goe on, to doe it much more, and be carefull to send godly men, though they want some of that worldly policie which this world hath in her owne generation, and so though you loose, the Lord shall gayne. I rejoyce greatly in your free and readie mindes to your powers, yea, and beyond your powers to further this worke, that you thus honour God with your riches, and I trust you shall be repayed againe double & treble in this world, yea, and the memory of this action shall never die, but above all adding unto this (as I trust you doe) like freenesse in all other Gods services, both at home and abroad, you shall finde a reward with GOD, ten thousand fold surpassing all that you can doe or thinke, be not therefore discouraged, for no labour is lost, nor money spent, which is bestowed for God, your ends were good, your successe is good, and your profit is comming, even in this life, and in the life to come much more; And what shall I say now, a word to men of understanding sufficeth, pardon I pray you my boldnesse, reade over the ensuing Treatise, and judge wisely of the poore weakling, and the Lord, the God of Sea and Land, stretch out his arme of protection over you and us, and over all our lawfull and good enterprises, either this, or any other way.

Plimmoth in *New-England,*
    December 12. 1621.

A Sermon Preached at Plimmoth, in New-England.

1. COR. 10. 24.
Let no man seeke his owne, But every man anothers wealth.

The
connexion. THE OCCASION of these words of the Apostle *Paul*, was because of the abuses which wert in the Church of *Corinth*. Which abuses arose cheifly thorow swelling pride, selfe-love and conceitednes, for although this Church were planted by *Paul*, and watred by *Apollo*, and much increased by the Lord; yet the sower of tares was not wanting to stirre up evill workers and fleshly minded hypocrites, under a shew of godlines, and with Angellike holinesse in appearance to creepe in amongst them to disturbe their peace, trie their soundnesse, and prove their constancie. And this the Apostle complaines of very often: as first, in their carnall devisions, Chap. 1. then in their extolling their eloquent teachers, and despising *Paul*, Chap. 4. Then in their offensive going to Law, before the heathen Judges Chap. 6. Then in eating things offered to Idols, to the destroying of the tender consciences of their Brethren, Chap. 8. Then in their insatiable love-feastes, in the time and place of their Church meetings, the rich which could together feede to fulnes, despising and contemning the poore, that had not to lay it on as they had, Chap 11. Finally in both the Epistles, hee very often nippeth them for their pride, and selfe-love, straitnesse and censoriousnes, so that in the last Chapter hee willeth them againe and againe to prove, trie and examine themselves, to see whether Christ were in them or not, for howsoever many of them seemed as thousands doe at this day, to soare aloft, and goe with full sayle to heaven: yet as men

Similie. that row in Boats, set their faces earnestly one way, when yet their whole body goeth apace another way: so there are many which set such a face uppon Religion, and have their mouthes full of great swelling words: as if they would even blow open the doores of heaven, despising all humble minded and broken hearted people, as weake, simple, sottish &c. when yet notwithstanding, these Blusterers, which seeme to goe so fast, and leave all others behind them, if like these glosing *Corinthians* they carry affectedly their owne glory with them, and seeme thus to stand for the glory of God, What doe they else but joyne flesh to spirit, serving not God for nought, but for wages, and so serving their bellies, whose end will be damnation, except a speedie and sound remedie be thought of, which remedie is even that which our Saviour teacheth the rich young gallant, and which *Paul* heere prescribeth, in willing them not to seeke their owne, but everie man anothers wealth, which Physicke is as terrible to carnall professors, as abstinence from drinke is to a man that hath the dropsie: and it is a sure note, that a man is sicke of this disease of self-love, if this be grievous to him, as appeareth in the man whom Christ bid sell that hee had, and hee went away very sorrowfull, yet surely this veine must bee pricked, and this humor let out, els it will spoyle all, it will infect both soule and body, yea and the contagion of it is such (as wee shall see anone) as will even hazard the welfare of that societie, where selfe seekers and selfe lovers are.

As God then did direct this Apostle to lay downe this briefe direction as a remedy for that evill in *Corinth*, so you may thinke it is by Gods speciall providence, that I am now to speake unto you from this text: and say in your hearts surely some thing is amisse this way: let us know it and amend it.

DIVISION   The parts of this text are two. 1. a *Dehortation*, 2. an *Exhortation*. The Dehortation. *Let no man seeke his owne*. The Exhortation *But every man anothers wealth*.

In handling of which, I will first, open the   Order of wordes. Secondly, gather the Doctrine. Thirdly,   handling. illustrate the Doctrine by Scriptures, experience and Reasons. Fourthly, apply the same, to every one his portion.

The proper drift of the Apostle heere is not   The Apostles to taxe the *Corinthians*, for seeking their owne   drift. evill endes in evill actions, but for aiming at themselves, and their owne benefits in actions lawfull, and that appeareth in the former verse, where he sayth, *All things are lawfull &c.* viz. all such thinges as now wee speake of, to eate any of Gods creatures, offered to Idols or not, to feast and bee merrie together, to shew love and kindnesse to this or that person, &c. but when by such meanes wee seeke our selves, and have not a charitable loving and reverent regard of others, then they are unexpedient, unprofitable, yea unlawfull, and must

bee forborne, and hee that hath not learned to denie himselfe
even the very use of lawfull things, when it tendeth to the
contempt, reproch, greife offence, and shame of his other
Brethren and Associats, hath learned nothing aright, but is
apparently a man that seekes himselfe, and against whom the
Apostle heere dealeth most properly.

EXPOSITION The maner of the speech may seeme as
counsell left at libertie: as Mat. 27. 49. and in our ordinary
speech, wee thinke they be but weake charges, which are thus
delivered, let a man doe this, or let him doe that. But wee
must learne the Apostles modestie, and know that whatsoever
the termes seeme to imply, yet even this and other the like in
this Epistle, are most absolute charges: as *Let a man esteeme
of us, as the ministers of Christ*, that is, a man ought so to esteeme of us. *Let a man examine himselfe*, that is, as if he sayd
a man must examine himselfe, *Let your women keepe silence in
the Churches*, that is, they ought so to doe.

The meaning then summarily is, as if hee sayd, the bane of
all these mischeifes which arise amongst you is, that men are
to cleaving to themselves, and their owne matters, and disre-
garde and contemne all others: and therefore I charge you, let
this selfe-seeking be left off, and turne the streame another
way, namely, seeke the good of your Brethren, please them,
honor them, reverence them, for otherwise it will never goe
well amongst you.

OBJECT. But doth not the Apostle else where say? *That
hee, which careth not for his owne, is worse than an Infidell.*

RESP. True but by (owne) there, he meaneth properly, a
mans kindred, and heere by (owne) hee meaneth properly a
mans selfe.

Secondly, Hee there especially taxeth such as were negligent in their labours and callings, and so made themselves
unable to give releife and entertainement to such poore
Widowes and Orphans as were of their owne flesh and bloud.

Thirdly, Be it so that some man should even neglect his
owne selfe, his owne wife, children, friends, &c. and give that
hee had to strangers, that were but some rare vice, in some
one unnaturall man, and if this vice slay a thousand, selfe-love
slayeth ten thousand.

And this the wisedome of God did well forsee, and hath set

no caveats in the Scriptures either to taxe men, or forewarne them from loving others, neither sayth God any wher, let no man seeke the good of another, but let no man seeke his owne, and everie where in the Scriptures he hath set watch words against selfe-good, selfe-profit, selfe-seeking, &c. And thus the sence beeing cleared, I come to the doctrine.

DOCT. 1   All men are to apt and readie to seeke themselves to much, and to preferre their owne   Amplific. matters and causes beyond the due and lawfull measure, even to excesse and offence against God, yea danger of their owne soules, and this is true not onely in wicked men which are given over of God to vile lusts, as *Absolon* in getting favour in his Fathers Court: *Jeroboam*, in setling his kingdome fast in *Samaria*, *Ahab* in vehement seeking *Naboths* vineyard, but men, otherwise godly, have through frailtie beene soyled heerein, and many thousands which have a shew of godlinesse, are lovers of themselves: *David* was about to seeke himselfe when he was going to kill *Naball*; *Asa* in putting *Hanani* in prison; *Josiah* when hee would goe warre with *Necho*, against the counsell of God and reason; *Peter* when hee dissembled about the Ceremonies of the Law, yea and *Paul* complaines of all his followers (*Timothie* excepted) that they sought their owne to inordinately.

And why else are these caveats in the Scriptures, but to warne the godly that they bee not tainted herewith? as *looke not every man on his owne things, but on the things of another: Love seeketh not her owne things. Be not desirous of vaine glory, &c.*

Yea and doth not experience teach, that even amongst professors of Religion, almost all the love and favour that is shewed unto others is with a secret ayme at   Illustration experimentall. themselves, they will take paines to doe a man good, provided that he will take twise so much for them they will give a penny so as it may advantage them a pound, labor hard so as all the profite may come to themselves, else they are hartlesse and feeble. The vaine and corrupt   Simile. heart of man cannot better be resembled then by a belly-god, Host, or Inkeeper, which welcommeth his guests with smilings, and salutations, and a thousand welcomes, and rejoyceth greatly to have their companie to dice, card, eate,

drinke, and bee merrie, but should not the box be paid, the
pot be filling, and the money telling, all this while the
Epicures joy would soone be turned into sorrow, and his
smiles turned into frownes, and the doore set open, and their
absence craved: even so men blow the bellowes hard, when
they have an Iron of their owne a heating, worke hard whilest
their owne house is in building, dig hard whilest their owne
garden is in planting, but is it so as the profit must goe wholy
or partly to others, their handes waxe feeble, their hearts waxe
faint, they grow churlish and give crosse answers like *Naball*,
they are sowre, discontent, and nothing will please them. And
where is that man to be found, that will sparse abroad, and
cast his bread upon the waters, that will lend looking for
nothing againe, that will doe all duties to others freely and
cheerefully in conscience of God, and love unto men without
his close and secret ends, or ayming at himself? such a man,
out of doubt, is a blacke Swanne, a white Crowe almost, and
yet such shall stand before God with boldnesse at the last day,
when others which have sought themselves, though for love
of themselves they have sought heaven, yea and through selfe-
love perswaded themselves they shoulde finde it, yet wanting
love unto others, they will be found as sounding brasse, and
as a tinkling Cimbale, and whilst they have neglected others,
and not cared how others live, so as themselves may fare well,
they will be found amongst them, that the Lord will say unto,
I know you not, depart ye cursed into everlasting fire.

But that I may not walke in generalities, the
particular wayes by which men seeke their owne
are these, First such as are covetous, seeke their
owne by seeking riches, wealth, money, as *Fælix* pretending
love unto *Paul*, sent for him often, but it was in hope of
mony. Many there are who say, *who will shew us any good*, and
pretend Religion, as some of the Jewes did the keeping of the
Sabboth, which yet cryed out when will the Sabboth bee
done, that wee may sell corne and gaine, if a man can tell
them how to get gold out of a flint, and silver out of the
Adamant, no paines shalbe spared, no time shall bee neglected, for gold is their hope, and the wedge of gold is their
confidence, their hearts are set upon the pelfe of this world,
and for love of it, all thinges are let slipp, even all duties to

Particular
amplific. 1.

God or men, they care not how basely they serve, how wretchedly they neglect all others, so as they may get wealth: pinch who will? and wring who will, all times are alike with them, and they runne for the bribe like *Gehazie*, and this is the first way that men seeke their owne.

Now the contrary is seene in *Nehemiah*, who when the people were hard put to it, and the land raw, he tooke not the dueties which were due to him being a Magistrate, he bought no land, nor grewe not rich, for it was no time: but he maintained at his table many of his breathren the Jewes, and so spent even his owne proper goods. And *Paul* sought no mans gold nor silver, but though hee had authoritie, yet he tooke not bread of the Churches, but laboured with his hands: And why? It was no time to take, some Churches were poore and stood in want, as *Thessalonica*, others were in danger to be preyed upon by covetous belly-gods, as *Corinth*: and therefore hee saw it no fit time now to take any thing of them.

And indeede heere is the difference betweene a covetous worldling, and an honest thriftie Christian, it is lawfull sometimes for men to gather wealth, and grow rich, even as there was a time for *Joseph* to store up corne, but a godly and sincere Christian will see when this time is, and will not hord up when he seeth others of his brethren and associates to want, but then is a time, if hee have any thing to fetch it out and disperse it, but the covetous gather good, he like *Achan* covets all that he seeth, and neglects no time, but gathers still and holds all fast, and if it were to save the life of his brother, his baggs must not be minished, nor his chestes lighted, nor his field set to sale, gather as much as he can, but its death to diminish the least part of it.

The second way by which men seeke their owne, is when they seeke ease, or pleasure, as the 2.
Scribes and *Pharisies*, who would not touch the burthen with one of their fingers; so, there is a generation, which thinke to have more in this world then *Adams* felicitie in Innocencie, being borne (as they thinke) to take their pleasures, and their ease, let the roofe of the house drop thorow, they stirre not; let the field be over-growne with weeds, they care not, they must not soile their hand, nor wet their foote, its enough for them to say, Goe you, not let us goe, though never so much

need; such idle Droanes are intollerable in a setled Common-wealth, much more in a Common-wealth which is but as it were in the bud; of what earth I pray thee art thou made, of any better then other of the sonnes of *Adam*? And canst thou see other of thy brethren toile their hearts out, and thou sit idle at home, or takest thy pleasure abroad? Remember the example of *Uriah*, who would not take his ease, nor his plea-sure, though the King required him, and why? Because his brethren, his associates, better men then himselfe (as he es-teemed them) were under hard labours and conditions, lay in the fields in tents, caves, &c.

3. The third way is when men seeke their owne bellies, as some did in the Apostles times, which went about with new doctrines and devices, knowing that the people had itching eares, and would easily entertaine, and willingly feede such novelists, which brought in dissensions, schismes, and contentions, and such were rocks, or pillars in their love-feasts, as *Jude* speaketh, they were shaddowes in Gods service, but when feasting came, then they were sub-stances, then they were in their element. And certainely there are some men which shape even their Religion, humaine state, and all, even as the belly cheare is best, and that they must have, els all heart and life is gone, let all conscience, care of others goe, let *Lazarus* starve at the gate, let *Josephs* af-fliction be increased, they must have their dishes, their dain-ties, or no content. The contrary was seene in *Nehemiah*, who would not take his large portion alotted to the governour, be-cause he knew it went short with others of his brethren; and *Uriah* would not receive the Kings present and goe banquet with his wife, because he knew the whole Hoast his brethren were faine to snap short in the fields.

And the difference betweene a temperate good man, and a belly-God is this: A good man will not eate his morsels alone, especially if he have better then other, but if by Gods provi-dence, he have gotten some meate which is better then ordi-nary, and better then his other brethrens, he can have no rest in himselfe, except he make other partaker with him. But a belly-God will slop all in his owne throat, yea, though his neighbour come in and behold him eate, yet his griple gut shameth not to swallow all. And this may be done sometimes, as well in meane fare as in greater dainties, for all countries afford not alike.

The fourth way by which men seeke their owne, 4. is by seeking outward honour, fame, and respect with men, as King *Saul* when he had lost all respect and favour with God, then thought to give content to his heart by being honoured before the Elders of the people; and it is wonderfull to see how some men are *desirous of vaine glory*, and how earnestly they seeke prayse, favour, and respect with men, and can have no quiet longer then their worldly favour lasteth, and that they will have what dishonour soever come to God, or disgrace unto men, yea, they will disgrace, reproch, and disdaine others, to gaine honour and advancement to themselves, yea, they will make bold with the Scriptures and word of God, to wrest and wring, and slight it over for their credits sake. And let a man marke some mens talke, stories, discourses, &c. and he shall see their whole drift is to extoll and set out themselves, and get praise and commendations of men.

Now the contrary was seene in *Paul*, he sayth, *He needed no letters of commendations*. And againe, *He is not affected with mens prayse*; and here is indeed the difference betweene an humble minded Christian, and a proud selfe-lover; an humble man often hath prayse, as *David*, *Hezekiah*, and *Josiah*, but he seekes it not, he desires it not, he is content to goe without it, he loves not the prayse of men, for he knowes it is but froth and vanitie: But a proud selfe-lover, he seekes it still, get it or not get it, and if he get it he is fully satisfied, if he get it not he hangs the head like a Bull-rush, and hath no comfort.

The fift way by which men seeke their owne, is 5. by seeking to have their wils, as the wrong doers in *Corinth*, who thought it not enough to doe wrong and harme to their brethren, but to have their wills enough of them, drew them before the Heathen Magistrates.

And truely, some men are so Prince-like, or rather Papall, that their very will and word is become a law, and if they have said it, it must be so, els there is no rest nor quietnesse to be had, let never so many reasons be brought to the contrary, its but fighting with the winde. They are like the obstinate *Jewes*,

who, when against Gods law & reason, they had askcd a
King, though *Samuel* shewed them that it would turne in the
end to their owne smart, yet still held the conclusion, and
sayd, nay, *But we will have a King*. Thus men are caught by
their owne words, and insnared by the straitnes of their owne
hearts, and it is death to them not to have their wils, and
howsoever sometimes (like *Jezabell*) they are cut short of their
purposes, yet selfe-willed men will strout and swell like
Absolon, saying neither *good nor bad*, but hope for the day,
and threaten like prophane *Esau*: Now the contrary is seene in
David, though a Prince, a Captaine, a Warriour, who having
sayd, yea, sworne, that he would kill *Naball*, and all his family that day, yet upon reasonable counsell given, and that but
by a weake woman, he changed his minde, altered his purpose, and returned, without striking one stroake, an example
rare, and worthy imitation; and when men are sicke of will, let
them thinke of *David*, it was his grace and honour to goe
backe from his word and practise, when reason came; So was
it *Herods* disgrace and shame to hold his word and will against
reason and conscience.

QUEST.   But some man happily will say unto me, It is true,
that men seeke their owne by all these wayes, But what
should be the reason and cause of this? that men seeke so
earnestly themselves, in seeking riches, honour, ease, belly-
cheare, will, &c. something there is that carrieth them.

RESP.   True, and the reasons and causes are specially these
three;

REASON I.   First, pride and high conceitednes, when men
over-value themselves: And this made *Absolon* to seeke his
Fathers kingdome, because he thought himselfe worthy of it.:
This made *Haman* so sore vexed, because *Mordecai* bowed
not to him, because he highly valued himselfe.

And surely, that which a man valueth as much, he giveth
much respect to, and so it is a sure signe that a man loves
himselfe most when he giveth most to himselfe, and some intollerable proud persons even thinke all the world is for them,
and all their purposes and endevours shew what a large conceit they have of themselves.

REASON 2.   Secondly, want of due consideration and

valuation of other mens endowments, abilities, and deserts, when men passe those things by, though they have both seene, heard, and felt them, as *Pharaohs* Butler forgat *Josephs* eminency when he was restored to his place, so men use to write their owne good actions in Brasse, but other mens in Ashes, never remembring nor considering the paynes, labour, good properties, &c. which others have, and so they have no love to them, but onely to themselves; as if God had made all other men unreasonable Beasts, and them onely reasonable men.

REASON 3.   Thirdly, want of a heavenly conversation, and spirituall eye to behold the glory, greatnesse, and majestie, and goodnesse of God, as the Queene of *Sheba* thought highly of her own glory, wisedome, and happinesse, till she saw *Salomons* wisdome and glory, and then she cryed out, not of the happinesse of her owne servants, but of his servants that stood before him; and verily, if men were conversant Courtiers in heaven, they would cry out with *Paul, Oh the deepnesse of the riches, wisedome, and knowledge of God, &c.* and would be ashamed of their owne sinfulnesse, nakednesse, and misery; for, as country men which never saw the state of Cities, nor the glory of courts, admire even their owne countrey orders: And as the Savages here which are clad in skinnes, and creepe in woods and holes, thinke their owne brutish and inhumane life the best, which if they saw and did rightly apprehend the benefit of comely humanity, the sweetnes of Religion, and the service of God, they would even shamefully hide themselves from the eye of all noble Christians.

Similies.

Even so, if men in serious contemplation, by the eye of faith, would behold the glory of God, and what great riches, beautie, fulnesse, perfection, power, dignitie, and greatnesse is in God, they would leave admiring of themselves, and seeking of themselves, and would say with *David, What am I? And what is my Fathers house? that thou shouldest thus blesse me?* Yea, *What is man? or the sonne of man that thou so regardest him?*

But it is time that we now come to apply these things more particularly to ourselves, and see what use is to be made of them.

USE 1.   Is it so that God seeth a proannes in all the sonnes of *Adam*, to seeke themselves too much, and hath given them warnings and watch words thereof, as we have heard, and doth experience confirme it? Then hence are reproved a number of men, who thinke they can never shew love enough to themselves, nor seeke their own enough, but thinke all cost, charges, cheerishing, prayse, honour, &c. too little for them, and no man needeth say to them, as *Peter* did to Christ, *favour thy selfe*, but if they doe a little for another man, they account it a great matter, though it be but a morsell of bread, or a single penny; but no varieties of dainties is too good for them, no silke, purple, cloth, or stuffe is too good to cloth them, the poore mans idlenesse and ill husbandry is oft throwne in his dish, but their owne carnall delights and fleshly wantonnesse is never thought upon: and why? Because they thinke even God and man owes all to them, but they owe nothing to none. Why, thou foolish and besotted man, hath not the holy Ghost read it in the face of every sonne of *Adam*, that he is too apt to seeke his owne, and art thou wiser then God, to thinke thou never seekest thine owne enough? or dreamest thou that thou art made of other, and better mettall then other men are? Surely, I know no way to escape, having of corruption to thy Father, and the worme to thy sister and brother. And if God had any where in all the Scriptures sayd, love thy selfe, make much of thy selfe, provide for one, &c. there were some reason for thee to take up the Nigards Proverbs, *Every man for himselfe, and God for us all; Charitie beginneth at home, &c.* But God never taught thee these things; No, they are Sathans positions: Doth God ever commend a man for carnall love of himselfe? Nay, he brands it, and disgraceth it, as *selfe-love; taking thought for the flesh; loving of pleasure, &c.*

OBJECT.   It is a point of good naturall policie, for a man to care and provide for himselfe.

RESP.   Then the most fooles have most naturall policie, for see you not the greatest droanes and novices, either in Church, or Common-wealth, to be the greatest scratchers, and scrapers, and gatherers of riches? Are they not also, for the most part, best fed and clad? and live they not most easily? What shall I say? Even hoggs, doggs, and bruit Beasts know their own ease, and can seeke that which is good for themselves; And what doth this shifting, progging, and fat feeding which some use, more resemble any thing then the fashion of hoggs? and so let it be what naturall policie it will.

USE 2. If God see this disease of selfe-love so dangerous in us, then it standeth us all in hand to suspect ourselves, and so to seeke out the roote of this disease, that it may be cured. If a learned Physitian, shall see by our counte- _{Simile.} nance and eye, that we have some dangerous disease growing on us, our hearts will smite us, and we will bethinke our selves, where the most griefe lieth, and how it should come, whether with cold, heate, surfeit, over-flowing of bloud, or thorow griefe, melancholy, or any such way, and every man will bestirre himselfe to get rid of it, and will prevent all wayes that feed the disease, and cherish all courses that would destroy it.

Now, how much more ought we to bestirre our selves, for this matter of selfe-love, since God himselfe hath cast all our waters, and felt all our pulses, and pronounced us all dangerously sicke of this disease? beleeve it, God cannot lie, nor be deceived; He that made the heart, doth not he know it? Let every mans heart smite him, and let him fall to examination of himselfe, and see first, whether he love not riches and worldly wealth too much, whether his heart be not too jocand at the comming of it in, and too heavie at the going of it out, for if you find it so, there is great danger; if thou canst not buy as if thou possessedst not, and use this world as thou usedst it not, thou art sicke and haddest need to looke to it. So, if thou lovest thine ease and pleasure, see whether thou canst be content to receive at Gods hands evill as well as good; whether thou have learned as well to abound as to want, as well to endure hard labour, as to live at ease; and art as willing to goe to the house of mourning as to the house of mirth; for, els, out of doubt, thou lovest thy carnall pleasure and ease too much.

Againe, see whether thine heart cannot be as merry, and thy mind as joyfull, and thy countenance as cheerefull, with course fare, with poulse, with bread and water (if God offer thee no better, nor the times afford other) as if thou hadst great dainties: So also whether thou canst be content as well

with the scornes of men, when thou hast done well, as with
their prayses, so if thou canst with comfort and good conscience say, I passe little for mans judgement, whether thou
canst doe thy duety that God requireth, and despise the
shame, referring thy selfe unto God, for if thou be dishartned,
discouraged, and weakened in any duety because of mens dis-
prayses, its a signe thou lovest thyselfe too much.

So for the will, if thou canst be content to give way even
from that which thou hast sayd shalbe, yea vowed shalbe,
when better reason commeth, and hast that reverence of
other men, as that when it standeth but upon a matter of will,
thou art as willing their wils shall stand as thine, and art not
sad, churlish, or discontent, but cheerefull in thine heart,
though thy will be crossed, it is a good signe, but if not, thou
art sicke of a selfe will, and must purge it out. I the rather
presse these things, because I see many men both wise and religious, which yet are so tainted with this pestilent selfe-love,
as that it is in them even as a dead flie to the Apothecaries
ointment, spoyling the efficacie of all their graces, making
their lives uncomfortable to themselves, and unprofitable to
others, being neither fit for Church nor common wealth, but
have even their very soules in hazard thereby, and therefore
who can say too much against it?

A faire warning.   It is reported, that there are many men gone
to that other Plantation in *Virginia*, which,
whilest they lived in England, seemed very religious, zealous,
and conscionable; and have now lost even the sap of grace,
and edge to all goodnesse; and are become meere worldlings:
This testimonie I beleeve to be partly true, and amongst
many causes of it, this selfe-love is not the least; It is indeede
a matter of some commendations for a man to remove himselfe out of a thronged place into a wide wildernesse; to take
in hand so long and dangerous a journey, to be an instrument
to carry the Gospell and humanitie among the bruitish heathen; but there may be many goodly shewes and gloses and
yet a pad in the strawe, men may make a great appearance of
respect unto God, and yet but dissemble with him, having
their owne lusts carying them: and, out of doubt, men that
have taken in hand hither to come, out of discontentment,
in regard of their estates in England; and ayming at great

matters heere, affecting it to be Gentlemen, landed men, or hoping for office, place, dignitie, or fleshly liberty; let the shew be what it will, the substance is nought, and that bird of selfe-love which was hatched at home, if it be not looked to, will eate out the life of all grace and goodnesse: and though men have escaped the danger of the sea, and that cruell mortalitie, which swept away so many of our loving friends and brethren; yet except they purge out this selfe-love, a worse mischeife is prepared for them: And who knoweth whether God in mercy have delivered those just men which heere departed, from the evils to come; and from unreasonable men, in whom there neither was, nor is, any comfort but greife, sorrow, affliction, and miserie, till they cast out this spaune of selfe-love.

But I have dwelt too long upon this first part; I come now to the second, which concernes an Exhortation, as I shewed you, in the Division.

TEXT.   *But every man anothers wealth.*

EXPLI.   In direct opposition, he should say, *Let every man seeke anothers*, but the first part being compared with the latter, and (*seeke*) being taken out of the former and put to the latter, and (*wealth*) taken out or rather implied, in the former, the whole sentence is thus resolved, *Let no man seeke his owne wealth, but let every man seeke anothers wealth.*

And the word here translated *wealth*, is the same with that in *Rom.* 13. 4. and may not be taken onely for riches, as English-men commonly understand it, but for all kind of benefits, favours, comforts, either for soule or body; and so here againe, as before, you must understand an Affirmative Commandement, as the Negative was before: and least any should say, If I may not seeke my owne good, I may doe nothing; Yes, sayth *Paul*, Ile tell thee, thou shalt seeke the good of another, whereas now all they seeking helps but one, by this meanes thou shalt helpe many: and this is further enforced by these two circumstances, (no man) may seeke his owne, be he rich, learned, wise, &c. *But every man must seeke the good of another.*

DOCT. 2.   The point of instruction is taken from the very letter and phrase, *viz.* A man must seeke the good, the wealth, the profit of others, I say, he must seeke it, he must seeke the

comfort, profit, and benefit of his neighbour, brother, associate, &c. His owne good he need not seeke, it will offer it selfe
to him every houre, but the good of others must be sought,
a man must not stay from doing good to others till he is
sought unto, pulled and haled (as it were) like the unjust
Judge, for every benefit that is first craved, commeth too late.
And thus the auncient Patriarkes did practise, when the
travayler and way-faring man came by, they did not tarry till
they came and asked reliefe and refreshing, but sat at the
gates to watch for such, and looked in the streets to find
them, yea, set open their doores that they might freely and
boldly enter in. And howsoever, some may thinke this too
large a practice, since, now the world is so full of people, yet
I see not but the more people there is, the larger charitie
ought to be.

But be it so as a man may neglect, in some sort the generall world, yet those to whom he is bound, either in naturall,
civill, or religious bands, them he must seeke how to doe
them good: A notable example you have in *David*, who, because there was twixt him & *Jonathan* a band and covenant,
therefore he enquired, *Whether there was any left of the house
of Saul, to whom he might shew mercy for Jonathans sake;* So,
this people of *Corinth*, to whom *Paul* writeth, they were in a
spirituall league and covenant in the *Gospell*, and so were a
body; Now for one member in the body to seeke himselfe,
and neglect all other, were, as if a man should cloth one arme
or one leg of his body with gold and purple, and let all the
rest of the members goe naked.

Now brethren, I pray you, remember your selves, and
know, that you are not in a retired Monasticall course, but
have given your names and promises one to another, and
covenanted here to cleave together in the service of God, and
the King; What then must you doe? May you live as retired
Hermites? and looke after no body? Nay, you must seeke still
the wealth of one another; And enquire as *David*, how liveth
such a man? How is he clad? How is he fed? He is my
brother, my associate; we ventered our lives together here,
and had a hard brunt of it, and we are in league together, is
his labour harder then mine? surely, I will ease him; hath
he no bed to lie on? why, I have two, Ile lend him one; hath he

no apparel? why, I have two suits, Ile give him one of them; eates he course fare, bread and water, and I have better? why, surely we will part stakes: He is as good a man as I, and we are bound each to other, so that his wants must be my wants, his sorrowes my sorrowes, his sicknes my sicknes, and his welfare my welfare, for I am as he is. And such a sweet sympathie were excellent, comfortable, yea, heavenly, and is the onely maker and conserver of Churches and common-wealths, and where this is wanting, ruine comes on quickly, as it did here in *Corinth.*

REASONS.   But besides these motives, there are other reasons to provoke us not onely to doe good one to another; but even to seeke and search how to doe it.

1 REASON.   As first, to maintaine modestie in all our associates, that of hungrie wanters they become not bold beggers and impudent cravers, for as one sayth of women, that, when they have lost their shamefastnes, they have lost halfe their honestie, so may it truely be sayd of a man, that when he hath lost his modestie, and puts on a begging face, he hath lost his majestie, and the Image of that noble creature, and man should not begge and crave of man but onely of God; true it is, that as Christ was faine to crave water of the Samaritan woman, so men are forced to aske sometimes rather then starve, but indeede in all societies it should be offered them, men often complaine of mens boldnes in asking, but how commeth this to passe, but because the world hath beene so full of selfe-lovers, as no man would offer their money, meate, garmentes, though they saw men hungrie, harborlesse, poore, and naked in the streetes; and what is it that makes men brazen faced, bold, bruitish, tumultuous, mutinous, but because they are pinched with want, and see others of their Companions (which it may be have lesse deserved) to live in prosperitie and pleasure?

2 REASON.   It wonderfully encourageth men in their dueties, when they see the burthen equally borne; but when some withdraw themselves and retire to their owne particular ease, pleasure, or profit; what heart can men have to goe on in their businesse? when men are come together, to lift some weighty peece of tymber or vessell; if one stand still and doe not lift, shall not the rest be weakned and dishartned? will not

a few idle droanes spoyle the whole stocke of laborious Bees: so one idle belly, one murmurer, one complainer, one selfe-lover will weaken and disharten a whole Colonie. Great matters have beene brought to passe, where men have cheerefully as with one heart, hand, and shoulder, gone about it both in warres, buildings, and plantations, but where every man seekes himselfe, all commeth to nothing.

3 REASON. The present necessitie requireth it, as it did in the dayes of the *Jewes*, returning from captivitie, and as it was here in *Corinth*. The Countrey is yet raw, the land untilled, the Cities not builded, the Cattell not setled, we are compassed about with a helplesse and idle people, the natives of the Countrey, which cannot in any comely or comfortable manner helpe themselves, much lesse us. Wee also have beene very chargeable to many of our loving friends, which helped us hither, and now againe supplyed us, so that before we thinke of gathering riches, we must even in Conscience thinke of requiting their charge, love, and labour, and cursed be that profit and gaine which aymeth not at this. Besides, how many of our deare friends, did here die at our first entrance, many of them no doubt for want of good lodging, shelter, and comfortable things, and many more may goe after them quickly, if care be not taken. Is this then a time for men to begin to seeke themselves? *Paul* sayth, that men in the last dayes shall be lovers of themselves, but it is here yet but the first dayes, and (as it were) the dawning of this new world, it is now therefore no time for men to looke to get riches, brave clothes, daintie fare, but to looke to present necessities; it is now no time to pamper the flesh, live at ease, snatch, catch, scrape, and pill, and hoord up, but rather to open the doores, the chests, and vessels, and say, brother, neighbour, friend, what want yee, any thing that I have? make bold with it, it is yours to command, to doe you good, to comfort and cherish you, and glad I am that I have it for you.

4 REASON. And even the example of God himselfe, whom we should follow in all things within our power and capacitie, may teach us this lesson, for (with reverence to his Majestie be it spoken) he might have kept all grace, goodnesse, and glory to himselfe, but he hath communicated it to us, even as farre as we are capable of it in this life, and will communicate

his glory in all fulnesse with his Elect in that life to come; even so his Sonne Christ Jesus left his glory eclipsed for a time, and abased himselfe to a poore and distressed life in this world, that he might, by it, bring us to happinesse in the world to come. If God then have delighted in this doing good and relieving frayle and miserable man, so farre inferior to himselfe, what delight ought man to have to relieve and comfort man, which is equall to himselfe?

5 REASON. Even as we deale with others, our selves and others shall be dealt withall, carest thou not how others fare, how they toile, are grieved, sicke, pinched, cold, harborlesse, so as thou be in health, livest at ease, warme in thy nest, farest well? The dayes will come when thou shalt labour and none shall pittie thee, be poore and none relieve thee, be sicke, and lie and die and none visit thee, yea, and thy children shall lie and starve in the streets, and none shall relieve them, for *it is the mercifull that shall obtaine mercy;* and *the memory of the Just shall be blessed* even in his seede; and a mercifull and loving man when he dies, though he leave his children small and desolate, yet every one is mercifully stirred up for the Fathers sake to shew compassion, but the unkindnesse, currishnesse, and selfe-love of a Father, is thorow Gods just judgement recompenced upon the children with neglect and crueltie.

6 REASON. Lastly, that we may draw to an end; A mercilesse man, and a man without naturall affection or love, is reckoned among such as are given over of God to a reprobate minde, and (as it were) transformed into a beast-like humor; for, what is a man if he be not sociable, kinde, affable, free hearted, liberall; He is a beast in the shape of a man; or rather an infernall Spirit, walking amongst men which makes the world a hell what in him lieth; for, it is even a hell to live where there are many such men: such the Scripture calleth *Nabals,* which signifieth *fooles* and decayed men, which have lost both the sap of grace and nature; and such merciles men are called *Goats,* and shall be set at Christs left hand at the last day; *Oh therefore seeke the wealth one of another.*

OBJECT. But some will say, it is true, and it were well, if men would so doe, but we see every man is so for himselfe, as that if I should not doe so, I should doe full ill, for if I have it not of my owne, I may snap short sometimes, for I see no body sheweth me any kindnesse, nor giveth me any thing; if I have gold and silver, that goeth for payment, and if I want it, I may lie in the streete, therefore I were best keepe that I have, and not be so liberall as you would have me, except I saw others would be so towards me.

RESP. This Objection seemeth but equall and reasonable, as did the Answere of *Naball* to *Davids* men, but it is most foolish and carnall, as his also was; for, if we should measure our courses by most mens practises, a man should never doe any godly dutie; for, doe not the most, yea, almost all, goe the broad way that leadeth to death and damnation? who then will follow a multitude? It is the word of God, and the examples of the best men that we must follow. And what if others will doe nothing for thee, but are unkinde, and unmercifull to thee? Knowest thou not that they which will be the children of God must be kinde to the unkinde, loving to their enemies, and blesse those that curse them? If all men were kinde to thee, it were but *Publicans* righteousnesse to be kinde to them; If all men be evill, wilt thou be so too? When *David* cryed out; *Helpe Lord, for not a godly man is left.* Did he himselfe turne ungodly also? Nay, he was rather the more strict: So, if love and charitie be departed out of this world, be thou one of them that shall first bring it in againe.

And let this be the first rule, which I will with two others conclude for this time.

1 RULE. Never measure thy course by the most, but by the best, yea, and principally by Gods word; Looke not what others doe to thee, but consider what thou art to doe to them; seeke to please God, not thy selfe: did they in *Mathew* 25. 44. plead, that others did nothing for them? No such matter, no such plea will stand before God, his word is plaine to the contrary, therefore, though all the world should neglect thee, disregard thee, and contemne thee, yet remember thou hast not to doe with men, but with the highest God, and so thou must doe thy dutie to them notwithstanding.

2 RULE. And let there be no Prodigall person to come forth and say, Give me the portion of lands and goods that appertaineth to me, and let me shift for my selfe; It is yet too soone to put men to their shifts; *Israel* was seaven yeares in *Canaan*, before the land was divided into Tribes, much

longer, before it was divided into Families: And why wouldest thou have thy particular portion, but because thou thinkest to live better then thy neighbour, and scornest to live so meanely as he? but who, I pray thee, brought this particularizing first into the world? Did not Sathan, who was not content to keepe that equall state with his fellowes, but would set his throne above the Starres? Did not he also entise man to despise his generall felicitie and happinesse, and goe trie particular knowledge of good and evill? And nothing in this world doth more resemble heavenly happinesse, then for men to live as one, being of one heart, and one soule; neither any thing more resembles hellish horror, then for every man to shift for himselfe; for if it be a good minde and practise, thus to affect particulars, *mine* and *thine*, then it should be best also for God to provide one heaven for thee, and another for thy neighbour.

OBJECT. But some will say, if all men would doe their endevour as I doe, I could be content with this generalitie, but many are idle and sloathful, and eate up others labours, and therefore it is best to part, and then every man may doe his pleasure.

RESP. First, This, indeed, is the common plea of such as will endure no inconveniences, and so for the hardnesse of mens hearts, God and man doth often give way to that which is not best, nor perpetuall, but indeede if wee take this course, to change ordinances and practises, because of inconveniences, wee shall have, every day, new lawes.

Secondly, If others be idle, and thou diligent, thy fellowship, provocation, and example may well helpe to cure that maladie in them, being together, but being asunder, shall they not be more idle, and shall not *Gentrie* and *Beggerie* be quickly the glorious Ensignes of your Common-wealth?

Thirdly, Construe things in the best part, be not too hastie to say, men are idle and slouthfull, all men have not strength, skill, facultie, spirit, and courage to worke alike; it is thy glory and credit, that canst doe so well, and his shame and reproach, that can doe no better; and art not these sufficient rewards to you both?

Fourthly, if any be idle apparantly, you have a Law and Governours to execute the same, and to follow that rule of the Apostle, to keepe backe their bread, and let them not eate, goe not therefore whisperingly, to charge men with idlenesse; but goe to the Governour and prove them idle; and thou shalt see them have their deserts.

And as you are a body together, so hang not together by skins and gymocks, but labour to be joynted together and knit by flesh and synewes; away with envie at the good of others, and rejoyce in his good, and sorrow for his evill, let his joy bee thy joy, and his sorrow thy sorrow: let his sicknesse be thy sicknesse: his hunger thy hunger: his povertie thy povertie: And if you professe friendship, be friends in adversities: for then a friend is knowne, and tryed, and not before.

3 RULE. Lay away all thought of former thinges and forget them, and thinke upon the things that are, looke not gapingly one upon other, pleading your goodnesse, your birth, your life you have lived, your meanes you had and might have had, heere you are by Gods providence, under difficulties, be thankfull to God, it is no worse, and take it in good part that which is, and lift not up your selves because of former priviledges, when *Job* was brought to the dunghill, he sate downe upon it. And when the Almightie had beene bitter to *Naomie*, shee would bee called *Marah*, consider therefore what you are now, and where you are, say not I could have lived thus and thus; but say, thus and thus I must live: for God, and naturall necessitie requireth, if your difficulties be great, you had neede to cleave the faster together, and comfort and cheere up one another, laboring to make each others burden lighter, there is no griefe so tedious as a churlish companion, and nothing makes sorrowes easie more then cheerefull associates: Beare ye therefore one anothers burthen, and be not a burthen one to another, avoide all factions, frowardnes, singularitie, and withdrawings, and cleave fast to the Lord, and one to another continually; so shall you bee a notable president to these poore Heathens, whose eyes are upon you, and who very bruitishly and cruelly doe dayly eate and consume one another, through their emulations, warres, and contentions; bee you therefore ashamed of it, and winne them to peace both with your selves, and one another, by your peaceable examples, which will preach louder to them, then if you could crie in their Barbarous language: So also shall you bee an en-

couragement to many of your Christian friendes in your native Countrey, to come to you, when they heare of your
peace, love, and kindnesse that is amongst you: But above all,
it shall goe well with your soules, when that GOD of peace
and unity shall come to visite you with death, as hee hath
done many of your associates, you being found of him, not in
murmurings, discontent and jarres, but in brotherly love, and
peace, may bee translated from this wandring wildernesse,
unto that joyfull and heavenly *Canaan*.

FINIS.

JOHN WINTHROP

A Modell of Christian Charity

Written
On Boarde the Arrabella,
On the Attlantick Ocean.
By the Honorable John Winthrop Esquire.

In His passage, (with the great Company of
Religious people, of which Christian Tribes he was
the Brave Leader and famous Governor;) from the Island
of Great Brittaine, to New-England in the North America.
Anno 1630.

———

Christian Charitie.

A MODELL HEREOF.

GOD Almightie in his most holy and wise providence hath soe disposed of the Condicion of mankinde, as in all times some must be rich some poore, some highe and eminent in power and dignitie; others meane and in subjeccion.

THE REASON HEREOF.

1. REAS. *First*, to hold conformity with the rest of his workes, being delighted to shewe forthe the glory of his wisdome in the variety and differance of the Creatures and the glory of his power, in ordering all these differences for the preservacion and good of the whole, and the glory of his greatnes that as it is the glory of princes to have many officers, soe this great King will have many Stewards counting himselfe more honoured in dispenceing his guifts to man by man, then if hee did it by his owne immediate hand.

2. REAS. *Secondly*, That he might have the more occasion to manifest the worke of his Spirit: first, upon the wicked in

moderateing and restraineing them: soe that the riche and mighty should not eate upp the poore, nor the poore, and dispised rise upp against theire superiours, and shake off theire yoake; 2ly in the regenerate in exerciseing his graces in them, as in the greate ones, theire love mercy, gentlenes, temperance etc., in the poore and inferiour sorte, theire faithe patience, obedience etc:

3. REAS. *Thirdly*, That every man might have need of other, and from hence they might be all knitt more nearly together in the Bond of brotherly affeccion: from hence it appeares plainely that noe man is made more honourable then another or more wealthy etc., out of any perticuler and singuler respect to himselfe but for the glory of his Creator and the Common good of the Creature, Man; Therefore God still reserves the propperty of these guifts to himselfe as Ezek: 16. 17. he there calls wealthe his gold and his silver etc. Prov: 3. 9. he claimes theire service as his due honour the Lord with thy riches etc. All men being thus (by divine providence) rancked into two sortes, riche and poore; under the first, are comprehended all such as are able to live comfortably by theire owne meanes duely improved; and all others are poore according to the former distribution. There are two rules whereby wee are to walke one towards another: JUSTICE and MERCY. These are allwayes distinguished in theire Act and in theire object, yet may they both concurre in the same Subject in eache respect; as sometimes there may be an occasion of shewing mercy to a rich man, in some sudden danger of distresse, and allsoe doeing of meere Justice to a poor man in regard of some perticuler contract etc. There is likewise a double Lawe by which wee are regulated in our conversacion one towardes another: in both the former respects, the lawe of nature and the lawe of grace, or the morrall lawe or the lawe of the gospell, to omitt the rule of Justice as not propperly belonging to this purpose otherwise then it may fall into consideracion in some perticuler Cases: By the first of these lawes man as he was enabled soe withall is commaunded to love his neighbour as himselfe upon this ground stands all the precepts of the morrall lawe, which concernes our dealings with men. To apply this to the works of mercy this lawe requires two things first that every man afford his help to

another in every want or distresse Secondly, That hee performe this out of the same affeccion, which makes him carefull of his owne good according to that of our Saviour Math: 7. 12 Whatsoever ye would that men should doe to you. This was practised by Abraham and Lott in entertaineing the Angells and the old man of Gibea.

The Lawe of Grace or the Gospell hath some differance from the former as in these respectes first the lawe of nature was given to man in the estate of innocency; this of the gospell in the estate of regeneracy: 2ly, the former propounds one man to another, as the same fleshe and Image of god, this as a brother in Christ allsoe, and in the Communion of the same spirit and soe teacheth us to put a difference betweene Christians and others. Doe good to all especially to the household of faith; upon this ground the Israelites were to putt a difference betweene the brethren of such as were strangers though not of the Canaanites. 3ly. The Lawe of nature could give noe rules for dealeing with enemies for all are to be considered as freinds in the estate of innocency, but the Gospell commaunds love to an enemy proofe. If thine Enemie hunger feede him; Love your Enemies doe good to them that hate you Math: 5. 44.

This Lawe of the Gospell propoundes likewise a difference of seasons and occasions there is a time when a christian must sell all and give to the poore as they did in the Apostles times. There is a tyme allsoe when a christian (though they give not all yet) must give beyond theire abillity, as they of Macedonia. Cor: 2. 6. likewise community of perills calls for extraordinary liberallity and soe doth Community in some speciall service for the Churche. Lastly, when there is noe other meanes whereby our Christian brother may be releived in this distresse, wee must help him beyond our ability, rather then tempt God, in putting him upon help by miraculous or extraordinary meanes.

This duty of mercy is exercised in the kindes, Giveing, lending, and forgiveing.

QUEST. What rule shall a man observe in giveing in respect of the measure?

ANS. If the time and occasion be ordinary he is to give out of his aboundance—let him lay aside, as god hath blessed him. If the time and occasion be extraordinary he must be ruled by them; takeing this withall that then a man cannot likely doe too much especially, if he may leave himselfe and his family under probable meanes of comfortable subsistance.

OBJECTION. A man must lay upp for posterity, the fathers lay upp for posterity and children and he is worse then an Infidell that prouideth not for his owne.

ANS. For the first, it is plaine, that it being spoken by way of Comparison it must be meant of the ordinary and usuall course of fathers and cannot extend to times and occasions extraordinary; for the other place the Apostle speakes against such as walked inordinately, and it is without question, that he is worse then an Infidell whoe throughe his owne Sloathe and voluptuousnes shall neglect to provide for his family.

OBJECTION. The wise mans Eies are in his head (saith Salomon) and foreseeth the plague, therefore wee must forecast and lay upp against evill times when hee or his may stand in need of all he can gather.

ANS. This very Argument Salomon useth to perswade to liberallity. Eccle: 11. 1. cast thy bread upon the waters etc.: for thou knowest not what evill may come upon the land Luke 16. make you freinds of the riches of Iniquity; you will aske how this shall be? very well. for first he that gives to the poore lends to the lord, and he will repay him even in this life an hundred fold to him or his. The righteous is ever mercifull and lendeth and his seed enjoyeth the blessing; and besides wee know what advantage it will be to us in the day of account, when many such Witnesses shall stand forthe for us to witnesse the improvement of our Tallent. And I would knowe of those whoe pleade soe much for layeing up for time to come, whether they hold that to be Gospell Math: 16. 19. Lay not upp for yourselves Treasures upon Earth etc. if they acknowledge it what extent will they allowe it; if onely to those primitive times lett them consider the reason whereupon our Saviour groundes it, the first is that they are subject to the moathe, the rust the Theife. Secondly, They will steale away the hearte, where the treasure is there will the heart be allsoe. The reasons are of like force at all times therefore the exhortacion must be generall and perpetuall which applies allwayes in respect of the love and affeccion to riches and in

regard of the things themselves when any speciall service for
the churche or perticuler distresse of our brother doe call for
the use of them; otherwise it is not onely lawfull but necessary to lay upp as Joseph did to have ready uppon such occasions, as the Lord (whose stewards wee are of them) shall call
for them from us: Christ gives us an Instance of the first,
when hee sent his disciples for the Asse, and bidds them answer the owner thus, the Lord hath need of him; soe when
the Tabernacle was to be builte his servant sends to his people to call for their silver and gold etc.; and yeildes them noe
other reason but that it was for his worke, when Elisha comes
to the widowe of Sareptah and findes her prepareing to make
ready her pittance for herselfe and family, he bids her first provide for him, he challengeth first gods parte which shee must
first give before shee must serve her owne family, all these
teache us that the lord lookes that when hee is pleased to call
for his right in any thing wee have, our owne Interest wee
have must stand aside, till his turne be served, for the other
wee need looke noe further then to that of John 1. he whoe
hath this worlds goodes and seeth his brother to neede, and
shutts upp his Compassion from him, how dwelleth the love
of god in him, which comes punctually to this Conclusion: if
thy brother be in want and thou canst help him, thou needst
not make doubt, what thou shouldst doe, if thou lovest god
thou must help him.

QUEST.   What rule must wee observe in lending?

ANS.   Thou must observe whether thy brother hath present or probable or possible meanes of repayeing thee, if ther
be none of these, thou must give him according to his necessity, rather then lend him as hee requires; if he hath present
meanes of repayeing thee, thou art to looke at him, not as an
Act of mercy, but by way of Commerce, wherein thou arte to
walke by the rule of Justice, but, if his meanes of repayeing
thee be onely probable or possible then is hee an object of thy
mercy thou must lend him, though there be danger of loose-
ing it Deut: 15. 7. If any of thy brethren be poore etc. thou
shalt lend him sufficient that men might not shift off this duty
by the apparant hazzard, he tells them that though the Yeare
of Jubile were at hand (when he must remitt it, if hee were
not able to repay it before) yet he must lend him and that

chearefully: it may not greive thee to give him (saith hee) and because some might object, why soe I should soone impover-ishe my selfe and my family, he adds with all thy Worke etc. for our Saviour Math: 5. 42. From him that would borrow of thee turne not away.

QUEST. What rule must wee observe in forgiveing?

ANS. Whether thou didst lend by way of Commerce or in mercy, if he have noething to pay thee thou must forgive him (except in cause where thou hast a surety or a lawfull pleadge) Deut. 15. 2. Every seaventh yeare the Creditor was to quitt that which hee lent to his brother if hee were poore as appeares ver: 4: save when there shall be noe poore with thee. In all these and like Cases Christ was a generall rule Math: 7. 22. Whatsoever ye would that men should doe to you doe yee the same to them allsoe.

QUEST. What rule must wee observe and walke by in cause of Community of perill?

ANS. The same as before, but with more enlargement to-wardes others and lesse respect towards our selves, and our owne right hence it was that in the primitive Churche they sold all had all things in Common, neither did any man say that that which he possessed was his owne likewise in theire returne out of the Captivity, because the worke was greate for the restoreing of the church and the danger of enemies was Common to all Nehemiah exhortes the Jewes to liberallity and readines in remitting theire debtes to theire brethren, and disposeth liberally of his owne to such as wanted and stands not upon his owne due, which hee might have demaunded of them, thus did some of our forefathers in times of persecu-cion here in England, and soe did many of the faithfull in other Churches whereof wee keepe an honourable remem-brance of them, and it is to be observed that both in Scrip-tures and latter stories of the Churches that such as have beene most bountifull to the poore Saintes especially in these extraordinary times and occasions god hath left them highly Commended to posterity, as Zacheus, Cornelius, Dorcas, Bishop Hooper, the Cuttler of Brussells and divers others ob-serve againe that the scripture gives noe causion to restraine any from being over liberall this way; but all men to the lib-erall and cherefull practise hereof by the sweetest promises as to instance one for many, Isaiah 58. 6: Is not this the fast that I have chosen to loose the bonds of wickednes, to take off the heavy burdens to lett the oppressed goe free and to breake every Yoake, to deale thy bread to the hungry and to bring the poore that wander into thy house, when thou seest the naked to cover them etc. then shall thy light breake forthe as the morneing, and thy healthe shall growe speedily, thy righteousnes shall goe before thee, and the glory of the lord shall embrace thee, then thou shalt call and the lord shall Answer thee etc. 2. 10: If thou power out thy soule to the hungry, then shall thy light spring out in darknes, and the lord shall guide thee continually, and satisfie thy Soule in draught, and make fatt thy bones, thou shalt be like a watered Garden, and they shall be of thee that shall build the old wast places etc. on the contrary most heavy cursses are layd upon such as are straightened towards the Lord and his people Judg: 5. 23. Cursse ye Meroshe because they came not to help the Lord etc. Pro: 21. 13. Hee whoe shutteth his eares from hearing the cry of the poore, he shall cry and shall not be heard: Math: 25. 41. Goe ye curssed into everlasting fire etc. 42. I was hungry and ye fedd mee not. Cor: 2. 9. 6. He that soweth spareingly shall reape spareingly.

Haveing allready sett forth the practise of mercy according to the rule of gods lawe, it will be usefull to lay open the groundes of it allsoe being the other parte of the Commaundement and that is the affeccion from which this exercise of mercy must arise, the Apostle tells us that this love is the fullfilling of the lawe, not that it is enough to love our brother and soe noe further but in regard of the excellency of his partes giveing any motion to the other as the Soule to the body and the power it hath to sett all the faculties on worke in the outward exercise of this duty as when wee bid one make the clocke strike he doth not lay hand on the hammer which is the immediate instrument of the sound but setts on worke the first mover or maine wheele, knoweing that will certainely produce the sound which hee intends; soe the way to drawe men to the workes of mercy is not by force of Argument from the goodnes or necessity of the worke, for though this course may enforce a rationall minde to some present Act of mercy as is frequent in experience, yet it cannot worke such a habit in a Soule as shall make it prompt upon all occasions to produce the same effect but by frame-ing these affeccions of love in the hearte which will as natively bring forthe the other, as any cause doth produce the effect.

The diffinition which the Scripture gives us of love is this Love is the bond of perfection. First, it is a bond, or ligament. 2ly, it makes the worke perfect. There is noe body but con-sistes of partes and that which knitts these partes together gives the body its perfeccion, because it makes eache parte soe contiguous to other as thereby they doe mutually participate with eache other, both in strengthe and infirmity in pleasure and paine, to instance in the most perfect of all bodies, Christ and his church make one body: the severall partes of this body considered aparte before they were united were as dispropor-tionate and as much disordering as soe many contrary qualli-ties or elements but when christ comes and by his spirit and love knitts all these partes to himselfe and each to other, it is become the most perfect and best proportioned body in the world Eph: 4. 16. Christ by whome all the body being knitt together by every joynt for the furniture thereof according to the effectuall power which is in the measure of every perfec-cion of partes a glorious body without spott or wrinckle the ligaments hereof being Christ or his love for Christ is love 1 John: 4. 8. Soe this definition is right Love is the bond of perfeccion.

From hence wee may frame these Conclusions.

1 first all true Christians are of one body in Christ 1. Cor. 12. 12. 13. 27. Ye are the body of Christ and members of your parte.

2ly. The ligamentes of this body which knitt together are love.

3ly. Noe body can be perfect which wants its propper liga-mentes.

4ly. All the partes of this body being thus united are made soe contiguous in a speciall relacion as they must needes par-take of each others strength and infirmity, joy, and sorrowe, weale and woe. 1 Cor: 12. 26. If one member suffers all suffer with it, if one be in honour, all rejoyce with it.

5ly. This sensiblenes and Sympathy of each others Con-dicions will necessarily infuse into each parte a native desire

and endeavour, to strengthen defend preserve and comfort
the other.

To insist a little on this Conclusion being the product of all
the former the truthe hereof will appeare both by precept and
patterne 1. John. 3. 10. yee ought to lay downe your lives for
the brethren Gal: 6. 2. beare ye one anothers burthens and
soe fulfill the lawe of Christ.

For patterns wee have that first of our Saviour whoe out of
his good will in obedience to his father, becomeing a parte of
this body, and being knitt with it in the bond of love, found
such a native sensiblenes of our infirmities and sorrowes as
hee willingly yeilded himselfe to deathe to ease the infirmities
of the rest of his body and soe heale theire sorrowes: from the
like Sympathy of partes did the Apostles and many thousands
of the Saintes lay downe theire lives for Christ againe, the like
wee may see in the members of this body among themselves.
1. Rom. 9. Paule could have beene contented to have beene
seperated from Christ that the Jewes might not be cutt off
from the body: It is very observable which hee professeth of
his affectionate partakeing with every member: whoe is weake
(saith hee) and I am not weake? whoe is offended and I burne
not; and againe. 2 Cor: 7. 13. therefore wee are comforted
because yee were comforted. of Epaphroditus he speaketh
Phil: 2. 30. that he regarded not his owne life to do him service soe Phebe. and others are called the servantes of the
Churche, now it is apparant that they served not for wages or
by Constrainte but out of love, the like wee shall finde in the
histories of the churche in all ages the sweete Sympathie of affeccions which was in the members of this body one towardes
another, theire chearfullnes in serveing and suffering together
how liberall they were without repineing harbourers without
grudgeing and helpfull without reproacheing and all from
hence they had fervent love amongst them which onely makes
the practise of mercy constant and easie.

The next consideracion is how this love comes to be
wrought; Adam in his first estate was a perfect modell of
mankinde in all theire generacions, and in him this love was
perfected in regard of the habit, but Adam Rent in himselfe
from his Creator, rent all his posterity allsoe one from another, whence it comes that every man is borne with this prin-

ciple in him, to love and seeke himselfe onely and thus a man continueth till Christ comes and takes possession of the soule, and infuseth another principle love to God and our brother. And this latter haveing continuall supply from Christ, as the head and roote by which hee is united get the predominency in the soule, soe by little and little expells the former 1 John 4. 7. love cometh of god and every one that loveth is borne of god, soe that this love is the fruite of the new birthe, and none can have it but the new Creature, now when this quallity is thus formed in the soules of men it workes like the Spirit upon the drie bones Ezek. 37. 7. bone came to bone, it gathers together the scattered bones or perfect old man Adam and knitts them into one body againe in Christ whereby a man is become againe a liveing soule.

The third Consideracion is concerning the exercise of this love, which is twofold, inward or outward, the outward hath beene handled in the former preface of this discourse, for unfolding the other wee must take in our way that maxime of philosophy, Simile simili gaudet or like will to like; for as it is things which are carved with disafeccion to eache other, the ground of it is from a dissimilitude or   ariseing from the contrary or different nature of the things themselves, soe the ground of love is an apprehension of some resemblance in the things loved to that which affectes it, this is the cause why the Lord loves the Creature, soe farre as it hath any of his Image in it, he loves his elect because they are like himselfe, he beholds them in his beloved sonne: soe a mother loves her childe, because shee throughly conceives a resemblance of herselfe in it. Thus it is betweene the members of Christ, each discernes by the worke of the spirit his owne Image and resemblance in another, and therefore cannot but love him as he loves himselfe: Now when the soule which is of a sociable nature findes any thing like to it selfe. it is like Adam when Eve was brought to him, shee must have it one with herselfe this is fleshe of my fleshe (saith shee) and bone of my bone shee conceives a great delighte in it, therefore shee desires nearenes and familiarity with it: shee hath a great propensity to doe it good and receives such content in it, as feareing the miscarriage of her beloved shee bestowes it in the inmost closett of her heart, shee will not endure that it shall want any

good which shee can give it, if by occasion shee be with-
drawne from the Company of it, shee is still lookeing towardes the place where shee left her beloved, if shee heare it
groane shee is with it presently, if shee finde it sadd and disconsolate shee sighes and mournes with it, shee hath noe such
joy, as to see her beloved merry and thriveing, if shee see it
wronged, shee cannot beare it without passion, shee setts noe
boundes of her affeccions, nor hath any thought of reward,
shee findes recompence enoughe in the exercise of her love
towardes it, wee may see this Acted to life in Jonathan and
David. Jonathan a valiant man endued with the spirit of
Christ, soe soone as hee Discovers the same spirit in David
had presently his hearte knitt to him by this linement of love,
soe that it is said he loved him as his owne soule, he takes soe
great pleasure in him that hee stripps himselfe to adorne his
beloved, his fathers kingdome was not soe precious to him as
his beloved David, David shall have it with all his hearte, himselfe desires noe more but that hee may be neare to him to rejoyce in his good hee chooseth to converse with him in the
wildernesse even to the hazzard of his owne life, rather then
with the greate Courtiers in his fathers Pallace; when hee sees
danger towards him, hee spares neither care paines, nor perill
to divert it, when Injury was offered his beloved David, hee
could not beare it, though from his owne father, and when
they must parte for a Season onely, they thought theire
heartes would have broake for sorrowe, had not theire affeccions found vent by aboundance of Teares: other instances
might be brought to shewe the nature of this affeccion as of
Ruthe and Naomi and many others, but this truthe is cleared
enough. If any shall object that it is not possible that love
should be bred or upheld without hope of requitall, it is
graunted but that is not our cause, for this love is allwayes under reward it never gives, but it allwayes receives with advantage: first, in regard that among the members of the same
body, love and affection are reciprocall in a most equall and
sweete kinde of Commerce. 3ly, in regard of the pleasure and
content that the exercise of love carries with it as wee may see
in the naturall body the mouth is at all the paines to receive,
and mince the foode which serves for the nourishment of all
the other partes of the body, yet it hath noe cause to com-

plaine; for first, the other partes send backe by secret passages a due proporcion of the same nourishment in a better forme for the strengthening and comforteing the mouthe. 2ly the labour of the mouthe is accompanied with such pleasure and content as farre exceedes the paines it takes: soe is it in all the labour of love, among christians, the partie loveing, reapes love againe as was shewed before, which the soule covetts more then all the wealthe in the world. 4ly. noething yeildes more pleasure and content to the soule then when it findes that which it may love fervently, for to love and live beloved is the soules paradice, both heare and in heaven: In the State of Wedlock there be many comfortes to beare out the troubles of that Condicion; but let such as have tryed the most, say if there be any sweetnes in that Condicion comparable to the exercise of mutuall love.

From the former Consideracions ariseth these Conclusions.

1 First, This love among Christians is a reall thing not Imaginarie.

2ly. This love is as absolutely necessary to the being of the body of Christ, as the sinewes and other ligaments of a naturall body are to the being of that body.

3ly. This love is a divine spirituall nature free, active strong Couragious permanent under valueing all things beneathe its propper object, and of all the graces this makes us nearer to resemble the virtues of our heavenly father.

4ly, It restes in the love and wellfare of its beloved, for the full and certaine knowledge of these truthes concerning the nature use, and excellency of this grace, that which the holy ghost hath left recorded 1. Cor. 13. may give full satisfaccion which is needfull for every true member of this lovely body of the Lord Jesus, to worke upon theire heartes, by prayer meditacion continuall exercise at least of the speciall power of this grace till Christ be formed in them and they in him all in eache other knitt together by this bond of love.

It rests now to make some applicacion of this discourse by the present designe which gave the occasion of writeing of it. Herein are 4 things to be propounded: first the persons, 2ly, the worke, 3ly, the end, 4ly the meanes.

1. For the persons, wee are a Company professing our selves fellow members of Christ, In which respect onely though wee

were absent from eache other many miles, and had our im-
ploymentes as farre distant, yet wee ought to account our
selves knitt together by this bond of love, and live in the excercise of it, if wee would have comforte of our being in
Christ, this was notorious in the practise of the Christians in
former times, as is testified of the Waldenses from the mouth
of one of the adversaries Aeneas Sylvius, mutuo solent amare
penè antequam norint, they use to love any of theire owne religion even before they were acquainted with them.

2ly. for the worke wee have in hand, it is by a mutuall consent through a speciall overruleing providence, and a more
then an ordinary approbation of the Churches of Christ to
seeke out a place of Cohabitation and Consorteshipp under a
due forme of Goverment both civill and ecclesiasticall. In
such cases as this the care of the publique must oversway all
private respects, by which not onely conscience, but meare
Civill pollicy doth binde us; for it is a true rule that perticuler
estates cannott subsist in the ruine of the publique.

3ly. The end is to improve our lives to doe more service to
the Lord the comforte and encrease of the body of christe
whereof wee are members that our selves and posterity may
be the better preserved from the Common corrupcions of this
evill world to serve the Lord and worke out our Salvacion under the power and purity of his holy Ordinances.

4ly for the meanes whereby this must bee effected, they are
2fold, a Conformity with the worke and end wee aime at,
these wee see are extraordinary, therefore wee must not content our selves with usuall ordinary meanes whatsoever wee
did or ought to have done when wee lived in England, the
same must wee doe and more allsoe where wee goe: That
which the most in theire Churches maineteine as a truthe in
profession onely, wee must bring into familiar and constant
practise, as in this duty of love wee must love brotherly
without dissimulation, wee must love one another with a
pure hearte fervently wee must beare one anothers burthens,
wee must not looke onely on our owne things, but allsoe on
the things of our brethren, neither must wee think that the
lord will beare with such faileings at our hands as hee dothe
from those among whome wee have lived, and that for 3
Reasons.

1. In regard of the more neare bond of mariage, betweene him and us, wherein he hath taken us to be his after a most strickt and peculiar manner which will make him the more Jealous of our love and obedience soe he tells the people of Israell, you onely have I knowne of all the families of the Earthe therefore will I punishe you for your Transgressions.

2ly, because the lord will be sanctified in them that come neare him. Wee know that there were many that corrupted the service of the Lord some setting upp Alters before his owne, others offering both strange fire and strange Sacrifices allsoe; yet there came noe fire from heaven, or other sudden Judgement upon them as did upon Nadab and Abihu whoe yet wee may thinke did not sinne presumptuously.

3ly When God gives a speciall Commission he lookes to have it strictly observed in every Article, when hee gave Saule a Commission to destroy Amaleck hee indented with him upon certaine Articles and because hee failed in one of the least, and that upon a faire pretence, it lost him the kingdome, which should have beene his reward, if hee had observed his Commission: Thus stands the cause betweene God and us, wee are entered into Covenant with him for this worke, wee have taken out a Commission, the Lord hath given us leave to drawe our owne Articles wee have professed to enterprise these Accions upon these and these ends, wee have hereupon besought him of favour and blessing: Now if the Lord shall please to heare us, and bring us in peace to the place wee desire, then hath hee ratified this Covenant and sealed our Commission, and will expect a strickt performance of the Articles contained in it, but if wee shall neglect the observacion of these Articles which are the ends wee have propounded, and dissembling with our God, shall fall to embrace this present world and prosecute our carnall intencions, seekeing great things for our selves and our posterity, the Lord will surely breake out in wrathe against us be revenged of such a perjured people and make us knowe the price of the breache of such a Covenant.

Now the onely way to avoyde this shipwracke and to provide for our posterity is to followe the Counsell of Micah, to doe Justly, to love mercy, to walke humbly with our God, for this end, wee must be knitt together in this worke as one man, wee must entertaine each other in brotherly Affeccion, wee must be willing to abridge our selves of our superfluities, for the supply of others necessities, wee must uphold a familiar Commerce together in all meekenes, gentlenes, patience and liberallity, wee must delight in eache other, make others Condicions our owne rejoyce together, mourne together, labour, and suffer together, allwayes haveing before our eyes our Commission and Community in the worke, our Community as members of the same body, soe shall wee keepe the unitie of the spirit in the bond of peace, the Lord will be our God and delight to dwell among us, as his owne people and will commaund a blessing upon us in all our wayes, soe that wee shall see much more of his wisdome power goodnes and truthe then formerly wee have beene acquainted with, wee shall finde that the God of Israell is among us, when tenn of us shall be able to resist a thousand of our enemies, when hee shall make us a prayse and glory, that men shall say of succeeding plantacions: the lord make it like that of New England: for wee must Consider that wee shall be as a Citty upon a Hill, the eies of all people are uppon us; soe that if wee shall deale falsely with our god in this worke wee have undertaken and soe cause him to withdrawe his present help from us, wee shall be made a story and a by-word through the world, wee shall open the mouthes of enemies to speake evill of the wayes of god and all professours for Gods sake; wee shall shame the faces of many of gods worthy servants, and cause theire prayers to be turned into Cursses upon us till wee be consumed out of the good land whether wee are goeing: And to shutt upp this discourse with that exhortacion of Moses that faithfull servant of the Lord in his last farewell to Israell Deut. 30. Beloved there is now sett before us life, and good, deathe and evill in that wee are Commaunded this day to love the Lord our God, and to love one another to walke in his wayes and to keepe his Commaundements and his Ordinance, and his lawes, and the Articles of our Covenant with him that wee may live and be multiplyed, and that the Lord our God may blesse us in the land whether wee goe to possesse it: But if our heartes shall turne away soe that wee will not obey, but shall be seduced and worshipp other Gods our pleasures, and proffitts, and serve them; it is propounded

unto us this day, wee shall surely perishe out of the good
Land whether wee passe over this vast Sea to possesse it;

Therefore lett us choose life,
that wee, and our Seede,
may live; by obeyeing his
voyce, and cleaveing to him,
for hee is our life, and
our prosperity.

JOHN COTTON

The Way of Life

Or,
Gods Way and Course, in Bringing the Soule into,
keeping it in, and carrying it on, in the wayes
of life and peace.

Laid downe in foure severall Treatises on foure
Texts of Scripture.

COLOS. 3. 3, 4.
For yee are dead and your life is hid with Christ in God;
when Christ who is our Life shall appeare, then shall yee
also appeare with him in glory.

4
The Life of Faith

———

GAL. 2. 20.
Yet not I, but Christ liveth in me.

Now he corrects, or indeed rather explaines himselfe, how or what kind of life it is that he lives; Not hee, how then? Christ lives in him.

So that in these words, you have a deniall of himselfe, to be the author and roote of his owne life; he denies himselfe to live, even then when he doth live.

Secondly, You have an acknowledgement of the Author and roote of his life; Christ lives in his life.

DOCTRINE. *A living Christian lives not himselfe, but Christ in him.*

Or thus:

The life of a Christian is not his owne life, but the life of Christ Jesus.

Either of both these expresse these two parts of the verse;

A living Christian lives not himself, not his own life, but Christ lives in him.

First, See how a living Christian lives not his owne life, after once he hath had part in the death of Christ, and hath thereby beene initiated into the life and power of Christs death, and so become a mortified and crucified Christian in some measure, such a Christian lives not his own life in this world.

There is a threefold life, *A carnall life, a spirituall life, and a naturall life*; and in some respect, a living Christian lives none of these lives.

A carnall life is expressed in three things, in living to a mans *lusts*, in living to the *world*, and in living to a mans *owne wisedome and reason*.

Now a Christian man lives to none of these; He lives not to his owne lusts: *How shall we that are dead to sin live any longer therein? Rom.* 6. 2. He looks at it as an absurdity, and indeed in some measure monstrous, *ver.* 6. *The body of sin is dead in us, that we should no more serve sin*; and ver. 7. he that is dead with Christ, is *free from sinne*: arme your selves with the same minde; now you live *no longer to the lusts of men*, but to the will of God; this life *Paul* doth not live, he is not lively at his lusts, they are death to him; for though a Christian man may be defiled, and sometimes overtaken, yet so farre as he is a living Christian, so farre he is a dead man to those lusts, they are the deadnesse of his heart, the discouragement of his spirit, the hell of his soule, that he is compassed about with such evils as these be; *Oh wretched man that I am, &c. Rom.* 7. 23, 24. as if it were the death of his life, that he carried about such *a body of death* with him. Now then, saith the Apostle, if I doe that which I hate, *It is no more I that doe it, but sin that dwelleth in me, Rom.* 7. 20. It is the misery of my spirituall life, that I am at any time deadhearted to spirituall duties, and somewhat apt to close with temptations to sinne, whether darted by Satan, or stirred up by my owne corrupt heart; and therefore if there be any life of sin in me, in the least measure, it is the death of my heart.

And secondly, so neither lives he in regard of the *world*, for though you may have a godly man busie in his calling from Sunne rising to Sunne setting, and may by Gods providence fill both his hand and head with businesse, yet a living Christian when he lives a most busie life in this world, yet he lives not a worldly life.

There are foure or five severall differences between a Christian his living to the world, and another mans that is not yet alive to God, and hath no fellowship with Christ in his death.

First, A Christian man principally seeks Christ above and before the world, *Mat.* 6. 33. He doth first look for spirituall things, he had rather have his part in Christ, then in all the blessings of this life, he would first order his heart to Christ, his principall care is about that, and if he doe not so, he looks at it as his death, which a worldly man doth not.

Secondly, As he first and principally seekes Christ, so all the good things he hath, he lookes for them from Christ, he goes not about his businesse in his owne strength, but what he wants he seeks it from Christ, and what he hath he receives it from Christ, *Gen.* 33. 5, 11. If God blesse him with children, with health, or with estate, or what ever other comfort of this life, he lookes at it as a free gift of Gods grace; he doth not sacrifice to his owne nets, nor to the dexterity of his owne hands, but these are the blessings God hath graciously given to his servant, though common, and such as every one hath, yet not so to him.

Thirdly, A Christian man, as he receives the world from Christ, so he enjoyes them all in Christ; I meane he enjoyes it not in the sense of his owne desert, but he lookes at himselfe lesse then the least of them all, *Gen.* 32. 10. *I am lesse then the least of all thy faithfulnesse to thy servant.* This is to enjoy all in Christ, not in his own worth, but in the merit of Christ.

Now this a Christian doth, whatever his businesse be, in his worldly businesse, he doth not lead a worldly life.

Fourthly, Hee useth and imployeth all for Christ, In our gates, saith the Church, are all manner of pleasant fruits, my Beloved I have kept them all for thee: When he hath many blessings, he considers what he shall doe with them. This is the frame of a living Christian, one whose heart is given to Christ. I have indeed all manner of these things, faire houses, well furnished roomes, pleasant provision of all sorts, but my Beloved I have kept them all for thee, though I have never so much, yet it is all for Christ, 1 *Cor.* 10. 31. That God may be glorified in Jesus Christ; this is the summe of his eating and drinking, and buying and selling, &c. this is the upshot of all, this is all for Christ, and this is so to live in the world, as not to live like a man of the world, and so he makes good work of his worldly businesse, though in themselves never so intricate.

Fiftly, A living Christian lives unto God, even then when he lives in the world, in that he is willing to leave worldly businesse, and worldly things for Christ, leave them all, rather then part with Christ; this is the resolution of his spirit, and his practise when he is put to it, *Psal.* 45. 10. Hearken O daughter and consider, *forget thy kindred and thy Fathers house;* let them all goe, forget thy pleasures and treasures in *Pharaohs* Court, so shall the King have pleasure in thy beauty, that if any thing stand betweene obtaining of Christ, and the enjoying of the world, let all goe; were the comfort of this life never so precious and glorious, yet forget them all, let them all be as a *dead commodity for a living Christ, Matth.* 16. 27. *We have forsaken all and followed thee;* and if afterward the world and Christ should fall out, as sometimes they will, and ere long it will be that a man cannot keep his heart in a comfortable plight with Christ, but it will cost him losse of friends, and sometimes losse of estate, and sometimes losse of life, why yet a Christian will forsake all for Christ, if once the world and Christ come to fall out; and in this case a Christian thinks it no hard choyce, though *Demas* did, 2 *Tim.* 4. 10. *I passe not at all,* saith a Christian, *so that I may but finish my course with joy, Acts* 20. 23, 24. This is the true life of a Christian in respect of his Christian life, and wherein he differs from a worldly man; for there is no worldly man that lives a worldly life, but his first care is for his estate to settle that well, and when he hath thus provided for him and his, in the remanent of his time he will seek Christ.

And when he gets any thing, he depends much upon his trade, he lives unto himself, and what he hath he thinks he hath deserved it, and he will be much offended with Gods providence if he be crossed in his designs and labours. And that which he hath, for whom doth he keep it? He will say for wife, and children, and kindred; but how they will use it, that is no matter. And if it come to a parting blow, that either the world or Christ we must lose, they think men very unwise that will part with a bird in the hand for two in the bush. They may goe away sorrowfull, but away they will goe, if there bee no remedy, rather let Christ provide for himselfe; for their part, they will beare no such burthens for him; but now a Christian lives not to the world, and if hee should so live, it were rather a swoune of Christianity, then any life and power of Christ.

For *a carnall life*, which is a life of living to a mans owne wisdome and reason, he lives not that life neither, *If any man would be wise in this world, let him become a foole that hee may bee wise*, 1 *Corinth.* 3. 18, 19, 20. No living Christian but he must deny his owne wisedome, judgement, and understanding, that he may be wise in Christ; You say, what, would you have men senslesse, and mopish, and not understand themselves? No, no, here is the point, True grace doth not destroy a mans wisdome, but rather enlargeth and enlightneth it wonderfully; so as that men by nature are blinde, but spirituall wisedome enlightens the eyes of the blinde. It is an excellent speech, that in the *Heb.* 11. 1. *Faith is the substance*; in the Originall it is, Faith is the *subsistence of things not seene*; The meaning is, that if wee should tell many a man, that the favour of God is more worth then any blessing of this world, the blood of Christ more precious then gold, the spirit of grace the best companion for the soule, &c. these seeme to many a man but fained things, no subsistence in these things: This is but some strong imagination of some melancholy braines, he sees no such matter in them, and he is perswaded there is no such thing, it is onely faith that sees subsistence in these things; To a faithfull Christian there is subsistence in al the promises, there is waight in the examples, threatnings, and Commandements of the word, subsistence in the favour of God, and in the blood of Christ, and in fellowship with the spirit, and in other things there is none at all. Now in this case a man must see all his wisedome to be but folly, all the high thoughts hee had of the world and himselfe, hee must looke at them all as vain; and all the low thoughts he had of Religion and the wayes of grace, hee must looke at them all as folly and madnesse; So that here a Christian is dead to his owne wisedome; that which sometimes hee thought to have beene his chiefest good, is now nothing but vanity and vexation of spirit, but when hee comes to see spirituall things have onely true subsistence in them, then he leads a wiser life then ever hee did before.

Now for his *spirituall life*: A living Christian, his whole spirituall life is Christ, and not himselfe, his spirituall life is not his owne life.

There be three parts of spirituall life, which a Christian lives in this world, the fourth (which is the life of glory) he lives in that which is to come.

A life of Justification, a life of Sanctification, a life of spirituall Consolation.

1. A life of Justification, *Rom.* 5. 18. Now a Christian man lookes for Justification, not from all his spirituall performances, prayer, preaching, receiving Sacraments, &c. He lookes at all these as losse, that hee might winne Christ, *Not having his owne righteousnesse, Philip.* 3. 6, 7, 8, 9.

2. For his life of Sanctification, he doth not make account that himself is sufficient, as of himselfe, to thinke a good thought, 2 *Cor.* 3. 5. When God hath given him grace, yet *he can doe nothing* in any lively manner, unlesse Christ assist him, and help him at every turne, 1 *Cor.* 15. 10. *By the grace of God I am that I am, and the grace in mee was not in vaine*; but I laboured more abundantly then they all; *yet not I*, it is not I that have took all this paines; though he had a good calling, and an honest heart, *yet not I*, nay, neither was it the grace of Christ that was in him, but the *grace of God that was with him*; it was the spirit of God breathing in his grace, that made *these spices thus flow forth, Cant.* 4. *ult.* Though he had many precious graces bestowed on him yet not he, nor any grace in him, but the grace of God *with him*, that wrought with him, and acted, and did all he did wherever he came; Now blessed be God that makes manifest the savor of his grace, 2 *Cor.* 2. 12. *to* 15.

3. And thirdly, for his life of Consolation, there goe two things for the making up of a mans consolation, partly Gods favour, and that is better then life, *Psal.* 63. 3 *Psal.* 30. 5. *In thy favour is life.*

Secondly, The prospering of Gods work in themselves and

others, 1 *Thess.* 3. 8. *Now we live, if ye stand fast in the Lord*: they were his joy, and his crown and glory; But was that his life of Justification, think you? No, nor of his Sanctification neither; though the Church had falne, yet *Paul* his work had been glorious in Gods sight, and he had still been justified and sanctified; but it was the life of his consolation: this is our life, and the crowne of our rejoycing if you stand fast in the Lord.

Now for a mans *naturall life*, how can a man be said not to live his owne naturall life? Yet a Christian may say, that in some measure he lives not his owne naturall life, but Christ lives in him, *Acts* 17. 28. *In him we live, move, and have our being*: You say, so hath a carnall man his life from Christ; True, but he acknowledgeth it not; In him was life, and that was the life of men, *Joh.* 1. 3, 4. A Christian man hath his naturall life from Christ, as from an head that gives both spirituall and naturall life; In him thou hast given me life and breath, and thy visitation hath preserved my being, *Job* 12. 10. Christ gave us our life, and he preserves it, wee cannot better explaine it then thus; A wind-mill moves not onely by the wind, but in the wind; so a water-mill hath its motion, not onely from the water, but in the water; so a Christian lives, as having his life from Christ, and in Christ, and further then Christ breathes and assists, he stirs not; *Psal.* 104. 29, 30. *My times are in thy hands, Psal.* 31. 5. *Dan.* 5. 23. Thou hast not honoured thy God, *in whose hand thy breath is, and all thy wayes*, it was the sinne of the prophane King not to regard it; All his wayes and turnings, his sicknesse and health, and all his changes, they are all in Gods hands; *Jer.* 10. 23. *I know that the way of man is not in himselfe;* upon thee have I beene cast, from my mothers wombe, thou hast poured me out like milke, and by thee I was curdled in my mothers wombe, so that I live; What you *Paul?* No, not I; as if it were too broad a word for a Christian man to speake, *Though I live, yet not I.*

Now secondly, how may it be said, that Christ lives in a living Christian; How? as a roote of his life, as the Author both of his spirituall and naturall life: for his carnall life, that he is wholly dead unto; but for his other, Christ is the Actor and roote of all, for God hath given him above all *to be head of the Church*; as the members live a reasonable life from the head, so doth the Church from Christ; *Without me you can doe nothing, John* 15. 1, 2. he is called the *Prince of life, Acts* 3. 15. 1 *Cor.* 15. 45. And this comes to passe partly by Gods acceptance of him as our head; God hath appointed him to bee our head; and also by the communication of his Spirit to us, 1 *Cor.* 6. 17.

And thirdly, by faith, for it is faith that receives Christ to dwell in us, *Ephes* 3. 17. so that by these we dwell in Christ, and so live in him, and he in us, for by this meanes Christ is made our roote, *Rom.* 11. 17. so as we that were by nature *branches of the wild Olive*, are now made partakers *of the good Olive*: and hence it is, that wee bring forth savoury fruit; some fruits there bee, which if you never transplant them, they will grow wild, but transplant them, and they will bring forth fruit; so take any man that is wild by nature, and let him be crucified with Christ, cut him off from fellowship with *Adam*, and his lusts, and implant him into Christ, and then he is made partaker of the true Olive, and so will bring forth good fruit.

USE. It may be first an evident signe of tryall to every one of us, of our owne estates, whether we have part in Christs death yea or no, whether wee be living Christians, or no; Christians we are, wee cannot denie, and so have an outward right to partake with the rest of Gods people; But would you know whether you bee living Christians, or no? Consider, a living Christian lives not himselfe, but Christ lives in him; Christian signifies one *Anointed with the grace of Christ*, 1 *John* 2. 27. Now for this consider what hath beene said; If thou beest a living Christian, thou livest, yet not thou, but Christ in thee; And let me say this to every Christian soule, and take it as an eternall truth, if to this day thou livest to thy lusts, and livest in any knowne sin, and it is the delight of thy soule to live in pride, and covetousnesse, &c. if you live in any sinne, and desire so to doe, thou maiest be called a Christian, but thou art a dead Christian. But you say, you thank God, you have bid adieu to all your lusts: but it was a shrewd saying of old, *Licitis perimus omnes*, we most of us perish by lawfull things; and therefore I say further, Dost thou not live to the world? Thou sayest, Is it not lawfull for a man to be diligent in his calling, thou canst not leave thy businesse, as such

and such as are bankrupts; Well, God forbids thee not to be
diligent in thy calling; let me tell thee, if thou canst so live in
the world, as that thy first care is to seeke Christ, before the
doing of any worke of thine owne, and if to manage thy calling thou looke for helpe from him, and looke at thy selfe, as
unworthy of any mercy from God, and aske thy heart, who is
all this for? is it for Christ? canst thou say, I have kept them
all for thee? and canst thou come to this resolution, that if
Christ and thy calling come to be at variance, yet thou canst
part with all to keepe fellowship with Christ? then thou livest
in the World, but art not a man of the World; Christ sits next
to thy heart all this while, and then thou art well; but otherwise let mee tell thee, if thou canst first be busie about thy
calling, and thinke you have wit enough for your owne businesse, and you think you deserve all you have, else you would
not bee so much disturbed when you are crossed in it; and if
you use them not for Christ, but you lose him in the use of
them, and you keepe it, that you and yours may bee some
great ones in the World; and if a crosse way come, that Christ
and your estates must part, you turne your back upon Christ,
and upon all that professe his name; then bee not a lyer
against the truth, thou art of the world, and livest to the
world, and the Lord Jesus hath yet no hold of thee; and
therefore bee sure if it bee so with you, you have failed in one
of these; you have stirred about worldly businesse, before you
looked for Christ, and gone about them in your owne
strength, and in sense of your owne worthinesse of them,
which makes you discontent when you are crossed in them,
and you consider not for what end you laid up all these; and
hence it is, that when it comes to a parting blow, many a
Christian is foiled about the world: and therefore looke seriously to it, and if you conceive worldly things have some subsistence in them, but not so of the things of GOD, then it is
not Christ that lives in you, but you live to your selves.

  USE 2.   To cast a just reproofe upon living Christians, that
Christian men should not live like Christian men; a shame for
Christian men still to live in pride, and uncleannesse, committing the works of darknesse; and therefore bee ashamed
that ever you should take up the life of a Christian, and still
bee more forward for the world, then for Christ; still to bee

impatient for worldly crosses, and still to want serious thoughts for whom is all this, and yet not come to consider how you must part from all these. This may cast much confusion upon the face of a Christian man, that to this day they cannot say that they live unto Christ. Some there be, who say, that they live unto Christ, and some that say, they will not have Christ to reigne over them, *Luke* 19. 14. some there be that say; Let us breake his bonds asunder, and cast his cords from us, *Psal.* 2. but it were a shame that any Christian should do so.

USE 3. To teach us all, in the name of the Lord Jesus Christ, to desire to make knowne to our owne consciences, and to the world, that wee are crucified with Christ, and live to God; let us say, it is not enough for a Christian to live besides his lusts, or that the world is lesse to be regarded then Christ, &c. but I pray you practise this resolution daily, unlesse you have some thoughts of this daily, you will lose your spiritual life daily, and you never finde your hearts lost in worldly businesse; but when you want a heart daily to consider what God cals you to, you must therefore have these thoughts daily. And further, take this counsell, if thou beest troubled about thy justification and peace with God, let this comfort thee, that thou knowest thou livest not by thine owne graces, but by Christ.

USE 4. Of comfort and consolation, to every soule as can truly say, this is the frame of their hearts, they doe not live themselves, but Christ in them; bee not you discouraged at your owne weaknesse, but make account your living in Christ will beare you out, and therefore labour to be loose to the World, and live like those that have a living fountaine to run unto, for supply of what ever you stand in need of, that so all the rest of our time may not be a life of our owne lusts, but of Christ in us.

THOMAS HOOKER

The Paterne of Perfection

*Exhibited in Gods Image on Adam:
And Gods Covenant made with him.*

*Remember from whence thou art fallen, and repent, and
do the first works, or else I will come unto thee quickly,
and will remove thy Candlestick out of his place, except
thou repent,* REV. 2/5.

———

7.
Of Gods Image in the Affections

Now wee proceed to the image of God in the affections of
Adam, as love, joy, delight, sorrow, feare, which are seated in
the sensitive soule; for all sensitive creatures have them. The
poore creature feares the whip; and the creature againe, sports
and delights it selfe. Now these *Adam* had, and in these was
the image of God.

Qu. What was the image of God in the affections of
Adam?

Ans. It appeared in that serviceable subjection, sweet
agreement, and submission which they did yeeld unto holy
will, and right reason. The Understanding directed what should bee done, the Will imbraced
that, and the Affections yeelded serviceably to the command
of Reason and Holinesse. Herein appeared the difference between these affections in *Adam*, and in other creatures. The
creature is carried by the rule of appetite; the horse rusheth
into the battell, the wild asse snuffeth up the winde. The
Psalmist saith, *Bee not like the horse and mule, which have no
understanding, Psal.* 32. Here was the excellency of *Adam*;
that wisdome that God had imprinted in his understanding,
that holinesse that hee had implant in his will, commanded

(margin) What it is

54

his affections, and they did sweetly yeeld thereto. *Adams* soule was like a well-tuned instrument, all the strings (the affections) being rightly tuned, make a sweet harmony. In a well governed common-wealth, the Councel directs, the King enacts lawes, and the subjects obey: so there was wisdome in *Adams* understanding, and that counselled; there was holinesse in the will, and that commanded; and all the affections were like loyall subjects, imbracing what reason and holy will commanded. In this common-wealth there were no traitors; no, in *Adams* heart there were no tumultuous disorders, as now we finde; but what the reason said, and the will chused, that the affections embraced.

QUEST.   Wherein doth this subjection discover it selfe? How shall wee see *Adams* affections submitting to reason?

ANS.   In foure particulars.

1. The affections of *Adam* were willing to entertaine every command which wisedome and holinesse gave. The affections are but so many servants that attend on the understanding. 1 *Pet.* 5. 9. *Bee sober and watch*: There is a sobriety required in the soul; namely, a man should not lavish out his affections on other things, and so unfit himself to be under the subjection of the Truth. This sobriety was abundant in *Adam*; he had a sweet easinesse and softnesse of affection, like waxe, to take the print of Gods Seale: whereas it is with our affections as with drunken servants, who, when their Masters call them, are not themselves: for there is a drunkennesse in mans heart, when it is inordinately carried with too eager a pursuit after vaine things; & though reason commands, yet it obeyeth not. *Adams* affections were in a sweete frame: for if God revealed any command, love embraced it. *Ephes.* 6. 15. *Having your feet shod with the preparation of the Gospel of peace.* The feet are the affections; the shooing of the feet, is the preparing of the affections to entertaine all the conditions of the Gospel of peace. A man that is shod, is fit to goe a journey: so when the affections are thus shod, they are fit to walke in any way that God requires. Since *Adam* lost this sobriety of affections, what awkwardnesse doe wee finde to duty! when a man should love an enemy, how hardly is hee brought to it! when a man ought to reforme a sinne, what a difficulty is there in it!

(margin note: Wherein the affections submitted to reason.)

2. They were speedy in the performance of what was in-joyned them. A wise understanding could no sooner reveale a duty to be done, but they eccohed answerably, This all of us would have *Psalm.* 40. mark how speedy Christ was in per-forming of duty: *Behold I come, thy law is within mine heart.* And *Psal.* 27. 8. *The Lord saith, seek yee my face*: and his affec-tions answered, *Thy face (Lord) will I seeke.* Also in *Psal.* 119. 4, 5. Gods voice saith, *I charge you diligently, keepe my Com-mandements*: and they eccho again, *Oh that our wayes were made so direct, that we might keep thy Statutes!* 1 *Pet.* 1. 13. *Gird up the loyns of your mind.* And in *Luk.* 12. 35. it is said, *Let your loynes bee girded about, and your lights burning.* The loynes of our mindes are our affections. They are compared to loose garments, such as they wore in the East Countries, which they girded up, when they went on a journey. Our af-fections hang like loose garments about us, wee must gird them up, that we may with more speed goe in the pathes of Gods Statutes. Thus *David* prayeth: *Set mine heart at liberty, that I may runne the wayes of thy commandements.* But we find the contrary: for though many times the minde so yeelds, that the course is holy, yet what a base wearinesse hangs on the heart! what slow hearts have we! how doe we draw our loyns after us! We feele this; and the ground of it is the want of Gods image.

3. They continued in the speed they made. *Adams* affec-tions were to hold themselves in an holy bent, without warp-ing. Wee finde the contrary. In *Gal.* 6. the Apostle saith, *Bee not weary in well doing.* Sometimes a man is hot at first, and then his affections coole; this is the bane of Religion. Hee *was* holy; so they may say of a man-devill, an Angell of light. But *Adam* was able to hold himselfe in a right pitch. This *David* prayed for, *Psal.* 51. 12. when he had wounded his affections, *Oh stablish mee with thy free spirit!* as if he should say: Time was, when I did love thy Word, mine heart did feare evill, and I did hate uncleannesse; but now, how unstedfast are my af-fections! therefore *stablish mee with thy free spirit.* If you finde your hearts giving way to any base lusts, you shall finde them easily giving back from holy duties. *Rev.* 2. 31. *Thou hast for-saken thy first love*: O woe to that declining condition; that those who heretofore expressed forwardnesse in a good

course, and could cry for mercy as for life, are now key-cold: But *Adams* affections were able to keep themselves in full strength: and so did the Saints of God. *Num.* 14. 24. Caleb *followed God fully. Psalm.* 63. 9. *My soule followes hard after thee.* Hee pursued God with eagernesse, as the creature the prey. *David* stands not still, nor delayes, but pursueth; and as the phrase is, (*Esa.* 51. 1) *follows after righteousnesse.* Thou that hast a stubborne heart by nature, if thou beest once righteous, thou wilt then follow after meeknesse.

4. His affections were in an orderly tractablenesse to the rule of reason and holinesse. Reason and holinesse gave not only direction to the affections, but moderation in all things, and upon all occasions. The affections would not bee carried out of order nor measure upon any thing, nor stay longer then they should upon any object. An Embassador goes no farther then his Commission, stayes no longer then his Commission gives leave: so reason and holinesse were the commanders of *Adams* affections; they received a command therefrom, and went no further then reason and holinesse allowed them. It is lawfull for a man to love the world; but no more then reason and holinesse allowes: if God should say, I will take away these things from thee, love and joy should willingly part with them. The souldier, if he be loyall, when the Commander biddeth battell, hee goes; when hee soundeth a retrait, he returnes home againe: so the reason and will sanctified, were the commanders of *Adams* course. When reason and holinesse saith it, a man may delight in the things of this life; but when they say, grieve no more for the losse of them, the affections should yeeld to the command of reason. It is quite contrary in us; a mans affections, though they are set upon a lawfull object, yet they goe so amaine like unruly colts, that they cast the rider: delight and desire outbid reason, and sometimes transgresse the bounds of honesty, most commonly of holinesse. It is marvellous hard to have our affections at command. *Lot* goes into Sodom, and God could not get him out againe, but that the Angel was faine to carry him out by force: so when a man gets into Sodom, lets loose his affections on shoppe, or children, or the like, oh what an hard matter is it to say, No more of that! But *Adams* affections were so ordered, that if reason should say, Love

that now, and then leave it; hee would love it now, and leave it then. *Philip.* 4. 12. *I know how to abound, and how to bee poore*; his meaning is, if God would bestow these things, he had an heart to love them; if hee would take them away, he was content to leave them. *Job* 1. 21. *The Lord hath given, and the Lord hath taken away, blessed be the name of the Lord*; whereas wee sit *Rachel*-like, disquieted, because our comforts are not.

USE 1.   The first Use is of examination. A man may here plainely perceive what measure of grace hee hath, and whether hee hath any or no: See what tractablenesse there is in thy affections, to submit unto the authority of holinesse. So much boysterousnesse as thou findest against the evidence of reason, and frame of holinesse; so much corruption there is in thy heart. I speak this the rather, to take off the conceit of many, who use to commend a man in this manner; Hee is an holy man, but that hee hath one fault, hee is as dogged as may be: it is but a poor commendation. So much boyling as is in thine heart, so much want of grace is there. He is a good Christian (they will say) but wonderfull outragious: surely then there is but little good in him. The servant is stubborne against his Master, the master againe is quarrelsome for every word: if there bee grace in these, it is well; yet there is a great deale of the want of Gods image upon such a soule: 1 *Cor.* 3. 3. *When there are strifes and envyings amongst you, are ye not carnall?* When the heart is boysterous and full of envie, is it not carnall? There is a great deal of rubbish in thy heart, which grace, if it were there, would remove. The Philosopher observes, that all stormes are here below in these baser bodies, there is none of them in the highest heavens: so, hadst thou an heavenly heart, all thunderings and lightenings, all crosse, dogged, and malicious distempers would bee gone, there would bee no newes of them. *The fruits of the Spirit are love, meeknesse, &c.* But when men runne abreast, the Master his way, and the Servant his way, where are the fruits of the Spirit? Are ye not carnall?

OB.   But may not a man by education or misery bee tempered, and cooled from these things?

[margin note: By order in thy affections, esteeme what grace thou hast.]

ANSW. Yes, he may have the ruggednesse of his affections smoothed, and the edge of furiousnesse blunted. But though a man may have these somewhat abated, and want grace, yet if a man have these, it is somewhat suspicious, whether hee have grace. There may bee a root, and yet no blossomes, and yet it is certaine, where there are blossomes there is a root. If a man expresse envie in his life, there is sure a treasure of it in his heart. If there be so much filth in the streames, there is more in the fountaine: if there be good in thee, there is but a little.

Here we may also see, whether wee have any truth of grace: judge of it by the works. No fire but will burn: fire will heate the whole house; so grace will frame the whole soule. Art thou able to tame those jarring affections, and to stifle them? Art thou able, when they would transport thee, to allay them, and bring thy soule to a calme frame? Then it is a signe thou hast grace. God is the God of order, not only in the Church, but in the house, and every where. If thou canst master those boysterous affections, that they may be subject unto wisdome and holinesse, then it is certaine, there is some grace in thee.

QUEST. But are not the best men troubled with passions and distempers?

ANSW. There are such in the best, upon whom the Lord hath beene pleased to look graciously: but they are in a farre different manner in them, then in the wicked. Their spots are different: *Deut.* *Differences of distempers in the godly and others.*
32. 5. *Their spot is not like the spot of my children*: as who should say, the Saints have their spots, and the wicked have their spots; but they are not the same. The spots of the purples are dangerous, but the spots of the plague are deadly. The wicked have the spots of the plague; the Lord have mercy on them, they are but dead men. Though a Common-wealth bee subject to conspiracies, yet a wise King can discover them; but when there is no King, (as in Israel) every man doth what he list: so in the heart of an ungodly man, corruptions do what they list, they make him as proud, and as covetous as they list. The Saints have many mutinies in their hearts, yet they have a wise King, a gracious will that quels these, and submits to God, and the power of his grace.

The difference betweene the distempers of the Saints and the wicked, appeares in three particulars.

1. The Saints make those distempers and unruly affections which lye upon them, their greatest burthen; it is their heart-smart, though other sins are greater: and the reason is, because they break the union between God and the soule, and they breed a distance between Gods good Spirit and it. 2 *Cor.* 12. 7. God suffered Sathan to buffet St. *Paul*, which was some distemper, and provocation to sin; now this made him grone and sigh to the Lord, yea, it brought him on his knees thrice. As it is with an enemie, if his use bee to come suddenly upon a Towne, a wise Captaine will gather his forces together to hinder his designes: So must the Saints, because their corruptions surprize them suddenly. These make them cry out, This will be my bane; the least sin will damne me as well as the greatest; *I shall perish one day by the hand of Saul, &c.* whereas a carnall man maketh nothing of these, but beares all with a Pish, it is not such a great matter as some make it: I confesse I am passionate and cholerick; but I would I had no worse to answer for, and the like. Oh, how doth this argue a gracelesse heart, that can thus digest gracelesse courses. A toad will feede upon poison; but if a man take two or three drops, it will kill him: it is a signe thou hast a toadish nature, that canst digest these lusts. *Gen.* 15. *ult. Esau* went away carelesly, when hee saw that hee lost his birthright. I confesse, it is possible for a carnall heart to grieve for these distempers, but it is either when a man hath monstrously befooled himselfe, or when conscience flies in his face; What, you go to heaven? Therefore a man on these termes may crouch, not because of sin, but of disgrace, or the sting of conscience, that lies in his bosome.

2. The Saints, when they are thus, it is but a pang, they come to their cold temper againe, and they then will welcomly entertain the word, and desire that it would discover their sinne. A gracious heart cares not what the man bee that discovers his sinne, whether he bee friend or enemy, whether a good man or a bad man. Hee lookes not at the man, but at the goodnesse of the command. 1 *Sam.* 1. 17. *Eli*, when he had been indulgent, and the Lord threatned him for it, hee saith to *Samuel, Hide nothing from mee. Jonah* being in a sullen fit,

forsakes Gods command; but this is but in a push; in cold
blood hee is otherwise. *David*, that had the heart of a Lyon,
he would not leave a man alive in *Nabals* house; yet *Abigail*,
a woman, makes him say, *Blessed be thou, & thy counsell*: here
was a gracious heart, that could submit to the counsell of so
mean a person. But a wicked man cannot abide to have his
corruption crossed: they are so incorporated into it, that they
cannot live without it: This was it that made the young man
go away sorrowfull. They murmure against their instructers,
as the Hebrew said to *Moses, Exod.* 2. 14. *What, wilt thou slay
mee, as thou didst the Egyptian yesterday*? Let every cup stand
upon his owne bottome; what have you to doe with mee? &c.
A wicked man may bite the lip for the present, and say, I
thanke you for your counsell; yet he will goe away, and fit you
an evill turne. But the godly come, and acknowledge plainely,
These passages and grace cannot stand together, and therefore they will submit to the truth with all their heart. A
wicked man will use all means to undermine the truth, and
misconstrue it; and if any man will joyn side with him, hee
will fly out desperately: but if hee cannot avoid it, hee will
(like the dogge) bite the stone; if hee cannot have his will of
the man, hee will owe him a grudge. The Saints will say, *The
Word of the Lord is good*, strike here at this sin, smite home.

3. The Saints are not only carefull to have their sinnes outwardly mortified, but their lives reformed; they do not complain of this and that, and yet maintaine it: no, hee that is
burthened with sinne, will part with it. *Luk.* 2. 8. When Christ
came, *crooked things were made straight*: not onely mountaines
were brought low, but *rough things* were made *smooth*: So in
the Saints of God, there is not onely a new tongue, to talke
of religion; but a new heart, and new affections. It is possible
for a godly man by the power of tentation to bee led aside,
yet you shall alwayes finde him on the mending hand, and so
in conclusion forsakes sin. I do not say, he will bee now and
then drunk, and the like; (for we doe not read of those, that
after they accustome themselves to gross sins, do ordinarily
rise again;) but I speake of some boysterous distemper which
breaks out, yet I say, hee will bee of the mending hand. As a
man in an Ague, when nature growes strong, his Ague will
leave him: so if a man bee overtaken with these, if grace grow

strong, hee will leave them, else hee erres from the nature of true repentance. You know what God calls for, when hee requires repentance, *Isa.* 1. 24. *Cease to doe evill, learne to doe well. Jer.* 26. 3. *Isa.* 55. 7. *Let the wicked forsake his way, and the imaginations of his heart.* This is repentance; this the Saints have done, as holy *Job* speaks, chap. 34. 32. *If I have done iniquity, I will doe so no more. Psalm.* 18. 23. *I have kept my selfe from mine iniquity. Gal.* 5. 24. *They that are in Christ, have crucified the flesh with the lusts thereof:* the flesh is sin, the lusts thereof are the violent distempers thereof; hee that hates sinne, kils these. Can any man kill the roote, and the blossome flourish? so, can the root of sinne bee killed, and the fruit thrive? It cannot be. Again, morality can make a man somewhat qualified, and cannot grace much more? shall a Heathen bridle himselfe, and not a gracious man? That cannot be. But a wicked man gives way to, and continues in his course without any amendment, and that's the reason why they fall to day, and fall to morrow, and continue in it. *Jer.* 8. 6. He takes fast hold of iniquity, and rusheth into it, *as the horse rusheth into the battell*: for a man customarily, usually to bee transported with these boysterous distempers, this is the spot of the wicked; no righteous man can alwaies bee thus: for hee hath not that depth of wickednesse in him; yet upon some occasion hee may and doth fall into sin. You see how the godly are, and how the wicked behave themselves. The wife railes, and the husband, out of a kind of sottish *Nabalnesse*, if any thing fall crosse, makes the wife and child pay for it. This is ordinary, these are the plague-sores of our townes; also the servant, if hee be admonished, then hee flies out, and warning must bee given presently to be gone. These are the spots of profession now-adaies.

Grace, ordering the affections, brings the most quiet life.   USE 2. It is a word of instruction, That a gracious heart brings most quiet to a mans life: that takes away the greatest troubles: that is most peaceable. Nothing can trouble a gracious heart, unlesse hee trouble himselfe. It is not the blowing of the winde that shakes the earth; but the wind is got into some hollow of the earth, and the shaking comes from within: so, when there is envie & malice within, these breed hatred without, and these shake our holds: whereas, were these removed, were a man quiet at home, hee should never be troubled from without. It is not a mans condition, but his corruption that breeds discontent; therefore St. *Paul* saith, *I can abound, and be poor*; hee had quiet within him. Looke, as it was with our Saviour, *Math.* 8. when the winds arose, hee commands them to cease; so it is in the Lords power to rule these distempers: nothing under heaven can quiet a man thus enraged, but grace. Goe to God to take away thy unrulinesse. Grace makes a man on Gods side, and therefore there can bee no dissention: if God takes away any thing, the good soule is content; if hee will have any thing, the soule yeelds it, and so here is no trouble.

THOMAS HOOKER

The Application of Redemption

By the Effectual Work of the Word, and Spirt of Christ, for the bringing home of lost Sinners to God.

Book X.

On Acts, 2. 37.
When they heard this, they were pricked to the heart, and said to Peter, *and the rest of the Apostles, Men and Brethren, what shall we do?*

DOCT. 3.
APPLICATION OF SPECIAL SINS BY THE MINISTRY, IS A MEANS TO BRING MEN TO SIGHT OF, AND SORROW FOR THEM.

———

The description of contrition stood of two parts wherby the nature of the work was especially discoverd.

Partly in the
{
  Causes of it, { *Sight of sin,*
  Sorrow for sin.

  Effects of it, { *Detestation of sin.*
  Sequestration from sin.
}

CONCERNING the sight of sin so far as it serves our turn in a true conviction of it, in that they stood here as accused by *Peter* and condemned in their own Consciences as guilty of no less than the blood of Jesus, we have already spoken.

The second thing in the text to be considered is the means how this was wrought. And these are two.

The first, *is a particular Application of their special corruption,* the Apostle doth not hover in the general and shoot at rovers, but comes close to them, chargeth them expresly in a special manner, and lets fly in the very faces of them, *this Jesus whom yee have crucified*, he names not, he blames not any other, he sayes not *Judas* was a wretch that betrayed him, the souldiers cruel that took him, *Pilate* base and fearful and unjust that condemned him, no this is the *Jesus and you are the men that have committed this villany*, A person could not be more innocent, a practice more bloody, you are men that stand guilty of this horrible abomination of *Crucifying the Lord of Glory*. The Doctrine from hence is this.

DOCT. *A plain and particular Application of special sins by the Ministry of the word is a special means to bring the soul to a sight of, and sorrow for them.*

Plain Application and powerful conviction go together. *Let the house of Israel know that God hath made him Lord and Christ whom ye have crucifyed;* you are the men I mean, this is your sin I mention. Thus our saviour the great Prophet of His Church, who spake as never man spake and best knew how to deal with deceitful hearts, he layeth his finger upon the sore, and mark how he pincheth with particulars, as his ordinary manner of dispensation was to the Churches; *Rev.* 3. 2. *I know thy works, thou hast a name to be alive but thou art dead.* I say thou art hypocritical, and I know what I say, and I tell thee openly what I know, thou hast a form of profession but thou hast no heart nor life nor power of religion in thy course; He that could not erre in what he did teach, he teacheth what Ministers should do in their dispensation; And there was nothing more usual with our Saviour, then to point out particular sins and sinners; *Woe be to you Scribes, Pharisees, Hypocrites. Math.* 23. and therefore he doth not closly and covertly as it were give a kind of intimation, afar off what he would, and leaves men to pick and search out his meaning; but tells them their own in English as we say: plucks them out by the pole goes not behind the dore to tel men their faults, but gives in testimony against their sin and that to their teeth; *Luke.* 16. 15. when the Pharisees in an impudent manner, began to mock at him, he lets fly poynt blanck, *You are they that justefy your selves but the Lord knows your hearts;* Yea it was the charge he gives to al his prophets, when they were to deal with the Jewes and to dispense his counsels unto them,

Hos. 2. 1. 2. *Plead with your Mother plead, tell her she is not my Wife.* [Plead] is a Law term, cal her by name, summon her into the court of Conscience, follow the suit against her Lay the charge and plead the Acton against her particular sins. Thus *Stephen Acts.* 7. 51. *Yee stiff-necked and hard hearted, yee have alwayes resisted the holy Ghost, as your Fathers did so do yee.* So the Apostle frequently *Acts,* 4. 10. 11. *be it known to you and to all the people of Israel, that in the name of Jesus &c. whom ye have crucifyed, This is the stone refused by you builders,* you are the men, and this is your evil.

The Reasons shall be touched in a word.

REASON I. *The place and duty of a Minister requires this,* who hath a special charge, and therefore should have a particular care to foresee, and so to prevent the particular and special evils, which he perceives to blemish the Christian course, and endanger the spiritual comforts of the people under his guidance and of whose safety he must give an account; and this wil not be done unless a man single out the persons and set home their sins in special. The steward is not only to know the several conditions of the persons in the family but to provide a portion suitable for each, if ever the safety of the whol be provided for; and the cordials for the weak, milk for the little ones, and stronger meat for those who are of able strength; the Skil of the Physitian & the onely way to cure a settled and inward distemper as the dropsy or falling sickness, is not to give the patient an ordinary purge, a common receit; that every Quack-salver wil do and do no good at al; But he must have that wisdom to hit the humor, and to provide ingredients that wil suit the temper of the party and the particular nature of the disease; So it is the part of a skilful Minister to hit the humor of the heart of a sinner; to make a receipt on purpose to meet with the particular distemper such as wil worke upon, or sluggishness pride hypocrisie, perversness and as the medicine doth upon the spleen or choller, and so the Lord to the Prophet *Ezek.* 16. 2. *Cause the house of Israel to know their abominations;* The Sedulous shepheard who indeed would provide for the wellfare of his sheep, its not enough that by common survey he casts his eye upon them, but he must pen them, and handle them, search them and dress them, according to their several ayls, and such

Maladies unto which they are subject. So a faithful Minister must deal with poor sinners, as with the Sheep commended to his care and custody; he must find them in their particular evils, and follow them with application of special helps.

REAS. 2. *The necessity of sinners requires this:* For this manner of the delivery of the Truth, it awakens and stirs up the mind and heart of the Hearer to a more serious attention to that which is spoken, and settles the heart upon a more through consideration of himself and his waies; unto both which the soul of a sinner rocked as it were asleep in the security of a sinful course, is loth to come; not willing to hear any thing that would trouble him in his sins, and very ready to lay aside the consideration of that he hears in that behalf. Whereas particular application provokes to the practice of both, cals a man by name as it were, that he must come to his Answer; he cannot avoid it, it wil not suffer him to make an escape before he give in his Answer: This flings in the light so ful into mens faces that it forceth them to look about them. General Truths generally do little good. That which is spoken to all, is spoken to none at al. No man heeds more than needs he must to such things he hath little heart unto, or takes little delight in. An Inditement or Attachment without a name, read, published, and proclaimed in the face of the World, no man is either troubled at it, or reclaimed by it; but when the name is recorded, and the man challenged, it makes him bethink himself how to get a Surety, or pay the debt, or prevent the danger. So is it with a general reproof, no man will own it, and therefore no man reforms by it, or is forced to seek out. Thus *Nicodemus* never left cavilling before the Lord came home to his own person, and touched him to the quick, *John,* 3. 20. *Art thou a Master in Israel, and knowest thou not these things?* See and be ashamed; a Master not to know that which a Scholler might and should. It's not enough that we be stirring in the house, and people be up, but we must knock at mens doors, bring a Candle to their bed-sides, and pinch the sluggard, and then if he have any life he wil stir. While the Ministers of the Lord are preaching and publishing the Mind and Counsel of God in the Assemblies, there is some stirring in Gods house, but yet the secure person sits and sleeps on the stool as the sluggard in his bed, unless some special

Application pinch him to the quick: then he begins to look up, and ask who is there? So it was with *David, thou art the man* did prevail more with him than al *the Parable*, 2 *Sam*. 12. As the noise of a piece afar off makes the Fowl listen, but one scattered shot that fals upon the wing or leg makes them cry and stir. All the common discourse came not neer *David*, but *thou art the man*; three words like three smal shot awakened him with a witness.

REAS. 3. *The Nature of the Word calls for this manner of dispensation as that which suits and serves best for the end and work of it.* It makes it hit sooner, and pierce more deeply and prevailingly into the heart: The speech of the Minister and his words are like darts and arrows, the right and particular applying them is the level carriage of them to the heart, and so they hit unavoidably, and fasten strongly thereupon. General discourses are like arrows shot a cock-height at al adventures without aim, and so without success or special profit, or powerful work upon the hearer; men come and go away not touched, not troubled, not affected with any thing. The word is compared to a *Sword*, the Explication is like the drawing of it. So the Truth in the naked Nature and vertue of it comes to be discovered; but the florishing of the Sword wil never do the deed. But he that handles it suitable to the end and work of it, he must follow the blow if he purpose to force his Enemy either to fly or yield. So it is with the Truth: downright blows puts sometimes the most cunning Fencer past his Sence; so these cunning Hypocrites beyond all their Shifts. See how the Woman of *Samaria, John*, 4. 18, 19. Put off our Savior with fond Cavils, sawcy and contemptuous Speeches, until our Savior met with her in particular, *Go call thy Husband*, she answers, *I have no Husband*; our Savior comes within her, *Thou hast had five Husbands, and he whom now thou hast is not thine Husband, in that thou sayest right*, thou poor sinful Adulteress; then she fel before our Savior. It is in a mans Spiritual as it is with a mans outward estate. The Bond lies forfeited, and the careless Debtor or Bankerupt he looks not out to pay. He hears the news of a Writ out for him, but sees none to arrest, and therefore he grows fearless. But when the Sergeant arrests him, and drags him to prison, you wil not provide for your debt to pay, provide then to go to prison, that makes him begin to send to friends, to gather up his debts, sel his Commodities, crave Baile and Surety. So it is with careless prodigal sinners which suffer their souls and salvations to lie forfeit, and yet look not out, until some particular word meet and make an arrest upon the soul, and the Minister by his Commission like the Sergeant seizeth upon him, you wil not forsake your sins, you must therefore perish in your sins. He then begins to bethink himself what to do.

USE I. *We here see the reason why there is so little good done by the Ministry of the Word upon the hearts of ungodly men:* Many Hypocrites lie skulking under the covers of deceit, and are not discovered; many proud hearts not humbled, but go on in their sturdy distempers; many sleepers sit and snort in their security, and go hood-winked down to destruction, and see nothing before they sink into the pit. We do not knock at mens doors, we do not bring the light to their bed-sides, we do not pinch them indeed with sharp and particular reproofs, and those set on to purpose; we do not put them beyond their fence, we do not keep them under the arrest of some conviction, so that they cannot make an escape; but each carnal reason rescues them from the hold of some common Truths that happily are delivered. Oh we level not, we hit not, we apply not the Word so home, so particularly as the occasions, conditions, corruptions of men require; and therefore it prevails not with that power, finds not that success which otherwise it might. Common Reproofs are like the confused noise in the Ship when the Marriners were rowing *Jonah* to the shore, notwithstanding all which, *Jonah* lies and sleeps under hatches: But when they go down to him, and laid hold upon him, and awakened him with a witness, *Arise thou sluggard, and call upon thy God, lest we all perish, Jonah,* 1. 5. He then began to bethink himself where he was, and what he had done; and then remembred that though he had feared and served the God of Heaven, yet by his rebellion he had departed away from him. So here, all the while we take up mens minds, and exercise their Ears and thoughts with some hovering Discourses, and common words of course, *We are all sinners, In many things we offend all, All flesh is frail;* but I hope better things of you, I hope there is none such amongst you.

Those daubing discourses and roving reproofes, toothless, powerless dispensations, like arrowes shot a cock-height, they touch not, trouble not, and in the issue profit no man at all. They come proud and stubborn and perverse and careless, they sit so and returne so, day after day and year after year. But you should shake up a sinner, go down under the hatches to *Jonah* set upon the hearts of men in particular *Awake thou sluggard*. Thou a master of a family and teachest not, instructest not those that are under thee? Thou a servant yet stubborn and perverse, and submits not to those that are set over thee in the Lord? Art thou a Wife and dost not reverence and obey with fear him whom God hath made thy head and guide? Art thou a member of a Christian Congregation, and hast the name of Christ called upon thee, and art thou treacherous to the Covenant of Christ, opposest the government and spirit of Christ, and despisest the ordinances of the Lord Jesus? Awake you careless masters and rebellious servants, perverse wives, treacherous and faithless members; Know that your Religion is vain and your selves also while these distempers rest in your bosom; cal upon your own hearts for Humiliation and repentance, and unto God for mercy that you perish not. Thus when *Peter* was recovered out of his fal, and had the blood of Christ running warm in his veynes, and the power of the spirit of the Lord now setting on the right hand of the Father filling his heart with love to his Saviour and zeal for his glory; see how sharply he applies the keenest reproofes to cut the Consciences of al to whom he speaketh without fear or partiality, *Acts.* 4. 10. 11. Be it known to you, *Oh ye rulers and all yee people of Israel, that by the name of Jesus of Nazareth whom yee have crucified, you have slayn the just and innocent one and desired a murderer to be given to you &c.* and see the success, *God added daily to the Church such as should be saved.* It's *Cartwrights* expression, when our saviour sent out *the sons of thunder then Satan fel like lightening from Heaven*, the right levelling the ordinances of Christ wil undoubtedly make battery in the kingdom of Satan; sharp reproofs make sound Christians. It's a course which God commends in scripture, and hath not fayled to bless. *Judges* 2. 4. When the Angel pleaded the inditement so punctually so plainly against the people, their hearts brake al in pieces under such blowes, *they lift up their voyces and wept,* they left cavilling and replying, and fell to weeping bitterly.

USE 2. *Here see the reason why the best preaching finds the least and worst acceptance at the hands of rebellious sinners,* that which works, and troubles most, that they most distast, that which gives the least quiet to them, so that they give the least respect and liking. Like children they love raw fruit which wil breed worms and sickness, rather then worme-seed though that would prevent both. So men love raw and windy discourses to please sinful humors, and corrupt hearts, rather than some bitter and particular reproofs which would make them sound in the Faith. *Ahab* wil nourish *four hundred false Prophets at his Table,* feed them with Dainties, and make choyce provision for them, that they may feed his humor, and speak good things to him, when he is not able to abide the sight, scarce to hear the name of *Micaiah* the Prophet of the Lord, who would speak the Counsel of the Lord without fear and partiality, 1 *Kings,* 22. So they in *Isai.* 30. 10. *They say to the Seers, see not; and to the Prophets, prophesie not unto us right things; prophesie smooth things:* such as might suit their sensual Appetites, and would down without chewing. And it's strange to see when such men have told a grave tale, and vented a heartless, toothless discourse, neither pith nor power in it; I say, it's strange to see what admiration and esteem such carnal hearts wil set upon such persons and expressions; great their parts, prudence, and discretion: Oh how sweet and seasonable their discourse, how glad to hear, and how unweariable to attend such: And al the while they may sit and sleep in their sinful condition, and neither have their Consciences awakened, nor their corruption discovered. Squeamish Stomachs had rather take Sugar-sops a whol week together than a bitter Potion one day. This is the Disease which *Paul* complains of as incident to the last Age of the World; and therefore adviseth his Scholler *Timothy,* 2 *Tim.* 4. 2, 3. *To be instant in season, out of season, convince, rebuke, exhort, for the time will come that men will not endure sound Doctrine; but according to their proper lusts, having itching Ears, will heap to themselves Teachers:* itching Ears must be scratched, not boxed.

USE 3. Information: *It's not only in the Liberty, but it's the*

Duty of a Minister, according as the Text suits, and the condition of the Hearers answer, to aim at the sins of the persons and people to whom he speaks. Particular application implies a special intendment of the parties, 1 *Kings*, 21. 20. When *Ahab* met *Elijah*, he salutes him on this manner, *Hast thou found me, O mine Enemy?* He answers him, *I have found thee*, q.d. It was my duty to do so, and therefore I have endeavored it, and according to my desire and endeavor I have accomplished it, I came on purpose. *Ezek.* 33. 8. *If the Watch-man do not warn the wicked from his way, that wicked man shall die in his iniquity; but his blood will I require at his hand.* The necessity of the people, the nature of the work which he intends, and the charge of his place which lies upon him, cals for this at the hands of a Minister. Will not common Sense conceive it reasonable, that the Physitian discover the Nature of the Disease that troubles the Patient, and put in such Ingredients as may purge the particular Humor; it's the choycest skil he can use, and the chiefest good he can do; and therefore he should intend it and endeavor it in a special manner: Would you not have the Commander in the Field search the particular disorder in the Camp, and pursue the reformation of it in each special passage thereof. Herein the Faithful Execution of his place appears.

This I speak the rather to crush that vain Cavil of captious Spirits; Why did not the Minister mean me, intend me? if the Word meet with their corruptions, and begin to ransack and search the festered sores of their guilty Consciences?

I Answer four things:

1. If thy heart misgive thee that thou art guilty, he did mean thee, he should mean thee. If thy heart condemn thee, know that God is greater than thy Conscience, and knows more than he can express, or thou perceive in thy self.

2. However it is, He had thee in his intendment in what he said; If thou wert faulty, to reform the evil; if not faulty, to forewarn thee: For a faithful Minister should intend the good of all in al it delivers, and they should receive it.

3. If happily thou be freed from the outward practice of the evil, yet thou hast the spawn of it in thy soul, and that which wil provoke thee unto it, and that corrupt part hath given approbation to the evil; thou hast not set thy self so

much against the evil, and that hath made thee so far share in the evil, and so justly subject to share in the reproof. Thus the Apostle chargeth the Jew, *Rom.* 2. 1. When the Jew would plead his Innocency from such evils of the Gentiles, because he is ready to condemn and judg them in that behalf, saies the Apostle, *Thou therefore that judgest another, thou condemnest thy self, for thou thy self dost the same things;* but it might have been replyed, We do not, we are not whisperers, back-biters, guilty of fornication, malice, covetousness, &c. Interpreters answer, that the Apostles meaning is, Though they committed not such evils, yet the corruption of their Nature suited with them, and so shared in them, and therefore justly liable to the like Censure of the Law more or less.

4.   He meant what he said, and what his words meant, *If there be any evil in them, bear witness of the evil, John,* 18. 23. and it's just a man should bear his blame. Would'st thou fish more out of a mans meaning than thou canst find in his words? I fear thou meanest to be a Caviller. It's a certain Argument of a captious and contentious disposition, and commonly of a man that carries a galled Conscience, that seeks waies and means to make a fault when he cannot find one.

USE 4.   *It's a word of Exhortation, 1. To Ministers, 2. To People. To Ministers, what they should do: To the People, what they should desire.*

To the Ministers: *They have a pattern here for their Practice.* If we wil be faithful to our Places,   1. and the Work commended to our Care, faithful to the souls of the People; if we would further the Work of the Lord, and the Word, and see the fruit of our labors to the conviction and conversion of such as belong unto Gods Council: This is Gods way in which we must walk if we purpose to find Gods blessing, that others may reap the profit, and we the comfort of our pains at the great Day of our Account; we must by particular Application make men see their sins, if ever we hope they shal see the Salvation of the Lord.

How to stere our course in this so tickle a Channel, and so tender a Work, these following   Directions. *Directions* will not be unseasonable.

1.   First, *We must learn to bottom our Application upon the blessed Word of the Lord rightly apprehended, and opened*

plainly by undeniable Evidence. Then our Application wil come with uncontroulable power to the Conscience, when it comes guarded with Authority and demonstration of the Truth; and men cannot but give way to those Reproofs, when they cannot gainsay the evidence of Gods mind and Counsel therein. That however carnal hearts wil secretly be weary of them, yet they wil not dare openly to oppose them, because they perceive that they must oppose the Counsel of God plainly dispensed therein, and in their own Conscience also. Therefore I have ever judged it most seasonable, if I would pursue a sinful course breaking out, not by the by to pull it into a discourse, but to take a Text on purpose, wherein it is plainly condemned. That the people may hear God in his Word speaking before we speak; this is to shew our Commission before we do Execution, and this wil stop mens mouths. Never balk any thing that is in the Text, never wrest any thing out of the Text that is not there, for that favors too much of a mans own spirit or passion, or private ends, al which must be avoided as much as Hell. *If any man speak, let him speak as the Oracles of God,* 1 *Pet.* 4. 11. not our fancies, or passions, or conceits, but let Gods Oracles be heard only.

2.   It's lawful for a Minister so to cast the mould, and carry the frame of his Application that the guilty parties may conceive it, and their Consciences find and feel it, that they be the parties that the Lord points out, and intends of purpose to indite and pursue, *Matth.* 21. 41. 45. Thus our Savior laies out the corrupt carriages of the Scribes and Pharisees, and paints them out so lively that they felt him, and were forced to give in evidence of their own condemnation against themselves; as in verse 41. They say, *he will miserably destroy those wicked men*; and verse 45. *When the chief Priests heard this, they perceived that he spake of them.*

3.   In case either some false Opinions are spreading, or some corrupt and sinful practices are like to grow and leven and that speedily and dangerously, It's lawful in way of caution and prevention to discover mens sins and errors in their own words, that others may avoyd them the better, and they be ashamed of them the more. Thus *Peter* discovers the faults and wretched behaviour of the Jewes to our saviour in their own words. *Acts.* 3. 14. *you denyed that holy and just one and*

desired a murderer to be granted to you: Not him but Barabbas.
1. *Cor.* 15. 22. *How say some among you, that there is no resur-*
rection? Nay its lawful to name special persons in an evil, if
there may thereby be special warning given to others from
falling. So *Paul* to *Timothy* 2. *Tim.* 1. 15. *of whom is* Phygellus
and Hermogenes it's *Calvins* note upon the place, they were
more famous, and therefore their Apostacy might be a means
to draw others, therefore he gives warning concerning them.
If any man say this is to shame men, I answer their sins should
be made shameful, & they should take shame for them, that
they may sorrow for them and forsake them.

4. Let our Application go so wel guarded and fensed
against al exceptions and cavils that a sinner may not be able
to rescue himself or make an escape by carnal reason. As *Acts.*
6. 10. *It's said they were not able to resist the wisdome and the*
spirit by which he spake. Math. 22. 34. our saviour Christ *put*
the Sadducees *to silence.*

5. Let it be done with pity and tender compassion to mens
souls, though with zeal and indignation against their sins.
2. *Tim.* 2. 24. 25. *the servant of the Lord must be patient and*
gentle towards al in meekness instructing those that oppose them-
selves. As a Chirurgeon may be most compassionate when he
cuts most deep even to fetch up the core, and therefore the
Apostle adds both to Titus, *shew all meekness to all men,* and
therefore to the Cretians and yet *rebukes them sharply. Titus.* 1.
13. He that is truly meek, and pities the souls of men most he
wil shew least pity to their sins, all sharpness of rebuke and yet
al meekness of spirit do wel accord.

The exhortation to the people is that as ever
you desire to see your sins and have your hearts
brought to sorrow for them, you must desire it
and delight in it, that you may have the light brought home
to your souls in way of particular applycation to your own
sins, there is no means so effectual as this, therefore desire
God that your ministers may take such paines that they may
speak to your Consciences.

Take three considerations here.

1. Weigh sadly that when the Minister speaks in way of
Applycation so as to discover thy sins, he doth no more than
he may, nay no more than he should in point of Conscience,

Second part of exhortation

his life lyes at stake if he should not deal plainly and faithfully, and therefore know its unreasonable for thee to quarrel with the Minister, or with that he speaks when he hath the word for his warrant in what he does.

2. Look at the good of the dispensation of an ordinace and overlook the tartness of it. As some would not see but drink of the Physick minding the wholsomness and bearing with the unpleasantness of it for the present. As it's wearisom to the Surgeon to be raking in the sore, so it is to the Minister, but it is for thy good, and therfore though it be painful and cross to thy carnal affection yet thou shouldest take contentment in such a dispensation of the word as is such an effectual means of thy good.

3. When thou findest thy heart skittish, consider that an under quiet taking in sharp reproof its a sound argument of the sincerity of thy heart and truth of thy love to God and his word. When a man beginns to be shaken in his Comforts, and a sharp and keen reproof comes home to a man, to force him to see and be humbled & reform his evil wayes, if he can willingly receive and yield himself to such a reproof it's a sign his heart is sincere in the sight of God when he saies as they did *Zach.* 13. 6. *these are the wounds I received in the house of my friends.*

THOMAS SHEPARD

The Parable of the Ten Virgins Opened & Applied

Being the Substance of divers Sermons on Matth. 25. 1,–13.

Wherein, the Difference between the Sincere Christian and the most Refined Hypocrite, the Nature and Characters of Saving and of Common Grace, the Dangers and Diseases incident to most flourishing Churches or Christians, and other Spiritual TRUTHS of greatest importance, are clearly discovered, and practically Improved

LUKE 21. 36.
Watch ye therefore and pray alwaies, that ye may be accounted worthy to escape all these things that shall come to passe, and to stand before the Son of man.

———

Second Part, Chap. I.
Of Carnal Security in Virgin Churches

SECT. I.
Matth. 25. 5. *Whilst the Bridegroom tarried, they all slumbered and slept.*

IN this Parable were noted two things;

First, The Churches preparation to meet Christ from vers. 1. to 5.

Secondly, The Bridegrooms coming out to meet them, from vers. 5. to 12.

In this second part, which now we are to open, three things are to be attended unto;

1. The delay of Christs coming, or the long-suffering of Christ before he come, vers. 5.

2. The preparation he makes for his coming, a little before

it, from verse 6. to vers. 10. by an awakening cry, which makes all the Virgins look about them.

3. The coming it self; where those that were ready, were with joy let in; and those that were unready were with shame shut out.

1. *The delay of Christs coming.*

Whence note First, What happened in the interim of his delay, and that is *Carnal Security*, expressed and set out from the lowest and highest degree of it. 1. They *Slumbered*; *i.e.* fell a nodding or winking, as the word most properly signifies. 2. They *Slept*; *i.e.* now they were buried in their sleep, overcome by it.

Secondly, Upon whom these sleeps and slumbers fell; and that is, *They All slumbered and slept*; *i.e.* though for a time they were both awake, yet good and bad, wise and foolish fell into this senceless and stupid, dull and dead, sluggish and sleepy condition.

Observ. I. *That in the last days Carnal Security either is or will be the universal sin of Virgin Churches.*

Observ. II. *That Carnal Security falls by degrees upon the hearts of men.*

Observ. III. *That the spirit of sloath and security is the last sin that befals the people of God.*

Observ. IV. *That Christs tarrying from the Churches, is the general occasion of all security in the Churches; or the not coming of the Bridegroom when the Saints expect him, is the general cause of that security which doth befall them.*

Sect. II.

Observ. 1. *That in the last days Carnal Security either is or will be the universal sin of Virgin Churches:* When the Churches are purged from the gross pollutions of the world, and Antichristian fornications and bondage, then either there is or will be general Security: For these Virgins, when they first made profession of their Virginity by their burning lamps, were for a time all awakened, but at last they all slumbered and slept: This is the temper of the body of the Churches.

Matth. 24. 38. *As it was in the days of Noah, so shall it be in the days of the coming of the Son of man.*

Luk. 18. 8. *When the Son of man cometh, shall he find faith in the earth? i.e.* an awakening faith.

Hence the Lord forewarns his people of this, *Deut.* 6. 12. *When thou comest to such a land, beware lest thou forget the Lord thy God.*

QUEST. *But what is this their general Security?*

ANSW. Look as it is in our ordinary sleep, so it is in this general Security: There are these six things in it.

1. A man forgets his business, his work he was about, or is to be exercised about; so in a carnal security, men forget the Lord, his works, and his will; that which we most think of while we be awake, we least think of indeed when we be asleep: Take a man awakened indeed, O then the worst remember the Lord and his Covenant, *Psal.* 78. 47. But when asleep, the Lord and his errand is least thought of; and hence security is exprest by *forgetting God, Psal.* 50. 21. And hence *Jerusalems* security was in this, *they remembred not their latter end.*

2. A man in sleep fears no evill until it be upon him, awakening of him; so this is another ingredient into carnal security, though sin lies upon them, they fear not till evil comes; as *Josephs* brethren, though warning is given them, they fear not: Like them in the days of *Noah* and *Lot.* And hence *Job* 21. 9. *their houses are free from fear*; the misery for the same sin is lighted upon another; yet the secure soul fears not, as in *Belshazar, Dan.* 5. 22.

3. In sleep all the sences are bound up, the outward sences especially, the eye watcheth not, the ear hears not, the tongue tastes not, the body feels not; so this is an ingredient of carnal security, it binds up all the sences, as it did the Prophet *Jonah* his in the storm; when misery was upon him, he heard not, he saw not, he felt not; so when misery, outward or spiritual, is upon a man, he that had quick sences before, his eye sees not, watcheth not; Christians neglect their watchfulness for their friends, the Lord, and his Spirit, and coming; nor watch against their enemies that daily besiege them; the ear hears not the voice of the Ministry, the voyce of Providences, the voyce of the spirit within; the soul smels not, tastes not the sweet of any promise, any Ordinance, no! or of the grace of the Lord himself; hence it commends them not; nay the

soul feels nothing, no evil, no good the Lord doth him; that look as the Lord there said, *Isa.* 29. 9, 10. *The Lord hath poured upon you a spirit of sleep, and hath closed your eyes;* so the Lord closeth up all the sences, that a man is now stupid, when he is fallen asleep in security.

4. In sleep there is a cessation from speaking and motion: there a man keeps silence and lies still; so in carnal security, the spirit of prayer is silent, *Isa.* 64. 7. *Psal.* 32. 1, 2, 3. *David* calls it a keeping of silence; *up, why sleepest thou? seek to thy God*, say the Mariners; indeed men may talk in their sleep, so men may pray in their deep security, yet not throughly awakened: And there is a lying still, no progress; so in carnal security the soul stands at a stay, goes not backward, grows not worse, but goes not forward; such a one is compared to the door on the hinge.

5. In sleep the sences being stupified, and motion ceased, a man falls a dreaming; some dreams he forgets, some he remembers, and in his sleep fully and firmly believes them; so in carnal security, now a mans mind dreams of that which is not, and of that which never shall be; a mans mind is grown vain, and full of fancies and dreams; those things which never entered into Gods thoughts, something a man dreams of the Lord that this is his will and mind, which is not; of the world, that it is a goodly thing; of things to come which shall never be.

6. In deep sleep, though a man be awakened, yet he presently is overcome by his sleep again; so that is another ingredient into spiritual slumber; sleepiness is predominant over his watchfulness; and thus it was with the Disciples in the garden, they slept; the Lord came once and twice, and awakens them, yet they slept till temptation surprized them; scarce any Christian so secure in the chambers of Christ, but he hath some knocks of conscience, some cries of the Ministry, some woundings from the Lord, and they do awake him, but yet he falls to sleep again.

Sect. III.

We shall now shew the Reasons why Virgin Churches in the last days are or will be overcome by security.

Reason i. First, Because that in Virgin Churches there

are the strongest provocations to this sin: Which are chiefly three.

1. Rest and places of peace, and freedom from hard bondage; *Jacob* may sleep with his stone under his head, but much more easily under his own Vine and Figtrees. A man may be secure in the times of trouble, but much more in times of peace, when we have our beds made soft for us, and easie pillows. Friends can boldly desire us to rest, where there is lodgings for us: The world thrusts us out of lodging: While the prick is at the brest the Nightingale awakes and sings, but when that is taken away it sleeps in the day. In times of persecution *Paul* is preaching till midnight, and the Lord is remembred in the songs, and sighs, and prayers of the night-season; but in times of peace, peace like *Jaels* milk and butter stupifies all the sences, though destruction be near; Hence *Deut.* 6. 12. *Then forget not the Lord*. Do you think that *Noah* in the Ark, when the waters swelled above the mountains, was secure? no, but when the waters ceased, and he had his Vineyard planted, now he sleeps in his drunkenness, because he knew not the strength of wine. In the Virgin-Church, where this sleep is, we suppose this freedom from evil.

2. Because there men are most free from inward pain; for where there is much grief and pain, there's no rest, though all the house about be still; but when the house is still, and the body well, now tis hard but there may be rest; Whiles the Christian doth live under Antichristian pollution, his Conscience hath no rest, and hence 'tis awake there; here (saith the soul) I want the Ordinances of God, Oh that I had them! Here I see sin and wickedness abounding, that my childe is like to be poisoned therewith; here are such and such superstitions that my Conscience cannot bear: Hence Conscience is kept waking. But in Virgin-Churches, where the house is swept of these, now Conscience is quiet and at rest; now I have got a Levite into my house, God is now blessing me, &c. Now Conscience hath laid down its burthen, it falls down to sleep; now they cry, *The Temple of the Lord*, &c.

3. Because in such Churches there is most aptitude in men to spiritual fulness, *viz.* plenty of the means; there is all the Ordinances; in this mountain, *Isa.* 25. 1. Gods feast is made, and fulness of spiritual gifts and graces, because they have

now escaped the pollutions of the world, conquered the enmity of the world; now have come to a good measure of grace, and conquered the way of their enemies, got the better of them; hence, as the *Israelites* made peace with the *Canaanites*, not when they were too strong but too weak for them: So now the Soul comes to be at rest, to lay down its Warfare, and to yield to a truce, to a league to his lusts and distempers for a time. When men are kept short of food, now they awake, so when the Word of the Lord and his Ordinances be rare and precious, and hard to finde, now a Christian can trudge after them; but when men are full, now they desire rest; so 'tis here.

4. Because in Virgin-Churches, there men are most apt to be overtaken with weariness; A man that never walkt on in a holy way, may at first setting out delight in Christ; but after he hath done walking in it, now he is apt to faint; especially, if he sows much, and reaps for the present but little. And hence *Gal.* 6. 9. *You shall reap in due season, if you faint not*: Now in Virgin-Churches, these Virgins are such persons as have begun to make a profession, and have made a fair progress; O how difficult now is it not to be weary! it's strange to see what short spirits after the Lord, what large after the Creatures we have.

REASON 2. Because they are the more easily overcome by this sin, than by any other.

1. Because it's a sin which a man least foresees or fears: The Apostle saith, *They that are drunk, and that sleep, sleep in the night;* and yet here men sleep in the open light; Why so? Men see it not, men know it not; sleep steals upon a man: It's lawful to sleep; carnal security arises chiefly from the use of lawful things, on which a mans heart and thoughts are spent; they eate, drank, gave in marriage, they could see no hurt therein. When a man is had before Councels, now a man fears to sin, he knows he shall be tempted unto sin; but when the Lord brings the shoulder from under such burdens, now to fear our Tables, our Beds, our Wives, our Children, our Callings, our Professions and the snares of these, Oh it is exceeding hard!

2. Because Security is so sweet a sin; O sleep is sweet; meat is sweet, but men may be soon full of that; but when sleep

comes, many hours are little enough to entertain that: Some sins are sweet for a time, as a short meal and away; but sloth is a sweeter sin than any else besides. Let a Christian ask his heart, when he can take no content in Pots, or loose company, or Queans, and can find none in the Lord, yet this will give him ease, *viz.* his sloth; When he is weary of the World, and of walking with God also, yet sloth is his delight; and hence he crys, *A little more slumber and sleep, untill destruction comes as an armed man:* When a man delights not in his Wife, Children, Riches, Honors, yet is he sometimes contentedly swallowed up with his sleep and rest.

3. Because Satan doth make his strongest forces ready alway to bring a man first into this sin; because this makes way for the entrance of all sin and misery; no people so happy as the *Israelites,* while they were awakened and up with God; no misery could hurt them, *Jer.* 2. 1, 2, 3. but when they forgot him, all misery came in; *While the strong man keeps the Palace, his goods be at peace;* it's his care to keep men secure and still.

SECT. IV.

USE 1.   Let us therefore now examine whether this sin be not our sin in this Country, if it be not begun among us; if we be not sleeping, yet are we not slumbering? if we are not Virgin-Churches, why have we the name of it? if we be Virgin-Churches, then make search if this be not our sin; we have all our beds and lodgings provided, the Lord hath made them easie to us; We never looked for such days in *New-England,* the Lord hath freed us from the pain and anguish of our Consciences; we have Ordinances to the full, Sermons too long, and Lectures too many, and private meetings too frequent, a large profession many have made, but are you not yet weary? if weary, not sleepy, not slumbering? it may be on you before you are aware, and you not know it; and when so it is, it may be so sweet that you may be loth to see it, that so you may forsake it. Let me knock again, is it not so? Let me come to every mans bed side, and ask your consciences.

1. Have you not forgot your God, and forgot your work also? the business for which you made this great undertaking?

Psal. 106. 12. When they were saved from the Sea they soon forgat the Lord: Hath not the Lord by a stretched-out arm brought thee and thine through seas and dangers, and delivered you wonderfully? are not all his kindnesses forgotten? all your promises forgotten? When the Lord had brought the *Israelites* out of their captivity, and some hopeful beginnings were, they came for the Temple; the dust was precious, but Gods house did lie waste, *Hag.* 1. 5, 6. *Consider your ways;* no man prospered scarce in his estate; God did blow upon their corn because they forgat their end. What was your end of coming hither? the Ordinances of God, the presence of God; and oh one day there better than a thousand elsewhere; hath it been so? No, but as it is vers. 9. *Every man turns to his own house:* Every man for himself, to their own house, lot, accommodation, provision for children; and in the mean while the Lords house lies waste, you build not up that; the Souls of thy Brethren in Church-fellowship, yea, of thy family are not built up; the Lords house is despised now; and it's like the Schools of the Prophets, and much more. Oh thought we, if we had such priviledges, how would we improve them! but when we have them, have we the same thoughts? do we not forget them, like men that come to a place for gold, and find it not without digging, they fall to lade their ship with wood or coal, that which it will bear.

2. Have we not shaken off all fear almost of sin and misery? *Go to the Ant thou sluggard, she fears and provides against a winter:* Do not men think that we have fled too far for the cross to finde us, or as if the Temple of the Lord was such a Den as no Foxes or Wolves could follow us into? especially when there are causes of fear, when War is proclaimed, and the causes known, and yet they are never feared: How many men have the hand-writing of death in their Consciences against them! this they confess is naught, they have lived careless, sluggish, and have had some sence of it, yet no awakening fear of the terror of the Lord; when a Prince is nigh us, now to commit a little lewdness is great wickedness: where is the man that trembles at the nearness of God to us? when a breach is made, then fear enemies. Divisions and breaches go before falls of Churches; where is that spirit of *Jehosaphat*, that feared and proclaimed a fast? When God hath begun to smite,

what cause is there to fear! we have been hurt, and yet not laid it to heart; the Lion roars, shall not the people fear? I believe we should not have had those Pequot furies upon us, but God saw we began to sleep: Where is the man that, with *Paul*, knows the terror of the Lord, and hence perswades men? when the enemy is ever about us, there is always cause of fear, and yet we fear but now and then.

3. Are not our sences bound up? look upon men in their fields and conversings, buyings and sellings; where is a daily, weekly watchfulness over our thoughts and tongues? Look to mens closets, do men there call themselves to account? can they finde leisure or need of it? are not mens eyes closed up, that the glory of God in the Scripture is a sealed thing? Men have eyes but see not; are not mens ears sealed up? Some Sermons men can sleep them out; mans voyce is heard, but not the voyce of the Son of God: Oh how many men are there that become quite Sermon-proof now adays! Are not men blockish, dull, senceless, heavy under all means! they taste not, smell not, whereas elsewhere, O how lively and spiritual are they!

4. Is not the spirit of Prayer, that lamp going out in the Church of God? the blessedness of all flourishing Plantations in the world began by means of that, and shall not continue but as it continues; and if ever cause to seek for prosperity of Plantations, these have need. If God should take away this generation of Magistracy and Ministery, what would this despised Country do? and what would become of your children? then no Schools for them, when no Gospel left among them; then every mans sword shall be against his brother, and God spreading the place with darkness, which through his presence is made light; what little hope of a happy generation after us, when many among us scarce know how to teach their children manners? How apt are we, like to those *Asian* Churches, to fall into those very sins which overwhelmed them, and ruined them? how many fall off, and in time break forth, that it would make men sick to hear of their pranks? what place more open to temptations of persecution and worldly delusion? go up and down the Plantations, where is the man that lays things to heart? who hath the condition of the Country written upon his heart, and presenting it before the Lord,

rather than his own good? Oh men are silent because asleep! How do sins run thorough men as water thorough a mill, and men regard it not? what means, what deliverances have we had! but oh what little thankfulness? 2. Do we make progress; nay, is not our shadow gone back? *I sleep, but my heart waketh;* it should be so, but it is not so indeed.

5. Have we not fallen a dreaming here? what meaneth else the delusions of mens brains? what a swarm of strange opinions, which (like flies) have gone to the sores of mens heads and hearts, and these are believed also? and more dreams men have that are never spoken; every man hath some drunken conceit that rocks him asleep; dreams are quite contrary to the truths. What meaneth these, if men are not sleeping? First, Drunken dreams of the world. Secondly, golden dreams of grace; that these things advance grace which indeed destroy grace; that there is no grace in the Saints, no grace in Christ, no humane Nature, no promise to evidence grace; no Law to be a Rule to them that have received grace: Who would think that ever any should so fall by a simple woman? But if this be not general; yet look how do men begin to dream concerning the world? scarce a man but finds want, or is well; if he wants, Oh then, if I had such a lot about me, such an estate, how well then were I? and *è contra*, They that have it, and now they take their rest: *Take heed*, saith the Lord, *your hearts be not overcome with cares;* So say I to you.

6. Doth not the Lord oft awaken us, yet we fall to sleep again? the Lord awakened us by the Pequot Hornet, yet what use is there made of that? doth not the Lord oft meet us in an Ordinance, but he is soon lost and gone again? Is there a man that hath not had his cross since he came hither, as loss in cattel and estate, a dear Husband, Childe, Wife dead? a sore and sharp sickness, *&c.* he hath been exercised with, *&c.* but do we not sleep still? if it be not thus, it will come; fear it for time to come; but if it be thus, then I say no more, but know it, you are in your enemies hand; and in such an enemies hand, that if you mourn not under it, will open the door either to the entrance of some gross sin and temptation, or for some heavy and sudden wrath. It's sufficient for me this day to shew you where your hurt lyeth.

SECT. V.

USE 2. Hence see the reason why men are worse in
Virgin-Churches, than in polluted places, and why it is so
generally; Because here are more temptations to make them
all slumber and sleep; here their beds are made soft, here the
storms are past, here they are under the shadow, and out of
the sun, and security opens the door for an enemy: No wonder if the City be taken though never so strong, if it grow
once secure: no wonder if the world be entred, and men are
grown more worldly; and if Satan be entred, and men grow
more passionate than ever before; no wonder a mans work be
neglected, if he be asleep, Ordinances more slighted than ever
before: Never shall you see Security fall upon a man alone,
but it brings its train with it; when the Husbandmen sleep,
tares will be sown, and when the Disciples sleep, temptations
will enter; This is that which the Lord testifies of his people,
Jer. 2. 2, 3, 4. I remember what thou didst in times of
streights, in a land not sown; every one that touched you did
offend; but in the seventh and eighth verses, when brought to
a plentiful Country, they did not so much as say, Where is the
Lord that hath done this for us! But yet the Lord questions
his people for this, *What iniquity have you found in me?* which
question you cannot answer without grief here, or confusion
another day. You that are the Lords, often have heard this
complaint (for this may be your condition as well as *Noah*'s
and *Lot*'s) but now see the cause of it, how hard to awake on
hour? how hard to walk with God one day? short awakenings
you have, but long sleeps (this may be your condition for a
time) but you cannot continue so for ever if you are the
Lords. But if you do continue so, especially without bemoan-
ing this unto the Lord, 'tis a question whether ever there was
that oyl in your vessel, which others have, when not only a
mans acts grow worse, but the very spirit of a man degenerates; when not only the leaves of the Vine fall, but the Vine it
self groweth degenerate, and hence continueth so; this is a
sore evidence of a woful state, *Jer.* 2. 20, 21. *When the yoke was
upon thy neck, thou saidst, Thou wouldst not transgress; but the
Lord hath broken thy bands; and now thou art becom a strange
Vine:* Remember, it will be an heavy indictment against thee,

to be good in *Mesheck*, but base in *Sion*; to be then worst
when the Lord is best.

USE 3.   Hence see one reason why the Lord pursueth
many a Soul with inward terrors and outward sorrows. Those
that are fast asleep, because soft speechs cannot awaken
them, hence we lay our hands upon them, and sometimes
knock them, because this is the way to awaken them, and
then they hear; so the Word and Spirit speak to a man, but
such soft still winds rock them asleep rather than awaken
them; hence the Lord layeth his iron hands upon a man, and
knocks by blows, and now when affliction is upon you, now
you can hear; When as the winds and water were ready to
tear the ship in pieces, now they enquire, Why were they
sent? *And the lot fell upon Jonah*, who was then sleeping; it is
easie to awaken out of natural sleep, but very hard out of
spiritual security: All the terrors of God on *Jonah* within
and without are little enough; but at last he could hear, and
run on his errand. *Psal.* 30. 6, 7. Why did God hide his face
from *David*? *he said in prosperity he should not be moved*; this
was the reason of it; the Lord sees you have need of it;
seldom shall one see an awakening Christian without inward
temptations and terrors, or outward sorrows: Oh consider
then if the Lord do meet with thee! consider thy own security thou hast been in, or art apt to fall into! This is the sin
you must enquire after and finde out; and do not account it
hard, though long, though bitter; for never greater misery
than for the Lord to say *Sleep on*; it is one of the heaviest
Judgements, for the Lord to let a man go on in a secure condition without blows; mark therefore unto the end of those
blows, to be throughly awakened by them: For sometimes
when the Lord sends them, a man (if they be not very bitter,
if he hath any rest) lays them not to heart, *Isa.* 42. 25.
Fire burnt about him; and in this Country I know not what
curse befalls men; peace makes men secure, and sorrow
makes men discontented, and sunk, and discouraged, which
may be for a fit in a Saint; but to continue so, this is that
Ahab: Oh when as thou feelest the blow, look now that thou
dost awaken, and be thankfull for it, that you met with that
you did never reckon upon, *viz.* to be frighted out of security thereby.

Sect. VI.

Use 4.   To watch over one another, by *ex-horting one another while it is called to day,* Heb.
3. 13. Let both the Watchmen and Members of

Of Exhortation

Churches do this; for this is one means appointed by the Lord
to preserve the soul from sleeping, 1 *Thes.* 5. 1, 5, 6. *Exhorting
one another;* as it is in Cities, when the Watch is apt to sleep,
they have their companies that are passing up and down the
walls the greatest part of the night, and so they are kept waking; and we shall finde, that as it is in a Town where men are
all asleep, one Bell-man, one waking Christian will keep life,
and spirit, and the power of godliness in many; and when he
sleeps, all are fast. Nothing in the world brings security
sooner upon men than sleepy company: Officers of Churches
watch not over members, nor they one over another, exhorting and crying one unto another to their work, while it is
called to day: Oh then let every man get up, and fall to this
work of mutual exhorting! go and visit one another, go and
speak oft to one another; and if thou be a childe of the light,
see that thou endure not thy fellow servants to sleep in the
open day in one duty or another. Know, if God stirs thee,
thou wilt awaken others, 2 *Cor.* 5. 10. *We knowing the terrors
of the Lord perswade men.*

2. Consider thy labor cannot be in vain here; the best met-
talled horse needs spurs; others are asleep.

You will say if I knew such a sin I would speak, but I dare
not.

Answ.   It is the case of all the Virgins, they have need of
it, *Jude* 23. *Some save with fear, pulling them out of the fire,*
Matth. 3.

3. Consider this is one part of your Warfare, to keep your
watch whereby you may be made conquerors; You complain
you have many sins and temptations arising and prevailing;
never do they usually prevail, but when you are secure; first
the Watch is taken, and then the City is suddenly taken; now
look as *Paul,* 2 *Tim.* 4. 6, 7. *he hath finished his course, and
fought his fight, and now expects the crown;* how can you end
your days in peace, that cannot in some measure finde and
feel this? The Church is the City of the living God, this is
taken, and every man in it, unless you be watchful, and *exhort*

one another daily, while it is called to day: And that I may not speak in the clouds,

4. Their sin will be yours.

First, Labor to know the state of thy Brethren whom thou art to exhort; what their sleepy neglects be, and sins are; it may be thou hast known one hath been very humble, tender, affected under Ordinances, made many fair shews and promises of growing, and thriving, and sensibly complaining of his own vileness, and now he is in a silent sleep; Dost thou know this, and wilt not speak a word to awaken him, for whom Christ shed his blood, who it may be will do thee as good a turn, and make many a prayer for thee? *Barnabas when he saw the grace of God, exhorted them with full purpose of heart to cleave unto him;* much more should you when you see grace dying, 2 *Thes.* 3. 11. *Paul* heard that some were idle, them he exhorts to work; what good might one word do?

Secondly, if you do not know, enquire with a spirit of much love, how it is with them; as *David* of his Brethren when they were gone into the fields; do you not decline, do you not stand still? how have you found your heart since last Sermon, Sabbath, Fast, Affliction? have you got any ground against that sin you complained of last year? *&c.* Suppose you cannot do this to all, yet why not to some? Suppose you have no other place than when you meet them in the fields, do it there, *Jude* 20. *Build up your selves, &c.* Now here a man must know the height, how high they are built already, how can they lay their stones else? It is one of the heavey curses of God upon the Idol Shepherd, *He shall not visit the hidden, nor seek the young, Zach.* 11. 16.

[sidenote: Christians are to give up accounts one to another of their gains and losses.]

Thirdly, If thou knowest nothing from them, then relate thy own condition, this is a most lovely provocation, and exhortation unto another frame; for one great cause that hardeneth men in their security, is because they see no such living Christianity in the world: But when they do, *now (Zach.* 8) *many shall take hold of the skirt of a Jew, for they shall say God is with you; Agrippa* was almost perswaded and awakened when he heard *Paul* relate his conversion; although there be many impostors in the world that do so. Tell me, are all things in peace with you? the Devil is in you then: What? hast no temptations? yet many; Dost not observe how they prevail? yes; dost never get strength against them? yes; hast no good days after them? yes, much peace and life, and presence of God! Hath the Lord given these talents to thee to be hid in a Napkin, this treasure to keep and not to spend? who knows but that the speaking of these may awaken others? these temptations, and this condition is mine, these sins I find he makes a great matter of them; Lord what will become of me that am hardned under them? this peace they finde, my Soul is a stranger to it; Conscience will work thus: Women should speak thus to women, and men to men; others were provoked by the example of the *Corinthians*, to help others; so there is a provoking power here.

Fourthly, If this prevail not, speak often to them, of the sins of others; in condemning others you condemn them; and this will make them look about them; view the fields, and shew them the tares that are grown up by security; and laying down these sins you strike at the root of theirs; It may be, you cannot tell certainly, *Acts* 2. 40. The Lord made this one means to awaken a *Belshazzar*, *Dan* 5. 22. God turned thy Father into a beast, *&c.* to live in the woods, yet thou humbledst not thy self, *&c.* How many Professors doth God deal so withal?

Fifthly, Enter into Covenant and brotherly promise to exhort one another, as *David* and *Jonathan*; If any hurt be toward *David*, *Jonathan* will speak of it, 1 *Sam.* 20. Some may in Church-fellowship be more nearly knit than others, to call one another to account, to tell one another their fears, to know of one another their progress. Canst not give an account to man? how wilt thou give an account to God of it? I am perswaded many a man lies smoothered to death by means of this. Canst not come to the light of a candle? Oh how then canst thou appear before the light of the Sun.

Sixthly, Provoke one another to frequency in Ordinances, *Heb.* 10. 23, 24. and therein consider one another; dost see thy Brother in doubts or complaints? call him to pray with thee; dost see things go ill in Churches, and men bite the bit? call to fasting and prayer, three or four together, as *Paul*, when he saw the ship sinking, then he exhorted them, *Act.* 27. 22. Especially when you see danger near mens hearts, ready to be lost in the World: In these times suppose only two, or three, or four should go and pray one half hour together, and tell one another their wants, now help here; in our times it hath been so, one living Christian helps others dying.

But yet how is this neglected, as if men were resolved not only to dye sleeping themselves but to let others sleep also? No, you will say, not my self; yet it may be in your family it is so, and before the Lord.

What art alive to God and family, where thou canst do but little common good, and art dead to thy Brother? it is made a sad sign of a man forsaken of God, if when he thinks he shall sleep his last, and be damned himself, yet he would have others damned also. Tell me, would you have all *New England* lye in security as well as your selves? No! do you not desire it when you use not the means that prevent it; and that is mutual exhortation; Oh therefore do it; Ministers may preach, and every man sleep still, unless some awake and rouse up the rest (as some, when others are abed and fast asleep) that lye a dreaming: Some there be, that though Doomsday were to morrow, they would sleep; Oh therefore let me perswade some one or two to fall to his work, lest their security prove your undoing; therefore speak oft one to another, forsake not your assembling, visit one another, pray one for another, warning one another, that you may awake with the Lord one hour.

SECT. VII.

USE 5. Let every man not only exhort his brother, but fear this himself; You have a race to run, many enemies to conquer, sleep not lest you fall short, sleep not lest you be taken captive: lest in exhorting others, your selves proves Reprobates: I will not tell you what I fear, but *Luk.* 21. take heed lest your hearts be overcome; be not drunk with some delight, be not filled with vain cares; Hence, prevent it, as *Noah moved with fear made an Ark.*

First, Set a high price upon those awakenings and revivings of heart that God sometimes giveth you; I am sure you finde these sometimes. A man that hath nothing to lose, will sleep with his doors open in the night; when a man hath a treasure he will be watchful to keep it; all security comes from an under-valuing of the Spirit of grace, and its presence among us,

Prov. 4. 13. keep her, for it is thy life; and when it is lost, what are you but dead?

Secondly, Consider thy continual danger; if enemies be at the gates, all the Town is watching; one would not think the depth of security that is in a careless heart, *Psal.* 30. 6. *I said I should never be moved;* he had good days and a thankful heart; then God did hide his face: A man would think *Sampson* should awake when the Philistines ate upon him; but here Devils be upon thee, 1 *Pet.* 5. 10. If all be well now, yet remember evil days; would you know when? even then when men say peace.

Thirdly, Know the work you have to do, and make it your main business; when men have weighty business of the world in hand, they cannot sleep in their beds; and as the wicked, *Prov.* 4. 16. *They sleep not without doing mischief;* and so 'tis their main work.

Fourthly, Call thy self to account daily, let not thy Soul long go on without reflecting, What do I do? Harts and Hawks kept from sleep lose their wildeness, but they must be constantly tended and kept watching: So consider the account you must give to God, 2 *Cor.* 5. 9. with 11. Hence *Hag.* 1. 5. Sins were upon them, and they repented not; miseries, and those were not removed; because they considered not their ways, especially before the great Tribunal of God. I am perswaded the reason why men walk in their sleep, and go dreaming up and down the world, is this, they consider not, nor reflect upon themselves to any purpose; what do I? whether go I? no Sermons awaken, you consider not of them.

THOMAS SHEPARD

Of Ineffectual Hearing the Word

*How we may know whether we have heard the same
effectually: And by what means it may be come
effectual unto us*

————

JOHN 5. 37.
*Ye have neither heard his voice at any time,
nor seen his shape.*

FROM the 31. *Vers.* to the end of this *Chapter*. Our Saviour proves that he was the *Messiah* to come, from four testimonies.

1. From the testimony of *John*; the first, yet the least, yet very strong and full, *vers.* 32. 33.

2. From the testimony of his works, greater then that of *John*, *vers.* 35.

3. From the testimony of the Father, by his voice from heaven, *vers.* 37.

4. From the voice of the Scriptures, the highest of all, and surer then a voice from heaven. (2 *Pet.* 1. 19.) *v.* 39, 46.

Now these words are annexed to the third testimony, which I told you is the voice of God from heaven, set down *Mat.* 3. 17. For this testimony of the Father is not the inward testimony of the spirit only; Because Christ speaks of publick, and evident testimonies in this place; nor is it meant of the testimony of the Father in the Scripture; for that is a distinct testimony: and though the Father doth testifie of Christ in the Scriptures; yet 'tis not as his testimony, no more then the testimony of *John*, and of his works, whereby the Father did testifie also: Nor is it probable that our Saviour would at this time, omit that famous testimony of the Father at his Baptisme; which if it be not here, is no where in this *Chapter*.

Beside, how is this testimony the Fathers more then the Spirits; but then, being called his Son, he did evidently declare himself to be the Father that spake. Lastly, the Spirits testimony is spoken of, as the testimony of *Moses* and the Prophets. *Vers.* 46, 47. *For had ye beleeved* Moses, *ye would have beleeved me, for he wrote of me,* vers. 47. *For if ye beleeve not his writings how shall he beleeve my words.*

Now our Saviour in these words answers an *Objection*, which the Jewes (ever conceited of their own knowledge) might make. We know the Father as well as you; and yet we know no such testimony that he gives. Christ answers, You do not know him; for the certain knowledge of a thing, is either by seeing or hearing; now you never saw him nor heard him; you have therefore no acquaintance with him.

So that the words contain 1. Christs fearful accusation of the Jews to be ignorant of God. 2. The aggravation and extent of it, at no time, *i.e.* not only at Baptisme, but at no other time, in any Ministery, or in any Scripture, &c.

QUEST. 1. *What is it not to see his shape nor hear his voice?*

ANSW. Some think they are metaphorical speeches, to expresse their ignorance of God; Now though this be the scope, and the general truth, yet I conceive, the Lord speaking particularly, and knowing what he spake, intends something particularly: and it is a rule, never to flie to metaphors, where there can be a plain sense given. There is therefore two degrees of true knowledge of God in this life, or 'tis attained unto by a double meanes.

1. By hearing of him, for hence our faith comes by the Word.

2. By hearing thus from him, the mind also comes to have a true *Idea* of God, as he reveals himself in the Word and Means by the Spirit, *Job* 42. 5. *I have heard of thee by the hearing of the ear, but now mine eye seeth thee;* and this is the *shape* here spoken of, not bodily and carnal. Now Christ doth professe that they did want both. Carnal and unregenerate hearts, neither hear Gods voice, nor have a right *Idea* of God in their mindes but become vain in their mindes, though they have meanes of knowing, and their foolish hearts are darkned; the wiser they be, the more foolish they grow.

2. *At no time, i.e.* neither at baptism, nor else in any mans

Ministery, nor in any of the Scriptures which you read, and where the Lord speaks.

3. But did they not hear the voice of God at Christs baptism, and at the Mount when Christ preach't, when the Scriptures were opened every Lords day and at other times amongst them?

ANSW. No, they never heard it. It's a strange thing, that such men that read, heard, preach't, remembred the Scriptures and could tell you mysteries in titles, never heard the voice of God; and yet it is most true.

OBSERVAT. *That many men may a long time together know and heare the Word of God written and spoken, yet never hear the Lord speaking that Word, no not so much as one word, title or syllable; no not so much as once, at any time.* This was the estate of the Jewes, and this is the estate of all unregenerate men. Hence Christ, *Luke* 19. 41. laments and weeps over *Jerusalem*, saying, *Oh that thou hadst known in this thy day, &c.*

1. QUEST. *How did the Jewes heare, and yet not heare God speaking?*

ANSW. There is a twofold word, or rather a double declaration of the same word. 1. There is Gods external or outward word, containing letters and syllables, and this is his external voice. 2. There is Gods internal word and voice, which secretly speaks to the heart, even by the external word, when that only speaks to the eare. The first the Jewes did hear at Christs Baptism, in Christs Ministery, and in reading the Scriptures, and when they did hear it, it was Gods word they heard, full of glory, and so they heard the word spoken, but only man speaking it: the other comes to few, who hear not only the word spoken, but God speaking the word, *Rom.* 10. 18, 19. *Israel did hear*, but *Israel did not know.* Christ speaks in parables; Hence *in seeing they did not see, Luke* 8. 10. And this is one way, how 'tis true that Christ sayes, *They never heard his voice.* As 'tis with a painted Sun on the wall, you see the Sun and Stars, but there is a difference between seeing this and the Sun and Starres themselves, wherein is an admirable glory: go to a painted Sun, it gives you no heat, nor cherisheth you not; so it is here, &c.

2. This inward word is double. 1. Ineffectual, (though in-

ward.) 2. Effectual. 1. Ineffectual, is that which hath some inward operation upon the heart, but it attaines not Gods end to bring a man into a state of life; and thus, *Heb.* 6. 2, 5. *Many tasted of the good word of God, yet fell away.* And such a heart is compared to a field which a man plowes and sowes, and raine falls on it, and yet the end is not attained, *it brings forth thistles*; and this many Jewes did hear, and hence had some kinde of faith in Christ. 2. Effectual, is that which hath such an inward efficacy upon mens hearts, as that God attaines his end thereby, *Isa.* 55. 11. and brings men to a state of life, of which Christ speaks, *John.* 6. 45. and this voice none but the Elect hear; and of this Christ speaks here, as appears, *verse* 38. *Him whom he sent, ye beleeve not.* Hence it is you have heard God at no time. Hence he speaks of such a hearing and knowing, such a hearing outwardly, as is accompanied with such a hearing inwardly, *Joh.* 14. 17. so that many men may hear the word spoken outwardly, but never inwardly: they may hear it inwardly, but never effectually, translating them from state to state, from death to life, from life to life and glory. No sense of the Majesty of God speaking, nor effectual hearing of the word spoken. When the Sun is down the Moon may arise, but yet a man is cold and dark; but when the Sun ariseth, on it warmes, nourisheth and cherisheth, &c. *nothing is hid from it*; so it is here, when the Lord speaks inwardly and effectually to the heart.

REAS. 1. From that great distance and infinite separation of mens soules from God, that though God cals, yet they can't hear no more then men a 1000 mile off. *Eph.* 2. 1. *men are dead in sin.* Now what is spiritual death, but separation of the soul from God, & God from it. A dead man cannot hear one word at no one time, he was not dead if he could. Mens minds are far from God, & hearts also, that they are neither stricken with the sight of his glory, nor sense and savour of his goodnesse, but must be vaine, and have worldly hearts in the Church, nay adulterous eyes, or if they listen, God is gone from them, and from his Word also, *Hos.* 5. 6.

REAS. 2. From the mighty and wonderful strange power of Satan, which blindes their eyes they cannot see nor hear, 2 *Cor.* 4. 4. never such clear light, never such an effectual Word, as that of the Apostles, yet it was *hid*; why? *The God of this*

world blinded them, either he will keep such a noise and lumber in their heads, that they cannot hear God speaking for the
noise, or else turn himself into an Angel of light, and speak,
and by their light will blinde them, that the light in them shall
be darknesse. *Rom.* 1. 22. When men with natural light began
to be most wise, then they became the greatest fooles: so 'tis
with other knowledge of Scripture, and things they heare.
Happy were it for many a man if he had never heard nor seen;
for that which he hath heard and seen keeps him from hearing. *Tyre* and *Sidon* would hear sooner then *Capernaum* that
heard most.

REAS. 3.   From the righteous judgment of God, in leaving
men to be blinded and made deaf, from and by the means
whereby they should hear and know; that as it is with the
Saints, all evil things are for their good, so all good things are
for their hurt, *Isa.* 6. 10. the meriting cause is unbelief and sin,
but the deep and hidden rise of all is Gods eternal dereliction
of them, God never intended love, special love to them, hence
he never speaks one word to them, 2 *Cor.* 4. 3. *John* 6. 65.
Many were offended at his words and forsook him. Now to take
off this offence, I said, *None can come to me, except it be given
him of the Father,* what is that? see *vers.* 45. *and* 37.

USE 1.   Hence see the reason, why the Word is so wonderfully ineffectual to the soules of many men, that it never
stirs them, that it's a strange thing to them; it's *Heb.* 12. 19.
like the law, *a voice of words*, a sound of words, so they hear
men spake but understand no more then if they speak in a
strange language, or if they do, it concernes not them; or if it
stirs, 'tis but as the blowing of the winde upon a rock, which
blusters for a time; but when the winde is down they are still.
Truly they hear the word spoken, but they do not hear God
speaking. They heard *Latimer* speak, but not God speaking,
they hear a sound, which every one sayes, and they think is
the word, but they hear not God speaking it.

One would wonder that those Jewes that heard *John* and
his disciples, *Moses* and the Prophets, nay Gods voice from
heaven, saying, *This is my sonne*, that they should not hear
this, and receive him with all their hearts, but they did not
hear his voice. One would wonder to see, that such things
which a gracious heart thinks, this would draw every heart,

yet remaine not stir'd, things which the devils tremble at, and others which Angels wonder at, yet they hear not. Oh they hear not God speak, they are dead in their graves, farre from God; and there they are kept by the mighty power of Satan, like one in a deep dark cave, kept by fiery dragons under the ground, and the tombstone is laid upon them. If Christ spake he would make the dead to heare, and the blinde to see.

USE 2. Hence see why the Saints finde such changes and alterations in themselves when they come to heare; sometimes their hearts are quickned, fed and cherished, healed and comforted, relieved and visited; sometime again dead and senselesse, heavy and hardned. *Mark* 8. 17, 18, 21. *How is it ye do not understand?* Nay which is more, that the same truth which they hear at one time, should affect them, and at another time doth not; the same thing which they have heard a hundred times, and never stir'd them, at last should. The reason is, they heard the Word of God spoken at one time, but not God speaking; and they heard the Lord speaking that same Word at another time; the Lord is in his Word at one time, the Word goes alone at another time; as in *Eliah*, the Lord was not in the whirlwinde, but he spake in the *still voice*, and hence there he was to *Elijah, Luke* 24. 25. *with* 32. not that you are to lay blame on the Lord; for he blows where he listeth; but to make us see 'tis not in outward meanes, nor 'tis not in our own spirits to quicken our selves; and to make us ashamed of our own darknesse, that when he speaks, yet we cannot hear, there is so much power of spiritual death and Satan yet within us, only out of his pity he speaks sometimes; not that you should despise the outward word; No, no, the Lord is there shining in Perfection of glory, and that which doth thee no good, the Lord makes powerful to some others. But prize the Spirit of God in that Word, which alone can speak to thee.

USE 3. Of dread and terrour to all unregenerate men. Hence see the heavy wrath of God against them: they have indeed the Scriptures, and the precious Word of God dispensed to them; but the Lord never speaks one word unto them. If any one from whom we expect and look for love, passe by us and never speak; What not speak a word? and we call to him and he will not speak, we conclude he is angry and displeased with us. You look for love, do you not? you that heare every Sabbath, and come to Lectures, and you must out; tis well: yes, you will say, *His love is better then life*, and frownes more bitter then death; Love? wo to me if the Lord do not love me, better never been born. I hope he loves me. Happy I if the mountains might fall on me, to crush me in pieces if he loves me not, &c. but consider if he loves, he will then speak peace unspeakable to thy conscience when humbled, life to thy heart, joy in the Holy Ghost, *Isa.* 57. 19. *John* 6. 63. 1 *Thes.* 1. 6. but look upon thy soul, and see this day in the sight of God, whether ever the Lord spake one word to thee: outwardly indeed he hath, but not inwardly; inwardly also, but not effectually, *to turn them from darknesse to light, and the power of Satan to God, &c.* The voice of God is full of Majesty, it shakes the heart; 'tis full of life, it quickens the dead, and light, and peace, and gives wisdom to the simple. *Ps.* 119. *Opening of thy word gives light to the eyes.* How many women, ever learning and never knowing, and many men learning and knowing what is said, but never heare God speak? Then know the wrath of the Lord, see and go home mourning under it. There is a fourefold wrath in this.

1. 'Tis the Lords sore wrath and displeasure, *Zach.* 1. 2. with *ver.* 4. If one should expect love from another to do much for him, and he did not, it may be he would not take it as a signe of displeasure: but if he will not do a small thing, not speak a word to him, oh this is bitter; what will not the Lord speak a word, not one word, especially when thy life lies on it, thy soule lies on it, eternity lies on it, especially the Lord that is so merciful and pitiful? this is a signe of sore anger.

2. 'Tis a token of Gods old displeasure, eternal displeasure; I know you cannot heare; hence though God speaks, you hear him not: but why doth not the Lord remove that deafnesse? you old hearers, that have eares fat with hearing, but heavy, he never intended love, else he would speak there would be some time of love. *Rom.* 11. 7, 8. *The Elect have had it, others are blinded, as 'tis written, God hath given them the spirit of slumber, eyes that they should not see, and eares that they should not hear to this day.*

3. 'Tis the Lords present displeasure. When a man looks for love and speech, and he doth not speak at those times he is

not wont to speak; one may take it as no signe of anger: but when the Lord shall speak usually, and then he speaks not, this is a sad signe. 1 *Sam.* 28. 6, 15. He cries out of this, *He answers me not by* Urim *nor dreames,* nor thee by the Gospel nor Law, neither where he useth to answer. If this anger were to come, it were some comfort: but when 'tis now upon thee, even that very Sermon and Word whereby he speaks to others, but not a word to thee.

4. 'Tis his insensible anger: for a fat heart and an heavy eare ever go together; for you will say, I feel no hurt in this, I have heard and been never the better, but yet that hath made me never the worse. Oh poor creature! 'tis because you feel it not; but when the time of misery shall come, you will say, This is wo and load enough, for the Lord to give no answer. *Psal.* 74. 9. *We see not our Prophets, nor any to tell us how long:* so you that despise meanes you shall then lament and say, none can tell how long. Oh therefore, lament this thy condition now, that the Lord may hear some of your cries, &c.

USE 4. Hence examine whether ever you heard the Lords voice or no: not only outwardly (for that you know you have often done) but inwardly; and not only so, for so ye may do, and yet your eares heavy; but effectually, that if it be not so, you may be humble and say, Lord how have I spent my time in vaine? and if it be so, you may be thankful, and say, Lord, what am I that the infinite God should speak to me?

There is great need of trial of this, for a man may reade, hear and understand externally, whatever another may; and yet the whole Scripture a sealed book.

There are therefore these three degrees, by which you shall discern the effectual voice of God, you must take them joyntly.

1. The voice of God singles a man out, and (though it be generally written or spoken) speaks particularly to the very heart of a man, with a marvellous kinde of Majesty and glory of God stamp't upon it; and shining in it.

When a man heares things generally delivered, the blessed estate of the Saints, the cursed estate of the wicked, consolations to the one, curses to the other, exhortations to faith and obedience, to both, and a man sits by, and never thinks the Lord is now speaking, and means me. Or if it doth so, yet thinks he intends me no more then others, he heares not the Lord speaking; for when he speaks, he speaks particularly to the very heart of a man: he doth so fit the word to him, whether it be the Word of the law to humble him, or of Gospel to comfort, or of command to guide, as if the Lord meant none but them.

The word is like an exact picture, it looks every man in the face that looks on it, if God speaks in it, *Heb.* 4. 12, 13. *It searcheth the heart, verse* 12. but *verse* 13. he speaks of God, how comes that in? because God, the Majesty of God comes with it when God speaks it; *With whom we have to do*, why is that put in? because when the Lord speaks, a man thinks now I have to do with God, if I resist I oppose a God. Before this a man thinks he hath nothing to do with God, they are such strangers. Hence it is one man is wrought on in a Sermon, another not. God hath singled out one, not the other that day. Hence take a man unhumbled, he hears many things, and it may be understands not; if so, yet they concern not him; if they do, and conscience is stir'd, yet they think man means them, and speaks by hap, and others are as bad as they, and his trouble is not much. At last he heares his secret thoughts and sins discovered, all his life is made known, and thinks 'tis the Lord verily that hath done this; now God speaks, 1 *Cor.* 14. 25. those things he did neither believe nor imagine; &c. *John* 4. 29. *See the man that hath told me all that ever I did.* Hence take a soul that is humbled, he heares of the free offer of grace, he refuseth it; why, this is to all and to hypocrites as well as to me. Apply any promise to it, it casts by all, it looks upon them as things generally spoken, and applied by man, but they hear not God speaking; but when the Lord comes, he doth so meet with their objections, and speaks what they have been thinking may be true, that they think this is the Lord, this is to me. *Hosea* 2. 14. *I'le speak to her heart*: and hence 'tis called *the ingraffed word*, James 1. 21. like one branch of many, applied to the stock, *Job* 33. 14, 16.

2. The voice of the Lord doth not only speak particularly, but it goes further; it comes not only with an Almighty power, but with a certain everlasting efficacy and power on the soul. Thus 'tis here, *verse* 38. *Ye have not his word in you*, they had it out of them; and not only in you, but abiding in

you, 1 *Pet.* 1. 23. *born of incorruptible seed*, the Apostle seems
to speak of a kinde of birth by corruptible seed, and such are
like goodly flowers which soon wither, but you are born of incorruptible seed, which hath an eternal savour, sweetnesse
and power. *Mat.* 13. of the foure grounds three of them fall
away. *John* 15. 16. Their fruit does not remain: they have some
living affection at the present, but they go away and it dies.
Look but upon particulars, doth the Lord once speak by the
Word, and humble the heart? it never lifts up its head more;
doth he reveal the glory of Christ? that light never goes out
more. *Isa.* 60. 19. 2 *Cor.* 4. 4, 5. As at the first Creation, there
was light, and so continues to this day; so doth he give life,
John 11. 26. You shall never die more; doth he give peace and
joy? no man shall take their joy from them. *Isa.* 32. 17. *Fruit
of Righteousnesse and Peace, and assurance for ever.* Doth he
give the Spirit of all these, which *Gal.* 3. comes by hearing of
faith? it shall abide for ever, *John* 14. 17.

That look as Gods love is everlasting, so his words have an
everlasting excellency and efficacy in them, and goodnes in
them, the sweetest token of his love: and as Christs purchase
is only of eternal good things; so the application of this purchase by the Word, 'tis of eternal worth: peace, but peace
eternal, life, light, favour, joy, but joy eternal; like mustard
seed, though very little, yet mighty in increase, and never subdued again; so that though it be but little, yet 'tis eternal: and
hence observe where God hath spoken effectually, the longer
the man lives, the more he growes in the vertue and power of
the word; another though wonderfully ravished for a time, yet
dies, most commonly outwardly in external Profession, but
ever in inward savour; so that when you hear the word, and it
moves you, affects you, and *John is a burning light, and you
rejoyce therein, but 'tis but for a season.* The evil Spirit comes
on you, and *David* plays upon his Harp, and Ministers
preach sweet things, but as soon as the Musick is done, the
evil Spirit returns, I say you never heard the Lords voice. The
peace and joy of the Lord enters into Eternity, and the
Apostle expresly calls him an unfruitful hearer, *James* 1. 24.
that sees his face and forgets himself. A gracious heart can say,
This peace shall go to heaven; and joy, and love, and fear, it's
part of eternal glory.

3. The voice of the Lord comes not only thus particularly, and with eternal efficacy, but with such efficacy as carries unto, and centers in Christ; so 'tis here: *For him whom God hath sent you believe not. John* 6. 41. *They shall be taught of God*: wherein doth that appear? *they shall hear and learn so as to come to me;* if the law humbles them, it's such a humbling as drives them unto Christ, poor and undone, *Rom.* 10. 4. if the Word gives peace to them, 'tis such a peace which at the last they finde in Christ, *Eph.* 2. 17, 18. with 14. if it live holily, it lives unto Christ, not meerly as to God, and to quiet conscience, unto a Creator as *Adam*, but for Christs sake. 2 *Cor.* 5. 14, 15. *We judge that if we were dead, and Christ died for us, we should then live unto him;* if they grow up by the word, 'tis in Christ, *Eph.* 4. 14. though Christ be not mentioned, yet it is strange to see, let the word speak what it will, whether terrour; Oh my need of Christ! mercy and grace; oh the love of Christ! oh the blood of Christ! Command; Oh that I may live to honour Christ, and wrong him no more! Duties; Oh the easie yoke of Christ! They look upon the whole Word rightly dispensed as the Bridegrooms voice, and truly his words are sweet.

For a man may have some such feare, reformation, affection, as may continue, but never carry him out of himself unto Christ. The Pharisees knew the law, were very exact even til their death, profited as *Paul* said he did; yet they had not the word abiding in them; because not driven out of themselves to Christ, to rest there.

Hence when men shall hear many things, but to what end do you heare, or what vertue have the things you hear? Do they only please fancy for a time? or do you hear to increase your knowledge and parts? or do you hear for custome and company, and to quiet conscience? or are you affected and sunk, but not driven by all to lay thy head on Christ? the Lord never spake yet to thee; when the word hath laid you on this foundation, truly it's office is done and ended, Gods end is now attained, &c.

Oh try your selves here, have you heard, but never heard the voice of the Lord, rushing upon thee with Majesty, speaking to thy heart, and the very secrets of it, but have said, This is for others, and when you have thought the man hath spoken to you, your hearts have then swollen against him? or have you thus heard, but all dies and withers like flowers, the same heart still? or have you had some powerful stroke which remaines, but it forceth you not out of your selves to Christ, there to rest, there to joy, there to live, there to die? truly your time hath been spent in vain, you never yet heard the Lord speak. Oh mourn for it, thou art still in thy blood, if he never said Live; in thy bondage, if the Lord never said, Come forth. This is the condition of many to be lamented with teares. But if thou hast thus heard particularly, and though but little light, life and peace, yet it is of eternal efficacy, and all to draw thee to Christ; then blesse the Lord: *For blessed are your eares that hear,* and I say as *Moses* said, *Deut.* 4. 32. *Ask if ever People heard God speaking and live.* The Apostle, *Heb.* 12. 24. makes it a greater matter to come to hear God on *Mount Sion,* and yet live; Blessed be God I live.

OBJECT. But may not many of the Saints hear, and hear the Lord speak; but not feel this everlasting power and efficacy?

ANSW. I would not lay a foundation of unthankfulnesse, nor discourage any; and therefore, note for answer these particulars.

1. There may be an eternal efficacy of the Word, and yet ly hid, and not felt for a time. The Word is compared, you know, to seed, and that in this respect; the seed it is cast under the clod in the winter-time, and it hath a vertue in it to grow; but it is hid, and comes not to blade of a good while; and when it doth blade, yet it beares not fruit of a long time: So here, the Lord may cast the seed of his Word into the heart; but it is hidden for a time, it is not felt as yet, but there it is; a word of threatning, a word of promise, a word of Command; a man may cast it by, and say, It belongs not to me; a man may slight the command for a time: Yet notwithstanding, the Lord having cast his seed into the heart; it shall spring up. As many a childe, the father speaks to it, and applies the word home to it, when it is of some years; the childe regards it not: But now stay some time, till the Lord do bring it into some sad affliction; now a man begins to think, I remember what my father spake to me once, & I regarded it not then: Now this seed which was cast when the childe was

young, it shall spring up twenty years after. *John* 2. 22. Christ had said, *He would destroy the Temple, and raise it againe in three dayes:* Now *when he was risen from the dead, his disciples remembred that which he had spoken to them,* but they regarded it not before; *These things,* saith Christ, *have I spoken to you whiles I was with you; but when the comforter is come, he shall bring all these words to your remembrance that I have said unto you.* One sentence it may be that hath discovered a mans sin, it lyes hid; but when the time of ripening drawes near, you shall see the word will have marvelous increase; and that sin it may be will bring to minde twenty sins; and that promise of God which gives but a little consolation, consider'd in it self, it shall give marvelous consolation. One would wonder to see what one word will do, when the Lords time of blessing it is come.

2. After that a Christian hath had the feeling of the efficacy of the word, he may lose the feeling of it again, and yet the being of it may remain; and the reason is this, partly because there is not alwayes need of feeling the like efficacy in the word. A man may have by the word a marvelous deal of assurance of Gods love, and sense of mercy and joy in the holy Ghost, he may have this in the feeling of it: This word, it did ly hid for a time; afterward it springs up and gives him peace. But he loses his peace again, his Sun do's set, and it is midnight with him within twenty four hours, and he is as much in the dark as before; Now the being of this peace is there, but he hath no need of the feeling of it at all times; the Lord he will reserve that till some time of tentation, that he shall meet withall. As *Paul,* he had marvelous Revelations; but *Paul* had more need of humiliation, then exaltation; and there was not that use of *Pauls* having those glorious manifestations to him; *I will glory in my infirmities:* There was need for *Paul* to know the evils of his heart, that he might walk humbly; and it did not make so much for the glory of the Lord, as this that *Paul* should say; I have this misery and darknesse, and sins, and yet Jesus Christ he will take away all: There was not need for *Paul* to have those joyes at all times, that he had at one time. So the Lord he gives a Christian joy and peace, now there is no need for a Christian to have it alwayes. *I will pour floods of water on dry ground:* Beloved, if

there should be nothing but raine, raine every day and night, the ground would be glutted with raine, and so turned into a puddle; but when the land is dry and thirsty, now the ground hath need of raine: Let the Earth make use of that raine it hath: and when it is dry and thirsty, I will give more, saith the Lord. So the Lord he gives the soul joy and peace; Now, if it should continue, the very peace and joy of God, would not be pleasant to the soul; or at least, not so pleasant as it will be, when the Lord takes it away, and gives it the soul again. A Christian comes to the meeting-house, and the Lord fills the sailes of a poor soul, that he wonders the Lord should meet him, and speak so suitably to him: But as soone as he is gone out again, this is the complaint of the soul, all is lost again; now the soul it falls a mourning again. It is not for the glory of God to give the soul such peace out of his Ordinances, as he doth in them; the soul it would not prize the Ordinances of the Lord so much; yet there it is; and when they come again, the Lord, he either gives them the same refreshings again, or else there is a new spring.

3. The eternall efficacy of the word and voice of God; it may be preserved in an internall spirit of prayer, for the con-tinuance of it while a man hath it, and for the return of it when it is lost. *Ps.* 119. 4, 5. *Thou hast commanded us to keep thy precepts diligently. David* he knew his own weaknesse; yet he intimates with what power it came on his heart: *Oh that my soul were directed to keep thy statutes;* When the soul sees the beauty of a command, and the good will of God, how sweet it is, and how amiable the way and work of God is; *Oh that my heart were directed to keep thy statutes.* And so when it is gone, *Psal.* 63. 3. *My soul thirsteth after thee, Lord,* saith *David, that I may see thy glory and power, as I have seen thee in thy Sanctuary.* He doth not say, that I may see thy glory and power in thy sanctuary, though that might be too; no, but *that I may see thy glory and power, as I have seen thee in thy sanctuary. David* he did finde a want of seeing him as he had done; yet the vertue of it did remaine in a spirit of thirsting, and desire: *My soul thirsteth for thee, as in a dry land where no water is, that I may see thee.* A Christian may have at sometime such a glimpse (in hearing the word) of Gods grace, of the ex-ceeding riches of Gods grace, and the love of God to him,

that he may be in a little heaven at that time; ravished in the admiration of that mercy, that ever God should look to him. It is so, and the word sayes so, and the soul is ravished with wonderment at it; yet God is gone again, and the soul loses it. Now the soul thinks, I have lost the efficacy of Gods word, but it is not so; for thus it may be preserved. Oh that I may see this God as I have done: And all his life-time the soul may finde the want of this, and yet it may be preserved in a spirit of prayer. For whom the Lord hath given once a glimpse of his glory; the soul it cannot be at rest, but it breatheth for more of that mercy and presence; a Christian may finde his spirit marvelously refreshed at the word, he may taste how good the Lord is, and he may lose it again: but this may be preserved in a spirit of longing after this God, and presence again. And I will say this, Brethren, A Christian may finde no good by the word to his apprehension; he sees the admirable blessed estate of the Saints, and exceeding riches of God in Christ, sees the swetnesse of the wayes of God; goes home and thinks within himself, Happy they that are in this condition: Blessed are they that can walk thus with God; But I cannot, saith the soul. I say it may finde it thus, when he cannot finde the reall efficacy of the word as he would do; he may receive the benefit of that word, if the Lord do but only give him a heart to desire it. Oh that the Lord would but thus manifest himself to me; the soul may go away poor and hungry from the word, and the Lord may yet reserve a spirit of thirsting after that good which a man desires to finde; and there is the efficacy of the word there.

As now there are two golden vessels; one a man fills, and it is every day dropping, and he preserves it; another vessel he do's not fil, but with something that he hath, he is every day widening of it. So some Christians, the Lord he's a filling of them; others, the Lord he do's not fill them with such peace and joy; ay, but though the Lord is not filling of them, he is a widening of them: there is such a vertue that the Lord do's enlarge the heart; with secret desires and longings after more of Gods grace, and Christs: The Lord he saith, I intend to make this man a vessel of glory; and I intend he shall have a great deal of glory and peace at the last. The Lord he leaves such an impression of the word upon him, as that thereby he enlargeth the heart; *Open thy mouth wide, and I will fill it.*

4. A Christian may have the everlasting efficacy of the word and voice of God preserved in a spirit of thankfulnesse and love to the Lord, for those joyes and good that it findes by the word sometimes. When it feels that the sweet and savour of the word is gone, a spirit of thankfulnesse and love to the word that doth remaine; The Lord he preserves the efficacy of the word in this way. *Psal.* 119. 7. *I shall,* saith *David, then praise thee with uprightnesse of heart, when I shall have learned thy righteous judgements.* The Lord he may teach his people his righteous judgements; and the savour and feeling, and strength of them to their feeling may be gone, and yet it is preserved in a spirit of thankfulnesse and praise, that ever the Lord should shew it such mercy. When the Spirit is gone, the spirit of love and thankfulnesse remaines. As now a man hath heard the word, the Lord he hath effectually wrought on him, and changed his heart, and drawn him to himself; a Christian it may be he may lose those sorrowes and humiliations, and the remembrance of those things; yet there remaineth to his dying day this Spirit, he blesseth God, and wondereth at God, that ever he should make the word effectual; that he should leave so many thousands in the world, and cast his skirt over him, and say to him, Live; this do's remain still.

Brethren, the Lord do's sometimes let light into a mans minde to discover his sin: now this light it do's not sensibly overcome the power of sinne: But now the soul blesseth God for that word which hath convinced it; had I never seen my sinne, saith the soul, I should never a sought for power against it, and pardon of it; and this continues now, and cannot but continue; here is the efficacy of the word, the word of Gods grace; though the flower of it be gone, yet there is an eternal power of the word; that the soul can say, It hath come to me, and helped me against these sins; and the soul wonders at the Lord, it should be so much as it is. So again, a Christian he findes marvelous refreshings and affection whiles he is a hearing; when he is gone away, he findes not the same, but he blesseth God for those affections he findes, and there remains an eternall efficacy of the word.

5. The eternall efficacy of the word, it may be and is preserved, by nourishing, increasing and restoring the new man that is eternall. There is a double efficacy that the word hath; the first is to beget a Christian to life, and this new man is eternall. I conceive all the actions of the new man may be suspended, and the increasings of the new creature may be decayed, though God doth renew it again: But this never do's decay, it never dies: *He that is born of God cannot sin, because he is borne of God; and because the seed of God remaines in him.*

2. There is efficacy in the word when it hath begotten a man to nourish him up; and so the word it is food to him, that was seed to him to beget him, which food is eternal. How is it eternal? Is it in this, that now the sweetnesse, savour and remembrance of every thing that doth refresh him, shall last in it self? No, but in this respect it is eternall, in that it leaveth its secret vertue in the nourishing of that which is eternall. As now *Adam* when he was in innocency, and had an immortall body, his food it should have been an immortal food to him; but how should that have been? should he alwayes have had the same strength, from the same diet, which he ate long before? No, but in this respect it should have been an immortall food to him, in that it was to nourish that which was to be eternal: So it is here, the word of Gods grace it begets a man, it humbles a man, and drawes the soul to Christ; but afterwards, there are many things that God speaks to the soul in the word, that hath an eternall vertue, in that it doth nourish up the new creature; the word hath a secret vertue in it for this end. I will shew it you thus; *Isa.* 58. 11. The Lord he professes to his People, *Thy soul shall be as a watered garden:* The Lord will make the souls of his people like watered gardens, in peace, and joy, and life. Now look as if so be trees by water or by some springs that run by it, and slide away, and ye cannot tell, which it is that makes them to grow; yet ye know this, there is in all of them joyned together, a secret insensible vertue; that every one of them addes something to the flourishing of the tree: So it is here, the Saints of God, the word of God it comes to them, and passes by them; and ye cannot tell whether this part or that part of the word leave any vertue, but many times a man feels no vertue; yet it is manifest, here is a flourishing Christian, here is heart, and

life, and peace that it hath with God, and the soul it remains flourishing; there is a secret vertue, all the words that run by and passe by the souls of Gods people, they do leave a marvellous vertue, to make the soules of Gods people like watered gardens, and to increase in grace. Note it by the way you that live under the means of grace, *your soules shall be like watered gardens;* if God have spoken to you first or last, the Lord speaks many times to you, sometimes affecting, and sometimes warning, sometimes convincing and humbling, and speaking Peace, and there is a vertue that remaines, and if ye finde it not, know that God hath not spoken to you.

6. The eternal efficacy of the word may be preserved in a power of Conflict against the power of sin: for therein the Lords power of the Word does principally appear in this life, though not in a power of victory, I mean a compleat victory, yet an imperfect and incompleat victory, there ever is first or last, whereever there is a power of Conflict. I mean thus, the Word it singles a man out, and speaks to his heart, and sets him at variance with his sin, and with himself for his sin, and he joynes side with God in the use of all meanes, that his unbelieving heart and proud Spirit may be subdued; it sets him at variance with his sin; now there is many a Christian thinks there is no power of the Word: oh my unbelief continues still, and my vain minde, and I can finde little strength; no, ye must not look for a power of compleat victory, but yet there is a power of Conflict; God he sets the soul at an everlasting distance with his sin, never to be reconciled, and looks to the Lord, that by his Word and Spirit he would subdue them, that so he may see the death of them, and he sides with the Lord in the use of all means, comes to the Word, and comes to Prayer, and sayes, Speak against my sin, Lord; Lord, waste these distempers: and so the soul is thus at variance with his sin, although his temptations do get winde and hill of him, he goes again, and to them again: and though he perisheth, and never have mercy from the Lord; yet, Lord, that I may never sin against thee more, help therefore, Lord, by this promise, and mercy and meanes; and here he keeps him, and here he holds. Truly, brethren, here is an eternal vertue, and such a vertue as no hypocrites have, that have some sting of conscience, and after they have some peace, they are at truce with

their sins. No, there is an everlasting conflict and warfare, and I do assure you there is an everlasting power gone forth. *Mat.* 12. 20. *Christ will not break the bruised reed, nor quench the smoaking flax, till judgement come to victory;* Therefore there may be judgement, but it may not come to victory, there may be smoak and fire, and it may almost go out, and the Lord he blowes it up again, and at the last, though it be weak and little, and he think with himself he shall never get strength again, yet the Lord will give victory in his time.

Only be cautious here; I told you there is an incompleat victory, the Lord never sets his people at variance with their sin, but they have victory, but it is an incompleat victory, Saith the Lord, *I will drive out the Hittites, and Canaanites, and Perizzites before you, but I will do it by little and little.* There is many a Christian that findes within himself a Spirit of warfare against his sin, and did he examine himself, he should finde a Spirit of victory; but he thinks he hath none because his victory is not compleat. If he had a heart so to believe as never to doubt more, and such quickning as never to be dead more, never to depart from God more, now I should think the Word comes with power; but I finde that these evils prevaile against me. There is many a one does scorn the kindnesse of Christ, because he findes not compleat victory, but darknesse remaines still, and sinful lusts remaine still, therefore the Word doth me no good at all, saith he. The Lord he hath given thee a Spirit of Conflict, and hath set thee at an everlasting distance with thy sin, and he doth give thee some victory. Beloved, a Christian may decay in the power of the grace of Christ, which he hath received from the Word, and voice of God in the Word, and he may decay and grow to a very low estate; yet he shall finde this, the Word of the Lord hath come with power to him, it will recover his soul again, and so the efficacy of the Word is eternal. *Psal.* 72. its said of Christ, that *his People shall feare him so long as Sun and Moon shall endure,* that is, continually, all their life-time. It may be said, there be many that finde decay of their service and obedience, and they lose their feare of the Lord, and their dread, and their humble walking before him, *He shall come as the raine on the mowen grasse:* many times a Christian hath his flourishing time as the grasse, but when the grasse is mowen, it is as a dry chip; so the soul it may grow dry, as dry as a chip. Now where is your sap and savour? but I tell you, if you belong to the Lord Jesus, the raine it will fall again, the Word of God set on by the Spirit of Christ, it shall fall upon you as the raine on the mowen grasse, and you know that it recovers little by little, and puts on a green coat again. Here is the eternal love of the Lord Jesus to his People, and thus the eternal efficacy of the word does continue.

3. USE is of exhortation. Oh Brethren and beloved in the Lord Jesus, may a Christian heare the Word of God spoken, and yet never hear God speak? may he hear it externally and not internally? then rest not in external hearing, and with some little movings, and affections, and stirrings of the Word of Gods grace in hearing. Let not the Word be to you as the sound of many waters, and a noise, no efficacy of the Word that do remaine on your soules. Brethren and beloved in Christ, I lay my finger on the sore in these times. Oh the contempt of the Gospel of Christ, though I believe it hath its efficacy in the heart of the Elect: that is the thing that I presse, never be content with external hearing, though thou mayest have some affection, and know new things, unlesse thou finde the Lord speaking with an eternal efficacy to thy soul. I conceive two things are to be done, that the word may come with an everlasting efficacy; although something is to be done by Ministers; that is, to preach truth, and Gospel-truth, fetch't from heaven with many prayers, and soaked truth with many teares. *Ye shall know the truth, and that truth shall make you free.* Convicting truth. *We preach,* saith the Apostle, *in the demonstration of the Spirit. The Spirit of God when he cometh, he convinceth the world of sin.* Let Ministers do so. Preach convincing truth and Gospel-truth, fetch'd from heaven, and bathed in teares. Oh brethren, let the fire burn clear, let there not be more smoake then fire, it will never come with power then; convincing Gospel-truth, set on by the demonstration of the Spirit of the Lord, and this will set a Christian at liberty; there is never such a Sermon that the faithful ones of God preach to you; if it come not with a power to loosen you and call you home; it comes with a power to blinde you: it is

an axe at the root of the trees, but I leave this. What means ought the people to use, that the Word of God may come with efficacy?

Them that are in their unregenerate estate, the Lord only knowes how to work on their hearts; they must come to the outward meanes. I speak to the Saints of God, I leave others to the infinite mercy of the Lord; *It is not in him that willeth or runneth, but in the Lord that sheweth mercy.* In the use of meanes.

1. Meanes. Do not only see they infirmities and weakness, but pray to God to give thee a heart bleeding under the sense of thy many infirmities. Many times men slight them, and are not sensible of them; I do not say wickednesses and wilfulnesses, but thy infirmities and weaknesses, get a heart mourning under them. A Christian is made up of infirmities and weaknesses, a man would not think there is that in another, which he knowes by himself. Oh brethren, labour for a broken heart in the sense of your many infirmities and weaknesses, darknesse and enmity, vanity and unsavourinesse, the Lord will have his time to speak to such a soul. *Break up the fallow ground of your hearts,—lest my wrath break out with fire:* the Lord hath promised *to dwell with the poor and contrite.* Look as it was with our Saviour Christ, they brought the sick and the lame ones to him, and vertue went out from Christ to heal them all. Bring thy sick and blinde heart to Christ, and vertue shall go forth from Christ to heal it.

2. Draw near to God in the Word, by looking on it as God speaking to thee. We are far from God, and therefore we cannot hear him: draw near to him when you come to the external Word, when you come to heare the Word, heare it as the voice of God; *You heard the Word as the Word of God,* which you felt in you. I do not speak that the soule should take every thing that Ministers speak as the Word of God, but that which is the Word of God, take it as God speaking. I am not able to expresse the infinite unknown sweetnesse, and mercy, and presence of God, that you shall finde thus coming. I know it is a common truth, but I am not ashamed to tell you, I have not for many a year understood this truth, and I see but little of it yet; ye have heard of it, but ye do not understand what it is to hear God speaking. When God hath an

intent to harden a mans heart and to damn him, either he
shall have a prejudice against the man, or else if he hath not a
prejudice against the man, there is a secret loathing of the
truth, in regard of the commands of it, and that is all, and the
Lord he hardens, and blindes, and prepares for eternal ruine,
all the men in the world by this meanes, that live under the
meanes. When the Lord spake to *Samuel, Samuel* heard a
voice, but he heard it not as spoken by God, but when he
took *Elies* counsel, and saw it was the Lord that spoke; now
he listens to the voice of the Lord, and now the Lord opens
all his minde to him.

3. Do not trust to the external word. It is a heaven on earth
to hear the Word exalted, a glorious thing to hear the Word
of God as Gods Word; but trust to the free grace of God in
it, and the Spirit of God in Christ to set on that Word. When
they brought the lame, and blinde, and halt to Christ, they
looked for the Word and the Power of it; *Speak the Word,
Lord, and thy servants shall be whole;* so bring your blinde,
lame, and halt soules to Christ, and trust to the free grace of
the Lord Jesus Christ. *The Work of the Lord it shall prosper in
his hand;* so the Word of the Lord it shall prosper in his hand
also.

Lastly, so seek the Lord, and so heare the Word, to see the
truth, and so heare the truth, as that you lay up your happinesse in this world, in closing with the truth and with the
word. Brethren, what is a mans happinesse in heaven, but to
close with God and Christ? I cannot come to God now, the
most that I can have of God now is in his word; if it be happinesse in heaven to close with God in Christ, truly then it is
a mans happinesse to close with God in his word on earth;
and if it be your happinesse, lay up your happinesse in it. *My
son,* saith Solomon, *if thou wilt hear my word, let them not
depart from thine eyes; keep them in the middest of thy heart;*
place thy happinesse in them. *So shall they be life to thy soul.*
Neverthelesse Brethren, let a mans soul be set upon any thing
in the world, when he comes to hear, besides the word; if he
lay not up his happinesse in closing with the word; truely, the
word it will be like a song to him. The Prophet *Ezekiel* tells
them, *Their hearts were gone after their covetousnesse.* When a
man comes to hear a Sermon, there is a Sermon and the

Market, there is a Sermon and a friend to speak withall; and
so many young people will go abroad to hear Sermons; What
is the end of it? It is, that ye may get wives and husbands
many of you; but it is not your blessednesse to close with the
Lord in his word. I have known some men that have had a
distaste against the truth of the Lord; and I have known them
for many a day, they have not been able to understand the
truth of the Lord. When it shall be thus with a man, that a
mans heart is set on something else besides the word of the
Lord, that it is not my happinesse to close with the truth of
the Lord; such a man shall never understand the truth of the
Lord. Though the word be sweet to you sometimes, if your
blessednesse do not lye in this, to enjoy God; Oh this Gospel
of God, and these Commands of God, that your blessednesse
do not lye in cleaving to the Lord in his word; I say, it is a certain truth, you shall be blinded and hardned by the word: For
here is a Rule; Whatsoever a mans heart is set on, as his
chiefest good, the presence of that good it comes with power:
So here, the precious Gospel of Christ, when the presence of
it commands the heart, nothing is good enough for it, and it
closeth with it, and with Christ in it.

I beseech you therefore, Beloved in Christ, set upon the
use of these meanes, think within your selves; What if the
Lord had left me without the word? I will tell you what ye
would have been. Look upon these poor *Indians*, herds of
Beasts; look upon others on their Ale-benches, enemies to the
Lord, such a one thou hadst been.

This blessed word and voice of God, every tittle of it cost
the blood of Christ; written all the lines of it in the blood of
Christ. Oh, make much of it, and it will make much of you;
it will comfort you, and strengthen you, and revive you; and
if the word come not with power, ye shall be under the power
of something else; if not under the power of the word, then
under the power of some lust. What is the reason that these
poor creatures, that are come to the tryall for life and death,
that have fallen into such sins as were never heard of? What is
the reason that they are under the power of their lusts? I will
tell you what *Solomon* saith, *My son, if wisdome enter into thy
heart, and discretion be pleasant to thy soul, it shall keep thee
from the strange woman,* & sinful companion. If it be pleasant,

here is the reason, the word of Gods grace it never came with power, or if it came with power, powerless the word of Gods grace hath been to them; and because it hath not come with power, the Lord he hath given them over to the power of their lusts, and sinfull distempers. Oh Brethren, truely I cannot see how any man can maintaine any evidence of Gods electing love; that shall hear and hear, and good dayes mend him not, nor bad dayes paire him: that can commend a Sermon, and speak of it; but that efficacy is not known to him, neither doth he mourne for the want of it; but the eternall efficacy thereof is a stranger to it. 1 *Thes.* 1. 5. *Knowing*, saith the Apostle, *your election of God*; How did he know it? For, saith he, *Our Gospel came not to you in word, but in power*; ye will rejoyce the hearts of your Ministers, when the word comes with power. Let me say this, and so I conclude.

I remember the Lords threatning; *I will take away the staffe of bread, and ye shall eat, and shall not be satisfied;* When the Lord shall let men have the word, when the Lord shall not take away the word, but the staffe of the word. Suppose you poor Parents, Fathers, and Mothers; your families should have good Corne, but when you come to eat it, no strength at all, but ye dye and weare away; and others that are about you, they have planted the same Corne, and eat and are satisfied; What will ye do in this case? You would set apart a day of fasting and prayer; and say, Good Lord, what a curse is upon me? my poor children are dying before me, others have the staffe of Corne; but my Family have no strength at all. Ye would mourne if it were thus with your poor Cattell. Oh, for poor Creatures to have the word, but the efficacy of it to be taken away; no blessing, no power at all. Oh poor Creatures, go and say! Oh the the curse of God that lyes on me, the wrath of God that lyes on my servants, it is a heavy plague. But Oh the sweetnesse and excellency of it, when a Christian shall finde everlasting vertue and efficacy conveyed to him by the word.

All you that are before the Lord this day, ye shall see an end of all perfection; but eternall things are not they worth something? You shall see an end of all delights and contentments; but this shall comfort you when you are a dying, that the word which you attended upon the Lord in, such peace, and such consolations I have found by it; and the efficacy of that word then remaines with you; nay, goes to heaven with you. *I commend you therefore to the word of his grace, which is able to build you up unto an eternall inheritance amongst them that are sanctified, Acts* 20. 32.

FINIS

JONATHAN MITCHEL

Nehemiah on the Wall in Troublesom Times

Or,

*A Serious and Seasonable Improvement of that great
Example of Magistratical Piety and Prudence, Self-denial
and Tenderness, Fearlesness and Fidelity, unto
Instruction and Encouragement of present
and succeeding Rulers in our Israel.*

*As it was delivered in a Sermon Preached at
Boston in N. E. May 15. 1667. being the
Day of Election there.*

Psal. 78. 70–72. *He chose David his servant—He brought
him to feed Jacob his people, and Israel his inheritance.
So he fed them according to the integrity of his heart,
and guided them by the skilfulness of his hands.*

Josh. 7. 10. *And the Lord said to Joshua, Get thee up:
wherefore liest thou thus upon thy face?*

Isa. 32. 1, 2.—*Princes shall rule in judgement. And a
man shall be as an hiding-place from the wind, and a
cover from the tempest, as rivers of water in a dry place,
as the shadow of a great rock in a weary land.*

———

AT THE ELECTION AT BOSTON,
MAY 15. 1667.

Nehemiah 2. 10.
There was come a man to seek the welfare of the children of Israel.

THE *Occasion* of these words, and frame of the *Context*, is
known and obvious to every Reader, we need not take up
time in that.

The words are a short, but notable *Character* or description of good *Nehemiah*, when appointed to be *Governour* or
Ruler in *Judah*, and that in a time of trouble (of great

Affliction and Reproach, as *ver.* 3. of *Chap.* 1. and the whole frame of the Story tells us) then he willingly undertakes the Charge, and comes with this design, this was his aim and *spirit*, (as it was afterward his *practise*) to seek the *Welfare* of the Children of *Israel*. If you ask who or what *Nehemiah* was, that was now come to be Ruler in *Judah*, (for so he was, *Chap.* 5. 14.) or what his business or design was? You are answered in this *Periphrasis, There was come a man to seek the welfare of the children of Israel*. It is brought in here as that that was the grief of the *back-friends* of *Judah*, (*Sanballat* and *Tobiah, when they heard of it, it grieved them exceedingly*, saith the Text) but it was a truth in it self; (that is it that I aim at) this was the *News* that was then to be heard at *Jerusalem*: and it was no small joy to them, that there was come a man (*viz. Nehemiah*) whose aim, business and spirit *was to seek the welfare*, (or *the good*, as the word is) *of*, or that *that was good for, the children of Israel*.

But without further *Preface*, the words plainly afford us this Truth:

DOCT. *It is the Work and Spirit of faithful Rulers, to seek the welfare of the People, especially when as they are the People of the God of Israel*. Or,

It is the Duty and the Spirit of faithful Rulers, even in difficult and troublesome Times, (you may adde that, for that was *the case* of the *Text*) *to seek the good* (or *welfare*) *of the People, especially when as they are the People of God.*

Thus *Nehemiah* did, this was his *Spirit* and *Character*, and he made it his business all the time he was Ruler in *Judah*, as the whole after-story shews, which is a large *Comment* on the *Text*; and his commended Example is here set forth in the Book of God, for others *Instruction* and *Imitation*. Rulers (I say) *are to seek the welfare, the good of the People*: *Rom.* 13. 4. *He is the Minister of God to thee for good*; speaking of the *Civil Magistrate*: he is so by his *Place*, and he ought to be so in his *Practice*; *Esth.* 10. 3. *Wealth-good* (the word is) or *welfare*: the same word is there in the *Hebrew*, with this in the Text. *Luk.* 22. 25. Civil Rulers are called *Benefactors*, (saith Christ) and such they ought to be, as they may justly and truly be so called; Benefactors, ἐνεργέται, *doers of good*, to and for the people they rule over, especially when they are the *people* of

God; so we know *Israel* (the children of *Israel*) were Gods *Covenant people*, 2 *Sam.* 7. 24. and to seek the welfare of such a people (the children and people of *Israel*) that hath an *Emphasis* in the Text, was emphatically the *design* and *desire* of good *Nehemiah*; that consideration moved his heart when he was in the Court of *Persia*, both to *pray* for them, and to *endeavour* their help, *Chap.* 1. 10. The safety of *Jerusalem*, the holy City, by his building up the Wall thereof, was his main design, *Nehem.* 2. 13, 17. So *Psal.* 78. 71, 72. great is the Trust and Obligation upon *David*, when set to *feed* (to *Rule*) *Jacob*, that are the people of God, and *Israel* his inheritance: *Psal.* 122. 9. so speaks *David*, a Ruler, to *Jerusalem*. For the Religious Interests thereof (Because of the House of God that is in it) he is eminently affected *to seek its good*.

For a little *Explication*. The *Object*, [the Peoples welfare] and the *Act*, [Seek] are here considerable.

QUEST. I. *What is that good, or welfare of the people, which Rulers ought to seek? or wherein doth it consist?*

ANSW. Take it in the Example of *Nehemiah*, the improvement whereof the Text leads us unto.

1. They are to seek the Maintenance and furtherance of true *Religion* amongst a people. *Nehemiah* did not think himself unconcern'd in that; or that he being a *Civil Ruler*, had nothing to do in matters of *Religion*: He encouraged and assisted *Ezra* in the Reformation of Religion, *Chap.* 8. & 10. He put forth his Authority to *restrain* and *redress* sundry abuses therein; as *Nehem.* 13. *The defiling of the Temple*, ver. 7, 8, 9. *Neglect of the Levites*, ver. 10–13. *Prophanation of the Sabbath*, ver. 15–22. *Religion* is the chief and principal thing, wherein the *welfare* of a people stands; it is impossible they should *be well* and *do well* without this, whereby they may come to serve God and glorifie him, and attain Salvation for their own Souls. The weal, the excellency, end and happiness of Mankinde, lyes in true Religion: and therefore if Rulers seek the weal of a people, they must needs seek the advancement and establishment of this. Hence *Religio est summus politicæ finis*; Religion is the chief and last end of Civil Policy. *Alsted. Encyclop. p.* 1389. Gods Commandments are the Rule of man's good, *Deut.* 6. 24. & 5. 29. so is the *first* Table as well as the *second*: hence they must be *keepers* of *both Tables*.

2. In *subordination* to Religion, they are to seek also the external, temporal welfare of the people:

1. Consisting in their *Safety*, that *Nehemiah* taketh care for in the first place; (the preservation and safety of their persons and enjoyments, both Publick and Personal, Religious and Civil). To that end he builds the Wall of *Jerusalem*, for their safety, that they might not be a prey unto, or reproach amongst their Adversaries, *Nehem.* 2. 17. This is fundamentally necessary to the welfare, or well-being of a people, they cannot possibly have *well being*, without the *preservation* of their *Being*, both Personal and Political. When *Nehemiah* came to seek the welfare of the children of *Israel*, his great business was to build the Wall of *Jerusalem*, in which place their principal Concernments, both of Religion and Government, were laid up, *Psal.* 122. 3, 4, 5. That *Jerusalem* have a Wall for the safety and preservation of it, (and of what is contained in it) is requisite to the welfare of *Israel*.

2. Their *Honesty*. Rulers are to seek to maintain, cherish and preserve *Civil Honesty* amongst a people, by restraining and redressing Injuries between man and man, and other Crimes and Misdemeanours, by the Administration and Execution of *Justice*; by the free passage of *Righteousness*, which assigneth to every one his own; and of *Equity* also, abating the rigour and extremity of strict Justice, where need is. *Nehemiah* left an eminent Example of this, *Neh.* 5. 7–13. causing them to deal honestly, yea mercifully with their poor brethren, according as the distress of the time required, suppressing the biting *Usury* that was among them; he frees the oppressed from their oppressions, and taketh care that *Righteousness* and *Equity* may obtain amongst the people; this also is a part of his care for the good of *Israel*. That people may live together in *all honesty* as well as *godliness*, is the care and the benefit of good Rulers, 1 *Tim.* 2. 1, 2. and so that *Judgement* and *Justice* may be faithfully administred, which is a main *Basis* of the welfare of a people, and a main part of the work of Rulers, 1 *Kings* 10. 9. *Jer.* 22. 3, 15, 16. *Amos* 5. 24. 1 *Pet.* 2. 14.

3. Their *Prosperity*, in matters of outward Estate and Livelyhood, by such help as the care of Government may contribute to that end. That that we commonly call (*Wealth*) is a part of the wealth or welfare of a people, though not the

greatest part, as the world is apt to esteem it. Good Rulers will gladly be a furtherance thereunto, what in them lyes, that the *Commonwealth* may flourish and prosper in that respect, but especially in reference to necessary livelyhood, when it is a time of distress and poverty, or special scarcity in this or that, of food or clothing: when the people are in a low condition (or many of them at least) wrestling with many and great difficulties, or in a dearth, *Chap.* 5. 3. how careful is *tender-hearted Nehemiah* of the people at such a time, *Nehem.* 5. he took great care that things might be so carried on, that *poor people* might be provided of *necessaries*, and be able to sustain their Families, that they might not perish in a time of dearth and scarcity, *vers.* 2, 3, *&c.* this was part of the good he did for the people, *ver.* 19. So *Gen.* 41. 33–36.

4. Their *Tranquility*, *Quietness* (or Peace) in the enjoyment of all those, (both Religious and Civil good things.) That was the scope of *Nehemiahs* care and endeavours in many of his actings. That the people might enjoy Peace and Tranquility, he doth endeavour to prevent and hinder both *Disturbances* from *without*, (hence he built the Wall of *Jerusalem*) and also to establish *Unity*, Love and Peace *among themselves*; to that end he took care to quiet Complaints and Contentions, and to heal dissatisfactions that arose among them, *Neh.* 5. 1, 2–6, 7. It is the great fruit and *benefit* of good *Government*, that the people *may lead a quiet and peaceable life*, in the wayes both of true *Religion*, and civil *Honesty*, (or in respect both of their Religious and Civil Concernments) 1 *Tim.* 2. 2. That of *Tertullus* was a great commendation of *Felix* his government, had it been true, and spoken without flattery, *Acts* 24. 2. the enjoyment of Quietness (Peace and Tranquility) is an excellent fruit of good Government. Thus of what the *welfare* of a *People* is. Now

2. To [Seek] a peoples welfare, is to put forth utmost and best Endeavours to procure, promote and maintain it; to *study* it, and to *speak* for it; to *act* for it, as occasion is. It is not an empty *wishing* and *woulding*, (I could be glad, saith a man, *to see it go well with such a People*) nor yet to *talk* of it onely, and *speak* great words, but to *do* (effectually and vigorously to do) for it what in us lies, as the *case* requires. *Seeking* implies positive and industrious Endeavours, in the use of all

due means, to obtain a thing; as the use of the Word, in other places shews: See *Psal.* 34. 14. *Prov.* 11. 27. *&* 15. 14. *&* 18. 1. *Mat.* 13. 45. Take a man that seeks Wealth, or seeks Honour, how diligent, active, sedulous is he in his way, he layes out himself in industrious pursuit after it: so doth a faithful Ruler seek the welfare of the people, so *Nehemiah* did (as the story tells us.) But I may not enlarge here.

REAS. 1.   Why it is the Work or Duty of Rulers to seek the good and welfare of the people; 1. *Because this is the way whereby the Ruler, as such, glorifies God;* viz. by seeking the good and welfare of the people. To glorifie God, is the last end and great duty of every man, and thither we are to refer all we do, 1 *Cor.* 10. 31. Now we serve and glorifie God in our several stations, (and as placed amongst men in this world) in a way of seeking and serving the good of men: hence the *Law*, which is the *Rule* of our serving and *glorifying God*, we know *one Table* of it is taken up in enjoyning of us to do good to men, to seek and further the good and welfare of our *Neighbour*, in all that concerns him, (*in his Honour, Life, Estate, &c.*) Would you *serve God*? then saith the Lord, *Love your Neighbour*, seek the good and welfare of your Neighbour as your own: this is that Eternal, Immutable, Moral Rule that lies upon all men. Hence it lies upon the Ruler, that he do in his place, and according to his *capacity* and *compass*, (which is greater then that of a private person, and therefore more is expected from him) seek the good of the people he stands related to. For [*our Neighbour*] is any one or more of Man-kinde, whom we have any opportunity or capacity to do good unto, *Luk.* 10. 29–37. and the more Spiritual opportunity, advantage and obligation we are under to do good to another, the nearer Neighbour he is. Hence the *People* are the *Rulers* next Neighbour, (as I may say) they are the direct and eminent Object of his love, and of the fruits thereof, whom his Place gives him the highest advantages and obligations to do good unto. Hence to seek the good of the people, is the great work and duty which the Eternal Law of God layes on those that are called to place of Rule and Government.

REAS. 2.   Hence, *The next end of the Ruler, as such, is to be for the people, and to promote their good and welfare:* As the last end is the glory of God, so the next end is the good of the people, *Rom.* 13. 4. As 1 *Cor.* 11. 9. *i.e.* Woman is lastly and as *Homo* (or one of mankinde) for God; but nextly and as *Mulier* (in her proper place and Sex) for the man, to be an Help to him, *Gen.* 2. 18. So the Ruler is (as every man is) lastly for God, but nextly, and as a *Ruler*, for the *People*. The people are not for the Rulers, but the Rulers for the people, to minister to their welfare. Now it is the *excellency* (the goodness) of every thing, and the *duty* of the rational creature, to serve to its End; and the more aptly and fully that any do serve to their End, the better and more excellent they are.

Jun. Brut. pag 74. Buean. pag. 751.

REAS. 3.   *From the Trust that is committed unto Rulers:* They are *betrusted* by God (yea by *God* and *Man*) with the Publick Weal, and God will call for an Account of it, they are his *Ministers*, his Trustees for that business, *Rom.* 13. 4. No man can wholly excuse himself from being his *Brothers keeper, Gen.* 4. 9. but the keeping of the Common-weal of all their Brethren, is in a particular manner committed to Rulers, they are called in Scripture *Shepherds, Psal.* 78. 71. & 77. 20. *Ezek.* 34. 23. *Mic.* 5. 5. *Jer.* 23. 14. who are betrusted with the *Flock*; *Nursing-fathers*, who are betrusted with the care of the *Childe, Numb.* 11. 12. *Isa.* 49. 23. These and such like *Titles* import the Trust they are charged with. If the people or their welfare should ever miscarry in their hands, through their default, it will be required of them by the Lord. The peoples welfare is a *depositum* committed to them to keep. If but one Neighbour commit a thing to another to keep, *care* and *fidelity* in that *Trust* will be required, *Exod.* 22. 7–12. much more when a whole People, and God by them, do commit their whole common welfare unto such and such to keep.

QUEST. 2.   *Why they are especially to seek the welfare of the people of God;* or to seek the welfare of the people over whom they are Rulers, especially when as they are the Lords people.

REAS. 1.   From the *Preciousness* of such a people, and of the things that are laid up with them: The *Lord* hath but one *Darling* in all the world, and that is his *People, Jer.* 12. 7. the *dearly beloved of my Soul*, even sinful *Israel* is so called; *Israel is his Son, his first-born, Exod.* 4. 22. and such an one he puts to you to nurse, who are Rulers in *Israel*; they are his Portion, his Inheritance, his *peculiar Treasure, Deut.* 32. 9. even *when found in a desert land*, ver. 10. there he leads them about as a *Flock, by the hands of Moses and Aaron*; and they are to him as *the Apple of his Eye*, ver. 11. *Psal.* 135. 4. *Exod.* 19. 4, 5. *His Vineyard, Isa.* 5. 7. and this he commits to your care and keeping (as *Cant.* 1. 6.) With what care is such a Trust to be managed and looked unto? and how solemn would the account be if neglected? as 1 *King.* 14. 7. *&* 16. 2. They are the Brethren of Christ, and what is done to or for them, yea for the least, for a despised handful of them, he accounts as done to himself, *Mat.* 25. 40, 45. They are the Spouse of Christ, of whom he is very tender, for whose welfare he is exceeding jealous, *Zech.* 1. 14. They are the *Houshold of Faith*, and there is a specialty of duty and obligation to do good to such, to seek their good and welfare, *Gal.* 6. 10. The nearer that any are to God, the nearer they are and ought to be to us. Gods people are precious and honourable in Gods sight; yea if any part of his people be more holy, more reformed, more conformable to his Will and Image then others, they are the more precious: and so they should be in our sight, and will be so with all that

Vi. Dutch &
Engl. Annot.
in loc.

have a heart after the heart of God, and that love the righteous as such, *Isa.* 43. 4. *Jer.* 2. 3. When and *while Israel was Holiness to the Lord*, (an holy people) not onely by *designation*, but also in measure *actually* so, the Lord was more then ordinary tender and chary of them.

Remember also the precious things that are laid up with and among the people of God; as *viz.* The holy Ordinances of God, The Truth of Religion, The dispensation of the glorious Gospel, The helps of everlasting Salvation: These things are high and strong obligations to seek the good of such a people, *Psal.* 122. 9. and to maintain, preserve and promote these Enjoyments, wherein the choicest part of their welfare is contained. When the Ship is loaden with Plate and Treasure, it highly concerns the Master and Pilot to be very careful of her, that she miscarry not.

REAS. 2. The *glory of Gods Name* is eminently bound up and concerned in the welfare of his people; and therefore, if Rulers seek the glory of God, they must intensely seek the welfare of his people. It is true, that God who brings good out of evil, can and doth make the adversity and sufferings of

his people turn to his glory; but that it doth so, is but by accident, and a working by contraries. The peace and welfare of
the Lords people, hath a more proper and direct tendency to
the glory of God, as well as their own comfort. Indeed if you
speak of bare outward quiet and prosperity, singly considered,
that hath not so near connexion with the glory of God
(though that was an outward blessing, and was accounted a
great favour in *Solomons* time, 1 *Kings* 5. 4) but take the whole
welfare and peace of a Religious people together, that com-
priseth the flourishing of Religion, the open exercise of Gods
Worship, the free passage of the Gospel, the most advantageous enjoyment of all the helps of Salvation, and of all encouragement in the wayes of God: and there is a very near
and direct connexion between this and the glory of God; his
glory is eminently bound up in it. So *Psal.* 102. 16. when *Zion*
is pull'd down, laid in the dust, as *ver.* 14. lies in rubbish,
the glory of Gods Name suffers, and is eclipsed, (*Ezek.* 36. 20.
Isa. 52. 5.) But when *Zion* is built up, and restored from her
Captivity into a condition of welfare, then the Lords glory
appears, shines out, and is advanced. So also under the *New
Testament*, when deliverance, peace, rest, and visible welfare is
given and granted to the Church, it is counted and spoken of
as a great glory to God, and his Name is thereby lifted up
amongst men. So in the time of *Constantine*, as that is commonly taken in *Rev.* 12. 10. (The Kingdome of God is after a
sort visibly seen, saith *Brightman* on the place, when God set-
teth up godly Rulers to govern his people.) And so upon the
more full and final deliverance and restauration of the
Church, and peaceable flourishing of Religion therein yet to
come, (the great issue and scope of the *Providence* of God, of
the *Promises* and *Prophesies* of his Word, and of the *Prayers*
and *Hopes* of his people) the peace and welfare of his people
will be matter of great and wonderful glory to God, and
an exaltation to his Name and Kingdome in the world, *Rev.*
19. 1, 2, 5, 6. &* 11. 15–18. It is therefore no carnal thing, but an
holy duty to desire, and in our places to seek and endeavour
the Peace and Tranquility of *Israel*, not for low and sensual
ends, but that God might have glory by his mercy to us, and
by more abundant and fruitful service from us. And look as it
is in the Body *Natural*, though God can and doth turn

Sickness, Diseases, and other like Afflictions, into great good
to his people, and glory to his Name; yet notwithstanding
Health is to be prized, prayed for, and by all lawful means
sought after: and it is a duty of the sixth Commandment so to
do. The same may be said of *political* health and welfare: God
is to be submitted to, and glorified in Affliction and Tribulation, if he please to bring it; but he is to be waited on in all
regular wayes (in the use of all lawful means) for welfare, even
outward peace and welfare: and it is a great glory to his
Name, where he bestows it upon a people of his, (publick
peace and welfare upon a whole people especially) and he is
to be glorified for it. And hence to act against the welfare of
the people of God, is (in Scripture account) to act against the
Lord himself, and against his Name and Glory, (which shews
how eminently the same is concerned in them, and in their
welfare) *Psa.* 83. 3, 4, 5. (such are enemies to God, therefore
to his glory, *ver.* 2.) *&* 74. 7, 8, 22, 23. *Zech.* 2. 8. And on the
contrary, all that *Nehemiah* did for this people, and for their
welfare, he did it for God, and the Lord accepted it, *Neh.* 5. 19.
& 13. 14. And so *Heb.* 6. 10. you shew love to Gods Name,
when you minister to his Saints.

REAS. 3.   The Rulers *own good* and *comfort* will eminently
hereby be promoted; God will graciously remember *Nehemiah for good*, for all the good turns that he doth for his
people, *Neh.* 5. 19. *&* 13. 31. So *Heb.* 6. 10. God will in a Gospel
way (by his rich grace) richly reward every such service; *Moses*
had the *recompence of reward* to look unto, and so hath every
faithful Ruler, *Heb.* 11. 25, 26. If you would study for your own
welfare, and contrive to finde out a way how you may be well,
and do well enough (for one) whatever comes, there is no
way in all the world like this, Faithfully to seek the welfare of
the Lords people: Be and do for God and for his people, and
you shall be sure to do well whatever come. *Ebed melech* that
did but do for one *Jeremiah*, found a reward even in those
saddest times, *Jer.* 39. 16, 17, 18. much more shall they (one
way or other) that do for a whole Body of the Lords people.
Dan. 4. 27. the poor, *i.e.* specially the poor people of God
(the afflicted *Jews*) then in his Dominions in Captivity, if there
was any way in the world to lengthen out his Tranquility, that
was it. As *Numb.* 10. 29, 32. the Lord hath spoken good

concerning *Israel*, if you faithfully seek their good, you shall partake in the good and blessing that the Lord hath laid up for them; you shall be blessed with them and among them, not in this onely, but in another world: for *they shall prosper that love Jerusalem*, and faithfully seek the peace thereof, *Psal.* 122. 6.

USE I.   This Point shews us what ought to be the general End and Rule of all the Motions and Actions of Rulers, *viz.* the welfare of the people. To that scope *Nehemiah* bends all his Actions and Endeavours; and *Finis est mensura mediorum*, the End serves to measure, regulate, direct and limit the means, and shew what should be done. That *Maxime* of the *Romans* was and is a Principle of right Reason, *Salus Populi Suprema Lex*, [The welfare of the People is the Supreme Law] and is engraven on the Forehead of the Law and Light of *Nature*. Hence it is owned and confirmed by the *Scriptures*, as we see in the Text; and it is easily deducible from the Law of God: for that that is indeed the Law of Nature, is a part of the Eternal Law of God; and the Law of God enjoyns, that in Humane Civil Affairs, things be managed according to right Reason and Equity; and that Rulers, as they are for the people, so they are to make it their main business, and the scope of all their Actions, Laws and Motions, to seek the welfare of the people. There is Sun-light for this Maxime, and it was never doubted nor denied by any that held but to Rational and Moral Principles. Hence this Law being Supreme, it limits all other Laws and Considerations. Hence it is impossible that a people or their Rulers should be bound by any other Law, or Custome, or Consideration whatsoever, to do any thing that is really and evidently contrary to this. If it be indeed contrary or destructive to the welfare of the people, (of the Community they stand charged with) it is impossible they should be bound in *Conscience* to do it.

This is the *Compass* that Rulers are to steer by, and the *Touch-stone* of Right and Wrong in all their Motions, *viz.* What is for or against the Publick good, and the Welfare of the people, *Rom.* 13. 14. That bounds and regulates his whole Ministration. What is for the *Common good*, that and that only you are to do; and all that are set in place of Rule and Government (be they of higher or of lower quality) do stand charged with the welfare of that people, whom they are Rulers over.

I know when it comes to particulars, the doubt will still be, What is for the welfare of the people. One will say, this is most for the common good, another that. But

1. It will help much if this Principle be setled and acknowledged, That in Civil Affairs, the Consideration of the welfare of the whole, is that which shews and determines what is right, and weighs down all other Considerations whatsoever. Men will say, We must do what is right, whatsoever comes of it: *Fiat Justitia ruat Cœlum.* True, but it is most certain it is not right, if it be against the welfare of the people. It is impossible that any thing should be truly right, that is destructive to the common good: for it will constantly hold, *Salus Populi Suprema Lex.*

2. Consider the things wherein the welfare of a people does consist, which are above-mentioned, [*viz.* Religion in the first place, and then their Safety, or the Preservation of their Being, both Personal and Political, and their participation in the Rules and Fruits of Righteousness, Equity, Order and Peace] and that will help to discover and discern what is for the welfare of the people, or for the common good, and what not. There is need of much prudence and wariness in particular Applications and Cases; but those general Principles will hold, That a peoples welfare lies in such things as these, and that Rulers are bound in all their Motions and Actions to seek the welfare of the people, and to do nothing contrary thereunto.

USE II.   Hence see, that difficulties and troubles do not *excuse*, nor should *discourage* Rulers from doing the work of their Places which God calls them unto, or from seeking the welfare of the people: Such things do not excuse, nor should discourage from taking and accepting the Place of Rule when called to it. As they did not *Nehemiah*, though he heard before that their condition was a condition of great affliction and reproach, *Neh.* 1. 3. yet he voluntarily left the Court of *Persia*, to embarque with the *Jews* at *Jerusalem*, when in so stormy a time as this was; and how is he honoured in the Book of God for it? It was a difficult time and task that *Moses* was sent upon, accompanied also with a deep sense of his own infirmity and unfitness, *Exod.* 3. 4. he could not but be slow and backward to such a work; but yet when he was over-backward the Lord grew angry, and chides him into a consent: but (I say) difficulties and troubles should not discourage nor hinder Rulers from doing the work of their Places when set therein, *i.e.* from faithful seeking and acting for the welfare of the people, which is (as we have said) the summary work of the Rulers Place. Consider a little the difficulties that lay upon the *Jews* and their Rulers at this time in *Jerusalem*, after their return from Captivity, and in the dayes of *Nehemiah*.

1. They were a small, weak and despised people, *Nehem.* 4. 1, 2, 4. & 1. 3. & 2. 19. Contempt and reproach is a bitter and killing thing to ingenuous Spirits; yet this they were fain to bear and pass through. It was a *day of small things*, which others, yea even themselves are apt to despise, *Zech.* 4. 10.

2. They were in the midst of Enemies, and Adversaries round about them, of several sorts and Nations; *Sanballat* a *Moabite*, (from *Horonaim* a chief City of *Moab*, *Isa.* 15. 5. *Jer.* 48. 3, 5, 34. called the *Horonite*) and *Tobiah* the Servant, the *Ammonite*, on the East, *Neh.* 2. 10. (*The Servant*, he was Governour of the *Ammonites*, but of a base and servile spirit; some think that of a mean man, he was got into Place, and therefore is called *Tobiah the Servant*: such are often worst, *Prov.* 30. 21, 22.) *Geshem* the *Arabian* (Neh. 6. 1. & 4. 7.) and others on the *South*; and the *Samaritans* on the *North*, *Neh.* 4. 2. *Ezra* 4. 9, 10. Thus they were beset round with Adversaries, and Ill-willers, and many Informers and Complainers there were against them, as before in the dayes of *Zerubbabel*, *Ezra* 4. & 5.

3. Their Adversaries did labour to affright them with the Accusation of *Rebellion*, *Neh.* 2. 19. an old *Artifice*, but it was an injurious Calumny, and most groundless Accusation. The building of the Wall of *Jerusalem* for *self-preservation*, had nothing in it of *Rebellion*: but many clamours and stories they raised of that nature, *Neh.* 6. 6, 7, 8. and see their end therein, *ver.* 9. to weaken and discourage them from their work, that their hearts and hands might fail them therein, that was it they aimed at.

4. There were Discontents and Divisions among themselves, *Neh.* 5. 1. Great Complaints of the *Inferiour* sort against

their *Superiours*, of the Poor against the Rich; of Brethren against Brethren: yea, there were among themselves that were helpers to their Adversaries, and complied with them, even some *chief men* and others, *Neh.* 6. 17, 18. and thereby, among other evils, it came to pass that nothing could be kept within its due compass, but every thing was carried and reported to their Adversaries, *ver.* 19. *They uttered my words* (or my matters) *unto him*; and that doubtless not in the fairest dress. Yea, there were some of the Prophets that endeavoured to weaken the hands of faithful *Nehemiah*, and to put discouragement upon him, *Neh.* 6. 10, (This *Shemaiah* is conceived to be the same that is mentioned *Ezra* 8. 16.) 11, 12, 13. (By the way, who would have said that that would have been a sin, which might seem to be a prudent retirement for safety? yea, but for *Nehemiah*, in a case so circumstanced, to act fear and discouragement to the prejudice of his Cause and Work, would have been a sin.) But *ver.* 14. there were also that raised Slanders of others of their *Prophets*, those it's like who were of another minde, *ver.* 7.

Vid Engl Annot.

5. They were poor, and low, and weak as to outward estate, conflicting with wants and straits, and many difficulties in that respect, very unable to support themselves, and to bear the Publick Burthens that were then upon them, *Neh.* 5. 2–5. and *ver.* 18. *The bondage was heavy upon this people: Neh.* 9. 37. *We are in great distress.*

6. Hence there was *hard* Work, and *weak* Instruments, ready many times to be discouraged, *Neh.* 4. 10. the Workmen themselves, and those that should joyn hands together to labour and carry on the work, began to mutter and be discouraged, by the difficulty of the work, and their own weakness; *We are not able,* say they, *to carry it on:* At the same time when the Adversaries were high, *prefident* and threatning, *ver.* 11. their own workmen began to be disheartned and *diffident*, ver. 10. Here was a juncture of discouraging trial. Hence hard shifts they were fain to make to carry on the work, and to put forth themselves to the utmost, and beyond an ordinary measure, by the care and courage and conduct of good *Nehemiah*, *ver.* 16, 17. Every one had both his hands full, and they were fain to do two works at once, the work of a *Souldier*, and of a *Labourer*, ver. 18, 21, 22, 23.

7. It was a time of many *fears*, wherein they had many fears among them, and many that heightned those fears: many Reports, Threatnings and fore-speakings of this, and that, to that purpose, *Neh.* 4. 12. *&* 6. 9, 13, 14, 19. It is observeable, that that was the drift and endeavours of Adversaries and Ill-willers, *Fear, fear, fear*; a discouraging *Heart* and *Hand-weakning* carnal *fear*. The great word of *God* to godly Rulers is, *Be strong, and of a good courage*, fear not when in Gods way and work, *Josh.* 1. 6, 7, 9. But the word of *Satan* and his Instruments is, *Fear*, be *afraid*, look upon the danger of be-ing faithful: But (as to man and second Causes) they had many very great causes of fear, many dangers round about them, and to be faithful in duty in a time of fear, proves a dif-ficult task to flesh and blood.

8. Which was worst of all, Among this people of the *Jews* af-ter Captivity, when engaged in Reforming work, there were many sins, disorders and miscarriages, which were provoking unto God, and a great exercise of discouragement to their faithful Leaders; such in *Ezra*'s time as made him *blush before* God, and fear what God would do with them, *Ezra* 9. 6, 10, 14. And before that in *Haggai*'s time, such neglects of carry-ing on Temple-work, and of finishing what was begun, as he sharply reproves, yea as God reproved from Heaven, by Drought, Blastings, *&c. Hag.* 1. 2, 5, 6, 9, 10, 11. *&* 2. 16, 17. And here in *Nehemiahs* time there were faults, evils and dis-tempers found among them, as *Neh.* 5. 1, 6, 7, 9. *&* 13. 4, 5, 10, 15, 18, 23, 24, 26, 27. not onely matter of *Affliction*, but sin-ful *Corruptions* and Distempers do sprout up among a Reforming people, and those they have to wrestle with: yet neither did these take them or their Leaders off from their Work, nor utterly overturn it; nor did the Lord cast them off (though he chastened them) but helped them along, though in much infirmity. He was with them at many a dead lift, (*Hag.* 2. 4.) and after *frowns*, yet *smiled* on them again: espe-cially while the Leaders were faithful to search out and testifie against *evil*, and to set upon *duty* when called to it; and the people were willing to hearken to them, and to be reduced and reformed by them: both which may be observed of them all along in the story, *Hag.* 1. 12, 13. *Ezra* 10. 2, 3, 4, 7, 8, 12, 14.

9. Lastly, we may remember the long time wherein this poor people were conflicting and labouring under Difficulties and Infirmities, and what a succession of Difficulties and Troubles did attend them in the Reforming, and Rebuilding work they were upon. From their first Grant by *Cyrus*, unto the beginning of *Nehemiahs* Government (in the twentieth year of *Artaxerxes*) according to the shortest Account, were 82 years (so *Usher* in his *Annals. Junius* saith 146. *Lightfoot* saith but 37, but few embrace that *.) Almost all that time, & so afterward in the time of *Nehemiahs* Government, they were followed with various Troubles and Exercises (as the story at large tells us) though they had their lucid Intervals, and the Lord still helping in the issue.

*Vid. Apud Tillinghast knowl. of Times, p. 226, to 251.

Thus that word was made good, *Dan.* 9. 25. that *Jerusalem*, both City and Wall, *should be built again in troublous times.* Yet notwithstanding all this, they went on in their Work with *Courage*, and *Constancy*, and *Confidence* in God, *Neh.* 2. 20. and he did prosper them, not by preventing Difficulties, but by carrying on the Work in their hands through all Difficulties, and in the midst of all their Infirmities. And it is observeable, That every *Tragedy* they passed through, had a glad *Catastrophe*; every stress had a comfortable issue: God still helped them in the conclusion and upshot of every business, that they came off well at last, though with much tugging and wrestling, much exercise of Faith and Patience. So in the Building of the Temple, (thus it went on heavily, and met with many obstructions, and many Adversaries; yet they got through at last, to their great joy) *Ezra* 6. 15, 16, 22. So here in the building of the Wall, *Neh.* 6. 15, 16. & 12. 27, 43. And so in the Reformation of Abuses, *Ezra* 10. *Neh.* 5. & 13. The story of the *Church* in all Ages, & especially in the Scripture, informs us, that the best and greatest works God hath delighted to carry on through many Difficulties and Oppositions, and in much felt infirmity of Instruments. The time of *Moses*, of *David*, of *Israel*, all along in the *Old Testament*, will furnish us with many Instances of it; yea and also of the *Apostles* in their Work under the *New Testament*, *Act.* 20. 19. 1 *Cor.* 16. 9. & 3. 3. 2 *Cor.* 11. 23–28, 29, 30. *Gal.* 4. 13, 14. the glorious Gospel must be preached & carried

on *through Infirmity of the flesh*, i.e. through outward meanness and affliction of Instruments, yet not therefore to be despised. The whole Church of God, and every particular
concernment thereof, is in a *Militant* conflicting condition in
this world, and it must be no stumbling to us to see it so: it
occasions the more exercise of *Faith, Patience, Prayer, &c.* in
the work (as we see in the example of *Nehemiah* all along)
and the more of God to appear in the issue of it, *Neh.* 6. 16.

Go on therefore in the Work of the Lord, and in the
Service of your several Places, and be not taken off by trouble, difficulties, oppositions, felt infirmities in your selves,
weaknesses and distempers in persons and things round about
you, (which will alwayes be.) When were there work for
Patience, Faith, Fortitude, Self-denial, and for the Spirit of a
Souldier, Wrestler, *&c.* if it were not for such things? We must
none of us say, of one Order or other, I will serve God in my
place, and help build the Wall of *Jerusalem*, if I may do it with
ease and tranquility, without trouble, without hazard, without
reproaches, and ill requitals from men, *&c.* Christ is little be-
holden to us, if that be all we will do for him; that is too low
for the Spirit of a *good Souldier of Christ Jesus*, 2 *Cor.* 6. 4, 5, 8.
Yea, now you look like the Ministers of God, when you cheerfully discharge your Places, though surrounded and loaden
with Afflictions, Distresses, Labours, false Reproaches, *&c.*
Now you are drest like a Minister, like a Servant of God, and
of his people in Publick Work; and through such things as
these, you must go on in your Work, as the Apostles then did.

USE III. A threefold Exhortation: 1. To our *Rulers* and
Leaders. 2. To the *People.* 3. To both joyntly, or to the *Whole.*

1. To Rulers and Leaders, who are betrusted with the
Government of this people; Let them be Exhorted by the
Word, and in the *Name* of the Lord, to follow the Example of
good *Nehemiah*, and to be of this Spirit, to make it your work
and business to seek the welfare of the Lords people. The
Concernments of a People framed into a Body Politick, are
put into your hands, and of such a people as are the people of
God (that no Christian Spirit can deny) a part of Gods *Israel*,
though but a part, yet no inconsiderable part of the people of
God at this day in the world: such a part of Gods people as
are retired into these Ends of the Earth, for known ends of

Religion and Reformation, to serve God in his *Temple* and *Ordinances* according to his appointment: You are betrusted with as precious an Interest as is this day upon the Earth; *viz.* with the Lives, Estates, Liberties, and Religious Enjoyments of some thousands whose Names are written in Heaven, and bound upon the Breast and Heart of Christ Jesus: yea, with so much of the Interest of Christ, his Truth, Wayes, Worship, Gospel, Name and Kingdome, as is to be found here amongst this people. This part of *Israel* do under God confide in you, and betrust you with their Welfare: To be Instrumentally the *Saviours* and Preservers hereof, is a thing more *honourable* and excellent (yea and more *profitable* too, as will appear one day) then to be Owners of all the Wealth of both the *Indies*. Poor *Nehemiah*, who sought and maintained the welfare of the children of *Israel*, when but an handful, a poor small and despised people, is more honourable in the Book of God, then all the great Ones of the Earth in his time. The Lord Jesus Christ, having *ask'd* and obtained this piece of the *uttermost ends of the Earth for his possession*, doth commit it unto you, as Instruments under him, to keep and maintain his possession in it. The eyes of the whole *Christian World* are upon you; yea which is more, the eyes of *God* and of his holy *Angels* are upon you, to see and observe how you Manage and Discharge this Trust now at such a time. And though your Obligations and Encouragements from men, from the people over which you Rule, are but small, there is little outward advantage you have by them to engage you to them, or their welfare, (and hence they that look no higher then the world, will never do much for such a people) yet to men of *Religion*, and *Conscience*, and *Faith*, there is enough to be said to oblige and encourage them: the Charge and *Commandment* of God, and *Duty* to him, is the highest *Obligation*. Remember that the Lord, the great God, layes this solemn Charge and Injunction upon you (*Honoured Fathers*) as you will answer it at the great Day, That you seek the good, and be tender of the welfare of this people: and God may be bold with you, though we may not; he speaks not without Authority to *Command*, nor without Riches and Power to *Reward* you; he hath given an *Advantage* to set before you, and *encourage* you by, though we your poor people have not; he hath the

Promise to *encourage*, as well as the *Precept* to *binde* and oblige: they that can really believe the Promise, will never stick at any Duty, and so not at this duty of the Precept. When *Moses* chose to suffer affliction with the people of God, he made the best *bargain* for himself that ever man did. *Paul* never *gain'd* so much, as when he *lost all* for Christ. The Lord will not let you be losers by any thing you do for his people, *Neh.* 5. 19. Every *peny-worth* of such Service shall have many *pounds* of reward, *Mark* 10. 29, 30. God in Christ is a rich and *gracious* Rewarder, as well as a *soveraign* Commander; and therefore when you are before the Lord, and look to him (as it is before him, and in his Name that we now speak) the Exhortation mentioned is strong and powerful, and wants no strength of *Argument* to back it, to perswade and constrain (encourage and oblige) to seek the welfare of such a people.

And some Helps to this purpose (or useful Directions) we may readily gather from the Example of *Nehemiah*.

DIRECT. 1. *Put on bowels of Compassion*, so as to have a lively sense of the Condition and Concernments of this people: So *Neh.* 1. 4. & 2. 3. & 5. 18. Think not that it is well enough if I can shift for one; *Nehemiah* was not of that minde, he took a view of their case, (in special to see where ought was broken down and out of order in the Wall of *Jerusalem*, that he might stir up himself and them to mend it) *Neh.* 2. 13, 15, 17.

2. Be studious and solicitous about the *Publick Welfare*; bestow intense thoughts, study and care concerning it, what may be needful or expedient for it. *Neh.* 5. 7. *My heart consulted* (took counsel, the phrase is) *in me*; his minde wrought about the business: he is also very vigilant and industrious to *foresee* evils, and to use means to *prevent* the same, and to order things in their time and place; as may be seen in special in *Chap.* 4. at large.

3. Practise *Self-denial* and *Patience*; faithful Rulers will finde much need of that, especially among a people that are poor and full of infirmities: *Neh.* 5. 14, 15, 16, 18. *He requires not the bread of the Governour*, (i.e. the Maintenance belonging and sutable to such a Place) because many heavy burthens were upon that poor people. This was a voluntary departing from his own Right, and it cannot be urged as binding where the

case is not alike (though where, or so far as the case is alike, the fear of God will teach it, as it did him, *ver.* 15.) We may fear indeed that there is not that done by the people with us, that should be, and might be in this particular; it may be time will teach us more of our duty in that matter: But to be sure great things cannot be done by this poor people; and where so it is, Rulers shall honour God and themselves much by Self-denial, and condescending to mean things, and to do that out of *love* to God and his people, for the which they are not *rewarded* by men: (Oh there are but a few such *Nehemiahs* in the world, we have cause to prize and be thankful for such, you cannot finde the people upon earth that have so *Self-denying* and condescending a *Magistracy*, as the Lord hath given unto us.) But the less your reward is on *Earth*, the greater it shall be in *Heaven*. As you are to practise *Self-deniall*, so also *Patience*. When God chose a Ruler for *Israel* in the *Wilderness*, he chose the *meekest* man in all the Earth, (*Numb.* 12. 3.) a man of patience, and he had need be so, to bear the Infirmities, Murmurings, Unthankfulness, and the Distempers of the people. *Moses* was a *Nursing-father*, *Numb.* 11. 12. The Nurse had need have more patience then the Childe, else what will become of it? If when the *Childe* is froward and unquiet, the *Nurse* should be so too, what work would there be? Though it be a time of strife (the great distemper) of the Congregation, *Moses* and *Aaron* must carry it with *patience* and *moderation*, else God will not take it well, *Numb.* 27. 14.

4. *Courage* and *Constancy* was another imitable excellency in *Nehemiah*, and without which he could never have done his work, nor stood up for the welfare of that people, especially at such a time. Many sought to drive him from his work by *fear*, but he abode *undaunted* and couragious in the Lord, *Neh.* 6. 9, 11, (he counts that such an act of *fear* was very *unsuitable* to one in such a Place) 13, 14, 19. Threatnings, Letters, Prophets, all cannot discompose him by fear: yea, he hath such a Courage, Faith and Presence of Spirit, as to encourage others in time of danger, *Neh.* 4. 14, 20. (*Our God shall work for us.*) If the Spirits of Leaders fail when Difficulties and Troubles come, all fails; but God hath appointed them to Spirit all about them, to be both the *Head* and the *Heart* of

a people, 2 *Chron*. 32. 6, 7, 8. That (I say) is the great word of God to good Rulers, onely *be strong, and of a good courage*, viz. in the way of the Rule, *Josh*. 1. 6, 7, 9. and they have a strong word to build upon, (*ver*. 5.) *I will not fail thee, nor forsake thee*.

5. *Wisdome* and *Prudence* in the management of Affairs; as it is mentioned in Scripture as a Requisite in Civil Rulers, *Deut*. 1. 13, 15. 2 *Chron*. 1. 10. so it was not wanting in *Nehemiah*, as the whole frame of the story shews us. I might instance in some acts & fruits of his Wisdom; as in his practising the lesson that we have since had from Christs own mouth, *Beware of men*, (*Mat*. 10. 16, 17.) *Neh* 6. 2, 3, 4. in his not being carried with pretences, and taking plausible shews of Reason, no not from *Prophets* themselves, *Neh*. 6. 10, 11, 12. nor with great words from others, *Neh*. 2. 19, 20. His putting great Trust into the hands of faithful men, *Neh*. 7. 2. *&* 13. 13, *&c*. We may here remember, That *Religion* is the truest *Reason*; *Honesty* the best *Policy*; and to keep in the way of the *Rule*, in the fear of God, is the highest *Wisdome*: and all sinful *deviation* or turning to crooked wayes, is *folly*, *Job* 28. 28. *Psal*. 111. 10. *Prov*. 10. 9. But Religion doth not take away, but establish the prudent managing of Affairs, as to the manner and circumstances of Actions. How often may the same thing be done, and the same end attained, in a discreet, moderate, comely and prudent way, as well as in a way that is less expedient? *David guided them with the skilfulness of his hands*, as well as *with integrity of heart*, *Psal*. 78. 72. Leaders are to exert a skilfulness and prudence in the manner of the Conduct of Affairs.

6. Be much in *Prayer* on all occasions: *Nehemiah* was a praying Magistrate, and therefore so helped and blessed in his way and work, *Neh*. 6. 9. *&* 4. 8, 9. *&* 1. 4, 11. (He laid the ground-work and *beginning* of his work and business on *Prayer*, and so he carried it on.) He will have an *Ejaculation* to Heaven, even when he is upon *Action*, and hath not time for more, *Neh*. 2. 4. The Prayers of Rulers and Leaders for the People, are a precious means of the peoples welfare. That is one good way of seeking their good, to set God on work by Prayer, and engage him to do them good, *Psal*. 51. 18. When *Hezekiah* and *Isaiah* do both cry and pray to Heaven, there is

good hopes it shall go well with that people, and that God will appear for them, as he did, 2 *Chron.* 32. 20, 21, 22. How oft did the Prayer of *Moses* and *Aaron* for *Israel* in the Wilderness, slip in between them and *destruction, Numb.* 14. 12, 13–19, 20. *&*

V. Clark
Martyr.
pag. 274. 16. 20, 21, 22, 45. *&* 21. 7. It was an exemplary passage of that worthy *Prince* of *Orange*, who when he had but *one breath* to draw, spent *half* of it on the *people* in *prayer* for them, crying (as he fell down slain) *Oh my God, take pity of my Soul, and of this poor people.*

2. This Point may afford several *Instructions* to the *People*.

1. It gives a Direction whom to make *Choice* of for their *Rulers*; viz. Such as may be most fit and likely, faithfully to seek the good and welfare of the people; and of such a people of God as through grace are in this *Wilderness*, and so circumstanced as they are. But I shall not insist on this.

2. Learn and be exhorted hence highly to *prize* and *honour* such *Rulers* when Chosen, and called to Place of Government. Such as have it upon their heart, and make it their business faithfully to seek your best welfare; such as are in measure of *Nehemiahs* Spirit; those whose *design* it is to seek not themselves, nor great things for themselves, (alas they are not to be had here) but the *welfare* of the people, their Safety, Peace and Prosperity, (and the Prosperity of *Religion*, which is the principal part of our welfare) out of *love* to God and to his people; Be assured your welfare is bound up in such. It is God that works and maintains a peoples weal, but he does it by means, and especially by this means of faithful Rulers and Leaders. It was the great work of Gods mercy to the *Jews* after the Captivity, (which the story is taken up in) that he raised up for them, and among them, faithful Leaders to be Instruments of their good; *Zerubbabel, Ezra* and *Nehemiah*, to rebuild both the Temple and City of *Jerusalem*, and settle things in the Church and Common-wealth. When God means well to a people, (hath thoughts of peace, *Jer.* 29. 11. *&* 32. 41.) he gives them such Leaders as shall cordially seek their welfare; when ever he hath good dayes for his people, he layes in this, *Isa.* 1. 26. *&* 60. 17. *Jer.* 23. 4. (See 1 *Kings* 10. 9.) So of old in the Wilderness, *Psal.* 77. 20. Which Text of Scripture we heard well improved in a Sermon on the like occasion now Seven years ago; wherein it was said, That that was the Thir-

tieth year currant that God had given us godly *Magistrates*: if so, this is the Thirty seventh year currant, wherein we have enjoyed that mercy. Whereupon it was then solemnly added (by that Reverend Servant of God who then Preached) That the Sun shines not upon an happier people then we are in regard of this mercy: The Lord make us thankful for it, and give us to know and prize the things of our peace, and faithfully to adhere thereunto, (not medling with them that are given to change) as also to love, honour, and acknowledge those that are and have been the Instruments of our peace and welfare, as doth become us.

3. Pray much for Rulers, that God may dispose and assist them to seek and promote your welfare, 1 *Tim.* 2. 1, 2. (that it may be well with us, that we may enjoy welfare under their Government) their work is great and weighty, and you are concern'd therein unspeakably, [*viz.* to be Instrumental under God of your whole welfare] and therefore you had need to pray hard for them. It was a good speech of *Bugenhagius*, (*apud Gerhard. de Magistr. Polit. pag.* 924.) *Si tam prompti essemus*, &c. If we were but as forward to *pray* for Magistrates, as we are to *censure* and blame them, things would be better with us then they are.

4. Let people be friends and *Helpers* to their own welfare; or every one in your several places seek the common good of the whole. If Rulers are to *seek* the welfare of the people, then surely people themselves are not to *prejudice* or neglect their own welfare. The *Patient* must contribute Endeavours towards his own health, as well as the *Physician*, else there will be but little good done. It is the Rulers work eminently, as his Place is more eminent; but it is also the work of every one, according to the compass of his capacity and opportunity, to seek the welfare of the place and people, where & among whom he lives, *Jer.* 29. 7. So the Lord speaks to Captives in *Babylon*, during the time of Gods patience with it; much more doth that duty lie on those that dwell in *Zion*, to seek the good and the peace of the place, both by Prayer to God, and by all other due means within their power. Love thy Neighbour, much more a whole *Community*, a multitude of thy Neighbours, is the Lords charge to every one. A little more particularly,

1. Be sure (every particular person, I now speak to even them that are in private capacity) to do no *hurt* to *Israel*, (to the Lords people among whom you live) either *directly*, or *indirectly*; either wilfully or carelesly: that is just contrary to seeking the welfare of the place and people where you live; which is a Moral and great duty lying upon every Soul. Woe to that person, whosoever he be, that shall be a willing or blameable cause of hurt or harm to the *Lords people* here, whom he that toucheth will be found to touch the *Apple of his Eye, Psal.* 34. 21. When God called *Abraham* forth to follow him in a way of Reformation, he gave that word along with him, *Gen.* 12. 3. and so to *Jacob* or *Israel, Gen.* 27. 29. and he did and will make it good. If you love your Souls, take heed of touching *Israel* to their hurt: yea even words that tend to the reproach or prejudice of the people of God, or Builders in *Jerusalem*, is not a small matter, *Neh.* 4. 2, 3, 4, 5. (such *Imprecations* tell us, what will be the portion of such except they repent, though not that ordinary and private Spirits should be forward to wish that it might be so to particular persons). *They have provoked anger* (*Thee* is not in the Hebrew) irritated and raised spirits (by their Scoffs and Reproaches) *before*, or in respect of *the Builders.* The words may carry that meaning.

2. Think it not enough to do *no hurt*, but according to your place and opportunity do *good* to *Israel*, to that part of it in special in which the Lord hath cast you. Be willing to put forth thy self for the publick good according to thy *Talent.* Hast thou Estate which the Lord hath blessed thee with, (and gotten, it may be, here under the shadow of the Government?) let not the Publick suffer for want, when as thou hast it by thee. Hast thou Ability to serve the Country any other way? be ready thereunto: Do not onely *pray*, but put forth *endeavours* according to capacity and opportunity for the peace and good of *Jerusalem*; else you do but dally in praying, if you will do nothing for it, *Psal.* 122. 9. Seek it in the use of all due means. A *publick* Spirit even in a *private* person is a precious thing; *i.e.* according to the compass of his place to be ready to do for the common good. Could the Heathen (the *Romans* and others) produce such Sayings as these; *That man was not born for himself, but for his Country; That even to die*

for it is sweet: Dulce & decorum pro Patriâ mori; and boast of those among them that practised accordingly: and shall Christians be strangers to such a Publick Spirit, or be backward to act for the common welfare. Here in *Nehemiahs* time every one set his hand to, to build up the Wall of *Jerusalem,* and the *particular* persons and companies that did their parts therein, are to their honour *recorded* in the holy story, *Neh.* 3. Oh that is a pleasant sight, to see all sorts contributing to the Safety, Peace, Welfare of *Jerusalem,* and joyning *Hearts* and *Hands* therein, *Neh.* 4. 6. Oh! have you a minde to *build* or to save the Wall and Welfare of *Jerusalem?* Are you *cheerful, cordial, forward, industrious* therein? not a man to *talk* onely, but to *work* when the case requires it.

3. Keep Order: keep in your places, acknowledging and attending the Order that God hath established in the place where you live. *Numb.* 2. 2. the *Israelites* were commanded to pitch every man by his own Standard; the LXX. render it κατὰ τάγμα, *According to order.* So 1 *Thess.* 4. 11. Act *orderly* if you would act any thing for the *publick* welfare; leave the guidance of the Ship to those that sit at Helm, and are by God and his people set there, and whom you are immediately stated under: onely pray for them. And if there be place for a modest Suggestion, tender it as becomes you, but justle not into their Places, nor refuse to acquiesce in their Conclusions. This people of the *Jews* after the Captivity, we finde them ready and willing to be ordered by those the Lord set over them; and by that means things went well, or when ought was amiss it found amendment, *Ezra* 10. 2, 3, 4, 8, 12, 14. *Neh.* 5. 12, 13. &13. It was a good time in *Issachar,* when as, 1 *Chron.* 12. 32.

3. The third Branch of the Exhortation. Let me *speak* a few words unto *All,* to Rulers and People both together. The Command is (as we see) that we all ought to aim at, and be studious of the common good, the *weal* and *welfare* of the *whole*; the *Lines* of every ones wayes and actings should meet in that *Center.* In the fear of God be faithful and careful herein. And to this end, let me adde a few general Helps and Directions from the Word of God, such as may concern both Rulers and People in their several capacities, though more eminently the former, as having the main stroke in the Conduct of Affairs.

1. Be sure to fix upon a right *Basis*, or settle upon a right *Interest*, even the true Interest of Christ Jesus; *i.e.* Be found in, and cleave to the way of the Rule, the way of Gods Word, in those things especially that are of publick and general Concernment. Faithfully keep with God, and then he will be with you; as we well heard the last Year, from 2 *Chron.* 15. 2. That therefore is the sure and certain *way* to *welfare*, *Deut.* 5. 29. In matters of Religion and Reformation in a special manner (which is our main Interest) keep close to the right way, turn not from it to the right hand or left; not in those things especially that concern your publick *Profession* and *Practice* in the sight of the World. Take heed of Corruption here.

(1.) Do not wrong and marre an excellent Work and *Profession*, by mixing and weaving in spurious *Principles* or *Practises*; as those of *Separation*, *Anabaptism*, *Morellian* (Anarchical) *Confusion*, and Licentious *Toleration*. If any would secretly twist in and espouse such things as those, and make them part of our Interest, we must needs renounce it as none of our Cause, no part of the End and Design of the Lords faithful Servants, when *they followed him into this Land that was not sown*. *Separation* and *Anabaptism* are wonted Intruders, and seeming *Friends*, but secret fatall *Enemies* to Reformation; as *Paul* in a case not much unlike, 1 *Cor.* 3. 10–15. In this Work here on foot, there was a good Foundation laid, *viz.* Christ as the onely Law-giver in his Church, and *Reformation* designed according to his Will and *Apostolical pattern*; but take heed how you *build* thereupon. If you should build the *Hay* and *Stubble* of such things as those, then verily (though sincere persons will be saved, and the main of the Work may be saved and revived at last), yet verily sooner or later there will come a *Fire* that will *burn* up this *Stubble*, and then your poor Leaders that would have led you the right way, may be remembred when it is too late. Do not on pretence of avoiding *Corruption*, run into sinful *Separation* from any of the true *Churches* of God, (and what is good therein) or from the Children of the Covenant. Prize and hold fast the Covenant of God to you and yours. Keep with God in his Covenant, and walk up to it, and you may boldly trust him, God All-sufficient will keep you. If we will own Gods Covenant but for one generation onely, (when as *Gen.* 17. 7.

the *Covenant* runs *to us and our seed after us in their genera-tions*) how justly may the Lord tarry with us but for *one gen-eration*, and then break up house, and leave us to *confusion*.

(2.) On the other hand, do not so avoid *Separation*, as to neglect or prejudice *Reformation*. The good old *Non-Conformists* were very zealous for *Reformation*, and yet al-wayes stedfast Enemies to *Separation*: those two may well consist, and they left us a good example therein. Such things as are or have been known Corruptions in other Churches, it is no part of sinful *Separation*, but a part of just *Reformation* to avoid them, or refuse to propagate, practise or continue them. Christ would not separate from (or cast off) the *Temple*, but he was zealous to *purge* the Temple, and so should we be. And it is our Errand into the Wilderness to study and practise true Scripture-*Reformation*, and it will be our Crown (in the sight of God and man) if we finde it, and hold it without Adulterating *deviations*. Oh seek and keep it, and hold it fast, *Rev.* 3. 11. To leave the *Children* of non-scan-dalous Orthodox Christians *Unbaptized*, will (I doubt not) be one day found a thing displeasing unto Jesus Christ. But on the other hand, to Baptize in such a lax and licentious way, as serves to dress men in the *Livery*, without bearing the *Yoke* of Christ; to have his *Name* upon them, with rejection of his *Government*, this will not suit either the *Principles* of Re-formers, or the *Rules* of Scripture. So though Rigid *Severity* in Admissions to the Lords Table is to be avoided; yet to be lax and slight therein, to admit all sorts to full Communion, or upon very slight *Qualifications*, is against the Principles and against the Interest of *Reformation*. Again, to put *Election* of Church-Officers into the hands of All, (though matters ought to be so unblameably carried, as none may have any just *Objection* against the person Chosen, without matter of *satis-faction* given them) is such a piece of ruining Confusion, as none of the Wayes or *Models* of *Church Government* that have been of any repute in the world, would ever admit of. *That is an Anabaptistical Tenet*; Spanhem. Disput. 1. *Thes.* 53. Take heed of Extremes, and of passing from one Extreme to an-other, (or from flying from *Papall* or *Prelaticall Tyranny*, into *Morellian Anarchy*) which mans weakness is very apt to do. Pray and study to find and keep the true Scripture way, and be not hurried from it on one hand or other, by the Devices of our cunning Adversary (*Satan*) whose wiles we should not be ignorant of.

So also in Civil Concernments, fix upon a right *Basis*, upon Foundations and Principles that are Righteous and *Rational*, and that will hold, and let not one thing justle out another. But I forbear to meddle there.

In all avoid Irregular *Extremes*, and wilde *Extravagancies*; be for safe and sober *Principles* and *Practices*. It was a wise mans *Motto*, (viz. Sir *Nicholas Bacons*) *Mediocria Firma*: Things carried with Moderation and Mediocrity are firm and stable; Extremes soon run themselves out of breath, tumble down of themselves, and so end in Confusion.

2. Study *Unity*, (and to that end *Order*,) *i.e.* Unity in the Lord, and in his Truth and Fear. Unity in Sin, Errour and Evil is a piece of *Hell*; but Unity in Peace and Righteousness is no little part of *Heaven*, and a main Ingredient in a peoples welfare, *Psal.* 133. 3. To this end,

(1.) Let all that fear God heartily Unite in the main; yea all that fear God will Unite therein: *i.e.* in the main Concernments both of things of Religion, and of the good of the People. He that fears and loves God, will love his *Truth*, love his *Word*, (the Rule of Faith and Life) and love his *people*, and love their best *welfare*: and the main Concernments of all these things are so plain and palpable, as he that cordially loves them will (unless transported in a pang of Temptation which will not hold) see and close with them, and unite therein.

(2.) Let not them that *Unite* in the main, be *dis-united* by lesser Differences, but therein attend the means of *Help*, and be set down by *Order*.

1. Attend the Means of discerning and finding out the right way even in lesser matters, and of agreeing therein. There is nothing so little in the things of *Religion*, or of the *publick Welfare*, (especially in matters of practice, wherein we must of necessity act and practise one way or other) as that we may neglect it, or neglect our best Endeavours to finde it out, and attend the minde of God therein. We must not disregard *the least of Gods Commandments, nor teach men so to do, Mat.* 5. 19. Though the Points of *Baptism*, *Church-Order*, and such

like, be not Fundamentals of *Salvation*, yet they are matters of necessary *practice*, (and of no small moment neither) wherein we ought to use all the means that God hath appointed, and gives opportunity to know and do his Will, and to labour to agree therein, that *we may speak the same thing*, 1 *Cor.* 1. 10. We should not think it a light thing to be of *many mindes*, but diligently use the utmost means to *agree*.

2. If after the use of all Means, some smaller and lesser Differences do remain, (as some there will be while we dwell in the flesh) *Agree* not to *Disagree* about them, but to manage them with Love and Meekness. Agree, I say, not in order to *Separation*, that is a strange *Agreement* to *agree* to *Divide* and *Disunite*, but in order to Union and Communion: and in the issue, let Order carry it; be set down by Order, submitting *one to another in the Lord*, 1 *Cor.* 14. 32, 33. There cannot be *peace* (but *confusion*) if there be not an orderly *subjection* one to another.

You will say these are but *generals*. It is not easie to speak more then so here: but yet they are such generals as (I humbly conceive) admit an easie application to *particulars*.

3. Let every one take heed of *Sin*, and study *Holiness*, and practical *Piety*, or close walking with God, *Prov.* 14. 34. *Joel* 3. 17. Be an *holy*, and you shall be an *happy* People. If any sin be *sprouting* up or getting head, timely observe it, and *weed* it out of your Souls, Churches, Families, Towns, Country. Let *Ministers reprove* sin, and spare not, *Isa.* 58. 1. Let *Magistrates* impartially *punish* it, (and God forbid that should ever be found with us, as *Amos* 5. 10.) And let all sorts of men stand up against sin in their several places, and in all regular wayes, (for a *disorderly* ungrounded and ill-managed *Zeal* often doth more hurt then good.) Keep out *Sin*, and that will keep out *Sorrow*. *Isa.* 4. 3, 5. when *Jerusalems* remnant are *holy*, and thereby a beauty and glory to God, *then upon all that glory there shall be a defence.* We in these places are eminently *obliged*, and eminently *advantaged* to be an holy people; and God expects it from us: If we be not so, we may expect his Rod, *Amos* 3. 2. yet if *we bear his Rod*, and be improving of it unto holiness and amendment, he will not cast us off.

4. In this way (of regular walking before God) put your *trust in the Lord God Almighty*, *Zeph.* 3. 12. Be *humble* and

believing. Carry it humbly before God and man; be not *haughty* because of the holy Mountain, nor in any other regard. I wish our whole course, garb and guise might speak *Humility* and *Humilation*, in so humbling a time as this is. Carry it in all things as becomes a poor and afflicted people: But if you be the people of God, and God Almighty be your God, then put your trust in him. *Psal.* 62. 8. that was the great duty of *Israel* in the Wilderness of old, and the want of that the great Controversie, *Psal.* 78. 22. Never did God take person or people into Covenant and near fellowship with himself, but he put them upon this sooner or later, to venture all upon God, and to relie upon his Mercy, Power and Faithfulness, having no other *string* to their *Bow* but Faith in him: So *Abraham* and *Jacob* often: so *Israel* at the Red-Sea, and in the Wilderness, where they were called openly to *act* and *live* by *Faith* in the sight of the world, both as to Protection and Provision. And never was God known to fail a people, that in a way of well-doing did trust themselves with him. We have sundry times read of *weapons formed*, but never of any that *prospered* against a *Reforming* people, and *relying* upon God. The story of *Asa*, of *Jehoshaphat*, of *Hezekiah* may easily be remembred, 2 *Chron.* 14. *&* 20. *&* 32. and of *Nehemiah* also, *Neh.* 4. 11, 15. *&* 6. 16. & so in the Promise, *Isa.* 54. 17. That *denomination* [of a Reforming people] may (I hope) in some comfortable measure be given to this people. Reformation is that that we are engaged upon, & are labouring in, though with much infirmity and trouble, and sometime ready to say as they, *Neh.* 4. 10. yet the Work is in hand, and not quite given over: And there is a *desire* to fear Gods Name, and do his Will, as *Neh.* 1. 11. I hope the greatest and swaying part do sincerely say, *Thy Will be done*, though through weakness we cannot reach it; we should not *despise*, as *Zech.* 4. 10. God may chasten us for neglects and faults, as he did them when they were upon Reforming work after the Captivity, *Hag.* 1. [And indeed there are such faults among us, as do give matter of *fear* as well as *hope*; I mean, fear of very sore and smart Chastisements: we have no cause to flatter our selves, or to be secure.] But yet God will be slow to cast off his poor people; though he *chasten* us, yet he will not *kill* us, nor destroy, but *save* in the issue, *Psal.* 118. 18. and therefore we should be slow to cast off our hope. Lay aside Security, and be awakened. (If there be things of moment amiss among us, and we will neither *mend*, nor *endeavour* it in good earnest, but it may be fall out with those that would mend us, verily God will make us know that he is in good earnest, and will not be dallied with; it is a jealous God with whom we have to do) but do not lay aside your Hope and Faith. Yea, whatever the Lord do with us, we ought with humble reliance on him, to leave our selves with him. You that have *Faith*, put it forth; *pray* down, and *believe* down Mercy for the Lords people, (all manner of mercy, *preventing* mercy, *reforming* mercy, *pardoning sanctifying* mercy, and *delivering* mercy.) That of *Asa, Help us, for we rest on thee*, (2 *Chron.* 14. 11.) is wont to bring a good issue.

5. Lastly, Let every one be and do for *God* and for his *people* now, as they would wish to have done, when the great Day of Account shall come. *For God*, and *For His People*, is the *Motto* of every gracious Soul, 2 *Cor.* 5. 13. and he that is indeed for God, is for his People, (that is certain, 1 *Joh.* 5. 1. & 4. 20, 21.) and doth sincerely seek their good and welfare. Why now hearken to this word, all you that stand before the Lord this day; we must ere long meet in a farre greater *Assembly* then this is, where we must give *Account* of our *speaking*, and of our *hearing* and *doing*; when *Christ shall break out of the Clouds, who is the onely Potentate, King of kings, and Lord of lords*, and sit him down on the Throne of his Glory, and call all Nations, and us all before him; and when it shall be said, What you did to my *Brethren*, to my *People*, yea *to the least of these my Brethren*, you did it unto me? and what good you *did not do*, what you neglected, or had no heart, no affection to do, nor courage *to do for these, you did it not to me, Mat.* 25. 40, 45. How will these things look then? when all worldly Interests shall be worth nothing; when Estates, and Friends, yea *Crowns* and Kingdomes shall appear to be but *pebble stones*, compar'd with one good look from Christ Jesus! Will it not then be a comfort to have sought the welfare of the children of *Israel*? and will it not then be more bitter and terrible then many deaths, not to have done it, or to have done the contrary thereunto? What the Apostle saith to *Ecclesiastical*, I may say to *Civil Rulers*, 1 *Pet.* 5. 2, 4. *Feed*

and rule the Lords people, and seek their good in the integrity of your hearts, and *when the chief Shepherd,* and chief Ruler *shall appear, then shall you receive a Crown of Glory that fadeth not away!* And so all the people of God in your several places, the Lord is *with you,* while you be *with him;* as we excellently heard the last year: and if you be with him, you must and will be with and for his people; yea *chuse to suffer affliction with them,* if that be their condition, as *Moses* did, *Heb.* 11. 25. And you will every one say, as you sometimes had that word on such a day as this, sweetly left with you, by that faithful *Nathaniel* now with God, *Psal.* 122. 8. *For my Brethren, and companions sake, I will now say to Jerusalem, Peace be within thee: and because of the house of the Lord our God, I will seek thy good;* that is thy voice of every Soul that *loves our Lord Jesus in sincerity.* In that Spirit and way persist, act and walk in your several places, and *hold on* therein against all Temptations, *in faith and love through Christ Jesus.* And at *that day,* when every Cup of cold *water* to a Disciple shall be rewarded; when *the house of Onesiphorus shall be remembred;* when every act of love to the faithful shall be honourably acknowledged: Then shall you *stand in the Congregation of the righteous,* (in the same company then, that you cleave unto now) *And the Lord the Righteous Judge shall give you a Crown of Righteousness, and unto all that love his appearing.*

FINIS

SAMUEL DANFORTH

A Brief Recognition of New-Englands Errand into the Wilderness

Made in the Audience of the General Assembly of the Massachusets Colony, at Boston in N. E. on the 11th of the third Moneth, 1670. being the Day of Election there.

Jer. 2. 2.   *Go, and cry in the ears of Jerusalem, saying, Thus saith the Lord, I remember thee, the kindness of thy youth, the love of thine espousals, when thou wentest after me in the wilderness, in a Land that was not sown.*

    3. *Israel was Holiness unto the Lord, and the first-fruits of his increase—*

    5. *Thus saith the Lord, What iniquity have your fathers found in me, that they are gone far from me, and have walked after vanity, and are become vain?*

———

Matth. 11. 7, 8, 9.

—*What went ye out into the wilderness to see? A reed shaken with the wind?*

But what went ye out for to see? A man clothed in soft raiment? behold, they that wear soft clothing, are in Kings houses.

But what went ye out for to see? A Prophet? yea, I say unto you, and more then a Prophet.

THESE WORDS are our Saviour's *Proem* to his illustrious Encomium of *John* the *Baptist*. *John* began his Ministry, not in *Jerusalem*, nor in any famous City of *Judea*, but in the *Wilderness*, i.e. in a woody, retired and solitary place, thereby withdrawing himself from the envy and preposterous zeal of such as were addicted to their old Traditions, and also taking the people aside from the noise and tumult of their secular occasions and businesses, which might have obstructed their ready and cheerful attendance unto his Doctrine. The Ministry of *John* at first was entertained by all sorts with singular affection: There *went out to him Jerusalem and all Judea, and all the region round about Jordan, Mat.* 3. 5. but after awhile, the people's fervour abated, and *John* being kept under restraint divers moneths, his authority and esteem began to decay and languish, *John* 5. 35. Wherefore our Saviour, taking occasion from *Johns* Messengers coming to him, after their departure, gives an excellent *Elogie* and Commendation of *John*, to the intent that He might ratifie and confirm his Doctrine and Administration, and revive his Authority and Estimation in the hearts and consciences of the people.

This *Elogie* our Saviour begins with an elegant *Dialogism*, which the Rhetorician calleth *Communication*: gravely deliberating with his Hearers, and seriously enquiring to what purpose they went out into the Wilderness, and what expectation drew them thither. Wherein we have, 1. *The general Question, and main subject of his Inquisition.* 2. *The particular Enquiries.* 3. *The Determination of the Question.*

The general Question is, *What went ye out into the Wilderness to see?* He saith not, Whom went ye out to *hear*, but what went ye out to *see*? Θεάσασθω. The phrase agrees to Shows and Stage-playes; plainly arguing that many of those, who seemed well-affected to *John*, and flock'd after him, were *Theatrical* Hearers, *Spectators* rather than *Auditors*; they went not to *hear*, but to *see*; they went to gaze upon a new and strange Spectacle.

This general Question being propounded, the first particular Enquiry is, whether they went to see *A reed shaken with the wind?* The expression is Metaphorical and Proverbial. A reed when the season is calm, lifts up itself and stands upright, but no sooner doth the wind blow upon it, but it shakes and trembles, bends and bows down, and then gets up again: and again it yields and bows, and then lifts up it self again. A notable *Emblem* of light, empty and inconstant persons, who in times of peace and tranquillity, give a fair and plausible Testimony to the Truth; but no sooner do the winds of Temptation blow upon them, and the waves of Troubles roll over them, but they incline and yield to the prevailing Party: but when the Tempest is over, they recover themselves and assert the Truth again. The meaning then of this first Enquiry is, Went ye out into the Wilderness to see a light, vain and inconstant man, one that could confess and deny, and deny and confess the same Truth? This Interrogation is to be understood negatively and ironically; *q.d.* Surely ye went not into the desert to behold such a ludicrous and ridiculous sight, *A man like unto a reed shaken with the wind*. Under the negation of the contrary levity, our Saviour sets forth one of *John*'s excellencies, *viz.* his eminent *Constancy* in asserting the Truth. The winds of various temptations both on the right hand and on the left, blew upon him, yet he wavered not in his testimony concerning Christ, *He confessed and denied not, but confessed* the truth.

Then the general Question is repeated, *But what went ye out for to see?* and a second particular Enquiry made, Was it to see *a man clothed in soft raiment?* This Interrogation hath also the force of a negation, *q.d.* Surely ye went not into the Wilderness to see a man clothed in silken and costly Apparel. The reason of this is added, *Behold, they that wear soft clothing, are in Kings houses.* Delicate and costly Apparel is to be expected in Princes Courts, and not in wilde Woods and Forrests. Under the negation of *John*'s affection of Courtly delicacy, our Saviour sets forth another of *John*'s excellencies, *viz.* his singular *gravity* and *sobriety*, who wore rough garments, and lived on course and mean fare, *Mat.* 3. 4. which austere kinde of life was accommodated to the place and work of his Ministry. *John* Preached in the Wilderness, which was no fit place for silken and soft raiment. His work was to prepare a people for the Lord, by calling them off from worldly pomp and vanities, unto repentance and mourning for sin. His peculiar habit and diet was such as became a penitentiary Preacher.

Thirdly, the generall Question is reiterated, *But what went ye out for to see?* and a third particular Enquiry made, Was it to see a *Prophet?* This Interrogation is to be understood affirmatively, *q.d.* no doubt but it was to see a *Prophet.* Had not *John* been a rare and excellent Minister of God, you would never have gone out of your Cities into the desert to have seen him. Thus our Saviour sets forth another of *John*'s admirable excellencies, *viz.* his *Prophetical* Office and Function. *John* was not an ordinary Interpreter of the Law, much less a Teacher of Jewish Traditions, but *a Prophet*, one who by the extraordinary Inspiration of the holy Ghost, made known the Mysteries of Salvation, *Luke* i. 76, 77.

Lastly, our Saviour determines and concludes the Question, He, whom ye went out to see was *more then a Prophet*, περισσότερον προφήτου, *much more*, or *abundantly more then a Prophet*. This he confirms by his wonted Asseveration, *Yea, I say unto you*, and much more then a Prophet. How was *John* much more then a Prophet? *John* was *Christs Herauld* sent immediately before his face, to proclaim his Coming and Kingdome, and prepare the people for the reception of him by the Baptism of Repentance, *ver.* 10. Hence it follows *ver.* 11. *Among all that are born of women, there hath not risen a greater Prophet then John.* *John* was greater then any of the Prophets that were before him, not in respect of his personal graces and virtues, (for who shall perswade us that he excelled *Abraham* in the grace of *Faith*, who was the father of the faithful, or *Moses* in *Meekness*, who was the meekest man on earth, or *David* in *Faithfulness*, who was a man after Gods own heart, or *Solomon* in *Wisdome*, who was the wisest man that ever was or shall be?) but in respect of the manner of his dispensation. All the *Prophets* foretold Christs Coming, his Sufferings and Glory, but the *Baptist* was his *Harbinger* and *Forerunner*, that bare the Sword before him, Proclaimed his Presence, and made room for him in the hearts of the people. All the *Prophets* saw Christ afar off, but the *Baptist* saw him present, baptized him, and applied the Types to him personally. *Behold the Lamb of God. He saw and bare record that this is the Son of God, Joh.* i. 29, 34. *But he that is least in the Kingdome of Heaven, is greater then John.* The least Prophet in the Kingdome of Heaven, *i.e.* the least Minister of the Gospel since Christ's Ascension, is greater then *John*; not in respect of the measure of his personal gifts, nor in respect of the manner of his Calling, but in respect of the *Object* of his Ministry, *Christ on the Throne*, having finished the work of our Redemption, and in respect of the *degree* of the revelation of Christ, which is far more clear and full. *John* shewed Christ in the flesh, and pointed to him with his finger, but the Ministers of the Gospel declare that he hath done and suffered all things necessary to our Salvation, and is risen again and set down at the right hand of God.

DOCT. *Such as have sometime left their pleasant Cities and Habitations to enjoy the pure Worship of God in a Wilderness, are apt in time to abate and cool in their affection thereunto: but then the Lord calls upon them seriously and throughly to examine themselves, what it was that drew them into the Wilderness, and to consider that it was not the expectation of ludicrous levity, nor of Courtly pomp and delicacy, but of the free and clear dispensation of the Gospel and Kingdome of God.*

This Doctrine consists of two distinct Branches; let me open them severally.

Branch I. *Such as have sometime left their pleasant Cities and Habitations, to enjoy the pure Worship of God in a Wilderness, are apt in time to abate and cool in their affection thereunto.* To what purpose did the Children of *Israel* leave their Cities and Houses in *Egypt*, and go forth into the Wilderness? was it not to *hold a Feast to the Lord*, and to *sacrifice to the God of their fathers?* That was the onely reason, which they gave of their motion to *Pharaoh, Exod.* 5. 1, 3. but how soon did they forget their Errand into the Wilderness, and corrupt themselves in their own Inventions? within a few moneths after their coming out of *Egypt, they make a Calf in Horeb, and worship the molten Image, and change their glory into the similitude of an Ox that eateth grass, Psal.* 106. 19, 20. *Exod.* 32. 7, 8. yea for the space of forty years in the Wilderness, while they pretended to Sacrifice to the Lord, they indeed worshipped the Stars and the Host of Heaven, and together with the Lords Tabernacle, carried about with them the Tabernacle of *Moloch, Amos* 5. 25, 26. *Acts* 7. 42, 43. And how did they spend their time in the Wilderness, but in tempting God, and in murmuring against their godly and faithful Teachers and Rulers, *Moses* and *Aaron? Psal.* 95. 8. To what purpose did the Children of the Captivity upon *Cyrus* his Proclamation, leave their Houses which they had built, and their Vineyards and Oliveyards which they had planted in the Province of *Babylon*, and return to *Judea* and *Jerusalem*, which were now become a Wilderness? was it not that they

might build the House of God at *Jerusalem*, and set up the
Temple-worship? But how shamefully did they neglect that
great and honourable Work for the space of above forty years?
They pretended that Gods time was not come to build his
House, because of the rubs and obstructions which they
met with; whereas all their difficulties and discouragements
hindred not their building of stately houses for themselves,
Hag. 1. 2, 3, 4. To what purpose did *Jerusalem* & all *Judea*, &
all the region round about *Jordan*, leave their several Cities
and Habitations, and flock into the *Wilderness of Judea*? was it
not to see that *burning and shining light*, which God had
raised up? To hear his heavenly Doctrine, and partake of that
new Sacrament, which he administred? O how they were affected with his rare and excellent gifts! with his clear, lively
and powerful Ministry! *The Kingdome of Heaven pressed in*
upon them *with* a holy *violence, and the violent*, the zealous
and affectionate hearers of the Gospel, *took it by force, Mat.*
11. 12. *Luk.* 16. 16. They leapt over all discouragements and im-
pediments, whether outward, as Legal Rites and Ceremonies,
or inward, the sense of their own sin and unworthiness, and
pressed into the Kingdome of God, as men rush into a
Theatre to see a pleasant Sight, or as Souldiers run into a be-
sieged City, to take the Spoil thereof: but their hot fit is soon
over, their affection lasted but for an *hour*, i.e. a short season,
Joh. 5. 35.

    Reas. 1. Because the *affection* of many to the Ministry of
the Gospel and the pure Worship of God, is built upon *temporary* and *transitory* grounds, as the *novelty* and *strangeness
of the matter, the rareness and excellency of Ministerial Gifts,
the voice of the people, the countenance of great men, and the
hope of worldly advantage.* The Jews had lien in ignorance
and darkness a long time, being trained up under the superstitious observances of their old Traditions, which were vain,
empty and unprofitable Customes, and the Church wanted
the gift of Prophecy about four hundred years, and therefore
when *John* the *Baptist* arose like a bright and burning light,
shining amongst them with admirable gifts of the Spirit, and
extraordinary severity and gravity of manners, proclaiming the
Coming and Kingdome of the Messias, (which had been oft

promised and long expected) and pressing the people to
Repentance and good works; O how they admire and reverence him? especially, when grown popular, and countenanced
by *Herod* the *Tetrarch.* What sweet affections are kindled!
what great expectations are raised! what ravishing joy is conceived! Hoping (as its probable) to make use of his Authority
to cast off the *Roman* yoke, and recover their Civil Liberties,
Riches and Honours. But after a little acquaintance with *John*,
(for he was a publick Preacher but a year and half) his
Doctrine, Administrations and Prophetical Gifts, grew common and stale things, and of little esteem with them; especially, when they saw their carnal hopes frustrated, the Rulers
disaffected, and *Herods* countenance and carriage toward him
changed.

Reas. 2. Because *Prejudices* and *Offences* are apt to arise in
the hearts of many against the *faithful Dispensers* of the
Gospel. The *Pharisees* and *Lawyers* came among others to the
Baptism of *John*, but when they hear his sharp reprehensions
of their *Viperous* Opinions and Practices, they nauseate his
Doctrine, repudiate his Baptism, calumniate his Conversation,
Luke 7. 30. *Herodias* hath an inward grudge and a quarrel
against him, because he found fault with her incestuous
Marriage, *Mar.* 6. 19. Yea, that very Age and Generation of
the Jews, were like to a company of surly, sullen and froward
children, whom no Musick can please, they neither dance
after the Pipe, nor make lamentation after the mourner. They
inveigh against *John's* austerity, saying that he was transported
with diabolical fury, and was an enemy to humane society:
and they do as much distaste and abhor *Christ's* gentleness
and familiarity, traducing him, as being a sensual and volup-
tuous person, given to intemperance and luxury, and a Patron
and Abettor of looseness and profaneness, *Mat.* 11. 16–19.
Thus doth the frowardness and stubbornness of man, resist
and oppose the wisdome and goodness of God, who useth
various wayes and instruments to compass poor sinners, but
they through their folly and perverseness, frustrate, disanul
and abrogate the counsel of God against themselves. The evil
spirit that troubled *Saul*, was quieted and allayed by the sweet
Melody of *David's* Harp: but the mad and outragious fury

that transports men against the Truth and the Ministry thereof, cannot be quieted and allayed by the voice of the Charmers, charm they never so wisely.

Branch II. *When men abate and cool in their affection to the pure Worship of God, which they went into the Wilderness to enjoy, the Lord calls upon them seriously and throughly to examine themselves, what it was that drew them into the Wilderness, and to consider that it was not the expectation of ludicrous levity, nor of Courtly pomp and delicacy, but of the free and clear dispensation of the Gospel and Kingdome of God.* Our Saviour knowing that the people had lost their first love and singular affection to the revelation of his grace by the Ministry of his Herauld *John,* He is very intense in examining them, what expectation drew them into the Wilderness: He doth not once nor twice, but thrice propound that Question, *What went ye out into the Wilderness to see?* Yea, in particular he enquires whether it were to see a man that was like to *a Reed shaken with the wind?* or whether it were to see *a man clothed like a Courtier,* or whether it were to see a *Prophet,* and then determines the Question, concluding that it was to see a great and excellent Prophet, and that had not they seen rare and admirable things in him, they would never have gone out into the Wilderness unto him.

The Reason is, Because the serious consideration of the inestimable grace and mercy of God in the free and clear dispensation of the Gospel and Kingdome of God, is a special means to convince men of their folly and perverseness in undervaluing the same, and a sanctified remedy to recover their affections thereunto. The Lord foreseeing the defection of *Israel* after *Moses* his death, commands him to write that Prophetical Song, recorded in *Deut.* 32. as a Testimony against them: wherein the chief remedy, which he prescribes for the prevention and healing of their Apostacy, is their calling to remembrance Gods great and signal love in manifesting himself to them in the Wilderness, in conducting them safely and mercifully, and giving them possession of their promised Inheritance, *ver.* 7–14. And when *Israel* was apostatized and fallen, the Lord to convince them of their ingratitude and folly, brings to their remembrance his deliverance of them out of *Egypt,* his leading them through the Wilderness

for the space of forty years, and not onely giving them possession of their Enemies Land, but also raising up, even of
their own Sons, *Prophets*, faithful and eminent Ministers, and
of their young men *Nazarites*, who being separated from
worldly delights and encumbrances, were Paterns of Purity
and Holiness: all which were great and obliging mercies. Yea,
the Lord appeals to their own Consciences, whether these his
favours were not real and signal, *Amos* 2. 10, 11. The Prophet
Jeremiah, that he might reduce the people from their back-
slidings, cries in the ears of *Jerusalem*, with earnestness and
boldness declaring unto them, that the Lord remembred how
well they stood affected towards him, when he first chose
them to be his people and espoused them to himself, how
they followed him in the Wilderness, and kept close to him in
their long and wearisome passage through the uncultured
Desert; how they were then consecrated to God, and set apart
for his Worship and Service; as the first-fruits are wont to be
sequestred and devoted to God: and thereupon expostulates
with them for their forsaking the Lord, and following after
their Idols, *Jer.* 2. 2, 3, 5, 6. Surely our Saviour's *Dialogism*
with his Hearers in my Text, is not a meer Rhetorical
Elegancy to adorn his Testimony concerning *John*, but a clear
and strong conviction of their folly in slighting and despising
that which they sometime so highly pretended unto, and a
wholesome admonition and direction how to recover their
primitive affection to his Doctrine and Administration.

USE I. Of solemn and serious Enquiry to us all in this
general Assembly, Whether we have not in a great measure
forgotten our Errand into the Wilderness. You have solemnly
professed before God, Angels and Men, that the Cause of
your leaving your Country, Kindred and Fathers houses, and
transporting your selves with your Wives, Little Ones and
Substance over the vast Ocean into this waste and howling
Wilderness, was *your Liberty to walk in the Faith of the Gospel
with all good Conscience according to the Order of the Gospel,
and your enjoyment of the pure Worship of God according to his
Institution, without humane Mixtures and Impositions.* Now
let us sadly consider whether our ancient and primitive affections to the Lord Jesus, his glorious Gospel, his pure and
Spiritual Worship and the Order of his House, remain, abide

and continue firm, constant, entire and inviolate. Our Saviour's reiteration of this Question, *What went ye out into the
Wilderness to see?* is no idle repetition, but a sad conviction of
our dulness and backwardness to this great duty, and a clear
demonstration of the weight and necessity thereof. It may be
a grief to us to be put upon such an Inquisition; as it is said
of *Peter, Joh.* 21. 17. *Peter was grieved, because he said unto him
the third time, Lovest thou me?* but the Lord knoweth that a
strict and rigid examination of our hearts in this point, is no
more then necessary. Wherefore let us call to remembrance
the former dayes, and consider whether *it was not then better
with us, then it is now.*

   In our first and best times the Kingdome of Heaven brake
in upon us with a holy violence, and every man pressed into
it. What mighty efficacy and power had the clear and faithful
dispensation of the Gospel upon your hearts? how affectionately and zealously did you entertain the Kingdome of God?
How careful were you, even all sorts, young and old, high
and low, to take hold of the opportunities of your Spiritual
good and edification? ordering your secular affairs (which
were wreathed and twisted together with great variety) so as
not to interfere with your general Calling, but that you might
attend upon the Lord without distraction. How diligent and
faithful in preparing your hearts for the reception of the
Word, *laying apart all filthiness and superfluity of naughtiness,*
that you might *receive with meekness the ingrossed word, which
is able to save your souls; and purging out all malice, guile,
hypocrisies, envies, and all evil speakings, and as new-born babes,
desiring the sincere milk of the Word, that ye might grow
thereby?* How attentive in hearing the everlasting Gospel,
*watching daily at the gates of Wisdome, and waiting at the posts
of her doors, that ye might finde eternal life, and obtain favour
of the Lord?* Gleaning day by day in the field of Gods Ordinances, even among the Sheaves, and gathering up handfuls,
which the Lord let fall of purpose for you, and at night going
home and beating out what you had gleaned, by Meditation,
Repetition, Conference, and therewith feeding your selves
and your families. How painful were you in recollecting, repeating and discoursing of what you heard, whetting the
Word of God upon the hearts of your Children, Servants and

Neighbours? How fervent in Prayer to Almighty God for his divine Blessing upon the Seed sown, that it might take root and fructifie? O what a reverent esteem had you in those dayes of Christ's faithful Ambassadors, that declared unto you the Word of Reconciliation! *How beautiful* were *the feet of them, that preached the Gospel of peace, and brought the glad tidings of Salvation!* you *esteemed them highly in love for their works sake.* Their Persons, Names and Comforts were precious in your eyes; you counted your selves blessed in the enjoyment of a Pious, Learned and Orthodox Ministry: and though you ate the bread of adversity and drank the water of affliction, yet you rejoyced in this, that your eyes saw your Teachers, they were not removed into corners, and your ears heard a word behinde you, saying, This is the way, walk ye in it, when you turned to the right hand and when you turned to the left, *Isa.* 30. 20, 21. What earnest and ardent desires had you in those dayes after Communion with Christ in the holy Sacraments? *With desire you desired* to partake of the Seals of the Covenant. You thought your Evidences for Heaven not sure nor authentick, unless the Broad-Seals of the Kingdome were annexed. What solicitude was there in those dayes to *seek the Lord after the right Order*? What searching of the holy Scriptures, what Collations among your Leaders, both in their private Meetings and publick Councils and Synods, to finde out the Order, which Christ hath constituted and established in his House? What fervent zeal was there then against Sectaries and Hereticks, and all manner of Heterodoxies? *You could not bear them that were evil,* but tried them that pretended to New Light and Revelations, and found them *liars.* What pious *Care* was there of *Sister-Churches,* that those that wanted *Breasts,* might be supplied, and that those that wanted *Peace,* their Dissentions might be healed? What readiness was there in those days to call for the help of Neighbour-Elders and Brethren, in case of any Difference or Division that could not be healed at home? What reverence was there then of the Sentence of a Council, as being *decisive* and issuing the Controversie? According to that ancient Proverbial Saying, *They shall surely ask counsel at Abel, and so they ended the matter,* 2 *Sam.* 20. 18. What holy Endeavours were there in those dayes to *propagate* Religion to your Children and Posterity, training them up in the nurture and admonition of the Lord, keeping them under the awe of government, restraining their enormities and extravagancies; charging them to know the God of their fathers, and serve him with a perfect heart and willing minde; and publickly asserting and maintaining their interest in the Lord and in his holy Covenant, and zealously opposing those that denied the same?

And then had the Churches *rest* throughout the several Colonies, and were *edified: and walking in the fear of the Lord, and in the comfort of the holy Ghost, were multiplied.* O how your *Faith* grew exceedingly! you proceeded from faith to faith, from a less to a greater degree and measure, growing up in Him, who is our Head, and receiving abundance of grace and of the gift of righteousness, that you might reign in life by Jesus Christ. O how your *Love and Charity* towards each other abounded! O what comfort of Love! what bowels and mercies! what affectionate care was there one of another! what a holy Sympathy in Crosses and Comforts, weeping with those that wept, and rejoycing with those that rejoyced!

But who is there left among you, that saw these Churches *in their first glory,* and how do you see them *now?* Are they not in your eyes in comparison thereof, *as nothing? How is the gold become dim! how is the most fine gold changed!* Is not the Temper, Complexion and Countenance of the Churches strangely altered? Doth not a careless, remiss, flat, dry, cold, dead frame of spirit, grow in upon us secretly, strongly, prodigiously? They that have Ordinances, are as though they had none; and they that hear the Word, as though they heard it not; and they that pray, as though they prayed not; and they that receive Sacraments, as though they received them not; and they that are exercised in the holy things, using them by the by, as matters of custome and ceremony, so as not to hinder their eager prosecution of other things which their hearts are set upon. Yea and in some particular Congregations amongst us, is there not *in stead of a sweet smell, a stink? and in stead of a girdle, a rent? and in stead of a stomacher, a girding with sackcloth? and burning in stead of beauty?* yea *the Vineyard is all overgrown with thorns, and nettles cover the face thereof, and the stone-wall thereof is broken down, Prov.* 24. 31. yea, and that which is the most sad and certain sign of calamity approaching, *Iniquity aboundeth, and the love of many waxeth cold, Mat.* 24. 12. Pride, Contention, Worldliness, Covetousness, Luxury, Drunkenness and Uncleanness break in like a flood upon us, and good men grow cold in their love to God and to one another. If a man be cold in his bed, let them lay on the more clothes, that he may get heat: but we are like to *David* in his old age, *they covered him with clothes, but he gat no heat,* 2 *Sam.* 1. 1. The Lord heaps mercies, favours, blessings upon us, and loads us daily with his benefits, but all his love and bounty cannot heat and warm our hearts and affections. Well, the furnace is able to heat and melt the coldest Iron: but how oft hath the Lord cast us into the hot furnace of Affliction and Tribulation, and we have been scorched and burnt, yet not melted, but hardened thereby, *Isa.* 63. 17. How long hath God kept us in the furnace day after day, moneth after moneth, year after year? but all our Afflictions, Crosses, Trials have not been able to keep our hearts in a warm temper.

Now let me freely deliberate with you, what may be the *Causes* and *Grounds of such decayes and languishings* in our affections to, and estimation of that which we came into the Wilderness to enjoy? Is it because *there is no bread, neither is there any water, and our soul loatheth this light bread? Numb.* 21. 5. *Our soul is dried away, and there is nothing at all, besides this Manna, before our eyes, Numb.* 11. 6. What, is Manna no bread? Is this Angelical food, light bread, which cannot satisfie, but starves the Soul? Doth our Soul loath the bread of Heaven? The Lord be merciful to us: The full soul loatheth the honey-comb, *Prov.* 27. 7.

What then is the cause of our decayes and languishings? Is it because the Spirit of the Lord is straitned and limited in the dispensers of the Gospel, and hence our joyes and comforts are lessened and shortned? *O thou that art named the house of Jacob, is the Spirit of the Lord straitned? are those his doings? Do not my words do good to him that walketh uprightly? Mic.* 2. 7. Surely it is not for want of fulness in the Spirit of God, that he withholds comforts and blessings from any; neither doth he delight in threatnings and judgements, but his words both promise and perform that which is good and comfortable to them that walk uprightly. The Spirit is able to enlarge it self unto the reviving and cheering of every man's heart; and that should we experience, did not our iniquity put a barre. 2 *Cor.* 6. II, 12. *O ye Corinthians, our mouth is open unto you, our heart is enlarged: Ye are not straitned in us, but ye are straitned in your own bowels.* The Spirit of God dilateth and enlargeth the heart of the faithfull Ministry for the good of the people; but many times the people are straitned in their own bowels, and cannot receive such a large portion, as the Lord hath provided for them. *What then is the cause of our coolings, faintings and languishings?* The grand and principal cause is our *Unbelief.* We believe not the Grace and Power of God in Christ. Where is that lively exercise of faith, which ought to be, in our attendance upon the Lord in his holy Ordinances? Christ came to *Nazareth* with his heart full of love and compassion, and his hands full of blessings to bestow upon his old Acquaintance and Neighbours, among whom he had been brought up, but their *Unbelief* restrained his tender mercies, and bound his Omnipotent hands, that he could not do any great or illustrious Miracle amongst them. *Mat.* 13. 58. *Mark* 6. 5, 6. *He could do there no mighty work—and he marvelled because of their unbelief.* Unbelief straitens the grace and power of Christ, and hinders the communication of divine favours and special mercies. The word preached profits not, when it is not mixed with faith in them that hear it, *Heb.* 4. 2. We may pray earnestly, but if we ask not in faith, how can we expect to receive any thing of the Lord? *Jam.* 1. 6, 7.

But though Unbelief be the principal, yet it is not the sole cause of our decayes and languishings: *Inordinate worldly Cares, predominant Lusts, and malignant Passions and Distempers* stifle and choak the Word, and quench our affections to the Kingdome of God, *Luke* 8. 14. The Manna was gathered early in the morning, when the Sun waxed hot, it melted, *Exod.* 16. 21. It was a fearful Judgement on *Dathan* and *Abiram*, that the earth opened its mouth and swallowed them up. How many Professors of Religion, are swallowed up alive by earthly affections? Such as escape the *Lime-pit of Pharisaical Hypocrisie*, fall into the *Coal-pit of Sadducean Atheism and Epicurism*. Pharisaism and Sadduceism do almost divide the Professing World between them. Some split upon the *Rock* of affected ostentation of singular Piety and Holiness, and others are drawn into the *Whirlpool*, and perish in the *Gulf* of Sensuality and Luxury.

If any question how seasonable such a Discourse may be upon such a Day, as this; let him consider, *Hag.* 2. 10–14. *In the four and twentieth day of the ninth moneth, in the second year of Darius, came the word of the Lord by Haggai the Prophet, saying, Thus saith the Lord of Hosts, Ask now the Priests concerning the law, saying, If one bear holy flesh in the skirt of his garment, and with his skirt do touch bread, or pottage, or wine, or oyl, or any meat, shall it be holy? And the Priests answered and said, No. Then said Haggai, If one that is unclean by a dead body, touch any of these, shall it be unclean? And the Priests answered and said, It shall be unclean. Then answered Haggai and said, So is this people, and so is this nation before me, saith the Lord; and so is every work of their hands, and that which they offer there is unclean.* It was an high and great day, wherein the Prophet spake these words, and an holy and honourable Work, which the people were employed in. For this day they laid the Foundation of the Lords Temple, *ver.* 18. nevertheless, the Lord saw it necessary this very day to represent and declare unto them, the pollution and uncleanness both of their persons and of their holy Services, that they might be deeply humbled before God, and carry on their present Work more holily and purely. What was their uncleanness? Their eager pursuit of their private Interests, took off their hearts and affections from the affairs of the House of God. It seems they pleased themselves with this, that the Altar stood upon its Bases, and Sacrifices were daily offered thereon, and the building of the Temple was onely deferred untill a fit opportunity were afforded, free from disturbance and opposition: and having now gained such a season, they are ready to build the Temple: but the Lord convinceth them out of the Law, that their former negligence was not expiated by their daily Sacrifices, but the guilt thereof rendred both the *Nation* and this *holy and honourable Work*, which they were about, *vile and unclean* in the sight of God. And having thus shewn them their spiritual uncleanness, he encourageth them to go on with the work in hand, the building of the Temple, promising them from *this day* to bless them, *ver.* 18.

USE II. Of Exhortation, To excite and stir us all up to attend and prosecute our Errand into the Wilderness. *To what purpose came we into this place, and what expectation drew us hither?* Surely, not the expectation of *ludicrous Levity.* We came not hither to see *a Reed shaken with the wind.* Then let us not be *Reeds*, light, empty, vain, hollow-hearted Professors, shaken with every wind of Temptation: but solid, serious and sober Christians, constant and stedfast in the Profession and Practice of the Truth, *Trees of Righteousness, the planting of the Lord, that he may be glorified*, holding fast the profession of our Faith without wavering.

Alas, there is such variety and diversity of Opinions and Judgements, that we know not what to believe.

Were there not as various and different Opinions touching the Person of Christ, even in the dayes of his flesh? Some said that He was *John the Baptist*, some *Elias*, others *Jeremias*, or one of the old *Prophets.* Some said he was a gluttonous man, and a wine-bibber, a friend of publicans and sinners: others said He was a *Samaritan*, and had a Devil; yet the Disciples knew what to believe. *Whom say ye that I am? Thou art Christ, the Son of the living God, Mat.* 16. 15, 16. The various heterodox Opinions of the people, serve as a *foil* or tinctured leaf to set off the lustre and beauty of the Orthodox and Apostolical Faith. This is truly commendable, when in such variety and diversity of Apprehensions, you are not byassed by any sinister respects, but discern, embrace and profess the Truth, as it is in Christ Jesus.

But to what purpose came we into the Wilderness, and what expectation drew us hither? Not the expectation of *Courtly Pomp and Delicacy.* We came not hither to see men clothed like *Courtiers.* The affectation of Courtly Pomp and Gallantry, is very unsuitable in a Wilderness. Gorgeous Attire is comely in Princes Courts, if it exceed not the limits of Christian Sobriety: but excess in Kings houses, escapes not divine Vengeance. *Zeph.* 1. 8.—*I will punish the Princes and the Kings children, and all such as are clothed with strange Apparel.* The pride and haughtiness of the Ladies of *Zion* in their superfluous Ornaments and stately gestures, brought wrath upon themselves, upon their Husbands, and upon their Children, yea and upon the whole Land, *Isa.* 3. 16–26. How much more intolerable and abominable is excess of this kinde in a

Wilderness, where we are so far removed from the Riches and Honours of Princes Courts?

To what purpose then came we into the Wilderness, and what expectation drew us hither? Was it not the expectation of the *pure and faithful Dispensation* of the Gospel and Kingdome of God? The times were such that we could not enjoy it in our own Land: and therefore having obtained *Liberty* and a gracious *Patent* from our *Soveraign*, we left our Country, Kindred and Fathers houses, and came into these wilde Woods and Deserts; where the Lord hath planted us, and made us *dwell in a place of our own, that we might move no more, and that the children of wickedness might afflict not us any more,* 2 *Sam.* 7. 10. What is it that *distinguisheth New-England* from other Colonies and Plantations in *America*? Not our transportation over the *Atlantick* Ocean, but the *Ministry* of Gods faithful Prophets, and the fruition of his holy *Ordinances*. Did not the Lord bring *the Philistines from Caphtor, and the Assyrians from Kir,* as well as *Israel from the land of Egypt? Amos* 9. 7. But *by a Prophet the Lord brought Israel out of Egypt, and by a Prophet was he preserved, Hos.* 12. 13. What, is the Price and Esteem of Gods Prophets, and their faithful Dispensations, now fallen in our hearts?

The hardships, difficulties and sufferings, which you have exposed your selves unto, that you might dwell in the House of the Lord, and leave your Little Ones under the shadow of the wings of the God of *Israel*, have not been few nor small. And shall we now withdraw our selves and our Little Ones from under those *healing Wings*, and lose that full Reward, which the Lord hath in his heart and hand to bestow upon us? Did we not with *Mary* choose this for our *Part, to sit at Christs feet and hear his word*? and do we now repent of our choice, and prefer the Honours, Pleasures and Profits of the world before it? *You did run well: who doth hinder you, that you should not obey the truth? Gal.* 5. 7.

Hath the Lord been wanting to us, or failed our expectation? *Micah* 6. 3. *O my people, what have I done unto thee, and wherein have I wearied thee? testifie against me. Jer.* 2. 5. *What iniquity have your fathers found in me, that they are gone far from me?* and *ver.* 31. *O generation, see ye the word of the Lord: have I been a wilderness unto Israel? a land of darkness?* May not the Lord say unto us, as *Pharaoh* did to *Hadad*, 1 *King.* 11. 22. *What hast thou lacked with me, that behold, thou seekest to go to thine own Country?* Nay, *what could have been done more*, then what the Lord hath done for us? *Isa.* 5. 4.

How sadly hath the Lord testified against us, because of our *loss* of our *first love*, and our *remissness* and negligence in his Work? Why hath the Lord smitten us with Blasting and Mildew now seven years together, superadding sometimes severe Drought, sometimes great Tempests, Floods, and sweeping Rains, that leave no food behinde them? Is it not because the Lords House lyeth waste? Temple-work in our Hearts, Families, Churches is shamefully neglected? What should I make mention of *Signes* in the Heavens and in the Earth, *Blazing-Stars, Earthquakes*, dreadful *Thunders* and *Lightnings*, fearful *Burnings*? What meaneth the heat of his great Anger, in calling home so many of his *Ambassadors*? In plucking such burning and shining *Lights* out of the Candlesticks; the principal *Stakes* out of our Hedges; the *Cornerstones* out of our Walls? In removing such faithful *Shepherds* from their Flocks, and breaking down our *defenced Cities, Iron Pillars*, and *Brazen-Walls*? Seemeth it a small thing unto us, that so many of Gods *Prophets* (whose Ministry we came into the Wilderness to enjoy) are taken from us in so short a time? Is it not a Sign that God is making a way for his Wrath, when he removes his *Chosen* out of the *Gap*? Doth he not threaten us with a *Famine* of the Word, the *Scattering* of the Flock, the *Breaking* of the Candlesticks, and the turning of the *Songs* of the Temple into *howlings*?

It is high time for us to *remember whence we are fallen, and repent, and do our first works*. Wherefore let us *lift up the hands that hang down, and strengthen the feeble knees, and make straight paths for our feet, lest that which is lame be turned out of the way, but let it rather be healed, Heb.* 12. 12, 13. Labour we to redress our Faintings and Swervings, and address our selves to the Work of the Lord. Let us arise and build, and the Lord will be with us, and from this day will he bless us.

Alas, we are feeble and impotent; our hands are withered, and our strength dried up.

Remember the man that had a withered hand: Christ saith

unto him, *Stretch forth thy hand; and he stretched it forth, and it was restored whole, like as the other, Mat.* 12. 13. How could he stretch forth his hand, when it was withered, the Blood and Spirits dried up, and the Nerves and Sinews shrunk up? The Almighty Power of Christ accompanying his Command, enabled the man to stretch forth his withered hand, and in stretching it forth, restored it whole, like as the other. Where the Soveraignty of Christ's Command takes place in the Conscience, there is effectual grace accompanying it to the healing of our Spiritual Feebleness and Impotency, and the enabling of us to perform the duty incumbent on us. Though we have no might, no strength, yet at Christ's Command, make an essay. Where the word of a King is, there is power.

But alas, our Bruise is incurable and our Wound grievous, there is none to repair the Breach, there is no healing Medicine.

The Lord Jesus, the great Physician of *Israel*, hath undertaken the Cure. *I will restore health unto thee, and I will heal thee of thy wounds, saith the Lord, Jer.* 30. 17. No case is to be accounted desperate or incurable, which Christ takes in hand. If he undertake to heal *Jairus* his daughter, he will have her *death* esteemed but *a sleep*, in reference to his power. *She is not dead, but sleepeth, Mat.* 9. 24. When Christ came to *Lazarus* his grave, and bade them take away the stone, *Martha* saith, *Lord, by this time he stinketh; for he hath been dead four dayes.* But Christ answereth, *Said I not unto thee, that if thou wouldest believe, thou shouldest see the glory of God? Joh.* 11. 40. Let us give glory to God by believing his word, and we shall have real and experimental manifestations of his *glory* for our good and comfort.

But alas, our hearts are sadly prejudiced against the Means and Instruments, by which we might expect that Christ should cure and heal us.

Were not the hearts of *John's Disciples* leavened with carnal emulation and prejudices against *Christ* himself? They would not own him to be the Messias, nor believe their Master's Testimony concerning him: insomuch that the Lord saw it necessary that *John* should decrease and be abased, that *Christ* might encrease and be exalted: and therefore suffered *Herod* to shut up *John* in Prison, and keep him in durance about twelve moneths, and at length to cut off his head, *that so these fondlings might be weaned from their Nurse;* and when *John* was dead, his Disciples resort to Jesus, acquaint him with the calamity that befell them, and were perfectly reconciled to him, passing into his School, and becoming his Disciples, *Mat.* 14. 12.

But alas, the Times are difficult and perillous; the Wind is stormy, and the Sea tempestuous; the Vessel heaves and sets, and tumbles up and down in the rough and boisterous waters, and is in danger to be swallowed up.

Well, remember that *the Lord sitteth upon the flood, yea the Lord sitteth King for ever, Psal.* 29. 10. *His way is in the sea, and his path in the great waters, and his footsteps are not known, Psal.* 77. 19. *He stilleth the noise of the seas, the noise of their waves, and the tumult of the people, Psal.* 65. 7. He saith to the raging Sea, *Peace, be still: and the wind ceaseth, and there is a great calm, Mark* 4. 39. Yea, he can enable his people to tread and walk upon the waters. To sail and swim in the waters, is an easie matter; but to walk upon the waters, as upon a pavement, is an act of wonder. *Peter* at Christ's call *came down out of the ship and walked on the water to go to Jesus, Matth.* 14. 29. and as long as his Faith held, it upheld him from sinking; when his Faith failed, his body sunk: but he *cried to the Lord, and he stretched forth his hand and caught him, and said unto him, O thou of little faith, wherefore didst thou doubt?*

But what shall we do for bread? The encrease of the field and the labour of the Husbandman fails.

Hear Christ's answer to his Disciples, when they were troubled, because there was but one Loaf in the ship. *O ye of little faith, why reason ye, because you have no bread? perceive ye not yet, neither understand? have ye your heart yet hardened? having eyes, see ye not? and having ears, hear ye not, and do ye not remember? Mark* 8. 17, 18. *Mat.* 16. 8, 9. Those which have had large and plentiful experience of the grace and power of Christ in providing for their outward Sustenance, and relieving of their Necessities, when ordinary and usual Means have failed, are worthy to be severely reprehended, if afterward they grow anxiously careful and solicitous, because of the defect of outward supplies. In the whole Evangelicall History, I finde not that ever the Lord Jesus did so sharply rebuke his

Disciples for any thing, as for that fit and pang of Worldly care and solicitude about Bread. Attend we our Errand, upon which Christ sent us into the Wilderness, and he will provide Bread for us. *Matth.* 6. 33. *Seek ye first the Kingdome of God, and his Righteousness, and all these things shall be added unto you.*

But we have many Adversaries, and they have their subtile Machinations and Contrivances, and how soon we may be sur-prized, we know not.

Our diligent Attention to the Ministry of the Gospel, is a special means to check and restrain the rage and fury of Adversaries. The people's assiduity in attendance upon Christ's Ministry, was the great obstacle that hindred the execution of the bloody Counsels of the Pharisees. *Luk.* 19. 47, 48. *He taught daily in the Temple, but the chief Priests and the Scribes, and the chief of the people, sought to destroy him, and could not finde what they might do: for all the people were very attentive to hear him.* If the people cleave to the Lord, to his Prophets, and to his Ordinances, it will strike such a fear into the hearts of enemies, that they will be at their wits ends, and not know what to do. However, In this way we have the promise of divine Protection and Preservation. *Revel.* 3. 10. *Because thou hast kept the word of my Patience, I also will keep thee from the hour of Temptation, which shall come upon all the world, to try them that dwell upon the earth.* Let us with *Mary* choose this for our Portion, *To sit at Christ's feet and hear his word;* and whosoever complain against us, the Lord Jesus will plead for us, as he did for her, and say, They *have chosen that good part, which shall not be taken away from* them, *Luk.* 10. 42. *AMEN.*

INCREASE MATHER

Sermon Occasioned by the Execution of a Man Found Guilty of Murder

Preached at Boston in New-England, March 11th 168 $\frac{5}{6}$.
(Together with the confession, Last Expressions, and Solemn
Warning of that Murderer, to all Persons; especially to
Young Men, to beware of those Sins which brought
him to his Miserable End.)

> Deut. 19. 20, 21. *And those which remain shall hear, and*
> *fear, & shall henceforth commit no more any such evil*
> *among you. And thine eye shall not pity, but life shall go*
> *for eye for eye, tooth for tooth, hand for hand, foot for*
> *foot.*
> Prov. 28. 17. *A man that doth violence to the blood of any*
> *person, shall flee to the Pit, let no man stay him.*

———

NUMB. 35. 16.
And if he smite him with an instrument of iron (so
that he die) he is a murderer, the murderer shall
surely be put to death.

A GREAT part of this Chapter is taken up in declaring who
should have benefit by *the City of Refuge*; and who might not
expect advantage thereby. There are two sorts of *Man-slayers*,
(1) One may kill his Neighbour accidentally, though he had
no design of hurt to him—nor any displeasure against him.
The *City of Refuge* was for such. (2.) A Man may in hatred or
in passion kill another, and then the *City of Refuge* could not
secure or save him from the hand of Justice; To intimate
which is the scope of the Words which have been now read:
wherein we have two things: 1. A Criminal. 2. The Punishment to be inflicted on such a Criminal.

1. A Criminal   *He is a Murderer:* there are three Particulars mentioned, which if they concur the person is guilty of Murder: 1. If he smites another man, *h.e.* if he does so, not accidentally but designedly. 2. If the *Instrument* which he smites him with be of *Iron*, that makes the Murder to be the more evident. In the verses following it is added, *That if he smite him mortally with a Stone, or with Wood, he shall be accounted a Murderer.* The *Jewish* Writers tell us, (*a*) That if a Man were slain, there was diligent enquiry made concerning the *Instrument*, whereby he was killed. If it was with a Stone, or with Wood, they examined whether the Stone or Wood were of that bigness as that the dead man might probably receive his deaths Wound thereby: But (they say) if it were with an *Instrument of Iron*, no enquiry was made as to the greatness of it, because the least nail of Iron might easily kill. And it is to be presumed, that a man will not strike another with an *Instrument of Iron*, except Blood and Murder be in his Heart. 3. If the Wound prove mortal, then the striker is guilty of Murder. Though a Man should smite another, and that with an Instrument of Iron, if death does not follow, he is not guilty of that high degree of Murder which the Text speaks of; but if he smite his Neighbour so that he die, then he is a Murderer.

2. Here is the punishment to be inflicted on such a *Criminal. The Murderer shall surely be put to death.* Only Gods Order was to be observed. The Murderer was to be put to death in a judiciary way. Amongst the *Jews, the avenger of blood was to be the Executioner*, as the nineteenth verse in this Chapter shews, where it is said, *that the avenger of blood himself shall slay the Murderer.* The Hebrew Word for the *Avenger of Blood* is *GOEL*, which is sometimes translated a *Redeemer.* The Word properly signifies one that is *near a kin.* The next kinsman had right to Redeem, he also was to be the Avenger of blood. Only before Execution could be done, the Magistrate was to pass a Judgment. The Man-slayer was sent from the City of Refuge whither he fled, unto the place where the Fact was done, there to have his Trial. If the Magistrates of that place found him not Guilty, he was returned to the

(*a*) Vide *Grotium* & *Ainsworth* in Locum.

City of Refuge, there to be in safety till the death of the High Priest, and then to be set at liberty: But if he was found guilty of Murder, he was to be put to death publickly by the hand of Justice.

The *Doctrine* then before us, as suited to the present Occasion is,

That Murder is a Sin so great and hainous as that whoever shall be found Guilty of it, must be put to Death by the hand of Publick Justice.

The Explication and Confirmation of this Doctrine may be set before us in three *Propositions.*

PROPOS. I. *Murder, is when a Man does voluntarily and unjustly take away the life of another person.*

So that there are three things implied in Murder:

1. *The Object slain must be one of man-kind.* To take away the life of another Creature is not Murder. The eighth Commandment saith, *Ye shall not Kill.* The Hebrew words are LO TIRTZACH, *i.e. Thou shalt not Murder.* It was vain opinian of the *Manichees,* whom *Austin* confutes, That the Life of no Creature might be taken away, because the Commandment of God saith, *Thou shalt not kill.* God has given express leave to all the Sons of *Noah, i.e.* to Mankind, that they should take away the Lives of other Creatures, as they should see cause; only Man being a more Divine Creature, his Life is to be Sacred. It may not be medled with, except in cases where the Great and Soveraign God, who has an absolute Power of Life and Death, has appointed.

2. *Capital Murder is wilful.* There is a difference between Murder, and *Casual Homicide,* or Accidental Man slaughter. If a Man shoots an Arrow, or throws a Stone, or the like, not thinking that any one will be hurt thereby; in case it should happen to kill a man, it is not Murder. If that he did it ignorantly, unawares, and no way *sought the harm* of the slain Man, he is not to be punished as a Murderer: This we see in the Context. *ver.* 15, 23, 24, 25. The City of Refuge was for such an one; *Deut.* 19. 4, 5. *And this is the case of the Slayer, which shall flee thither, that he may live: whosoever killeth his Neighbour ignorantly, whom he hated not in time past; as when a man goes into the Wood with his Neighbour to hew wood, and his hand fetcheth a stroke with the Ax, to cut down the Tree,*

and the head slippeth from the helve, and lighteth upon his Neighbour that he die, he shall flee unto one of those Cities and live. Not but that a man may be guilty of Murdering his Neighbour: tho' he did not intend to kill him; namely, if he did smite him in anger, or intend to *harm* him, as the expression is in the Twenty Third Verse of this Chapter. And it is here expresly declared, not only that he who *shall lye in wait*, or watch for an opportunity to destroy his Neighbour, or that did *formerly hate him*, shall be judged a Murderer, but if he *smite him in enmity that he dye*, verse 21. *i.e.* in an hostile way; though he had no quarrel with him before, if he fall out with him, and in his passion smite him a mortal blow, he hath murdered his Neighbour, and is guilty of death. This is presumptuous Murder, the heart was in it, nor can it be said to be done ignorantly. There is another clear Scripture, which proveth, that if persons fall out, and in the strife one shall strike the other a deadly blow *Life shall go for Life*, See *Exod.* 21. 14, 21, 22.

But then Thirdly, In Murder the Life of a Man is taken away *unjustly*. In some cases it is lawful to take away the Life of another. Yea, matters may be so cimcumstanced, as it would be a great sin not to do it: There are Three Cases, wherein the Life of a Man may be taken away, and yet no Sin, no Murder committed.

1. *In case of a Just War.* There is a great difference between Blood shed in War, and in a time of Peace. *Joab* was guilty of Murder, because he *Shed the Blood of War in Peace*, 1 *Kings* 2. 5. Had he Killed *Abner* and *Amasa* in the War-Time, before *David* had made Peace with them, he had not been guilty of Murder; but because he shed Blood after a Peace was concluded, he was a Murderer. Sometimes in War, they that take away Lives do an Acceptable Service to God. *Abigail* told *David*, that God would certainly bless him, because he *fought the Battles of the Lord*, 1 *Sam.* 25. 28. And we know that *Abraham* was blessed, after he returned from *the Slaughter of the Kings*, with whom he had a just War, *Heb.* 7. 2. In these Cases the not shedding of Blood may possibly expose to a Curse. *Jer.* 48. 10. *Cursed be he that does the work of the Lord deceitfully, and cursed be he that keeps back his Sword from Blood.*

2. *They that are in Civil Authority, may and ought to take away the Lives of Men, that shall commit Crimes, by the Law of God worthy of Death.* The Apostle therefore saith concerning the Magistrate: *He is the Minister of God to thee for good: But if thou do that which is evil, be afraid; for he beareth not the Sword in vain; for he is the Minister of God: a Revenger, to execute Wrath upon him that does Evil. Rom.* 13. 4. Private Revenge is evil, but publick Revenge on those that violate the Laws of God, is good. The Magistrate is Gods Vice gerent. As none can give Life but God, so none may take it away, but God or such as he has appointed. It is their work to see that the Lives of Men be taken from them, when God has said, *That they shall surely be put to Death.* Hence *David* speaks, as in *Psal.* 101. 8. *I will early destroy all the Wicked of the Land, that I may cut off all the Wicked Doers from the City of the Lord.* God had put the Sword into his hand for that end, that so he might clear the Land of wicked Malefactors, who were worthy of Death, and he was resolved to see Justice done. But private persons are not to arrogate to themselves that which is the Magistrates proper work. Men must have lawful Authority for what they do, else in taking away Life, they become guilty of Murder. Suppose a person to have committed never such Capital Crimes, if a private person, or one that has no Legal Authority, shall take away his Life, he is guilty of Murder.

Except 3. *In case of a mans own just defence.* So a private person may take away the Life of another: The light of Nature teacheth men self preservation. If a Murderer assault him he may kill rather than be killed. We cannot say that *Abner* was guilty of Murder when he slew *Asahal* in his own defence. (*b*) If a man be contrary to Justice, invaded or set upon by another in an hostile manner, and there be no other way for him to preserve his own Life, but by killing the Assailant: The Law of Nature, and of all Nations acquit him from the guilt of Murder. But he that *has shed Blood causeless,* or that has Avenged himself is a Murderer. 1 *Sam.* 25. 31.

PROPOS. II. *Murder is an exceeding great Sin.* It is an expression in the Scriptures, *he is as if he slew a man, Isa.* 66. 3. Implying, that to slay a man is a thing most horrid and hate-

(*b*) Alsted Theol. Cas. Cap. 15. *p.* 350.

ful; it is indeed the greatest Sin against the Second Table of the Moral Law, and is therefore set in the first place, amongst negative Precepts therein. God forbids the greatest Sin in the first place: It is a Crying Sin. The Lord said to *Cain, The voice of thy Brothers Blood cryeth to me from the ground, Gen.* 4. 10. In the original, the word is in the Plural Number, the voice of thy Brothers *Bloods.* Every drop of *Abels* Blood had as it were a *voice*, a tongue in it, crying for Vengeance against his Brother, that had Murdered him. But that this is a grievous Sin is manifest: 1. *In that it is a most unnatural thing.* Creatures of the same kind are not wont to destroy one another. Naturalists observe concerning Wolves, that though they be cruel creatures, they will never kill one another; therefore if men do so, they are worse then Wolves and Tygers; so that Murder is an unnatural and a monstrous wickedness. 2. *The Vengeance which is wont to follow this Sin, proveth that it is an horrid and hainous Transgression.* There is a peculiar Vengeance that does pursue this Sin at the heels of it. The *Gentiles* had the notion of this fixed in their minds: Hence those Barbarians could say, *No doubt this Man is a Murderer, whom tho' he escaped the Seas, yet vengeance suffereth not to live, Act.* 28. 4. The Heathen (†) Esteemed δικη (which is the Word there used for Vengeance) as a *Deity* that would not suffer great Sinners, and in special Murderers to go unpunished. Temporal Vengeance pursueth this sin. Hence they that have been guilty of it seldom live long in quiet. *Bloody and deceitful men shall not live out half their dayes, Psal.* 55. 23. Either they are cut off by the Sword of Civil Justice, or if their Murders happen to be undiscovered, a secret Curse of God follows them: oftentimes they are themselves Murdered, as both Divine and Humane Records do abundantly declare: Nay, though men should truly Repent of this sin, and are then through the merit of Christ saved from everlasting punishment, yet not from temporal Judgment. I cannot tell whither ever any Man that was found guilty of this sin did escape temporal Judgment at last. When *David* had caused *Uriah* to be Murdered, he did repent of it most deeply and unfeignedly,

---

† Ethnici *dicen* tanquam Deam & Filiam *Jovis* colebant in *Plut.* lib. de sera vindicta *dice Dæmon* dicitur.

yet God punished him severely as to outward Judgments; he saw but few comfortable days after that, the Sword never departed from his House. I have read of a Man that (c) fought a Duel & Murdered his Adversary, who afterwards was very penitent, and for several years an eminent instance of exemplary piety; but at last he was smitten by the immediate hand of God, so as that Blood gushed out of all the passages of his Body, and he died suddenly. The Relator notes upon it, that though God forgave him as to Eternal, yet not as to Temporal Vengeance. But especially Spiritual Vengeance follows this Sin: The Murderers Soul is filled with hellish horror of heart; so that he is as it were Damned above ground, and in Hell whilst he is yet alive. *The Avenger of Blood pursueth his Soul*; Murderers have confessed, that as soon as ever they had committed the Bloody Fact, they felt the Flames of Hell-fire in their Consciences, and this we see in *Cain*. Therefore after he had murdered his Brother, he cried and roared out, that his sin was greater than could be forgiven, his punishment greater than could be endured. And some think that the mark which the *Lord* set upon *Cain*, was a ghastly, guilty Countenance, that he had Hell and Horror in his Countenance as well as in his Conscience. And without Repentance, everlasting Vengeance will follow that Sin. It is said, *No Murderer has Eternal Life*, 1 *John* 3. 15. that is, without true Repentance. And if he has not Eternal Life, then I am sure he has Eternal Death and Damnation. If the Murderer were only to have the Life of his Body taken from him, tho in a painful, shameful and accursed way, that were a light matter; but there is an eternal curse, a weight of everlasting vengeance, heavier than Mountains of Lead, that shall press his immortal Soul to death, world without end. Murder then is a fearful Sin.

PROPOS. III. *The Murderer is to be put to death by the hand of Publick Justice.* And this confirms the former Proposition concerning the greatness of this Sin: Men may not pardon or remit the punishment of that Sin. Among the *Jews* there was no City of Refuge for a wicked or wilful *Man slayer*; and it is said in the one and thirtieth verse of this Chapter, *You shall take no satisfaction for the Life of a Murderer, which is guilty of death, but he shall surely be put to Death.* This Sin shall not be satisfied for, with any other punishment, but the death of the

Murderer: There are some Crimes, that other punishment less then death may be accepted of as a Compensation for the wrong done; either some mulct or Fine in their Estates, or some other corporal punishment less than death, but in case of Murder, no Fine or Imprisonment, or Banishment or Corporal Punishment less than death can be accepted: *You shall take no satisfaction for the Life of a Murderer.* And indeed equity requires this; by the Law of Retaliation, it is meet that men should be done unto, as they have done to others; and that as Limb should go for Limb, so Life for Life. But besides that, there are two Reasons mentioned in the Scripture, why the Murderer must be put to death.

REAS. I. *That so the Land where the Murder is committed, may be purged from the guilt of Blood.* For Murder is such a Crime as does pollute the very Land where it is done; not only the person that has shed blood is polluted thereby, but the whole Land lieth under pollution until such time as Justice is done upon the *Murderer*; thus in the thirty third verse of this Chapter; this is given as the reason why no satisfaction might be taken for the Life of a Murderer, *so shall ye not pollute the Land wherein you are; for blood it defileth the Land, and the Land cannot be cleansed of the blood that is shed therein but by the blood of him that shed it.* One Murder unpunished may bring guilt and a Curse upon the whole land, that all the Inhabitants of that Land shall suffer for it; so that mercy to a Murderer is cruelty to a people. Therefore is it said concerning the Murderer, *Thine Eye shall not pity him, but thou shalt put away the guilt of innocent Blood from Israel, that it may go well with thee.* If the Murderer be not punished, it may go ill with the whole, all may fare the worse for it; if the sin be not duly punished there is a partaking in the guilt of it.

REAS. II. *Because Man is made in the image of God.* This Reason is mentioned *Gen.* 9. 6. *Whosoever sheddeth mans blood, by man, h.e.* by some man in Authority, proceeding in an orderly way of Judicature, as the Hebrew Expositors do rightly interpret the words, *shall his blood be shed, for in the image of God made he him.* Hence there is sacriligious guilt in this sin; Amongst the *Romans* (*d*) if a man did but strike his Servant

(*d*) *Sueton.* in tiber. cap. 58.

near the place where one of their Emperors lay, he was to die for it, because that was looked upon as an affront put upon his *Imperial Majesty*; so he that shall kill a man that is made after the image of God, puts a Contempt upon the *Divine Majesty*, there is Treason against God contained in the bloody bowels of this Sin. Upon this account it is indeed a greater sin to kill a good man that has the Image of God renewed in him, then to kill a wicked man. Nevertheless, that also is a Capital Crime; for all men have something (*e*) of Gods Image remaining in them, not only in that every man has an immortal Soul, and is in that respect more like the *Immortal God* than any other Creature in the world, and in that men have a dominion over the Creatures, which is one part of Gods image; on that account does the Apostle say, *That Man is the Image and Glory of God*, 1 *Cor.* 11. 7. But also, in that the Law is written in the hearts of men by nature; (*f*) though God has executed spiritual death upon mankind for Adams Apostacy, after a dreadful manner, yet he has moderated that punishment; hence men in a natural estate, yet close with some *Practical Principles* of Piety and Righteousness, as that God ought to be worshipped, that men should do as they would be done by, and the like; and many *natural men*, yet have an *Image of vertue*, they have something like Grace; a shadow of it, they hate flagitious Crimes, and approve of a morally honest Conversation; these things shew that there are some remainders of the Image of God in men: Therefore he that shall murder such a Creature is worthy of death.

But thus for the Doctrinal handling of the Truth before us. I proceed to make some Application.

1. By way of Information.

2. For Exhortation.

INFOR. 1. *This Doctrine justifieth the Authority here, in respect of the Sentence of death which has been passed on the Murderer, who is this day to be executed.*

There is a man standing before the Lord, and amongst his people this day, who has done just as my Text expresseth, He has smitten his Neighbour, and that *with an Instrument of*

(*e*) Calvin *Rivet.* & *Pareus* in Gen. 9. 6.
(*f*) *Ames. Theol.* lib. 1 *cap.* 14.

Iron too, with a cruel Spit made of Iron; the thing proved by several Witnesses, and the man that was hurt dyed by that wound; therefore he that has smitten him is a Murderer, and must surely be put to death; though for a long time he denied it, nevertheless since his Condemnation he has acknowledged it, and yesterday he confessed to me, that he had in his rage murdered the man, whose death and blood has been laid to his charge; he told me that the other gave him some ill language whereby he was provoked, and that he said to him, if he came within the door, he would run the Spit into his bowels, and he was as wicked as he said he would be, so that he is guilty of Murder. Therefore none ought to blame those in Authority for causing the Murderer to be put to death; conscience to God, and to the people under their charge, and to their own Souls also, has necessitated them to do what they have done in this matter. Let every one remember that Scripture, *Prov.* 28. 17. *A man that doth violence to the blood of any person, shall flee to the Pit, let no man stay him*; if he has shed blood, to the Pit let him go, and flie thither, let all convenient speed be used in the execution of Justice; that so the Land may be cleared from blood, and let no man in Authority stay him, let no private person Solicit for him. But let us be thankful to God, that we are under such Magistrates, as will do Justice, and Execute Judgment, and punish Sin according as the Word of God requireth that it should be done.

INF. 2. *Hence those things which have a tendency to, and a degree of Murder in them, must needs be evil. e.g.* Rash sinful anger is an evil thing, Murder begins there. It was said of those Brethren in iniquity, *Simeon and Levi, That Instruments of Cruelty were in their Habitations, for in their anger they slew a man, Cursed be their wrath, for it was cruel, Gen.* 49. 5, 6. And our Lord Jesus Christ in his Exposition of the sixth Commandment, sheweth that rash anger is a degree of Murder, *Matth.* 5. 21, 22. *You have heard that it was said by them of old time, Ye shall not kill, and whosoever shall kill, shall be in danger of the Judgment, but I say unto you, that whosoever is angry with his Brother without a cause, shall be in danger of the Judgment.* There is Mans Judgment-seat, and Gods Judgment seat: murder makes a man be in danger of the former; sinful anger exposeth him to the latter; not that all anger is sinful, there is an anger that is good, when a man is angry in Gods Cause, moved with zeal and indignation, because God is dishonoured; that's very good; and a man may sometimes be angry in his own Cause too and yet not sin. *Be angry and sin not*, but when men are angry without a just cause, that's evil. When they are angry more than they have cause for, that they are all on a Flame for a meer trifle, when (as one well expresseth it) (*g*) Man shall *suffer the Beacon of his Soul to be set all on fire at the landing of every small Boat*, thats a foolish and evil thing, or when men shall be angry longer than they ought to be; an implacable Spirit is a vile Murderous Spirit: Anger rests in the bosome of Fools; sinful anger is poyson, which as soon as ever a man has taken it into his mouth, he should spit it out again. And when anger shall break out into Curses and wicked imprecations, thats wicked Anger. This Condemned man that stands here, confesseth that he was wont in his passion to Curse all near him. He murdered many a man with his bloody tongue, before he was left of God to murther any with his hand. His mouth was full of Cursing and bitterness before he shed blood; and when men in their rage imprecate and curse themselves, it is a very evil thing; there are some that will say, *They wish they may be hanged*, if such a thing be so, and many times the Righteous Judgment of God brings that very evil upon them.

There is a Printed Relation concerning (*h*) a person of Quality that was hanged for a Crime laid to his charge; and when he came to die, he confessed that he had been much addicted to that sinful Recreation of *Card-playing*; and that many times when the Game went otherwise than he wished for, he should in his Passion, wish that he might be hanged if it were so, and once he wished he might be hanged if ever he played again; and therefore (said he) God is just in bringing me to such a death as that. And when anger shall break out into blows, quarrelling and fighting between Neighbours that ought to live in peace, there is great evil in it. This miserable Creature before us, acknowledgeth that it was so with him. In

(*g*) See Mr. *Cradocks* Supplement chap. 9. *p.* 368.

(*h*) Sir *Gervase Elwayes* mentioned by *Howel* in his Londinopolis, and by Mr. *Ball* of the power of Godliness L. 4. C. 3. P 329. And by Mr. *Leigh* in his Body of Divinity, Book 4, C. 16. P. 445.

his mad passions he cared not whom he did strike or hurt. It is not good for them that have lawful power to strike others, to do it in passion. It is not good for Parents to strike their Children, or Masters their Servants, or School masters their Scholars in heat of anger, lest they become guilty of breaking the sixth Commandment. A moral Heathen, when his Servant had committed a fault that greatly incensed him, said to him, *If I were not angry with thee I would strike thee; but I will stay till my passion is over before I punish thee*. Again, a spirit of Revenge is an evil thing: it is Murder in Gods sight, 1 *Joh*. 3. 15. *He that hates his Brother, is a Murderer*. Hatred never rests but in the destruction of the thing hated. To say no more here; *Cruelty* is a degree of Murder and a great Evil. And most of all for men to be cruel to those that stand in nearest relation to them (as this Malefactor owns that he has been) whom they ought to love dearly; is an high degree of inhumanity. *No man* that acted like a man, *ever hated his own flesh*. To be cruel, though to a Servant or Slave, is a very sinful thing. Nay *Cruelty* though to a Beast argueth a murderous, bloody disposition. The Scripture saith *that a good man is merciful to his Beast*. They then that make themselves sport with putting dumb creatures to misery, do very sinfully. Yet that has been practised here of later years in the open Streets, especially on one day of the Year.(†) To do it at such a time is vanity and Heathenish Superstition; besides to make sport with exercising cruelty on dumb Creatures, which had never been miserable had not the sins of men made them so; it is a wicked thing, and ought not to be amongst those that call themselves Christians.

INF. 3. *If Murder be such a crime as has been shewed, it is then a sorrowful thing that so many of the Children of men should be found guilty of this evil.*

There are some places of the World where Murder is a common Sin. The dark corners of the Earth are full of the habitations of cruelty. And there are many in the World that call themselves Christians, who nevertheless delight in shedding innocent Blood. Persecutors are Murderers. Bloody Papists are in the Scripture charged with Murder on this

† *I* intend the Cock-scalings of *Shrove Tuesday.*

account: It is said of them, *they repented not of their Murders,* *Rev.* 9. 21. namely of their Murdering the Saints of God for their Religion, for the truths sake; and because they would not comply with their Superstitions and Idolatries. That *Mother of Harlots* the Church of *Rome*, she has made her self drunk with blood; many millions of Saints have been murdered by her. Persecuters are *Cains* Children. O how many are there going up and down the World with *Cain*'s bloody Club in their hands to this day! It was *Luther's* sayings, *Cain* will kill *Abel* to the end of the World. But besides this, that which the Civil Laws of Nations make to be Murder is frequent in some places. A late Historian reports, that in the Kingdom of *France*, (*) within the space of ten years, there were known to be no less than six thousand Murders committed. And in Popish Countries, they have Sanctuaries for Murderers. (*k*) A man that has been guilty of a wilful Murder, if he does but run into a *Church* (as they call it) or into a *Monastery*, he is protected in those bloody places of Refuge. Their Writers plead for this. And though no convicted Murderer did ever escape the stroke of Justice in this Land (which is matter of rejoycing) yet it is a very sad thing, that any in such a place as this should be found guilty of such a Crime. That men should do so wickedly in a Land of uprightness: but so it has been. Divers have been Executed for this sin formerly, and one that is to be *put to death* for it this day. And there have been several Murders committed amongst us, the Authors of which are not as yet known. Some that have been so monstrously Wicked and Unnatural, as to embrew their hands in the Blood of their own Children: who they are God knoweth, and will find a time to judge them; and one day we and all the World shall know who they are. Besides these, several others have been under vehement suspicion, and tryed for their lives, on the account of this Sin. We have all cause to Pray for *New-England*, as the Lords People of old were directed for to do, in case of an uncertain Murder, *Deut.* 21. 7, 8. *They shall Answer and say, our hands have not shed this Blood, neither have our eyes seen it; Be merci-*

*See *Trap* on *Gen.* 9. 6.
(*k*). v. *Corn a Lapide* in *Deut.* 19.

ful O Lord to thy People Israel, whom thou hast Redeemed, and lay not innocent Blood unto the people of Israels charge; and the blood shall be forgiven them. Be merciful O Lord, to thy People in *New-England*, and lay not innocent Blood to their charge.

USE II. For *Exhortation*:

There is a double Exhortation before us.

1. *Hence men should beware that they do not become guilty of this Sin.* It is in Man's corrupt nature. Nothing is more natural than a spirit of Revenge, as we see in little Children, which discovers that the Children of Men bring murderous Natures into the World with them. Hence the Apostle declaring, what men by nature are, saith, *That their feet are swift to shed blood, Rom.* 3. 15. because there is a marvelous propensity in mans Nature unto this sin. Should not the Lord either by special or common Grace restrain them, how many would soon become guilty of Murder it self? Yea, and those too that do not believe any such thing concerning themselves. When the Prophet *Elisha* told *Hazael* what a prodigious Murderer he would be, what (said he) *Am I a Dog*, that thou shouldest have such thoughts of me? But in a little time he appeared to be as curst a Blood hound as ever the Prophet had said to him. O then beware of this sin. And therefore take heed of giving way to wicked passions. Lesser sins make way for greater. And especially take heed of great Sins: For many a Man by being guilty of other great sins, has provoked the Holy God to leave him unto this Sin too. The poor condemned Malefactor who stands here in the sight of this Congregation, does acknowledg, that he has by living in other sins provoked God to leave him unto this, which he must now dy for, & warns others especially Young men to take heed of those Sins as they love their lives or souls. I know not but that it may be for edification, and tend to Gods Glory, if I should read in this great Assembly, what I received in Writing from this dying and distressed Creature. It is this which followeth;

I James Morgan, *being Condemned to die, must needs own to the glory of God, that he is Righteous, and that I have by my Sins provoked him to destroy me before my time. I have been a great sinner, guilty of Sabbath-breaking, of Lying, and of Uncleanness; but there are especially two Sins: whereby I have offended the Great God; one is, that Sin of* Drunkenness, *which has caused me to commit many other Sins; for when in drink, I have been often guilty of Cursing and Swearing, and quarelling, and striking others: But the Sin which lieth most heavy upon my Conscience, is, that* I have despised the Word of God, and many a time refused to hear it preached. *For these things, I believe God has left me to that which has brought me to a shameful and miserable Death. I do therefore beseech and warn all persons, young men especially, to take heed of these Sins, lest they provoke the Lord to do to them as he has justly done by me. And for the further peace of* my *own Conscience, I think* my *self obliged to add this unto* my *foregoing Confession, That I own the Sentence which the Honoured Court has passed upon me, to be exceeding just, in as much as though I had no former grudge and malice against the man whom I have Killed, yet my passion at the time of the fact was so outragious, as that it hurried me on to the doing of that which makes me justly now proceeded against as a Murderer.*

Thus does this miserable man confess: but how many are there in the Congregation, that this may strike terror and trembling into their Souls.

O Lord, how many are there in this great Assembly, who have lived and do live in those very Sins, for which this man confesseth that God has been provoked to destroy him! Let Sinners hear and take warning this day; this man now that the Terrors of God have awakened his distressed Soul bitterly complains of two Sins especially; one is that of *Drunkenness.* And indeed, *Drunkenness* has been a bloody Sin; it has been the cause of many a Murder. The man here who is now flying to the Pit, confesseth that in his drink, he was wont to curse and swear, and to quarrel, and strike those near him; and he acknowledged to me, that he had made himself grievously drunk the day before he was left of God to commit the Murder which he now must dye for; yea, and that he had that very night been drinking to excess, and that he was not clear of drink at the time when he did the bloody Fact? And does not the Scripture say, *Who has Wo, Who has Sorrow, Who has Contentions! who has Babling? who has Wounds without Cause! They that tarry long at the Wine—Prov.* 23. 29, 30. Wicked men when they are in drink, will fall to quarrelling; words will bring on blows, and those blows will cause wounds, and those wounds may perhaps prove mortal. And then what Wo and Sorrow followeth: Oh how many have by means of this Sin, been guilty of *Interpretative Murder!* They have caused others to die by making them drunk; There has been an horrible thing done in this place; some wicked persons (who they are God knows) have given or sold Strong Liquors to the *Indians*, and made them drunk also, and several of them have dyed in that condition; let such know, that the Lord will judg them; yea, he will judg them as men that have shed blood shall be judged; they must answer for the blood of Souls and Bodies too. Most wicked and miserable Creatures they are, that to gain a few pence, will bring upon themselves the guilt of the blood of Souls and Bodies too. And *this bloody sin of drunkenness* has been the cause of many a self Murder; how many have made themselves the woful *Martyrs of Bacchus* thereby: by Drunkenness and intemperance, they have brought their Bodies to the Grave, and their Souls to Hell before their time. It is an unhappy thing that of later years, a kind of Strong * Drink has been common amongst us, which the poorer sort of people, both in Town and Country, can make themselves drunk with, at cheap and easy rates. They that are poor and wicked too (Ah most miserable Creatures!) can for a peny or two pence make themselves drunk: I wish to the Lord, some Remedy might be thought of, for the prevention of this evil. It is a very sad thing, that so many Bodies and Souls should be eternally ruined, and no help for it. How few are there, that if once they be addicted to this vice, do ever truly repent of it, or turn from it. There was a man, who hearing that his Son took evil courses, and that he followed such a vice, well (said he) I hope he'll leave that; and that he was given to another vice, I hope (said he) he'll leave that too; but it was told him his Son was given to Drunkenness also: Nay, then (said he) *I have no hope of him.* I will not say (as he did) there is no hope that ever a Drunkard should repent, but I say, there have been but few such

(*) Reverend Mr. *Wilson* once sayd in a Sermon, *there is a sort of drink come into the Country, which is called,* Kill Devil, *but it should be called,* Kill men for the Devil.

instances in the world. How rarely have any of you known a man that has been addicted to this Body-destroying, and Soul-murdering iniquity, that has truly repented of it, or turned from it again. O then, let men that have any love for their Lives or Souls, beware of this bloody Sin.

But the other evil which this undone man, does especially cry out of, and which now that he seeth his Soul going into Eternity, he saith, *lieth most heavy upon his Conscience*, is *his despising the Word of God*. I do not wonder to hear him speak so, for I have known several Condemned Persons, who have made the same out-cry. *O nothing terrifieth our Consciences, like the thought of this, that we have neglected the means of Grace!* And what think you of Sinners in Hell, who are wayling for this with tears of Blood for ever and ever; whose doleful and bitter cry, is, *O the Sermons which we once heard, or might have heard but would not: Ten Thousand Worlds would we give for an opportunity, to hear one of those Sermons again with any hope of finding mercy with God!* O you that have lived under the Gospel, but despised it, think of this. Verily I say unto you, all the sins in the world will not Damn like this: Suppose a man to have been guilty of Adultery, or Murder, or the most horrid Transgressions against the Law of God, these will not Damn his Soul like that of despising the Word of God. *For this is* the *Condemnation that light is come into the world, and men love darkness rather than light. And how shall we escape, if we neglect so great Salvation:* They that shall be found guilty of neglecting the great Salvation offered in the Gospel, cannot escape the Wrath of God to the utmost of it. And this is true, not only concerning such as have lived under the constant preaching of the Gospel, and yet remain, and live and dye in a natural unconverted estate; but of them also, that might hear the Word of God, but will not; concerning such Christ saith, *it shall be more tolerable for* Sodom *and* Gomorrah *at the day of Judgment, than for them, Mat.* 10. 15. This dying man, now that his Conscience is awakened, saith, it is a terror to him to think, *I might have heard the Word of God Preached many a time, but refused it;* he neglected to hear Sermons, not only on Lecture-dayes, but on Lords-days too; when he was a Servant, he was wont (as himself saith) on the Sabbath-days, to go out into the Fields, and there to profane the Lords-day, at the very time when he might, and ought to have been hearing the Word of God; and since he had a Family, his custom was to keep at home, when others were attending the Publick Worship of God; and he told me, that he did foolishly please himself, and think he had a sufficient reason to stay at home, because he had not Cloaths good enough to appear publickly in; when as the mony that he misspent in drink, would have procured him cloathing. Let others then by his example, be warned against this evil, lest they provoke God, and feel sorrow for it, as he has done. I doubt there are very many in this great Town guilty of his Sin in this particular, perhaps some that are Professors of Religion, which is dreadful to think on. I hear some say, that there are many hundreds, nay, some thousands in this place, that seldome hear a Sermon Preached, from one end of the year to the other; if that be so, it is very lamentable. What is like to become of the Souls of such profane persons? If they that are in place of Power (be they Superior, or inferior Officers) can possibly redress this evil, they will certainly do a Service acceptable to God, and to the Lord Jesus Christ.

But I proceed to the second *Exhortation.*

If Murder be such a Crime as has been declared, then, *let whoever has been guilty of this sin, be humbled for it, and repent of it.* As for *Interpretative Murder*, many are guilty of that. O how many that have by debauchery and intemperance, shortned the lives of themselves or others; let such repent, and turn from their sins unto God. But I hope there is none in this vast Assembly, that has been guilty of that Murder which is by the Law of God, and of the Land a Capital Crime, excepting one man, and one such person where is here present, unto whom I shall now particularly apply my self. Do you then hear, that your Soul may live: This is the last Sermon that ever you shall hear. Time was when you might have heard Sermons, but would not; and now you shall not hear them, tho' you would. For, as God said to him, *This night thy Soul shall be required of thee;* so I say to you in his Name, *This night thy Soul shall be taken from thee:* This night your Soul shall be either in Heaven or in Hell for ever. You are appointed to die this day, and after death, cometh the Judgment; as soon as your Body

is dead, your immortal Soul shall appear before the Great
God and Judge of all, and a Sentence of Everlasting Life, or
Everlasting Death shall be passed upon you. Are you willing
when those Chains, which are about you, shall be taken off,
that your immortal Soul should be hanged in Everlasting
Chains? Are you willing that when your Body is removed
from the Prison, your Soul should go to the Spirits that are in
Prison: You have complained that you have been in a
Dungeon, and had little light there; but are you willing to go
where you shall never see light? Are you willing that when
your Body is delivered from this Dungeon, your Soul should
go into that Dungeon, where is blackness of darkness for
ever? If not, I charge you in the Name of God to hear and
obey his Word: Yea, that Word which you have many a time
despised: I have spoken so often to you in private, since your
being Apprehended, that I shall not need to say much now,
only a few words.

1. *Consider what a Sinner you have been:* The sin which you
are to die for, is as red as Scarlet; and many other sins has
your wicked life been filled with. You have been a Stranger to
me, I never saw you, I never heard of you, until you had committed the Murder, for which you must die this day; but I
hear by others, that have known you, how wicked you have
been; and you have your self confessed to the world, that you
have been *guilty* of Drunkenness, *guilty* of Cursing and
Swearing, *guilty* of Sabbath-breaking, *guilty* of Lying, *guilty*
of secret Uncleanness; as *Solomon* said to *Shimei, Thou knowest the wickedness which thine own heart is privy unto*; so I say
to you. And that which aggravates your guiltiness not a little,
is, that since you have been in Prison, you have done
wickedly; you have made your self drunk several times since
your Imprisonment; yea, and you have been guilty of Lying
since your Condemnation: It was said to a Dying man *Dost
not thou fear God, seeing thou art under Condemnation.* O
what a sinner have you been! for since you have been under
Condemnation, you have not feared God. And how have you
sinned against the Gospel? What Unbelief? What Impenitency
have you been guilty of?

Consider 2. *What misery you have brought upon yourself,* on
your body, that must die an accursed death; you must hang

between Heaven and Earth, as it were forsaken of both, and unworthy to be in either; and what misery have you brought upon your poor Children, you have brought an everlasting reproach upon them. How great will their shame be, when it shall be said to them, that their Father was hanged, not for his goodness, as many in the world have been, but for his wickedness: Not as a Martyr, but as a Malefactor, truly so? But that which is ten thousand times worse then all this, is, that you have (without Repentance) brought undoing misery upon your poor, yet precious Soul: Not only death on your Body, but a *second death*, on your never dying Soul: It is said in the Scripture, that *Murderers shall have their part in the Lake, which burns with fire and Brimstone, which is the Second Death: Rev.* 21. 8. O tremble at that! I remember a man that was Condemned and Executed in this place some years ago, that had been a Souldier, and as stout a spirited man as most in the world, who when he came to die, thus expressed himself to a Minister, that treated with him about his Soul, *I* (said he) *never knew what fear meant, tho' I have been amongst Drawn Swords, and before the Canons mouth; I feared not death; but now you tell me of a Second Death, it makes my Soul to shake within me.* That's a death, the thought whereof may make the Soul of the stoutest Sinner in the world to tremble; for that's a death which is eternal: *The things which are seen are temporal, but the things which are not seen are eternal.* The death of the body, that's seen, and it is soon over; but what becomes of the Soul when a sinner dieth, they that stand by him do not see, but if he die impenitent, the death which is not seen takes hold on him, and it is eternal: The God against whom he has sinned, liveth for ever to punish him. And a fearful thing it is, to fall into the hands of the everliving God: O run not into the mouth of the Second Death; into the wide mouth of the fiery Pit, which has devoured millions of millions of immortal Souls; and know you for certain, that if you die impenitent, your Damnation will be no ordinary one; for you have not only transgressed against the Law of God, with an high hand, but sinned against the Gospel too. The Sermons which you have heard formerly, or might have done, will be as so many witnesses against you, before the Judgment seat of Christ: the three Sermons which have been Preached to you in Publick, since your Condemnation; the pains which has been taken with you in private, by one or other of the Lords Servants; all these will aggravate your Condemnation, when you shall be Judged again before all the world, at the last day if you die impenitent.

Consider 3. *There is yet a possibility that your Soul may be saved;* notwithstanding all that has been spoken to you, do not despair; repent but do not despair. I would not have you say as *Cain* did, *My sin is greater than can be forgiven:* The Lord is a merciful God; though men cannot forgive you, God can; and he will do it, if you unfeignedly repent, and believe on the Lord Jesus. There is infinite merit in the death of Christ; if your bloody Soul be washed in his blood, it shall be made whiter than the Snow: That sin which you must now dye for, God has forgiven to others upon their true Repentance: *Manasseh* filled the streets of *Jerusalem* with innocent blood, but when he humbled himself, and besought the Lord for mercy, God was entreated of him. O therefore repent, and then tho your Body must die, your Soul shall live, and not die.

I have but two words more to say to you, and then I shall take my leave of you forever.

1. *Be sure that you be sincere in your Repentance.* Many times men under fears, will seem very penitent, when as they do but flatter God with their mouths, and lie unto him with their Tongues: Thus it was with *Pharaoh*, and with many a Sinner, whose hard heart was never broken nor changed; we see often, that Sinners on sick-beds, when they behold Death and Eternity before their eyes, will confess their sins, and promise Reformation; but if the Lord spare and restore them, they are the same that they were before: And we have known instances among our selves, of men that when they have been Captives, and in *Turkish* slavery, they have pretended to a sense of those sins which provoked the Most High to bring that misery upon them, and have written seemingly pious and penitent Letters to their friends, but now God has delivered them, they are as vain as profane, as ungodly as ever in their lives before; nay, some of them worse: for the truth is, if men be not humbled and converted by such signal dispensations, many times they are judicially and everlastingly hardned. They never leave sinning until they have sinned themselves into Hell, past

all hopes of mercy, or of recovery. To come nearer to you, I have known some, more than one, or two, or three, that have been Condemned to die, and whilst they remained under that Sentence, they seemed very penitent, but they were pardoned (for they had not been guilty of Murder as you have) and since that, have been as wicked as ever. O then look to your self, that you do not dissemble with God and man, and your own Soul too. And let not the fear of punishment only, but the sense of mercy break your heart.

2. *In this way of sincere Repentance, betake your self to the City of Refuge;* go to Christ for life. The wilful Manslayer had (as you heard but now) no benefit by the City of Refuge; so shall impenitent Sinners have no Salvation by Christ; but they that have a real sight of their sins, and flie from the Avenger of Blood, unto Christ for Life, he is ready to succour them. Poor man! has the fiery Serpent bitten and stung thy Soul; then look unto the Brazen Serpent, look unto the Lord Jesus, that you may live and not die for ever. Build your hopes of Salvation on Christ and his Righteousness alone: Do not think you shall be saved, only because Good Men have prayed for you, or for the Confession of your sins, which you have now made; or for the sake of *any* thing but Christ. And I pray the Son of God to have Compassion on you.

———

THE LAST EXPRESSIONS AND SOLEMN
WARNING OF *JAMES MORGAN,*
AS THEY WERE IN SHORT-HAND TAKEN
FROM HIS MOUTH, AT THE PLACE OF
EXECUTION:
MARCH 11. 168$\frac{5}{6}$.

I Pray God that I may be a warning to you all, and that I may be the last that ever shall suffer after this manner: in the fear of God I warn you to have a care of taking the Lords Name in vain; mind and have a care of that Sin of Drunkenness, for that is a sin that leads to all manner of sins and wickedness: mind, and have a care of breaking the sixth Commandment, where it is said, Thou shalt do no Murder, *for when a Man is in Drink he is ready to commit all manner of sin till he fill up the cup of the wrath of God, as I have done by committing that Sin of Murder: I beg of God, as I am a dying man, and to appear before the Lord within a few minutes, that you may take notice of what I say to you; Have a care of Drunkenness, and ill Company, and mind all good Instruction, and don't turn your back upon the Word of God as I have done. When I have been at Meeting, I have gone out of the Meeting-house to commit sin, and to please the Lust of my flesh; and don't make a mock at any poor object of pity, but bless God that he hath not left you as he hath justly done me to commit that horrid sin of Murder. Another thing that I have to say to you, is to have a care of that House where that Wickedness was committed, and where I have been partly ruined by: But here I am, and know not what will become of my poor Soul which is within a few moments of Eternity; I, that have Murdered a poor Man, who had but a little time to Repent, and I know not what's become of his poor Soul; O that I may make use of this opportunity that I have; Oh that I may make improvement of this little little time before I go hence and be no more: O let all mind what I am a saying now, I am a going out of this World; O take warning by me, and beg of God to keep you from this Sin which hath been my ruine. His last words were,* O Lord receive my Spirit, I come unto thee O Lord, I come unto thee O Lord; I Come, I Come, I Come.

COTTON MATHER

The Wonders of the Invisible World

*Observations as well Historical as Theological, upon the
Nature, the Number, and the Operations of the DEVILS*

AN HORTATORY AND NECESSARY ADDRESS.
TO A COUNTRY NOW EXTRAORDINARILY ALARUM'D
BY THE WRATH OF THE DEVIL. TIS THIS,

LET US now make a Good and a Right use, of the Prodigious
Descent, which the *Devil*, in *Great Wrath*, is at this day
making upon our Land. Upon the Death of a Great Man
once, an Orator call'd the Town together, crying out, *Con-
currite Cives, Dilapla sunt vestra Mania!* that is, *Come together, Neighbours, your Town-Walls, are fallen down!* But such
is the Descent of the Devil at this day upon ourselves, that I
may truly tell you, *The Walls of the whole World are broken
down!* The usual *Walls* of Defence about mankind have such
a Gap made in them, that the very *Devils* are broke in upon
us, to Seduce the *Souls*, Torment the *Bodies*, Sully the *Credits*,
and consume the *Estates* of our Neighbours, with Impressions
both as *Real* and as *Furious*, as if the *Invisible* World were becoming *Incarnate*, on purpose for the vexing of us. And what
use ought now to be made of so Tremendous a dispensation?
We are engaged in a *Fast* this day; but shall we try to fetch,
Meat out of the Eater, and make the *Lion* to afford some *Hony*
for our *Souls*.

That the Devil, is *Come down unto us with great Wrath*, we
find, we feel, we now deplore. In many wayes, for many years,
hat the Devil been assaying to Extirpate the Kingdom of our
Lord Jesus here. *New-England* may complain of the Devil, as
in *Psal.* 129. 1, 2. *Many a time have they Afflicted me, from my
Youth, may*, New-England *now say; many a time have they
Afflicted me from my Youth; yet they have not prevailed against*

me. But now there is a more than Ordinary *Affliction*, with which the *Devil* is Galling of us: and such an one as is indeed Unparallellable. The Things Confessed by *Witches* and the Things Endured by *Others*, laid together, amount unto this account of our Affliction. The *Devil*, Exhibiting himself ordinarily as a small *Black man*, has decoy'd a fearful Knot of Proud, Froward, Ignorant, Envious, and Malicious Creatures, to List themselves in his Horrid Service, by Entring their Names in a *Book* by him Tendred unto them. These *Witches*, whereof above a Score have now *Confessed, and shown their Deeds*, and some are now Tormented by the Devils, for *Confessing*, have met in Hellish *Randezvouzes*, wherein the Confessors do say, they have had their Diabolical Sacraments, imitating the *Baptism* and the *Supper* of our Lord. In these Hellish Meetings, these Monsters have associated themselves to do no less a Thing than, *To Destroy the Kingdom of our Lord Jesus Christ, in these parts of the World;* and in order hereunto, First, they each of them have their *Spectres*, or Devils, Commission'd by them, and Representing of them, to be the Engines of their Malice. By these wicked *Spectres*, they Sieze poor people about the Country, with Various and bloody *Torments*; and of those Evidently Preternatural Torments there are some have Dy'd. They have bewitched some, even so far as to make them *Self-Destroyers*: and others are in many Towns here and there Languishing under their *Evil Hands*. The People thus Afflicted, are miserably Scratched and Bitten, so that the Marks are most *Visible* to all the World, but the causes utterly *Invisible*; and the same *Invisible* Furies, do most Visibly stick *Pins* into the Bodies of the Afflicted, and *Scald* them, & hideously Distort, and Disjoint all their members, besides a thousand other sorts of Plagues beyond these of any Natural Diseases which they give unto them. Yea, they sometimes drag the poor People out of their Chambers, and Carry them over *Trees* and *Hills*, for diverse Miles together. A large part of the Persons tortured by these Diabolical *Spectres*, are horribly Tempted by them, sometime, with fair Promises, and sometimes with hard Threatenings, but alwayes with felt Miseries, to sign the *Devils Laws*, in a Spectral *Book* laid before them; which two or three of these poor Sufferers, being by their Tiresome Sufferings overcome to do, they have immediately been released from all their Miseries, & they appear'd in *Spectre* then to Torture those that were before their Fellow-Sufferers. The *Witches* which by their Covenant with the Devil, are become Owners of *Spectres*, are oftentimes by their own *Spectres* Required and Compelled to give their Consent, for the Molestation of some, which they had no mind otherwise to fall upon; and Cruel Depredations are then made upon the Vicinage. In the Prosecution of these *Witchcrafts*, among a thousand other unaccountable Things, the *Spectres* have an odd Faculty of Cloathing the most Substantial and Corporeal Instruments of Torture, with *Invisibility*, while the Wounds thereby given have been the most palpable Things in the World; so that the Sufferers assaulted with Instruments of Iron wholly *unseen* to the Standers-by, tho' to their cost seen by themselves, have upon snatching, wrested the Instruments out of the *Spectres* Hands, and every one has then immediately not only *beheld*, but *handled*, an Iron Instrument taken by a Devil from a Neighbour. These wicked *Spectres* have proceeded so far, as to Steal several Quantities of Mony from divers people, part of which Money has before sufficient Spectators been dropt out of the Air into the Hands of the Sufferers, while the *Spectres* have been urging them to Subscribe their *Covenant with Death*. In such extravagant wayes, have these Wretches propounded, the *Dragooning* of as many as they can, into their own Combination, and the *Destroying* of others, with Lingring, Spreading, Deadly Diseases; till our Country should at last become too hot for us. Among the Ghastly Instances of the *Success* which those Bloody Witches have had, we have seen even some of their own *Children*, so Dedicated unto the Devil, that in their Infancy, it is found, the *Imps* have Sucked them, and Rendred them Venemous to a Prodigy. We have also seen the Devils *First* Batteries, upon the Town, where the *First* Church of our Lord in this Colony was Gathered, producing those Distractions, which have almost Ruined the Town. We have seen likewise the *Plague* reaching afterwards into other Towns far and near, where the Houses of *Good Men* have the Devil, filling of them with terrible Vexations!

This is the *Descent* which, as it seems, the Devil has now made upon us. But that which makes this Descent the more

formidable is; The *Multitude* and *Quality* of Persons Accused
of an Interest in this *Witchcraft*, by the Efficacy of the *Spectres*
which take their Name and Shape upon them; causing very
many Good and Wise, men to fear, That many *Innocent*, yea,
and some *Vertuous* Persons, are by the Devils in this matter
Imposed upon; That the Devils have obtain'd the power,
to take on them the *Likeness* of Harmless People, and in
that *Likeness* to Afflict other People, and be so abused by
Præstigious *Dæmons*, that upon their *Look* or *Touch*, the Afflicted shall be oddly Affected. Arguments from the *Providence* of *God*, on the one side, and from our *Charity* towards
Man, on the other side, have made This now to become a
most Agitated Controversy among us. There is an *Agony* produced in the minds of men, Lest the *Devil* should sham us
with *Devices*, of perhaps a finer Thred, than was ever yet practised upon the World. The whole Business is become hereupon so *Snarled*, and the Determination of the Question one
way or another, so *Dismal*, that our Honourable Judges, have
a Room for *Jehoshaphats* Exclamation, *We know not what to
do!* They have used, as Judges have heretofore done, the
Spectral Evidences, to introduce their further Enquiries into
the *Lives* of the Persons Accused; and they have thereupon, by
the wonderful Providence of God, been so strengthened with
Other Evidences, that some of the *Witch Gang* have been fairly
Executed. But what shall be done, as to those against whom
the *Evidence* is chiefly founded in the *Dark World*? Here they
do solemnly demand our Addresses to the, *Father of Lights*,
on their Behalf. But in the mean time, the Devil improves the
Darkness of this Affair, to push us into a *Blind Mans Buffet*,
and we are even ready to be *Sinfully*, yea, Hotly, and Madly,
Mauling one another, in the *Dark*.

The Consequence of these things, every *Considerate* man
trembles at; and the more, because the frequent Cheats of
Passion, and Rumour, do precipitate so many, that I wish I
could say, The most were *Considerate*.

But that which carries on the Formidableness of our Trialls,
unto that which may be called, *A wrath unto the uttermost*, is
this: It is not without the *wrath* of the Almighty *God* Himself,
that the *Devil* is permitted thus to come down upon us in
wrath. It was said, in *Isa.* 9. 19. *Thro the wrath of the Lord of*

Hosts, the Land is Darkned. Our Land is *Darkned* indeed; since the *Powers of Darkness* are turned in upon us, tis a *Dark Time*, yea, a Black Night indeed, now the *Ty-Dogs* of the Pitt, are abroad among us: but, *It is thro the wrath of the Lord of Hosts!* Inasmuch as the *Fire-brands* of *Hell* it self are used for the Scorching of us, with cause Enough may we cry out, *What means the Heat of this Anger?* Blessed Lord! Are all the other Instruments of thy Vengeance, too Good for the chastisement of such transgressors as we are? Must the very *Devils* be sent out of *Their own place,* to be our Troublers? Must we be lash'd with *Scorpions,* fetch'd from the *Place of Torment?* Must this *Wilderness* be made a Receptacle for the *Dragons of the Wilderness?* If a *Lapland* should nourish in it vast numbers, the Successors of the old *Biarmi,* who can with looks or words bewitch other people, or Sell Winds to Marriners, and have their *Familiar Spirits* which they bequeath to their Children when they dy, and by their Enchanted Kettle-Drums can learn things done a Thousand Leagues off; If a *Swedeland* should afford a Village, where some scores of Haggs, may not only have their Meetings with *Familiar Spirits,* but also by their Enchantments drag many scores of poor Children out of their Bed-Chambers, to be spoiled at those meetings; This, were not altogether a matter of so much wonder! But that *New-England* should this way be harassed! They are not *Chaldeans,* that *Bitter, and Hasty Nation,* but they are, *Bitter and Burning Devils;* They are not *Swarthy Indians,* but they are *Sooty Devils;* that are let loose upon us. Ah, Poor *New-England*! Must the plague of *Old Egypt* come upon thee? Whereof we read in *Psal.* 78. 49. *He cast upon them, the fierceness of his Anger, Wrath, and Indignation, and Trouble, by sending Evil Angels among them.* What? O what must next be looked for. Must that which is there next mentioned, be next encountered? *He spared not their soul from death, but gave their life over to the Pestilence.* For my part, when I consider what *Melancthon* saies, in one of his Epistles, *That these Diabolical Spectacles are often Prodigies;* and when I consider, how often people have been by *Spectres* called upon, just before their Deaths; I am verily afraid, Lest some wasting *Mortality,* be among the things, which this plague is the *Forerunner* of. I pray God, prevent it!

But now, *What shall we do?*

I. Let the Devils *coming down* in *great wrath* upon us, cause us to *come down* in *great grief* before the Lord. We may truly and sadly say, *We are brought very low! Low*, indeed when the Serpents of the dust, are crawling and coyling about us, and Insulting over us. May we not say, *We are in the very belly of Hell*, when *Hell* it self is feeding upon us? But how *Low* is that! O let us then most Penitently lay ourselves very *Low*, before the God of Heaven, who has thus Abased us. When a Truculent *Nero*, a *Devil* of a man, was turned in upon the World, it was said in, 1. *Pet.* 5. 6, *Humble yourselves under the mighty hand of God.* How much more now ought we to *Humble ourselves*, under that *Mighty Hand* of that God who indeed has the Devil in a *Chain*, but has horribly lengthened out the *Chain*! When the Old People of God, heard any *Blasphemies* tearing of his Ever-Blessed Name to pieces, they were to *Rend their Cloaths* at what they heard. I am sure that we have cause to *Rend our Hearts* this Day, when we see what an High Treason has been committed against the most High God, by the Witchcrafts in our Neighbourhood. We may say; and shall we not be *Humbled* when we say it? *We have seen an horrible thing done in our Land!* O 'tis a most humbling thing, to think, that ever there should be such an abomination among us, as for a Crue of Humane Race, to renounce their *Maker*, and to unite with the *Devil*, for the Troubling of Mankind, and for people to be, (as is by some confess'd) *Baptized* by a *Fiend* using this form upon them, *Thou art mine, and I have a full power over thee!* afterwards communicating in an Hellish *Bread* and *Wine*, by that Fiend Admnistred unto them. It was said in *Deut.* 18. 10, 11, 12. *There shall not be found among you an Inchanter, or a Witch, or a Charmer, or a Consulter with Familiar Spirits, or a Wizzard or a Necromancer; For all that do these things are an Abomination to the Lord, and because of these Abominations, the Lord thy God doth drive them out before thee.* That *New-England* now should have these *Abominations* in it, yea, that some of no mean *Profession*, should be found guilty of them: Alas, what *Humiliations* are we all hereby oblig'd unto? O 'Tis a *Defiled Land*, wherein we Live; Let us be Humbled for these *Defiling Abominations*, Lest we be driven out of our Land.

It's a very *Humbling* Thing to think, what Reproaches will be cast upon us, for this Matter, among, *The Daughters of the Philistines*. Indeed, enough might easily be said for the Vindication of *this* Country from the *Singularity* of this Matter, by Ripping up, what has been discovered in *others*. *Great Britain* alone, and this also in our Dayes of *Greatest Light*, has had that in it, which may divert the Calumnies of an Ill-natured World, from Centring here. They are the words of the Devout Bishop *Hall, Satan's Prevalency in this Age, is most clear in the marvellous Number of Witches abounding in all places. Now Hundreds are discovered in one Shire; and, if Fame Deceive us not, in a Village of Fourteen Houses in the North, are found so many of this Damned Brood. Yea, and these of both Sexes, who have Professed much Knowledge, Holiness, and Devotion, are drawn into this Damnable Practice.* I suppose the Doctor in the first of those Passages, may refer to what happened in the Year 1645. When so many Vassals of the Devil were Detected, that there were *Thirty* Try'd at one time, whereas about *Fourteen* were Hang'd, and an Hundred more Detained in the Prisons of *Suffolk* and *Essex*. Among other things which many of these Acknowledged, one was, That they were to undergo certain *Punishments*, if they did not such and such *Hurts*, as were appointed them. And, among the Rest that were then Executed, there was an Old Parson, called, *Lowis*, who Confessed, that he had a Couple of *Imps*, whereof *One* was alwayes putting him upon the doing of Mischief; Once particularly, that *Imp* calling for his Consent so to do, went immediately and Sunk a *Ship*, there under Sail. I pray, Let not *New-England* become of an Unsavoury and a Sulphurous Resentment in the Opinion of the World Abroad for the Doleful Things which are now fallen out among us, while there are such *Histories* of other places abroad in the World. Nevertheless, I am sure that *one*, the People of *New-England* have cause enough to *Humble* our selves under our most *Humbling* Circumstances. We must no more, be, *Haughty, because of the Lords Holy Mountain among us*; No, it becomes us rather to be, *Humble, because we have been such an Habitation of Unholy Devils!*

II. Since the Divel is *come down* in *great wrath* upon us, let not us in our *great wrath* against one another provide a

Lodging for him. It was a more wholesome caution, in *Eph.* 4. 26, 27. *Let not the Sun go down upon your wrath: Neither give place to the Divel.* The Divel is come down to see what *Quarter* he shall find among us: and, if his coming down, do now fill us with *wrath* against one another; and if between the cause of the *Sufferers* on one hand, and the cause of the *Suspected* on t'other, we carry things to such extreames of *Passion* as are now gaining upon us, the Devil will Bless himself to find such a convenient *Lodging* as we shall therein afford unto him. And it may be that the *wrath* which we have had against one another has had more then a little Influence upon the coming down of the Divel in that *wrath* which now amazes us. Have not many of us been *Devils* one unto another for Slanderings, for Backbitings, for Animosities? For *this*, among other causes, perhaps, God has permitted the *Devils* to be Worrying, as they now are, among us. But it is high time to leave off all *Devilism*, when the *Devil* himself is falling upon us: and it is *no time* for us to be Censuring and Reviling one another, with a *Devilish Wrath*, when the *Wrath* of the *Devil* is annoying of us. The way for us to out-wit the Devil, in the *Wiles* with which he now *Vexes* us, would be for us, to join as one man in our cries to God, for the Directing, and Issuing of this Thorny Business; but if we do not *Lift up* our Hands to Heaven, *Without Wrath*, we cannot then do it *without Doubt*, of speeding in it. I am ashamed when I read French Authors giving this Character of Englishmen [*Ils se haissent Les uns les autres, et sont en Division Continuelle.*] *They hate one another, and are always Quarrelling one with another.* And I shall be much more ashamed, if it become the Character of *New-Englanders*; which is indeed, what the Devil would have. *Satan* would make us *Bruise* one another, by breaking of the *Peace* among us; but O let us disappoint him. We read of a thing that sometimes happens to the *Devil* when he is foaming with his *Wrath*, in *Mat.* 12. 43. *The unclean Spirit seeks rest, and finds none.* But we give *Rest* unto the Devil, by *Wrath* one against another. If we would lay aside all fierceness, and keeness, in the disputes which the Devil has raised among us; and if we would use to one another none but the, *Soft Answers, which Turn away Wrath,* I should hope that we might light upon such Counsels, as would quickly Extricate us out of our *Labyrinths*. But the Old *Incendiary* of the world, is come from Hell, with *Sparks* of Hell-Fire Flashing on every side of him; and we make ourselves *Tynder* to the Sparks. When the Emperour *Henry* III. kept the Feast of *Pentecost*, at the City *Mentz*, there arose Dissension among some of the People there, which came from words to Blows, and at last it passed on to the Shedding of blood. After the Tumult was over, when they came to that clause in their Devotions, *Thou hast made this day Glorious;* the Devil to the unexpressible Terrour of that vast Assembly, made the Temple Ring with the Outcry *But I have made this Day Quarrelsome!* We are truly come into a day, which by being well managed might be very *Glorious*, for the exterminating of those, *Accursed Things*, which have hitherto been the Clogs of our Prosperity; but if we make this day *Quarrelsome*, thro' any *Raging Confidences*, Alas, *O Lord, my Flesh Trembles for fear of thee, and I am afraid of thy Judgments. Erasmus*, among other Historians, tells us, that at a Town in *Germany*, a Witch or Devil, appear'd on the Top of a Chimney, Threatning to set the Town on *Fire*: and at length, Scattering a Pot of Ashes abroad, the Town was presently and Horribly Burn't unto the Ground. Methinks, I see the *Spectres*, from the Tops of the Chimneys to the North ward, threatning to Scatter *Fire*, about the Countrey; but let us Quench that *Fire* by the most amicable Correspondencies: Lest, as the *Spectres*, have, they say, already most Literally Burn't some of our Dwellings, there do come forth a further *Fire* from the *Brambles* of Hell, which may more terribly *Devour* us. Let us not be like a *Troubled House*, altho we are so much haunted by the *Devils*. Let our *Long Suffering* be a Well-placed piece of *Armour*, about us, against the *Fiery Darts* of the wicked ones. History informs us, That so long ago, as the year, 858. a certain Pestilent and Malignant sort of a *Dæmon*, molested *Caumont* in *Germany* with all sorts of methods to stir up Strife among the Citizens. He uttered Prophecies, he detected Villanies, he branded people with all kind of Infamies. He incensed the Neighbourhood against one Man particularly, as the cause of all the mischiefs: who yet proved himself innocent. He threw stones at the Inhabitants, and at length burn't their Habitations, till the Commission of the *Dæmon* could go no further. I say, Let us be well aware lest such *Dæmons* do, *Come hither also!*

III. Inasmuch as the Devil is come down in *Great Wrath*, we had need Labour, with all the Care and Speed we can to Divert the *Great Wrath* of Heaven from coming at the same Time upon us. The God of Heaven has with long and loud Admonitions, been calling us to, *A Reformation of our Provoking Evils*, as the only way to avoid that *Wrath* of His, which does not only *Threaten*, but *Consume* us. 'Tis because we have been Deaf to those *Calls*, that we are now by a provoked God, laid open to the *Wrath* of the Devil himself. It is said in *Prov.* 16. 7. *When a mans ways please the Lord, He maketh even his Enemies to be at peace with him.* The Devil is our Grand *Enemy*: and tho' we would not be at peace *with* him, yet we would be at peace *from* him; that is, we would have him unable to Disquiet our *Peace*. But inasmuch as the *Wrath* which we Endure from this *Enemy*, will allow us no *Peace*, we may be sure, *Our Ways have not pleased the Lord*. It is because we have *broken the Hedge* of Gods *Precepts*, that the Hedge of Gods *Provodence* is not so Entire as it uses to be about us; but *Serpents* are *Biting* of us, O let us then set our selves to make our *Peace* with our God, whom we have *Displeased* by our Iniquities: and let us not imagine that we can Encounter the *Wrath* of the Devil while there is the *Wrath* of God Almighty to set that Mastiff upon us. REFORMATION! REFORMATION! has been the Repeated *Cry*, of all the Judgments, that have hitherto been upon us: because we have been as *Deaf Adders* thereunto, the *Adders* of the Infernal Pit are now hissing about us. At length, as it was of old said in *Luc.* 16. 30. *If one went unto them, from the Dead, they will Repent;* Even so, There are some come unto us from the *Damned*. The Great God has Loosed the Bars of the Pit, so that many *Damned Spirits* are come in among us, to make us *Repent* of our Misdemeanours. The means which the Lord had formerly Employ'd for our *Awakening*, were such, that he might well have said, *What could I have done more?* and yet after all, He has done *more*, in some regards, than was ever done for the Awakening of any People in the World. The

Things now done to Awaken our Enquiries after our *Provoking Evils*, and our Endeavours to Reform those Evils; are most EXTRAORDINARY Things; For which cause I would freely speak it, If we now do not some EXTRAORDINARY Things in Returning to God, we are the most *Incurable*, and I wish it be not quickly said, the most *Miserable*, People under the Sun. Believe me, 'tis a Time for all people to do something EXTRAORDINARY *In Searching and in Trying of their Ways, and in Turning to the Lord*. It is at an EXTRAORDINARY Rate of *Circumspection* and *Spiritual Mindedness*, that we should all now maintain a *Walk with God*. At such a Time as This, ought *Magistrates* to Do something EXTRAORDINARY in promoting of what is Laudable, and in Restraining and Chastising of *Evil Doers*. At such a Time as This, ought *Ministers* to Do something EXTRAORDINARY in pulling the Souls of men out of the *Snares* of the Devil, not only by publick Preaching, but by personal Visits and Counsels, *from House to House*. At such a Time as This, ought *Churches* to Do something EXTRAORDINARY, in *Renewing* of their Covenants, and in *Remembring*, and *Reviving* the Obligations of what they have Renewed. Some Admirable Designs about the *Reformation* of Manners, have lately been on foot in the English Nation, in pursuance of the most Excellent Admonitions, which have been given for it, by the Letters of Their Majesties. Besides the vigorous Agreements of the *Justices* here and there in the Kingdom; assisted by Godly Gentlemen and Informers, to Execute the *Laws* upon Profane Offenders: there has been started, A PROPOSAL, for the well-affected people in every Parish, to enter into orderly *Societies*, whereof every Member shall bind himself, not only to *Avoid* Profaneness in himself, but also according unto their Place, to do their utmost in first *Reproving*, and, if it must be so, then *Exposing*, and so *Punishing*, as the Law directs, for, others that shall be guilty. It has been observed, That the English Nation has had some of its greatest Successes, upon some special, and signal *Actions* this way; and a Discouragement given unto Legal Proceedings of this Kind, must needs be very exercising to the, *Wise that observe these Things*. But, O why should not *New-England* be the most forward part of the English Nation in such *Reformations*? Methinks, I hear the Lord from Heaven saying over us, *O that my People had hearkened unto me; Then* I *should soon have subdued the Devils, as well as their other Enemies!* There have been some feeble Essays towards *Reformation*, of late in our *Churches*; but, I pray, what comes of them? Do we stay till the *Storm* of his *Wrath* be over? Nay, let us be Doing what we can as fast as we can, to divert the *Storm*. The Devil, having broke in upon our World, there is great Asking, *Who is it that have brought them in?* and many do by *Spectral* Exhibitions come to be *cry'd out* upon. I hope in Gods Time, it will be found, that among those that are thus *Cry'd out* upon, there are persons yet *Clear from the Great Transgression*; but indeed, all the *Unreformed* among us, may justly be *Cry'd out* upon, as having too much of an Hand in letting of the Devils in to our Borders; 'tis *our* Worldliness, *our* Formality, *our* Sensuality, and *our* Iniquity, that has help'd this Letting of the Devils in. O Let us then at last, *Consider our Wayes.* 'Tis a strange passage recorded by Mr. *Clark*, in the Life of his Father, That the People of his Parish refusing to be Reclaimed from their *Sabbath Breaking*, by all the zealous Testimonies which that Good man bore against it; at last, on a Night after the people had Retired Home from a Revelling Profanation of the *Lords Day*, there was heard a Great Noise, with Rattling of Chains, up and down the Town, and the horrid Scent of Brimstone fill'd the Neighbourhood. Upon which the *Guilty Consciences* of the Wretches, told them, the Devil was come to fetch them away: and it so terrify'd them, that an Eminent *Reformation* follow'd the Sermons which that man of God Preached thereupon. Behold, Sinners, Behold, and *Wonder*, lest you *Perish*; the very *Devils* are Walking about our Streets, with Lengthened *Chains*, making a dreadful Noise in our Ears, and *Brimstone*, even without a Metaphor, is making an Hellish and Horrid Stench in our Nostrils. I Pray, Leave off all those things, whereof your *Guilty Consciences* may now accuse you, lest these Devils do yet more direfully fall upon you. *Reformation* is at this Time, our only *Preservation*.

IV. When the Devil is come down in *Great Wrath*, Let every *Great Vice* which may have a more Particular Tendency to make us a Prey unto that *Wrath*, come into a due Discredit with us. It is the General Concession of all men, who are not become too *Unreasonable* for Common Conversation, That the Invitation of *Witchcrafts* is the Thing that ha's now Introduced the Devil into the midst of us. I say then, Let not only all *Witchcrafts* be duely abominated with us, but also Let us be duely Watchful against all the *Steps* Leading thereunto. There are Lesser *Sorceries* which, they say, are too frequent in our Land. As it was said in 2 *King.* 17. 9. *The Children of Israel did Secretly those things that were not Right against the Lord their God.* So tis to be feared, The Children of *New-England* have *Secretly* done many things that have been pleasing to the Devil. They say, That in some Towns, it ha's been an usual Thing for People to Cure Hurts with *Spells,* or to use Detestable Conjurations, with *Sieves,* & *Keyes,* and *Pease,* and *Nails,* and *Horse-Shooes,* and I know not what other Implements, to Learn the Things, for which they have a Forbidden, and an Impious *Curiositie.* 'Tis in the Devils Name, that such Things are done; and in Gods Name I do this Day Charge them, as vile Impieties. By these Courses 'tis, that people play upon *The Hole of the Asp;* till that cruelly venemous *Asp* has pull'd many of them, into the Deep *Hole,* of *Witchcraft* it self. It has been acknowledged by some who have sunk the deepest into this *Horrible Pit,* that they began, at these Little *Witchcrafts;* on which 'tis pitty but the Laws of the English Nation, whereby the Incorrigible Repetition of those *Tricks,* is made *Felony,* were severally Executed. From the like Sinful *Curiosity* it is, that the Prognostications of *Judicial Astrology,* are so Injudiciously Regarded by multitudes among us; and although the Jugling *Astrologers* do scarce ever hit Right, except it be in such *Weighty Judgments,* forsooth, as that many *Old Men* will Dy such a year, and that there will be many *Losses* felt by some that Venture to Sea, and that there will be much *Lying* and *Cheating* in the World; yet their Foolish Admirers, will not be perswaded, but that the Innocent *Stars* have been concern'd in these Events. It is a Disgrace to the English Nation that the Phamphlets of such Idle, Futil, Trifling *Star-gazers* are so much Considered; and the Countenance hereby given to a Study, wherein at Last, all is done by *Impulse,* if any thing be done to any purpose at all, is not a little perilous to the Souls of men. It is, (*a Science,* I dare not call it, but) a *Juggle,* whereof the Learned *Hall,* well says, *It is presumptuous and unwarrantable, & cry'd ever down by Councils and Fathers, as unlawful, as that which Lies in the mid-way between Magick, and Imposture, and partakes not a little of both.* Men Consult the Aspects of Planets, whose Northern or Southern Motions receive Denominations from a *Cælestial Dragon*, till the *Infernal Dragon* at length insinuate into them, with a *Poyson* of *Witchcraft* that can't be cured. Has there not also been a world of *Discontent* in our Borders? 'Tis no wonder, that the *Fiery Serpents* are so Stinging of us; We have been a most *Murmuring Generation.* It is not Irrational, to ascribe the late Stupendous Growth of *Witches* among us, partly to the Bitter *Discontents*, which Affliction and Poverty has fill'd us with: it is inconceivable, what Advantage the Devil gains over men, by *Discontent.* Moreover, The Sin of *Unbelief* may be reckoned as perhaps the chief *Crime* of our Land. We are told, *God Swears in Wrath, against them that believe not*; and what follows then but this, *That the Devil comes unto them in wrath*? Never were the Offers of the *Gospel,* more freely Tendered, or more basely Despised, among any people under the whole Cope of Heaven, then in This *New-England.* Seems it at all marvellous unto us, that the *Devil* should get such Footing in our Country? Why, 'tis because the *Saviour* has been slighted here, perhaps more than any where. The Blessed Lord Jesus Christ has been profering to us, *Grace, and Glory, and every good thing,* and been alluring of us to Accept of Him, with such Terms as these; *Undone Sinner, I am All; Art thou willing that I should be thy All?* But, as a proof of that Contempt which this Unbelief has cast upon these proffers, I would seriously ask of the so many Hundreds above a Thousand People within these Walls; Which of you all, O how few of you, can indeed say, *Christ is mine, and I am his, and He is the Beloved of my Soul?* I would only say thus much: When the precious and glorious Jesus, is Entreating of us to Receive *Him,* in all His *Offices,* with all His *Benefits*; the Devil minds what Respect we pay unto that Heavenly Lord; if we *Refuse Him that speaks from Heaven,* then he that, *Comes from Hell,* does with a sort of claim set in, and cry out, *Lord, since this Wretch is not willing that thou shouldst have him, I pray, let me have him.* And thus, by the just vengeance of Heaven, the Devil

becomes a *Master*, a *Prince*, a *God*, unto the miserable Unbelievers: but O what are many of them then hurried unto!
All of these Evil Things, do I now set before you, as *Branded*
with the Mark of the Devil upon them.

V. With *Great Regard*, with *Great Pitty*, should we Lay to
Heart the Condition of those, who are cast into Affliction, by
the *Great Wrath* of the Devil. There is a Number of our
Good Neighbours, and some of them very particularly noted
for Goodness and Vertue, of whom we may say, *Lord, They
are vexed with Devils.* Their Tortures being primarily Inflicted
on their *Spirits*, may indeed cause the Impressions thereof
upon their Bodies to be the less *Durable*, tho' rather the more
Sensible: but they Endure Horrible Things, and many have
been actually Murdered. Hard *Censures* now bestow'd upon
these poor Sufferers, cannot but be very Displeasing unto our
Lord, who, as He said, about some that had been Butchered
by a *Pilate*, in *Luc.* 13. 2, 3. *Think ye that these were Sinners
above others, because they suffered such Things? I tell you No,
But except ye Repent, ye shall all likewise Perish:* Even so, he
now says, *Think ye that they who now suffer by the Devil, have
been greater Sinners than their Neighbours.* No, Do you
Repent of your *own Sins*, Lest the Devil come to fall foul of
you, as he has done to *them*. And if this be so, How *Rash* a
thing would it be, if such of the poor Sufferers, as carry it
with a Becoming Piety, Seriousness, and Humiliation under
their present Suffering, should be unjustly *Censured*; or have
their very *Calamity* imputed unto them as a *Crime*? It is an
easy thing, for us to fall into, the Fault of, *Adding Affliction
to the Afflicted*, and of, *Talking to the Grief of those that are already Wounded*: Nor can it be Wisdom to slight the Dangers
of such a Fault. In the mean time, We have no Bowels in us,
if we do not Compassionate the Distressed County of *Essex*,
now crying to all these Colonies, *Have pitty on me, O ye my
friend, Have pitty on me, for the Hand of the Lord has Touched
me, and the Wrath of the Devil has been therewithal turned
upon me.* But indeed, if an hearty *pitty* be due to any, I am
sure, the Difficulties which attend our Honourable *Judges*,
doe demand no Inconsiderable share in that *Pitty*. What a
Difficult, what an Arduous Task, have those Worthy Person-
ages now upon their Hands? To carry the *Knife* so exactly,

that on the one side, there may be no Innocent Blood Shed,
by too unseeing a *Zeal for the Children of Israel*; and that on
the other side, there may be no Shelter given to those Diabolical *Works of Darkness*, without the Removal whereof we
never shall have *Peace*; or to those *Furies* whereof several have
kill'd *more people* perhaps than would serve to make a Village:
Hic Labor, Hoc Opus est! O what need have we, to be concerned, that the Sins of our *Israel*, may not provoke the God
of Heaven to leave his *Davids*, unto a wrong Step, in a matter of such Consequence, as is now before them! Our Disingenuous, Uncharitable, Unchristian Reproching of such
Faithful Men, after all, *The Prayers and Supplications, with
strong Crying and Tears*, with which we are daily plying the
Throne of Grace, that they may be kept, from what *They Fear*,
is none of the way for our preventing of what We *Fear*. Nor
all this while, ought our *Pitty* to forget such *Accused* ones, as
call for indeed our most Compassionate *Pitty*, till there be
fuller Evidences that they are less worthy of it. If *Satan* have
any where maliciously brought upon the *Stage*, those that
have hitherto had a just and good stock of Reputation, for
their just and good Living, among us; If the *Evil One* have
obtained a permission to *Appear*, in the Figure of such as we
have cause to think, have hitherto *Abstained*, even from the
Appearance of Evil: It is in Truth, such an Invasion upon
Mankind, as may well Raise an Horror in us all: But, O what
Compassions are due to such as may come under such
Misrepresentations, of the *Great Accuser*! Who of us can say,
what may be shown in the *Glasses* of the Great *Lying Spirit*?
Altho' the *Usual Providence* of God [we praise Him!] keeps us
from such a Mishap; yet where have we an *Absolute Promise*,
that we shall every one alwayes be kept from it? As long as
Charity is bound, to Think *no Evil*, it will not Hurt us that
are *Private Persons*, to forbear the *Judgment* which belongs
not unto us. Let it rather be our Wish: May the Lord help
them to Learn the *Lessons*, for which they are now put unto
so hard a School.

VI. With a *Great Zeal*, we should lay hold on the *Covenant*
of God, that we may Secure *Us* and *Ours*, from the *Great
Wrath*, with which the Devil Rages. Let us come into the
Covenant of Grace, and then we shall not be hook'd into a

Covenant with the Devil, nor be altogether unfurnished with armour, against the Wretches that are in the *Covenant*. The way to come under the Saving Influences of the *New Covenant*, is, to close with the Lord Jesus Christ, who is the All-sufficient *Mediator* of it: Let us therefore do *that*, by Resigning up ourselves unto the Saving, Teaching, and Ruling, Hands of this Blessed *Mediator*. Then we shall be, what we read in *Jude*, 1. *Preserved in Christ Jesus:* That is, as the *Destroying Angel*, could not meddle with such as had been distinguished, by the Blood of the *Passeover* on their Houses, Thus the Blood of the Lord Jesus Christ, Sprinkled on our Souls, will *Preserve* us from the Devil. The *Birds of prey* (and indeed the *Devils* most literally in the shape of great *Birds!*) are flying about: Would we find a Covert from these *Vultures:* Let us then Hear Our Lord Jesus from Heaven Clocqing unto us, *O that you would be gathered under my Wings*. Well; When this is done, Then let us own the *Covenant*, which we are now come into, by joining ourselves to a Particular *Church*, walking in the Order of the Gospel; at the doing whereof, according to that *Covenant* of God, We give up Ourselves unto the Lord, and in Him unto One Another. While others have had their Names Entred in the *Devils Book*; let our Names be found in the *Church Book*, and let us be, *Written among the Living in Jerusalem*. By no means let, *Church-Work* sink and fail in the midst of us; but let the Tragical Accidents which now happen, exceedingly Quicken that *Work*. So many of the *Rising Generation*, utterly forgetting the Errand of our Fathers to build Churches in this Wilderness, and so many of Our *Cottages* being allow'd to Live, where they do not, and perhaps can not, wait upon God with the Churches of His People! tis as likely as any one thing to procure the swarmings of *Witch-crafts* among us. But it becomes us, with a like Ardour, to bring our poor *Children* with us, as we shall do, when we come ourselves, into the *Covenant* of God. It would break an heart of Stone, to have seen, what I have lately seen; Even poor Children of several Ages, even from seven to twenty more or less, *Confessing* their Familiarity with Devils; but at the same time, in Doleful bitter Lamentations, that made a Little Pourtraiture of *Hell* it self, Expostulating with their execrable Parents, for *Devoting* them to the Devil in their Infancy, and so *Entailing* of Devillism upon them! Now, as the Psalmist could say, *My Zeal hath Consumed me, because my Enemies have forgotten thy Words:* Even so, let the nefarious wickedness of those that have Explicitly dedicated their Children to the Devil, even with Devillish Symbols, of such a Dedication, Provoke our *Zeal* to have our Children, Sincerely, Signally, and openly *Consecrated* unto God; with an *Education* afterwards assuring and confirming that Consecration.

VII. Let our *Prayer* Go up with *Great Faith*, against the Devil, that comes down in *Great Wrath*. Such is the Antipathy of the Devil to our *Prayer*, that he cannot bear to stay long where much of it is: indeed it is *Diaboli Flagellum*, as well as, *Miseriæ Remedium*; the Devil will soon be Scourgd out of the Lords Temple, by a *Whip*, made and used, with the, *Effectual Fervent Prayer of Righteous Men*. When the Devil by Afflicting of us, drives us to our Prayers, he is, *The Fool making a Whip for his own Back*. Our Lord said of the Devil, in *Mat.* 17. 21. *This Kind goes not out, but by Prayer and Fasting*. But, *Prayer and Fasting* will soon make the Devil be gone. Here are *Charms* indeed! Sacred and Blessed *Charms*, which the Devil cannot stand before. A *Promise* of God, being well managed in the *Hands* of them, that are much upon their *Knees*, will so, *Resist the Devil*, that he will *Flee from us*. At every other Weapon, the *Devils* will be too hard for us; the *Spiritual Wickednesses in High Places*, have manifestly the Upper Hand of us; that *Old Serpent* will be too Old for us, too cunning, too subtil; they will soon *out-wit* us, if we think to Encounter them with any *Wit* of our own. But when we come to *Prayers*, Incessant and Vehement *Prayers* before the Lord, *there* we shall be too hard for them. When well-directed *Prayers*, that great Artillery of Heaven, are brought into the Field, *There*, methinks I see, *There are these Workers of Iniquity fallen, all of them!* And who can tell, how much the most *Obscure Christian* among you all, may do towards the Deliverance of our Land from the Molestations which the Devil is now giving unto us. I have Read, That on a Day of Prayer kept by some Good People for and with a Possessed Person, the Devil at last flew out of the Window, and referring to a Devout, plain, mean Woman then in the Room, he cry'd out, *O the Woman behind the Door! 'Tis that Woman that forces me away!* Thus, the Devil that now Troubles us, may be forced within a while to Forsake us: and it shall be said, *He was driven away by the prayers of some Obscure and Retired Souls, which the world has taken but little notice of!* The Great God, is about a *Great Work* at this Day among us; now there is extream Hazzard left the Devil who by *Compulsion* must submit unto that *Great Work,* may also by *Permission* come to Confound that *Work*: both in the *Detections* of some, and in the *Confessions* of others, whose *Ungodly Deeds* may be brought forth, by a *Great Work* of God, there is Hazzard lest the Devil intertwist some of his Delusions. 'Tis PRAYER, I say, 'tis PRAYER, that must carry us well thro' the Strange Things that are now upon us. Only that *Prayer* must then be, *The Prayer of Faith*: O where is our *Faith* in Him, Who *hath Spoiled these Principalities and Powers, on His Cross Triumphing over them!*

VIII. Lastly, Shake off, every Soul, Shake off the *Hard Yoke* of the Devil, if you would not perish under the *Great Wrath* of the Devil. Where 'tis said, *The whole World lies in Wickedness,* 'tis by some of the Ancients rendred, *The whole world lies in the Devil.* The Devil is a *Prince,* yea, the Devil is a *God* unto all the Unregenerate; and alas, there is, *A whole world of them.* Desolate Sinners, Consider what an Horrid *Lord* it is that you are Enslav'd unto; and Oh shake off your Slavery to such a *Lord.* Instead of *him,* now make your Choice of the Eternal God in Jesus Christ; Choose *Him* with a most unalterable Resolution; and unto *Him* say, with *Thomas, My Lord, and my God!* Say with the Church, *Lord, other Lords have had the Dominion over us, but now thou alone shalt be our Lord for ever.* Then instead of your perishing under the *wrath* of the Devils, God will fetch you to a place among those that fill up the *Room* of the Devils, left by their Fall from the Ethereal Regions. It was a most awful Speech made by the Devil, Possessing a young Woman, at a Village in *Germany, By the Command of God, I am come to Torment the Body of this young Woman, though I cannot hurt her Soul; and it is that I may warn men, to take heed of Sinning against God.* Indeed (said he) *'tis very sore against my will that I do it; but the command of God forces me to declare what I do; However I know that at the Last Day, I shall have more Souls than God*

Himself. So spoke that horrible Devil! But O that none of our *Souls* may be found among the Prizes of the Devil, in the Day of God! O that what the Devil has been *forc'd to Declare*, of his Kingdom among us, may prejudice our Hearts against him for ever!

My Text saies, *The Devil is come down in Great Wrath, for he has but a short Time.* Yea, but if you do not by a Speedy and Thorough Conversion to God, Escape the *Wrath* of the Devil, you will yourselves Go *down*, where the Devil is to be, and you will there be sweltring under the Devils *Wrath*, not for a *Short Time*, but, *World without End*; not for a *Short Time*, but for, *Infinite Millions of Ages.* The smoke of your Torment under that *Wrath*, will *Ascend for ever and ever*! Indeed the Devils Time for his *Wrath* upon you in this World, can be but short, but his *Time* for you to do his *Work*, or, which is all one, to delay your turning to God, that is a *Long Time.* When the Devil was going to be Dispossessed of a Man, he Roar'd out, *Am I to be Tormented before my Time.* You will *Torment* the Devil, if you Rescue your Souls out of his hands, by true Repentance; if once you begin to look that way, hee'll Cry out, *O This is before my Time, I must have more Time, yet in the service of such a guilty Soul.* But, I beseech you, let us join thus to *Torment* the Devil, in an Holy Revenge upon him, for all the Injuries which he has done unto us; let us tell him, *Satan, Thy Time with me is but short, Nay, thy Time with me shall be no more; I am unutterably sorry that it has been so much; Depart from me thou Evil-Doer, that would'st have me to be an Evil-Doer Like thy self; I will now for ever keep the Commandments of that God, in whom I Live, and Move, and have my Being!* The Devil has plaid a fine Game for himself indeed, if by his Troubling of our Land, the souls of many People should come to, *Think upon their Wayes, till they turn their Feet into the Testimonies of the Lord.* Now that the Devil may be thus outshot in his own Bow, is the Desire of all that *Love the Salvation of God* among us, as well as of him, who has thus Addressed You. *Amen.*

SOLOMON STODDARD

The Tryal of Assurance

Set forth in a Sermon;
Preached at Boston upon a Lecture day.
July 7th. 1698.

2 Pet. I. 10. *Brethren give diligence to make your Calling*
and Election sure.

———

JOHN 21. 17.
Simon son of Jonas, lovest thou Me?

THE FALLS of the People of God do darken their sincerity: they are as a Cloud covering their uprightness: they do make their sincerity questionable unto others: some that take notice of their falls are ready to suspect, and others are ready to deny their sincerity; standers by are apt to impute their falls to their Hypocrisy and the reigning power of sin; as if they had now proved themselves to be Hypocrites. They are ready to say of them, as *David* said of *Doeg, Lo this is the man that made not God his trust.* And their falls make their sincerity questionable to themselves: if they have seen something of uprightness in themselves before, now they fear, they were mistaken: they think if there had been any Grace, that would have preserved them from falling: their falls wound their Consciences and disturb their Peace. They think if God had loved them, he would not have suffered them to fall into such sin: it seems to them to be the fruit of Gods hatred: they are apt to think that their sins have turned away the heart of God from them, and that he cannot delight in them: they think moreover that if they had loved God, they could not have been drawn to sin so against him. Satan is wont to improve their falls unto their discouragement; and raises such mists, that day is turned into night unto them. Upon this occasion Christ puts this question to *Peter*: the Disciples might be unsatisfyed with him, because of his fall; and he might be dissatisfyed with himself: but hereby Christ is leading of him into the Examination of his own sincerity. You may conceive Christs meaning thus: *Peter* you have made a Profession many years; but in the time of my affliction, you shamefully denied me, you formerly professed that you would dye with me, before you would deny me, but as soon as the Temptation came; you presently denyed me: and as if it were not enough to do it once, you did it a second and a third time: and as if plain denying had not been enough, you did it with Cursing and Swearing: is there any love in your heart unto me? you shewed some affection but now, in throwing your self into the Sea, but is it real love? have I your heart? am I the object of your love? you professed more love than other Disciples; but do you indeed love me?

DOCTRINE.   *If a man do's not certainly know, that he has performed one act of Saving Grace, he cannot be certain of his Sincerity from his Walk.*

The Tryal of sincerity is a great and weighty work. Ministers had need be careful in giving Rules of Tryal; and People had need be careful in applying Rules of Tryal: the Doctrine is propounded to prevent mistakes in this matter. Godly men are described in the Scripture to be men, *that walk in the law of the Lord; men that walk not after the flesh but after the Spirit*: but it is impossible for any man to evidence his sincerity from hence; unless he certainly knows that he has performed some act or acts of saving Grace. A man may have a probable knowledge of his sincerity, though he do not certainly know that he has performed any act of saving Grace: but this is all that he can attain to by his walk; he do not know that he has performed any one act of saving Grace. There be many acts of saving Grace; as to believe in Christ, to love God and Christ, to hate sin, to make the Glory of God one's end: and if a man don't certainly know any such thing by himself: he will never be able from his walk to prove himself to be a Saint. If a thing shine like fire in the night, yet you cannot know it to be fire from thence; unless you see in it some property of fire. If a thing acts as if it had life, yet you cannot know from thence, that it has life, unless you know some action to be a Vital action. You cannot know that a man do's miracles, unless you know some one action to be miraculous: So here.

In order to the clearing of this, I shall first premise three things.

1. They that walk in a way of holiness are sincere: all that walk in a way of obedience are upright. Walking in Gods ways is the Character of a Saint. *Psal.* 119. 1. *Blessed are the undefiled in the way, who walk in the law of the Lord.* An holy life is a certain sign of a holy heart. A life of obedience shows a principal of Grace: they that live a life of humility, love and faith are real Saints; they are such indeed as they do profess themselves to be: though they have many infirmities and corruptions, yet they are sincere Saints. An holy life is more than any Hypocrite can attain unto: he may counterfeit Holiness and have the image of it; but falls utterly short of an holy life: an holy life is a life of sincerity and flows from a principle of sincerity: other principles may make a man live a moral and religious life: Prudence, Pride and slavish fear may produce much out-ward conformity, and many inward affections: but only a principle of Grace can inable a man to live an holy life: all that live holily are regenerate men. *Eph.* 2. 10. *Created in Christ Jesus unto good works.*

2. They that walk in a way of unholiness are not sincere: they that lead an unholy life are not upright: a principle of Grace will keep a man from ways of sin. 1 *Joh.* 3. 9. *He that is born of God, doth not commit sin, for his seed remaineth in him, and he cannot sin, because he is born of God*: he has so much fear that he can't live a life of sin, he hates sin so that he cannot live a life of sin: Some that are sincere have a less degree of sincerity than others; but the least degree of sincerity will preserve a man from an unholy life. *Psal.* 18. 23. *I was also upright before him and I kept my self from mine iniquity.* An unholy life shews the reigning power of sin. *Job.* 8. 34. *He that committeth sin, is the servant of sin.* They that are serving any Lust are not serving of the Lord: if men make great pretensions of sincerity, yet lead unholy lives, there is no sincerity in them: if they have great affections and hopes, yet they have no sincerity: they profess one thing and practise another. If men serve their Pride or their Coveteousness, or

their Voluptuousness, they are not sincere, they are utterly destitute of a principle of Grace: if they have shews of Grace, yet they are but Hypocrites, and will be damned at the last day. *Luke* 13. 27. *Depart from me, all ye workers of iniquity.*

3. Many men seem to themselves to walk in a way of Holiness, yet don't certainly know that ever they did perform an act of saving grace; though all that make an high profession don't seem to themselves to lead an holy life, yet abundance of them do: they are consciencious of all their ways, have many religious affections; mourn for sin, rejoyce in Sabbaths, are thankful for mercies; are afflicted under the Tokens of Gods Anger, are desirous of the Conversion of others: it seems to them, that they live in some degree as Saints of old did: they think they walk holily, yet many of these persons don't certainly know that ever they did perform one act of saving grace, several of them never did perform one act of saving grace, therefore they cannot know that they have: and some that have done it, are in the dark about it; they are under doubts and uncertainties about it: the Question is, Whether such persons can know from their Walk, that they are sincere. This the Doctrine does deny, and it may thus be cleared up.

Argument 1. It is the acting of Grace that makes and shews the Walk to be holy: it is not the orderliness of mens walk that shews it to be holy; nor the affectionateness of mens hearts in Religion, that shews their walk to be holy; nor the long continuance of good carriages, nor a good behaviour in a day of temptation; not a savoury spirit; these things may all be, yet the walk not be holy: if there be the acting of love, faith and repentance, then the walk is holy: but all that men do is done in hypocrisy, if there be not the acting of grace: if there be no grace in their prayers, in their fastings, in their discourses; all is in hypocrisy: conscienciousness don't prove their walk to be sincere: the young man in the Gospel was conscientious: *Mat.* 19. 20. *all these things have I done from my youth.* Zeal don't prove it, a man may be zealous, yet not upright: *Rom.* 10. 2. they be the actings of grace that make and shew the walk to be holy; if it be not a life of faith and love, it is not a holy life: *Gal.* 2. 20. *the life that I live in the flesh, I live by the faith of the Son of God*: therefore he that don't know that he has performed an act of grace, can't know that he has an holy walk: he that don't know that he has that which is the life of an holy walk, and essential to it, can't know that his walk is holy.

2. It is harder to know an holy walk than one act of grace: it is harder for any man to discern that he leads an holy life, then that he performs a gracious act: for an holy life does consist of many gracious actions; and it is harder to discern that a man has done many, then that he has done one: it is harder to find out many profitable herbs in the field than one; harder to discern many grains of Wheat among the Chaff, than one: it is harder to find many Evidences of a good Estate than one; to the discerning of many acts of grace, there is required more observation and examination, then to the discerning of one act of grace; if it be difficult to find one, it will be more difficult to find two, ten, an hundred: therefore he that don't know that he has performed one act of grace, does not know that he leads an holy life. I may allude to that, *Jer.* 12. 5. *if thou hast run with the footmen and they have wearied thee, how wilt thou contend with horses.*

3. If the holiness of mens actions can't be discerned severally, it can't be discerned in conjunction: if a man looks upon his actions severally, and cannot say that this or that or any one was an holy action; he cannot say concerning any action, that it was an act of saving faith, or saving love; how can he when he looks upon his carriages together, say they are holy, if there be no one action that he can say is sincere; how can he say that his walk is sincere: if a man sees an heap of corn, how can he say, it is an heap of wheat, when he does not know, that there is one grain of wheat there: the sincerity of his walk depends upon the sincerity of particular actions; and if that be hidden from him, how can he say his walk is sincere: if for ought he knows every prayer and duty be done in hypocrisy; then for ought he knows, his whole life is a life of hypocrisy; if he can instance in no action that is certainly otherwise, it may be so for ought that he knows; if he can't answer to this question. *Joh.* 21. 17. *Lovest thou me?* or to that, *Joh.* 9. 35. *dost thou believe on the Son of God?* or some such like; he cannot tell that he lives an holy life: therefore such a man can't prove his sincerity from his walk. No walk can be

evidential, but what is made up of acts of grace; therefore if he feel none, he can have no evidence from his walk.

4. If there be no act of grace, there is no sincerity; therefore if he sees no act of grace, he sees no sincerity; when there is no act of grace, there is no principle of grace: though a man walk in print, yet there is no sincerity; many carry themselves very fairly, but if there be no grace, there is no uprightness in them, *Joh.* 5. 42. *I know you, that you have not the love of God in you;* it is all counterfeit walk: they are like men upon the Stage, that personate other kind of men; so these men walk like Saints, and talk like Saints; but if there be no act of grace, they are no Saints, they want that which does constitute a Saint; therefore if a man do not know any act of grace in himself, he can't know himself to be a Saint, though he walk like an Angel.

5. The multiplication of such acts as are common to Saints and hypocrites, don't shew him to be sincere; prayer is common to Saints and hypocrites. *Psal.* 78. 34. *When he slew them, then they fought him, they returned and enquired early after God;* therefore if a man do this a thousand times, it don't prove him to be a Saint; so morality is common to Saints and hypocrites. *Mat.* 19. 20. and if a man carries morally, twenty years together, it don't shew him to be a Saint; so zeal, so delight in Sabbaths; if an hypocrite may do these things, then the multiplication of them, and walking in such a way is no evidence; that which is common, let it be multiplied never so often, don't become saving: multiply cyphers, and they make no number: therefore there can be no evidence of a good estate from a mans walk, unless he knew some act of grace; if he can't discern some act of saving grace, he must be at a loss about his sincerity.

USE I.   See the reason why many Professors are unsatisfied about their sincerity; though they have a pretty good conversation, are conscientious, affectionate, zealous, yet they are full of fears, they are often perplexed, and don't know what to make of themselves; it seems to them that their walk is pretty much according to rule, but they do not know that ever they did perform any act of saving grace; they can't answer to such questions, *Lovest thou me? Joh.* 21. 17. *Or dost thou believe on the Son of God? Joh.* 9. 35. this does create a deal of perplexity to them; and they are afraid what will become of themselves, after all their profession. And there are three sorts of them.

1. Some Professors never did see any act of grace in themselves: they never had any: and therefore could not see any: they have had affection, but no love; sorrow, but not godly sorrow, encouragement, but no faith. There be many Professors that are utterly destitute of gracious carriages, they have the resemblance of them, but they never had any exercise of grace; they are *spiritually dead*, and never did perform any act of *spiritual life*; thus it was with *Saul, Doeg, Achitophel, Judas* and *Demas*, they were only the pictures of Saints, and imitated the actions of Spiritual Life, but did not perform them; *an evil tree can't bring forth good fruit, men can't gather grapes of thorns, or figs of thistles: Mat. 7. 16, 18.* they can't see acts of grace: men cannot see that which is not.

2. Some Professors never did certainly know that they have performed any act of saving grace; they have discovered the workings of grace sometimes in themselves, but not so plainly, as to be able to speak roundly up to it, as *Peter* did, *Lord, thou knowest all things; thou knowest that I love thee? Joh.* 21. 17. they understand that there is a great deal that does resemble grace, that is not grace; and so they doubt whether it be of the right kind: they know that there is a temporary faith, *Luk.* 8. 13. *some believe for a time, and then fall away*; and there may be strong desires and delight, where there is no sincere love; here may be great pangs of affection, without any uprightness, and the acts of grace were not so clear, as some others do speak of; hence they are not fully satisfied; as when one sees a man at a great distance, he is at some loss whether it be a man.

3. Some have certainly seen the workings of grace, but through temptations since, they have lost the certainty of that knowledge; at the time they knew they did believe in Christ, and that they loved God, and could say as *David, Psalm* 116. 1. *I love the Lord*; and as, *Psal.* 46. 1. *The Lord is my strength and refuge*: but afterwards they have not so full and clear a remembrance of it: and God brings them into affliction, and unbelief prevails, and now they are suspicious that they were mistaken; besides, God don't hear their prayers, they have sought him many a time for such & such a mercy, and he has denied them at last: besides, they find a dead heart,

corruption strong, and have had no such plain working of Grace a pretty while, accordingly they are full of fears whether they are not mistaken: they say, if there were no deceit in it, how comes it to be so and so with me?

USE II. Others cannot be certain of a mans sincerity from his Conversation: if others see men carry well, they presently say, they are good men: but they don't know it from thence; there is indeed ground enough for Charity; but not for Assurance: for whatever mens Conversation be, if they don't see the actings of Grace, they cannot be assured that the man is a Godly man. It is not good to depend upon the judgment of others, for they do not know, whether a man be sincere or not. All the external acts of Charity, Piety, Justice and Sobriety, may be performed by a man that has no Grace; Prudence and Conscience may produce them all: and one that has no Grace may carry as well in the eye of the world, as he that has it. *Peter* does but suppose *Silvanus* to be faithful. 1. *Pet.* 5. 12.

Consider 1. The inward actings of Grace are invisible to others. A man may look into his own heart, and see the actings and workings that are there; but he can't look into the hearts of others; men can't tell what actings there be in their understandings and wills: men can't see when they act, nor what they act, nor what they act upon; nor how they act: men can't tell whether they chuse or refuse. *Jer.* 17. 9. *The heart is deceitful above all things, who can know it?*

2. Men cannot by words or actions make the actings of grace so visible to others, that they can distinguish them: if a man talk graciously and walk graciously, he can't make another certain that he does so: another that sees the external action, can't certainly distinguish it from a formal action; if he satisfy another, yet he can't assure another, that it is a gracious action; a man may speak like an Angel, yet not have charity; *he may give all his goods to feed the poor, and his body to be burned, and yet not have charity,* 1 *Cor.* 3. 1, 2, 13.

USE III. *Of Warning,* That you be not confident of your sincerity from your walk, without the certain knowledge that you have performed any act of saving grace: some men will be confident that they are in a good estate, though they do not know that ever they believed in Christ, or have exercised any true love to God: all that they have to say for themselves is, that they have a consciencious care to do their duty, and are many times affected in a religious way, and hope, they do trust in Christ and make the glory of God their end; and they find affection to the people of God: but this you may be sure of, you can't conclude your sincerity from your walk, unless you know that you have performed some act or acts of saving grace: if you do know that, then you have reason to conclude your walk to be holy: where there is one act of saving grace, there will be more: there is the principle, but without this you cannot conclude it.

Consider 1. If you be sincere, this confidence is meer flattery; good men sometimes think they are good upon such foundations as will not hold: as because God does the things that they have prayed for; because he smiles upon them in his Providence; because others think they are Saints: so this is one way of flattery: if you be upright, yet you can't tell it from your walk, if you do not know that you exercise grace: for ought any thing that you know, your life is a life of hypocrisy: men may do all that you know you do, and yet be hypocrites; your walk can't be evidential to you, if you do not see the acts of grace, your confidence is presumption; men must go upon a sure bottom, 2 *Cor.* 13. 5. *Examine your selves, prove your own selves,* & this flattering & sleep that you are fallen into does you much hurt: this makes you neglect a good confidence, and exposes you to live a careless life, without any great matter of the life of religion.

2. If you be not sincere, it may prove your ruine; some men that take notice of their conscientiousness do conclude themselves godly, when they are ungodly: and fall short of a principle of grace: they are destitute of faith and love, *Joh.* 5. 42. *I know you, that you have not the love of God in you*: but because they imagine that they are sincere, they rest in their present attainments, *Joh.* 9. 41. *because you say we see, therefore your sin remaineth*: when they are stirred up to get sincerity, they hope they have it already, they hope others will take the warning, and that their children will hearken, but they think themselves are out of danger: counsels and warnings are lost upon them, they bless themselves in their present estate, they think their disease is cured, and so give over the use of means; they think

they are provided for Eternity, and so they are at rest: they are under some endeavours to get more knowledge and more grace, but not to be Converted: hence this work is neglected; when once they have taken up such a conceit that they are godly, they have got their deaths wound, if mercy do not prevent: they live carelesly, and when they come to dye, they will be shut out of the Kingdom of God: there will be no room for them in heaven, *Mat.* 25. 12. *Depart from me I know you not. Isa.* 50. 11. *all you that kindle a fire and compass your selves about with sparks; walk in the light of your fire, and in the sparks which you have kindled, this shall ye have of mine hand, ye shall lie down in sorrow.*

USE IV. *Of Direction*: To Saints how to get the knowledge of your sincerity; by getting such visible actings of grace, that you may know them certainly to be the acts of saving grace: it is a great exercise to some Saints, whether they be sincere Saints, they labour in it for many years; and one Minister gives signs, and they try themselves by them, and another gives signs, and they try themselves by them; and sometimes they think they see the signs of Saints, and sometimes the sign of hypocrites: and they don't know what to make of themselves: the best way is to get such exercise of grace, that you may know it to be grace; don't let grace lie in a withering condition: let it flourish, that it may act visibly: that you may certainly know it: your walk without this, will never clear up your good condition.

Consider 1. There is good use of signs provided they be true signs warranted by right interpretation of the Scripture; though many signs that men give are very fallible: but if the signs be good, there is very good use to be made of them; though a man may ask signs of signs endlessly; yet they are of good advantage to beget a probable knowledge of a mans good estate; many persons are incouraged and supported by them. 1 *Joh.* 3. 14. *Hereby we know that we are passed from death to life, because we love the brethren*: and they are a further confirmation to those that have had Assurances of their sincerity: when they find Scripture signs falling in with those evidences, which they have formerly received, they are further established thereby.

2. But the visible actings of Grace will satisfy all sorts of Christians. We may distinguish Christians into two sorts; some are persons of great understanding and knowledge, they have a deep insight into those ways of deceit and hypocrisy that the heart is subject to: and they are apt to be puzled with questions and doubts, that fly over the heads of others; they are afraid of such deceits as other men don't suspect: but when they have plain visible workings of Grace, that they know to be Grace, this fully satisfyes them: *Thou knowest that I love thee. Joh.* 21. 17. Others are weak and ignorant and can't give many signs of true Grace, nor distinctly take them up, when they are laid down: yet when they plainly see the visible actings of saving Grace, the thing is put beyond question. A weak woman is as well satisfyed that she loves her child as the wisest man in the land, though she can't make a large discourse upon it, nor prove it by infallible signs, because she feels her love: so it is in this case.

3. Though the visible actings of Grace may be counterfeited, yet they that have them, may know that they have them. There is nothing but may be counterfeited, men may counterfeit themselves to be great men and holy men: Gold and Silver, and Jewels may be counterfeited. So these visible actings of Grace; men may have very strong affections; where there is no love or godly sorrow. *Matt.* 8. 19. *Master I will follow thee whither soever thou goest.* 1 *Sam.* 24. 16. *Saul lift up his voice and wept.* Men may say Hosanna to day, and Crucify to morrow. Yet those that have the visible actings of Grace know it. He that dreams thinks he is awake, but he that is awake, knows he is awake: though there be counterfeits, yet the visible actings may be known at the time.

4. If men have such visible actings of Grace but now and then, they will be of great use to them as long as they live: though they may be after that Exposed to great Temptations, yet these actings of Grace that they have seen, will be a stay to them: they will work on abiding hope in the heart; they will often have occasion to call to mind the years of the right hand of the most high, and their Song in the night. If a man should live many years after, he will not forget this. *Psal.* 63. 2. *That I may see thy power and glory, so as I have seen thee in*

the Sanctuary. If he has great Temptations from deadness and from Gods withdrawings; this will come to mind, and so he will have hope: and the more such acts are repeated, the more advantage he is under to have a settled Assurance of his sincerity.

COTTON MATHER

A Man of Reason

A Brief Essay to demonstrate,
That all Men should hearken to Reason;
and,
What a World of Evil would be prevented in the World,
if Men would once become so Reasonable.

Nam et Communis Intelligentia nobis Res notas efficit, ea
quæ in Animis nostris inchoavit, ut Honesta in Virtute
Ponantur, in Vitiis Turpia.   Cic.

———

JOB XIII. 6.
Hear now my REASONING.

I WILL without any delay at all, Declare what I Design. My
Design is to inculcate a *Doctrine* of this Importance; *That
Men ought to hearken to Reason*. I confess it seems a strange,
and a sad Thing, and little short of a *Satyr* upon Mankind,
That there should be any occasion to inculcate such a *Doctrine*. But I am well *Assured*, and why should I not say, as
much *Ashamed*, That I know not the *Doctrine*, which there is
more occasion to insist upon.

They were *Wise* Men, and they were *Good* Men, whom the
Afflicted *Job* has to do withal; and they were Men of *Reason*
too. But it was a very sensible part of his Affliction, That they
dealt *Unreasonably* with him. He does accordingly take pains
to convince them of their *Unreasonableness*. His Discourse is
introduced with this Preface; *Hear now my Reasoning*. The
Word signifies *A Reasonable Demonstration*; such a *Demonstration* as ought to be brought by a Man, that would hope
to *convince* another Man; an Irrefragable, an unanswerable
Argument. What he says amounts to this; *If I speak reason, I
think, I ought to be heard*. Yea, syr, so you ought, if you had

been the meanest Man in all the *Arabias.* I suppose, No Man will be so Unreasonable as to deny the *Justice* of the Demand. I conclude, Every Man, will pay so much Homage to *Reason,* as to grant me my DOCTRINE, with which I do now again come upon you;

That he that would approve himself a Reasonable Man, must hearken to Reason.

That we may prosecute this *Doctrine* to some Effect, we may first settle the matter, in Two *Self-Evident Propositions.* We shall *speak after the manner of Men,* in delivering of them.

I. There is a *Reasonable Spirit in Man, and the Inspiration of the Almighty has given him an understanding*; and there are certain *Principles of Reason,* which every Man does *naturally* and *ordinarily* bring with him into the World. This is not spoken *without Book*: The *Book* of GOD, has in express Terms asserted it, [*Job* 32. 8.]

There is in every Man an admirable *Spirit.* In that *Spirit,* there is a Faculty called *Reason.* 'Tis that Faculty which is called, *Prov.* 20. 27. *The Spirit of a Man, which is the Candle of the Lord.* By the *Light* of this precious and wondrous *Candle* it is, that we discern the *Connection* & *Relation* of Things to one another. There are certain *Idea's* imprinted on the Spirit of Man, by the GOD, who *forms the Spirit of Man within him.* It is an *Irrational,* as well as an *Unscriptural* Opinion, that we have no *Ideas* in our minds, but what are introduced from abroad, by Observation. There are a rich cluster of *Ideas* which we are born withal, and which are only awakened, and brought into Exercise by Observation. The *Ideas* which I mean, are those, which we call, the *Principles of Reason.* According to these *Principles,* the *Reason* of Men, does pronounce on Things that are plainly brought unto it. *Reason* proceeds according to these *Common* and *Innate Principles,* in passing a *Judgment* on what is plainly laid before it. *Reason* Judges of what is *Mathematically True* or *False.* But this is not all; It Judges as often, and as clearly, what is *morally Good,* or what is *morally Evil*; what is *Right* and what is *Wrong,* in *morality* too. Indeed, there are very many, who do not actually discern, what is morally *Good* or *Evil, Right* or *Wrong*; But so there are many, who do not actually discern *Mathematical Truth* from *Falshood.* There were *Sixscore Thousand*

Persons in *Nenive*, at one time, who did not actually discern, That an Hundred & Twenty would make *Six score*, or twice Five Hundred make a *Thousand*. This is no Objection. For the *Faculty* to discern such Things is in them; The *Principles* upon which these Objects are to be judged of, are already in their minds. When the Objects are laid near enough, and *Reason* comes into play, and the *Sentence* of *Reason* is called for; you may depend upon it, *Reason* which cannot but own, *This is true*; in *Mathematical* points: it will in *Moral* points, as readily own, *This is Good; This is Right; The contrary is not so.*

There is a *Foolish* and *Cursed* Opinion, which has *taken Root*, in a Debauched Generation of Men; who pretend indeed that they *magnify Reason*; Perhaps, their *Brasen Heads* will publish pretended, *Oracles of Reason*: but they go really to *extinguish Reason*, and chase it out of the World. The Opinion is, That nothing is *Good* or *Evil, Right* or *Wrong*, antecedent unto the *Compact* of *Humane Society* upon it: That all the *Difference* between *Good* and *Evil, Right* & *Wrong*, lies in the *Agreement* of *Humane Society* thereupon. These wicked Sons of the *Leviathan* do confute themselves. For they themselves must own, That antecedently unto all *Compact*, it is *Good* & *Right*, that a *Compact* should be kept; It is *Evil* and *Wrong* to break a *Compact*, else they say nothing. But it is too much *Honour* put upon such Wretches, to *Argue* with them; I doubt, whether it be *Prudence* to argue with them.

In brief; There is an *Eternal Difference* between *Good* & *Evil*; between *Right* and *Wrong*. 'Tis constituted by GOD: GOD has inwrought those *Principles* in the *Reasonable Spirit* of Man, which will necessitate him to acknowledge this *Difference*, when it is evidently set before him.

II. There is all possible *Reason* [Excuse the *Pleonasm* of the Expression,] why every Man should *Hearken to Reason*; or do nothing against the *Principles of Reason*. There are many *Principles of Reason*; But, I take this to be the very *First* of them; *That a Man ought to act according to them*; Or, *That a Reasonable Man must hearken to Reason*.

It were a very *unreasonable* Thing to put me upon the *Proof* of this Assertion; Or, demand of me a *Reason*, why a Man should *hearken to Reason*. Yet I will, for a *Reason*, by' and by to be mention'd, proceed upon it.

First; The Man who does not *Hearken to Reason*, does
Rebel against the Glorious GOD, who has placed Man under
the Guidance of *Reason*. It were mightily for the *Honour* of
GOD, and for the *Welfare* of Men, if Men were apprehensive,
That they have to do with GOD, in the affairs of Humane
Life, oftner than is commonly imagined. I will particularly entreat, that this may be received as a very certain position; We
have to do with GOD, as often as we have *Right Reason*
calling upon us. I shall have opportunity anon to clear this
Position, from the Infection which the *Heresies* of corrupt
minds may give unto it. And I will now say, We never *Transgress* any *Law of Reason*, but we do at the same time, *Transgress* the *Law of GOD*. Now, there is always a *Sin*, the blackest
thing in the World! in such a *Transgression*. GOD sets up
Reason in Man. If we do not keep *Reason* in the *Throne*, we
go to *Dethrone* the Infinite GOD Himself. The voice of
Reason, is the *Voice of GOD*. GOD speaks, as often as *Reason*
and *Wisdom utters its Voice*. GOD who has furnished us with
Reason, has required us, to be obedient unto the *Dictates of
Reason*. To Man, He says, *Let Reason be thy Guide; Never go
against thy well-enlightened Reason*. We have received this
Order from GOD our Maker; *Isai*. 46. 8. *Show your selves
Men*. That is to say, Act *Reasonably*; Do like *Reasonable Men*.
How many *Appeals to Reason*, do we find in the Word of
GOD? Ever now and then, we have a passage of that impor-
tance; 1 *Cor*. 11. 13. *Judge in your selves*. And, *Act*. 4. 19.
Whether it be Right, Judge ye. Such Things had never been
spoken, if this were not incontestable; That if we shake off the
Government of *Reason*, we shake off the *Government* of our
Great *Creator*, who has put *Reason* into us, as the *Grand
Instrument* of His *Government* over us. When we don't
Hearken to Reason, we say, *GOD Himself shall not Reign over
us!* A *Rebellion*, Horrible to be thought upon!

Secondly. The Man who does not *Hearken to Reason*, is
very *Unthankful* to GOD, for Endowing, Enriching, Ennobling of him with *Reason*. So dreadfully do they stand stig-
matized, who do not *Hearken to Reason*; *Rom*. 1. 21. *Neither
were they thankful. Reason*, 'Tis a *Noble* Thing; It makes *Man*
a *Noble* Creature. It is the *Glory* of Man; It is the *Glorious
Image* of GOD upon him. *Reason*, 'Tis That wherein we

excel the *Beasts of the Field*. Thou, *Reason*, dwellest with *Prudence*; and thou findest out the *knowledge of witty Inventions; Counsel is thine, and sound Wisdom & Strength*. By Thee, Man is able to Rule over other *Men*, as well as over the *Beasts* of the Earth: Thou art the *Sword* in the Hand of *all the Judges of the Earth*. GOD giving *Reason* to Man, his *Privilege* is inexpressible. *Reasonable* and *Priviledged* MAN, should *Thankfully* say upon it; *Isai*. 28. 26, 29. *God does instruct him to Discretion, & does teach him. This cometh forth from the Lord of Hosts, who is wonderful in Counsel, & excellent in Working*. To do *Unreasonably* is to do most *Unthankfully*. When a Man will not *Hearken to Reason*, he despises the *peculiar Advantage of Mankind*; He that won't go *according to Reason*, blasphemes and proclaims, That it is better to *Go without Reason*. He debases the *Nature* of MAN. He treads under foot the most illustrious *Jewel* in the World. He says, He had rather GOD had made him a *Beast*, than made him a *Man*. O monstrous *Ingratitude*!

Thirdly. The Man who does not *Hearken to Reason*, does the part of a *Brute*, yea, he does worse than a *Brute*, that is destitute of *Reason*. We read of *Bruitish Men*; and of those who are, *Jude* 10. *As Brute Beasts*: Men, who as far as they can, quit the order of *Men*, & rank themselves with *Brutes*. Verily, A *Man* who does not *Hearken to Reason*, so far *Unmans* himself; Transforms himself so far into a *Brute*. It is a *Bruitish* Thing, to refuse the Direction of *Reason*. A *Man* who abandons the *Rules of Reason* in what he does,—Pardon me, wretch, that I *miscall'd* thee, A *Man*; I will *Recall* it— Such a *Brute* is worthy to be addressed with nothing but *Sarcasm*, and *Satyr*; Go, Thou *Brute*, Get a little more *Hair*, and crawl upon *all Four*, and come not among the *Children of Reason* any more. Don't count me too severe; I will speak a thing, which to me seems but *Reasonable*. When it shall be with all convenient Solemnity put unto a Man, Whether he do not own such or such a thing to be *Reasonable*? He *does* own it; He *must* own it: And yet he will not *Hearken to Reason*; he will deliberately go against it, act *Unreasonably*. Such a Man *deserves* to be chased out of the Conversation of Men: The *Desert* of such a Man would be, to be sent a grazing with *Nebuchadnezzer*, among the *Brutes* of the Field.

How bitterly were the People upbraided of old! *Isai.* 1. 3. *The Ox knows his owner, & the Ass his Masters crib; but my people does not consider.* A Man that will not *consider* what is *Reasonable*, is like the Ox and the *Ass*; yea, he is much worse than they. To go *Against Reason*, is worse than to be *Without Reason.* For a *Man* to *Bruitify* himself:—*Oh! Do not this Abominable thing!*

Fourthly, There is a *Conscience* in the Case. The Man that will not *Hearken to Reason*, goes against the *Light* of his *Conscience.* There is a *Conscience* in Man, which commends unto him, what is *Reasonable*; which condemns him to suffer the Vengeance of GOD, if he do that which is not *Reasonable.* We read, *Rom.* 2. 15. *There is the work of the Law written in their Hearts, their Conscience also bearing witness.* What is *Conscience*, but, *Reason submitting to the Judgment of GOD?* When a Man will not *Hearken to Reason*, he is one of those, who, *Job.* 24. 13. *Rebel against the Light.* The *Conscience* of a Man, forewarns him, and assures him, of a *Punishment* reserved in another World; *A Strange punishment for the workers of Iniquity.* His *Reason* will give him some warning of it. Hence we read; *Act.* 24. 25. *As Paul Reasoned of Righteousness, Temperance, & Judgment to come, Felix trembled.* The *Reason* of the miserable Man, being minded of his *Bribery*, & his *Drusilla*, told him such uneasy things, that he had no way to be quiet, but by never hearing the Servant of GOD Preach any more. A Mans *Reason* will tell him, that he ought to live *Righteously*, and live *Temperately*; Not *Abuse* others, nor himself. His *Reason* will tell him, that he must give unto the GOD of his Life, an *Account* of his Life; in which he shall be Judged according to the *Law* that GOD has given him. The *Conscience* of the Sinner, is operating all this while; And if he will not *Hearken to Reason* in these things his *Conscience* will employ dreadful Scourges upon him. A Man will be dreadfully Scourged & Scalded by an enraged *Conscience* in another World, for doing such things, as his *Reason* forbad his doing of.

The *Reason* of my speaking these things is, that I may come out the better armed for the Expedition which I am now to make, against an *Host* of *Unreasonable things*, which are every day doing among us. You see, my Hearers, what *Thick-Bosses of a Buckler* you have to run upon, if you will not *Suffer that*

Word of Exhortation, with which I am now to call upon you. *Hearken to Reason*; That is the EXHORTATION. You see there is abundance of *Reason*, that you should *hearken* to it.

There are certain *Maxims of Reason*, which I am now to set before you. But they shall be every one of them, Glorious *Maxims of Religion*. They shall every one of them call upon you, as he once did upon his Countrymen; *Hearken to me, that GOD may hearken to you another Day.*

First. *Hear now my Reasoning.* We are to *Distinguish* between what is, *Against Reason*; & what is, *Above Reason.* We must not call a Thing *Unreasonable*, meerly because unto us, it is *Incomprehensible.* We must not so *Hearken to Reason*, as to make an *Idol* of *Reason*: or to admit nothing as a *Revelation* from GOD, but what we can fathom, with our little *Reason.* There is no *Reason* for *That.* There are *Mysteries* in the *Christian Religion*; incomprehensible *Mysteries: Three Persons* United in ONE GOD; *Two Natures* United in the ONE PERSON of our *Immanuel*: The *Resurrection* of the Dead, into a Life of Immortality, in the cælestial *City*: and the like *Mysteries*, that carry with them their *Astonishments.* We read; *Job.* 11. 7. *Canst thou by searching find out GOD? Canst thou find out the Almighty unto Perfection?* Even so; Canst thou by *Searching find out* the *Mysteries* in the Religion of GOD? Canst thou *find out the Great Mysteries of Godliness unto Perfection?* It must not be pretended unto!

There was of late Years a Notable Experiment of this matter. The *Pelagians* every where decried the *Doctrines of Grace*; yea, tho' they subscribed them, they decried them. The cry was; *Reason* could not comprehend them; They did not square well with *Reason.* Well; when this cry for a while had carried all before it, anon the *Socinians* begun theirs. Gentlemen, we hope you won't oblige us to believe the *Trinity* of Persons in GOD, & the *Godhead* and *Sacrifice* of our Saviour; why *Reason* cannot comprehend them; They don't square well with *Reason.* This made Men see, how presumptuously the *Gospel* may be betray'd by pretences of *Reason*, too far insisted on.

This *Reason* will do. It will demonstrate it unto us, That the *Scriptures* are the *Word of GOD*, & the *Book of Truth.* If you will *Hearken to Reason*, you must confess, That Writings full of such *Holiness*, and *Wisdom*, & *Grandeur*, & exquisite *contrivance* and Heavenly *Intention*, as compose our Bible, must needs be of Divine Originat. But there are many things in the *Scriptures* which are, *Above Reason*. Our shallow *Reason* must not be set up, as the measure of what is to be Received, as a *Faithful Saying*, & *Worthy of all Acceptation*. *Faith, Faith* is here to interpose. *Reason*, Stand thou by, with an humble *Reverence*, an awful *Silence*. In the *Scriptures*, there is nothing *Against Reason*, tho' there be some things *Above Reason*. It must also be remembred, that by our Fall from GOD, the strength of *Reason* is much impaired in us; the Eye of *Reason* is darkened, is depraved, is miserably wounded. We are prone to take some things, as according to *Reason*, which are not so. If then there be any thing prescribed in the Sacred *Scriptures*, which our *carnal Reason*, may be ready to cavil at, say not, *I can't see Reason for this*. There is a famous Instance, for this caution. The way prescribed in the Gospel, for the *Justification of a Sinner*: O Sinner, 'Tis, that thou repair with all thy *Sinfulness*, and without any *Righteousness* of thy own, unto the Lord JESUS CHRIST; hoping to be *Justified* before GOD, only by pleading of that wonderful *Righteousness*. Proud Man will try to make his *Reason* invent a World of objections against this *Glorious Gospel of the Blessed GOD*. But if there be *Scripture* for any thing, lay this down for a Maxim, There is *Reason* for it. Perhaps we can't see the *Reason*: But *Reason* says, The *Scripture* is a *Revelation* from GOD: And *Reason* says, what GOD has *Revealed* must be *Reasonable*. But then also, Vain Man, Do not imagine, That they *Light within*, or the *Light* of *Reason*, is a *Sufficient Guide* without the *Scripture*, to bring thee unto Salvation: much more, To make a *Christ*, and a *God* of that *Light*, it is a dangerous *Idolatry*. We must *Hearken to Right Reason*: but beware, Lest we ascribe too much, to our own *broken Faculties*.

Secondly. *Hear now my Reasoning*, There is a *Golden Rule of Reason*, which well-applied, would wonderfully rectify the Conversation of Mankind: Even that Rule, *For a Man to do unto others, as he would own it reasonable for others to do unto him*. Our Saviour has Honoured & Confirmed this *Rule* with His own Royal Stamp upon it; *Matth.* 7. 12. *All things whatsoever ye would that Men should do to you, do ye even so to them*.

Yea; but it is a *Rule* engraven by the Hand of GOD, upon the *Reason* of Mankind. There is no *Reasonable* Man, but what will fall down before this *Rule*, and say, *'Tis an Excellent Rule! Happy, Happy would the World be, if this Rule might bear Rule in the World.* You may as easily bring a Man to own this *Rule*, as to own that *Three* and *Four* make *Seven*. And the Man that will say, 'Tis *unjust* for another Man to do so & so unto me, but it is not *unjust* in me to do the same unto him, will presently prove himself as great a *Sott*, as he that shall say, *Three* & *Four* make *Seven*, but *Four* & *Three* won't do so. The *Rule* has been acknowledged, both among *Jews* & *Gentiles.* They have sometimes expressed it positively; *Quod tibi fieri non vis, alteri ne feceris.* The *Talmuds* of the *Jews*, have those words, *Do not that unto another, which thou hatest, when it is done unto thy self.* 'Tis also in the *Apocrypha.* Among the *Gentiles*, how often do their moral Writers recommend it? I might bring an *Army* of them. Their *General* shall be that *Roman Emperour*, who had it in his mouth continually, and made the Officers of the Empire to put it into publick Proclamations.

A very considerable part of our Duty, is, *What we owe to one another.* Might this *One Rule* be *hearkened* unto, what a vast influence would it have upon the Discharge of our Duty! In our Treating of other People, their *Place*, their *Peace*, their *Bed*, their *Wealth*, their *Name*, any Article of their *Prosperity*, Syrs, *Hear now my Reasoning*; we should come to think, *Should others do by me, just as I do by them, Say, O my Reason, Say Impartially, would it be my Duty to think it Reasonable?*

There is a most notorious violation of this *Golden Rule*, in those *Persecutions* which at any time worry the *Churches* and *Servants* of GOD. *Persecutors* are called, 2 *Thes.* 3. 2. *Unreasonable Men.* Those *Unreasonable Men*, while they are uppermost, what vile Things will they do? Things that the very *Hottentots* of *Africa* would cry, *Shame* upon. Let there be any *Turn* of the Times, & let them have no other *Harm* done them, except only to Restrain them from doing *Harm* to others, what an outcry do they make, as if they were the most oppressed People that ever were in the World. They rage, & roar, & bring Heaven & Earth together. *Come not into their secret, O my Soul! O my Tongue, speak not a word for their Assembly.*

But, *Hear now my Reasoning*: Whatever would seem *Hard* in others towards *ourselves*, Nothing, Nothing of that should be found, in what we do towards *others*. I press this Advice, with the greatest Importunity; & I will a little particularize it.

This Advice, ought very particularly to take place, in the *Business* which Men have with one another; their *Traffic*, their *Commerce*. There are those *Dealers*, who may provoke this Expostulation; 'Man, wouldest not thou complain of it, if another Man should use that *Fraudulence* or *Extortion* towards thee, which thou dost put upon him? Wouldest thou not be full of Complaints, if another Man should *withold* from thee thy Dues, or *Delay* to make up Accompts with thee, or deny or obstruct thy *Just Satisfaction*, as thou dost unto him? *Hear now my Reasoning*; For thee to persist in this way, 'tis Abominable, 'tis Inexcusable!'

Again, This Advice ought mightily to Regulate the Carriage of *Relatives* to one another. We sustain several *Relations* to one another. Now let us in our Thoughts *Change Relations* with our *Correlates*; put our selves into *their Circumstances*. *Consorts*, Think, what *Goodness* you would wish from your *Consorts*, if *you* were *They*, and *They* were *you*. *Parents*, make your selves *Children*; *Children*, make your selves *Parents*. *Masters* & *Servants*, *Rulers* & *Subjects*, enterchange Conditions with one another. Think; *What would I expect, if I were he! What should I Resent, if I were what he now is?* My Friend, *Hear now my Reasoning*; Certainly, it becomes *thee* to do, as thou wouldest have *him* to do; For *thee* to do, what thou wouldest be vex'd if *he* should do, 'tis against all the *Reason* in the World.

Yea; This Incomparable *Rule of Reasoning*, you will find it applicable to the Government of all your *Actions*, and of all your *Passions*. When I examine it over again, I find it *Exceeding Broad*; extendible to a much Broader Application, than I at first imagined. In the case of Sorrow for a *Dead Friend*: Suppose, I were *Dead*; would I have my Friend mourn for me, with an Excessive, Oppressive, Destructive *Sorrow*. No, sure. Why then let my *Sorrow* for my *Friend*, be discreetly moderated. Yea, I find a Person of Quality observing, That without offence, our Duty towards our Creator, may from this very *Rule of Reason* receive some Direction.

For, if we had *Power to Create*, we should certainly expect from our *Creatures*, all the Love, all the Reverence, all the Obedience imaginable. Then, O Man, Render it unto *thy Creator*!

Thirdly, *Hear now my Reasoning*. It stands to *Reason*, that in passing of *Censures*, we should not make *Flesh* of one, & *Fish* of another. We read; 1 *Tim.* 5. 21. Of, *Doing nothing by Partiality*. The Greek Word, for, *Partiality, Procklisis*, is as much as to say, *A Tilting the Ballance on one side*. Unreasonable *Partiality*! How often, how often, is the Ballance of *Justice* turned with it!

One Man shall suffer, I know not what, Exclamations. *Another* Man shall come, and do the same thing, yea, much worse; and not a Word must be spoken of it: or perhaps, 'tis laudable in *him*. This is not *Reasonable*!

If a thing be decried as a *Folly*, or a *Baseness*, in a Man of another Party, 'tis but *Reason*, that it should be decried in one of our own Party too. And so, If old *Eli*, can see Faults in other People, & their Families, 'tis but *Reason*, that he should not wink at the same Faults in his *own Children*. If Sinners of an *Inferiour Quality* must be punished for their misdemeanours, 'tis but *Reason*, that the *Bigger sort* of Sinners also should not pass unpunished. There is no *Reason*, for *Laws* to be *Cobwebs*, only to catch the *Little Flies*, and let the *Greater Birds* break through them.

Fourthly. *Hear now my Reasoning*. It is but *Reason*, that a Man should not be *Condemned*, without any *Hearing* of what may be pleaded for him. It was of old said; *Act.* 25. 16. *It is not the manner of the Romans to deliver any Man to dye, before that he which is Accused, have Licence to answer for himself, concerning the Crime laid against him.* Even so; It is not the manner of the *Reasonable*, to condemn a Man as a *Criminal*, without first Hearing, or Knowing, what may be said in his Defence. If this one Demand of *Reason* might be hearkened unto, what would become of the *Defamations*, with which we commonly keep wounding one another! We *Curse the Deaf*: we Accuse, we Expose, we Revile, those who can't speak for themselves. They are *Absent*. We have not understood, what *Reason* they might have to do, what we are so ready to blame them for. O *Unreasonable*! *Reason* says, *Audi alterum partem*.

A Man has *Two Ears.* 'Tis *monstrous* to have both of them on *one side.* Reserve one of them; it may be 'tis that *Reserved Ear,* that *Reason* is to enter at.

Fifthly. *Hear now my Reasoning:* Methinks, 'Tis no more than *Reason* that Men should curb their *Passion,* and not let that usurp the place of *Reason.* If Men are of a boisterous, raging, raving, (I will not say, *Temper,* but rather) *Distemper,* there is little of *Reason* to be expected in their Doings. The *Bridle* of *Reason* is cast off, and *Passion,* Headstrong *Passion* will precipitate them, into very unreasonable Exorbitancies & Enormities. Ah, *Fury,* how *unseemlily* dost thou *Behave thy self!* The bravest Man in the World, once in a *Passion,* broke both *Tables* of the *Law.* Fearful Breaches are made upon the *Law* of *Reason,* when *Men* let their *Passion* govern them. How loathsome then will be the Behaviour of those *Cholerick* Folks, that are almost always in a *Fury!* We read, *Eccl.* 9. 17. *The words of Wise Men are heard in Quiet.* The *Rules of Reason,* & of *Wisdom,* are not heard, but when *Passion* lies *Quiet.* We are forbidden to make any *Friendship* with a *Furious Man.* Why so? Because he is a Man that will not *Hearken to Reason.* We are told, *The Wrath of Man will not work,* that *Righteousness,* and *Reasonableness,* which GOD would have His People always maintain among them. Oh! moderate, & mortify all uncomely *Passion.* Let *Reason,* calm *Reason,* cool *Reason* have the upper-hand.

Sixthly. *Hear now my Reasoning:* In the *Churches* of GOD, when matters of *Prudence* occur, why should *Plain Reason* be laid aside, meerly because Men do not see *Express Institution?* A Church of the Lord JESUS CHRIST, must keep close to His *Institution;* & no parts or means of *Divine Worship* are to be introduced there, without His *Institution.* Our *Loyalty* to the Son of GOD, in this Point, is with Infinite *Reason,* to be preserved Inviolable. But yet, our Lord JESUS CHRIST, when He *Instituted* particular *Churches,* did presuppose them, to Consist of *Reasonable* People. The *Common Law* of *Reason,* whereto all *Societies* as such, are to conform themselves, is always *presupposed.* There was no need at all, of any *Institution* for such Things to be done in Churches, as *Reason* tells us are to be done in all *Societies.* This will give no advantage to *Superstitions* & *Ceremonies*, of *Will-Worship*, *Usur-pations* which have no *Warrant* in the Word of GOD. But then it will rebuke some *Unreasonable Practices*, that creep into Churches, & have a tendency to render them *Unreasonable Societies*, which they ought not to be. When some *Irregularities* did show their *Heads* in the Church of *Corinth*, our Apostle so rebuked them; 2 *Cor.* 11. 14. *Doth not even Nature it self teach you otherwise?* Thus, I will say; Shall a Member of One Church, have his *Relation* to it fully transferred unto another, without some *Declared Allowance* of the Church to which he formerly belonged, where it can be obtained? *Nature itself teaches otherwise.* Shall any *One Church* refuse to show any Respect unto the countenance of any *Neighbouring Churches*, and yet require to be countenanced as such, in all the Churches? *Nature itself teaches otherwise.* And, I think, I do more than *think*; a *Covenant* is to be look'd upon as *mutual.* There is a *Covenant* between the *Pastor* & the *People.* The *Pastor* must not leave the *People*, must serve them Day and Night; But it seems, the *People* owe no Regards unto the *Pastor.* They may without saying one word unto him, utterly withdraw from his *Ministry*, & his *Communion*; yea, tho' they continue to live in the same Town with him. This is *Reason*; is it? No, 'Tis a *Scandal. Nature itself teaches otherwise.*

Seventhly. *Hear now my Reasoning: Reason* says, That it is a most aggravated Wickedness, for a *Christian* to do that, which a sober *Pagan* would blush to do. I remember, That *Festus*, would not permit a barbarous thing to be done unto a Famous Minister of the Gospel; and the *Reason* he gave was this; *Act.* 25. 27. *It seems to me unreasonable.* This Ruler was a *Pagan*; & he was not the best Man in the World. Yet an oppressed Servant of GOD, found more *fair dealing* from this *Pagan*, than he did from his own Countrymen, who called themselves, *The People of GOD.* They would have done such *Things*, as Governour *Festus* would abhor to do. A Man shall sometimes be more fairly dealt withal among *Pagans* themselves, than among some that would be call'd, *The People of GOD.* Professed *Christians* will sometimes deal more basely than many *Infidels.* They will be called, *Most Christian*, and yet the *Turks* be *Saints* to 'em. *Church-Members* will sometimes more basely shuffle with you, & abuse you more *ungratefully* & *unreasonably*, than People that make no Profession at all. They will before the Face of the *Court* itself, be detected in such Actions, that were *Festus* the Judge, & *Plutarch* the Foreman of the Jury, they would be cried out upon. Syrs, Is this *Reasonable*? The *Pagans* have only the Light of *Reason*. We have the Light of *Reason*, & the much brighter Light of the *Gospel*. But, as it was said, *Go to the Ant, thou Sluggard*: So, shall it be said, *Go to the Pagan, thou Christian, & receive thy Condemnation!* Would *Aristides* have so play'd the knave; whom they Syrnamed, *The Just*? Would *Fabritius* have been so *Covetous*, who would not receive a *Bribe* on any terms? Would *Regulus* have been so *Treacherous*, who would not break his *Word* unto his very Enemies? *Regulus*, a Man so true to his Country, that rather than have it hurt, he would expose himself to all the *Tortures* that his Enemies could inflict upon him! Alas, That the *Pagan* should condemn the *Christian*! *Reason*! *Reason*, makes a fearful cry on this occasion: *Oh! Let it not be so!*

Lastly. Behold, An Engine, to batter all *Impiety*! *Hear now my Reasoning.* It is from a prodigious Hardness of Heart, if Men will not be *Reasoned* out of all *Impiety*. Of all ungodly Men, we read, *Psal*. 14. 4. *They have no Knowledge*; They act, as if they had *no Reason* in them. We may strike all *Impiety*, with the *Lightning* of *Reason* as well as with the *Thunder* of *Scripture*. It is a most flaming Aggravation, [and, Oh! that it were more considered!] of the *Impiety* committed in the World, That the Plain *Rules of Reason* are therein boldly contradicted, grosly superseded. There are certain *Principles of Religion*, which must be acknowledged by the *Reason* of all Men, as much as any *Principles of the Mathematicks*. A *Reasonable Creature*, you may compel him to acknowledge, That *Two* & *Two* make *Four*; or, That a *Square* is double to a *Triangle*, of Equal *Base* and *Heighth*. The proportions in *Arithmetic* and *Geometry*, he must needs acknowlege them. You may as easily compel him, to acknowledge, That there is a GOD, who must be *Ador'd* & *Obey'd*: you may compel him, to acknowledge, That he ought not to offer unto his *Neighbour*, any thing which if he himself were in the *State* of that

Neighbour, he would count an *Injury*. Now, upon Transgressions on these *Two Points*, there turns all the Wickedness of the World.

I must then arraign all *Wickedness* before the Bar of *Reason*. Ah! *Shameful* wickedness! Ah! wicked Man; when *Reason* does come, as it must one day come, to be heard, it must be said of the Things done by thee; *Rom.* 6. 21. *They are the Things, whereof you are now ashamed.*

It is an awful Work, which I am now upon. *Hear now my Reasoning.* I must call upon you, as the Prophet of old; 1 *Sam.* 12. 7. *Now stand still, that I may Reason with you, before the Lord.* I will propound unto you some Assertions of *Practical Religion*, which you must every one of you, acknowledge to be *Reasonable*. The Man who does not acknowledge them, does cast off, and Slander, & Smother his own *Reason*. The Man who does acknowlege them, & yet will *Practically Renounce* them; GOD will, with the *Briars* & *Thorns* of his Affronted *Reason, tear him in pieces*, & there shall be *none to deliver him*.

First. *Reason* says, There is a GOD, the *Maker* & *Ruler* of the World. *Hear now my Reasoning.* It is but *Reasonable*, That this GOD should be *Sought* & *Serv'd* by all the Men in the World. For a Man, to live without *Prayer* to GOD: For a Man to *Do* any thing, which he knows, that GOD has forbidden him to do; I will add, For a *Family* which depends on GOD for His Blessings, to live without any Homage to GOD: certainly, There is not one Man among you, but what will acknowledge, 'Tis against *Reason*, that it should be so.

Secondly. *Reason* says, That all our *Enjoyments*, are the *Blessings* and *Favours* of GOD. The *Devil* himself will say so much: We read, *Job.* 1. 10. *Satan said, Thou hast blessed the work of his hands, and his substance is increased in the Land.* A Man who when he has the comfortable *Things* of an *Increased Substance* about him, will not own, *These are the Blessings of GOD*: Such a Man is in this, worse than a *Devil*. But; *Hear now my Reasoning*: Surely, 'Tis but *Reasonable*, That a Man should study how to use his *Blessings* and *Comforts*, for the Service of GOD. That GOD should *Bless* a Man, and the Man *Serve* none but himself: I beseech you, Syrs, What *Reason* for that!

Thirdly. *Reason* says, That the *Soul* of a Man requires as much care to be well provided for, as his *Body*. We *Rise up Early*, we *Sit up Late*, we *Eat the Bread of Sorrows*. All to provide for a *Body*, that can't be kept long undissolved. *Hear now my Reasoning*. It is but *Reasonable* sure, That we should be more sollicitous, about the Happiness of a *Soul*, which must be Happy or Undone, after the Death of the *Body*. Our Lord Redeemer spoke a most *Reasonable* Thing; *Matth.* 16. 26. *What is a Man profited, if he gain the whole World, and lose his own Soul?* A Thing so *Reasonable*, that it is in the Writings of the Heathens themselves to be met withal! For a Man to be so taken up with the World, as to do nothing for his *Reasonable Soul*; Verily, 'Tis a thing against all the *Reason* in the World.

Fourthly. We all say, *We desire the Grace of GOD. Reason* says, we ought then to attend the *Means of Grace; Means* in our use of which we may hope, that he will dispense His *Grace. Hear now my Reasoning*; To think, That GOD should give us *Faith* in His Christ, without our Attentive *Hearing* of His Word, when *Faith comes by Hearing*: To think, That GOD should give us *Help* against *Sin*, without our *Asking*, & Crying, & Weeping to Him, for His *Help*; To think, That GOD should *Save us*, & we never set apart any Time to *work out our own Salvation*; What *Reason* have we to look for such Things? For, *Ezek.* 36. 37. *Thus saith the Lord God, I will yet for this be Enquired of.*

Fifthly. *Hear now my Reasoning*; 'Tis *Unreasonable*, O our Young People, 'Tis *Unreasonable*, to give the *Prime* of your Strength, to *Sin* and *Satan*, and reserve only an *Uncertain Old Age* for your only *SAVIOUR*. A Glorious CHRIST Exhibits Himself unto you. In His *Gospel* He has done enough to assure the *Reason* of all Mankind. That He is what He is; The *Son of GOD*, the *Prince of Life*, the *Lord of all*. 'Tis but *Reason*, That you should immediately Embrace Him, and Resign and Devote your selves unto Him. There is all the *Reason* imaginable in that Exhortation; *Eccl.* 12. 1. *Remember now thy Creator, in the days of thy Youth*. To continue in the Drudgeries of the *Devil*, and think; *Hereafter, But I know not when, I will hearken to my SAVIOUR*: Oh! Say, Is not this

Unreasonable? Then in the Name of GOD, we charge you, Don't venture upon a thing so *Unreasonable.* What would you do, if you could see the *Heavens opened,* and have a view of the Glories there? would you not say, *Nothing would be so Reasonable, as for me Betimes to lay hold on Eternal Life!* What would you do, if you could look down into the *Horrible Pit,* and see the Torments of the Damned in the Place of Dragons! would you not say, *Nothing would be so Reasonable as for me to flee from this Wrath to come?* Oh! why will you not now do, what you could not but own to be *Reasonable,* if you saw things as they are? Or, when a *Dying Hour* comes upon you, will you not pronounce *Early Religion,* the most *Reasonable* thing in the World? My Children, your *Dying Hour* is hastning upon you. But this is what I am in the last place to advise you of.

Lastly. My Hearers; You are *Dying;* you are *Dying;* you will *Dye Speedily;* you may *Dye Suddenly.* You are called, you know not how soon, out of the World. Presently, presently, to make *Ready* for it, is the most *Reasonable* Thing in the World. You make *Ready* for *Death,* by *Repenting* of all *Sin,* and Renouncing all your Sinful Vanities; by *Embracing* of the Great GOD, for your GOD, His CHRIST for your compleat and only Redeemer; *by Resolving* upon a Life of Serious PIETY. Till you are thus made *Ready,* you are every Day in a Danger, wherein a *Reasonable* Man would not Sleep a Night, for a Thousand Worlds! Awake, O *Reason,* Awake! And Oh! That Men would *Reasonably* consider, *That* they are a *Dying,* and *What* they would chuse and wish, when they come to *Dye.* I have read of one, who at once performed a great *Exploit,* and committed a great *Offence.* He was therefore honoured with the Sword of *Knighthood;* but at the same time a *Burning Match* was laid by him, and he was condemned to suffer a terrible Death as soon as that *Match* was burnt out. Syrs, you enjoy your Delights and Honours; Oh! but the *Burning Match!* Your Lives are that *Burning Match.* Do you know what will become of you, when that *Match* is burnt out? What an horrible Punishment is reserved for you, if you are found in ill Terms with Heaven! *Hear now my Reasoning.* Something should be done about the matter, Effectually done, & Immediately done. I beseech you, delay not the doing of it.

But the *Crooked Things*, that are against *Reason*, among us, cannot be Numbred! However, let these be *Reformed*, these be *Redressed*; and the rest will of course quickly be so too.

FINIS

BENJAMIN COLMAN

The Case of Satan's Fiery Darts in Blasphemous Suggestions and Hellish Annoyances

As they were considered in Several Sermons,
Heretofore preach'd to the Congregation in Brattle-Street,
Boston, May 1711. and lately repeated to them May 1743.
And now publish'd at the Desire of some, who having
suffer'd by such Temptations, would thus (by the Will of
GOD) minister to the Direction and Support of Others in
like spiritual Trouble and Distress.

Rom. xvi. 20. *The* GOD *of Peace shall bruise Satan under*
your Feet shortly: The Grace of our LORD JESUS
CHRIST *be with you: Amen.*

———

JOB II. 9, 10.
Then said his Wife unto him, Dost thou still retain thine
Integrity? curse GOD and die: But he said unto her,
Thou speakest as one of the foolish Women speaketh;
what? shall we receive good at the Hand of GOD, and
shall we not receive evil? In all this did not Job sin with
his Lips.

WE HAVE HEARD of the *Patience of Job*, and seen the *End of
the* LORD; which some excellent *Expositors* have said was to
give an early and *illustrious Type* of the *Humiliation of*
CHRIST, and *his Sufferings*, in his Way to Glory and
Exaltation, as our *Intercessor* at the right Hand of GOD.

Among the many excelling Examples and *Patterns* given us
thro' the *Holy Scriptures*, of *Suffering* Affliction and Patience,
no One is more remarkable, noble and illustrious, teaching
and affecting than that of JOB's; in the surprising *first and second* Assault of *Satan* upon his *Family, Estate* and *Person.*

The Sovereign and gracious GOD had prov'd *his Grace* in

this his Servant in a long *prosperous State*; and now was pleas'd to make a sudden *Change* upon him, for an equal *Display* of the Power and Glory of his Grace in a State of *deepest Affliction.*

Satan was greedy of a Permission to tempt and *sift* him, as he afterward was to try *Peter.* The cruel *Devil* spoil'd him of his Substance, and bereaved him of his *Children* and Servants in one Day; and that in so terrible and *judicial* a Manner as might speak most dreadfully the immediate Hand and utmost Indignation of *Heaven*: But failing of his *Wish*, hereby to provoke him to *curse* GOD; he ask'd a further Permission to *smite his Body* from Head to Foot, with *Boils* and fiery *Ulcers*, extreamly *painful* and tormenting, as well as *filthy* and loathsome. It was the Pleasure of *Sovereign Grace*, to permit *this* also, that the *Trial of Faith* in his *chosen Servant* might be found to *Praise* and *Honour and Glory* thro' all Generations of the *Church* on Earth, and at the *Day* of the Coming of CHRIST to Judgment.

But no Word *amiss* falling from the afflicted *Saint*, in this his *destitute and tormented* State; no Words but of *profound* Humility, Resignation, Worship and Thanksgiving, dropping from his Lips; the subtle *Tempter* having spent all his outward *Forces*, betook himself to his hellish *Craft* and Policy, and annoy'd his gracious *Soul* with diabolical *Suggestions* and *blasphemous* Thoughts against GOD; to second him in which he excited his *Wife*, whom the spiteful *Fiend* seems to have left to him on Design to make *her* his *Tempter* and Tormentor.— So he afterward grieved our blessed SAVIOUR; against whom not prevailing by more immediate Assaults in the *Wilderness*, he us'd the unwary and rash Lips of *Peter*, and got him that just Rebuke, "*Get thee behind me, Satan.*"

Her Words in my *Text* are very *gross*, and smell rank of *Hell; Then said his Wife to him, Dost thou still retain thy Integrity? curse GOD and die.*

I am not ignorant that the *Hebrew* is capable of another *Sense*, and that some make it a Piece of *gracious Advice*, "*Bless God, and expire*": But I adhere to our *Translation*, which perfectly agrees with *Job's Reply* to her; "*Thou speakest as a foolish Woman! What, shall we receive Good at the Hand of GOD, and shall we not receive Evil?*"

Some think her Words spoken in Way of profane *Sarcasm*, from a vext and inraged Heart; q.d. "Yes, *keep on blessing GOD!* for *what* I pray! for *Plagues* and Want? and to what *Fruit?* to *perish* praising! persist then, and *die as a Fool dieth.*" —But more *simply* taken, and as our *Translators* give 'em, they are a Piece of *profane and furious Counsel*; cast off thy Reverence of the DIVINE MAJESTY, and dare to reproach that GOD who can deal so hardly and *unjustly* by thee; notwithstanding all thy religious Services and Worship, thy Devotion and Integrity; "*Curse* him tho' thou die for it; curse and *provoke him to strike thee dead* at once, and put an *End* to all thy Misery."

I confess *this* Sense sounds very *horrid*! but not beyond the *Devil*; who *dar'd* to demand of the SON OF GOD himself, to fall down and *worship him*: And as HE then turn'd and rebuked the *Tempter* and drove him away; "*Get thee hence Satan!*" Matth. iv. 10. So *Job* in the Spirit and Strength of his REDEEMER turn'd to his *Wife* and rebuked *her; Thou speakest as a foolish* wicked *Woman! What? Shall we receive Good at the Hand of GOD, and shall we not receive Evil?*

These are Words of high and merited *Anger* and severe *Reproof*; but like those of the *Arch-Angel* when contending with the *Devil*, there is no *railing* in them: The holy Man kept a Guard on his *Lips*, tho' no doubt his Soul was *pierced* with Horror at her Words. He detested the impious Motion, and rejected it with Abhorrence, without a Moment's Hesitation. He might well call her a *foolish Woman, rash* and inconsiderate, and also *profane*; as the *Fool* means in the *Phrase* of Scripture.—And then he more *mildly argues* with her; yet with a sufficient *Resentment: What? shall we receive Good*, and so *much* Good as *we* have done, in a long Course of *high* worldly Prosperity! and *shall we not receive Evil?* even *such* Evils, so *many* and *mighty* ones together; and breaking in upon us all *at once*, bereaving us of *Children* and *Houshold, Substance* and *Estate, Ease* and *Health*; in such a *sudden* and *awful* Manner. Can any Thing be *wrong* or unjust that a *good* GOD orders to befall us? The Evil of *Affliction* comes from *Him* now, as much as all the *Affluence* of worldly Prosperity that has heretofore distinguish'd us! and weigh now the *one* against the other; what *Good* we have receiv'd all the Days of our Life, and comparatively how few and *light Afflictions*; and then say, if we ought not to *bear* silently and patiently, and with adoring Submission, the *Evils* which He *now* pleases to lay upon us?

This was *Job's* gracious Way of *Reasoning*; these *Thoughts* had kept his own Spirit *calm*, and with the same he would *lay* the roil'd Spirit of his Wife, and *stop* her muttering and *blaspheming* Mouth.—The *Good* and the *Evil* of this *Life* are both *from GOD*; his *Sovereignty* (abstracted from every other Consideration) accounts for *both* in our State of *Trial*: The *least* of the *Good* is not deserved, the *Evil* is *all* merited and much *more*; the *Good* is much *more* for Kind, Measure and Continuance, thro' our whole Lives, than the Evil; the *Good* is at least necessary and what we could not *subsist* without, the Evil what may be *liv'd* under and outliv'd. The most *common* Mercies of this Life are usually the *greatest* and most needful. The *Good* is not only for Necessity, but also for Delight; the *Evil* is no more than we *need*, and what we could not do *well* without: The Evil and the Good both come according to GOD's *Covenant-Faithfulness* to his own People; the Evil is improvable to the *best Good*, and 'tis the Will and Meaning of GOD that we so improve it; and (to have done) the *Good* which we receive from the Hand of GOD doth not always give to particular *Graces* an equal *Lustre*, as does the *Evil*.— Should we not then *receive the Evil* in this State of our *Trial* and Probation? Surely 'tis calculated for *it*; the Honour of GOD requires it; there are *passive Graces* which our *fallen* State calls for the Exercise of; and CHRIST *the Captain of our Salvation was made perfect thro' Suffering.*

But to return.—In the Words of my *Text* we have one of the most *diabolical Motions* that was ever made to a *holy Soul* against the blessed GOD; and also one of the *noblest Resentments* that *such* a Soul is capable of. No Wonder therefore that we find so express and full a *Divine Approbation* of *Job's* gracious and holy *Return* to his *Wife's* outrageous Words: "*In all this did not Job sin with his Lips.*"

Satan assaulted him *by her*: He us'd and acted her, and *spake* by her Lips: So in the Beginning he *beguiled Eve*, and by her prevail'd on *Adam*. It is one of his cursed *Policies* which he yet continues to assault us in the *weakest* Place, and by them we *love*. "He sends Temptations by unsuspected Hands; theirs that have most Interest in us and Influence upon us." Profaness in such a *Relative*, or Discontent, *Passion*, Rage in 'em, is an *unknown* (yet *too well* known) Provocation to Evil.

The cursed Motion in the *Text* is 1. to *hard Thoughts* of the blessed GOD and his holy Providence; and 2. to outrageous and *blasphemous Words*: "Dost thou still retain thy Integrity? *curse GOD and die!*" What could be more furious and extravagant, *impious* and detestable. Well might he with *Horror* hear, and *spue out* the hellish *Suggestion* with high Indignation and *Detestation*; and well is the *Judgment of GOD* given strongly in his *Favour*, on his doing so. GOD justifies and *honours* him, GOD acquits and *absolves* him, upon a *first* and *second* fiery *Trial*. He approv'd himself to be the *perfect and upright Man*. By *not offending in Word*, Jam. iii. 2. Not an *impatient* Word fell from him, under so many *surprising Blows* and *Breaches* upon his Person, Family and Estate! not a Word, but of *Humiliation and Adoration*, when urg'd to *Rebellion* by all the Force and Stratagems of Hell: mov'd as he was to *curse*, he still kept on *blessing*; the cursed Suggestion enter'd only his *Ear*, not into his *Soul*; that *abhorr'd* from it.

Let the DOCTRINE therefore, for our *Instruction* and Warning, and also for *Comfort* and Support as there may be Occasion, be this,

"That many of GOD's *dear Children* are often annoy'd with cursed and *diabolical Suggestions*, which He will never *reckon to them as their Sin*, because they do in their Souls *abhor and reject them* with utmost *Detestation*."

This was *Job's* Case, and so it is of many a gracious *Saint* in our *own* Time: We see 'em terrify'd and pierc'd with *hellish* Suggestions, which they abhor, and are ready to *shriek* out at: they look on 'em as *their own* Wickedness, and so at themselves as *Devils* almost: they *loathe* themselves on this Account, and *cry* to GOD for Deliverance, and are in *Anguish*, that ever such *foul* Thoughts should have *Access* to them, and as they apprehend *lodge* within them: But what says my *Text* to 'em? even as GOD in it did to *Job*; "in *all this* they have *not sinned*."

I am then in the following *Discourse* to speak to these *three Propositions*: 1. That the most *upright* and dearest of the

Children of GOD in his Church on Earth, may be sometimes *annoy'd* and tormented with some of the most cursed and *diabolical Suggestions*, most injurious and dishonourable to the blessed GOD. 2. That these *hellish* Thoughts and *Injections* should be most *grievous* and *abhorred* to their holy Souls, and *rejected* with utmost Detestation. 3. That then they are not *their Sin*, nor will ever be imputed to them by the *Holy GOD*.

I. The dearest of GOD's *Children* in his Church on Earth may be at Times *annoy'd and terrified*, pursu'd and haunted by some of the most *cursed* and diabolical *Suggestions*, most injurious and dishonourable to the blessed GOD.

If *Job* suffered thus in his Day, why not the most dear and pleasant *Child* of GOD in ours? Who among *us* shall be exempt from *this*, or any other Kind of *fiery Trial*? Nay, a greater *than Job* presents HIMSELF to us in the Front of the *New Testament*: Matth. iv. 1. *Then was* JESUS *led up of the* SPIRIT *into the Wilderness, to be tempted of the Devil: And when the Tempter came to Him he said, "If thou be the* SON OF GOD—!"* And again, *"If thou wilt fall down and worship me!"—Then* JESUS *saith unto him, "Get thee hence Satan."* What an impudent, impure and *damnable* Motion was this of the *Devil's* to the SON OF THE HIGHEST when He took the *Likeness of sinful Flesh!* Not only was he mov'd to *distrust* and tempt GOD, but even to *worship the Devil*. Surely then there can be *no Sin so foul and monstrous*, but the *best of Saints* may be tempted to it. And *whom* may not *Satan* use as a *Tempter* to another, when the *Wife of Job* was so abused by him, and afterward the Lips of *Peter* to blaspheme the Purpose and *Decree* of GOD, respecting the *Sufferings* of CHRIST, as unjust and impossible, to the very Face of CHRIST, and in the Presence of his *Fellow-Apostles*;* before *whom* he receiv'd a like *Rebuke* that the *Devil* had in the *Wilderness*; *"Get thee behind me Satan, thou art an Offence to me; for thou savourest not the Things that be of GOD."*

When we consider *Satan's* using *Job's Wife* to *vex* his righteous Soul, and draw him into Sin and Rebellion against GOD; it forces into our *Remembrance* his Malice and Subtilty

---

*Matth. xvi. 22. For he seems not so to have *taken him aside*, as to be out of their *Sight and Observation*, if out of *hearing*.

from the Beginning, when he took the Form of the *Serpent* in his *first* Temptation, so *fatal* to Mankind through all Generations. The *Woman* was first in the Transgression; the *Devil* gat into *her*, and by her into *Adam*; he shock'd her by a *horrid Suggestion* against the Goodness and *Truth* of GOD and prevailed! *Has God indeed said* (said the blasphemous lying *Spirit*) *ye shall not eat, least ye die? Whereas he knows that in the Day you eat, your Eyes will be opened, and you will be like* HIMSELF *for Knowledge* and Understanding. The malicious and false *Fiend* suggests to her, that from *Ill-will* and Envy GOD had forbid them the delicious and *improving* Fruit, and that the *Threatning*, by which he had restrain'd them, was a *Lye*. In all his *modern* Temptations he takes the *same Course*; "he questions the *Precept*, he denies the *Danger*, and he suggests some great *Advantage*." So the Devil began with *belying* and reproaching the blessed GOD, to alienate Man's Heart from him.

I might mention *two Instances* more, which are *famous* in Scripture Story, of the *Wives of good Men*, used by the *Devil* to tempt them into *ill Thoughts* of GOD. The first is that of *Zipporah* to *Moses*, when she was terrified into the *Circumcision* of her Son; for she saw her *Husband* struck *sick* on his Journey, and threatned with *Death* for the *Omission*, and hereby *disabled* for the Duty; she therefore cast the *Foreskin* at his Feet and said, "*A bloody Husband art thou to me.*" This is vulgarly interpreted in Way of *Passion* and Wrath; and for ought I know 'tis the *right* Sense of the Words, after all the fine *Criticism* that has been bestowed on them, to make them bear another Sense. Now, in this *literal* Sense,—if *Moses* was a *bloody Husband* for obliging her to execute the Command of GOD in that *bleeding Rite* of Circumcision; then what a bloody *Imputation* is here suggested against the good GOD, that He should institute and require it, as the *Sign* and Seal of his *Covenant*, threaten now to spill the Blood of *Moses* for his daring to *omit* it so long, from his *Indulgence* to her! If this were the real *Meaning* and Language of angry *Zipporah*, what a *virulent Reproach* do her Words imply against GOD and his gracious Law?

The other *Instance* I pointed at is *Michal* the Wife of *David*, when she saw him in his *Transport* of holy Zeal and

Joy *dancing* before the *Ark* of GOD: She blasphemed the religious *Act* as *leud* and shameful; and as if it were below the
Dignity and State of the *King of Israel* to disrobe and *uncover*
himself so before the DIVINE MAJESTY.—Was it *Michal's*
Pride, or was it *Satan's* Envy and Rage, that we must *impute*
these Reproaches against GOD unto? Doubtless she was *possess'd*, the Devil was in her, and he fill'd her *Heart* with
Contempt, and her *Mouth* with Railings. She vilify'd GOD
and his *Ark*, in reviling *David*, his Zeal and Devotion; and
GOD laid her under Reproach, and made her *vile* for the rest
of her Life.

But to *return* again: The *Devil* needs no *Instruments* by
whom to tempt: He has Access to our *Minds*, if GOD do not
restrain and forbid him, to raise and move evil Thoughts in
us. He *shoots* his fiery Darts, and they *enter* we know not how;
but we *feel* 'em pierce and fasten in our Souls. For *how* one
Spirit acts on another we know not; but *this* we know, that
Satan can fill the Heart against the HOLY GHOST; as in the
Case of *Ananias* and *Sapphira*.

Sometimes the *Devil has hurried* poor Souls with
Atheistical Thoughts; for he finds *an evil Heart of Unbelief*
within us, and foments it at Times, to high Degrees of
Infidelity, so as not only to question the *Mystery* of the *Trin-
ity*, and therein of JESUS, *GOD manifest in Flesh*; but also the
very *Being* and incomprehensible necessary *Perfections* of the
DEITY; his *Eternity*, perfect *Prescience* and *Decrees*, which are
indeed as the *thick Darkness*, or rather *unapproachable Light*
wherein the ETERNAL dwells; and into which it may be the
Angels of Heaven are no more allow'd to *pry* with any
Thought of searching them out, than the *Church* of old in the
Wilderness was permitted to come near unto the *Bounds* about
the *Mount* to *gaze*; into which if they had *look'd*, what could
they have *seen* but Cloud and Lightning?

The *Word* and *Providence* of GOD are also special Objects
of *Satan's* furious Attack, in his Assaulting the *Faith* and *Love*
of GOD's Saints. And herein he does by the *Members*, as
he did by the HEAD, in the forty Days of our LORD's
Temptation.

Thus *Asaph* was almost *born away* headlong into Unbelief
and *Despondency*; though he had thrown out his *strong*

Anchor and Cable, "*Truly GOD is good to Israel, even to them that are of a clean Heart!*" Yet could he scarce *outride* the furious *Storm*: Psal. lxxiii.—*But as for me, my Feet were almost gone, for I was envious at the foolish, when I saw the Prosperity of the Wicked:—Verily I have cleansed my Heart in vain, and washed my Hands in Innocence! But should I speak thus, I shall offend against the Generation of thy Children!*—Yet *was my Heart grieved and I was pricked in my Reins; so foolish was I and ignorant, I was even as a Beast before Thee!* For *never the less I am continually with thee, thou hast holden me by my right Hand; and whom have I in Heaven but Thee, and there is none upon Earth that I desire besides thee, &c.*

The Rage and Blasphemy of the *Devil* is especially spent against the *Faithfulness and Truth of GOD, in his Promises* and *Threatnings*: he inrages the *wicked* very often by accursed *Misrepresentations* of the *one*, and would drive the *Godly* into *Despondencies* and *Desperation*, by impudent Denials of the *other*. He has a furious *Antipathy* to that *Name* of GOD which is the strong *Tower* of the righteous, and into which they are ever *flying*; for in it *all his Glory* passes before sinful Man; Exod. xxxiv. 6, 7. *The LORD, the LORD GOD, merciful and gracious, long-suffering, and abundant in Goodness and Truth; keeping Mercy for Thousands*, &c. The Devil *stabs* a Child of GOD to the Heart, and *pierces* him in the most *sensible* and tender Part, while he *reproaches* him, and makes him but seem to *doubt* the *Goodness and Truth* of GOD, his *Covenant-Kindness* and *Faithfulness*. No Wonder therefore if we find the most *Eminent Saints* on holy Record thus afflicted and tormented by the *Blasphemer* and *Avenger*.—As *Job* was thus outrag'd in my *Text*, so were *David* and *Asaph* and *Heman* in their times, long after; for the *Tempter* is the *same* to all that are living *godly* in every Age; as *they* are much the *same* in respect of Faith and Infirmity. *David* tells us in Psalm xlii. how he went *mourning because of the Oppression of the Enemy*, who insultingly *reproach'd him from Day to Day*, "*Where is thy GOD?*" It was a *Sword in his Bones*, more for the *Name* of his GOD than the *Scorn* cast on himself; *the Voice of Him that reproacheth and blasphemeth! why art thou cast down O my Soul, and why disquieted within me? hope thou in GOD, for I shall yet praise Him.*—*Asaph* was a like suffering *Saint* by like violent Temptations to *Despondency*; Psal. lxxvii. *His Sore ran in the Night and ceased not; his Soul refused to be comforted; he remembred GOD* (his Name, Perfections, Promises and Works) and yet his *Trouble* remained or increased; *his Spirit was overwhelmed* while it *made diligent Search*; "*Will the* LORD *cast off forever? and will he be favourable no more? is his* MERCY *clean gone forever, and doth his* PROMISE *fail forevermore? hath GOD forgotten to be gracious, hath he in Anger shut up his tender Mercies?—I said, this is my Infirmity, I will remember the Years of the right Hand of the most High! Thy Way is in the Sea, thy Path as in the great Waters, and thy Footsteps are not known.*"—*Heman* also was a Man of like *Sorrows*, and of like *Faith and Devotion*: He has given us a *Psalm of Instruction* to Souls *in the lowest Pit, in Darkness, in the Deeps*; Psal. lxxxviii. "*O* LORD *GOD of my Salvation, I have cried Day and Night before Thee; let my Prayer come before thee, incline thine Ear unto my Cry; for my Soul is full of Troubles, and my Life draweth nigh unto the Grave;—why castest thou off my Soul, why hidest thou thy Face from me? LORD, I have called daily upon thee, I have stretched out my Hands to thee;* and still *in the Morning shall my Prayer prevent thee*: After all the Tossings of the *Night*, the Light of the *Morning* shall find me praying."

In fine, it has often been the *Complaint* of humble and gracious Persons, that they have found themselves annoy'd with *unaccountable irreverent, foolish, vile, filthy, base*, abominable Thoughts; They know not *what, how* or *why*! but they seem to *buzz* about 'em like *Swarms of Flies*, or break about 'em like *Sparkles of Fire*; more especially when they would set themselves to *meditate* and *pray*, and have their Minds most *solemn* and *composed* and *close* with GOD in holy Exercises.— Now what shall we say to these *Satanical* Molestations and Disturbances? On the *Serpent's* part it is more *easy* to account for it, from his *Spite* and Malignity against GOD and his Grace; but on the part of GOD, his Permission of *Baalzebub* herein, and the *holy Ends* of his gracious Government; it may be more *difficult* for us to conceive aright.

1. On the part of *Satan* it is obvious to account for it from his implacable *Hatred* of GOD, and of *Souls recovering* into his Holiness and Favour; from which he is himself utterly and

forever *excluded*. He *hates* GOD because of his *Holiness*, and for his righteous *Judgment*, his Power and *Vengeance*; which it is his *Torment* to think of, and know it *coming* on him. So when the *fierce Devils*, "exceeding fierce from the *Tombs*," whither they had driven the *two possessed*, beheld their *Judge, the* HOLY ONE OF GOD in their Way, and were corrected by his Power and stopt; Matth. viii. 29. *They cried out saying,* "*What have we to do with thee*; *Jesus thou Son of GOD! art thou come to torment us before the Time?*" It is the Devil's *Torment* to behold Angels or Men holy and *happy*, while he is miserable. He hates GOD because he is *unlike* him, and under his *Wrath*; he spitefully hates to see GOD *serv'd* and glorify'd by others; he would pollute and damn our Souls, that we may be as *he is*, impure and odious to GOD. He affects a *Kingdom* of his own on Earth, in Opposition to the Kingdom of GOD and of Grace. He could not bear to see *Man* in *Paradise*, and be himself in *Hell*; to see *Adam* in the Likeness and Love of GOD and worshipping before Him, and *himself* cast from those Felicities. *Curs'd* in his Rage on this Account, beyond a common damned *Ghost* I may suppose, he wishes for *Millions* and *Worlds* to follow by his Means into the State of eternal Miseries; and having beguiled our miserable *first Parent* into an Apostacy from GOD, and finding *himself* only the *more damned*, and a SAVIOUR revealed for the *Sons of Men*; and Him a singular and eminent SEED of that very *Woman* whom he had deceived into Sin and Misery; his *Envy* and *Hatred* against all her natural *Seed*, but more especially against the blessed and *promised* ONE Himself, and those that should *believe* on his Name, has been so *inflam'd*—that *as a roaring Lion* he drives thro' the World, (and is *going up and down in it*, which are his own Words) *seeking whom he may devour*; And whom he cannot *destroy* he loves to *distress*, affright and scare, *terrify* and wound; or *worry* if he cannot *rend*; and no wonder if he *roar* the more, when he *sees* and cannot *reach* his Prey; as in the *Case* of *Job*, and Souls *upright* like him:— Or like a *Dog* rather he goes *about the City*, and haunts the Villages like the *Wolf* by night; grinning and barking at the *Flock of* CHRIST and his *Lambs*, whose *Blood* he thirsts after. So the HOLY GHOST has represented to us our *Adversary the Devil*, I Peter v. 8. shown us our *Enemy* and Danger: So that on the *Tempter's* part it is *easy* to say, *why* he annoys *Souls* with his hellish *Suggestions* against the blessed GOD; he hates both GOD and them, and desires nothing more than to see GOD *dishonoured* and *them* polluted, that they may be damned.— This was his Wish and *Hope* in his Attempt on holy *Job*; to bring the *Man of boasted Integrity to curse his GOD*; and for the same Reason he desired to have the *Sifting of Peter* who was too ready to *boast* in himself; *though all Men forsake thee, yet will not I:* Luke xxii. 31. *Satan has desired to have thee, to sift thee as Wheat:* to have him for *his own* if it might be, and carry him off an *easy Prey*, if CHRIST had not *pray'd for him that his Faith should not fail;* but if *that* may not be, he desires however by *winnowing* to *shake and toss him furiously*, and show his *Chaff*.

In short, as Dr. *Tillotson* has it: "*Malice* against GOD and *Envy* to Men account for *Satan's* Tempting us; to *spoil* (if he can) GOD of his Subjects and *debauch* them from their Allegiance, into his own *Condemnation*, Malignity and Misery."—A *Ghost in Hell* does not presently commence *Devil*, in this Height of Malignity against GOD and Cruelty toward Fellow-Sinners; if we may take Leave to form an Idea to our selves by the Words which the *Parable* puts into the Mouth of the *rich Man* there; "*Nay Father Abraham, but if one went to them from the Dead they would repent! Send Lazarus therefore to my Father's House, for I have five Brethren; that he may testify unto them, lest they come* also *into this Place of Torment!*"— The *best Thing*, I suppose, that was ever intimated with Respect to a *lost Soul* in Hell: but such a *parabolical* Representation means not to *affirm* any Thing with Respect to *Hell* itself, but only to *affect* and move the *Bowels of Sinners*, to themselves and others, in our *present State* of Probation and Repentance.

2. It may be more *difficult* for us to *dive* into the wise and holy *Ends* of GOD, in his *Permission* of these *fiery* Assaults of *Satan* upon the Children of his *Love*.

It was a most *dark* Dispensation to pious *Job* and his *Friends*, when it was *his* Case: his *Wife* broke out even into *Blasphemy* upon it, and his *Friends* afterward *rent their Garments*, and sat down by him *silent* and astonied, *wailing* and in Fears: It amaz'd *Job himself* under the *Conscience of his*

Integrity, and it threw his *Friends* into horrid Tears and *Suspicions* of some heinous *Iniquity* by which he had provoked the *Wrath* and Judgment of GOD in so *many* and heavy Instances of it at once: But while He now stands in the Eyes of some, as the "*Hero* of an inspir'd *Epic. Poem,** brave in Distress, valiant in Affliction, maintaining his Character for Vertue and Piety under the most powerful Temptations, and exasperating Provocations, that the Malice of Hell could invent;" let us take a more *adoring View* of the *End of the* LORD herein; to represent unto his *Chosen and Sanctified* through all Generations, in every Part of his visible Church; that he should in *like Manner,* here and there, call *one and another* of them, as unto *single Combat* with the *Enemy* of their Salvation; arming 'em beforehand with the *Shield of Faith, the Breast-plate of Righteousness, the Sword of the Spirit,* whereby they should be able to *quench* the fiery Darts of the *wicked One;* and *stand* as *Job* did in the *evil Day,* and come off Conquerors and *more than Conquerors thro'* JESUS that *has loved them.* Ephes. vi. 10, 11, 12. Rom. viii. 37, 38.

1. The *Sovereignty* of GOD must set us down *silent* under such *astonishing Dispensations, Trials and Exercises* of his most *gracious Saints;* nor may his *Will,* Wisdom, *Goodness* and Faithfulness be doubted, *question'd* or disputed by *Them* or others. It was (without Doubt) the *Error* of *Job* and his *Friends* that they enter'd *so far* into an *Argument* and Dispute about the *Reasons* of the *Divine Conduct* respecting him; which may seem too much verging toward *a Saying unto GOD, what dost thou?* or *why* hast thou done this? which *who shall say?* Eccles. viii. 4. Therefore *Job* and his *Friends* receiv'd no other *Answer* from Heaven, either first by *Elihu* who spake under a Divine Impulse and *Inspiration,* nor afterward by the more immediate *Voice out of the Whirlwind,* but the *unaccountable Greatness, Majesty* and most certainly *wise and perfect Dominion* and Government of GOD *most High and Holy.* All Flesh must be *silent* before Him; be *dumb* and not open their *Mouth* because GOD does it! be *still* and know that it is of GOD; like *Aaron* hold their *Peace,* like *Eli* say "*It is the LORD!*"—*Job* and his *Friends* did but *darken Counsel by Words*

*Sir *Richard Blackmore.*

without Knowledge, while they were ready to fix *one Rule* and Measure in all Providential Dispensations. We are let into the *Secret* and Reason in the *Case of Job*, that we may learn to rest *satisfied* in the Will of GOD, and the Dispositions of Providence, *whatever* befals our selves or others. GOD is wise and holy, and his *Work perfect*, in all Things that respect either his *Children* or his *Enemies*. We may neither say, "*Why does the Way of the Wicked prosper?*" Or wherefore does GOD seem to *look favourably* upon the Way of them *that deal treacherously?* And why do they *devour the Man that is more righteous?* without laying down to our selves, and that strongly, an immoveable Foundation, as the *Prophet* does, Hab. i. 12, 13. "*Art thou not from Everlasting, O* Lord *my GOD, my* Holy One? *thou art of purer Eyes than to behold Iniquity.*" So when the Prophet *Jeremiah* was ready to have *pleaded with GOD*, and was tempted to *talk with him of his Judgments*, he was *inspir'd* first to lay down this Principle, never to be departed from, but ever kept in Mind, "*righteous art thou O* Lord!"

2. As GOD will not suffer his *upright* Servants to be *tempted* above what they are *able* to bear, but will with the *Temptation* find a Way for their *Escape*, so his gracious *Purpose* in permitting *Satan's fiery Assaults* on their Souls, is to *glorify his Grace* in their *holy bearing* and resisting them, and so by the *Weakness of Man* to make the *Triumphs of Grace* the more glorious over the Subtlety, Malice and *Wrath of Satan*. So it was in the Conflict of *Job*,—"Let me try his *boasted Grace* (said the *Tempter*) and he'll curse thee to thy Face;" "He is in *thy Hand* (said GOD) and *my Grace* in him shall *triumph* gloriously over *thy* Spite and Power." Therefore when he held fast his *Integrity* under the *first Scene* of dreadful Trials, the Almighty even gloried in him over his false and cruel Enemy, Job ii. 3. "*And still he holdeth fast his Integrity; although thou movedst me against him.*" And in the *Record* of these Sufferings and Patience of *Job*, the *Grace* of GOD is glorified to his *Church* forever in the Power, the Riches and *Alsufficiency* thereof. The *perfect Man* came out of his *first* and *second* Fire, as the *three Worthies* did out of the *fiery Furnace*, without the least *Smell* upon him, or his *Raiment* so much as scorch'd: And as the Lord GOD of Hosts, the *GOD of Israel* was magnified in the Sight of

Nebuchadnezzar and all the *Princes* of his vast Empire, in the one *Miracle* of Power; so is the Power of *Faith*, Patience, Penitence, Adoration, Submission glorified to the *Saints* of GOD in *all Ages* by the History of *Job*; and perpetual Glory is *render'd* by the Church on *his* Account from Age to Age. And how abundantly *crowned* then is that *Trial of Faith*, whatever it be, by *manifold Temptations for a Season*, tho' it be tried by *Fire*, which shall be *found to Praise Honour and Glory* unto the *Day of Christ*, and *in* that glorious Day, and unto all *Eternity?*—Thus has the LORD *set apart* some *for Himself!* And "they *shall be mine* says the LORD in the Day when *I make up my Jewels!*" "*Thou shalt tread upon the Lion and Adder, the young Lion and the Dragon shalt thou trample under Foot! because he hath set his Love upon me*, (and shewn it by *trusting* in me) *therefore will I deliver him; I will set him on High, because he hath known my Name; he shall call upon me and I will answer him; I will be with him in Trouble, I will deliver him and honour him*": Psalm xci. Thus GOD did by his Servant *Job*, and so he often *glorifies his Grace* in the suffering Members of a tempted *Saviour*, that they may *glorify him*, by being *Types* of Him.

3. *Satan* may be permitted to distress the Souls of GOD's Children by his foul Suggestions, to *show them the Corruption that is in them by Nature*, and the sad *Remains* of it after their Regeneration, their *Weakness* and *Danger*, and absolute *Dependance* in their best Estate on his *free Grace* for Preservation and Safety. GOD lets 'em *see* what they are *liable* to, and *capable* of, if he should *leave* 'em; what Enemies beset them and whither they would hurry 'em. GOD shews 'em *Themselves* and effectually *abases* 'em, makes 'em low and *vile* in their own Eyes, fills 'em with *Shame* and *Fear*, and makes 'em to know that they are but *Dust* and Pollution: This makes 'em *watch and pray* with a holy *Jealousy* of themselves, lest as *Satan beguiled Eve* he prevail over them her *Offspring*, conceived in *Sin*, and shapen in Iniquity. GOD brings them to *Despair* in themselves, and to *trust* only in CHRIST for Righteousness and Strength, for *present* as well as *future* and eternal Salvation. Psalm xvii. 7, 8, 9. "Shew thy marvellous *Loving Kindness*, O thou that *savest* by thy right Hand them which put their *Trust* in Thee, from those that *rise* up against

them: Keep me as the *Apple of the Eye*, hide me under the *Shadow of thy Wings*; from the *Wicked that oppress me*, from my *deadly Enemies* that compass me about! like *as a Lion* that is greedy of his Prey,—*arise O* LORD, disappoint him, cast him down."

Satan sees the natural Profaness, *Atheism* and Infidelity of our evil Hearts; that there are the *Seeds* of all Impiety, *Blasphemy* and Malignity in us, he makes his Advantage of this *natural* Propensity in us, and while he watches to *inflame* the Soul from *within* it self, GOD *frustrates* him in his mischievous Device, by discovering to the *Soul* its own *native Viciousness* and Impurity; with its absolute *Need* of the Succours of *Almighty Grace*; and that *self-loathing* and abhorring, with *Fear* and Trembling, it must only go and *cast it self* upon sovereign *Mercy*. Psalm cxliii. *I flee unto Thee to hide me, quicken me O* LORD *for thy Name Sake; for thy Righteousness sake bring my Soul out of Trouble; and of thy Mercy cut off mine Enemies, and destroy all them that afflict my Soul; for I am thy Servant.* Thus the *Result* of all is,

4. GOD permits and uses the foul and furious *Assaults of Satan* upon the Souls of his Children unto the *most kind and gracious Event and Issue*, to be truly the *Means* of a *great Increase of Grace* in them, and of *their Establishment and Perseverance* in Grace, and very often of much *Light and Comfort, Peace and Joy* in believing. "The *grievous Chastning* yields the *peaceable Fruits* of Righteousness to them that are exercised thereby; wherefore *lift up* the Hands that hang down and the feeble Knees; and make *strait Paths* for your Feet; lest that which is *lame* be turned out of the Way, but rather let it be *healed*."

The *Temptation* in it self tends only to *defile and pollute*, but GOD makes it *purifying*; its natural and designed Tendency is only to darken and *torture*, but GOD *turns the Shadows of Death into the Light of the Morning*. It has been, I doubt not, the *first Means* of saving *Conversion* to many a *Soul*, the *Means* also of *Growth* and *Increase* to many a *regenerate* Person, and the *Forerunner* of a *confirmed Peace* to many a happy *Penitent* and true *Believer* in CHRIST. I say,

1. The Means of the first *saving* effectual *Conviction* and true *Awakening* to many a *Sinner*. GOD holds the *Devil* in

those *Chains of Darkness* as to make him against his *Will*, and contrary to his own wicked *Design*, to serve and *minister* in bringing some of his *Elect* into a saving *Fight* to the Blood of CHRIST, and *Subjection* to him as *Prince and Saviour*. So the *Shepherd* uses the barking of his *Dog* to bring back a *stray Sheep* to the Fold. "*The wicked is snared in the Work of his own Hands; Higgaion Selah!*" i.e. put a special *Remark* on this; it is a *Point* that deserves our deepest *Attention*. Psal. ix. 16.

Satan would not *chuse* (we may well think) to *disrest* a Soul that is at *Ease* in Sin, but rather would *soothe* and rock him into a sounder *Sleep*: but the Tempter may be so *infatuated* at times, for ought we know, as to raise those Fears and *Horrors* in some under their *first* (and but common) Conviction, which he can *never* lay again, and which free Grace makes to *issue* in their saving *Conversion*. Or rather may we not think, that GOD having awaken'd the Soul, and *Satan* fearing to *lose* his hold of it, his *Rage* is over ruled to *promote* and carry on the good Work of GOD begun, and to *drive* the Soul faster and closer to its SAVIOUR.

2. It may be a more sensible and *evident* thing in the *Kingdom of* GOD's *Grace within Men*, that the *Assaults of Hell* upon them are frequently made the *Means of Increase* in Grace, and of the *Progress* of Sanctification. The *Tempter* attempts, again and again, to *blast* the Work of Grace begun, to bring it to a *stop*, to deter and *dishearten* the pious Soul in its Way: "there is a *Lion* in the street, an *Adder* in the Path! desist or turn back!"—but GOD *turns* the affrighting Suggestion to Unbelief and *Despondency*, into an *Alarm* unto *Faith*, holy *Fear*, Prayer and Fortitude; so that what was meant to affright astonish and *deter*, is made to *quicken* unto Prayer, Watchfulness and Diligence, in a more earnest Flight to the SPIRIT of Grace for Succour, and to the atoning cleansing Blood of a great SAVIOUR and INTERCESSOR: by which means you may have often found, O buffetted *Child* of GOD, that you had been less *humble*, careful, *sollicitous* and anxious about your spiritual State, and in your Walk with GOD, if you had never *felt* those *Conflicts* with your spiritual Adversaries, which a holy GOD has mercifully call'd you to endure, and has carried you through. These are the *Beginnings of Revenges upon the Enemy*, which call upon all *around* the suffering *Children* of

GOD to *rejoice with them*, and on their Account.—Shall I *say to them* what I have *tho't*, and been *perswaded* from what I have *heard and seen* from such distressed *Christians* under the Persecutions of some unseen evil Adversary; "You *love* GOD much the more, and *fear* him more, and *adore* him better, and *walk* the more *humbly and closely* with Him, and *hate Sin* the more, and *pray the better*, and are the more *circumspect meek and lowly* in Heart, and have really much the more *Communion* with GOD, from what you have *suffer'd* by the Malice and Wrath of *Satan*. So *his Wrath* shall praise GOD by *your Lips*, as long as you live; and the *Remainder thereof* GOD *will restrain*."

Upon all

3. The fiery *Assaults of Hell* upon the dear *Children of GOD* prove the *Means*, as of their greater *Purification* from Sin and Growth in *Holiness*, so of all *Joy and Peace in believing* to them. The Affliction for the present is very *grievous*, but it yields the *peaceable Fruits of Righteousness to them that are exercised thereby*. So *blessed is the Man that has endured Temptation*, for after the *Conflict* comes the *Crown*: *Light is sowing* through all the Clouds and Darkness, Rain or Tempest, *for the Righteous, and Gladness for the Upright in Heart*: As *Job* found it in the Day when GOD *justified* him, after he had *humbled* him and made him *viler* than the Dust in his own Eyes; "*Go to my Servant* (said the HOLY ONE) *and he shall pray for you*." The *Joy of Victory* follows upon *Satan's* Assault and *Defeat*. GOD *crowns* the humble *Overcomer* with Garlands of Joy here sometimes, and will with those of Glory hereafter; for *when he is tried he shall receive the Crown of Life*. *Job* shone the *brighter* all his After-life in the Eyes of all about him; and it was to him the same Thing as if he had only been in the *Mount with Moses*, and came down with his *Face*. *His* restored *Prosperity* was doubly *serene* and pleasant, both to *himself* and his *Friends*. He was seen and lov'd like *David* long after, when he came back with the *Sword and Head of the Giant* in his Hand. So shall it be *done* to *Him* whom the *King of Saints delights to honour*.—When *Asaph* also had got *through* his Temptation, hear how he *triumph'd* in his GOD and over the Enemy: Psalm lxxiii. 23, 24. *Never the less I am continually with Thee, thou hast holden me by my right*

Hand; thou shalt guide me by thy Counsel, and afterward receive me to Glory: Whom have I in Heaven but thee, and there is nothing on Earth that I desire beside thee: my Heart and my Flesh faileth, but thou art the Strength of my Heart and my Portion for ever. Asaph's sore *Dejections* clear'd the Way to these his *Exultations;* which bring to Mind the *Words of* CHRIST *to his Disciples,* when they return'd from their *more easy Acquests* over *Satan,* "LORD, *the very Devils are subject to us through thy Name*:" " 'Tis so, replied the late *tempted* JESUS,—*I beheld Satan as Lightning fall from Heaven! but in this rejoice not that the Devils are subject to you; but that your Names are written in Heaven.*" Victory over *Satan's Temptations,* in some of his remarkable and violent, but more especially in the *Course* of his ordinary Assaults, may minister unto us the *joyous Hope* of our *Election* of GOD, and of our final *Perseverance* in Grace. No doubt but holy *Job* spent the latter Part of his Life in the more blessed *Assurance* of his Interest in the Love of GOD, and in the *Joys* thereof; by the *Breaches* which *Satan* was permitted to make on him for a *Season.* 1. Pet. i. 6, 7. "Wherein ye *greatly rejoice,* though now for a *Season* (if need be) ye are in *Heaviness* thro' *manifold Temptations,* that the *Trial of Faith,* tho' tried as with *Fire,* may be found unto *Praise and Honour and Glory in the Day of* CHRIST." This is but as CHRIST himself suffer'd, being *tempted,* and the *Consolations of* GOD flow'd down upon him. Matth. iv. 11. *Get thee hence Satan, and the Devil left him, and Angels came and minister'd to him.* Those holy *benevolent Spirits are ministring Spirits to the Heirs of Salvation;* and never so more *gladly,* than when they have seen *'em combatting* with the *Powers of Darkness,* and stedfastly *resisting* them. So the *Darkness* of the *Night* makes the *Light* of the *Morning* pleasant, and even *Dirt and Sand* are us'd to *scour* and brighten the Vessel, and the *scullions* foul Hands to *wash* and cleanse it. So *Silver* and *Gold* pass through *Fire* and are *refined*: only the *Dross* is purged away.

Thus we have look'd a little into this *dark Dispensation* of *Divine Providence;* this *mysterious Conduct of Sovereign Grace,* in the *Permission* of the *fiery Assaults* of *Satan* upon some of the *dearest* Children of GOD: Altho' they are *dear to GOD,* and *He so to them,* yet are they sometimes *annoy'd* with

hideous hateful *Suggestions* against his *Holiness and Glory.*
GOD has his wise, most holy and gracious *Ends* in this
Permission; *Glory to Himself,* and much *Spiritual Good* to
these his *favourite* Sufferers.

I will only add,—When our LORD gave the *Tempter* his last
Rebuke, upon his most *horrid* Assault, He *passed* immediately
upon his *public Ministry.* And his *Apostle* St. *Paul* was *established* and *enlarged* in his *abundant Labours* and extensive
Services, by the *Messengers of Satan* of one kind and another,
that *dogg'd* and set upon him, where ever he went: I'll read
you some Account of it, and *conclude* on this Head, 2 Cor. iv.
8, 9, &c. "We are *troubled* on every side, yet not *distressed,* we
are *perplexed* but not in *Despair; persecuted* but not *forsaken,*
cast *down,* but not *destroyed;* always *bearing* about in the *Body*
the *Dying* of the LORD JESUS, that the *Life also of* JESUS may
be made *manifest* in our Body;—For which Cause we *faint
not,* but though our *outward Man perish,* yet the *inward Man
is renewed* Day by Day: For our *light Affliction,* which is but
for a *Moment* worketh for us a *far more exceeding and eternal
Weight of Glory.* While we *look,* not to the Things that are
seen, but at the Things which are *not seen;* for the Things
which are *seen* are *temporal,* but the Things which are *not* seen
are *eternal.*"

I come now to the *second* Thing proposed, which is,

II. These hellish *Suggestions,* and horrid *diabolical*
Thoughts, as they should and will be most *grievous* and abhorred to a holy Soul, so ought they to be *rejected* and cast
out with utmost *Detestation.*

It is not only Matter of *Fact* and Experience, but also of
Necessity, that they are thus *grievous* to and abhorred by a *holy
Mind*: As it is *Duty* to GOD, so where *Grace* is in Exercise it
is in the Nature of Things necessary.—*Job* appears in the *Text*
as if *stab'd* to the Heart by his *Wife's* hideous Words; he *answers* the foul Temptation with Abhorrence, he *ejects* the
cursed Thought, he *reprehends* her with Indignation, and calls
her a *foolish* wicked Woman; and *argues* on GOD's Behalf,
why utmost Reverence, Love, Fear, Gratitude, Adoration
Submission was *due* from him to the *blessed* GOD, and should
ever be *render'd* by him, by the Help of his Grace: *What?
Shall we receive Good at the Hand of the LORD, and shall we*

not receive Evil? Thus *Grace* will direct, urge and *constrain us* to think and speak in any like Case; as we know it was exhibited by our blessed SAVIOUR in his Temptations.

But let us take the *Truth* before us, the *Duty* propounded to us, in its several *Parts*, and briefly speak to each of them: These *infernal* Thoughts and *Injections*, should be very *grievous* and distressing to us, we should heartily *detest* 'em, *reject* and spue 'em out as soon as they arise in us, if we can; and at the same Time *fortify* our selves with holy *Reasoning* and Argument, as we are able; as *Job* piously and wisely did under the Direction and Assistance of GOD.

1. They should be very *grievous* and distressing to our Souls, and they necessarily *are* so to a gracious Heart. *As a Sword in our Bones* it should be to us as it, was to *David*: Psal. xlii.—It is hard to hear our *selves*, a *Parent* or a *Friend*, any whom we esteem and reverence, spoken evil of or *reviled*; but how much more dear and *sacred* is the Name and *Glory* of *GOD most High*, good and holy, wise and just, to a pious Heart? *"Holy and reverend is his Name! Him thou shalt fear, to him thou shalt cleave and Him thou shalt serve! He is thy Praise and He is thy GOD."* Deut. x. 20. *That glorious and fearful Name, the* LORD *thy GOD.* xxxviii. 58.

It should be *grievous* to apprehend the *Enemy of GOD and of all Righteousness* so *nigh* us, and that by our *Apostacy* from GOD he has such *Access* to us. It may well *scare* us to think that he is or has been (as it were) *at our right Hand*, and whispering into our *Ear* with a *contagious* filthy Breath; Things so *impious* in themselves, and to us *pernicious* without the Succours of preserving Grace.

It should be *horrible* to imagine (but that the Heart is *conscious* to its own Wickedness) that *Satan* should see any Way of *Entrance* into us for his hellish *Blasphemies*, and Profaness! or that he should conceive the least *Hope of Success* against us, in such barefac'd Infidelity, *Atheism* and Devilism! that he should seem to *see* us *so like* himself! or that any of the *Humane Race*, but especially under the Light of the *Gospel*, could be really *such incarnate Devils*, as this would render them.

We may well *tremble* with Horror from a pious *Self-Love*, lest those hellish Suggestions should make any Impression, find the least Entertainment in us, or Compliance from us. For sooner should we chuse *to cease to be*, then to be capable of *regarding* and yielding to a *Thought* of this Nature, against the Being, Holiness and Glory of the GOD that made us! which were to *bring up Hell* from beneath, and *act the Devil* in open Day-Light.

In a Word, It should grieve us to think or know that there is any such Degree of *Malignity* against GOD in any *Creature* whatsoever! That even *Hell* it self can show any Thing so vile and unclean. As one would be scar'd to see a *Devil*, so this *Idea* of diabolical *Spleen* and Hatred, and of *spiritual Filthiness*, may justly make our *Blood* run *cold* thro' every Vein, and the *Hair* of our Head to *rise* up an End!

So grievous and terrifying have the *blasphemous Suggestions of Satan* been to holy Souls, in whom the HOLY SPIRIT of GOD dwells and rules, having fill'd them with *Faith and Love, Reverence and godly Fear*.

2. We must therefore in our Souls *detest* and *loathe*, feel and express a vehement *Abhorrence* of such *hellish Suggestions*. "*Do I not hate them, that hate thee?* (said holy *David*, teaching us to *feel* and speak *thus* after him, Psalm cxxxix) *and am I not grieved with them that rise up against Thee? I hate 'em with perfect Hatred,—I count them my Enemies: Search me O GOD and know my Heart, try me and know my Thoughts, and see Thou* and show to *me* if it be not thus."

What should our Souls equally *detest*, as this expressed open Enmity, Hatred, Contempt and *Spite* against the Holy GOD? At what should they equally *rise*, bursting with Anger *Disdain* and Wrath? *Meekness*, I had well nigh said, were here a *Vice*; and *Mildness* the Want of *Zeal*; did I not call to Mind the *Arch-Angel's* Words when *contending with the Devil*; how far he kept from any *railing Accusation*, but only said "*the LORD rebuke thee.*" Provok'd *Abishai* could not preserve a *like* Government of himself when *Shimei* only railed against his *Earthly King*; "*Shall this dead Dog curse my Lord?*" said he: But what would *David* himself have said, had the *Curse* been utter'd against his *King* and GOD, the LORD *of Glory?* The blasphemous *Being* and his *Act* had equally been the *hated of David's Soul*, and should be of *ours?* Although there *needs* no imprecating any *Curse* upon the *Devil, curs'd* as he is long since from the Mouth of GOD, and under the Sentence of eternal Death.—"If any Man *love not our* LORD JESUS CHRIST *let him be Anathema, Maran-atha,*" says the *Apostle* 1 Cor. xvi. 22. Which is to say, *cursed* in the *highest Manner* and *Degree*! how *accursed* then to us should the *Devil* and his *blasphemous* Suggestions be, which breathe implacable and *furious Hatred* against the *Being*, Blessedness and *Grace* of God to us thro' JESUS CHRIST our LORD?

An *Idolater* won't suffer his *dumb* and dead *Idol* to be spoken against; if he calls it his *God* he will not bear to hear it despised; an *Egyptian* of old would have *ston'd* the Man that should have sacrificed his *Abomination* before his Eyes; nor would One of all the *rout at Ephesus* endure a Blasphemer of their *Goddess Diana*! Nor is there a modern *Zealot* of *Rome Antichristian*, but thinks it *meritorious* to be the *Death* of you if you affront their *Wafer-Idol* the *Host*, when elevated in the *Church*, or when carried through the *Streets* in Form and Pomp. Can then the least Thought be *whisper'd* in our *Minds* against the Honour of our GOD and SAVIOUR, and not wound and pierce them? should not that be *execrable* to us, which is reproachful and *contemptuous* of HIM? What *Devotion*, what Love or Fear of GOD, can there be in us, if this Resentment and *Indignation* be wanting in us, when his Name is *blasphemed*? And when the *Endeavour* is to make us *Partners in the Blasphemy?*—Well was it made a *Law* to the *Israel of GOD*, Levit. xxiv. 15. *Whosoever curseth his GOD shall bear his Sin, and he that blasphemeth the Name of the* LORD *shall surely be put to Death, and all the Congregation shall certainly stone him with Stones.*

3. To express our Detestation of a *blasphemous Injection* we should *instantly reject* and *spue out the Abomination*, and not *suffer the vile Thought to lodge* in us. As it is but *rising* and *entring*, we must *rebuke*, suppress, forbid and *curse* it in the Name of the LORD. Let us vehemently turn away, and neither *hearken* nor *argue*; as *Calvin** advises. The *cloven Foot* is seen

*Caveamus itaque, ne *Satanæ* his Flabellis nos adversus DEUM sollicitanti Aures præbeamus; ne ab illo circumveniamur: Monemur, eiusmodi Blasphemias, ut quæ *Satanæ* Vomitus, acriter esse redarguendas: Vehementiam opponere debemus; non enim ludendum est cum furioso Hoste—So the *Jews* were won't to *rend* their Clothes at the hearing of *Blasphemy*.

here at once, and there needs not a Moment's Thought what to do. "Be *gone* from me thou cursed Thought," *thou Child of the Devil, and Enemy of all Righteousness!* I detest and *defy* thee, thou art none of *mine,* but art *execrable* to me! my GOD *impute it not* unto me! my GOD I will *adore* thee! raise now my Adorations of Thee *more* than ever! I would even *loathe* my own Soul, that the hated *Foe* could think to find any *liking* in me! my GOD forbid it! and get thee hence *Satan!*—So the blessed *Apostle,* filled with the HOLY GHOST, set his Eyes on the Sorcerer *Elymas,* who sought to *turn away the Deputy from the Faith;* and said, "*O full of all Subtlety and Mischief, thou Child of the Devil,* thou *Enemy of all Righteousness! will thou not cease to pervert the right Ways of the LORD!*" Acts xiii. 10.

4. After the Repulse and *Rejection* of the vile *Temptation,* we may *fortify* our Souls against every Return of it, by holy *Reasonings* and Argument, Meditation and *Prayer,* religious *Discourse,* and setting our selves to the *immediate Duties* incumbent on us in our present State and Circumstances; from which we should not suffer any *Temptation* to divert us, or keep us.

So when *Job had rebuk'd his Wife,* and spoke his *Detestation* of her Words; he then proceeded to give the *Reason* of his doing so; saying, "*What? Shall we receive Good from the Hand of the LORD? and shall we not receive Evil?*" q.d. "Shall I *curse GOD* to Day, because he pleases in his *Sovereignty,* or for the *Punishment of my Sins,* which have daily made the *Forfeiture* of all the Affluence of *good Things* with which his Providence had distinguish'd me, now to *bereave* me of them? or be it for the *Trial* Exercise and Increase of *his Grace* bestowed on me, which He may *prove* and require the *Exercise* of as he pleases! or if He *has prov'd* it in a State of outward *Prosperity* for so many Years together; shall he not now *call me* to express the same *Faith and Love,* Adoration and Praise, Devotedness and Subjection in a State of *Humiliation* and *Adversity; destitute, afflicted, tormented?* I will lie therefore *silent and adoring* before him in the *Dust* where his *wise* and *holy* and *righteous* PROVIDENCE has laid me, and go on to worship, *Naked came I out of my Mother's Womb, and naked shall I return; the LORD gave and the LORD has taken; blessed be the Name of the LORD.* I will therefore still go on to *bless*, and call upon my GOD, and the LORD shall *save* me! He is still the same *Good*, gracious and holy GOD to me; and by his Grace I will be the *same* humble thankful abased *Worshipper* before Him; trusting in Him and waiting on Him for his Salvation:—As He has had my daily *Thanksgivings* and Praises in the *Months past* wherein the LORD preserv'd me; when his *Candle* shone upon my Head and by his *Light* I walked through Darkness; when his *Secret* was upon my Tabernacle and my *Children were about me!* As I then *sent and sanctified* them when the Days of their *Feasting* were gone about, and early rose up in the Morning to offer *Sacrifices* according to the *Number* of them all; so Morning and Evening, and through the waking *painful* Hours of every Day and Night, will I (by his Grace) now ly *adoring my GOD* in my Sores and Ashes!—I then *fear'd for them* and for my self, and said, *It may be my Sons have sinned* in their Rejoicings *and cursed GOD in their Hearts;* (for out of the *Heart* proceed evil *Thoughts and Blasphemies*)—but if it were only I might fear my Sons had *neglected* to render unto GOD the *Praise and Glory* of his Mercies as became them; I therefore fail'd not to offer for 'em my *Burnt-Offerings:*—And shall I now *curse* HIM, whom I have been all my Life *blessing*? because I have neither *Child* to offer for, nor a *Sheep* or *Ox* out of my *Thousands* and *Hundreds* to bring unto his *Altar;* nor *Strength* to rise and go to it *as my exceeding Joy?*—No, *Thou* art my *Hope O LORD GOD*! thou art my *Trust* from my *Youth!* by *Thee* have I been holden up from the *Womb*, my *Praise* shall be continually of thee! I am a *Wonder* unto many, but thou my strong *Refuge*! let my Mouth be filled with thy *Praise* and with thy *Honour* all the Day."

I have put this *Run* of Scripture together, and as it were into the Mouth of tempted *Job*, to assist *others* when tempted to *hard Thoughts* of the blessed GOD, in strengthning and confirming themselves in their *Adorations* before Him. In much *fewer* Words *Job* set the *Temptation* in its true Colours, as most unjust and *base*, ungrateful and *impious;* and what his Soul should *never* come into, GOD helping him; but keep at the greatest *Distance* from it.

It was the SPIRIT and Grace of CHRIST that thus *animated Job* and fill'd his Mouth with *Arguments;* for when JESUS was *himself* led by the SPIRIT into the Wilderness to be tempted of the *Devil*, he *rebuk'd* the filthy and impudent *Suggestions* of *Satan* once and again, by giving his holy and irresistible *Reasons* from the *Word* of GOD; "*It is written*, said he, and again—*it is written*:" So it became *Him* who took our *Nature*, therein to be made *under the Law*, and to *fulfil* it; and whose *Glory* it was to say "*Thy Law is within me.*"

Joseph was the princely *Type* of CHRIST both in his *resolute Repulse* of the *Tempter*, the Devil in his *Mistress*; refusing to see or hear her; and yet *arguing* too *the great Wickedness, and Sin against GOD*; and also the foul *Ingratitude* Injustice and Villany to his *Master*. And when nothing would do with the impudent *Creature* he *fled*: An *Act* as *heroic* in its Circum-stances, as *David's* facing the *Monster* of a Man, the *Defier of the Host of GOD.*—In like manner, when *David* was outrag'd by *Michal* for the *Transports of his Devotion*, he bid her think if it were not *grateful* in him to *dance before the LORD* and his *Ark*, who had prefer'd him to her *Father's* House, and made him the *King of Israel*; "the devout will *honour me* said he, *and I will be yet more vile than thus, and base in my own Eyes.*" 1 Sam. v. 22.

In short, *Sin* is never to be *parly'd with*, but at once and resolutely to be *denied*; yet is it the *Act of Wisdom* and Grace to *reason with our selves* for our Confirmation and Estab-lishment in just and holy Resolutions; and with *others* for their Reproof and Conviction. The *Holy Scripture* is our *Armory* or *Magazine* to supply us *with Helmet and Shield, Sword and Buckler*, for our Defence against the *Darts of Hell*; and for *Offence* and Wounding to the *Enemy*, who flies before the holy hated WORD. From this *Artillery* discharge upon the *Hosts of Hell*, and they will *flee from you.*

Thus *rebuke* the Tempter and *refuse* to sin: and when this is done, *clench* the Denial with the *Word of Truth*, which sets be-fore you the impious Nature of *Sin*, and the cursed Nature and End of the *Tempter*; our Relation and natural Subjection to GOD and infinite Obligations to Him; his *Laws* Promises and Threatnings; and *be* the *Christian fixed in his Post, strong in the* LORD *and in the Power of his Might, to withstand the Wiles of the Devil, and wrestle against Principalities and Powers, the Rulers of the Darkness of this World, and spiritual*

Wickedness in high Places. Think, what is *holy* and righteous, wise and good, Duty and Interest; and there *fix your Foot*, and *stand*, having your *Loins girt about with Truth* and having on *the Breastplate of Righteousness.* Commit yourself thus to GOD and to the *Word of his Grace, which is able to keep you from falling.*

So far we have seen under the *two first Propositions;* that the *dearest* Children of GOD may be call'd to *endure* the most *foul* and accursed Annoyances from the *Devil;* which will be unspeakably *grievous* to them and abhorred, and ought to be infinitely detested and instantly *rejected* by them.—Yet if they cannot get *rid* of them, as they desire and *strive* to do, they must *beware* of a too *intense contending* with them; but *turn away* as from a barking *Dog*, or from an abusive raving *Scold*, or from a *cursing Shimei.*—As the heavenly Mr. *Janeway* advises in this Case, "Let not *such Thoughts* have any Time of *Abode* in your Mind, but *turn 'em out* with all the *Loathing* and Abhorrence that you can; and with as *little Trouble and Disturbance* as you can; or else *it pleases the Devil* if he can but make you your *own Tormentor.*—*Divert* your Thoughts therefore to something good and *holy*, and let those very *Injections* be constantly the Occasion of some *spiritual Meditation*, and *that* the *quite contrary* to the Blasphemy or infidel Suggestion: Or fall a *praying* with Earnestness; and the *Devil* will be *weary* if he finds his *Designs thus broken;* and that those *Sparks of Hell* which he *strikes* into Souls to *kindle* and *inflame Corruption*, do but put *Warmth into Grace*, and set Faith and Prayer a working: He will be *beat* with his own *Weapon* when it is *turn'd* upon him, what he intended as *Water* to cool or *quench* your Love to GOD, proves like *Oil* to make it *flame* the more vehemently."

I go on now to show in the *last* place,

III. That these grievous and *abhorred Injections are not the Sin of the dear Saints of GOD*, nor will be *reckoned* so by their *holy and gracious GOD;* nor do they *defile and pollute* their Souls, nor bring them under *Guilt*, when they are detested and rejected. This the *Text* is plain and positive in, "*In all this Job sinned not.*"

It is *strange* to observe the dreadful *Fears* of many *melancholly Christians*, who are *hurried* and distressed with evil and wicked Thoughts which their Souls abhor; That 'tis *altogether* (or very *much*) their *own Wickedness* and Guilt; and they are ready to account and call themselves the most *unbelieving and profane*, the most *polluted and vile* of any in the World; and to think that *none have Hearts* and Minds so *alienated from GOD*, and turn'd against Him as *theirs*: they *impute* all to themselves, and think themselves *twofold* more the Children of *Hell* than others!—Why is it *thus*? they are ready to *ask*, if there is not a *Fountain of Impurity* in *Me* more than in others, casting up *such Mire and Dirt*? Or if the Hand of *Satan* be in the *troubling of the Waters*, yet is it not plain he *finds* all this odious *Filth* at the Bottom in me? for which I should *abhor* my self and fear lest GOD abhor me!—And yet verily *GOD sees not Iniquity or Perverseness* in them, but is *pleas'd* in the Struggle and *Victory* of *his own Grace* within them.

The Support and *Relief* of such distressed Souls, and to *convince* them of their *Error*, I had principally in Mind in the Choice of this *Subject*; although I take it not to have been the very *State* of the *Case* with *Job*, who was too *intelligent* and establish'd a Worshipper of GOD to be driven from the happy *Confidence* of his *Integrity* and Uprightness, by the Assaults of *Satan* or by the *Arguments* of his *Friends*: He *appeal'd* from *them* unto GOD the Searcher of the *Heart*, and who knows all Things, that He *knew he loved Him*: Chap. x. v. 7. *Thou knowest that I am not wicked!* and in his *last Reply*, he finish'd with a long *Train* of noble *Appeal* to GOD and Affirmations to Men: Chap. xxvii. "As GOD *liveth* who hath taken away my Judgment, and the ALMIGHTY who hath vexed my Soul; all the while my *Breath* is in me and the *Spirit* of GOD is in my Nostrils; my *Lips* shall not speak Wickedness, nor my Tongue utter *Deceit*: GOD forbid that I should *justify* you; *'till I die I will not deny my Integrity*: My Righteousness I *hold fast* and will not let it go; my Heart shall *not reproach* me as long as I live."

But alas! how *few* of the dear *Children of GOD* in our Days arrive at like *steddy* full *Assurance* of Faith as *Job* had, respecting their *Integrity*! they are too often *soon shaken in Mind*; though we are admonished by the HOLY GHOST *not* to be so on one Account and another. 2 Thess. ii. 2. Even *Ministers* as well as common *Disciples* may be too justly likened to *Reeds shaken with the Wind!* and no wonder, when *Peter* himself was so easily carried away as the dry *Stubble* by a sudden *Blast* of Temptation, in his *Self-Confidence*, and after Warning given him by his LORD.

But what now lies before us, is to affirm and *prove* that there may be the *foulest Motions* to Sin, made by *Satan* to the Minds and Hearts of the most *sincere* and *pious* among the People of GOD; as *this* in the *Text* was to *Job*, "*Curse GOD and die!*" and yet if their Soul *abhors from* the cursed Motion, consent not to it, but detest it; it is *not their Sin*, but only *Satan's*:—"in all this *they have not sinned.*"

If we *receive the Witness of Man*, the *Witness of GOD is greater.* My *Text* is the *Witness of GOD* concerning *Job*; and by it the SPIRIT OF GOD witnesses the same concerning *You, O afflicted and tossed in Spirit and not comforted*; if you are enabled by *Him* to detest and eject like *blasphemous* and diabolical *Injections*, as odious and abominable to you. GOD, the righteous and gracious *Judge*, is then so far from beholding this Iniquity *in you*, that on the contrary He will in the great and *last Day*, before Men and Devils, in the most free and open manner *own accept* and *reward* it as the Power of his *Grace* in You, and an Instance of the sincere *Devotion* of your Souls towards Him*.

But to put this matter yet in a *clearer Light*, and give the utmost *Demonstration* of it, let us again recur to the horrid Motion of the *Devil* to the *Man* CHRIST JESUS our LORD; who was *in all Points tempted as we are, yet without Sin:* Heb. iv. 15. *For we have not a High Priest which cannot be touched with the feeling of our Infirmities: let us therefore come boldly to the Throne of Grace, that we may obtain Mercy and find Grace*

* *Van Mastricht* de Suggestionibus blasphemis. "Sunt Tentationes *Satanæ*, quibus Menti etiam pientissimorum obtrudit Cogitationes adversus Maiestatem DEI, Sufficientiam CHRISTI &c; non esse *DEUM*, vel Providentiam particularem; quibus etiam egregii pii exagitantur, ad hoc tantum ut conturbentur, et in Officiis Cultus Divini fatigentur. Sunt quidem in his Suggestionibus horrenda Scelera, sed *nequaquam in tentatis*, quippe qui ab eis abhorrent; sed in *tentante* solo.—Communis est Sors optimorum, huiusmodi Insultus *Santanæ* sustinere, quin et ipsius CHRISTI, *Matth.* iv.—Id a quo ingenue abhorret, et cui fortiter obnititur, non esse suum Peccatum; quin potius durissimam *Crucem*, sibi portatu longe molestissimam."

to help in Time of need.—For was not the LORD *of Glory*, the
HOLY ONE of GOD annoy'd by *Satan* with as cursed
Suggestions respecting the blessed GOD, as ever *You* were? and
yet *in Him was no Sin.*

He was tempted to a *Distrust* and Disbelief of his FATHER's
Care & kind Providence; "He lets thee *starve* and *famish*, and
casts thee here, where no *Bread* is to be got; *care* now for thy
Self, and if thou art the SON and *Prophet*, the promised
Messiah, as thou hast been declared at thy *Baptism, command
that these Stones be made Bread:*" q.d. thy FATHER is unnatural
and *cruel*, thy Dependance on Him *vain*; thy *Hunger* is natural necessary and *innocent* after so long Abstinence and
Devotion; Self-preservation is thy *Duty*, and 'tis a Case of
Necessity, and calls thee to go out of the *ordinary* Way for thy
Supply.—But our LORD in effect bid the *Tempter* remember
how the *Church* of old had been *fed* in the *Wilderness* by the
care of his FATHER; nor without *his Blessing* could the miraculous Bread *nourish* Him.

Again, the Devil's *last* Temptation of our SAVIOUR was
more *foul* and horrid than the *first*: In some visionary Representation of all the *Glories* of the *Kingdoms* of this *World*, he
set them before Him; and impudently call'd them *all his own*,
and told him he would *give 'em all* unto him, if he would *fall
down and worship him.* What a *Landskip* is here of the *Devil's*
drawing in a Wilderness? becoming the *Father of lies* and the
Pride of *Lucifer*, with the Subtlety of the *Old Serpent*! and
equally impudent his *Claim* and *Promise.* May I be permitted
to *paraphrase* the hellish Suggestion: q.d. "You have been led
up into this horrid *Wilderness*, and are you not here miserably
abandon'd by Him you call your *Father*! I the *God of this
World* appear to succour you! your *Father* has *little* in it to call
his *own*! *Rome* and all the Glories of it are all mine! this poor
Judea and the Wilderness about it he may call *his*! My *Idols* fill
Italy and *Greece*! there I am *worshiped* with utmost Pomp and
Glitter! the Earth and all its Learning and *Phylosophy* bows to
me! to Me the *Poets* sing, and *Cesar* with all the *Potentates* are
my Votaries: the *Powers* that be are ordained by me, and their
Dominions are by *me* distributed! to *whomsoever I will, I give
them*! are you not now poor *desolate*, empty in your great
Title the *Son of* GOD! do you deserve to be so abandon'd! be

mine and see what I will do for you! this *World* and all its *Glories* shall immediately be *yours*! its Rule, its Riches, its Homage and all its *Worship*! render me *only* this small Acknowledgment, this *single* Act of Homage, *fall down and worship me*!"

Thus the *evil One*, the *Prince of this World* came first with *Flatteries* and Allurements, and afterward with *Rage* and Terrors, with all the *Powers of Darkness* surrounding our blessed LORD, and *found nothing in him; for in Him was no Sin*. And if JESUS was thus *tempted*, yet *without Sin*; so if any of his dear *Members* are in like Manner tempted, and by his Grace are *kept* from yielding; by his *Power* are enabled to resist and *rebuke* the Temptation, it is by no Means *Sin* in them; but they are *more than Conquerors thro' Him*.

Let us *reason* and argue a little on this *Point*.

1. The meer *thinking* on Sin, or the Contemplation of it with *Aversion* of Soul, can by no Means *defile* the Mind. GOD Himself *beholds* Sin, *thinks* of it, yet is infinitely *holy*, and of *purer Eyes than to behold Evil, and cannot look on Iniquity*. Hab. i. 13. i.e. He beholds it with *Abhorrence*, his *Soul* hates it, his *Word* forbids, condemns and threatens it. The holy *Angels* also see our Sins, open and secret, consider and detest 'em; are offended at and grieved by them; and it is their *Holiness.—Good Men* make *diligent Search* and Enquiry into the Nature of *Sin*, their own and others among whom they dwell; discern the moral *Evil*, Guilt and Pollution of it; its Turpitude, Baseness and Malignity; yet are they not *defiled* hereby, no but the more *purified* both in Heart and Life.— Regenerate Persons and sincere *Penitents* find it absolutely necessary for them often to call their *past* Sins to Remembrance; they can neither shew themselves *Men* nor *Christians* without doing so, for a renewed *Repentance* on the Account of 'em, to increase their *Humiliation* and Abasement before GOD, to quicken themselves in the *Mortification* of the Body of Sin and Death which they carry about with them, to fix their *Abhorrence* of it and of themselves for it, and to strengthen their *Watch* against every Motion to it, from within or from without;—but all this is according to *Godliness*, and *purifying* to the Soul in *obeying the Truth*.— Now it is the same Thing in the Event, thro' the *Grace of*

GOD with and in his *Saints*, if vile and wicked Thoughts arise *involuntarily* in 'em, or are thrown and cast in upon them by *Satan* without and against their Will: If the Soul in either Case rise against them in *Fear*, in Mourning, in Hatred and *loathing* of them; Iniquity is but *purged away* hereby, and the Soul *confirmed* in holy Disposition, and the *Habit* of Grace is strengthned. As if you *rinse* a very foul Vessel, though it be in *dirty* Water, yet it will be something the *cleaner* for it; the *Dirt* at the Bottom will be in Part (at least) loosned, and cast out with the Water; so here, though the Injection of *Satan* be never so unclean and defiling in it self, yet the Soul *spuing out* the foul Thought, *casts up* also something further of its natural Impurity together with it.

Indeed there is a Contemplation or *thinking* of Sin that is most *impure* and defiling: To think of it with *liking* and Complacency or Desire is highly so; to *crave*, intend, and project it, to muse and dwell on it with Pleasure, to *roll it as a sweet Morsel under our Tongue* with Taste and Relish; to recollect it with Delight and *chaw* it over again as the *Cud*, (which is to *injure* the wholsome Property of the *clean* Creatures) this is to *listen* to the Tempter with Inclination and Consent, and call the forbidden Fruit *good* for Sight and Taste, and is *grosly* polluting to the Soul; as also in a *Degree* it is, not to have our Hearts *rise against*, and *fly from* every Motion within us to known Sin. For in this Case *Lust lodges*, is *harbour'd* and entertained, *conceives* and brings forth; and is so much *real* Adultery, Murder, Profaness of the Heart: Matth. v. 12. But on the contrary, to think of *Sin* with Grief and *Mourning*, Fear and Confusion, Indignation and Rejection, this is *purgative* and purifying, *wholsome* and healthful, *medicinal* and restorative, nourishing and *strengthning* to a *Principle of Grace*, in *Act* and Exercise.

2. Let it be moreover consider'd, that the very *Argument* I am upon *supposes* the abhorred detested Thoughts *injected by another*, and that they do *not come* or proceed from the *Soul it self*, nor are originally its *own*, and that the Soul is *grieved* by 'em, *offended* at 'em, *disowns* and rejects 'em: they are therefore some *spurious Births* from abroad, laid *secretly* and basely at our *Door*, or within it, and *falsly father'd on us*, if we

are *so foolish* as to receive and *own* them. If we consent not, 'tis only the *Devil's Sin*; his Act, his Guilt and he must answer for it. If for Instance, the first *Adam* had done as the SECOND did; if our *first* Parents, had *rebuk'd* the Tempter and *detested* his Motion to them, when he persuaded them to *disbelieve* and disobey GOD; the *Sin* had rested only on the *Devil*; they had remained *innocent* and been *confirm'd* in Holiness; but they *yeilded* to his cursed Suggestion, took *part* in his Act and in his *Apostacy* from GOD.

Indeed, now in our *fallen* State we have just *Reason* to suspect our Selves and *fear always*, sometimes *more* than at other, whether the vile *Motions* to Sin within us be not from our *own Hearts, which are deceitful above all things* and desperately wicked; *who can know them?* No wonder therefore if the *holiest* Child or Servant of GOD be sometimes ready to say, "I fear it is *Sin dwelling* and reigning in me, and the Hand of the *Devil* is it may be *little* in it;" for as St. *James* says "*Every Man is tempted when he is drawn away of his own Lust and enticed*: and how shall I *know* but that it is *thus* with me?"

But let us call in the *Aid* of the blessed St. *Paul* to set this matter in its true Light; and it is well for the *Church* that it has these *two Apostles* to give Light into each others Meaning. In the vii. *Chap.* to the *Romans*, the *Apostle* gives a Description of the *Conflict between Grace and Corruption* which he experienced in *himself!* and no doubt but every *renewed* sanctified Soul has more or less the *like* Experience. The *Apostle* calls himself *carnal and sold under Sin*, because he at Times did that which he *allowed not*, but truly *hated*: but his Support and *Relief* was, "that it was *no more He that did it, but Sin that dwelt in him*: for, the *Good* that he *would* he too often did *not*, but the *Evil* that he would not, that he *did*: Now (says he again) if I *do* that I *would not*, it is no more *I* that do it, but *Sin* that dwelleth in me:" He goes on, "I find then a *Law* that when I *would do good, Evil is present* with me: For I *delight* in the *Law of GOD* after the *inward Man*; but I see *another Law* in my Members *warring against* the Law of my *Mind*, and bringing me into *Captivity* to the Law of Sin! *O wretched Man* that I am, who shall *deliver me from the Body of this Death?*"—The like spiritual *Conflict* and *lusting* of the

Flesh against the *Spirit*, and of the *Spirit against the Flesh*, was found in the *Christians* at *Galatia*, so that *they could not do the Things that they would.* Gal. v. 17.

We see here that a *good Man* may have this *Rejoicing*, "the Testimony of his *Conscience* to his *Complacency* in the *Law* of GOD, and that his highest *Pleasure* in Life is, when *Heart and Life* are in the strictest Conformity to the Law and *Will of GOD*; and that with *his Mind* he is *serving the Law of GOD*; and yet at Times, *hold himself* no better than one brought into *Captivity* to the Law of *Sin*, a *carnal Creature, and sold under* it:" And yet he must *not impute* to his *own Will* and allowance the *Evils* which he *bewails, groans* out under, *strives* against and *hates* himself for. To this *he* must recur, "It is *no more I* that do it, but *Sin* which dwelleth in me; a *Body of Death* which I am hourly *groaning* for a *full* Deliverance from."—It is the Experience and *Confession* of the *holiest Saints* on Earth, that there are sad *Remains of Impurity* and Uncleanness cleaving to them; the *Filthiness both of Flesh and Spirit*, which are *defiling* to their best *Frames* and Duties; and too often *lusting* strongly and at Times *prevalently*; so that the *Good* which they *desire* to do they too often *do not*, and the *Evil* which they *wou'd not* they at Times *do*: Their *Souls delight in GOD, after the inward Man*, but yet they *find another Law*, Power or Principle of *Corruption, warring* against the *Law of GOD* and the *Law* that *bears Rule* in their Minds.— Now suppose this *carnal* Principle (*mortified* but not yet *slain* and extinguished) *lusts* and tempts to *blasphemous* and diabolical Tho'ts of it *self* alone or by the Instigation of *Satan*; and at the same Time suppose the *sanctified Spirit lusting against these hellish Motions, and groaning within it self for Deliverance* from them, and *Victory* over 'em; ready to *abhor it self* on the Account of them, and *crying out* of its *own* Captivity and *Bondage*,—we may be then *assured*, that whatever be the *Rise* of the cursed Temptation; be it from *Job's* own corrupt *Nature*, or from his *Wife*, or from his *Adversary the Devil*; it is not at all his *own Sin* and Act; it is *no more He that does it*, though it may be from *Sin that dwelleth in him*; Sin which he *allows not*, Sin which he is daily labouring to *mortify*, and from which he is earnestly *seeking* Deliverance.

In short, All *Sin* is voluntary; the *Will* is in it, the *Choice* is of it, the Soul *likes* it, and hence *Guilt* arises.—All that I shall further *add* on this Argument, to carry it to the utmost *Evidence* and Demonstration, is

3. There is not only *no Sin*, but *much Vertue*; a notable Exercise of *Grace*, and *Victory* over Temptation, in the *Case* supposed; when *blasphemous* Tho'ts arising in us, or violently suggested to us, are *abhorred* by us, detested and *rejected*. Violent Temptations to hideous Sin are hereby resisted, refused and *overcome*: And how *far* is this from the committing Sin, or *contrasting Guilt*? GOD, the righteous *Judge* reckon'd it to *Job* for *Righteousness*, and his *Triumph over Satan*; *still he holdeth fast his Integrity! although thou movedst me against him, to destroy him without a Cause.*

"This added to his *Character*, (says Mr. *Henry* on the Place) turn'd to his *Praise and Glory*! GOD himself speaks of it with a kind of Pleasure and *Wonder*, and of *Triumph* in the Power of his own *Grace*! He stands the *faster*, and *holds* the faster, for being shaken! *still* he does so; after so *violent* an Assault upon him! he has *got Ground* instead of losing any! his *Constancy* shows proves and *crowns* his Integrity! He is more hearty and *lively* than ever in *blessing Me.*"

Thus *Job* approv'd himself the perfect and *upright Man*, one that feared GOD and *eschewed Evil*; and that there was *none like him* on the Earth: None *tried*, tempted and afflicted like him in his Day, or since among meer Men, or that *bore* Temptations of like Kind and Degree, so many and great, with like *Heroic* Piety and Fortitude.—The *Tempter* could not but own himself *beat*, and GOD *justified* in all that He had said of his penitent, patient, believing faithful *Servant*.

GOD meant and allow'd the *Trial*, that it might stand on *Record* for the Comfort of his *tempted Saints*, and for the Edification of his *Church* for ever. It is a *Banner display'd* for others to *fight* under, in the Cause of *Truth* and Holiness, to the End of the World. *Job* has help'd many a weak and strong *Believer* to beat the Devil again and again, down to our own Days. He still *sits as a King in the Army*, and *what Hosts* of suffering Saints are *still fighting* under and after him, and conquering by *Faith in his* REDEEMER.

And by every Fight and *Victory* they certainly get some further *Strength* and Power against Sin, and *Confirmation* in

Grace; even as *the Testimony of* CHRIST *was confirmed* in the *Corinthians,* and they *confirmed to the End*; that they might be *blameless in the Day of* CHRIST: 1 Cor. i. 6, 8. *Satan* also is more and more *bruised under the Feet* of GOD's People; and like the conquering *Israelites* they will be *call'd by* JESUS to set their *Feet* on the *Necks* of the *Principalities and Powers of Darkness*; and the *Promises* of both *Testaments* will be fulfilled to them and in them; "*thou shalt tread upon the Lion and the Adder; on Serpents and Scorpions, and over all the Power of the Enemy,*" Psal. xci. Luk. x. So *Light is sowing for the righteous,* in the Hours of greatest *Darkness*; and the humble *Disciples of* JESUS will one Day like the *Seventy* return with *Joy* to Him, saying, "LORD, *even the Devils are subject to us thro' thy Name*!"—And he said to them, "*I beheld Satan as Lightning fall from Heaven*! and in *this* rejoice, *that your Names are written in Heaven.*"

The Day is coming when *the Saints shall judge the World, shall judge Angels*! Then they shall see *their Enemy,* the *Old Serpent,* the *Devil and Satan* at the *Bar* of CHRIST their *Saviour,* and *damn'd* and cast into the *Lake of Fire*! Then having follow'd CHRIST in the *Regeneration* they shall *sit down with him on his Throne*! Then having drank of *his Cup* and been baptized with *his Baptism,* they shall sit on his *right Hand* and on his *left* in his Kingdom!—Let 'em realize now by *Faith* how full will be their *Joy,* how bright their *Glory,* how high their *Honour,* how *wide* their *Fame* and *Renown* in that illustrious *Day*! They *Conquerors* and *more* than Conquerors! and so their *Triumphs* more than *August* or *Roman*; Divine, Cælestial and Eternal!—Wherefore "my beloved *Brethren,* count it *all Joy* when ye fall into diverse *Temptations,* yea the most *fiery* Trials; for blessed is the Man that *endureth* them; for when he is *tried* he shall receive the *Crown of Life,* which the LORD hath *promised* to them that love Him: But let *Patience* have its *perfect* Work, that ye may be perfect and *entire* wanting nothing." James i. 2, 3, 4, 12.

I close with some Words of the very Reverend and pious Dr. *Horneck* on this Argument: "*Unallowed blasphemous* and other *wicked* Thoughts in the Heart *do not defile it*. This *Doctrine* must be often inculcated, because of the great Number of *pious Souls* who look upon themselves as the *vilest*

Wretches in the World, and are ready to run into *Desperation*, because so many *horrid* Tho'ts and *filthy* Suggestions present themselves to their Minds; more especially disturbing them in their *Devotions* and religious Exercises: But not being *allow'd* of, nor *consented* to; however dreadful and *hainous* they are in themselves, they *no more defile the Heart* than *boisterous Winds*, and the *Commotion* of the Water sully the *Pearls* that ly at the Bottom.—That they are not their *own* Tho'ts is evident, because their *Will* is contrary to them, their Understanding is convinced of the Iniquity of them, and their Hearts *Desire* is to be rid of 'em. The *Soul* in this Case is like the *young Men in the fiery Furnace*; while a thousand *Sparks* fly about them, not a hair of their Head is singed."

To have done,—In every *Congregation* almost there are some whose *Case* this is: Some are *known* to us, and there may be others: To *all such* I have bro't the *Mind* of GOD and they must make *Conscience* of receiving it as *from Him*: Wherefore *comfort* your selves together, and *edify* one another: *Comfort the Feeble-minded, and support the Weak: And the very GOD of Peace sanctify you wholly; and I pray GOD your whole Spirit Soul and Body be preserved blameless unto the Coming of our* LORD JESUS CHRIST: *Faithful is He that calleth you, who also will do it. Amen.*

CHARLES CHAUNCY

Man's Life Considered Under the Similitude of a Vapour, That Appeareth for a Little Time, and Then Vanisheth Away

A Sermon on the Death of that Honorable & Vertuous
Gentlewoman Mrs. Sarah Byfield,
The amiable Consort of the Honorable
Nathanael Byfield, Esq;
Who died Decemb. 21st. 1730.
In the 58th Year of her Age.

1 Chron. xxix. 15.— *Our days on earth are as a shadow,*
and there is none abiding.

Psal. xxxix. 4. *LORD, make me to know mine end, and*
the measure of my days what it is: that I may know how
frail I am.

———

To the Honourable Nathanael Byfield Esq;
Honoured SIR,

When I had fallen in with Your Desire *to Print this* Sermon, *I could not prevail with my self to let it go to the* Press, *without first paying* Public *regards to so good a* Friend: *whom, I have Reason to love & reverence as a* Father.

The Sermon *was Preach'd on the lamented* Death *of your dear & amiable* Consort. *I tho't it proper to take special Notice of such a* Providence: *and as I endeavour'd to improve it for the* Benefit *of all my* Hearers; *so for* Your's *in particular. In the* Character *I have given* Madam Byfield, *I have not affected Niceness & Acuracy; yet have had a* strict *regard to* Truth & Uprightness. *And I doubt not, but all that were acquainted with* her, *will judge, that her* Memory *is worthy to be transmitted to* Posterity, *with more* Honour, *than I have been able to do it.*

I heartily joyn with You, Sir, *in rendring Thanks to a good GOD,* who *directed you to a* Person, *every way so agreable: and that He continued* her, *so long a Blessing and Comfort to you; the pleasant Companion of your* Age; *your Crown & Ornament. 'Tis the same most Wise & Merciful GOD, that has taken* her *away from you. And 'tis for your* Good, *He has* thus *afflicted you. This* Correction *of your Heavenly Father, was* necessary *in that* Chain *of* Events, *by which, He had* ordained *to bring you to* Glory: *which is the highest Motive to Patience & Submission.*

May this, *and all* other *Divine Dispensations be Sanctify'd to You! and bless'd as a* Means *to make you still more* meet *for* that *World, where there is no* Sin *nor* Sorrow; *where* all Tears shall be wip'd from your Eyes, *and you shall be compleatly happy in the Sight and Fruition of the blessed GOD. And may your* Children, *(already Propagated to the fourth Generation, and) throughout all Generations, follow you into the* Heavenly State, *and be an Eternal Spring of Joy to You!*

So Prays,

Your much oblig'd and
Affectionate Servant in CHRIST,

Charles Chauncy.

Man's Life Consider'd Under the Similitude of a Vapour

JAMES IV. 14.
For what is your Life? It is even a Vapour, that appeareth for a little time, and then vanisheth away.

I HAVE made Choice of this *Text,* to lead you into some proper Meditations on *humane Frailty:* a subject *never* unsuitable for *dying* Men to employ their Tho'ts upon; and *particularly* seasonable, after any fresh, affecting Instance of *Mortality.*

We are here presented with a very instructive Description of *Life.* It's consider'd under the Similitude of *a Vapour, that appeareth for a little time, and then vanisheth away.* A true and lively Representation of the *State,* of *Man's Life* upon Earth!

which is of but short Continuance, inconstant and uncertain: The effect whereof shou'd be, our *living* after the best and wisest manner; to the purposes of another World, & so as to secure to our selves, an *Interest* in that *future & eternal Life*, which the *Gospel* has reveal'd, and promises *to them, who, by patient continuance in well doing, seek for Glory, Honour and Immortality.*

And that we may be excited and quicken'd, in making such an *Improvement* of the *present Life*, I shall beg your Attention, while I am discoursing to you, upon the two following important Points; agreable to the *Scope* of the *Apostle* in the words, I have sed to you.

I. I shall consider the Representation that is here given us of *Man's Life.*

II. I shall show, What *Influence*, such a Representation, *ought, in all reason, to have upon us.*

I. I am to consider the Representation, that is here made of *Man's Life. It is even a Vapour, that appeareth for a little time, and then vanisheth away.*

I have no Design to pursue this *Metaphor*, in *all* the *little* Resemblances, which one's Imagination might easily suggest: but shall confine my self to a few Particulars; which lie open to common View, and were, no doubt, the *things* intended by the *Apostle.* And they are such as these. 1. That *Man's Life*, upon Earth, is *Short.* 2. *Uncertain.* 3. *Inconstant.* 4. *Irrecoverable*, when once gone.

1. *Man's Life* may be represented by a *Vapour*, to signifie the *exceeding Shortness of it.* A *Vapour* is of but *short* Continuance. It may for a while "wander upon the Surface of the Earth or Water;" but is soon driven away by the Wind: or spends it self, and *vanishes away.* Just the same thing may be said of the *Life* of *Man*: which, whatever it is, and however active and buisie it may for a while appear, is yet soon extinguished: or of it self languishes and expires. The *Scriptures* are full of affecting Illustrations to this purpose. They sometimes comprehend *Man's Life*, within the narrow compass of an *Hand-breadth*; which is one of the most inconsiderable Measures. Psal. 39. 5. *Behold, thou hast made my Days as an Hand-breadth.* Sometimes they limit it to the Time a Man takes in *telling a Story*, which soon passes away, and is gone.

Psal. 90. 9. *For all our Days are passed away in thy Wrath: We spend our Days as a Tale that is told.* At other times, they measure *Life*, by some of the *Swiftest Motions*; to signify how soon it arrives at it's determin'd Period. Our Days are said to be *swifter* than a *Weaver's Shuttle**, which is no sooner thrown in at one side of the Web, but it is out at the other; to pass away as the *swift Ships*, which with a brisk Gale, are quickly carried out of Sight; to be *swifter* than a *Post*, who hurries along, with all possible Speed: And the *Eagle* that maketh towards *her Prey*, does not *fly* more *swiftly*, than the *Life* of *Man* passes away: As these things are elegantly express'd, Job. 9. 25, 26. *Now my days are swifter than a Post: they flee away:—they are passed away as the swift Ships: as the Eagle that hasteth to her prey.*

And there is a *certain* Justness and Propriety in these *Scripture* Representations of *Man's Life*; tho' borrow'd from things, some of which are but of few Days, and others of but few Moments Continuance: and that, if at the same Time, we should suppose *it* to reach the *utmost Bounds* of it's appointed *Duration*. For what are *threescore* or *fourscore Years*? As the *Psalmist's* Expression is,† they are soon cut off, and we fly away. Indeed, when we look *forward* from *Youth* or *Childhood*, to *Old age*; it appears at a vast Distance: and as tho' we should scarce ever arrive at it. But by only changing the *Scituation* of our selves, how different will the Prospect appear! Let a Person look back from *Age* to *Youth*, and it will seem but a very small Space: those *Thirty* or *Forty* Years, which were judged by him in his *Childhood* unattainable, how short do they seem, now he has *passed thro' them*! So true is that Observation, That *a Day to come shews longer to us than a Year that is gone.* And it is the universal Sense of all that are *grown* into *Years* concerning it. They are even surpriz'd, when they look back to find, how insensibly their *Days* are rolled away. If they extend their *View* forty, fifty, or threescore Years *backwards*; they can scarce believe they have *Liv'd* so long, it appears such a *Moment* of time. And generally speaking, the longer Persons live, the *shorter* their *past* Days and Years seem

*Job 7. 6.
†Psalm 90. 10.

to them: And when they are in a serious turn of Tho't, they more thoroughly realize, what a *small* part of *Duration*, the *Term* of *Humane Life* contains.

And if the *Life* of *Man* appears thus *short* even to *Men* themselves, when set in a due light: how much more *inconsiderable* must it seem in GOD's Eye! with whom there is no *Beginning of Days*, nor *End of Years*; and in whose Sight *a thousand Years are but as one Day*. Surely in this View of *Life*, it must sink into the *smallest* Point of Time. Yea, as the *Psalmist* phrases it, *our Age is as nothing before GOD.** Nay, if our *Lives*, like *Methusalah's*, were protracted to near a *Thousand* Years; in GOD's Account, and in compare with his *Eternal* Duration, they would seem but as a single Moment. And yet, how many of our *Ages* go to make up a *Thousand* Years! and yet further, how *few* live to what we call the *full Age* of a Man! Perhaps the greatest part of *Mankind* die within the *Space* of the *first Seven Years*. And where one arrives at the general *Period* affix'd to *Humane Life*, a *thousand* die in *Youth* or *Middle age*. Such a Justness and Propriety is there in these *Scripture* Representations of *Man's Life*: like a *Vapour, it appears* but *for a little time, and then vanishes away.*

If any shou'd now feel themselves *uneasie* at this Representation of *Life*, and be tempted to think *hardly* of GOD, for making the *Limits* of it so exceeding *narrow*; it will at once satisfy all their *Objections*, to consider *Life* in the true and proper *Notion* of it: *as a Probation season for Eternity.*

The GOD that gave us our *Beings*, design'd them for an *End* worthy of Himself, and those noble *Powers, He* has endow'd us with. But this *End* is not to be obtain'd in *this* World. There is nothing *here*, that can satisfy the *Desires* of our Souls, or be a commensurate *Happiness* for them. We must look beyond the *Grave* for this, to the unseen unutterable Glories of the *Heavenly* State. And if we take a View of the *present Life*, as referring to *this State*, and a *Tryal* for our Entrance into it, it will sufficiently justify, both the Wisdom and Goodness of GOD in the *Shortness* of it.

Especially, if we go on and consider, that the Time of *Life* is a *Space* full *long* enough for the *Business* we were sent into

*Psalm 39. 5.

the World upon; *viz.* to make *Preparation* for *Eternity.* For thro' the LORD JESUS CHRIST, *who* has obey'd the *Law*, and suffer'd the *Penalty* of it, for *us* and in *our* stead; the *Terms* of Salvation are bro't down to our present *fallen* State: and nothing more is *absolutely* requir'd of us, but FAITH in JESUS CHRIST, as the SON of the *living* GOD, including in it the *Seeds & Principles* of sincere *Repentance*, and a true *Gospel Obedience.* And no sooner is such a *Faith* wrought in our Souls, but our *main Work* is done, and the *great Design* of *Life* answered. And Persons not only may, but often are, even in the *beginning* of Life, thus endow'd with *Faith.* And a *little* Time, if it be well improv'd, in the diligent Use of proper Means, will serve for this purpose. And *all* that is *afterwards* necessary, will be *only* to give proof of our good Estate; to *continue* in the *Faith* of CHRIST; to *grow* in *Grace*; to *shine* in the World by our *good Examples*; and in a word, to *glorify* GOD by our holy *Carriage* of our selves under whatever Condition He shall please to order out unto us. And when our Lives come to be thus employ'd, the *shorter* they are the *better*; inasmuch as we shall hereby the sooner obtain *the End of our Faith, the Salvation of our Souls.* And this is the Tho't of all that are truly wise. They would not willingly have the Term of Life set at a *further* Distance, least the Tryal of their Graces should be *too* heavy and tedious; and the *full* Reward of their Faith and Good works *too* long detain'd from them.

And on the other hand, when Persons do pervert the grand Design of Life; neglecting their Souls, and taking no Care to prepare themselves for the future State; 'tis unreasonable to expect their Lives should be protracted, beyond what the Lives of Men ordinarily are, that so they might have a *longer* Space of Tryal, before their Condition is unalterably determined. For if they should live over the present Life, as bounded by GOD, tho'tless of Eternity, and unconcern'd to make Preparation for it; and instead hereof, should spend their Days in Vanity, or the Gratification of their Fleshly Lusts, there would be but little Hope of their Amendment and returning to a better Mind, if their Time should be lengthned out to the *longest* Period: But on the contrary, great reason to fear, that they would only grow more bold and obstinate in Wickedness, and get still at a further Distance from GOD and Happiness. Besides, the *ordinary* Duration of Man's Life, is full long enough for such Persons to be continued *Plagues* to Mankind, by their evil Practices and bad Examples. And 'tis in *Mercy* to the World in general, that the Time of their Life is limited to *threescore* or *fourscore* Years.

But I must not enlarge here. To proceed,

II. By the *Metaphor* in the *Text*, we have represented to us, the *utter Uncertainty of Humane Life*. What more *uncertain* than the Appearance of a *Vapour*? It sometimes continues a *longer*, and sometimes a *shorter* Time: is sometimes *suddenly* extinguished, and sometimes *slowly* and by *degrees*. Alike *uncertain* is the *Life* of *Man*. 'Tis *certain* indeed, that *all Men shall once die*. And there is no Man living but knows that he shall die. We know likewise, that we are surrounded with an infinite Variety of Distempers, and every moment lie expos'd to innumerable Accidents, which may put a Period to our Days. So that there is no *Point* of Time, in which we are free from Danger, and may be sure of not falling by the Stroke of Death. Yet, *the precise Time when*, and *particular Means* and *manner how*, remain, as to us, *absolute Uncertainties. Man knoweth not his Time**. This is the *Sole* Prerogative of *the most high GOD*. Nothing, to Him, is either contingent or uncertian. And in a very particular manner, He is the *Supream* LORD of *Life* and *Death*. And as *such*, He hath appointed the *Day* and *Hour*, nay, the very *Moment*, when every *Son* and *Daughter* of *Adam*, shall undergo the Change of Death. *Job* seems to have put this Matter beyond Dispute, Job. 7. 1. *Is there not an appointed time to Man upon Earth? Are not his Days also like the Days of an Hireling?* An *Hireling*, we all know, hath his *fix'd* Time of Service: and when this is expired, he is discharg'd from his Labour. The same thing may be said of *Man*: he has his *determin'd* Time of Duration; and whenever this comes, in a moment he expires. This Matter is further illustrated, Chap. 14. 5. *Man's days are determined, the Number of his Months are with thee: thou hast appointed his Bounds, that he cannot pass.* So that, let our Character be what it will; if we are never so desireable, or never so useful: or let

---

*Eccles. 9. 12.

our State be what it will; be we prepar'd or unprepar'd, we must at such a particular Point of Time, which GOD from Eternity, has pitch'd upon, be dismis'd from the Body. And He will so order it in his *Active Providence*, that all necessary natural Causes shall *unitedly* concur, to put a Period to our Life, not only at the *very Time*, but after the *same manner*, that he has decreed.

GOD has not indeed alotted to all Men the *same* Number of Months and Years: nor determin'd to accomplish his *Decree* upon them, by the *same* Means and after the *same* manner; but has *variously* fix'd the *Periods* of Life in different Persons, and uses as great a *Variety* in the *Means* and *manner* of their Death. And upon this Account it is, that both the *Time* and *Means & manner* of our going out of the World, are, as to us, Matters of the *greatest Uncertainty*.

We know not *when* we shall die: whether in Infancy or Childhood, while our Natures are weak and tender; before we are instructed in the Worth of Life, or are capable of exerting ourselves to any valuable purposes? Or in *Youth*, our Constitutions being strong & healthy; our Powers active and sprightly, and in the best Capacity of serving the Ends of Life? Or whether we shall continue, till *the evil Days come, and the Years draw nigh, when we shall say, we have no Pleasure in them*?

We Know not the *Manner* in which we shall die: Whether on a Sudden, or by slow & leisurly Steps? in the Height of Prosperity, or Depth of Adversity? in a Throng of worldly Business, or free from outward Cares and Incumberances? *Death* will most certainly seize upon us: but where will it be? In the Closet, or the Street? in the Shop, or the Field? at Sea, or on dry Land?—These things are *Secrets* in the Breast of GOD alone—.

In fine, We are absolutely ignorant by what *Means* GOD will take us out of the World: whether by Disease, or Accident? according to Nature, or by Force & Violence? He will doubtless make use of natural Causes: But what will they be? A Fever, or a Frenzy? the Teeth of an Insect, or a blast of Wind? a Morsel of Meat, or a Hair from our Heads? a fall from a Horse, or the hand of Malice? Or will *He* suffer us to live, till Nature is Spent, & we die of ourselves?—

Thus *Uncertain* a thing is the *Life* of Man.—And it is an Argument of great Wisdom and Goodness in GOD, that 'tis so. For if we Knew the *determinate* Space of Life, or that it would surely expire at such a *particular* Term, it would have a very unhappy Influence upon us. For, on the one hand, if it was at a *considerable* Distance, we should be in utmost Hazard of allowing our selves Liberty, to *live according to the Course of this World; fulfilling the desires of the Flesh & Mind.* And this we shou'd be apt to do, till we came within the near Prospect of our Dissolution: and then having so habituated ourselves to Sin as to be harden'd in it; it would be *almost* a Miracle, if we were ever prevail'd upon, to *break off our Sins by Righteousness, and our Iniquities by turning to* GOD. For as the Prophet argues, Jer. 13. 23. *Can the Ethiopian change his Skin, or the Leopard his Spots? Then may ye also do good, that are accustom'd to do evil.* And on the other hand, if the Time of Life was *Short*, and to be terminated in the space of a few Years: tho' it might awaken our Consideration, & put us on Endeavours to make our Peace with GOD, and secure an Interest in Christ; yet how melancholy & uncomfortable, would it be like to make our Abode upon Earth? We should enjoy no Pleasure in the World: neither in Friends, nor Relatives; nor any of the good things, GOD has provided for our present Happiness. Such would be our Concern & Fear; such our dark and gloomy Apprehensions, as would not only unfit us to converse with one another; but even to live in such a World, as GOD has made this to be.

But now that the *Time* remains *Uncertain*, both these Inconveniences are avoided. Instead of being encourag'd in a Course of Sin for the *present*, we have one of the strongest Arguments to engage us in an *immediate* Care, about the Business of Religion, and our Soul's Salvation; and at the same time, there is room left for the Exercise of *Hope*, which layes a Foundation for the Enjoyment of ourselves and the Comforts of Life.

We shou'd therefore thankfully acknowledge and admire the Wisdom & Goodness of GOD, in keeping us ignorant of the *Time & Circumstances* of our Death: the Knowledge of which, could not be of any real Service to us; but very hurtful upon many Accounts. We shou'd be content to be in the dark, as to these *Futurities*, and improve our Ignorance as a Motive to Zeal and Industry in *working out our own Salvation with Fear and Trembling*.

III. The *Metaphor* in the *Text* signifies to us, *the inconstant, unsettled State of the present Life*. A *Vapour* is an *inconstant variable* Meteor. *One while* it extends it self far & wide, *anon* it dwindles away into Nothing. *Now* it appears thick & dense, *presently* it becomes so thin & rarify'd as not to fall within Reach of Observation. Just such an *inconstant variable* thing is the *Life* of *Man*.

We seldom continue *long* in the same State; but are constantly passing under innumerable Changes. *This* Moment we are well and in Health; the *next* we are seiz'd with some fatal Distemper. *Now* we abound in Riches and Plenty; *on a sudden* we are reduced to Poverty and Penury. In the *Morning* we are in Honour and Dignity; before *Night*, we wear the Character of Men of low Degree. To *Day* we are respected and well spoken of; by to *Morrow*, we are hated, despis'd and evil spoken against. This *Week* we are surrounded with Friends and Acquaintance; the *next* we have reason to make that Complaint, Psal. 88. 18. *Lover and Friend, thou hast put far from me, and mine Acquaintance into Darkness*. And so whatever our present State is, we quickly pass out of it into another; that is sometimes better, and sometimes worse.

And it is in a sort necessary, the *present State* of *Man's Life* should be thus *variable*. For so perverse & depraved are our Tempers, since our *Fall* from GOD, that it would be scarce possible for us, to carry it suitably, under *any one* invariable Condition of Life.

If, on the other hand, we were bless'd with a constant *Run* of Prosperity; for a long time together enjoying our Health & Friends, and all the Comforts and good things of Life: ten to one, but it would be the Means of our being ruined for ever. We could not bear such an *uninterrupted* Series of Worldly Happiness. We should be apt to grow proud & insolent; forgetful of GOD & our own Souls: & instead of being the more strongly engaged in His Love & Service, it would be likely we should *Kick* against Him; contemn His Law, slight his Goodness, and by our *hard & impenitent Heart, treasure up to ourselves Wrath against the day of Wrath*. And on the other hand, if we were frown'd upon in Providence, and kept under poor, difficult and afflictive Circumstances; and this was to be our Condition *invariably*; it would sink our Spirits, discourage our Endeavours, and unfit us for every thing. We shou'd have no Heart to engage in any Affair, neither respecting our Souls nor Bodies: or if we had, we shou'd not be able to pursue it, with Zeal and Resolution.

It is therefore a Wise disposal of Providence, that our *present* State is *variable*, that we are sometimes in one Condition & sometimes in another; sometimes in Adversity & sometimes in Prosperity. Such a *mixt inconstant* State is best suited to the *present* Frame of our Minds; and no doubt was design'd by GOD as a *Kindness* to the World in general; as being a *Means* wisely adapted, to serve the *End* of *Life*, which is the Glory of GOD, in such a Temper & Behaviour of ourselves, as He has made necessary, in order to our Future & Eternal well being.

IV. The *Metaphor* in the *Text* represents to us, the *Irrecoverableness of Man's Life*, when once gone. A *Vapour* when once vanish'd away, is *irrecoverably* gone. The same must be said of *Life*: When once expir'd, it can *never* be *recall'd*. The Extinction of Life is therefore described, Psal. 39. ult. *As agoing hence, & being here no more.* And *Job* speaking of Man's Death, expresses himself in such Language as that, Job 14. 12. *Man lieth down, and riseth not till the Heavens be no more: they shall not awake, nor rise out of their Sleep.* And in the 14. v. *If a Man die, shall he live again?* The Question does not infer a Doubt, whether such as die, shall return back to live their Lives over again: But is the strongest *Negation. They shall not live again.* They shall never return back to any of the Employments or Enjoyments of the present Life. When Death hath once passed upon Men, their Probation season is over, and State made *Unalterable* for Eternity. Eccl. 11. 3.—*If the Tree fall towards the South, or towards the North: in the Place where the Tree falleth, there shall it be.* An awful Consideration! It should surely affect us to think, that as Death leaves us, so Judgment will find us; that as soon as ever this frail Life of our's is ended, our Condition from *that Moment* is for ever determined; our Place of Abode so fix'd, as that if we have misimprov'd the present season, we can never amend or correct our Mistake. O how shou'd our Attention be awaken'd at this! and our Hearts animated with Zeal & Resolution in doing the work, we were sent into the World upon! *Beloved*, seeing things are thus, *What manner of Persons ought we to be in all holy Conversation & Godliness?* With what Diligence should we labour, *that we may be found* of our Judge, *in Peace, without spot and blameless.* Which brings me to our next general Head of Discourse, *viz.*

II. To show what *Influence*, the Representation, the *Text* gives of Life, *ought, in all Reason to have upon us.* And here that I might not *Exceed* the Limits of my *Hour*, I must confine my self to *only* a few general Hints. As,

1. It shou'd put us upon *Weaning our Affections from the World, and Moderating our Endeavours after it.* And are there any, whose Hearts are too much set upon the World, & that employ too much Pains in the Pursuit of it? It shou'd seem incredible, that *Men*, whom GOD has endow'd with Reason & Understanding, shou'd be so little govern'd, by a sense of their own Frailty, the exceeding Shortness & Uncertainty of the present Life. And yet alas! so it is. Yea, and the Generality of Persons are so strangely fond of the World as to think, they can never love it too well, nor endeavour too much after it. They will rise up early, and sit up late; go thro' Difficulties and Hardships; expose themselves to Hazards; run all Risques; submit to any thing, and do any thing, for the Obtaining *only* of a few Scraps or Portions of it. If we were to judge by the Temper & Behaviour of some Men, we must suppose they imagin'd, that both themselves and *their Houses would continue for ever, and their Dwelling-places to all Generations.* When alas! *Their Life, like a Vapour, appeareth* but *for a little Time, and then vanisheth away.* How shou'd this Tho't beat down the Price of the World in our Esteem, and check our Endeavours after it? For if at the *longest* we must *quickly* leave the World; and may in a *Moment*, at any Time, be snatch'd away from all the Enjoyments of it: Why shou'd our Hearts be wedded to it, and our whole Time and Souls employ'd about it! Is it not far more reasonable to loosen our Affections from the Earth? to set light by the good things of it? and spend no more Pains in the Pursuit of them, than is realy necessary for our present Comfort?

Perhaps we look upon the World, as our only Place of Happiness: and entertain in our Minds such exalted Apprehensions of the Value of outward Enjoyments, as to desire & aim at nothing higher. But O! let us remember, we shan't always have such Tho'ts of the World. We are hastening apace to the Grave. It won't be long, however far we may put from us the evil Day, before we shall find ourselves in the Agonies of Death. And when this comes to be our Case; what think we, will our Apprehensions about the World be? As we shall View it in a different Light, so will it certainly appear in quite different Colours. It will seem altogether Vanity. We shall see nothing desirable in it: but shall be amaz'd at our former Folly, in setting so high a Price on it, and making it the chief Object of our sollicitous Concern. And at such a Time as this: of what great Advantage will it be to us, if we have gain'd even as much of this World, as we could possibly desire? Has our *highest* Ambition been gratified, in being honour'd and perferr'd among Men?—Our Honour must now be laid in the Dust; all our Marks of Distinction drop'd at the Mouth of the Grave: and when we appear in the other World, it will be upon a Level with the most ignoble Slave.—Or have we indulg'd our selves in Ease & Pleasure? taking all the carnal Delight we could wish for, or are capable of enjoying?—It is now all over and gone. And what remains, but cutting Reflections; restless Fears and Convulsions of Soul?—Or have we *heap'd up Riches; joyning House to House, and Field to Field*, till *we are placed alone in the midst of the Earth*?—Yet let us consider, That *Riches are not for ever*,* and that, "of all our Possessions, we shall *now* need no more than will but suffice to bury us. Silver & Gold are too heavy Laden, to be carried into another World. And what is it to a *dying* Man, whether his Chamber be richly furnish'd or not; whether he breath out his Soul in a Palace, or a Cottage"†. In an Hour of Death, "We shall not take Pleasure in summing up our Estates, and counting how much we shall die worth, and how many Hundreds or Thousands we shall leave behind us." Alas! the Concerns of *dying* Persons are usually of a quite different

*Prov. 27. 24.
†Bp. Hopkins's Works Sermon 2 d.

Nature. The Necessities of our Souls will now crowd themselves upon us. An accusing Conscience, and a fearful Expectation of approaching Torments, will shake out of our
Minds all Tho'ts of the World, and fill us with the greatest
Sollicitude to obtain the Favour of GOD, the Pardon of Sin,
Peace of Conscience, and an Interest in the great SAVIOUR
of Sinners. And of what Service will the World be to us, in
these Respects? What Suitableness is there in it to supply these
Wants of our Souls? "Food may satisfy Hunger, and Raiment
fence off the Injuries of the Weather": There is a Suitableness
in them to do so. But what will all worldly Enjoyments avail
towards appeasing GOD's Anger, or giving us a comfortable
Hope of future Blessedness? What Suitableness is there in a
Bag "of Gold, or a sumptuous Building, to satisfy a Man's
Mind, when perplex'd with Fears of Wrath & Hell? You may
as well seek to cure a Wound in the Body, by applying a
Plaister to the Garment, as seek to ease a wounded Spirit, by
all the Treasures, Pleasures & Enjoyments of this World."*
Riches profit not in the Day of Wrath.† There is no Aptness in
them to bring any true solace to the Soul. O let us not then
suffer the World to engross our Affections, and take off our
Tho'ts & Care from things of infinitely more Weight &
Importance: But remembring, that we are *dying* Creatures,
and that our Life, like a *Vapour, will appear* but *for a little
Time*; let us make no other use of the World, nor put a higher
Value upon it, than is reasonable for such kind of Creatures.
The Apostle directs us, after what manner to use this World;
with whose words, I shall finish this Head. *But this, I say
Brethren, the Time is Short. It remaineth, that both they that
have Wives, be as tho' they had none; and they that weep, as tho'
they wept not; and they that rejoyce, as tho' they rejoyced not;
and they that buy, as tho' they possess'd not; and they that use this
World, as not abusing it: for the Fashion of this World passeth
away*, I Cor. 7. 29–31.

2. The Account, we have had of *Life*, should *reconcile our
Tho'ts to whatever Condition, it shall please GOD to order out
to us in the World*; It is not a Matter of much Concernment,

*Bp. Hopkins's Works. Sermon 1 st.
†Prov. 11. 4.

what our outward Circumstances are: provided, we make use of them, as a Means, to our better Preparation for Eternity. For whatever our Condition is, if we are contented with it, and make it our Care to glorify GOD under it, it will be no Hindrance to our future & everlasting well-being. And in order to this, we should Meditate upon the present Life, under the Representation, our *Text* gives of it. And the Influence of such Meditations, shou'd be to compose our Minds, and make us perfectly calm and resign'd to the Will of Heaven.

Has it pleased GOD to allow us but a *small Portion* of this World's Goods. Why, a *little* shou'd content us for a *little while*: and tis but for a *short Time*, we shall have our Abode here. Or are our Circumstances *strait & difficult*? Are we *hard* put to it, and *often suffering for want*? It cannot last *long*. Our Lives will *soon* come to their appointed Period. And this is a Consideration, that shou'd restrain Discontent, check all Misgivings of Heart, & silence our Murmurings. Or does GOD call us to undergo great *Tryals & Afflictions*? It shou'd make us easy, to think they shall *Shortly* have an End: when, if we have behav'd suitably under them, our Reward will be great, far beyond the Proportion of our sufferings. In a word, however *undesirable* our *present Circumstances* are, & what ever *Troubles & Inconveniences* we may meet with, we shou'd solace our selves with this, that if we *despise not these Chastenings of the Lord, nor faint when rebuked of him*: but are patient, humble and submissive; it won't be *long*, before we shall be deliver'd out of all our Difficulties, and translated to a World that is free from all kind of Evil; where we shall be compleatly happy, without Interruption for ever.

3. The Representation we have had of *Life*, should *make us good Husbands of our Time, and put us upon improving it to the wisest purposes*. For since, like a *Vapour*, it is so *exceeding short* and *uncertain*: we ought in all reason to *redeem* our *Time*, and improve the whole of it to the *best* Advantage; in mortifying our Lusts, restraining our Appetites, governing our Passions, rectifying our Tempers; and in a word, accomplishing the great Work, for which our Life is designed. We should improve all Opportunities of doing and getting as much Good as we can; and should avoid all Occasions, either of doing Hurt to others, or receiving any our selves. We

should always employ ourselves about something; and *some-thing* that shall some how or other turn to a good Account. We should beware of squandering away our Time in Idleness; unprofitable Chat; too frequent Diversions & Visits: than which nothing more tends to wear off that serious Temper of Mind, that becomes such *dying* Creatures. In a Word, we should labour that our Life may be filled up with Work, and that it be *such*, both as to *Matter* and *Manner*, as shall subserve the Interest of our Souls and their eternal Salvation: and as that we may have Peace in our latter End. And indeed what more comfortable in an Hour of Death, than to be able to look back into a well spent Life; carefully employ'd to the Honour of GOD, the true Service of ourselves, and the Benefit of our fellow Creatures? As on the contrary, what more cutting and stinging, than to be forced to reflect upon a useless and unprofitable Life? spent to no purpose at all: or worse than none, in the Service of Sin and Satan? These Considerations, if there were no other, make it highly worth Men's while, to husband their Time well and so improve it to the best Advantage.

4. The Consideration of *Life as a Vapour, that appeareth* but *for a little Time, and then vanishes away, should put us upon frequent Examination into our State.* Serious *Self-examination* can never be an unsuitable Exercise for such *frail short liv'd* Creatures as we are. And we should be often calling ourselves to an Account; looking into our Hearts and Lives, and inquiring what would become of us, if we should die within a few Days, and be called to give up our Account. Suppose our Case to be like *Hezekiah's,* who received such a Message as that from GOD,* *Thus saith the* LORD, *set thine House in order, for thou shalt die, and not live.* Or suppose GOD should say to us, as He did to the *rich Fool* in the *Gospel,*† *This Night, shall thy Soul be required of thee.* What Provision have we made for an amazing Eternity? Are we secure of the Friendship of GOD? Are we interested in the Merits of the *great* REDEEMER? Is our Account ready for our LORD and JUDGE? Or is GOD our Enemy, and

*Isai. 38. 1.
†Luk. 12. 20.

CHRIST our Enemy? Are we wholly unprepared to die? and unmeet for an Appearance before the SON of MAN? These are very serious and solemn Inquiries. And whatever the loose and unthinking Part of the World, may imagine; they are very proper and seasonable Inquiries, for such to make, whose *Lives*, like a *Vapour*, are exceeding *short* and *uncertain*. And the Consideration that they are so, should put us upon frequent questioning with our selves, after some such manner as this: What if my Life should expire within a *few* Months, or Days? Yea, what if I should be seiz'd with Death, *this very* Day or Hour? Where would my poor Soul take up its everlasting Abode? in Heaven or in Hell? O let none of us rest satisfy'd, till we know, what our Condition is with respect to the eternal World, & how it would fare with us forever, if GOD should speedily & suddenly call us hence! Can we with Ease lie down to Sleep, & not know but we may awake in everlasting Burnings! Surely we must be dreadfully stupify'd and harden'd, if we can live in Quiet, while Uncertain what our Eternal State is!—

5ly & finally, The Representation that has been given of *Life, should put us upon particular and immediate Endeavours to prepare for the Time of its Expiration*. And this is the best Improvement, we can make of it. And tis not a Matter of *Indifferency*, whether we will make this Use of it, yea or no: but of the *nearest* Concern; yea, of *absolute* Necessity. Our well being forever depends upon it. For the present is the only State, wherein we can make Provision for Eternity. And if we are negligent in an Affair of such infinite Importance, and leave it undone, we shall perish without any Remedy.

And the *sooner* we set about this great Work the *better*: because when we have in any good Measure accomplish'd it, we shall at once have freed ourselves, from that *Spirit of Bondage*, which otherwise we might, all our Days, have been *subject to*, by reason of *continual Fears of Death*. Besides, the *sooner* we begin upon this Work, the *more fit* we shall be to engage in it, the *better* dispos'd to it, and the *easier* we shall find it. But above all, the *utter Uncertainty of Life* discovers the Wisdom of a *speedy* Preparation for Death.

O let us not then Procrastinate in a Work of such infinite and everlasting Moment! but immediately set about it, and in

GOD's Strength pursue it with the utmost Vigour & Resolution; giving ourselves no Rest, till we are in a fair way of going thro' with it.

But Perhaps we imagine *Death* to be *afar off*, and that tis Time eno'uh *hereafter* to think of *dying*, & in earnest to set about getting ready for it. Multitudes have tho't thus, and have acted under the Power of such a vain Imagination, to their eternal Undoing. GOD grant this may not be the Case of any of us! There is infinite *Danger* of it, while we put off the Tho'ts of Death. And yet alas! how apt are we all to do so! We can; but few of us, bear the Prospect of dying; and because we are inclin'd to live a great while; we *hope* we shall; and so live and act, as tho' we certainly *should*. What *Madness* is this! At what a dreadful *Hazard*, do we put our Soul's Salvation! Is it not altogether *Uncertain*, how *long* we shall live? Are we sure of living *another* Day? Yea, can any particular Person say, that he shall go alive out of *this Assembly*? And shall we then run Ventures in a Case, where our everlasting well being is dependant! Is not this infinite & amazing Folly! Do we manage thus in the common Affairs of Life? Should we not be condemned for *Fools* and *Madmen* if we did? And shall we act after this manner, *only* in that Case, wherein if we are surpriz'd in our *Folly* by Death, it will be too late to repent of it for ever! Surely we an't appriz'd of the *desperate* Folly we bewray! If we were *duly* sensible of it, we could not be *easy* with ourselves; but should, being filled with Agony of Soul, immediately betake ourselves to GOD, & peirce even Heaven it self with ardent Cries for pardoning Mercy—.

Or it may be we think a few of our *latest* Days are enough, to be employ'd about the Work of preparing ourselves for another World! and that, if we have Time, upon a *Death-bed*, to cry to GOD for Mercy, it will be *Sufficient* for our Admission into Heaven.

To expose the Folly of this Pretence, I dare not say, as some have done, that a *Death-bed Repentance* is impossible; and that, if Persons ever obtain Salvation in such a Case, it must be thro' the *Uncovenanted* Mercy of GOD. Such an Opinion as this; as it seems contrary to the Tenure of the *Bible*, so it very much *lessens* the Riches and Glory of free Grace—.

There is no *truly* humble Penitent, but is a *qualify'd* Object of pardoning Mercy; and shall, according to the *Gospel Covenant*, certainly obtain it. And tho' a Person, who has been no ways concern'd about his Soul, till he comes to lie upon a Death-bed, is very *unfit* for the Work of Salvation, and has but *little* reason, *comparatively* speaking, to expect the *Aids* of Divine Grace: Yet, who can say, but GOD may dissolve such a Sinner into Grief & Shame; give him a *true* sight and sense of his Sins, and cause him to repent in Dust & Ashes: and so pluck him, as a Fire-brand out of the Fire.

This is what the most merciful GOD *may* do, if He should so please. Yea, and He has encouraged us to hope, this is what He *will* do; if we have not *out sinned* the Day of His Grace, and are not wanting to our selves. And no Sinner, tho' he may have rolled away his Days in Vanity, and is *now* just dropping into Eternity, has reason to despair of Divine Mercy. The Case of the *Penitent Thief* on the Cross, seems to have been recorded as an *Encouragement* to such Sinners—. And it must be *constantly affirmed*, that the Grace of GOD, is not confin'd to any particular *Age* or *Time* of Life. He may bestow his Grace, as upon *whomsoever*, so *whensoever* He pleases. And tis past doubt, many have experienced *the Loving-Kindness of* GOD *in* CHRIST, in some of their *last* Moments; and instead of *going away into Everlasting Punishment, have inherited Eternal Life*.

But let no Sinner encourage himself from the Mercy of GOD, to *continue* in his evil Courses, and *put off* the Business of Religion, till a *dying Hour*. What can be more base & disingenuous than this? To live in Sin all our Days, dishonouring and offending GOD, because He is so merciful and compassionate, as to accept *even* our *latest* Repentance, rather than we should perish forever; wherein could we discover a more vile ungenerous Temper of Mind! Surely this Goodness of GOD should work upon our Ingenuity, lead us to Repentance, & immediately engage us in the Divine Love & Service. This ought to be the Influence of such wonderful Grace & Mercy: Nor unless it is, shall we be able to free ourselves from the Charge of the greatest Baseness, the blackest Ingratitude.

Or if there was nothing of Disingenuity in such a Proceedure: Yet how infinitely unreasonable is it: "What strange

Tho'ts must Men have of GOD & Heaven, & what extravagant Conceits of the *little* Evil of Sin, and the *great* Easiness of Repentance, that can impose upon themselves at this rate?" And how shall we be able to apply our selves to GOD *now*, when we have scarce ever had a serious Tho't of Him all our Lives? "Can we have the Face to bespeak Him in this manner? LORD, now the World and my Lusts have left me, and I feel my self ready to sink into eternal Perdition, I lay hold upon thy Mercy to deliver my Soul from going down into the Pit. I have heard strange things of thy Goodness, and that thou art merciful even to a Miracle. This is that which I always trusted to, that after a long Life of Sin & Vanity thou wouldest at last be satisfy'd with a few penitent Words & Sighs at the Hour of Death. Let me not, I pray thee, be disappointed of this Hope, and put to Confusion. Is this an Address fit to be made to a wise Man, much less to the all-wise and just Judge of the World? and yet this seems to be the plain Interpretation of the late & forced Application of a great & habitual Sinner to *Almighty* GOD in his last Extremity, and when he is just giving up the Ghost & going to appear before his dreadful Tribunal."*

Besides, is a Time of Sickness and Death the most fit season, in which to make Preparation for Eternity, that we put it off till then? Certainly, if we have had Occasion to visit sick Chambers, and have taken a View of the Circumstances of *dying* Persons, we can never imagine thus! they have now enough to graple with their Illness. The whole strength of their Nature is laid out in sustaining the Infirmities of it. And they have little or no Heart to think of their Souls, or make Provision for their future Happiness. Or if they have, they are less fit for this now, than they ever were before. For either their Senses are stupify'd, their Tho'ts confused and shatter'd, their Frame discompos'd: Or else their Pains are so extream, or their Bodies so very weak and faint, as to incapacitate them for the Work of getting ready to go out of the World. And O! how many, when upon a Death-bed, have, with Tears in their Eyes, most bitterly lamented their Folly, in deferring to make their Peace with GOD till then; they have *now* found so many

---

*Dr. *Tillitson*, Vol. I. Ser. 54.

Difficulties & Inconveniences in the way, beyond what they would have done, if they had engaged in this Business sooner, and in a more proper Time of Life.

Furthermore, there is nothing more precarious than a *Death-bed* Preparation for another World. Sinners indeed, at such a time, are often in great Consternation of Mind; their Cries for Mercy serious & affecting, & their Vows & Promises particular and solemn.—Yet, tis to be fear'd their *Concern* about their State most frequently arises, *only* from an awaken'd Sense *of what a fearful thing it is to fall into the Hands of the living GOD*. They can't bear to think of going away, *to dwell with devouring Fire, and to inhabit everlasting Burnings*. And because they are in Distress & Agony of Soul, they themselves, and perhaps their Friends too, are ready to hope for the best, and willing to believe that their Sorrows are the Sorrows of a *Repentance unto Life*: When alas! it may be, they are no ways troubled, that they have offended GOD and rejected CHRIST and acted all their Days unworthy of themselves, and below the Glory of their Natures; but are fill'd with Horrour at the Prospect, of what is like to be the Consequence of their evil doings. Many while under Apprehensions of Death approaching, have been as much terrify'd and as heartily troubled; and have made as fair pretences & as solemn Promises: and yet, when GOD has ransom'd their Lives from Destruction, they have forgot the Anguish of Spirit they were in, and return'd to their former Folly & Wickedness: Yea, they have made themselves seven-fold more the Children of the Devil: whereby they have evidently discovered it to the World, that their Repentance was not sincere; and that if they had died, they would have perish'd forever. And no doubt, this is the Case of many, whose Lives were not spared to them. If they had been raised up again, their Repentance would have prov'd it self to have been, nothing more than the Terrours of a guilty Conscience. In a word, tis a Matter of the greatest Niceness and Difficulty, to determine concerning any *Death-bed* Repentance in *particular*, whether it be sincere and such as GOD will accept: And after all that can be said, it must & will remain very precarious and uncertain.

Moreover, when we come to lie upon a Sick bed, we shan't find the Business of getting ready for Death and Judgment such an easie thing, as at present we may imagine it to be. I doubt not, but most Sinners have slight Tho'ts of the Work of Repentance & Salvation. They suppose it is but confessing their Sins with external signs of Sorrow, and putting up a few Prayers to GOD for Mercy, *and so an Entrance shall be ministred unto them abundantly into the everlasting Kingdom of our* LORD *and* SAVIOUR JESUS CHRIST: and they imagine they can do this as well, just at the Point of Death, as at any Time, and so put it off till then. But O! what amazing Folly is this! and how dreadfully do we impose upon ourselves in a Matter of the highest Moment! Is the Work of Salvation such an easie one, and so dependant on our own Pleasure, that we may thus dally with it? Alas! if GOD ever give us a true Sight and Sense of things, we shall have quite different Tho'ts of it, and find that we were miserably mistaken. Heaven is not so easily obtained. Tis a great and difficult work to prepare ourselves for it, and we shall certainly find it to be so. And to convince us of this Truth, I tho't now to have gone on to tell you, what is included in that Preparation for Death, that I have been thus long urging upon you. But I see the Time will allow me only to observe in General,

That there is a two fold Preparation for Death, the one *habitual*, the other *actual*. The Ingredients that constitute the *former*, are true Faith in CHRIST, an inward rooted Aversion to all Sin, & a prevailing Disposition to universal Holiness: in order to which, generally Speaking, it is necessary, that we take a great deal of Pains in the use of Prayer, Meditation, reading & hearing GOD's Word, &c. which are the ways, in which He ordinarily *makes known the exceeding Greatness of his Power*, in putting Persons into a State of Salvation. But besides this, there is an *actual* Preparation; which, tho' not of absolute Necessity, yet is highly requisite, as tending to a peaceful & comfortable Death. And the best way in order to our obtaining this, is to familiarize to ourselves the Tho'ts of Death; to keep a constant sense of our own Frailty upon our Minds; to mortify our Affections to the World, and place them upon those things that are above: and in a word, to look upon every Day of our Lives, as not Knowing but it may be our Last; and to live & act every Day, as tho' we were certain, before the next, our eternal State would be determin'd.

I have now done with my Text: and shall only add a few Words on the mournful Occasion of my discoursing to you upon such a Subject at this Time, *viz.* the Lamented Death of that Honourable and vertuous Gentlewoman, Mrs. *SARAH BYFIELD*, whom, last Week, we follow'd to the Grave.

For her Character, I think my self, in Justice to her Memory, oblig'd to say,—That as she was honoured by her Birth; being *Daughter* to a *renowned* FATHER* *of this Country*, who, for several Years, with *universal* Love and Reverence, sat in the FIRST CHAIR of Government over it; so that her Temper & Conduct were every way worthy of such a *distinguished* Parentage.

She had *naturally* a weak & tender Body; but a strong & noble Soul: which, being cultivated & enrich'd by a good Education and great Industry, render'd her truly amiable & desirable; and fitted her to be a Blessing in the Station Providence had assign'd her.

Her Temper was lively & chearful; yet far from light & vain: being well *ballast* by a *singular* Discretion. In her most pleasant Hours, She was never unfit to enter upon a Serious Subject, and always treated it with a becoming Gravity and Reverence.

She had a good Taste in Conversation, and was excellently well turn'd for it: having a ready Wit; a sprightly Genius; an easy smooth way of expressing herself; and being able, without Stiffness or Ostentation, to be both entertaining and profitable.

She was a *Person* of great Sincerity & Plainheartedness; meek & humble; patient & resign'd: which she had frequent Opportunities of discovering, by reason of those many Indispositions, that were inseparable from so *brittle* a Constitution.

In a Word, She was an *Honour* to her *Sex*, in her exemplary Deportment under all the various Characters & Relations of Life: As a Neighbour, Kind & Pitiful: As a Friend, true &

*Gov. LEVERETT.

hearty; without Disguise & abhorrent to Flattery and Deceit: As a Wife, tender & dutiful; engaging in her Carriage; reverent & respectful: As Mistress in a Family, discreet in her Management; a Lover of good Order; neat & cleanly; tho't-ful of all under her Care; indulgent & compassionate to her Servants: especially concern'd about their Souls, and frequent in teaching them the good Knowledge of the LORD; in her Treatment of Strangers, hospitable; courteous, pleasant, obliging & edifying to those that came to visit her.

But her *chief* Excellency, & what *most* recommended to all that knew her, was her *undissembled* Piety. She had an habitual prevailing Awe and Reverence of GOD upon her Heart: which *early* discovered it self, and *all along* thro' the Course of her Life, not only in an utter Abhorrence of every thing that savour'd of Prophanness & Irreverence; but in a due Treatment of those things, wherein the *Divine Honour* is nearly concern'd. She lov'd the House, & Sanctify'd the Day of God; gave her constant devout Attendance on the Publick Worship, and *all* Gospel Ordinances; paid a singular Regard to the *Holy Scriptures*; valued the Ministers of Religion; and had an universal Regard to all good Men. But above all, CHRIST was the *Object* of her Love, her Faith, her Hope. It was in her Account *a faithful saying*, and the esteem'd it *worthy of all Acceptation, that* CHRIST JESUS *was come into the World to save Sinners.* HIM therefore she embrac'd as the *alone* REDEEMER of Souls; HIM she trusted with the great Affair of her Eternal Salvation; HIM she lov'd with her whole Heart; HIM she made it her Care to please in all things; HIS Image she was Adorn'd with; & the Graces of HIS SPIRIT she liv'd in the daily Exercise of: And we charitably believe she is gone to be with CHRIST, which is best of all.

I doubt not, but the Mourning Friends & Relatives have often refresh'd their Souls, by looking back to her past Conversation in CHRIST; and then by turning their View forward to those unutterable Glories, she is now possess'd of, in the Place GOD has ordain'd for the *Spirits* of Believers, in their *separate State.* And while by *Faith*, they are beholding her, as in the Bosome of JESUS, I may well suppose, they grieve not for *her*; but rather rejoyce, that she is got beyond the Reach of Sorrow, the Power of Temptation and the

Possibility of Sinning; and that she is entred upon the Reward of Righteousness, which is *Joy & Peace, Quietness & Assurance for ever*. Yet upon their *own* Accounts, they may have Reason to Mourn, and stand in need of Consolation.

We heartily wish, for all the Relatives, Divine Support under this *Tryal of their Faith*; the comforting Presence of the *Holy* GHOST; and the sanctifying Influences of supernatural Grace, whereby they may be enabled, so to behave themselves, as that GOD may be honour'd their own Holiness increased, and their future & *eternal Weight of Glory* inhanced.

And particularly, we would sympathize with that Aged & Honourable Servant of GOD, who was most nearly related to the Person deceased. You little tho't to appear in mourning for one, you expected and desir'd shou'd follow you to the Grave. Yet so the Sovereign GOD has order'd it! He has taken from you the pleasant Companion of your Age, who might have been the Helper of it's Griefs, and render'd it far more easie and desirable to you! But be dumb with Silence;—meekly bear this *Chastening of the* LORD;—take a realizing View of it, as coming from your Covenant GOD and FATHER, *who never afflicts willingly, nor grieves his Children*:—Adore the Sovereignty, the Wisdom, the Righteousness and Holiness of this Providence.—Let it be your chief Care so to carry your self under it, as to give a bright Example of *Subjection to the Father of Spirits*; of Humility, Patience, Resignation—And may it serve to make you a *Partaker of the Divine Nature* in still greater Measures, and so advance you yet further in your Preparedness for that Eternal *happy* State, you hope and long for, and are arrived at the Confines of!—We heartily pray GOD to be the Staff of your Age, your Joy and Comfort thro' the remaining part of your Life; your Guide thro' Death, and *when your Flesh and Heart faileth, the Strength of your Heart and your GOD forever*.

To Conclude: The Death even of Women of so distinguish'd a Character is a publick Loss: and we shou'd resent it as such;—and be importunate in our Cries to the GOD of all Grace, that as He removes them away by Death, so that He would raise up others of the same excellent Spirit to supply their Place, and make good their Ground—We should *all* lay the Deaths of such Persons to Heart.—Particularly *our*

Women shou'd do so, and labour to imitate them in those things that were vertuous and praise-worthy. And it is to be wish'd for all our Women, that they may *be well reported of for good Works** being *in Behaviour as becometh Godliness; not false Accusers; not given to much Wine: Teachers of good things; Sober, Lovers of their Husbands; Lovers of their Children; discreet; chast; Keepers at Home; good; obedient to their own Husbands, that the Word of GOD be not blasphemed.*† *In like manner also, that they adorn themselves in modest Apparel, with shame-facedness & Sobriety;—and (which becometh Women professing Godliness) with good Works.*‡ Amen.

*I. Tim. 5. 10.
†Titus 2. 3,–6.
‡I. Tim. 2. 9, 10.

MATHER BYLES

A Discourse on the Present Vileness of the Body
and
Its Future Glorious Change by Christ

Deliver'd at Dorchester April 23. 1732.

Hic neque concepto fetu, nec semine surgit:
secunda morte reformat
Et petit alternam totidem per funera vitam.
CLAUD. PHŒNIX.

———

PREFACE

If any enquire into the Reasons of this Publication; the Importunity of some Friends, and the Judgment of others, together with some Desire to do good, are the general Arguments of a modern Preface: And the Author hopes he has some Right to this common and useful Train of Thoughts.

The Sermons are Plain, & adapted to a popular Audience. They were composed without any Tho't of the Press, and when they were perswaded out of the Author's Hands, he could not find Leasure from his other Studies to transcribe them: for which Cause the Reader will not expect to find any thing laboured or uncommon. The Author imagines that lively Descriptions, a clear Method, and pathetick Language best become the Desk: And this possibly may be one Reason why he insisted no more upon Philosophical Arguments in his Discourse upon the vile Body changed. *Tho' he believes the Doctrine of the* Stamen *will as easily account for a Resurrection, as for Generation, yet he supposes such Talk in the Pulpit serves more to amuse the Auditory, and complement the Preacher himself, than to honour CHRIST, or do good to Souls.*

If by looking over the ensuing Pages, any Christian shall have one more holy or proper Tho't, the Writer will think his Pains well rewarded.

The Glorious Change of the Vile Body

PHILIP. iii. 21.
*Who shall change our vile body, that it may be
fashioned like unto his glorious body.*

THE Apostle *Paul* in the Chapter open before us, after some
Precepts laid down, concludes with Two Motives to perswade
Men to the Practice of them: And these are, the *Coming of*
CHRIST, in the Verse preceeding my Text; and the *Resurrec-
tion of the Saints* now read unto you. Both of them are very
solemn and sublime Thoughts: But it is only the latter which
comes immediately within the Compass of our present
Meditation.

The *Resurrection of the Dead*, and, which is much the same
thing, the *Transformation of these found alive* at the coming of
CHRIST, are very clearly revealed in the New Testament,
especially by the Apostle *Paul*. But the Glory of a Believer's
Raised Body is not, nor indeed can it be any where more fully
express'd, than in the Words under our immediate View. *Who
shall change our vile body, that it may be fashioned like unto his
glorious body.*

The Apostle tells us, Our Bodies are now *vile*; our vile
Bodies shall be *changed*; it is our Lord JESUS CHRIST *who*
shall change them; and they shall be *fashion'd like unto his glorious body*. How much is crowded into a few Words! how emphatical are they! how copious! how sublime! How amply do
they fill the Mind, and exhaust the Imagination, inspire our
Faith, and awaken our Joy!

In handling these Words, I shall only have Time to speak to
Three of the Four Articles (or if you please, *Doctrines*) which
you see are plainly contained in them.

I. *These Bodies of ours, in their Present State, are* VILE
BODIES. *Who shall change our vile bodies?* Shall we here let
our Thoughts loose upon a few Particulars, which will render
it plain, and humble us with the sad Conviction. These
Bodies, of whose Beauty and Vigour we are so apt to boast,
alas, they are vile Bodies.

1. Their *Original* is mean and despicable. In the Sense of the
Greek Text, our Body was vile, even in the Purity of its first

Creation. The Word which we translate *vile*, is ταπεινώσεως: The Body of our *Humility*. 'Tis a *humble* Body. It carries *Humiliation* even in its Origin and Constitution. It comes from *Humus*; the *moist Ground*; The *Clay*, the *low Earth*. The First Principle of *Humans*, is *Humus*. Humiliation and Vileness is thus entail'd upon our Body, even from the primitive Materials out of which it was framed. Even *Adam* in Paradise and Innocence, might in this sacred sense, have own'd a Vile Body.

And now, Let the Proud Creature look down to the Earth, & view the Dust from which he sprung, & then confess his Body Vile. *And the Lord God formed man out of the dust of the ground**. Out of the Clay was this living Frame fashioned; here it had its humble Original; and from this abject Earth, did it arise and shoot up, thus curious in its Form and Constitution. This beauteous Arrangement of finer Dust, was taken from the common Glebe, into which it must quickly fall, and resolve again. The Limbs which now shew the exactest Symmetry and Proportion, the Pulses which beat with the strongest Energy and Life, and the Aspect that is flush'd with Health and Beauty, owe all their Existance to the same Clods of Earth which harbour our Brethren, the Worms: The Worms, which wait to Feast upon our moulding Carcase; and riot in our wasting Flesh. The Body *is of the Earth, earthy. Dust it is, and to Dust it shall return*. Let us reflect thus, & then confess, This VILE BODY.

2. It is a *sinful* Body, and therefore a vile Body. It has in it a Body of Death; and no wonder it looks ghastly, and loathsome, and vile. All its Appetites are vitiated, and disorder'd, and it leads the Soul about like a Malefactor in Chains. The Spirit which God *infuses* is depraved and polluted by it: and Original Sin is *communicated* thro' the Veins of the guilty Parent. The several *Senses* of the Body, prove so many Traitors to the nobler Faculties of the Mind, and continually captivate and debase it. How many Sins enter at the *Eyes*? and how many idle Ideas pass in at the *Ears*, *forever open* to the Vanity of empty and corrupted Air. The Luxuries of the *Palate* de-

*Gen. ii. 7.

bauch the enslaved Mortal, and drag him on to Excess and Intemperance. He wanders among sensible Appearances, and forgets spiritual and divine Reallities. He is hardly brought to consider, that the *things which are SEEN are temporal, but the things which are not seen are eternal.* Is not the Body, that thus abuses the Soul, the Rational principle within, a vile Body? The Body, the beautiful Workmanship of an Alwise Artificer, how is it sunk beneath the Level of the brutal World, by its Sin against God? *O wretched that we are! who shall deliver us from the Body of this Death?*

3. Our Body is a weak, *infirm* Body, and therefore a vile Body. It is a feeble House of Clay, that totters to every Blast. Disease and Mortality lurk in every Member, and Vein, and Muscle. It is liable to Contagions and Distempers of all Sorts. They March silent and unseen, in the fine Air about us. They lie brooding in their Venom, thro' all the Fluids within: Latent Destruction! Death in Ambuscade! A Thousand different Fevers stand ready to seize this Body; to torment it, and to burn away its Life: To lick up the finer Spirits, and snap the Vital Cord. It may be at once *blinded* by a Defluxion of Rheum, fetter'd with the Tortures of the *Gout*, and broken in the Agonies of the *Stone*: Like *Sampson* in the Philistian Prison-house, at the same Time *blinded*, and *shackled*, and *grinding*. Every Nerve about us, is capable of Pains too great for us to bear, too strong for us to resist, and too subtil for us to escape. The Strength of the most athletick Body, is still on the Wing; may fly away suddenly; will do it speedily; and must at last wholly leave it. The Beauty of the most amiable Body, is every Day hasting to fade, and go out in obscure Darkness. Our daily eating and drinking, proclaim a feeble Body, that would faint and die if these were omitted. Every Time we set down to a Table, or take a Cup in our Hand, we confess we are Creatures that need constant Support and Nourishment. When we lie down to the necessary Sleep of the Night, we own the Sleep of the Night must relieve us a little from the long Slumber of the Grave. Every Breath we draw insinuates, in a silent Whisper, our Frailty, our Dependance on God, and our short Continuance: It warns us that our *Life is Wind.*—So Weak is our Body, that it take away much of our Thought

from our Souls, to contrive for its Life, and Health, and Sustenance.—Let us look now upon the brittle Frame, and exclaim, O the vile Body!

4. It is a *dying* Body, & therefore a vile Body. Here our Bodies now stand, perhaps flourishing in all the Pride and Bloom of Youth: Strong our Sinews; moist our Bones; active and supple our Joints; our Pulses beating with Vigour, and our Hearts leaping with a Profusion of Life and Energy. But oh! Vain Appearance and gaudy Dream! Surely every Man at his best Estate, is altogether Vanity. He walks in a vain Show; he glitters with delusive Colours; he spends his Years as an Idle Tale. What avails it, that he is now hardy and robust, who must quickly pant upon a Death-bed. What avails it, that his Limbs are sprightly in their easy Motions, which must quickly stretch in the dying Agony. The Lips now flush'd with a Rosey Colour, will anon quiver and turn pale. The Eyes that roll with a sparkling Vivacity, will fix in a ghastly Horror. The most musical Voice will be stop'd; and the tuneful Breath fly away. The Face where Beauty now triumphs, will appear cold, and wan, and dismal, rifled by the Hand of Death. A Cold Sweat will chill the Body; a hoarse Rattling will fill the Throat; the Heart will heave with Pain and Labour, and the Lungs catch for Breath, but gasp in vain. Our Friends stand in Tears about our Bed: They weep; but they cannot help us. The very Water with which they would cool and moisten our pearched Mouths, we receive with a hollow Groan. Anon we give a Gasp, and they shriek out in Distress, *'Oh! He's gone,— He's dead!'* The Body in that Instant stretches on the Sheets, an awful Corpse. This is the End of our Body for this World: Pronounce now; Is it not a Vile Body? But this brings me to the last Article.

5. Our Body will quickly be a *dead* Body, and this proclaims it a vile Body. The Silks and soft Linnen which now fold and adorn these Bodies, must be changed for a winding Sheet. The Applause and Complement which now flatter us, are not heard in the Retirements of the Grave, to disturb its aweful Silence: Nor shall Reproaches and Revilings break in upon our Rest there. Our pleasant Habitations will be left for others, while we have no Apartment left us, but a Coffin, or a Tomb at most. We shall forsake our Dishes and our Tables;

and our selves become Food for the crawling Vermin of the Dust. How quickly shall we hasten to Clay and Ashes, in the solitary, and dark, and cold Grave?

In a few Years, the most beautious, or learned, or pious Head will grin a hideous Skull. Our broken Coffins will show nothing but black Bones, and black Mould, and Worms & Filth. The Places that knew us shall know us no more. The Persons who were most intimate in our Acquaintance; who sooth'd us with their Visits, or caress'd us in their Bosoms, will now forget us. When they shall perhaps enter our Tombs and take up our Bones in their Hand, they'll not suspect the frightful Carcase to be Ours, save by the Letters on the broken Coffin, or the Inscription on the mouldring Monument.

And now, *Man giveth up the Ghost, and where is he?* What becomes of the Dream of Worldly Happiness? Where are the Houses, and the Coffers? The Great Name, the loud Applause, and the Brutal Pleasure? His Riches are left to others: And to whom he knows not; whether a Wise Man or a Fool. He forsakes his numerous Houses, and is confined to a narrow Coffin, in a lonely Vault. Out of all his Lands he retains but a few Foot of Earth to cover him from the Sight. His boasted Name is forgot among the living, and scarce once in an Age casually read upon his Grave-stone. *His Breath goeth forth, he returneth to his Earth, in that very Day his Thoughts perish.**

The Spirit is given up; and see the Body drops down, pale, and stiff, and cold. The Eyes are fixt; the Teeth are set; the Breath is fled. Is this the Face we once gaz'd upon with so much Pleasure? Are these the Cheeks that glow'd so fresh, and bloom'd so lovely? Are these the Lips that smil'd so graceful, and pour'd out such a gliding Stream of Eloquence and Musick? Where's the tuneful Voice that once held the listening Ear, and rais'd the attentive Eye? Where are the proportioned Limbs, the supple Joints, the vigorous Pulses, the beating Heart, the working Brain, and the breathing Breast? Lo, the Body is laid in the Dust, and the Worms cover it. Polluted Vermine crawl over every Part of the elegant Form, and the beautious Face. It is folded in a winding Sheet, it is

*Psal. xlvi. 4.

nailed in a black Coffin, and it is deposited in a silent Vault, amidst Shades and Solitude. The Skin breaks and moulders away; the Flesh drops in Dust from the Bones; the Bones are covered with black Mould, and Worms twist about them. The Coffins break, and the Graves sink in, and the disjointed Skelliton strows the lonely Vault. This shapely Fabrick must leave its Ruins among the Graves; lie neglected and forgot; moulder away without a Name, and scatter among the Elements. 'And were these Bones once living like ours? and must ours be as they'? This hideous Skull, the frightful Jaw fallen, and the black Teeth naked to the Eye, was it once a thinking Frame, covered with a beauteous Skin? Strange Alteration made by Death! And are not our Burying-Grounds full of such Spectacles? What do they but illustrate and confirm the Doctrine? Methinks every Grave, with open Mouth, preaches upon my Text, *This Vile Body*. O Vile Body! under what infamous Dishonours of Loathsomeness and Corruption art thou? Thou must be laid away in the dusty Galleries of the Grave, the gloomy Chambers of Death, unregarded and unknown; lost in deep Retirement, and awful Silence. O Vile Body!

Thus we have seen with what Propriety Vileness belongs to these Bodies. How suitable and emphatical the degrading Epithet? Let us here pause, and improve, and set Limits to the Description.

Is this Body so Vile and Wretched? *How vain and foolish is it to be Proud of our Body.* τὸ σῶμα τῆς ταπεινώσεως ἡμῶν: *The Body of our Humiliation.* Vain Men! Proud of the very Body of Humiliation; Vile, debasing, sinful Clay. Why should we set our Eyes upon that which is not; or in a little Time will not be? Why should we prefer our Bodies, and forget our Souls? Cloath and adorn those, while we are regardless of the Salvation of these? Why, ye *Fair*, should ye be proud of a Beauty destin'd to the embrace of Worms? Or why, ye *Strong*, should ye boast the hardy Nature, which must quickly faint, and drop down breathless. O far be the Tho'ts from us, to be vain of such vile Bodies! Away, the haughty Mein, and the disdainful Glance; the conscious Smile, and the assuming Brow. Away the artful Movements and manag'd Airs of Wantonness and Pride. No more let airy Fashions and looser Modes of Dress expose the Body. Nor let it be lost in the studied Disproportions of an ambitious Garb. Why need we affect an Apparel, fantastically Demure, on the one hand; or choose on the other, Pomp, and Glitter, and empty Show? We may appear decent in the Polite World, without running thro' all the quick Succession of Fopperies: The *round Attyre like the Moon*, in a perpetual Circle of Changes. Let the vile Body, *be* CLOATHED *with* HUMILITY:* Modesty and Sobriety are the best Ornaments.

But let us set Limits to the Exclamation, and not carry it too far. No; our Bodies, vile as they are, are to be honoured and respected by us. They are the wonderful Production of Omnipotence, the curious Workmanship of an alwise Artificer. Let the Body of the Sinner be as vile as it will, your Bodies, ye happy Believers, are raised above the common Clay in a nobler Honour. *What, know ye not,* (says the Apostle) *that your Bodies are the Members of* JESUS CHRIST?—*Know ye not, that your Bodies are the Temples of the holy Ghost, that dwelleth in you.*† Our Bodies, it is true, are in many respects vile; But yet, under all their Humble Circumstances, they are the Members of our Lord JESUS. Let us always then, when we call our Bodies vile, remember that they are noble too, and intituled to the sublimest Honours. Let us take Care of them, cherish them, view them in the Light in which CHRIST looked upon his own Body. For he *spake concerning the Temple of his Body*, Joh. ii. 21. Let us respect and reverence our Bodies, as the Temples of the HOLY SPIRIT; the Members of JESUS CHRIST, and the Candidates of a glorious Resurrection. When we wash, or feed, or cloath, or adorn our Bodies, let such Meditations as these, produce, and sanctify the Act.

But we come to the second Doctrine.

II. *These vile Bodies of ours shall be* CHANGED. The greatest Part of Believers on CHRIST shall be changed at a Resurrection from the Dead: But not all. Some shall never die, but be found alive at the Appearance of CHRIST: These shall be caught up to meet the descending Judge, and shall be changed in the shining Ascent. See in the 1st Epist. Cor. xv.

*1 Pet. v. 5.
†1 Cor. vi. 15, 19.

Chap. where the Apostle treats this Subject at large, ver. 51, 52. *Behold I shew you a mystery; we shall not all sleep, but we shall all be changed, in a moment, in the twinkling of an Eye, at the last Trumpet, (for the Trumpet shall sound) and the dead shall be raised incorruptable, and we shall be changed.* So that in the End, there will be very little Difference between the dead Believers, and those whom our Lord finds alive at his coming. Both shall be changed at our Lord's descent; caught up to meet him in the Regions of Air, as his fiery Chariot rolls down amidst Thunder, and Clouds, and Whirlwinds. The Living Saints shall be snatched from the Earth, and changed from the feeble State they are now in: Those who are Dead, and sleep among the Tombs, shall shake off the Dishonours of the Graves, and be changed from the Vileness of Dust and Worms. Of these in their Order.

1. This vile Body shall be changed from the STATE *of* DEATH. What though our Bodies die; they shall revive from the Condition of Curse and Corruption. *If a man die, shall he live again?* Yes; at the Resurrection of the Dead shall he be raised. GOD shall raise the Dead, by the Man whom he hath ordained, whereof he has given Assurance unto all Men in that he raised him from the Dead. So long ago as the Time of *Job*, the holy Man could look to a Redeemer, who should call him from the corruptions of the Grave, and renew his consumed Limbs to Strength, and his Eyes to Light. [Job xix. 25, 26, 27.] *For I know that my Redeemer liveth, and that he shall stand at the latter Day upon the Earth. And tho' after my Skin, Worms destroy this Body, yet in my Flesh shall I see GOD; whom I shall see for my self, and my Eyes behold, and not another, tho' my Reins be consumed within me.* We must die, but what then, we are as sure of a Resurrection as we are of Death. But Oh! what a blessed Change will the Resurrection make upon our dead Bodies. Perhaps the Worms have feasted themselves upon our Last Dust; But they shall refund it, and give back every Attom: All that really belongs to our numerical Body. The Fishes perhaps have eaten the Carcase, buried in the Waves, and lost in the Depths of the Ocean: But *the Sea* also shall return it back,* and *give up the Dead that is in it.* These

*Rev. xx. 13.

Bodies may dissolve, and scatter among the Elements. Our Fluids may forsake their Vessels; the Solid contract, and fold up in its primitive Miniature. And even after that the little invisible Bones may moulder to finer Dust, the Dust may refine to Water, wander in a Cloud, float in a River, or be lost in the wide Sea, and undistinguished Drop among the Waves. They may be again sucked up by the Sun, and fall in a Shower upon the Earth; They may refresh the Fields with Dew, flourish in a Spire of Grass; look green in a Leaf, or gaudy in a Flower or a Blossom. For we know Matter is continually changing, and one Element perpetually loosing it self in another. But let our Dust wander where it will, thro'out the whole material Creation, yet at the first Blast of the last Trumpet, it shall all at once rush together, and start up a compleat Man. The vile Body shall be changed, where-ever it lay hid: The Dust shall be called together; the Bones shall harden, and the Joynts connect; a new, unknown, incorruptible Fluid suddenly fill the Vessels; the Sinews shall brace with an immortal Strength, no more to be parted; and the Skin cover all with everlasting Beauty, never to fade any more. This shall be the Change from the *State of Death*, which our vile Bodies shall pass through.—The prophetick Vision of *Ezekiel*, shall be litterally fulfilled at that day. *Ezek.* xxxvii, 14.

2. This vile Body shall be changed from its PRESENT STATE. Tho' it shall be raised from the Dead, it shall *not* revive to its *present* mean and dishonourable Condition, but shall be changed. Now it is a Body full of Uncleanness and Corruption, Disease and Death. But it shall be changed. *Tho' it is sown in corruption, it shall be raised in incorruption.** Now our Body is mean and vile, and upon many Accounts dishonourable; But it shall be changed. *Tho' it is sown in Dishonour, it is raised in Glory.* Now they are weak, and faint, and soon exhausted, and spent with long and close Labour. But they shall be changed from their feeble state. *It is sown in Weakness, it is raised in Power.* Now how gross and heavy are our Bodies? How sluggish and unactive the unweildy Flesh? But it shall be changed. *This I say Brethren, Flesh and Blood cannot inherit the Kingdom of God; neither doth Corruption*

*1 Cor. xv. 42. 50, 44, 53.

inherit Incorruption, ver. *It is sown a natural Body, it is raised a Spiritual Body,* ver. What can we say more to illustrate the blessed Change? Our Body is now in a thousand respects an infirm and dying Body: But, O glorious Transformation! *This corruptible must put on Incorruption; and this mortal must put on Immortality,* ver. This is the Change from the *present State,* of which these very vile Bodies are the Candidates. But we will not prevent our selves from saying

III. *This vile Body of ours shall be* FASHIONED LIKE UNTO CHRIST's GLORIOUS BODY. They shall be changed from the corrupt and unclean State of Death. More than this: they shall be changed from all the Dishonours and Meanness of the Present Life: But O sublimest Glory of all! O divine Expectation, and sacred Hope! They shall be *fashioned like unto his glorious Body.* Like the illustrious and immortal Body of our blessed LORD JESUS CHRIST. Observe; CHRIST still has a Body. His Body has a Form and Shape belonging to it. It is not our Bodies shall be *made* like unto CHRIST's glorious Body; but shall be *fashioned*; σύμμορφον, shall receive a like *Figure* and *Shape,* and be *changed into the same Image.* So says the Apostle, 1 Cor. xv. 47, 49. *The first man is of the Earth earthy; the second Man is the Lord from Heaven. And as we have born the Image of the Earthy, we shall also bear the Image of the Heavenly.*

But what is this Image? and what is implied in that most expressive Idea, our vile shall be changed; and fashioned like unto CHRIST's glorious Body? I shall just hint at a few Particulars very briefly.

1. To have the vile Body fashioned like unto CHRIST's glorious Body, implies in it, that it be made *splendid and illustrious.* The Body of CHRIST is a shining Body, and *scatters Light and Glory round about it. Saul* was struck blind, dazled with the unsufferable Blaze, that rush'd in a Tempest upon his Eyes, from the Body of the Son of GOD. *John* beheld him, with his Face shining like the Sun in its meridian Flame, and his Body beaming in an answerable Glory. The Angels and the glorified Saints beheld him, as the great Ornament and the Light of Heaven: *For the Lamb is the Light of it, and they need no Sun, or Moon, or Candle.**

---

*Rev. xxi. 23.

If CHRIST's Body be thus splendid, our's shall be so too; for they shall be fashioned like unto his glorious Body. They shall put on a shining Form; shoot like a Flame from the Grave, and glitter like a Ray of Light up the Ether. Dan. xii. 3. *They that be wise, shall shine as the brightness of the Firmament, and they which turn many to Righteousness, as the Stars for ever and ever.*

2. It implies that our Bodies shall be *immortal.* CHRIST's Body is immortal; *Being raised from the Dead, he dieth no more,* Rev. vi. 9. He pronounces with a Voice of Triumph, Rev. i. 18. *I am he that liveth, and was dead, and behold, I am alive for evermore; Amen.*

Is the Body of CHRIST immortal? our Bodies shall be fashioned like unto his own immortal Body. *This Mortal must put on Immortality.* We must all die; we shall die but once. Being raised from the Dead, Death shall be swallowed up in Victory; and *there shall be no more Death.**

3. It implies that our Bodies shall be glorified with very *mysterious and astonishing Powers.* The Body of Christ could ascend and descend with equal ease. It could stand aloft in the Air, without any visible Support; So he looked down thro' the opened Heavens, upon the expiring *Stephen*; Act. vi. 56. So he dazled the Eyes of *Saul* in the Road to *Damascus*; Act. ix. 3. It could rise up gradually from the Ground, and tower away thro' the upper Skies, to the World above. So he ascended in the View of the Men of *Galilee*, till a Cloud sail'd under his Feet, and ravished him from their gazing Eyes; Act. i. 9. The Body of CHRIST could shift its form as their was Occasion, and vary its Shape and Dress, according to the Disposition of his Soul. To *Mary Magdalene* he assumed the Form and Habit of a Gardener; Joh. xx. 15. While the same Day, the Two Disciples going to *Emmaus*, mistook him for a Traveller, from his Air and Dress.† *For after that he appeared in another Form unto two of them as they walked, and went into the Country.* In a Word, the Body of CHRIST could appear or vanish just as he pleased, and it should seem without Resistance from grosser Matter. Thus to his Disciples met together, with the

*Rev. xxi. 4.
†Luk. xxiv. 13. Mark xvi. 12.

Door shut, on a sudden, he stood confess'd in the midst of them, to their Wonder and Amazement.* I can see nothing tending to Heresy in this conjecture: Nor do I think we have any reason to read the Passage, *after the Time of shutting the Door.* But it is indifferent to our present Head, whether the Body of our Lord penetrated thro' the Pores of the Wood, as Light, which is a Body, does thro' the much finer Pores of Glass; or whether it had a power so marvellous, as to open and shut the Door, at once so swift, and so soft, as to be entirely unperceived both by their Sight and Hearing. Either the one or the other, shows the wondrous Powers of the raised Body.

And are these the Glories of CHRIST's Body? our's shall be fashioned like it. When we are raised from the Dead, our Bodies will be active as the Flames, and vigorous as the Sunbeams. They will be able to command their Shape, or to shift their Place as they please. To glide over Oceans, rise thro' the Clouds, dart like a Stream of Lightning from East to West, and range suddenly over the whole Creation.

4. It implies, That our Bodies shall be renewed, *holy* Bodies. CHRIST's Body is holy, and always was so. *He knew no Sin*; and tho' he was made in the likeness of sinful Flesh, yet without Sin. He was *holy, harmless, undefiled, seperate from Sinners.* His Body was sacred, and consecrate, and perfectly holy from its Birth. So the Angel blessed the Womb of the pregnant Virgin, *The Holy thing which shall be born of thee, shall be called the Son of GOD.*†

Is the Body of CHRIST holy? our's shall be so too; shall be fashioned like unto his own holy Body. These Senses shall be refined, these Passions rectified, and these Appetites adjusted to a perfect Order and Oeconomy. O divine Felicity, when this sinful Flesh, shall be changed into a perfectly holy Temple! Our Sanctification displays it self upon Spirit, Soul, and Body. But in this Life, we are sanctified but in Part, in each of these. But our Souls are wholly sanctified, upon the last happy Gasp of Death: Our Bodies will be so too, at the final Note of the great Trumpet, that shall call them from the

*Joh. xx. 19, 26. Luk. xxiv. 36, 37.
†Luk. i. 35.

dusty Bosom of the Grave. Then shall they be raised holy Bodies, fashioned like unto CHRIST's most glorious Body.

But why should we proceed any further? Shall our Bodies be fashioned like to CHRIST's glorious Body? It is enough! We can go no higher; can wish no more! We make a vain essay to describe the Glory, which the Fancy cannot paint, nor the Heart conceive. Our raised Bodies will shine with a Splendour, which, at present, we can have no equal Idea of. *Beloved, now are we the Sons of* GOD; *and it doth not appear what we shall be: But we know, that when he shall appear, we shall be like him, for we shall see him as he is.** *It does not* yet *appear what we shall be:* We can't imagine or conceive the Brightness of our future Glory. No matter; It is enough for us, that we shall with these Eyes behold the beauteous and majestick Face of JESUS, and *see him as he is.* If we may but *with open Face behold the Glory of the Lord,* we shall irresistibly catch the Beams, and be *changed into the same Image from Glory to Glory.* The Vision will be a transforming Vision. *We shall be like Him, for we shall see him as he is.* Be like Him; How? who can say how? It is above our mortal Language to declare how. *It does not appear what we shall be, but we know that when he shall appear we shall be like him, for we shall see him as he is.* O happy Vision! O blissful Change! O mysterious Glory!

The Fourth Proposition of the Text, is, It is our LORD JESUS CHRIST *who* shall change our vile Body, and fashion it like His glorious Body. This is the Work of the great GOD our SAVIOUR. He *can* do it, and he *will* do it, Here is the *Power*; here is the *Goodness* of a GOD. He is *able* and he *will* keep, and raise, and glorify, even the Dust committed to Him. From the Hints of the Context I might fetch Arguments enough to enlarge here.—But I see the Time expires, and I desist.

I come now to make a short Improvement of the noble Doctrines.

I. *How unhappy are Wicked Men!* He *shall change OUR vile Body that it may be fashioned like* his. *Ours;* none but *ours.* The Unbeliever and Impenitent has no Interest at all in this

*Joh. iii. 2.

blessed hope; none but the sincere Christian can apply it to himself. It is true, the wicked must be raised from the Dead, as well as the holy. But Oh! how wide the Difference between the one and the other, at the great decisive Day! The wicked shall be *raised to shame and everlasting Contempt.* No Glory shall shine about them, no Image of CHRIST shall appear upon them. They shall be changed, 'tis true, but O the dreadful Change! Their *feeble* Bodies must be changed into Bodies *strong* to bear the Wrath of an Almighty GOD. Their *dying* and *dead* Bodies shall be changed into Bodies of an *immortal* Constitution; Bodies that must live forever in unsufferable Anguish! That must measure Eternal Ages with Groans and Out-cries, and Execrations and Despair. Their *corrupt* and *filthy* Bodies shall be changed into ten thousand Times more *hideous* and *loathsome* Figures: Fit to be Inhabitants of Hell, and Companions for Devils. Their *healthy* and *pleasurable* Bodies shall be changed, be seized and rack'd with an unknown Variety of Pains and Torments; shall feed the Flames of the horrible Furnace; kindled with the Wrath of GOD, that burneth as an Oven, and endureth for ever. And Oh! *who can dwell with devouring Fire? who can inhabit everlasting Burnings?* The *darkness of a Grave* shall be changed for the *outer Darkness, where shall be weeping and gnashing of Teeth.* Instead of being fashioned like unto CHRIST's glorious Body; they shall be blacken'd with the finish'd Image of the Devil, and be consigned over to *everlasting Fire, prepared for the Devil and his Angels.* O the fearful Change, which the Resurrection will make upon the Bodies of the wicked!

II. *Let us learn to set a due Value upon our Bodies.* Tho' we may not idolize them, as the Crime generally is, we ought to honour them, and cherish them with a proper Care. What Honours are they coming to in a future State? They shall be raised, and changed, and fashioned like to CHRIST's glorious Body.

III. *Learn the Honours of our Lord* JESUS CHRIST. 'Tis HE who shall raise these vile Bodies, and fashion them like his glorious Body. Herein is the dear Saviour *mighty* as a GOD; Herein he is *good* as a GOD too. Not only *can* he, but he *will* do this for us. O what Love should beat in the Hearts of these Bodies, to him who shall change them, and be the Strength of *these* very Hearts, and their Portion for ever. What Thanks shall we pay this adored JESUS! What grateful Returns shall we make him! Let every Breath arise tuneful in his Honours, who shall quickly inspire these Nostrils with Breath that will never scatter or gasp away. Let every Pulse in our Blood, beat Time to Musick of his Praise, who will anon give the Pulses to leap thro' this living Frame, unfainting and immortal. Let every Member of these vile Bodies, grow honourable, by Employment in his Service, who shall change our vile Bodies, and fashion them like his own. Our *Eyes*, be ye exhausted in viewing the Works of GOD, in Reading his Word, and be lifted up to Heaven in his Praise! These Eyes which shall see GOD! Our *Ears*, employ all your curious Organs in hearing his dear Voice. These Ears which shall quickly be changed; which shall hear the Voice of the Son of GOD, in the Graves where they lie, and be transported with endless *Hallelujahs*. Shall not these *Tongues* of ours be redeemed from the silent Grave, and utter the Anthems of Heaven? Awake up then, our Tongue, our Glory; and bless and praise the LORD. These *Lips* shall forget the Pale of Death, and be changed, and bloom afresh: what can we do less than praise thee aloud with joyful Lips, who shall renew their faded Beauty. O Let *all* the Body which shall be changed by CHRIST, be employed in the Service of CHRIST. How was CHRIST's Body employed upon Earth? Let our Bodies be *employed* like *his now*, which shall be *fashioned* like *his hereafter*.

IV. And to conclude. *Rejoyce*, O Believer. *Thy dead men shall live, together with my dead Body shall they arise; Awake, and sing ye that dwell in the Dust: for thy dew is as the dew of Herbs, and the Earth shall cast out her dead.* Shall our Body be raised from the Grave, let us not be afraid to put off this Body; Let us meet Death with Triumph! Death! which shall only change this vile Body for a glorious one. What glories are to come even upon this vile Body of ours. Our Souls, the noblest Parts, they are safe. Nay, but our body too, the vile Body, shall be all glorious. Now, perhaps, these Bodies are in Pain; but quickly they shall know no more Pain. Now they are weary with Labour; quickly, they shall rest from their Labour,

*Isai. xxvi. 19.

and rise to constant Exercise without Weariness. Now they weep and sigh in many Sorrows: Quickly, all Tears shall be wiped from our Eyes, and Sorrow and Sighing shall flee away. Now they shall die, and go down to the Graves which wait for us: But tho' we die, yet shall we live; we shall be redeemed from the Power of the Grave, and arise to die no more. *Therefore my heart is glad, and my glory rejoyceth; my flesh also shall rest in hope. For thou wilt not leave my Soul in the* Grave; *nor suffer thy holy one* always *to see corruption. Thou wilt shew me the path of Life,* in a Resurrection from the Dead; *In thy Presence is Fulness of Joy, and at thy Right hand are Pleasures for evermore.*

AMEN.

JONATHAN EDWARDS

A Divine and Supernatural Light

*Immediately imparted to the Soul by the Spirit of God,
Shown to be both a Scriptural, and Rational
Doctrine;*

*In a Sermon Preach'd at Northampton,
And Published at the Desire of some of the Hearers.*

Job 28. 20.—*Whence then cometh wisdom? and where is
the place of understanding?*
Prov. 2. 6. *The LORD giveth wisdom.*
Isa. 42. 18. *Look ye blind that ye may see.*
2 Pet. 1. 19.—*Until the day dawn and the day-star arise
in your hearts.*

———

THE PREFACE.

*I am sensible that my consenting that the following Discourse
of mine should be published, needs Excuse; but yet don't think it
worth the while for me, here, to excuse my self, by declaring how
backward I was to it, and how much I was urged, and that I
was prevail'd with to do it, more to gratify others, and from an
Aim at promoting the Interest of Religion, and the Good of
Souls, than by any thought I had of any Honour that I should
get by it: for such things, I apprehend, ordinarily make less
Impression upon the Readers, to alter their thought of the
Author, and his Design, than the Authors generally think for.
They at whose desire, and upon whose Account chiefly, this
Sermon is printed, are already acquainted with the Circumstances of the Matter; and if any others should happen to see it,
and should think it worth their while to read it, I shall only desire of them, that they would put as favourable a Construction
upon my herein appearing in Print, as they can; and that they
would read the following Discourse with Candour, and without*

Prejudice against it, either from an Idea of the Author's Forwardness and Ostentation, or the Unfashionableness of the Subject. As to you, that are the People of the Flock, of which CHRIST hath called me to the Oversight, I have no Reason to be jealous that you will have any Prejudice against this Discourse, upon either of those mention'd Accounts, to stand in the way of your duly weighing, and considering, and suitably entertaining the things treated of in it. I have Reason to bless GOD, that there is a more happy Union between us, than that you should be prejudiced against any thing of mine, because 'tis mine; And however the subject is out of Mode in the World, 'tis doubtless your peculiar Happiness, that you have been so thoroughly instructed in such like Doctrines, even from your Beginning: and I rejoice in it, that Providence, in this Day of Corruption and Confusion, has cast my Lot where such Doctrines, that I look upon so much the Life and Glory of the Gospel, are not only own'd, but where there are so many, in whom the Truth of them is so apparently manifest, in their Experience, that any one who has had the Opportunity of Acquaintance with them in such matters, that I have had, must be very unreasonable to doubt of it. It is pleasant to me to read discourses on such Subjects, and to see such Doctrines well treated of in Books, but much more pleasant, to see them clearly exemplified. If what is here offered to you, shall be a means further to establish you in such Truths, and to make those among you, that yet remain in spiritual Darkness and Blindness, sensible of their Misery, and stir them up earnestly to seek after this spiritual and divine Illumination; and shall be for the Comfort and Edification of those that have Experienced it, I shall have great Reason to rejoice, and be thankful: and I desire your earnest and continual Prayers for me, that I may be the Instrument of much such Good to you, and Glory to GOD therein.

J.E.

The Reality of Spiritual Light

MATTHEW XVI. 17.

And JESUS answered and said unto him, blessed art thou Simon Barjona; *for Flesh and Blood hath not revealed it unto thee, but my Father which is in Heaven.*

CHRIST says these Words to *Peter*, upon Occasion of his professing his faith in him as the Son of GOD. Our Lord was enquiring of his Disciples, who Men said he was; not that he needed to be informed, but only to introduce and give Occasion to what follows. They answer, that some said he was *John* the *Baptist*, and some *Elias*, and others *Jeremias* or one of the Prophets. When they had thus given an Account, who others said he was, CHRIST asks them, who they said he was. *Simon Peter*, whom we find always zealous and forward, was the first to answer; he readily replied to the Question, *Thou art CHRIST the Son of the living GOD.*

Upon this Occasion CHRIST says as he does *to* him and *of* him in the Text: In which we may observe,

1. That *Peter* is pronounced blessed on this Account. *Blessed art thou*— "Thou art an happy man, that thou art not ignorant of this, that I am *CHRIST the Son of the living God.* Thou art distinguishingly happy. Others are blinded, and have dark and deluded Apprehensions, as you have now given an Account, some thinking that I am *Elias*, and some that I am *Jeremias*, and some one thing, and some another; but none of them thinking right, all of them misled. Happy art thou, that art so distinguished as to know the Truth in this Matter."

2. The Evidence of this his Happiness declared; *viz*. That GOD and he *only* had *revealed it* to him. This is an Evidence of his being *blessed*.

First, as it shows how peculiarly favoured he was of GOD, above others. *q.d.* "How highly favoured art thou, that others that are wise and great Men, the Scribes, Pharisees, and Rulers, and the Nation in general, are left in Darkness, to follow their own misguided Apprehensions, and that thou should'st be singled out, as it were by Name, that my heavenly Father should thus set his Love on *thee Simon Bar-jona*. This argues thee *blessed*, that thou should'st thus be the Object of GOD's distinguishing Love."

Secondly, it evidences his Blessedness also, as it intimates that this Knowlege is above any that *Flesh and Blood* can *reveal.* "This is such Knowlege as my *Father which in Heaven* only can give: It is too high and excellent to be communicated by such Means as other Knowlege is. Thou art *blessed,* that thou knowest that which GOD alone can teach thee."

The Original of this Knowlege is here declared; both negatively and positively. *Positively,* as GOD is here declared the Author of it. *Negatively,* as 'tis declared that *Flesh and Blood* had *not revealed it.* GOD is the Author of all Knowlege and Understanding whatsoever: He is the Author of the Knowlege, that is obtained by human Learning: He is the Author of all moral Prudence, and of the Knowlege and Skill that Men have in their secular Business. Thus it is said of all in *Israel* that were *wise-hearted,* and skill'd in Embroidering, that GOD had *fill'd* them *with the spirit of Wisdom.* Exod. 28. 3.

GOD is the Author of such Knowlege; but yet not so but that *Flesh and Blood reveals* it. Mortal Men are capable of imparting the Knowlege of human Arts and Sciences, and Skill in temporal Affairs. GOD is the Author of such Knowlege by those Means: *Flesh and Blood* is made use of by GOD as the *mediate* or *second* Cause of it; He conveys it by the Power and Influence of natural Means. But this spiritual Knowlege, spoken of in the Text, is what GOD is the Author of, and none else: He *reveals it* and *Flesh and Blood reveals it not.* He imparts this Knowlege immediately, not making use of any intermediate natural Causes, as he does in other Knowlege.

What had passed in the preceeding Discourse, naturally occasioned CHRIST to observe this; because the Disciples had been telling, how others did not know him, but were generally mistaken about him, and divided and confounded in their Opinions of him: but *Peter* had declared his assured Faith that he was the *Son of GOD.* Now it was natural to observe, how it was not *Flesh and Blood,* that had *revealed it to* him, but GOD; for if this knowlege were dependent on natural Causes or Means, how came it to pass that they, a Company of poor Fishermen, illiterate Men, and Persons of low Education, attain'd to the knowlege of the Truth; while the Scribes and Pharisees, Men of vastly higher advantages, and greater knowlege and sagacity in other matters, remain'd in Ignorance?

This could be owing only to the gracious distinguishing Influence and Revelation of the SPIRIT of GOD. Hence, what I would make the Subject of my present Discourse from these Words, is this

DOCTRINE, viz.

That there is such a thing, as A SPIRITUAL and DIVINE LIGHT, immediately imparted to the Soul by GOD, of a different Nature from any that is obtain'd by natural Means.

In what I say on this Subject at this Time, I would

I. Show what this *divine Light* is.

II. How it is given *Immediately by GOD*, and not *obtain'd by natural Means.*

III. Show the Truth of the Doctrine.

And then conclude with a brief Improvement.

I. I would show *what this* spiritual and divine Light *is.* And in order to it would shew,

First, in a few things *what it is not.* And here,

1. *Those Convictions that natural Men may have of their Sin and Misery* is not *this* spiritual and divine Light. Men in a natural Condition may have Convictions of the Guilt that lies upon them, and the anger of GOD, and their Danger of divine Vengeance. Such Convictions are from *Light* or Sensibleness of Truth: that some Sinners have a greater Conviction of their Guilt and Misery than others, is because some have more *Light*, or more of an Apprehension of Truth, than others. And this *Light* and Conviction may be from the Spirit of GOD; *the SPIRIT convinces* Men *of Sin*: but yet nature is much more concern'd in it than in the Communication of that *spiritual and divine Light*, that is spoken of in the *Doctrine*; 'tis from the Spirit of GOD only as assisting *natural Principles*, and not as infusing any new *Principles. Common Grace* differs from *special*, in that it influences only by assisting of *Nature*; and not by imparting *Grace*, or bestowing any thing *above* Nature. The *Light* that is obtain'd, is wholly *natural*, or of no superiour *Kind* to what meer *Nature* attains to; tho' more of *that kind* be obtained, than would be obtained if Men were left wholly to themselves. Or *in other Words, Common Grace* only assists the Faculties of the Soul to do that more fully, which they do by *Nature*; as *natural* Conscience, or Reason, will by meer *Nature* make a Man

sensible of Guilt, and will accuse and condemn him when he has done amiss. Conscience is a *Principle natural* to Men; and the Work that it doth *naturally*, or of it self, is to give an Apprehension of *right* and *wrong*; and to suggest to the Mind the Relation that there is between right and wrong, and a Retribution. The Spirit of GOD, in those Convictions which unregenerate Men sometimes have, assists Conscience to do this Work in a further Degree, than it would do if they were left to themselves: He helps it against those Things that tend to stupify it, and obstruct its Exercise. But in the *renewing* and *sanctifying* work of the HOLY GHOST, those things are wrought in the Soul that are *above* Nature; and of which there is nothing of the like kind in the Soul *by* Nature; and they are caused to exist in the Soul habitually, & according to such a stated Constitution or Law, that lays such a Foundation for Exercises in a continued Course, as is called a *Principle* of nature. Not only are remaining *Principles* assisted to do their work more freely and fully, but those *Principles* are restored that were utterly destroyed by the Fall; and the mind thenceforward habitually exerts those acts that the Dominion of Sin had made it as wholly destitute of, as a dead Body is of vital Acts.

The Spirit of GOD acts in a very different manner in the one Case, from what he doth in the other. He may indeed act *upon* the Mind of a natural Man; but he acts *in* the Mind of a Saint as an *indwelling vital Principle*. He acts upon the Mind of an unregenerate Person as an *extrinsick occasional Agent*; for in acting upon them he doth not unite himself to them; for notwithstanding all his Influences that they may be the Subjects of, they are still *sensual having not the Spirit.* Jude 19. But he unites himself with the Mind of a Saint, takes him for his Temple, actuates and influences him as a new, *supernatural Principle* of Life and Action. There is this Difference; that the Spirit of GOD in acting in the Soul of a Godly Man, exerts and communicates himself there in his own proper Nature. Holiness is the proper Nature of the Spirit of GOD. The HOLY SPIRIT operates in the Minds of the Godly, by uniting himself to them, and living in them, and exerting his own Nature in the Exercise of their Faculties. The Spirit of GOD may act upon a Creature, and yet not, in acting communicate himself. The Spirit of GOD may act upon inanimate Creatures; as *the Spirit moved upon the Face of the Waters*, in the Beginning of the Creation: So the Spirit of GOD may act upon the minds of Men, many ways, and communicate himself no more than when he acts upon an inanimate Creature. *For Instance.* He may excite Thoughts in them, may assist their natural Reason and Understanding, or may assist other natural Principles, and this without any Union with the Soul, but may act, as it were, as upon an external Object. But as he acts in his holy Influences, and spiritual Operations, he acts in a way of peculiar Communication of himself; so that the Subject is thence denominated *Spiritual*.

2. *This* spiritual and divine Light *don't consist in any Impression made upon the Imagination*. 'Tis no *Impression* upon the Mind, as tho' one saw any thing with the bodily Eyes: 'Tis no *Imagination* or *Idea* of an outward *Light* or Glory, or any Beauty of Form or Countenance, or a visible Lustre or Brightness of any Object. The *Imagination* may be strongly impress'd with such things; but this is not *spiritual Light*. Indeed when the Mind has a lively Discovery of spiritual things, and is greatly affected by the Power of divine Light, it may, and probably very commonly doth, much affect the *Imagination*: So that *Impressions* of an outward Beauty or Brightness, may accompany those spiritual Discoveries. But *spiritual Light* is not that *Impression upon the Imagination*, but an exceeding different thing from it. Natural Men may have lively *Impressions* on their *Imaginations*; and we cant determine but that the Devil, *who transforms himself into an Angel of Light*, may cause *Imaginations* of an outward Beauty, or visible Glory, and of Sounds and Speeches, and other such Things; but these are Things of a vastly inferiour Nature to *Spiritual Light*.

3. *This* spiritual Light *is not the suggesting of any new Truths, or Propositions not contain'd in the Word of GOD*. This suggesting of new Truths or Doctrines to the Mind, independent of any antecedent Revelation of those Propositions, either in Word or Writing, is Inspiration; such as the Prophets and Apostles had, and such as some Enthusiasts pretend to. But this *spiritual Light* that I am speaking of, is quite a different thing from Inspiration: It reveals no new Doctrine, it suggests

no new Proposition to the Mind, it teaches no new thing of GOD, or CHRIST, or another World, not taught in the Bible; but only gives a due Apprehension of those things that are taught in the word of GOD.

4. *'Tis not every affecting View that Men have of the Things of Religion, that is this* spiritual and divine Light. Men by meer Principles of Nature are capable of being *affected* with Things that have a special Relation to Religion, as well as other Things. A Person by meer Nature, for Instance, may be liable to be *affected* with the Story of JESUS CHRIST, and the sufferings he underwent, as well as by any other tragical Story: He may be the more *affected* with it from the Interest he conceives Mankind to have in it: Yea he may be *affected* with it without believing it; as well as a Man may be *affected* with what he reads in a Romance, or see's acted in a Stage Play. He may be *affected* with a lively and eloquent description of many pleasant things that attend the state of the Blessed in Heaven; as well as his Imagination be entertain'd by a romantick description of the pleasantness of Fairy Land, or the like. And that common belief of the truth of *the things of Religion*, that Persons may have from Education, or otherwise, may help forward their *affection*. We read in Scripture of many that were greatly *affected* with things of a religious nature, who yet are there represented as wholly graceless, and many of them very ill Men. A Person therefore may have *affecting views of the things of Religion*, and yet be very destitute of *spiritual Light*. *Flesh* and *Blood* may be the Author of this: One Man may give another an *affecting view* of divine things with but common assistance; but GOD alone can give a *spiritual* Discovery of them.

But I proceed to show,

Secondly, Positively, *WHAT this* spiritual and divine Light *is*.

And it may be thus described, *A true sense of the divine Excellency of the things revealed in the Word of GOD, and a conviction of the truth and reality of them, thence arising.*

This *spiritual Light* primarily consists in the former of these, *viz.* a real sense and apprehension of the divine Excellency of things revealed in the Word of GOD. A spiritual and saving Conviction of the truth and reality of these things, arises from such a sight of their divine Excellency and Glory;

so that this Conviction of their truth is an effect and natural consequence of this sight of their divine Glory. There is therefore in this *spiritual Light*,

I. *A true sense of the divine and superlative excellency of the things of Religion*; a real sense of the excellency of GOD, and JESUS CHRIST, and of the work of Redemption, and the ways and works of GOD revealed in the Gospel. There is a *divine* and *superlative* Glory in these things; an Excellency that is of a vastly higher Kind, and more sublime Nature, than in other things; a Glory greatly distinguishing them from all that is earthly and temporal. He that is spiritually *enlightened* truly apprehends and sees it, or has a sense of it. He don't meerly rationally believe that GOD is Glorious, but he has a sense of the Gloriousness of GOD in his Heart. There is not only a rational belief that GOD is holy, and that Holiness is a good thing; but there is a sense of the Loveliness of GOD's Holiness. There is not only a speculatively judging that GOD is gracious, but a sense how amiable GOD is upon that Account; or a sense of the Beauty of this divine Attribute.

There is a twofold Understanding or Knowledge of Good, that GOD has made the Mind of Man capable of. The *First*, that which is meerly *speculative* or *notional*: As when a Person only speculatively judged, that any thing is, which by the Agreement of Mankind, is called Good or Excellent, *viz.* that which is most to general Advantage, and between which and a Reward there is a suitableness; and the like. And the *other* is that which consists in the sense of the Heart: As when there is a sense of the Beauty, Amiableness, or Sweetness of a thing; so that the Heart is sensible of Pleasure and Delight in the presence of the *Idea* of it. In the *former* is exercised meerly the speculative Faculty, or the Understanding strictly so called, or as spoken of in Distinction from the Will or Disposition of the Soul. In the *latter* the Will, or Inclination, or Heart, are mainly concern'd.

Thus there is a Difference between *having an Opinion* that GOD is holy and gracious, and *having a sense* of the Loveliness and Beauty of that Holiness and Grace. There is a Difference between *having a rational Judgment* that Honey is sweet, and *having a sense* of its sweetness. A Man may have the *Former*, that knows not how Honey tasts; but a Man can't have the *Latter*, unless he has an *Idea* of the tast of Honey in his Mind. So there is a difference between *believing* that a Person is Beautiful, and *having* a sense of his Beauty. The *Former* may be obtain'd by hear-say, but the *Latter* only by seeing the Countenance. There is a wide difference between meer *speculative, rational Judging* any thing to be excellent, and *having* a sense of its Sweetness, and Beauty. The *Former* rests only in the Head, Speculation only is concern'd in it; but the Heart is concern'd in the *Latter*. When the Heart is sensible of the Beauty and Amiableness of a Thing, it necessarily feels Pleasure in the Apprehension. It is implied in a Persons being heartily sensible of the Loveliness of a thing, that the *Idea* of it is sweet and pleasant to his Soul; which is a far different thing from having a rational Opinion that it is excellent.

2. *There arises from this* sense of divine Excellency of Things contain'd in the Word of GOD, *a Conviction of the Truth and Reality of them: and that either* indirectly, *or* directly.

First, *Indirectly*, and that two ways.

1. *As the Prejudices that are in the Heart, against* the truth of divine things, *are hereby removed; so that the Mind becomes susceptive of the due Force of rational Arguments for their Truth.* The Mind of Man is naturally full of *Prejudices against the Truth of divine Things.* It is full of Enmity against the Doctrines of the Gospel; which is a disadvantage to those *Arguments* that prove their *Truth*, and causes them to lose their Force upon the Mind. But when a Person has discovered to him the divine excellency of Christian Doctrines, this destroys the Enmity, removes those *Prejudices*, and sanctifys the Reason, and causes it to lie open to the *Force of Arguments for their Truth.*

Hence was the different Effect that CHRIST's Miracles had to convince the Disciples, from what they had to convince the Scribes and Pharisees. Not that they had a stronger Reason, or had their Reason more improved; but their Reason was sanctified, and those blinding *Prejudices*, that the Scribes and Pharisees were under, were removed by the sense they had of the Excellency of CHRIST, and his Doctrine.

2. *It not only removes the Hindrances of Reason, but positively helps Reason.* It makes even the speculative Notions the more

lively. It engages the attention of the Mind, with the more Fixedness and Intenseness to that Kind of Objects; which causes it to have a clearer View of them, and enables it more clearly to see their mutual Relations, and occasions it to take more Notice of them. The *Ideas* themselves that otherwise are dim, and obscure, are by this Means impress'd with the greater Strength, and have a Light cast upon them; so that the Mind can better judge of them. As he that beholds the Objects on the Face of the Earth, when the Light of the Sun is cast upon them, is under greater Advantage to discern them in their true Forms, and mutual Relations, than he that sees them in a dim Star-light or Twilight.

The Mind having a sensibleness of the Excellency of divine Objects, dwells upon them with Delight; and the Powers of the Soul are more awaken'd, and enliven'd to employ themselves in the Contemplation of them, and exert themselves more fully and much more to Purpose. The Beauty and Sweetness of the Objects draws on the Faculties, and draws forth their Exercises: So that Reason it self is under far greater Advantages for its proper and free Exercises, and to attain its proper End, free of Darkness and Delusion. But,

Secondly, A true sense of the divine Excellency of the Things of GOD's Word doth more *directly* and *immediately* convince of the Truth of them; And that because the Excellency of these Things is so superlative. There is a Beauty in them that is so divine and Godlike, that is greatly and evidently distinguishing of them from things meerly human, or that Men are the Inventors and Authors of; a Glory that is so high and great, that when clearly seen, commands Assent to their Divinity, and Reality. When there is an actual and lively Discovery of this Beauty and Excellency, it won't allow of any such Thought as that it is an human Work, or the Fruit of Mens Invention. This Evidence, that they, that are spiritually *enlightned*, have of the Truth of the things of Religion, is a Kind of *intuitive* and *immediate* Evidence. They believe the Doctrines of GOD's Word to be divine, because they see Divinity in them, i.e. They see a divine, and transcendent, and most evidently distinguishing Glory in them; such a Glory as, if clearly seen, don't leave Room to doubt of their being of GOD, and not of Men.

Such a Conviction of the Truth of Religion as this, arising, these Ways, from a sense of the divine Excellency of them, is that true spiritual Conviction, that there is in saving Faith. And this Original of it, is that by which it is most essentially distinguished from that common assent, which unregenerate Men are capable of.

II. I Proceed now to the second Thing proposed, *viz.* To show *how this Light is Immediately given by GOD, and not obtain'd by natural Means.* And here,

1. *'Tis not intended that the natural Faculties are not made Use of in it.* The *natural Faculties* are the Subject of this Light: And they are the Subject in such a Manner, that they are not meerly pasive, but active in it; the Acts and Exercises of Man's Understanding are concern'd and made use of in it. GOD in letting in this *Light* into the Soul, deals with Man according to his Nature, or as a rational Creature; and makes Use of his human *Faculties.* But yet this *Light* is not the less *immediately* from GOD for that; tho' the *Faculties are made Use of,* 'tis as the Subject and not as the Cause; and that acting of the *Faculties* in it, is not the Cause, but is either implied in the Thing it self, (in the *Light* that is imparted) or is the Consequence of it. As the Use that we make of our Eyes in beholding various Objects, when the Sun arises, is not the Cause of the Light that discovers those Objects to us.

2. *'Tis not intended that outward Means have no Concern in this Affair.* As I have observed already, 'tis not in this Affair, as it is in Inspiration, where new Truths are suggested: for here is by this *Light* only given a due Apprehension of the same Truths that are revealed in the Word of GOD; and therefore it is not given without the Word. The Gospel is made Use of in this Affair: This *Light* is the *Light of the Glorious Gospel of CHRIST* 2 Cor. 4. 4. The Gospel is as a Glass, by which this *Light* is conveyed to us. 1 Cor. 13. 12. *Now we see through a Glass—* But,

3. When it is said that this *Light* is given immediately by GOD, and not obtained by natural Means, *hereby is intended, that 'tis given by GOD without making Use of any Means that operate by their own Power, or a natural Force.* GOD makes Use of Means; but 'tis not as mediate Causes to produce this Effect. There are not truly any second Causes of it; but it is

produced by GOD *immediately*. The Word of GOD is no proper Cause of this Effect: It don't operate by any *natural Force* in it. The Word of GOD is only made Use of to convey to the Mind the Subject matter of this saving Instruction: And this indeed it doth convey to us by *natural Force* or Influence. It conveys to our Minds these and those Doctrines; it is the Cause of the Notion of them in our Heads, but not of the sense of the divine Excellency of them in our Hearts. Indeed a Person can't have *spiritual Light* without the Word. But that don't argue, that the Word properly causes that *Light*. The Mind can't see the Excellency of any Doctrine, unless that Doctrine be first in the Mind; but the seeing the Excellency of the Doctrine may be immediately from the Spirit of GOD; tho' the conveying of the Doctrine or Proposition it self may be by the Word. So that the Notions that are the Subject matter of this *Light*, are conveyed to the Mind by the Word of GOD; but that due sense of the Heart, wherein this *Light* formally consists, is immediately by the Spirit of GOD. As *for Instance*, that Notion that there is a CHRIST, and that CHRIST is holy and gracious, is conveyed to the Mind by the Word of GOD: But the sense of the Excellency of CHRIST by reason of that Holiness and Grace, is nevertheless immediately the Work of the HOLY SPIRIT.

I come now,

III. To show *the Truth of the Doctrine*; that is to show *that there is such a Thing as that spiritual Light that has been described, thus immediately let into the Mind by GOD*. And here I would shew briefly, that this Doctrine is both *scriptural*, and *rational*.

First, 'tis *SCRIPTURAL*. My Text is not only full to the Purpose, but 'tis a Doctrine that the Scripture abounds in. We are there abundantly taught, that the Saints differ from the Ungodly in this, that they have the Knowlege of GOD, and a sight of GOD, and of JESUS CHRIST. I shall mention but few Texts of many; 1 John 3. 6. *Whosoever sinneth hath not seen him, nor known him.* 3 John 11. *He that doth Good, is of GOD; but he that doth Evil, hath not seen God.* John 14. 19. *The world seeth me no more; but ye see me.* John 17. 3. *And this is Eternal Life, that they might know thee, the only true GOD, and JESUS CHRIST whom thou hast sent.* This Knowlege, or sight of

GOD and CHRIST, can't be a meer speculative Knowlege; because it is spoken of as a seeing and knowing, wherein they differ from the Ungodly. And by these Scriptures it must not only be a different Knowlege in Degree and Circumstances, and different in its Effects; but it must be entirely different in Nature and Kind.

And this Light and Knowlege is always spoken of as immediately given of GOD Mat. 11. 25, 26, 27. *At that time JESUS answered and said, I thank thee O Father Lord of Heaven and Earth, because thou hast hid these things from the wise and prudent, and hast revealed them unto Babes; even so Father, for so it seemed good in thy sight. All things are delivered unto me of my Father; and no Man knoweth the Son but the Father; neither knoweth any Man the Father, save the Son, and he to whomsoever the Son will reveal him.* Here this Effect is ascribed alone to the arbitrary Operation, and Gift of GOD, bestowing this Knowlege on whom he will, and distinguishing those with it, that have the least natural Advantage or Means for Knowlege, even *Babes*, when it is denied to the *Wise* and *Prudent*. And the imparting the Knowlege of GOD is here appropriated to the Son of GOD, as his sole Prerogative. And again, 2 Cor. 4. 6. *For GOD who commanded the Light to shine out of Darkness, hath shined in our Hearts, to give the Light of the Knowlege of the Glory of GOD in the Face of JESUS CHRIST.* This plainly shows, that there is such a thing as a discovery of the divine superlative Glory and Excellency of GOD and CHRIST; and that peculiar to the Saints: and also that 'tis as immediately from GOD, as Light from the Sun: and that 'tis the immediate Effect of his Power and Will; for 'tis compared to GOD's creating the Light by his powerful Word in the beginning of the Creation; and is said to be by the Spirit of the LORD, in the eighteenth verse of the preceeding Chapter. GOD is spoken of as giving the Knowlege of CHRIST in Conversion, as of what before was hidden and unseen in that Gal. 1. 15, 16. *But when it pleased GOD, who separated me from my Mothers Womb, and called me by his Grace, to reveal his Son in me—.* The Scripture also speaks plainly of such a Knowlege of the Word of GOD, as has been described, as the immediate gift of GOD. Psal. 119. 18. *Open thou mine Eyes, that I may behold wondrous things out of thy Law.* What could the Psalmist mean, when he begged of GOD to *open* his *Eyes*? was he ever blind? might he not have Resort to the Law and see every Word and Sentence in it when he pleased? And what could he mean by those *wondrous Things*? was it the wonderful Stories of the Creation, and Deluge, and Israel's passing thro' the red Sea, and the like? were not his Eyes open to read these strange things when he would? Doubtless by *wondrous Things in GOD's Law*, he had Respect to those distinguishing and wonderful Excellencies, and marvellous Manifestations of the divine Perfections, and Glory, that there was in the Commands and Doctrines of the Word, and those Works and Counsels of GOD that were there revealed. So the Scripture speaks of a Knowlege of GOD's Dispensation, and Covenant of Mercy, and Way of Grace towards his People, as peculiar to the Saints, and given only by GOD, Psal. 25. 14. *The Secret of the LORD is with them that fear him; and he will shew them his Covenant.*

And that a true and saving Belief of the Truth of Religion is that which arises from such a Discovery, is also what the Scripture teaches. As John 6. 40. *And this is the will of him that sent me, that every one that SEETH the Son, and BE-LIEVETH on him, may have everlasting Life.* Where it is plain that a true Faith is what arises from a spiritual sight of CHRIST. And John 17. 6, 7, 8. *I have manifested thy Name unto the Men which thou gavest me out of the World—. Now they have known that all things whatsoever thou hast given me, are of thee; for I have given unto them the words which thou gavest me, and they have received them, and known surely that I came out from thee, and they have believed that thou didst send me.* Where CHRIST's *manifesting* GOD's *Name* to the Disciples, or giving them the Knowlege of God, was that whereby they knew that CHRIST's Doctrine was *of GOD*, and that CHRIST himself was *of* him, proceeded *from* him, and was *sent* by him. Again John 12. 44, 45, 46 *JESUS cried and said, he that* believeth *on me*, believeth *not on me, but on him that sent me; and he that* seeth *me* seeth *him that sent me. I am come a Light into the World, that whosoever* Believeth *on me should not abide in* Darkness. There Believing in CHRIST and spiritually Seeing him, are spoken of as running parallel.

CHRIST condemns the Jews, that they did not know that

he was the MESSIAH, and that his Doctrine was true, from an inward distinguishing Tast and Relish of what was divine, in Luke 12. 56, 57. He having there blamed the Jews, that though they could *discern the Face of the Sky and of the Earth*, and Signs of the Weather, that yet they could not *discern* those *Times*; or as 'tis expressed in *Matthew*, *the Signs of* those *Times*; He adds, *yea and why even of your own selves, judge ye not what is right?* i.e. without extrinsick *Signs*. "Why have ye not that sense of true Excellency, whereby ye may distinguish that which is holy and divine? Why have ye not that savour of the things of GOD, by which you may see the distinguishing Glory, and evident Divinity of me and my Doctrine?"

The Apostle *Peter* mentions it as what gave them (the Apostles,) good and well grounded Assurance of the Truth of the Gospel, that they had seen the divine Glory of CHRIST. 2 Pet. 1. 16. *For we have not followed cunningly devised Fables, when we made known unto you, the Power and Coming of our Lord JESUS CHRIST, but were Eye-witnesses of his Majesty.* The Apostle has Respect to that visible Glory of CHRIST which they saw in his Transfiguration: That Glory was so divine having such an ineffable Appearance and semblance of divine Holiness, Majesty, and Grace, that it evidently denoted him to be a divine Person. But if a sight of CHRIST's outward Glory might give a rational Assurance of his Divinity, why may not an Apprehension of his spiritual Glory do so too. Doubtless CHRIST's spiritual Glory is in itself as distinguishing, and as plainly shewing his Divinity, as his outward Glory; and a great deal more: for his spiritual Glory is that wherein his Divinity consists; and the outward Glory of his Transfiguration shew'd him to be divine, only as it was a Remarkable Image or Representation of that spiritual Glory. Doubtless therefore he that has had a clear sight of the spiritual Glory of CHRIST, may say, I *have not followed cunningly devised Fables, but* have been *an Eye-witness of his Majesty*, upon as good Grounds as the Apostle, when he had Respect to the outward Glory of Christ, that he had seen. But this brings me to what was proposed next *viz.* to show that,

Secondly, this Doctrine is RATIONAL.

1. 'Tis rational *to suppose that there is really such an Excellency in divine things, that is so transcendent and exceed-*

ingly different from what is in other things, that if it were seen would most evidently distinguish them. We can't *rationally* doubt but that Things that are *divine*, that appertain to the supreme Being, are vastly different from Things that are *human*; that there is that Godlike, high, and glorious Excellency in them, that does most remarkably difference them from the things that are of Men; insomuch that if the difference were but seen, it would have a convincing, satisfying influence upon any one, that they are what they are, viz. *divine.* What Reason can be offered against it? Unless we would argue that GOD is not remarkably distinguished in Glory from Men.

If CHRIST should now appear to any One, as he did on the Mount at his Transfiguration; or if he should appear to the World in the Glory that he now appears in in Heaven, as he will do at the Day of Judgment; without doubt, the Glory and Majesty that he would appear in, would be such as would satisfy every One, that he was a divine Person, and that Religion was true: And it would be a most reasonable, and well grounded Conviction too. And why may there not be that Stamp of Divinity, or divine Glory on the word of GOD, on the Scheme and Doctrine of the Gospel, that may be in like manner distinguishing and as *rationally* convincing, provided it be but seen? 'Tis rational to suppose, that when GOD speaks to the World, there should be something in his Word or Speech vastly different from Men's Word. Supposing that GOD never had spoken to the World, but we had Notice that He was about to do it; that he was about to Reveal himself from Heaven, and speak to us immediately himself, in divine Speeches or Discourses, as it were from his own Mouth; or that he should give us a Book of his own inditing; after what manner should we expect that he would speak? Would it not be *rational* to suppose, that his Speech would be exceeding different from Men's Speech, that he should speak like a GOD; that is, that there should be such an Excellency and sublimity in his Speech or Word, such a Stamp of Wisdom, Holiness, Majesty, and other divine Perfections, that the word of Men, yea of the wisest of Men, should appear mean and base in Comparison of it? Doubtless it would be thought *rational* to expect this, and *unreasonable* to think otherwise. When a wise Man speaks in the Exercise of his Wisdom, there is something in every thing he says, that is very distinguishable from the Talk of a little Child. So, without doubt, and much more, is the Speech of GOD, (if there be any such Thing as the Speech of GOD,) to be distinguished from that of the wisest of Men; agreable to Jer. 23. 28, 29. GOD having there been reproving the false Prophets that prophesied in his Name, and pretended that what they spake was his Word, when indeed it was their own Word, says, *The Prophet that hath a Dream, let him tell a Dream; and he that hath my Word, let him speak my Word faithfully: WHAT IS THE CHAFF TO THE WHEAT? Saith the LORD. Is not my Word like as a Fire, saith the LORD, and like a Hammer that breaketh the Rock in Pieces?*

2. *If there be such a distinguishing Excellency in divine things; 'tis* rational *to suppose that there may be such a thing as seeing it.* What should hinder but that it may be seen? 'Tis no Argument that there is no such Thing as such a distinguishing Excellency, or that, if there be, that it can't be seen, that some don't see it; tho' they may be discerning Men in temporal Matters. It is not *rational* to suppose, if there be any such Excellency in divine Things, that wicked Men should see it. 'Tis not *rational* to suppose, that those whose Minds are full of spiritual Pollution, and under the Power of filthy Lusts, should have any Relish or Sense of divine Beauty, or Excellency; or that their Minds should be susceptive of that *Light* that is in its own Nature so pure and heavenly. It need not seem at all strange, that Sin should so blind the Mind, seeing that Mens particular natural Tempers and Dispositions will so much blind them in secular Matters; as when Mens natural Temper is melancholly, jealous, fearful, proud, or the like.

3. *'Tis* rational *to suppose that this Knowlege should be given immediately by GOD, and not be obtain'd by natural means.* Upon what account should it seem *unreasonable*, that there should be any *immediate* Communication between GOD and the Creature? 'Tis strange that Men should make any matter of difficulty of it. Why should not He that made all things, still have something *immediately* to do with the Things that he has made? Where lies the great difficulty, if we own the Being of a GOD, and that he created all things out of

Nothing, of allowing some immediate Influence of GOD on the Creation still. And if it be *reasonable* to suppose it with Respect to any Part of the Creation, 'tis Especially so with Respect to reasonable intelligent Creatures; who are next to GOD in the Gradation of the different Orders of Beings, and whose Business is most *immediately* with GOD; who were made on Purpose for those Exercises that do respect God, and wherein they have *nextly* to do with God: for *Reason* teaches that Man was made to serve and glorify his Creator. And if it be *rational* to suppose that GOD immediately communicates himself to Man in any Affair, it is in this. 'Tis *rational* to suppose that GOD would reserve that Knowlege and Wisdom, that is of such a divine and excellent Nature, to be bestowed *immediately* by himself, and that it should not be left in the Power of second Causes. Spiritual Wisdom and Grace is the highest and most *excellent* Gift that ever GOD bestows on any Creature: In this the highest Excellency and Perfection of a rational Creature consists. 'Tis also immensely the most *important* of all divine Gifts: 'Tis that wherein Mans Happiness consists, and on which his everlasting Welfare depends. How *rational* is it to suppose that GOD, however he has left meaner Goods and lower Gifts to second Causes, and in some sort in their Power, yet should reserve this most excellent, divine, and important of all divine Communications, in his own Hands, to be bestowed *immediately* by himself, as a thing too great for second Causes to be concern'd in? 'Tis *rational* to suppose that this Blessing should be *immediately* from GOD; for there is no Gift or Benefit that is in itself so nearly related to the divine Nature, there is nothing the Creature receives that is so much *of* GOD, *of* his Nature, so much a Participation of the Deity: 'Tis a Kind of Emanation of GOD's Beauty, and is related to GOD as the Light is to the Sun. 'Tis therefore congruous and fit, that when it is given of GOD, it should be nextly from himself, and by himself, according to his own Sovereign Will.

'Tis *rational* to suppose, that it should be beyond a Man's Power to obtain this Knowlege, and *Light*, by the meer Strength of natural Reason; for 'tis not a Thing that belongs to Reason, to see the Beauty and Loveliness of spiritual things; it is not a speculative thing, but depends on the Sense of the Heart. Reason indeed is necessary in order to it, as 'tis by Reason only that we are become the Subjects of the means of it; which means I have already shown to be necessary in order to it, though they have no proper causal Influence in the Affair. 'Tis by Reason, that we become possessed of a notion of those Doctrines that are the Subject Matter of this *divine Light*; and Reason may many ways be indirectly, and remotely an Advantage to it. And Reason has also to do in the Acts that are immediately consequent on this Discovery: A seeing the Truth of Religion from hence, is by Reason; though it be but by one step, and the Inference be immediate. So Reason has to do in that accepting of, and trusting in CHRIST, that is consequent on it. But if we take Reason strictly, not for the Faculty of mental Perception in general, but for Ratiocination, or a Power of Inferring by Arguments; I say if we take Reason thus, the perceiving of spiritual Beauty and Excellency no more belongs to Reason, than it belongs to the Sense of feeling to perceive Colours, or to the Power of seeing to perceive the Sweetness of Food. It is out of Reason's Province to perceive the Beauty or Loveliness of any thing: Such a Perception don't belong to that Faculty. Reason's Work is to perceive Truth, and not Excellency. 'Tis not Ratiociation that gives Men the Perception of the Beauty and Amiableness of a Countenance; tho' it may be many ways indirectly an advantage to it; yet 'tis no more Reason that immediately perceives it, than it is Reason that perceives the Sweetness of Honey: It depends on the Sense of the Heart. Reason may determine that a Countenance is Beautiful to others, it may determine that Honey is sweet to others; but it will never give me a Perception of its Sweetness.

I will conclude with a very brief *Improvement* of what has been said.

First. This Doctrine may lead us *to reflect* on the Goodness of GOD, that has so ordered it, that a saving Evidence of the Truth of the Gospel is such, as is attainable by Persons of mean Capacities, and Advantages, as well as those that are of the greatest Parts and Learning. If the Evidence of the Gospel depended only on History, and such Reasonings as learned Men only are capable of, it would be above the Reach of far the greatest part of Mankind. But Persons, with but an ordinary Degree of Knowlege, are capable without a long and subtil Train of Reasoning, to see the divine Excellency of the things of Religion: They are capable of being taught by the Spirit of GOD, as well as learned Men. The Evidence that is this Way obtained, is vastly better and more satisfying, than all that can be obtain'd by the Arguings of those that are most Learned, and greatest Masters of Reason. And Babes are as capable of knowing these things, as the wise and prudent; and they are often hid from these, when they are revealed to those. 1 Cor. 1. 26, 27. *For ye see your Calling Brethren, how that not many wise Men, after the Flesh, not many mighty, not many noble are called. But GOD hath chosen the foolish things of the World—.*

Secondly. This Doctrine may well put us upon *examining* our selves, whether we have ever had his *divine Light*, that has been described, let into our Souls. If there be such a thing indeed, and it ben't only a Notion, or Whimsy of Persons of weak and distempered Brains, then doubtless 'tis a thing of great Importance, whether we have thus been taught by the Spirit of GOD; whether *the Light of the Glorious Gospel of CHRIST, who is the Image of GOD hath shined into us, giving us the Light of the Knowlege of the Glory of GOD, in the Face of JESUS CHRIST;* whether we have *seen the Son, and believed on him,* or have that Faith of Gospel Doctrines that arises from a spiritual Sight of CHRIST.

Thirdly. All may hence be *exhorted,* earnestly *to seek* this *spiritual Light.* To influence and move to it, the following things may be consider'd.

1. This is the most *excellent and divine* Wisdom, that any Creature is capable of. 'Tis more excellent than any human Learning; 'Tis far more excellent, than all the Knowlege of the greatest Philosophers, or States-men. Yea the least Glimpse of *the Glory of GOD in the Face of CHRIST* doth more exalt and enoble the Soul, than all the Knowlege of those that have the greatest speculative Understanding in Divinity, without Grace. This Knowlege has the most noble Object that is, or can be, *viz.* the divine Glory, and Excellency of GOD, and CHRIST. The Knowlege of these Objects is that wherein consists the most excellent Knowlege of the Angels, yea, of GOD himself,

2. This Knowlege is that which is above all others *Sweet and Joyful*. Men have a great deal of Pleasure in human Knowlege, in Studies of natural things; but this is nothing to that Joy which arises from this *divine Light* shining into the Soul. This *Light* gives a View of those things that are immensely the most exquisitely Beautiful, and capable of delighting the Eye of the Understanding. This *spiritual Light* is the dawning of the Light of Glory in the Heart. There is nothing so powerful as this to support Persons in Affliction, and to give the Mind Peace and Brightness, in this stormy and dark World.

3. This Light is such as *effectually influences the Inclination, and changes the Nature of the Soul*. It assimilates the Nature to the divine Nature, and changes the Soul into an Image of the same Glory that is beheld. 2 Cor. 3. 18. *But we all with open Face beholding as in a Glass the Glory of the Lord, are changed into the same Image, from Glory to Glory, even as by the Spirit of the Lord*. This Knowlege will wean from the World, and raise the Inclination to heavenly things. It will turn the Heart to GOD as the Fountain of Good, and to choose him for the only Portion. This *Light*, and this only, will bring the Soul to a saving Close with CHRIST. It conforms the Heart to the Gospel, mortifies its Enmity and Opposition against the Scheme of Salvation therein revealed: It causes the Heart to embrace the joyful Tidings, and entirely to adhere to, and acquiesce in the Revelation of CHRIST as our Saviour: It causes the whole Soul to accord and Symphonize with it, admitting it with entire Credit and Respect, cleaving to it with full Inclination and Affection. And it effectually disposes the Soul to give up it self entirely to CHRIST.

4. This Light and this only *has its Fruit in an universal Holiness of Life*. No meerly notional or speculative Understanding of the Doctrines of Religion, will ever bring to this. But this *Light* as it reaches the bottom of the Heart, and changes the Nature, so it will effectually dispose to an universal Obedience. It shews GOD's worthiness to be obeyed and served. It draws forth the Heart in a sincere Love to GOD, which is the only Principle of a true, gracious and universal Obedience. And it convinces of the Reality of those glorious Rewards that GOD has promised to them that obey him.

JONATHAN EDWARDS

Sinners in the Hands of an Angry God

*A Sermon Preached at Enfield, July 8th 1741.
At a Time of great Awakenings; and attended with
remarkable Impressions on many of the Hearers.*

Amos ix. 2, 3. *Though they dig into Hell, thence shall
mine Hand take them; though they climb up to Heaven,
thence will I bring them down. And though they hide
themselves in the Top of Carmel, I will search and take
them out thence; and though they be hid from my Sight
in the Bottom of the Sea, thence I will command the
Serpent, and he shall bite them.*

———

DEUT. XXXII. 35.
—Their Foot shall slide in due Time.—

In this Verse is threatned the Vengeance of God on the
wicked unbelieving Israelites, that were God's visible People,
and lived under Means of Grace; and that, notwithstanding all
God's wonderful Works that he had wrought towards that
People, yet remained, as is expressed, *ver.* 28. void of Counsel,
having no Understanding in them; and that, under all the
Cultivations of Heaven, brought forth bitter and poisonous
Fruit; as in the two Verses next preceeding the Text.

The Expression that I have chosen for my Text, *Their Foot
shall slide in due Time;* seems to imply the following Things,
relating to the Punishment and Destruction that these wicked
Israelites were exposed to.

1. That they were *always* exposed to Destruction, as one
that stands or walks in slippery Places is always exposed to fall.
This is implied in the Manner of their Destruction's coming
upon them, being represented by their Foot's sliding. The
same is express'd, Psal. 73. 18. *Surely thou didst set them in slippery Places; thou castedst them down into Destruction.*

2. It implies that they were always exposed to *sudden* un-expected Destruction. As he that walks in slippery Places is every Moment liable to fall; he can't foresee one Moment whether he shall stand or fall the next; and when he does fall, he falls at once, without Warning. Which is also expressed in that, Psal. 73. 18, 19. *Surely thou didst set them in slippery Places; thou castedst them down into Destruction. How are they brought into Desolation as in a Moment?*

3. Another Thing implied is that they are liable to fall *of themselves*, without being thrown down by the Hand of an-other. As he that stands or walks on slippery Ground, needs nothing but his own Weight to throw him down.

4. That the Reason why they are not fallen already, and don't fall now, is only that God's appointed Time is not come. For it is said, that when that due Time, or appointed Time comes, *their Foot shall slide.* Then they shall be left to fall as they are inclined by their own Weight. God won't hold them up in these slippery Places any longer, but will let them go; and then, at that very Instant, they shall fall into Destruc-tion; as he that stands in such slippery declining Ground on the Edge of a Pit that he can't stand alone, when he is let go he immediately falls and is lost.

The Observation from the Words that I would now insist upon is this,

> *There is nothing that keeps wicked Men, at any one*
> *Moment, out of Hell, but the meer Pleasure of GOD.*

By the meer Pleasure of God, I mean his sovereign Plea-sure, his arbitrary Will, restrained by no Obligation, hinder'd by no manner of Difficulty, any more than if nothing else but God's meer Will had in the least Degree, or in any Respect whatsoever, any Hand in the Preservation of wicked Men one Moment.

The Truth of this Observation may appear by the following Considerations.

1. There is no Want of *Power* in God to cast wicked Men into Hell at any Moment. Mens Hands can't be strong when God rises up: The strongest have no Power to resist him, nor can any deliver out of his Hands.

He is not only able to cast wicked Men into Hell, but he can most *easily* do it. Sometimes an earthly Prince meets with a great deal of Difficulty to subdue a Rebel, that has found Means to fortify himself, and has made himself strong by the Numbers of his Followers. But it is not so with God. There is no Fortress that is any Defence from the Power of God. Tho' Hand join in Hand, and vast Multitudes of God's Enemies combine and associate themselves, they are easily broken in Pieces: They are as great Heaps of light Chaff before the Whirlwind; or large Quantities of dry Stubble before devouring Flames. We find it easy to tread on and crush a Worm that we see crawling on the Earth; so 'tis easy for us to cut or singe a slender Thread that any Thing hangs by; thus easy is it for God when he pleases to cast his Enemies down to Hell. What are we, that we should think to stand before him, at whose Rebuke the Earth trembles, and before whom the Rocks are thrown down?

2. They *deserve* to be cast into Hell; so that divine Justice never stands in the Way, it makes no Objection against God's using his Power at any Moment to destroy them. Yea, on the contrary, Justice calls aloud for an infinite Punishment of their Sins. Divine Justice says of the Tree that brings forth such Grapes of Sodom, *Cut it down, why cumbreth it the Ground*, Luk. 13. 7. The Sword of divine Justice is every Moment brandished over their Heads, and 'tis nothing but the Hand of arbitrary Mercy, and God's meer Will, that holds it back.

3. They are *already* under a Sentence of Condemnation to Hell. They don't only justly deserve to be cast down thither; but the Sentence of the Law of God, that eternal and immutable Rule of Righteousness that God has fixed between him and Mankind, is gone out against them, and stands against them; so that they are bound over already to Hell. Joh. 3. 18. *He that believeth not is condemned already.* So that every unconverted Man properly belongs to Hell; that is his Place; from thence he is. Joh. 8. 23. *Ye are from beneath.* And thither he is bound; 'tis the Place that Justice, and God's Word, and the Sentence of his unchangeable Law assigns to him.

4. They are now the Objects of that very *same* Anger & Wrath of God that is expressed in the Torments of Hell: and the Reason why they don't go down to Hell at each Moment, is not because God, in whose Power they are, is not then very

angry with them; as angry as he is with many of those miserable Creatures that he is now tormenting in Hell, and do there feel and bear the fierceness of his Wrath. Yea God is a great deal more angry with great Numbers that are now on Earth, yea doubtless with many that are now in this Congregation, that it may be are at Ease and Quiet, than he is with many of those that are now in the Flames of Hell.

So that it is not because God is unmindful of their Wickedness, and don't resent it, that he don't let loose his Hand and cut them off. God is not altogether such an one as themselves, tho' they may imagine him to be so. The Wrath of God burns against them, their Damnation don't slumber, the Pit is prepared, the Fire is made ready, the Furnace is now hot, ready to receive them, the Flames do now rage and glow. The glittering Sword is whet, and held over them, and the Pit hath opened her Mouth under them.

5. The *Devil* stands ready to fall upon them and seize them as his own, at what Moment God shall permit him. They belong to him; he has their Souls in his Possession, and under his Dominion. The Scripture represents them as his *Goods*, Luk. 11. 21. The Devils watch them; they are ever by them, at their right Hand; they stand waiting for them, like greedy hungry Lions that see their Prey, and expect to have it, but are for the present kept back; if God should withdraw his Hand, by which they are restrained, they would in one Moment fly upon their poor Souls. The old Serpent is gaping for them; Hell opens its Mouth wide to receive them; and if God should permit it, they would be hastily swallowed up and lost.

6. There are in the Souls of wicked Men those hellish *Principles* reigning, that would presently kindle and flame out into Hell Fire, if it were not for God's Restraints. There is laid in the very Nature of carnal Men a Foundation for the Torments of Hell: There are those corrupt Principles, in reigning Power in them, and in full Possession of them, that are Seeds of Hell Fire. These Principles are active and powerful, and exceeding violent in their Nature, and if it were not for the restraining Hand of God upon them, they would soon break out, they would flame out after the same Manner as the same Corruptions, the same Enmity does in the Hearts of damned Souls,

and would beget the same Torments in 'em as they do in them. The Souls of the Wicked are in Scripture compared to the troubled Sea, *Isai.* 57. 20. For the present God restrains their Wickedness by his mighty Power, as he does the raging Waves of the troubled Sea, saying, *Hitherto shalt thou come, and no further*; but if God should withdraw that restraining Power, it would soon carry all afore it. Sin is the Ruin and Misery of the Soul; it is destructive in it's Nature; and if God should leave it without Restraint, there would need nothing else to make the Soul perfectly miserable. The Corruption of the Heart of Man is a Thing that is immoderate and boundless in its Fury; and while wicked Men live here, it is like Fire pent up by God's Restraints, when as if it were let loose it would set on Fire the Course of Nature; and as the Heart is now a Sink of Sin, so, if Sin was not restrain'd, it would immediately turn the Soul into a fiery Oven, or a Furnace of Fire and Brimstone.

7. It is no Security to wicked Men for one Moment, that there are no *visible Means* of *Death* at Hand. 'Tis no Security to a natural Man, that he is now in Health, and that he don't see which Way he should now immediately go out of the World by any Accident, and that there is no visible Danger in any Respect in his Circumstances. The manifold and continual Experience of the World in all Ages, shews that this is no Evidence that a Man is not on the very Brink of Eternity, and that the next Step won't be into another World. The unseen, unthought of Ways and Means of Persons going suddenly out of the World are innumerable and inconceivable. Unconverted Men walk over the Pit of Hell on a rotten Covering, and there are innumerable Places in this Covering so weak that they won't bear their Weight, and these Places are not seen. The Arrows of Death fly unseen at Noon-Day; the sharpest Sight can't discern them. God has so many different unsearchable Ways of taking wicked Men out of the World and sending 'em to Hell, that there is nothing to make it appear that God had need to be at the Expence of a Miracle, or go out of the ordinary Course of his Providence, to destroy any wicked Man, at any Moment. All the Means that there are of Sinners going out of the World, are so in God's Hands, and so universally absolutely subject to his Power and Determination,

that it don't depend at all less on the meer Will of God, whether Sinners shall at any Moment go to Hell, than if Means were never made use of, or at all concerned in the Case.

8. Natural Men's *Prudence* and *Care* to preserve their own *Lives*, or the Care of others to preserve them, don't secure 'em a Moment. This divine Providence and universal Experience does also bear Testimony to. There is this clear Evidence that Men's own Wisdom is no Security to them from Death; That if it were otherwise we should see some Difference between the wise and politick Men of the World, and others, with Regard to their Liableness to early and unexpected Death; but how is it in Fact? Eccles. 2. 16. *How dieth the wise Man? as the Fool.*

9. All wicked Men's *Pains* and *Contrivance* they use to escape *Hell*, while they continue to reject Christ, and so remain wicked Men, don't secure 'em from Hell one Moment. Almost every natural Man that hears of Hell, flatters himself that he shall escape it; he depends upon himself for his own Security; he flatters himself in what he has done, in what he is now doing, or what he intends to do; every one lays out Matters in his own Mind how he shall avoid Damnation, and flatters himself that he contrives well for himself, and that his Schemes won't fail. They hear indeed that there are but few saved, and that the bigger Part of Men that have died heretofore are gone to Hell; but each one imagines that he lays out Matters better for his own escape than others have done: He don't intend to come to that Place of Torment; he says within himself, that he intends to take Care that shall be effectual, and to order Matters so for himself as not to fail.

But the foolish Children of Men do miserably delude themselves in their own Schemes, and in their Confidence in their own Strength and Wisdom; they trust to nothing but a Shadow. The bigger Part of those that heretofore have lived under the same Means of Grace, and are now dead, are undoubtedly gone to Hell: and it was not because they were not as wise as those that are now alive: it was not because they did not lay out Matters as well for themselves to secure their own escape. If it were so, that we could come to speak with them, and could inquire of them, one by one, whether they expected when alive, and when they used to hear about Hell, ever to be the Subjects of that Misery, we doubtless should hear one and another reply, 'No, I never intended to come here; I had laid out Matters otherwise in my Mind; I thought I should contrive well for my self; I thought my Scheme good; I intended to take effectual Care; but it came upon me unexpected; I did not look for it at that Time, and in that Manner; it came as a Thief; Death outwitted me; God's Wrath was too quick for me; O my cursed Foolishness! I was flattering my self, and pleasing my self with vain Dreams of what I would do hereafter, and when I was saying Peace and Safety, then sudden Destruction came upon me.'

10. God has laid himself under *no Obligation* by any Promise to keep any natural Man out of Hell one Moment. God certainly has made no Promises either of eternal Life, or of any Deliverance or Preservation from eternal Death, but what are contained in the Covenant of Grace, the Promises that are given in Christ, in whom all the Promises are Yea and Amen. But surely they have no Interest in the Promises of the Covenant of Grace that are not the Children of the Covenant, and that don't believe in any of the Promises of the Covenant, and have no Interest in the *Mediator* of the Covenant.

So that whatever some have imagined and pretended about Promises made to natural Men's earnest seeking and knocking, 'tis plain and manifest that whatever Pains a natural Man takes in Religion, whatever Prayers he makes, till he believes in Christ, God is under no manner of Obligation to keep him a *Moment* from eternal Destruction.

So that thus it is, that natural Men are held in the Hand of God over the Pit of Hell; they have deserved the fiery Pit, and are already sentenced to it; and God is dreadfully provoked, his Anger is as great towards them as to those that are actually suffering the Executions of the fierceness of his Wrath in Hell, and they have done nothing in the least to appease or abate that Anger, neither is God in the least bound by any Promise to hold 'em up one moment; the Devil is waiting for them, Hell is gaping for them, the Flames gather and flash about them, and would fain lay hold on them, and swallow them up; the Fire pent up in their own Hearts is struggling to break out; and they have no Interest in any Mediator, there are no Means within Reach that can be any Security to them.

In short, they have no Refuge, nothing to take hold of, all that preserves them every Moment is the meer arbitrary Will, and uncovenanted unobliged Forbearance of an incensed God.

APPLICATION.

The USE may be of *Awakening* to unconverted Persons in this Congregation. This that you have heard is the Case of every one of you that are out of Christ. That World of Misery, that Lake of burning Brimstone is extended abroad under you. *There* is the dreadful Pit of the glowing Flames of the Wrath of God; there is Hell's wide gaping Mouth open; and you have nothing to stand upon, nor any Thing to take hold of: there is nothing between you and Hell but the Air; 'tis only the Power and meer Pleasure of God that holds you up.

You probably are not sensible of this; you find you are kept out of Hell, but don't see the Hand of God in it, but look at other Things, as the good State of your bodily Constitution, your Care of your own Life, and the Means you use for your own Preservation. But indeed these Things are nothing; if God should withdraw his Hand, they would avail no more to keep you from falling, than the thin Air to hold up a Person that is suspended in it.

Your Wickedness makes you as it were heavy as Lead, and to tend downwards with great Weight and Pressure towards Hell; and if God should let you go, you would immediately sink and swiftly descend & plunge into the bottomless Gulf, and your healthy Constitution, and your own Care and Prudence, and best Contrivance, and all your Righteousness, would have no more Influence to uphold you and keep you out of Hell, than a Spider's Web would have to stop a falling Rock. Were it not that so is the sovereign Pleasure of God, the Earth would not bear you one Moment; for you are a Burden to it; the Creation groans with you; the Creature is made Subject to the Bondage of your Corruption, not willingly; the Sun don't willingly shine upon you to give you Light to serve Sin and Satan; the Earth don't willingly yield her Increase to satisfy your Lusts; nor is it willingly a Stage for your Wickedness to be acted upon; the Air don't willingly serve you for Breath to maintain the Flame of Life in your Vitals, while you spend your Life in the Service of God's Enemies. God's Creatures are Good, and were made for Men to serve God with, and don't willingly subserve to any other Purpose, and groan when they are abused to Purposes so directly contrary to their Nature and End. And the World would spue you out, were it not for the sovereign Hand of him who hath subjected it in Hope. There are the black Clouds of God's Wrath now hanging directly over your Heads, full of the dreadful Storm, and big with Thunder; and were it not for the restraining Hand of God it would immediately burst forth upon you. The sovereign Pleasure of God for the present stays his rough Wind; otherwise it would come with Fury, and your Destruction would come like a Whirlwind, and you would be like the Chaff of the Summer threshing Floor.

The Wrath of God is like great Waters that are dammed for the present; they increase more and more, & rise higher and higher, till an Outlet is given, and the longer the Stream is stop'd, the more rapid and mighty is it's Course, when once it is let loose. 'Tis true, that Judgment against your evil Works has not been executed hitherto; the Floods of God's Vengeance have been with-held; but your Guilt in the mean Time is constantly increasing, and you are every Day treasuring up more Wrath; the Waters are continually rising and waxing more and more mighty; and there is nothing but the meer Pleasure of God that holds the Waters back that are unwilling to be stopped, and press hard to go forward; if God should only withdraw his Hand from the Flood-Gate, it would immediately fly open, and the fiery Floods of the Fierceness and Wrath of God would rush forth with inconceivable Fury, and would come upon you with omnipotent Power; and if your Strength were ten thousand Times greater than it is, yea ten thousand Times greater than the Strength of the stoutest, sturdiest Devil in Hell, it would be nothing to withstand or endure it.

The Bow of God's Wrath is bent, and the Arrow made ready on the String, and Justice bends the Arrow at your Heart, and strains the Bow, and it is nothing but the meer Pleasure of

God, and that of an angry God, without any Promise or
Obligation at all, that keeps the Arrow one Moment from
being made drunk with your Blood.

Thus are all you that never passed under a great Change of
Heart, by the mighty Power of the SPIRIT of GOD upon
your Souls; all that were never born again, and made new
Creatures, and raised from being dead in Sin, to a State of
new, and before altogether unexperienced Light and Life,
(however you may have reformed your Life in many Things,
and may have had religious Affections, and may keep up a
Form of Religion in your Families and Closets, and in the
House of God, and may be strict in it,) you are thus in the
Hands of an angry God; 'tis nothing but his meer Pleasure
that keeps you from being this Moment swallowed up in everlasting Destruction.

However unconvinced you may now be of the Truth of
what you hear, by & by you will be fully convinced of it.
Those that are gone from being in the like Circumstances
with you, see that it was so with them; for Destruction came
suddenly upon most of them, when they expected nothing of
it, and while they were saying, *Peace and Safety*: Now they
see, that those Things that they depended on for Peace and
Safety, were nothing but thin Air and empty Shadows.

The God that holds you over the Pit of Hell, much as one
holds a Spider, or some loathsome Insect, over the Fire, abhors you, and is dreadfully provoked; his Wrath towards you
burns like Fire; he looks upon you as worthy of nothing else,
but to be cast into the Fire; he is of purer Eyes than to bear
to have you in his Sight; you are ten thousand Times so
abominable in his Eyes as the most hateful venomous Serpent
is in ours. You have offended him infinitely more than ever a
stubborn Rebel did his Prince: and yet 'tis nothing but his
Hand that holds you from falling into the Fire every
Moment: 'Tis to be ascribed to nothing else, that you did not
go to Hell the last Night; that you was suffer'd to awake
again in this World, after you closed your Eyes to sleep: and
there is no other Reason to be given why you have not
dropped into Hell since you arose in the Morning, but that
God's Hand has held you up: There is no other Reason to be
given why you han't gone to Hell since you have sat here in

the House of God, provoking his pure Eyes by your sinful wicked Manner of attending his solemn Worship: Yea, there is nothing else that is to be given as a Reason why you don't this very Moment drop down into Hell.

O Sinner! Consider the fearful Danger you are in: 'Tis a great Furnace of Wrath, a wide and bottomless Pit, full of the Fire of Wrath, that you are held over in the Hand of that God, whose Wrath is provoked and incensed as much against you as against many of the Damned in Hell: You hang by a slender Thread, with the Flames of divine Wrath flashing about it, and ready every Moment to singe it, and burn it asunder; and you have no Interest in any Mediator, and nothing to lay hold of to save yourself, nothing to keep off the Flames of Wrath, nothing of your own, nothing that you ever have done, nothing that you can do, to induce God to spare you one Moment.

And consider here more particularly several Things concerning that Wrath that you are in such Danger of.

1. *Whose* Wrath it is: It is the Wrath of the infinite GOD. If it were only the Wrath of Man, tho' it were of the most potent Prince, it would be comparatively little to be regarded. The Wrath of Kings is very much dreaded, especially of absolute Monarchs, that have the Possessions and Lives of their Subjects wholly in their Power, to be disposed of at their meer Will. Prov. 20. 2. *The Fear of a King is as the Roaring of a Lion: whoso provoketh him to Anger, sinneth against his own Soul.* The Subject that very much enrages an arbitrary Prince, is liable to suffer the most extream Torments, that human Art can invent or human Power can inflict. But the greatest earthly Potentates, in their greatest Majesty and Strength, and when cloathed in their greatest Terrors, are but feeble despicable Worms of the Dust, in Comparison of the great and almighty Creator and King of Heaven and Earth: It is but little that they can do, when most enraged, and when they have exerted the utmost of their Fury. All the Kings of the Earth before GOD are as Grashoppers, they are nothing and less than nothing: Both their Love and their Hatred is to be despised. The Wrath of the great King of Kings is as much more terrible than their's, as his Majesty is greater. Luke 12. 4, 5. *And I say unto you my Friends, be not afraid of them that kill*

the Body, and after that have no more that they can do: But I will forewarn you whom ye shall fear; fear him, which after he hath killed, hath Power to cast into Hell; yea I say unto you, fear him.

2. 'Tis the *Fierceness* of his Wrath that you are exposed to. We often read of the *Fury* of God; as in Isai. 59. 18. *According to their Deeds, accordingly he will repay Fury to his Adversaries.* So Isai. 66. 15. *For behold, the Lord will come with Fire, and with Chariots like a Whirlwind, to render his Anger with Fury, and his Rebukes with Flames of Fire.* And so in many other Places. So we read of God's *Fierceness.* Rev. 19. 15. There we read of *the Winepress of the Fierceness and Wrath of Almighty God.* The Words are exceeding terrible: if it had only been said, *the Wrath of God*, the Words would have implied that which is infinitely dreadful: But 'tis not only said so, but *the Fierceness and Wrath of God*: the Fury of God! the Fierceness of Jehovah! Oh how dreadful must that be! Who can utter or conceive what such Expressions carry in them! But it is not only said so, but *the Fierceness and Wrath of ALMIGHTY GOD.* As tho' there would be a very great Manifestation of his almighty Power, in what the fierceness of his Wrath should inflict, as tho' Omnipotence should be as it were enraged, and excited, as Men are wont to exert their Strength in the fierceness of their Wrath. Oh! then what will be the Consequence! What will become of the poor Worm that shall suffer it! Whose Hands can be strong? and whose Heart endure? To what a dreadful, inexpressible, inconceivable Depth of Misery must the poor Creature be sunk, who shall be the Subject of this!

Consider this, you that are here present, that yet remain in an unregenerate State. That God will execute the fierceness of his Anger, implies that he will inflict Wrath without any Pity: when God beholds the ineffable Extremity of your Case, and sees your Torment to be so vastly disproportion'd to your Strength, and sees how your poor Soul is crushed and sinks down, as it were into an infinite Gloom, he will have no Compassion upon you, he will not forbear the Executions of his Wrath, or in the least lighten his Hand; there shall be no Moderation or Mercy, nor will God then at all stay his rough Wind; he will have no Regard to your Welfare, nor be at all careful lest you should suffer too much, in any other Sense than only that you shall not suffer beyond what strict Justice requires: nothing shall be with-held, because it's so hard for you to bear. Ezek. 8. 18. *Therefore will I also deal in Fury; mine Eye shall not spare, neither will I have Pity; and tho' they cry in mine Ears with a loud Voice, yet I will not hear them.* Now God stands ready to pity you; this is a Day of Mercy; you may cry now with some Encouragement of obtaining Mercy: but when once the Day of Mercy is past, your most lamentable and dolorous Cries and Shrieks will be in vain; you will be wholly lost and thrown away of God as to any Regard to your Welfare; God will have no other Use to put you to but only to suffer Misery; you shall be continued in Being to no other End; for you will be a Vessel of Wrath fitted to Destruction; and there will be no other Use of this Vessel but only to be filled full of Wrath: God will be so far from pitying you when you cry to him, that 'tis said he will only *Laugh and Mock*, Prov. 1. 25, 26, &c.

How awful are those Words, Isai. 63. 3. which are the Words of the great God, *I will tread them in mine Anger, and will trample them in my Fury, and their Blood shall be sprinkled upon my Garments, and I will stain all my Raiment.* 'Tis perhaps impossible to conceive of Words that carry in them greater Manifestations of these three Things, *viz.* Contempt, and Hatred, and fierceness of Indignation. If you cry to God to pity you, he will be so far from pitying you in your doleful Case, or shewing you the least Regard or Favour, that instead of that he'll only tread you under Foot: And tho' he will know that you can't bear the Weight of Omnipotence treading upon you, yet he won't regard that, but he will crush you under his Feet without Mercy; he'll crush out your Blood, and make it fly, and it shall be sprinkled on his Garments, so as to stain all his Raiment. He will not only hate you, but he will have you in the utmost Contempt; no Place shall be thought fit for you, but under his Feet, to be trodden down as the Mire of the Streets.

3. The Misery you are exposed to is that which God will inflict to that End, that he might *shew* what that *Wrath* of JEHOVAH is. God hath had it on his Heart to shew to Angels and Men, both how excellent his Love is, and also how

terrible his Wrath is. Sometimes earthly Kings have a Mind to shew how terrible *their* Wrath is, by the extream Punishments they would execute on those that provoke 'em. *Nebuchadnezzar*, that mighty and haughty Monarch of the *Chaldean* Empire, was willing to shew *his* Wrath, when enraged with *Shadrach*, *Meshech*, and *Abednego*; and accordingly gave Order that the burning fiery Furnace should be het seven Times hotter than it was before; doubtless it was raised to the utmost Degree of Fierceness that humane Art could raise it: But the great GOD is also willing to shew *his Wrath*, and magnify his awful Majesty and mighty Power in the extream Sufferings of his Enemies. Rom. 9. 22. *What if God willing to shew HIS Wrath, and to make his Power known, endured with much Long-suffering the Vessels of Wrath fitted to Destruction?* And seeing this is his Design, and what he has determined, to shew how terrible the unmixed, unrestrained Wrath, the Fury and Fierceness of JEHOVAH is, he will do it to Effect. There will be something accomplished and brought to pass, that will be dreadful with a Witness. When the great and angry God hath risen up and executed his awful Vengeance on the poor Sinner; and the Wretch is actually suffering the infinite Weight and Power of his Indignation, then will God call upon the whole Universe to behold that awful Majesty, and mighty Power that is to be seen in it. Isai. 33. 12, 13, 14. *And the People shall be as the burning of Lime, as Thorns cut up shall they be burnt in the Fire. Hear ye that are far off what I have done; and ye that are near acknowledge my Might. The Sinners in Zion are afraid, fearfulness hath surprized the Hypocrites &c.*

Thus it will be with you that are in an unconverted State, if you continue in it; the infinite Might, and Majesty and Terribleness of the OMNIPOTENT GOD shall be magnified upon you, in the ineffable Strength of your Torments: You shall be tormented in the Presence of the holy Angels, and in the Presence of the Lamb; and when you shall be in this State of Suffering, the glorious Inhabitants of Heaven shall go forth and look on the awful Spectacle, that they may see what the Wrath and Fierceness of the Almighty is, and when they have seen it, they will fall down and adore that great Power and Majesty. Isai. 66. 23, 24. *And it shall come to pass, that from one new Moon to another, and from one Sabbath to another, shall all Flesh come to Worship before me, saith the Lord; and they shall go forth and look upon the Carcasses of the Men that have transgressed against me; for their Worm shall not die, neither shall their Fire be quenched, and they shall be an abhorring unto all Flesh.*

4. 'Tis *everlasting* Wrath. It would be dreadful to suffer this Fierceness and Wrath of Almighty God one Moment; but you must suffer it to all Eternity: there will be no End to this exquisite horrible Misery: When you look forward, you shall see a long Forever, a boundless Duration before you, which will swallow up your Thoughts, and amaze your Soul; and you will absolutely despair of ever having any Deliverance, any End, any Mitigation, any Rest at all; you will know certainly that you must wear out long Ages, Millions of Millions of Ages, in wrestling and conflicting with this almighty merciless Vengeance; and then when you have so done, when so many Ages have actually been spent by you in this Manner, you will know that all is but a Point to what remains. So that your Punishment will indeed be infinite. Oh who can express what the State of a Soul in such Circumstances is! All that we can possibly say about it, gives but a very feeble faint Representation of it; 'tis inexpressible and inconceivable: for *who knows the Power of God's Anger?*

How dreadful is the State of those that are daily and hourly in Danger of this great Wrath, and infinite Misery! But this is the dismal Case of every Soul in this Congregation, that has not been born again, however moral and strict, sober and religious they may otherwise be. Oh that you would consider it, whether you be Young or Old. There is Reason to think, that there are many in this Congregation now hearing this Discourse, that will actually be the Subjects of this very Misery to all Eternity. We know not who they are, or in what Seats they sit, or what Thoughts they now have: it may be they are now at Ease, and hear all these Things without much Disturbance, and are now flattering themselves that they are not the Persons, promising themselves that they shall escape. If we knew that there was one Person, and but one, in the whole Congregation that was to be the Subject of this Misery, what an awful Thing would it be to think of! If we knew who it was, what an awful Sight would it be to see such a Person! How might all the rest of the Congregation lift up a lamentable and bitter Cry over him! But alass! instead of one, how many is it likely will remember this Discourse in Hell? And it would be a Wonder if some that are now present, should not be in Hell in a very short Time, before this Year is out. And it would be no Wonder if some Person that now sits here in some Seat of this Meeting-House in Health, and quiet & secure, should be there before to morrow Morning. Those of you that finally continue in a natural Condition, that shall keep out of Hell longest, will be there in a little Time! your Damnation don't slumber; it will come swiftly, and in all probability very suddenly upon many of you. You have Reason to wonder, that you are not already in Hell. 'Tis doubtless the Case of some that heretofore you have seen and known, that never deserved Hell more than you, and that heretofore appeared as likely to have been now alive as you: Their Case is past all Hope; they are crying in extream Misery and perfect Despair; but here you are in the Land of the Living, and in the House of God, and have an Opportunity to obtain Salvation. What would not those poor damned, hopeless Souls give for one Day's such Opportunity as you now enjoy!

And now you have an extraordinary Opportunity, a Day wherein CHRIST has flung the Door of Mercy wide open, and stands in the Door calling and crying with a loud Voice to poor Sinners; a Day wherein many are flocking to him, and pressing into the Kingdom of God; many are daily coming from the East, West, North and South; many that were very lately in the same miserable Condition that you are in, are in now an happy State, with their Hearts filled with Love to Him that has loved them and washed them from their Sins in his own Blood, and rejoycing in Hope of the Glory of God. How awful is it to be left behind at such a Day! To see so many others feasting, while you are pining and perishing! To see so many rejoycing and singing for Joy of Heart, while you have Cause to mourn for Sorrow of Heart, and howl for Vexation of Spirit! How can you rest one Moment in such a Condition? Are not your Souls as precious as the Souls of the

People at * *Suffield*, where they are flocking from Day to Day to Christ?

Are there not many here that have lived *long* in the World, that are not to this Day born again, and so are Aliens from the Common-wealth of Israel, and have done nothing ever since they have lived, but treasure up Wrath against the Day of Wrath? Oh Sirs, your Case in an especial Manner is extreamly dangerous; your Guilt and Hardness of Heart is extreamly great. Don't you see how generally Persons of your Years are pass'd over and left, in the present remarkable & wonderful Dispensation of God's Mercy? You had need to consider your selves, and wake throughly out of Sleep; you cannot bear the Fierceness and Wrath of the infinite GOD.

And you that are *young Men*, and *young Women*, will you neglect this precious Season that you now enjoy, when so many others of your Age are renouncing all youthful Vanities, and flocking to CHRIST? You especially have now an extraordinary Opportunity; but if you neglect it, it will soon be with you as it is with those Persons that spent away all the precious Days of Youth in Sin, and are now come to such a dreadful pass in blindness and hardness.

And you *Children* that are unconverted, don't you know that you are going down to Hell, to bear the dreadful Wrath of that God that is now angry with you every Day, and every Night? Will you be content to be the Children of the Devil, when so many other Children in the Land are converted, and are become the holy and happy Children of the King of Kings?

And let every one that is yet out of Christ, and hanging over the Pit of Hell, whether they be old Men and Women, or middle Aged, or young People, or little Children, now hearken to the loud Calls of God's Word and Providence. This acceptable Year of the LORD, that is a Day of such great Favour to some, will doubtless be a Day of as remarkable Vengeance to others. Men's Hearts harden, and their Guilt increases apace at such a Day as this, if they neglect their Souls: and never was there so great Danger of such Persons

*The next neighbour Town.

being given up to hardness of Heart, and blindness of Mind. God seems now to be hastily gathering in his Elect in all Parts of the Land; and probably the bigger Part of adult Persons that ever shall be saved, will be brought in now in a little Time, and that it will be as it was on that great out-pouring of the SPIRIT upon the *Jews* in the Apostles Days, the Election will obtain, and the rest will be blinded. If this should be the Case with you, you will eternally curse this Day, and will curse the Day that ever you was born, to see such a Season of the pouring out of God's Spirit; and will wish that you had died and gone to Hell before you had seen it. Now undoubtedly it is, as it was in the Days of *John the Baptist*, the Ax is in an extraordinary Manner laid at the Root of the Trees, that every Tree that brings not forth good Fruit, may be hewen down, and cast into the Fire.

Therefore let every one that is out of CHRIST, now awake and fly from the Wrath to come. The Wrath of almighty GOD is now undoubtedly hanging over great Part of this Congregation: Let every one fly out of *Sodom: Haste and escape for your Lives, look not behind you, escape to the Mountain, least you be consumed.*

FINIS.

SAMUEL JOHNSON

A Sermon Concerning the Intellectual World

In Advent 1747.

A Prospect through Sensible Things into the Intellectual World

2 Cor. IV, 18. *While we look not at the things which are seen but at the things which are not seen; for the things which are seen are temporal, but the things which are not seen are eternal.*

———

THE CHIEF POINT which the Apostle has in view in this Epistle is to vindicate himself against the aspersions he labored under from those false teachers who were for blending Judaism with Christianity; and because he endeavored to vindicate the liberty of Christians from the yoke of the Mosaic law, which they were for imposing upon them, especially those from among the Gentiles, they did all they could to discredit him and his ministry, and to render both his person and labors contemptible. In order therefore to do himself justice, he is obliged tho' with great reluctance to say many things of himself and his proceedings in a manner, which otherwise might savor of boasting. And among other things he is here speaking of his great labors and sufferings in the cause of the Gospel, and asserting his sincerity and disinterestedness, and explaining the views upon which he acted, having no eye at any motives or considerations taken from this visible and transitory world, but being solely governed by the views of the invisible and eternal things of the world to come. For which cause, says he, we faint not, v. 16, but though our outward man perish, yet our inward man is renewed day by day. For our light affliction, which is but for a moment worketh for us a far more exceeding and eternal weight of glory; while we look not at things which are seen but at the things which are not seen, for the things which are seen are temporal, but the things which are not seen are eternal. And what those are he goes on to explain more particularly in the next chapter. For we know, says he, that if our earthly house of this tabernacle were dissolved we have a building of God, an house not made with hands eternal in the heavens, v. 1, etc., etc., v. 10. We must all appear before the judgment seat of Christ, etc. So that the certainty of another life after this, and the account to be given of ourselves to God, and these apprehended by the eye of faith, as not being objects of sight, are the unseen things which he speaks of in my text under the influence of which he faithfully labored to fulfil his ministry; for as he had said, v. 7, We walk by faith not by sight, which words do in effect import the very same thought with those in my text.

Now the principles upon which the Apostle tells us he acted are those upon which it concerns us all, and all Christians, as such, in all ages and nations, always to act in all our deportment, throughout the whole course of our lives, *viz.*, to look through things seen and temporal to the things which are unseen and eternal, and to be principally governed by them in all our conduct. For this is the grand business and design of the Gospel, to acquaint us with intellectual objects, to inure us to them that we may chiefly be governed by them. We are born children of flesh (3 John), time and sense, but are designed for immortality, and for a spiritual intellectual and eternal happiness, and consequently by the discipline of the Gospel into which we are brought by baptism, to be gradually disengaged from sensible pleasures and transitory engagements, which must shortly cease of course and to be trained up to the exercises of reason faith and virtue to place our happiness in the things which are entirely of another nature, things spiritual, intellectual, stable and eternal. We consist of a sensible and rational or intellectual nature in strict union with each other. We begin with sense, and from thence are to take our rise to the objects and exercises of reason and faith, and so gradually go on to that highest spiritual and moral perfection for which we are ultimately designed which is the perfection and happiness of our better part, our rational and immortal nature. Now the Gospel is the great engine to raise us above the objects and pleasures of sense, which are those of our animal nature, with which we begin, and to lead us on to that spiritual and moral perfection which is the happiness of that reasonable and immortal part of our nature; that when we have done with this sensible and transitory state, we may be qualified for that intellectual and eternal happiness, for which we were ultimately designed. This is an affair of that vast importance to us, that God thought fit to send his son into this world upon that very errand to establish a most excellent institution to disengage us from this present world, of sense and time, and recover us from the many errors we had fallen into, and the guilt we had contracted by our too great attachment to sensible things; to open and ascertain to us the views of the intellectual invisible and eternal world, and to train us up to those spiritual, intellectual and moral exercises and practices that would fit and qualify us for the everlasting happiness thereof. It is therefore my design from this text to trace out the method of this heavenly institution, the Gospel, in accomplishing this end. In order to which I must a little more particularly define the terms of the text.

By the things seen are meant all the objects of sense signified by those of the most comprehensive and pleasing sense of seeing, which according to the style of the Hebrews, is put for all the senses. This expression therefore, comprehends all the objects, pleasures and enjoyments of our present animal state. The objects and pleasures of seeing, hearing, feeling, tasting, and smelling, the objects of which senses constitute what we call the whole natural world, and the gratification of them implies all the pleasures of sense. These are designed for a very good end, *viz.*, to direct and employ our active powers for attaining an agreeable and comfortable subsistence while it should please God to continue us in this present state, which is our first entrance into being, and a state of childhood and discipline in order for a more mature state which may be called a state of manhood in another life after this, which is to endure forever, when we come to be perfect men in Christ Jesus. And in this state we are to take our rise from these sensible things, and gradually learn the exercises of reason and faith and the practices of holiness and virtue in order to our being qualified for that more perfect state of being. And the chief of our discipline in this immature state consists in not suffering these objects of sense to hinder or interrupt the more noble exercises of reason, faith, and virtue, but rather in making them subservient to those purposes. Our heavenly Father deals with us in this as we do with our children. He gives us these sensible things as baubles and playthings to divert and amuse us while we are children. But as a wise and good parent contrives the diversity and amusements of his children so as to make them the means of exercising and improving their minds and their active powers and training them up by degrees to things more manly and of greater importance, pleasing and improving them at the same time. So our Heavenly Father gives us these sensible things, the things of this world, so to subsist, please and divert us, as that at the same time they may be means of exercising and improving our reason and our active powers, and gradually perfecting them, and thereby fitting us for that more perfect state of being in the life to come. And as our present state is to continue but for a short space of time, so these sensible objects and enjoyments are but transient and temporal. The things which are seen are temporal. As this world is not designed for our perpetual abode, but only for a short state of discipline, so these things which are seen, these sensible objects and amusements are fitted for such a transitory state, they are only of a temporary and transient nature. They are perpetually fluctuating and changing, and in a little time they are to cease and be no more.

But the things which are not seen are eternal. Where by the things which are not seen, are meant the objects of pure intellect, of the mind and understanding, of reason and faith, in opposition to those of sense and imagination, and they are objects of quite another kind from the others. We are apt to think these objects of sense the only real solid stable things, and that these things unseen are only mere notional airy things, and the men of this world are wont to consider them as mere phantoms, and whimsies; whereas in truth they are the only real, firm, stable, and unchangeable things and the others are, compared with them, but little better than shadows. Now what are these things unseen, these objects of intellect, reason and faith? I answer they are, in the first place, God, the being of beings in whom is all reality, all perfection and excellency, from whom all things else have all that they are and have, and on whom they all depend. He is absolute real being itself, and all other things are in effect but the shadows of being, compared with Him, as they merely depend upon the incessant exertion of his will and power. He is all knowledge and wisdom, all power and goodness, all holiness, justice, truth and benevolence. He is the life and support of the whole creation; in a word, He is All in All. In the next place, among these invisible things, are our own souls and all other intelligent beings, which so far forth partake of the Father and Fountain of all being, and perfection, as to be intelligent, free, active, beings, as He is, and to be capable of resembling Him in holiness justice and goodness, and by his decree, will and power shall always exist and never cease to be or to be happy, in proportion as they resemble Him and be obedient to Him, tho' they must be otherwise unavoidably miserable. And lastly to these invisible things must be reckoned the whole conduct and management of Almighty God in the government of the world, and particularly with regard to his rational creatures in rewarding or punishing them according as they behave themselves, and all the great principles of truth, justice, equity and benevolence on which the whole conduct of his government is founded, and more especially the whole economy of his grace in the dispensation of his Gospel with regard to the sinful race of mankind, by his blessed son Jesus Christ, for their recovery from sin and death and restoration to his image, favor, and immortality. These are the things, which being not seen, being not the objects of sense but apprehended by the faculties of reason and faith, are of a stable, eternal and unchangeable nature.

My method therefore in treating on this subject shall be to open to you the invisible world, and to represent to you more particularly those spiritual eternal and invisible things which the Gospel recommends to our chief concern, and to show under each head how God designs by sensible to lead us up to spiritual things, and to teach us not to look upon, not to rest in, or be too much pleased with the things which are seen and are temporal, but through them to look forward, and to be chiefly delighted in the things unseen represented by them, which are eternal. And

1. The first, and chief unseen intelligible and eternal object of our reason and faith to be here considered, God, the sovereign and chief good, who is all in all. We are placed here, in the midst of a glorious sensible scene of visible things, a world which is truly amiable, and beautiful, and may in some sort be said to be the image of the invisible God. Everything is so far beautiful and amiable as it is pleasing, useful, and advantageous to the reasonable and intelligent nature, to its real happiness or enjoyment of itself in the whole of its nature, and duration. This world therefore is beautiful and amiable as it subsists and pleases us while we continue here in our present state, but (as we are reasonable and immortal creatures) more especially as it represents and leads us to the eternal God, our chief good. It subsists us while we are here, and everything at the same time contributes to our pleasure and comfort; but as our animal nature is but short lived and very uncertain, while we consider it only in this light tho' it is so far forth valuable and we ought to give God thanks for it, yet it must be considered as a very fading and transitory thing. It is therefore designed that we should consider it in another light, that we should look on it, as at the same time to look through it and look beyond it. That we should consider it as not only a means for the subsistence and pleasure of our bodies, but as a means for the instruction and improvement of our souls, by leading us to the acknowledgement and adoration of that glorious being who is the Author of it, and at the same time the true father and former of our immortal spirits and their sole, their chief and sovereign good. Because as they are immortal, so He is a being who is eternal and unchangeable.

Now therefore what the Gospel requires of us is not absolutely to disregard these visible or sensible things, as being what they are; for in the view wherein I have represented them, they are to be regarded, but comparatively (according to the genius of the Hebrew language) to make light of them, *i.e.*, in comparison with God and the spiritual Heavenly things represented by them, according to the Psalmist in the 73rd Ps. where he says, v. 25. 26. Whom have I in Heaven but Thee, and there is none upon earth that I desire in comparison of Thee? My flesh and my heart faileth, but Thou O God, art the strength of my heart and my portion forever.

Let us then according to the Gospel consider this visible world chiefly in this view, as an emblem of things invisible, and a means to lead us by reason and faith to the sight of God our great, our chief good. For according to the Apostle's philosophy in the 17th of Acts, v. 24, etc., God hath to that end made the world and all things therein, and hath made of one blood all nations of men to dwell on all the face of the earth, that they should seek the Lord, and that they might feel after Him, and find Him whose offspring they are, and in whom they all live, move and have their being. For, says he, Rom. 1, 20, the invisible things of Him from the creation of the world are clearly seen, being understood from the things that are made, even his eternal power and Godhead. Let me then from the visible things before our eyes, direct you to look to the invisible things of Him who is the Father and Lord of all things. Let us consider the objects of our sight as leading us directly to Him who is invisible. We know they are effects produced in our minds whereof we are not the cause and yet nothing that is an effect can exist without a cause. The Father of Lights, therefore must be the cause of all that light that is let into our minds, and consequently of all the objects of our sight. We certainly find that light and all these visible objects serve to guide and direct us in every thing that it concerns us to do for avoiding things hurtful and procuring things advantageous to us; we must therefore conclude that the great and good author of them designs by them to guide and direct us in every thing that concerns us, and consequently is ever present with us in them, and ever watching over us and speaking to us and directing us in everything that concerns us thereby enlightening our eyes from without us, while He enlighteneth our minds within us. Can we then behold the sun in the firmament every day, by his light incessantly flowing from him opening to our view the whole visible world about us, in all which we behold innumerable and inimitable displays of wisdom unsearchable, of power ineffable, and of goodness immense, and by which we are continually directed in all our actions, and in the management of all our affairs, and by his heat and influences pervading and perfecting all its productions, being as it were, the life and soul of the whole creation. Can we, I say, thus daily behold him without considering him as representative of that infinitely more glorious being who is truly the author of all his light and heat and all his sweet influences, who being every where covered with his light as with a garment perpetually worketh all in all? Can we look upon him with an eye of sense, without looking beyond him and through him with an eye of reason and faith to the eternal and invisible God, who is the father of the intellectual world of spirits, as the sun is, as it were, the father of the sensible world of bodies? Do we not behold and in some sort, feel the Deity in the light and heat of the sun, thrusting himself upon us and forcing a sense of himself upon our minds, and fitly representing his co-eternal Son and Spirit, the light and life of our souls?

And when we have thus been looking outward upon the things that are seen, can we not then turn the eye of our minds inward and there behold the same invisible Father of our spirits enlightening them from within, enabling us to discern the various relations and connections of things both sensible and intellectual? For instance, between causes and their effects, subjects and their accidents, wholes and their parts, things equal and unequal, like and unlike, agreeing and disagreeing, diverse and opposite, etc., from which intellectual apprehensions we are directly led to a sense of true and false, and of right and wrong, and are conscious to ourselves when we know the truth or are deceived, and when we do well or ill, and enjoy unspeakable satisfaction in the one and uneasiness and remorse in the other. In all which cases do we not find there are a great number of necessary and eternal truths, and duties which force our assent, and of which we are intuitively certain, and our minds, are merely as passive to them as our eyes to the light of the sun? From which we are necessarily and directly led to the sense and acknowledgment of that necessarily existent and eternal being, from whom all intellectual or spiritual light perpetually flows, irradiates our minds, as the sensible light of the sun irradiates our eyes. And the more we consider and contemplate the eternal God and eternal truth thus discovered with the eye of our mind, the more sensible we shall be of his reality and stability, and of his immutability and eternity, and consequently that he is our sole and supreme good, and the more firm and stable we ourselves shall be in adhering to him and our duty while we endure like Moses as seeing Him who is invisible and the more indifferent we shall grow towards the things which are seen, which we find to be perpetually fluctuating, unstable, and temporal, and the more we shall admire and love this invisible being, his infinite knowledge, wisdom, and power, and his infinite holiness, justice, and goodness, while we keep the eye of our faith fixed upon these things which are not seen, but are unchangeable and eternal.

2. And in the next place, while we are thus considering these things that are seen and from them arguing and proceeding to the invisible God, we naturally proceed further to reflect and consider ourselves; that perceiving, thinking, and active being, which we call ourselves; our souls which are properly our persons, whereof these bodies of ours are but mere sensible representatives and engines. By these it is that we perceive all these things, that are seen, while they themselves are among the things that are not seen. By these we see, hear, feel, taste, and smell, and become acquainted with all visible and sensible things, and by these we go on and reason from these things that are seen to the spiritual intellectual and eternal things that are not seen. By these we not only know things visible and invisible, but are conscious of our own existence and all our faculties, of all our enjoyments, and all our hopes, and by these we are able to look forward to eternal ages, and not only see that we may, but be convinced that we must subsist forever, and fare well or ill according as we behave ourselves in this life. These immortal souls of ours, being not objects of sense any more than the Deity, the father and former of them, we scarce know how to reckon them, as well as Him, among real beings. They seem to our weak minds such airy, fleeting (fugacious) beings that we are sometimes almost tempted to doubt of their existence, independent of these gross tangible bodies. Whereas if we would accustom ourselves to withdraw our thoughts from the things that are seen and raise them as much as we can above them, we might soon be convinced that their existence is so far from depending on the existence of the body (that on the other hand, the existence of body depends entirely on the existence of mind, and that its existence can have no sense or meaning

in it separate from its being perceived and acted by mind: and consequently that) it is these bodies that are really the empty uncertain, unstable fleeting (fugacious) things, and that it is mind soul or spirit, that is the real stable and certain thing. Bodies are the things seen which are temporal, and minds are the things unseen which are eternal. What are all the objects and pleasures of sense but mere fleeting, fugacious, unstable and uncertain things, I had almost said, but mere imaginary things, and but little better than dreams? Whereas the objects of reason and faith and the pleasures and joys that attend them, with the conscience of being governed by them, in delighting in and acting what is reasonable, fit and right, on all occasions; these are solid, stable, durable things; which the wise man calls durable riches and righteousness. And so with regard to the pains of body, and mind, he says the spirit of man may bear his infirmity, but a wounded spirit who can bear? The pains of sense are indeed many times great, but by how much the greater, by so much the shorter, but the remorse of conscience from having done ill, is a most insupportable anguish; under the other we may have peace, a peace that passeth all understanding, if we do well and trust in God. But under these we can have no peace, no ease, nothing but horror and vexation, unless we turn about and alter our conduct, and return to what is fit, right, and our bounden duty. This abundantly speaks the reality and stability of our souls, our reason and consciences and their spiritual and peculiar interests. Thus, as St. John says, The world passeth away and the lusts thereof; the things that are seen are temporary, fleeting, and transitory, but he that doeth the will of God abideth forever. Doing the will of God, *i.e.,* what is reasonable, fit and right, with all the satisfaction and joys attending it, is a stable thing and can never fail us; the things that are not seen are eternal.

And such as these souls of ours are, such we must conceive all others to be; what we find their natures and interests to be, we must unavoidably conceive to be the nature and interest of all other intelligent beings throughout the universe, reason and intellect being in the nature of them in general everywhere the same. We find here a vast number of them of this family upon this globe of ours. And by analogy from what we find here in the various gradation of creatures below us, and the mighty extent and variety of the works of God which come within our ken, we may reasonably conclude, and by faith we must believe, that there are multitudes of other tribes and innumerable other creatures of the same intelligent active nature with us, many of whom may be vastly more perfect than we in the same faculties and powers that we have, and others may have faculties and powers of a higher kind and of much greater perfection than ours, tho' agreeing in the same general intelligent active nature which we are furnished with. But be they ever so numerous or ever so various, they must all be alike the creatures of God and all alike subject to his universal dominion and government; all of his family and household, of whom the whole family of heaven and earth are named. He is the one King and Lord of all, and they all constitute his one universal Kingdom, and must be reckoned among the things not seen which are eternal.

3. And lastly, to these unseen things which are eternal, must be also reckoned, the whole conduct of Almighty God in the government of the world, and especially of his intelligent or rational creatures. Verily, Thou art a God that hidest thyself, says the prophet. It is the unseen God that continually works all in all, behind the curtain, in all the productions of nature, as we commonly call them, tho' strictly speaking they are truly the operations of his almighty will and power, giving them being, actuating all their motions, and making them answer their several ends in their subserviency to the subsistence and well-being of his reasonable creatures, which are more properly his own offspring, whose happiness is his greatest care. And it is the same invisible God, their great common Father and Lord, who governs and presides over all his offspring, his whole family of heaven and earth, pursuing that great end of their being, their true happiness by all the dispensations of his providence towards them, and by all the instructions, laws and injunctions he gives them, and the various pleasures or pains he causes them to meet with. Indeed as these creatures of his are a visible system, sensible to each other, and their social life depends upon a sensible intercourse with each other, he hath rendered himself visible to them in the glorious person of his Son, whom he hath

established his visible representative and vicegerent in the government of the world; not only men, but angels, authorities, and powers being made subject unto Him, and accountable to him as their head, lord, and judge. But tho' his person be visible yet his government is purely of an invisible spiritual and intellectual nature, as it is properly a spiritual and intellectual society, and their visible appearances to each other are only sensible means of conveying to them the notices of each other's invisible persons. The laws of this spiritual and eternal society or kingdom, are entirely of a spiritual nature, being designed to govern our hearts as well as our lives and actions, to regulate our thoughts, appetites, and affections, and direct all our actions in relation to spiritual objects, God, ourselves and one another. They prescribe the spiritual and eternal laws of humility, temperance, meekness, patience, and contentment in regard to ourselves, piety and devotion with respect to God, and justice and charity with respect to our neighbors, all which are spiritual exertions, and invisible so far forth as they are moral, *i.e.,* the free voluntary exertions of our souls, and done from a sense of duty to Him that made us. And lastly the sanctions to these laws are moreover of the spiritual and invisible kind. The pleasures or pains that will attend our obedience or disobedence which are intellectual and spiritual perceptions; the unspeakable spiritual joys and satisfactions that attend our being conscious of doing our duty and pleasing our God and securing our happiness, and the amazing horror and remorse attending the known violation of our duty, our reason and consciences, the displeasing God and exposing ourselves to his wrath and vengeance; these are the general principles upon which the government of the whole rational world must turn, and which you see are all of a spiritual nature, not objects of sense or imagination, but of reason and faith.

And with respect to us men in particular, while we were in a state of innocence God taught us from the beginning to look through things seen to the things not seen; He made use of this sensible world as the visible means and emblem to lead us to the knowledge of Himself, and our duty and happiness. The tree of the knowledge of good and evil was made use of to teach our first parents duty and sin, and to lead them to a sense of God's dominion over them, and the tree of life, to teach them that immortality and happiness that should attend their obedience, as their exclusion from it, if they were disobedient, would be attended with their death and destruction. As the others were natural, so these and all that follows were instituted visible means to represent invisible things. And when they had sinned and were expelled from Paradise, as God assured them of pardon upon their repentance, and that if they would yet do well they should be accepted, so he probably instituted the visible emblems of the cherubims, and sacrifice, to be means for instructing them in the spiritual invisible things of the Gospel, and to teach them to keep the way of the tree of life; *i.e.,* how to recover that immortality which they had lost by their disobedience.

This was the beginning of that whole series of dispensations which God used from that day to this in his conduct towards mankind, for their recovery, which all turn upon the principle in my text of looking through things seen to things unseen. The whole Mosaic dispensation, which seems to be a revival of, or at least founded upon those original visible emblems, the cherubim and sacrifices, a system of visible typical institutions, designed to represent and teach the future spiritual and invisible things of the Gospel. The cherubims were symbols of the divine presence exhibiting mercy to penitents. The sacrifices were types representative of the sacrifice of Christ, and emblems to represent the heinousness of sin, to induce the sinner to repentance, and ascertain pardon to the penitent. The priesthood was a type of the priesthood and intercession of Christ; circumcision of the flesh represented and obliged to the circumcision of the heart and the mortification of base lusts; the purifications of the flesh, to the moral purity of heart and life; the Passover was a type of the death of Christ, and the earthly of the heavenly Canaan; and so of the rest. In all which they were taught not to look at those things, that were seen so as to rest in them, but at the things of the Gospel which were not seen, whereof they were shadows and emblems, which when Christ the body, the substance, the archetype came of course ceased and were done away.

Now the Gospel is the spirit whereof they were the letter, being the spiritual invisible things then not seen, but are, since Christ came, visible to us, being a vastly more spiritual dispensation than that of Moses. Life and immortality are brought to light by the Gospel. And when we are admitted by baptism into the fellowship of Christ's religion, we are made free, of that invisible spiritual and heavenly society, the Kingdom of Heaven. We are come to the spiritual Mount Zion and the heavenly Jerusalem. To an innumerable company of angels, to the spirits of just men made perfect, to the Church of the firstborn, which are written in heaven, to Jesus the mediator of the New Covenant, and to God the judge of all. By our natural birth we were born into this visible animal state, but by this spiritual birth, we are born into that invisible spiritual heavenly society. And yet even now we are still taught by the things that are seen to look further to the things that are not seen. From hungering and thirsting after bodily food, we are taught to hunger and thirst after righteousness; from the health and nourishment of the body we are led to understand the spiritual health and nourishment of the soul, and in all our Savior's discourses and parables, He makes use of temporal things to resemble and shadow forth to us the things that are eternal. And he has in particular instituted two visible ordinances fitted to the present state of his visible church, the one for a rite of our admission into it, the other for our improvement in it. Baptism or the washing of our bodies in water to represent and engage us to all purity of heart and life, and to seal the renewing and purifying influences of God's Holy Spirit, and the Lord's Supper to represent the body and blood of Christ and the spiritual benefits purchased thereby and to seal and convey them for their spiritual nourishment to all that receive with a truly penitent heart and lively faith and the heavenly temper of universal charity. In all which we are still not to look on the things that are seen, these visible ordinances, so as to rest in them, but by an eye of faith to look through them and beyond them to the spiritual things which are not seen that are represented by them. For what is faith but the substance of things hoped for and the evidence of things not seen. This was the faith of all the ancient patriarchs from the beginning of the world and this is still the faith of us Christians, and in all our worship our prayers and praises, and in all the actions and conduct of our lives, without this faith of spiritual and invisible things it is impossible to please God. For he that cometh unto God must believe that He is and that He is the rewarder of all them that diligently seek him.

Thus my brethren I have explained to you as briefly and as clearly as I could the full force and purport of this text. Let us then rouse us and vigorously exert both our reason and faith to look through and beyond the things visible and temporal to the things invisible and eternal, and so to realize them to our minds, not only as things of the most stable substantial reality, but also as of the greatest importance to us, who are shortly to quit this short-lived sensible scene, and to enter into the eternal invisible world. Let us enter into it as far as possible beforehand by the frequent exercise of reason and faith that it may have such a powerful influence on our hearts and lives as may qualify us to be eternal happy in that eternal invisible state, while we look not at the things which are seen. Which God of His infinite mercy grant through Jesus Christ.

JONATHAN MAYHEW

A Discourse Concerning Unlimited Submission and Non-Resistance to the Higher Powers

*With some Reflections on the Resistance made to King Charles I.
And on the Anniversary of his Death:*

In which the Mysterious Doctrine of that Prince's Saintship and Martyrdom is Unriddled:

The Substance of which was delivered in a Sermon preached in the West Meeting-House in Boston the Lord's Day after the 30th of January, 1749/50.

Published at the Request of the Hearers.

Fear GOD, honor the King.   SAINT PAUL.

He that ruleth over Men, must be just, ruling in the Fear of GOD.   PROPHET SAMUEL.

I have said, ye are Gods—but ye shall die like Men, and fall like one of the PRINCES.   KING DAVID.

Quid memorem infandas cædes? quid facta TYRANNI Effera? Dii CAPITI ipsius GENERIQUE reservent— Necnon Threïcius *longa cum veste* SACERDOS Obloquitur—   *Rom. Vat. Prin.*

———

PREFACE

The ensuing discourse is the last of three upon the same subject, with some little alterations and additions. It is hoped that but few will think the subject of it an improper one to be discoursed on in the pulpit, under a notion that this is preaching politics, instead of CHRIST. However, to remove all prejudices of this sort, I beg it may be remembered, that "all scripture—is prof-

itable for doctrine, for reproof, for CORRECTION, for instruction in righteousness." Why, then, should not those parts of scripture which relate to civil government, be examined and explained from the desk, as well as others? Obedience to the civil magistrate is a christian duty: and if so, why should not the nature, grounds and extent of it be considered in a christian assembly? Besides, if it be said, that it is out of character for a christian minister to meddle with such a subject, this censure will at last fall upon the holy apostles. They write upon it in their epistles to christian churches: And surely it cannot be deemed either criminall or impertinent, to attempt an explanation of their doctrine.*

It was the near approach of the Thirtieth *of* January, *that turned my thoughts to this subject: on which solemnity the* slavish *doctrine of passive obedience and non-resistance is often warmly asserted; and the dissenters from the established church, represented, not only as scismatics, (with more of triumph than of truth, and of choler than christianity) but also as persons of seditious, traiterous and rebellious principles—GOD be thanked one may, in any part of the* british *dominions, speak freely (if a decent regard be paid to those in authority) both of government and religion; and even give some broad hints, that he is engaged on the side of Liberty, the BIBLE and Common Sense, in opposition to Tyranny, PRIEST-CRAFT and Non-sense, without being in danger either of the* bastile *or the* inquisition:—Though *there will always be some interested politicians, contracted bigots, and hypocritical zealots for a party, to take offence at such freedoms. Their censure is praise; Their praise is infamy— A spirit of domination is always to be guarded against both in church and state, even in times of the greatest security, such as the present is amongst US, at least as to the latter. Those nations who are now groaning under the iron scepter of tyranny, were once free. So they might, probably, have remained, by a seasonable precaution against despotic measures. Civil tyranny is usually small in its beginning, like "the drop of a bucket,"† till at length, like a mighty torrent, or the raging waves of the sea, it bears down all before it, and deluges whole countries and*

*2 Pet. iii. 16.
†Isai. xl. 15.

empires. Thus it is as to ecclesiastical tyranny also,—the most cruel, intolerable and impious, of any. From small beginnings, "it exalts itself above all that is called GOD and that is worshipped."* People have no security against being unmercifully priest-ridden, *but by keeping all imperious BISHOPS, and other CLERGYMEN who love to "lord it over God's heritage," from getting their foot into the stirrup at all. Let them be once fairly mounted, and their "beasts, the laiety,"† may prance and flounce about to no purpose: And they will, at length, be so jaded and hack'd by these reverend jockies, that they will not even have spirits enough to complain, that their backs are galled; or, like Balaam's ass, to "rebuke the madness of the prophet."‡*

"The mystery of iniquity began to work"§ even in the days of some of the apostles. But the kingdom of Antichrist was then, in one respect, like the kingdom of heaven, however different in all others.—It was "as a grain of mustard-seed."‖ This grain was sown in Italy, that fruitful field: And though it were "the least of all seeds," it soon became a mighty tree. It has, long since, overspread and darkned the greatest part of Christendom, so that we may apply to it what is said of the tree which Nebuchadnezzar saw in his vision—"The height thereof reacheth unto heaven, and the sight thereof to the end of all the earth—And THE BEASTS OF THE FIELD have shadow under it." Tyranny brings ignorance and brutality along with it. It degrades men from their just rank, into the class of brutes. It damps their spirits. It suppresses arts. It extinguishes every spark of noble ardor and generosity in the breasts of those who are enslaved by it. It makes naturally-strong and great minds, feeble and little; and triumphs over the ruins of virtue and humanity. This is true of tyranny in every shape. There can be nothing great and good, where its influence reaches. For which reason it becomes every friend to truth and human kind; every lover of God and the christian religion, to bear a part in opposing this hateful monster. It was a desire to contribute a mite towards

*2 Thes. ii. 4.
†Mr. *Leslie.*
‡2 Pet. ii. 16.
§2 Thes. ii. 7.
‖Mat. xiii. 31.

carrying on a war against this common enemy, that produced the following discourse. And if it serve in any measure, to keep up a spirit of civil and religious liberty amongst us, my end is answered.—There are virtuous and candid men in all sects; all such are to be esteemed: There are also vicious men and bigots in all sects; and all such ought to be despised.

"To virtue only and her friends, a friend;
The world beside may murmur or commend.
Know, all the distant din *that* world can keep
Rolls o'er my grotto, and but sooths my sleep."

POPE.

Concerning Unlimited Submission and Non-Resistance to the Higher Powers.

ROM. XIII. 1–8.

1. *Let every soul be subject unto the higher powers. For there is no power but of God: the powers that be, are ordained of God.*

2. *Whosoever therefore resisteth the power, resisteth the ordinance of God: and they that resist, shall receive to themselves damnation.*

3. *For rulers are not a terror to good works, but to the evil. Wilt thou then not be afraid of the power? do that which is good, and thou shalt have praise of the same:*

4. *For he is the minister of God to thee for good. But if thou do that which is evil, be afraid; for he beareth not the sword in vain: for he is the minister of God, a revenger to execute wrath upon him that doth evil.*

5. *Wherefore ye must needs be subject, not only for wrath, but also for conscience sake.*

6. *For, for this cause pay you tribute also: for they are God's ministers, attending continually upon this very thing.*

7. *Render therefore to all their dues: tribute to whom tribute is due; custom, to whom custom; fear, to whom fear; honour, to whom honour.*

IT IS EVIDENT that the affair of civil government may properly fall under a *moral* and *religious* consideration, at least so far forth as it relates to the general nature and end of magistracy, and to the grounds and extent of that submission which persons of a private character, ought to yield to those who are vested with authority. This must be allowed by all who acknowledge the divine original of christianity. For although there be a sense, and a very plain and important sense, in which Christ's *kingdom is not of this world;** his inspired apostles have, nevertheless, laid down some general principles concerning the office of civil rulers, and the duty of subjects, together with the reason and obligation of that duty. And from hence it follows, that it is proper for all who acknowledge the authority of Jesus Christ, and the inspiration of his apostles, to endeavour to understand what is in fact the doctrine which they have delivered concerning this matter. It is the duty of *christian* magistrates to inform themselves what it is which their religion teaches concerning the nature and design of their office. And it is equally the duty of all *christian* people to inform themselves what it is which their religion teaches concerning that subjection which they owe to *the higher powers.* It is for these reasons that I have attempted to examine into the scripture-account of this matter, in order to lay it before you with the same *freedom* which I constantly use with relation to other doctrines and precepts of christianity; not doubting but you will *judge* upon every thing offered to your consideration, with the same spirit of *freedom* and *liberty* with which it is *spoken.*

The passage read, is the most full and express of any in the new-testament, relating to rulers and subjects: And therefore I thought it proper to ground upon it, what I had to propose to you with reference to the authority of the civil magistrate, and the subjection which is due to him. But before I enter upon an explanation of the several parts of this passage, it will be proper to observe one thing which may serve as a key to the whole of it.

It is to be observed, then, that there were some persons

*John xviii. 36.

amongst the *christians* of the apostolic age, and particularly those at *Rome*, to whom St. *Paul* is here writing, who seditiously disclaimed *all* subjection to civil authority; refusing to pay taxes, and the duties laid upon their trafic and merchandize; and who scrupled not to speak of their rulers, without any due regard to their office and character. Some of these turbulent *christians* were converts from *judaism*, and others from *paganism*. The *jews* in general had, long before this time, taken up a strange conceit, that being the *peculiar* and *elect* people of God, they were, therefore, exempted from the jurisdiction of any *heathen* princes or governors. Upon this ground it was, that some of them, during the public ministry of our blessed Saviour, came to him with that question—*Is it lawful to give tribute unto* Cesar *or not?** And this notion many of them retained after they were proselyted to the *christian* faith. As to the *gentile* converts, some of them grosly mistook the nature of that *liberty* which the gospel promised; and thought that by virtue of their subjection to Christ, the *only* King and Head of his church, they were wholly freed from subjection to any other prince; as tho' Christ's *kingdom had been of this world*, in such a sense as to interfere with the civil powers of the earth, and to deliver their subjects from that allegiance and duty, which they before owed to them. Of these visionary *christians* in general, who disowned subjection to the civil powers in being where they respectively lived, there is mention made in several places in the new-testament: The apostle *Peter* in particular, characterizes them in this manner—*them that—despise government—presumptuous are they, self-willed, they are not afraid to speak evil of dignities.*† Now it is with reference to these doting *christians*, that the apostle speaks in the passage before us. And I shall now give you the sense of it in a paraphrase upon each verse in its order, desiring you to keep in mind the character of the persons for whom it is designed, that so, as I go along, you may see how just and natural this address is; and how well suited to the circumstances of those against whom it is levelled.

*Matth. xxii. 17.
†2 Pet. ii. 10.

The apostle begins thus—*Let every soul* be subject unto the higher powers;†* *for there is no power‡ but of God: the powers that be§ are ordained of God‖* ver. 1. q. d. "Whereas some professed *christians* vainly imagine, that they are wholly excused from all manner of duty and subjection to civil authority, refusing to honour their rulers, and to pay taxes; which opinion is not only unreasonable in itself, but also tends to fix a lasting reproach upon the *christian* name and profession, I now, as an apostle and ambassador of Christ, exhort every one of you, be he who he will, to pay all dutiful submission to those who are vested with any civil office. For there is, properly speaking, no authority but what is derived from God, as it is only by his permission and providence that any possess it. Yea, I may add, that all civil magistrates, as such, altho' they may be *heathens*, are appointed and ordained of God. For it is certainly God's will, that so useful an institution as that of magistracy, should take place in the world, for the good of civil society." The apostle proceeds—*Whosoever, therefore, resisteth the power, resisteth the ordinance of God; and they that resist shall receive to themselves damnation.* ver. 2. q. d. "Think not,

---

* *Every soul.* This is an *hebraism*, which signifies *every man*; so that the apostle does not exempt the *clergy*: such as were endowed with the gift of prophesy, or any other miraculous powers which subsisted in the church at that day. And by his using the *hebrew* idiom, it seems that he had the *jewish* converts principally in his eye.

† *The higher powers*: more literally, the *over-ruling powers*: which term extends to all civil rulers in common.

‡ By *power*, the apostle intends not lawless *strength* and brutal *force*, without regulation or proper direction; but just *authority*, for so the word here used properly signifies. There may be *power* where there is no *authority*. No man has any *authority* to do what is wrong and injurious, though he may have *power* to do it.

§ *The powers that be*: those persons who are in fact vested with authority; those who are in possession. And who those are, the apostle leaves christians to determine for themselves; but whoever they are, they are to be obeyed.

‖ *Ordained of God*: as it is not without God's providence and permission, that any are clothed with authority; and as it is agreeable to the positive will and purpose of God, that there should be *some persons* vested with authority for the good of society: not that any rulers have their commission immediately from God the supreme Lord of the universe. If any assert that kings, or any other rulers, are ordained of God in the latter sense, it is incumbent upon them to show the commission which they speak of, under the broad seal of heaven. And when they do this, they will, no doubt, be believed.

therefore, that ye are guiltless of any crime or sin against God, when ye factiously disobey and resist the civil authority. For magistracy and government being, as I have said, the ordinance and appointment of God, it follows, that to resist magistrates in the execution of their offices, is really to resist the will and ordinance of God himself: And they who thus resist, will accordingly be punished by God for this sin in common with others." The apostle goes on—*For rulers are not a terror to good works, but to the evil.* * *Wilt thou then, not be afraid of the power? Do that which is good, and thou shalt have praise of the same. For he is the minister of God to thee for good,* ver. 3d, and part of the 4th. q. d. "That you may see the truth and justness of what I assert, (*viz.* that magistracy is the ordinance of God, and that you sin against him in opposing it,) consider that even *pagan* rulers, are not, by the nature and design of their office, enemies and a terror to the good and virtuous actions of men, but only to the injurious and mischievous to society. Will ye not, then, reverence and honor magistracy, when ye see the good end and intention of it? How can ye be so unreasonable? Only mind to do your duty as members of society; and this will gain you the applause and favour of all good rulers. For while you do thus, they are, by their office, as ministers of God, obliged to encourage and protect you; it is for this very purpose that they are clothed with power." The apostle subjoins—*But if thou do that which is evil, be afraid, for he beareth not the sword in vain. For he is the minister of God, a revenger, to execute wrath upon him that doth evil.*† ver. 4. latter part. q. d. "But upon the other hand, if ye

---

* *For rulers are not a terror to good works, but to the evil.* It cannot be supposed that the apostle designs here, or in any of the succeeding verses, to give the true character of *Nero*, or any other civil powers then in being, as if they were in fact such persons as he describes, a terror to evil works only, and not to the good. For such a character did not belong to them; and the apostle was no sycophant, or parasite of power, whatever some of his pretended successors have been. He only tells what rulers would be, provided they acted up to their character and office.

†It is manifest that when the apostle speaks of it, as the office of civil rulers, to encourage what is *good*, and to punish what is evil, he speaks only of *civil good* and *evil*. They are to consult the good of society *as such*; not to dictate in religious concerns; not to make laws for the government of men's consciences; and to inflict civil penalties for religious crimes. It is sufficient to

refuse to do your duty as members of society; if ye refuse to bear your part in the support of government; if ye are disorderly, and do things which merit civil chastisement, then, indeed, ye have reason to be afraid. For it is not in vain that rulers are vested with the power of inflicting punishment. They are, by their office, not only the ministers of God for good to those that do well; but also his ministers to revenge, to discountenance and punish those that are unruly, and injurious to their neighbours." The apostle proceeds—*Wherefore ye must needs be subject not only for wrath, but also for conscience sake,* ver. 5. q. d. "Since therefore, magistracy is the ordinance of God; and since rulers are, by their office, benefactors to society, by discouraging what is bad, and encouraging what is good, and so preserving peace and order amongst men; it is evident that ye ought to pay a willing subjection to them; not to obey merely for fear of exposing yourselves to their wrath and displeasure, but also in point of reason, duty and conscience: Ye are under an indispensable obligation, as *christians,* to honour their office, and to submit to them in the execution of it." The apostle goes on—*For, for this cause pay you tribute also: for they are God's ministers, attending continually upon this very thing,* ver. 6. q. d. "And here is a plain reason also why ye should pay tribute to them; for they are God's ministers, exalted above the common level of mankind, not that they may indulge themselves in softness and luxury, and be entitled to the servile homage of their

---

overthrow the doctrine of the authority of the civil magistrate, in affairs of a spiritual nature, (so far as it is built upon any thing which is here said by St. *Paul,* or upon any thing else in the new-testament) only to observe, that all the magistrates then in the world were *heathen,* implacable enemies to christianity: so that to give them authority in religious matters, would have been, in effect, to give them authority to extirpate the christian religion, and to establish the idolatries and superstitions of paganism. And can any one reasonably suppose, that the apostle had any intention to extend the authority of rulers, beyond concerns merely civil and political, to the overthrowing of that religion which he himself was so zealous in propagating! But it is natural for those whose religion cannot be supported upon the footing of reason and argument, to have recourse to power and force, which will serve a bad cause as well as a good one; and indeed much better.

fellow men; but that they may execute an office no less laborious than honourable; and attend continually upon the public
welfare. This being their business and duty, it is but reasonable, that they should be requited for their care and diligence
in performing it; and enabled, by taxes levied upon the subject, effectually to prosecute the great end of their institution,
the good of society." The apostle sums all up in the following
words—*Render therefore to all their dues: tribute,* * to whom
tribute is due; custom,* * to whom custom; fear, to whom fear;
honour, to whom honour,* ver. 7. q. d. "Let it not, therefore, be
said of any of you hereafter, that you contemn government,
to the reproach of yourselves, and of the *christian* religion.
Neither your being *jews* by nation, nor your becoming the
subjects of Christ's kingdom, gives you any dispensation for
making disturbances in the government under which you
live. Approve yourselves, therefore, as peaceable and dutiful
subjects. Be ready to pay to your rulers all that they may, in
respect of their office, justly demand of you. Render tribute
and custom to those of your governors to whom tribute and
custom belong: And chearfully honor and reverence all who
are vested with civil authority, according to their deserts."

The apostle's doctrine, in the passage thus explained, concerning the office of civil rulers, and the duty of subjects, may
be summed up in the following observations;† *viz.*

That the end of magistracy is the good of civil society, *as
such*:

That civil rulers, *as such*, are the ordinance and ministers of
God; it being by his permission and providence that any bear
rule; and agreeable to his will, that there should be *some persons* vested with authority in society, for the well-being of it:

That which is here said concerning civil rulers, extends to

**Grotius* observes that the greek words here used, answer to the *tributum*
and *vectigal* of the *Romans*; the former was the money paid for the soil and
poll; the latter, the duties laid upon some sorts of merchandize. And what the
apostle here says, deserves to be seriously considered by all christians concerned in that common practice of carrying on an *illicit trade*, and *running
of goods*.

†The several observations here only mentioned, were handled at large in
two preceeding discourses upon this subject.

all of them in common: it relates indifferently to monarchical, republican and aristocratical government; and to all other forms which truly answer the sole end of government, the happiness of society; and to all the different degrees of authority in any particular state; to inferior officers no less than to the supreme:

That disobedience to civil rulers in the due exercise of their authority, is not merely a *political sin*, but an heinous *offence against God* and *religion*:

That the true ground and reason* of our obligation to be subject to the *higher powers*, is the usefulness of magistracy (when properly exercised) to human society, and its subserviency to the general welfare:

That obedience to civil rulers is here equally required under all forms of government, which answer the sole end of all government, the good of society; and to every degree of authority in any state, whether supreme or subordinate:

(From whence it follows,

That if unlimited obedience and non-resistance, be here required as a duty under any one form of government, it is also required as a duty under all other forms; and as a duty to subordinate rulers as well as to the supreme.)

---

*Some suppose the apostle in this passage inforces the duty of submission, with *two* arguments quite distinct from each other; one taken from this consideration, that rulers are the ordinance, and the ministers of God, (ver. 1. 2. and 4.) and the other, from the benefits that accrue to society, from civil government, (ver. 3, 4, and 6.) And indeed these may be distinct motives and arguments for submission, as they may be separately viewed and contemplated. But when we consider that rulers are not the ordinance and the ministers of God, but only so far forth as they perform God's will, by acting up to their office and character, and so by being benefactors to society, this makes these arguments coincide, and run up into *one* at last: At least so far, that the former of them cannot hold good for submission, where the latter fails. Put the supposition, that any man bearing the title of a magistrate, should exercise his power in such a manner as to have no claim to obedience by virtue of that argument which is founded upon the usefulness of magistracy; and you equally take off the force of the other argument also, which is founded upon his being the ordinance and the minister of God. For he is no longer God's ordinance and minister, than he acts up to his office and character, by exercising his power for the good of society—This is, in brief, the reason why it is said above, in the *singular* number, *that the true ground and reason,* &c. The use and propriety of this remark may possibly be more apparent in the progress of the argument concerning resistance.

And lastly, that those civil rulers to whom the apostle injoins subjection, are the persons *in possession*; *the powers that be*; those who are *actually* vested with authority.*

There is one very important and interesting point which remains to be inquired into; namely, the *extent* of that subjection *to the higher powers*, which is here enjoined as a duty upon all christians. Some have thought it warrantable and glorious, to disobey the civil powers in certain circumstances; and, in cases of very great and general oppression, when humble remonstrances fail of having any effect; and when the publick welfare cannot be otherwise provided for and secured, to rise unanimously even against the sovereign himself, in order to redress their grievances; to vindicate their natural and legal rights: to break the yoke of tyranny, and free themselves and posterity from inglorious servitude and ruin. It is upon this principle that many royal oppressors have been driven from their thrones into banishment; and many slain by the hands of their subjects. It was upon this principle that *Tarquin* was expelled from *Rome*; and *Julius Cesar*, the conqueror of the world, and the tyrant of his country, cut off in the senate house. It was upon this principle, that king *Charles* I, was beheaded before his own banqueting house. It was upon this principle, that king *James* II. was made to fly that country which he aim'd at enslaving: And upon this principle was that *revolution* brought about, which has been so fruitful of happy consequences to *Great-Britain*. But, in opposition to this principle, it has often been asserted, that the scripture in

*This must be understood with this *proviso*, that they do not grosly *abuse* their power and trust, but exercise it for the good of those that are governed. Who these persons were, whether *Nero*, &c. or not, the apostle does not say; but leaves it to be determined by those to whom he writes. God does not interpose, in a miraculous way, to point out the persons who shall bear rule, and to whom subjection is due. And as to the unalienable, indefeasible right of *primogeniture*, the scriptures are intirely silent: or rather plainly contradict it: *Saul* being the first king among the *Israelites*; and appointed to the royal dignity, during his own father's life-time: and he was succeeded, or rather superseded, by *David*, *the* last *born among many brethren*—Now if *God* has not invariably determined this matter, it must, of course, be determined by *men*. And if it be determined by *men*, it must be determined either in the way of *force*, or of *compact*. And which of these is the most *equitable*, can be no question.

general (and the passage under consideration in particular) makes all resistance to princes a crime, in any case whatever— If they turn tyrants, and become the common oppressors of those, whose welfare they ought to regard with a paternal affection, we must not pretend to right ourselves, unless it be by prayers and tears and humble intreaties: And if these methods fail of procuring redress, we must not have recourse to any other, but all suffer ourselves to be robbed and butchered at the pleasure of the *Lord's anointed*; lest we should incur the sin of rebellion, and the punishment of damnation. For he has God's authority and commission to bear him out in the worst of crimes, so far that he may not be withstood or controuled. Now whether we are obliged to yield such an absolute submission to our prince; or whether disobedience and resistance may not be justifiable in some cases, notwithstanding any thing in the passage before us, is an inquiry in which we are all concerned; and this is the inquiry which is the main design of the present discourse.

Now there does not seem to be any necessity of supposing, that an absolute, unlimited obedience, whether active or passive, is here injoined, merely for this reason, that the precept is delivered in *absolute terms*, without any *exception* or *limitation* expresly mentioned. We are enjoined, (ver. 1.) to be *subject to the higher powers*: and (ver. 5.) to be *subject for conscience sake*. And because these expressions are absolute and unlimited, (or more properly, general) some have inferred, that the subjection required in them, must be absolute and unlimited also: At least so far forth as to make passive obedience and non-resistance, a duty in all cases whatever, if not active obedience likewise. Though, by the way, there is here no distinction made betwixt active and passive obedience; and if either of them be required in an unlimited sense, the other must be required in the same sense also, by virtue of the present argument; because the expressions are equally absolute with respect to both. But that unlimited obedience of any sort, cannot be argued merely from the indefinite expressions in which obedience is enjoined, appears from hence, that expressions of the same nature, frequently occur in scripture, upon which it is confessed on all hands, that no such absolute and unlimited sense ought to be put. For example, *Love not* *the world; neither the things that are in the world;* Lay not up for yourselves treasures upon earth;† Take therefore no thought for the morrow;‡* are precepts expressed in at least equally absolute and unlimited terms: but it is generally allowed that they are to be understood with certain restrictions and limitations; some degree of love to the world, and the things of it, being allowable. Nor, indeed, do the *Right Reverend Fathers in God*, and other *dignified clergymen* of the established church, seem to be altogether averse to admitting of restrictions in the latter case, how warm soever any of them may be against restrictions, and limitations, in the case of submission to authority, whether civil or ecclesiastical. It is worth remarking also, that patience and submission under private injuries, are injoined in much more peremptory and absolute terms, than any that are used with regard to submission to the injustice and oppression of civil rulers. Thus, *I say unto you, that ye resist not evil; but whosoever shall smite thee on the right check, turn to him the other also. And if any man will sue thee at the law, and take away thy coat, let him have thy cloke also. And whosoever shall compel thee to go a mile with him, go with him twain.§* Any man may be defied to produce such strong expressions in favor of a passive and tame submission to unjust, tyrannical rulers, as are here used to inforce submission to private injuries. But how few are there that understand those expressions literally? And the reason why they do not, is because (with submission to the *quakers*) common sense shows that they were not intended to be so understood.

But to instance in some scripture-precepts, which are more directly to the point in hand.—Children are commanded to obey their parents, and servants, their masters, in as absolute and unlimited terms as subjects are here commanded to obey their civil rulers. Thus this same apostle—*Children obey your parents in the Lord; for this is right. Honour thy father and mother,—which is the first commandment with promise.— Servants, be obedient to them that are your masters according to the flesh, with fear and trembling, with singleness of your heart*

*1 John ii. 15.
†Matt. vi. 19.
‡Matt. vi. 34.
§Mat. v. 39, 40, 41.

as unto Christ. * Thus also wives are commanded to be obedient to their husbands—*Wives, submit your selves unto your own husbands, as unto the Lord. For the husband is head of the wife, even as* CHRIST IS THE HEAD OF THE CHURCH—*Therefore, as the church is subject unto Christ, so let the wives be to their own husbands* IN EVERY THING.† In all these cases, submission is required in terms (at least) as absolute and universal, as are ever used with respect to rulers and subjects. But who supposes that the apostle ever intended to teach, that children, servants and wives, should, in all cases whatever, obey their parents, masters and husbands respectively, never making any opposition to their will, even although they should require them to break the commandments of God, or should causelesly make an attempt upon their lives? No one puts such a sense upon these expressions, however absolute and unlimited. Why then should it be supposed, that the apostle designed to teach universal obedience, whether active or passive, to *the higher powers*, merely because his precepts are delivered in absolute and unlimited terms? And if this be a good argument in one case, why is it not in others also? If it be said that resistance and disobedience to *the higher powers*, is here said positively to be a sin, so also is the disobedience of children to parents; servants, to masters; and wives, to husbands, in other places of scripture. But the question still remains, whether in all these cases there be not some exceptions? In the three latter, it is allowed there are. And from hence it follows, that barely the use of absolute expressions, is no proof, that obedience to civil rulers, is, in all cases, a duty; or resistance, in all cases a sin. I should not have thought it worth while to take any notice at all of this argument, had it not been much insisted upon by some of the advocates for passive obedience and non-resistance: For it is, in itself, perfectly trifling; and render'd considerable, only by the stress that has been laid upon it for want of better.

There is, indeed, one passage in the new-testament, where it may seem, at first view, that an unlimited submission to civil rulers, is injoined.—*Submit your selves to every ordinance*

*Eph. vi. 1, &c.
†Eph. v. 22, 23, 24.

of man for the Lord's sake.*—To *every ordinance of man.*— However, this expression is no stronger than that before taken notice of, with relation to the duty of wives—*So let the wives be subject to their own husbands*—IN EVERY THING. But the true solution of this difficulty (if it be one) is *this*: by *every ordinance of man,*† is not meant every command of the civil magistrate without exception; but *every order of magistrates appointed by man*;—whether *superior* or *inferior*. For so the apostle explains himself in the very next words— *Whether it be to the king as supreme, or to governors, as unto them that are sent,* &c. But although the apostle had not subjoined any such explanation, the reason of the thing itself would have obliged us to limit the expression [*every ordinance of man*] to such human ordinances and commands, as are not inconsistent with the ordinances and commands of God, the supreme lawgiver; or with any other higher, and antecedent, obligations.

It is to be observed, in the next place, that as the duty of universal obedience and non-resistance to the *higher powers*, cannot be argued from the absolute unlimited expressions which the apostle here uses; so neither can it be argued from the scope and drift of his reasoning, considered with relation to the persons he was here opposing. As was observed above, there were some professed *christians* in the apostolic age, who disclaimed all magistracy and civil authority in general, *despising government*, and *speaking evil of dignities*, some under a notion that *jews* ought not to be under the jurisdiction of *gentile* rulers; and others, that they were set *free* from the temporal powers, by Christ. Now it is with persons of this licentious opinion and character, that the apostle is concerned. And all that was directly to his point, was to show, that they were bound to submit to magistracy *in general*. This is a circumstance very material to be taken notice of, in order to ascertain the sense of the apostle. For this being considered, it is sufficient to account for all that he says concerning the duty of subjection, and the sin of resistance, to the *higher powers*,

---

*1 Pet. 2. 13.

†Literally, *every human institution, or appointment*. By which manner of expression the apostle plainly intimates, that rulers derive their authority *immediately*, not from *God*, but from *men*.

without having recourse to the doctrine of unlimited submission and passive obedience, in all cases whatever. Were it known that those in opposition to whom, the apostle wrote, allowed of civil authority in general, and only asserted that there were *some cases* in which obedience and non-resistance, were not a duty; there would, then, indeed, be reason for interpreting this passage as containing the doctrine of unlimited obedience, and non-resistance, as it must, in this case, be supposed to have been levelled against such as denied that doctrine. But since it is certain that there were persons who vainly imagined, that civil government in general, was not to be regarded by them, it is most reasonable to suppose, that the apostle designed his discourse only against *them*. And agreeably to this supposition, we find that he argues the usefulness of civil magistracy in general; its agreeableness to the will and purpose of God, who is *over all*; and so deduces from hence, the obligation of submission to it. But it will not follow, that because civil government, is, in general, a good institution, and necessary to the peace and happiness of human society, therefore there are no supposeable cases in which resistance to it can be innocent. So that the duty of unlimited obedience, whether active or passive, can be argued, neither from the manner of expression here used, nor from the general scope and design of the passage.

And if we attend to the nature of the argument with which the apostle here inforces the duty of submission to *the higher powers*, we shall find it to be such an one as concludes not in favor of submission to all who bear the *title* of rulers, in common; but only, to those who *actually* perform the duty of rulers, by exercising a reasonable and just authority, for the good of human society. This is a point which it will be proper to enlarge upon; because the question before us turns very much upon the truth or falshood of this position. It is obvious, then, in general, that the civil rulers whom the apostle here speaks of, and obedience to whom he presses upon christians as a duty, are *good rulers*,* such as are, in the exercise of their office and power, benefactors to society. Such they are

---

*By *good rulers*, are not intended such as are good in a *moral* or *religious*, but only in a *political*, sense; those who perform their duty so far as their office extends; and so far as civil society, as such, is concerned in their actions.

described to be, thro'out this passage. Thus it is said, that they are not *a terror to good works, but to the evil*; that they are *God's ministers for good; revengers to execute wrath upon him that doth evil*; and that *they attend continually upon this very thing*. St. *Peter* gives the same account of rulers: They are *for a praise to them that do well, and the punishment of evil doers.** It is manifest that this character and description of rulers, agrees only to such as are rulers in fact, as well as in name: to such as govern well, and act agreeably to their office. And the apostle's argument for submission to rulers, is wholly built and grounded upon a presumption that they do in fact answer this character; and is of no force at all upon supposition of the contrary. If *rulers are a terror to good works, and not to the evil*; if they are not *ministers for good to society*, but for evil and distress, by violence and oppression; if they *execute wrath upon* sober, peaceable persons, who do their duty as members of society; and suffer rich and honourable knaves to escape with impunity; if, instead of *attending continually upon* the good work of advancing the publick welfare, they *attend* only upon the gratification of their own lust and pride and ambition, to the destruction of the public welfare; if this be the case, it is plain that the apostle's argument for submission does not reach them; they are not the same, but different persons from those whom he characterizes; and who must be obeyed according to his reasoning.—Let me illustrate the apostle's argument, by the following *similitude*: (it is no matter how far it is from any thing which has, in fact, happened in the world.) Suppose, then, it was allowed, in general, that the *clergy* were an useful order of men; that they ought to be *esteemed very highly in love for their works sake*;† and to be decently supported by those whom they serve, *the labourer being worthy of his reward*.‡ Suppose farther, that a number of *Reverend* and *Right Reverend Drones*, who *worked not*; who preached, perhaps, but *once a year*, and *then*, not the *gospel* of Jesus Christ; but the *divine right of tythes*;—the *dignity of their office as ambassadors of Christ*, the equity of *sine-cures*, and a *plurality of benefices*;—the excellency of the *devotions* in

---

*See the marginal note, page 387. See also the marginal note, p. 387–388.

†1 Thes. v. 13.

‡1 Tim. v. 18.

that prayer-book, which some of them hired *chaplains to use for them;*—or some favourite point of *church-tyranny,* and *anti-christian* usurpation; suppose such men as these, spending their lives in effeminacy, luxury and idleness; (or when they were not idle, doing that which is worse than idleness; suppose such men) should, merely by the merit of *ordination* and *consecration,* and a *peculiar, odd habit,* claim great respect and reverence from those whom they civilly called *the beasts of the laiety;** and demand thousands *per annum,* for that good service which they—*never performed;* and for which, if they had performed it, this would be much more than a *quantum meruit:* suppose this should be the case, (it is only by way of *simile,* and surely it will give no offence) would not every body be astonished at such insolence, injustice and impiety? And ought not such men to be told plainly, that they could not reasonably expect the esteem and reward, due to the ministers of the gospel, unless they did the duties of their office? Should they not be told, that their *title* and *habit* claimed no regard, reverence or pay, separate from the *care* and *work* and various *duties* of their *function?* And that while they neglected the *latter,* the *former* served only to render them the more ridiculous and contemptible?—The application of this *similitude* to the case in hand, is very easy.—If those who bear the title of civil rulers, do not perform the duty of civil rulers, but act directly counter to the sole end and design of their office; if they injure and oppress their subjects, instead of defending their rights and doing them good; they have not the least pretence to be honored, obeyed and rewarded, according to the apostle's argument. For his reasoning, in order to show the duty of subjection to the *higher powers,* is, as was before observed, built wholly upon the supposition, that they do, *in fact,* perform the duty of rulers.

If it be said, that the apostle here uses another argument for submission to the *higher powers,* besides that which is taken from the usefulness of their office to civil society, when properly discharged and executed; namely, that their *power is from God;* that they *are ordained of God;* and that they *are God's ministers.* And if it be said, that this argument for sub-

*Mr. *Leslie.*

mission to them will hold good, although they do not exercise their power for the benefit, but for the ruin, and destruction of human society; this objection was obviated, in part,
before.* Rulers have no authority from God to do mischief.
They are not *God's ordinance*, or *God's ministers*, in any other
sense than as it is by his permission and providence, that they
are exalted to bear rule; and as magistracy duly exercised, and
authority rightly applied, in the enacting and executing good
laws,—laws attempered and accommodated to the common
welfare of the subjects, must be supposed to be agreeable to
the will of the beneficent author and supreme Lord of the
universe; whose *kingdom ruleth over all*;† and whose *tender
mercies are over all his works.*‡ It is blasphemy to call tyrants
and oppressors, *God's ministers.* They are more properly *the
messengers of satan to buffet us.*§ No rulers are properly *God's
ministers*, but such as are *just, ruling in the fear of God.*‖ When
once magistrates act contrary to their office, and the end of
their institution; when they rob and ruin the public, instead
of being guardians of its peace and welfare; they immediately
cease to be the *ordinance* and *ministers of God*; and no more
deserve that glorious character than common *pirates* and
highwaymen. So that whenever that argument for submission,
fails, which is grounded upon the usefulness of magistracy to
civil society, (as it always does when magistrates do hurt to society instead of good) the other argument, which is taken
from their being the ordinance of God, must necessarily fail
also; no person of a civil character being *God's minister*, in the
sense of the apostle, any farther than he performs God's will,
by exercising a just and reasonable authority; and ruling for
the good of the subject.

This in general. Let us now trace the apostle's reasoning in
favor of submission to the *higher powers*, a little more particularly and exactly. For by this it will appear, on one hand, how
good and conclusive it is, for submission to those rulers who
exercise their power in a proper manner: And, on the other,

*See the margin, page 390.
†Psal. ciii. 19.
‡Psal. cxlv. 19.
§2 Cor. xii. 7.
‖2 Sam. xxiii. 3.

how weak and trifling and inconnected it is, if it be supposed to be meant by the apostle to show the obligation and duty of obedience to tyrannical, oppressive rulers in common with others of a different character.

The apostle enters upon his subject thus—*Let every soul be subject unto the higher powers; for there is no power but of God: the powers that be, are ordained of God.* Here he urges the duty of obedience from this topic of argument, that civil rulers, as they are supposed to fulfil the pleasure of God, are the ordinance of God. But how is this an argument for obedience to such rulers as do not perform the pleasure of God, by doing good; but the pleasure of the devil, by doing evil; and such as are not, therefore, *God's ministers,* but the devil's! *Whosoever, therefore, resisteth the power, resisteth the ordinance of God; and they that resist, shall receive to themselves damnation.*† Here the apostle argues, that those who resist a reasonable and just authority, which is agreeable to the will of God, do really resist the will of God himself; and will, therefore, be punished by him. But how does this prove, that those who resist a lawless, unreasonable power, which is contrary to the will of God, do therein resist the will and ordinance of God? Is resisting those who resist God's will, the same thing with resisting God? Or shall those who do so, *receive to themselves damnation! For rulers are not a terror to good works, but to the evil. Wilt thou then not be afraid of the power? Do that which is good; and thou shalt have praise of the same. For he is the minister of God to thee for good.*‡ Here the apostle argues more explicitly than he had before done, for revereing, and submitting to, magistracy, from this consideration, that such as really performed the duty of magistrates, would be enemies only to the evil actions of men, and would befriend and encourage the good; and so be a common blessing to society. But how is this an argument, that we must honor, and submit to, such magistrates as are not enemies to the evil actions of men; but to the good; and such as are not a common blessing, but a common curse, to society! *But if thou do that which is evil, be afraid: For he is the minister of God, a revenger, to*

*Ver. 1.
†Ver. 2.
‡Ver. 3d. and part of the 4th.

*execute wrath upon him that doth evil.** Here the apostle argues from the nature and end of magistracy, that such as did evil, (and such only) had reason to be afraid of the *higher powers*; it being part of their office to punish evil-doers, no less than to defend and encourage such as do well. But if magistrates are unrighteous; if they are *respecters of persons*; if they are partial in their administration of justice; then those who do well have as much reason to *be afraid*, as those that do evil: there can be no safety for the good, nor any peculiar ground of terror to the unruly and injurious. So that, in this case, the main end of civil government will be frustrated. And what reason is there for submitting to that government, which does by no means answer the design of government? *Wherefore ye must needs be subject not only for wrath, but also for conscience sake.*† Here the apostle argues the duty of a chearful and conscientious submission to civil government, from the nature and end of magistracy as he had before laid it down, i. e. as the design of it was to punish evil doers, and to support and encourage such as do well; and as it must, if so exercised, be agreeable to the will of God. But how does what he here says, prove the duty of a chearful and conscientious subjection to those who forfeit the character of rulers? to those who encourage the bad, and discourage the good? The argument here used no more proves it to be a sin to resist such rulers, than it does, to *resist the devil*, that he may *flee from us.*‡ For one is as truly the *minister of God* as the other. *For, for this cause pay you tribute also; for they are God's ministers, attending continually upon this very thing.*§ Here the apostle argues the duty of paying taxes, from this consideration, that those who perform the duty of rulers, are continually attending upon the public welfare. But how does this argument conclude for paying taxes to such princes as are continually endeavouring to ruin the public? And especially when such payment would facilitate and promote this wicked design! *Render therefore to all their dues; tribute, to whom tribute is due; custom, to whom custom; fear, to whom fear; honor, to*

*Ver. 4th. latter part.
†Ver. 5.
‡James iv. 7.
§Ver. 6.

*whom honor.** Here the apostle sums up what he had been saying concerning the duty of subjects to rulers. And his argument stands thus—"Since magistrates who execute their office well, are common benefactors to society; and may, in that respect, be properly stiled *the ministers and ordinance of God*; and since they are constantly employed in the service of the public; it becomes you to pay them tribute and custom; and to reverence, honor, and submit to, them in the execution of their respective offices." This is apparently good reasoning. But does this argument conclude for the duty of paying tribute, custom, reverence, honor and obedience, to such persons as (although they bear the title of rulers) use all their power to hurt and injure the public? such as are not *God's ministers*, but *satan's*? such as do not take care of, and attend upon, the public interest, but their own, to the ruin of the public? that is, in short, to such as have no natural and just claim at all to tribute, custom, reverence, honor and obedience? It is to be hoped that those who have any regard to the apostle's character as an inspired writer, or even as a man of common understanding, will not represent him as reasoning in such a loose incoherent manner; and drawing conclusions which have not the least relation to his premises. For what can be more absurd than an argument thus framed? "Rulers are, by their office, bound to consult the public welfare and the good of society: therefore you are bound to pay them tribute, to honor, and to submit to them, even when they destroy the public welfare, and are a common pest to society, by acting in direct contradiction to the nature and end of their office."

Thus, upon a careful review of the apostle's reasoning in this passage, it appears that his arguments to enforce submission, are of such a nature, as to conclude only in favour of submission *to such rulers as he himself describes*; i. e. such as rule for the good of society, which is the only end of their institution. Common tyrants, and public oppressors, are not intitled to obedience from their subjects, by virtue of any thing here laid down by the inspired apostle.

I now add, farther, that the apostle's argument is so far from proving it to be the duty of people to obey, and submit

*Ver. 7.

to, such rulers as act in contradiction to the public good,* and so to the design of their office, that it proves *the direct contrary*. For, please to observe, that if the end of all civil government, be the good of society; if this be the thing that is aimed at in constituting civil rulers; and if the motive and argument for submission to government, be taken from the apparent usefulness of civil authority; it follows, that when no such good end can be answered by submission, there remains no argument or motive to enforce it; and if instead of this good end's being brought about by submission, a *contrary end* is brought about, and the ruin and misery of society effected by it, here is a plain and positive reason against submission in all such cases, should they ever happen. And therefore, in such cases, a regard to the public welfare, ought to make us with-hold from our rulers, that obedience and subjection which it would, otherwise, be our duty to render to them. If it be our duty, for example, to obey our king, merely for this reason, that he rules for the public welfare, (which is the only argument the apostle makes use of) it follows, by a parity of reason, that when he turns tyrant, and makes his subjects his prey to devour and to destroy, instead of his charge to defend and cherish, we are bound to throw off our allegiance to him, and to resist; and that according to the tenor of the apostle's argument in this passage. Not to discontinue our allegiance, in this case, would be to join with the sovereign in promoting the slavery and misery of that society, the welfare of which, we ourselves, as well as our sovereign, are indispensably obliged to secure and promote, as far as in us lies. It is true the apostle puts no case of such a tyrannical prince; but by his grounding his argument for submission wholly upon the good of civil society; it is plain he implicitly authorises, and even requires us to make resistance, whenever this shall be necessary to the public safety and happiness. Let me make use of this easy and familiar *similitude* to illustrate the point in hand—Suppose God requires a family of children, to obey their father and not to resist him; and

---

*This does not intend, their acting so in *a few particular instances*, which the best of rulers may do through mistake, &c. but their acting so *habitually*, and in a manner which plainly shows, that they aim at making themselves great, by the ruin of their subjects.

inforces his command with this argument; that the superintendence and care and authority of a just and kind parent, will contribute to the happiness of the whole family; so that they ought to obey him for their own sakes more than for his: Suppose this parent at length runs distracted, and attempts, in his mad fit, to cut all his children's throats: Now, in this case, is not the reason before assigned, why these children should obey their parent while he continued of a sound mind, namely, *their common good*, a reason equally conclusive for disobeying and resisting him, since he is become delirious, and attempts their ruin? It makes no alteration in the argument, whether this parent, properly speaking, loses his reason; or does, while he retains his understanding, that which is as fatal in its consequences, as any thing he could do, were he really deprived of it. This similitude needs no formal application—

But it ought to be remembred, that if the duty of universal obedience and non-resistance to our king or prince, can be argued from this passage, the same unlimited submission under a republican, or any other form of government; and even to all the subordinate powers in any particular state, can be proved by it as well: which is more than those who alledge it for the mentioned purpose, would be willing should be inferred from it. So that this passage does not answer their purpose; but really overthrows and confutes it. This matter deserves to be more particularly considered.—The advocates for unlimited submission and passive obedience, do, if I mistake not, always speak with reference to kingly or monarchical government, as distinguished from all other forms; and, with reference to submitting to the will of the king, in distinction from all subordinate officers, acting beyond their commission, and the authority which they have received from the crown. It is not pretended that any persons besides kings, have a divine right to do what they please, so that no one may resist them, without incurring the guilt of factiousness and rebellion. If any other supreme powers oppress the people, it is generally allowed, that the people may get redress, by resistance, if other methods prove ineffectual. And if any officers in a kingly government, go beyond the limits of that power which they have derived from the crown, (the supposed original source of all power and authority in the state) and attempt, illegally, to take away the properties and lives of their fellow-subjects, they may be *forcibly* resisted, at least till application can be made to the crown. But as to the sovereign himself, he may not be resisted in any case; nor any of his officers, while they confine themselves within the bounds which he has prescribed to them. This is, I think, a true sketch of the principles of those who defend the doctrine of passive obedience and non-resistance. Now there is nothing in scripture which supports this scheme of political principles. As to the passage under consideration, the apostle here speaks of civil rulers in *general*; of all persons in *common*, vested with authority for the good of society, without any particular reference to one form of government, more than to another; or to the supreme power in any particular state, more than to subordinate powers. The apostle does not concern himself with the different forms of government.* This he supposes left intirely to human prudence and discretion. Now the consequence of this is, that unlimited and passive obedience is no more enjoined in this passage, under monarchical government; or to the supreme power in any state, than under all other species of government, which answer the end of government; or, to all the subordinate degrees of civil authority, from the highest to the lowest. Those, therefore, who would

---

*The essence of government (I mean *good* government; and this is the *only* government which the apostle treats of in this passage) consists in the *making* and *executing of good laws*—laws attempered to the common felicity of the *governed*. And if this be, *in fact*, done, it is evidently, in it self, a thing of no consequence at all, what the *particular* form of government is;—whether the legislative and executive power be lodged in *one and the same* person, or in *different* persons;—whether in *one* person, whom we call an *absolute monarch*;—whether in a *few*, so as to constitute an *aristrocrasy*;—whether in *many*, so as to constitute a *republic*; or whether in *three coordinate branches*, in such manner as to make the government *partake* something of *each* of these forms; and to be, at the same time, *essentially different* from them *all*. If the *end* be attained, it is enough. But no form of government seems to be so unlikely to accomplish this *end*, as *absolute monarchy*.—Nor is there any one that has so little pretence to a *divine original*, unless it be in this sense, that God *first* introduced it into, and thereby overturned, the common wealth of *Israel*, as a *curse* upon that people for their *folly* and *wickedness*, particularly in *desiring* such a government. (See 1 *Sam*. viii. chap.) Just so God, before, sent *Quails* amongst them, as a *plague*, and a *curse*, and not as a *blessing*. *Numb*. chap. xi.

from this passage infer the guilt of resisting kings, in all cases whatever, though acting ever so contrary to the design of their office, must, if they will be consistent, go much farther, and infer from it the guilt of resistance under all other forms of government; and of resisting *any petty officer* in the state, tho' acting beyond his commission, in the most arbitrary, illegal manner possible. The argument holds equally strong in both cases. All civil rulers, as such, are the *ordinance* and *ministers of God*; and they are all, by the nature of their office, and in their respective spheres and stations, bound to consult the public welfare. With the same reason therefore, that any deny unlimited and passive obedience to be here injoined under a republic or aristocrasy, or any other established form of civil government; or to subordinate powers, acting in an illegal and oppressive manner; (with the same reason) others may deny, that such obedience is enjoined to a king or monarch, or any civil power whatever. For the apostle says nothing that is *peculiar to kings*; what he says, extends equally to *all* other persons whatever, vested with any civil office. They are all, in exactly the same sense, the *ordinance of God*; and the *ministers of God*; and obedience is equally enjoined to be paid to them all. For, as the apostle expresses it, *there is* NO POWER *but of God*: And we are required to *render to* ALL *their* DUES; and not MORE than their DUES. And what these *dues* are, and to *whom* they are to be *rendered*, the apostle *sayeth not*; but leaves to the reason and consciences of men to determine.

Thus it appears, that the common argument, grounded upon this passage, in favor of universal, and passive obedience, really overthrows itself, by proving too much, if it proves any thing at all; namely, that no civil officer is, in any case whatever, to be resisted, though acting in express contradiction to the design of his office; which no man, in his senses, ever did, or can assert.

If we calmly consider the nature of the thing itself, nothing can well be imagined more directly contrary to common sense, than to suppose that *millions* of people should be subjected to the arbitrary, precarious pleasure of *one single man*; (who has *naturally* no superiority over them in point of authority) so that their estates, and every thing that is valuable in life, and even their lives also, shall be absolutely at his disposal, if he happens to be wanton and capricious enough to demand them. What unprejudiced man can think, that God made ALL to be thus subservient to the lawless pleasure and phrenzy of ONE, so that it shall always be a sin to resist him! Nothing but the most plain and express revelation from heaven could make a sober impartial man believe such a monstrous, unaccountable doctrine, and indeed, the thing itself, appears so shocking—so out of all *proportion*, that it may be questioned, whether all the *miracles* that ever were wrought, could make it credible, that this doctrine *really* came from God. At present, there is not the least syllable in scripture which gives any countenance to it. The hereditary, indefeasible, divine right of kings, and the doctrine of non-resistance, which is built upon the supposition of such a right, are altogether as fabulous and chimerical, as transubstantiation; or any of the most absurd reveries of ancient or modern visionaries. These notions are fetched neither from divine revelation, nor human reason; and if they are derived from neither of those sources, it is not much matter from *whence they come, or whither they go*. Only it is a pity that such doctrines should be propagated in society, to raise factions and rebellions, as we see they have, in fact, been both in the *last*, and in the *present*, REIGN.

But then, if unlimited submission and passive obedience to the *higher powers*, in all possible cases, be not a duty, it will be asked, "How far are we obliged to submit? If we may innocently disobey and resist in some cases, why not in all? Where shall we stop? What is the measure of our duty? This doctrine tends to the total dissolution of civil government; and to introduce such scenes of wild anarchy and confusion, as are more fatal to society than the worst of tyranny."

After this manner, some men object; and, indeed, this is the most plausible thing that can be said in favor of such an absolute submission as they plead for. But the worst (or rather the best) of it, is, that there is very little strength or solidity in it. For similar difficulties may be raised with respect to almost every duty of natural and revealed religion.—To instance only in two, both of which are near akin, and indeed exactly parallel, to the case before us. It is unquestionably the duty of children to submit to their parents; and of servants, to their masters. But no one asserts, that it is their duty to obey, and submit to them, in all supposeable cases; or universally a sin to resist them. Now does this tend to subvert the just authority of parents and masters? Or to introduce confusion and anarchy into private families? No. How then does the same principle tend to unhinge the government of that larger family, the body politic? We know, in general, that children and servants are obliged to obey their parents and masters respectively. We know also, with equal certainty, that they are not obliged to submit to them in all things, without exception; but may, in some cases, reasonably, and therefore innocently, resist them. These principles are acknowledged upon all hands, whatever difficulty there may be in fixing the exact limits of submission. Now there is at least as much difficulty in stating the measure of duty in these two cases, as in the case of rulers and subjects. So that this is really no objection, at least no reasonable one, against resistance to the *higher powers*. Or, if it is one, it will hold equally against resistance in the other cases mentioned.—It is indeed true, that turbulent, vicious-minded men, may take occasion from this principle, that their rulers may, in some cases, be lawfully resisted, to raise factions and disturbances in the state; and to make resistance where resistance is needless, and therefore, sinful. But is it not equally true, that children and servants of turbulent, vicious minds, may take occasion from this principle, that parents and masters may, in some cases be lawfully resisted, to resist when resistance is unnecessary, and therefore, criminal? Is the principle in either case false in itself, merely because it may be abused; and applied to legitimate disobedience and resistance in those instances, to which it ought not to be applied? According to this way of arguing, there will be no true principles in the world; for there are none but what may be wrested and perverted to serve bad purposes, either through the weakness or wickedness of men.*

---

*We may very safely assert these two things in general, without undermining government: One is, That no civil rulers are to be obeyed when they enjoin things that are inconsistent with the commands of God: All such disobedience is lawful and glorious; particularly, if persons refuse to comply with any *legal establishment of religion*, because it is a gross perversion and

A PEOPLE, really oppressed to a great degree by their sovereign, cannot well be insensible when they are so oppressed. And such a people (if I may allude to an ancient *fable*) have, like the *hesperian* fruit, a DRAGON for their *protector* and *guardian*: Nor would they have any reason to mourn, if some

---

corruption (as to doctrine, worship and discipline) of a pure and divine religion, brought from heaven to earth by the *Son of God*, (the only King and Head of the *christian* church) and propagated through the world by his inspired apostles. All commands running counter to the declared will of the supreme legislator of heaven and earth, are null and void: And therefore disobedience to them is a duty, not a crime. (See the marginal note, pages 387–388.)—Another thing that may be asserted with equal truth and safety, is, That no government is to be submitted to, at the *expence* of that which is the *sole end* of all government,—the common good and safety of society. Because, to submit in this case, if it should ever happen, would evidently be to set up the *means* as more valuable, and above, the *end*: than which there cannot be a greater solecism and contradiction. The only reason of the institution of civil government; and the only rational ground of submission to it, is the common safety and utility. If therefore, in any case, the common safety and utility would not be promoted by submission to government, but the contrary, there is no ground or motive for obedience and submission, but, for the contrary.

Whoever considers the nature of civil government must, indeed, be sensible that a great degree of *implicit confidence*, must unavoidably be placed in those that bear rule: this is implied in the very notion of authority's being originally a *trust*, committed by the people, to those who are vested with it, as all just and righteous authority is; all besides, is mere lawless force and usurpation; neither God nor nature, having given any man a right of dominion over any society, independently of that society's approbation, and consent to be governed by him—Now as all men are fallible, it cannot be supposed that the public affairs of any state, should be always administered in the best manner possible, even by persons of the greatest wisdom and integrity. Nor is it sufficient to legitimate disobedience to the *higher powers* that they are not so administred; or that they are, in some instances, very ill-managed; for upon this principle, it is scarcely supposeable that any government at all could be supported, or subsist. Such a principle manifestly tends to the dissolution of government; and to throw all things into confusion and anarchy.—But it is equally evident, upon the other hand, that those in authority may abuse their *trust* and power *to such a degree*, that neither the law of reason, nor of religion, requires, that any obedience or submission should be paid to them; but, on the contrary, that they should be totally *discarded*; and the authority which they were before vested with, transferred to others, who may exercise it more to those good purposes for which it is given.—Nor is this principle, that resistance to the *higher powers*, is, in some extraordinary cases, justifiable, so liable to abuse, as many persons seem to apprehend it. For although there

HERCULES should appear to dispatch him—For a nation thus abused to arise unanimously, and to resist their prince, even to the dethroning him, is not criminal; but a reasonable way of vindicating their liberties and just rights; it is making use of the means, and the only means, which God has put into their power, for mutual and self-defence. And it would be highly criminal in them, not to make use of this means. It would be stupid tameness, and unaccountable folly, for whole nations to suffer *one* unreasonable, ambitious and cruel man, to wanton and riot in their misery. And in such a case it would, of the two, be more rational to suppose, that they did NOT *resist*, than that they who did, would *receive to themselves damnation.*

---

will be always some petulant, querulous men, in every state—men of factious, turbulent and carping dispositions,—glad to lay hold of any trifle to justify and legitimate their caballing against their rulers, and other seditious practices; yet there are, comparatively speaking, but few men of this *contemptible character.* It does not appear but that mankind, in general, have a disposition to be as submissive and passive and tame under government as they ought to be.— Witness a great, if not the greatest, part of the known world, who are now groaning, but not murmuring, under the heavy yoke of tyranny! While those who govern, do it with any tolerable degree of moderation and justice, and, in any good measure act up to their office and character, by being public benefactors; the people will generally be easy and peaceable; and be rather inclined to flatter and adore, than to insult and resist, them. Nor was there ever any *general* complaint against any administration, *which lasted long*, but what there was good reason for. Till people find themselves greatly abused and oppressed by their governors, they are not apt to complain; and whenever they do, in fact, find themselves thus abused and oppressed, they must be stupid not to complain. To say that subjects in general are not proper judges when their governors oppress them, and play the tyrant; and when they defend their rights, administer justice impartially, and promote the public welfare, is as great *treason* as ever man uttered;—'tis treason,—not against one *single* man, but the state—against the whole body politic;—'tis treason against mankind;—'tis treason against common sense;—'tis treason against God. And this impious principle lays the foundation for justifying all the tyranny and oppression that ever any prince was guilty of. The people know for what end they set up, and maintain, their governors; and they are the proper judges when they execute their *trust* as they ought to do it;—when their prince exercises an equitable and paternal authority over them;—when from a prince and common father, he exalts himself into a tyrant—when from subjects and children, he degrades them into the class of slaves;—plunders them, makes them his prey, and unnaturally sports himself with their lives and fortunes——

And

This naturally brings us to make some reflections upon the resistance which was made about a century since, to that unhappy prince, KING CHARLES I; and upon the ANNIVERSARY of his death. This is a point which I should not have concerned myself about, were it not that *some men* continue to speak of it, even to this day, with a great deal of warmth and zeal; and in such a manner as to undermine all the principles of LIBERTY, whether civil or religious, and to introduce the most abject slavery both in church and state: so that it is become a matter of universal concern.—What I have to offer upon this subject, will be comprised in a short answer to the following *queries; viz.*

For what reason the resistance to king *Charles* the *First* was made?

By whom it was made?

Whether this resistance was REBELLION,* or not?

How the *Anniversary* of king *Charles's* death came *at first* to be solemnized as a day of fasting and humiliation?

And lastly,

Why those of the episcopal clergy who are very high in the principles of *ecclesiastical authority*, continue to speak of this unhappy man, as a great SAINT and a MARTYR?

For what reason, then, was the resistance to king *Charles*, made? The general answer to this inquiry is, that it was on account of the *tyranny* and *oppression* of his reign. Not a great while after his accession to the throne, he married a *french catholic*; and with her seemed to have *wedded* the politics, if not the religion of *France*, also. For afterwards, during a reign, or rather a tyranny of many years, he governed in a perfectly wild and arbitrary manner, paying no regard to the constitution and the laws of the kingdom, by which the power of the crown was limited; or to the solemn oath which he had taken at his coronation. It would be endless, as well as needless, to give a particular account of all the illegal and despotic measures which he took in his administration;—partly from

---

*N. B. I speak of rebellion, treason, saintship, martyrdom, &c. throughout this discourse, only in the *scriptural* and *theological sense*. I know not how the *law* defines them; the study of *that* not being my employment——

his own natural lust of power, and partly from the influence of wicked councellors and ministers.—He committed many illustrious members of both houses of parliament to the *tower*, for opposing his arbitrary schemes.—He levied many taxes upon the people without consent of parliament;—and then imprisoned great numbers of the principal merchants and gentry for not paying them.—He erected, or at least revived, several arbitrary courts, in which the most unheard-of barbarities were committed with his knowledge and approbation— He supported that more than fiend, arch-bishop *Laud* and the clergy of his stamp, in all their church-tyranny and hellish cruelties—He authorised a book in favor of *sports* upon the *Lord's day*, and several clergymen were persecuted by him and the mentioned *pious* bishop, for not reading it to the people after *divine service*—When the parliament complained to him of the arbitrary proceedings of his corrupt ministers, he told that *august body*, in a rough, domineering, unprincely manner, that he wondred any one should be so foolish and insolent as to think that he would part with the meanest of his servants *upon their account*—He refused to call any parliament at all for the space of twelve years together, during all which time, he governed in an absolute lawless and despotic manner—He took all opportunities to encourage the *papists*, and to promote them to the highest offices of honor and trust—He (probably) abetted the horrid massacre in *Ireland*, in which two hundred thousand protestants were butchered by the roman catholics.—He sent a large sum of money, which he had raised by his arbitrary taxes, into *Germany*, to raise foreign troops, in order to force more arbitrary taxes upon his subjects.—He not only by a long series of *actions*, but also in *plain terms*, asserted an absolute uncontroulable power; saying even in one of his speeches to parliament, that as it was blasphemy to dispute what God might do; so it was sedition in subjects to dispute what the king might do.— Towards the end of his tyranny, he came to the house of commons with an armed force,* and demanded five of its

---

*Historians are not agreed, what number of soldiers attended him in this monstrous invasion of the priviledges of parliament—Some say 500, some 400: And the author of *The history of the kings of Scotland*, says 500.

principal members to be delivered up to him—And this was a prelude to that unnatural war which he soon after levied against his own dutiful subjects; whom he was bound by all the laws of honor, humanity, piety, and I might add, of *interest* also, to defend and cherish with a paternal affection—I have only time to hint at these facts in a general way, all which, and many more of the same tenor, may be proved by good authorities: So that the *figurative* language which St. *John* uses concerning the just and beneficent deeds of our blessed Saviour, may be applied to the unrighteous and execrable deeds of this prince, *viz. And there are also many other things which* king Charles *did, the which, if they should be written every one, I suppose that even the world itself, could not contain the books that should be written.** Now it was on account of king *Charles's* thus assuming a power above the laws, in direct contradiction to his coronation oath, and governing the greatest part of his time, in the most arbitrary oppressive manner; it was upon this account, that that resistance was made to him, which, at length, issued in the loss of his crown, and of *that head* which was unworthy to wear it.

But by whom was this resistance made? Not by a private *junto*;—not by a small seditious *party*;—not by a *few desparadoes*, who, to mend their fortunes, would embroil the state;—but by the LORDS and COMMONS of *England*. It was they that almost unanimously opposed the king's measures for overturning the constitution, and changing that free and happy government into a wretched, absolute monarchy. It was they that when the king was about levying forces against his subjects, in order to make himself absolute, commissioned officers, and raised an army to defend themselves and the public: And it was they that maintained the war against him all along, till he was made a prisoner. This is indisputable. Though it was not properly speaking the parliament, but the army, which put him to death afterwards. And it ought to be freely acknowledged, that most of their proceeding, in order to get this matter effected; and particularly the court by which the king was at last tried and condemned, was little better than a mere mockery of justice.—

*John xxi. 25.

The next question which naturally arises, is, whether this resistance which was made to the king *by the parliament*, was properly *rebellion*, or not? The answer to which is plain, that it was not; but a most righteous and glorious stand, made in defence of the natural and legal rights of the people, against the unnatural and illegal encroachments of arbitrary power. Nor was this a rash and too sudden opposition. The nation had been patient under the oppressions of the crown, even to *long-suffering*;—for a course of many years; and there was no rational hope of redress in any other way—Resistance was absolutely necessary in order to preserve the nation from slavery, misery and ruin. And who so proper to make this resistance as the lords and commoners—the whole representative body of the people;—guardians of the public welfare; and each of which was, in point of legislation, vested with an equal, co-ordinate power, with that of the crown?* Here were *two* branches of

---

*The *english* constitution is originally and essentially *free*. The character which *J. Cæsar* and *Tacitus* both give of the ancient *Britains* so long ago, is, That they were extremely *jealous of their liberties*, as well as a people of a *martial* spirit. Nor have there been wanting frequent instances and proofs of the same glorious spirit (in both respects) remaining in their posterity ever since,—in the struggles they have made for liberty, both against foreign and domestic tyrants.—Their kings hold their title to the throne, solely by grant of parliament; i. e. in other words, by the voluntary consent of the people. And, agreably hereto, the prerogative and rights of the crown are stated, defined and limited by law; and that as truly and strictly as the rights of any inferior officer in the state; or indeed, of any private subject. And it is only in this respect that it can be said, that "the king can do no wrong." Being restrained by the law, he cannot, while he confines himself within those just limits which the law prescribes to him as the measure of his authority, injure and oppress the subject.—The king, in his coronation oath, swears to exercise only such a power as the constitution gives him: And the subject, in the oath of allegiance, swears only to obey him in the exercise of such a power. The king is as much bound by his oath, not to infringe the legal rights of the people, as the people are bound to yield subjection to him. From whence it follows, that as soon as the prince sets himself up above law, he loses the king in the tyrant: he does to all intents and purposes, unking himself, by acting out of, and beyond, that sphere which the constitution allows him to move in. And in such cases, he has no more right to be obeyed, than any inferior officer who acts beyond his commission. The subjects obligation to allegiance *then* ceases of course: and to resist him, is no more *rebellion*, than to resist any foreign invader. There is an essential difference betwixt *government and tyranny*; at least under such a constitution as the *english*. The former consists in ruling according to law and equity; the latter, in ruling contrary to law and

the legislature against *one*;—two, which had law and equity and the constitution on their side, against one which was impiously attempting to overturn law and equity and the constitution; and to exercise a wanton licentious *sovereignty* over the properties, consciences and lives of all the people:—Such a *sovereignty* as some inconsiderately ascribe to the supreme Governor of the world.—I say, inconsiderately; because God himself does not govern in an absolutely arbitrary and despotic manner. The power of this Almighty King (I speak it not without caution and reverence; the power of this Almighty King) is *limited by law*; not, indeed, by *acts of parliament*, but by the eternal *laws* of truth, wisdom and equity; and the everlasting *tables* of right reason;—tables that cannot be *repealed*, or *thrown down* and *broken* like those of *Moses*.—But king *Charles* sat himself up above all these, as much as he did above the written laws of the realm; and made mere humor and caprice, which are no rule at all, the only rule and measure of his administration. And now, is it not perfectly ridiculous to call resistance to such a tyrant, by the name of *rebellion?—the grand rebellion?* Even that—parliament, which brought king *Charles* II. to the throne, and which run *loyally mad*, severely reproved one of their own members for condemning the proceedings of that parliament which first took up arms against the former king. And upon the same principles that the proceedings of this parliament may be censured as wicked and rebellious, the proceedings of those who, since, opposed king *James* II, and brought the prince of *Orange* to the throne, may be censured as wicked and rebellious also. The cases are parallel.—But whatever *some* men may *think*, it is to be hoped that, for their own sakes, they will not dare to *speak* against the REVOLUTION, upon the justice and legality of which depends (in part) his present MAJESTY's right to the throne.

---

equity. So also, there is an essential difference betwixt resisting a tyrant, and rebellion; The former is a just and reasonable self-defence; the latter consists in resisting a prince whose administration is just and legal; and this is what denominates it a crime.—Now it is evident, that king *Charles's* government was illegal, and very oppressive, through the greatest part of his reign: And, therefore, to resist him, was no more rebellion, than to oppose any foreign invader, or any other domestic oppressor.

If it be said, that although the parliament which first opposed king *Charles's* measures, and at length took up arms against him, were not guilty of rebellion; yet certainly those persons were, who condemned, and put him to death; even this perhaps is not true. For he had, in fact, *unkinged* himself long before, and had forfeited his title to the allegiance of the people. So that those who put him to death, were, at most only guilty of *murder*; which, indeed, is bad enough, if they were really guilty of *that*; (which is at least disputable.) *Cromwell*, and those who were principally concerned in the (*nominal*) king's death, might possibly have been very wicked and designing men. Nor shall I say any thing in vindication of the reigning *hypocrisy* of those times; or of *Cromwell's* male-administration during the *interregnum*: (for it is *truth*, and not a *party*, that I am speaking for.) But still it may be said, that *Cromwell* and his adherents were not, properly speaking, guilty of *rebellion*; because he, whom they beheaded was not, properly speaking, *their king*; but a *lawless tyrant.*—much less, are the whole body of the nation at that time to be charged with rebellion on that account; for it was no *national act*; it was not done by a *free* parliament. And much less still, is the nation at present, to be charged with the great sin of rebellion, for what their *ancestors* did, (or rather did NOT) a century ago.

But how came the *anniversary* of king *Charles's* death, to be solemnized as a day of fasting and humiliation? The true answer in brief, to which inquiry, is, that this fast was instituted by way of *court* and *complement* to king *Charles* II, upon the *restoration*. All were desirous of making their court to him; of ingratiating themselves; and of making him forget what had been done in opposition to his *father*, so as not to revenge it. To effect this, they ran into the most extravagant professions of affection and loyalty to him, insomuch that he himself said, that it was a *mad* and *hair brain'd* loyalty which they professed. And amongst other strange things, which his first parliament did, they ordered the *Thirtieth* of *January* (the day on which his father was beheaded) to be kept as a day of solemn humiliation, to deprecate the judgments of heaven for the rebellion which the nation had been guilty of, in that which was no national thing; and which was not rebellion in them that did it—Thus they soothed and flattered their new king, at the expence of their liberties:—And were ready to yield up *freely* to *Charles* II, all that enormous power, which they had justly resisted *Charles* I, for usurping to himself.

The last query mentioned, was, Why those of the *episcopal clergy* who are very high in the principles of *ecclesiastical authority*, continue to speak of this unhappy prince as a *great Saint* and a *Martyr*? This, we know, is what they constantly do, especially upon the 30th of *January*;—a day sacred to the *extolling* of *him*, and to the *reproaching* of those who are not of the *established church. Out of the same mouth* on this day, *proceedeth blessing and cursing*;* *there-with bless they their God,* even Charles, *and therewith curse they* the dissenters: And their *tongue can no man tame; it is an unruly evil, full of deadly poison.* King *Charles* is, upon this solemnity, frequently compared to our Lord Jesus Christ, both in respect of the *holiness* of his life, and the greatness and injustice of his *sufferings;* and it is a wonder they do not add something concerning the *merits* of his death also—But *blessed saint* and *royal martyr,* are as humble titles as any that are thought worthy of him.

Now this may, at first view, well appear to be a very strange *phenomenon.* For king *Charles* was really a man black with guilt and *laden with iniquity,*† as appears by his crimes before mentioned. He liv'd a tyrant; and it was the oppression and violence of his reign, that brought him to his untimely and violent end at last. Now what of saintship or martyrdom is there in all this? What of saintship is there in encouraging people to *profane* the *Lord's Day*? What of saintship in falshood and perjury? What of saintship in repeated robberies and depredations? What of saintship in throwing real saints, and glorious patriots, into goals? What of saintship in overturning an excellent civil constitution;—and proudly grasping at an illegal and monstrous power? What of saintship in the murder of thousands of innocent people; and involving a nation in all the calamities of a civil war? And what of martyrdom is there, in a man's bringing an immature and violent

*Jam. iii. 8, 9, 10.
†Isai i. 4.

death upon himself, by *being wicked overmuch*?* Is there any such thing as grace, without goodness? As being a follower of Christ, without following him? As being his disciple, without learning of him to be just and beneficent? Or, as saintship without sanctity?† If not, I fear it will be hard to prove this man a saint. And verily one would be apt to suspect that *that church* must be but *poorly stocked* with saints and martyrs, which is forced to adopt such enormous sinners into her *kalendar*, in order to swell the number.

But to unravel this *mystery of* (*nonsense* as well as of) *iniquity*, which has *already worked* for a *long time* amongst us;‡ or, at least, to give the most probably solution of it; it is to be remembred, that king *Charles*, this *burlesque* upon saintship and martyrdom, though so great an oppressor, was a true friend to the *Church*;—so true a friend to her, that he was very well affected towards the *roman catholics*; and would, probably, have been very willing to unite *Lambeth* and *Rome*. This appears by his marrying a true *daughter* of that true *mother of harlots*;§ which he did with a dispensation from the *Pope*, that supreme BISHOP; to whom when he wrote, he gave the title of MOST HOLY FATHER. His queen was extremely bigotted to all the follies and superstitions, and to the *hierarchy*, of *Rome*; and had a prodigious ascendency over him all his life. It was, in part, owing to this, that he (probably) abetted the massacre of the protestants in *Ireland*; that

*Eccles. vii. 17.

†Is it any wonder that even persons who do not *walk after their own lusts*, should *scoff* at *such saints* as this, both in the *first* and in the *last days*, even *from everlasting to everlasting*? 2 Pet. iii. 3, 4.—But perhaps it will be said, that these things are MYSTERIES, which (although very true in themselves) *lay-understandings* cannot comprehend: Or, indeed, any other persons amongst us, besides those who being INWARDLY MOVED BY THE HOLY GHOST, have taken a trip across the *Atlantic* to obtain *episcopal ordination* and *the indelible character*.—However, if these *consecrated gentlemen* do not quite despair of us, it is hoped that, in the abundance of their charity, they will endeavour to *illucidate* these *dark* points; and, at the same time, explain the creed of *another of their eminent saints*, which we are told, that unless we *believe faithfully*, (i. e. *believingly*) *we cannot be saved*: which creed, (or rather *riddle*) notwithstanding all the labours of the *pious*—and *metaphysical* Dr. *Waterland*, remains somewhat *enigmatical* still.

‡2 Thess. ii. 7.

§Rev. xvii. 5.

he assisted in extirpating the *french* protestants at *Rochelle*; that he all along encouraged *papists*, and popishly effected *clergymen*, in preference to all other persons, and that he upheld that monster of wickedness, ARCH-BISHOP LAUD, and the bishops of his stamp, in all their church-tyranny and diabolical cruelties. In return to his kindness and indulgence in which respects, they caused many of the pulpits throughout the nation, to ring with the divine absolute, indefeasible right of kings; with the praises of *Charles* and his reign; and with the damnable sin of resisting the *Lord's anointed*, let him do what he would. So that not *Christ*, but *Charles*, was commonly preached to the people.—In *plain english*, there seems to have been an impious bargain struck up betwixt the *scepter* and the *surplice*, for enslaving both the *bodies* and *souls* of men. The king appeared to be willing that the clergy should do what they would,—set up a monstrous hierarchy like that of *Rome*,—a monstrous inquisition like that of *Spain* or *Portugal*,—or any thing else which their own pride, and the devil's malice, could prompt them to: *Provided always*, that the clergy would be *tools* to the crown; that they would make the people believe, that kings had God's authority for breaking God's law; that they had a commission from heaven to seize the estates and lives of their subjects at pleasure; and that it was a damnable sin to resist them, even when they did such things as deserved more than damnation.—This appears to be the true key for explaining the *mysterious* doctrine of king *Charles's* saintship and martyrdom. He was a saint, not because he was in his life, a good *man*, but a good *churchman*; not because he was a lover of *holiness*, but the *hierarchy*; not because he was a friend to *Christ*, but the *Craft*. And he was a martyr in his death, not because he bravely suffered death in the cause of truth and righteousness, but because he died an enemy to liberty and the rights of conscience; i. e. not because he died an enemy to *sin*, but *dissenters*. For these reasons it is that all bigotted clergymen, and friends to church-power, paint this man as a saint in his life, though he was such a mighty, such a *royal sinner*; and as a martyr in his death, though he fell a sacrifice only to his own ambition, avarice, and unbounded lust of power. And from prostituting their praise upon king *Charles*, and offering him that incense which is not his due, it is natural for them to make a transition to the dissenters, (as they commonly do) and to load them with that reproach which they do not deserve; they being generally professed enemies both to civil and ecclesiastical tyranny. WE are commonly charged (upon the *Thirtieth of January*) with the guilt of putting the king to death, under a notion that it was our ancestors that did it; and so we are represented in the blackest colours, not only as scismaticks, but also as traitors and rebels and all that is bad. And these *lofty* gentlemen usually rail upon this head, in such a manner as plainly shows, that they are either grosly ignorant of the history of those times which they speak of; or, which is worse, that they are guilty of the most shameful prevarication, slander and falshood.—But every *petty priest*, with a *roll* and a *gown*, thinks he must do something in imitation of his *betters*, in *lawn*, and show himself a *true son* of the church: And thus, through a foolish ambition to appear *considerable*, they only render themselves *contemptible*.

But suppose *our* fore-fathers did kill their *mock* saint and martyr a century ago, what is that to *us* now? If I mistake not, these gentlemen generally preach down the doctrine of the *imputation of Adam's sin to his posterity*, as absurd and unreasonable, notwithstanding they have solemnly subscribed what is equivalent to it in *their own articles of religion*. And therefore one would hardly expect that they would lay the guilt of the king's death upon *us*, altho' *our fore-fathers* had been the only authors of it. But this conduct is much more surprising, when it does not appear that *our* ancestors had any more hand in it than *their own*.—However, bigotry is sufficient to account for this, and many other *phenomena*, which cannot be accounted for in any other way.

Although the observation of this *anniversary* seems to have been (at least) superstitious in its *original*; and although it is often abused to very bad purposes by the established clergy, as they serve themselves of it, to perpetuate strife, a party spirit, and divisions in the christian church; yet it is to be hoped that one good end will be answered by it, quite contrary to their intention: It is to be hoped, that it will prove a standing *memento*, that *Britons* will not be *slaves*; and a warning to all corrupt *councellors* and *ministers*, not to go too far in advising to arbitrary, despotic measures——

To conclude: Let us all learn to be *free*, and to be *loyal*. Let us not profess ourselves vassals to the lawless pleasure of any man on earth. But let us remember, at the same time, government is *sacred*, and not to be *trifled* with. It is our happiness to live under the government of a PRINCE who is satisfied with ruling according to law; as every other *good prince* will—We enjoy under his administration all the liberty that is proper and expedient for us. It becomes us, therefore, to be contented, and dutiful subjects. Let us prize our freedom; but not *use our liberty for a cloke of maliciousness.** There are men who strike at *liberty* under the term *licentiousness*. There are others who aim at *popularity* under the disguise of *patriotism*. Be aware of both. *Extremes* are dangerous. There is at present amongst *us*, perhaps, more danger of the *latter*, than of the *former*. For which reason I would exhort you to pay all due Regard to the government over us; to the KING and all in authority; and to *lead a quiet and peaceable life.*† —And while I am speaking of loyalty to our *earthly Prince*, suffer me just to put you in mind to be loyal also to the supreme RULER of the universe, *by whom kings reign, and princes decree justice.*‡ To which king eternal immortal, invisible, even to the ONLY WISE GOD,§ be all honor and praise, DOMINION and thanksgiving, through JESUS CHRIST our LORD. AMEN.

*1 Pet. ii. 16.
†1 Tim. ii. 2.
‡Prov. viii. 15.
§ 1 Tim. i. 17.

FINIS.

SAMUEL DAVIES

The Nature and Universality of Spiritual Death

EPHES. II. 1, and 5.
—*Who were dead in trespasses and sins.—Even when
we were dead in sins.*

THERE IS a kind of death which we all expect to feel that carries terror in the very sound, and all its circumstances are
shocking to nature. The ghastly countenance, the convulsive
agonies, the expiring groan, the coffin, the grave, the devouring worm, the stupor, the insensibility, the universal inactivity,
these strike a damp to the spirit, and we turn pale at the
thought. With such objects as these in view courage fails, levity looks serious, presumption is dashed, the chearful passions
sink, and all is solemn, all is melancholy. The most stupid and
hardy sinner cannot but be moved to see these things exemplified in others, and when he cannot avoid the prospect, he
is shocked to think that he himself must feel them.

But there is another kind of death little regarded indeed,
little feared, little lamented, which is infinitely more terrible,
the death, not of the body, but of the soul: a death which
does not stupify the limbs but the faculties of the mind: a
death which does not separate the soul and body, and consign
the latter to the grave, but that separates the soul from GOD,
excludes it from all the joys of his presence, and delivers it
over to everlasting misery: a tremendous death indeed! "a
death unto death." The expression of St *Paul* is prodigiously
strong and striking; Θανατος εις Θανατον, Death unto
death, death after death, in a dreadful succession, and the last
more terrible than the first (*a*); and this is the death meant in
my text, "dead in trespasses and sins."

To explain the context and shew you the connection I shall
make two short remarks.

(*a*) 2 Cor. ii. 16.

The one is, that the apostle had observed in the nineteenth and twentieth verses of the foregoing chapter that the same almighty power of GOD which raised CHRIST from the dead, is exerted to enable a sinner to believe. "We believe, says he, according to the working or energy (*a*) of his mighty power which he wrought in CHRIST, when he raised him from the dead." The one as well as the other is an exploit of omnipotence. The exceeding greatness of his mighty power is exerted towards us that believe, as well as it was upon the dead body of CHRIST to restore it to life, after it had been torn and mangled upon the cross, and lain three days and three nights in the grave. What strong language is this! what a forcible illustration! Methinks this passage alone is sufficient to confound all the vanity and self-sufficiency of mortals, and entirely destroy the proud fiction of a self-sprung faith produced by the efforts of degenerate nature. In my text the apostle assigns the reason of this. The same exertion of the same power is necessary in the one case and the other; because, as the body of CHRIST was dead, and had no principle of life in it, so, says he, "ye were dead in trespasses and sins;" and therefore could no more quicken yourselves than a dead body can restore itself to life. "But GOD, verse 4th, who is rich in mercy, for his great love wherewith he loved us;" that GOD, who raised the entombed Redeemer to life again, that same almighty GOD, by a like exertion of the same power, "hath quickened us, verse 5th, even when we were dead in sins;" dead, senseless, inactive, and incapable of animating ourselves. Let any man carefully read these verses, and consider their most natural meaning, and I cannot but think common sense will direct him thus to understand them. The Scriptures were written with a design to be understood; and therefore that sense which is the most natural to a plain unprejudiced understanding is most likely to be true.

The other remark is, That the apostle having pronounced the *Ephesians* dead in sin, while unconverted, in the first verse, passes the same sentence upon himself and the whole body of the *Jews*, notwithstanding their high privileges in the fifth verse. The sense and connection may be discovered in the

(*a*) Ενεργειαν.

following paraphrase: "You *Ephesians* were very lately Heathens, and, while you were in that state you were spiritually dead, and all your actions were *dead works.* In time past ye walked in trespasses and sins, nor were you singular in your course: though it be infinitely pernicious, yet it is the common course of this world, and it is also agreeable to the temper and instigation of that gloomy prince, who has a peculiar power in the region of the air; that malignant spirit who works with dreadful efficacy in the numerous children of disobedience; but this was not the case of you Heathens alone: we also who are *Jews,* notwithstanding our many religious advantages, and even I myself, notwithstanding my high privileges and unblameable life as a Pharisee, we also, I say, had our conversation in times past among the children of disobedience; we *all,* as well as they, walked in the lusts of the flesh, fulfilling the desires and inclinations (*a*) of our sensual flesh, and of our depraved minds; for these were tainted with spiritual wickedness, independent upon our animal passions and appetites, and we were all, even *by nature,* children of wrath, even as others: in this respect we *Jews* were just like the rest of mankind, corrupt from our very birth, transgressors from the womb, and liable to the wrath of GOD. Our external relation and privileges as the peculiar people of GOD, distinguished with a religion from heaven, makes no distinction between us and others in this matter. As we are all children of disobedience by our lives, so we are all, without exception, children of wrath by nature: but when we were all dead in sins, when *Jews* and *Gentiles* were equally dead to GOD, then, even then, GOD who is rich in mercy had pity upon us; 'he quickened us;' he inspired us with a new and spiritual life by his own almighty power, which raised the dead body of CHRIST from the grave. 'He quickened us together with CHRIST:' We received our life by virtue of our union with him as our vital head, who was raised to an immortal life that he might quicken dead souls by those influences of his Spirit, which he purchased by his death; and therefore by grace are ye saved. It is the purest, richest, freest grace, that ever such dead souls as we were made alive to GOD, and not suffered to remain dead for ever."

(*a*) Θελήματα.

This is the obvious meaning and connection of these verses, and we now proceed to consider the text, "Dead in trespasses and sins:" you dead, we dead, *Jews* and *Gentiles*, all "dead together in trespasses and sins." A dismal, mortifying character! "This one place, says *Beza*, like a thunderbolt, dashes all mankind down to the dust, great and proud as they are; for it pronounces their nature not only hurt but *dead* by sin, and therefore liable to wrath (*a*)."

Death is a state of insensibility and inactivity, and a dead man is incapable of restoring himself to life, therefore the condition of an unconverted sinner must have some resemblance to such a state in order to support the bold metaphor here used by the apostle. To understand it aright we must take care on the one hand that we do not explain it away in flattery to ourselves, or in compliment to the pride of human nature: and on the other hand that we do not carry the similitude too far, so as to lead into absurdities, and contradict matter of fact.

The metaphor must be understood with several limitations or exceptions; for it is certain there is a wide difference between the spiritual death of the soul, and the natural death of the body, particularly in this respect, that death puts an entire end to all the powers, actions, and sensations of our animal nature universally with regard to all objects of every kind; but a soul dead in sin is only *partially* dead; that is, it is dead only with regard to a certain *kind* of sensations and exercises, but in the mean time it may be all life and activity about other things. It is alive, sensible, and vigorous about earthly objects and pursuits; these raise its passions and engage its thoughts. It has also a dreadful power and facility of sinning, though this is not its life but its disease, its death, like the tendency of a dead body to corruption. It can likewise exercise its intellectual powers, and make considerable improvements in science. A sinner dead in trespasses and sins may be a living treasury of knowledge, an universal scholar, a profound philosopher, and even a great divine, as far as mere speculative knowledge can render him such, nay, he is capable of many

(*a*) Hoc uno loco, quasi fulmine, totus homo, quantus quantus est prosternitur. Neque enim naturam dicit læsam, sed *mortuam*, per peccatum; ideoque iræ obnoxiam.

sensations and impressions from religious objects, and of per-
forming all the external duties of religion. He is able to read,
to hear, to pray, to meditate upon divine things; nay, he may
be an instructor of others, and preach perhaps with extensive
popularity: he may have a form of godliness, and obtain a
name to live among men: he is in some measure able, and it
is his duty to attend upon the means GOD has instituted for
quickening him with spiritual life, and GOD deals with him as
with a rational creature, by laws, sanctions, promises, expos-
tulations, and invitations: these concessions I make, not only
to give you the sense of the text, but also to prevent the abuse
of the doctrine, and anticipate some objections against it, as
though it were an encouragement to continue idle, and use
no means to obtain spiritual life; or as tho' it rendered all the
means of grace needless and absurd, like arguments to the
dead to restore themselves to life. But, notwithstanding all
these concessions, it is a melancholy truth that an unregenerate sinner is dead. Though he can commit sin with greediness,
though he is capable of animal actions, and secular pursuits,
nay, though he can employ his mind even about intellectual
and spiritual things, and is capable of performing the external
duties of religion, yet there is something in religion with regard to which he is entirely dead: there is a kind of spiritual
life of which he is entirely destitute: he is habitually insensible
with regard to things divine and eternal: he has no activity, no
vigour in the pure, spiritual, and vital exercises of religion: he
has no prevailing bent of mind towards them: he has not
those views and apprehensions of things which a soul spiritually alive would necessarily receive and entertain: he is destitute of those sacred affections, that joy, that love, that desire,
that hope, that fear, that sorrow, which are as it were the innate passions of the new man. In short, he is so inactive, so
listless, so insensible in these respects, that death, which puts
an end to all action and sensation, is a proper emblem of his
state; and this is the meaning of the apostle in my text. He is
also utterly unable to quicken himself. He may indeed use
means in some sort, but to implant a vital principle in his
soul, to give himself vivid sensations of divine things, and
make himself alive towards GOD, this is entirely beyond his
utmost ability: this is as peculiarly the work of almighty power

as the resurrection of a dead body from the grave. As to this death it is brought upon him by, and consists in "trespasses and sins." The innate depravity and corruption of the heart, and the habits of sin contracted and confirmed by repeated indulgences of inbred corruption, these are the poisonous, deadly things that have slain the soul; these have entirely indisposed and disabled it for living religion. "Trespasses and sins" are the grave, the corrupt effluvia, the malignant damps, the rottenness of a dead soul: it lies dead, senseless, inactive, buried "in trespasses and sins." "Trespasses and sins" render it ghastly, odious, abominable, a noisome putrefaction before an holy GOD, like a rotten carcass, or a mere mass of corruption: the vilest lusts, like worms, riot upon and devour it, but it feels them not, nor can it lift a hand to drive the vermin off. Such mortifying ideas as these may be contained in the striking metaphor, "dead in trespasses and sins;" and I hope you now understand its general meaning.

If you would know what has turned my thoughts to this subject I will candidly tell you, though with a sorrowful heart. I am sure, if any objects within the compass of human knowledge have a tendency to make the deepest impressions upon our minds, they are those things which Christianity teaches us concerning GOD, concerning ourselves and a future state; and if there be any exercises which should call forth all the life and powers of our souls into action, they are those of a religious nature: but, alas! I often find a strange, astonishing stupor, and listlessness about these things. In this I am not singular; the best among us complain of the same thing; the most *lively* Christians feel this unaccountable languor and insensibility; and the generality are evidently destitute of all habitual concern about them: they are all alive in the pursuit of pleasure, riches, or honours; their thoughts are easily engaged, and their affections raised by such things as these; but the concerns of religion, which above all other things are adapted to make impressions upon them, and stir up all the life within them, seem to have little or no effect. When I have made this observation with respect to others, and felt the melancholy confirmation of it in my own breast, I have really been struck with amazement, and ready to cry out, "Lord what is this that has befallen me, and the rest of my fellow-mortals? what can be the cause of such a conduct in a rational nature, to be active and eager about trifles, and stupid and careless about matters of infinite importance? O whence is this strange infatuation!" Thus I have been shocked at this astonishing fact, and I could account for it no other way but by reflecting that we have all been "dead in trespasses and sins." In such a solemn hour the apostle's expression does not seem at all too strong. I have no scruple at all to pronounce, not only from the authority of an apostle, but from the evidence of the thing, that I, and all around me, yea, and all the sons of men have been dead, in the spiritual sense utterly dead. Multitudes among us, yea, the generality are dead still; hence the stillness about religion among us; hence the stupor, the carelessness about eternal things, the thoughtless neglect of GOD, the insensibility under his providential dispensations, the impenitence, the presumption that so much prevails. GOD has indeed, out of the great love wherewith he loved us, quickened some of us, even when we were dead in sins, and we have a little life, some vital sensations and impressions at times, but O! how little, how superficial, how much of a deadly stupor yet remains! how little life in prayer, in hearing, or in the nearest approach to the living GOD! The reflection is shocking, but, alas, it is too true; consult your own hearts and you will find it even so. Animal life seems to be a gradual thing; it gradually grows in an infant, it is perfect in mature age, and in old age it gradually decays, till all is gone; but how small is the degree of life, when the fœtus is just animated, or the infant born into the world! but little superior to that of a plant or an oyster: what faint sensations, what obscure and languid perceptions, what feeble motions! Such are the children of grace in the present state. Spiritual life is gradual; it is infused in regeneration; but O! how far from perfection while on this side heaven! Alas! the best of us are like the poor traveller that fell among thieves, and was left half dead: however, it is an unspeakable mercy to have the least principle of spiritual life, and we should prize it more than crowns and empires.

If you would know my design in choosing this subject, it is partly for the conviction of sinners, that they may be alarmed with their deplorable condition, which is the first step towards their being quickened; partly to rouse the children of grace to seek more life from their vital head; and partly to display the rich grace of GOD in quickening such dead sinners, and bestowing upon them a spiritual and immortal life; and surely nothing can inflame our gratitude and raise our wonder more than the consideration that we were dead in trespasses and sins! If I may but answer these ends it will be an unspeakable blessing to us all. And O that divine grace may honour this humble attempt of a poor creature, at best but half alive, with success! I hope, my brethren, you will hear seriously for it is really a most serious subject.

You have seen that the metaphorical expression in my text is intended to represent the stupidity, inactivity, and impotence of unregenerate sinners about divine things. This truth I might confirm by argument and scripture-authority, but I think it may be a better method for popular conviction to prove and illustrate it from plain instances of the temper and conduct of sinners about the concerns of religion, as this may force the conviction upon them from undoubted matters of fact and their own experience. This therefore is the method I intend to pursue, and my time will allow me to particularize only the following instances.

I. Consider the excellency of the divine Being, the sum total, the great original of all perfections. How infinitely worthy is he of the adoration of all his creatures! how deserving of their most intense thoughts, and most ardent affections! If majesty and glory can strike us with awe and veneration does not *Jehovah* demand it, who is clothed with majesty and glory as with a garment, and before whom all the inhabitants of the earth are as grasshoppers, as nothing, as less than nothing, and vanity? If wisdom excites our pleasing wonder, here is an unfathomable depth. O the depth of the riches of the wisdom and knowledge of GOD! If goodness, grace, and mercy attract our love and gratitude, here these amiable perfections shine in their most alluring glories. If justice strikes a damp to the guilty, here is justice in all its tremendous majesty. If veracity, if candor, if any, or all of the moral virtues engage our esteem, here they all center in their highest perfection. If the presence of a king strikes a reverence, if the eye of his judge awes the criminal, and restrains him from offending, certainly we should fear before the Lord all the day, for we are surrounded with his omnipresence, and he is the Inspector and Judge of all our thoughts and actions. If riches excite desire, here are unsearchable riches: if happiness has charms that draw all the world after it, here is an unbounded ocean of happiness; here is the only complete portion for an immortal mind. Men are affected with these things in one another, tho' found in a very imperfect degree. Power awes and commands; virtue and goodness please; beauty charms; justice strikes with solemnity and terror; a bright genius is admired; a benevolent merciful temper is loved: thus men are affected with created excellencies. Whence it is then they are so stupidly unaffected with the supreme original excellencies of *Jehovah*? Here, my brethren, turn your eyes inward upon yourselves, and enquire, are not several of you conscious that, though you have passions for such objects as these, and you are easily moved by them, yet, with regard to the perfections of the supreme and best of beings, your hearts are habitually senseless and unaffected. It is not an easy thing to make impressions upon you by them; and what increases the wonder, and aggravates your guilt, is, that you are thus senseless and unaffected, when you believe and profess that these perfections are really in GOD, and that in the highest degree possible. In other cases you can love what appears amiable, you revere what is great and majestic, you eagerly desire and pursue what is valuable, and tends to your happiness; and all this you do freely, spontaneously, vigorously, by the innate inclination and tendency of your nature, without reluctance, without compulsion, nay without persuasion; but as to GOD and all his perfections you are strangely insensible, backward, and averse. Where is there one being that has any confessed excellency in the compass of human knowledge that does not engage more of the thoughts and affections of mankind than the glorious and ever-blessed GOD? The sun, moon, and stars have had more worshippers than the uncreated fountain of light from which they derive their lustre. Kings, and ministers of state, have more punctual homage, and frequent applications made to them than the King of kings, and Lord of lords. Created enjoyments are more eagerly pursued than the supreme good. Search all the world over, and you will find but very little motions of heart towards GOD; little love, little desire, little searching after him. You will often indeed see him honoured with the compliment of a bended knee, and a few heartless words under the name of a prayer, but where is the heart, where are the thoughts, where the affections? These run wild through the world, and are scattered among a thousand other objects. The heart has no prevailing tendency toward GOD, the thoughts are shy of him, the affections have no innate propensity to him. In short, in this respect the whole man is out of order: here he does not at all act like himself; here are no affectionate thoughts, no delightful meditations, no ardent desires, no eager pursuits and vigorous endeavours, but all is listless, stupid, indisposed, inactive, and averse; and what is the matter? "Lord! what is this that has seized the souls of thine own offspring, that they are thus utterly disordered towards thee!" The reason is, they are dead, "dead in trespasses and sins." It is impossible a living soul should be so stupid and unaffected with such an object: it must be a dead soul *that* has no feeling. Yes, sinners, this is the melancholy reason why you are so thoughtless, so unconcerned, so senseless about the GOD that made you: you are dead. And what is the reason that you who have been begotten again to a spiritual life, and who are united to CHRIST as your vital head, what is the reason that you so often feel such languishments, that the pulse of spiritual life beats so faint and irregular, and that its motions are so feeble and slow? All this you feel and lament, but how comes it to pass? what can be the cause that you who have indeed tasted that the Lord is gracious, and are sensible that he is all-glorious and lovely, and your only happiness, O! what can be the cause, that you, of all men in the world, should be so little engaged to him! Alas! the cause is you have been dead, and the deadly stupor has not yet left you: you have (blessed be the quickening spirit of CHRIST!) you have received a little life; but, alas! it is a feeble spark; it finds the principles of death still strong in your constitution; these it must struggle with, and by them it is often borne down, suppressed, and just expiring. Walk humbly then, and remember your shame, that you were once dead, and children of wrath, even as others. The carelessness and indisposition of the soul toward the supreme excellence will appear yet more evident and astonishing, if we consider,

II. The august and endearing relations the great and blessed GOD sustains to us, and the many ways he has taken to make dutiful and grateful impressions upon our hearts. What tender endearments are contained in the relation of a *Father*! This he bears to us: "he made us, and not we ourselves." Our bodies indeed are produced in a succession from *Adam* by generation, but who was it that began the series? It was the Almighty, who formed the first man of the dust: it was he who first put the succession of causes in motion, and therefore he is the grand original cause, and the whole chain depends upon him. Who was it that first established the laws of generation, and still continues them in force? It is the all-creating Parent of nature, and without him men would have been no more able to produce one another than stones or clods of earth. As to our souls, the principal part of our persons, GOD is their immediate author, without the least concurrence of secondary causes. Hence he is called the Father of your spirits in a peculiar sense (*a*), and he assumes the endearing name of "the GOD of the spirits of all flesh (*b*)." Now the name of a father is wont to carry some endearment and authority. Children, especially in their young and helpless years, are fond of their father; their little hearts beat with a thousand grateful passions towards him; they love to be with him, to be dandled on his knees, and fondled in his arms, and they fly to him upon every appearance of danger; but if GOD be a father, where is his honour? here, alas! the filial passions are senseless and immovable. It is but a little time since we came from his creating hand, and yet we have forgotten him. It seems unnatural for his own offspring to enquire "where is GOD my Maker?" They shew no fondness for him, no affectionate veneration, and no humble confidence; their hearts are dead towards him, as though there were no such being, or no such near relation subsisting between them. In childhood a rattle, or a straw, or any trifle, is more thought of than their

(*a*) Heb. xii. 9.
(*b*) Numb. xvi. 22.

heavenly Father: in riper years their vain pleasures and secular pursuits command more of their affections than their divine original and only happiness. Compare your natural temper towards your heavenly Father, and towards your earthly parents, and how wide is the difference! Nature works strong in your hearts towards them, but towards him all the filial passions are dull and dead; and why? alas! the reason is, you "are dead in trespasses and sins." But this relation of a Father is not the only relation our GOD sustains to you; he is your supreme *King*, to whom you owe allegiance; your *Lawgiver*, whose will is the rule of your conduct; and your *Judge*, who will call you to an account, and reward or punish you according to your works, but how unnatural is it to men to revere the most high GOD under these august characters! Where is there a king upon earth, however weak or tyrannical, but is more regarded by his subjects than the King of heaven by the generality of men? Were ever such excellent laws contemned and violated? Did ever criminals treat their Judge with so much neglect and contempt? And are these souls alive to GOD who thus treat him? No. Alas! "they are dead in trespasses and sins:" however lively they are towards other things, yet in this respect they are seized with a deadly stupor. GOD is also our *Guardian* and *Deliverer*, and from how many dangers has he preserved us, from how many calamities has he delivered us! Dangers, distresses, and deaths crowd upon us and surround us in every age and every place: the air, the earth, the sea, and every element are pregnant with numberless principles of pain and death ready to seize and destroy us: sickness and death swarm around us; nay, they lie in ambush in our own constitution, and are perpetually undermining our lives, and yet our divine *Guardian* preserves us for months and years unhurt, untouched; or if he suffers the calamity to fall, or death to threaten, he flies to our deliverance; and how many salvations of this kind has he wrought for us, salvations from accidents, from sicknesses, from pain, from sorrows, from death; salvations for our persons and our possessions, for ourselves, and for our friends and relations; salvations from dangers seen and unseen; salvations in infancy, in youth, and in maturer years! These things we cannot deny without the most stupid ignorance, and an atheistical disbelief of divine Providence. Now such repeated, such long-continued, such unmerited favours as these would not pass for nothing between man and man. We have hearts to feel such obligations; nay, the ten thousandth, the millionth part of such gracious care and goodness would be gratefully resented, and thankfully acknowledged. Indeed it is impossible we should receive even this small, this very small proportion of favours from men in comparison of what we receive from GOD; and even when they are the instruments of our deliverance he is the original author. But after all, is there a natural aptitude in the hearts of men to think of their gracious Guardian and Saviour? Does the principle of gratitude naturally lead them to love him, and to make thankful acknowledgments to him? Alas! no. They may indeed feel some transient, superficial workings of gratitude when under the fresh sense of some remarkable deliverance, but these impressions soon wear off, and they become as thoughtless and stupid as ever. But let a man, like yourselves, save you from some great distress, you will always gratefully remember him, think of him often with pleasure, and take all opportunities of returning his kindness, especially if your deliverer was much your superior, and independent upon you, if you had forfeited his favour, provoked him, and incurred his displeasure: great favours from such an one would make impressions upon the most obdurate heart. But tho' GOD be infinitely superior to us, and it is nothing to him what becomes of us, though we have rebelled against him, and deserve his vengeance, yet ten thousand deliverances from his hands have little or no effect upon the hearts of men: all these cannot bring them to think of him, or love him as much as they do a friend, or a common benefactor of their own species: and does such stupid ingratitude discover any spiritual life in them? No; they are dead in this respect, tho' they are all alive to those passions that terminate upon created objects. Farther, GOD is the *Benefactor* of mankind, not only in delivering them from dangers and calamities, but in bestowing unnumbered *positive* blessings upon them. Here I cannot pretend to be particular, for the list of blessings is endless, and it will be the happy employment of an eternity to recollect and enumerate them. What an extensive and well-furnished world has our GOD formed for our accommodation! For us he has enriched the sun with light and heat, and the earth with fruitfulness. The numerous inhabitants of every element, the plants, minerals, and beasts of the earth, the fishes of the sea, the fowls of the air, are all rendering their service to man; some afford him food, and others work for him: the winds and seas, fire and water, stones and trees, all conspire to be useful to him. Our divine Benefactor crowns us with the blessings of liberty, of society, of friendship, and the most endearing relations: he preserves our health, gives us "rain from heaven, and fruitful seasons, and fills our hearts with food and gladness." In short, he gives us life, and breath, and all things; every day, every hour, every moment has arrived to us richly freighted with blessings; blessings have resided with us at home, and attended us abroad; blessings presented themselves ready for our enjoyment as soon as we entered into the world; then GOD provided hands to receive us, knees to support us, breasts to suckle us, and parents to guard and cherish us; blessings have grown up with us, and given such constant attendance, that they are become familiar to us, and are the inseparable companions of our lives. It is no new or unusual thing to us to see an illustrious sun rising to give us the day, to enjoy repose in the night, to rise refreshed and vigorous in the morning, to see our tables spread with plenty, the trees covered with fruit, the fields with grain, and various forms of animals growing up for our support or service. These are such familiar blessings to us, that they too often seem things of course, or necessary appendages of our being. What a crowd of blessings have crowned the present morning! You and yours are alive and well, you have not come hither ghastly and pining with hunger, or agonizing with pain. How many refreshing draughts of air have you drawn this morning, how many sprightly and regular pulses have beat through your frame, how many easy motions have you performed with hands, feet, eyes, tongue, and other members of your body, and are not all these favours from GOD? yes undoubtedly; and thus has he gone on blessing you all your days, without any interruption at all in many of these particulars of kindness, and with but very little in the rest. Sinful and miserable as this world is it is a treasury rich in blessings, a store-house full of provisions, a dwelling well furnished for the accommodation of mortals, and all by the care, and at the expence of that gracious GOD who first made and still preserves it what it is. Lord, whence is it then that the inhabitants forget and neglect thee, as though they were not at all obliged to thee? O whence is it that they love thy gifts, and yet disregard the giver; that they think less of thee than of an earthly father or friend, or an human benefactor; that there should be so little gratitude towards thee, that of all benefactors thou shouldst be the least acknowledged, that the benefactors of nations, and even of private persons, in instances unworthy to be mentioned with those of thy goodness, should be celebrated, and even adored, while thou art neglected, thine agency overlooked, and thy goodness forgotten? O whence is this strange phœnomenon, this unaccountable, unprecedented stupidity and ingratitude in reasonable creatures! Surely, if they had any life, any sensation in this respect, they would not be capable of such a conduct; but they are dead, dead to all the generous sensations of gratitude to GOD: and as a dead corpse feels no gratitude to those that perform the last friendly office, and cover it with earth, so a dead soul stands unmoved under all the profusion of blessings which heaven pours upon it.

The blessings I have mentioned, which are confined to the present state, are great, and deserve our wonder and thanksgiving, especially considering that they are bestowed upon a race of rebellious, ungrateful creatures, who deserve the severest vengeance: but there is a set of blessings yet unmentioned, of infinitely greater importance, in which all others are swallowed up, by the glory of which they are obscured, like the stars of night by the rising sun. To some of our race GOD has given crowns and kingdoms. For *Israel* JEHOVAH wrought the most astonishing miracles; seas and rivers opened to make way for them; rocks burst into springs of water to quench their thirst; the clouds poured down manna and fed them with bread from heaven: their GOD delivered *Daniel* from the jaws of hungry lions, and his three companions from the burning fiery furnace. He has restored health to the sick, sight to the blind, and life to the dead. These blessings and deliverances have something majestic and striking in them, and had we been the subjects of them we could not but have regarded them as great and singular, but what are these in comparison of GOD's gift of his Son, and the blessings he has purchased? his Son, who is of greater value, and dearer to him than ten thousand worlds; his beloved Son, in whom he is well pleased; him has he given for us, given up to three and thirty years of the most mortifying abasement, and an incessant conflict with the severest trials, given up to death, and all the ignominy and agonies of crucifixion. Thus has GOD loved our world! and never was there such a display of love in heaven or on earth. You can no more find love equal to this among creatures than you can find among them the infinite power that formed the universe out of nothing. This will stand upon record to all eternity, as the unprecedented, unparalelled, inimitable love of GOD. And it appears the more illustrious when we consider that this unspeakable gift was given to sinners, to rebels, to enemies, that were so far from deserving it, that, on the other hand, it is a miracle of mercy that they are not all groaning for ever under the tremendous weight of his justice. O that I could say something becoming this love; something that might do honour to it! but, alas! the language of mortals was formed for lower subjects. This love passes all description and all knowledge. Consider also what rich blessings CHRIST has purchased for us; purchased not with such corruptible things as silver and gold, but with his own precious blood: the price recommends and endears the blessings, though they are so great in themselves as to need no such recommendation. What can be greater or more suitable blessings to persons in our circumstances, than pardon for the guilty, redemption for slaves, righteousness and justification for the condemned, sanctification for the unholy, rest for the weary, comfort for mourners, the favour of GOD for rebels and exiles, strength for the impotent, protection for the helpless, everlasting happiness for the heirs of hell, and, to sum up all, grace and glory, and every good thing, and all the unsearchable riches of CHRIST for the wretched and miserable, the poor, and blind, and naked! These are blessings indeed, and in comparison of them all the riches of the world are impoverished, and vanish to nothing; and all these blessings are published, offered freely, indefinitely offered to you, to me, to the greatest sinner on earth, in the gospel; and we are allowed,— *allowed* did I say? we are *invited* with the utmost importunity,

intreated with the most compassionate tenderness and conde-
scension, and *commanded* by the highest authority upon pain
of eternal damnation to accept the blessings presented to us:
and what reception does all this love meet with in our world!
I tremble to think of it. It is plain these things are proposed to
a world dead in sin; for they are all still, all unmoved, all senseless under such a revelation of infinite grace; mankind know
not what it is to be moved, melted, transported with the love
of a crucified Saviour, till divine grace visits their hearts, and
forms them into new creatures: they feel no eager solicitude,
nay, not so much as a willingness to receive these blessings, till
they become willing by almighty power: and judge ye, my
brethren, whether they are not *dead* souls that are proof even
against the love of GOD in CHRIST, that are not moved and
melted by the agonies of his cross, that are careless about such
inestimable blessings as these? Has that soul any spiritual life
in it, that can sit senseless under the cross of JESUS, that can
forget him, neglect him, dishonour him, after all his love and
all his sufferings; that feels a prevailing indifference and languor towards him; that loves him less than an earthly friend,
and seeks him with less eagerness than gold and silver? Is not
every generous passion, every principle of gratitude quite extinct in such a spirit? It may be alive to other objects, but towards this it is dead, and alas! is not this the common case! O
look round the world, and what do you see but a general neglect of the blessed JESUS, and all the blessings of his gospel?
How cold, how untoward, how reluctant, how averse are the
hearts of men towards him; how hard to persuade them to
think of him and love him! Try to persuade men to give over
their sins which grieve him, dishonour him, and were the
cause of his death; try to engage them to devote themselves
entirely to him, and live to his glory, alas! you try in vain; their
hearts still continue cold and hard as a stone; try to persuade
them to murder or robbery, and you are more likely to prevail.
Suffer me, in my astonishment, to repeat this most melancholy truth again; the generality of mankind are habitually
careless about the blessed JESUS; they will not seek him, nor
give him their hearts and affections, tho' they must perish for
ever by their neglect of him! Astonishing, and most lamentable, that ever such perverseness and stupidity should seize

the soul of man! Methinks I could here take up a lamentation over human nature, and fall on my knees with this prayer for my fellow-men. "Father of spirits, and Lord of life, quicken, O quicken these dead souls!" O, sirs, while we see death all around us, and feel it benumbing our own souls, who can help the most bitter wailing and lamentation; who can restrain himself from crying to the great Author of life for a happy resurrection! While the valley of dry bones lies before me, while the carnage, the charnel-house of immortal souls strikes my sight all around me far and wide, how can I forbear crying, "Come from the four winds, O breath; breathe upon these slain, that they may live?" But to return from this digression, into which I was unavoidably hurried by the horror of the subject, I would observe farther, that kind usage and pleasing treatment may not be always best for such creatures as we are: fatherly severities and chastisements, though not agreeable to us, yet may be necessary and conducive to our greatest good. Accordingly GOD has tried the force of chastisements to make impressions upon our hearts: these indeed have been but few in comparison of his more agreeable dispensations; yet recollect whether you have not frequently felt his rod. Have you not languished under sickness and pain, and been brought within a near view of the king of terrors? Have you not suffered the bereavement of friends and relations, and met with losses, adversity, and disappointments? Others have felt still greater calamities in a closer succession, and with fewer mercies intermixed. These things, one would think, would immediately bring men to regard the hand that smites them, and make them sensible of their undutiful conduct, which has procured the correction: these are like the application of fire to one in a lethargy, to awaken him to life; but alas! under all these afflictions, the stupor and insensibility still remain. Sinners groan by reason of oppression, but it is not natural for them to enquire, "Where is GOD my Maker, that giveth songs in the night?" It is not natural for them to repent of their undutiful conduct and amend; or, if they are awakened to some little sense, while the painful rod of the Almighty is yet upon them, as soon as it is removed they become as hardened and senseless as ever. And is not a state of death a very proper representation of such sullen, incorrigible stupidity? Living souls have very tender sensations; one touch of their heavenly Father's hand makes deep impressions upon them; they tremble at his frown, they fall and weep at his feet, they confess their offences, and mourn over them; they fly to the arms of his mercy to escape the impending blow; and thus would all do were they not quite destitute of spiritual life.

I have materials sufficient for a discourse of some hours, but at present I must abruptly drop the subject: however, I cannot dismiss you without making a few reflections. And

1. What a strange affecting view does this subject give us of this assembly! I doubt not but I may accommodate the text to some of you with this agreeable addition, "You hath he quickened, though you were once dead in trespasses and sins." Though the vital pulse beats faint and irregular, and your spiritual life is but very low, yet, blessed be GOD, you are not entirely dead: you have some living sensations, some lively and vigorous exercises in religion. On the other hand, I doubt not but some of you not only were, but still are "dead in trespasses and sins." It is not to be expected in our world, at least not before the millennium, that we shall see such a mixed company together, and all living souls. Here then is the difference between you; some of you are spiritually alive, and some of you are spiritually dead: here the living and the dead are blended together in the same assembly, on the same seat, and united in the nearest relations: here sits a dead soul, there another, and there another, and a few living souls are scattered here and there among them: here is a dead parent and a living child, or a dead child and a living parent: here life and death (O shocking!) are united in the bonds of conjugal love, and dwell under the same roof: here is a dead servant and a living master; and there a dead master (O terrible!) commands a living servant. Should I trace the distinction beyond this assembly into the world we shall find a family here and there that have a little life; perhaps one, perhaps two discover some vital symptoms; but O what crowds of dead families! all dead together, and no endeavours used to bring one another to life; a death-like silence about eternal things, a deadly stupor and insensibility reign among them; they breathe out no desires and prayers after GOD; nor does the vital pulse of love beat in their hearts towards him; but, on the contrary, their souls are putri-

fying in sin, which is very emphatically called *corruption* by the sacred writers; they are over-run and devoured by their lusts, as worms insult and destroy the dead body. Call to them they will not awake; thunder the terrors of the Lord in their ears they will not hear; offer them all the blessings of the gospel they will not stretch out the hand of faith to receive them: lay the word of GOD, the bread of life, before them, they have no appetite for it. In short, the plain symptoms of death are upon them: the animal is alive, but alas! the spirit is dead towards GOD. And what an affecting, melancholy view does this give of this assembly, and of the world in general! "O that my head were waters, and mine eyes fountains of tears, that I might weep day and night for the slain of the daughter of my people!" Weep not for the afflicted, weep not over ghastly corpses dissolving into their original dust, but O weep for dead souls. Should GOD now strike all those persons dead in this assembly whose souls are "dead in trespasses and sins," should he lay them all in pale corpses before us, like *Ananias* and *Sapphira* at the apostle's feet, what numbers of you would never return from this house more, and what lamentations would there be among the surviving few! One would lose a husband or a wife, another a son or a daughter, another a father or a mother, and alas! would not some whole families be swept off together, all blended in one promiscuous death! Such a sight as this would strike terror into the hardiest heart among you. But what is this to a company of rational spirits slain and dead in trespasses and sins? How deplorable and inexpressibly melancholy a sight this! Therefore,

2. "Awake thou that sleepest, and arise from dead, that CHRIST may give thee light." This call is directed to you dead sinners, which is a sufficient warrant for me to exhort and persuade you. The principle of reason is still alive in you; you are also sensible of your own interest, and feel the workings of self-love. It is GOD alone that can quicken you, but he effects this by a power that does not exclude, but attends rational instructions and persuasions to your understanding. Therefore, though I am sure you will continue dead still if left to yourselves, yet with some trembling hopes that his power may accompany my feeble words, and impregnate them with life, I call upon, I intreat, I charge you sinners to rouse yourselves

out of your dead sleep, and seek to obtain spiritual life. Now, while my voice sounds in your ears, now, this moment waft up this prayer, "Lord, pity a dead soul, a soul that has been dead for ten, twenty, thirty, forty years, or more, and lain corrupting in sin, and say unto me, Live: from this moment let me live unto thee." Let this prayer be still upon your hearts: keep your souls always in a supplicating posture, and who knows but that he, who raised *Lazarus* from the grave, may give you a spiritual resurrection to a more important life? But if you wilfully continue your security expect in a little time to suffer the second death; the mortification will become incurable; and then, though you will be still dead to GOD, yet you will be "tremblingly alive all over" to the sensations of pain and torture. O that I could gain but this one request of you, which your own interest so strongly enforces! but alas! it has been so often refused that to expect to prevail is to hope against hope.

3. Let the children of GOD be sensible of their great happiness in being made spiritually alive. Life is a principle, a capacity necessary for enjoyments of any kind. Without animal life you would be as incapable of animal pleasures as a stone or a clod, and without spiritual life you can no more enjoy the happiness of heaven than a beast or a devil. This therefore is a preparative, a previous qualification, and a sure pledge and earnest of everlasting life. How highly then are you distinguished, and what cause have you for gratitude and praise!

4. Let us all be sensible of this important truth that it is entirely by grace we are saved. This is the inference the apostle expressly makes from this doctrine; and he is so full of it, that he throws it into a parenthesis (verse 5th) though it breaks the connection of his discourse, and as soon as he has room he resumes it again, (verse 8th) and repeats it over and over in various forms in the compass of a few verses. "By grace are ye saved.—By grace are you saved through faith.—It is the gift of GOD;—not of yourselves,—not of works," (ver. 9th). This, you see, is an inference that seemed of great importance to the apostle, and what can more naturally follow from the premises? If we were once dead in sin, certainly it is owing to the freest grace that we have been quickened, therefore, when we survey the change, let us cry "Grace, grace unto it."

SAMUEL FINLEY

The Madness of Mankind

Represented in a Sermon Preached
in the New Presbyterian Church in Philadelphia
on the 9th of June, 1754.

ECCLES. ix. 3.
*—And Madness is in their Heart while they live,
and after that they go to the Dead.*

WHOEVER seriously views and wisely considers the Manners of Mankind, and brings them to the Test of right Reason, will be forced to receive the same melancholy Idea of them, represented in this Text. The Words are *Solomon's*, who was not only an indefatigable Student of Nature, but an accurate Observer of divine Providence, of the Conduct of Men, and the several Consequences of Actions, divine and human. He here tells us the Result of his Researches respecting these. As to *Providence*, that though God has a special Regard to the Holy and Good; yet in external Things he makes no Difference; but *all Things come alike to all.* As to *Mankind*, that they take Occasion from these promiscuous Dispensations to commit Wickedness without Reserve: *Their Heart is full of Evil*: for they observe, that *such as work Wickedness are set up, and they who tempt God are even delivered.* Mal. iii. 15. This has sometimes been puzzling to the Pious, but has struck the Ungodly with Madness. Hence it comes that *Madness is in their Heart while they live.*

Madness is a State of Irregularity and Discomposure. The Person affected with it, is not fixed in his Purpose; is not influenced in his Conduct by the most engaging Motives; pays no Regard to the Dictates of right Reason; nor is careful about what is decorous, profitable, disadvantageous, or dangerous.

Now we are assured, by unerring Truth, that this is the

State of the *Sons of Men*. 'Tis true, they make high Pretences to Wisdom, and have a Shew of it; but *the Wisdom of this World is Foolishness with God*. 1. Cor. iii. 19. If Madness were concealed in the Heart we could not discover it: But *out of the Abundance of the Heart the Mouth speaketh*; Matth. xii. 34. and so by Men's Words and Actions we come to know what is in their Hearts. Hence, a Course of Life, contrary to right Reason, and just Rules of Conduct, will evidence Heart-Madness.

In treating this Subject, I am naturally led to shew wherein the Madness of human Hearts discovers itself. This cannot be done, but by mentioning particular Instances of human Conduct.

And as I apprehend, that the Method of such a Narration is in a great Measure arbitrary, I shall not attempt a nice Arrangement of the general Heads in natural Order; but propose them as they occur. And,

I. Precipitant Conclusions concerning Persons, Things, or Opinions, formed without Evidence, and often in Defiance of Demonstration to the contrary, discover a Degree of Madness. The Croud of Mankind determine the most important Points, without weighing the Reasons on both Sides of the Question. In their own Imagination they quickly penetrate Matters, which to the more Judicious are abstruse and intricate. If they embrace Truth, it is by Accident. They contend not for Religion, because they see its proper Evidence; but because they have been accustomed to it: And thus they may be orthodox and regular Christians, from no better Principles than those from which the *Turks* are *Mahometans*. Nay, they form their Judgment of Religion, the highest Concern of all, with more Indifference than of the small Affairs of this Life. From hence arise the many sottish Opinions, wild Reveries, and destructive Heresies, that pass for pure Religion with their respective Votaries, divide the christianized World into so many opposite Parties, are contended for with a Peremptoriness that knows not to yield to Argument, and promoted frequently with a bitter, sometimes with a bloody, Zeal. What intelligent Christian is there, who, without a Mixture of Pity and Contempt, can observe the *Professors of Wisdom become Fools?* Rom. i. 22. Hear the Dictates of eternal Wisdom pronounced Folly, with a supercilious Air? and fanciful Chimeras substituted in its Room? It would seem as though the Faculty of Reasoning was, to many, given in vain; while one asserts the *Uselessness* of it in Religion, another its *Sufficiency*, in our lapsed State. This denies the Necessity of any divine Revelation; that asserts, every Circumstance must be immediately revealed. One thinks Saving Grace consists in moral Honesty, another places it in the Observation of invented Forms. One is a Libertine, who fancies he serves GOD while he gratifies his Lusts; another is superstitious, and thinks to please *him* by monkish Austerities. One is content with a dead Faith, which neither *purifies the Heart*, nor *works by Love*; another is persuaded he shall be saved by his good Works, though imperfect, without Faith in the Righteousness of Christ. This lays the whole Stress on orthodox Principles; that thinks it indifferent what we believe. Some doubt not their Safety, because they are of such a particular religious Denomination; others are of Opinion, that all Denominations stand alike fair for Salvation. Here is a Bigot who esteems every Circumstance in Religion to be essential, and whatever he believes to be right and true must be a Term of Communion; there is a Latitudinarian whose Religion has little or nothing in it that is important, or worthy to be earnestly contended for. Here unaffecting Speculation is triumphant; there Ignorance is the Mother of Devotion. Here Religion is dressed in gaudy Attire, with *Jewish* worldly Pomp, insomuch that its first Institution is hardly at all discernable; there the pure external Ordinances of God himself are rejected with Scorn, from a swoln Conceit of Spirituality. Now all these contradictory Parties will be equally stiff and positive in their Notions; yet are all equally extravagant and monstrous: all opposite to divine Revelation, and the Reason of Things. And are all these, O my Soul! are *all these* the rational Sons of Men! Are all these *sure* they are wise! Can Truth, divine Truth, be a System—a *System* did I say? a *Heap* of Dotages! Can Reason, strict Reason, approve Contradictions! or rather, must we not assuredly conclude, that *Madness is in their Heart while they live*?

Nor shall we find more Wisdom in their Judgment of Men than of Things. They conclude of Characters in the Lump:

can hardly see any thing amiable and good where some Things displease; nor are Blemishes apt to be disgustful where some good Qualities shine. Superficial Defects hide substantial Excellencies from the vulgar Eye; whilst the Absence of all valuable Accomplishments is easily supplied by meer Sound, and empty Show. Wisdom and Virtue, meanly cloathed, are despised; whilst Ignorance and Vice, dressed in Purple, are honoured. An easy Air and genteel Address, often recommend Nonsense, and make Flattery appear sincere; but an uncouth Mode will cause the same Persons, to disrelish undissembled Regard, and solid Discretion. Even learned Criticks do sometimes defend the very Absurdities of a favourite Author; and censure what is truly sublime in another. Whole Communities, nay, whole Nations, lie under the Censure which belongs only to a Part, and, perhaps, a small Part of them. Thus Mankind judge as though Reason taught them to make the Conclusion universal, when the Premises are only particular.

II. Men judge not more precipitantly, than speak and act inconsiderately. How frequently may we see proper and improper confused? No Respect had to Time, or Place, or Person; nor a Thought of the obvious and unavoidable Consequences? How many live as if there was no need of Caution, no possible Danger of missing the Right, nor any Extreme to be feared?—As if nothing could follow from any Course of Conduct, and a necessary Cause would not produce its genuine Effect?—As if Prudence and Circumspection were mere Names, and no Power of Deliberation had ever been given? They live at random, and seem to consider Right and Wrong with absolute Indifference. In the religious Life, some are offensive, others stumble and fall, and some take Offence when none is given. In the civil Life, many ruin themselves in their worldly Affairs, and others too, by Indiscretion. Some live above their Ability, engage in Matters too high for them, and fall by those Means by which they thought to rise. The imprudent Pursuit of Grandeur brings others into Contempt, whilst they industriously seek to obtain a Character which they cannot support; and climb to a Pinnacle where their Brains are turned, and they cannot stand.

Many, in a devout Qualm, engage in a Course of strict

Religion, without a rational Sense of its Importance, or *counting the Cost.* Luke xiv. 28. They think not what Offences and stumbling Blocks are in the Way—What Artifices of Satan, what Allurements of the Flesh, and what Terrors of the World, are combined to turn them aside.—How *strait the Gate,* how *narrow the Path,* Matth. vii. 14. how arduous the Ascent, and how deceitful and impotent their Souls.—What Self-denial, what Humbleness of Mind, what Watchfulness and Care, and what Courage and determinate Resolution, are requisite for the Purpose. They assure themselves that they will stand firm against all Assaults, though they were at no Pains to *dig deep,* and *found themselves on a Rock:* Hence, when the *Rain descends,* when the *Floods come,* and the *Winds blow,* and *beat upon them, they fall,* Matth. vii. 26, 27. and are carried headlong down the Stream. Hence their *Goodness is as a Morning-Cloud,* and vanishes *like the early Dew.* Hos. vi. 4. They either become profane, or are taken in the Snare of some delusive Opinion, or Heresy: *They turn away their Ears from the Truth, and are turned into Fables:* 2 Tim. iv. 4. And thus ends their Religion.

III. Many appear to have false Views of what is advantageous, or hurtful; and draw false Inferences from Actions and Event. In how strange a Light do they look on strict Piety, who disdain it as mean, or avoid it as unpleasant; and how come the Paths of Sin to appear honourable and blissful? Religious Persons, and spiritual Conversation, are by many shunned as though they were dangerous, while the Loose and Profane are chosen for Companions, as though they were most safe. They are not afraid to violate the Laws of God; yet they dread his threatned Vengeance. Hell is their Terror, Sin their Sport and Entertainment. They tremble at the Effect, yet delight in its proper Cause. But how absurd is it, mentally to separate Misery from Sin, when they can never be separated in Fact? The eternal Reason of Things has made their Connexion inviolable.

What false Apprehensions have many of their own Cases? The Aged and Infirm think of Years to come, and hence defer their intended Preparation for Death. The Drunkard never knows his Capacity, but thinks he may safely venture to take the other Glass: nor does the covetous Miser ever judge truly of his Necessity, and therefore lives poor in the Midst of Plenty.

Every Occurrence is perverted. The Goodness of GOD, which would seem sufficient to melt hard Hearts, and form them according to his Will, becomes a Mean of hardening them against him. If he gives to some Abundance of worldly Wealth, they use it as though it were a Licence given them to indulge Wantonness, Excess of Riot, Luxury, and all those sensual Pleasures, which to others are forbidden. If Honour and Power are conferred on them, they act as though they were advanced above a scrupulous Regard to the divine Commands. They seem to say, *Who is the Lord, that we should obey him?* Exod. v. 2. Because the Wicked prosper, they conclude it is quite safe to follow their Ways: And *because Sentence against an evil Work is not speedily executed*, Eccles. viii. 11. they are bold in Impiety, presuming on perpetual Impunity. They see Men despise Piety, and even sit in the Scorner's Chair, yet no visible Evil befals them; hence some are tempted to think divine Threats are but Bug-bears, and Religion but a Fancy. On the contrary, pious People are distressed, often severely reproached and run down, and no visible Regard manifested for all their Care to please God: Upon this others readily determine, that *it is vain to serve him.* Mal. iii. 1. Some, who made a plausible Profession of strict Religion, fall away, and prove themselves, by their After-conduct, to have been but Hypocrites: Therefore, others carefully avoid every Appearance of Piety, that they may avoid Hypocrisy: They expect to be counted honest and upright, when they are openly wicked, and glory in their Shame.

IV. There are Numbers who do not so much as attempt to form their Judgment, or regulate their Practice, by Reason. They follow the Vogue without Scruple. They seek no other Test of Truth, than that it is said by the *Great* or the *Many;* nor any other Proof of the Propriety and Goodness of their Behaviour, but that it is modish. Custom is to them instead of Reason, and influences them much more powerfully than the Authority of GOD himself. Let their Conduct be irrational, let it be wicked too, provided only it be fashionable. Has it a Multitude to patronize it? then 'tis no Matter though it cannot stand the Test of Scripture; no, nor of common Sense.

The Croud, like a Torrent, carries these along, and they lose themselves in it. Their weak Minds are confused with the Tumult, and made *giddy with the Glare of worldly Pomp.* Sedate Thought and calm Reason, by Means of numberless airy Vanities, lose their Weight, and are resolved into Fume and Vapour. In this Plight, it is no Wonder that they esteem those contemptibly weak who chuse rather to expose themselves to the Censure of the World, than to offend God. They judge of Religion itself by the Fashion. By that they determine which of the divine Commands it is proper to obey; and which of them, for the sake of Decency, is to be laid aside. If religious Discourse is reckoned unpolite, a serious Expression will shock a gay Company, and a few would go near to disperse them. Though it is the Will of God, that Sin should be reproved, and the Sinner made ashamed; yet we would offend against modern Politeness, should we discover even a calm Disapprobation of what is wickedly spoken or acted in Company. They who would be quite acceptable to this World, must, *at least seem,* to approve what GOD condemns, that so none may ever be made uneasy by their Presence. They must *say to every one that despises the LORD,* and *that walks after the Imagination of his Heart, ye shall have Peace, and no Evil shall come upon you.* Jer. xxiii. 17. But surely, *the Friendship of the World is Enmity with God.* Jam. iv. 4.

But let us proceed further, and take a View of Men who mistake not their Duty; who acknowledge the Things *that are excellent, being instructed out of the Law;* and we cannot but conclude that they exceed in Madness. For,

V. Multitudes continually counteract their Judgment and Conscience, when rightly informed. They own the Soul to be more excellent than the Body, yet are most anxious to provide for the latter. They spare not Cost and Pains to cure a bodily Distemper, while the immortal Spirit, all disordered, is quite neglected. Remedies are carefully sought for an Head-ach; but none for an hard Heart. A Fever is deplored; irregular and distorted Passions are indulged. The Body is gorgeously cloathed, and delicately fed, while the Soul is naked, without Righteousness, and no Bread of Life sought after for its Nourishment. It is of more Value than the *the whole World,* yet is bartered away for a very small Part of it; for Vanity, for

Songs, for Triffles. That Heaven is infinitely preferable to this Earth, eternal Glory to temporal Felicity, is not disputed; yet Sinners chuse to live here always. They are conscious to themselves, that they would desire no other Kind of Blessedness than this World affords, could they but *still* enjoy it, and enjoy it *fully*; and hence grasp the Present, regardless of the Future. They acknowledge, that they should make it the very Business of their Life to please God, and that his Favour is more valuable than the Favour of all Mankind; yet they gratify their Appetites and Humours, when they know they displease him in so doing: and if they stand fair in the Opinion of Men, are quite careless about his Approbation. They commend Virtue, but practise Vice; and while they own, that Wickedness is the Way to Hell, walk boldly on in that Way at all Adventures.

They confess, that Reason should guide, and the Passions should be governed by its Dictates; yet when their Passions become clamorous, the Voice of Reason is drowned, and its loudest Remonstrances no more heard. The covetous Man is drawn into Absurdities by the Love of Money, the Voluptious hurries on in Pursuit of ruining Pleasures, and Thirst of Praise carries the Ambitious headlong.

They make no suitable Improvement of their own Experiences, nor correct past Follies by After-observation. The World and its evil Customs are infectious; they have been often caught in the same Snare, yet never learn to be guarded and circumspect. The Review of past Scenes of guilty Pleasures gives griping Remorse; the present do not satisfy, yet many Trials convince them not that the future will surely disappoint them. After drinking to Excess, the Heart is thirsty; and Hunger succeeds the most plenteous Repast. *In the midst of Laughter the Heart is sorrowful, and the End of that Mirth is Heaviness.* Prov. xiv. 13. For oftentimes Reason is debauched, the Conscience seared, the Passions inflamed, the Constitution broken, Estate ruined, and the Person despised. Guilt is contracted, Time wasted, and the Spirits flag by means of an immoderate Elevation. Sensual Joys cloy and surfeit, but do not content: they gratify the Brute, but starve the Man, and frequently ruin the Christian. Yet, see Multitudes of Mortals eagerly fluttering to grasp Joys, which, like airy

Phantoms, still elude their Embraces; and are hardly the Shadows of Realities!—disappointed, they nevertheless still pursue, still go the tiresome Round, and tread the same beaten Path, in vain! In fine, after numberless Experiments, they neither learn the Emptiness of earthly Things, nor the Deceitfulness of their own Hearts.

VI. It is well known, that Madness hurries Persons, who are affected with it, into most desperate Courses: And this is the Case of Mankind. *They know the Judgment of God, that they who commit such Things are worthy of Death;* Rom. i. 32. yet they do them, and delight in them. They sin against plainest Precepts, guarded with most awful Threatnings. In the very Sight of *Sinai's* burning Mount, amidst the Thunders of offended *Jehovah*, hardy Rebels durst form a God of Gold. Sinners are still the same. They sin against shocking Terrors, felt by themselves; and disregard alluring Offers of Pardon, and charming Promises of eternal Salvation. They sin, while they are receiving tender Mercies, never considering, *that the Goodness of God should lead them to Repentance*; Rom. ii. 4. and while they suffer the Inflictions of severe Judgments. Examples of Despair, the fearful Ends of wretched Offenders, deter them not; nor are they persuaded to be religious by the Death-bed Joys of pure and living Piety. Let their dearest Friends, and the most learned and godly Ministers, convince and beseech them, yet will they not *yield themselves to God.* SOLOMON with all his Wisdom, the royal Authority, joined with the sublimest Strains, of the *sweet Singer of* ISRAEL, the persuasive Oratory of APOLLOS, with *Peter's* burning Zeal, could not turn Sinners from their Course. Let Miracles be wrought, the Mountains removed, the Dead raised, the Deaf made to hear, and the Blind to see; even these Things will not have the Force of Argument with them. *Uncover Destruction, and make Hell naked* before them, with open Eyes they rush into those Flames. Let Angels come from Heaven, and Fiends from the Infernals; let eternal Raptures, and endless Horrors, be presented lively to their View, they will hardly so much as make a Pause. Tell them, nay shew them, how sottish and foolish their Way is, yet they will not be ashamed. Conscience speaks, but is not heard; commands, but is not obeyed. What shall I say more?—They *rush on God himself, on the thick Bosses of his Buckler*, Job. xv. 26.—They provoke incensed Omnipotence to unequal Engagement; defy his Power, despise his Wrath, and, like LEVIATHAN, *laugh at the Shaking of his Spear*, Job. xli. 29. They cannot successfully contend, nor is it possible to escape, yet they will not submit;—will be broken rather than bow, and *dashed in Pieces like a Potter's Vessel*, Psalm ii. 9. rather than comply with the confessedly righteous Will of God. They are told, that eternal Damnation cannot be avoided, nor eternal Glory obtained, but only by the Merits of JESUS CHRIST; yet many, (could it have been thought!) many *make light even of a Saviour*! despise the Redeemer! most horrid, most desperate Thought! His exquisite Agonies, his exceedingly sorrowful Soul, his bloody Sweat, the Soldiers Scourges, the Crown of Thorns, the cruel Mockings, the painful and accursed Death he endured for Sin, instead of affecting them with Reverence and Love to his Person, are the Matter of their Scorn; or, at best, received with the coldest Indifference. *O my Soul! come not thou into their Secret; unto their Assembly, mine Honour, be not thou united!* Gen. xlix. 6.—*Be astonished, O ye Heavens*, at the Madness, the daring Impiety, of guilty Mortals! *be horribly afraid! be ye very desolate!* Jer. ii. 12.

VII. Madness discovers itself in *absurd and unreasonable Hopes.* Earthly-minded and sensual Persons hope to content their lustful Appetites, by gratifying them to the full; whereas it is plain, that all vicious Passions, like the Dropsy, increase by Indulgence: Endeavours to satisfy them, and by that Means to get rid of their importunate Cravings, is the same as heaping Fuel on Fire, in order to extinguish it, which yet only serves to heighten and perpetuate the Flame. There is no Mean that has a proper Tendency to quell irregular Desires, but only Self-denial.

Some hope to obtain Heaven without Holiness; to *be glorious in the Eyes of the Lord*, Isai. xlix. 5. though quite unlike Him; to dwell with Pleasure for ever in his Presence, though *Enemies in their Minds by wicked Works*, Col. i. 21. and to enjoy spiritual Blessedness, while they carnalize their Affections, and more and more indispose themselves to relish it. Thus they separate *what GOD has joined together*, while they expect the End without the appointed Means. They hope to be pardoned without an Heart-purifying Faith, and accepted of God without the imputed Righteousness of Christ:—to be embraced by that Mercy which they grossly abuse, and spared by that Patience which they continue to provoke. Nay, they propose what is obviously impossible; to live with the Wicked, the Worldly, and Debauched, and yet to die with the Holy and Self-denied:—to be Followers of the meek and humble Jesus, and yet indulge Wrath and Ambition:—and to be happy without friendly Intercourse with the Father of their Spirits, and Fountain of Bliss; and hence live contented without *having Fellowship with the Father and his Son Jesus Christ.* 1 John i. 3. Though all fallible, and prone to deceive, they nevertheless depend more firmly on each others Word, than on the Promise and Oath of God, *who cannot lie.* Tit. i. 2. They hope to get Victory over Sin by slothful Wishes, without striving earnestly against it, and to become *some how* good, without ever *exercising themselves unto Godliness.* 1 Tim. iv. 7. O! what shocking Disappointments will such Hopes meet with! The higher they rise, the more dreadful their Fall! They will all be *cut down like a Tree,* Job. xix. 10. and end in certain Despair.

VIII. Madness appears in the *precarious Fickleness* of human Hearts. Mankind are blown hither and thither, like withered Leaves in Autum, or like Chaff, the Sport of Winds. They are not only contradictory to each other, but the same Individual is discordant with himself. One Thing is approved in the Morning, the Contrary in the Evening. Now Love is predominant, but the next Pulse beats Disaffection to the same Object. *This Hour* the Sinner, disturbed in Mind, rejects a favourite Lust with Abhorrence; the *next* he recalls and embraces it. He now resolves to be religious in Earnest, but presently defers it till To-morrow; and when the Morrow is come, he has forgotten the Whole. Now the Judgment is clear, and Things appear in comely Order; now it is covered with Clouds, and what was Order becomes Confusion. Now the Heart is calm, easy, and pliant; now a Tempest ruffles the Bosom, and Obstinacy that cannot bend, takes Place. Now Mercy and Kindness sweeten the Temper, which is presently soured by Revenge and Moroseness. Now he steers a steady Course this Way, but turns to a different Point with the next veering Gale. Excellent Sentiments are quickly blotted, and the last Impressions still razed out by the next succeeding. A determinate and fixed Resolve but mocks the Observer, and seems more like the Effect of Chance, than of Judgment and Deliberation.

How ludicrous are the quick Changes of Customs and Fashions! yet each of them approved, and each of them censured in its Turn, by the very same Persons! Now it pleases; now it gives Disgust; and now it pleases again. The Gay and Fashionable, and they who live in affluent Circumstances, are busied too, and even perplexed, in the Variety of Vanity; and wearied in the giddy Chace,—and though many of them are, in some lesser Points, more polished than others, yet they afford us a prospect, not more rational, nor less wild, than those they despise. Worldly Prosperity, perverted from its Use by human Depravity, makes their Passions impetuous, their Impatience violent, and their Judgment weak. This being the Character, though *not of all*, yet of the *greater Part* of those who glory in *high Life*, what can follow from it but a wild Inconstancy!—O my Soul! how evanid are human Thoughts, and human Things! How delusive the Scenes of mortal Pleasures! and how little Reason is there to depend on the Power, or Wisdom, or Fidelity of the fallen human Race! *Trust not in Princes* themselves, *nor in the Son of Man, in whom there is no Help:* Psal. cxlvi. 3. but rather, *cease from Man, whose Breath is in his Nostrils; for wherein is he to be accounted off?* Isai. ii. 22. These Characters are no Fictions, nor Exaggerations of the Truth, but are all taken from the Life: And though the half is not told, yet in what a shocking Point of Light do even these rough and imperfect Sketches set Mankind!

But what aggravates this Madness to the highest Degree, is, that *after all they go to the Dead.* Solemn Consideration!—The Gay and Jovial, the Rich, the Great, the Poor and Mean, the Sorrowful and Afflicted,—all depart hence, and are seen no more among the Living! See whole Ages swept away by the *Besom of Destruction*! Isai. xiv. 23. noisy and bustling Millions silent in the Dust! and all their mortal Honours, their sensual Joys, and earthly Cares, are for ever departed with them. What Authority or Empire have *Alexander* the *Great*, *Cyrus*, or *Cæsar*, now? Where are their Favourites, their Friends, their Flatterers, and their Subjects? Who fears their Frowns, trembles at their Threats, or courts their Favour, in the House of Silence? And what do their Triumphs and Spoils avail them now? Implacable Enemies are hushed into everlasting Peace. *Are these the Men that made the Earth tremble? that shook Kingdoms?* Isai. xiv. 16. they are *become weak* as the meanest; (*v.* 10.) their *Pomp is brought down to the Grave*; the *Worm* is spread *under them, and the Worms cover them.* ver. 11. Thus Mankind, in every Age, bustle and die. Like Bubbles, they are blown up, glitter, and break: like Flowers, they spring, bloom, and are cut down: and like *Shadows they pass away*, and *continue not.* Job xiv. 2. But whither do they pass? Where shall our curious, or rather sollicitous Thoughts follow them? Is Death the End of their Existence? No. *After that* comes the *Judgment.* Heb. ix. 27. They are summoned to appear before the august, the impartial, and sovereign Judge; they stand at his Bar, and hear an irrevocable Doom. What Doom? Can we bear to contemplate the State of those, who madly provoked their Judge, and persisted impenitent? Does not the Heart recoil, the Imagination startle, at the direful Thought of an horrible Gloom,—Regions of eternal Despair,—the Steam of Sulphur mixed with unquenchable Fire,—the torturing Gripes, the relentless Lashes of a guilty Conscience, that gnawing, never-dying Vulture,—the insufferable Impressions of almighty Wrath,—and the hideous Shrieks of damned Souls? Are the bare Thoughts of these Things shocking? what then will it be to endure them? And can we judge those to be sober, and in their right Minds, who are in continual Danger of plunging into these Miseries, and yet are secure and careless about any Endeavours to *escape from the Wrath to come*? What an amazing Scene do the Sons and Daughters of Pleasure exhibit to us? They are daily exposed to a thousand Deaths; are easily broken by numberless unforeseen Accidents; and if they die impenitent, they are for ever undone: yet are no more alarmed than if they were immortal. All thoughtless, all volatile, hating serious Things, and Lectures of Death, which therefore surprizes them, finds them unprovided, hurries them away, and pushes them reluctant down the dreadful Precipice,—from Time into Eternity. O the hardy Adventure! to take a *Leap in the Dark* into an endless, unalterable State! Merry Company, Balls, Assemblies, and Plays, amuse them so, that they forget they are mortal, till they die; and see not their Danger, till they are beyond Relief. They live in Jest, *and after that they go to the Dead* in Earnest. What Degree of Folly is it, to catch a Feather, and let go a Crown! to gain a Toy, and lose a Kingdom! for a Morsel to barter a Birthright! and for a Moment's Pleasure to part with everlasting Joys, and suffer eternal Woes! And are these your *Men of Sense*, who look indignant on those who are so weak as to be deeply concerned about such important Affairs? *Vain Man*, forsooth, *would be wise, though he is born like the wild Asse's Colt.* Job xi. 12. It is an inexpressible Absurdity, that temporal Things, whether Riches, Honour, or Pleasures, should ingross the intensest Thoughts of Beings bound for Eternity: And it is an eternal Solecism in Religion, to be engaged about the Concerns of it in a cold and indifferent Manner. *The Kingdom of Heaven suffereth Violence, and the Violent take it by Force.* Matth. xi. 12.

After considering all these Things, will it seem an Abuse of Mankind, if I compare this World to a great *Bedlam*, filled with Persons strangely and variously distracted? Some are so desperate, as to refuse all salutary Medicines; and the Habit so inveterate, as to non-plus the Physician's Skill, and make him almost despair of their Cure: Some appear hopeful for a while, but relapse, and their Case is more dangerous than before: And some are actually recovered in a less, some in a greater Degree; but not so much as one perfectly well. My Text will warrant the Comparison: and I may not flatter Mankind by soothing Expressions, when their Case requires plain Dealing; nor be so polite as not to learn of God how to speak, when I deliver his Message.

From the Whole we are taught,

1. How little Reason any one has to be puffed up with popular Applause, or dispirited when he does not obtain it. For, consider who are the Judges? Are they all Persons of sound Minds, whose Conclusions are according to Truth? Far from it. It is true, all fancy themselves mighty good Judges of Merit: but I speak charitably, when I say, perhaps one in an Hundred can distinguish. That Soul, therefore, is lighter than

Vanity, that is tossed hither and thither, according to the ebbing and flowing Tides of inconstant Affections. The favourable Opinion of Mankind is chiefly to be valued as it gives an Opportunity to serve their best Interests more successfully.

2. How much Reason there is in that divine Exhortation, *Be not conformed to this World.* Rom. xii. 2. Do not act upon its Principles, nor accommodate yourselves to its evil Customs and Modes. For this World is at Variance with God, and *no Man can serve two Masters.* Matth. vi. 24. It is here modish to make light of Religion, and treat it, if treated at all, with an Air of the most absolute Indifference, and Unconcern.—Nay, with many it is polite, to sneer at solemn Devotion, and *make a Mock of Sin.* He appears big, who dares trample on sacred and inviolable Authority, and laugh at divine Threatnings; and wise, who can ridicule the Mysteries of the Gospel. He who is *a Companion of* such *Fools, shall be destroyed.* Prov. xiii. 20.

Lastly, Let the Follies of others be a Motive to engage your more earnest Pursuit of saving Wisdom. *Seek her as Silver, search for her as for hidden Treasure.* Prov. ii. iv. *Happy is the Man that finds her; for she is more precious than Silver, than fine Gold and Rubies.—Her Ways are Ways of Pleasantness, and all her Paths are Peace.* chap. iii. ver. 13, 14, 15, and 17. If any of you *lack* this spiritual *Wisdom, ask it of GOD, who gives liberally, and upbraids not*: and let it ever be a small Matter with you, to be judged weak and foolish by a mad World, provided always that you are *wise to Salvation.*

ANON.

A Sermon in Praise of Swearing

DEUT. vi. 13. The latter Part of the Verse.
And SHALT *swear by his name.*

THERE is a set of men in the world, who need only be known
in order to be despised; men, who are a constant subject for
ridicule, and justly the derision of the gay and more refined
part of the human species: men who are so stupid, as to be
more enamoured with the pleasure of a benevolent action,
more charmed with giving joy to the helpless and miserable,
with drying up the tears of the distressed, or soothing the agonies of the bursting heart, than with the lordly pride of wanton power, than in rendering the wretched more wretched,
than with spurning at patient merit, or even the satisfaction of
racking tenants, hoarding wealth, or all the high gratification
of a debauch; more delighted with the visionary pleasure of
indulging their own reflections, and the applause of a good
conscience, than with the charms of a bottle, the transports
afforded by the lascivious wanton, or all the high-wrought indulgences of a luxurious appetite. And, in one word, to sum
up their character, more afraid of a false, or even an unnecessary oath, than of the point of a sword.

It is with these poor mean-spirited wretches, that I am now
to combat, in order to shew the great advantages that attend
a strict compliance with the injunction in my text, *And thou
shalt swear by his name.* I shall not here take up your time in
examining the context, or even in considering what is meant
by the command in my text, which some would confine to
the necessary oaths, taken in a court of judicature; but, like all
sound divines, and in compliance with the custom of all good
commentators and disputants, consider the passage before us,
in that latitude, which is most adapted to answer my particular design.

One man takes his text, and endeavours, with the most elaborate eloquence, to prove, that the bible he preaches from is a work not fit to be read; that it never was designed for the instruction of such blockheads as his audience, who, by looking into it, incur damnation. What concerns all to know, must be read by none but the priest, or whom he shall appoint. How glorious that revelation, which, in the hands of the multitude, points the way to misery, but, in those of the church, to eternal life! It is she alone, who can infallibly inform us, that love, and charity, and compassion, and tenderness, so often mentioned in that old book, the bible, mean spite, and hatred, and inquisition, and burning faggots.

Another, with pious snuffle, and all the moving force of sighs and groans, proves, that the God of truth is the God of falsehood; and, finding his scheme contradicted, by the language of scripture, from scripture nicely distinguishes between a revealed and a secret will, both opposite, both contradictory to each other. Scripture he proves to be a lye; his opinion he proves to be true from scripture. He wisely turns out common sense, to make room for grace. He degrades reason, as being in league with the devil, and, in the pious ardour of his heart, saves himself the trouble of thinking, and cries out—*I believe, because it is impossible.* Ye deists rejoice in these your friends! Admit them into your societies! They, like you, can darken truth, they have assisted you in setting fragment against fragment; and, when the dazzling sunbeams shine too bright, can wisely close their eyes. Let me too be permitted to rank myself on this side, and, countenanced by such great authorities, to take a text that suits my present purpose, regardless of every other passage that may be supposed to contradict it: nay, regardless of the text itself, any further than as it may serve for a plausible introduction to what I have to offer.

It is sufficient, therefore, that we have here a command to swear by the name of God; which I shall take, in the common and vulgar sense of the word swearing, to mean, not only all manner of oaths, but whatever goes under the denomination of swearing in conversation, as oaths, curses, and imprecations.

In treating this subject I shall consider,

I. The many advantages attending the frequent use of

oaths, curses, and imprecations: in which will be sufficiently proved, the falseness of that assertion, that swearing is attended with neither pleasure nor profit.

II. Answer some objections. And,

III. Make a suitable application.

I. I am to consider the many advantages arising from a frequent use of oaths, curses, and imprecations.

In the *first* place, this genteel accomplishment is a wonderful help to discourse; as it supplies the want of good sense, learning, and eloquence. The illiterate and stupid, by the help of oaths, become orators; and he, whose wretched intellects would not permit him to utter a coherent sentence, by this easy practice, excites the laughter, and fixes the attention, of a brilliant and joyous circle. He begins a story, he is lost in a vacuity of thought, and would instantly, to his eternal dishonour, become silent, did not a series of oaths and imprecations give him time to gather up, or rather seek the thread of his discourse: he begins again, again he is lost, but having complimented his friends, by calling for eternal damnation on them all, he has thought what to say next, and finds himself able to proceed with a sentence or two more. Thus he still talks on, while thought follows slowly after. Blest expedient! by the use of which, polite conversation glides on uninterupted, while sound is happily substituted in the place of sense: by this, mankind communicate familiar noises to each other, with as little intellectual ability and labour, as a pack of well-matched hounds; so often the object of their delight and admiration! O how preposterously absurd then! how false, and contrary to experience, is that ridiculous assertion, that swearing is attended with neither pleasure nor profit! For what higher pleasure, what greater profit and advantage can a man enjoy, than to find, that, *in spight of nature, who has directed him to be silent*, he can hear himself talk—talk without stammering, or drawling out each heavy sentence, that lags behind to wait on thought. Ye idiots rejoice! ye coxcombs, whose costive brain ne'er dictated the flowing sentiment, be glad! Ye, whom learning never fired, in stupid ignorance lost, exult! Blest with ease and indolence, you talk, and those, like you, admire; while listening demons clap their wings, and grin applause.

Forgive me, Sirs, if, fired with my subject, I lose my usual moderation; for who can help being warmed at the mention of such glorious advantages as these? Advantages, which level the conversation of the mighty, and raise the oratory of the carman and porter. Here the lowest frequently excel; the plowman, with clouted shoon, outvies his competitors, and practises the vices of the gentleman, with more success than the lord of the manor, or the splendid courtier, though adorned with star and garter. Here no abilities, no learning, are necessary, no studious hours are required to attain perfection. Tropes and figures, all the flowers of oratory, all the pedantry of the schools, are vain and useless trumpery, compared to these ornaments: they require pains and study, nor can be applied without judgment, and the toil of reading what are foolishly called, the ingenious and polite authors: but swearing is, as I have said, learning to the ignorant, eloquence to the blockhead, vivacity to the stupid, and wit to the coxcomb.

Secondly, Oaths and curses are a proof of a most heroic courage, at least in appearance, which answers the same end. For who can doubt the valour, the intrepidity of him who braves the thunder of heaven, who affronts the most formidable being in the universe, and treats with contempt, that all enlivening principle, which sustains and animates the whole creation? To what a noble elation is the heart of the coward conscious, when he thus defies the Almighty, and imprecates the fires of hell! Let the blustering bully domineer, let him roar out his curses, and threaten all who dare provoke the vengeance of his potent arm; let him terrify by a surly frown, and intimidate when, with portly gait, he vents ten thousand oaths and curses on the wretch, who impudently presumes to oppose his mighty will—who dares doubt his courage? Who can believe, that the cane, or the toe, when duly applied, have such magic power, as to make him twist and writhe himself like a serpent, till, with this excercise, his joints, and his mind, become so supple, that he can bend and cringe and ask pardon? Let the meek soldier boast his deeds of war, and, with oaths and execrations lace the self-flattering tale; who can believe that so great a hero should have an antipathy to the sight of steel? Or that he, who challenges the blasting lightning to fall on his head, would tremble, and turn pale, at the flash of a pistol? No, this must never be imagined; for can it be supposed that he has less bravery in the field than in the tavern? With these blustering expletives, then, the coward may strut and look big, and every minute give fresh proofs of an invincible courage: he may bravely sport with that being, whose frown would make the heavens and earth to tremble: he may seem to snatch the vengeance from his uplifted hand, and throw it on his foe: he may invoke the wrath of heaven: and who can imagine that he is afraid of death, when he is continually calling for all the horrors of hell?

Thirdly, He hereby not only gives a proof of his courage, but informs the world, that he is intirely divested of all the foolish prejudices of education, and has unlearned

All that the nurse, and all the priest have taught:

that he has not only shook off the shackles of enthusiasm, but has banished from his mind, that reverence of the deity, which is the foundation of every system of religion. He is not suspected of being such a fool as to want instruction, since it cannot be imagined, that he has so dull a taste as to go to church, unless, if he be a gentleman, to ogle the ladies; if a clown, to sleep; or, if a tradesman, in complaisance to the sober old women of both sexes, who happen to be his customers: and he has this additional advantage, that he will never be taken for a pious churchman, a presbyterian, a quaker, or a methodist. And, in reality, he is so far from being a bigot to any religious principles, that he belongs to no religious society upon earth. That he is not, nor cannot be a christian, is evident; for, what is christianity? It is extensive benevolence, humanity, and virtue, to which he bids defiance with every curse. He cannot be a deist, because they openly profess the utmost reverence for the deity; and, for the same reason, he can neither be a Jew, or a Mahometan, or a follower of Confucius. No, nor even an atheist; since we cannot conceive, that he would so often call upon God, if he was thoroughly convinced there was no such being in the universe; however, he every minute lets us see, that he does not fear him. How unlicenced is his freedom, how glorious and unconstrained! Let the wretches, who meanly bend their wills, and regulate their actions, by the sage dictates of reason and conscience; who stoop to follow the rules of religion, and call them sacred; let these bridle their tongues, let these confine themselves within the narrow limits prescribed by reason and good sense; the swearer knows better; sense, and reason, and religion, are all subservient to his will, he disdains their fetters, and rules those which rule all the world beside.

Fourthly, and lastly, Another advantage which attends this vice of the gentleman, this noble accomplishment, is, that it sometimes raises him to dignity and honour. Under this head, indeed, I take a greater latitude and advert to a remote consequence of the practice of swearing: but, as there is such a close concatenation in all our habits, and virtue and vice are progressive in their very nature, I should not do complete justice to my subject, if I omitted the consideration of it in this particular view. When a man, therefore, by a happy association of ideas, joins to the other advantages of this vice, ideas of wealth and grandeur; when he sees no argument, that appears of any weight, to bind him down to the unthrifty rules of honesty, and his regard for his own private advantage is too strong to let him have any for the private property of his neighbour; what should hinder him, when a fair opportunity offers, from raising himself, by the ruin of his neighbour, his companion, or his dearest friend? He has swore to a thousand lyes in company, without any view of private advantage; what should prevent him then from taking one false oath, when the advantage is so considerable? Surely, neither conscience, nor reason, nor religion, can do this: no, that is impossible; for I, who am as infallible as any dignified priest, that ever mounted a pulpit, have asserted, that these are all subservient to his will.

Here the swearer, with an unbounded ambition, aspires to seize on wealth, and boldly to grasp at those riches, which fortune has foolishly given to a more deserving person; and this, in spite of JUSTICE and EQUITY, who are his professed enemies. Thus he rises above the multitude, and gains a lasting fame; not by blood and slaughter, but by cunning, deceit, and artifice; by bursting through the most solemn engagements, breaking in sunder the bonds of society, and only violating what all honest men hold sacred. Suppose, that he fails in his attempt, and the property of the person he has attacked remains inviolate: he is conveyed to a castle, strong as that of a crowned head where no impertinent intruders dare appear to disturb his repose: for in the day time, he has a porter to stand at his gate; in the night his faithful attendants lock and bar his doors.

Surrounded with guards, he pays a solemn visit at the seat of JUSTICE; he has the honour of being admitted to the royal bench; he converses with that sovereign personage herself, and for a considerable time, takes up the whole attention of her prime ministers, the lords of her court, who, assiduous to pay all due respect, wait his coming in their proper habiliments; and, though it be ever so early in the day, he is never received with the disrespectful negligence of an undress. The ceremony being over, he is reconducted by the same guards who brought him thither, and who dare not presume to leave him, till he is safe within his palace. He now soon receives the reward of his baffled dexterity, the glorious fruit of his ambition. The day arrives, devoted to mirth and jollity; business and care are laid aside, and every labouring hand has now a holy day. He walks, or rides in his triumphal car, attended by a numerous throng of gazing spectators: he is mounted above their heads, and his neck, not his temples, adorned with a civic wreath, and his wrists with an embrasure, composed of a matter, something coarser, indeed, than that of pearls and diamonds. This is no sooner done, than gaping thousands send forth shouts of joy, and bending low, even to the ground, pay him homage; then rising up, with loud acclamations, present their tribute, striving who most shall pay, who oftenest bend. He is covered, he is loaded, with their gifts, and sensibly touched with their bounty. The more he gains, the more unenvied here he stands, while all rejoice, and give the applause that is his due. But let his modesty be ever so great, let his blushes be like the trickling drops of crimson, painting his bashful cheek, and prompting a willingness to retire from these honours; yet one hour, at least he is restrained to stay, to receive the willing offerings of the multitude. Thrice happy man! had conscience, or bad reason sway'd, thou never hadst thus been blest; unknown thou mightest have lived, unknown have died.

II. I come now in the second place, to answer some objections: but as these, after what has been said, must appear extremely trifling, I shall be as concise as possible, and hasten to a conclusion. It is said,

In the first place, That the swearer acts in direct opposition to all the rules of right reason.

But how can this be called an objection against swearing? What have we to do with right reason?—We leave it to the dull wretches, the men of reflection: and yet there are some of these, who attempt to mimic us: but if they act inconsistently with their own abilities, let them look to that. An upright man is a downright fool, if he swears at all. Let those who can talk without it, extol their wonderous talents; they have no need of this polite vice to recommend them to the world. The squeamish wretch, who is afraid of a lye, has no need to swear to what he says, for he is certain that his word will be readily taken. But away with these *yea and nay* wretches, men born to be pointed at; the sheepish, the sober fools, who, regardless of the boundless liberty we enjoy, talk of rectitude of manners, religion, and conscience.

Secondly, and lastly, it is objected, that it is one of the most senseless, unnatural, rude, and unmannerly vices, that ever was invented.

This, it must be confessed, is paying a fine compliment to, at least, half the polite world. How can that be *rude* and *unmannerly*, which gives such a grace to conversation? 'Tis true, we express ourselves strongly, and use none of those languid, sneaking, epithets in our discourse, which your modest men, your men of humanity make use of: but as we talk without meaning, nobody can say that we mean ill. And, indeed, it is a very injurious expression, to say that this is *unnatural*, when so many of us have the honour of being universally deemed to be little better than *naturals*.

And now, Sirs, I have proved, so effectually, the great advantages, attending the practice of this genteel and fashionable vice, that there needs but one word by way of application.

Consider, O consider, how inestimable are the advantages I have mentioned! If there is any one here desirous of obtaining these, and yet is troubled, and intimidated, with the impertinence of a restless conscience, flying in his face, and threatning to haunt him, like a ghost, let him but follow my advice, and conscience will fall asleep. Would he steel his heart against compunction, let him advance by degrees; if he is afraid of an oath, let him come as near it as he can, let him cry, *egad*, *ramnation*, and *o'dram ye*; let him thus chip and carve a few common-place expressions, to fit them to his conscience, and the business will be done. This, practice will render familiar, and the coward, who first trembled, at the thought of hell, will soon have the courage to call for damnation.

And now, ye who have long indulged this vice, who have arrived at perfection in this great accomplishment, and by this means, have gained that applause, which nature would have denied you, which reason refused, and conscience condemned: you, I say, who, by the assistance of this vice, have distinguished yourselves, either as the orator, the pimp, or the bully: you who, with more distinguished glory have graced the lofty pillory; and you who, under specious oaths of speedy marriage, have violated virgin innocence, and rewarded the maid, that loved you, with eternal infamy; consider these noble advantages, applaud, congratulate yourselves, and rejoice: you have not stopped at the most flagrant impieties; you have challenged, and defied, the blasting power of heaven to do its worst, and with a disinterestedness, peculiar to yourselves, have generously sold the reversion of eternal, inexhaustible happiness, merely for the pleasure of affronting that great beneficent being, who has prepared it for you, your indulgent creator, and almighty friend. How nobly ungrateful! how unselfish your conduct! Boast your bravery, and consider the wisdom of the exchange: for how blind must you be to every self-interested view, how deaf to the calls of self-love, while infinite unbounded felicity has no charms, when standing in competition with the delight of affronting a benefactor, with the pleasure of a curse, and the satisfaction of hearing your own impertinence! STUPIDITY, IGNORANCE, and FOLLY, are on your side: act therefore, like men, who profess to be their friends; and like the true enemies to REASON, RELIGION, VIRTUE, and COMMON SENSE. You have seen your practice justified with advantages, which you have never before thought of: if these have any weight, if these have any charms, let them have all their influence. To sum up all, let every man act consistently with his real character, and, by his indulgence of this practice, or his forbearance, let his abilities, or his follies, stand confessed.

SAMUEL COOKE

A Sermon Preached at Cambridge

in the Audience of His Honor
Thomas Hutchinson, Esq;
Lieutenant-Governor and Commander in Chief;
The Honorable His Majesty's Council, and the Honorable
House of Representatives, of the Province of the
Massachusetts-Bay in New-England,
May 30th, 1770.
Being the Anniversary for the Election of His Majesty's
Council for the said Province.

———

An Election-Sermon.

2 SAM. XXIII. 3, 4.
—*He that ruleth over Men, must be just, ruling in the fear of GOD.*
And he shall be as the light of the morning when the sun riseth, even a morning without clouds: as the tender grass springing out of the earth by clear shining after rain.

THE solemn introduction to the words now read, Respectable Hearers, is manifestly designed to engage your attention and regard;—as given by inspiration from God,—and as containing the last—the dying words, of one of the greatest and best of earthly rulers;—who by ruling in the fear of God, had served his generation according to the Divine will.—Transporting reflection!—when his flesh and his heart failed, and his glory was consigned to dust.

From this, and many other passages, in the sacred oracles, it is evident, that the supreme Ruler, tho' he has directed to no particular mode of civil government, yet allows and approves of the establishment of it among men.

The ends of civil government, in Divine revelation are clearly pointed out—The character of rulers described,—and the duty of subjects asserted and explained. And in this view, civil government may be considered as an ordinance of God; and when justly exercised, greatly subservient to the glorious purposes of divine providence and grace.—But the particular form is left to the choice and determination of mankind.

In a pure state of nature, government is in a great measure unnecessary; private property in that state is inconsiderable, men need no arbiter to determine their rights,—they covet only a bare support,—their stock is but the subsistence of a day,—the uncultivated desarts are their habitations,—and they carry their all with them, in their frequent removes—they are each one a law to himself, which in general, is of force sufficient for their security, in that course of life.

It is far otherwise when mankind are formed into collective bodies, or a social state of life;—here, their frequent mutual intercourse, in a degree, necessarily leads them to different apprehensions, respecting their several rights, even where their intentions are upright.—Temptations to injustice and violence increase, and the occasions of them multiply, in proportion to the increase and opulence of the society.

The laws of nature, though enforced by Divine revelation, which bind the conscience of the upright, prove insufficient to restrain the sons of violence, who have not the fear of God before their eyes.

A society cannot long subsist in such a state—Their safety, —their social being depends upon the establishment of determinate rules or laws, with proper penalties to enforce them; to which individuals shall be subjected:—The laws, however wisely adapted, cannot operate to the public security, unless they are properly executed;—The execution of them, remaining in the hands of the whole community, leaves individuals to determine their own rights, and in effect, in the same circumstances, as in a state of nature.

The remedy in this case is solely in the hands of the community.

A society emerging from a state of nature, in respect to authority, are all upon a level,—no individual can justly challenge a right to make, or execute the laws, by which it is to be governed, but only by the choice, or general consent of the community.—The people, the collective body, only have a right, under God, to determine who shall exercise this trust for the common interest, and to fix the bounds of their authority.

And consequently, unless we admit the most evident inconsistence, those in authority, in the whole of their public conduct, are accountable to the society, which gave them their political existence.

This is evidently the natural origin, and state of all civil government,—the sole end and design of which is, not to ennoble a few, and enslave the multitude, but the public benefit,—the good of the people,—that they may be protected in their persons, and secured in the enjoyment of all their rights,—and be enabled to lead quiet and peaceable lives in all godliness and honesty.

While this manifest design of civil government, under whatever form, is kept in full view; the reciprocal obligations of rulers and subjects are obvious, and the extent of prerogative and liberty, will be indisputable.

In a civil state, that form is the most eligible which is best adapted to promote the ends of government,—the benefit of the community;—reason and experience teach that a mixed government is most conducive to this end.

In the present imperfect state, the whole power cannot with safety be entrusted with a single person; nor with many, acting jointly in the same public capacity.

Various branches of power, concentring in the community from which they originally derive their authority, are a mutual check to each other, in their several departments, and jointly secure the common interest: This may indeed, in some instances, retard the operations of government, but will add dignity to its deliberate counsels, and weight to its dictates.

This, after many dangerous conflicts with arbitrary power, is now the happy constitution of our parent state.—We rejoice in the gladness of our nation,—may no weapon formed against it prosper—may it be preserved inviolate till time shall be no more.

This, under God, has caused Great Britain to exalt her head above the nations—restored the dignity of royal authority—and rendered our Kings truly benefactors.

The Prince upon the British throne can have no real interest distinct from his subjects; his crown is his inheritance—his kingdom his patrimony, which he must be disposed to improve, for his own, and his family's interest—his highest glory is to rule over a free people, and reign in the hearts of his subjects—The Peers who are lords of parliament, are his hereditary council.—The Commons, elected by the people, are considered as the grand inquest of the kingdom; and while incorrupt, are a check upon the highest offices in the state.

A constitution thus happily formed and supported, as a late writer has observed, cannot easily be subverted, but by the prevalence of venality in the representatives of the people.

How far septennial parliaments conduce to this, time may further shew.—Or whether this is not an infraction upon the national constitution, is not for me to determine.

But the best constitution, separately considered, is only as a line which marks out the inclosure, or as a fitly organized body without spirit or animal life.

The advantages of civil government, even under the British form, greatly depend upon the character and conduct of those to whom the administration is committed.

When the righteous are in authority, the people rejoice; but when the wicked beareth rule, the people mourn.

The Most High, therefore, who is just in all his ways—good to all—and whose commands strike dread, has strictly enjoined faithfulness upon all those who are advanced to any place of public trust.

Rulers of this character, co-operate with God, in his gracious dispensations of providence, and under him, are diffusive blessings to the people:—and are compared to the light of the morning, when the sun riseth, even a morning without clouds.

By the ruler in the text, is intended not only the King as supreme; but also every one in subordinate place of power and trust, whether they act in a legislative or executive capacity, or both:—In whatever station men act for the public, they are included in this general term—and must direct their conduct by the same upright principle.

Justice as here expressed, is not to be taken in a limited

sense, but as a general term, including every quality necessary to be exercised for the public good, by those who accept the charge of it.

Justice must be tempered with wisdom, prudence and clemency; otherwise it will degenerate into rigor and oppression.

This solemn charge given to rulers, is not an arbitrary injunction imposed by God; but is founded in the most obvious laws of nature and reason.

Rulers are appointed for this very end—*to be ministers of God for good.*—The people have a right to expect this from them, and to require it, not as an act of grace, but as their unquestionable due.—It is the express or implicit condition, upon which they were chosen, and continued in public office,—that they attend continually upon this very thing.

Their time—their abilities—their authority, by their acceptance of the public trust, are consecrated to the community, and cannot, in justice, be with-held;—they are obliged to seek the welfare of the people, and exert all their powers to promote the common interest.

This continual solicitude for the common good, however depressing it may appear, is what rulers of every degree have taken upon themselves; and in justice to the people,—in faithfulness to God, they must either sustain it with fidelity, or resign their office.

The first attention of the faithful ruler will be to the subjects of government, in their specific nature;—He will not forget that he ruleth over *Men*—Men, who are of the same species with himself, and by nature equal—Men who are the offspring of God, and alike formed after his glorious image—Men of like passions and feelings with himself, and as men, in the sight of their common Creator of equal importance—Men who have raised him to power, and support him in the exercise of it—Men who are reasonable beings, and can be subjected to no human restrictions, which are not founded in reason; and of the fitness of which they may be convinced—Men, who are moral agents, and under the absolute controul of the High Possessor of heaven and earth; and cannot, without the greatest impropriety and disloyalty to the King of kings, yield unlimited subjection to any inferior power—Men whom the Son of God hath condescended to ransom, and dignified their nature, by becoming the son of man.

Men, who have the most evident right, in every decent way, to represent to rulers their grievances, and seek redress.

The people forfeit the rank they hold in God's creation, when they silently yield this important point, and sordidly, like Issachar, couch under every burden wantonly laid upon them.

And rulers greatly tarnish their dignity, when they attempt to treat their subjects otherwise than as their fellow-men,—Men who have reposed the highest confidence in their fidelity; and to whom they are accountable for their public conduct.—And in a word, Men, among whom they must, without distinction, stand before the dread tribunal of heaven.

Just rulers therefore in making and executing the laws of society, will consider who they are to oblige, and accommodate them to the state and condition of men.

Fidelity to the public, requires that the laws be as plain and explicit as possible; that the less knowing may understand and not be ensnared by them—while the artful evade their force.

Mysteries of law and government may be made a cloak of unrighteousness.

The benefits of the constitution, and of the laws, must extend to every branch, and each individual in society, of whatever degree; that every man may enjoy his property, and pursue his honest course of life with security.

The just ruler, sensible he is in trust for the public, with an impartial hand, will supply the various offices in society:—his eye will be upon the faithful—merit only in the candidate, will attract his attention.

He will not, without sufficient reason, multiply lucrative offices in the community; which naturally tends to introduce idleness and oppression.

Justice requires, that the emoluments of every office, constituted for the common interest, be proportioned to their dignity, and the service performed, for the public:—Parsimony in this case, enervates the force of government, and frustrates the most patriotic measures. A people therefore for their own security, must be supposed willing to pay tribute to whom it is due, and freely support the dignity of those under whose protection they confide.

On the other hand, the people may apprehend they have just reason to complain of oppression and wrong, and to be jealous of their liberties, when subordinate public offices are made the surest step to wealth and ease.

This not only encreases the expences of government, but is naturally productive of dissipation and luxury—of the severest animosities among candidates for public posts,—and of venality and corruption; the most fatal to a free state.

Rulers are appointed guardians of the constitution, in their respective stations; and must confine themselves within the limits by which their authority is circumscribed.

A free state will no longer continue so, than while the constitution is maintained entire, in all its branches and connections.—If the several members of the legislative power become entirely independent of each other, it produceth a schism in the body politic; and the effect is the same, when the executive is in no degree under the controul of the legislative power,—the balance is destroyed, and the execution of the laws left to arbitrary will.

The several branches of civil power, as joint pillars, each bearing its due proportion, are the support, and the only proper support of a political structure, regularly formed.

A constitution which cannot support its own weight, must fall—It must be supposed essentially defective in its form or administration.

Military aid has ever been deemed dangerous to a free civil state; and often has been used as an effectual engine to subvert it.

Those, who in the camp, and in the field of battle, are our glory and defence; from the experience of other nations, will be thought, in time of peace, a very improper safe-guard, to a constitution, which has Liberty—British Liberty, for its basis.

When a people are in subjection to those, who are detached from their fellow citizens,—under distinct laws and rules—supported in idleness and luxury—armed with the terrors of death—under the most absolute command—ready and obliged to execute the most daring orders—What must!—what has been the consequence!—

Inter arma silent leges.—

Justice also requires of rulers, in their legislative capacity, that they attend to the operation of their own acts; and repeal whatever laws, upon an impartial review, they find to be inconsistent with the laws of God—the rights of men—and the general benefit of society.

This the community hath a right to expect. And they must have mistaken apprehensions of true dignity, who imagine they can acquire or support it, by persisting in wrong measures; and thereby counteracting the sole end of government.

It belongs to the all-seeing God alone, absolutely to be of one mind. It is the glory of man, in whatever station, to perceive and correct his mistakes.

Arrogant pretences to infallibility in matters of state or religion, represent human nature in the most contemptible light.

We have a view of our nature in its most abject state, when we read the senseless laws of the Medes and Persians, or hear the impotent thunders of the Vatican.

Stability in promoting the public good, which justice demands, leads to a change of measures, when the interest of the community requires it; which must often be the case in this mutable—imperfect state.

The just ruler will not fear to have his public conduct critically inspected; but will choose to recommend himself to the approbation of every man.—As he expects to be obeyed for conscience sake, he will require nothing inconsistent with its dictates; and be desirous that the most scrupulous mind may acquiesce in the justice of his rule.

As in his whole administration, so in this, he will be ambitious to imitate the supreme Ruler—who appeals to his people, Are not my ways equal?

Knowing therefore that his conduct will bear the light, and his public character be established by being fully known—He will rather encourage than discountenance a decent freedom of speech, not only in public assemblies, but among the people.

This liberty is essential to a free constitution, and the ruler's surest guide.

As in nature we best judge of causes by their effects—So rulers, hereby—will receive the surest information of the fitness of their laws, and the exactness of their execution,—the success of their measures—and whether they are chargeable with any mistakes, from partial evidence or human frailty—and whether, all acting under them, in any subordinate place, express the fidelity, becoming their office.

This decent liberty the just ruler will consider not as his grant, but a right inherent in the people, without which their obedience is rendered merely passive.

And tho', possibly, under a just administration, it may degenerate into licentiousness, which in its extreme, is subversive of all government; yet the history of past ages, and of our nation, shews, that the greatest dangers have arisen from lawless power.

The body of a people are disposed to lead quiet and peaceable lives—and it is their highest interest to support the government under which their quietness is ensured—They retain a reverence for their superiors, and seldom foresee or suspect danger, till they feel their burdens.

Rulers of every degree, are in a measure above the fear of man; but are equally with others under the restraints of the Divine law.

The Almighty has not divested himself of his own absolute authority, by permitting subordinate government among men—He allows none to rule, otherwise, than under him, and in his fear.—And without a true fear of God, justice will be found to be but an empty name.

Though reason may in some degree investigate the relation and fitness of things, yet I think it evident, that moral obligations are founded wholly in a belief of God and his superintending providence.

This belief deeply impressed on the mind, brings the most convincing evidence, that men are moral agents,—obliged to act, according to the natural and evident relation of things—and the rank they bear in God's creation—That the Divine will, however made known to them, is the law by which all their actions must be regulated, and their state finally determined.

Rulers may in a degree be influenced to act for the public good, from education—from a desire of applause—from the natural benevolence of their temper: But these motives are feeble and inconstant, without the superior aids of religion. They are men of like passions with others, and the true fear of God only, is sufficient to controul the lusts of men; and especially the lust of dominion—to suppress pride—the bane of every desirable quality in the human soul—the never-failing source of wanton and capricious power.

So did not I—said the renowned governor of Judah—*because of the fear of God.*

He had nothing to fear from the people:—His commission he received from the luxurious Persian court, where the voice of distress was not heard—where no sad countenance might appear.—But he feared his God.—This moved him to hear the cries of his people, and without delay, redress their wrongs.—He knew this was pleasing to his God, and while he acted in his fear, trusted he would think upon him for good.

This fear doth not intend, simply, a dread of the Almighty, as the supreme Ruler and Judge of men—but especially, a filial reverence, founded in esteem and superlative love implanted in the heart:—This will naturally produce a conformity to God in his moral perfections—an inclination to do his will—and a delight in those acts of beneficence which the Maker of all things displays throughout his extended creation.

This fear of God is the beginning, and also the perfection of human wisdom.

And tho' dominion is not, absolutely, founded in grace; yet a true principle of religion must be considered as a necessary qualification in a ruler.

The religion of Jesus teacheth the true fear of God, and marvellously discloseth, the plan of Divine government;—

In his gospel, as thro' a glass, we see heaven opened—the mysteries of providence and grace unveiled—Jesus sitting on the right hand of God,—to whom all power is committed,—and coming to judge the world in righteousness.

Here is discovered to the admiration of angels—the joy of saints, and the terror of the wicked; the government of the man Christ Jesus, founded in justice and mercy; which in his glorious administration meet together in perfect harmony.

The sceptre of his kingdom is a right sceptre; he loveth righteousness and hateth wickedness.

And tho' his throne is on high—prepared in the heavens; yet he makes known to the sons of men his mighty acts, and the glorious majesty of his kingdom.—By him kings reign, and princes decree justice, even all the nobles and judges of the earth.—His eyes are upon the ways of men—His voice which is full of majesty, to earthly potentates, is, be wise now, O ye kings; be instructed, ye judges of the earth—serve the Lord with fear, and rejoice in your exalted stations with submissive awe—embrace the Son, lest he be angry, and ye perish from the way.

The christian temper, wro't in the heart by the Divine Spirit, restores the human mind to its primitive rectitude,—animates every faculty of the soul—directs every action to its proper end—extends its views beyond the narrow limits of time, and raises its desires to immortal glory.

This makes the face of every saint to shine; but renders the ruler, in his elevated station, gloriously resplendent.

This commands reverence to his person—attention to his counsels—respect to the laws—and authority to all his directions.—And renders an obedient people easy and happy under his rule.

Which leads to the consideration of the last thing suggested in the text, viz. The glorious effects of a just administration of government.

And he shall be as the light of the morning when the sun riseth, even a morning without clouds—as the tender grass springing out of the earth, by clear shining after rain.

This includes, both the distinguishing honor and respect acquired by rulers of this character; and the unspeakable felicity of a people thus favored of the Lord.

Justice and judgment are the habitation of the throne of the Most High; and he delighteth to honor those who rule over men in his fear—He has dignified them with a title of divinity—and called them in a peculiar sense, the children of the Highest.

And we are not to wonder, that in the darker ages of the world, from worshipping the host of heaven, the ignorant multitude were led to pay divine honors to their beneficent rulers—whom they esteemed as demi-gods.

The light of Divine revelation has dispelled these mists of superstition and impiety, and opened to the pious ruler's view, the sure prospect of unfading glory in the life to come:—And in the present state he is not without a reward.

To find that his conduct meets with public approbation,—that he is acceptable to the multitude of his brethren, greatly corroborates his internal evidence of his own integrity and impartiality,—and especially, of his ability for public action.—And which is the height of his ambition in this state of pro-bation,—enlarges his opportunity of doing good.

The shouts of applause, not from sordid parasites, but the grateful,—the artless multitude, the pious ruler receives as the voice of nature—the voice of God.—This is his support under the weight of government, and fixes his dependence upon the aid of the Almighty, in whose fear he rules.

How excellent in the sight of God and man, are rulers of this character!

Truly the light is good, and a pleasant thing it is to behold the sun—Thus desirable—thus benign, are wise and faithful rulers to a people. The beautiful allusion in the text naturally illustrates this.

The Sun, as the center of the solar system, connects the planetary worlds, and retains them in their respective orbits: They all yield to the greater force of his attractive power,—and thus with the greatest regularity observe the laws, im-pressed upon the material creation.

The Ruler of the day, as on a throne, shining in his strength, nearly preserves his station, and under the prime agent, di-rects all their motions—imparting light and heat to his several attendants, and the various beings which the Creator has placed upon them. His refulgent rays dispel the gloomy shades, and cause the cheerful light to arise out of thick dark-ness, and all nature to rejoice.

The Planets, with their lesser attendants, in conformity to their common head, mutually reflect with feebler beams their borrowed light, for the common benefit; and all, in propor-tion to their distance and gravity bear their part, to support the balance of the grand machine.

By this apposite metaphor, the Divine Spirit has represented the character and extensive beneficence of the faithful ruler—who with a God-like ardor employs his authority and influence, to advance the common interest.

The righteous Lord, whose countenance beholdeth the upright, will support and succeed rulers of this character: And it is an evidence of his favor to a people, when such are appointed to rule over them.

The natural effect of this is quietness and peace, as showers upon the tender grass, and clear shining after rain.

In this case a loyal people must be happy, and fully sensible that they are so—while they find their persons in safety—their liberties preserved—their property defended,—and their confidence in their rulers entire.

The necessary expences of government will be born by the community with pleasure, while justice holds the balance, and righteousness flows down their streets.

Such a civil state, according to the natural course of things, must flourish in peace at home, and be respectable abroad—private virtues will be encouraged, and vice driven into darkness—industry in the most effectual manner promoted—arts and sciences patronized—the true fear of God cultivated,—and his worship maintained.

This,—this is their only invaluable treasure.—This is the glory, safety and best interest of rulers—the sure protection and durable felicity of a people.—This, thro' the Redeemer, renders the Almighty propitious, and nigh unto a people in all they call upon him for.

Happy must the people be, that is in such a case—Yea, happy is the people whose God is the Lord.

But the affairs of this important day demand our more immediate attention.

With sincere gratitude to our Almighty Preserver, we see the return of this Anniversary; and the leaders of this people assembled, (tho' not according to the general desire, in the city of our solemnities)—to ask counsel of God; and as we trust, in the integrity of their hearts, and by the skillfulness of their hands, to lead us in ways of righteousness and peace.

The season indeed is dark; but God is our sun and shield.

When we consider the days of old, and the years of ancient time,—the scene brightens,—our hopes revive.

Our Fathers trusted in God,—He was their help and their shield.

These ever memorable worthies, nearly a century and an half since, by the prevalence of spiritual and civil tyranny, were driven from their delightful native land, to seek a quiet retreat in these uncultivated ends of the earth.

And however doubtful it might appear to them or others, whether the lands they were going to possess, were properly under the English jurisdiction; yet our ancestors were desirous of retaining a relation to their native country, and to be considered as subjects of the same prince.

They left their native land, with the strongest assurances, that they and their posterity should enjoy the privileges of free natural-born English subjects; which they supposed fully comprehended in their charter. The powers of government therein confirmed to them, they considered as including English liberty in its full extent.

And however defective their charter might be in form, a thing common in that day,—yet the spirit and evident intention of it, appears to be then understood.

The reserve therein made of passing no laws contrary to those of the parent state, was then considered as a conclusive evidence of their full power, under that restriction only, to enact whatever laws they should judge conducive to their benefit.

Our Fathers supposed their purchase of the aboriginals, gave them a just title to the lands—that the produce of them by their labour, was their property, which they had an exclusive right to dispose of—that a legislative power, respecting their internal polity, was ratified to them—and that nothing short of this, considering their local circumstances, could entitle them or their posterity to the rights and liberties of free, natural-born English subjects.

And it does not appear but that this was the general sentiment of the nation, and parliament.

They did not, then, view their American adventurers, in the light ancient Rome did, her distant colonies; as tributaries, unjustly subjected to arbitrary rule; by the dread or force of her victorious arms—But as sons, arrived to mature age— entitled to distinct property,—yet connected, by mutual ties of affection and interest, and united under the common supreme head.—

The New-England Charter, was not considered, as an act of grace, but a compact, between the Sovereign and the first patentees.

Our Fathers plead their right to the privilege of it, in their address to King Charles the second;—wherein they say—"It was granted to them, their heirs, assigns, and associates for ever; not only the absolute use and propriety of the tract of land therein mentioned; but also full and absolute power of governing all the people of this place, by men chosen from among themselves, and according to such laws as they shall from time to time see meet to make and establish, not being repugnant to the laws of England—They paying only the fifth part of the oar of gold and silver, that shall be found here— for and in respect of all duties, demands, exactions and services whatsoever". And from an apprehension, that the powers given by the crown to the four commissioners sent here, were in effect subversive of their rights and government—they add,—"We are carefully studious of all due subjection to your Majesty, and that not only for wrath, but for conscience sake."

"But it is a great unhappiness to be reduced to so hard a case, as to have no other testimony of our subjection and loyalty offered us but this, viz. to destroy our own being, which nature teacheth us to preserve; or to yield up our liberties, which are far dearer to us than our lives—and which, had we any fears of being deprived of, we had never wandered from our fathers houses into these ends of the earth—nor laid out our labors and estates therein."

But all their humble addresses were to no purpose.

As an honorable historian observes—"At this time Great-Britain, and Scotland, especially, was suffering under a prince inimical to civil liberty: And New-England, without a miraculous interposition, must expect to share the same judgments." And indeed of this bitter cup, the dregs were reserved for this people, in that and the succeeding happily short, but inglorious reign.

Our Charter was dissolved, and despotic power took place.

Sir Edmund Andros—a name never to be forgotten—in

imitation of his Royal Master, in wanton triumph, trampled upon all our laws and rights.—And his government was only tolerable, as it was a deliverance from the shocking terrors of the more infamous Kirk.

Sir Edmund at first made high professions of regard to the public good—But it has been observed,—"that Nero concealed his tyrannical disposition more years than Sir Edmund and his creatures did months."

But the triumphing of the wicked is often short.

The glorious revolution, under the Prince of Orange, displayed a brighter scene to Great-Britain, and her colonies. And tho' no part of its extended empire did bear a greater part in the joy of that memorable event than this province, yet it was then apprehended we were not the greatest sharers in the happy effects of it.

I trust we are not insensible of the blessings we then received, nor unthankful for our deliverance from the depths of woe.

We submitted to the form of government established under our present Charter—trusting, under God, in the wisdom and paternal tenderness of our gracious Sovereign—That in all appointments reserved to the crown, a sacred regard would be maintained to the rights of British subjects;—and that the royal ear would always be open to every reasonable request and complaint.

It is far from my intention to determine whether there has been just reason for uneasiness or complaint on this account—But with all submission, I presume the present occasion will permit me to say,—That the importance of his Majesty's Council to this people appears in a more conspicuous light, since the endeavors which have been used, to render this invaluable branch of our constitution, wholly dependent upon the chair.

Should this ever be the case, which God forbid—Liberty here will cease.—This day of the gladness of our hearts, will be turned into the deepest sorrow.

The authority and influence of his Majesty's Council, in various respects, while happily free from restraints, is momentous: our well-being greatly depends upon their wisdom and integrity.

The concern of electing to this important trust, wise and faithful men, belongeth to our Honored Fathers now in General Assembly convened.

Men of this character we trust are to be found, and upon such, and only such, we presume will the eye of the electors be this day.

It is with pleasure that we see this choice in the hands of a very respectable part of the community, and nearly interested in the effects of it.

But our reliance, Fathers, under God, is upon your acting in his fear.

God standeth in the assembly of the mighty, and perfectly discerns the motives by which you act—May his fear rule in your hearts, and unerring counsel be your guide.

You have received a sure token of respect, by your being raised to this high trust;—but true honor is acquired only by acting in character.

Honor yourselves, Gentlemen,—Honor the council-board —your country—your king—and your God, by the choice you this day make.

You will attentively consider the true design of all civil government; and without partiality, give your voice for those you judge most capable and disposed to promote the public interest.—Then you will have the satisfaction of having faithfully discharged your trust—and be sure of the approbation of the Most High.

The chief command, in this province, is now devolved upon one of distinguished abilities, who knows our state, and naturally, must care for us—One, who in early life has received from his country the highest tokens of honor and trust, in its power to bestow. And we have a right to expect, that the higher degrees of them conferred by our gracious Sovereign, will operate thro' the course of his administration, to the welfare of this people.

His Honor is not insensible, that as his power is independent of the people, their safety must depend, under providence, upon his wisdom,—justice, and paternal tenderness, in the exercise of it.

It is our ardent wish and prayer, that his administration may procure ease and quietness to himself, and the province.—

And having served his generation according to the Divine will,—he may rise to superior honors in the kingdom of God.

When the elections of this important day are determined—what farther remains to be undertaken for the securing our liberties—promoting peace and good order—and above all—the advancement of religion—the true fear of God thro' the land, will demand the highest attention of the General Assembly.

We trust the fountain of light, who giveth wisdom freely, will not scatter darkness in your paths—and that the day is far distant, when there shall be cause, justly to complain—The foundations are destroyed; what can the righteous do?

Our present distresses, Civil Fathers, loudly call upon us all, and you in special, to stir up ourselves in the fear of God—Arise, this matter belongeth unto you, we also will be with you, be of good courage and do it.

Whether any other laws are necessary for this purpose; or whether there is a failure in the execution of the laws in being, I presume not to say.—But with all due respect, I may be permitted to affirm, that no human authority can enforce the practice of religion with equal success to your example.

Your example, Fathers, not only in your public administrations, but also in private life, will be the most forcible law—the most effectual means to teach us the fear of the Lord, and to depart from evil.

Then, and not till then, shall we be free indeed—being delivered from the dominion of sin, we become the true sons of God.

The extent of the secular power, in matters of religion, is undetermined;—but all agree,—that the example of those in authority, has the greatest influence upon the manners of the people.

We are far from pleading for any established mode of worship; but an operative fear of God—the honor of the Redeemer, the everlasting King—according to his gospel.

We whose peculiar charge it is to instruct the people, preach to little purpose, while those in an advanced state, by their practice say—the fear of God is not before their eyes.—Yet will we not cease to seek the Lord, till he come and rain down righteousness upon us.

I trust, on this occasion, I may, without offence—plead the
cause of our African slaves; and humbly propose the pursuit of
some effectual measures, at least, to prevent the future importation of them.

Difficulties insuperable, I apprehend, prevent an adequate
remedy for what is past.

Let the time past more than suffice, wherein we, the pa-
trons of liberty, have dishonored the christian name,—and degraded human nature, nearly to a level with the beasts that
perish.

Ethiopia has long stretched out her hands to us—Let not
sordid gain, acquired by the merchandize of slaves, and the
souls of men—harden our hearts against her piteous moans.
When God ariseth, and when he visiteth, what shall we answer!

May it be the glory of this province—of this respectable
General Assembly—and we could wish, of this session, to lead
in the cause of the oppressed.—This will avert the impending
vengeance of heaven—procure you the blessing of multitudes
of your fellow men ready to perish—be highly approved by
our common Father, who is no respecter of persons—and we
trust, an example which would excite the highest attention of
our sister colonies.

May we all, both rulers and people, in this day of doubtful
expectation, know and practice the things of our peace—and
serve the Lord our God without disquiet, in the inheritance
which he granted unto our fathers.

These adventurous worthies, animated by sublimer prospects, dearly purchased this land with their treasure.—They
and their posterity have defended it with unknown cost,*—in
continual jeopardy of their lives—and with their blood.

Thro' the good hand of our God upon us, we have for a
few years past been delivered from the merciless sword of the
wilderness, and enjoyed peace in our borders—and there is in
the close of our short summer the appearance of plenty in our
dwellings; but from the length of our winters, our plenty is

---

*Be it far from me, O Lord, said the ancient Hero, that I should do this;
is not this the blood of the men that went in jeopardy of their lives? therefore he would not drink it.—Will not the like sentiments rise in a generous
mind, thrust into our possessions?—

consumed, and the one half of our necessary labour is spent in dispersing to our flocks and herds, the ingatherings of the foregoing season: And it is known to every person of common observation, that few—very few, except in the mercantile way,—from one generation to another, acquire more than a necessary subsistence, and sufficient to discharge the expences of government, and the support of the gospel—yet content, and disposed to lead peaceable lives.

From misinformations, only, we would conclude, recent disquiets have arisen—they need not be mentioned—they are too well known—their voice is gone out thro' all the earth—and their sound to the end of the world.—The enemies of Great-Britain hold us in derision—while her cities and colonies are thus perplexed.

America now pleads her right to her possessions—which she cannot resign, while she apprehends she has truth and justice on her side.

Americans esteem it their greatest infelicity, that thro' necessity, they are thus led to plead with their parent state—the land of their fore-father's nativity, whose interest has always been dear to them*—and whose wealth they have increased by their removal, much more than their own.

They have assisted in fighting her battles, and greatly enlarged her empire—and God helping, will yet extend it thro' the boundless desert, untill it reach from sea to sea.

They glory in the British constitution, and are abhorrent, to a man, of the most distant thought of withdrawing their allegiance from their gracious Sovereign, and becoming an independent state.

And tho' with unwearied toil, the colonists can now subsist upon the labors of their own hands—which they must be driven to, when deprived of the means of purchase,—yet they are fully sensible of the mutual benefits of an equitable commerce with the parent country; and chearfully submit to regulations of trade, productive of the common interest.

These their claims, the Americans consider, not as novel, or wantonly made, but founded in nature—in compact—in their

*Their losses, and private expences, in watches, guards and garrisons for their defence, and from continual alarms—in all their former wars—have greatly exceeded the public charges.

right as men—and British subjects—The same which their fore-fathers the first occupants made, and asserted, as the terms of their removal with their effects into this wilderness* —and with which the glory and interest of their King, and all his dominions, are connected.

May these alarming disputes be brought to a just and speedy issue—and peace and harmony be restored.

But, while in imitation of our pious forefathers, we are aiming at the security of our liberties; we should all be concerned to express, by our conduct, their piety and virtue. And in a day of darkness, and general distress,—carefully avoid every thing offensive to God, or injurious to men.

It belongs not only to rulers—but subjects also, to set the Lord always before their face, and act in his fear.

While under government, we claim a right to be treated as men;—we must act in character, by yielding that subjection which becometh us as men.

Let every attempt to secure our liberties be conducted with a manly fortitude; but with that respectful decency, which reason approves, and which alone gives weight to the most salutary measures.

Let nothing divert us from the paths of truth and peace, which are the ways of God—and then we may be sure that he will be with us as he was with our fathers—and never leave nor forsake us.

Our Fathers, where are they?—They looked for another and better country, that is an heavenly. They were but as sojourners here; and have long since resigned these their transitory abodes, and are securely seated in mansions of glory. —They hear not the voice of the oppressor.

We also are all strangers on earth; and must soon, without distinction, lie down in the dust; and rise not, till these heavens and earth are no more.

May we all realize the appearance of the Son of God, to

---

*It is apprehended, a greater sacrifice of private interest to the public good, both of Great-Britain and the Colonies, hath at no time been made, than that of the patriotic merchants, of this, and all the considerable colonies, by their non-importation agreement—And whatever the effects may be, their names will be remembered with gratitude to the latest generations, by all true friends to Britain and her Colonies.

judge the world in righteousness;—and improve the various talents committed to our trust; that we may then lift up our heads with joy—and thro' grace, receive an inheritance which cannot be taken away—even life everlasting.

AMEN.

NATHANAEL EMMONS

The Dignity of Man

*A Discourse Addressed to the Congregation in Franklin,
Upon the Occasion of their receiving from Dr. Franklin,
the Mark of his Respect, in a rich Donation of Books,
Appropriated to the Use of a Parish-Library.*

———

TO HIS EXCELLENCY
BENJAMIN FRANKLIN, Esq.
PRESIDENT OF THE STATE OF PENNSYLVANIA;
THE ORNAMENT OF GENIUS, THE PATRON OF SCIENCE,
AND THE BOAST OF MAN;
THIS DISCOURSE IS INSCRIBED, WITH THE GREATEST
DEFERENCE, HUMILITY AND GRATITUDE, BY HIS MOST
OBLIGED, AND MOST OBEDIENT SERVANT,

THE AUTHOR.

Franklin, in Massachusetts,
March 1, 1787.

A Discourse Addressed to the Congregation in Franklin.

1 KINGS II. 2.
—Shew thyself a Man.

DAVID closed the scene of life, with that propriety of conduct, and that composure of mind, which at once displayed the beauty of religion, and the dignity of human nature. When the time of his departure drew nigh, he had nothing to do to prepare for death, but only, like other pious and illustrious Patriarchs, to converse with his friends, and to give them his last and best advice. And, as he had, some time before, committed to Solomon the care of his Family and government of his Kingdom; so he felt a strong and ardent desire, that this beloved Son, in whom he had reposed such important trusts, should appear with dignity, and act a noble and worthy part upon the stage of life. Accordingly he called him into his presence, and with equal solemnity and affection, addressed him in these memorable words, "I go the way of all the earth: be thou strong therefore, and shew thyself a man." This appellation sometimes signifies the dignity, and sometimes the meanness of our nature. Job makes use of it to express our meanness and turpitude in the sight of God. "How can man be justified with God? or how can he be clean that is born of a woman? Behold, even to the moon and it shineth not, yea the stars are not pure in his sight. How much less man that is a worm, and the Son of Man which is a worm." But Isaiah employs this same appellative to represent the dignity of human nature, when he calls upon stupid idolaters to "remember this, and shew themselves men." So here, David in his dying address to Solomon, "shew thyself a man," evidently means to use the term in the best sense, and to urge him to act up to the dignity of his nature, and the end of his being.

Agreeably therefore to the spirit and intention of the text, the subject which now properly lies before us, is the dignity of man. And, I hope, the observations which shall be made upon this subject, will do honour to our nature in one view, and pour contempt upon it in another, and so lead us all into a clear and just apprehension of ourselves, which is the most useful, as well as the most rare and high attainment in knowledge.

The dignity of man appears from his bearing the *image* of his Maker. After God had created the heavens and the earth, and furnished the world with a rich profusion of vegetive and sensitive natures, he was pleased to form a more noble and intelligent Creature, to bear his image, and to be the lord of this lower creation. "And God said, Let us make man in our image, after our likeness. And the Lord God formed man of the dust of the ground, and breathed into his nostrils the breath of life; and man became a living soul." This allows us to say, that man is the offspring of God, a ray from the fountain of light, a drop from the ocean of intelligence. Though, man, since the fall, comes into the world destitute of the *moral* image of God, yet, in the very frame and constitution of his nature, he still bears the *natural* image of his Maker. His soul is a transcript of the *natural* perfections of the Deity. God is a spirit, and so is the soul of man; God is intelligence and activity, and so is the soul of man. In a word, man is the living image of the living God, in whom is displayed more of the divine nature and glory, than in all the works and creatures of God upon earth. Agreeably therefore to the dignity of his nature, God hath placed him at the head of the world, and given him the *dominion* over all his works. Hence says the Psalmist, "Thou hast made him a little lower than the Angels, and hast crowned him with glory and honour. Thou madest him to have *dominion* over the works of thy hands; thou hast put all things under his feet: all sheep and oxen, yea the beasts of the field; the fowls of the air; and the fish of the sea." How wide is the kingdom of man! how numerous his subjects! how great his dignity!

God has, besides, instamped a dignity upon man by giving him not only a rational, but an immortal existence. The soul, which is properly the man, shall survive the body and live forever. This might be argued from the nature, the capacity, and the desires of the human mind, and from the authority of the wiser Heathens, who have generally supposed the soul to be a spiritual and immortal principle in man. But, since the Heathen Moralists might derive their opinion from a higher source than the light of nature, and since every created object necessarily and solely depends, for continued existence, upon the will of the Creator; we choose to rest the evidence of this point upon the authority of the sacred Oracles. Here indeed we find the immortality of the soul sufficiently established. Solomon saith, "Who knoweth the spirit of man that goeth upward, and the spirit of the beast that goeth downward to the earth?" And, in another place, after describing the frailty and mortality of the body, he adds, "Then shall the dust return to the earth as it was, and the spirit shall return unto God who gave it." Agreeably to this, our Lord declares that men are able to kill the body, but are not able to kill the soul. And God has told us that he will, at the last day, separate the righteous from the wicked, and fix the latter in a miserable, but the former in a blessed immortality. Hence immortality appears to be the common property and dignity of the human kind.

The creatures and objects, with which we are now surrounded, have but a short and momentary being. One species of insects, we are told, begin and end their existence in twenty-four hours. Others live and flutter a few hours longer, and then drop into their primitive dust. The larger animals, which people the air, the earth, and the sea do, day after day, in a thick and constant succession, die and dissolve in their own elements. And even the whole material system will, after a few ages, either by the immediate hand of God, or by the gradual operation of the laws of nature, be rolled together as a scroll, and tumbled into one vast and promiscuous ruin. But *we* shall survive all these ruins and ravages of time, and live the constant spectators of the successive scenes of Eternity. And this renders us infinitely superior, in point of dignity and importance, to all the objects and creatures, whose existence expires with time.

The dignity of man also appears, from the great attention and regard, which God hath paid to him. God indeed takes care of all his creatures, and his tender mercies are over all his works: But man has always been the favorite child of Providence. God, before he brought him into being, provided a large and beautiful world for his habitation; and ever since the day of his creation, he has commanded all nature to contribute to his support and happiness. For his good, he has appointed the Sun to rule the day, and the Moon to rule the night. Into his bosom, he has ordered the Earth and the Sea to pour all their rich and copious blessings. And for his use and comfort, he has given the fowls of the mountains, the beasts of the forests, and the cattle upon a thousand hills. He has also given his Angels charge over him, to keep him in all his ways. Accordingly they have appeared from time to time, to instruct him in duty, to deliver him from danger, to bring him good tidings, to attend his dissolution, and to convey his departing spirit to the mansions of rest. But, the most distinguishing and most astonishing display of the divine mercy, is the Incarnation and Death of the Son of God for the salvation of man. By the Incarnation of Christ, our nature was united with the divine, and the dignity of man with the dignity of

Christ. Hence all the sufferings, which Christ hath endured on earth, and all the honours, which he hath received in heaven, have displayed the dignity of man. And for the same reason, the dignity of man will be eternally rising, with the rising honour and dignity of Christ.

But, we must furthermore observe, that the large and noble capacities of the human mind, set the dignity of our nature in the clearest and strongest light. Let us therefore consider, in this place, several of these with particular attention.

First, Man hath a capacity for constant and perpetual progression in knowledge. Animals, indeed, appear to have some small degree of knowledge. "The ox knoweth his owner, and the ass his master's crib." But, as all the lower species are destitute of the power of reasoning, or the faculty of arranging and comparing their ideas; so they are totally incapable of enlarging their views, by intellectual improvements. The bee cannot improve her skill, nor the ant her prudence, by observation or study. All their knowledge is the mere gift of God, which he bestows upon them without any application or exertion of theirs.

But, man is capable of improving in knowledge as long as he enjoys the means or materials of improvement. Indeed he has power to improve the smallest stock forever. The faculty of Reason, with which he is endowed, enables him to proceed from one degree of knowledge to another, in a constant and endless progression. The grounds of this are obvious. As a certain chain, or connection runs through all branches of knowledge; so the acquisition of one degree of knowledge facilitates the acquisition of another, and the more a man knows, the more he is capable of knowing. And, as all the powers and faculties of the mind brighten and expand by exercise; so a man's capacity for improvement increases, as the means and thirst for improvements increase. Accordingly the path of knowledge, has resembled the path of the Just, which shineth more and more unto the perfect day. One generation have been improving upon another, from age to age. And the improvements and discoveries of the last and present Century are truly surprizing, and justify this grand and bold description,

"Earth's disembowell'd, measured are the skies,
  Stars are detected in their deep recess,
  Creation widens, vanquish'd nature yields,
  Her secrets are extorted, art prevails.
What monuments of genius, spirit, pow'r!"

But to show that reality in this case surpasses description, let me here mention Solomon, that great man, who is addressed in our text, and whose astonishing improvements in knowledge are recorded by the pen of Inspiration, for the encouragement, as well as the instruction of all future ages. "And Solomon's wisdom excelled the wisdom of the East country, and all the wisdom of Egypt. For he was wiser than all men: than Ethan the Ezrahite, and Heman, and Chalcol, and Darda, the sons of Mahol: and his fame was in all nations round about. And he spake three thousand proverbs, and his songs were a thousand and five. And he spake of trees, from the cedar-tree that is in Lebanon, even unto the hyssop that springeth out of the wall: he spake also of beasts, and of fowls, and of creeping things, and of fishes." The children of the East country were the Chaldeans, who, after the flood, made the first advances in Astronomy, Philosophy and other abstruse sciences. Next to them the Egyptians turned their attention to Learning, and soon outrivalled all other nations in literary fame. Solomon therefore surpassed all the Priests and Poets, all the Physicians and Historians, and all the Naturalists, Philosophers, and Astronomers of the two most antient, and most refined nations in the world. What an exalted idea does this exhibit of his wisdom and learning! And, as we must suppose that he made these improvements by reading, by observation, and study; so he stands a lasting ornament of human nature, and a perpetual monument of man's capacity for constant and endless advances in knowledge.

Secondly, Man hath a capacity for holiness as well as knowledge. The horse and mule which have no understanding, and indeed all the lower animals, are utterly incapable of holiness; and even Omnipotence himself, to speak with reverence, cannot make them holy, without essentially altering the frame and constitution of their natures. But man is capable of holiness. His rational and moral faculties both capacitate and oblige him to be holy. His perception and volition, in connection with his reason and conscience, enable him to discern and feel the *right* and *wrong* of actions, and the *beauty* and *deformity* of characters. This renders him capable of doing justly, loving mercy, and walking humbly with God. In a word, this renders him capable of every holy and virtuous affection. And, as he is capable of growing in knowledge, so he is capable of growing in grace, in a constant and endless progression. What a dignity does this give to man, and how near does it place him to principalities and powers above! This leads me to observe,

Thirdly, That man hath a capacity for happiness, equal to his capacity for holiness and knowledge. Knowledge and holiness are the grand pillars which support all true and substantial happiness; which invariably rises or falls, accordingly as these are either stronger or weaker. Knowledge and holiness in the Deity are the source of all his happiness. Angels rise in felicity as they rise in holiness and knowledge. And saints here below grow in happiness as they grow in grace, and in the knowledge of holy and divine objects. Of this, we have a beautiful and striking instance in Solomon. View him at the Dedication of the Temple, when he fell upon his knees, and lifted up his hands and his heart to God, and poured into the ear of the divine Majesty the voice of prayer and supplication, the voice of joy, of gratitude and praise. How near did he approach to God! how high did he rise in felicity! how much did he anticipate the joys of the blessed! And, if we now follow him to the Temple above, where his views, his affections, and his joys are incessantly enlarging; we may form some faint conception of that amazing height, to which man is capable of rising in pure and divine enjoyments. What a vessel of honour and dignity will man appear, when all his capacities for knowledge, for holiness, and for happiness, shall be completely filled! And to all this we must add,

Fourthly, That man hath a capacity for great and noble actions. Of this, we might find numerous monuments, if we had time to survey the land of Shinar, where Babel, Babylon, and Ninevah stood; or the land of Egypt, where so many grand and costly Pyramids, Tombs, and Temples were erected; or the famous cities of Greece and of Rome, where the nobler efforts of human power and genius, have been still more amply displayed. But, the bounds of this discourse will allow us only to mention a few Individuals of our race, who, by their great and noble exertions, have done honour to human nature. Noah, the second Father of mankind, saved the world from total extinction. Joseph preserved two nations from temporal ruin. Moses delivered the People of God from the house of bondage, and led them through hosts of enemies and seas of blood to the land of promise. David settled the kingdom of Israel in peace; and Solomon raised it to the summit of national glory. Paul, in spite of Pagan superstition, laws and learning, established Christianity in the Heathen world. Luther, by the tongue and pen of controversy, brought about a great and glorious revolution in the christian Church. Newton, by his discoveries in the *material*, and Locke, by his discoveries in the *intellectual* world, have enlarged the boundaries of human knowledge, and of human happiness. And, to name no more, Franklin in the Cabinet, and Washington in the Field, have given Independence and Peace to America. But greater things than these remain to be done. The kingdom of Antichrist is to be destroyed, the Mahomedans are to be subdued, the Jews are to be restored, the Barbarous nations are to be civilized, the Gospel is to be preached to all nations, and the whole face of things in this world, is to be beautifully and gloriously changed. These things are to be done by the instrumentality of man. And by these, his capacity for great and noble actions, will be still more illustriously displayed. Thus the image, which man bears of his Maker, the immortal spirit which resides within him, the distinguishing favours, which he has received from the Father of mercies, and all his noble powers and faculties, unite to stamp a dignity upon his nature, and raise him high in the scale of Being.

It now remains to make a few Deductions from the subject, and to apply it to the happy occasion of our present meeting.

First, We may justly infer from the nature and dignity of man, that we are under indispensible obligations to Religion. Our *moral* obligations to religion are interwoven with the first principles of our nature. Our minds are so framed, that we are capable of knowing, of loving, and of serving our

Creator; and this lays us under *moral* obligation to worship
and obey him. Nor is there one of our race, who is incapable
of feeling his *moral* obligations to religion. Only draw the
character of the Supreme Being, and describe his power, wisdom, goodness, justice, and mercy, before the most ignorant
and uncultivated Savage; and, as soon as he understands the
character of God, he will feel that he *ought*, that he is *morally
obliged* to love and obey the great Parent of all. He will feel
himself under the same *moral* obligation to pay *religious
homage* to God, as to speak the truth, or to do justice to man.
Every man in the world is capable of seeing that the worship
of God is a reasonable service. Religion therefore takes its rise
and obligation not from the laws of Politicians, nor from the
ignorance and superstition of Priests; but from the immutable
laws of nature, and the frame and constitution of the human
mind. Hence it is utterly impossible for men wholly to eradi-
cate from their minds all sense of *moral* obligation to religion,
so long as they remain moral agents, and are possessed of
common sense.

And, as man is formed for religion, so religion is the ornament and perfection of his nature. The man of religion is, in
every supposable situation, the man of dignity. Pain, poverty,
misfortune, sickness and death, may indeed *veil*, but they cannot destroy his dignity, which sometimes shines with more resplendent glory, under all these ills and clouds of life. While
the soul is in health and prosperity; while the mind is warmed
with holy and religious affections, the man appears with
dignity, whether he is in pain, or in sickness, or even in the
agonies of death. But, Atheism and Infidelity, with their evil
offspring, serve more than all other causes put together, to
defile the nature, and sink the dignity of man. This appears
from the black description, which the great Apostle Paul has
drawn of those nations, who *liked not to retain God in their
knowledge.* "They changed the glory of the uncorruptible
God into an image made like to corruptible man, and to
birds, and to four-footed beasts, and creeping things. They
changed the truth of God into a lie, and worshipped and
served the creature more than the Creator. They *dishonoured*
their own bodies by the most mean and infamous vices. And
they became of a *reprobate mind*, being filled with all un-

righteousness, fornication, covetousness, maliciousness; full of envy, murder, debate, deceit, malignity; whisperers, back-biters, haters of God, despiteful, proud, boasters, inventors of evil things, disobedient to parents, without understanding, covenant-breakers, without natural affection, implacable, un-merciful." These are things which defile the nature, and de-grade the dignity of man.

And these too are prejudicial to all learning and mental im-provements. These debilitate the mind, cloud the imagina-tion, and cramp all the noble powers and faculties of the soul. These degraded the Alexanders, the Pompeys, and the Cæsars of the world, below the human kind. Had they been influ-enced by truly virtuous and religious motives, their great ex-ertions would have done honour to human nature, but now they have stained the glory of all flesh. Nay, even a *declension* in religion hath left indelible stains upon the brightest Characters recorded in sacred story; I mean Noah, David, and Solomon. Solomon was at the height of his glory, when at the height of religion; but when he declined into vice and idola-try, he fell into shame and disgrace, and lost that dignity, which had filled the world with his fame.

Now there is nothing that can wipe off from human nature these blemishes, and restore the dignity of man, but true reli-gion. That charity which seeketh not her own, that love which is the fulfilling of the law, is the essence of religion and the bond of perfection. This cures the mind of Atheism, Infidelity and Vice. This fills the soul with noble views and sentiments, and directs all its powers and faculties to their proper use and end. This exalts the dignity of human nature, and spreads the greatest glory around any human character. This rendered Noah superior to Nimrod, Moses superior to Pharaoh, David superior to Saul, Solomon superior to Socrates, Daniel superior to the wise men of Babylon, and Paul superior to Plato, and all the Sages of the Pagan world. "Happy is the man who findeth *religion*: For the merchandise of it is better than the merchandise of silver, and the gain thereof than fine gold. She is more precious than rubies; and all the things thou canst desire, are not to be compared to her. Length of days are in her right hand; and in her left hand riches and honour. Her ways are ways of pleasantness, and all her paths are peace. She is a tree of life to them that lay hold upon her; and happy is the man that retaineth her." Let us all then put on this rich and beautiful ornament, and shew ourselves men.

Secondly, This subject may help us to ascertain the only proper and immutable boundaries of human knowledge. I mean such boundaries of our knowledge, as arise from the frame and constitution of our nature, and not from any particular state or stage of our existence. Our rational powers, it is often said, are limited, and therefore all our intellectual pursuits and improvements must be equally limited. This is doubtless true in a certain sense, but not in the sense in which it is generally understood. It appears from what has been observed in this discourse, concerning the powers and faculties of the human mind, that men are capable of making constant and eternal progression in knowledge. The only bounds therefore that can be set to their intellectual improvements, must be such as have respect to the *kinds*, and not to the *degrees* of their knowledge. There are, indeed, certain *kinds* of knowledge, which men are totally incapable of understanding; but these are only such *kinds* of knowledge, as require more than *created* faculties to understand. For, whatever *kinds* of knowledge any *created* beings are capable of understanding, *men* are also capable of understanding, though with more difficulty, and less rapidity. As Newton knew nothing, which any man is now incapable of knowing, in a certain time, and under certain circumstances; so there is nothing, which any intelligent creatures now know, that men are incapable of knowing, in a given time, and under proper advantages. The truth is, rationality is the same in all intelligent beings. Reason is the same thing in God, in Angels, and in Men. As men therefore bear the *image* of God, in point of Rationality; so they possess all the *rational* powers and faculties, which bear any analogy to the divine intelligence; or, which can be communicated to *created* beings. Accordingly Angels are superior to men in the same sense, and perhaps nearly in the same degree, that Newton was superior to most of his own species. As Newton had no *rational* power or faculty peculiar to himself; so Angels have no rational powers or faculties which are not common to all intelligent creatures. Every man therefore is capable of learning all that any man, or any intelligent creature has learned, or can learn. Hence the only natural and necessary distinction between Angels and men, and between one man and another is this; that Angels are capable of acquiring knowledge more easily, and more swiftly than men; and some men are capable of acquiring knowledge more easily, and more swiftly than others. And this difference between Angels and men, and between man and man, to whatever cause it may be owing, will probably continue forever; and forever keep up a distinction in their knowledge and improvements for the time being.

Now this being a settled point, we may easily, perhaps, fix the proper boundaries of human knowledge, or determine the proper subjects of human enquiry. It is a caveat given to men, but especially to inquisitive men, not to pry into things above their measure. This caveat, undoubtedly, in some cases, may be very proper and necessary; but generally, I imagine, it is not only needless but absurd. For, unless men attempt to pry into things which surpass *created* powers and faculties, I do not know that they transgress the boundaries of human knowledge. There are some things, which, in a moment, we know cannot be understood by *creatures*. And there may be many others, which, by a little attention, we may perceive come under the same predicament. All therefore that Divines and Metaphysicians, as well as Philosophers have to do, in order to know where to *begin*, and, where to *end* their researches, is only to determine whether or not, the proposed subjects require more than *created* abilities to investigate them. If they do require more than *created* abilities, it is vain and absurd to proceed: but if they do not, we have the same grounds to proceed, that men have ever had, to attempt new discoveries.

Thirdly, This subject gives us reason to suppose, that men, in the present state, may carry their researches into the works of nature, much further than they have ever yet carried them. The fields of Science, though they have been long traversed by strong and inquisitive minds, are so spacious, that many parts remain yet undiscovered. There may be therefore room left in Divinity and Metaphysics, as well as in Philosophy and other sciences, to make large improvements. The large and growing capacities of men, and the great discoveries and improvements of the last and present Century, give us grounds to hope, that human learning and knowledge will increase from generation to generation, through all the remaining periods of time. Men have the same encouragements now, that Bacon, Newton and Franklin had, to push their researches further and further into the works of nature. It is, therefore, as groundless, as it is a discouraging sentiment, which has been often flung out, that all the subjects of Divinity, all of human inquiry, are nearly exhausted, and that no great discoveries or improvements, at this time of day, are either to be expected or attempted. The present Generation have superior advantages, which, with capacities no more than equal to their Fathers, may enable them to surpass all who have gone before them in the paths of Science. Let this thought rouse their attention, and awaken their exertions, to shew themselves men.

Fourthly, The observations, which have been made upon the noble powers and capacities of the human mind, may embolden the Sons of Science to aim to be Originals. They are strong enough to go alone, if they only have sufficient courage and resolution. They have the same capacities and the same original sources of knowledge, that the Antients enjoyed. All men are as capable of thinking, of reasoning, and of judging for themselves in matters of Learning, as in the common affairs and concerns of life. And would men of Letters enjoy the pleasures of knowledge, and render themselves the most serviceable to the world, let them determine to think and judge for themselves. Their progress may perhaps, in this way, not be so rapid; yet it will be much more entertaining and useful. When I say their progress may not be so rapid, I mean with respect to those only, who possess moderate abilities; for as to those of superior powers, they will make much swifter progress by going alone out of the common, beaten track. The way to outstrip those who have gone before us, is not to tread in their steps, but to take a nearer course. What Philosopher can expect to overtake Newton, by going over all the ground, which he travelled? What Divine can expect to come up with Mede, Baxter, or Edwards, while he pursues their path? Or, what Poet can hope to transcend Homer and

Milton, so long as he sets up these men as the standards of perfection? If the Moderns would only employ Nature's powers, and converse freely and familiarly with Nature's objects, they might rise above the Antients, and bear away the Palm from all who have gone before them in the walks of Science.

Fifthly, What has been said concerning the nature and dignity of man, shows us, that we are under indispensable obligations to cultivate and improve our minds in all the branches of human knowledge. All our natural powers are so many talents, which, in their own nature, lay us under *moral* obligation to improve them to the best advantage. Being men, we are obliged to act like men, and not like the horse or the mule which have no understanding. Besides, knowledge, next to religion, is the brightest ornament of human nature. Knowledge strengthens, enlarges, and softens the human soul, and sets its beauty and dignity in the fairest light. Learning hath made astonishing distinctions among the different nations of the earth. Those nations, who have lived under the warm and enlightening beams of science, have appeared like a superior order of beings, in comparison with those, who have dragged out their lives under the cold and dark shades of ignorance. The Chaldeans and Egyptians, as well as the Greeks and Romans, while they cultivated the arts and sciences, far surpassed, in dignity and glory, all their ignorant and barbarous neighbours. Europe, since the resurrection of Letters in the sixteenth Century, appears to be peopled with a superior species. And the present Inhabitants of North-America owe all their superiority to the Aboriginals, in point of dignity, to the cultivation of their minds in the civil and polite arts. Learning has also preserved the Names, Characters, and mighty Deeds of all antient nations from total oblivion. A few learned men in each nation, have done more to spread their national fame, than all their Kings and Heroes. The boasted glory of Britain is more to be ascribed to her Newtons, her Lockes, and her Addisons, than to all her Kings, and Fleets, and Conquerors.

But the cultivation and improvement of the mind is more necessary for use, than for ornament. We were made for usefulness and not for amusement. We were made to be the servants of God, and of each other. We were made to live an active, diligent, and useful life. As men therefore we cannot reach the end of our being, without cultivating all our mental powers, in order to furnish ourselves for the most extensive service in our day and generation. Knowledge and learning are useful in every station; and in the higher and more important departments of life, they are absolutely and indispensibly necessary.

Permit me now, therefore, My Hearers, to suggest several things, which may serve to excite you to improve your minds in every branch of useful knowledge, which, either your callings, or your circumstances require.

I am happy to congratulate you, my Countrymen, that we live in an age, which is favourable to mental and literary improvements. In the present age, our Country is in a medium between Barbarity and Refinement. In such an age, the minds of men are strong and vigorous, being neither enfeebled by luxury, nor shackled by authority. At such an happy period, we have come upon the stage, with the fields of science before us opened but not explored. This should rouse our dormant faculties, and call up all our latent powers in the vigorous pursuit of knowledge. Those, who have gone before us in these pursuits, have only set us an example, and facilitated our progress, without damping our hopes, or forbidding our success.

Again, we live under that Form of government, which has always been the friend of the Muses, and parent and nurse of Arts. It was while Greece and Rome were free, republican States, that Learning there sprang up, flourished, and rose to its height; and enrolled their Names in the annals of Fame. Liberty, which is the birth-right of man, and congenial with his nature, ennobles and exalts the mind; inspires it with great and sublime sentiments; and, at the same time invites and encourages its highest exertions, with hopes of success and the promises of reward. For, in free Republics, where liberty is equally enjoyed, every man has weight and influence in proportion to his abilities, and a fair opportunity of rising, by the dint of merit, to the first offices and honours of the State.

Another motive to improvement, you will allow me to say, may be taken from your past singular and laudable efforts to cultivate and diffuse useful knowledge in this place. It is now more than Thirty years, since this single and then small Congregation collected a very considerable Parish-Library, in order to improve their minds in useful and divine knowledge. This was such an effort to promote mental improvements as, I imagine, cannot be easily found in this Country. The benefit of this Library you have all perhaps more or less experienced; and, to its happy influence owe, in a measure, your general Character as a Religious and Intelligent People. May this consideration have all its weight upon you, since our Lord hath said in the Parable of the Talents, "Whosoever hath, to him shall be given, and he shall have more abundance."

In this respect, how wonderful the smiles of Providence upon you! Whose heart doth not glow with gratitude for the auspicious occasion which hath now brought us together! How great our obligations to God for the unmerited and unexpected Favour of a rich Collection of Books now received, as a mark of Respect of the first literary Character in America, his Excellency President FRANKLIN! This well chosen and very valuable Library, while it sets the divine kindness in a high and engaging light, lays you under the strongest ties of gratitude to improve the means of cultivating your minds for the service of God and of your fellow-men. Should you second the views of that great Man, and build upon the broad foundation which he has generously laid, you may enjoy ample advantages, in point of Books, to improve your mental powers, and furnish yourselves for usefulness in all your various stations and employments of life. Nor can you neglect or abuse such advantages, without drawing upon yourselves the reproach of the world, and which is infinitely more, the reproach of your own consciences. Be entreated then to improve to the best advantage, every price put into your hands to get wisdom.

There are three grand sources of knowledge before you, Nature, Men, and Books. Attentively read each of these great Volumes.

Read Nature, which is truly an original author. King David, studying this large and instructive volume, which filled his mind with the noblest views and sentiments, broke forth in a rapture of praise, "The heavens declare the glory of God; and the firmament sheweth his handy work. Day unto day uttereth speech, and night unto night sheweth knowledge."

Read Men. "For as in water face answereth to face, so the heart of man to man." This volume David perused and digested in the Court and Camp of Saul, where human nature, with, and without a veil, was very visible to his critical and discerning eye.

But the design of this discourse more directly leads me to urge the reading of Books in particular. These are a grand magazine of knowledge, and contain the Learning and Wisdom of ages. But, you must know, that Books are a peculiar fountain, from whence may be drawn either *sweet* waters or *bitter*, the waters of *life*, or the waters of *death*. For this reason, you will allow me here to advise you, to take heed *how* you read.

And, in the first place, read with Caution. A person may be undone by a single volume. Nothing contains such secret and fatal poison as Books. Though they profess a kind and friendly intention, yet they often bite like a serpent and sting like an adder. Be careful what books you read. There are many, which the young and inexperienced at least, should totally avoid. In this particular, if you are wise, and faithful to yourselves, you will endeavour to obtain and follow good advice.

Read with Judgment. This is, in every view, indispensibly necessary, in order to read to advantage. This will enable you to discover and ascertain the main object of your Author, which will be a key to all he says in the various parts and branches of his subject. This will help you to distinguish truth from error, good sentiments from bad, and sound reasoning and strict demonstration, from mere conjectures and bold assertions. But if you read without judgment, you will be in danger of imbibing error as well as truth, of always believing the last Author you read, and of never having any fixed and settled sentiments of your own.

Read for Use and not for Amusement. The time is worse than thrown away, which is spent in reading for amusement, without any particular end or object in view. We should be careful how we take up a Book, especially, if it be an entertaining one, with which we have no particular concern; for it will require a considerable effort of the mind to throw it aside, and if we do not throw it aside it will steal away our time, and prevent our being better employed. Almost any book, if read for use, may be of advantage. We may read amusing, and, even corrupting books to advantage, if we read them in order to make a good use of them. The bee can suck honey from the same flowers, from which other insects suck poison. But we may read all our lives to very little purpose, if we read every book which happens to fall in our way for amusement and not for use. We should always read with reference, either to our own particular profession, or to the particular state and situation of our own minds. When we read with either of these objects in view, we shall be apt both to understand and digest what we read. There is great and singular advantage in reading proper books at a proper time, when we really stand in need of them. This is of the same happy tendency, as eating and drinking at the proper seasons, when it serves to nourish and strengthen, instead of clogging and surfeiting the body.

Read with Patience. Many Authors are both prolix and obscure in conveying their ideas; and after all, have much more chaff than wheat in their writings. In reading such, we must go over a great deal of ground in order to reap a small harvest of ideas. It is difficult, however, for any man to treat any subject in a method entirely new. We must expect therefore to find many common and familiar thoughts in every Author, which we must patiently read, if we would *properly* come at those which are more new, entertaining and instructive. And for this reason it is generally best perhaps, if Authors are of any tolerable size, to read them through, with patience and attention. This is but justice to them, and prudence to ourselves.

Read with Confidence. In our first essays after knowledge, we are obliged, by the laws of our nature, to depend upon the assistance and instruction of others, and in consequence of this, we are apt to feel, through life, too great a sense of our own weakness and imbecility, and to despair of going a step further than we are led. This, however is very unfriendly to all improvement by reading. We ought therefore to feel that we are men, and place a proper degree of confidence in our own strength and judgment. We ought to fix it in our minds that we are capable of improvement. Such a confidence in ourselves as this, will embolden us to read with a view not only of understanding, but of improving upon the Authors we read. Very few Authors have exhausted the subjects upon which they have treated, and therefore have generally left us ample room to improve upon what they have written. And by reading with this view, if we fail of improving upon those we read, we shall, however, more clearly and fully understand *their* meaning, and more thoroughly make *their* ideas and sentiments our own.

Yet, at the same time, every one should read with Humility. Reading, more than any other method of improvement, is apt to puff up the mind with pride and self-conceit. For, persons of reading are very prone to estimate their knowledge more according to the number of books which they have read, than according to the number of ideas which they have collected and digested. And so are ready to imagine, that they have engrossed to themselves all knowledge; though, in reality, they have not read enough, to learn their own ignorance. This should teach us to take the Poet's advice.

> "A little learning is a dangerous thing:
> Drink deep, or taste not the Pierian spring.
> There shallow draughts intoxicate the brain;
> And drinking largely sobers us again."

Nor is pedantry peculiar to those only, who begin to read and study late in life; for it is too often found among those, who have enjoyed a regular and liberal education. Do not Physicians and Attorneys, by reading a few books in Divinity, sometimes fancy themselves masters of that sacred and sublime science? And, on the other extreme, do not Divines, by reading a few books in Law and Physic, sometimes fancy themselves masters of those two learned professions? But this is rank pedantry. It is an easy matter to gain a superficial acquaintance with the general objects of science; but it is a laborious task to acquire a deep and thorough acquaintance with any single branch of knowledge. It is easy to know *something* about *every thing*; but it is difficult to know *every thing* about *any thing*. If men of reading would collect the whole stock of their knowledge, and the whole force of their genius more to a point, and aim to be complete masters of their own professions; they would become at once, much less pedantic, and much more useful to the world. Many men of real abilities and learning, have defeated their own usefulness, by attempting to know, and to do too much.

In the last place, read *prayerfully*. "If any of you lack wisdom, says the Apostle, let him ask of God, that giveth to all men liberally, and upbraideth not; and it shall be given him." This Solomon found to be true, by happy experience. "In Gibeon the Lord appeared to Solomon in a dream by night; and God said, Ask what I shall give thee. And Solomon said, Thou hast shewed unto thy servant David my father great mercy, according as he walked before thee in truth, and in righteousness, and in uprightness of heart with thee; and thou hast kept for him this great kindness that thou hast given him a son to sit on his throne, as it is this day. And now, O Lord my God, thou hast made thy servant king instead of David my father; *and I am but a child; I know not how to go out or come in.* And thy servant is in the midst of thy people which thou hast chosen, a great people that cannot be numbered nor counted for multitude. *Give therefore thy servant an understanding heart,* to judge thy people, that I may discern between good and bad: for who is able to judge this thy so great a people? *And the speech pleased the Lord, that Solomon had asked this thing.* And God said unto him, Because thou hast asked this thing, and hast not asked for thyself long life; neither hast asked riches for thyself, nor hast asked the life of thine enemies, but hast asked for thyself *understanding* to discern judgment; behold, I have done according to thy words: lo, I have given thee *a wise and understanding heart.*" It was Dr. Doddridge, I think, who never used to take up a new book to read, without an ejaculatory prayer for divine influence and direction. This example is worthy of universal imitation. Let us therefore always accompany our essays after knowledge with a humble and prayerful spirit; and then we may hope to read and study with safety and success.

To all these directions, I might now add, Diligence and Perseverance, which always have had, and always will have, a mighty influence, in all the great things done by mankind.

But I shall only add a few words to those, who are very immediately and deeply interested in the things which have been said in this discourse.

This subject calls upon Parents in particular, to shew themselves men. You are, my respectable Hearers, men in years, be men also in virtue, in religion, and in understanding. Let the dignity of man appear in all your conduct, and especially in your conduct towards your children. Let them see the dignity of human nature exemplified before their young and attentive minds. They are every day, and every hour, watching your conduct, and looking up to you for example and instruction. Take heed, that none of your words, none of your actions, none of your pursuits, be unworthy of men. But, let all your conversation and behaviour be such as your children may follow with propriety, with safety, and dignity. And while you are teaching them by example, teach them also by precept. Give them good instruction; and for this purpose, provide them good instructors. These are of great importance to your children, whose progress in knowledge, will generally bear a very exact proportion to the abilities and fidelity of their Teachers. The education of children has always been an object of great attention among all wise nations, and especially among all wise and good Parents. Let this then be the object of your attention. Consider the dignity of man. Consider the worth of the soul. Consider the rich and invaluable treasure put into your hands. Consider how much the dignity and happiness of your children both in time and in Eternity, depend upon your care and fidelity. And let the ties of nature, the authority of God, and your own solemn vows, engage you to bring them up in the nurture and admonition of the Lord, and to cultivate and embellish their opening minds in every branch of useful and ornamental knowledge. Admit not the thought, that such little, such weak, and to appearance, such useless creatures, are of small importance; but remember that they are men in miniature, and may, one day, surprize the world with their dignity. When a young Prince is born, all the Kingdom feel the importance of his education, and are anxiously concerned to have the ablest instructors employed, to form him for great and noble actions. But you have more than Princes, even young Immortals, committed to your care, whose powers and capacities, whose dignity and importance, will astonish you, at the great Day, if not before. How happy will that parent be, who shall then be found to have been faithful to his children! "He will then join, as a celebrated Writer observes, his virtuous offspring in the habitations of the just, and there see them rise up and call him blessed. But if a parent neglects his duty to his children; if he sets before them an example of irreligion, and suffers them to grow up loose and unprincipled, he may expect that their blood will be required at his hands, and he should tremble to think of that period of retribution, when probably they will curse him for that negligence which has ruined them."

Finally, Let this subject awaken the attention of the Youth, to the dignity of their nature and the end of their being. My dear young Friends, you will soon be called to act your various parts upon the stage of life. You are now the Hope of your Parents, of your Pastors, and of your Country. The eyes of the world are upon you. Be entreated then to cultivate all your noble powers, and to shew yourselves men, in whatever departments of life, divine Providence shall place you. Piety and Knowledge will prepare you for a useful and honourable life, and for a peaceful and triumphant death. Let these then be the supreme objects of your pursuit. Early consecrate all your time and all your talents to the service of God, and of your fellow-men. Seek for knowledge, as for silver, and search for it, as for hid treasures; and sacrifice every object which obstructs your pursuit of it. "Through desire a man having *separated himself*, says Solomon, seeketh and intermeddleth with all wisdom." If you would make progress in learning, and rise to any distinguishing degrees of knowledge, you must separate yourselves from the vanities of youth, and devote those vacant hours to mental improvements, which, too many of your age trifle away in folly and vice. In particular, flee youthful lusts, which war against both the body and the mind. Shun that all-devouring monster, Intemperance, by which so many *strong minds* have been cast down and destroyed. Avoid bad company and unmanly diversions, which are an inlet to every vice. Hold in steady contempt, *Beaus* and *Fops*, those butterflies which live upon the filth and dregs of the earth. Diogenes walking the streets of Athens at noon-day with a lanthorn in his hand; and being asked, as he intended to be, what he was searching after, tartly replied, "I am looking for Men." A severe satire upon the luxury and effeminacy of that once manly and virtuous People. The dignity of man appears in the ornaments of the mind, and not in those of the body. Seek therefore to adorn and embellish your minds both by reading and observation, and your gifts and abilities will make room for you, and bring you before great men. You have peculiar advantages and encouragements to animate you to great and noble exertions. *Therefore set your Mark of intellectual attainments as high as you please, and, according to the common course of events, you will, by uniformity, diligence, and perseverance, infallibly reach it.* Your generous Benefactor hath set you an example, as well as given you the means of intellectual improvements. That Great Man, in the morning of life, was surrounded with uncommon difficulties and embarrassments, but by the mere dint of genius and of application, he surmounted every obstacle thrown in his way, and by his rapid and astonishing progress in knowledge, he hath risen, step by step, to the first offices and honours of his Country, hath appeared with dignity in the Courts of Britain and of France, and now fills more than half the globe with his Fame. Keep this illustrious example in your eye, and shew yourselves men.

DEVEREUX JARRATT

*The Nature of Love to Christ,
and the Danger of Not Loving Him,
Opened and Explained*

1. Cor. xvi. 22. *If any man love not the Lord JESUS
CHRIST, let him be Anathema, Maran-atha.*

LOVE is the spring of all acceptable obedience, and the most
essential ingredient in true religion. Without it, all our pretensions to virtue and morality are vain and fruitless.

Should we give all our goods to feed the poor, and deliver
up our bodies to be burnt, in defence of religion itself; had
we the knowledge of all mysteries; the gift of prophecy, and
could speak with all the eloquence of angels; yet with all these
qualifications and high improvements, we should be nothing
without love.

Love to God and the Saviour, is a thing not only essentially
necessary, in order to render most religious performances
acceptable, but also a thing infinitely fit and reasonable in itself, as every one who acknowledges the existence of a God,
will confess. If perfect beauty and unbounded goodness; if the
greatest benefactor and most generous friend, infinite excellency and tender compassion, should be loved, then, without
all doubt, we should love *the Lord Jesus Christ*, in whom every
thing that is great and good, beautiful, excellent, tender and
compassionate meets and centers. And because he ought to
be loved, and it is so infinitely fit and reasonable that all his
rational creatures should love him, therefore the wretch, who
dares withhold his love from him, or refuses to bestow his
supreme affection upon him;—and, though he calls himself a
christian, yet maintains a secret enmity of heart towards him;
and prefers the pleasures and profits of this world to him, is
judged worthy the most dreadful of all curses, even to be
anathematized from the presence of Christ when he cometh

to sit in judgment, and pronounce sentence of damnation upon the whole Christ-despising and impenitent world. To this purpose speaks the apostle in my text: If any man love not the Lord Jesus Christ, let him be *Anathema, Maran-atha*; Let him be bound over to eternal punishment, and depart accursed into everlasting fire prepared for the devil and his angels, those malignant and irreconcileable enemies to the Lord and his Christ.

Various are the opinions of commentators about these words, "Let him be Anathema, Maran-atha"—but the more probable and satisfactory to me, is that of Dr. Doddridge. He supposes, that when the Jews lost the power of life and death, they used nevertheless to pronounce an anathema on persons, who according to the law of Moses should have been executed: and such a person became an anathema and *accursed*. They had a full pursuasion the *curse* that was pronounced, would not be in vain, but that some judgment correspondent to the sentence, would certainly befal the offender. For instance, a man to be stoned would be killed by the fall of a stone or some heavy body upon him: One whom the law sentenced to be burnt, would be burnt in his house. Now to express their faith, that God would, one way or other, interpose to add that efficacy to their own sentence, which they could not give it, they might use the words, maran-atha, that is, *the Lord cometh*: or he will surely and quickly come to put this sentence in execution, and to shew that the person on whom it falls, is indeed anathema, accursed.—* Viewing the words in this light, the apostle's allusion to them is very beautiful, when he was speaking of a *crime*, not capable of being convicted or punished by the church; that is, a secret alienation of heart from Christ maintained under the form, or by any of the professors of christianity: and therefore he reminds them that the Lord Jesus Christ, will come at length, and point out such a person and punish him in a proper manner.

That this awful sentence might be the more attentively regarded by the Corinthian brethren, as well as to let them see that the whole epistle was genuine, the apostle writes it with his own hand. *The salutation of me Paul with mine own hand.*

* *See Doddridge in Loc.*

It is supposed that St. Paul, having no great dexterity in the use of the pen, used to employ an Emanuensis to write for him, as he dictated: but, for the purposes already mentioned, he might choose to write this sentence with his own hand. If any man love not the Lord Jesus Christ, let him be anathema maran-atha. As if he had said; if any man, be his station in church or state, what it will; be his gifts ever so great, his profession ever so plausible, his life ever so upright in the eyes of men, yet if he is destitute of sincere love to the Lord Jesus Christ, let him be *accursed**—he is worthy of the most fearful curse, which will be put in full execution upon him when *the Lord cometh,*† in the day of his appearing and glory, to judge the quick and dead.

In the prosecution of this subject I shall observe this method,

I. Shew what is implied in loving the Lord Jesus Christ; or, what love to Christ is.

II. I shall consider the reasonableness of loving him.

III. Consider the danger of not loving him, &c.

IV. Conclude with some application.

I. I am to shew what is implied in loving the Lord Jesus Christ, or what love to Christ is.

Love to Christ, or God, (for there needs no distinction, since Christ is God, as well as man.) Love to Christ, I say, may be thus described: "It is a gracious and supernatural principle, or habit, wrought in the soul by the power of the holy spirit; whereby the creature is inclined supremely to delight in, and esteem the Lord Jesus, so that his thoughts freely go out after him, and his meditation of him is sweet; it excites earnest desires after communion with him in his ordinances; and to please him by walking before him in holiness and righteousness all our days." Where there is the least spark of divine love there will also be an earnest desire for an interest in God's favour as the highest happiness, and a willingness to resign the whole soul to the Redeemer, and to receive him for all the purposes for which he is offered in the gospel. The true lover of Christ is willing and desirous to learn of him as his

* *Avadupua.*
† *Maqav-ada.*

prophet, and cheerfully submit to the teachings of his word and spirit;—to rely upon him as a priest to make an atonement for his sin by the blood of his cross; and to choose him for his Lord to reign over him, renouncing every Lord and Saviour beside; and lastly, he endeavours to do all the good he can for his sake, and especially to those who are of the household of faith. This is evidently implied in loving the Lord Jesus Christ. For rendering this more clear, and also that you may have an opportunity of enquiring whether the love of Christ be in you, I shall enlarge upon each particular in the definition.

1st. "Love to Christ is a supernatural principle wrought in the soul by the power of the holy spirit."

Would you know then whether you love the Lord Jesus Christ, you should examine how you came by this love; since it is not the spontaneous growth of nature, but the effect of divine power and influence. If you are strangers to a supernatural power working it in you, you may be assured, that whatever pretensions you may make of loving Christ, they are all vain and delusive. By nature we do not love him, but are strangely indisposed and disaffected to him, as experience might have fully taught us, had we carefully looked into our own hearts. We have abundant proof from scripture of our uncreaturely disaffection to our Creator. St. Paul tells us, "that the carnal mind of man in a state of nature, is enmity to God;" that "we are enemies to him in our minds, and by wicked works;" and, "that while we were yet enemies, Christ died for us." The whole gospel indeed, points out this truth; or why is it called, "the ministry of reconciliation." Why are we so earnestly intreated "*to be reconciled to God;*" or why does the apostle say, "that when we were enemies we were reconciled to God by the death of his Son?"—Brethren we were all by nature guilty of this monstrous crime of being enemies to the ever-blessed God in our hearts and ways. And you who are now the sincere lovers of God, do really know, that you were once implacable enemies to him. The question then is, who among you have been brought out of this wretched state? Surely a turn from a state of enmity to a state of love, must be a thing plainly perceivable. If you are now the lovers of Christ, you must have been the subjects of converting grace, and have consequently experienced a great and mighty change wrought upon your hearts and affections: and you cannot, sure, be altogether insensible how this change was brought about. Surely you can now recollect how you were shocked when a view of your disaffection to God first appeared to you, and you made a discovery of the dire secrets of wickedness which lurked in your hearts, unperceived before. Were you not made to cry out, "Oh! is this my heart! I once flattered myself that my heart was good, though I knew my life was not; but now I see it to be a sink of pollution indeed!" O then, you cried out with the greatest importunity, that the merciful Lord God would change your inward temper and disposition, and shed abroad his love in your hearts, by the Holy Ghost. In a word, if you are the lovers of God, you have been made new-creatures; old things are done away, and all things are become new. And now, brethren, who among you are the sincere lovers of the Lord Jesus Christ? Who among you have had this great change wrought in you?

Methinks I hear some honest, but doubting soul reply,— "For my part I am afraid to say that I have any true love to my Lord and Saviour, I feel so little of it in my heart, and am so cold and languid in his service. But this I know, that there has been a change wrought in me, so that I am not altogether what I once was. I am confident that I do not love the Lord Jesus, as I know I ought; but this is the grief of my soul, that I do not love him as he deserves; and nothing would give me greater pleasure than to feel my heart burn with his love, and to find my whole soul going out after him with ardent affection." This is an honest confession, and your complaint is no more than what thousands of sincere christians have cause to utter. I speak this for your comfort: yet I would have you to be jealous over your own hearts, and still seek for greater degrees of love.

But do not the consciences of many of you plainly tell you that you are utter strangers to this great change; you know nothing of any love, but what was always natural to you. Some of you, perhaps, are so blind to this day, that you would insist upon it that you always loved the Lord, and never was an enemy to him in all your life. O sirs, if this be the case of any of you, there is all the reason in the world to conclude that you are indeed strangers to yourselves and to every divine principle and affection. I must honestly tell you, that if you have never experienced a work of divine grace upon your hearts, and a change in the temper of your minds, though you may be outwardly, decent and moral people, and have a glaring profession of religion, yet you have not the love of God in you: I know you, saith our Saviour to the Jews, who were zealous for religion, I know you, that you have not the love of God in you. How should you have it? it is not natural: and you know not any thing of its being implanted by grace. It is plain, my dear brethren, that you are destitute of divine love; and O that you would but admit the conviction, and never rest till you obtain this heaven-born principle from God.

2d. "Love to the Lord Jesus Christ inclines the creature supremely to delight in and affectionately to esteem him, so that his thoughts freely go out after him."

It is natural for the thoughts to fix upon the object beloved; and we find sweet delight in contemplating the excellencies which are discovered in it. If therefore we love the Lord Jesus Christ, we shall find our thoughts frequently through the day going out after him and affectionately entering upon him. Thus it was with the Psalmist.—"How precious are the thoughts of thee unto me, O God, how great is the sum of them; if I should count them, they are more than the sand, when I wake I am still with thee. I remember thee upon my bed and meditate upon thee in the night watches." Those that love the Lord will find their warm and affectionate thoughts making frequent excursions toward him; and they find great pleasure therein;—while those that are his enemies, forget the Lord and do not like to retain God in their thoughts. A thousand other objects meet their hearts and affections and carry away their thoughts and pursuits after them, while the Lord Jesus Christ is only complimented with an empty profession.

From this property or effect of love, I would again ask; "Who among you are the lovers of the Lord Christ?"—Who can give a comfortable answer to the question from this scriptural characteristic of divine love? Some of you I hope can do it. You are indeed often jealous of your love; but yet you have reason to conclude that you do love him. If you love him not, why are you so frequently thinking of him. Why cannot your thoughts and affections dwell on things below and fly round in a circle of vanity as they once could? why do your thoughts so often hover around the cross of your crucified Jesus, and cling to him as your only trust? Why do you grieve because you cannot love him with that ardor as you know his excellencies demand, and as you desire to do? Why are you uneasy when you hear his dear name blasphemed, by the tongues of daring mortals, and see his laws trampled under foot? And why are you sorry because you serve so good a master with so much langour and inconstancy? Do not all these things shew that you really love him, though not so much as you would and ought? Therefore take comfort ye humble jealous-hearted creatures, you have at least a spark of divine love enkindled in your hearts; and though the spark at times seems just ready to expire, yet he that first kindled it will protect and recruit it with the oil of his grace; so that all the storms raised against it from earth and hell shall never be able entirely to extinguish it: But—

On the other hand, may not many of you be convinced by these things, that the love of Christ is not in you? Are not your hearts and affections rivitted to the present world and expressively set on things below? You do not naturally and freely delight to think of God, and Christ, and things eternal. Your conversation seldom takes a turn upon divine matters; you talk of any thing more freely and pleasantly than you do of God, and the wonders of redeeming love and goodness. Here it is that you rather choose the company of those whose conversation savours of the world and its vanities; and when the name of God and Christ is seldom mentioned, unless in a trifling or profane manner. And what is the reason of this? Does not this shew that you are disaffected to God, and that you are conscious that your behaviour toward him, is not such as he approves? Surely you cannot pretend to be lovers of God or the Lord Jesus Christ, while such is your temper and disposition. No, brethren, such earthly souls, who are so indifferent about divine things, and affect so little to think or hear of Jesus, and talk of the wonders of his love and mercy displayed in the gospel, must be strangely disaffected to him, and they are accounted his enemies now, and will be treated as such.

III. "True love to Christ creates in the soul an ardent desire of holding communion with him in his ordinances."

It is natural for a man to delight in and desire the company and conversation of one he loves; and he will take every opportunity to enjoy his society. Thus the lovers of the Lord Jesus Christ are anxious to embrace and improve every opportunity of seeking and enjoying holy communion with him. And as the ordinances of the gospel, the word, sacrament and prayer, are the places of appointment, where the Lord meets his people and communicates the influence of his grace, to quicken their souls and to inflame their hearts with love; therefore they are diligent in their attendence upon these, and esteem one day spent in the sanctuary better than a thousand spent in the tents of wickedness. The house of the Lord is the place where they delight to resort; and O! what sacred pleasure do they often enjoy here, when they get an interview with the Lord Jesus, and have liberty in pouring out their hearts into the ears of their indulgent Father, and feel his love shed abroad in their hearts by the Holy Ghost. This, to them, is a little heaven upon earth. But when at any time they miss these sweet communications in the ordinances, and the Lord seems to hide his face, then they languish and pine and return disappointed; moaning like the turtle for his cooing mate. These things may sound strange in some of your ears, and may be thought to savour strongly of enthusiasm; but they are well known and experienced by all the friends and lovers of Jesus. And if you are strangers to them, it is because you are strangers to the sacred passion of divine love. For truly, says the apostle, (speaking in his own and in the name of his fellow christians,) *truly our fellowship is with the Father and the Son Jesus Christ.* And, *if any man love me,* says our Lord, *my Father will love him, and we will come and make our abode with him.*

And now, my brethren, I would again put the question. Have you discovered in yourselves this mark, of your being the lovers of the Lord Jesus Christ? Do you understand what I have said with regard to communion with the Father and the Son, by your own experience. Can you say, with the Psalmist, it is good for me to draw near to God? Do you attend upon the ordinances of the gospel constantly, because there you hope to enjoy the pleasure of meeting your God and holding communion with him? For this purpose also you pray to and worship God in your families and in your secret retirements, that you may get greater discoveries of the glory of the Lord, and have your hearts more suitably affected towards him. But because the Lord loveth the gates of Zion more than all the dwellings of Jacob, therefore you make the house of God, and the place where his honour dwelleth, the place of your greatest delight: and would not on any occasion let slip an opportunity of approaching the Lord with the great congregation. If you can say, that thus it is with you, then have ye reason to draw the welcome conclusion, that you do indeed love the Lord and his Christ.

But are there not many of you, who might be convinced, by this time that they are destitute of this divine principle. You are strangers to that sacred communion with God, which his children enjoy, and therefore you neither seek it nor desire it—you attend indeed at the house of God, when your worldly concerns will give you leave, but this is more out of custom, and to satisfy conscience, than from any real delight you find in the ordinances. In short you will do no more this way than what you are forced to; and hence religious duties are rather drudgery than a sacred pleasure. But I must hasten,

IV. To the last thing I mentioned in the definition. "That love to Christ will necessarily lead him that is possessed of it, to study and endeavour with all his heart to walk in all holy obedience to the commandments of Jesus our Lord and King."

This earnest desire to please the object beloved, is also a natural passion: and therefore if you love the Lord Jesus Christ, it will be your constant and unwearied endeavour to please him. Let others follow their own inclinations and seek the gratification of their lusts and appetites; let them inquire, who will show us any earthly good, that they may indulge themselves in what is pleasing to the flesh; but as for you, your inquiry will be, what shall we do to please the Lord and promote his glory in the world. And so cautious will you be lest you offend, that you shun all places of temptation, as much as in you lies; and avoid every thing that is either sinful in itself, or has an apparent tendency to seduce your hearts and affections from God; or may be a means of seducing you to fall into sin. And in this respect the christian is mindful of that apostolic injunction, To *abstain from all appearance of evil.* The genuine test of divine love, is sincere obedience to all the commands. "If any man love me," says Christ, "he will keep my words, and he that loveth me not, keepeth not my sayings. He that hath my commandments and keepeth them, he it is that loveth me."—And the beloved apostle says, "This is the love of God that ye keep his commandments." And again, "He that saith, I know him, and keepeth not his commandments is a liar."

In vain then do you pretend to love God, if you allow yourselves in the breach of his commandments. And yet, alas! do not the drunkards and swearers, liars and sabbath-breakers, and even whoremongers and adulterers presume that they are lovers of God? Strange indeed!

And now let me ask you, who name the name of Christ, and profess love to the Lord Jesus; does your love stand this test? Have you respect to all God's commandments? and do you utterly abhor every false way? Do you make it the labour and business of your lives to approve yourselves in the sight of God, and to please him well in all things? Do you cautiously avoid whatever you know would displease him; and vigorously resist every temptation to sin? Some of you, I hope, can give comfortable answers to these questions. But as for others, if you have been honest in putting these questions to your hearts and consciences, you must have discovered that the love of God is not in you. Strong and clear evidence is against you, and you stand convicted of the horrid crime of *not loving* the Lord Jesus Christ. You are proved to be his enemies in your hearts by the wickedness of your lives. And however you may flatter yourselves, and muffle yourselves up in the darkness of ignorance, in order to keep out the painful light of conviction, yet the Lord knoweth your hearts; he can see through all false disguises, and penetrate into the secrets of wickedness which lurk within; and will one day bring you forth, with the workers of iniquity, and treat you as enemies and persons disaffected to his crown and dignity. And a fearful destruction you must expect, since you refuse to love the Lord Jesus Christ, the Saviour of a lost world, and are guilty of a crime so uncreaturely and unreasonable,—Which leads me

II. To shew the reasonableness of loving the Lord Jesus Christ.

Here I need not be long; for full evidence turns upon us at first sight. If infinite holiness, unbounded goodness, and perfect beauty demand our love and esteem; then the Lord Christ ought to be loved and esteemed; since all these excellencies meet and center in him, in the highest degree. He is the chiefest among ten thousand, and altogether lovely.

If our creator, preserver, and liberal benefactor, deserves to be loved and adored by his creatures and dependents; then it is fit and reasonable that we should love and adore the Lord Jesus: since we, as well as all things in heaven and earth, were created by him, and are still daily supported by the bounties of his hand.

If we should love what is good in itself, and what is good to us, then Jesus the Saviour claims the chief place in our hearts and affections, for he is good and doth good, and his tender mercies are over all his works.

If it be fit and reasonable that we should render love for love; then it is highly fit and reasonable that we should love him, whose love to us brought him from heaven and the bosom of his Father, down into our wretched world, where he endured every species of trouble and affliction, which human or diabolical cruelty could invent. It was in love for us, that he became an exile from his Father's throne;—for us did he agonize in the garden of Gethsamine, till all his garments were dyed red in his own sacred gore;—for us was his back harrowed by the tormenting scourge;—for us was he maltreated by the Jewish rabble, and unjustly condemned as a malefactor, at Pilate's bar;—for us did he toil up the bloody steep of Calvary, under the load of his fatal cross;—for us was he nailed to the accursed tree, and O! for us he expired in agonies unknown, giving his own life a ransom for ours. Herein is love beyond degree. Greater love hath no man than this, that a man lay down his life for his friend; but Christ hath manifested the supereminency of his love, by laying down his life for those that were enemies.—Judge ye brethren; should not our hearts burn with his love, and should not our whole souls be engaged to give evidences of our gratitude, by doing all in our power to please such a bountiful benefactor and generous friend?—And that heart that is so dead to every generous sentiment and principle of gratitude, as to refuse to love him, after all, must be possessed with such an invincible malignity, as would render him fit, only for the society of the malignant powers of darkness. And the crime in itself is so base and unreasonable, that whosoever is guilty of it, does justly deserve to be *anathema maran-atha.* And this leads me to

III. Where I was to consider the danger of not loving the Lord Jesus Christ. And this is expressed in the latter part of the text: Let him be anathema maran-atha.

A soul destitute of the love of Christ must be exposed to the greatest of dangers, inasmuch as he is guilty of the greatest of sins. Want of love to him is a crime of the deepest die, because it is sinning against the strongest obligations that possibly can be. He therefore, who is guilty of it, is in danger of the most intollerable vengeance, proportionable to the demerit of his guilt. A crime so unnatural, so inexcusable, must expose a man to the most aggravated condemnation. He that is an enemy to the Lord Jesus, in his heart and by wicked works, is in danger every moment, lest that God, to whom vengeance belongeth, should no longer bear with his monstrous disaffection, under a mark of friendship, but cut him off and sink him down to hell among devils and hypocrites, whom he so much resembles in his temper and disposition. The heart, which is not seasoned with the love of Christ, must be a sink of abomination, odious and detastable in the eyes of divine purity; *a vessel of wrath filled to destruction.* O how many thousands of souls that profess to be the followers of Christ;—have been baptized into, and are called after his name; who are so far from loving him, that they openly proclaim themselves his enemies by their unholy lives and conversations. There are others who carry their mark more secretly; they profess great friendship to Christ, and may go so far in things external as to impose upon their fellow mortals, who cannot explore the secrets of the heart. But what of all this? the Lord whose eyes are as a flaming fire, sees through all your false disguises; is perfectly acquainted with the secrets of iniquity that lurk in the deep recesses of your hearts and souls, and counts you his enemy, while you are not actuated by the spirit of love. All your performances that spring not from a principle of love, are nothing worth. Consider, dear immortal souls, the danger, the awful danger you are in, while you are strangers to the love of Christ. The Lord counts you enemies to him, and he is an enemy to you, and is angry with you every day. And though he bears with you for a while, and heaps those mercies upon you, which might gain your affections and turn the inveterate enmity of your hearts into love; yet as long as his benefits fail to have this effect upon you, you abide under the *anathema*, the curse of God. "Cursed are ye in the city, and cursed in the field; cursed in your basket, and in your store; cursed in the fruit of your body, and the fruit of your land, and in your kine; cursed when you go out, and cursed when ye come in. Yea, cursed in every thing ye set your hands to do."

Thus O sinners, you are cursed in the present time, and are treasuring up wrath against the day of wrath and revelation of the righteous judgment of God. You are every moment in danger of the arrest of death, which will put you beyond all possibility of altering your present condition, and God will remain your enemy for ever. Think, O think of this, O ye Christ-despising sinners, what an enemy you have to contend with. He is wise in heart and mighty in strength, and none that set themselves against him can prosper. Have ye strength to contend with him? Are ye mightier than he? Have ye an arm like God, or can ye thunder with a voice like him? Can ye resist his determinations and elude his judgments? If you are so vain as to think ye can perform such exploits, then gird up your loins like men, and, as ye have already by practice, now by words declare war against him. Summon the whole band of your fellow-sinners upon earth, and call the stubborn powers of hell to join in confederacy with you; and go forth to meet the Lord, when he cometh forth against you in all the terrors of an enraged enemy. See if you can withstand the right-aiming thunder-bolts of his power, or quench the lightnings of his wrath. I know that you would shudder at the very thoughts of such a desperate enterprize: you confess your weakness in words: and why then, in the name of God, do you not drop your present unnatural rebellion against him by your practice; and divest yourselves of your uncreaturely disaffection and enmity of heart toward him! For while you retain these, you are in danger every moment to be crushed down by the weight of his Almighty hands, into everlasting misery and destruction. The Lord has borne with you a long time; he has patiently waited for your return, and his goodness may induce him to bear with you a while longer. But he will not bear always. He will ere long commission the king of terrors to tear your guilty souls from your bodies, and cite them before his awful bar; to hear their doom and sink to hell. And at the appointed time, the same Lord Jesus, who once bled in sacrifice for sin, and so richly deserved your love and obedience, will come again in all the pomp and majesty of a God, to render vengeance to his adversaries and his rebukes with flaming fire. Then, O then it will appear to the whole congregated universe, that you had ever retained a secret alienation of heart to the blessed Jesus, and will accordingly be pronounced anathema maran-atha, accursed when the Lord comes to judgment.

Oh! that you would think of that awful day, when Christ the Lord shall be revealed from heaven with his mighty angels, in flaming fire—when he shall appear in the clouds and the trump of God shall be blown, with the strength of an archangel's breath, to summon the nations to appear before the judgment-seat.—The judge seated, and ten thousand times ten thousand standing before him—See! his enemies seperated from his friends, and placed upon the left hand! See, what dire astonishment seizes upon them, and trembling and amazement take hold of them—Pale horrors appear in every face, the joints of their loins are loosed and their knees smite one against another;—while the judge, the Lord Jesus, rises, with solemn aspect, and pronounces the decisive sentence; "Those mine enemies that would not that I should reign over them, let them be taken and bound over to everlasting destruction, from the presence of the Lord and the glory of his power;—let them be bound hand and foot and cast into utter darkness, where there is weeping, and wailing, and gnashing of teeth." Or, "Go ye cursed into everlasting fire, prepared for the devil and his angels." This is the awful import of that sentence in my text, Let him be anathema maran-atha.

O that you, my *dear people*, would think of that decisive day and solemn appearance of the great God. Realize it;—make it present to your view; that your hearts and minds being duly impressed therewith, you may no longer continue to rebel against that Almighty Lord God, the breath of whose displeasure will blast you in everlasting ruin.

Of all these dreadful things are you in danger, while you persist in sin, and love not the Lord Jesus Christ in sincerity. —I proceed

IV. To make some application. I shall improve this subject with an use of examination and exhortation.

Is it so, that those who love not the Lord Jesus Christ, are in such emminent danger—Hence see, that it highly becomes us to examine ourselves whether we love him or not.— Suppose the Lord Jesus should this day, put the same question to each one of us; as he did to Peter—"Simon, son of Jonas, lovest thou me?" Who among you could appeal to the all-seeing eye of God, and answer, "Lord thou knowest all things, thou knowest that I love thee."

There is the more reason to push home this inquiry, because in nothing are mankind more apt to deceive themselves, than in this particular point of loving the Lord. On the one hand, some who do really love him are so apt to be jealous over themselves, that they are afraid to draw the conclusion, that they have one spark of sincere love to him; and this, that they do indeed love him, they do not enjoy the comfort of it. While on the other hand, those who are intirely destitute of this heaven-born principle, are unapt to call their love in question, and thus deceive themselves and are ready to perish through presumption. Therefore put the question home to your hearts and examine closely, and do not give over till you have brought the matter to some certain issue.—

Q. But how shall I know whether I love the Lord Jesus or not?

A. I have already described the marks and characters of genuine love, under the first head of discourse, and by these I would have you examine yourselves. You may remember, I told you (1) that divine love was not the spontaneous growth of nature, but a principle implanted by a supernatural power; and that such as do now love God and Christ, have been sensibly convinced of their want of love, and have been made to cry heartily to heaven for it, and that it might be shed abroad in their hearts by the Holy Ghost.—(2) I told you that this love inclined and disposed a creature to delight in and highly esteem Christ, so that his thoughts would make frequent excursions toward him through the day. He would think of him with delight, and love to meditate upon the wonders of his redeeming mercy and goodness.—(3) That this love would excite the professor of it, to seek communion with Christ, and to make use of all the means and ordinances of grace to obtain it—And (4) That true love would constrain him to do every thing pleasing to Christ and abstain from every thing displeasing. Whatever the Lord forbids, that he cautiously avoids; whatever he commands, that he honestly endeavours to perform. By these marks, I request you to examine yourselves.—

To assist you further in this inquiry, I shall lay down three other marks and characters to examine yourselves by.

1st. If you love the Lord Jesus Christ, you will love his people. The saints, to you, are the excellent ones of the earth, in whom is your delight. For every one that loveth him that begat, loveth him also, who is begotten of him. "And by this we know that we are passed from death unto life, because we love the brethren." Do you find this to be the case with you? are the saints, or such as you have reason to believe are the true lovers and worshippers of Jesus; are these, I say, lovely in your eyes? And do you make those your chosen companions and intimate friends, who love to talk of Christ and the glorious mysteries of redemption, and to tell what God has done for their souls?

2d. If you love Christ, you choose him and love him, in all his offices. To you, that believe, he is precious. As a prophet he is lovely and precious to you, because by his word and spirit you are taught and enlightened.—As a priest he is precious, because by the blood of his cross, he made an atonement for sin, and you choose him as your only Saviour and deliverer from the wrath of God and the curse of the law, renouncing every other trust and dependence whatever.—As a king, you choose him to reign over you, you love his government, and are grieved that you serve him not better.

3d. If you love the Lord Jesus Christ you will endeavour and pray for the increase of his kingdom on earth. It will rejoice your hearts to hear of any new subjects listing under his banner and flocking to his standard: you will chearfully do all in your power to gain souls to Christ. And you cannot but grieve when you see your dear master's interest getting ground so slowly in the world; while so many thousands are crouding the devil's camp.

These marks must suffice at present for you to examine yourselves by, with regard to your love to Christ Jesus our Lord—And who among you can lay claim thereto?—If you can claim these characters as your own, then fear not to conclude, that you do indeed love the Lord Jesus Christ.—But if not.—Though you should flatter yourselves ever so much, yet, I tell you, ye have not the love of God in you. He that loveth me not, keepeth not my sayings. The case is quite plain with regard to such as live in the practice of any overt acts of sin; such as swearing, lying, drunkenness and such like. Or in the omission of plain commanded duty to God and man. Would to God you would admit the conviction and take the alarm: seeing you stand exposed to all the dreadful things contained in that awful sentence in this text, if any man love not the Lord Jesus Christ, let him be anathema maran-atha.

What remains then, but that I exhort you by all that is dear and important, to lay the sad state of your souls to heart, and no longer continue enemies to God and your own everlasting interest.

I have told you already of the sad state your souls are in, and the more awful danger they are exposed to. But if a sense of your own danger and misery will not prevail with you to seek reconciliation with God, surely the love of Jesus must constrain you to it. And it is in his dear name that I beseech you to be reconciled to God. Is your enmity so inveterate and your disaffection to the best of beings so fixed and immoveable, as to be proof against the almighty attraction of redeeming love and goodness? Shall Jesus pour out his soul and expire in agony and blood, in love for you; and is it not strange that you cannot find it in your hearts to render love for love!—There is something so disingenuous and uncreaturely in such a temper and disposition, that I wonder you are not shocked at it yourselves. Does not Jesus richly deserve your most ardent love? Had any creature done the thousandth part of what Jesus has done for you, and you should still continue to despise him and use him ill; would you not be deemed a monster of ingratitude? What then must we think of those men, who live daily upon the bounties of Christ, and owe all that they enjoy or hope for in time or in eternity to his mediation, suffering, and death, and yet continue enemies to him in their minds and wicked works! If these be not worthy of condemnation, who is?—To conclude. If any of you are sensible of your want of love to the Saviour, and would desire to be possessed of it, I would advise you as the best expedient to enkindle that sacred passion in your hearts, to think seriously, and often, of the great love of Christ, in so freely submitting to die for a lost world;—dwell upon the many instances of his goodness and mercy, and beg of God to open your eyes to see these things, in a suitable manner, so that they may have a proper effect upon your minds;—persevere in this course, till you can say with the apostle, we love him, because he first loved us. Which may God grant, for Jesus sake, *Amen.*

LEMUEL HAYNES

Universal Salvation: A Very Ancient Doctrine

With Some Account of the Life and Character of Its Author

A Sermon, Delivered at Rutland, West-Parish, in the Year 1805.

————

PREFACE

There is no greater folly than for men to express anger and resentment because their religious sentiments are attacked. If their characters are impeached by their own creed, they only are to blame. All that the antagonists can say, cannot make falshood truth, nor truth falshood.

The following discourse was delivered at Rutland, Vt. June, 1805, immediately after hearing Mr. BALLOU, an Universal Preacher, zealously exhibit his sentiments. The author had been repeatedly solicited to hear and dispute with the above Preacher; and had been charged with dishonesty and cowardice for refusing. He felt that some kind of testimony, in opposition to what he calls error, ought to be made; and has been urged to let the same appear in print. But whether, on the whole, it is for the interest of truth, is left to the judgment of the candid.

Rutland, December 30, 1805.

A Sermon, &c.

GENESIS III. 4.
And the Serpent said unto the Woman, Ye shall not surely die.

THE holy Scriptures are a peculiar fund of instruction. They inform us of the origin of creation; of the primitive state of

531

man; of his fall, or apostacy from God. It appears that he was placed in the garden of Eden, with full liberty to regale himself with all the delicious fruits that were to be found, except what grew on one tree—if he eat of that he should surely die, was the declaration of the Most High.

Happy were the human pair, amidst this delightful paradise, until a certain preacher, in his journey, came that way, and disturbed their peace and tranquility, by endeavoring to reverse the prohibition of the Almighty, as in our text—"Ye shall not surely die."

> "She pluck'd, she ate:
> Earth felt the wound; nature from her seat,
> Sighing through all her works, gave signs of woe,
> That all was lost."
>
> MILTON

We may attend

To the *character* of the preacher—To the *doctrine* inculcated—To the *hearer* addressed—To the *medium* or *instrument* of the preaching.

I. As to the preacher, I would observe, he has many names given him in the sacred writings, the most common is the *Devil*. That it was he that disturbed the felicity of our first parents, is evident from 2. *Cor.* xi. 3. and many other passages of Scripture. He was once an angel of light, and knew better than to preach such doctrine; he did violence to his own reason.

But to be a little more particular, let it be observed,

1. He is an *old* preacher. He lived above one thousand seven hundred years before Abraham—above two thousand four hundred and thirty years before Moses—four thousand and four years before Christ. It is now five thousand eight hundred and nine years since he commenced preaching. By this time he must have acquired great skill in the art.

2. He is a very *cunning* artful preacher. When Elymas, the sorcerer, came to turn away people from the faith, he is said to be *full of all subtlety, and a child of the devil*—not only because he was an enemy of all righteousness, but on account of his carnal cunning and craftiness.

3. He is a very *laborious* unwearied preacher. He has been in the ministry almost six thousand years; and yet his zeal is

not in the least abated. The apostle Peter compares him to a roaring lion, *walking* about, seeking whom he may devour. When God enquired of this persevering preacher, *Job* ii. 2. "From whence camest thou?" he answered the Lord, and said, "From *going to and fro* in the earth, and from *walking up and down in it.*" He is far from being circumscribed within the narrow limits of parish, state, or continental lines; but his haunt and travel is very large and extensive.

4. He is a *heterogeneous* preacher, if I may so express myself. He makes use of a Bible when he holds forth, as in his sermon to our Saviour, *Matthew* iv. 6. He mixes truth with error, in order to make it go well, or to carry his point.

5. He is a very *presumptuous* preacher. Notwithstanding God had declared in the most plain and positive terms, "Thou shalt surely die"—or "In dying thou shalt die"—yet, this audacious wretch had the impudence to confront Omnipotence, and says, "Ye shall not surely die!"

6. He is a very *successful* preacher. He draws a great number after him. No preacher can command hearers like him. He was successful with our first parents—with the old world. Noah once preached to those spirits that are now in the prison of hell; and told them from God, that they should surely die: but this preacher came along and declared the contrary—"Ye shall not surely die." The greater part, it seems, believed him, and went to destruction. So it was with Sodom and Gomorrah—Lot preached to them; the substance of which was, "Up, get ye out of this place; for the Lord will *destroy* this City." *Gen.* xix. 14. But this old declaimer told them, No danger! no danger! "Ye shall not surely die." To which they generally gave heed; and Lot seemed to them as one who *mocked*—they believed the Universal preacher, and were consumed—agreeably to the declaration of the apostle Jude, "Sodom and Gomorrah and the cities about them, suffering the vengeance of eternal fire."

II. Let us attend to the doctrine inculcated by this preacher, "Ye shall not surely die." Bold assertion! without a single argument to support it. The death contained in the threatening, was doubtless *eternal* death,—as nothing but this would express God's feelings towards sin, or render an infinite atonement necessary. To suppose it to be spiritual death, is to blend crime and punishment together. To suppose temporal death to be the curse of the law, then believers are not delivered from it, according to *Gal.* iii. 13. What Satan meant to preach was, that there is no hell; and that the wages of sin is not death, but eternal life.

III. We shall now take notice of the hearer addressed by the preacher. This we have in the text—"And the serpent said unto the WOMAN," &c. That Eve had not so much experience as Adam, is evident; and so not equally able to withstand temptation. This doubtless was a reason why the tempter chose her, with whom he might hope to be successful. Doubtless he took a time when she was separated from her husband.

That this preacher has had the greatest success in the dark and ignorant parts of the earth, is evident: his kingdom is a kingdom of darkness. He is a great enemy to light. St. Paul gives us some account of him in his day—2. *Tim.* iii. 6. "For of this sort are they which creep into houses, and lead captive *silly* women, laden with sins, led away with diverse lusts." The same apostle observes, *Rom.* xvi. 17, 18. "Now I beseech you brethren, mark them which cause divisions and offences contrary to the doctrine which ye have learned, and avoid them. For they that are such serve not our Lord Jesus Christ, but their own belly; and by good words and fair speeches deceive the hearts of the *simple.*"

IV. The instrument or medium made use of by the preacher, will now be considered. This we have in the text—"And the SERPENT said," &c. But how came the devil to preach through the serpent?

1. To save his own character, and the better to carry his point. Had the devil come to our first parents personally and unmasked, they would have more easily seen the deception. The reality of a future punishment is at times so clearly impressed on the human mind, that even Satan is constrained to own that there is a hell; altho' at other times he denies it. He does not wish to have it known that he is a liar; therefore he conceals himself, that he can the better accomplish his designs, and save his own character.

2. The devil is an enemy to all good, to all happiness and excellence. He is opposed to the felicity of the brutes. He

took delight in tormenting the swine. The serpent, before he set up preaching Universal Salvation, was a cunning, beautiful and happy creature; but now his glory is departed. "And the Lord said unto the serpent, because thou hast done this, thou art cursed above all cattle, and above every beast of the field: upon thy belly shalt thou go, and dust shalt thou eat all the days of thy life." There is therefore, a kind of duplicate cunning in the matter—Satan gets the preacher and hearers also.

> "And is not this triumphant treachery,
> And more than simple conquest in the foe!"
> YOUNG.

3. Another reason why Satan employs instruments in his service is, because his empire is large, and he cannot be every where himself.

4. He has a large number at his command, that love and approve of his work, delight in building up his kingdom, and stand ready to go at his call.

INFERENCES.

1. The devil is not dead, but still lives; and is able to preach as well as ever, "Ye shall not surely die."

2. Universal Salvation is no new fangled scheme, but can boast of great antiquity.

3. See a reason why it ought to be rejected, because it is an ancient devilish doctrine.

4. See one reason why it is that Satan is such a mortal enemy to the Bible, and to all who preach the Gospel, because of that injunction, *Mark* xvi. 15, 16. "And he said unto them, Go ye into all the world, and preach the Gospel to every creature. He that believeth and is baptized shall be saved; but he that believeth not shall be *damned*."

5. See whence it was that Satan exerted himself so much to convince our first parents that there was no hell—because the denunciation of the Almighty was true, and he was afraid that Adam and Eve would continue in the belief of it. Was there no truth in future punishment, or was it only a temporary evil, Satan would not be so busy in trying to convince men that there is none. It is his nature and element to lie. "When

he speaketh a lie, he speaketh of his own; for he is a liar, and the father of it." *John* viii. 44.

6. We infer that ministers should not be proud of their preaching. If they preach the true Gospel, they only, in substance, repeat Christ's sermons. If they preach "Ye shall not surely die," they only make use of the Devil's old notes, that he delivered almost six thousand years ago.

7. It is probable that the doctrine of Universal Salvation will still prevail, since this preacher is yet a live, and not in the least superanuated; and every effort against him only enrages him more and more, and excites him to new inventions and exertions to build up his cause.

To close the subject.—As the author of the foregoing discourse has confined himself wholly to the character of Satan, he trusts no one will feel himself personally injured by this short sermon: But should any imbibe a degree of friendship for this aged divine, and think that I have not treated this Universal Preacher with that respect and veneration that he justly deserves, let them be so kind as to point it out, and I will most cheerfully retract; for it has ever been a maxim with me, *"Render unto all their dues."*

The following Hymn, taken from the Theological Magazine, was repeated after the delivery of the preceding discourse.—

A late writer in favor of Universal Salvation, having closed his piece with these last lines of Pope's Messiah,

> The seas shall waste, the skies in smoke decay,
> Rocks fall to dust, and mountains melt away;
> But fixt his word, his saving power remains,
> Thy realm forever last, thy own Messiah reigns;

his antagonist made the following addition to them:—

UNIVERSALISM INDEED.

> "When seas shall waste, and skies in smoke decay,
> Rocks fall to dust, and mountains melt away;
> In adamantine chains shall death be bound,
> And hell's grim tyrant feel the eternal wound."

But all his children reach fair Eden's shore,
Not e'er to see their father Satan more.
The tottering drunkards shall to glory reel,
And common strumpets endless pleasure feel.
Blest are the haughty, who despise the poor,
For they're entitled to the heavenly store.
Blest all who laugh and scoff at truth divine,
For bold revilers endless comfort find.
Blest are the clam'rous and contentious crew,
To them eternal rest and peace are due.
Blest all who hunger, and who thirst to find
A chance to plunder and to cheat mankind:
Such die in peace—for God to them has giv'n,
To be unjust on earth, and go to heaven.
Blest is the wretch whose bowels never move
With gen'rous pity, or with tender love;
He shall find mercy from the God above.
Blest all who seek to wrangle and to fight;
Such mount from seas of blood to worlds of light.
Go riot, drink, and ev'ry ill pursue,
For joys eternal are reserv'd for you.
Fear not to sin, till death shall close your eyes;
Live as you please, yours is th' immortal prize.
Old Serpent, hail! thou mad'st a just reply
To mother Eve, "Ye shall not surely die!"
But, Reader, stop!—and in God's holy fear,
With sacred truth these tenets first compare;
Our Saviour's Sermon on the mount peruse—
Read with attention, and the bane refuse!

ABSALOM JONES

A Thanksgiving Sermon

Preached January 1, 1808,
In St. Thomas's, or the African Episcopal, Church,
Philadelphia:
On Account of
The Abolition of the African Slave Trade,
On That Day, by the Congress of the United States

———

EXODUS, iii. 7,–8.
*And the Lord said, I have surely seen the affliction
of my people which are in Egypt, and have heard
their cry by reason of their task-masters; for I know
their sorrows; and I am come down to deliver them
out of the hand of the Egyptians.*

THESE WORDS, my brethren, contain a short account of some of the circumstances which preceded the deliverance of the children of Israel from their captivity and bondage in Egypt.

They mention, in the first place, their *affliction*. This consisted in their privation of liberty: they were slaves to the kings of Egypt, in common with their other subjects; and they were slaves to their fellow slaves. They were compelled to work in the open air, in one of the hottest climates in the world: and, probably, without a covering from the burning rays of the sun. Their work was of a laborious kind: it consisted of making bricks, and travelling, perhaps to a great distance, for the straw, or stubble, that was a component part of them. Their work was dealt out to them in tasks, and performed under the eye of vigilant and rigorous masters, who constantly upbraided them with idleness. The least deficiency, in the product of their labour, was punished by beating. Nor was this all. Their food was of the cheapest kind, and contained but little nourishment: it consisted only of leeks and onions, which grew almost spontaneously in the land of Egypt. Painful and distressing as these sufferings were, they constituted the smallest part of their misery. While the fields resounded with their cries in the day, their huts and hamlets were vocal at night with their lamentations over their sons; who were dragged from the arms of their mothers, and put to death by drowning, in order to prevent such an increase in their population, as to endanger the safety of the state by an insurrection. In this condition, thus degraded and oppressed, they passed nearly four hundred years. Ah! who can conceive of the measure of their sufferings, during that time? What tongue, or pen, can compute the number of their sorrows? To them no morning or evening sun ever disclosed a single charm: to them, the beauties of spring, and the plenty of autumn had no attractions: even domestick endearments were scarcely known to them: all was misery; all was grief; all was despair.

Our text mentions, in the second place, that, in this situation, they were not forgotten by the God of their fathers, and the Father of the human race. Though, for wise reasons, he delayed to appear in their behalf for several hundred years; yet he was not indifferent to their sufferings. Our text tells us, that he saw their affliction, and heard their cry: his eye and his ear were constantly open to their complaint: every tear they shed, was preserved, and every groan they uttered, was recorded; in order to testify, at a future day, against the authors of their oppressions. But our text goes further: it describes the Judge of the world to be so much moved, with what he saw and what he heard, that he rises from his throne—not to issue a command to the armies of angels that surrounded him to fly to the relief of his suffering children—but to come down from heaven, in his own person, in order to deliver them out of the hands of the Egyptians. Glory to God for this precious record of his power and goodness: let all the nations of the earth praise him. *Clouds and darkness are round about him,* but *righteousness and judgment are the habitation of his throne. O sing unto the Lord a new song, for he hath done marvellous things: his right hand and his holy arm hath gotten him the victory. He hath remembered his mercy and truth toward the house of Israel, and all the ends of the earth shall see the salvation of God.*

The history of the world shows us, that the deliverance of the children of Israel from their bondage, is not the only instance, in which it has pleased God to appear in behalf of oppressed and distressed nations, as the deliverer of the innocent, and of those who call upon his name. He is as unchangeable in his nature and character, as he is in his wisdom and power. The great and blessed event, which we have this day met to celebrate, is a striking proof, that the God of heaven and earth is *the same, yesterday, and to-day, and for ever*. Yes, my brethren, the nations from which most of us have descended, and the country in which some of us were born, have been visited by the tender mercy of the Common Father of the human race. He has seen the affliction of our countrymen, with an eye of pity. He has seen the wicked arts, by which wars have been fomented among the different tribes of the Africans, in order to procure captives, for the purpose of selling them for slaves. He has seen ships fitted out from different ports in Europe and America, and freighted with trinkets to be exchanged for the bodies and souls of men. He has seen the anguish which has taken place, when parents have been torn from their children, and children from their parents, and conveyed, with their hands and feet bound in fetters, on board of ships prepared to receive them. He has seen them thrust in crowds into the holds of those ships, where many of them have perished from the want of air. He has seen such of them as have escaped from that noxious place of confinement, leap into the ocean, with a faint hope of swimming back to their native shore, or a determination to seek an early retreat from their impending misery, in a watery grave. He has seen them exposed for sale, like horses and cattle, upon the wharves, or, like bales of goods, in warehouses of West India and American sea ports. He has seen the pangs of separation between members of the same family. He has seen them driven into the sugar, the rice, and the tobacco fields, and compelled to work—in spite of the habits of ease which they derived from the natural fertility of their own country—in the open air, beneath a burning sun, with scarcely as much clothing upon them as modesty required. He has seen them faint beneath the pressure of their labours. He has seen them return to their smoky huts in the evening, with nothing to satisfy their hunger but a scanty allowance of roots; and these, cultivated for themselves, on that day only, which God ordained as a day of rest for man and beast. He has seen the neglect with which their masters have treated their immortal souls; not only in withholding religious instruction from them, but, in some instances, depriving them of access to the means of obtaining it. He has seen all the different modes of torture, by means of the whip, the screw, the pincers, and the red hot iron, which have been exercised upon their bodies, by inhuman overseers: overseers, did I say? Yes: but not by these only. Our God has seen masters and mistresses, educated in fashionable life, sometimes take the instruments of torture into their own hands, and, deaf to the cries and shrieks of their agonizing slaves, exceed even their overseers in cruelty. Inhuman wretches! though You have been deaf to their cries and shrieks, they have been heard in Heaven. The ears of Jehovah have been constantly open to them: He has heard the prayers that have ascended from the hearts of his people; and he has, as in the case of his ancient and chosen people the Jews, *come down to deliver* our suffering countrymen from the hands of their oppressors. He *came down* into the United States, when they declared, in the constitution which they framed in 1788, that the trade in our African fellow-men, should cease in the year 1808: He *came down* into the British Parliament, when they passed a law to put an end to the same iniquitous trade in May, 1807. He *came down* into the Congress of the United States, the last winter, when they passed a similar law, the operation of which commences on this happy day. Dear land of our ancestors! thou shalt no more be stained with the blood of thy children, shed by British and American hands: the ocean shall no more afford a refuge to their bodies, from impending slavery: nor shall the shores of the British West India islands, and of the United States, any more witness the anguish of families, parted for ever by a publick sale. For this signal interposition of the God of mercies, in behalf of our brethren, it becomes us this day to offer up our united thanks. Let the song of angels, which was first heard in the air at the birth of our Saviour, be heard this day in our assembly: *Glory to God in the highest*, for these first fruits of *peace upon earth, and good-will to man*: O! let us *give thanks unto the Lord*: let us *call upon his name*, and *make known his deeds among the people*. Let us *sing psalms unto him and talk of all his wondrous works*.

Having enumerated the mercies of God to our people, it becomes us to ask, What shall we render unto the Lord for them? Sacrifices and burnt offerings are no longer pleasing to him: the pomp of public worship, and the ceremonies of a festive day, will find no acceptance with him, unless they are accompanied with actions that correspond with them. The duties which are inculcated upon us, by the event we are now celebrating, divide themselves into five heads.

In the first place, Let not our expressions of gratitude to God for his late goodness and mercy to our countrymen, be confined to this day, nor to this house: let us carry grateful hearts with us to our places of abode, and to our daily occupations; and let praise and thanksgivings ascend daily to the throne of grace, in our families, and in our closets, for what God has done for our African brethren. Let us not forget to praise him for his mercies to such of our colour as are inhabitants of this country; particularly, for disposing the hearts of the rulers of many of the states to pass laws for the abolition of slavery; for the number and zeal of the friends he has raised up to plead our cause; and for the privileges we enjoy, of worshiping God, agreeably to our consciences, in churches of our own. This comely building, erected chiefly by the generosity of our friends, is a monument of God's goodness to us, and calls for our gratitude with all the other blessings that have been mentioned.

Secondly, Let us unite, with our thanksgiving, prayer to Almighty God, for the completion of his begun goodness to our brethren in Africa. Let us beseech him to extend to all the nations in Europe, the same humane and just spirit towards them, which he has imparted to the British and American nations. Let us, further, implore the influence of his divine and holy Spirit, to dispose the hearts of our legislatures to pass laws, to ameliorate the condition of our brethren who are still in bondage; also, to dispose their masters to treat them with kindness and humanity; and, above all things, to favour them with the means of acquiring such parts of human knowledge, as will enable them to read the holy scriptures, and understand the doctrines of the Christian religion, whereby they may become, even while they are the slaves of men, the freemen of the Lord.

Thirdly, Let us conduct ourselves in such a manner as to furnish no cause of regret to the deliverers of our nation, for their kindness to us. Let us constantly *remember the rock whence we were hewn, and the pit whence we were digged. Pride was not made for man*, in any situation; and, still less, for persons who have recently emerged from bondage. The Jews, after they entered the promised land, were commanded, when they offered sacrifices to the Lord, never to forget their humble origin; and hence, part of the worship that accompanied their sacrifices consisted in acknowledging, *that a Syrian, ready to perish, was their father*: in like manner, it becomes us, publickly and privately, to acknowledge, that an African slave, ready to perish, was our father or our grandfather. Let our conduct be regulated by the precepts of the gospel; let us be sober minded, humble, peaceable, temperate in our meats and drinks, frugal in our apparel and in the furniture of our houses, industrious in our occupations, just in all our dealings, and ever ready to honour all men. Let us teach our children the rudiments of the English language, in order to enable them to acquire a knowledge of useful trades, and, above all things, let us instruct them in the principles of the gospel of Jesus Christ, whereby they may become *wise unto salvation*. It has always been a mystery, Why the impartial Father of the human race should have permitted the transportation of so many millions of our fellow creatures to this country, to endure all the miseries of slavery. Perhaps his design was, that a knowledge of the gospel might be acquired by some of their descendants, in order that they might become qualified to be the messengers of it, to the land of their fathers. Let this thought animate us, when we are teaching our children to love and adore the name of our Redeemer. Who knows but that a Joseph may rise up among them, who shall be the instrument of feeding the African nations with the bread of life, and of saving them, not from earthly bondage, but from the more galling yoke of sin and satan.

Fourthly, Let us be grateful to our benefactors, who, by enlightening the minds of the rulers of the earth, by means of their publications and remonstrances against the trade in our countrymen, have produced the great event we are this day celebrating. Abolition societies and individuals have equal claims to our gratitude. It would be difficult to mention the names of any of our benefactors, without offending many whom we do not know. Some of them are gone to heaven, to receive the reward of their labours of love towards us; and the kindness and benevolence of the survivors, we hope, are recorded in the book of life, to be mentioned with honour when our Lord shall come to reward his faithful servants before an assembled world.

Fifthly, and lastly, Let the first of January, the day of the abolition of the slave trade in our country, be set apart in every year, as a day of publick thanksgiving for that mercy. Let the history of the sufferings of our brethren, and of their deliverance, descend by this means to our children, to the remotest generations; and when they shall ask, in time to come, saying, What mean the lessons, the psalms, the prayers and the praises in the worship of this day? let us answer them, by saying, the Lord, on the day of which this is the anniversary, abolished the trade which dragged your fathers from their native country, and sold them as bondmen in the United States of America.

Oh thou God of all the nations upon the earth! we thank thee, that thou art *no respecter of persons*, and that thou *hast made of one blood all nations of men*. We thank thee, that thou hast appeared, in the fulness of time, in behalf of the nation from which most of the worshipping people, now before thee, are descended. We thank thee, that the sun of righteousness has at last shed his morning beams upon them. *Rend* thy *heavens*, O Lord, and *come down* upon the earth; and grant that *the mountains*, which now obstruct the perfect day of thy goodness and mercy towards them, may *flow down at thy presence*. Send thy gospel, we beseech thee, among them. May the nations, which now *sit in darkness*, behold and rejoice in its *light*. May *Ethiopia soon stretch out her hands unto thee*, and lay hold of the gracious promise of thy everlasting covenant. Destroy, we beseech thee, all the false religions which now prevail among them; and grant, that they may soon *cast* their *idols, to the moles and the bats* of the wilderness.

O, hasten that glorious time, when the knowledge of the gospel of Jesus Christ, shall cover the *earth, as the waters cover the sea;* when *the wolf shall dwell with the lamb, and the leopard shall lie down with the kid and the calf and the young lion and the fatling together, and a little child shall lead them;* and, *when, instead of the thorn, shall come up the fir tree, and, instead of the brier, shall come up the myrtle tree: and it shall be to the Lord for a name and for an everlasting sign that shall not be cut off.* We pray, O God, for all our friends and benefactors, in Great Britain, as well as in the United States: reward them, we beseech thee, with blessings upon earth, and prepare them to enjoy the fruits of their kindness to us, in thy everlasting kingdom in heaven: and dispose us, who are assembled in thy presence, to be always thankful for thy mercies, and to act as becomes a people who owe so much to thy goodness. We implore thy blessing, O God, upon the President, and all who are in authority in the United States. Direct them by thy wisdom, in all their deliberations, and O save thy people from the calamities of war. Give peace in our day, we beseech thee, O thou *God of peace!* and grant, that this highly favoured country may continue to afford a safe and peaceful retreat from the calamities of war and slavery, for ages yet to come. We implore all these blessings and mercies, only in the name of thy beloved Son, Jesus Christ, our Lord. And now, O Lord, we desire, with angels and arch-angels, and all the company of heaven, evermore to praise thee, saying, *Holy, holy, holy, Lord God Almighty: the whole earth is full of thy glory.* Amen.

JOHN COMLY

Sermon Delivered at Darby, April 15, 1827

THERE WAS a watch-word which forcibly impressed my attention in the early gathering of this meeting; and apprehending that it was designed for the benefit of my own mind, I was quite disposed to profit by it myself, and there to keep it; but it does not seem as if this was the only object; it may, therefore, possibly be of use to some other minds on future occasions. I have often needed it, and there is no doubt that every serious mind may need also, that kind of exercise, to get into the closet, into that state, that was comprised in the expression, "Every man to his tent." It implies to my mind a state of quietude, a state of calmness, in which the mind is susceptible of divine instruction; of hearing the intimation that is conveyed to every one of us, individually, when the divine spirit stands at the door and knocks. "If any man hear my voice and open the door, I will come in to him." We often need this state of quietness and retirement.

"Adam where art thou?" An inquiry is raised in us, when there is a state like being gathered into the tent, into the quiet, or into the closet. And hence the excellency of the privilege of silent waiting, or, of what we call silent worship, wherein every one may attain to that instruction conveyed by the spirit of truth, as suited to his particular state, without interfering with that of another.

This watch word, or call to this quiet and retired state of mind, was succeeded by another inquiry, which has occupied my attention in a renewed investigation, that I hope, in conformity with the preceding testimony, may take hold of every mind present. It is an address of the apostle James, to a state, in which, I have hoped there were few or none present—a state included in the answer of the apostle to that question, "What is your life?" This is a question, which every one may ask who is retired into his own closet, where the mind is quieted and brought under that kind of feeling, in which a living exercise is felt, as to the object of our being associated and gathered. And it not only applies to us when seated in our silent, solemn assemblies; but it will apply to us through the whole course of our lives. And in our daily transactions, we ought ever to keep in view, the consideration; what is our life? And wherein does our life consist? It consists not in the abundance of our possessions. For we are told that, it is even a "vapour, that appeareth for a little time, and then vanisheth away." And it is so with every thing under the sun—every thing created, must thus pass away. And yet there is in the New Testament, as it is called, the term eternal life, and this must stand decidedly opposed to that which is but vapour, and breath, which after a little while vanisheth away; for eternal life does not vanish away, it must last for ever.

Now if this eternal life is our life, we come to understand within ourselves the nature of that living fountain that was preached to the Samaritan woman—it is that living water, and fountain of life, of eternal life, or life in the soul of man. Now "what is your life?" "Where your treasure is there will your heart be also." "A good man out of the good treasure of the heart, bringeth forth good things;" and "herein is your Heavenly Father glorified, that ye bring forth much fruit." Now is not this the fruit of divine love in the soul? and has it not been portrayed in lively colours to our understanding in the preceding communication, in the fruits of that love that was manifested in the tenderness of feeling, and compassion shown to the poor man who had fallen into difficulties and trials, who was not dead but was left in a deplorable condition, and said to be half dead? Now where was the love of the priest, and what was his life? Now by this we may measure and compare ourselves—we may come to a certain evidence in ourselves respecting the feelings in our minds. For it is from the feeling, and the life that are in the soul, that the works and fruits will always proceed. "Every good tree bringeth forth good fruit, but a corrupt tree bringeth forth evil fruit." Neither "do men gather grapes of thorns, or figs of thistles." It is impossible in the nature of things, that such contrarieties should be produced.

Wherefore, "Ye shall know them by their fruits." Apply this unto thyself, and by thy fruits thou mayest be known to thyself; for "where your treasure is, there will your heart be also," and what thy heart is fixed on, that will be set above every thing else and whatever it may be, it will be uppermost, as the thing that thou lovest best, profession to the contrary notwithstanding. It is in a state of retirement that we are to see and read—and it will be an easy matter clearly to read ourselves in this quiet, retired state of mind, if we are only willing to be searched. And here we should be willing to examine ourselves, to prove our ownselves whether we be in the faith or not, that faith which works by love; for all other faith may be overcome of the world, whereas the faith which works by love purifies the heart; and the fountain being pure, the streams will be of a like nature.

Now "what is your life?" and where is your life? where are those feelings, those heavenly feelings, or feelings with which the good Samaritan was clothed, and which distinguished him as neighbour to the one that fell among thieves? How forcible, how instructive must that parable be, to one that is thus circumstanced to inquire, who is my neighbour? Let us then inquire, who is my neighbour? It is an investigation and inquiry profitable to be raised in the youthful mind; and if the operation of this gift leads to that inquiry, don't quench it, I entreat it of you, dear children, but simply regard and cherish it, and here you will be instructed and taught by that teacher, which is the grace of God in your own hearts. This is an all-sufficient teacher, who will show you with clearness and certainty whether you are in the faith, whether you are in that living, practical faith, which stands not in words, letters, books, papers, or in any thing of the kind; for it is that which operates in the soul, that constitutes a practical, living faith, which brings forth the fruits of righteousness, and those feelings of the mind which lead to do good one to another, as comprehended in the first and great commandment. Thus when we rightly consider the subject, and when love to our Heavenly Father is the supreme object of our attention— when our life is employed to do that which is good, and when we delight in feeling a sense of it in our own minds, then it is, that we can love every body—and when we feel any thing like hardness or disrespect arising in the mind, toward a fellow creature, we immediately suppress it, and counteract it; and in the room thereof set up the cross to our natural propensities, as animals and men. And when we take up the cross to these, and suppress those feelings which would go to harm one another, there will rise up in their stead, feelings of good will to men, and glory to God in the highest—this is the result—the fruit brought forth by such a disposition as this. And when there is no action to be performed in an external sense, such as the Samaritan performed for the suffering man, yet in the disposition that we feel, we are accepted. And if this disposition be felt and lived in, we become prepared for any occasion which may offer for our active duty; and the disposition being already in the soul, feelings of love and good-will predominate, and we shall be prepared for those works of righteousness which have their origin and their foundation in this eternal spirit; and here it is that we can say, "glory to God in the highest, and on earth peace, good will toward men."

Now the profession of Christianity so far as it produces this effect in individual minds,—so far as it rises and prevails, gives demonstration where we are, and if we act to the contrary, still we have an evidence; for by their fruits shall ye know them—so by our fruits we may know ourselves, and see what our life is. And one of our greatest delights in this state will be, to feel no evil in the heart toward our fellow creatures; and so will it be our greatest happiness, to feel the heart glowing in love to our Heavenly Father, and in peace and good will to men. And this, when uninterrupted, constitutes a life of God in the soul of man; and when this life of God in the soul of man rises so as to have dominion over every contrary disposition, it is the kingdom of heaven in man; which, as we come to know it, will enable us to feel and realize, and we shall give forth an evidence in our lives, and a demonstration in our conduct, that we are the disciples of Jesus Christ. And herein as there is a death to every thing that is contrary to this eternal life in the soul, we know what it is to be "buried by baptism into death; that like as Christ was raised up from the dead by the glory of the Father, even so we also should walk in newness of life."

Now I would, that encouragement might be administered to every mind present, to press after this; for it is by pressing, striving, and labouring, that we shall in due time attain to it, if we faint not. There is, therefore, no cause for being discouraged, though the conflict may seem long, and we may seem to gain but little. Keep thy eye on the object, the standard raised in thy view, as a mark to aim at, and the prize of enjoyment will be obtained.

Fear not, therefore, nor shrink back at the difficulties, trials, and troubles which you may have to pass through in this journey. Dwell in littleness and simplicity, and learn a daily lesson of meekness and lowliness of heart, and thou wilt find rest to thy soul, and also, that this eternal life is the life in thee, and that every inferior life will be absorbed and swallowed up in this. Then follow it up; I intreat you, dear children, to flee from the dangerous snares of custom which are surrounding you.

You have great need to be watchful; you have great need to be careful; you have need often to retire into your tents, and to sit as Mary did, when it was said she had "chosen that good part, which should not be taken away from her." And it will never be taken from you, unless you deprive yourselves of it. Then sit at the feet of your divine instructer, and hear the gracious words that proceed from his mouth, and then will your strength be renewed from day to day, and you will know a feeding on that divine food, which will nourish this life in the soul.

WILLIAM ELLERY CHANNING

A Discourse at the Ordination of
the Rev. Frederick A. Farley

———

EPHESIANS V. I.
Be ye therefore followers of God, as dear children.

To PROMOTE true religion is the purpose of the Christian ministry. For this it was ordained. On the present occasion, therefore, when a new teacher is to be given to the church, a discourse on the character of true religion will not be inappropriate. I do not mean, that I shall attempt, in the limits to which I am now confined, to set before you all its properties, signs, and operations; for in so doing I should burden your memories with divisions and vague generalities, as uninteresting as they would be unprofitable. My purpose is, to select one view of the subject, which seems to me of primary dignity and importance; and I select this, because it is greatly neglected, and because I attribute to this neglect much of the inefficacy, and many of the corruptions, of religion.

The text calls us to follow or imitate God, to seek accordance with or likeness to him; and to do this, not fearfully and faintly, but with the spirit and hope of beloved children. The doctrine which I propose to illustrate, is derived immediately from these words, and is incorporated with the whole New Testament. I affirm, and would maintain, that true religion consists in proposing, as our great end, a growing likeness to the Supreme Being. Its noblest influence consists in making us more and more partakers of the Divinity. For this it is to be preached. Religious instruction should aim chiefly to turn men's aspirations and efforts to that perfection of the soul, which constitutes it a bright image of God. Such is the topic now to be discussed; and I implore Him, whose glory I seek, to aid me in unfolding and enforcing it with simplicity and clearness, with a calm and pure zeal, and with unfeigned charity.

I begin with observing, what all indeed will understand, that the likeness to God, of which I propose to speak, belongs to man's higher or spiritual nature. It has its foundation in the original and essential capacities of the mind. In proportion as these are unfolded by right and vigorous exertion, it is extended and brightened. In proportion as these lie dormant, it is obscured. In proportion as they are perverted and overpowered by the appetites and passions, it is blotted out. In truth, moral evil, if unresisted and habitual, may so blight and lay waste these capacities, that the image of God in man may seem to be wholly destroyed.

The importance of this assimilation to our Creator, is a topic which needs no labored discussion. All men, of whatever name, or sect, or opinion, will meet me on this ground. All, I presume, will allow, that no good in the compass of the universe, or within the gift of omnipotence, can be compared to a resemblance of God, or to a participation of his attributes. I fear no contradiction here. Likeness to God is the supreme gift. He can communicate nothing so precious, glorious, blessed, as himself. To hold intellectual and moral affinity with the Supreme Being, to partake his spirit, to be his children by derivations of kindred excellence, to bear a growing conformity to the perfection which we adore, this is a felicity which obscures and annihilates all other good.

It is only in proportion to this likeness, that we can enjoy either God or the universe. That God can be known and enjoyed only through sympathy or kindred attributes, is a doctrine which even Gentile philosophy discerned. That the pure in heart can alone see and commune with the pure Divinity, was the sublime instruction of ancient sages as well as of inspired prophets. It is indeed the lesson of daily experience. To understand a great and good being, we must have the seeds of the same excellence. How quickly, by what an instinct, do accordant minds recognise one another! No attraction is so powerful as that which subsists between the truly wise and good; whilst the brightest excellence is lost on those who have nothing congenial in their own breasts. God becomes a real being to us, in proportion as his own nature is unfolded within us. To a man who is growing in the likeness of God, faith begins even here to change into vision. He carries within himself a proof of a Deity, which can only be understood by experience. He more than believes, he feels the Divine presence; and gradually rises to an intercourse with his Maker, to which it is not irreverent to apply the name of friendship and intimacy. The Apostle John intended to express this truth, when he tells us, that he, in whom a principle of divine charity or benevolence has become a habit and life, 'dwells in God and God in him.'

It is plain, too, that likeness to God is the true and only preparation for the enjoyment of the universe. In proportion as we approach and resemble the mind of God, we are brought into harmony with the creation; for, in that proportion, we possess the principles from which the universe sprung; we carry within ourselves the perfections, of which its beauty, magnificence, order, benevolent adaptations, and boundless purposes, are the results and manifestations. God unfolds himself in his works to a kindred mind. It is possible, that the brevity of these hints may expose to the charge of mysticism, what seems to me the calmest and clearest truth. I think, however, that every reflecting man will feel, that likeness to God must be a principle of sympathy or accordance with his creation; for the creation is a birth and shining forth of the Divine Mind, a work through which his spirit breathes. In proportion as we receive this spirit, we possess within ourselves the explanation of what we see. We discern more and more of God in every thing, from the frail flower to the everlasting stars. Even in evil, that dark cloud which hangs over the creation, we discern rays of light and hope, and gradually come to see, in suffering and temptation, proofs and instruments of the sublimest purposes of Wisdom and Love.

I have offered these very imperfect views, that I may show the great importance of the doctrine which I am solicitous to enforce. I would teach, that likeness to God is a good so unutterably surpassing all other good, that whoever admits it as attainable, must acknowledge it to be the chief aim of life. I would show, that the highest and happiest office of religion is, to bring the mind into growing accordance with God; and that by the tendency of religious systems to this end, their truth and worth are to be chiefly tried.

I am aware that it may be said, that the Scriptures, in speaking of man as made in the image of God, and in calling us to imitate him, use bold and figurative language. It may be said, that there is danger from too literal an interpretation; that God is an unapproachable being; that I am not warranted in ascribing to man a like nature to the Divine; that we and all things illustrate the Creator by contrast, not by resemblance; that religion manifests itself chiefly in convictions and acknowledgments of utter worthlessness; and that to talk of the greatness and divinity of the human soul, is to inflate that pride through which Satan fell, and through which man involves himself in that fallen spirit's ruin.

I answer, that, to me, scripture and reason hold a different language. In Christianity particularly, I meet perpetual testimonies to the divinity of human nature. This whole religion expresses an infinite concern of God for the human soul, and teaches that he deems no methods too expensive for its recovery and exaltation. Christianity, with one voice, calls me to turn my regards and care to the spirit within me, as of more worth than the whole outward world. It calls us to 'be perfect as our Father in heaven is perfect;' and everywhere, in the sublimity of its precepts, it implies and recognises the sublime capacities of the being to whom they are addressed. It assures us that human virtue is 'in the sight of God of great price,' and speaks of the return of a human being to virtue as an event which increases the joy of heaven. In the New Testament, Jesus Christ, the Son of God, the brightness of his glory, the express and unsullied image of the Divinity, is seen mingling with men as a friend and brother, offering himself as their example, and promising to his true followers a share in all his splendors and joys. In the New Testament, God is said to communicate his own spirit, and all his fulness to the human soul. In the New Testament man is exhorted to aspire after 'honor, glory, and immortality'; and Heaven, a word expressing the nearest approach to God, and a divine happiness, is everywhere proposed as the end of his being. In truth, the very essence of Christian faith is, that we trust in God's mercy, as revealed in Jesus Christ, for a state of celestial purity, in which we shall grow for ever in the likeness, and knowledge, and enjoyment of the Infinite Father. Lofty views of the nature of man are bound up and interwoven with the whole Christian system. Say not, that these are at war with humility; for who was ever humbler than Jesus, and yet who ever possessed such a consciousness of greatness and divinity? Say not that man's business is to think of his sin, and not of his dignity; for great sin implies a great capacity; it is the abuse of a noble nature; and no man can be deeply and rationally contrite, but he who feels, that in wrong doing he has resisted a divine voice, and warred against a divine principle, in his own soul.—I need not, I trust, pursue the argument from revelation. There is an argument from nature and reason, which seems to me so convincing, and is at the same time so fitted to explain what I mean by man's possession of a like nature to God, that I shall pass at once to its exposition.

That man has a kindred nature with God, and may bear most important and ennobling relations to him, seems to me to be established by a striking proof. This proof you will understand, by considering, for a moment, how we obtain our ideas of God. Whence come the conceptions which we include under that august name? Whence do we derive our knowledge of the attributes and perfections which constitute the Supreme Being? I answer, we derive them from our own souls. The divine attributes are first developed in ourselves, and thence transferred to our Creator. The idea of God, sublime and awful as it is, is the idea of our own spiritual nature, purified and enlarged to infinity. In ourselves are the elements of the Divinity. God, then, does not sustain a figurative resemblance to man. It is the resemblance of a parent to a child, the likeness of a kindred nature.

We call God a Mind. He has revealed himself as a Spirit. But what do we know of mind, but through the unfolding of this principle in our own breasts? That unbounded spiritual energy which we call God, is conceived by us only through consciousness, through the knowledge of ourselves.—We ascribe thought or intelligence to the Deity, as one of his most glorious attributes. And what means this language? These terms we have framed to express operations or faculties of our own souls. The Infinite Light would be for ever hidden from us, did not kindred rays dawn and brighten within us. God is another name for human intelligence raised above all error and imperfection, and extended to all possible truth.

The same is true of God's goodness. How do we understand this, but by the principle of love implanted in the human breast? Whence is it, that this divine attribute is so faintly comprehended, but from the feeble development of it in the multitude of men? Who can understand the strength, purity, fulness, and extent of divine philanthropy, but he in whom selfishness has been swallowed up in love?

The same is true of all the moral perfections of the Deity. These are comprehended by us, only through our own moral nature. It is conscience within us, which, by its approving and condemning voice, interprets to us God's love of virtue and hatred of sin; and without conscience, these glorious conceptions would never have opened on the mind. It is the lawgiver in our own breasts, which gives us the idea of divine authority, and binds us to obey it. The soul, by its sense of right, or its perception of moral distinctions, is clothed with sovereignty over itself, and through this alone, it understands and recognises the Sovereign of the Universe. Men, as by a natural inspiration, have agreed to speak of conscience as the voice of God, as the Divinity within us. This principle, reverently obeyed, makes us more and more partakers of the moral perfection of the Supreme Being, of that very excellence, which constitutes the rightfulness of his sceptre, and enthrones him over the universe. Without this inward law, we should be as incapable of receiving a law from Heaven, as the brute. Without this, the thunders of Sinai might startle the outward ear, but would have no meaning, no authority to the mind. I have expressed here a great truth. Nothing teaches so encouragingly our relation and resemblance to God; for the glory of the Supreme Being is eminently moral. We blind ourselves to his chief splendor, if we think only or mainly of his power, and overlook those attributes of rectitude and goodness, to which he subjects his omnipotence, and which are the foundations and very substance of his universal and immutable Law. And are these attributes revealed to us through the principles and convictions of our own souls? Do we understand through sympathy God's perception of the right, the good, the holy, the just? Then with what propriety is it said, that in his own image he made man!

I am aware, that it may be objected to these views, that we receive our idea of God from the universe, from his works, and not so exclusively from our own souls. The universe, I know, is full of God. The heavens and earth declare his glory. In other words, the effects and signs of power, wisdom, and goodness, are apparent through the whole creation. But apparent to what? Not to the outward eye; not to the acutest organs of sense; but to a kindred mind, which interprets the universe by itself. It is only through that energy of thought, by which we adapt various and complicated means to distant ends, and give harmony and a common bearing to multiplied exertions, that we understand the creative intelligence which has established the order, dependencies, and harmony of nature. We see God around us, because he dwells within us. It is by a kindred wisdom, that we discern his wisdom in his works. The brute, with an eye as piercing as ours, looks on the universe; and the page, which to us is radiant with characters of greatness and goodness, is to him a blank. In truth, the beauty and glory of God's works, are revealed to the mind by a light beaming from itself. We discern the impress of God's attributes in the universe, by accordance of nature, and enjoy them through sympathy.—I hardly need observe, that these remarks in relation to the universe apply with equal, if not greater force, to revelation.

I shall now be met by another objection, which to many may seem strong. It will be said, that these various attributes of which I have spoken, exist in God in Infinite Perfection, and that this destroys all affinity between the human and the Divine mind. To this I have two replies. In the first place, an attribute, by becoming perfect, does not part with its essence. Love, wisdom, power, and purity do not change their nature by enlargement. If they did, we should lose the Supreme Being through his very infinity. Our ideas of him would fade away into mere sounds. For example, if wisdom in God, because unbounded, have no affinity with that attribute in man, why apply to him that term? It must signify nothing. Let me ask what we mean, when we say that we discern the marks of intelligence in the universe? We mean, that we meet there the proofs of a mind like our own. We certainly discern proofs of no other; so that to deny this doctrine would be to deny the evidences of a God, and utterly to subvert the foundations of religious belief. What man can examine the structure of a plant or an animal, and see the adaptation of its parts to each other and to common ends, and not feel, that it is the work of an intelligence akin to his own, and that he traces these marks of design by the same spiritual energy in which they had their origin?

But I would offer another answer to this objection, that God's infinity places him beyond the resemblance and approach of man. I affirm, and trust that I do not speak too strongly, that there are traces of infinity in the human mind; and that, in this very respect, it bears a likeness to God. The very conception of infinity, is the mark of a nature to which no limit can be prescribed. This thought, indeed, comes to us, not so much from abroad, as from our own souls. We ascribe this attribute to God, because we possess capacities and wants, which only an unbounded being can fill, and because we are conscious of a tendency in spiritual faculties to unlimited expansion. We believe in the Divine infinity, through something congenial with it in our own breasts. I hope I speak clearly, and if not, I would ask those to whom I am obscure, to pause before they condemn. To me it seems, that the soul, in all its higher actions, in original thought, in the creations of genius, in the soarings of imagination, in its love of beauty and grandeur, in its aspirations after a pure and unknown joy, and especially in disinterestedness, in the spirit of selfsacrifice, and in enlightened devotion, has a character of infinity. There is often a depth in human love, which may be strictly called unfathomable. There is sometimes a lofty strength in moral principle, which all the power of the outward universe cannot overcome. There seems a might within, which can more than balance all might without. There is, too, a piety, which swells into a transport too vast for utterance, and into an immeasurable joy. I am speaking, indeed, of what is uncommon, but still of realities. We see however the tendency of the soul to the infinite in more familiar and ordinary forms. Take for example the delight which we find in the vast scenes of nature, in prospects which spread around us without limits, in the immensity of the heavens and the ocean, and especially in the rush and roar of mighty winds, waves, and torrents, when, amidst our deep awe, a power within seems to respond to the omnipotence around us. The same principle is seen in the delight ministered to us by works of fiction or of imaginative art, in which our own nature is set before us in more than human beauty and power. In truth the soul is always bursting its limits. It thirsts continually for wider knowledge. It rushes forward to untried happiness. It has a deep want which nothing limited can appease. Its true element and end is an unbounded good. Thus God's infinity has its image in the soul, and through the soul much more than through the universe, we arrive at this conception of the Deity.

In these remarks I have spoken strongly. But I have no fear of expressing too strongly the connexion between the divine and the human mind. My only fear is, that I shall dishonour the great subject. The danger to which we are most exposed, is that of severing the Creator from his creatures. The propensity of human sovereigns to cut off communication between themselves and their subjects, and to disclaim a common nature with their inferiors, has led the multitude of men, who think of God chiefly under the character of a king, to conceive of him as a being who places his glory in multiplying distinctions between himself and all other beings. The truth is, that the union between the Creator and the creature surpasses all other bonds in strength and intimacy. He penetrates all things, and delights to irradiate all with his glory. Nature, in all its lowest and inanimate forms, is pervaded by his power; and when quickened by the mysterious property of life, how wonderfully does it show forth the perfections of its Author! How much of God may be seen in the structure of a single leaf, which, though so frail as to tremble in every wind, yet holds connexions and living communications with the earth, the air, the clouds, and the distant sun; and, through these sympathies with the universe, is itself a revelation of an omnipotent mind. God delights to diffuse himself everywhere. Through his energy, unconscious matter clothes itself with proportions, powers, and beauties, which reflect his wisdom and love. How much more must he delight to frame conscious and happy recipients of his perfections, in whom his wisdom and love may substantially dwell, with whom he may form spiritual ties, and to whom he may be an everlasting spring of moral energy and happiness. How far the Supreme Being may communicate his attributes to his intelligent off-spring, I stop not to inquire. But that his almighty goodness will impart to them powers and glories, of which the material universe is but a faint emblem, I cannot doubt. That the soul, if true to itself and its Maker, will be filled with God, and will manifest him, more than the sun, I cannot doubt. Who can doubt it, that believes and understands the doctrine of human immortality?

The views which I have given in this discourse, respecting man's participation of the divine nature, seem to me to re-ceive strong confirmation, from the title or relation most fre-quently applied to God in the New Testament; and I have reserved this as the last corroboration of this doctrine, be-cause, to my own mind, it is singularly affecting. In the New Testament God is made known to us as a Father; and a brighter feature of that book cannot be named. Our worship is to be directed to him as our Father. Our whole religion is to take its character from this view of the Divinity. In this he is to rise always to our minds. And what is it to be a Father? It is to communicate one's own nature, to give life to kindred beings; and the highest function of a Father is to educate the mind of the child, and to impart to it what is noblest and hap-piest in his own mind. God is our Father, not merely because he created us, or because he gives us enjoyment; for he cre-ated the flower and the insect, yet we call him not their Father. This bond is a spiritual one. This name belongs to God, because he frames spirits like himself, and delights to give them what is most glorious and blessed in his own na-ture. Accordingly, Christianity is said, with special propriety, to reveal God as the Father, because it reveals him as sending his Son, to cleanse the mind from every stain, and to replen-ish it for ever with the spirit and moral attributes of its Author. Separate from God this idea of his creating and train-ing up beings after his own likeness, and you rob him of the paternal character. This relation vanishes, and with it vanishes the glory of the Gospel, and the dearest hopes of the human soul.

The great use which I would make of the principles laid down in this discourse, is to derive from them just and clear views of the nature of religion. What, then, is religion? I answer; it is not the adoration of a God with whom we have no common properties; of a distinct, foreign, separate being; but of an all-communicating Parent. It recognises and adores God, as a being whom we know through our own souls, who has made man in his own image, who is the perfection of our own spiritual nature, who has sympathies with us as kindred beings, who is near us, not in place only like this all surrounding atmosphere, but by spiritual influence and love, who looks on us with parental interest, and whose great design it is to communicate to us for ever, and in freer and fuller streams, his own power, goodness, and joy. The conviction of this near and ennobling relation of God to the soul, and of his great purposes towards it, belongs to the very essence of true religion; and true religion manifests itself chiefly and most conspicuously in desires, hopes, and efforts corresponding to this truth. It desires and seeks supremely the assimilation of the mind to God, or the perpetual unfolding and enlargement of those powers and virtues by which it is constituted his glorious image. The mind, in proportion as it is enlightened and penetrated by true religion, thirsts and labors for a godlike elevation. What else, indeed, can it seek, if this good be placed within its reach? If I am capable of receiving and reflecting the intellectual and moral glory of my Creator, what else in comparison shall I desire? Shall I deem a property in the outward universe as the highest good, when I may become partaker of the very mind from which it springs, of the prompting love, the disposing wisdom, the quickening power, through which its order, beauty, and beneficent influences subsist? True religion is known by these high aspirations, hopes, and efforts. And this is the religion which most truly honors God. To honor him, is not to tremble before him as an unapproachable sovereign, not to utter barren praise which leaves us as it found us. It is to become what we praise. It is to approach

God as an inexhaustible Fountain of light, power, and purity. It is to feel the quickening and transforming energy of his perfections. It is to thirst for the growth and invigoration of the divine principle within us. It is to seek the very spirit of God. It is to trust in, to bless, to thank him for that rich grace, mercy, love, which was revealed and proffered by Jesus Christ, and which proposes as its great end the perfection of the human soul.

I regard this view of religion as infinitely important. It does more than all things to make our connexion with our Creator ennobling and happy; and, in proportion as we want it, there is danger that the thought of God may itself become the instrument of our degradation. That religion has been so dispensed as to depress the human mind, I need not tell you; and it is a truth which ought to be known, that the greatness of the Deity, when separated in our thoughts from his parental character, especially tends to crush human energy and hope. To a frail dependent creature, an omnipotent Creator easily becomes a terror, and his worship easily degenerates into servility, flattery, self-contempt, and selfish calculation. Religion only ennobles us, in as far as it reveals to us the tender and intimate connexion of God with his creatures, and teaches us to see in the very greatness which might give alarm, the source of great and glorious communications to the human soul. You cannot, my hearers, think too highly of the majesty of God. But let not this majesty sever him from you. Remember, that his greatness is the infinity of attributes which yourselves possess. Adore his infinite wisdom; but remember that this wisdom rejoices to diffuse itself, and let an exhilarating hope spring up, at the thought of the immeasurable intelligence which such a Father must communicate to his children. In like manner adore his power. Let the boundless creation fill you with awe and admiration of the energy which sustains it. But remember that God has a nobler work than the outward creation, even the spirit within yourselves; and that it is his purpose to replenish this with his own energy, and to crown it with growing power and triumphs over the material universe. Above all, adore his unutterable goodness. But remember, that this attribute is particularly proposed to you as your model; that God calls you, both by nature and revelation, to a fellowship in his philanthropy; that he has placed you in social relations for the very end of rendering you ministers and representatives of his benevolence; that he even summons you to espouse and to advance the sublimest purpose of his goodness, the redemption of the human race, by extending the knowledge and power of Christian truth. It is through such views, that religion raises up the soul, and binds man by ennobling bonds to his Maker.

To complete my views of this topic, I beg to add an important caution. I have said that the great work of religion is to conform ourselves to God, or to unfold the divine likeness within us. Let none infer from this language, that I place religion in unnatural effort, in straining after excitements which do not belong to the present state, or in anything separate from the clear and simple duties of life. I exhort you to no extravagance. I reverence human nature too much to do it violence. I see too much divinity in its ordinary operations, to urge on it a forced and vehement virtue. To grow in the likeness of God, we need not cease to be men. This likeness does not consist in extraordinary or miraculous gifts, in supernatural additions to the soul, or in anything foreign to our original constitution; but in our essential faculties, unfolded by vigorous and conscientious exertion in the ordinary circumstances assigned by God. To resemble our Creator, we need not fly from society, and entrance ourselves in lonely contemplation and prayer. Such processes might give a feverish strength to one class of emotions, but would result in disproportion, distortion, and sickliness of mind. Our proper work is to approach God by the free and natural unfolding of our highest powers, of understanding, conscience, love, and the moral will.

Shall I be told that by such language, I ascribe to nature the effects which can only be wrought in the soul by the Holy Spirit? I anticipate this objection, and wish to meet it by a simple exposition of my views. I would on no account disparage the gracious aids and influences which God imparts to the human soul. The promise of the Holy Spirit is among the most precious in the sacred volume. Worlds could not tempt me to part with the doctrine of God's intimate connexion with the mind, and of his free and full communications to it. But these views are in no respect at variance with what I have taught, of the method, by which we are to grow in the likeness of God. Scripture and experience concur in teaching, that by the Holy Spirit, we are to understand a divine assistance adapted to our moral freedom, and accordant with the fundamental truth, that virtue is the mind's own work. By the Holy Spirit, I understand an aid, which must be gained and made effectual by our own activity; an aid, which no more interferes with our faculties, than the assistance which we receive from our fellow beings; an aid, which silently mingles and conspires with all other helps and means of goodness; an aid, by which we unfold our natural powers in a natural order, and by which we are strengthened to understand and apply the resources derived from our munificent Creator. This aid we cannot prize too much, or pray for too earnestly. But wherein, let me ask, does it war with the doctrine, that God is to be approached by the exercise and unfolding of our highest powers and affections, in the ordinary circumstances of human life?

I repeat it, to resemble our Maker we need not quarrel with nature or our lot. Our present state, made up, as it is, of aids and trials, is worthy of God, and may be used throughout to assimilate us to him. For example, our domestic ties, the relations of neighbourhood and country, the daily interchanges of thoughts and feelings, the daily occasions of kindness, the daily claims of want and suffering, these and the other circumstances of our social state, form the best sphere and school for that benevolence, which is God's brightest attribute; and we should make a sad exchange, by substituting for these natural aids, any self-invented artificial means of sanctity. Christianity, our great guide to God, never leads us away from the path of nature, and never wars with the unsophisticated dictates of conscience. We approach our Creator by every right exertion of the powers he gives us. Whenever we invigorate the understanding by honestly and resolutely seeking truth, and by withstanding whatever might warp the judgment; whenever we invigorate the conscience by following it in opposition to the passions; whenever we receive a blessing gratefully, bear a trial patiently, or encounter peril or scorn with moral courage; whenever we perform a disinterested deed; whenever we lift up the heart in true adoration to God; whenever we war against a habit or desire which is strengthening itself against our higher principles; whenever we think, speak, or act, with moral energy, and resolute devotion to duty, be the occasion ever so humble, obscure, familiar, then the divinity is growing within us, and we are ascending towards our Author. True religion thus blends itself with common life. We are thus to draw nigh to God, without forsaking men. We are thus, without parting with our human nature, to clothe ourselves with the divine.

My views on the great subject of this discourse have now been given. I shall close with a brief consideration of a few objections, in the course of which I shall offer some views of the christian ministry, which this occasion and the state of the world, seem to me to demand.—I anticipate from some an objection to this discourse, drawn as they will say from experience. I may be told, that I have talked of the godlike capacities of human nature, and have spoken of man as a divinity; and where, it will be asked, are the warrants of this high estimate of our race? I may be told that I dream, and that I have peopled the world with the creatures of my lonely imagination. What! Is it only in dreams, that beauty and loveliness have beamed on me from the human countenance, that I have heard tones of kindness, which have thrilled through my heart, that I have found sympathy in suffering, and a sacred joy in friendship? Are all the great and good men of past ages only dreams? Are such names as Moses, Socrates, Paul, Alfred, Milton, only the fictions of my disturbed slumbers? Are the great deeds of history, the discoveries of philosophy, the creations of genius, only visions? Oh! no. I do not dream when I speak of the divine capacities of human nature. It was a real page in which I read of patriots and martyrs, of Fenelon and Howard, of Hampden and Washington. And tell me not that these were prodigies, miracles, immeasurably separated from their race; for the very reverence, which has treasured up and hallowed their memories, the very sentiments of admiration and love with which their names are now heard, show that the principles of their greatness are diffused through all your breasts. The germs of sublime virtue are scattered liberally on our earth. How often have I seen in the obscurity of domestic life, a strength of love, of endurance, of pious trust, of virtuous resolution, which in a public sphere would have attracted public homage. I cannot but pity the man, who recognises nothing godlike in his own nature. I see the marks of God in the heavens and the earth; but how much more in a liberal intellect, in magnanimity, in unconquerable rectitude, in a philanthropy which forgives every wrong, and which never despairs of the cause of Christ and human virtue. I do and I must reverence human nature. Neither the sneers of a worldly scepticism, nor the groans of a gloomy theology, disturb my faith in its godlike powers and tendencies. I know how it is despised, how it has been oppressed, how civil and religious establishments have for ages conspired to crush it. I know its history. I shut my eyes on none of its weaknesses and crimes. I understand the proofs, by which despotism demonstrates, that man is a wild beast, in want of a master, and only safe in chains. But injured, trampled on, and scorned as our nature is, I still turn to it with intense sympathy and strong hope. The signatures of its origin and its end are impressed too deeply to be ever wholly effaced. I bless it for its kind affections, for its strong and tender love. I honor it for its struggles against oppression, for its growth and progress under the weight of so many chains and prejudices, for its achievements in science and art, and still more for its examples of heroic and saintly virtue. These are marks of a divine origin and the pledges of a celestial inheritance; and I thank God that my own lot is bound up with that of the human race.

But another objection starts up. It may be said, 'Allow these views to be true; are they fitted for the pulpit? fitted to act on common minds? They may be prized by men of cultivated intellect and taste; but can the multitude understand them? Will the multitude feel them? On whom has a minister to act? On men immersed in business, and buried in the flesh; on men, whose whole power of thought has been spent on pleasure or gain; on men, chained by habit, and wedded to sin. Sooner may adamant be riven by a child's touch, than the human heart be pierced by refined and elevated sentiment.

Gross instruments will alone act on gross minds. Men sleep, and nothing but thunder, nothing but flashes from the everlasting fire of hell, will thoroughly wake them.'

I have all along felt that such objections would be made to the views I have urged. But they do not move me. I answer, that I think these views singularly adapted to the pulpit, and I think them full of power. The objection is that they are *refined*. But I see God accomplishing his noblest purposes by what may be called refined means. All the great agents of nature, attraction, heat, and the principle of life, are refined, spiritual, invisible, acting gently, silently, imperceptibly; and yet brute matter feels their power, and is transformed by them into surpassing beauty. The electric fluid, unseen, unfelt, and everywhere diffused, is infinitely more efficient, and ministers to infinitely nobler productions, than when it breaks forth in thunder. Much less can I believe, that in the moral world, noise, menace, and violent appeals to gross passions, to fear and selfishness, are God's chosen means of calling forth spiritual life, beauty, and greatness. It is seldom that human nature throws off all susceptibility of grateful and generous impressions, all sympathy with superior virtue; and here are springs and principles to which a generous teaching, if simple, sincere, and fresh from the soul, may confidently appeal.

It is said, men cannot *understand* the views which seem to me so precious. This objection I am anxious to repel, for the common intellect has been grievously kept down and wronged through the belief of its incapacity. The pulpit would do more good, were not the mass of men looked upon and treated as children. Happily for the race, the time is passing away, in which intellect was thought the monopoly of a few, and the majority were given over to hopeless ignorance. Science is leaving her solitudes to enlighten the multitude. How much more may religious teachers take courage to speak to men on subjects, which are nearer to them than the properties and laws of matter, I mean their own souls. The multitude, you say, want capacity to receive great truths relating to their spiritual nature. But what, let me ask you, is the Christian religion? A spiritual system, intended to turn men's minds upon themselves, to frame them to watchfulness over thought, imagination, and passion, to establish them in an intimacy with their own souls. What are all the Christian virtues, which men are exhorted to love and seek? I answer, pure and high motions or determinations of the mind. That refinement of thought, which, I am told, transcends the common intellect, belongs to the very essence of Christianity. In confirmation of these views, the human mind seems to me to be turning itself more and more inward, and to be growing more alive to its own worth, and its capacities of progress. The spirit of education shows this, and so does the spirit of freedom. There is a spreading conviction that man was made for a higher purpose than to be a beast of burden, or a creature of sense. The divinity is stirring within the human breast, and demanding a culture and a liberty worthy of the child of God. Let religious teaching correspond to this advancement of the mind. Let it rise above the technical, obscure, and frigid theology which has come down to us from times of ignorance, superstition, and slavery. Let it penetrate the human soul, and reveal it to itself. No preaching, I believe, is so intelligible, as that which is true to human nature, and helps men to read their own spirits.

But the objection which I have stated not only represents men as incapable of understanding, but still more of being moved, quickened, sanctified, and saved, by such views as I have given. If by this objection nothing more is meant, than that these views are not alone or of themselves sufficient, I shall not dispute it; for true and glorious as they are, they do not constitute the whole truth, and I do not expect great moral effects from narrow and partial views of our nature. I have spoken of the godlike capacities of the soul. But other and very different elements enter into the human being. Man has animal propensities as well as intellectual and moral powers. He has a body as well as mind. He has passions to war with reason, and self-love with conscience. He is a free being and a tempted being, and, thus constituted he may and does sin, and often sins grievously. To such a being, religion, or virtue, is a conflict, requiring great spiritual effort, put forth in habitual watchfulness and prayer; and all the motives are needed, by which force and constancy may be communicated to the will. I exhort not the preacher, to talk perpetually of man as 'made but a little lower than the angels.' I would not narrow him to any class of topics. Let him adapt himself to our whole and various nature. Let him summon to his aid all the powers of this world, and the world to come. Let him bring to bear on the conscience and the heart, God's milder and more awful attributes, the promises and threatenings of the divine word, the lessons of history, the warnings of experience. Let the wages of sin here and hereafter be taught clearly and earnestly. But amidst the various motives to spiritual effort, which belong to the minister, none are more quickening than those drawn from the soul itself, and from God's desire and purpose to exalt it, by every aid consistent with its freedom. These views I conceive are to mix with all others, and without them all others fail to promote a generous virtue. Is it said, that the minister's proper work is, to preach Christ and not the dignity of human nature? I answer, that Christ's greatness is manifested in the greatness of the nature which he was sent to redeem; and that his chief glory consists in this, that he came to restore God's image where it was obscured or effaced, and to give an everlasting impulse and life to what is divine within us. Is it said, that the malignity of sin is to be the minister's great theme? I answer, that this malignity can only be understood and felt, when sin is viewed as the ruin of God's noblest work, as darkening a light brighter than the sun, as carrying discord, bondage, disease, and death into a mind framed for perpetual progress towards its Author. Is it said, that terror is the chief instrument of saving the soul? I answer, that if by terror, be meant a rational and moral fear, a conviction and dread of the unutterable evil incurred by a mind which wrongs, betrays, and destroys itself, then I am the last to deny its importance. But a fear like this, which regards the debasement of the soul as the greatest of evils, is plainly founded upon and proportioned to our conceptions of the greatness of our nature. The more common terror, excited by vivid images of torture and bodily pain, is a very questionable means of virtue. When strongly awakened, it generally injures the character, breaks men into cowards and slaves, brings the intellect to cringe before human authority, makes man abject before his Maker, and, by a natural reaction of the mind, often terminates in a presumptuous confidence, altogether distinct from virtuous self-respect, and singularly hostile to the unassuming, charitable spirit of Christianity. The preacher should rather strive to fortify the soul against physical pains, than to bow it to their mastery, teaching it to dread nothing in comparison with sin, and to dread sin as the ruin of a noble nature.

Men, I repeat it, are to be quickened and raised by appeals to their highest principles. Even the convicts of a prison may be touched by kindness, generosity, and especially by a tone, look, and address, expressing hope and respect for their nature. I know, that the doctrine of ages has been, that terror, restraint, and bondage are the chief safeguards of human virtue and peace. But we have begun to learn that affection, confidence, respect, and freedom are mightier as well as nobler agents. Men *can* be wrought upon by generous influences. I would that this truth were better understood by religious teachers. From the pulpit generous influences too seldom proceed. In the church men too seldom hear a voice to quicken and exalt them. Religion, speaking through her public organs, seems often to forget her natural tone of elevation. The character of God, the principles of his government, his relations to the human family, the purposes for which he brought us into being, the nature which he has given us, and the condition in which he has placed us, these and the like topics, though the sublimest which can enter the mind, are not unfrequently so set forth as to narrow and degrade the hearers, disheartening and oppressing with gloom the timid and sensitive, and infecting coarser minds with the unhallowed spirit of intolerance, presumption, and exclusive pretension to the favor of God. I know, and rejoice to know, that preaching in its worst forms does good; for so bright and piercing is the light of Christianity, that it penetrates in a measure the thickest clouds in which men contrive to involve it. But that evil mixes with the good, I also know; and I should be unfaithful to my deep convictions, did I not say, that human nature requires for its elevation, more generous treatment from the teachers of religion.

I conclude with saying, let the minister cherish a reverence for his own nature. Let him never despise it even in its most forbidding forms. Let him delight in its beautiful and lofty manifestations. Let him hold fast as one of the great qualifications for his office, a faith in the greatness of the human soul, that faith, which looks beneath the perishing body, beneath the sweat of the laborer, beneath the rags and ignorance of the poor, beneath the vices of the sensual and selfish, and discerns in the depths of the soul a divine principle, a ray of the Infinite Light, which may yet break forth and 'shine as the sun' in the kingdom of God. Let him strive to awaken in men a consciousness of the heavenly treasure within them, a consciousness of possessing what is of more worth than the outward universe. Let hope give life to all his labors. Let him speak to men, as to beings liberally gifted, and made for God. Let him always look round on a congregation with the encouraging trust, that he has hearers prepared to respond to the simple, unaffected utterance of great truths, and to the noblest workings of his own mind. Let him feel deeply for those, in whom the divine nature is overwhelmed by the passions. Let him sympathize tenderly with those, in whom it begins to struggle, to mourn for sin, to thirst for a new life. Let him guide and animate to higher and diviner virtue those, in whom it has gained strength. Let him strive to infuse courage, enterprise, devout trust, and an inflexible will, into men's labors for their own perfection. In one word, let him cherish an unfaltering and growing faith in God as the Father and quickener of the human mind, and in Christ as its triumphant and immortal friend. That by such preaching he is to work miracles, I do not say. That he will rival in sudden and outward effects what is wrought by the preachers of a low and terrifying theology, I do not expect or desire. That all will be made better, I am far from believing. His office is to act on free beings, who after all must determine themselves; who have power to withstand all foreign agency; who are to be saved, not by mere preaching, but by their own prayers and toil. Still I believe, that such a minister will be a benefactor beyond all praise to the human soul. I believe, and know, that on those, who will admit his influence, he will work deeply, powerfully, gloriously. His function is the sublimest under heaven; and his reward will be, a growing power of spreading truth, virtue, moral strength, love, and happiness, without limit, and without end.

RALPH WALDO EMERSON

Sermon Delivered September 9, 1832

The kingdom of God is not meat and drink; but righteousness and peace and joy in the holy ghost.
ROMANS 14:17

IN THE HISTORY of the Church no subject has been more fruitful of controversy than the Lord's Supper. There never has been any unanimity in the understanding of its nature nor any uniformity in the mode of celebrating it. Without considering the frivolous questions which have been hotly debated as to the posture in which men should partake or whether mixed or unmixed wine should be served, whether leavened or unleavened bread should be broken, the questions have been settled differently in every church, who should be admitted to partake, and how often it should be prepared. In the Catholic Church once infants were permitted and then forbidden to partake. Since the ninth Century, bread only is given to the laity and the cup is reserved to the priesthood. So as to the time. In the fourth Lateran Council it was decreed that every believer should communicate once in a year at Easter. Afterwards three times—But more important have been the controversies respecting its nature. The great question of the Real Presence was the main controversy between the Church of England and the Church of Rome. The doctrine of the Consubstantiation maintained by Luther was denied by Calvin. In the Church of England Archbishops Laud and Wake maintained that it was a Eucharist or sacrifice of thanksgiving to God, Cudworth and Warburton that it was not a sacrifice but a feast after a sacrifice, and Bishop Hoadly that it was a simple commemoration.

If there seem to you an agreement in this last opinion among our churches it is only but of yesterday and within narrow limits.

And finally it is now near 200 years since the society of

Quakers denied the authority of the supper altogether and gave good reasons for disusing it.

I allude to these facts only to show that so far from the Supper being a tradition in which all are fully agreed, there has always been the widest room for difference of opinion upon this particular.

Having recently paid particular attention to this subject, I was led to the conclusion that Jesus did not intend to establish an institution for perpetual observance when he ate the passover with his disciples; and further to the opinion that it is not expedient to celebrate it as we do. I shall now endeavour to state distinctly my reasons for these two opinions.

An account of the last Supper of Christ with his disciples is given by the four Evangelists, Matthew, Mark, Luke and John.

In St. Matthew's Gospel (26:26) are recorded the words of Jesus in giving bread and wine on that occasion to his disciples but no expression occurs intimating that this feast was hereafter to be commemorated.

In St. Mark the same words are recorded and still with no intimation that the occasion was to be remembered (14:22).

St. Luke, after relating the breaking of the bread, has these words: 'This do in remembrance of me' (22:15).

In St. John, although other occurrences of the same evening are related, this whole transaction is passed over without notice.

Now observe the facts. Two of the evangelists (namely, Matthew and John) were of the twelve disciples and were present on that occasion. Neither of them drops the slightest intimation of any intention on the part of Jesus to set up any thing permanent. John especially, the beloved disciple, who has recorded with minuteness the conversation and the transactions of that memorable evening, has quite omitted such a notice.

Neither did it come to the knowledge of St. Mark, who relates the other facts. It is found in Luke alone, who was not present. There is no reason, however, that we know for rejecting the account of Luke. I doubt not that the expression was used by Jesus. I shall presently consider its meaning. I have only brought these accounts together that you may judge whether it is likely that a solemn institution to be continued to the end of time, by all mankind, as they should come, nation after nation, within the influence of the Christian religion, was to be established in this slight manner, in a manner so slight that the intention of remembering it should not have caught the ear or dwelt in the mind of the only two among the twelve, who wrote down what happened!

Still we must suppose that this expression—This do in remembrance of me—had come to the ear of Luke from some disciple present. What did it really signify? It is a prophetic and an affectionate expression. Jesus is a Jew sitting with his countrymen celebrating their national feast. He thinks of his own impending death and wishes the minds of his disciples to be prepared for it and says to them, "When hereafter you shall keep the passover it will have an altered aspect in your eyes. It is now a historical covenant of God with the Jewish nation. Hereafter it will remind you of a new covenant sealed with my blood. In years to come, as long as your people shall come up to Jerusalem to keep this feast (forty years) the connexion which has subsisted between us will give a new meaning in your eyes to the national festival as the anniversary of my death."—I see natural feeling and beauty in the use of such language from Jesus, a friend to his friends. I can readily imagine that he was willing and desirous that when his disciples met, his memory should hallow their intercourse, but I cannot bring myself to believe that he looked beyond the living generation, beyond the abolition of the festival he was celebrating and the scattering of the nation, and meant to impose a memorial feast upon the whole world.

But though the words *Do this in remembrance*, to which so much meaning has been given, do not occur in Matthew, Mark, or John, yet many persons are apt to imagine that the very striking and formal manner in which this eating and drinking is described intimates a striking and formal purpose to found a festival. This opinion would easily occur to any one reading only the New Testament, but the impression is removed by reading any narrative of the mode in which the ancient or the modern Jews kept the passover. It is then perceived at once that the leading circumstances in the gospel are only a faithful account of that ceremony. Jesus did not

celebrate the passover and afterwards the supper, but the supper *was* the passover. He did with his disciples exactly what
every master of a family in Jerusalem was doing at the same
hour with his household. It appears that the Jews ate the lamb
and the unleavened bread and drank wine after a prescribed
manner. It was the custom for the Lord or master of the feast
to break the bread and to bless it, using this formula, which
the Talmudists have preserved to us, 'Blessed be thou O Lord
who givest us the fruits of the earth', and to give it to every
one at the table. It was the custom for the master of the family to take the cup which contained the wine and to bless it
saying, 'Blessed be thou O Lord who givest us the fruit of the
vine,' and then to give the cup to all. Among the modern
Jews, a hymn is sung after this ceremony, specifying the
twelve great works done by God for the deliverance of their
fathers out of Egypt. And Jesus did the same thing.

But why did he use expressions so extraordinary and emphatic as these: This is my body which is broken for you.
Take, Eat. This is my blood which is shed for you. Drink it.
They are not extraordinary expressions from him. They were
familiar in his mouth. He always taught by parables and symbols. It was the national way of teaching and was largely used
by him. Remember the readiness which he always showed to
spiritualize every occurrence. He stooped and wrote on the
sand. He admonished his disciples respecting the leaven of the
Pharisees. He instructed the woman of Samaria respecting living water. He permitted himself to be anointed, declaring it
was for interment. He washed the feet of his disciples. These
are admitted to be symbolical actions and expressions. Here
in like manner he calls the bread his body and bids the disciples eat. He had used the same expression repeatedly before.
The reason why St. John does not repeat the words here,
seems to be that he had narrated a similar discourse of Jesus
to the people of Capernaum more at length already (John
6:27). He there tells the Jews—'Except ye eat the flesh of the
Son of Man and drink his blood ye have no life in you.'

And when the Jews on that occasion complained that they
did not comprehend what he meant, he added for their better understanding, and as if for our understanding, that we
might not think that his body was to be actually eaten, that

he only meant we should live by his commandment. He closed his discourse with these explanatory expressions: "The flesh profiteth nothing;—the *words* that I speak to you, they are spirit and they are life."

Whilst I am upon this topic I cannot help remarking that it is very singular we should have preserved this rite and insisted upon perpetuating one symbolical act of Christ whilst we have totally neglected others, particularly one other which had at least an equal claim to our observance. Jesus washed the feet of his disciples and told them that 'As he had washed their feet, they ought to wash one another's feet, for he had given them an example that they should do as he had done to them.' I ask any person who believes the Supper to have been designed by Jesus to be commemorated forever, to go and read the account of it in the other gospels, and then compare with it the account of this transaction in St. John and tell me if it is not much more explicitly authorized than the supper. It only differs in this, that we have found the Supper used in New England and the washing of the feet not. If we had found this rite established, it would be much more difficult to show its defective authority. That rite is used by the Church of Rome and the Sandemanians. It has been very properly dropped by other Christians. Why? 1. Because it was a local custom and unsuitable in western countries, and 2. because it was typical and all understand that humility is the thing signified. But the passover was local too and does not concern us; and its bread and wine were typical and do not help us to understand the love which they signified.

These views of the original account of the Lord's Supper lead me to esteem it an occasion full of solemn and prophetic interest but never intended by Jesus to be the foundation of a perpetual institution.

It appears however from Paul's Epistle to the Corinthians that the disciples had very early taken advantage of these impressive words of Christ to hold religious meetings where they broke bread and drank wine as symbols.

I look upon this fact as very natural in the circumstances of the Church. The disciples lived together; they threw all their property into a common stock; they were bound together by the memory of Christ and nothing could be more natural

than that this eventful evening should be affectionately remembered by them; that they, Jews like Jesus, should adopt
his expression and his type, and furthermore that what was
done with peculiar propriety by them, by his personal friends,
should come to be extended to their companions also. In this
way religious feasts grew up among the early Christians. They
were readily adopted by the Jewish converts who were familiar with religious feasts, and also by the Pagan converts whose
idolatrous worship had been made up of sacred festivals and
who very readily abused these to gross riot as appears from
the censures of St. Paul. Many persons consider this fact, the
observance of such a memorial feast by the early disciples, decisive of the question whether it ought to be observed by us.
For my part I see nothing to wonder at in its originating
there; all that is surprizing is that it should exist amongst us.
It had great propriety for his personal friends to remember
their friend and repeat his words. It was but too probable that
among the half-converted Pagans and Jews any rite, any form
would be cherished whilst yet unable to comprehend the spiritual character of Christianity.

The circumstance however that St. Paul favors these views
has seemed to many persons conclusive in favor of the institution. I am of opinion that it is wholly on this passage and
not upon the gospels that the ordinance stands. A careful examination of that passage will not I think make that evidence
so weighty as it seems. That passage, the eleventh chapter
I Corinthians, appears to be a reproof to the Corinthian converts of certain gross abuses that had grown up among them,
offending against decency not less than against Christianity:
accusing their contentiousness; the fanaticism of certain of
their women; and the intemperance into which they had
fallen at the Lord's supper. The end he has in view, in that
Chapter, and this is observable, is not to enjoin upon them to
observe the supper, but to censure their abuse of it. *We* quote
the passage nowadays as if it enjoined attendance on the supper, but he wrote it merely to chide them for drunkenness. To
make their enormity plainer he goes back to the origin of this
religious feast to show what that feast was out of which this
their riot came and so relates the transactions of the Lord's
supper. *I have received of the Lord*, he says. By this expression

it is often thought that a miraculous communication is implied, but certainly without good reason if it is remembered that St. Paul was living in the lifetime of all the apostles who could give him an account of the transaction, and it is contrary to all experience to suppose that God should work a miracle to convey information that might be so easily got by natural means. So that the import of the expression is that he had got the account of the Evangelists, which we also possess.

But the material circumstance which diminishes our confidence in the correctness of the apostle's view is the observation that his mind had not escaped the prevalent error of the primitive Church, the belief namely that the second coming of Christ would shortly occur, until which time, he tells them, this feast was to be kept. At that time the world would be burnt with fire, and a new government established in which the Saints would sit on thrones; so slow were the disciples during the life and after the ascension of Christ to receive the idea which we receive that his Second Coming was a spiritual kingdom, the dominion of his religion in the hearts of men to be extended gradually over the whole world.

In this manner I think we may see clearly enough how this ancient ordinance got its footing among the early Christians and this single expectation of a speedy reappearance of a temporal messiah upon earth, which kept its influence even over so spiritual a man as St. Paul, would naturally tend to preserve the use of the rite when once established.

We arrive then at this conclusion: 1. That it does not appear from a careful examination of the account of the Last Supper in the Evangelists that it was designed by Jesus to be perpetual. 2. It does not appear that the opinion of St. Paul, all things considered, ought to alter our opinion derived from the Evangelists.

I have not attempted to ascertain precisely the purpose in the mind of Jesus. But you will see that many opinions may be entertained of his intention all consistent with the opinion that he did not design the ordinance to be perpetual. He may have foreseen that his disciples would meet together to remember him and seen good in it. It may have crossed his mind that this would be easily continued a hundred or a thousand years, as men more easily transmit a form than a virtue, and yet have been altogether out of his purpose to fasten it upon men in all times and all countries.

Admitting that the disciples kept it and admitting Paul's feeling of its perpetuity, that does not settle the question for us. I think it was good for them. I think it is not suited to this day. We do not take them for guides in other things. They were, as we know, obstinately attached to their Jewish preju- dices. All the intercourse with the most persuasive of teachers seems to have done very little to enlarge their views. On every subject we have learned to think differently, and why shall not we form a judgment upon this, more in accordance with the spirit of Christianity than was the practice of the early ages?

But it is said, Admit that the rite was not designed to be perpetual. What harm doth it? Here it stands generally ac- cepted under some form by the Christian world, the un- doubted occasion of much good; is it not better it should remain? This is the question of Expediency.

I proceed to notice a few objections that in my judgment lie against its use in its present form.

1. If the view which I have taken of the history of the insti- tution be correct, then the claim of authority should be dropped in administering it. You say, every time you celebrate the rite, that Jesus enjoined it, and the whole language you use conveys that impression. But if you read the New Testament as I do, you do not believe he did.

2. It has seemed to me (yet I make the objection with dif- fidence) that the use of this ordinance tends to produce con- fusion in our views of the relation of the soul to God. It is the old objection to the doctrine of the Trinity that the true wor- ship was transferred from God to Christ or that such confu- sion was introduced into the soul that an undivided worship was given nowhere. Is not that the effect of the Lord's Supper? I appeal now to the convictions of communicants and ask such persons whether they have not been occasionally conscious of a painful confusion of thought between the wor- ship due to God and the commemoration due to Christ. For the service does not stand upon the basis of a voluntary act, but is imposed by authority. It is an expression of gratitude to him enjoined by him. There is an endeavour to keep Jesus in mind whilst yet the prayers are addressed to God. I fear it is

the effect of this ordinance to clothe Jesus with an authority which he never claimed and which distracts the mind of the worshipper. I know our opinions differ much respecting the nature and offices of Christ and the degree of veneration to which he is entitled. I am so much a Unitarian as this, that I believe the human mind cannot admit but one God, and that every effort to pay religious homage to more than one being goes to take away all right ideas. I appeal, brethren, to your individual experience. In the moment when you make the least petition to God, though it be but a silent wish that he may approve you, or add one moment to your life—do you not—in the very act—necessarily exclude all other beings from your thought? In that act the soul stands alone with God, and Jesus is no more present to the mind than your brother or your child.

But is not Jesus called in Scripture the Mediator? He is the Mediator in that only sense in which possibly any being can mediate between God and man, that is an Instructer of man. He teaches us how to become like God. And a true disciple of Jesus will receive the light he gives most thankfully, but the thanks he offers and which an exalted being will accept are not compliments, commemorations—but the use of that instruction.

3. To pass by other objections, I come to this: that the *use of the elements*, however suitable to the people and the modes of thought in the East where it originated, is foreign and unsuited to affect us. Whatever long usage and strong association may have done in some individuals to deaden this repulsion I apprehend that their use is rather tolerated than loved by any of us. We are not accustomed to express our thoughts or emotions by symbolical actions. Most men find the bread and wine no aid to devotion and to some persons it is an impediment. To eat bread is one thing; to love the precepts of Christ and resolve to obey them is quite another. It is of the greatest importance that whatever forms we use should be animated by our feelings; that our religion through all its acts should be living and operative.

The statement of this objection leads me to say that I think this difficulty, wherever it is felt, to be entitled to the greatest weight. It is alone a sufficient objection to the ordinance. It is my own objection. This mode of commemorating Christ is not suitable to me. That is reason enough why I should abandon it. If I believed that it was enjoined by Jesus on his disciples, and that he even contemplated to make permanent this mode of commemoration every way agreeable to an Eastern mind, and yet on trial it was disagreeable to my own feelings, I should not adopt it. I should choose other ways which he would approve more. For what could he wish to be commemorated for? Only that men might be filled with his spirit. I find that other modes comport with my education and habits of thought. For I chuse that my remembrances of him should be pleasing, affecting, religious. I will love him as a glorified friend after the free way of friendship and not pay him a stiff sign of respect as men do to those whom they fear. A passage read from his discourses, the provoking each other to works like his, any act or meeting which tends to awaken a pure thought, a glow of love, an original design of virtue I call a worthy, a true commemoration.

4. In the last place the importance ascribed to this particular ordinance is not consistent with the spirit of Christianity. The general object and effect of this ordinance is unexceptionable. It has been and is, I doubt not, the occasion of indefinite good, but an importance is given by the friends of the rite to it which never can belong to any form. My friends, the kingdom of God is not meat and drink. Forms are as essential as bodies. It would be foolish to declaim against them, but to adhere to one form a moment after it is outgrown is foolish. That form only is good and Christian which answers its end. Jesus came to take the load of ceremonies from the shoulders of men and substitute principles. If I understand the distinction of Christianity, the reason why it is to be preferred over all other systems and is divine is this, that it is a moral system; that it presents men with truths which are their own reason, and enjoins practices that are their own justification; that if miracles may be said to have been its evidence to the first Christians they are not its evidence to us, but the doctrines themselves; that every practice is Christian which praises itself and every practice unchristian which condemns itself. I am not engaged to Christianity by decent forms; it is not saving ordinances, it is not usage, it is not what I do not understand

that engages me to it—let these be the sandy foundation of falsehoods. What I revere and obey in it is its reality, its boundless charity, its deep interior life, the rest it gives to my mind, the echo it returns to my thoughts, the perfect accord it makes with my reason, the persuasion and courage that come out of it to lead me upward and onward.

Freedom is the essence of Christianity. It has for its object simply to make men good and wise. Its institutions should be as flexible as the wants of men. That form out of which the life and suitableness have departed should be as worthless in its eyes as the dead leaves that are falling around us.

And therefore, though for the satisfaction of others I have labored to show by the history that it was not intended to be perpetual, though I have gone back to weigh the expressions of Paul, I feel that here is the true way of viewing it. In the midst of considerations as to what Paul thought and why he so thought, I cannot help feeling that it is labor misspent to argue to or from his convictions or those of Luke or John respecting any form. I seem to lose the substance in seeking the shadow. That for which Paul lived and died so gloriously; that for which Jesus was crucified; the end that animated the thousand martyrs and heroes that have followed him, was to redeem us from a formal religion, and teach us to seek our wellbeing in the reformation of the soul. The whole world was full of idols and ordinances. The Jewish was a religion of forms; the Pagan was a religion of forms; it was all body, it had no life,—and the Almighty God was pleased to qualify and send forth a man to teach men that they must serve him with the heart; that only that life was religious which was thoroughly good, that sacrifice was smoke and forms were shadows, and this man lived and died true to this purpose, and now, with his blessed words and life before us, Christians must contend that it is a matter of vital importance, really a duty, to commemorate him by a certain form, whether that form be agreeable to their understandings or not.

Is not this to make vain the gift of God? Is not this to turn back the hand on the dial? Is not this to make men, to make ourselves, forget that not forms but duties, not names but righteousness and love are enjoined and that in the eye of

God there is no other measure of the value of any one form than the measure of its use?

There remain some practical objections to the ordinance which I need not state. There is one on which I had intended to say a few words, the unfavorable relation in which it puts those persons who abstain from it merely from disinclination to that rite.

Influenced by these considerations, I have proposed to the brethren of the church to drop the use of the elements and the claim of authority in the administration of this ordinance, and have suggested a mode in which a meeting for the same purpose might be held, free of objection.

They have considered my views with patience and candor, and have recommended unanimously an adherence to the present form. I have therefore been compelled to consider whether it becomes me to administer it. I am clearly of opinion that I ought not. This discourse has already been so far extended that I can only say that the reason of my determination is shortly this—It is my desire, in the office of a Christian minister, to do nothing which I cannot do with my whole heart. Having said this, I have said all. I have no hostility to this institution. I am only stating my want of sympathy with it. Neither should I ever have obtruded this opinion upon other people, had I not been called by my office to administer it. That is the end of my opposition, that I am not interested in it. I am content that it stand to the end of the world if it please men and please heaven, and shall rejoice in all the good it produces.

As it is the prevailing opinion and feeling in our religious community that it is an indispensable part of the pastoral office to administer this ordinance, I am about to resign into your hands that office which you have confided to me. It has many duties for which I am feebly qualified. It has some which it will always be my delight to discharge according to my ability wherever I exist. And whilst the thought of its claims oppresses me with a sense of my unworthiness, I am consoled by the hope that no time and no change can deprive me of the satisfaction of pursuing and exercising its highest functions.

JOSEPH SMITH

Sermon Delivered April 7, 1844

Beloved Saints, I will call the attention of this congregation while I address you on the subject of the dead. The decease of our beloved brother Elder King Follett, who was crushed in a well by the falling of a tub of rock, has more immediately led to that subject. I have been requested to speak by his friends and relatives, but inasmuch as there are a great many in this congregation who live in this city as well as elsewhere, who have lost friends, I feel disposed to speak on the subject in general, and offer you my ideas, so far as I have ability, and so far as I shall be inspired by the Holy Spirit to dwell on this subject.

I want your prayers and faith that I may have the instruction of Almighty God and the gift of the Holy Ghost, so that I may set forth things that are true and which can be easily comprehended by you and that the testimony may carry conviction to your hearts and minds of the truth of what I shall say. Pray that the Lord may strengthen my lungs, stay the winds, and let the prayers of the Saints to heaven appear, that they may enter into the ears of the Lord of Sabaoth, for the effectual prayers of the righteous avail much. There is strength here, and I verily believe that your prayers will be heard. Before I enter fully into the investigation of the subject which is lying before me, I wish to pave the way and bring up the subject from the beginning, that you may understand it. I will make a few preliminaries, in order that you may understand the subject when I come to it. I do not intend to please your ears with superfluity of words or oratory or with much learning; but I intend to edify you with the simple truths from heaven.

In the first place, I wish to go back to the beginning—to the morn of creation. There is the starting point for us to look to, in order to understand and be fully acquainted with the mind, purposes and decrees of the Great Elohim, who sits in yonder heavens as he did at the creation of this world. It is necessary for us to have an understanding of God himself in the beginning. If we start right it is easy to go right all the time; but if we start wrong, we may go wrong, and it be a hard matter to get right.

There are but a very few beings in the world who understand rightly the character of God. The great majority of mankind do not comprehend anything, either that which is past, or that which is to come, as it respects their relationship to God. They do not know, neither do they understand the nature of that relationship; and consequently they know but little above the brute beast, or more than to eat, drink and sleep. This is all man knows about God or his existence, unless it is given by the inspiration of the Almighty.

If a man learns nothing more than to eat, drink and sleep, and does not comprehend any of the designs of God, the beast comprehends the same things. It eats, drinks, sleeps, and knows nothing more about God; yet it knows as much as we, unless we are able to comprehend by the inspiration of Almighty God. If men do not comprehend the character of God, they do not comprehend themselves. I want to go back to the beginning, and so lift your minds into a more lofty sphere and a more exalted understanding than what the human mind generally aspires to.

I want to ask this congregation, every man, woman and child, to answer the question in their own heart, what kind of a being God is? Ask yourselves; turn your thoughts into your hearts, and say if any of you have seen, heard, or communed with him. This is a question that may occupy your attention for a long time. I again repeat the question—What kind of a being is God? Does any man or woman know? Have any of you seen him, heard him, or communed with him? Here is the question that will, peradventure, from this time henceforth occupy your attention. The scriptures inform us that "This is life eternal that they may know thee, the only true God, and Jesus Christ whom thou hast sent."

If any man does not know God, and inquires what kind of a being he is—if he will search diligently his own heart—if the declaration of Jesus and the apostles be true, he will realize that he has not eternal life; for there can be eternal life on no other principle.

My first object is to find out the character of the only wise and true God, and what kind of a being he is; and if I am so fortunate as to be the man to comprehend God, and explain or convey the principles to your hearts, so that the Spirit seals them upon you, then let every man and woman henceforth sit in silence, put their hands on their mouths, and never lift their hands or voices, or say anything against the man of God or the servants of God again. But if I fail to do it, it becomes my duty to renounce all further pretensions to revelations and inspirations, or to be a prophet; and I should be like the rest of the world—a false teacher, be hailed as a friend, and no man would seek my life. But if all religious teachers were honest enough to renounce their pretensions to godliness when their ignorance of the knowledge of God is made manifest, they will all be as badly off as I am, at any rate; and you might as well take the lives of other false teachers as that of mine, if I am false. If any man is authorized to take away my life because he thinks and says I am a false teacher, then, upon the same principle, we should be justified in taking away the life of every false teacher, and where would be the end of blood? And who would not be the sufferer?

But meddle not with any man for his religion: and all governments ought to permit every man to enjoy his religion unmolested. No man is authorized to take away life in consequence of difference of religion, which all laws and governments ought to tolerate and protect, right or wrong. Every man has a natural, and, in our country, a constitutional right to be a false prophet, as well as a true prophet. If I show, verily, that I have the truth of God, and show that ninety-nine out of every hundred professing religious ministers are false teachers, having no authority, while they pretend to hold the keys of God's kingdom on earth, and was to kill them because they are false teachers it would deluge the whole world with blood.

I will prove that the world is wrong, by showing what God is. I am going to enquire after God; for I want you all to know him, and to be familiar with him; and if I am bringing you to a knowledge of him, all persecutions against me ought to cease. You will then know that I am his servant; for I speak as one having authority.

I will go back to the beginning before the world was, to show what kind of being God is. What sort of a being was God in the beginning? Open your ears and hear all ye ends of the earth for I am going to prove it to you by the Bible, and to tell you the designs of God in relation to the human race, and why He interferes with the affairs of man.

God himself was once as we are now, and is an exalted man, and sits enthroned in yonder heavens! That is the great secret. If the veil were rent today, and the great God who holds this world in its orbit, and who upholds all worlds and all things by his power, was to make himself visible—I say, if you were to see him today you would see him like a man in form—like yourselves in all the person, image, and very form as a man; for Adam was created in the very fashion, image and likeness of God, and received instruction from, and walked, talked and conversed with him, as one man talks and communes with another.

In order to understand the subject of the dead, for consolation of those who mourn for the loss of their friends, it is necessary we should understand the character and being of God and how he came to be so; for I am going to tell you how God came to be God. We have imagined and supposed that God was God from all eternity. I will refute that idea, and take away the veil, so that you may see.

These are incomprehensible ideas to some, but they are simple. It is the first principle of the Gospel to know for a certainty the Character of God, and to know that we may converse with him as one man converses with another, and that he was once a man like us; yea, that God himself, the Father of us all, dwelt on an earth, the same as Jesus Christ himself did; and I will show it from the Bible.

I wish I was in a suitable place to tell it, and that I had the trump of an archangel, so that I could tell the story in such a manner that persecution would cease for ever. What did Jesus say? (Mark it, Elder Rigdon!) The Scriptures inform us that Jesus said, As the Father hath power in Himself, even so hath the Son power—to do what? Why, what the Father did. The answer is obvious—in a manner to lay down His body and take it up again. Jesus, what are you going to do? To lay down my life as my Father did, and take it up again. Do we believe it? If you do not believe it, you do not believe the Bible. The Scriptures say it, and I defy all the learning and wisdom and all the combined powers of earth and hell together to refute it.

Here, then, is eternal life—to know the only wise and true God; and you have got to learn how to be Gods yourselves, and to be kings and priests to God, the same as all Gods have done before you, namely, by going from one small degree to another, and from a small capacity to a great one; from grace to grace, from exaltation to exaltation, until you attain to the resurrection of the dead, and are able to dwell in everlasting burnings, and to sit in glory, as do those who sit enthroned in everlasting power. And I want you to know that God, in the last days, while certain individuals are proclaiming his name, is not trifling with you or me.

These are the first principles of consolation. How consoling to the mourners when they are called to part with a husband, wife, father, mother, child, or dear relative, to know that, although the earthly tabernacle is laid down and dissolved, they shall rise again to dwell in everlasting burnings in immortal glory, not to sorrow, suffer, or die any more; but they shall be heirs of God and joint heirs with Jesus Christ. What is it? To inherit the same power, the same glory and the same exaltation until you arrive at the station of a God, and ascend the throne of eternal power, the same as those who have gone before. What did Jesus do? Why; I do the things I saw my Father do when worlds came rolling into existence. My Father worked out his kingdom with fear and trembling, and I must do the same; and when I get my kingdom, I shall present it to my Father, so that he may obtain kingdom upon kingdom, and it will exalt him in glory. He will then take a higher exaltation, and I will take his place, and thereby become exalted myself. So that Jesus treads in the tracks of his Father, and inherits what God did before; and God is thus glorified and exalted in the salvation and exaltation of all his children. It is plain beyond disputation, and you thus learn some of the first principles of the Gospel, about which so much hath been said.

When you climb up a ladder, you must begin at the bottom, and ascend step by step, until you arrive at the top; and so it is with the principles of the Gospel—you must begin with the first, and go on until you learn all the principles of exaltation. But it will be a great while after you have passed through the veil before you will have learned them. It is not all to be comprehended in this world; it will be a great work to learn our salvation and exaltation even beyond the grave. I suppose I am not allowed to go into an investigation of anything that is not contained in the Bible. If I do, I think there are so many over-wise men here, that they would cry "treason" and put me to death. So I will go to the old Bible and turn commentator today.

I shall comment on the very first Hebrew word in the Bible; I will make a comment on the very first sentence of the history of creation in the Bible—Berosheit. I want to analyze the word. Baith—in, by, through, and everything else. Rosh —the head. Sheit—grammatical termination. When the inspired man wrote it, he did not put the baith there. An old Jew without any authority added the word; he thought it too bad to begin to talk about the head! It read first, "The head one of the Gods brought forth the Gods." That is the true meaning of the words. Baurau signifies to bring forth. If you do not believe it, you do not believe the learned man of God. Learned men can teach you no more than what I have told you. Thus the head God brought forth the Gods in the grand council.

I will transpose and simplify it in the English language. Oh, ye lawyers, ye doctors, and ye priests, who have persecuted me, I want to let you know that the Holy Ghost knows something as well as you do. The head God called together the Gods and sat in grand council to bring forth the world. The grand councilors sat at the head in yonder heavens and contemplated the creation of the worlds which were created at the time. When I say doctors and lawyers, I mean the doctors and lawyers of the Scriptures. I have done so hitherto without explanation, to let the lawyers flutter and everybody laugh at them. Some learned doctors might take a notion to say the Scriptures say thus and so; and we might believe the Scriptures; they are not to be altered. But I am going to show you an error in them.

I have an old edition of the New Testament in the Latin,

Hebrew, German and Greek languages. I have been reading the German, and find it to be the most correct translation, and to correspond nearest to the revelations which God has given to me for the last fourteen years. It tells about Jacobus, the son of Zebedee. It means Jacob. In the English New Testament it is translated James. Now, if Jacob had the keys, you might talk about James through all eternity and never get the keys. In the 21st of the fourth chapter of Matthew, my old German edition gives the word Jacob instead of James.

The doctors (I mean doctors of law, not physic) say, "If you preach anything not according to the Bible, we will cry treason." How can we escape the damnation of hell, except God be with us and reveal to us? Men bind us with chains. The Latin says Jacobus, which means Jacob; the Hebrew says Jacob, the Greek says Jacob and the German says Jacob; here we have the testimony of four against one. I thank God that I have got this old book but I thank him more for the gift of the Holy Ghost. I have got the oldest book in the world; but I have the oldest book in my heart, even the gift of the Holy Ghost. I have all the four Testaments. Come here, ye learned men, and read, if you can. I should not have introduced this testimony, were it not to back up the word rosh—the head, the Father of the Gods. I should not have brought it up, only to show that I am right.

In the beginning, the head of the Gods called a council of the Gods; and they came together and concocted a plan to create the world and people it. When we begin to learn this way, we begin to learn the only true God, and what kind of a being we have got to worship. Having a knowledge of God, we begin to know how to approach him, and how to ask so as to receive an answer. When we understand the character of God, and know how to come to him, he begins to unfold the heavens to us, and to tell us all about it. When we are ready to come to him, he is ready to come to us.

Now, I ask all who hear me, why the learned men who are preaching salvation, say that God created the heavens, and the earth out of nothing? The reason is, that they are unlearned in the things of God, and have not the gift of the Holy Ghost; they account it blasphemy in any one to contradict their idea. If you tell them that God made the world out of something, they will call you a fool. But I am learned, and know more than all the world put together. The Holy Ghost does, anyhow, and He is within me, and comprehends more than all the world; and I will associate myself with Him.

You ask the learned doctors why they say the world was made out of nothing; and they will answer, "Doesn't the Bible say He created the world?" And they infer, from the word create, that it must have been made out of nothing. Now, the word create came from the word baurau, which does not mean to create out of nothing; it means to organize; the same as a man would organize materials and build a ship. Hence, we infer that God had materials to organize the world out of chaos—chaotic matter, which is element, and in which dwells all the glory. Element had an existence from the time he had. The pure principles of element are principles which can never be destroyed; they may be organized and re-organized, but not destroyed. They had no beginning, and can have no end.

I have another subject to dwell upon, which is calculated to exalt man; but it is impossible for me to say much on this subject. I shall therefore just touch upon it, for time will not permit me to say all. It is associated with the subject of the resurrection of the dead—namely, the soul—the mind of man—the immortal spirit. Where did it come from? All learned men and doctors of divinity say that God created it in the beginning; but it is not so; the very idea lessens man in my estimation. I do not believe the doctrine; I know better. Hear it, all ye ends of the world; for God has told me so; and if you don't believe me, it will not make the truth without effect. I will make a man appear a fool before I get through if he does not believe it. I am going to tell of things more noble.

We say that God himself is a self-existent being. Who told you so? It is correct enough; but how did it get into your heads? Who told you that man did not exist in like manner upon the same principles? Man does exist upon the same principles. God made a tabernacle and put a spirit into it, and it became a living soul. (Refers to the old Bible.) How does it read in the Hebrew? It does not say in the Hebrew that God created the spirit of man. It says "God made man out of the earth and put into him Adam's spirit, and so became a living body."

The mind or the intelligence which man possesses is co-equal with God himself. I know that my testimony is true; hence, when I talk to these mourners, what have they lost? Their relatives and friends are only separated from their bodies for a short season: their spirits which existed with God have left the tabernacle of clay only for a little moment, as it were; and they now exist in a place where they converse to-gether the same as we do on earth.

I am dwelling on the immortality of the spirit of man. Is it logical to say that the intelligence of spirits is immortal, and yet that it had a beginning? The intelligence of spirits had no beginning, neither will it have an end. That is good logic. That which has a beginning may have an end. There never was a time when there were not spirits; for they are co-equal with our Father in heaven.

I want to reason more on the spirit of man; for I am dwelling on the body and spirit of man—on the subject of the dead. I take my ring from my finger and liken it unto the mind of man—the immortal part, because it has no begin-ning. Suppose you cut it in two; then it has a beginning and an end; but join it again, and it continues one eternal round. So with the spirit of man. As the Lord liveth, if it has a be-ginning, it will have an end. All the fools and learned wise men from the beginning of creation, who say that the spirit of man had a beginning, prove that it must have an end; and if that doctrine is true, then the doctrine of annihilation would be true. But if I am right, I might with boldness proclaim from the house-tops that God never had the power to create the spirit of man at all. God himself could not create himself.

Intelligence is eternal and exists upon a self-existent prin-ciple. It is a spirit from age to age, and there is no creation about it. All the minds and spirits that God ever sent into the world are susceptible of enlargement.

The first principles of man are self-existent with God. God himself, finding he was in the midst of spirits and glory, because he was more intelligent, saw proper to institute laws whereby the rest could have a privilege to advance like himself. The relationship we have with God places us in a situation to advance in knowledge. He has power to institute laws to instruct the weaker intelligences, that they may be exalted with himself, so that they might have one glory upon another, and all that knowledge, power, glory, and intelligence, which is requisite in order to save them in the world of spirits.

This is good doctrine. It tastes good. I can taste the principles of eternal life, and so can you. They are given to me by the revelations of Jesus Christ; and I know that when I tell you these words of eternal life as they are given to me, you taste them, and I know that you believe them. You say honey is sweet, and so do I. I can also taste the spirit of eternal life. I know it is good; and when I tell you of these things which were given me by inspiration of the Holy Spirit, you are bound to receive them as sweet, and rejoice more and more.

I want to talk more of the relation of man to God. I will open your eyes in relation to your dead. All things whatsoever God in his infinite wisdom has seen fit and proper to reveal to us, while we are dwelling in mortality, in regard to our mortal bodies, are revealed to us in the abstract, and independent of affinity of this mortal tabernacle, but we are revealed to our spirits precisely as though we had no bodies at all; and those revelations which will save our spirits will save our bodies. God reveals them to us in view of no eternal dissolution of the body, or tabernacle. Hence the responsibility, the awful responsibility, that rests upon us in relation to our dead; for all the spirits who have not obeyed the Gospel in the flesh must either obey it in the spirit or be damned. Solemn thought!—dreadful thought! Is there nothing to be done?— no preparation—no salvation for our fathers and friends who have died without having had the opportunity to obey the decrees of the Son of Man?

Would to God that I had forty days and nights in which to tell you all! I would let you know that I am not a "fallen prophet."

What promises are made in relation to the subject of the salvation of the dead? and what kind of characters are those who can be saved, although their bodies are mouldering and decaying in the grave? When his commandments teach us, it is in view of eternity; for we are looked upon by God as though we were in eternity. God dwells in eternity, and does not view things as we do.

The greatest responsibility in this world that God has laid upon us is to seek after our dead. The Apostle says, "They without us cannot be made perfect;" (Hebrews 11:40) for it is necessary that the sealing power should be in our hands to seal our children and our dead for the fulness of the dispensation of times—a dispensation to meet the promises made by Jesus Christ before the foundation of the world for the salvation of man.

Now I will speak of them. I will meet Paul half way. I say to you, Paul, you cannot be perfect without us. It is necessary that those who are going before and those who come after us should have salvation in common with us; and thus hath God made it obligatory upon man. Hence, God said, I will send you Elijah the prophet before the coming of the great and dreadful day of the Lord: and he shall turn the heart of the fathers to the children, and the heart of the children to their fathers, lest I come and smite the earth with a curse." (Malachi 4:5.)

I have a declaration to make as to the provisions which God hath made to suit the conditions of man—made from before the foundation of the world. What has Jesus said? All sin, and all blasphemies, and every transgression, except one, that man can be guilty of, may be forgiven; and there is a salvation for all men, either in this world or the world to come, who have not committed the unpardonable sin, there being a provision either in this world or the world of spirits. Hence God hath made a provision that every spirit in the eternal world can be ferreted out and saved unless he has committed that unpardonable sin which cannot be remitted to him either in this world or the world of spirits. God has wrought out a salvation for all men, unless they have committed a certain sin; and every man who has a friend in the eternal world can save him, unless he has committed the unpardonable sin. And so you can see how far you can be a savior.

A man cannot commit the unpardonable sin after the dissolution of the body, and there is a way possible for escape. Knowledge saves a man; and in the world of spirits no man can be exalted but by knowledge. So long as a man will not

give heed to the commandments, he must abide without salvation. If a man has knowledge, he can be saved; although, if
he has been guilty of great sins, he will be punished for them.
But when he consents to obey the Gospel, whether here or in
the world of spirits, he is saved.

A man is his own tormentor and his own condemner.
Hence the saying, They shall go into the lake that burns with
fire and brimstone. The torment of disappointment in the
mind of man is as exquisite as a lake burning with fire and
brimstone. I say, so is the torment of man.

I know the Scriptures and understand them. I said, no man
can commit the unpardonable sin after the dissolution of the
body, nor in this life, until he receives the Holy Ghost; but
they must do it in this world. Hence the salvation of Jesus
Christ was wrought out for all men, in order to triumph over
the devil; for if it did not catch him in one place, it would in
another; for he stood up as a Savior. All will suffer until they
obey Christ himself.

The contention in heaven was—Jesus said there would be
certain souls that would not be saved; and the devil said he
could save them all, and laid his plans before the grand council, who gave their vote in favor of Jesus Christ. So the devil
rose up in rebellion against God, and was cast down, with all
who put up their heads for him. (Book of Moses—Pearl of
Great Price, Chap. 4:1–4; Book of Abraham, Chap. 3:23–28.)

All sins shall be forgiven, except the sin against the Holy
Ghost; for Jesus will save all except the sons of perdition.
What must a man do to commit the unpardonable sin? He
must receive the Holy Ghost, have the heavens opened unto
him, and know God, and then sin against Him. After a man
has sinned against the Holy Ghost, there is no repentance for
him. He has got to say that the sun does not shine while he
sees it; he has got to deny Jesus Christ when the heavens have
been opened unto him, and to deny the plan of salvation with
his eyes open to the truth of it; and from that time he begins
to be an enemy. This is the case with many apostates of the
Church of Jesus Christ of Latter-day Saints.

Whan a man begins to be an enemy to this work, he hunts
me, he seeks to kill me, and never ceases to thirst for my
blood. He gets the spirit of the devil—the same spirit that

they had who crucified the Lord of Life—the same spirit that sins against the Holy Ghost. You cannot save such persons; you cannot bring them to repentance; they make open war, like the devil, and awful is the consequence.

I advise all of you to be careful what you do, or you may by-and-by find out that you have been deceived. Stay yourselves; do not give way; don't make any hasty moves, you may be saved. If a spirit of bitterness is in you, don't be in haste. You may say, that man is a sinner. Well, if he repents, he shall be forgiven. Be cautious: await. When you find a spirit that wants bloodshed—murder, the same is not of God, but is of the devil. Out of the abundance of the heart of man the mouth speaketh.

The best men bring forth the best works. The man who tells you words of life is the man who can save you. I warn you against all evil characters who sin against the Holy Ghost; for there is no redemption for them in this world nor in the world to come.

I could go back and trace every subject of interest concerning the relationship of man to God, if I had the time. I can enter into the mysteries; I can enter largely into the eternal worlds; for Jesus said, "In my Father's house are many mansions; if it were not so, I would have told you. I go to prepare a place for you" (John 14:2). Paul says, "There is one glory of the sun, and another glory of the moon, and another glory of the stars; for one star differeth from another star in glory. So also is the resurrection of the dead" (1 Cor. 15:41). What have we to console us in relation to the dead? We have reason to have the greatest hope and consolations for our dead of any people on the earth; for we have seen them walk worthily in our midst, and seen them sink asleep in the arms of Jesus; and those who have died in the faith are now in the celestial kingdom of God. And hence is the glory of the sun.

You mourners have occasion to rejoice, speaking of the death of Elder King Follet; for your husband and father is gone to wait until the resurrection of the dead—until the perfection of the remainder; for at the resurrection your friend will rise in perfect felicity and go to celestial glory, while many must wait myriads of years before they can receive the like blessings; and your expectations and hopes are far above what man can conceive; for why has God revealed it to us?

I am authorized to say, by the authority of the Holy Ghost, that you have no occasion to fear; for he is gone to the home of the just. Don't mourn, don't weep. I know it by the testimony of the Holy Ghost that is within me; and you may wait for your friends to come forth to meet you in the morn of the celestial world.

Rejoice, O Israel! Your friends who have been murdered for the truth's sake in the persecutions shall triumph gloriously in the celestial world, while their murderers shall welter for ages in torment, even until they shall have paid the uttermost farthing. I say this for the benefit of strangers.

I have a father, brother, children and friends who have gone to a world of spirits. They are only absent for a moment. They are in the spirit, and we shall soon meet again. The time will soon arrive when the trumpet shall sound. When we depart, we shall hail our mothers, fathers, friends, and all whom we love, who have fallen asleep in Jesus. There will be no fear of mobs, persecutions, or malicious lawsuits and arrests; but it will be an eternity of felicity.

A question may be asked—"Will mothers have their children in eternity?" Yes! Yes! Mothers, you shall have your children; for they shall have eternal life, for their debt is paid. There is not damnation awaiting them for they are in the spirit. But as the child dies, so shall it rise from the dead, and be for ever living in the learning of God. It will never grow; it will still be the child, in the same precise form as it appeared before it died out of its mother's arms, but possessing all the intelligence of a God. Children dwell in the mansions of glory and exercise power, but appear in the same form as when on earth. Eternity is full of thrones, upon which dwell thousands of children, reigning on thrones of glory, with not one cubit added to their stature.

I will leave this subject here, and make a few remarks on the subject of baptism. The baptism of water, without the baptism of fire and the Holy Ghost attending it, is of no use; they are necessarily and inseparably connected. An individual must be born of water and the Spirit in order to get into the kingdom of God. In the German, the text bears me out the same as the revelations which I have given and taught for the last fourteen years on that subject. I have the testimony to put in their teeth. My testimony has been true all the time. You will find it in the declaration of John the Baptist. (Reads from the German.) John says, "I baptize you with water, but when Jesus comes, who has the power (or keys), he shall administer the baptism of fire and the Holy Ghost." Where is now all the sectarian world? And if this testimony is true, they are all damned as clearly as anathema can do it. I know the text is true. I call upon all you Germans who know that it is true to say, Aye. (Loud shouts of "Aye.")

Alexander Campbell, how are you going to save people with water alone? For John said his baptism was good for nothing without the baptism of Jesus Christ. "Therefore, not leaving the principles of the doctrine of Christ, let us go on unto perfection; not laying again the foundation of repentance from dead works, and of faith toward God, of the doctrine of baptisms, and of laying on of hands, and of resurrection of the dead, and of eternal judgment. And this will we do, if God permit." (Heb. 6:1–3).

There is one God, one Father, one Jesus, one hope of our calling, one baptism. All these three baptisms only made one. Many talk of baptism not being essential to salvation; but this kind of teaching would lay the foundation of their damnation. I have the truth, and am at the defiance of the world to contradict me, if they can.

I have now preached a little Latin, a little Hebrew, Greek, and German; and I have fulfilled all. I am not so big a fool as many have taken me to be. The Germans know that I read the German correctly.

Hear it, all ye ends of the earth—all ye priests, all ye sinners, and all men. Repent! repent! Obey the Gospel. Turn to God; for your religion won't save you, and you will be damned. I do not say how long. There have been remarks made concerning all men being redeemed from hell; but I say that those who sin against the Holy Ghost cannot be forgiven in this world or in the world to come; they shall die the second death. Those who commit the unpardonable sin are doomed to Gnolom—to dwell in hell, worlds without end. As they concoct scenes of bloodshed in this world, so they shall rise to that resurrection which is as the lake of fire and brimstone. Some shall rise to the everlasting burnings of God; for God dwells in everlasting burnings, and some shall rise to the damnation of their own filthiness, which is as exquisite a torment as the lake of fire and brimstone.

I have intended my remarks for all, both rich and poor, bond and free, great and small. I have no enmity against any man. I love you all; but I hate some of your deeds. I am your best friend, and if persons miss their mark it is their own fault. If I reprove a man, and he hates me, he is a fool; for I love all men, especially these my brethren and sisters.

I rejoice in hearing the testimony of my aged friends. You don't know me; you never knew my heart. No man knows my history, I cannot tell it: I shall never undertake it. I don't blame any one for not believing my history. If I had not experienced what I have, I could not have believed it myself. I never did harm any man since I was born in the world. My voice is always for peace.

I cannot lie down until all my work is finished. I never think any evil, nor do anything to the harm of my fellowman. When I am called by the trump of the archangel and weighed in the balance, you will all know me then. I add no more, God bless you all. Amen.

THEODORE PARKER

A Sermon of War

Preached at the Melodeon, on Sunday, June 7, 1846

———

"The Lord is a Man of War."—EXODUS, XV. 3.
"God is Love."—I JOHN, IV. 8.

I ASK your attention to a SERMON OF WAR. I have waited some time before treating this subject at length, till the present hostilities should assume a definite form, and the designs of the government become more apparent. I wished to be able to speak coolly and with knowledge of the facts, that we might understand the comparative merits of the present war. Besides, I have waited for others, in the churches, of more experience to speak, before I ventured to offer my counsel; and I have thus far waited almost in vain! I did not wish to treat the matter last Sunday, for that was the end of our week of Pentecost, when cloven tongues of flame descend on the city, and some are thought to be full of new wine, and others of the Holy Spirit. The heat of the meetings—good and bad—of that week, could not wholly have passed away from you or me, and we ought to come coolly and consider a subject like this. So the last Sunday I only sketched the back-ground of the picture, to-day intending to paint the horrors of war in front of that "Presence of Beauty in Nature," to which, with its "Meanings" and its "Lessons," I then asked you to attend.

It seems to me that an IDEA OF GOD as the Infinite is given us in our nature itself. But men create a more definite conception thereof in their own image. Thus a rude savage man, who has learned only the presence of Power in Nature, conceives of God mainly as a FORCE, and speaks of Him as a God of POWER. Such, though not without beautiful exceptions, is the character ascribed to Jehovah in the Old Testament. "The

Lord is a man of war." He is "the Lord of Hosts." He kills men, and their cattle. If there is trouble in the enemies' city, it is the Lord who hath caused it. He will "whet his glittering sword and render vengeance to his enemies. He will make his arrows drunk with blood, and his sword shall devour flesh!" It is with the sword that God pleads with all men. He encourages men to fight, and says "cursed be he that keepeth back his sword from blood." He sends blood into the streets; he waters the land with blood, and in blood he dissolves the mountains. He brandishes his sword before kings, and they tremble at every moment. He treads nations as grapes in a wine-press, and his garments are stained with their life's blood.*

A man who has grown up to read the older Testament of

---

*Isaiah, lxiii. 1–6. *Noyes's* Version.

The People.

1 Who is this, that cometh from Edom?
In scarlet garments from Bozrah?
This, that is glorious in his apparel,
Proud in the greatness of his strength?

Jehovah.

I, that proclaim deliverance,
And am mighty to save.

The People.

2 Wherefore is thine apparel red,
And thy garments like those of one that treadeth the wine-vat?

Jehovah.

3 I have trodden the wine-vat alone,
And of the nations there was none with me.
And I trod them in mine anger,
And I trampled them in my fury,
So that their life-blood was sprinkled upon my garments,
And I have stained all my apparel.

4 For the day of vengeance was in my heart,
And the year of my deliverance was come.

5 And I looked, and there was none to help,
And I wondered, that there was none to uphold,
Therefore my own arm wrought salvation for me,
And my fury, it sustained me.

6 I trod down the nations in my anger;
I crushed them in my fury,
And spilled their blood upon the ground.

God revealed in the Beauty of the Universe, and to feel the goodness of God therein set forth—sees Him not as FORCE only, or in chief, but as LOVE. He worships in love the God of Goodness and of Peace. Such is the prevalent character ascribed to God in the New Testament. He is the "God of Love and Peace;" "Our Father,"—"Kind to the unthankful and the unmerciful." In one word, God is Love. He loves us all, Jew and Gentile, bond and free; all are his children, each of priceless value in his sight. He is no God of Battles; no Lord of Hosts; no man of war. He has no sword, nor arrows; he does not water the earth nor melt the mountains in blood, but "he maketh his sun to rise on the evil and on the good, and sendeth rain on the just and the unjust." He has no garments dyed in blood; curses no man for refusing to fight. He is Spirit—to be worshipped in spirit and in truth! The commandment is: Love one another; resist not evil with evil; forgive seventy times seven; overcome evil with good; love your enemies; bless them that curse you; do good to them that hate you; pray for them that despitefully use you and persecute you.* There is no nation to shut its ports against another—all are men; no caste to curl its lip at inferiors—all are brothers, members of one body, united in the Christ, the ideal man and head of all. The greatest is the most useful. No man is to be master, for the Christ is our teacher. We are to fear no man, for God is our Father.

These precepts are undeniably the precepts of Christianity; equally plain is it that they are the dictates of man's nature, only developed and active; a part of God's universal revelation—His law writ on the soul of man, established in the nature of things; true after experience and true before all experience. The man of real insight into spiritual things sees and knows them to be true.

Do not believe it the part of a coward to think so. I have known many cowards; yes, a great many; some very cowardly, pusillanimous and faint-hearted cowards; but never one who thought so, or pretended to think so. It requires very little

*To show the differences between the Old and New Testament, and to serve as introduction to this discourse, the following passages were read as the morning lesson. Exodus, xv. 1–6; 2 Sam. xxii. 32. 35–43. 48; Ps. xlv. 3–5; Isa. lxvi. 15, 16; Joel iii. 9–17, and Matthew, v. 3–11. 38–39. 43–45.

courage to fight with sword and musket, and that of a cheap kind. Men of that stamp are plenty as grass in June. Beat your drum, and they will follow; offer them but eight dollars a month, and they will come—fifty thousand of them, and to smite and kill. Every male animal, or reptile, will fight. It requires little courage to kill; but it takes much to resist evil with good—holding obstinately out, active or passive, till you overcome it. Call that non-resistance, if you will; it is the stoutest kind of combat—demanding all the manhood of a man.

I will not deny that war is inseparable from a low stage of civilization; so is polygamy, slavery, cannibalism. Taking men as they were, savage and violent, there have been times when war was unavoidable. I will not deny that it has helped forward the civilization of the race, for God often makes the folly and the sin of men contribute to the progress of mankind. It is none the less a folly or a sin. In a civilized nation like ourselves, it is far more heinous than in the Ojibeways or the Camanches.

War is in utter violation of Christianity. If war be right then Christianity is wrong, false—a lie. But if Christianity be true—if Reason, Conscience, Religion, the highest faculties of man—are to be trusted, then war is the wrong, the falsehood, the lie. I maintain that war is a Sin; that it is national infidelity, a denial of Christianity and of God. Every man who understands Christianity by heart—in its relations to man, to society, the nation, the world—knows that war is a wrong. At this day, with all the enlightenment of our age, after the long peace of the nations, war is easily avoided. Whenever it occurs, the very fact of its occurrence convicts the rulers of a nation either of entire incapacity as statesmen, or else of the worst form of treason—treason to the people, to mankind, to God! There is no other alternative. The very fact of a war shows that the men who cause it must be either Fools or Traitors. I think lightly of what is called Treason against a government. That may be your duty to-day, or mine. Certainly it was our fathers' duty, not long ago; and it is our boast and their title to honor. But Treason against the People, against Mankind, against God, is a great Sin, not lightly to be spoken of. But the political authors of a war on this continent, and at this day, are either utterly incapable of a statesman's work, or else guilty of that sin. Fools they are, or Traitors they must be.

Let me speak, and in detail, of the EVILS OF WAR. I wish this were not necessary. But we have found ourselves in a war; the Congress has voted our money and our men to carry it on; the Governors call for volunteers; the volunteers come when they are called for. No voice of indignation goes forth out from the heart of the eight hundred thousand souls of Massachusetts; of the seventeen million freemen of the land how few complain; only a man here and there! The Press is well-nigh silent. And the Church, so far from protesting against this infidelity in the name of Christ, is little better than dead. The man of blood shelters himself behind its wall— silent, dark, dead and emblematic. These facts show it is necessary to speak of the evils of war. I am speaking in a city whose fairest, firmest, most costly buildings are warehouses and banks; a city whose most popular Idol is Mammon—the God of Gold; whose Trinity is a Trinity of Coin! I shall speak intelligibly, therefore, if I begin by considering war as a WASTE OF PROPERTY. *It paralyzes industry.* The very fear of it is a mildew upon commerce. Though the present war is but a skirmish, only a few random shots between a squad of regulars and some strolling battalions—a quarrel which in Europe would scarcely frighten even the Pope—yet see the effect of it upon trade. Though the fighting be thousands of miles from Boston, your stocks fall in the market; the rate of insurance is altered; your dealer in wood piles his boards and his lumber on his wharf, not finding a market. There are few ships in the great Southern mart to take the freight of many; exchange is disturbed. The clergyman is afraid to buy a book, lest his children want bread. So it is with all departments of industry and trade. In war the capitalist is uncertain and slow to venture, so the laborer's hand will be still and his child ill-clad and hungry.

In the late war with England many of you remember the condition of your fisheries, of your commerce; how the ships lay rotting at the wharf. The dearness of cloth, of provisions, flour, sugar, tea, coffee, salt, the comparative lowness of wages, the stagnation of business; the scarcity of money; the universal sullenness and gloom—all this is well remembered now. So is the ruin it brought on many a man.

Yet but few weeks ago some men talked boastingly of a war with England. There are some men who seem to have no eyes nor ears—only a mouth; whose chief function is talk. Of *their* talk I will say nothing,—we look for dust in dry places. But some men thus talked of war, and seemed desirous to provoke it, who can scarce plead ignorance and I fear not folly for their excuse. I leave such to the just resentment sure to fall on them from sober, serious men who dare be so unpopular as to think before they speak, and then say what came of thinking. Perhaps such a war was never likely to take place, and now—thanks to a few wise men—all danger thereof seems at an end. But suppose it had happened—what would become of your commerce, of your fishing smacks on the Banks or along the shore? what of your coasting vessels, doubling the headlands all the way from the St. Johns to the Nueces? what of your whale ships in the Pacific? what of your Indiamen, deep freighted with oriental wealth? what of that fleet which crowds across the Atlantic sea, trading with East and West and North and South? I know some men care little for the rich, but when the owners keep their craft in port, where can the "hands" find work or their mouths find bread? The shipping of the United States amounts nearly to 2,500,000 tons. At $40 a ton, its value is nearly $100,000,000. This is the value only of those sea-carriages; their cargoes I cannot compute. Allowing one sailor for every 20 tons burthen, here will be 125,000 seamen. They and their families amount to 500,000 souls. In war, what will become of them? A capital of more than $13,000,000 is invested in the fisheries of Massachusetts alone. More than 19,000 men find profitable employment therein. If each man have but four others in his family—a small number for *that* class—here are more than 95,000 persons in this State alone, whose daily bread depends on this business. *They* cannot fish in troubled waters, for they are fishermen, not politicians. Where could they find bread or cloth in time of war? In Dartmoor Prison? Ask that of your demagogues who courted war!

Then too the *positive destruction of property in war is*

monstrous. A ship of the line costs from $500,000 to $1,000,000. The loss of a fleet by capture, by fire, or by decay is a great loss. You know at what cost a fort is built, if you have counted the sums successively voted for Fort Adams in Rhode Island, or those in our own harbor. The destruction of forts is another item in the cost of war. The capture or destruction of merchant ships with their freight, creates a most formidable loss. In 1812 the whole tonnage of the United States was scarce half what it is now. Yet the loss of ships and their freight, in "the late war," brief as it was, is estimated at $100,000,000! Then the loss by plunder and military occupation is monstrous. The soldier, like the savage, cuts down the tree to gather its fruit. I cannot calculate the loss by burning towns and cities. But suppose Boston were bombarded and laid in ashes. Calculate the loss if you can. You may say this could not be, for 'tis easy to say No, as Yes. But remember what befel us in the last war; remember how recently the best defended capitals of Europe—Vienna, Paris, Antwerp—have fallen into hostile hands. Consider how often a strong place—like Coblentz, Maintz, Malta, Gibraltar, St. Juan d'Ulloa—has been declared impregnable, and then been taken; calculate the force which might be brought against this town—and you will see that in eight-and-forty hours, or half that time, it might be left nothing but a heap of ruins smoking in the sun! I doubt not the valor of American soldiers, the skill of their engineers, nor the ability of their commanders. I am ready to believe all this is greater than we are told. Still, such are the contingencies of war. If some not very ignorant men had had their way, this would be a probability and perhaps a fact. If we should burn every town from the Tweed to the Thames it would not rebuild our own city.

But on the supposition that nothing is destroyed, see the loss which comes from the *misdirection of productive industry.* Your fleets, forts, dock-yards, arsenals, cannons, muskets, swords, and the like, are provided at great cost, and yet are unprofitable. They don't pay. They weave no cloth; they bake no bread; they produce nothing. Yet from 1791 to 1832, in 42 years, we expended in these things, $303,242,576, viz., for the navy, &c., $112,703,933, for the army, &c., $190,538,643. For the same time, all other expenses of the nation came to but $37,158,047. More than eight-ninths of the whole revenue of the nation was spent for purposes of war. In four years, from 1812 to 1815, we paid in this way, $92,350,519.37. In six years, from 1835 to 1840, we paid annually on the average $21,328,903 in all $127,973,418. Our Congress has just voted $17,000,000 as a special grant for the army alone. The 175,118 muskets at Springfield are valued at $3,000,000. We pay annually $200,000 to support that arsenal. The navy yard at Charlestown, with its stores, &c., has cost $4,741,000. Now, for all profitable returns, this money might as well be sunk in the bottom of the sea. In some countries it is yet worse. There are towns and cities in which the fortifications have cost more than all the houses, churches, shops and other property therein. This happens not among the Sacs and Foxes, but in "Christian" Europe.

Then your soldier is the most unprofitable animal you can keep. He makes no railroads; clears no land; raises no corn. No, he can make neither cloth nor clocks! He does not raise his own bread, mend his own shoes, make his shoulder-knot of glory, nor hammer out his own sword. Yet he is a costly animal, though useless. If the President gets his fifty thousand volunteers—a thing likely to happen, for though Irish lumpers and hod-men want a dollar or a dollar and a half a day, your free American of Boston will 'list for twenty-seven cents, only having his livery, his feathers, and his "glory" thrown in—then at $8 a month, their wages amount to $400,000. Suppose the present government shall actually make advantageous contracts, and the subsistence of the soldier cost no more than in England, or $17 a month, this amounts to $850,000. Here are $1,250,000 to begin with. Then, if each man would be worth a dollar a day at any productive work, and there are 26 work days in the month, here are $1,300,000 more to be added, making $2,550,000 a month for the new army of occupation. This is only for the rank and file of the army. The officers, the surgeons, and the chaplains who teach the soldiers to *wad* their muskets with the leaves of the Bible, will perhaps cost as much more; or in all, something more than $5,000,000 a month. This of course does not include the cost of their arms, tents, ammunition, baggage, horses and hospital stores—nor the 65,000 gallons of whiskey which the government has just advertised for! What do they give in return? They will give us three things, "Valor," "Glory," and—Talk; which, as they are not in the price current, I must estimate as I can, and set them all down in one figure—0; not worth the whiskey they cost.

New England is quite a new country. Seven generations ago it was a wilderness; now it contains about 2,500,000 souls. If you were to pay all the public debts of these States, and then, in fancy, divide all the property therein by the population, young as we are, I think you would find a larger amount of value for each man than in any other country in the world, not excepting England. The civilization of Europe is old; the nations old,—England, France, Spain, Austria, Italy, Greece; but they have wasted their time, their labor and their wealth in war, and so are poorer than we upstarts of a wilderness. We have fewer fleets, forts, cannon and soldiers for the population, than any other "Christian" country in the world. This is one main reason why we have no national debt; why the women need not toil in the hardest labor of the fields, the quarries and the mines; this is the reason that we are well fed, well clad, well housed; this is the reason that Massachusetts can afford to spend $1,000,000 a year for her public schools! War, wasting a nation's wealth, depresses the great mass of the people, but serves to elevate a few to opulence and power. Every despotism is established and sustained by war. This is the foundation of all the aristocracies of the old world—aristocrats of blood. Our famous men are often ashamed that their wealth was honestly got by working, or peddling, and foolishly copy the savage and bloody emblems of ancient heraldry in their assumed coats of arms—industrious men seeking to have a Griffin on their seal! Nothing is so hostile to a true democracy as war. It elevates a few, often bold bad men, at the expense of the many, who pay the money and furnish the blood for war.

War is a most expensive folly. The revolutionary war cost the general government directly and in specie $135,000,000. It is safe to estimate the direct cost to the individual States also at the same sum, $135,000,000; making a total of $270,000,000. Considering the interruption of business, the waste of time, property and life, it is plain that this could not have been a fourth part of the whole. But suppose it was a third, then the whole pecuniary cost of the war would be $810,000,000. At the beginning of the revolution the population was about 3,000,000; so that war, lasting about eight years, cost $270 for each person. To meet the expenses of the war each year there would have been required a tax of $33.75 on each man, woman and child!

In the Florida war we spent between $30,000,000 and $40,000,000, as an eminent statesman once said, in fighting five hundred invisible Indians! It is estimated that the fortifications of the city of Paris, when completely furnished, will cost more than the whole taxable property of Massachusetts, with her 800,000 souls. Why, this year our own grant for the army is $17,000,000. The estimate for the navy is $6,000,000 more; in all $23,000,000. Suppose, which is most unlikely, that we should pay no more,—why that sum alone would support public schools, as good and as costly as those of Massachusetts, all over the United States, offering each boy and girl—bond or free—as good a culture as they get here in Boston, and then leave a balance of $3,000,000 in our hands! We pay more for ignorance than we need for education! But $23,000,000 is not all we must pay this year. A great statesman has said, in the Senate, that our war expenses at present are nearly $500,000 a day, and the President informs your Congress that $22,952,904 more will be wanted for the army and navy before next June!

For several years we spent directly more than $21,000,000 for war purposes, though in time of peace. If a railroad cost $30,000 a mile, then we might build 700 miles a year for that sum, and in five years could build a railroad therewith from Boston to the farther side of Oregon. For the war money we paid in 42 years, we could have had more than 10,000 miles of railroad, and with dividends at 7 per cent,—a yearly income of $21,210,000. For military and naval affairs, in eight years, from 1835 to 1843, we paid $163,336,717. This alone would have made 5,444 miles of railroad, and would produce at 7 per cent. an annual income of $11,433,569.19.

In Boston there are nineteen public grammar schools, a Latin and an English High School. The buildings for these schools—20 in number—have cost $653,208. There are also

135 primary schools, in as many houses or rooms. I know not their value, as I think they are not all owned by the city. But suppose them to be worth $150,000. Then all the school-houses of this city have cost $703,208. The cost of these 156 schools for this year is estimated at $172,000. The number of scholars in them is 16,479. Harvard University, the most expensive college in America, costs about $46,000 a year. Now the ship Ohio lying here in our harbor has cost $834,845, and we pay for it each year $220,000 more. That is, it has cost $31,637 more than these 155 school-houses of this city, and costs every year $2,000 more than Harvard University and all the public schools of Boston!

The military Academy at West Point contains two hundred and thirty-six cadets; the appropriation for it last year was $138,000, a sum greater, I think, than the cost of all the colleges in Maine, New Hampshire, Vermont and Massachusetts, with their 1,445 students.

The navy yard at Charlestown, with its ordnance, stores, &c., cost $4,741,000. The cost of the 78 churches in Boston is $3,246,500; the whole property of Harvard University is $703,175; the 155 school-houses of Boston are worth $703,208; in all $4,652,883. Thus the navy yard at Charlestown has cost $99,117 more than the 78 churches and the 155 school-houses of Boston, with Harvard College, its halls, libraries, all its wealth thrown in. Yet what does it teach?

Our country is singularly destitute of public libraries. You must go across the ocean to read the history of the church or state; all the public libraries in America cannot furnish the books referred to in Gibbon's Rome, or Gieseler's History of the Church. I think there is no public library in Europe which has cost three dollars a volume. There are six—the Vatican, at Rome; the Royal, at Paris; the British Museum, at London; the Bodleian, at Oxford; the University Libraries at Gottingen and Berlin—which contain, it is said, about 4,500,000 volumes. The recent grant of $17,000,000 for the army is $3,500,000 more than the cost of those magnificent collections!

There have been printed about 3,000,000 different volumes, great and little, within the last 400 years. If the Florida war cost but $30,000,000, it is ten times more than enough to have purchased one copy of each book ever printed, at one dollar a volume, which is more than the average cost.

Now all these sums are to be paid by the people, "the dear people," whom our republican demagogues love so well, and for whom they spend their lives, rising early, toiling late, those self-denying heroes, those sainted martyrs of the republic, eating the bread of carefulness for them alone! But how are they to be paid? By a direct tax levied on all the property of the nation, so that the poor man pays according to his little, and the rich man in proportion to his much, each knowing when he pays and what he pays for? No such thing; nothing like it. The people must pay and not know it; must be deceived a little or they would not pay after this fashion! You pay for it in every pound of sugar, copper, coal, in every yard of cloth; and if the counsel of some lovers of the people be followed, you will soon pay for it in each pound of coffee and tea. In this way the rich man always pays relatively less than the poor; often a positively smaller sum. Even here I think that three-fourths of all the property is owned by one-fourth of the people, yet that one-fourth by no means pays a third of the national revenue. The tax is laid on things men cannot do without,— sugar, cloth, and the like. The consumption of these articles is not in proportion to wealth but persons. Now the poor man, as a general rule, has more children than the rich, and the tax being more in proportion to persons than property, the poor man pays more than the rich. So a tax is really laid on the poor man's children to pay for the war which makes him poor and keeps him poor. I think your captains and colonels, those sons of thunder and heirs of glory, will not tell you so. They tell you so! they know it! Poor brothers, how could they? I think your party newspapers—penny or pound—will not tell you so; nor the demagogues, all covered with glory and all forlorn, who tell the people when to hurrah and for what! But if you cipher the matter out for yourself you will find it so, and not otherwise. Tell the demagogues—whig or democratic—that. It was an old Roman maxim, "The people wish to be deceived; let them." Now it is only practiced on; not repeated—in public.

Let us deal justly even with war, giving that its due. There is one class of men who find their pecuniary advantage in it. I mean army contractors, when they chance to be favorites of the party in power; men who let steamboats to lie idle at $500 a day. This class of men rejoice in a war. The country may become poor, they are sure to be rich. Yet another class turn war to account, get the "glory," and become immortal in song and sermon. I see it stated in a newspaper that the Duke of Wellington has received, as gratuities for his military services, $5,400,000, and $40,000 a year in pensions!

But the waste of property is the smallest part of the evil. THE WASTE OF LIFE IN WAR IS YET MORE TERRIBLE. Human life is a sacred thing. Go out into the lowest street of Boston; take the vilest and most squalid man in that miserable lane, and he is dear to some one. He is called Brother; perhaps Husband; it may be, Father; at least, Son. A human heart, sadly joyful, beat over him before he was born. He has been pressed fondly to his mother's arms. Her tears and her smiles have been for him; perhaps also her prayers. His blood may be counted mean and vile by the great men of the earth who love nothing so well as the dear people, for he has no "coat of arms," no liveried servant to attend him, but it has run down from the same first man. His family is ancient as that of the most long descended king. God made him,—made this splendid universe to wait on him and teach him; sent his Christ to save him. He is an immortal soul. To spill that man's blood is an awful sin. It will cry against you out of the ground—Cain! where is thy brother? Now in war you bring together 50,000 men like him on one side, and 50,000 of a different nation on the other. They have no natural quarrel with one another. The earth is wide enough for both—neither hinders the sun from the other. Many come unwillingly; many not knowing what they fight for. It is but accident which determines on which side the man shall fight. The cannons pour their shot—round, grape, canister; the howitzers scatter their bursting shells; the muskets rain their leaden death; the sword, the bayonet, the horses' iron hoof; the wheels of artillery grind the men down into trodden dust. There they lie—the two masses of burning valor—extinguished, quenched, and grimly dead, each covering with his body the spot he defended with his arms. They had no quarrel; yet they lie there, slain by a brother's hand. It is not old and decrepid men, but men of the productive age, full of lusty life.

But it is only the smallest part that perish in battle. Exposure to cold, wet, heat; unhealthy climates, unwholesome food, rum and forced marches—bring on diseases which mow down the poor soldiers worse than musketry and grape. Others languish of wounds, and slowly procrastinate a dreadful and a tenfold death. Far away, there are widows, orphans, childless old fathers, who pore over the daily news to learn at random the fate of a son, a father, or a husband! They crowd disconsolate into the churches, seeking of God the comfort men took from them,—praying in the bitterness of a broken heart, while the priest gives thanks for "a famous victory," and hangs up the bloody standard over his pulpit!

When ordinary disease cuts off a man, when he dies at his duty, there is some comfort in that loss. "'Twas the ordinance of God," you say. You minister to his wants; you smooth down the pillow for the aching head; your love beguiles the torment of disease, and your own bosom gathers half the darts of death. He goes in his time and God takes him. But when he dies in war, in battle, it is Man who has robbed him of life. It is a murderer that is butchered. Nothing alleviates that bitter, burning smart!

Others not slain are maimed for life. This has no eyes; that no hands; another no feet nor legs. This has been pierced by the lances, and torn with the shot, till scarce any thing human is left. The wreck of a body is crazed with pains God never meant for man. The mother that bore him would not know her child. Count the orphan asylums in Germany and Holland; go into the hospital at Greenwich, that of the Invalids at Paris, you see the "trophies" of Napoleon and Wellington. Go to the arsenal at Toulon, see the wooden legs piled up there for men now active and whole—and you will think a little of the physical horrors of war.

In Boston there are perhaps about 25,000 able-bodied men between 18 and 45. Suppose them all slain in a battle, or mortally hurt, or mown down by the camp-fever, *vomito*, or other diseases of war, and then fancy the distress, the heart-sickness amid wives, mothers, daughters, sons and fathers, here! Yet 25,000 is a small number to be murdered in "a famous victory;" a trifle for a whole "glorious campaign" in a great war. The men of Boston are no better loved than the men of Tamaulipas. There is scarce an old family, of the middle class, in all New England, which did not thus smart in the Revolution; many, which have not, to this day, recovered from the bloody blow then falling on them. Think, wives, of the butchery of your husbands: think, mothers, of the murder of your sons!

Here, too, the burthen of battle falls mainly on the humble class. They pay the great tribute of money; they pay also the horrid tax of blood. It was not your rich men who fought even the Revolution; not they. Your men of property and standing were leaguing with the British, or fitting out privateers when that offered a good investment, or buying up the estates of more consistent tories—making money out of the nation's dire distress! True, there were most honorable exceptions; but such, I think, was the general rule. Let this be distinctly remembered—that the Burthen of Battle is borne by the humble classes of men; they pay the vast tribute of money; they the awful tax of blood! The "glory" is got by a few; poverty, wounds, death, are for the people!

Military glory is the poorest kind of distinction, but the most dangerous passion. It is an honor to a man to be able to mould iron; to be skilful at working in cloth, wood, clay, leather. It is man's vocation to raise corn—to subdue the rebellious fibre of cotton and convert it into beautiful robes, full of comfort for the body. They are the heroes of the race who abridge the time of human toil and multiply its results; they who win great truths from God, and send them to a people's heart; they who balance the Many and the One into harmonious action—so that all are united and yet each left free. But the glory which comes of epaulets and feathers; that strutting glory which is dyed in blood—what shall we say of it? In this day it is not heroism; it is an imitation of barbarism long ago passed by. Yet it is marvellous how many men are taken with a red coat! You expect it in Europe—a land of soldiers and blood. You are disappointed to find that here the champions of force should be held in honor, and that even the lowest should voluntarily enrol themselves as butchers of men!

Yet more, WAR IS A SIN; A CORRUPTER OF THE PUBLIC MORALS. It is a practical denial of Christianity; a violation of God's eternal law of love. This is so plain that I shall say little upon it to-day. Your savagest and most vulgar captain would confess he does not fight as a Christian—but as a soldier; your magistrate calls for volunteers—not as a MAN loving Christianity, and loyal to God; only as GOVERNOR, under oath to keep the constitution, the tradition of the elders; not under oath to keep the commandment of God! In war the laws are suspended, violence and cunning rule everywhere. The battle of Yorktown was gained by a lie—though a Washington told it. As a soldier it was his duty. Men "emulate the tiger;" the hand is bloody, and the heart hard. Robbery and murder are the rule, the glory of men. "Good men look sad, but ruffians dance and leap." Men are systematically trained to burn towns, to murder fathers and sons; taught to consider it "glory," to do so. The government collects ruffians and cut-throats. It compels better men to serve with these and become cut-throats. It appoints chaplains to blaspheme Christianity; teaching the ruffians how to pray for the destruction of the enemy, the burning of his towns; to do this in the name of Christ and God. I do not censure all the men who serve: some of them know no better; they have heard that a man would "perish everlastingly" if he did not believe the Athanasian creed; that if he questioned the story of Jonah, or the miraculous birth of Jesus, he was in danger of hell-fire, and if he doubted damnation was sure to be damned. They never heard that war was a sin; that to create a war was treason, and to fight in it a wrong. They never thought of thinking for themselves; their thinking was to read a newspaper, or sleep through a sermon. They counted it their duty to obey the government without thinking if that government be right or wrong. I deny not the noble, manly character of many a soldier, his heroism, self-denial and personal sacrifice.

Still, after all proper allowance is made for a few individuals the whole system of war is unchristian and sinful. It lives only by evil passions. It can be defended only by what is low, selfish, and animal. It absorbs the scum of the cities, pirates, robbers, murderers. It makes them worse—and better men like them. To take a man's life is murder—what is it to practice killing as an art—a trade; to do it by thousands? Yet I think better of the hands that do the butchering than of the ambitious heads, the cold, remorseless hearts, which plunge the nation into war.

In war the State teaches men to lie, to steal, to kill. It calls for privateers—who are commonly pirates with a national charter—and pirates are privateers with only a personal charter. Every camp is a school of profanity, violence, licentiousness, and crimes too foul to name. It is so without sixty-five thousand gallons of whiskey. This is unavoidable. It was so with Washington's army, with Cornwallis's, with that of Gustavus Adolphus's—perhaps the most moral army the world ever saw. The soldier's life generally unfits a man for the citizen's! When he returns from a camp, from a war, back to his native village, he becomes a curse to society and a shame to the mother that bore him. Even the soldiers of the Revolution, who survived the war, were mostly ruined for life—debauched, intemperate, vicious and vile. What loathsome creatures so many of them were! They bore our burthen—for such were the real martyrs of that war, not the men who fell under the shot! How many men of the rank and file in the late war have since become respectable citizens?

To show how incompatible are War and Christianity, suppose that the most Christian of Christ's disciples, the well-beloved John, were made a navy-chaplain, and some morning, when a battle is daily looked for, should stand on the gun-deck, amid lockers of shot, his Bible resting on a cannon, and expound Christianity to men with cutlasses by their side! Let him read for the morning lesson, the Sermon on the Mount—and for text take words from his own Epistle—so sweet, so beautiful, so true: "Every one that loveth is born of God, and knoweth God, for God is Love." Suppose he tells his strange audience that all men are brothers; that God is their common father; that Christ loved us all—showing us how to live the life of love—and, then, when he had melted all those savage hearts by words so winsome and so true—let him conclude, "Blessed are the men-slayers! Seek first the glory which cometh of battle. Be fierce as tigers. Mar God's image in which your brothers are made. Be not like Christ, but Cain who slew his brother! When you meet the enemy, fire into their bosoms; kill them in the dear name of Christ; butcher them in the spirit of God. Give them no quarter—for we ought not to lay down our lives for the brethren—only the murderer hath eternal life!"

Yet great as are these threefold evils—there are times when the soberest men and the best men have welcomed it, coolly and in their better moments. Sometimes, a people long oppressed, have "petitioned, remonstrated, cast itself at the feet of the throne," with only insult for answer to its prayer. Sometimes there is a contest between a falsehood and a great truth; a war for freedom of mind, heart and soul; yes, a war for a man's body, his wife's and children's body, for what is dearer to men than life itself—for the inalienable Rights of man, for the idea that all are born free and equal. It was so in the American Revolution—in the English, in the French Revolution. In such cases men say, "Let it come." They take down the firelock in sorrow; with a prayer they go forth to battle, asking that the RIGHT may triumph. Much as I hate war I cannot but honor such men. Were they better, yet more heroic, even war of that character might be avoided. Still it is a colder heart than mine which does not honor such men, though it believes them mistaken. Especially do we honor them, when it is the few, the scattered, the feeble, contending with the many and the mighty; the noble fighting for a great idea, and against the base and tyrannical. Then most men think the gain, the triumph of a great Idea, is worth the price it costs, the price of blood. Still, without stopping to touch that question, if man may ever shed the blood of man, I think even such wars as that wholly unchristian; that they may now be avoided, and the result won in a manlier, yes, a wholly Christian way.

Now, to make the evils of war still clearer, and to bring them home to your door, let us suppose there was war between the counties of Suffolk, on the one side, and Middlesex on the other; this army at Boston, that at Cambridge.

Suppose the subject in dispute was the boundary line between the two—Boston claiming a pitiful acre of flat land, which the ocean at low tide disdained to cover. To make sure of that Boston seizes whole miles of flat, unquestionably not its own. The rulers on one side are Fools, and Traitors on the other. The two commanders have issued their proclamations; the money is borrowed; the whiskey provided; the soldiers—Americans, Negroes, Irishmen, all the able-bodied men—are enlisted. Prayers are offered in all the churches, and sermons preached, showing that God is a man of war, and Cain his first saint—an early Christian—a Christian before Christ. The Bostonians wish to seize Cambridge, burn the houses, churches, college-halls, and plunder the library. The men of Cambridge wish to seize Boston, burn its houses and ships, plundering its wares and its goods. Martial law is proclaimed on both sides. The men of Cambridge cut asunder the bridges, and make a huge breach in the mill-dam—planting cannon to enfilade all those avenues. Forts crown the hill-tops, else so green. Men, madder than lunatics, are crowded into the Asylum. The Bostonians re-build the old fortifications on the Neck, replace the forts on Beacon-hill, Fort-hill, Copps-hill, levelling houses to make room for redoubts and bastions. The batteries are planted, the mortars got ready; the furnaces and magazines are all prepared. The three hills are grim with war. From Copps-hill men look anxious to that memorable height the other side of the water. Provisions are cut off in Boston; no man may pass the lines; the aqueduct refuses its genial supply; children cry for their expected food. The soldiers parade—looking somewhat tremulous and pale; all the able-bodied have come, the vilest most willingly; some are brought by force of drink, some by force of arms. Some are in brilliant dresses—some in their working frocks. The banners are consecrated by solemn words.* Your church-towers are military posts of observation. There are Old Testament prayers to the "God of Hosts" in all the churches of Boston; prayers that God would curse the men of Cambridge, make their wives widows, their children fatherless, their houses

---

*See the appropriate forms of prayer for that service by the present Bishop of Oxford, in Jay's Address before the American Peace Society, in 1845.

a ruin, the men corpses, meat for the beast of the field and the bird of the air. Last night the Bostonians made a feint of attacking Charlestown, raining bombs and red hot cannon-balls from Copps-hill, till they have burnt a thousand houses, where the British burnt not half so many. Women and children fled screaming from the blazing rafters of their homes. The men of Middlesex crowd into Charlestown.

In the mean time the Bostonians hastily repair a bridge or two; some pass that way, some over the Neck—all stealthily by night—and while the foe expect them at Bunkers, amid the blazing town, they have stolen a march and rush upon Cambridge itself. The Cambridge men turn back. The battle is fiercely joined. You hear the cannon, the sharp report of musketry. You crowd the hills, the housetops; you line the Common, you cover the shore,—yet you see but little in the sulphurous cloud. Now the Bostonians yield a little—a reinforcement goes over. All the men are gone; even the gray-headed who can shoulder a firelock. They plunge into battle mad with rage, madder with rum. The chaplains loiter behind.

> "Pious men, whom duty brought,
>   To dubious verge of battle fought,
>   To shrive the dying, bless the dead,"

The battle hangs long in even scale. At length it turns. The Cambridge men retreat—they run—they fly. The houses burn. You see the churches and the colleges go up, a stream of fire. That library—founded 'mid want and war and sad sectarian strife, slowly gathered by the saving of two centuries, the hope of the poor scholar, the boast of the rich one—is scattered to the winds and burnt with fire, for the solid granite is blasted by powder, and the turrets fall. Victory is ours. Ten thousand men of Cambridge lie dead; eight thousand of Boston. There writhe the wounded; men who but few hours before were poured over the battle-field a lava-flood of fiery valor—fathers, brothers, husbands, sons. There they lie, torn and mangled; black with powder; red with blood; parched with thirst; cursing the load of life they now must bear with bruised frames and mutilated limbs. Gather them into hasty hospitals—let this man's daughter come to-morrow and sit by him, fanning away the flies; he shall linger out a life of wretched anguish unspoken and insupportable, and when he dies his wife religiously will keep the shot which tore his limbs. There is the battle field! Here the horse charged; there the howitzers scattered their shells, pregnant with death; here the murderous canister and grape mowed down whole the crowded ranks; there the huge artillery, teeming with murder, was dragged o'er heaps of men—wounded friends who just now held its ropes, men yet curling with anguish, like worms in the fire; hostile and friendly, head and trunk are crushed beneath their dreadful wheels. Here the infantry showered their murdering shot. That ghastly face was beautiful the day before—a sabre hewed its half away.

> "The earth is covered thick with other clay,
>   Which her own clay must cover, heaped and pent,
>   Rider and horse, friend, foe, in one red burial blent."

Again 'tis night. Oh, what a night, and after what a day! Yet the pure tide of woman's love—which never ebbs since earth began—flows on in spite of war and battle. Stealthily, by the pale moonlight, a mother of Boston treads the weary miles to reach that bloody spot; a widow she—seeking among the slain her only son. The arm of power drove him forth reluctant to the fight. A friendly soldier guides her way. Now she turns over this face, whose mouth is full of purple dust, bit out of the ground in his extremest agony—the last sacrament offered him by earth herself; now she raises that form, cold, stiff, stony and ghastly as a dream of hell. But, lo! another comes—she too a woman—younger and fairer, yet not less bold, a maiden from the hostile town to seek her lover. They meet—two women among the corpses; two angels come to Golgotha, seeking to raise a man. There he lies before them; they look,—yes, 'tis he you seek; the same dress, form, features too;—'tis he, the Son, the Lover. Maid and mother could tell *that* face in any light. The grass is wet with his blood. Yes, the ground is muddy with the life of men. The mother's innocent robe is drabbled in the blood her bosom bore. Their kisses, groans and tears recall the wounded man. He knows the mother's voice; that voice yet more beloved. His lips move only, for they cannot speak. He dies! The waxing moon moves high in heaven, walking in beauty 'mid the clouds, and murmurs soft her cradle song unto the slumbering earth. The broken sword reflects her placid beams. A star looks down and is imaged back in a pool of blood. The cool night wind plays in the branches of the trees shivered with shot. Nature is beautiful; that lovely grass underneath their feet; those pendulous branches of the leafy elm; the stars and that romantic moon lining the clouds with silver light! A groan of agony, hopeless and prolonged, wails out from that bloody ground. But in yonder farm the whippowil sings to her lover all night long; the rising tide ripples melodious against the shores. So wears the night away,—Nature, all sinless, round that field of wo.

> "The morn is up again, the dewy morn,
>   With breath all incense and with cheek all bloom,
>   Laughing the clouds away with playful scorn,
>   And living as if earth contained no tomb,
>   And glowing into day."

What a scene that morning looks upon! I will not turn again.—Let the dead bury their dead. But their blood cries out of the ground against the rulers who shed it,—Cain! where are thy brothers? What shall the Fool answer? what the Traitor say?

Then come thanksgiving in all the churches of Boston. The consecrated banners, stiff with blood and "glory," are hung over the altar. The minister preaches and the singer sings: "The Lord hath been on our side. He treadeth the people under me. He teacheth my hands to war, my fingers to fight. Yea, he giveth me the necks of mine enemies; for the Lord is His name;" and "'twas a famous victory!" Boston seizes miles square of land; but her houses are empty; her wives widows; her children fatherless. Rachel weeps for the murder of her innocents—yet dares not rebuke the rod. I know there is no fighting across Charles River, as in this poor fiction; but there was once, and instead of CHARLES say RIO GRANDE; for CAMBRIDGE read METAMORAS, and 'tis what your President recommended; what your Congress enacted; what your Governor issued his proclamation for; what your volunteers go to accomplish:—yes, what they fired cannon for on Boston Common t'other day. I wish *that* were a fiction of mine!

We are waging a most iniquitous war—so it seems to me. I know I may be wrong. But I am no partizan, and if I err, it is not wilfully, not rashly. I know the Mexicans are a wretched people—wretched in their origin, history and character. I know but two good things of them as a people—they abolished negro slavery, not long ago; they do not covet the lands of their neighbors. True, they have not paid all their debts, but it is scarcely decent in a nation with any repudiating States to throw the first stone at her for that!

I know the Mexicans cannot stand before this terrible Anglo-Saxon race, the most formidable and powerful the world ever saw; a race which has never turned back; which, though it number less than forty millions, yet holds the Indies, almost the whole of North America; which rules the commerce of the world; clutches at New Holland, China, New Zealand, Borneo, and seizes island after island in the farthest seas;—the race which invented steam as its awful type. The poor, wretched Mexicans can never stand before us. How they perished in battle! They must melt away as the Indians before the white man. Considering how we acquired Louisiana, Florida, Oregon, I cannot forbear thinking that this people will possess the whole of this continent before many years; perhaps before the century ends. But this may be had fairly; with no injustice to any one; by the steady advance of a superior race, with superior ideas and a better civilization; by commerce, trade, arts, by being better than Mexico, wiser, humaner, more free and manly. Is it not better to acquire it by the schoolmaster than the cannon; by peddling cloth, tin, any thing rather than bullets? It may not all belong to this Government—and yet to this race. It would be a gain to mankind if we could spread over that country the Ideas of America—that all men are born free and equal in rights, and establish there political, social, and individual freedom. But to do that we must first make real these ideas at home.

In the general issue between this race and theirs, we are

in the right. But in this special issue, and this particular war, it seems to me that we are wholly in the wrong; that our invasion of Mexico is as bad as the partition of Poland in the last century and in this. If I understand the matter—the whole movement, the settlement of Texas, the Texan revolution, the annexation of Texas, the invasion of Mexico has been a movement hostile to the American idea,—a movement to extend Slavery. I do not say such was the design on the part of the people, but on the part of the politicians who pulled the strings. I think the papers of the Government and the debates of Congress prove that. The annexation has been declared unconstitutional in its mode,—a virtual dissolution of the Union—and that by very high and well known authority. It was expressly brought about for the purpose of extending Slavery. An attempt is now made to throw the shame of this on the Democrats. I think the Democrats deserve the shame; but I could never see that the Whigs, on the whole, deserved it any less; only they were not quite so open. Certainly, their leaders did not take ground against it,—never as against a modification of the tariff! When we annexed Texas we of course took her for better or worse, debts and all, and annexed her war along with her. I take it every body knew that; though now some seem to pretend a decent astonishment at the result. Now one party is ready to fight for it as the other! The North did not oppose the annexation of Texas. Why not? They knew they could make money by it. The eyes of the North are full of cotton; they see nothing else, for a *web* is before them; their ears are full of cotton, and they hear nothing but the buzz of their mills; their mouth is full of cotton, and they can speak audibly but two words— Tariff, Tariff, Dividends, Dividends. Yes, the talent of the North is blinded, deafened, gagged with its own cotton. The North clamored loudly when the nation's treasure was removed from the United States Bank;—it is almost silent at the annexation of a slave territory big as the kingdom of France, encumbered with debts—loaded with the entailment of war! Northern governors call for soldiers; our men volunteer to fight in a most infamous war for the extension of slavery! Tell it not in Boston, whisper it not in Faneuil Hall, lest you

waken the slumbers of your fathers, and they curse you as
cowards and traitors unto men! Not satisfied with annexing
Texas and a war, we next invaded a territory which did not
belong to Texas, and built a fort on the Rio Grande, where, I
take it, we had no more right than the British, in 1841, had on
the Penobscot or the Saco. Now the Government and its
Congress would throw the blame on the innocent, and say
war exists "by the act of Mexico!" If a lie was ever told, I
think this is one. Then the "dear people" must be called on
for money and men, for "the soil of this free republic is invaded," and the Governor of Massachusetts, one of the men
who declared the annexation of Texas unconstitutional, recommends the war he just now told us to pray against, and appeals to our "patriotism," and "humanity," as arguments for
butchering the Mexicans, when they are in the right and we
in the wrong! The maxim is held up, "Our country, right or
wrong;" "Our country howsoever bounded;" and it might as
well be, "our country, howsoever governed." It seems popu-
larly and politically forgotten that there is such a thing as
RIGHT. The nation's neck invites a Tyrant. I am not at all astonished that Northern Representatives voted for all this work
of crime. They are no better than Southern Representatives;
scarcely less in favor of slavery, and not half so open. They
say: Let the North make money, and you may do what you
please with the nation; and we will choose governors that
dare not oppose you, for, though we are descended from the
Puritans, we have but one article in our creed we never flinch
from following, and that is—to make money; honestly, if we
can; if not, as we can!

Look through the action of your Government, and your
Congress. You see that no reference has been had in this affair to Christian ideas; none to Justice and the eternal Right.
Nay, none at all! In the Churches, and among the people,
how feeble has been the protest against this great wrong.
How tamely the people yield their necks—and say: "Take our
sons for the war—we care not, right or wrong." England
butchers the Sikhs in India—her generals are elevated to the
peerage, and the head of her church writes a form of thanksgiving for the victory—to be read in all the churches of that

Christian land.* To make it still more abominable, the blasphemy is enacted on Easter Sunday, the great Holiday of men
who serve the Prince of Peace. We have not had prayers in the
churches, for we have no political Archbishop. But we fired
cannon in joy that we had butchered a few wretched men—

Form of Prayer and Thanksgiving to Almighty God:
"O Lord God of Hosts, in whose hand is power and might irresistible, we,
thine unworthy servants, most humbly acknowledge thy goodness in the vic-
tories lately vouchsafed to the armies of our Sovereign over a host of barbarous invaders who sought to spread desolation over fruitful and populous
provinces enjoying the blessings of peace, under the protection of the British
Crown. We bless Thee, O Merciful Lord, for having brought to a speedy and
prosperous issue a war to which no occasion had been given by injustice on
our part, or apprehension of injury at our hands. To Thee, O Lord, we ascribe the glory. It was thy wisdom which guided the counsel. Thy power
which strengthened the hands of those whom it pleased Thee to use as Thy
instruments in the discomfiture of the lawless aggressor and the frustration of
his ambitious designs. From Thee alone, cometh the victory, and the spirit of
moderation and mercy in the day of success. Continue, we beseech Thee, to
go forth with our armies, whensoever they are called into battle in a righteous cause; and dispose the hearts of their leaders to exact nothing more
from the vanquished than is necessary for the maintenance of peace and security against violence and rapine.

"Above all, give Thy grace to those who preside in the councils of our
Sovereign, and administer the concerns of her widely extended dominions,
that they may apply all their endeavors to the purposes designed by Thy good
Providence in committing such power to their hands, the temporal and spiritual benefit of the nations entrusted in their care.

"And whilst Thou preserves our distant possessions from the horrors of
war, give us peace and plenty at home, that the earth may yield her increase,
and that we, Thy servants, receiving Thy blessings with thankfulness and
gladness of heart, may dwell together in unity, and faithfully serve Thee, to
Thy honor and glory, through Jesus Christ our Lord, to whom, with Thee
and the Holy Ghost, belong all dominion and power, both in heaven and
earth, now and for ever. Amen."—See a defence of this Prayer, &c., in the
London "Christian Observer" for May, p. 319, and for June p. 346, &c.

Would you know what he gave thanks for on Easter Sunday? Here is the
history of the Battle:

"This battle had begun at six, and was over at eleven o'clock; the hand-to-
hand combat commenced at nine, and lasted scarcely two hours. *The river
was full of sinking men.* For two hours, volley after volley *was poured in upon
the human mass*—the stream being *literally red with blood, and covered with
the bodies of the slain.* At last, the musket ammunition becoming exhausted,
the infantry fell to the rear, the horse artillery plying grape, till not a man was
visible within range. No COMPASSION WAS FELT OR MERCY SHOWN." But
"'twas a famous victory!"

half starved, and forced into the ranks by fear of death! Your
Peace-Societies, and your Churches, what can they do? What
dare they? Verily, we are a faithless and perverse generation.
God be merciful to us, sinners as we are!

But why *talk* forever? What shall we DO? In regard to this
present war, we can refuse to take any part in it; we can encourage others to do the same; we can aid men, if need be,
who suffer because they refuse. Men will call us traitors, what
then? That hurt nobody in '76! We are a rebellious nation;
our whole history is treason; our blood was attainted before
we were born; our Creeds are infidelity to the Mother-
church; our Constitution treason to our father-land. What of
that? Though all the Governors in the world bid us commit
treason against Man, and set the example, let us never submit.
Let God only be a Master to control our Conscience!

We can hold public meetings in favor of Peace, in which
what is wrong shall be exposed and condemned. It is proof of
our cowardice that this has not been done before now. We
can show in what the infamy of a nation consists; in what its
real glory. One of your own men, the last summer, startled
the churches out of their sleep, by his manly trumpet, talking
with us and telling that the true grandeur of a nation was
Justice not glory, Peace not war.

We can work now for future times, by taking pains to
spread abroad the Sentiments of Peace, the Ideas of Peace,
among the people in schools, churches—everywhere. At
length we can diminish the power of the National Government, so that the people alone shall have the power to declare
war, by a direct vote—the Congress only to recommend it.
We can take from the Government the means of war by raising only revenue enough for the nation's actual wants, and
raising that directly, so that each man knows what he pays,
and when he pays it, and then he will take care that it is not
paid to make him poor and keep him so. We can diffuse a real
practical Christianity among the people, till the mass of men
have courage enough to overcome evil with good, and look at
war as the worst of treason and the foulest infidelity!

Now is the time to push and be active. War itself gives
weight to words of peace. There will never be a better time,

till we make the times better. It is not a day for cowardice, but for heroism. Fear not that the "honor of the nation" will suffer from Christian movements for Peace. What if your men of low degree are a vanity, and your men of high degree are a lie? That is no new thing. Let true men do their duty, and the lie and the vanity will pass each to its reward. Wait not for the Churches to move, or the State to become Christian. Let us bear our testimony like men, not fearing to be called Traitors, Infidels; fearing only to BE such.

I would call on Americans, by their love of our country, its great ideas, its real grandeur, its hopes, and the memory of its fathers—to come and help save that country from infamy and ruin. I would call on Christians, who believe that Christianity is a Truth, to lift up their voice, public and private, against the foulest violation of God's law, this blasphemy of the Holy Spirit of Christ, this worst form of infidelity to Man and God. I would call on all men, by the one nature that is in you, by the great human heart beating alike in all your bosoms, to protest manfully against this desecration of the earth, this high treason against both Man and God. Teach your rulers that you are Americans, not Slaves; Christians, not Heathen; Men, not murderers, to kill for hire! You may effect little in this generation, for its head seems crazed and its heart rotten. But there will be a day after to-day. It is for you and me to make it better; a day of peace, when nation shall no longer lift up sword against nation; when all shall indeed be brothers, and all blest. Do this—you shall be worthy to dwell in this beautiful land; Christ will be near you; God work with you— and bless you forever!

This present trouble with Mexico may be very brief; surely it might be even now brought to an end with no unusual manhood in your rulers. Can we say we have not deserved it? Let it end, but let us remember that war, horrid as it is, is not the worst calamity which ever befalls a people. It is far worse for a nation to loose all reverence for Right, for Truth, all respect for Man and God; to care more for the freedom of trade than the freedom of Men! more for a tariff than millions of souls. This calamity came upon us gradually, long before the present war, and will last long after that has died away. Like People like Ruler, is a true word. Look at your rulers,

Representatives, and see our own likeness! We reverence
FORCE, and have forgot there is any Right beyond the vote of
a Congress or a people; any good beside Dollars; any God but
Majorities and Force. I think the present war, though it
should cost 50,000 men and $50,000,000, the smallest part of
our misfortune. Abroad we are looked on as a nation of
swindlers and men-stealers! What can we say in our defence?
Alas, the nation is a traitor to its great idea,—that all men are
born equal, each with the same inalienable rights. We are infidels to Christianity. We have paid the price of our shame.

There have been dark days in this nation before now. It was
gloomy—when Washington with his little army fled through
the Jerseys. It was a long dark day from '83 to 89. It was not
so dark as now; the nation never so false. There was never a
time when resistance to tyrants was so rare a virtue; when the
people so tamely submitted to a wrong. Now you can feel the
darkness. The sack of this city and the butchery of its people
were a far less evil than the moral deadness of this nation.
Men spring up again like the mown grass—but to raise up
saints and heroes in a dead nation, corrupting beside its
golden tomb, what shall do that for us? We must look not to
the many for that, but to the few who are faithful unto God
and Man.

I know the hardy vigor of our men, the stalwart intellect of
this people. Would to God they could learn to love the Right
and True. Then what a people should we be—spreading from
the Madawaska to the Sacramento—diffusing our great Idea,
and living our Religion, the Christianity of Christ! Oh, Lord!
make the vision true; waken thy prophets and stir thy people
till Righteousness exalt us! No wonders will be wrought for
that. But the voice of Conscience speaks to you and me—and
all of us; the Right shall prosper; the wicked States shall die,
and History responds her long Amen.

What lessons come to us from the past! The Genius of the
Old Civilization, solemn and sad, sits there on the Alps, his
classic beard descending o'er his breast. Behind him arise the
new nations, bustling with romantic life. He bends down over
the midland sea, and counts up his children—Assyria, Egypt,
Tyre, Carthage, Troy, Etruria, Corinth, Athens, Rome—once
so renowned, now gathered with the dead, their giant ghosts

still lingering pensive o'er the spot. He turns westward his face, too sad to weep, and raising from his palsied knee his trembling hand, looks on his brother Genius of the New Civilization. That young giant, strong and mocking, sits there on the Alleghanies. Before him lie the waters, covered with ships; behind him he hears the roar of the Mississippi and the far distant Oregon—rolling their riches to the sea. He bends down, and that far ocean murmurs pacific in his ear. On his left, are the harbors, shops and mills of the East, and a five-fold gleam of light goes up from Northern lakes. On his right, spread out the broad savannahs of the South, waiting to be blessed; and far off that Mexique bay bends round her tropic shores. A crown of stars is on that giant's head, some glorious with flashing, many-colored light; some bloody red; some pale and faint, of most uncertain hue. His right hand lies folded in his robe; the left rests on the Bible's opened page; and holds these sacred words—All men are equal, born with equal rights from God. The old says to the young: "Brother, BEWARE!" and Alps and Rocky Mountains say "BEWARE!" That stripling giant, ill-bred and scoffing, shouts amain: "My feet are red with the Indians' blood; my hand has forged the negro's chain. I am strong; who dares assail me? I will drink his blood, for I have made my covenant of lies and leagued with hell for my support. There is no Right, no Truth; Christianity is false, and God a name." His left hand rends those sacred scrolls, casting his Bibles underneath his feet, and in his right he brandishes the negro-driver's whip— crying again—"Say, who is God and what is Right." And all his mountains echo RIGHT. But the old Genius sadly says again: "Though hand join in hand, the wicked shall not prosper." The hollow tomb of Egypt, Athens, Rome, of every ancient State, with all their wandering ghosts, replies, "AMEN."

LUCRETIA MOTT

Abuses and Uses of the Bible

Sermon, Delivered at Cherry Street Meeting,
Philadelphia, November 4, 1849

Wʜᴀᴛ are the abuses and what are the proper uses of the
Bible and of this day of the week? This question is of some
importance for us to seek to answer aright lest we should fall
into the popular error that prevails upon this subject.
Mingling as we do in religious society generally, adopting
some of its forms and some of its theories, we have need to
be upon our guard lest we fall into the superstition and error
and before we are aware become bigoted in our opinions and
denunciatory in our conduct. We know well that in Christendom generally it is assumed that the Bible is the word of God,
while we from the earliest date of our religious society have
declared and believe we have been sustained by Scripture testimony in the view that the word of God is a quickening spirit
or as beautifully expressed in what are called the apocryphal
writings: "Thine incorruptible spirit Oh Lord filleth all things.
Therefore chastiseth thou them by a little and little that offend, and warnest them by putting them in remembrance
wherein they have offended, that leaving their wickedness
they may return unto thee O Lord." A portion of this
blessed, this divine and all pervading spirit of which there is
an acknowledgment to a greater or less extent everywhere, is
found wherever man is found, darkened to be sure and
clouded by very many circumstances. This divine and holy
spirit which is a quickening spirit and has even been believed
to be by this Society the word of God and the only word of
God; that it has been through the operation and inspiring
power of this word that the testimony to the truth has been
borne in various ages of the world; that this testimony wherever it be found either in Scriptures or out of them is but a
corroboration of the word and not the word itself and that

word of God, which is quick and powerful, which showeth
the thoughts and intent of the heart, that engrafted word
which is able to serve the soul, we find so spoken in the
Scriptures, but we no where find the Scriptures called the
word of God by themselves. We read of one of the ancient
Hebrew writers who after being converted to a purer faith,
commended the Scriptures as being able to give knowledge of
that which is to come, being able to make wise into salvation;
giving knowledge of a purer way, but only through the faith
of Jesus Christ. What is this faith of Jesus Christ; not as theologians define it, faith in the Trinity and a vicarious atonement, not faith in a system, a mere scheme of salvation, a plan
of redemption? Faith of Jesus Christ is faith in the truth, faith
in God and in man. The life that I now live in the flesh, said
the Apostle, I live by the faith of the son of God, who loved
me and gave himself for me. Well what is this other than a
faith similar to that which Jesus held, the faith of the Son of
God. How many chosen sons of God are there who have not
loved their lives unto death, who have given themselves for
their brethren even as the Apostle recommended; that as he,
Jesus, laid down his life for the brethren so do we also lay
down our lives one for another. This then perhaps is the more
intelligent reading of these Scriptures and of what is spoken
of as the word of God and as the saving faith of the Christian.
The great error in Christendom is that the Bible is called the
word, that it is taken as a whole, as a volume of plenary inspiration and in this way it has proved one of the strongest
pillars to uphold ecclesiastical power and hireling priesthood.
What has been the power of this book? Is it not uniformly
taken among all the professors to establish their peculiar
creeds, their dogmas of faith and their forms of worship, be
they ever so superstitious? Is not the Bible sought from beginning to end for its isolated passages wherewith to prove
the most absurd dogmas that ever were palmed off upon a
credulous people; dogmas doing violence to the divine gift of
reason with which man is so beautifully endowed; doing violence to all his feelings, his sense of justice and mercy with
which the Most High has seen fit to clothe him? The Bible
has been taken to make man from his very birth a poor corrupt sinful creature, and to make his salvation depend upon

the sacrifice of Jesus in order that he should be saved. When his understanding has been imposed on by a Trinity and Atonement in the manner that it has, well may we say that the abuse of the Bible has been a means of strengthening priest-craft, and giving sanction to sectarian ordinances and establishments. We find the religionist, especially those whose greater interest it is to build up sect than to establish truth and righteousness in the earth, and probably many of these in the main idea that by this means they shall do the other more effectually, ready to flee to the Bible for authority for all their mysteries, their nonsensical dogmas, that have been imposed as articles of belief, as essential doctrines of Christianity. But also my friends has there not been an unworthy resort to this volume to prove the rightfulness of war and slavery, and of crushing woman's powers, the assumption of authority over her, and indeed of all the evils under which the earth, humanity has groaned from age to age? You know as well as I do how prone the sectarian has been to flee to the Bible to find authority for war, and indeed in the very existence of war, and there is a disposition because of the undue veneration of these records, to regard our God, even now as a God of battles. We do not duly discriminate between that comparatively dark age, when they set up their shouts of victory for their successes in their wars, whether aggressive or defensive, and the present. There is not sufficient allowance for the state that they were in at that time. Because of the veneration paid to the Bible, we find, even down to the present time, the over-ruling providence of God is claimed as giving countenance to the most barbarous and horrid wars, that are even in this day, cursing and disgracing the nations of the earth. Slavery, you know how ready the apologists for slavery and these apologists, to the shame of the church be it spoken, have been abundantly found in the pulpit, have screened themselves behind their imaged patriarchal institution and what sanction has been given to this greatest of all oppressions, this most wicked system which the English language furnishes no words wherewith rightly to depict the enormity of its cruelty. And this is done even at the present time by these priests of sect, these monopolizers of the pulpit. These ecclesiastics of our day have sought authority from the Bible and made it the plea for the sabbath, by quotations there from, that it was of God's sanction, that it was a patriarchal institution. You know as regards sensual indulgence the great obstacles that were thrown in the way of the temperance reformation by the use that was made of the Bible, by authority sought, for indulging in the intoxicating cup. We may rejoice that truth has been found stronger than all these, that thus the great efforts that have been made in our day for peace, for human freedom, for temperance, for moral purity, for the removal of all oppressions and monopolies that are afflicting mankind, have been to a considerable extent successful notwithstanding such obstacles as a popular priesthood, a popular clergy and a popular belief and the use of the Bible, have placed in the way of these great reformations. See now the resort to the Bible to prove the superstitious observances of a day. The manner in which this day is observed is one of the strongholds of priestcraft. It forms one of the pillars which must be broken down and which will be broken down, before an enlightened Christian faith. But then it needs that there should be boldness to declare this faith. It needs there should be faith to act in accordance with this and to declare the abuse that is now made of the Bible, in seeking to establish forms of worship which long since should have passed away. Superstitions, baptism, communion tables and devotions of various kinds and orders, have there found their sanction by improper reference to this volume. Thus by taking the examples of the ancients, even though they may have been comparatively modern, though they may have been disciples of Jesus in his day, yet I believe there is no rightful authority, no Scripture authority, for taking their example as sufficient authority for the continuance of the practice in the present day. We are not thus to use the example or practice of the ancients. It may have been well for them, coming from under the cloud of superstition formerly. They may still have needed their outward school master to bring them to a higher position, a higher sphere, a higher understanding, a higher dispensation, but are we because we find that they continued their type under the law, or their baptism which was of John, because they continued in their Sabbath observances, are we to do these things? I tell you nay. This divine word which we believe to be our sufficient teacher, draws us away from a dependance upon books, or everything that is outward, and leads us onward and upward in the work of progress toward perfection. Were we to come to the light we should have less need of the ordinance, for it would lead us away from customs of the religious world. If we have come as a babe, like stated in the language of the Apostle, what need he says have we any more of these ordained; touch not, taste not, handle not for all are designed to punish with the using but the substance is of Christ. And if ye come to this then let no man judge you as regards meats and drinks or new moons, or Sabbath days.

Remember the Sabbaths are but a shadow of things to come but the substance is of Christ. Those whose dependance is upon apostolic authority cannot find it, but there is notwithstanding a superstitious veneration put in the clerical explanation of that authority which has led many most mournfully to pin their faith upon ministers sleeves. Therefore we see the religious world gone on satisfying itself with its mysteries, with its nice theories of religion. These they regard as useful but which are really anything but true religion. We see them going out satisfied with their forms and devotions, taking comparatively little interest in the great subject of truth and humanity.

But are those all or the only uses that are made of the Bible and of the first day of the week, for the day has been consecrated to the expounding of these dogmas and the enforcing of useless forms? Are there not also other uses of these, has there not been another reading of the Scriptures? The proper use of them I can verily believe has been understood and is increasingly understood by very many and that the day is a day also for strengthening good feelings, for exciting religious veneration in a profitable way. We can freely admit that the Bible, in the intelligent reading and growing intelligence with which it is pursued with proper discrimination, without taking it as a volume of inspiration but only acknowledging that which is inspired, the truth which is eternal and divine being of value to the soul, had used not a few with a proper appreciation of the day, it also had its uses. How many have found consolation in Scripture testimonials suited to their almost every state? When they were in the low dungeon, then the

Lord delivered his angels and those who are now in a similar state can understand these testimonies and they too sing their song on the banks of deliverance: These find true consolation in these corroborating testimonies for they have passed through similar scenes with those who are now suffering and who are now rejoicing. These are feelings leading to praises and acclamations unto the highest. How many are the testimonies of these Scriptures which suit the state of those who are desirous for truth and righteousness to prevail on the earth, how beautiful is the testimony from the beginning to the end of the Scriptures, to the discriminating servant of the highest that is born to righteousness, truth, uprightness, justice and mercy, peace and universal love? The law of the Lord is declared to be perfect, to be pure, upright and clear, and to abide forever and those who obey this word, are made clear sighted. This truth when heard and suffered to be as a law is as a candle, as a light leading and enlightening the path that leads into the right way. How satisfactory then are the corroborating testimonies of Scripture but not more so than the testimonies of many other servants of God. Why not regard all the testimonies of the good, as Scripture, recorded in every age and in every condition of life? These Scriptures are valuable because they bring together the testimonies of so many ages of the world, but are there not equal testimonies born to the truth that are not bound in this volume? Certainly there are and we do err not knowing the Scriptures, nor the power of God when we limit the Scriptures, when we limit the truth or indeed when we set so high a value on these Scriptures as to suffer our veneration to lead us to receive truth more from this source than from any other. There is one source which is higher than this, and when we come to it we are drawn away, to some extent from all external dependences, from all outward authorities. And further as regards these Scriptures, intelligently we shall not fasten upon ourselves any form of worship or conversion because those in ancient time were in the practice of them. We shall look at these and make all allowance for the state that they were in and suffer them to pass by. As regards days, we shall not be venerators of days because the ancients were, and indeed I have too often thought that the veneration which professing Christians paid to this day far exceeds that which was enjoined upon the Jews, among whom the observances were instituted. Well has a modern writer said, that the consecration of the Sabbath or one day in seven, indicates the desecration of the other six, that the consecration of our churches indicates the desecration of our homes, the consecration of a class leads to the desecration of the great mass of the people, the consecration of this leads to the desecration of others, rather than the dedication of them to holiness and sacredness. I knew a woman some years ago who would spend every day in the week reading all the novels that were issued from the press and on the first day she would take her Bible and read a chapter and one of Blair's sermons, then close up the books, and state what she had done, and look with a kind of religious horror upon those who would be engaged pursuing some innocent occupation, and whose every time was consecrated to truth and duty, God and humanity. This latter class find a portion of every day for religious devotion and instructive reading. Oh my Friends, the abuse that there is in this day; leading people to regard with a kind of pious horror anything which is innocent in itself. This is a superstition which we at least ought to be rid of. Our Fathers suffered enough in bearing their testimonies to the equality of days for us not to be found going back to the beggarly elements. Let us hail, in the present state of society, the existence of this day as set apart as a day of rest and it may be too of innocent recreation to the toil worn labourer, while there is a disposition to exact so much of him through the week, leaving little time for rest and innocent recreation, and for religious improvement, on other days. Let us hail this as a season that shall give such time though it may not be so used. Let us also hail it as a day furnishing opportunity for exciting the religious veneration of those who still require this for their better nature, be that either in psalmody, in melody and in prayer or in some other way suited to their views of what belongs to the day.

I also enjoy while I am coming down to my chosen place of gathering, the liberty, the freedom that is manifested in our fellow citizens, going each to his chosen place of worship. I also enjoy the cleanliness of our courts and alleys, and the little children who one day in a week have on what they call their Sunday clothes and go forth in a feeling of cleanliness and innocent enjoyment. While we feel that there may be these advantages let us earnestly protest against the superstition which had led to penal enactments to enforce the observance of this day. Let us protest against this spirit for it is a spirit of priestcraft. It is the clerical and ecclesiastical power that's gaining the ascendancy in this country so far as it is allowed by the public opinion of the country. It's gaining upon the people and it will make inroads upon us until our liberties are sapped, until we are brought under a yoke which neither we nor our fathers were able to bear. Let us then my friends cherish a religion which shall be rational and which shall be reasonable in its observances and in its requirements. Let us keep hold of the faith that is in accordance with reason and with the intelligent dictates of the pure spirit of God. Let us ever hold up the supremacy of this spirit, of this divine guidance, as far above all the leadings of men and the teaching of books or the veneration that is imposed by the observance of these, or by worship in meeting houses. We need to understand the worship that is more in our everyday life that is manifested more by efforts of love and of devotion to truth and righteousness. We need to consecrate ourselves more to God and to humanity and less to forms and ceremonies and to ritual faith. With the proper uses of the day and of the Bible and with the proper use of the church and of our religious institutions we may then be greatly benefited to improved. But there will be division and subdivisions until we come to fully to understand that truth which leadeth unto the liberty; That he that upholdeth truth designs that there should be no inspiration, no power delegated upon one portion of the people over another. Until we come to this, until there is an intelligent testimony born against ecclesiastical usurpations, against hierarchical institutions, against the favored few in the congregation, there must be divisions and subdivision among us. These things must needs be; therefore when we hear of wars and rumors of wars in our midst let us not be troubled but know full well that the end is not yet, but that we must trust in the growing light and intelligence which is spreading over the human family and which is marking those who are desirous to obtain the right,

who are hungering and thirsting after greater righteousness.
That in this growing intelligence, these evils which still cling
to sect, will be removed, and one great means of removing
these, is the diffusion of knowledge among both male and female. The usurpations of the church and clergy, by which
woman has been so debased, so crushed, her powers of mind,
her very being brought low, and a low estimate set upon
these, are coming to be seen in their true light. But woman
must avail herself of the increasing means of intelligence, education and knowledge. She must rise also in a higher sphere
of spiritual existence and suffer her moral nature to be developed, her mind to be made right in the sight of God. Then
will the time speedily come when the influence of the clergy
shall be taken off of woman, when the monopoly of the pulpit shall no more oppress her, when marriage shall not be a
means of rendering her noble nature subsidiary to man, when
there shall be no assumed authority on the one part nor admitted inferiority or subjection on the other. One of the
abuses of the Bible (for Apostolic opinion has been taken and
no doubt false opinion, for there have been abundant quotations and some mistranslations in order to make the Apostle
say what the priests declare he did say) has been to bind silence upon woman in the churches, fasten upon her that kind
of degrading obedience in the marriage relation which has led
to countless evils in society and indeed has enervated, and
produced for us a feeble race. Oh my friends, these subjects
are subjects of religious interest and of vast importance. I
would that there were successors coming forth in this great
field of reform. The Almighty is calling upon both man and
woman to open their mouths and judge righteously, to plead
the cause of the poor and needy and many sure are thus emphatically called to lift-up the voice and declare the truth of
God and this will give evidence of the divinity of their mission
just as Jesus did. The Spirit of the highest is upon me; The
Spirit of the Lord is upon me, because he hath anointed me
to preach the gospel, because he hath anointed me to bind up
the broken-hearted to preach deliverance to the captive, the
opening of the prison to them that are bound, and so preach
the acceptable ear of the Lord. May they then not be afraid,
may they not be ashamed to lift up their voices for the right

so let the sound be heard far and wide and let it go forth to the ends of the earth; The Spirit of the Lord is come upon them and they are called to go forth on this mission. A blessing will be to them for they will acknowledge that the highest has been their mouth and wisdom, their tongue and utterance have been of the Lord that whereas they were a few and feeble but that they have been made strong and mighty in him who is ever with his children. Whoever giveth them mouth and wisdom, tongue, and utterance to speak that which he commandeth, strength and perseverance in accordance with right; preaching and doing that which is right by a blessed example, by a pure life, for this is almost effectual preaching of righteousness.

BROTHER CARPER

The Shadow of a Great Rock in a Weary Land

as recorded by James V. Watson

Wʜᴀᴛ follows is scarcely an outline of his sermon, but rather a sketch of some of its most eloquent passages. He announced for his text these words:

"And a man shall be as a hiding-place from the wind, and a covert from the tempest; as rivers of water in a dry place, as the shadow of a great rock in a weary land." Isaiah xxxii, 2.

Dare be two kinds ob language, de literal and de figerative. De one expresses de tought plainly, but not passionately; de oder passionately, but not always so plainly. De Bible abounds wid bof dese mode ob talk. De text is an ensample of dat lubly stile of speech de figerative. De prophet's mind was as clear as de sea ob glass in de Rebalations, and mingled wid fire. He seed away down de riber ob ages glorious coming events. He held his ear to de harp ob prophecy, and heard in its fainter cadences, loudening as he listened, de birf-song ob de multitude ob de hebenly host on de meadows ob Bethlehem. He seed de hills ob Judea tipped wid hebenly light; de fust sermum mountin, and de transfigeration mountin, and de crucifixion mountin, and de mountin ob ascension, clapped dare hands in de prophet's wision ob gladness. Gray-bearded Time stretched his brawny sinews to hasten on de fullness of latter-day glory. Brederen, de text am as full ob latter-day glory as am de sun ob light. It am as full ob Christ as de body ob heben am ob God. De sinner's danger and his certain destruction; Christ's sabin lub; his sheltering grace and his feasting goodness am brought to view in de text, and impressed in de language ob comparison.

"And a man shall be as a hiding-place from de wind." Many parts ob de ancient countries (and it still am de case) was desert; wild wastes ob dreary desolation; regions ob fine blistering sands; just as it was leff when de flood went away, and which has not been suffered to cool since de fust sunshine dat succeed dat event. No grass, no flower, no tree dare be pleasant to de sight. A scene of unrelebed waste; an ocean made of powder, into which de curse ob angered heben had ground a portion ob earth. Now and den, a huge rock, like shattered shafts and fallen monuments in a neglected graveyard, and big enof to be de tombstone ob millions, would liff its mossless sides 'bove de 'cumulating sands. No pisnous sarpint or venemous beast here await dare prey, for death here has ended his work and dwells mid silence. But de traveler here, who adventures, or necessity may have made a bold wanderer, finds foes in de elements fatal and resistless. De long heated earth here at places sends up all kinds ob pisnous gases from de many minerals ob its mysterious bosom; dese tings take fire, and den dare be a tempest ob fire, and woe be to de traveler dat be obertaken in dis fire ob de Lord widout a shelter. Again, dem gases be pison, and dare be de pison winds, as well as de fire winds. Dey can be seen a coming, and look green and yeller, and coppery, spotted snake-like, and float and wave in de air, like pison coats on water, and look like de wing ob de death angel; fly as swift as de cloud shadow ober de cotton field, and when dey obertake de flying traveler dey am sure to prove his winding-sheet; de drifting sands do dare rest, and 'bliterate de faintest traces ob his footsteps. Dis be death in de desert, 'mid de wind's loud scream in your sand-filling ears for a funeral sermun, and your grave hidden foreber. No sweet spring here to weave her hangings ob green 'bout your lub-guarded dust. De dews ob night shall shed no tears 'pon your famined grave. De resurrection angel alone can find ye.

But agin dis fire wind and dis tempest ob pison dat widthers wid a bref, and mummifies whole caravans and armies in dare march, dare is one breast-work, one "hiding-place," one protecting "shadow" in de dreaded desert. It am "de shadow ob a great rock in dis weary land." Often has de weary traveler seen death in de distance, pursuing him on de wings ob de wind, and felt de certainty ob his fate in de darkness ob de furnace-like air around him. A drowsiness stronger 'most dan de lub ob life creeps ober him, and de jaded camel reels in de heby sand-road under him. A shout ob danger from de more resolute captin ob de caravan am sent along de ranks, prolonged by a thousand thirst-blistered tongues, commingled in one ceaseless howl ob woe, varied by ebery tone ob distress and despair. To "de great rock," shouts de leader as 'pon his Arab hoss he heads dis "flight to de Refuge." Behind dem at a great distance, but yet fearfully near for safety, is seed a dark belt bending ober de horizon, and sparkling in its waby windings like a great sarpint, air hung at a little distance from de ground, and advancing wid de swiftness ob an arrow. Before dem, in de distance, a mighty great rock spreads out its broad and all-resisting sides, lifting its narrowing pint 'bove the clouds, tipped wid de sun's fiery blaze, which had burnt 'pon it since infant creation 'woke from de cradle ob kaos at de call ob its Fader. [Here our sable orator pointed away to some of the spurs of the Ozark Mountains seen off to the northwest through a forest opening, at a distance of from ten to fifteen miles, and whose summits of barren granite blazed in the strength of a clear June sun, like sheeted domes on distant cathedrals.] Dat light be de light ob hope, and dat rock be de rock ob hope to de now flyin', weepin', faintin', and famishin' hundreds. De captin' has arrived dare. [Here a suppressed cry of "Thank God," escaped many of the audience.] See, he has disappeared behind it, perhaps to explore its cavern coverts. But see, he has soon reappeared, and wid joy dancing in his eye, he stands shoutin' and beckonin', "Onward, *onward*, ONWARD, ONWARD," when he reels from weariness and falls in behind de rock. ["Thank God, he's saved!" exclaimed a voice.] Onward dey rush, men, women, husbands, wives, parents and children, broders and sisters, like doves to de windows, and disappear behind dis rampart ob salvation. Some faint just as dey 'rive at de great rock, and dare friends run out and drag dem to de "hidin' place," when wakin' up in safety, like dat sister dare, dat lose her strength in de prayer-meetin', dey shout 'loud for joy. [Here many voices at once shouted "Glory."] De darknin' sand-plain ober which dese fled for life, now lies strewed wid beast, giben out in the struggle, and all useless burdens was trowed 'side. De waby sheet ob destruction, skimmin' the surface wid de swiftness ob shadow, now be bery near, and yet, a few feeble stragglers and lubbed friends ob dis sheltered multitude are yet a great way off. [Here words were uttered in a choked accent, the speaker seeming unable to resist the thrilling character of the analogy.] Yes, a great way off. But see, moders and broders from behind de rock are shoutin' to dem to hasten. Dey come, dey come. A few steps more, and dey are sabed. But O, de pison wind is just behind dem, and its choke mist already round dem! Dare one falls, and dare is a scream. No, he rises again and am sabed. But one still is exposed. It be de fader ob dat little nest ob sweet-eyed children, for which he had fled to de rear to hurry on. Dey have passed forward and are safe. He am but a little distance from de rock, and not a head dares to peep to him encouragement from behind it. Already de wings ob de death angel am on de haunches ob his strong dromedary. His beast falls, but 'pon de moment ob him falling, de rider leaps out ob his saddle into dis "hiding-place from de wind." His little boy crouched in a hole ob de rock, into which he thrusts his head, entwines his neck with his little arms and says, "Papa, you hab come, and we be all here." [Here the shouts of "Salvation," "Salvation," seemed to shake the place in which we were assembled.]

Now, de burnin' winds and de pison winds blow and beat 'pon dat rock, but dose who hab taken refuge behind it, in its overhanging precipices, are safe until de tempest am ober and gone.

And now, brederen, what does all dis represent in a figure? Dat rock am Christ; dem winds be de wrath ob God rabealed against de children ob disobedience. Dem that he sabed be dem dat hab fled to de refuge, to de hope set before dem in Christ Jesus de Lord. De desert am de vast howling wilderness ob dis world, where dare be so little ob lub, and so much ob hate; so little ob sincerity, and so much ob hypocrisy; so little ob good, and so much ob sin; so little ob heben, and so much ob hell. It seem to poor me, dat dis world am de battle-ground ob de debil and his angels against Christ and his elect, and if de debil hab not gained de victory, he hold possession because every sinner am a Tory. God ob de Gospel, open the batteries of heben to-day! [Here a volley of hearty "Amens."] Sinner, de wrath ob God am gathering against you for de great decisive battle. I already sees in de light ob Zina's lightnings a long embankment ob dark cloud down on de sky. De tall thunder heads nod wid dare plumes of fire in dare onward march. De day of vengeance am at hand. Mercy, dat has pleaded long for you wid tears of blood, will soon dry her eyes and hush her prayers in your behalf. Death and hell hang on your track wid de swiftness ob de tempest. Before you am de "hiding-place." Fly, *fly*, I beseeches you, from de wrath to come!

But, brederen, de joy ob de belieber in Jesus am set forth in a figerative manner in de text. It am compared to water to dem what be dying ob thirst. O, how sweet to de taste ob de desert traveler sweltering under a burning sun, as if creation was a great furnace! Water, sweet, sparklin', livin', bubblin', silvery water, how does his languid eye brighten as he suddenly sees it gushing up at his feet like milk from de fountain ob lub, or leaping from de sides ob de mountain rock like a relief angel from heben. He drinks long and gratefully, and feels again de blessed pulsations ob being. And so wid de soul dat experience joy in beliebing; de sweets ob pardon; de raptures ob peace; de witnessin' Spirit's communings, and de quiet awe ob adoption. Such a soul be obershadowed wid de Almighty; he linger in de shady retreats ob de garden ob God; he feed in de pastures ob his lub, and am led by still waters, and often visits de land ob Beulah, whare it always am light. But, my brederen, all comparison be too dispassionate, and an angel's words am too cold to describe de raptures ob salvation! It am unspeakable and full ob glory. De life ob innocence and prayer; de sweet, childlike smile and de swimmin' eye; de countenance so glorious in death, dat but for decay, de body ob de gone-home saint might be kept as a breathin' statue of peace and patience, smiling in victory ober all de sorrows ob life and de terrors ob death, are de natural language ob dis holy passion. O, glory to God! I feels it today like fire in my bones! Like a chained eagle my soul rises toward her native heben, but she can only fly just so high. But de fetters ob flesh shall fall off soon, and den,

> " 'I shall bathe my weary soul
> In seas ob hebenly rest,
> And not a wabe ob trouble roll
> Across my peaceful breast.' "

HENRY WARD BEECHER

Peace, Be Still

*A Sermon Preached at Plymouth Church, Brooklyn,
on the Day of the National Fast, Jan. 4, 1861*

*"And there arose a great storm of wind, and the
waves beat into the ship, so that it was now full. And
he was in the hinder part of the ship, asleep on a pillow: and they awake him, and say unto him, Master,
carest thou not that we perish? And he arose and
rebuked the wind, and said unto the sea, Peace, be
still. And the wind ceased, and there was a great
calm."*—MARK iv. 35–39.

AT THE CLOSE of a laborious day, our Saviour entered a ship,
upon the lake of Gennesaret, to cross to the other side.
Wearied by his great tasks of mercy, which had filled the day,
he fell asleep. Meantime, a sudden and violent wind, to which
that lake is even yet subject, swept down from the hills, and
well-nigh overwhelmed them. They were not ignorant of nav-
igation, nor unacquainted with that squally sea. Like good
men and true, doubtless, they laid about them. They took in
sail, and put out oars, and, heading to the wind, valiantly bore
up against the gale, and thought nothing of asking help till
they had exerted every legitimate power of their own. But the
waves overleaped their slender bulwarks, and filled the little
vessel past all bailing.

Then, when they had done all that men could do, but not
till then, they aroused the sleeping Christ and implored his
succor. Not for coming to him, did he rebuke them; but for
coming with such terror of despair, saying, Why are ye so
fearful? How is it that ye have no faith? He outbreathed upon
the winds, and their strength quite forsook them. He looked
upon the surly waves, and they hasted back to their caverns.
There is no tumult in the heavens, on the earth, nor upon the

sea, that Christ's word cannot control. When it pleases God to speak, tempestuous clouds are peaceful as flocks of doves, and angry seas change all their roar to rippling music.

This nation is rolling helplessly in a great tempest. The Chief Magistrate in despair calls us to go to the sleeping Saviour, and to beseech his Divine interference. It may be true that the crew have brought the ship into danger by cowardice or treachery; it may be true that a firm hand on the wheel would even yet hold her head to the wind, and ride out the squall. But what of that?

Humiliation and prayer are never out of order. This nation has great sins unrepented of; and whatever may be our own judgment of the wisdom of public men in regard to secular affairs, we cannot deny that in this respect they have hit rarely well. Instead of finding fault with the almost only wise act of many days, let us rather admire with gratitude this unexpected piety of men in high places.

This government is in danger of subversion; and surely, while the venerable Chief Magistrate of this nation, and all the members of his Cabinet, are doubtless this day religiously abstaining from food, according to their proclamation and recommendation to us, and humbly confessing their manifold sins, it would ill become us to go unconcerned and negligent of such duties of piety and patriotism. Nor need we be inconveniently frank and critical. What if some shall say that fasting is a poor substitute for courage, and prayer a miserable equivalent for fidelity to duty? What if the national authorities had not only appointed the Fast, but afforded sufficient material in their own conduct for keeping it? It is all the more necessary on that account that we should pause, and humble ourselves before God, and implore his active interference.

But however monstrous the pretence of trouble may be, the danger is the same. Government is in danger of subversion. No greater disaster could befal this continent or the world; for such governments fall but once, and then there is no resurrection. Since there is no famine in the land, no pestilence, no invasion of foreign foe, no animosity of the industrial classes against each other, or against their employers, whence is our danger? from what quarter come these clouds, drifting with bolts of war and destruction? Over the Gulf the storm hangs lurid! From the treacherous Caribbean sea travel the darkness and swirling tornadoes!

What part of this complicated Government has at last broken down? Is it the legislative? the judicial? the executive? Has experience shown us that this costly machine, like many another, is more ingenious than practicable? Not another nation in the world, not a contemporaneous government, during the past seventy-five years, can compare, for regularity, simplicity of execution, and for a wise and facile accomplishment of the very ends of government, with ours. And yet, what is the errand of this day? Why are we observing a sad Sabbath? a day of humiliation? a day of supplication? It is for the strangest reason that the world ever heard. It is because the spirit of liberty has so increased and strengthened among us, that the Government is in danger of being overthrown! There never before was such an occasion for fasting, humiliation, and prayer! Other nations have gone through revolutions to find their liberties. We are on the eve of a revolution to put down liberty! Other people have thrown off their governments because too oppressive. Ours is to be destroyed, if at all, because it is too full of liberty, too full of freedom. There never was such an event before in history.

But however monstrous the pretence, the danger is here. In not a few states of this Union reason seems to have fled, and passion rules. To us who have been bred in cooler latitudes and under more cautious maxims, it seems incredible that men should abandon their callings, break up the industries of the community, and give themselves up to the wildest fanaticism, at the expense of every social and civil interest, and without the slightest reason or cause in their relations to society and to the country, past or future.

Communities, like individuals, are liable to aberrations of mind. Panics and general excitements seem to move by laws as definite as those which control epidemics or the pestilence. And such an insanity now rules in one portion of our land. Cities are turned into camps. All men are aping soldiers. For almost a thousand miles there is one wild riot of complaint and boasting. Acts of flagrant wrong are committed against the Federal Government. And these things are but the prelude. It is plainly declared that this Government shall be broken up, and many men mean it; and that the President-elect of this great nation shall never come to the place appointed by this people. Riot and civil war, with their hideous train of murders, revenges, and secret villanies, are gathering their elements, and hang in ominous terror over the capital of this nation.

Meanwhile, we have had no one to stand up for order. Those who should have spoken in decisive authority have been—*afraid!* Severer words have been used: it is enough for me to say only that in a time when God, and providence, and patriotism, and humanity demanded courage, they had nothing to respond but fear. The heart has almost ceased to beat, and this Government is like to die for want of pulsations at the centre. While the most humiliating fear paralyzes one part of the Government, the most wicked treachery is found in other parts of it. Men advanced to the highest places by the power of our Constitution, have employed their force to destroy that Constitution. They are using their oath as a soldier uses his shield—to cover and protect them while they are mining the foundations, and opening every door, and unfastening every protection by which colluding traitors may gain easy entrance and fatal success. Gigantic dishonesties, meanwhile, stalk abroad almost without shame. And this Puritan land, this free Government, these United States, like old Rome in her latest imperial days, helpless at the court, divided among her own citizens, overhung by hordes of Goths and Barbarians, seem about to be swept away with the fury of war and revolution.

If at such a solemn crisis as this, men refuse to look at things as they are; to call their sins to remembrance; to confess and forsake them; if they shall cover over the great sins of this people, and confess only in a sentimental way, (as one would solace an evening sadness by playing some sweet and minor melody,) then we may fear that God has indeed forsaken his people. But if we shall honestly confess our real sins; if we propose to cleanse ourselves from them; if we do not make prayer a substitute for action, but an incitement to it; if we rise from our knees this day more zealous for temperance, for honesty, for real brotherhood, for pure and undefiled religion, and for that which is the sum and child of them all, regulating liberty to all men, then will the clouds begin to break, and we shall see the blue shining through, and the sun, ere long, driving away the tumultuous clouds, shall come back in triumph, and like one for a moment cast down but now lifted up for victory.

1. It is well, then, that every one of us make this day the beginning of a solemn review of his own life, and the tendencies of his own conduct and character. A general repentance of national sins should follow, rather than precede, a personal and private conviction of our own individual transgressions. For it has been found not difficult for men to repent of other people's sins; but it is found somewhat difficult and onerous to men to repent of their own sins. We are all of us guilty before God of pride, of selfishness, of vanity, of passions unsubdued, of worldliness in manifold forms, and of strife. We have been caught in the stream, and swept out into an ocean of thoughts and feelings which cannot bear the inquest of God's judgment-day. And we have lived in them almost unrebuked. Each man will find his own life full of repentable sins unrepented of.

2. We should take solemn account of our guilt in the great growth of social laxity, and vice, and crime, in our great cities. We have loved ease rather than duty. Every American citizen is by birth a sworn officer of State. Every man is a policeman. If bad men have had impunity; if the vile have controlled our municipal affairs; if by our delinquencies and indolence justice has been perverted, and our cities are full of great public wickedness, then we cannot put the guilt away from our own consciences. We have a partnership in the conduct of wicked men, unless we have exhausted proper and permissible means of forestalling and preventing it. And I think every citizen of such a city as this, looking upon intemperance, upon vice, upon lewdness, upon gambling, upon the monstrous wickednesses that ferment at the bottom of society, should feel that he has some occasion to repent of his own delinquency and moral indifference.

3. We may not refuse to consider the growth of corrupt passions in connection with the increase of commercial prosperity. Luxury, extravagance, ostentation, and corruption of morals in social life, have given alarming evidence of a

premature old age in a young country. The sins of a nation are always the sins of certain central passions. In one age they break out in one way, and in another age in another way; but they are the same central sins, after all. The corrupt passions which lead in the Southern States to all the gigantic evils of slavery, in Northern cities break out in other forms, not less guilty before God, because of a less public nature. The same thing that leads to the oppression of the operative, leads to oppression on the plantation. The grinding of the poor, the advantages which capital takes of labor, the oppression of the farm, the oppression of the road, the oppression of the shop, the oppression of the ship, are all of the same central nature, and as guilty before God as the more systematic and overt oppressions of the plantation. It is the old human heart that sins, always, North or South; and the nature of pride and of dishonesty are universal. Therefore we have our own account to render.

4. There is occasion for alarm and for humiliation before God, in the spread of avarice among our people. The intense eagerness to amass wealth; the growing indifference of morals as to methods; the gradual corruption of moral sense, so that property and interest supersede moral sense, and legislate and judge what is right and wrong; the use of money for bribery, for bribing electors and elected; the terrible imputations which lie against many of our courts, that judges walk upon gold, and then sit upon gold in the judgment-seat; the use of money in legislation; and the growing rottenness of politics from the lowest village concern to matters of national dimension, from constables to the Chief Magistrate of these United States—is this all to be confessed only in a single smooth sentence?

Such is the wantonness and almost universality of avarice as a corrupting agent in public affairs, that it behooves every man to consider his responsibilities before God in this matter. The very planks between us and the ocean are worm-eaten and rotting, when avarice takes hold of public integrity; for avarice is that sea-worm, ocean-bred, and swarming innumerable, that will pierce the toughest planks, and bring the stoutest ships to foundering. Our foundations are crumbling. The sills on which we are building are ready to break. We need reformation in the very beginnings and elements of society. If in other parts of our land they are in danger of going down by avarice in one form, we are in danger of going down by avarice in another form.

Our people are vain, and much given to boasting; and because they love flatteries, those deriving from them honor and trust, are too fond of feeding their appetite for praise. Thus it comes to pass that we hear the favorable side of our doings and character, and become used to a flattering portrait. Men grow popular who have flowing phrases of eulogy. Men who speak unpalatable truths are disliked; and if they have power to make the public conscience uncomfortable, they are said to abuse the liberty of free speech—for it is the liberty of fanning men to sleep that is supposed to be legitimate: the liberty of waking men out of sleep is supposed to be license! And yet we shall certainly die by the sweetness of flattery; and if we are healed, it must be by the bitterness of faithful speech. There is tonic in the things that men do not love to hear; and there is damnation in the things that wicked men love to hear. Free speech is to a great people what winds are to oceans and malarial regions, which waft away the elements of disease, and bring new elements of health. And where free speech is stopped miasma is bred, and death comes fast.

5. But upon a day of national fasting and confession, we are called to consider not alone our individual and social evils, but also those which are national. And justice requires that we should make mention of the sins of this nation on every side, past and present. I should violate my own convictions, if, in the presence of more nearly present and more exciting influences, I should neglect to mention the sins of this nation against the Indian, who, as much as the slave, is dumb, but who, unlike the slave, has almost none to think of him, and to speak of his wrongs. We must remember that we are the only historians of the wrongs of the Indian—we that commit them. And our history of the Indian nations of this country, is like the inquisitor's history of his own trials of innocent victims. He leaves out the rack, and the groans, and the anguish, and the unutterable wrongs, and puts but his own glozing view in his journal. We have heaped up the account of treachery and cruelty on their part, but we have not narrated the

provocations, the grinding intrusions, and the misunderstood interpretations of their policy, on our part. Every crime in the calendar of wrong which a strong people can commit against a weak one, has been committed by us against them. We have wasted their substance; we have provoked their hostility, and then chastised them for their wars; we have compelled them to peace ignominiously; we have formed treaties with them only to be broken; we have filched their possessions. In our presence they have wilted and wasted. A heathen people have experienced at the side of a Christian nation, almost every evil which one people can commit against another.

Admit the laws of race; admit the laws of advancing civilization as fatal to all barbarism; admit the indocility of the savage; admit the rude edges of violent men who form the pioneer advance of a great people, and the intrinsic difficulties of managing a people whose notions and customs and laws are utterly different from our own, and then you have only explained how the evil has been done, but you have not changed its guilt, nor fact. The mischief has been done, and this is simply the excuse. It is a sorry commentary upon a Christian nation, and indeed, upon religion itself, that the freest and most boastfully religious people on the globe are absolutely fatal to any weaker people that they touch. What would be thought of a man who, when he became converted to Christianity, was dangerous to the next man's pocket? What would be thought of a man who, when he became perfect, was a swindler and a robber? And what must be the nature of that Christianization which makes this Republic a most dangerous neighbor to nations weaker than ourselves? We are respectful to strength, and thieves and robbers to weakness. It is not safe for any to trust our magnanimity and generosity. We have no chivalry. We have avarice; we have haughty arrogance; we have assumptive ways; and we have a desperate determination to live, to think only of our own living, and to sweep with the besom of destruction whatever happens to be where we would put our foot.

Nor is this confined to the Indian. The Mexicans have felt the same rude foot. This nation has employed its gigantic strength with almost no moral restriction. Our civilization has not begotten humanity and respect for others' rights, nor a spirit of protection to the weak.

It is quite in vain to say that the land from which we sprung did the same as we are doing. A wicked daughter is not excused because she had a wicked mother. We boast of the Anglo-Saxon race; and if bone and muscle, an indomitable sense of personal liberty, and a disposition to do what we please, are themes for Christian rejoicing, then the Anglo-Saxon may well rejoice. There are sins that belong to races; there are sins that belong to peoples; there are sins that belong to generations of the same people; and the sins that I have enumerated, are sins that belong to our stock, to our kind.

But God never forgets what we most easily forget. Either the moral government over nations is apocryphal, or judgments are yet to be visited upon us for the wrongs done to the Indian.

6. But I am now come to the most alarming and most fertile cause of national sin—slavery. We are called by our Chief Magistrate to humble ourselves before God for our sins. This is not only a sin, but it is a fountain from which have flown so many sins that we cannot rightly improve this day without a consideration of them.

In one and the same year, 1620, English ships landed the Puritans in New England, and negro slaves in Virginia—two seeds of the two systems that were destined to find here a growth and strength unparalleled in history. It would have seemed almost a theatric arrangement, had these oppugnant elements, Puritan liberty and Roman servitude—(for, whatever men may say, American slavery is not Hebrew slavery; it is Roman slavery. We borrowed every single one of the elemental principles of our system of slavery from the Roman law, and not from the old Hebrew. The fundamental feature of the Hebrew system was that the slave was a man, and not a chattel, while the fundamental feature of the Roman system was that he was a chattel, and not a man. The essential principle of the old Mosaic servitude made it the duty of the master to treat his servants as men, and to instruct them in his own religion, and in the matters of his own household; while the essential principle of Roman servitude allowed the master to treat his servants to all intents and purposes as chattels, goods)—it would have seemed, I say, almost a theatric arrangement had these oppugnant elements, Puritan liberty and Roman servitude, divided the land between them, and, inspiring different governments, grown up different nations, in contrast, that the world might see this experiment fairly compared and worked out to the bitter end.

But it was not to be so. The same Government has nourished both elements. Our Constitution nourished twins. It carried Africa on its left bosom, and Anglo-Saxony on its right bosom; and these two, drawing milk from the same bosom, have waxed strong, and stand to-day federated into the one republic. One side of the body politic has grown fair, and healthy, and strong: the other side has grown up as a wen grows, and the wart, vast, the vaster the weaker. And this nation is like a strong man with one side paralyzed, but nourished and carried along by the help of the other side.

We who dwell in the North are not without responsibility for this sin. Its wonderful growth, and the arrogance of its claims, have been in part through our delinquency. And our business to-day is not to find fault with the South, I am not discussing this matter with reference to them at all, but only with reference to our own individual profit. Because the South loved money, they augmented this evil; and because the North loved money, and that quiet which befits industry and commerce, she has refused to insist upon her moral convictions, in days past, and yielded to every demand, carrying slavery forward in this nation. You and I are guilty of the spread of slavery unless we have exerted, normally and legitimately, every influence in our power against it. If we have said, "To agitate the question imperils manufacturing, imperils shipping, imperils real estate, imperils quiet and peace," and then have sacrificed purity and honesty; if we have bought the right to make money here by letting slavery spread and grow there, we have been doing just the same thing that they have; for they have held slaves for the sake of money, and we have permitted them to hold them for just the same reason—money, *money*. It has been one gigantic bargain, only working out in different ways, North and South. It is for us just as much as for them that the slave works; and we acquiesce. We clothe ourselves with the cotton which the slave tills. Is he scorched? is he lashed? does he water the crop with his sweat and tears? It is you and I that wear the shirt and consume the luxury. Our looms and our factories are largely built on the slave's bones. We live on his labor. I confess I see no way to escape a part of the responsibility for slavery. I feel guilty in part for this system. If the relinquishment of the articles which come from slave labor would tend even remotely to abridge or end the evil, I would without hesitation forego every one; but I do not see that it would help the matter. I am an unwilling partner in the slave system. I take to myself a part of the sin; I confess it before God; and pray for some way to be opened by which I may be freed from that which I hate bitterly.

But this state of facts makes it to-day eminently proper for us to confess our wrong and sin done to the slave. All the wrongs, the crimes of some, the abuse of others, the neglect, the misuse, the ignorance, the separations, the scourgings— these cannot be rolled into a cloud to overhang the South alone. Every one of us has something to confess. Those who have been most scrupulous, if God should judge their life, their motives, and their conduct, would find that they, too, had some account in this great bill of slavery. The whole nation is guilty. There is not a lumberman on the verge of Maine, not a settler on the far distant northern prairies, not an emigrant on the Pacific, that is not politically and commercially in alliance with this great evil. If you put poison into your system in any way, there is not a nerve that is not touched by it; there is not a muscle that does not feel it; there is not a bone, nor a tissue, nor one single part nor parcel of your whole body, that can escape it. And our body politic is pervaded with this black injustice, and every one of us is more or less, directly or indirectly, willingly or unwillingly, implicated in it. And when it comes to the question of confession, we have a great deal to confess before we cast reproaches upon the South. And while I hold Southern citizens to the full and dreadful measure of their guilt before God, and would, if I were settled there, tell them their sin as plainly as I tell you your sin, it is for us to-day, and here, to consider our own part in this matter; and to that I shall speak during the residue of my remarks.

Originally, we were guilty of active participation in slavery. It seems very strange to take up the old Boston books, and read the history of slavery in Boston. Not that they have not slaves there now; but they are white! Once they were African and involuntary: now they are political and voluntary. We of the North early abandoned the practice of holding slaves. But it is said that ours is a cheap philanthropy; that having got quit of our slaves by selling them, we turn round and preach to the South about the sin of holding theirs. There is nothing more atrociously false than such a charge as that. There is nothing more illustrious in the history of the state of New York, and of the Northern states generally, than the method by which they freed themselves from slavery. This state decreed liberty at a certain period, and then passed a most stringent act making it an offence, the penalty attached to which no one would willingly inherit, for a man to convey away, or in any manner whatsoever to sell out of the State, a person held as a slave; and if a man, anticipating the day of emancipation, wished to make a journey to the South with his slaves, he had to give bonds for their return before he went away, and had to give an account when he came back, if they did not come with him. Nothing could have been more humane than the provision that the slave should not be sold out of the state of New York, but should be emancipated in it. And what is true of New York in this respect, is true of the States generally that emancipated their slaves.

But we of the North participated in the beginnings, and we are in part guilty of the subsequent spread of the system of slavery. When our Government came into our hands, after the struggle of the Revolution, we had gone through such a school in order to assert our political independence, that the head, the conscience, and the heart of this nation, in the main, were right on the subject of human liberties. And at the adoption of the Federal Constitution, nearly seventy-five years ago, it might be said that, with local and insignificant exceptions, there was but one judgment, one wish, and one prophetic expectation—namely, that this whole territory should be dedicated to liberty, and that every compliance or compromise was not to be made in the interest of oppression, but was to be made only to give oppression time to die decently; and that was the spirit and intent of every compliance or compromise that was made.

The schools, the academies, the colleges, the intelligence, the *brain* of this nation, at that time, were in the North—and in the North I include all the territory this side of Mason's and Dixon's line. We were then the thinking part of this country. The church, the religious institutions, the moral elements that never parted from the posterity of the Puritans, were then, also, in the North. When our Constitution was adopted; when the wheels of our mighty confederacy were adjusted, and the pendulum began to swing—at that time the public sentiment was in favor of liberty. All the institutions were prepared for liberty, and all the public men were on the side of liberty. And to the North, because she was the brain; to the North, because she was the moral centre and heart of this confederacy, was given this estate—for in the first twenty-five or thirty years the North predominated in the counsels of the nation, and fixed the institutions, as the South have fixed their policy since. What, then, having this trust put into her hands, is the account of her stewardship which the North has to render? If now, after three-quarters of a century have passed away, God should summon the North to his judgment-bar, and say, "I gave you a continent in which, though there was slavery, it was perishing; I gave you a nation in which the sentiment was for liberty and against oppression; I gave you a nation in which the tendencies were all for freedom and against slavery; I gave you the supreme intelligence; I gave you the moral power in a thousand pulpits, a thousand books, a thousand Bibles; and I said, 'Take this nation, administer it, and render up your trust'"—if now, after three-quarters of a century have passed away, God should summon the North to his judgment-bar and say this, what would be the account which she would have to render—the North, that was strongest in the head and in the heart, and that took as fair a heritage as men ever attempted to administer? To-day, liberty is bankrupt, and slavery is rampant, in this nation. And do you creep out and say, "We are not to blame"? What have you been doing with your intelligence, your books, your

schools, your Bibles, your missionaries, your ministers?
Where, where is the artillery that God Almighty gave you,
park upon park, and what has become of this nation under
your care, that were provided and prepared for that special
emergency? I take part of the blame to myself. Much as I love
the North—(and I love every drop of Puritan blood that the
world ever saw; because it seems to me that Puritan blood
means blood touched with Christ's blood)—I take to myself
part of the shame, and mourn over the delinquency of the
North, that having committed to it the eminent task of preserving the liberties of this nation, they have sacrificed them.
For to-day there are more slave states than there were states
confederated when this nation came together. And instead of
having three or four hundred thousand slaves, we have more
than four millions; instead of a traffic suppressed, you and I
are witnesses to-day of a traffic to be reopened—of rebellion,
treasonable war, bloodshed, separate independence, for the
sake of reopening the African slave-trade. So came this country into the hands of the North in the beginning, and so it is
going out of her hands in the end. There never was such a
stewardship: and if this confederacy shall be broken up; if the
Gulf states shall demand a division of the country, and the intermediate states shall go off, and two empires shall be established, no steward that has lived since God's sun shone on the
earth, will have such an account to render of an estate taken
under such favorable auspices, as the North will have to render of this great national estate which was committed to her
trust. It is an astounding sin! It is an unparalleled guilt! The
vengeance and zeal of our hearts toward the South might be
somewhat tempered by the reflection that we have been so
faithless, so wicked, and that our account must stand before
God in the end, as it does stand, for delinquency in our duty.

That is not the worst. That is the material side. The next
step is this: that we have stood in the North with all the elements of power, boasting of our influence, and really swaying,
in many respects, the affairs of this continent; and yet we have
not only seen this tremendous increase of slavery, but we have
permitted the doctrines of liberty themselves to take paralysis
and leprosy. And to-day, *to-day*, TO-DAY, if you were to put it
to the vote of this whole people, I do not know as you could

get a majority for any doctrine of liberty but this: that each
man has a right to be free himself. The great doctrine of
liberty is concisely expressed by the Declaration of Independence; and it is this: that all men are free; born with equal
political rights, of life, liberty, and the pursuit of happiness.
And there is no true right that is not founded on this doctrine: "That liberty which is good for me, is indispensable for
everybody." A right love of liberty inspires a man to say, "I
will have it, and everybody shall have it." That is a poor love
of liberty that makes a man a champion for the liberty of
those that are capable of asserting their own liberty. But I
doubt whether, so corrupt are the times, you could get a popular vote for the liberty of all men. Why should you? I am
ashamed of what I must speak. The pulpit has been so prosti-
tuted, and so utterly apostatized from the very root and substance of Christianity, that it teaches the most heathen
notions of liberty; and why should you expect that the great
masses of men would be better informed on this subject than
they are? Do you believe that George Washington, were he
living, would now be able to live one day in the city of
Charleston, if he uttered the sentiments that he used to hold?
He would not. He would be denounced as a traitor, and
swung up on the nearest lamp-post. Do you suppose that one
single man that signed the Declaration of Independence, if
living, could go through the South to-day, repeating the sentiments contained in that document? The lives of the signers
of the Declaration of Independence would not be worth one
day's lease in Alabama, Louisiana, Carolina, or Florida, if they
were there to say the things plainly which they said when they
framed this government, so utterly have the South vomited
up their political views; so radically have they changed their
notions. Was this country committed to our care? and is such
the lesson that we have taught our pupils? Shall the schoolmaster render back the scholars that he undertook to teach,
with their minds debauched, and say that he was not responsible for what they learned? And if any part of the country was
responsible for the education of the whole, it was the free-
schooled, million-churched North. And the result of our instruction is this: slavery has spread gigantically, and the
doctrine of liberty is so corrupted, that to-day nothing is

more disreputable in the high places of this nation, than that very doctrine. And at last, when the sleeper, long snoring, having been awaked, raised himself up, and like all new zealots, somewhat intemperately made crusade for liberty, the land was so agitated, and with such surprise was this expression of the public sentiment of the North received, that the Chief Magistrate of this nation declared that we were the cause of all the trouble!

But this is not all. The most serious, the most grievous charge, is yet to be made upon the North. So far have we been delinquent in the trust that God committed to us, that the very centre of hope and expectation of success for humanity has been burned out; that from the very fountain out of which flowed, as from the heart of Christ, the first drops that were to cleanse men from oppressions, has been extracted in our day, and in our North very largely, the whole spirit of humanity which breathes freedom.

It ill becomes, I think, one profession to rail against another, or the members of the same profession to rail against each other. I have no accusations to make against any; but I will forsake my profession, for the time being, and stand as a man among men, to lift up my voice, with all my heart and soul, against any man who, professing to be ordained to preach, preaches out of Christ's Gospel the doctrines of human bondage. When the Bible is opened that all the fiends of hell may, as in a covered passage, walk through it to do mischief on the earth, I say, blessed be infidels! Where men take the Bible to teach me to disown childhood; where men take the Bible to teach me that it is lawful to buy and sell men, that marriage is an impossible state, that laws cannot permit it, and that customs cannot permit it; where the Bible is held as the sacred document and constitutional guarantee of a system which makes it impossible that a man should go up on the path of development; where the Bible is made to stand and uphold one man in saying to another, "You are good for me in that proportion in which you are able to use the spade and the hoe, and I forbid you to read and expand your mind because knowledge will render you unmarketable;" where, according to the Bible, men, women, and children are legal tenders in the market, and anything that lessens their value there is an impediment, so that marriage and its sanctities are regarded as over-refinements; where a man takes the Bible and lays it in the path over which men are attempting to walk from Calvary up to the gate of heaven—I declare that I will do by the Bible what Christ did by the temple: I will take a whip of cords, and I will drive out of it every man that buys and sells men, women, and children; and if I cannot do that, I will let the Bible go, as God let the temple go, to the desolating armies of its adversaries. And I do not wonder that after so long an experience of the world, men who bombard universal humanity, men who plead for the outrage of slavery, men who grope to find under crowns and sceptres the infamous doctrines of servitude—I do not wonder that they are pestered with the idea of man's individuality. Why, that minister who preaches slavery out of the Bible is the father of every infidel in the community! I tell you that the most intelligent people in the world are infidels. In Germany I will pick out nineteen out of every twenty democrats who are infidels. And why? Not because they do not believe really in the Bible, but because the priests that the kings ordain in Germany have built up the whole kingly fabric and the archepiscopal throne on the Bible; and when the democrat sees the oppression of the king, and feels the yoke of the priest, and protests against them, they stop his mouth by sticking the leaves of the Bible into it! So he comes to hate the Bible, not for what it is in reality, but because it is made the bulwark of oppression; and he spurns it that he may answer the call of God in his own nature—for to be free is a part of the sovereign call and election that God has given to every man who has a sense of his birthright and immortality. And in a community where the minister finds reason in the Bible for slavery, you may depend upon it that one of two things will take place: either there will be an inquisition to redeem the Bible from such abominable prostitution, or else the Bible will be spurned and kicked from under the feet of men, as it ought to be.

"I came to open the prison-doors," said Christ; and that is the text on which men justify shutting them and locking them. "I came to loose those that are bound;" and that is the text out of which men spin cords to bind men, women, and children. "I came to carry light to them that are in darkness, and deliverance to the oppressed;" and that is the Book from out of which they argue, with amazing ingenuity, all the infernal meshes and snares by which to keep men in bondage. It is pitiful.

A hunter scorns a pigeon-roost; because he would fain have some reward in skill and ingenuity; and he feels that to fire into a pigeon-roost is shocking butchery. But for that feeling I should like no better amusement than to answer the sermons of men who attempt to establish the right of slavery out of the Bible. It would be simple butchery! A man must be addicted to blood who would fire a twenty-four pounder into a flock of blackbirds or crows!

Now what has been the history of the Book but this: that wherever you have had an untrammeled Bible, you have had an untrammeled people; and that wherever you have had a trammeled Bible, you have had a trammeled people? Where you have had a Bible that the priests interpreted, you have had a king: where you have had a Bible that the common people interpreted; where the family has been the church; where father and mother have been God's ordained priests; where they have read its pages freely from beginning to end without gloss or commentary, without the church to tell them how, but with the illumination of God's Spirit in their hearts; where the Bible has been in the household, and read without hindrance by parents and children together—there you have had an indomitable yeomanry, a state that would not have a tyrant on the throne, a government that would not have a slave or a serf in the field. Wherever the Bible has been allowed to be free; wherever it has been knocked out of the king's hand, and out of the priest's hand, it has carried light like the morning sun, rising over hill and vale, round and round the world; and it will do it again! And yet there come up in our midst men that say to us that the Bible is in favor of slavery. And as men that make a desperate jump go back and run before they jump, so these men have to go back to the twilight of creation and take a long run; and when they come to their jump, their strength is spent and they but stumble!

It is in consideration of this wanton change which has taken place (and which ought never to have been permitted to take place, in view of the instruments that God put into our hands, and in view of the solemn responsibility that he has put upon us)—it is in consideration of this change which has taken place in the material condition of the country, and in the opinions of this people respecting the great doctrine of liberty, and the worse change which has corrupted in part the church at its very core, that I argue to-day the necessity of humiliation and repentance before God.

I shall first confess my own sin. Sometimes men think I have been unduly active. I think I have been indolent. In regard to my duty in my personal and professional life, I chide myself for nothing more than because I have not been more alert, more instant in season and out of season. If sometimes in intemperate earnestness I have wounded the feelings of any; if I have seemed to judge men harshly, for that I am sorry. But for holding the slave as my brother; for feeling that the Spirit of God is the spirit of liberty; for loving my country so well that I cannot bear to see a stain or a blot upon her; for endeavoring to take the raiment of heaven wherewith to scour white as snow the morals of my times, and to cleanse them to the uttermost of all spot and apsersion—for that I have no tears to shed. I only mourn that I have not been more active and zealous, and I do not wish to separate myself from my share of the responsibility. I am willing to take my part of the yoke and burden. I will weep my tears before God, and pray my prayers of sincere contrition and penitence, that I have not been more faithful to liberty and religion in the North and the whole land. And you must make this a day of penitence. You must do your part.

But be sure of one thing: He that would not come when the sisters sent, but tarried, has come, and the stone is rolled away, and he stands by the side of the sepulchre. He has called, "Liberty, come forth!" and, bound yet hand and foot, it has come forth; and that same sovereign voice is saying, "Loose him, and let him go!" and from out of the tomb, the dust, the night, and the degradation, the better spirit of this people is now emerging at the voice of God. We have heard his call, we know the bidding, and Death itself cannot hold us any longer; and there is before us, we may fain believe, a new lease of life, a more blessed national existence. That there will not be concussions, and perhaps some garments rolled in blood, I will not undertake to say: there may be some such things as these; but, brethren, this nation is not going to perish. This confederacy is not going to be broken and shivered like a crystal vase that can never be put together again. We are to be tested and tried; but if we are in earnest, and if we stand as martyrs and confessors before us have stood, bearing witness in this thing for Christ, know ye that ere long God will appear, and be the leader and captain of our salvation, and we shall have given back to us this whole land, healed, restored to its right mind, and sitting at the feet of Jesus.

Love God, love men, love your dear fatherland; to-day confess your sins toward God, toward men, toward your own fatherland; and may that God that loves to forgive and forget, hear our cries and our petitions which we make, pardon the past, inspire the future, and bring the latter-day glory through a regenerated zeal and truth, inspired by his Spirit, in this nation. Amen, and amen.

DAVID EINHORN

War With Amalek!

A Sermon Delivered on Sabbath P. Zachor, 5624.
(March 19th, 1864.)
in the Temple of the Congregation Keneseth Israel,
Philadelphia

———

TEXT:— *"God's is the war with Amalek from gen-*
eration to generation!" (EXODUS, chap. XVII, v. 16.)

AMALEK is represented in the Bible as the arch-foe of Israel, for he inflicted upon them the most unheard of cruelties, without having been in the least offended by the party attacked; he assaulted the champions of God when they were in a defenceless condition, in a state of utter exhaustion. To carry on a war against such a relentless foe is an act of self-defence, not of vengeance. Hence the war-cry: "War for God with Amalek from generation to generation!" It was a war for the existence of God's people, and hence a war for God Himself. In consequence of this arch-enmity against God and His people, Amalek has assumed the type of the evil principle among Israel. It is Amalek's seed, wherever the evil and wicked rule; wherever, especially, rude violence with cheaply bought courage makes war upon defenceless innocence, and wherever a majority in the service of falsehood directs its blows with ruthless fist against the very face of a weak minority. And thus even to-day the war-cry is heard: "God's is the war with Amalek from generation to generation!" Let us then consider how *this* war should be carried on in our own country and under existing circumstances.

FIRST,—the necessity is presented to us of a war against the *Enslavement of Race*, which has brought the Republic to the verge of destruction, against an Amalek-seed which is turned into a blood-drenched dragon-seed. Or is it anything else but

665

a deed of Amalek, rebellion against God, to enslave beings created in His image, and to degrade them to a state of beasts having no will of their own? Is it anything else but an act of ruthless and wicked violence, to reduce defenceless human beings to a condition of merchandize, and relentlessly to tear them away from the hearts of husbands, wives, parents, and children? We are told, that this crime rests upon a historical right! But, pray, can ancient custom indeed convert an atrocious wrong into right? Does a disease, perchance, cease to be an evil on account of its long duration? Is not the assertion that whatever our ancestors regarded as good, true and admissible, must be so also for us, however much reason and conscience may militate against it—is not that assertion an insult to all mental and moral progress of humanity? If such principles were true, could it ever have been possible to cease burning heretics and witches, aye! even to sacrifice the blood of one's own children? Does not the very establishment of our Republic rest upon the most emphatic protest against so-called Historic Right? Was not the enslavement of Israel in Egypt equally a historic right for Pharaoh and his mercenaries, and did God's judgment not burst upon Israel's oppressors just at the time when this reputed right had been transmitted through centuries? No! justice and truth may be perverted for a long space of time, but not forever. It is positive powers which sooner or later must triumph over ancient prejudices, over usurped titles and privileges, over hallowed atrocities. History is God's tribunal for the nations, and teaches us—often in the most awful manner—the ultimate fate of such usurped rights, a fate which Holy Writ proclaims even to infant mankind in the words: "God visiteth the transgressions of the fathers upon the children unto the third and fourth generation," meaning, as our Rabbins add by way of illustration, אוחזין כמעשי אבותיהם, when the children cling to the fatal inheritance.

But it is still further asserted: slavery is an institution sanctioned by the Bible, hence war against it is a war against, and not for God!

It has ever been a strategy of the advocate of a bad cause to take refuge from the spirit of the Bible to its letter, as criminals among the ancient heathen nations would seek protection near the altars of their gods. Can *that* Book hallow the enslavement of any race, which sets out with the principles, that Adam was created in the image of God, and that all men have descended from *one* human pair? Can *that* Book mean to raise the whip and forge chains, which proclaims, with flaming words, in the name of God: "break the bonds of oppression, let the oppressed go free, and tear every yoke!" Can *that* Book justify the violent separation of a child from its human mother, which, when speaking of birds' nests, with admirable humanity commands charitable regard for the feelings even of an animal mother? It is true, the institution of slavery was introduced, as legally existing, into the Mosaic Code; but only for this reason, because the deeply rooted evil could not be at once eradicated, and only with the intent to surround the detestable institution with ordinances mitigating the evil; as for instance, the provision according to which a slave should be free when his master had smitten out his tooth; and another, prohibiting the delivery of a fugitive slave to his master.

If it should be asserted that the Bible approves and sanctions everything it allows and tolerates, we would be compelled to the further assertion, that it approves, nay, hallows also polygamy, blood-revenge, and even royalty, which it emphatically repudiates; and thus irreconcilable contradictions would arise between its principles and practical provisions. There is an ancient maxim in Judaism: לא נתנה תורה למלאבי השרת "The law was not given for Angels;" the law of God was intended for human beings, and is, therefore, a law of education, affording to the human mind the most powerful impulse for development, and, in this spirit, expanding itself more widely and beautifully from its very innermost nature. It is only the slaves of the letter that deny this capability of development,—it is only they that convert the letter of the Bible into a slave-whip.

And what shall we say of that perversion which represents negro-slavery as sanctioned by the curse of Noah against a son of Ham? That the negroes are descendants of Ham is purely a fiction; and, besides, that curse is limited only upon Canaan, the progenitor of the Canaanites and Phenicians.

And even aside from all this—how can any command, or

even only a moral justification be derived from a curse or even a prophecy? Was the enslavement of Israel in Egypt less criminal, because God in a vision revealed to Abraham this bitter lot of his children? and did not God at the same time when He made this revelation, proclaim also the heavy punishment which was to be inflicted upon their oppressors? No! God commands no war against the black color, but against the dark deeds of Amalek.

But, alas! we have, in our own days, to struggle against Amalek also in another respect, namely: against the attempt at the *Enslavement of the Conscience*, against religious hatred and religious violence. Yes, my friends! however startling it may appear in this Republic, it is nevertheless true: a number of ministers of a Christian sect—the majority of Christian Ministers in this country no doubt condemn such attempt as much as we do—design nothing less than to convert our Constitution, the palladium of liberty of conscience, into a prison-fortress of religious tyranny. They desire, as they tell us, to improve the Constitution, but in reality to destroy its very inmost spirit, by an amendment recognizing the American nation as a Christian nation, the founder of the Christian Religion as the ruler of all, and his will as the highest law of the land; and that this principle should be the test for oaths of office and in all other matters! Would not the fathers of the Republic, if they could rise from their graves, utter a threefold woe! over such a devise;—would they not call unto the originators of such a detestable scheme with indignation and in a voice of thunder: "We have nourished and brought up children, and they have rebelled against us!"? If such a device should meet with success, the result would be, that not alone we, the professors of the One in Unity, but also the thousands, aye! the hundreds of thousands who, though bearing the name of Christians, yet cannot recognize the divine authority of the founder of Christianity, would become utterly disabled to take the oath on the Constitution and, consequently, to become citizens; America would become not merely a Christian State, but a real Church State, and Washington, a second Rome;—the President of the United States would be converted into a Pope, and the Congress, into an Ecclesiastical Tribunal! Aye! whenever such a theory shall have once been adopted, an irrepressible conflict to the death would, sooner or later, arise even between the different Christian sects. In that case also the majority would design to enslave the minority, considering that the public offices would be regarded as clerical prebends, and the most faithful believers—and as such those stronger in number always represent themselves—would claim for themselves the fattest benefices; and this country, hitherto the pride and glory of the world, would, sooner or later, behold a civil war, the horrors of which would compare with those of the present war as raging hurricanes with the soft whisper of a rustling leaf. Then the citizens would appear at the ballot-box with a Bible in one hand and a revolver in the other, and the blood-stained victors celebrate their triumphs by the bon-fires of burning churches. And yet, those men have the effrontery to demand their so-called amendment of the Constitution with the view of securing peace, tranquility, justice, and the welfare of the United States! As though the present bloody conflict and the ruling corruption owed their origin to a want of Christian belief;—as though the ministers of the South, in their sermons in defence of Slavery, did not refer to the authority of Christianity, just as the ministers of the North do in theirs against that institution; as though religion could at all gain in ennobling power, by presenting to those called upon to drink her heavenly dew, the fatness of the earth as an alluring bait,—by degrading it to a milk-yielding cow, to a net for office-fishing; in fine, to an article of trade, in order to open wide the gate for smuggling even in the most sacred domain! And what age is selected for such revolutionary schemes? The same age in which one state after another of Europe casts off the rusty chains of religious violence:—the very moment in which America arms herself to burst the ancient negro-fetters! While the dead rise again, the living are to be buried; the place of the so-called sons of Ham is to be assigned to the sons of Abraham, the sons of Shem, in whose tents Japhet dwells! Yea, it is but of recent date that the Haman cry was heard, that we had our peculiar customs, and hence, were a peculiar nation! It is true, we are a peculiar race, and indeed! we need not be ashamed of this peculiarity; for our race is the ancient depositary and mediator of civilization for the nations;

our race has given to the world its most precious spiritual treasures; and from our race have sprung the religions of all the civilized nations of the earth. But ever since the destruction of the Temple and our dispersion all over the globe, we have not been, nor do we desire to be, a peculiar *nation*; we do not desire to return to Palestine, but, as proclaimed by the prophet, be among the nations as the dew from God, as the showers upon the grass, that all of them may be blessed through the descendants of Abraham with the highest salvation. It is exclusively the bond of Religion that still holds our members entwined, and it is but natural that, in consequence, we should have also peculiar customs; but these customs have as little in common with a peculiar nationality as the common customs of the Christians of all countries. If to-day a war were to break out between America and England, the American Jew would as readily fight against his English fellow-believer, as in our day the Prussian Jew fights against his Danish coreligionist.

You are all—thus the Haman cry further maintains— *traders*, and this fact also testifies your peculiar nationality! Indeed! we do not know at which to be more astonished, at the narrow-mindedness or the ignorance with which that assertion passes such a condemnatory judgment over a whole religious community. To designate a race which is the guardian of the highest idea of mankind, which has a thousand times sacrificed life and fortune for that idea, and erected spiritual monuments which the world admires and worships; to designate a race that calls heroes of the spirit its own who reach far beyond centuries and thousands of years:—contemptuously to designate that race as a nation of traders is, to use a soft expression, an unmeasured absurdity. Moses, the greatest lawgiver of the world; David, the great king and bard, whose hymns even to this day resound in all Synagogues, Churches and Mosques; the Prophets, whose flaming speeches even to this day bear numberless hearts and souls up to heaven; the Maccabees, the most glorious heroes of the world in the struggle for truth and liberty; the Rabbi of Nazareth, who gave the moral laws of the Jews to numberless heathens, and is worshiped by millions of non-Israelites as their Savior; Jehuda Hallevi, Ibn Ezra, and Maimonides, in whom all the knowledge of their time was centred, and who were regarded as ornaments of their age; Baruch Spinoza, the founder of modern Philosophy, and Moses Mendelsohn, the German Socrates—are they all traders? And are, peradventure, all the modern Jews traders? There is hardly *one* branch in science and art, in the cultivation of which Jews have not distinguished themselves with honor; there is hardly *one* University in civilized Europe, in which Jews do not labor as respected teachers; there is hardly *one* political office—let me refer only to England, France and Holland—which Jews have not occupied, or do still occupy. In Europe the charge is raised against us, that Jewish minds rule the press and exercise their destructive influence upon art, literature and political life; and in this country we are called a nation of traders! Aye! the contemptuous charge is flung into our very faces, that even the founder of the Christian Religion, despite his omniscience, could not help receiving a Jewish thief and devil among his disciples! Why, should that race to which the honor is paid that it had given to the world a Divine Being, be contemptible, because it possessed also a thief and a devil? Do not many nations number among them thieves, and devils, and murderers, and yet, are not entitled to that honor? Should the Jewish race, with its great multitude of divine heroes, not be permitted to possess also moral caricatures without being visited therefor with a wholesale condemnation? Well then, let us make war upon this Amalek; let us meet this newly-budding religious animosity with all honorable weapons at our command! Let us seek to crush, at its very birth, the many-headed serpent which designs to clutch the Eagle in its coils and to kill him in the very hour of a hot and exhausting struggle, as Amalek attacked weary and exhausted Israel after his departure from Egypt! Let us not be lulled into inactivity by a foolish and pernicious feeling of security! Even Moses would not suffer his hands to rest until Amalek was conquered!

But in order to triumph in this struggle, we must not, above all, forget to make war upon the Amalek in our own midst, upon the *Enslavement of the Spirit*. Let us openly confess it, upon American Israel also the words of condemnation may in many regards be pronounced: "Jeshurun waxed fat and forsook the Rock of his salvation!" Crude worldliness has become so predominant among us, that one must often feel tempted to ask: are these members of that race, which once sacrificed everything for its spiritual treasures? There is indeed no want of Synagogues and Congregations; but many believe to have fulfilled all their obligations towards their congregation when they have paid in cash their dues, and take no further interest in its institutions. How many among us have become utterly indifferent to Israel's sublime mission, to carry the divine truths into all parts of the earth, and to glorify the name of God in the eyes of all nations! How many among us, driven on by a restless lust of earthly gain, have lost all sense for man's higher destination, all desire for spiritual elevation! Even young children are often violently torn from their schools to be tied to the yoke of business life, because they cannot too soon learn to worship the almighty dollar! The Sabbath, which again and again quickened ancient Israel with the spirit of God, which again and again protected our forefathers against fatigue and exhaustion, and girded them with strength and courage to break through the hosts of Amalek—the Sabbath has been banished from among us, and now bestows its blessings only upon other denominations, that have inherited it from us, and justly ask us: "Where is your God?" The staff of God has fallen from our hands, and, despite all pomp and glitter, we creep weary and exhausted, sighing and panting, through a vast desert affording no oasis, no refreshing well for us and our wives and children, to become a prey for Amalek. Can it under such circumstances be wondered at, that even domestic fervor, that ancient virtue of Israel, the self-sacrificing conjugal love, the careful attention to the moral and mental culture of those dear to our hearts, the profound reverence for parents, threatens to vanish from our homes? Must not every blossom of the heart and soul droop in such a drought, under such a parching glow? Can it then be wondered at, that the fear of חלול השם, "of the profanation of the name of God,"—a fear which once served the Jew for a mighty bulwark against the most alluring temptations to bring dishonor upon the name of Israel—is so often crushed by the wild boar of the lust of gain? If that fear still existed among us in its ancient power, Jewish smugglers—to adduce but one illustration—would indeed! belong to the greatest curiosities among the present, sad experiences in our country. I do not mean to say, that such great offences are not committed also by members of other denominations as often as, and perhaps oftener than by our own co-religionists; or that the old saying: "Little rogues are brought to punishment whereas big ones are allowed to escape," is not exemplified also in our country—; but the crime is far greater when committed by a Jew, because he must know, that the whole Jewish community is made accountable for his offence, that his act inflicts shame, disgrace and misfortune upon his fellow believers.

Let us then make war also upon the Amalek in our own midst! Let us meet them that bring shame and disgrace upon us and our religious faith, with the fullness of our moral indignation! Let us display, in this hard struggle for our national existence, sentiments of brilliant patriotism, in every respect, and let us never be found wanting whenever patriotism is appealed to for its gifts and for sacrifices. And above all, let us all rise again from the mire of worldliness unto the consciousness of our sublime world-historic mission, to glorify the One in Unity before the eyes of all the world! Then we shall be able to disperse now as in times of yore, with the war cry: ה' נסי "God is my banner!" the enemies of our race and our God, and unweary advance towards the exalted goal, to blot out the remembrance of Amalek, the reign of falsehood and darkness, from under heaven. Amen.

DWIGHT LYMAN MOODY

On Being Born Again

JOHN iii. 3: *"Jesus answered and said unto him, Verily, verily, I say unto thee, Except a man be born again, he can not see the kingdom of God."*

SUPPOSE I put the question to this audience, and ask how many believe in the Word of God, I have no doubt every man and every woman would rise and say, "I believe." There might be an infidel or skeptic here and there, but undoubtedly the great mass would say they believed. Then what are you going to do with this solemn truth, "Except a man be born again, he can not see the kingdom of God," much less inherit it? There are a great many mysteries in the Word of God. There are a great many dark sayings of which we have not yet discovered the depth. But God has put that issue so plainly and simply that he who runs may read if he will. This third chapter of St. John makes the way to Heaven plainer than any other chapter in the Bible; yet there is no truth so much misunderstood, and the church and the world are so troubled about, as this. Let me just say, before I go any further, what regeneration is not. It is not going to church. How many men think they are converted because they go to church! I come in contact with many men who say they are Christians because they go to church regularly. It is a wrong idea that the devil never frequents any place but billiard-halls, saloons, and theatres; wherever the Word of God is preached, He is there. He is in this audience to-day. You may go to church all the days of your life, and yet not be converted. Going to church is not being born again. But there is another class who say, "I don't place my hopes in going to church. I have been baptized, and I think I was regenerated when that took place." Where do those persons get their evidence? Certainly not in the Bible. You can not baptize men into regeneration. If you could, I would go up and down the world and baptize every man, woman, and child; and if I could not do it when they were awake, I would do it while they slept. But the Word says, "Except a man be born again"—born in the Spirit, born in righteousness from above—"he can not see the kingdom of God."

There is another class who say, "I was born again when I was confirmed. I was confirmed when I was five years old." But confirmation is not regeneration. A new birth must be the work of God, and not the work of man. Baptism, confirmation, and other ordinances are right in their place, but the moment you build hope on them instead of on new birth, you are being deceived by Satan. Another man says, "That is not what my hope is based upon; I say my prayers regularly." I suppose there was no man prayed more regularly than Paul did before Christ met him; he was a praying man. But saying prayers is one thing, and praying is another. Saying prayers is not conversion. You may pray from education; your mother may have taught you when you were a little boy. I remember that I could not go to sleep when I was a little boy unless I said my prayers, and yet perhaps the very next word I uttered might be an oath. There is just as much virtue in counting beads as in saying prayers, unless the heart has been regenerated and born again.

There is another class who say, "I read the Bible regularly." Well, reading the Bible is very good, and prayer is very good in its place; but you don't see anything in the Scriptures which says, "Except a man read the Bible he can not see the kingdom of God." There is still another class who say, "I am trying to do the best I can, and I will come out all right." That is not new birth at all; that is not being born of God. Trying to do the best you can is not regeneration. This question of new birth is the most important that ever came before the world, and it ought to be settled in every man's mind. Every one should inquire, Have I been born of the Spirit?—have I passed from death unto life?—or am I building my hopes of Heaven on some form? In the first chapter of Genesis we find God working alone; He went on creating the world all alone. Then we find Christ coming to Calvary alone. His disciples forsook Him, and in redemption He was alone. And when we get to the third chapter of John we find that the work of regeneration is the work of God alone. The Ethiopian can not change his spots; we are born in sin, and the change of heart must come from God. We believe in the good old Gospel.

What man wants is to come to God for this new heart. The moment he gets it he will work for the Lord. He can not help it; it becomes his second nature. Some say, "I would like to have you explain this new birth." Well, I might as well be honest, and own right up that I can not explain it. I have read a great many books and sermons trying to explain the philosophy of it, but they all fail to do it. I don't understand how it is done. I can not understand how God created earth. It staggers me and bewilders me when I think how God created nature out of nothing. But, say the infidels, He did not do it. Then how did He do it? A man came to me in Scotland, and said he could explain it, and I asked him how those rocks are made. He said, "They are made from sand." "What makes the sand?" "Oh!" he replied, "rocks." "Then," I asked him, "what made the first sand?" He couldn't tell. Notwithstanding the philosophy of some people, we do believe that God did create the world. We believe in redemption. We believe that Christ came from the Father, and that He grew up and taught men. We believe He went into the sepulchre and burst the bands of death. You may ask me to explain all this; but I don't know how to do it. You ask me to explain regeneration. I can not do it. But one thing I know—that I have been regenerated. All the infidels and skeptics could not make me believe differently. I feel a different man than I did twenty-one years ago last March, when God gave me a new heart. I have not sworn since that night, and I have no desire to swear. I delight to labor for God, and all the influences of the world can not convince me that I am not a different man. I heard some time ago about four or five commercial travelers going to hear a minister preach. When they got back to their hotel, they began to discuss the sermon. A good many people just go to church for the purpose of discussing those things, but they should remember that they must be spiritually inclined to understand spiritual things. Those travelers came to the wise conclusion that the minister did not know what he was talking about. An old man heard them say they would not believe anything unless they could reason it out, and he went up to them and said: "While I was coming down in the train this morning I noticed in a field some sheep, some geese, some swine, and cattle eating grass. Can you tell me by what process that grass is turned into hair, feathers, wool, and horns?" "No," they answered, "not exactly." "Well, do you believe it is done?" "Oh, yes, we believe that." "But," said the old man, "you said you could not believe anything unless you understood it." "Oh," they answered, "we can not help believing that; we see it." Well, I can not help believing that I am regenerated, because I feel it. Christ could not explain it to Nicodemus, but said to him, "The wind bloweth where it listeth, and thou hearest the sound thereof, but canst not tell whence it cometh and whither it goeth." Can you tell all about the currents of the air? He says it is every one that is born of the Spirit. Suppose, because I never saw the wind, I say it was all false. I have lived nearly forty years, and I never saw the wind. I never saw a man that ever did see it. I can imagine that little girl down there saying, "That man don't know as much as I do. Didn't the wind blow my hat off the other day? Haven't I felt the effects of the wind? Haven't I felt it beating against my face?" And I say you never saw the effects of the wind any more than a child of God felt the Spirit working in his heart. He knows that his eyes have been opened; that he has been born of the Spirit; that he has got another nature, a heart that goes up to God, after he has been born of the Spirit. It seems to me this is perfectly reasonable.

We have a law that no man shall be elected President unless he was born on American soil. I never heard any one complain of that law. We have Germans, Scandinavians, foreigners coming here from all parts of the world, and I never heard a man complain of that law. Haven't we got a right to say who shall reign? Had I any right when I was in England, where a Queen reigns, to interfere? Has a foreigner any right to interfere here? Has not the God of Heaven a right to say how a man shall come into His kingdom, and who shall come? And He says: "Except a man be born again, he can not see the kingdom." How are you going to get in? Going to try to educate men? That is what men are trying to do, but it is not God's way. A man is not much better after he is educated if he hasn't got God in his heart. Other men say, "I will work my way up." That is not God's way, and the only way is God's way—to be born again. Heaven is a prepared place for a prepared people. You take an unregenerated man in Chicago and put him on the crystal pavements of Heaven, and it would be hell! A man that can't bear to spend one Sunday among God's people on earth, with all their imperfections, what is he going to do among those who have made their robes white in the blood of the Lamb? He would say that was hell for him. Take the unregenerated man and put him into the very shadow of the Tree of Life, and he wouldn't want to sit there. A man who is born of the Spirit becomes a citizen of another world. He has been translated into new life, taken out of the power of darkness, and translated into the Kingdom of Light. Haven't you seen all around you men who had become suddenly and entirely changed?

Just draw a picture: Suppose we go down into one of these alleys—and I have been into some pretty dark holes down here in this alley that used to lie back of Madison street, and I have seen some pretty wretched homes. Go to one of those rooms, and you find a wife, with her four or five children. The woman is heart-broken. She is discouraged. When she married that man he swore to protect, love, and care for her, and provide for all her wants. He made good promises and kept them, for a few years, and did love her. But he got led away into one of these drinking saloons. He was a noble-hearted man by nature, and those are just the ones that are led astray. He has now become a confirmed drunkard. His children can tell by his footfall that he comes home drunk. They look upon him as a monster. The wife has many a scar on her body that she has received from that man's arm who swore to love and protect her. Instead of being a kind-hearted husband, he has become a demon. He don't provide for that poor woman. What a struggle there is! And may God have mercy upon the poor drunkard and his family is my prayer constantly! Suppose he is here in that gallery up there, or in the dark back there, and you can't see him. May be he is so ashamed of himself that he has got behind a post. He hears that he may be regenerated; that God will take away the love of strong drink, and snap the fetters that have been binding him, and make him a free man, and he says, "By the grace of God I will ask Him to give me a new heart." And he says, "O God, save me!" Then he goes home. His wife says, "I never saw my husband look so happy for years. What has come over him?" He says, "I have been up there to hear these strangers. I heard Mr. Sankey singing 'Jesus of Nazareth passeth by,' and it touched my heart. The sermon about being born again touched my heart, and, wife, I just prayed right there, and asked God to give me a new heart, and I believe He has done it. Come, wife, pray with me!" And there they kneel down and erect the family altar.

Three months hence you go to that home, and what do you find? All is changed. He is singing "Rock of Ages, cleft for me," or that other hymn his mother once taught him, "There is a fountain filled with blood." His children have their arms upon his neck. That is Heaven upon earth. The Lord God dwells there. That man is passed from death unto life. That is the conversion we are aiming at. The man is made better, and that is what God does when a man has the spirit of Heaven upon him. He regenerates them, re-creates them in His own image. Let us pray that every man here who has the love of strong drink may be converted. Unite in prayer with me now and ask God to save these men that are rushing on to death and ruin.

OCTAVIUS BROOKS FROTHINGHAM

The Dogma of Hell

HAD I BEEN TOLD, six months ago, that I should give a discourse on the subject of "hell," I should have received the information with absolute incredulity; incredulity as deep and scornful as the hunter would feel who was told that he should take his rifle and go forth to hunt the iguanodon, ichthyosaurus or other extinct monster of the pre-adamite epoch of the planet. A thousand years ago, the doctrine was alive and formidable. It stalked abroad, immense in size, terrible in aspect. Now it is rarely seen and when visible is but the shadow of its former self. It has left the world of philosophy and science, of literature and art, even in the wilderness of theology it is seldom met with. Its spectral image lingers near the tabernacle where the revival preacher endeavors to reproduce a system of religion that was natural in a departed era, but is unnatural in the present age—but there too it is altered, sadly changed from its former estate, a mere simulacrum, a ghost, which the people are allowed to look at, as forms are seen behind gauze curtains, or as "materialized" spirits are produced under "mediumistic" conditions.

All at once, this spectre becomes alive, is seen in the midst of us, terrifies women and children in the public places. We were mistaken in supposing the monster belonged to the Silurian epoch; or to speak more exactly, we were mistaken in thinking that the Silurian epoch was sunk beneath so many layers of rock. The Silurian epoch persists. In central New York, last summer, excellent persons were found who professed to believe in the lake of fire, and were surprised that any should be so audacious as to doubt it. In New England an ecclesiastical council demurred to the ordination of a minister, on the ground that he held unorthodox opinions on this point. In New York, an eminent divine and doctor of divinity, rector of a wealthy and fashionable church, expressed contempt for the opinion of Canon Farrar that no doctrine of everlasting suffering was taught in the Scripture. The doctrine is evidently not extinct. The majority of Congregational clergymen still maintain it, some in a qualified, others in an unqualified form.

How can such a surprising phenomenon as this be explained? We are forced to recognize the fact that the tenet in question has, at present, no substantial reason for being; that people who do not wish to believe it need not, may discard it, or let it alone. Those who cling to it, do so of their own free will, because they choose to, not because authority compels them, or evidence persuades. The disbelievers are in the ascendant. The doubter is in excellent company. He has the intelligence of centuries on his side.

In theology men of the highest eminence have repudiated the idea as inconsistent with the conception of a supreme justice. Origen in the third century declared it incredible, cleared the scriptures of it by resolving its language into allegory, and acquitted Deity of responsibility for it, by maintaining the evanescence of evil itself and teaching that Satan would at last be reclaimed. In the ninth century Scotus Erigena, one of the master minds of the Church, a man of genius, an acute and enterprising intellect, the prince of the scholastic philosophy advocated the same views with Origen, and defended them with unsurpassed vigor and subtlety of reasoning. Others, of less distinction might, if they would, take courage from these, especially in an age when no courage is needed, as it was in theirs. At present the courage is demanded of those who maintain the doctrine, not of those who reject it. The modern theologian is unwilling to commit himself to an opinion that has against it the suffrage of modern intelligence.

Philosophy suggested to theology its doubt. The office of philosophy is to present the unity of the world, to describe the universe as a whole, consistent and harmonious in all its parts; and in its attempt to do this, it inevitably suggested misgivings in regard to a doctrine so fatal to an intelligent order of the world as this. In the last century, Joseph Butler, "the most patient, original and candid of philosophic theologians," made a desperate stand for the belief in future punishment, and defended, or rather apologized for it, by arguing its complete accordance with the system of Nature, whose *divine author* inflicted unspeakable agonies on beings to all appearances innocent. Such reasoning may well be called desperate. That is indeed a hopeless cause that can be maintained only at the risk of atheism itself. To argue that God might be expected to punish people everlastingly in the future because, horribly and causelessly, he torments them in the present, may and does provoke men to ask whether it would not be better to deny the existence of God entirely, or to give the name Devil to the being who governs the world. Had bishop Butler deliberately gone to work to prove that the world was under the dominion of Satan, he could not have argued more successfully. The only criticism one feels disposed to make on such an argument is that it lacks subtlety. It is not cunning enough to persuade. It is barefaced. Origen and Scotus had no such audacity. They appealed to the conception of a supreme Being against what seemed to them a horrible imputation upon him. They attempted to relieve him from the guilt of inflicting *future* agonies on innocent souls. It never occurred to either of them to *defend* the atrocity of hell by bringing up the equally appalling atrocity of earth. It never occurred to them to give people their choice between atheism and diabolism.

The method of Butler has been repudiated by the more rational philosophy of a later day. There are now three alternatives presented to the philosophical mind. It may either accept the ancient theory of Dualism which allots the universe to two opposing powers, one good and one evil,—the evil power holding sway over the realm of anguish, whether temporal or eternal,—on which supposition, pain, death, hell are transferred from the dominion of Deity to the domain of Satan; or, maintaining the theory of Monism, which acknowledges but a single intelligent ruler of the universe, it may deny the existence of one spirit or the other, declaring for *optimism* with Leibnitz, and with him sustaining the opinion that good is the substantial principle, and evil the appearance, the apparition, the evanescent shadow, or for *pessimism* with Schopenhauer who contended that evil was the substantial principle and that good is the illusive semblance. Or again, as a third alternative, declining to answer dogmatically the question of the world's original authorship and essential control, it may hold to some form of the development theory, which describes the universe as unfolding gradually from organic germs, and as moving onward with or without the guidance of an intelligent being. Either of these suppositions variously tempered and modified, the philosopher of our day may accept; but the supposition of an everlasting hell for human beings is not admissible. That idea the philosophic mind discards, and they who seek the companionship of such minds must abandon it.

Of the belief in "hell" science knows nothing. As knowledge extends, the dominion of pure evil shrinks. Satan retreats from one department of Nature after another and leaves the high-ways and by-ways of creation free to the passage of serene, inexorable and regenerating law. Science discards the conception of the Devil, and the dogma of perdition. The scientific men who entertain these forms of opinion do so, not as men of science, but as members of the church, whose doctrines they do not presume to call in question.

The doctrine of future punishment as held by the creeds of Christendom, has always been rejected with abhorrence by the natural conscience of men, as fundamentally inconsistent with rational notions of justice. That men, even the worst men, could in their short life-time commit offences deserving everlasting punishment, the agonies of hell fire, for an eternity, or even for a hundred years, nay, for a single year, for a single day, is an idea that shocks every sentiment of equity. That the Being who is supremely, ideally, absolutely just, can inflict penalties for misdoing, such as no human being would lay on another, such as the most infernal cruelty never, even when maddened to insanity, devised, is a suggestion at which the natural conscience stands, always did stand and always must stand aghast. They who believed it when they could not help themselves, when church authority cowed their will, and silenced their protest, made this moral reservation. The voice of conscience was hushed. The moral sense was forbidden to assert itself.

That the human heart resents, repels with detestation the belief in future punishment, need not be said. Of course it does. Of course it always did. What pagan, what creature above the savage, ever cordially entertained the belief that one whom he loved, was howling in hell for deeds done in the body, for sentiments entertained, or for dispositions illustrated on earth? It is easy enough to profess doctrines in which one has no interest, with which one associates no feeling; but when feeling becomes enlisted, as, sooner or later it becomes, in a doctrine like this, the reaction against it is instantaneous and violent. There was a time when the heart dared not express its feeling. That time is past; now heartlessness is condemned. The voice of the heart is loud and imperative; it requires courage to resist it.

There remains the word of Scripture. Does this compel those who accept its authority, to receive the doctrine of future punishment against the protest of the heart, the remonstrance of the conscience, the reasoning of philosophy, the theologian's demur? This is a question which lack of space forbids my answering in full or arguing at length. To me, with whom the word of Scripture has no more authority than reason concedes to it, the discussion is without interest. At present, it satisfies my purpose to say that, in my honest and sober judgment, the language of Scripture does not warrant the christian doctrine. If it did, my opinion of the doctrine would be what it is. But honestly I think that it does not. At least, the essential thought, the true meaning of Scripture does not. More than this, I am not prepared to allow. The Universalists have not, in my judgment, fairly made out their case from the Bible. From the Old Testament they can easily, for to the Hebrew mind the doctrine is repugnant. But the New Testament contains expressions that have never been purged from the taint of the hideous thought. Language is put into the mouth of Jesus that conveys to the imagination the most horrible forebodings of doom. "Depart, ye cursed, into everlasting fire, prepared for the devil and his angels." It is hard for the grammarian to get over that.

Universalism has however, done this much; it has cast a grave doubt on the supposed teachings of Scripture in this matter. It has made it possible to doubt whether the Bible is chargeable with the belief in question. It has even made it easy for people who believe in the inspired authority of

Scripture and who are distressed because it teaches this disheartening dogma, to retain their faith in the Bible and at the
same time to indulge the sentiments which are native to their
hearts. This is much. Is it not as much as is demanded? Is it
not, practically, everything? None need entertain the dogma
on the authority of the Bible, who do not choose to. The
doubter has a valid excuse.

How then, to return to my original question, how then can
the revival of this monstrous doctrine be explained? Since
there are good reasons for discarding it, since the reasons that
once supported it are weakened if not wholly disposed of,
since to reject it is to be in the company of the best in repute,
since even Scripture permits merciful interpretations, why is
not the doctrine suffered to go unrestrained to its final account? The reply to the inquiry is close at hand.

*The doctrine is necessary to the integrity of the christian
scheme;* so necessary that its rejection would bring the whole
structure down. The christian scheme is a complete, logical
system, compactly fitted together. Its parts all cohere. The
dislodgement of one point endangers the security of the
structure. To deny the Trinity is to deny the deity of the
Christ. To deny the deity of the Christ is to deny the sufficiency of his atonement. To deny the atonement is to deny
the desperate need of man. To deny this, is to deny human
depravity, is to deny the necessity of Grace, is to vacate the offices of the Church, and reduce to nothing the significance of
Christendom. The dogma of future punishment is essential to
all the rest. It follows logically from the dogmas of Depravity
and Redemption. There must be a doom in reserve for the
unconverted. There must be a place for the unregenerate.
They are by nature depraved, heirs of death, children of
wrath; and their place must be the lowest and saddest conceivable. Their doom might be simply death, utter death, annihilation. But this doom would be rather negative than
positive. Death might be welcome. Annihilation might be a
boon. There must be something more appalling to the vulgar
imagination than that. With the idea of death must be cou-
pled the idea of agony. Hence, as life meant felicity, death
meant anguish. Hell was offset against Heaven. The two
were required to complete the series of conceptions which

constituted the "Plan of Redemption." The destruction of hell would deprive the system of its motive power. The good woman of Alexandria who went about with her bucket of water in one hand and her torch in the other—the water to extinguish hell, the torch to burn up heaven—was set down as a maniac. Had she succeeded, Christianity would have seen its last day. For the fires of perdition were as indispensible to the religion as was the divine love she wished to exalt.

Thus the tenacity of Christians to their dogma is accounted for. They may keep it in the background; they may conceal it beneath figures of speech; they may say little or nothing about it; they may even permit their neighbors to forget it. The revivalist preacher may speak of it with extreme reserve and reluctance, urging the persuasions of love instead of the former exasperations of fear. Still the doctrine is there, in its place, and when touched by the hand of criticism, it displays its vitality. They avow it who dare not disavow. They assent who dare not deny. Did the tenet stand by itself, alone, apart from the general scheme, there can scarcely be a doubt of its all but universal rejection. As it is, it is retained as a corner stone which the builders see no way to reject.

The strength, the bulwark of this doctrine has ever been the ecclesiastical spirit, the spirit of assumption and mental oppression. It grew up with the priesthood; and with the priesthood it prevailed, and with the power of the priesthood it declined. It never had much influence by reason of the moral consciousness of men. It is a remarkable fact that people have for the most part been consigned to hell for offences against ecclesiastical rule. The inhabitants of hell have been chiefly heretics sent there for the guilt of unbelief; skeptics who looked too deeply into the mysteries of dogma, infidels who abandoned the traditions of faith. A Parsee writing, it is said, describes a woman in hell, "beaten with stone clubs by two demons twelve miles high, and compelled to eat a basin of offal because some of her hair, as she combed it, fell into the sacred fire." A Brahmanic text, says Alger, tells of a man who for "neglecting to meditate on the mystic monosyllable OM, before praying, was thrown down on an iron floor in hell, and cloven with an ax, then stirred in a caldron of molten lead till covered all over with foam sweat, like a grain of rice in an

oven, and then fastened with head downwards and feet up-
wards to a chariot of fire, and urged onward with a red hot
goad." A general council of the Church condemned Origen
for teaching that the doctrine of eternal punishment in hell
did not comport with the idea of the infinite goodness of
God. An English cardinal, early in the thirteenth century,
wrote a book on the question: Is Origen saved or damned? In
Bayles' Dictionary is related the vision of a hermit who saw
hell uncovered, and in the midst of it, Origen in the company
of the damned, covered with flames and confusion.* The
pains of hell were reserved for offenders against the Church,
not for offenders against humanity. The hell of the Romanist
is full of Protestants. The hell of the Protestant is full of schis-
matics. Where theological hatred does not exist, there is no
hell, for there are none to put into it except murderers,
thieves and liars, and none of these deserve its frightful tortures. In the priests' eyes unbelief is the soul of guilt. So will
it be, so long as churches claim special revelations of truth, so
long as certain texts are revered as the word of God, so long
as ecclesiastical institutions and rites are held to be sacred
above human sanctities, so long as orders of men called religious assume the right to dictate thought and conduct to
mankind.

It is vulgarly thought that the belief in future punishment
is important as a check on the inordinate passions of men;
that it is valuable in keeping society in order, men being more
readily swayed by fear than by any other motive. This impression is, I am persuaded, quite mistaken. It is not probably
true that men are more powerfully affected by fear than by
love. The experiment has never been tried. The assumption
that fear is the only influence to which human beings respond
has been acted on from time immemorial and has begotten an
absolute skepticism in regard to the efficacy of any other sentiment. That men should be influenced for good by fear
seems to be something like an absurdity. Fear can do no more
for a moral nature, than darkness can do for a plant, or lightning for a tree. Sunshine alone quickens. Love alone warms.
Violence may *stimulate*, but how can it *nourish?* Fear may

*See Delapierre's "Enfer," p. 33, note.

create fear; can it create trust? Vitality is coincident with passionate desire, but fear produces apathy and repulsion. The substitution of rewards for penalties would probably be followed by a moral impulse towards goodness such as Christendom never experienced.

I heard, a short time since, the touching story of a drunkard. He had dragged himself and his wife down from a respectable position into the deepest pit of poverty and degradation. He was a beggar and a brute, and she was a wretched, sick, crushed creature, to whom existence was a burden. Reproaches had been rained upon his head for years; society had cast him into its outer darkness, shut its door upon him. The friend who told me the story found these people in a garret, and by the aid of some neighbors separated the husband from the wife. She, after a time, recovered herself sufficiently to do a little plain sewing; and when she had earned her first shilling, she placed half of it, sixpence, in her benefactor's hand saying, "When you see my husband, give him this, with my love." He did so. The wretched man took it, gazed at it, and broke into a sob of agony. "O God! I could bear threats, hunger and curses, but I cannot bear this. That sixpence breaks my heart!" Is a woman's love so powerful, and can the Supreme love be impotent?

But let this pass. It is enough for the present to know that the doctrine of future punishment has not been, to any considerable degree, employed as an agent in moral reformation. It has been used as an engine for the suppression of heresy. The free preachers who preceded Luther, did their best to galvanize sinners into good behavior by describing the terrors of hell. Very frightful their descriptions were; so grotesque and fantastical in their horror as to betray their weakness. None but the stupidest, the most credulous, the most animal could have been affected by threatenings so ludicrously violent. The preachers, one would say, felt the impotence of their method, and not being wise enough to change it for a better, heaped up the agony till it was amusing. It would be safe to say that the certainty of a good whipping to be inflicted immediately on the perpetration of the offence, would exert a more salutary effect on conduct than the most lurid prospect of imaginary flames.

The truth is that the threat of Hell even in its most miti-
gated form is so vastly in excess of any consciousness of guilt
as to be practically inoperative. The flames might as well be
painted, for any terror they carry. It is impossible to bring
such fantasies home to the practical sense. They who have
imagination to realize them are disgusted. They who have not
are confounded and stunned. Instead of apprehending a decline of morality from the popular disbelief in the doctrine of
hell torments, it will be more reasonable to apprehend such
decline from its continued profession, and the more sincere
the profession, the graver the cause for apprehension.
Whatever effect Christianity may have had in softening the
habits and sweetening the dispositions of men—and by all admission it has exerted a great deal—it has produced by its gra-
ciousness, in spite of this hideous doctrine. The benignant
character of Jesus, the human teachings of the Sermon on the
Mount, the lovely lessons of parables like the Good Samaritan
and the Prodigal Son, the touching suggestions of the Supper
the Garden and the Cross, the affecting mythology of the
Atonement, with its background of the Eternal Love and its
expression of self-sacrificing devotion on the part of the
purest and gentlest of the sons of men, all these combined
were perpetually dropping refreshing dew on the waste places
of the human heart and warming into life the seeds of kindness and purity. For one nature, hard and brutal, that the
terrors of the hereafter may have restrained, it has probably
deadened, discouraged or brutalized a hundred sensitive spirits that needed only a ray of hope to bloom in beauty and
shed a delicious fragrance on the air. If all were known, as all
never can be, it would probably appear that the doctrine of
future punishment has demoralized and dehumanized the
ages in which it prevailed, and has seriously retarded the
progress of virtue by hindering the natural play of motive and
preventing the standard of moral attainment. If all were
known it would probably appear that the doctrine reflected
the inhumanity of inhuman generations, and deepened it.

In measuring the moral influence of this dogma, due
weight must be allowed to a consideration which Mr. Lecky
makes prominent in his history of Rationalism in Europe. He
dwells at length on the disastrous effect it exerted on the

moral dispositions of churchmen, making them callous and cruel. He traces the connection between the horrible pictures of torment which they hung up and contemplated, which artists painted on walls and ceilings, which preachers colored with their ferocious rhetoric, which priests presented at the confessional, and mystics agonized over in their cell, and the frightful torments that were inflicted on heretics. The instruments of torture used in the middle ages, the wheels, rack, screws, pincers, were but material copies of the instruments which the fiends were believed to employ upon the damned in hell; and the cold-blooded ferocity with which the horrid enginery was plied, nay, the satanic glee of the *auto da fe*, was but such imitation as human creatures could make of the devils who executed on the cursed the mandates of the divine wrath. "If," says Lecky, "you make the detailed and exquisite torments of multitudes the habitual object of the thoughts and imaginations of men, you will necessarily produce in most of them a gradual indifference to human suffering, and in some of them a disposition to regard it with positive delight. If you further assure men that these sufferings form an integral part of a revelation which they are bound to regard as a message of good tidings, you will induce them to stifle every feeling of pity, and almost to encourage their insensibility as a virtue. If you end your teachings by telling them that the Being who is the ideal of their lives confines His affections to the members of a single church, that he will torture forever all who are not found within its pale, and that His children will forever contemplate those tortures in a state of unalloyed felicity, you will prepare the way for every form of persecution that can be directed against those who are without."

The bloody days are over. The instruments of torture are exhibited as curiosities in the castle dungeons of Europe. May we not hope, may we not reasonably expect that their diabolical counterparts will also be remanded to the mythological curiosity shop, to be marvelled at as the insane contrivances of a diseased fancy? Is it not melancholy, nay ludicrous to think, that men who cry over an attack of rheumatism, who will not permit a woman to be injured, who remonstrate against the execution of a criminal, who raise an outcry against the practice of vivisection whereby surgeons make studies in anatomy by cutting up frogs and cats, are standing out vigorously for a doctrine that condemns millions of their fellow creatures to agonies unspeakable and endless, and are defending the opinion in the name of the Supreme Goodness? Could there be a better illustration of the ease with which people allow themselves to use words without meaning? Could there be a better proof of hollowness and insincerity? Could there be a sharper admonition to the duty of making beliefs correspond with feelings, and of substituting for the gaudy card houses of rhetoric, the solid mansions of conviction? To *talk* about eternal torment is not difficult; to profess belief in it may be possible even for good natured people, but to *think* it, to *bring it home to reason or heart*, is what the stoutest cannot do. It may be questioned whether a single man, even a single priest, preacher or churchman, ever fully "realized" the import of the doctrine. We know the names of single men whom the far off contemplation of it drove to the madhouse. Nothing but dense ignorance, credulity, mental and moral apathy, wrapping human sensibility about as with the hide of a rhinoceros, enabled them to bear the suggestion of it, and still go on their way believing, hoping and rejoicing. In proportion as men become intelligent, conscientious and sensitive, they throw the incubus off, though, with it, they cast over creed, church, scripture, and all the associations of religion. For Reason is worth more than all.

That the doctrine of endless punishment will be fully, frankly, in every form discarded, while the popular religion—Christianity—survives, cannot be expected. For, as has been declared, the article is an essential part of that religion, and will be maintained, literally and figuratively, by those who are interested in keeping the system alive. But that it is vanishing away before the brighter intelligence and the better heart of the modern world, is very certain; and equally certain is it that into the shadow of oblivion will go the kindred tenets with which it is associated.

It is not enough, however, that the intelligent minds of a new age should reject the doctrine of *future* punishment, as held by the Christian Church. They must abandon the habit of associating any idea of *punishment* with the divine administration of the universe. Not the *physical* conception merely, but the *moral* conception must be discarded. Neither in the life after death, nor in the life before death, is the thought of punishment, of retribution, of vengeance to be entertained. It is the custom of the "liberal" sects, so called, to *spiritualize*, as they term it, the consequences of the divine wrath. They transfer the pains from the body to the soul, and imagine conscience as the agent in executing the avenging decree. They too, paint pictures of the torment of the damned which, they boast, are more lurid and awful even than those set forth by the calvinistic theology. They describe the agonies of the awakened conscience, as Spurgeon might describe the agonies of the resurrected frame. It is only another form of the old iniquity. It is but a continuation of the evil habit they so bitterly condemn in their fellow believers. Their doctrine, though less disgusting and revolting, is hardly more rational than the ancient dogma, which they repudiate.

The only rational alternative is, the omission of the word "punishment," from the vocabulary of religion. Speak of actions and their consequences; of conduct and its issues; of character and its laws; speak of moral cause and effect, and trace the connection between deeds and destinies, a vital, organic connection that cannot be broken or interrupted; but let the thought of retaliation be dropped. Then will life be ordered on rational principles; then will hopes and fears be reasonable; and then will our conceptions of providence and deity be worthy of intelligent beings.

T. DE WITT TALMAGE

The Ministry of Tears

"God shall wipe away all tears from their eyes."
—Rev. 7:17.

RIDING ACROSS a western prairie, wild flowers up to the hub of the carriage wheel, and while a long distance from any shelter, there came a sudden shower, and while the rain was falling in torrents, the sun was shining as brightly as ever I saw it shine; and I thought, What a beautiful spectacle this is! So the tears of the Bible are not midnight storm, but rain on pansied prairies in God's sweet and golden sunlight. You remember that bottle which David labelled as containing tears, and Mary's tears, and Paul's tears, and Christ's tears, and the harvest of joy that is to spring from the sowing of tears. God mixes them. God rounds them. God shows them where to fall. God exhales them. A census is taken of them, and there is a record as to the moment when they are born, and as to the place of their grave. Tears of bad men are not kept. Alexander, in his sorrow, had the hair clipped from his horses and mules, and made a great ado about his grief; but in all the vases of heaven there is not one of Alexander's tears. I speak of the tears of the good. Alas, me! they are falling all the time. In summer, you sometimes hear the growling thunder, and you see there is a storm miles away; but you know from the drift of the clouds that it will not come anywhere near you. So, though it may be all bright around about us, there is a shower of trouble somewhere all the time. You think it is the cannonading that you hear along the banks of the Danube. No. It is the thunder of clouds of trouble over the groaning hospitals, and over the desolated Russian and Turkish homes. Tears! Tears!

What is the use of them anyhow? Why not substitute laughter? Why not make this world where all the people are well, and eternal strangers to pain and aches? What is the use of an

693

eastern storm when we might have a perpetual nor'-wester? Why, when a family is put together, not have them all stay, or if they must be transplanted to make other homes, then have them all live? the family record telling a story of marriages and births, but of no deaths. Why not have the harvests chase each other without fatiguing toil, and all our homes afflicted? Why the hard pillow, the hard crust, the hard struggle? It is easy enough to explain a smile, or a success, or a congratulation; but, come now, and bring all your dictionaries and all your philosophies and all your religions, and help me this evening to explain a tear. A chemist will tell you that it is made up of salt and lime, and other component parts; but he misses the chief ingredients—the acid of a soured life, the viperan sting of a bitter memory, the fragments of a broken heart. I will tell you what a tear is; it is agony in solution.

Hear me, then, while I discourse to you of the ministry of tears, and of the ending of that ministry when God shall wipe them all away.

First. It is the ministry of tears *to keep this world from being too attractive.* Something must be done to make us willing to quit this existence. If it were not for trouble, this world would be a good enough heaven for me. You and I would be willing to take a lease of this life for a hundred million years, if there were no trouble. The earth cushioned and upholstered and pillared and chandeliered with such expense, no story of other worlds could enchant us. We would say: "Let well enough alone. If you want to die and have your body disintegrated in the dust, and your soul go out on a celestial adventure, then you can go; but this world is good enough for me." You might as well go to a man who has just entered the Louvre at Paris, and tell him to hasten off to the picture galleries of Venice or Florence. "Why," he would say, "what is the use of my going there? There are Rembrandts and Rubens and Raphaels here that I haven't looked at yet." No man wants to go out of this world, or out of any house until he has a better house.

To cure this wish to stay here, God must somehow create a disgust for our surroundings. How shall He do it? He cannot afford to deface His horizon, or to tear off a fiery panel from the sunset, or to subtract an anther from the water lily, or to banish the pungent aroma from the mignonette, or to drag the robes of the morning in the mire. You cannot expect a Christopher Wren to mar his own St. Paul's Cathedral, or a Michael Angelo to dash out his own "Last Judgment," or a Handel to discord his "Israel in Egypt;" and you cannot expect God to spoil the architecture and music of His own world. How then are we to be made willing to leave? Here is where trouble comes in. After a man has had a good deal of trouble, he says, "Well, I am ready to go. If there is a house somewhere whose roof doesn't leak, I would like to live there. If there is an atmosphere somewhere that does not distress the lungs, I would like to breathe it. If there is a society somewhere where there is no tittle-tattle, I would like to live there. If there is a home-circle somewhere where I can find my lost friends, I would like to go there." He used to read the first part of the Bible chiefly, now he reads the last part of the Bible chiefly. Why has he changed Genesis for Revelation? Ah! he used to be anxious chiefly to know how this world was made, and all about its geological construction. Now he is chiefly anxious to know how the next world was made, and how it looks, and who live there, and how they dress. He reads Revelation ten times now where he reads Genesis once. The old story, "In the beginning God created the heavens and the earth," does not thrill him half as much as the other story, "I saw a new heaven and a new earth." The old man's hand trembles as he turns over this apocalyptic leaf, and he has to take out his handkerchief to wipe his spectacles. That book of Revelation is a prospectus now of the country into which he is to soon immigrate; the country in which he has lots already laid out, and avenues opened, and trees planted, and mansions built. The thought of that blessed place comes over me mightily, and I declare that if this house were a great ship, and you all were passengers on board it, and one hand could launch that ship into the glories of heaven, I should be tempted to take the responsibility, and launch you all into glory with one stroke, holding on to the side of the boat until I could get in myself! And yet there are people here to whom this world is brighter than heaven. Well, dear souls, I do not blame you. It is natural. But, after a while, you will be ready to go. It was not until Job had been worn out with bereavements and carbuncles and a pest of a wife that he wanted to see God. It was not until the prodigal got tired of living among the hogs that he wanted to go to his father's house. It is the ministry of trouble to make this world worth less, and heaven worth more.

Again: it is the ministry of trouble *to make us feel our complete dependence upon God*. King Alphonso said that if he had been present at the Creation, he could have made a better world than this. What a pity he was not present! I do not know what God will do when some men die. Men think they can do anything until God shows them they can do nothing at all. We lay out great plans, and we like to execute them. It looks big. God comes and takes us down. As Prometheus was assaulted by his enemy, when the lance struck him it opened a great swelling that had threatened his death, and he got well. So it is the arrow of trouble that lets out great swellings of pride. We never feel our dependence upon God until we get trouble. I was riding with my little child along a road, and she asked if she might drive. I said, "Certainly." I handed over the reins to her, and I had to admire the glee with which she drove. But after a while we met a team, and we had to turn out. The road was narrow, and it was sheer down on both sides. She handed the reins over to me, and said: "I think you had better take charge of the horse." So, we are all children; and on this road of life we like to drive. It gives one such an appearance of superiority and power. It looks big. But after a while, we meet some obstacle, and we have to turn out, and the road is narrow, and it is sheer down on both sides; and then we are willing that God should take the reins and drive. Ah! my friends, we get upset so often because we do not hand over the reins soon enough.

Can you not tell when you hear a man pray, whether he has ever had any trouble? I can. The cadence, the phraseology indicate it. Why do women pray better than men? Because they have had more trouble. Before a man has had any trouble, his prayers are poetic, and he begins away up among the sun, moon, and stars, and gives the Lord a great deal of astronomical information that must be highly gratifying. He then comes on down gradually over beautiful tablelands to "for ever and ever, amen." But after a man has had trouble, prayer is with him a taking hold of the arm of God and crying out for help. I have heard earnest prayers on two or three occasions that I remember. Once, on the Cincinnati express train going at forty miles the hour, and the train jumped the track, and we were near a chasm eighty feet deep; and the men who, a few minutes before, had been swearing and blaspheming God, began to pull and jerk at the bell-rope, and got up on the backs of the seats, and cried out: "O God, save us!" There was another time, about eight hundred miles out at sea, on a foundering steamer, after the last lifeboat had been split finer than kindling wood. They prayed then. Why is it you so often hear people, in reciting the last experience of some friend, say: "He made the most beautiful prayer I ever heard"? What makes it beautiful? It is the earnestness of it. Oh, I tell you a man is in earnest when his stripped and naked soul wades out in the soundless, shoreless, bottomless ocean of eternity.

It is trouble, my friends, that makes us feel our dependence upon God. We do not know our own weakness or God's strength until the last plank breaks. It is contemptible in us, when there is nothing else to take hold of, that we catch hold of God only. A man is unfortunate in business. He has to raise a great deal of money, and raise it quickly. He borrows on word and note all he can borrow. After a while, he puts a second mortgage on his house. Then he puts a lien on his furniture. Then he makes over his life insurance. Then he assigns all his property. Then he goes to his father-in-law and asks for help! Well, having failed everywhere, completely failed, he gets down on his knees and says: "O Lord, I have tried everybody and everything, now help me out of this financial trouble." He makes God the last resort instead of the first resort. There are men who have paid ten cents on a dollar who could have paid a hundred cents on a dollar if they had gone to God in time. Why, you do not know who the Lord is. He is not an autocrat seated far up in a palace, from which He emerges once a year, preceded by heralds swinging swords to clear the way. No. But a Father willing, at our call, to stand by us in every crisis and predicament of life.

I tell you what some of you business men make me think of. A young man goes off from home to earn his fortune. He goes with his mother's consent and benediction. She has large wealth; but he wants to make his own fortune. He goes far away, falls sick, gets out of money. He sends to the hotel-keeper where he is staying, asking for lenience, and the answer he gets is, "If you don't pay up Saturday night you'll be removed to the hospital." The young man sends to a comrade in the same building. No help. He writes to a banker who was a friend of his deceased father. No relief. He writes to an old schoolmate, but gets no help. Saturday night comes, and he is moved to the hospital. Getting there he is frenzied with grief; and he borrows a sheet of paper and a postage stamp, and he sits down, and he writes home, saying: "Dear mother, I am sick unto death. Come." It is ten minutes of ten o'clock when she gets the letter. At ten o'clock the train starts. She is five minutes from the depot. She gets there in time to have five minutes to spare. She wonders why a train that can go thirty miles an hour cannot go sixty miles an hour. She rushes into the hospital. She says: "My son, what does all this mean? Why didn't you send for me? You sent to everybody but me. You knew I could and would help you. Is this the reward I get for my kindness to you always?" She bundles him up, takes him home, and gets him well very soon. Now, some of you treat God just as that young man treated his mother. When you get into a financial perplexity, you call on the banker, you call on the broker, you call on your creditors, you call on your lawyer for legal counsel, you call upon everybody, and when you cannot get any help then you go to God. You say: "O Lord, I come to Thee. Help me now out of my perplexity." And the Lord comes though it is the eleventh hour. He says: "Why did you not send for me before? As one whom his mother comforteth, so will I comfort you." It is to throw us back upon an all-comforting God that we have this ministry of tears.

Again: it is the ministry of tears *to capacitate us for the office of sympathy*. The priests under the old dispensation were set apart by having water sprinkled on their hands, feet, and head; and by the sprinkling of tears people are now set apart to the office of sympathy. When we are in prosperity, we like to have a great many young people around us, and we laugh when they laugh, and we romp when they romp, and we sing when they sing; but when we have trouble we like plenty of old folks around. Why? They know how to talk. Take an aged mother, seventy years of age, and she is almost omnipotent in comfort. Why? She has been through it all. At seven o'clock in the morning she goes over to comfort a young mother who has just lost her babe. Grandmother knows all about that trouble. Fifty years ago she felt it. At twelve o'clock of that day she goes over to comfort a widowed soul. She knows all about that. She has been walking in that dark valley twenty years. At four o'clock in the afternoon some one knocks at the door wanting bread. She knows all about that. Two or three times in her life she came to her last loaf. At ten o'clock that night she goes over to sit up with some one severely sick. She knows all about it. She knows all about fevers and pleurisies and broken bones. She has been doctoring all her life, spreading plasters and pouring out bitter drops, and shaking up hot pillows, and contriving things to tempt a poor appetite. Doctors Abernethy and Rush and Hosack and Harvey were great doctors; but the greatest doctor the world ever saw is an old Christian woman. Dear me! do we not remember her about the room when we were sick in our boyhood? Was there any one who could ever so touch a sore without hurting it? And when she lifted her spectacles against her wrinkled forehead so she could look closer at the wound, it was three fourths healed. And when the Lord took her home, although you may have been men and women thirty, forty, fifty years of age, you lay on the coffin lid and sobbed as though you were only five or ten years of age. O man, praise God, if, instead of looking back to one of these berouged and bespangled old people fixed up of the devil to look young, you have in your memory the picture of an honest, sympathetic, kind, self-sacrificing, Christ-like mother. Oh, it takes these people who have had trouble to comfort others in trouble. Where did Paul get the ink with which to write his comforting epistle? Where did David get the ink to write his comforting psalms? Where did John get the ink to write his comforting revelation? They got it out of their own tears. When a man has gone through the curriculum, and has taken a course of dungeons and imprisonments and shipwrecks, he is qualified for the work of sympathy.

When I began to preach, I used to write out all my

sermons, and I sometimes have great curiosity to look at the sermons I used to preach on trouble. They were nearly all poetic and in semi-blank verse; but God knocked the blank verse out of me long ago; and I have found out that I cannot comfort people except as I myself have been troubled. God made me the son of consolation to the people. I would rather be the means of soothing one perturbed spirit to-day, than to play a tune that would set all the sons of mirth reeling in the dance. I am a herb doctor. I put in the caldron the Root out of dry ground without form or comeliness. Then I put in the Rose of Sharon and the Lily of the valley. Then I put into the caldron some of the leaves from the tree of life, and the branch that was thrown into the wilderness Marah. Then I pour in the tears of Bethany and Golgotha; then I stir them up. Then I kindle under the caldron a fire made out of the wood of the cross, and one drop of that portion will cure the worst sickness that ever afflicted a human soul. Mary and Martha shall receive their Lazarus from the tomb. The damsel *shall* rise. And on the darkness shall break the morning, and God will wipe all tears from their eyes.

You know on a well-spread table, the food becomes more delicate at the last. I have fed you to-day with the bread of consolation. Let the table now be cleared, and let us set on the chalice of heaven. Let the King's cup-bearers come in. Good morning, Heaven! "Oh," says some critic in the audience, "the Bible contradicts itself. It intimates again and again that there are to be no tears in heaven, and if there be no tears in heaven, how is it possible that God will wipe any away?" I answer, have you never seen a child crying one moment and laughing the next; and while she was laughing, you saw the tears still on its face? And, perhaps, you stopped her in the very midst of her resumed glee, and wiped off those delayed tears. So, I think, after the heavenly raptures have come upon us, there may be the mark of some earthly grief, and while those tears are glittering in the light of the jasper sea, God will wipe them away. How well He can do that.

Jesus had enough trial to make Him sympathetic with all trial. The shortest verse in the Bible tells the story: "Jesus wept." The scar on the back of either hand, the scar on the arch of either foot, the row of scars along the line of the hair, will keep all heaven thinking. Oh, that great weeper is just the one to silence all earthly trouble and wipe out all stains of earthly grief. Gentle! Why His step is softer than the step of the dew. It will not be a tyrant bidding you to hush up your crying. It will be a Father who will take you on His left arm, His face gleaming into yours, while with the soft tips of the fingers of the right hand, He shall wipe away all tears from your eyes. I have noticed when the children get hurt, and their mother is away from home, they always come to me for comfort and sympathy; but I have noticed that when the children get hurt, and their mother is at home, they go right past me and to her; I am of no account. So, when the soul comes up into heaven out of the wounds of this life, it will not stop to look for Paul, or Moses, or David, or John. These did very well once, but now the soul shall rush past, crying: "Where is Jesus? Where is Jesus?" Dear Lord, what a magnificent thing to die if Thou shalt thus wipe away our tears. Methink it will take us some time to get used to heaven; the fruits of God without one speck; the fresh pastures without one nettle; the orchestra without one snapped string; the river of gladness without one torn bank; the solferinos and the saffron of sunrise and sunset swallowed up in the eternal day that beams from God's countenance!

"Why should I wish to linger in the wild,
    When Thou art waiting, Father, to receive Thy child?"

Sirs, if we could get any appreciation of what God has in reserve for us, it would make us so homesick we would be unfit for our every-day work. Professor Leonard, in Iowa University, put in my hands a meteoric stone, a stone thrown off from some other world to this. How suggestive it was to me. And I have to tell you the best representations we have of heaven are only aerolites flung off from that world which rolls on bearing the multitudes of the redeemed. We analyze these aerolites, and find them crystalizations of tears. No wonder, flung off from heaven. "God shall wipe away all tears from their eyes."

Have you any appreciation this evening of the good and glorious times your friends are having in heaven? How different it is when they get news there of a Christian's death from what it is here. It is the difference between embarkation and coming into port. Everything depends upon which side of the river you stand when you hear of a Christian's death. If you stand on this side of the river you mourn that they go. If you stand on the other side of the river, you rejoice that they come. Oh, the difference between a funeral on earth and a jubilee in heaven—between requiem here and triumphal march there—parting here and reunion there. Together! Have you thought of it? They are together. Not one of your departed friends in one land, and another in another land; but together in different rooms of the same house—the house of many mansions. Together! I never appreciated that thought so much as recently, when we laid away in her last slumber my sister Sarah. Standing there in the village cemetery, I looked around and said: "There is father, there is mother, there is grandfather, there is grandmother, there are whole circles of kindred;" and I thought to myself, "Together in the grave— together in glory." I am so impressed with the thought that I do not think it is any fanaticism when some one is going from this world to the next if you make them the bearer of despatches to your friends who are gone, saying: "Give my love to my parents, give my love to my children, give my love to my old comrades who are in glory, and tell them I am trying to fight the good fight of faith, and I will join them after a while." I believe the message will be delivered; and I believe it will increase the gladness of those who are before the throne. Together are they, all their tears gone. No trouble getting good society for them. All kings, queens, princes, and princesses. In 1751, there was a bill offered in your English Parliament, proposing to change the almanac so that the first of March should come immediately after the 18th of February. But, oh, what a glorious change in the calendar when all the years of your earthly existence are swallowed up in the eternal year of God!

My friends, take this good cheer home with you. Those tears of bereavement that course your cheek, and of persecution and of trial, are not always to be there. The motherly hand of God will wipe them all away. What is the use, on the way to such a consummation—what is the use of fretting about anything? Oh, what an exhilaration it ought to be in

Christian work. See you the pinnacles against the sky? It is the city of our God; and we are approaching it. Oh, let us be busy in the few days that shall remain for us. The Saxons and the Britons went out to battle. The Saxons were all armed. The Britons had no weapons at all; and yet history tells us the Britons got the victory. Why? They went into battle shouting three times "hallelujah!" and at the third shout of "hallelujah" their enemies fled panic struck; and so the Britons got the victory. And, my friends, if we could only appreciate the glories that are to come, we would be so filled with enthusiasm that no power of earth or hell could stand before us; and at our first shout the opposing forces would begin to tremble, and at our second shout they would begin to fall back, and at our third shout they would be routed forever. There is no power on earth or in hell that could stand before three such volleys of hallelujah.

I put this balsam on the recent wounds of your heart. Rejoice at the thought of what your departed friends have got rid of, and that you have a prospect of so soon making your own escape. Bear cheerfully the ministry of tears, and exult at the thought that soon it is to be ended.

> "There we shall march up the heavenly street,
> And ground our arms at Jesus' feet."

SAM P. JONES

Sermon Delivered August 2, 1885

A sermon, preached August 2, 1885, in presence of about 12,000 people, in the Camp-meeting, at Loveland, near Cincinnati. The preacher stood on the top of an old piano box. After a prayer and song from the choir he began as follows.

WE INVITE your prayerful attention to the nineteenth verse of the eleventh chapter of the Book of Proverbs: "As righteousness tendeth to life, so he that pursueth evil pursueth it to his own death."

When a good man dies he not only goes to heaven, drawn thither by the natural forces of spiritual gravity, by the approval of God and angels, but when a good man dies he goes to heaven by the common consent of every intelligent creature in the world. When a bad man dies he not only goes to hell, drawn thither by the natural forces of spiritual gravity, not only by the approval of God and His angels, but when a bad man dies he goes to hell by the common consent of every man in the world. You have attended the funeral of a doubtful character, and have been to the church he professed to, but did not possess religion, and his pastor on the occasion of the funeral read his text, and, as we say sometimes, "preached him to heaven." Haven't you left the church and heard on the sidewalk from saint and sinner about these words: "That preacher outraged every principle of truth; that man is not in heaven; he knows it, we know it, and all know that he has not gone to heaven." Have you ever left a good man's funeral, who was known and esteemed of all good men, and have you after hearing the eulogy of the preacher upon his life and character, and the preacher pointed to the sinners and said, "this man has gone to heaven;" and haven't you heard comment on the way from church, from saint and sinner, who all say "that was a truly good man, and he has gone home to God?" There is no other place in the universe for such a man.

When a good man goes to heaven he goes there just on the same principle this book would drop to the floor if I was to turn it loose. When this body of mine, when that body of yours, shall turn your spirit loose, if you be good, your spirit goes to God just as this book would drop to the floor; when a bad man dies his spirit goes to hell just as naturally and inevitably as this book would drop to the floor were I to turn it loose. A good man goes to heaven because he is good, and heaven is the centre of gravity for all that is good; a bad man goes to hell because he is bad—that's the nature of the whole matter.

Mark my word, brother, a good man is ready and destined for heaven before he dies. We seem to be far beyond the promised land, but heaven lets down low and hovers over the pallet of the good man, and he is in heaven before an angel could come to take him there. A good man goes to heaven because he is good, and a bad man goes to hell because he is bad. The demons of the pit, all of them, could not keep a good man out of heaven when he dies, and all the angels of heaven cannot keep a bad man out of hell when he dies. The natural and inevitable tendency of his nature and being and gravity cursed him in spite of all other forces in the universe. "Righteousness tendeth to life"—just as it is true for righteousness to lead to life and the light shines more and more into that perfect day, so the fate of the transgressor is hard and so the wicked shall be turned into hell. We have done good and shall see the resurrection, they that have done evil shall see the resurrection of damnation, and the question is not on general principles of general or effectual difficulties. It is not a question of how much God helps one man or another, but it is a question and the only question connected with it is, what sort of a man he may be? There is but one moral way in the universe of God, and every man in Kentucky is on that way. Heaven is at one end of the road—hell at the other, and the only question is which direction shall you go. A man on his way to hell, if he thinks a minute, and will turn around right on the road he is on, he is in the road to heaven; if he is on the way to heaven and turns around in that way he is in, he is on the road to hell in less than fifteen seconds. It is not a question of what your name is, or what church you may belong to, or how you have been baptized, but of which direction on this road you go. I used to think, when I was a little fellow, and heard it preached that the way to heaven was way over here and the way to hell over there, I didn't know they were the same road. Every sinner on this campground is on the road to heaven, and every Christian is on the road to hell, for the way to heaven is the way to hell—heaven is at one end and hell at the other. Which way are you going? Is your back on God and your face toward hell? And as long as this is so there are not enough angels in heaven and enough love in the heart of God to keep you out of perdition. As true as the right course will take you to heaven the man that goes the wrong course will go to hell. There is a great deal of discussion in pulpit and literature on the question of sin. Some profess to have found the origin of evil. My God, the question I am interested in, is there any way out of it? I never discuss the question of depravity as to whether personal or total, whether it is in the fall of Adam, or whether inherited, or whether it is progressive. I never discuss this feature. I look every man in the face and know he can be evil, and some are even more greedy than I was in this respect. The natural tendency of life is downward and hellward. That's true. We see this in the earliest development of childhood. Anger is almost the first expression of a child; covetousness is the next expression of its life, and so on; but whether it is inborn, or whether we are pure at birth—and then depravity is progressive—I have nothing to do with it. By the time you are twelve you are a solid lump of meanness. I found that out. Sin is fearful in this world. If I have been charged with anything, it is exaggeration.

They say Sam Jones speaks in hyperbole and Jones exaggerates; they charge me with that frequently. I will tell you what I will do: I will go to some homes in Kentucky, and some graveyards in Kentucky where the poor drunkards are buried, and I defy earth and hell to exaggerate the picture. Will words paint anything darker and more fearful than that? Things have happened in Lexington in the last ten years that I have referred to; are they exaggerated? Take that husband in his downward course and see him as he progresses in his ruin, he loses all his self-respect, his love for his wife, and then see the wife's feet gradually being brought to the grave day by day, and see the wife's heart as the blood trickles from it drop by drop, hour after hour, until its last crimson drop is exhausted, and she sinks into the grave, and the little children brought to shame, and desolation and want, and see that whole family, and when you have, bring it and throw its shadow into one picture before your eyes—a ruined man, a ruined soul, a broken-hearted wife and beggared children, and hope blasted forever. Is there a word painter in the universe of God who can exaggerate that picture? The only difference between the man who has done that and you, brother, is that he has gone a little further than you. You have the same disease, and unless it is arrested in its course you will reach the same point before long. I have been very strong in my denunciations of some things, and I denounce a thing in proportion as I see it is an evil; as I see it ruin humanity I denounce it in that proportion. I have said in the pulpit that no one but an infernal scoundrel would sell, and no one but an infernal fool would drink whiskey. "That is strong language," they say, "you ought not to say it." The liquor dealers at Chattanooga said: "Damn it, he insults a man to his face!" and have cussed about promiscuously about what I said in the pulpit, and I have been cussed about as much as I have been *dis*cussed, too. I told them, too, the next time they heard me to meet me the next morning, and go down a certain street with me until we arrived at the desolate home and see that pallid woman, and see themselves what a horrid wreck their trade has made of a once happy home. See the wrecked fireside, the wretched children on the floor, and then ask that woman who was her father and how was she raised, whom she married and what has become of her husband, and then place your ear to her heart and hear the blood dripping, dripping from it, and then see the besotted form and bleared eyes of the bloated man lying drunk on the floor in the back room, and then say if I exaggerate. A man in Tennessee wrote me the other day about as follows: "Jones, I understand you have offered $500 reward to any man who will take oath before a Justice of the Peace and sign his name that he doesn't want to go to heaven, and if you will write me, I'll meet you and take the oath, and get the money." I would be a fool to offer $500 for such a man and such an oath. I can get them all over this country for a dollar, and some even for fifty cents, and some would sell out for nothing and board themselves. Look at the picture! Of course I never made such a proposition. A fellow saw it in the newspapers! and the only thing I have against them is that everything they publish is true. That's the only objection I have in the world. You can bank on anything you see in the newspapers, that is Southern newspapers. That's a horrid picture there, isn't it? A man offers to sell his soul for $500, and sign, seal and deliver the instrument. My God! what farce is this? Every man that sells whiskey and every man that makes whiskey in this country is after the very same thing for which that fellow wanted to take an oath for $500. The worst enemy of God and the race, and the best friend of the devil is the man who makes whiskey. "They are generous," you say. Well, they ought to be. They will make a pauper out of a husband, widows out of wives, and send a man to hell, and then this generous whiskey dealer will send his widow a sack of flour! Ain't that generous? Ain't that nice? Don't you think it's the kindest thing you ever heard of in your life? They will take your members, and debauch them, and damn them and help pay you to preach!

My God, what sort of kindness is that? Let me tell you another thing. I have a good deal to say about the fellow who drinks whiskey, for the other fellows are rascals, while you are fools of the first water. Yes, you are. Aye, hear that? I've been thar; I know what I am talking about; nobody but a fool will touch it. No, there's a bigger fool than that, and that's the woman who will stir a toddy for her husband. [Laughter.]

Whenever you don't like my talk you can back out. A man is a fool that drinks whiskey. Yes, he is, too. In Gainesville, Ga., a few weeks ago the jailer walked into the jail one morning, and a man woke up and looking around said, "Where am I?" "You are in jail." "In Jail?" "Yes." "What for?" "For murder." "For murder?" "Yes." "Who have I killed?" "Your wife and sister." "My God, is that so? Tell them I don't want a judge, don't want a jury, don't want a trial: take me out and hang me to the first tree you can find." It looks like a fellow is a fool that will tamper with such stuff. Things are happening every day in Kentucky that is a demonstration of the fact

that a fellow who drinks whiskey is a fool of the first water.
Yes, he is.

I'll tell you another thing—nine-tenths of the sin in Kentucky is made by whiskey. Every one of your gambling houses
is founded on your bars; all your licentiousness floats upon
the river that flows from the worms of the still. With the
country debauched with whiskey what do you? Sin! Sin! It is
sin that hurts the race, and sin that damns the race, and we
have sin enough. I never meet a staggering drunkard but I
look him in the face and say, "Poor fellow, sin has wrecked
you." I never see a woman, a pallid, wretched woman, walking the streets of a city, but I say, "Poor woman, poor,
blighted, ruined creature, sin has doomed you forever!" And
I want to say right here that it is not right or human, for
when a woman falls she is lost forever. Our country is degraded, and the reason I fight whiskey is because whiskey is
my enemy, and I am going to fight for these wives, mothers
and children as long as God will let me stay above ground.
Yes, I am in full range of all the guns in this Blue Grass region. [Laughter.] I will tell you, from the worms of the stills
in Kentucky there is not as much water flows down yonder
Kentucky river as you pour out on this world in whiskey. It is
not only throwing its awful arms around your own State,
but it is trying to grasp other States around you, and send
them to hell and perdition with you. Yes, it is time you are
awakened.

Sometimes a state reaches that point where, that if a man is
not for whiskey and the whiskey party, you need not talk
about running him. God bless you, you cannot be elected for
Governor, Judge or Member of the Legislature now unless
you are of the whiskey crowd. God pity the unfortunate
wretch that floats upon this river, that's all I have to say about
him. I will declare before God, and write it in letters of blood
on every gate-post in this country, a man has to submit to debauchery of soul and body now to become a Democrat. I
hardly care to say I'm a Democrat. We are Democrats because
we say we don't want niggers settled on us. The niggers are
not on the side of whiskey always. I never had a nigger to do
me harm in my life, but whiskey was the cause of it. No nigger ever made my poor wife sick and drove the roses out of

her cheeks and made my little child almost a pauper. No, no nigger ever did that for me. If it is niggers or whiskey, knock your whiskey in the head and give me niggers every crack.

That's the only difference between the Republican Party and the Democrats, one is for niggers and the other for whiskey. I believe I'll join the Republicans.

Sin? I'll take no sin into my life, into my politics, into my family, into our world; let's away with it.   *   *   *

"He that pursueth evil pursueth it to his own death." I am practical, in one sense at least, and I always purpose to be practical. I am determined on one thing, and I don't care whether anybody agrees with me or not. I don't care if every person here goes off and calls me a fool and a fanatic. We'll meet in judgment and discuss that in the future. I don't care what your opinion of what I say is, and whether you endorse it or not, you are going to understand and see it. You can call Sam Jones a fool all you want to, and say you will never hear him preach again, but if I never preach the gospel again I'm going to give you the naked truth to-day. Take me down here and pitch me off the bluff, and as I fall you will say there goes that little tallow-faced fellow that told the truth while he was here.

"He that pursueth evil" pursueth it to the death of his conscience. That's what's the matter in this country, conscience has been stabbed to death. A man who sins deliberately against his conscience stabs his conscience, and it will breathe its last some of these days and be dead forever.

Sam Jones gave as an illustration of conscience, a man who joins the church, and yet, after a time, falls back into his old sins, and who, knowing he has not done right, feels it in his conscience, and it troubles him, until his conscience becomes so sin-hardened that nothing can affect it. A man joins the church, and next week is at the races. I have said it, and say it again, I love a fine horse next to a woman. I cannot help out-loving a woman above everything else in this country, and next to a woman I love a good horse—I like a grand horse—I can't help it. There is that magnificent blooded horse out there; I cannot help but admire him, and I would go to every fair in this country to look at him if it was not for one thing, and that's that low-down, trifling, pusillanimous fellow who says to everything you do or he does, "I bet you." I have a contempt for those cusses, and it's that sort that keeps me away from such places. I love blooded horses, but God help me, I'll never get on a horse and ride him to a race. I want that understood. There's many a Kentuckian gone to hell on a blooded horse, mark what I tell you. This little body sneers about a fair and I have a pronounced and supreme contempt for him.

Talk to me about no harm in these things. That old member of the church who will walk out of a grocery, and wipe his mouth, and say: "No harm in a dram." There is harm, but your conscience is dead! dead! dead! And I want to say right here, that if any of you are a member of any church and drink whiskey, you are a hypocrite of the deepest dye. An old Methodist demijohn. An old Baptist jug. An old Presbyterian decanter, half full all the time, and every time your poor wife wants to go to church, she has to stick her arm in the handle of an old demijohn and walk with that. I have a contempt for you—you old hog.

Lexington wants me, but she'll have to excuse me, as this sort of talk won't do for Lexington. If I do go there I tell you when I turn some of you lose you will hit ground a running. Conscience! conscience! dead! dead! all over this country. You may just as well be dead as without a conscience. They say they drink whiskey and dance and play cards because it's in the fashion. If that's the fashion, God bless you, I'm going to try to live out of it. I wish you preachers would say amen right there. Don't let anybody hear you—that's right.

Sam Jones then scathingly denounced the church people, who, being in control in certain cities, grant a license to sell whiskey and create devilment at so much per month— factories for making drunkards and ruining homes. Don't give them a license—close them up.

PHILLIPS BROOKS

The Seriousness of Life

Let not God speak to us, lest we die.—EX. xx. 19.

THE HEBREWS had come up out of Egypt, and were standing in front of Sinai. The mountain was full of fire and smoke.
Thunderings and voices were bursting from its mysterious
awfulness. Great trumpet-blasts came pealing through the
frightened air. Everything bore witness to the presence of
God. The Hebrews were appalled and frightened. We can see
them cowering and trembling. They turn to Moses and beg
him to stand between them and God. "Speak thou with us,
and we will hear; but let not God speak to us, lest we die."

At first it seems as if their feeling were a strange one. This
is their God who is speaking to them, their God who brought
them "out of the Land of Egypt, out of the House of
Bondage." Would it not seem as if they would be glad to have
Him come to them directly, to have Him almost look on
them with eyes that they could see, and make unnecessary the
interposition of His servant Moses, bringing them messages
from Him? Will they not feel their whole history of rescue
coming to its consummation when at last they find themselves
actually in the presence of the God who has delivered them,
and hear His voice?

That is the first question, but very speedily we feel how natural that is which actually did take place. The Hebrews had
delighted in God's mercy. They had come singing up out of
the Red Sea. They had followed the pillar of fire and the pillar of cloud. They had accepted God's provision for their
hunger. They had received Moses, whom God had made their
leader. But now they were called on to face God Himself. In
behind all the superficial aspects of their life they were called
on to get at its centre and its heart. In behind the happy
results, they were summoned to deal with the mysterious and
mighty cause. There they recoiled. "Nay," they said, "let us

go on as we are. Let life not become so terrible and solemn. We are willing to know that God is there. We are willing, we are glad, that Moses should go into His presence and bring us His messages. But we will not come in sight of Him ourselves. Life would be awful. Life would be unbearable. Let not God speak with us, lest we die!"

I want to bid you think this morning how natural and how common such a temper is. There are a few people among us who are always full of fear that life will become too trivial and petty. There are always a great many people who live in perpetual anxiety lest life shall become too awful and serious and deep and solemn. There is something in all of us which feels that fear. We are always hiding behind effects to keep out of sight of their causes, behind events to keep out of sight of their meanings, behind facts to keep out of sight of principles, behind men to keep out of the sight of God. Because that is such poor economy; because the only real safety and happiness of life comes from looking down bravely into its depths when they are opened to us, and fairly taking into account the profoundest meanings of existence; because not death but life, the fullest and completest life, comes from letting God speak to us and earnestly listening while He speaks,—for these reasons I think this verse will have something to say to us which it will be good for us to hear.

We have all known men from whom it seemed as if it would be good to lift away some of the burden of life, to make the world seem easier and less serious. Some such people perhaps we know to-day; but as we look abroad generally do we not feel sure that such people are the exceptions? The great mass of people are stunted and starved with superficialness. They never get beneath the crust and skin of the things with which they deal. They never touch the real reasons and meanings of living. They turn and hide their faces, or else run away when those profoundest things present themselves. They will not let God speak with them. So all their lives lack tone; nothing brave, enterprising, or aspiring is in them. Do you not know it well? Do you not feel it everywhere?

For we may lay it down as a first principle that he who uses superficially any power or any person which he is capable of using profoundly gets harm out of that unaccepted opportunity which he lets slip. You talk with some slight acquaintance, some man of small capacity and little depth, about ordinary things in very ordinary fashion; and you do not suffer for it. You get all that he has to give. But you hold constant intercourse with some deep nature, some man of great thoughts and true spiritual standards, and you insist on dealing merely with the surface of him, touching him only at the most trivial points of living, and you do get harm. The unused capacity of the man—all which he might be to you, but which you are refusing to let him be—is always there, demoralizing you. If you knew that a boy would absolutely and utterly shut his nature up against the high influences of the best men, would you not think it good for him to live not with them but with men of inferior degree, in whom he should not be always rejecting possibilities which he ought to take? A dog might live with a wise man, and remaining still a dog, be all the better for the wise man's wisdom, which he never rejected because he could not accept it. But a brutish man who lived with the sage and insisted that he would be still a brute, would become all the more brutish by reason of the despised and neglected wisdom.

Now we have only to apply this principle to life and we have the philosophy and meaning of what I want to preach to you this morning. It is possible to conceive of a world which should offer the material and opportunity of nothing but superficialness,—nothing but the making of money and the eating of bread and the playing of games; and in that world a man might live superficially and get no harm. On the other hand it is possible to conceive of a man who had no capacity for anything but superficialness and frivolity and dealing with second causes; and that man might live superficially even in this deep, rich world in which we live, and get no harm. But—here is the point—for this man with his capacities to live in this world with its opportunities and yet to live on its surface and to refuse its depths, to turn away from its problems, to reject the voice of God that speaks out of it, is a demoralizing and degrading thing. It mortifies the unused powers, and keeps the man always a traitor to his privileges and his duties.

Take one part of life and you can see it very plainly. Take the part with which we are familiar here in church. Take the religious life of man. True religion is, at its soul, spiritual sympathy with, spiritual obedience to God. But religion has its superficial aspects,—first of truth to be proved and accepted, and then, still more superficial, of forms to be practised and obeyed. Now suppose that a man setting out to be religious confines himself to these superficial regions and refuses to go further down. He learns his creed and says it. He rehearses his ceremony and practises it. The deeper voice of his religion cries to him from its unsounded depths, "Come, understand your soul! Come, through repentance enter into holiness! Come, hear the voice of God." But he draws back; he piles between himself and that importunate invitation the cushions of his dogma and his ceremony. "Let God's voice come to me deadened and softened through these," he says. "Let not God speak to me, lest I die. Speak thou to me and I will hear." So he cries to his priest, to his sacrament, which is his Moses. Is he not harmed by that? Is it only that he loses the deeper spiritual power which he might have had? Is it not also that the fact of its being there and of his refusing to take it makes his life unreal, fills it with a suspicion of cowardice, and puts it on its guard lest at any time this ocean of spiritual life which has been shut out should burst through the barriers which exclude it and come pouring in? Suppose the opposite. Suppose the soul so summoned accepts the fulness of its life. It opens its ears and cries, "Speak, Lord, for thy servant heareth." It invites the infinite and eternal aspects of life to show themselves. Thankful to Moses for his faithful leadership, it is always pressing through him to the God for whom he speaks. Thankful to priest and church and dogma, it will always live in the truth of its direct, immediate relationship to God, and make them minister to that. What a consciousness of thoroughness and safety; what a certain, strong sense of resting on the foundation of all things is there then! There are no closed, ignored rooms of the universe out of which unexpected winds may blow, full of dismay. The sky is clear above us, though we have not soared to its farthest height. The ocean is broad before us, though we have not sailed through all its breadth.

Oh, my dear friends, do not let your religion satisfy itself with anything less than God. Insist on having your soul get at Him and hear His voice. Never, because of the mystery, the awe, perhaps the perplexity and doubt which come with the great experiences, let yourself take refuge in the superficial things of faith. It is better to be lost on the ocean than to be tied to the shore. It is better to be overwhelmed with the greatness of hearing the awful voice of God than to become satisfied with the piping of mechanical ceremonies or the lullabies of traditional creeds. Therefore seek great experiences of the soul, and never turn your back on them when God sends them, as He surely will!

The whole world of thought is full of the same necessity and the same danger. A man sets himself to think of this world we live in. He discovers facts. He arranges facts into what he calls laws. Behind his laws he feels and owns the powers to which he gives the name of force. There he sets his feet. He will go no further. He dimly hears the depth below, of final causes, of personal purposes, roaring as the great ocean roars under the steamship which, with its clamorous machineries and its precious freight of life, goes sailing on the ocean's bosom. You say to him, "Take this into your account. Your laws are beautiful, your force is gracious and sublime. But neither is ultimate. You have not reached the end and source of things in these. Go further. Let God speak to you." Can you not hear the answer? "Nay, that perplexes all things. That throws confusion into what we have made plain and orderly and clear. Let not God speak to us, lest we die!" You think what the study of Nature might become, if, keeping every accurate and careful method of investigation of the way in which the universe is governed and arranged, it yet was always hearing, always rejoicing to hear, behind all methods and governments and machineries, the sacred movement of the personal will and nature which is the soul of all. Whether we call such hearing science or poetry, it matters not. If we call it poetry, we are only asserting the poetic issue of all science. If we call it science, we are only declaring that poetry is not fiction but the completest truth. The two unite in religion, which when it has its full chance to do all its work shall bring poetry and science together in the presence of a recognized God, whom the student then shall not shrink from, but delight to know, and find in Him the illumination and the harmony of all his knowledge.

The same is true about all motive. How men shrink from the profoundest motives! How they will pretend that they are doing things for slight and superficial reasons when really the sources of their actions are in the most eternal principles of things, in the very being of God Himself. I stop you and ask you why you give that poor man a dollar, and you give me some account of how his poverty offends your taste, of how unpleasant it is to behold him starve. I ask you why you toil at your business day in and day out, year after year. I beg you to tell me why you devote yourself to study, and you reply with certain statements about the attractiveness of study and the way in which every extension or increase of knowledge makes the world more rich. All that is true, but it is slight. It keeps the world thin. This refusal to trace any act back more than an inch into that world of motive out of which all acts spring, this refusal especially to let acts root themselves in Him who is the one only really worthy cause why anything should be done at all,—this is what makes life grow so thin to the feeling of men who live it; this is what makes men wonder sometimes that their brethren can find it worth while to keep on working and living, even while they themselves keep on at their life and work in the same way. This is the reason why men very often fear that the impulse of life may give out before the time comes to die, and shudder as they think how awful it will be to go on living with the object and the zest of life all dead. Such a fear never could come for a moment to the man who felt the fountain of God's infinite being behind all that the least of God's children did for love of Him.

I know very well how all this which I have undertaken to preach this morning may easily be distorted and misunderstood. It may seem to be the setting forth of a sensational and unnatural idea of life, the struggle after which will only result in a histrionic self-consciousness, a restless, discontented passion for making life seem intense and awful, when it is really commonplace and tame. "Let us be quiet and natural," men say, "and all will be well." But the truth is that to be natural is to feel the seriousness and depth of life, and that no man does come to any worthy quietness who does not find God and rest on Him and talk with Him continually. The contortions of the sensationalist must not blind us to the real truth of that which he grotesquely parodies. His blunder is not in thinking that life is earnest, but in trying to realize its earnestness by stirring up its surface into foam instead of piercing down into its depths, where all is calm. Yet even he, grotesque and dreadful as he is, seems almost better than the imperturbably complacent soul who refuses to believe that life is serious at all.

The whole trouble comes from a wilful or a blind underestimate of man. "Let not God speak to me, lest I die," the man exclaims. Is it not almost as if the fish cried, "Cast me not into the water, lest I drown," or as if the eagle said, "Let not the sun shine on me, lest I be blind." It is man fearing his native element. He was made to talk with God. It is not death, but his true life, to come into the divine society and to take his thoughts, his standards, and his motives directly out of the hand of the eternal perfectness. Man does not know his own vitality, and so he nurses a little quiver of flame and keeps the draught away from it, when if he would only trust it and throw it bravely out into the wind, where it belongs, it would blaze into the true fire it was made to be. We find a revelation of this in all the deepest and highest moments of our lives. Have you not often been surprised by seeing how men who seemed to have no capacity for such experiences passed into a sense of divine companionship when anything disturbed their lives with supreme joy or sorrow? Once or twice, at least, in his own life, almost every one of us has found himself face to face with God, and felt how natural it was to be there. Then all interpreters and agencies of Him have passed away. He has looked in on us directly; we have looked immediately upon Him; and we have not died,—we have supremely lived. We have known that we never had so lived as then. We have been aware how natural was that direct sympathy and union and communication with God. And often the question has come, "What possible reason is there why this should not be the habit and fixed condition of our life? Why should we ever go back from it?" And then, as we felt ourselves going back from it, we have been aware that we were growing unnatural again;

we were leaving the heights, where our souls breathed their truest air, and going down into the valleys, where only long habit and an educated distrust of our own high capacity had made us feel ourselves more thoroughly at home.

And as this is the revelation of the highest moments of every life, so it is the revelation of the highest lives; especially it is the revelation of the highest of all lives, the life of Christ. Men had been saying, "Let not God speak to us, lest we die;" and here came Christ, the man,—Jesus, the man; and God spoke with Him constantly, and yet he lived with the most complete vitality. He was the livest of all living men. God spoke with Him continually. He never did a deed, He never thought a thought, that He did not carry it back with His soul before it took its final shape and get His Father's judgment on it. He lifted His eyes at any instant and talked through the open sky, and on the winds came back to Him the answer. He talked with Pilate and with Peter, with Herod and with John; and yet his talk with them was silence; it did not begin to make His life, to be His life, compared with that perpetual communion with His Father which made the fundamental consciousness as it made the unbroken habit of His life. All this is true of Jesus. You who know the rich story of the Gospels know how absolutely it is true of Him. And the strange thing about it is that the life of which all this is true is felt at once to be the most natural, the most living life which the world has ever seen. Imagine Jesus saying those words which the Hebrews said: "Let not God speak to me, lest I die." You cannot put those words upon His lips. They will not stay there. "O God, speak to me, that I may live,"—that is the prayer with which He comes out of the stifling air of the synagogue or the temple, out of the half-death of the mercenary streets, out of the foolish rivalries and quarrellings of His disciples.

And every now and then a great man or woman comes who is like Christ in this. There comes a man who naturally drinks of the fountain and eats of the essential bread of life. Where you deal with the mere borders of things he gets at their hearts; where you ask counsel of expediencies, he talks with first principles; where you say, "This will be profitable," he says, "This is right." Remember I am talking about him now only with reference to this one thing,—that when men see him they recognize at once that it is from abundance and not from defect of vitality that this man lives among the things which are divine. Is there one such man—it may be one such boy—in the store where all the rest of you are working for rivalry or avarice? Is there one who works from principle, one who works for God; and will you tell me whether you do not all count him the most genuinely living of you all?

The student of history knows very well that there are certain ages and certain races which more than other ages seem to have got down to the fundamental facts, and to be living by the elemental and eternal forces,—ages and races which are always speaking with God. So we all feel about the Hebrews. The divine voice was always in their ears. Often they misunderstood it. Often they thought they heard it when it was only the echo of their own thoughts and wishes that they heard; but the desire to hear it, the sense that life consisted in hearing it,—that never left them. And so, too, we feel, or ought to feel, about the great Hebrew period of our own race, the Puritan century, in which everything was probed to the bottom, all delegated authorities were questioned, and earnestness everywhere insisted upon having to do immediately with God. Plenty of crude, gross, almost blasphemous developments of this insistence set themselves forth; but the fact of the insistence was and still is most impressive. It never frightened the Puritan when you bade him stand still and listen to the speech of God. His closet and his church were full of the reverberations of the awful, gracious, beautiful voice for which he listened. He made little, too little, of sacraments and priests, because God was so intensely real to him. What should he do with lenses who stood thus full in the torrent of the sunshine? And so the thing which makes the history of the Puritans so impressive is the sense that in them we come close to the great first things. We are back behind the temporary, special forms of living, on the bosom of the primitive eternal life itself.

When we turn suddenly from their time to our own time what a difference there is! At least what a difference there is between all their time and a part of ours. For our time is not capable of being characterized as generally and absolutely as theirs. It has many elements. Certainly it has much of Puritanism. The age which has had Carlyle for its prophet, and which has fought out our war against slavery has not lost its Puritanism. But the other side of our life, how far it is from the first facts of life, from God, who is behind and below everything! When I listen to our morals finding their sufficient warrant and only recognized authority in expediency; when I behold our politics abandoning all ideal conceptions of the nation's life and talking as if it were only a great mercantile establishment, of which the best which we can ask is that it should be honestly run; when I see society conceiving no higher purpose for its activities than amusement; when I catch the tone of literature, of poetry, and of romance, abandoning large themes, studiously and deliberately giving up principles and all heroic life, and making itself the servant and record of what is most sordid and familiar, sometimes even of what is most uncomely and unclean; when I think of art grown seemingly incapable of any high endeavor; when I consider how many of our brightest men have written the word Agnostic on their banner, as if not to know anything, or to consider anything incapable of being known, were a condition to shout over and not to mourn over,—when I see all these things, and catch the spirit of the time of which these things are but the exhibitions and the symptoms, I cannot help feeling as if out of this side, at least, of our time there came something very like the echoes of the old Hebrew cry, "Let not God speak to us, lest we die." We are afraid of getting to the roots of things, where God abides. What bulwarks have you, rich, luxurious men, built up between yourselves and the poverty in which hosts of your brethren are living? What do you know, what do you want to know, of the real life of Jesus, who was so poor, so radical, so full of the sense of everything just as it is in God? You tremble at the changes which are evidently coming. You ask yourself, How many of these first things, these fundamental things, are going to be disturbed? Are property and rank and social precedence and the relation of class to class going to be overturned? Oh, you have got to learn that these are not the first things, these are not the fundamental things! Behind these things stand justice and mercy. Behind everything stands God. He must speak to you. He will speak to you. Oh, do not try to shut out His voice. Listen to Him that you may live. Be ready for any overturnings, even of the things which have seemed to you most eternal, if by them He can come to be more the King of His own earth.

And in religion, may I not beg you to be vastly more radical and thorough? Do not avoid, but seek, the great, deep, simple things of faith. Religious people read thin, superficial books of religious sentiment, but do not meet face to face the strong, exacting, masculine pages of their Bibles. They live in the surface questions about how the Church is constituted, how it ought to be governed, what the forms of worship ought to be. They shrink from the profound and awful problems of the soul's salvation by the Son of God and preparation for eternity. Do we not hear—strangest of all!—in religion, which means the soul's relationship to God, do we not hear there—strangest of all—the soul's frightened cry, "Let not God speak with me, lest I die"? In all your personal life, my friends, it is more thoroughness and depth that you need in order to get the peace which if you spoke the truth you would own that you so wofully lack. You are in God's world; you are God's child. Those things you cannot change; the only peace and rest and happiness for you is to accept them and rejoice in them. When God speaks to you you must not make believe to yourself that it is the wind blowing or the torrent falling from the hill. You must know that it is God. You must gather up the whole power of meeting Him. You must be thankful that life is great and not little. You must listen as if listening were your life. And then, then only, can come peace. All other sounds will be caught up into the prevailing richness of that voice of God. The lost proportions will be perfectly restored. Discord will cease; harmony will be complete.

I beg you who are young to think of what I have said to you to-day. Set the thought of life high at the beginning. Expect God to speak to you. Do not dream of turning your back on the richness and solemnity of living. Then there will come to you the happiness which came to Jesus. You, like Him, shall live, not by bread alone, but by every word that proceedeth out of the mouth of God!

FRANCIS J. GRIMKÉ

A Resemblance and a Contrast

*Between the American Negro and the Children of Israel
in Egypt, or the Duty of the Negro to Contend Earnestly
for his Rights Guaranteed under the Constitution.*

*This Discourse was Delivered in the
Fifteenth Street Presbyterian Church.
October 12th, 1902.*

*In Connection with the Encampment of the Grand Army
of the Republic, in the City of Washington*

――――

EXODUS 1:9, 10.
*"And He said unto His people, Behold, the people
of the children of Israel are more and mightier than
we: Come, let us deal wisely with them; lest they
multiply, and it come to pass, that, when there
falleth out any war, they also join themselves unto
our enemies, and fight against us, and get them up
out of the land."*

IN THIS RECORD, there is a contrast suggested between our
people in this country, and the children of Israel in Egypt;
and also a resemblance to which I desire, for the moments
that I shall occupy, to call attention.

(1) The children of Israel went down into Egypt of their
own accord. Ten of the sons of Jacob, first went down to buy
corn, owing to a very severe famine that was raging in their
own country, and in all the surrounding countries. This journey was again repeated some time afterwards, at which time,
they were joined by Benjamin,—the man in charge of affairs
having made that a condition of their seeing his face. It was
during this second visit, that Joseph was made known to his
brethren, through whom an earnest invitation was sent to

his father, Jacob, and all the members of the family to come
and stay in the land, with the promise that all of their wants
would be supplied. It was in response to this invitation that
the family packed up everything which they had and went
down into Egypt. They went down from choice: it was a voluntary thing on their part. They were not forced against their
will.

The opposite of this was true in the case of the coming of
our forefathers to this country. It was not a voluntary act on
their part. They were seized by slave hunters and against their
will forced from the land of their birth. Left to themselves
they never would have sought these shores.

(2) The children of Israel were few in number when they
went down into Egypt. There were only about seventy odd
souls in all. During their sojourn, however, they greatly multiplied: so much so that at the time of the Exodus, 1491, B.C.,
according to the census that was taken under the divine direction, there were 603,550 men over twenty years of age who
were able to go to war. No mention is made of the male
members of the population under twenty, nor of the old men,
who were unfit for active military service; nor of the women
and female children. The whole number must have been between two and three millions. Assuming that Jacob went
down in the year 1706, B.C., and that the Exodus was in 1491,
this increase came about in a little over two centuries.

The same fact is noticeable in reference to our people in
this country. The first installment came in 1619, and the importation of slaves was prohibited in 1808. According to the
census for 1790, we numbered then 752,208. Fifty years afterwards, the number had increased to 2,873,648. In 1890, the
number had gone up to 7,470,040, while the last census
shows our present number to be 8,840,789. This is a very remarkable showing, when we remember the large mortality of
the race, and the fact that the increase has been purely a
natural one, without any accessions through immigration. It
shows that we are a very prolific race, and that there is no
danger of our dying out.

(3) The Egyptians were alarmed at the rapid increase of
the children of Israel, and sought in one way or another to
diminish their number, or to arrest their increase. The first

method was to work them to death, to kill them off by hard labor, and by cruel treatment. This method failed, however; instead of decreasing they went on steadily increasing, becoming more and more numerous. Then another method was resorted to,—the midwives were directed to strangle the male children to death at birth. This also failed. And a third and last method was devised: a decree was issued compelling parents to expose their own children to death. Under this decree, Moses, the great law-giver, would have perished had he not been providentially rescued by Pharaoh's daughter, from an untimely death.

The rapid increase of our people in this country has also been a source of disquiet, if not of positive alarm, to the white element of the population. In 1889, when the census showed an increase of over 22 per cent., you will remember, what an excitement it created, and what absurd predictions were made as to the possibility of the country being overrun by Negroes. In 1890, when the percentage was cut down owing to inaccuracies in the census of 1890, what a sense of relief was felt by the whites. The rapid increase of the colored population of this country is no more welcomed or relished by the white American than the rapid increase of the Jewish population was by the Egyptians. There has been no concerted action on the part of the whites to cut down our numbers, as was done in Egypt; the process of destruction, however, has gone on all the same. In the Southern section of our country, especially, the hand of violence has been laid upon our people, and hundreds and thousands of them have, in this way, been sent to untimely graves. The convict lease system has also had its influence in diminishing our numbers. Whether this was its intention originally or not, I am not prepared to say, but the fact is, it has had that effect. Through the Convict Camps, the exodus from this world to the next has been amazingly frequent. The avarice, the cupidity of the white man, as illustrated in the grinding conditions imposed upon the colored farmer, under the crop lease system, has also done much to increase the hardships of life for us and to shorten our days.

(4) The Egyptians were afraid that the children of Israel would get up and leave the land: and this, they didn't want them to do. They wanted them to remain, not because they

loved them, or because of any special interest which they felt in them as such; but from purely selfish considerations. They were valuable as laborers. From the narrative we learn that they worked in the fields, made bricks and built treasure cities for Pharaoh. It was a great thing to have at their disposal, a population of this kind, who could be pressed into service whenever they were needed. In those oriental monarchies, when great public works, like the building of the Pyramids, were carried on by the State, and when it required an enormous number of workmen, it was of the utmost importance to the State to have constantly at hand the means of supplying this want. And this they found in the rapidly increasing Jewish population, and accordingly, were not disposed to tolerate for a moment, the idea of their departure. How strongly they felt on this matter, is evident from the reply which Pharaoh made to the demand of Moses, "Thus saith the Lord, the God of Israel, Let My people go that they may hold a feast unto me in the wilderness." And Pharaoh said, "Who is the Lord, that I should hearken unto His voice to let Israel go? I know not the Lord, and moreover I will not let Israel go." The same is also evident from the fact, that it was not until the land had been visited by ten great plagues, ending with the death of the first-born, that they were willing to let them go.

When the children of Israel first went down into Egypt it was with no intention of remaining there permanently. It was intended to be only a temporary sojourn, during the continuance of the famine, which drove them there. Nor was it in accordance with the divine plan that they should remain permanently, as is evident from the record, in forty-six of Genesis. "And God spake unto Israel in the vision of the night, and said, Jacob, Jacob." And he said, "Here am I." And he said, "I am God, the God of thy fathers: fear not to go down into Egypt; for I will there make of thee a great nation: I will go down with thee into Egypt; and I will surely bring thee up again." And you will also remember what God said to Abraham, in response to the question, "Whereby shall I know that I shall inherit it," that is, the land of Canaan. "Know of a surety that thy seed shall be a stranger in a land that is not theirs, and shall serve them; and they shall afflict them four hundred years; and also that nation, whom they shall serve, will I judge: and afterwards they shall come out with great substance."

Now in both of these respects, things seem to be somewhat different with us in this country. If we may judge from the representations in the newspapers and magazines, which are made from time to time, it would appear that the white Americans would be very glad to have our people arise, and get out of the land. We hear a great deal about schemes for deporting the Negro, and in certain sections of the South, and even in certain parts of Illinois, the attempt has been made to forcibly drive him out. While I do not apprehend that there will ever be any general movement to get rid of us, to forcibly deport us from the country, nevertheless, I do not believe that there would be any regrets or tears shed on the part of the whites, if such a thing should occur. I think the great majority would be glad to get rid of us. With the Negro out of the country, what a love feast there would be between the North and the South: how they would rush into each others arms, and fondly embrace each other, and rejoice over the fact that at last the great barrier which has stood between them for so many years had been removed. With the Negro out of the country, what a bright prospect there would be of building up a respectable White Republican Party in the South; so we are told by some Republican fools, who lose sight of the fact that the glory of the Republican Party does not depend upon its getting rid of the Negro, but on the contrary, whatever of glory there is attached to it has come from its connection with the Negro. Why is it called the grand old party? What is it that has given it its pre-eminence; that has rendered it immortal; that has covered it with imperishable glory? Is it not the noble stand which it took for human rights; the magnificent fight which it made against slavery and rebellion, out of which came the great amendments to the Constitution, the Thirteenth, Fourteenth, and Fifteenth? It was the enactment of these great amendments that has given it its chief claim to distinction, and that will ever constitute its crowning glory. Yes, even the Republican party, I believe, would be glad to see us go. In two Southern States already, two Republican conventions have declined to receive or admit colored delegates. If some Moses should rise up to-day, as of old, and say to this nation, as was said to Pharaoh, "Let my people go," it would not be necessary to send any plagues in order to have the demand enforced. I believe from every part of the land—North, South, East and West, there would be but one voice, and that would be, Let them go.

The children of Israel wanted to go, while the Egyptians didn't want them to go; the reverse of that, I believe, is true in our case in this land. The white Americans would be glad to have us go, but there is no desire or disposition on our part to go. So far as I have been able to ascertain the sentiments of our people, it is our purpose to remain here. We have never known any other home, and don't expect, as a people, ever to know any other. Here and there an individual may go, but the masses of our people will remain where we are. Things are not exactly as we would like to have them; no, they are very far from being so, or from what we hope some time they will be, but bad as they are, we are nevertheless disposed to remain where we are. Besides, it would be cowardly to run away. Wherever we go we will have to struggle. Life is real, life is earnest everywhere. And since we are in the struggle here, we had just as well fight it out here as anywhere else. And that is what we are going to do. We are not going to retreat a single inch. We are not going to expatriate ourselves, out of deference to a Negro-hating public sentiment.

It was the *divine plan* that Israel's stay in Egypt should be only temporary; God's purpose was ultimately to lead them back to the land of Canaan, from which they had come. And it has been intimated, from certain quarters, that that is to be true of us; that God has providentially permitted us to be brought to this land, in order that we might be trained for future usefulness in the land of our forefathers. This is the view that has been taken by some white men, and also by some colored men. It may be so; but I confess, so far, I have not been able to discover any evidences of such a purpose. In the case of the Jews, the record showed what the purposes of God were in regard to that people; but we have no such revelation touching ourselves. God spoke to Abraham, and God spoke to Jacob, and showed them what was to be; but where are the Abrahams and Jacobs among us to whom he has spoken? There are those who are ready to speculate, but speculation amounts to nothing. What the divine purposes are touching this race no one knows. And therefore in the absence of any definite and positive information, we will assume, that this purpose is that we remain just where we are. Until we have very clear evidence to the contrary, we are not likely to take any steps to go elsewhere.

(5) The Egyptians were afraid that the children of Israel, in case of war with a foreign power, would join their enemies and fight against them. And well might they have feared. In the first place, the whole world at that time was in a state of war. It was might that made right. Wars of conquests were constantly going on. One nation or state felt perfectly justified in making war against another, if it was deemed to its interest to do so. As a matter of fact there was always liability of an invasion from some foreign power. This was a possibility, which Egypt, as well as every other country, had to take into consideration, and to provide against. At any moment the enemy might be seen approaching; at any moment their safety might be imperilled.

In the (2) place, with this possibility staring them in the face, their treatment of the Jews, in case of an invasion, would very naturally have led them to feel, that the sympathy of the Jews would be with the invaders instead of with them. The reason assigned in the narrative however for this fear is, lest through such an alliance with a foreign power, they succeed in getting out of the land. This shows conclusively that the Jews evidently wanted to get out of the land; and had possibly intimated that. The Egyptians didn't want them to go; and yet, strange to say, instead of setting themselves to work to make it so pleasant and agreeable for them that they would not want to go, the very opposite policy is pursued,—the policy of oppression, of injustice, of violence. Instead of seeking to win them by acts of kindness, they inaugurated a reign of terror; sought to intimidate them, to crush out of them every spark of manhood, to reduce them to the level of dumb, driven cattle. What a strange thing human nature is; how shortsighted, how blind, how utterly stupid men often are, and men from whom we might naturally, expect better things. If the Jews were to remain in Egypt, as the Egyptians desired to have them do, wasn't it a great deal better to have their love than their hatred, their friendship than their enmity? And even if they were going out, was it not better to have their good will than their ill will? For it was just possible, that some time in the future, they might need the help even of the descendants of Jacob, little and insignificant as they were at that time in their estimation. It was the day of small things with them; but there was no telling what the future might bring forth. As a matter of fact, we know that they did become a great and powerful nation.

It is just possible that the absurd and ruinous policy pursued by the Egyptians was due also to a sense of race superiority, and the assumption that if they were in any way civil, if they treated the Jews with the common courtesies that one human being owes to another, it might create within them a desire for social equality. It is possible that the fear of being overrun by an inferior race, may also have fired their imagination blinding their vision, and blunting their moral sensibilities. Whatever the reason may have been, the fact remains that the policy inaugurated by them was an utterly heartless and brutal one; and this policy they continued to pursue until it was reversed by the divine interposition, until God's righteous indignation was excited, and the angel of death was sent forth and smote the first-born throughout the land, and overthrew the tyrants in the Red Sea. It is only a matter of time when all such oppressors the world over, will meet a similar fate. God is not dead,—nor is he an indifferent onlooker at what is going on in this world. One day He will make requisition for blood; He will call the oppressors to account. Justice may sleep, but it never dies. The individual, race, or nation which does wrong, which sets at defiance God's great law, especially God's great law of love, of brotherhood, will be sure, sooner or later, to pay the penalty. We reap as we sow. With what measure we mete, it shall be measured to us again.

The absurdity of pursuing such a policy is evident from the disastrous consequences which followed. The voice of lamentation that was heard throughout the land of Egypt, the pall of death that hung over every home, and the appalling catastrophe at the Red Sea, which was the culmination of a series of terrible judgments, all came out of it. It was a policy which brought upon them only wretchedness and misery; from which they did not derive a single advantage, or reap a single benefit.

The policy pursued by them, not only did not benefit them, but did not in the least interfere with the divine purposes concerning the Jews. In spite of their policy of oppression, of injustice, of bitter hatred, God let the children of Israel out all the same, and safely conducted them to the Promised Land. The race that puts its trust in God, and is willing to be led by God, is safe. The heathen may rage and the people imagine a vain thing, but they will be powerless to stay its progress. They may worry and vex it for a while but they will not be able to do it any permanent injury, or seriously to interfere with its development, with its onward and upward march. The race that puts its trust in God has always, under all circumstances, more for it than against it. There is never therefore any reason for fear, or for becoming discouraged as long as it maintains its grip upon the Almighty, as long as its attitude is one of simple child-like trust and dependence.

This is not the point, however, that I had in view in referring to this aspect of the subject, which we are considering under this fifth general head. We were speaking under this head of the fear entertained by the Egyptians of the children of Israel joining their enemies, in case of an invasion, and fighting against them. And what I want to say, in this connection is, that there is no just ground for any such fear in regard to our people in this country. Whatever else may be said of the black man, the charge of disloyalty cannot be truthfully made against him. From the very beginning he has been loyal to the flag, and has always been willing to lay down his life in its defense. In the war of the Revolution; in the war of 1812; in the Mexican war; in the great Civil war; and in the war with Spain, he stood side by side with other citizens of the Republic facing the enemy; and in all of our national cemeteries may be found evidences of his patriotism and valor. It is only necessary to mention Milliken's Bend, Port Hudson, Fort Wagner, Olustee, during the great Civil war, and San Juan Hill, during the Spanish war, as evidences of his valor and patriotism. Joseph T. Wilson, who was himself a gallant soldier in the 54th Massachusetts, has written a book, entitled,

"The Black Phalanx," in which he traces the history of the Negro soldiers of the United States, from the earliest period through the great war of the Rebellion. It is a glorious record, and one that puts the patriotism of the Negro beyond all question. Whenever the call of danger has been sounded he has always been ready to respond, to bare his bosom to the bullets of the enemy.

This is all the more remarkable when we remember what his treatment has been in this country. Buffeted, spit upon, his most sacred rights trampled upon, without redress, discriminated against in hotels, restaurants, in common carriers, deprived of his political rights, shot down by lawless ruffians, every possible indignity heaped upon him, while the State and Nation look on, the one justifying the outrages, or at least doing nothing to prevent them, and the other protesting its inability to protect its own citizens from violence and injustice. Such treatment is not calculated to inspire one's patriotism, to kindle one's love for a government that permits such injustice and oppression to go on without, at least, the attempt to check them. And yet in spite of these monstrous wrongs that have gone on and are still going on, unrestrained by State or Federal authority, the record of the Negro for patriotism will compare with any other class of citizens. He has been just as constant, just as unswerving in his devotion to the Republic as the most favored class. Oppressed, downtrodden, discriminated against, denied even the common civilities of life, and yet, in the hour of danger, always ready to stretch forth his strong black arm in defense of the Nation. How to explain this, I do not know, nor is it necessary. It is with the fact alone that I am concerned. There it is, and it is true of no other element of the population. There is no other class of citizens, which, if treated as we have been and are still being treated, would evince any such patriotism, would show any such willingness to lay down their lives at the nation's call, as we have. The fear of the Egyptians cannot therefore be the fear of the white citizens of this country. The Negro has never shown any disposition to fight against the Republic, or to allay himself with a foreign foe. His sympathies have always been with the stars and stripes.

In our city we are now having what is known as the annual

encampment of the Grand Army of the Republic. This army is an organization made up of the surviving veterans of the great Civil War. It is called, The Grand Army. Mr. Gladstone used to be called The Grand Old Man, because he summed up in himself many great qualities. He was a matchless orator, a profound thinker, a great scholar, a man of encyclopedic information. The Republican Party is sometimes called The Grand Old Party, and the name is not inappropriately applied to it. There are many things connected with its history that justify that title. It has done some grand things, and it has had associated with it some of the bravest, truest, noblest, and brainiest men that this country has produced,—men, who were not afraid to do right; who felt, as Lowell has expressed it:

"Though we break our fathers' promise, we have nobler
        duties first;
  The traitor to Humanity is the traitor most accursed;
  Man is more than Constitutions; better rot beneath the sod,
  Than be true to Church and State while we are doubly false
        to God."

A party with such men, as it had in it years ago, may well be called, "The Grand Old Party." I take the term, grand, to apply to the old party—the party as it used to be, not to the party as it is to-day, with its petty little programme of a White Republican Party in the South; the elimination of Negro office-holders in the South, out of deference to white southern sentiment; white supremacy in the Philippines and Porto Rico; and the undue prominence that is given to material things; while it is indifferent to the rights of its citizens of color—caring more for dollars and cents, for material prosperity, than for righteousness, for simple, even-handed justice, which alone exalts a nation. It used to be the Grand Old Party. It is no longer such. There isn't a single thing about it, either in what it is at present doing, or in its purposes with reference to the future, to which the term "grand" can be truthfully applied. It has lost its fine sense of righteousness. It no longer gives evidence of those higher instincts, those nobler sentiments, that make nations and parties truly great. It grovels in the dust. Its aims and purposes are of the earth earthy. It is in the interest of commerce and trade and material development that it is bending its energies, and taxing its resources—forgetful of the fact, that it is true of a nation as of an individual, that its real true life does not consist in the abundance of the good things which it possesseth. Lowell, in his Ode on France, after describing the overthrow of the French tyrant during the great revolution, gives utterance to these significant words:

> "What though
> The yellow blood of trade meanwhile should pour
>   Along its arteries a shrunken flow,
> And the idle canvas droop around the shore?
>   These do not make a state, nor keep it great;
>   I think God made
>   The earth for man, not trade;
> And where each humblest human creature
> Can stand, no more suspicious or afraid
> Erect and kingly in his right of nature,
> To heaven and earth knit with harmonious ties,—
>   Where I behold the exaltation
>   Of manhood glowing in those eyes
>   That had been dark for ages,
>   Or only lit with bestial loves and rages,
>   There I behold a Nation;
>   The France which lies
>   Between the Pyrenees and the Rhine
>   Is the least part of France;
> I see her rather in the *soul* whose shine
> Burns through the craftsman's grimy countenance,
>   In the energy divine
>   Of toil's enfranchised glance."

Unfortunately neither Republicans nor Democrats in this country seem to recognize the great fact enunciated in these lines, but it is true nevertheless; and no party is entitled to the designation, "Grand," which does not accept it, and act in the light of it.

It is not of the Republican party that I started to speak, however, but of the Grand Army of the Republic. The term, "Grand," as applied to this army is a fitting tribute to the

great services which it has rendered to the Republic. It was
this army, the remnant of which is in our city to-day, that
saved the life of the Republic; that put down rebellion; and
that gave efficacy to Lincoln's great Proclamation of
Emancipation. Had he not had back of him this Army, his
proclamation would have been unavailing. An army that has
to its credit these great achievements may well be called,
Grand. It *is* the Grand Army of the Republic. There have
been other armies of the Republic,—the army of the Revolution, the army of 1812, the army of the war with Mexico,
and of the Spanish American war, but *the* Army of the Republic, both as to numbers and as to the importance of its
achievements, is the Army that put down the great Rebellion,
and with it the accursed system of slavery, which was like a
millstone about the neck of both races. All honor to these
brave men. Too much cannot be said in praise of their valor
and patriotism. As the years go by; as their numbers decrease,
as one by one they go to join their comrades on the other
side, the more and more should we honor those who still remain among us. I am glad of this annual encampment; glad of
the parade connected with it; glad to look into the faces, and
to have others look into the faces of the brave men who stood
by their guns, and stood watch over the nation, when
Rebellion sought to dissolve the Union and to rivet more
firmly the fetters upon four millions of bondmen. And, I am
especially glad to know that in these parades of the veterans
who saved the Nation, are to be found not only white men,
but black men as well. I hope that these representatives of our
race will always attend these annual gatherings, even though
it may entail some sacrifice on their part to do so. It is a splendid object lesson to the whole nation; and it is a fitting rebuke
to those recreant white Americans who say, "This is a white
man's country." If it is a white man's country, what are these
black heroes doing in these annual parades? If it is a white
man's country, why is it that in all of our national cemeteries
are the graves of Negroes? Why is it that in every war since
the beginning of the Republic, on sea and land, the blood of
the Negro has spurted in its behalf? Why is it that on the pen-
sion roll of the nation to-day are widows and orphans and
battle-scarred heroes of this race? If this is a white man's

country, why are Negroes ever called upon to take up arms in its defense? I am glad of these annual encampments, I say, and glad of the share which we have in them. Let every Negro veteran who can, always make it a point to be present at these gatherings, and always get into the ranks and march with the procession, in order that the multitudes who gather from all parts of the country may look on and take knowledge of the fact that the Negro is a man, and that he can do a man's part, and that he may be relied upon to do his part as a citizen of the Republic. It is a grand object lesson, I say, to the nation, to see these colored men in line under such circumstances. And so far, as we are concerned, we should never by our absence, permit that lesson to be lost.

In thinking of this Grand Army of the Republic I am painfully reminded of the fact, that though the War of the Rebellion is over, and has been over for more than thirty-five years; and though the great amendments to the Constitution have been enacted, making us freemen, and citizens, and giving us the right of the ballot, we have not yet been put in possession of these rights. We are still discriminated against, and treated as if we had no rights which white men were bound to respect. And I have called attention to this condition of things, in this connection, to remind us of the fact, that, though the Civil War is over, the battle for our rights in this country is not yet over. The great amendments are a part of the law of the land, but the same treasonable and Negro-hating spirit that sought to perpetuate our bondage, and to keep us in a state of hopeless inferiority, is still endeavoring to accomplish its purpose by seeking to nullify them. There is a spirit abroad in this land, which is determined that we shall never be accorded the rights of American citizens. And that spirit you have got to meet, and I have got to meet, and we have all got to meet. And it is from these old battle-scarred survivors of the Civil War, that we may learn how to meet it—with courage, with invincible determination; with the earnest purpose never to surrender. Be assured that these wrongs, from which we are suffering, will never be righted if we sit idly by and take no interest in the matter. If we are indifferent even those who might be disposed to assist us will also become indifferent. We must show the proper appreciation, the proper interest ourselves. We must agitate, and agitate, and agitate, and go on agitating. By and by, our very importunity will make itself felt. The people, in the midst of whom we are living, if not from a sense of justice, of right, of fair play, will on the principle of the unjust judge, who cared neither for God nor man, but who said, "I will right the widow's wrong, lest by her continual coming she weary me," be constrained to right our wrongs.

In the struggle which we are making in this country for the recognition of our rights as men and citizens, there is another thing which I want to say, There is little or nothing to be expected from those members of our race, whether in politics or out of it, who value their little petty personal interests above the interests of their race; whose first and last and only thought is, What is there in the struggle for me, what can I get out of it? And who, when they have gotten their little out of it, are perfectly willing to sacrifice the race, to turn it over to the tender mercies of its enemies; to stand by and see it despoiled of its rights without one word of protest. It is not from such men that anything is to be expected. It is rather from the men who are willing to make sacrifices, and to suffer, if need be, for principle; who cannot be satisfied, and cannot permit themselves to be silent in the presence of wrong, in order to ingratiate themselves into the favor of the dominant race, or that they might hold on to some petty office or position. If we are to succeed; if we are to make the proper kind of a fight in this country for our rights, we have got to develop a class of men who cannot be won over by a few offices, or by being patted on the shoulder; men, who, like John the Baptist, are willing to be clothed in camel's hair, and to subsist on locusts and wild honey,—to wear the coarsest clothing, and be content with the plainest food, in order that they might be free to follow the dictates of their own conscience; that they might be unhampered in the fight which they are making for their rights, and for the rights of their race. The men whose policy is to look out for self first, and to concern themselves about the race only so far as professing interest in it may be a help to them in working out their selfish ends and purposes, are men that are unworthy of our confidence. The men that we should honor, and that we may safely

follow, are those who are willing to lose themselves, to subordinate their selfish interests in order that the race may find
itself, may come into the full enjoyment of all of its rights.
That was the spirit exhibited by Garrison, though he was battling for the rights, not of white men, but of black men.

"In a small chamber, friendless and unseen,
    Toiled o'er his types one poor, unlearned young man;
The place was dark, unfurnitured, and mean;
    Yet there the freedom of a race began.
Help came but slowly; surely no man yet
    Put lever to the heavy world with less."

What a picture is that! We can see it all! The dingy little
room, dark, unfurnitured, and mean; and, we can understand
how difficult it must have been for him to keep soul and body
together; and yet he was willing to endure all, to suffer all, for
the sake of the cause to which he had dedicated his life. *That*
was a *white man* suffering for black men! What ought not
black men to be willing to suffer, to endure, for themselves?
If we are to succeed, I say, in the struggle through which we
are passing, we have got to develop within the race itself more
of the spirit which Garrison possessed,—the willingness to be
found, if necessary, in a small chamber, dark, unfurnitured
and mean, and to be friendless, in the struggle which we are
making for the new emancipation from the fetters of caste
prejudice, and from the injustice and oppression to which we
are at present subjected. We are still dragging the chain; and
we will go on dragging it until the race itself wakes up and
sets itself earnestly to work to break it. We are not sufficiently
in earnest; we are too easily lulled to sleep; we are too easily
satisfied; we are not sufficiently impressed with the gravity of
the situation—with the true inwardness of the motive which
is leading our enemies on, enemies within the race as well as
without it, in the assaults which they are making upon our
rights. Edwin Markham, in a little poem, entitled, "Thoughts
for Independence Day," asks the question:

"What need we, then, to guard and keep us whole?
    What do we need to prop the State?"

And the answer which he makes among others is:

> "We need the Cromwell fire to make us feel
> The public honor or the public trust
> To be a thing as sacred and august
> As some white altar where the angels kneel."

And that is what *we* need, "The Cromwell fire," to make us feel that the rights guaranteed to us under the Constitution, are

> "as sacred and august
> As some white altar where the angels kneel."

If we felt that way, we would not lightly surrender these rights, as too many are disposed to do.

At this Grand Army Encampment, when the issues of the great Civil War are brought vividly before us, it is a good time to look into each other's faces; to give each other the pass-word; and to pledge ourselves anew to stand by our colors. Mr. Webster, in his eulogy on Adams and Jefferson, represents John Adams as saying, on the question of independence, "Sink, or swim; live, or die; survive, or perish, I give my hand and heart to this vote." And in the same spirit let us say to-day, "Sink, or swim; live, or die, survive, or perish," we pledge our hands and hearts to each other, *never* to give up the struggle. Stanley is represented, while in Africa, as saying, "Nothing except the Bible gave me such comfort and inspiration as these lines from Browning:

> "'What on earth had I to do
> With the slothful with the mawkish, the unmanly?
> Being—who?
> One who never turned his back, but marched breast
> forward,
> Never doubted clouds would break,
> Never dreamed, though right were worsted, wrong
> would triumph,
> Held, we fall to rise, are baffled to fight better,
> Sleep to wake.'"

And that is what we must do, "March breast forward;" that is the kind of men that we must *be*;—the kind of men that we must seek more and more to develop among us,—men of courage, of faith, of steady purpose, of uncompromising fidelity to principle. Douglass was a man of that type. A majestic figure! A leader, who never turned his back; and who never compromised his race; a leader, who was always true; and who, down to the very last, stood empanoplied in its defense. It is the Douglass-type of leaders that we want—leaders who respect themselves, and to whom the interests of their race are above price. Long may the memory of this illustrious man linger with us, to stimulate our ambition; to arouse our slumbering energies; and to put within us the earnest purpose to continue the fight for equal civil and political rights in this land which we have helped to develop and to save.

"At the battle of Copenhagen, 1801, Nelson was vice-admiral, and led the attack against the Danish fleet. By accident one-fourth of the fleet were unable to participate, and the battle was very destructive. Admiral Parker, a conservative and aged officer, seeing how little progress was made after three hours conflict, signalled the fleet to discontinue the engagement. That signal was No. 39. Nelson continued to walk the deck, without appearing to notice the signal. 'Shall I repeat it?' said the lieutenant. No; acknowledge it. He turned to the Captain: 'You know, Forley, I have only one eye. I can't see it,' putting his glass to his blind eye. 'Nail my signal for close action to the mast,' cried Nelson." *That* was *his* order to continue the fight. And the fight was continued, and the battle was won. And so, when signals come to us, as they have come and are coming, from within the race, as well as from without it, bidding us give up the struggle; telling us to cease to agitate, to protest, to stand up for our rights; telling us not to trouble ourselves; that it doesn't do any good; that we had better let things go, which means, go the way our enemies want them to go; that all this agitation tends only to make things worse, to engender hard feelings;—to all such signals let us, like the intrepid Nelson, turn our blind eye towards them; let us not see them; and go right on fighting the battles of the race. If we are true to ourselves and to God the victory will be ours. It may be slow in coming, but come it will. Nothing is to be gained by withdrawing from the contest. Our duty is to remain firm; to plant ourselves squarely and uncompromisingly upon the rights guaranteed to us under the constitution, and to hold our ground. No backward step, should be our motto.

> "To-day is the day of battle,
>   The brunt is hard to bear;
> Stand back, all ye who falter,
>   Make room for those who dare."

Thank God there have always been among us men of this stamp; men who have realized the necessity of fighting, and who have been willing to go forward, regardless of personal consequences—brave men, true men, unselfish men.

Let us hope that the number of those who falter, who are disposed to stand back, to meekly surrender their rights, may be steadily on the decrease; and that the number of those who dare, who are resolved to go forward, to stand firmly for the right, may go on steadily increasing, until there shall not be left one lukewarm, indifferent, half-hearted, non-selfrespecting member of the race; until all shall be aroused, and shall be equally interested in a cause that ought to be dearer to us than life itself.

Let us be men; and let us stand up for our rights as men, and as American citizens.

> "Be strong!
> It matters not how deep entrenched the wrong,
> How hard the battle goes, the day, how long.
> Faint not, Fight on! To-morrow comes the song."

J. GRESHAM MACHEN

History and Faith

THE STUDENT of the New Testament should be primarily an historian. The centre and core of all the Bible is history. Everything else that the Bible contains is fitted into an historical framework and leads up to an historical climax. The Bible is primarily a record of events.

That assertion will not pass unchallenged. The modern Church is impatient of history. History, we are told, is a dead thing. Let us forget the Amalekites, and fight the enemies that are at our doors. The true essence of the Bible is to be found in eternal ideas; history is merely the form in which those ideas are expressed. It makes no difference whether the history is real or fictitious; in either case, the ideas are the same. It makes no difference whether Abraham was an historical personage or a myth; in either case his life is an inspiring example of faith. It makes no difference whether Moses was really a mediator between God and Israel; in any case the record of Sinai embodies the idea of a covenant between God and His people. It makes no difference whether Jesus really lived and died and rose again as He is declared to have done in the Gospels; in any case the Gospel picture, be it ideal or be it history, is an encouragement to filial piety. In this way, religion has been made independent, as is thought, of the uncertainties of historical research. The separation of Christianity from history has been a great concern of modern theology. It has been an inspiring attempt. But it has been a failure.

Give up history, and you can retain some things. You can retain a belief in God. But philosophical theism has never been a powerful force in the world. You can retain a lofty ethical ideal. But be perfectly clear about one point—you can never retain a gospel. For gospel means "good news", tidings, information about something that has happened. In other words, it means history. A gospel independent of history is simply a contradiction in terms.

We are shut up in this world as in a beleaguered camp. Dismayed by the stern facts of life, we are urged by the modern preacher to have courage. Let us treat God as our Father; let us continue bravely in the battle of life. But alas, the facts are too plain—those facts which are always with us. The fact of suffering! How do you know that God is all love and kindness? Nature is full of horrors. Human suffering may be unpleasant, but it is real, and God must have something to do with it. The fact of death! No matter how satisfying the joys of earth, it cannot be denied at least that they will soon depart, and of what use are joys that last but for a day? A span of life—and then, for all of us, blank, unfathomed mystery! The fact of guilt! What if the condemnation of conscience should be but the foretaste of judgment? What if contact with the infinite should be contact with a dreadful infinity of holiness? What if the inscrutable cause of all things should turn out to be a righteous God? The fact of sin! The thraldom of habit! This strange subjection to a mysterious power of evil that is leading resistlessly into some unknown abyss! To these facts the modern preacher responds—with exhortation. Make the best of the situation, he says, look on the bright side of life. Very eloquent, my friend! But alas, you cannot change the facts. The modern preacher offers reflection. The Bible offers more. The Bible offers news—not reflection on the old, but tidings of something new; not something that can be deduced or something that can be discovered, but something that has happened; not philosophy, but history; not exhortation, but a gospel.

The Bible contains a record of something that has happened, something that puts a new face upon life. What that something is, is told us in Matthew, Mark, Luke and John. It is the life and death and resurrection of Jesus Christ. The authority of the Bible should be tested here at the central point. Is the Bible right about Jesus?

The Bible account of Jesus contains mysteries, but the essence of it can be put almost in a word. Jesus of Nazareth was not a product of the world, but a Saviour come from outside the world. His birth was a mystery. His life was a life of perfect purity, of awful righteousness, and of gracious, sovereign power. His death was no mere holy martyrdom, but a sacrifice for the sins of the world. His resurrection was not an aspiration in the hearts of His disciples, but a mighty act of God. He is alive, and present at this hour to help us if we will turn to Him. He is more than one of the sons of men; He is in mysterious union with the eternal God.

That is the Bible account of Jesus. It is opposed today by another account. That account appears in many forms, but the essence of it is simple. Jesus of Nazareth, it maintains, was the fairest flower of humanity. He lived a life of remarkable purity and unselfishness. So deep was His filial piety, so profound His consciousness of a mission, that He came to regard himself, not merely as a prophet, but as the Messiah. By opposing the hypocrisy of the Jews, or by imprudent obtrusion of His lofty claims, He suffered martyrdom. He died on the cross. After His death, His followers were discouraged. But His cause was not lost; the memory of Him was too strong; the disciples simply could not believe that He had perished. Predisposed psychologically in this way, they had visionary experiences; they thought they saw Him. These visions were hallucinations. But they were the means by which the personality of Jesus retained its power; they were the foundation of the Christian Church.

There, in a word, is the issue. Jesus a product of the world, or a heavenly being come from without? A teacher and example, or a Saviour? The issue is sharp—the Bible against the modern preacher. Here is the real test of Bible authority. If the Bible is right here, at the decisive point, probably it is right elsewhere. If it is wrong here, then its authority is gone. The question must be faced. What shall we think about Jesus of Nazareth?

From the middle of the first century, certain interesting documents have been preserved; they are the epistles of Paul. The genuineness of them—the chief of them at any rate—is not seriously doubted, and they can be dated with approximate accuracy. They form, therefore, a fixed starting-point in controversy. These epistles were written by a remarkable man. Paul cannot be brushed lightly aside. He was certainly, to say the least, one of the most influential men that ever lived. His influence was a mighty building; probably it was not erected on the sand.

In his letters, Paul has revealed the very depths of a tremendous religious experience. That experience was founded, not upon a profound philosophy or daring speculation, but upon a Palestinian Jew who had lived but a few years before. That Jew was Jesus of Nazareth. Paul had a strange view of Jesus; he separated Him sharply from man and placed Him clearly on the side of God. "Not by man, but by Jesus Christ", he says at the beginning of Galatians, and he implies the same thing on every page of his letters. Jesus Christ, according to Paul, was man, but He was also more.

That is a very strange fact. Only through familiarity have we ceased to wonder at it. Look at the thing a moment as though for the first time. A Jew lives in Palestine, and is executed like a common criminal. Almost immediately after His death He is raised to divine dignity by one of His contemporaries—not by a negligible enthusiast either, but by one of the most commanding figures in the history of the world. So the thing presents itself to the modern historian. There is a problem here. However the problem may be solved, it can be ignored by no one. The man Jesus deified by Paul—that is a very remarkable fact. The late H. J. Holtzmann, who may be regarded as the typical exponent of modern naturalistic criticism of the New Testament, admitted that for the rapid apotheosis of Jesus as it appears in the epistles of Paul he was able to cite no parallel in the religious history of the race.*

The raising of Jesus to superhuman dignity was extraordinarily rapid even if it was due to Paul. But it was most emphatically not due to Paul; it can be traced clearly to the original disciples of Jesus. And that too on the basis of the Pauline Epistles alone. The epistles show that with regard to the person of Christ Paul was in agreement with those who had been apostles before him. Even the Judaizers had no dispute with Paul's conception of Jesus as a heavenly being. About other things there was debate; about this point there is not a trace of a conflict. With regard to the supernatural Christ Paul appears everywhere in perfect harmony with all Palestinian Christians. That is a fact of enormous significance.

*In *Protestantische Monatshefte*, iv (1900), pp. 465 ff., and in *Christliche Welt*, xxiv (1910), column 153.

The heavenly Christ of Paul was also the Christ of those who had walked and talked with Jesus of Nazareth. Think of it! Those men had seen Jesus subject to all the petty limitations of human life. Yet suddenly, almost immediately after His shameful death, they became convinced that He had risen from the tomb and that He was a heavenly being. There is an historical problem here—for modern naturalism, we venture to think, an unsolved problem. A man Jesus regarded as a heavenly being, not by later generations who could be deceived by the nimbus of distance and mystery, but actually by His intimate friends! A strange hallucination indeed! And founded upon that hallucination the whole of the modern world!

So much for Paul. A good deal can be learned from him alone—enough to give us pause. But that is not all that we know about Jesus; it is only a beginning. The Gospels enrich our knowledge; they provide an extended picture.

In their picture of Jesus the Gospels agree with Paul; like Paul, they make of Jesus a supernatural person. Not one of the Gospels, but all of them! The day is past when the divine Christ of John could be confronted with a human Christ of Mark. Historical students of all shades of opinion have now come to see that Mark as well as John (though it is believed in a lesser degree) presents an exalted Christology, Mark as well as John represents Jesus clearly as a supernatural person.

A supernatural person, according to modern historians, never existed. That is the fundamental principle of modern naturalism. The world, it is said, must be explained as an absolutely unbroken development, obeying fixed laws. The supernatural Christ of the Gospels never existed. How then explain the Gospel picture? You might explain it as fiction—the Gospel account of Jesus throughout a myth. That explanation is seriously being proposed to-day. But it is absurd; it will never convince any body of genuine historians. The matter is at any rate not so simple as that. The Gospels present a supernatural person, but they also present a real person—a very real, a very concrete, a very inimitable person. That is not denied by modern liberalism. Indeed it cannot possibly be denied. If the Jesus who spoke the parables, the Jesus who opposed the Pharisees, the Jesus who ate with publicans and sinners, is not a real person, living under real conditions, at a definite point of time, then there is no way of distinguishing history from sham.

On the one hand, then, the Jesus of the Gospels is a supernatural person; on the other hand, He is a real person. But according to modern naturalism, a supernatural person never existed. He is a supernatural person; He is a real person; and yet a supernatural person is never real! A problem here! What is the solution? Why, obviously, says the modern historian—obviously, there are two elements in the Gospels. In the first place, there is genuine historical tradition. That has preserved the real Jesus. In the second place, there is myth. That has added the supernatural attributes. The duty of the historian is to separate the two—to discover the genuine human traits of the Galilean prophet beneath the gaudy colors which have almost hopelessly defaced His portrait, to disentangle the human Jesus from the tawdry ornamentation which has been hung about Him by naïve and unintelligent admirers.

Separate the natural and the supernatural in the Gospel account of Jesus—that has been the task of modern liberalism. How shall the work be done? We must admit at least that the myth-making process began very early; it has affected even the very earliest literary sources that we know. But let us not be discouraged. Whenever the mythical elaboration began, it may now be reversed. Let us simply go through the Gospels and separate the wheat from the tares. Let us separate the natural from the supernatural, the human from the divine, the believable from the unbelievable. When we have thus picked out the workable elements, let us combine them into some sort of picture of the historical Jesus. Such is the method. The result is what is called "the liberal Jesus". It has been a splendid effort. I know scarcely any more brilliant chapter in the history of the human spirit than this "quest of the historical Jesus". The modern world has put its very life and soul into this task. It has been a splendid effort. But it has also been—a failure.

In the first place, there is the initial difficulty of separating the natural from the supernatural in the Gospel narrative. The two are inextricably intertwined. Some of the incidents, you say, are evidently historical; they are so full of local color; they could never have been invented. Yes, but unfortunately the miraculous incidents possess exactly the same qualities. You help yourself, then, by admissions. Jesus, you say, was a faith-healer of remarkable power; many of the cures related in the Gospels are real, though they are not really miraculous. But that does not carry you far. Faith-healing is often a totally in-adequate explanation of the cures. And those supposed faith-cures are not a bit more vividly, more concretely, more inimitably related than the most uncompromising of the mir-acles. The attempt to separate divine and human in the Gospels leads naturally to a radical scepticism. The wheat is rooted up with the tares. If the supernatural is untrue, then the whole must go, for the supernatural is inseparable from the rest. This tendency is not merely logical; it is not merely what might naturally be; it is actual. Liberal scholars are re-jecting more and more of the Gospels; others are denying that there is any certainly historical element at all. Such scep-ticism is absurd. Of it you need have no fear; it will always be corrected by common sense. The Gospel narrative is too inimitably concrete, too absolutely incapable of invention. If elimination of the supernatural leads logically to elimination of the whole, that is simply a refutation of the whole critical process. The supernatural Jesus is the only Jesus that we know.

In the second place, suppose this first task has been accom-plished. It is really impossible, but suppose it has been done. You have reconstructed the historical Jesus—a teacher of righteousness, an inspired prophet, a pure worshipper of God. You clothe Him with all the art of modern research; you throw upon Him the warm, deceptive, calcium-light of modern sentimentality. But all to no purpose! The liberal Jesus remains an impossible figure of the stage. There is a contradiction at the very centre of His being. That contradic-tion arises from His Messianic consciousness. This simple prophet of yours, this humble child of God, thought that He was a heavenly being who was to come on the clouds of heaven and be the instrument in judging the earth. There is a tremendous contradiction here. A few extremists rid them-selves easily of the difficulty; they simply deny that Jesus ever thought He was the Messiah. An heroic measure, which is generally rejected! The Messianic consciousness is rooted far too deep in the sources ever to be removed by a critical process. That Jesus thought He was the Messiah is nearly as certain as that He lived at all. There is a tremendous problem there. It would be no problem if Jesus were an ordinary fanatic or unbalanced visionary; He might then have deceived Himself as well as others. But as a matter of fact He was no ordinary fanatic, no megalomaniac. On the contrary, His calmness and unselfishness and strength have produced an indelible impression. It was such an one who thought that He was the Son of Man to come on the clouds of heaven. A contradiction! Do not think I am exaggerating. The difficulty is felt by all. After all has been done, after the miraculous has carefully been eliminated, there is still, as a recent liberal writer has said, something puzzling, something almost uncanny, about Jesus.* He refuses to be forced into the mould of a harmless teacher. A few men draw the logical conclusion. Jesus, they say, was insane. That is consistent. But it is absurd.

Suppose, however, that all these objections have been overcome. Suppose the critical sifting of the Gospel tradition has been accomplished, suppose the resulting picture of Jesus is comprehensible—even then the work is only half done. How did this human Jesus come to be regarded as a superhuman Jesus by His intimate friends, and how, upon the foundation of this strange belief was there reared the edifice of the Christian Church?

In the early part of the first century, in one of the petty principalities subject to Rome, there lived an interesting man. Until the age of thirty years He led an obscure life in a Galilean family, then began a course of religious and ethical teaching accompanied by a remarkable ministry of healing. At first His preaching was crowned with a measure of success, but soon the crowds deserted Him, and after three or four years, He fell victim in Jerusalem to the jealousy of His countrymen and the cowardice of the Roman governor. His few faithful disciples were utterly disheartened; His shameful death was the end of all their high ambitions. After a few days, however, an astonishing thing happened. It is the most

*Heitmüller, *Jesus*, 1913, p. 71.

astonishing thing in all history. Those same disheartened men suddenly displayed a surprising activity. They began preaching, with remarkable success, in Jerusalem, the very scene of their disgrace. In a few years, the religion that they preached burst the bands of Judaism, and planted itself in the great centres of the Graeco-Roman world. At first despised, then persecuted, it overcame all obstacles; in less than three hundred years it became the dominant religion of the Empire; and it has exerted an incalculable influence upon the modern world.

Jesus, Himself, the Founder, had not succeeded in winning any considerable number of permanent adherents; during His lifetime, the genuine disciples were comparatively few. It is after His death that the origin of Christianity as an influential movement is to be placed. Now it seems exceedingly unnatural that Jesus' disciples could thus accomplish what He had failed to accomplish. They were evidently far inferior to Him in spiritual discernment and in courage; they had not displayed the slightest trace of originality; they had been abjectly dependent upon the Master; they had not even succeeded in understanding Him. Furthermore, what little understanding, what little courage they may have had was dissipated by His death. "Smite the shepherd, and the sheep shall be scattered." How could such men succeed where their Master had failed? How could they institute the mightiest religious movement in the history of the world?

Of course, you can amuse yourself by suggesting impossible hypotheses. You might suggest, for instance, that after the death of Jesus His disciples sat quietly down and reflected on His teaching. "Do unto others as you would have others do unto you." "Love your enemies." These are pretty good principles; they are of permanent value. Are they not as good now, the disciples might have said, as they were when Jesus was alive? "Our Father which art in heaven." Is not that a good way of addressing God? May not God be our Father even though Jesus is now dead? The disciples might conceivably have come to such conclusions. But certainly nothing could be more unlikely. These men had not even understood the teachings of Jesus when He was alive, not even under the immediate impact of that tremendous personality. How much less would they understand after He had died, and died in a way that indicated hopeless failure! What hope could such men have, at such a time, of influencing the world? Furthermore, the hypothesis has not one jot of evidence in its favor. Christianity never was the continuation of the work of a dead teacher.

It is evident, therefore, that in the short interval between the death of Jesus and the first Christian preaching, something had happened. Something must have happened to explain the transformation of those weak, discouraged men into the spiritual conquerors of the world. Whatever that happening was, it is the greatest event in history. An event is measured by its consequences—and that event has transformed the world.

According to modern naturalism, that event, which caused the founding of the Christian Church, was a vision, an hallucination; according to the New Testament, it was the resurrection of Jesus from the dead. The former hypothesis has been held in a variety of forms; it has been buttressed by all the learning and all the ingenuity of modern scholarship. But all to no purpose! The visionary hypothesis may be demanded by a naturalistic philosophy; to the historian it must ever remain unsatisfactory. History is relentlessly plain. The foundation of the Church is either inexplicable, or else it is to be explained by the resurrection of Jesus Christ from the dead. But if the resurrection be accepted, then the lofty claims of Jesus are substantiated; Jesus was then no mere man, but God and man, God come in the flesh.

We have examined the liberal reconstruction of Jesus. It breaks down, we have seen, at least at three points.

It fails, in the first place, in trying to separate divine and human in the Gospel picture. Such separation is impossible; divine and human are too closely interwoven; reject the divine, and you must reject the human too. To-day the conclusion is being drawn. We must reject it all! Jesus never lived! Are you disturbed by such radicalism? I for my part not a bit. It is to me rather the most hopeful sign of the times. The liberal Jesus never existed—that is all it proves. It proves nothing against the divine Saviour. Jesus was divine, or else we have no certain proof that He ever lived. I am glad to accept the alternative.

In the second place, the liberal Jesus, after he has been re-constructed, despite His limitations is a monstrosity. The Messianic consciousness introduces a contradiction into the very centre of His being; the liberal Jesus is not the sort of man who ever could have thought that He was the Messiah. A humble teacher who thought He was the Judge of all the earth! Such an one would have been insane. To-day men are drawing the conclusion; Jesus is being investigated seriously by the alienists. But do not be alarmed at their diagnosis. The Jesus they are investigating is not the Jesus of the Bible. They are investigating a man who thought He was Messiah and was not Messiah; against one who thought He was Messiah and was Messiah they have obviously nothing to say. Their diag-nosis may be accepted; perhaps the liberal Jesus, if He ever existed, was insane. But that is not the Jesus whom we love.

In the third place, the liberal Jesus is insufficient to account for the origin of the Christian Church. The mighty edifice of Christendom was not erected upon a pin-point. Radical thinkers are drawing the conclusion. Christianity, they say, was not founded upon Jesus of Nazareth. It arose in some other way. It was a syncretistic religion; Jesus was the name of a heathen god. Or it was a social movement that arose in Rome about the middle of the first century. These construc-tions need no refutation; they are absurd. Hence comes their value. Because they are absurd, they reduce liberalism to an absurdity. A mild-mannered rabbi will not account for the ori-gin of the Church. Liberalism has left a blank at the begin-ning of Christian history. History abhors a vacuum. These absurd theories are the necessary consequence; they have sim-ply tried to fill the void.

The modern substitute for the Jesus of the Bible has been tried and found wanting. The liberal Jesus—what a world of lofty thinking, what a wealth of noble sentiment was put into His construction! But now there are some indications that He is about to fall. He is beginning to give place to a radical scep-ticism. Such scepticism is absurd; Jesus lived, if any history is true. Jesus lived, but what Jesus? Not the Jesus of modern naturalism! But the Jesus of the Bible! In the wonders of the Gospel story, in the character of Jesus, in His mysterious self-consciousness, in the very origin of the Christian Church, we discover a problem, which defies the best efforts of the naturalistic historian, which pushes us relentlessly off the safe ground of the phenomenal world toward the intellectual abyss of supernaturalism, which forces us, despite the resistance of the modern mind, to recognize a very act of God, which substitutes for the silent God of philosophy the God and Father of our Lord Jesus Christ, who, having spoken at sundry times and in divers manners unto the fathers by the prophets, hath in these last days spoken unto us by His Son.

The resurrection of Jesus is a fact of history; it is good news; it is an event that has put a new face upon life. But how can the acceptance of an historical fact satisfy the longing of our souls? Must we stake our salvation upon the intricacies of historical research? Is the trained historian the modern priest without whose gracious intervention no one can see God? Surely some more immediate certitude is required.

The objection would be valid if history stood alone. But history does not stand alone; it is confirmed by experience.

An historical conviction of the resurrection of Jesus is not the end of faith, but only the beginning; if faith stops there, it will probably never stand the fires of criticism. We are told that Jesus rose from the dead; the message is supported by a singular weight of evidence. But it is not just a message remote from us; it concerns not merely the past. If Jesus rose from the dead, as He is declared to have done in the Gospels, then He is still alive, and if He is still alive, then He may still be found. He is present with us to-day to help us if we will but turn to Him. The historical evidence for the resurrection amounted only to probability; probability is the best that history can do. But the probability was at least sufficient for a trial. We accepted the Easter message enough to make trial of it. And making trial of it we found that it is true. Christian experience cannot do without history, but it adds to history that directness, that immediateness, that intimacy of conviction which delivers us from fear. "Now we believe, not because of thy saying: for we have heard him ourselves, and know that this is indeed the Christ, the Saviour of the world."

The Bible, then, is right at the central point; it is right in its account of Jesus; it has validated its principal claim. Here, however, a curious phenomenon comes into view. Some men are strangely ungrateful. Now that we have Jesus, they say, we can be indifferent to the Bible. We have the present Christ; we care nothing about the dead documents of the past. You have Christ? But how, pray, did you get Him? There is but one answer; you got Him through the Bible. Without the Bible you would never have known so much as whether there be any Christ. Yet now that you have Christ you give the Bible up; you are ready to abandon it to its enemies; you are not interested in the findings of criticism. Apparently, then, you have used the Bible as a ladder to scale the dizzy height of Christian experience, but now that you are safe on top you kick the ladder down. Very natural! But what of the poor souls who are still battling with the flood beneath? They need the ladder too. But the figure is misleading. The Bible is not a ladder; it is a foundation. It is buttressed, indeed, by experience; if you have the present Christ, then you know that the Bible account is true. But *if* the Bible *were* false, your faith would go. You cannot, therefore, be indifferent to Bible criticism. Let us not deceive ourselves. The Bible is at the foundation of the Church. Undermine that foundation, and the Church will fall. It will fall, and great will be the fall of it.

Two conceptions of Christianity are struggling for the ascendency to-day; the question that we have been discussing is part of a still larger problem. The Bible against the modern preacher! Is Christianity a means to an end, or an end in itself, an improvement of the world, or the creation of a new world? Is sin a necessary stage in the development of humanity, or a yawning chasm in the very structure of the universe? Is the world's good sufficient to overcome the world's evil, or is this world lost in sin? Is communion with God a help toward the betterment of humanity, or itself the one great ultimate goal of human life? Is God identified with the world, or separated from it by the infinite abyss of sin? Modern culture is here in conflict with the Bible. The Church is in perplexity. She is trying to compromise. She is saying, Peace, peace, when there is no peace. And rapidly she is losing her power. The time has come when she must choose. God grant she may choose aright! God grant she may decide for the Bible! The Bible is despised—to the Jews a stumbling-block; to the Greeks foolishness—but the Bible is right. God is not a name for the totality of things, but an awful, mysterious, holy Person, not a "present God", in the modern sense, not a God who is with us by necessity, and has nothing to offer us but what we have already, but a God who from the heaven of His awful holiness has of His own free grace had pity on our bondage, and sent His Son to deliver us from the present evil world and receive us into the glorious freedom of communion with Himself.

AIMEE SEMPLE McPHERSON

The Baptism of the Holy Spirit

THE CURTAINS of the clouds which angelic hands had swept together when, the redemptive work of Jesus on earth completed, His ascending form disappeared from view, had again been parted, and the Holy Spirit, of whom Jesus had said—"He will abide with you forever"—had been sent forth from the presence of the Father. No sooner were they filled with the Holy Spirit than they began to speak with other tongues as the Spirit gave them utterance.

And *they were all filled with the Spirit.*

What was the immediate result and the outward evidence of that filling?—They began to speak with other tongues.

Is there any record of anyone ever having spoken in other tongues (languages which they had never learned and were unknown to themselves; see I Cor. 14:2), previous to the day of Pentecost and the opening of the dispensation of the Holy Spirit? NO.

The devout Jews who were gathered into Jerusalem at this time, for the religious feasts and ceremonies, came running together in multitudes, and, upon hearing the languages of the countries in which they had been born, spoken by these simple, unlearned Galileans, they were amazed, astonished, and in doubt.

At what were the people astonished? At what did they marvel? At the rushing mighty wind? No.

The tongues of fire? No; they are not again mentioned, and it is doubtful whether those who came together after the one hundred and twenty had been filled even saw them.

What then? They were amazed and marveled at the supernatural power that rested upon these men and women, causing them to reel and stagger, Acts 2:13, as though drunken with wine, and to speak with tongues unknown to themselves.

The spectators who looked upon the out-pouring of the Holy Ghost on the day of Pentecost were divided into two classes just as they are today.

One class were the mockers, who said in derision, "These men are full of new wine. Come on, let's have nothing to do with these people. They are fanatics. This is all excitement. 'Tis ridiculous to create so much noise and excitement over religion; the whole city is in an uproar; nothing but wildfire. They ought to be arrested," etc.

The other class were the thinkers—the thoughtful, intelligent men and women, who said:

"Wait a moment. There must surely be something behind all this. The ring in these people's voices—the shout in their souls—the joy and love, worship and adoration reflected in their faces—there must be some specific reason for it. They are certainly not reeling and staggering about like that for nothing. They must surely realize that the people who look on will make fun of them and think they have lost their senses.

"If they are not doing it for money nor for popularity, then why are they doing it? They are certainly not all fools. If there were only one or two we might think they were, but here are about one hundred and twenty; surely they cannot all be mad. I am going to investigate this matter and see what there is behind it all.

"Tell us, Oh, tell us, some of you good, happy people in there—stop your shouting and your rejoicing for a little space, and answer—WHAT MEANETH THIS?"

Then Peter, standing up—

"Peter, what are you rising up for? Are you frightened, Peter? Are you going to run away and seek to escape from this big, excited, questioning multitude as you did from the little girl that night you denied the Lord?"

"Run away? Oh, no! I will never run away any more now. I have been baptized with the Holy Ghost and fire. He has endued me with power from on high. He has taken fear away and put a holy boldness within my heart and words within my mouth, insomuch that out of my innermost being flow forth rivers of living water." Acts 4:13.

And Peter, standing up (ah, the Holy Spirit puts a real "stand up for Jesus" in the timid soul) with the eleven, lifted up his voice and said:

"Ye men of Judea, and all ye that dwell at Jerusalem, be this known unto you, and hearken to my words; for these are not drunken, as ye suppose, seeing it is but the third hour of the day, but this is that which was spoken of the prophet Joel. It shall come to pass in the last days, saith God, I will pour out My Spirit upon all flesh. Your sons and your daughters shall prophesy . . . on My servants and My handmaidens I will pour out in those days of My Spirit, and they shall prophesy. I will show wonders in the heavens above, signs in the earth beneath . . . and it shall come to pass that whosoever shall call on the name of the Lord shall be saved.

"Ye men of Israel, hear these words; Jesus of Nazareth . . . ye have taken, and by wicked hands have crucified and slain."

"Why, Peter, aren't you afraid to talk like that to this great mob of people? Do you not know that they gnash their teeth and hiss at the very name of Jesus? Are you not aware that you are laying yourself open to the danger of being seized upon, carried to the whipping post, stripped, beaten and stoned to death? I thought that you were a timid man who was ashamed to be known as one of them?"

"Oh, no, I will never be ashamed to be called one of the despised, persecuted, peculiar few any more. The Holy Ghost has come to abide in this life of mine, and the words that I speak I speak not of myself; the works that I do I do not of myself, but the Holy Spirit who has come to dwell within, He speaks the words; He does the works.

"This Jesus hath God raised up, whereof we are witnesses. Therefore being by the right hand of God exalted and having received of the Father the promise of the Holy Ghost, He hath shed forth this which you see (in the reeling bodies of those who appear to be drunken), and hear (in the speaking in other tongues)."

So boldly did this transformed man speak under the mighty power of the Holy Spirit that his hearers were pricked to their hearts and said unto Peter and the rest of the apostles:

"Men and brethren, what shall we do?"

Then Peter said unto them—"Repent, and be baptized, every one of you, in the name of Jesus Christ for the remission of sins, and ye shall receive the gift of the Holy Ghost.

"For the promise is unto you, and to your children, and to all that are afar off, even as many as the Lord our God shall call."

What promise is unto all that are afar off, even as many as the Lord God shall call, Peter?

The promise of the Holy Ghost—that which you see and hear.

But how much of the promise is unto us, Peter? Surely not all this mighty power, accompanied with the speaking in tongues. Was this not only the opening of the dispensation and for the Jews?

But no, says Peter, "The promise is unto them that are afar off, even as many as the Lord shall call, for now in Christ Jesus there is neither Jew nor Gentile; there is neither bond nor free. In Him we are one and are baptized into the one body."

Acts 10:44, eight years after the day of Pentecost, the door of salvation and the baptism of the Holy Spirit is opened unto the Gentiles. Walking into the home of Cornelius, in the 44th verse, we find a meeting in progress. Cornelius has gathered his household, his servants, and his neighbors together to hear the words which Peter is to speak, words whereby they may be saved.

"And while Peter yet spake these words, the Holy Ghost fell on all them which heard the Word.

"And they of the circumcision which believed were astonished, as many as came with Peter, because that on the Gentiles also was poured out the gift of the Holy Ghost.

"For they heard them speak with tongues, and magnify God."

In all these eight years the manner in which the Holy Spirit came in had not been changed—the same Bible evidence—speaking in tongues, remained. Even though there were no foreigners who came from other countries and spoke other languages, present to be benefited by the speaking in tongues, the Spirit spoke through them just the same, as He had on the day of Pentecost.

In Acts 19 a new voice is heard preaching Jesus Christ and the baptism of the Holy Spirit.

"Have you received the Holy Ghost since you believed?"

Why, that voice and face seems familiar. Have we seen or heard this man before?

"Excuse me, brother, but is your name not Saul of Tarsus?

Is this really you preaching the necessity of receiving the baptism of the Holy Spirit! I thought you condemned all this, thought it to be folly and not to be permitted. Did you not say that you were going to put an end to all this nonsense, when, after you had looked on approvingly at the stoning of Stephen, you rode away to Damascus with the intention of still further persecuting these Pentecostal Holy Ghost people?"

"Yes, I used to persecute these Christians. I thought that they were all wrong and should be wiped out of existence, but that was before my eyes were opened.

"Did you not hear how that, when riding on my way to do them greater hurt, the light of the Lord shone round about me and I was stricken from my horse and fell as one dead in the dust of the road, and how Jesus, whose face was brighter than the sun, and whose raiment was whiter than the light, came and spoke to me, saying:

" 'Saul, Saul, why persecutest thou Me?'

"Three days was I blind from the vision of His brightness. Then was I converted and my name was changed from Saul to Paul.

"Yes, I am one of them today. I will talk with you later, but now I must go on with my meeting."

After the baptismal service wherein the disciples are buried in the watery grave, in verse six, we see Paul laying his hands upon them, and read that the Holy Ghost came on them and they spoke with tongues and prophesied. Here, as in Jerusalem and in the house of Cornelius, the first thing that was mentioned of the souls that received the Holy Spirit was that they spoke with tongues.

In Acts 8:17, 18, we find sinful and wicked Simon the sorcerer, so impressed with the mighty power displayed when the believers received the Holy Ghost upon the laying on of the apostles' hands, that he offered money to the apostles in the hopes of being able to purchase the same power, saying:

"Give me also this power, that on whomsoever I lay my hands, he may receive the Holy Ghost." Without a doubt Simon saw and heard the same things that the onlookers saw and heard on the day of Pentecost. But Oh, this power could not be bought. All the money in the world could not have

BAPTISM OF THE HOLY SPIRIT

purchased it, but to those who humble themselves in lowliness and in sincerity before the Lord shall the Spirit be given freely without money and without price.

Oh, tell me, Peter and Paul, tell me John and James, and all you who received this mighty incoming of the Holy Ghost with its attendant power and glory, may we, in this 20th century, receive this like precious gift, or did the Holy Spirit empty Himself of all His power in the apostolic days? Did you consume all of these supernatural wondrous blessings, or did you leave enough to spare for us today?

"Yes, indeed," they answer in unison. "Heaven has not gone bankrupt. Heaven's storehouse still is full. The Holy Spirit has never lost His power, the promise is unto them that are afar off, even as many as the Lord our God shall call. Did not our Lord say: 'When He is come, He will abide with you forever'?

"Doubt no longer, but with open heart ask ye of the Lord rain in the time of the latter rain. Remember the words of Joel the prophet: 'It shall come to pass in the LAST days,' saith God, 'I will pour out My Spirit upon all flesh.' Remember, too, that when the high priest went in to the Holy of Holies the bells rang, and when the high priest came out the bells rang again.

"When Jesus ascended up on high the bells rang and the people spoke with tongues and magnified God. Now this same Jesus, our high priest, is coming forth again for His waiting church, and on earth the bells are ringing, the latter rain is falling, and again those who have received the old-time power speak with other tongues."

REUBEN ARCHER TORREY

The Most Wonderful Sentence Ever Written

*"For God so loved the world, that He gave His
only begotten Son, that whosoever believeth in Him
should not perish, but have everlasting life"*
(John 3:16).

My text is "The Most Wonderful Sentence That Was Ever Written." Of course that sentence is in the Bible. All the greatest sentences that were ever written are found in one book, God's Word, the Bible. The Bible is a book that abounds in illuminating, stirring, startling, marvelous, bewildering, amazing, and life-transforming utterances, utterances with which there is absolutely nothing to compare in all the other literature of the world. But I am inclined to think that the one we are to consider tonight is the most remarkable of them all. I think that after we have given it careful thought you will agree with me that this sentence is the most wonderful that was ever written.

You are all perfectly familiar with it. I doubt if there is a person in this audience who has not heard it again and again. Indeed our very familiarity with it has blinded many of us to the wonderful character of it and the stupendous significance of it. But we are going to look at it steadily and closely, turning it around and around—as one would turn around and scrutinize a diamond of unusual purity, beauty, brilliance, and play of prismatic colors—until its beauty, its profundity, its glory, its sublimity, and its amazing significance are more fully seen and appreciated by us.

The sentence is found in John 3:16, "For God so loved the world, that he gave his only begotten Son, that whosoever believeth in him should not perish, but have everlasting life." There are whole volumes of incomparably precious truth packed into that one sentence. Indeed many volumes have been devoted to the exposition of that one verse, but it is not exhausted yet and never will be. These marvelous words of God never become hackneyed or worn out or wearisome. We are always beholding new beauty and new glory in them. When all the millions of volumes that men have written in many languages throughout the many centuries of literary history have become obsolete and are forgotten, that imperishable sentence shall shine out in its matchless beauty and peerless glory throughout the endless ages of eternity.

Let me repeat it again. "For God so loved the world, that he gave his only begotten Son, that whosoever believeth in him should not perish, but have everlasting life." God Himself has used that statement to save thousands of souls, to lift men out of the sad—yes, appalling—ruin that sin had wrought into the glory of likeness to Himself. I trust that He may use it tonight to save many more.

The verse tells us five exceedingly important facts. First, God's attitude toward the world; second, God's attitude toward sin; third, God's attitude toward His Son; fourth, God's attitude toward all who believe in His Son; fifth, God's attitude toward all who refuse or neglect to believe in His Son.

First of all, *this verse from God's Word tells us what God's attitude is toward the world.* What is God's attitude toward the world? *LOVE.* The sentence reads, "God so *LOVED* the world." Love is the most wonderful thing in the world, and love is one of the most uncommon things in the world.

There is in the world today much that is called "love," but most of that which is called love is not love at all. We speak oftentimes of a young man's "love" for a young woman, and all we mean by it is that this young man wishes to get that young woman for his own pleasure and gratification. That is not love at all; it oftentimes has not the slightest semblance of love. It is oftentimes utter selfishness and not infrequently the vilest and most unbridled lust.

It is not at all unlikely that if the young woman refuses to accept him as a husband or so-called "lover," he will shoot her down or seek to blast her reputation. And that hideous thing we call "love!" He *"loved"* her so much that he killed her. It is really as remote from love as anything possibly can be, as remote from love as hell is from heaven. It is the very lowest order of selfishness and the grossest beastliness.

When a lawyer in this city week before last shot his former wife because she would not return to him and endure longer the outrages that he had inflicted upon her for years, was it love that prompted his amazingly cowardly, sneaking, cruel, ruffianly, devilish act? No, it was a passion that would have disgraced the lowest wild beast of the jungle.

We speak of one man's love for another. What do we usually mean? Only this—the two men are friendly because in many respects they are congenial and enjoy one another's society. But if one does some little thing that offends the other, the so-called love is turned into utter indifference or even into bitter hate. It was never "love." It was mere self-centered fondness.

All this is not love. What is love? *Love is the consuming, absorbing desire for and delight in another's highest good.* Real love is entirely unselfish. It loses sight utterly of self-interest and sets itself to seeking the interest of the person loved. This was God's attitude toward the world. He *loved* the world, really loved it.

He looked down upon this world, the whole mass of men living at any time upon it and that should live upon it in all times to come, and He loved them all. His whole being went out in infinite yearning to benefit and bless the world. Any cost to Himself would be disregarded if it would bless the world to pay the cost. "God so loved the world that *he gave his only begotten Son.*" Oh, men and women, stand and wonder! Oh, angels and archangel, cherubim and seraphim, stand and wonder! "God *so* loved the world *that he gave his only begotten Son.*"

Some men tell us that they cannot believe the Bible to be the Word of God because there are so many incredible statements in it. But that is the most incredible statement in the whole Book, and yet we know it is true. If I can believe that statement I ought not to have any difficulty with any other statement in the whole Book, and I can believe that statement. I do believe that statement. I know that statement is true. I have put it to the test of personal experience and found it true. "God so loved the world that He gave His only begotten Son"; that has been God's attitude toward the world from the beginning. That is God's attitude toward the world tonight.

God loves the *world*. There are men and women and children in this world whom you and I love, but God loves the whole world. There is not a man in it, not a woman in it, not a child in it whom God does not love. From the intellectually most rarely gifted and morally most saintly man and woman down to the most apelike and ignorant and the morally most degraded and brutelike man or woman, God loves each and every one. "God so loved the *world*."

There are hundreds and hundreds of people who gather in this church about whom you care absolutely nothing. You never saw them before; you will never see them again. If you should read in your paper tomorrow morning, "John Jones, who was at the Church of the Open Door, as he was going home from the meeting, got in front of a Sixth Street car and was instantly killed," you would hardly give it a second thought. John Jones is nothing to you.

But John Jones is something to God. God loves John Jones, and John Smith, and John Johnson, and every other man and woman and child. You may be a very lonely stranger in a great city's crowd. Perhaps you have been unfortunate and are penniless and friendless; perhaps you have gone down into some black depth of sin, and you say to yourself, "Not one person in this great crowd has the slightest interest in me." That may be true. But there is One who has an interest in you. There is One who so loved you that He "gave his only begotten Son" to die for you, and that One is God. God loves the world and every one in it. God loves the world in the purest, deepest, and highest sense of that word *love*. Yes, God loves you. "Whom do you mean by *you*?" someone asks. I mean every man, woman, and child.

There is nothing about the world that God should love it. It is a sinful world, it is a selfish world, it is a corrupt world. The more I get to know the world of which I am a part, and the more I get to know myself, the more I am humbled. John was entirely right when he said, "The whole world lieth in wickedness" (1 John 5:19).

I am an optimist, but I am not an optimist by painting a black world white. Look at the rich world. What a cruel thing it is. How it marches on, trampling down every one that lies in its path to obtain greater wealth. How are great fortunes usually built up? You know. I know—by the trampling of human hearts underfoot.

But look at the poor world. It is nearly as cruel as the rich world. One day in Chicago two men were working hard to make an honest living for themselves and their families, just four doors north of the church of which I was pastor. Four other poor men sneaked in, chopped their heads open with hatchets, and ran. Why did they do it? Simply because they wanted the jobs of those two men. The two men struck down by the four heartless cowards were guilty of no crime and no wrong against the ones that cut them down. They did not belong to the union, that was all.

If you wish to know the spirit of the rich world, look at some of the greedy, conscienceless trusts. If you wish to know the spirit of the poor world, look at the present day methods of the trades unions. The spirit of both is essentially the same—greed for gold; money must be secured at any cost, even the cost of murder of others by the slow process of starvation on the part of the rich or the rapid process of hatchet and bullet and dynamite on the part of the poor.

A cruel, selfish, bloodthirsty world is this. What the world really is we saw in the late war. But God loves it. God loves those four cowards who cut down their fellow laboring men. God loves those millionaires who, already having more than is for their own good or for the good of their families, are trying to increase their wealth by crowding competitors to the wall and their families to the poorhouse. God loves those moral monsters that made Europe flow with blood and gasp with poison gas. God loves the world.

As I come to know more and more of the cruelty, the greed, the selfishness, the falsehood, the villainy, the lust, the vileness, and the beastliness there is in this world—in the social world, high and low, in the business world in all its departments, and in the political world—I sometimes almost wonder why God does not blot out this whole world as He did Sodom and Gomorrah of old. Why does He not do it? I will tell you why. God *loves* the world. In spite of all its cruelty, in spite of all its greed, in spite of all its selfishness, in spite of all its lust, in spite of all its vileness in thought, word, and deed, God loves the world. Is it not wonderful, is it not amazing that a holy God should love a sinful world like this? But He does.

There is not a man whom God does not love. There is not a woman whom God does not love. There is not a thief whom God does not love. There is not a woman who has forgotten her modesty and her true womanhood that God does not love. There is not an adulterer whom God does not love, not a sinner, not an outcast, not a criminal of any kind whom God does not love. "God so loved the *world*."

Years ago I said to a woman, in deep despair because of the depths of iniquity and infamy into which she had fallen, "God loves you."

"Not me, Mr. Torrey. God doesn't love me. I have killed a man," she cried.

"Yes, I know that, but God loves you."

"No, not me. I have murdered innocent, unborn babes."

"Yes, I know that, but God loves you."

"Not me. My heart is as hard as a rock."

"Yes, but God loves you."

"Not me. I have prayed to the devil to take away all my convictions, and he has done it."

"Yes, I know all that, but God loves you."

Then I made that woman get down on her knees, and she came to believe in God's love to her and found a great peace. I saw her again last month when I was in Chicago. She came down to the platform to speak to me at the close of one of my meetings.

She said, "Do you know me?"

I replied, "Of course, I know you," and called her by name.

Her face was wreathed with smiles. "Oh," she said, "Mr. Torrey, I am still at the old work of winning others to Christ."

Ah, some of you self-righteous skeptics hold up your hands in holy horror and disgust and say, "I don't want to believe in a God who welcomes sinners so vile as that." You miserable pharisee, you old hypocrite, you are essentially as bad as she once was and infinitely worse than she now is. But God loves you, even you. God's attitude toward the whole wide world is love.

But what is God's attitude toward sin? Our text tells us, *God's attitude toward sin is HATE.* God loves the world with infinite love. God hates sin with infinite hate. How does our text show that? Listen. "God *so* loved the world, *that he gave his only begotten Son*, that whosoever believeth in him should not perish, but have everlasting life." How does that show that God hates sin? In this way: if God had not hated sin He could have saved the world He loved without an atonement, without the atonement that cost Him so much, the death and agony of His only begotten Son, who died as an atoning sacrifice on the cross.

Because God was holy and therefore hated sin, hated it with infinite hatred, His hatred of sin must manifest itself somehow, either in the punishment of the sinner—and the banishment of the sinner forever from Himself from life, and from hope—or in some other way. But God's love would not permit the just punishment of the sinner. So God in the person of His Son took the penalty of sin upon Himself and thus saved the world He loved. "All we like sheep have gone astray; we have turned every one to his own way; and Jehovah *hath made to strike on him* the iniquity of us all" (Isaiah 53:6, literal translation; italics added). In this way God made possible the salvation that He Himself purchased for men by the atoning death of His only begotten Son.

The cross of Christ declares two things: first, God's infinite love of the world; second, God's infinite hatred of sin. Oh, wicked man, do not fancy that because God loves you He will wink at your sin. Not for one moment. He hates your sin, He hates your greed, He hates your selfishness, He hates your lying, He hates your drunkenness, He hates your impure imagination, He hates your moral uncleanness, He hates your beastliness, He hates every sin, great and small, of which you are guilty. The hatred of a true man for all falsehood, the hatred of honest men for all dishonesty, the hatred of a true, pure woman for the unspeakable vileness of the woman of the street and gutter is nothing to the blazing wrath of God at your smallest sin. Nevertheless, God loves you.

This wonderful verse also tells of God's attitude toward His Son. What is God's attitude toward His Son? Listen. "God so loved the world that he gave *his only begotten son*." *God's attitude toward His Son, "his only begotten Son," is infinite love.* The Lord Jesus is the only Son of God. We become sons of God through our faith in Him, but He is the only Son of God by eternal and inherent right. He was the object of His Father's infinite love in the measureless ages before any one of the worlds was created—yes, before there was angel or archangel or any of the heavenly beings.

Let me speak to you, fathers. What is your attitude toward your son? How you love him! And if you have only one son, how intensely you love him. I have but one son. I have longed for more, but God in His wisdom has seen fit to give us but one son. How I love him! God only knows how I love him. But my love to my one son is nothing, nothing at all compared to God's love for His only begotten Son.

I sometimes think of my boy and fancy I know something of God's love for Jesus Christ, but it is only a little, a very little that I know. But though God thus loved His Son, God gave that Son whom He so infinitely loved, that Son who through all eternity had been the object of His delight, God gave that only begotten Son for the world, for you and for me. He gave Him to leave heaven and His own companionship to come down to earth to live a lonely stranger here. He gave Him to be spit upon and buffeted and "despised and rejected of men." He gave Him to be crowned with thorns, mocked at, and derided. He gave Him to be dragged through the streets before a howling, yelling, jeering mob. He gave Him to be nailed to the cross—yes, to a cross—and to hang there in misery, pain, and agony for hours, the object of the rude jests and jeers of the merciless mob. He gave Him to die of a "broken heart," a heart broken by the reproach of the men He loved (Psalm 69:20) and by grief over man's sins, which He had taken upon Himself. Yes, God gave Him *His only begotten Son*, thus to be separated from Himself, to suffer, and to die. Why? Because God loved you and me, and that was the only price that would purchase our salvation. And God paid that price, that awful price.

Oh, it is wonderful! I can think of but one other thing that is anywhere near as wonderful as the love of God for sinners. What is that? The way we treat that love. The way men treat it. The way some of you despise it. The way you reject it. The way you trample it underfoot. The way you even try to doubt it, disbelieve it, deny it, discredit it, and try to make yourself think that you have "intellectual difficulties about the doctrine of the atonement."

People, at least be honest. Your real difficulty is not intellectual—you want to save your pride and excuse the enormity of your ingratitude. To do that you do not hesitate at the gross sin of even denying the Lord that bought you, bought you by His atoning agony and death (2 Peter 2:1). Oh, be honest with the wondrous love of God, even if you are determined to spurn it. Your pretended "theological difficulties with the atonement" that Jesus Christ made upon the cross are simply your dishonest attempt to excuse your abominable ingratitude and damnable rejection of infinite love. Bear with me for talking thus plainly about your sin. I do it in love to you. You may not be willing to admit that tonight, but you will have to admit it in that day when you stand in the light of the great white throne where all lies and pretexts and deceptions and hypocrisies will be burned up.

Now let us look at another thing: *what the sentence teaches about God's attitude toward believers in the Lord Jesus Christ.* What is God's attitude toward all who believe in Jesus Christ? It can be put in a few words. *God's attitude toward all believers in Jesus Christ is to give them eternal life.* "God so loved the world, that he gave his only begotten Son, *that whosoever believeth in him should not perish, but have everlasting life.*" The death of Jesus Christ has opened for all who believe in Him a way of pardon and made it possible for a holy God to forgive sin and to give eternal life to the vilest sinner if only he will believe in Jesus Christ. "The wages of sin is death" (Romans 6:23), and these wages must be paid; but Jesus Christ paid the price, so life and not death is possible for you and me—"the gift of God is eternal life through Christ Jesus our Lord" (Romans 6:23). *Whosoever* believes on Jesus Christ, whom God gave to die for him, can have eternal life, yes, does have eternal life. Anyone can have eternal life. There is but one condition—just believe on Jesus Christ. You ought to do it anyhow, even if there were nothing to be gained by your believing in Him; you owe it to Jesus Christ to believe on Him. He is infinitely worthy of your faith.

But there *is* something to be gained by believing on Him, something of infinite worth—eternal life. Do you wish eternal life? You can have it. Anyone can have it, no matter what his past may have been. "God so loved the world, that he gave his only begotten Son, that *whosoever believeth* in him should not perish, but have everlasting life." Oh, if I offered you great honor it would be nothing compared with this. If I offered you enormous wealth it would be nothing compared with this. If I offered you exemption from all sickness and pain it would be nothing compared with this. *Eternal life!* That is what God offers. And God offers it to each one of you. Oh, how it makes the heart swell and throb with hope and joy and rapture—eternal life!

There is just one thing left to mention, and that is God's attitude toward all those who will not believe on Jesus Christ. What is it? Listen. "For God so loved the world, that he gave his only begotten Son, that *whosoever believeth in him should not perish*, but have everlasting life." *God's attitude toward those who will not believe in Jesus Christ, those who prefer sin and vanity and pride to the glorious Son of God, is simply this: God with great grief and reluctance withdraws from them the infinite gift He has purchased at so great cost and which they will not accept. God leaves them to perish.* There is no hope for any man who rejects God's gift of eternal life, obtained by simply believing in His only begotten Son. God has exhausted all the possibilities of a saving love and power in Jesus Christ's atonement on the cross of Calvary. Reject Him, neglect to accept Him, and you must eternally perish.

God's attitude toward the world is infinite love; God's attitude toward sin is infinite hatred. God's attitude toward His Son is unutterable love, but He gave up that Son to die for you and me. God's attitude toward the believer is to give him eternal life, regardless of what his past has been. God's attitude toward those who will not believe is to leave them to the perdition they so madly choose. Men and women, what will you choose tonight, life or death? Some of you will decide that question in a few minutes, decide it for all eternity. May God help you to decide it right.

One night in Minneapolis years ago, I knelt in prayer beside a young woman who was having an awful struggle. A fearful battle was going on in her soul between the forces of light and the forces of darkness. She heard God calling her to accept His love and to accept the eternal life that that love had purchased by the atoning death of His own Son. But she heard other voices too, voices of the world, and the voice of Satan himself, luring her to turn her back upon Jesus Christ and choose the world. It was awful to watch the battle, my heart ached as I watched the battle, and I kept crying to God that the Holy Spirit might gain the victory. Now and then I spoke to her. Finally I took out my watch and said, "This battle cannot last much longer. Continue to resist the Holy Spirit as you are resisting Him now, and you will seal your doom. I believe if you do not yield to God in the next ten minutes that you will never yield but will be lost forever." Then I prayed but said nothing more to her, but now and again looked at my watch. The fight went on. Which way would she decide! Before the ten minutes were up she yielded to God.

There is a like battle going on in the hearts of some who are reading these words. Some of you have been brought to realize the wondrous love of God for you as you have never realized it before. Some of you have been brought to see that eternal life is possible for you today if you will only choose Christ. But the power of the world and of sin and of Satan is strong upon you still, and the world, sin, and above all Satan will not let you go without making a mighty effort to keep you in his power, to blind you, and to forever destroy your soul.

Oh, men and women out of Christ, each and every one of you, look, look, look! Look once more at the cross of Christ. See Him hanging there in awful agony, paying the penalty of your sin, and as you look, listen once more to the precious words of the most wonderful sentence that was ever written, "God so loved the world, that he gave his only begotten Son, that whosoever believeth in him should not perish, but have everlasting life." What will you do with that love tonight? Will you yield to it and believe on the Savior and obtain eternal life? Or will you trample that wondrous love of God underfoot, and say again tonight as you have often said before, "I will not accept Christ," and go out to perish, perish eternally?

One night many years ago, I was preaching the first sermon

I ever preached in the city of Chicago. (It was some years before I went there to live.) I was at the first International Convention of Christian Workers. The morning the convention opened I entered a little late, and the nominating committee was just bringing in its report. To my amazement, I heard them announce my name as nominated for chairman of the convention and president of the International Christian Workers' Association. I was not yet thirty years old, and there were many workers there who knew far more about aggressive methods of Christian work than I had ever learned.

However, there was nothing to do but to accept the position, and during the days of that wonderful convention I occupied the chairman's seat. The convention was held in the old First Methodist Church in the heart of the city, at the corner of Washington and Clark streets.

When Sunday came, of course the church held its own services, but I was invited to preach at the evening service. There had been much prayer, and the Spirit of God was present in great power; when I gave the invitation many rose to say that they would accept Jesus Christ as their Savior and then came down to the altar. Among those who had risen I noticed a beautifully dressed lady near the front, an intelligent looking woman, but I noticed also that she did not come to the altar with the others. While the altar service was in progress I stepped down and urged her to come to the front, but she refused.

On Monday night at the regular session of the convention I saw her come in and take a seat just a few rows from the back of the building. When the meeting was drawing to a close I called Mayor Howland of Toronto (who was vice-president of the convention) to the chair and slipped down to the back of the church in order that I might speak with that lady before she got out of the building. The moment the benediction was pronounced I hastened to her side and asked if she would remain a few moments. As the others filed out she sat down, and I took a seat beside her and commenced to urge upon her an immediate and whole-hearted acceptance of Jesus Christ.

"Let me tell you my story," she replied. "I have attended a Sunday school in this city ever since I was a little girl. I scarcely missed a Sunday." (She told me what Sunday school it was—one of the aristocratic Sunday schools on the North Side.) "But," she continued, "though I have been going to Sunday school all these years, do you know that you are the first person in all my life that ever spoke to me personally about my accepting Christ?"

Then she went on to tell me the story of her life. She was unusually well-educated, occupying a high position of responsibility, but the story that she told me of her career was so shameless that I was amazed that a woman of sense, to say nothing of character, would dream of telling such a story to a man. Then she hurried on and told me how she had passed the preceding Easter Sunday. It was a story I could not repeat. Having finished, she said with a mocking laugh, "Funny way to spend Easter, wasn't it?"

I was astounded and shocked. I did not attempt to say anything in reply; I did not wish to. I simply opened my Bible to John 3:16, handed it to her, and asked her to read. It was a diamond print Bible, and she had to hold it close to her face to see the words. She began to read with a smile on her lips, "For God so loved the world"—the smile vanished as she read on—"that he gave his only begotten Son." She choked and broke down; the tears literally poured from her eyes on the page of the Bible and on the beautiful silk dress she wore. The love of God had conquered that sinful, hardened, trifling, seemingly shameless heart.

Oh, friend, I would that that love might break your heart, break down your hardness, unbelief, worldliness, and resistance to God and His love. See the Lord Jesus hanging on yonder cross in unutterable agony, in indescribable pain, His heart breaking for you, breaking for your sins, and hear again this most wonderful sentence that was ever written, "For God so loved the world, that he gave his only begotten Son, that whosoever believeth in him should not perish, but have everlasting life."

HARRY EMERSON FOSDICK

Shall the Fundamentalists Win?

A Sermon, Preached at the
First Presbyterian Church, New York
May 21, 1922

THIS MORNING we are to think of the Fundamentalist controversy which threatens to divide the American churches, as though already they were not sufficiently split and riven. A scene, suggestive for our thought, is depicted in the fifth chapter of the book of the Acts, where the Jewish leaders hale before them Peter and other of the apostles because they have been preaching Jesus as the Messiah. Moreover, the Jewish leaders propose to slay them, when in opposition Gamaliel speaks: "Refrain from these men, and let them alone: for if this counsel or this work be of men, it will be overthrown: but if it is of God ye will not be able to overthrow them; lest haply ye be found even to be fighting against God."

One could easily let his imagination play over this scene and could wonder how history would have come out if Gamaliel's wise tolerance could have controlled the situation. For though the Jewish leaders seemed superficially to concur in Gamaliel's judgment, they nevertheless kept up their bitter antagonism and shut the Christians from the Synagogue. We know now that they were mistaken. Christianity, starting within Judaism, was not an innovation to be dreaded; it was the finest flowering out that Judaism ever had. When the Master looked back across his racial heritage and said, "I came not to destroy, but to fulfill," he perfectly described the situation. The Christian ideas of God, the Christian principles of life, the Christian hopes for the future, were all rooted in the Old Testament and grew up out of it, and the Master himself, who called the Jewish temple his Father's house, rejoiced in the glorious heritage of his people's prophets. Only, he did believe in a living God. He did not think that God was dead,

having finished his words and works with Malachi. He had
not simply a historic, but a contemporary God, speaking now,
working now, leading his people now from partial into fuller
truth. Jesus believed in the progressiveness of revelation and
these Jewish leaders did not understand that. Was this new
Gospel a real development which they might welcome or was
it an enemy to be cast out? And they called it an enemy and
excluded it. One does wonder what might have happened had
Gamaliel's wise tolerance been in control.

We, however, face to-day a situation too similar and too urgent and too much in need of Gamaliel's attitude to spend
any time making guesses at supposititious history. Already all
of us must have heard about the people who call themselves
the Fundamentalists. Their apparent intention is to drive out
of the evangelical churches men and women of liberal opinions. I speak of them the more freely because there are no
two denominations more affected by them than the Baptist
and the Presbyterian. We should not identify the Fundamentalists with the conservatives. All Fundamentalists are
conservatives, but not all conservatives are Fundamentalists.
The best conservatives can often give lessons to the liberals in
true liberality of spirit, but the Fundamentalist program is essentially illiberal and intolerant. The Fundamentalists see, and
they see truly, that in this last generation there have been
strange new movements in Christian thought. A great mass of
new knowledge has come into man's possession: new knowledge about the physical universe, its origin, its forces, its laws;
new knowledge about human history and in particular about
the ways in which the ancient peoples used to think in matters of religion and the methods by which they phrased and
explained their spiritual experiences; and new knowledge,
also, about other religions and the strangely similar ways in
which men's faiths and religious practices have developed
everywhere. Now, there are multitudes of reverent Christians
who have been unable to keep this new knowledge in one
compartment of their minds and the Christian faith in another. They have been sure that all truth comes from the one
God and is his revelation. Not, therefore, from irreverence or
caprice or destructive zeal, but for the sake of intellectual and
spiritual integrity, that they might really love the Lord their

God not only with all their heart and soul and strength, but with all their mind, they have been trying to see this new knowledge in terms of the Christian faith and to see the Christian faith in terms of this new knowledge. Doubtless they have made many mistakes. Doubtless there have been among them reckless radicals gifted with intellectual ingenuity but lacking spiritual depth. Yet the enterprise itself seems to them indispensable to the Christian church. The new knowledge and the old faith cannot be left antagonistic or even disparate, as though a man on Saturday could use one set of regulative ideas for his life and on Sunday could change gear to another altogether. We must be able to think our modern life clear through in Christian terms and to do that we also must be able to think our Christian life clear through in modern terms.

There is nothing new about the situation. It has happened again and again in history, as, for example, when the stationary earth suddenly began to move and the universe that had been centered in this planet was centered in the sun around which the planets whirled. Whenever such a situation has arisen, there has been only one way out: the new knowledge and the old faith had to be blended in a new combination. Now, the people in this generation who are trying to do this are the liberals, and the Fundamentalists are out on a campaign to shut against them the doors of the Christian fellowship. Shall they be allowed to succeed?

It is interesting to note where the Fundamentalists are driving in their stakes to mark out the deadline of doctrine around the church, across which no one is to pass except on terms of agreement. They insist that we must all believe in the historicity of certain special miracles, pre-eminently the virgin birth of our Lord; that we must believe in a special theory of inspiration—that the original documents of the Scripture, which of course we no longer possess, were inerrantly dictated to men a good deal as a man might dictate to a stenographer; that we must believe in a special theory of the atonement—that the blood of our Lord, shed in a substitutionary death, placates an alienated Deity and makes possible welcome for the returning sinner; and that we must believe in the second coming of our Lord upon the clouds of heaven to set up a millennium here, as the only way in which God can bring history to a worthy dénouement. Such are some of the stakes which are being driven, to mark a deadline of doctrine around the church.

If a man is a genuine liberal, his primary protest is not against holding these opinions, although he may well protest against their being considered the fundamentals of Christianity. This is a free country and anybody has a right to hold these opinions or any others, if he is sincerely convinced of them. The question is: has anybody a right to deny the Christian name to those who differ with him on such points and to shut against them the doors of the Christian fellowship? The Fundamentalists say that this must be done. In this country and on the foreign field they are trying to do it. They have actually endeavored to put on the statute books of a whole state binding laws against teaching modern biology. If they had their way, within the church, they would set up in Protestantism a doctrinal tribunal more rigid than the Pope's. In such an hour, delicate and dangerous, when feelings are bound to run high, I plead this morning the cause of magnanimity and liberality and tolerance of spirit. I would, if I could reach their ears, say to the Fundamentalists about the liberals what Gamaliel said to the Jews, "Refrain from these men, and let them alone: for if this counsel or this work be of men, it will be overthrown: but if it is of God ye will not be able to overthrow them; lest haply ye be found even to be fighting against God."

That we may be entirely candid and concrete and may not lose ourselves in any fog of generalities, let us this morning take two or three of these Fundamentalist items and see with reference to them what the situation is in the Christian churches. Too often we preachers have failed to talk frankly enough about the differences of opinion that exist among evangelical Christians, although everybody knows that they are there. Let us face this morning some of the differences of opinion with which somehow we must deal.

We may well begin with the vexed and mooted question of the virgin birth of our Lord. I know people in the Christian churches, ministers, missionaries, laymen, devoted lovers of the Lord and servants of the Gospel, who, alike as they are in their personal devotion to the Master, hold quite different points of view about a matter like the virgin birth. Here, for example, is one point of view: that the virgin birth is to be accepted as historical fact; it actually happened; there was no other way for a personality like the Master to come into this world except by a special biological miracle. That is one point of view, and many are the gracious and beautiful souls who hold it. But, side by side with them in the evangelical churches is a group of equally loyal and reverent people who would say that the virgin birth is not to be accepted as an historic fact. To believe in virgin birth as an explanation of great personality is one of the familiar ways in which the ancient world was accustomed to account for unusual superiority. Many people suppose that only once in history do we run across a record of supernatural birth. Upon the contrary, stories of miraculous generation are among the commonest traditions of antiquity. Especially is this true about the founders of great religions. According to the records of their faiths, Buddha and Zoroaster and Lao-Tsze and Mahavira were all supernaturally born. Moses, Confucius and Mohammed are the only great founders of religions in history to whom miraculous birth is not attributed. That is to say, when a personality arose so high that men adored him, the ancient world attributed his superiority to some special divine influence in his generation, and they commonly phrased their faith in terms of miraculous birth. So Pythagoras was called virgin born, and Plato, and Augustus Cæsar, and many more. Knowing this, there are within the evangelical churches large groups of people whose opinion about our Lord's coming would run as follows: those first disciples adored Jesus—as we do; when they thought about his coming they were sure that he came specially from God—as we are; this adoration and conviction they associated with God's special influence and intention in his birth—as we do; but they phrased it in terms of a biological miracle that our modern minds cannot use. So far from thinking that they have given up anything vital in the New Testament's attitude toward Jesus, these Christians remember that the two men who contributed most to the church's thought of the divine meaning of the Christ were Paul and John, who never even distantly allude to the virgin birth.

Here in the Christian churches are these two groups of

people and the question that the Fundamentalists raise is this: shall one of them throw the other out? Has intolerance any contribution to make to this situation? Will it persuade anybody of anything? Is not the Christian church large enough to hold within her hospitable fellowship people who differ on points like this and agree to differ until the fuller truth be manifested? The Fundamentalists say not. They say that the liberals must go. Well, if the Fundamentalists should succeed, then out of the Christian church would go some of the best Christian life and consecration of this generation—multitudes of men and women, devout and reverent Christians, who need the church and whom the church needs.

Consider another matter on which there is a sincere difference of opinion among evangelical Christians: the inspiration of the Bible. One point of view is that the original documents of the Scripture were inerrantly dictated by God to men. Whether we deal with the story of creation or the list of the dukes of Edom or the narratives of Solomon's reign or the Sermon on the Mount or the thirteenth chapter of First Corinthians, they all came in the same way and they all came as no other book ever came. They were inerrantly dictated; everything there—scientific opinions, medical theories, historical judgments, as well as spiritual insight—is infallible. That is one idea of the Bible's inspiration. But side by side with those who hold it, lovers of the Book as much as they, are multitudes of people who never think about the Bible so. Indeed, that static and mechanical theory of inspiration seems to them a positive peril to the spiritual life. The Koran similarly has been regarded by Mohammedans as having been infallibly written in heaven before it came to earth. But the Koran enshrines the theological and ethical ideas of Arabia at the time when it was written. God an Oriental monarch, fatalistic submission to his will as man's chief duty, the use of force on unbelievers, polygamy, slavery—they are all in the Koran. The Koran was ahead of the day when it was written, but, petrified by an artificial idea of inspiration, it has become a millstone about the neck of Mohammedanism. When one turns from the Koran to the Bible, he finds this interesting situation. All of these ideas, which we dislike in the Koran, are somewhere in the Bible. Conceptions from which we now send missionaries to convert

Mohammedans are to be found in the Book. There one can find God thought of as an Oriental monarch; there, too, are patriarchal polygamy, and slave systems, and the use of force on unbelievers. Only in the Bible these elements are not final; they are always being superseded; revelation is progressive. The thought of God moves out from Oriental kingship to compassionate fatherhood; treatment of unbelievers moves out from the use of force to the appeals of love; polygamy gives way to monogamy; slavery, never explicitly condemned before the New Testament closes, is nevertheless being undermined by ideas that in the end, like dynamite, will blast its foundations to pieces. Repeatedly one runs on verses like this: "It was said to them of old time . . . but I say unto you"; "God, having of old time spoken unto the fathers in the prophets by divers portions and in divers manners, hath at the end of these days spoken unto us in his Son"; "The times of ignorance therefore God overlooked; but now he commandeth men that they should all everywhere repent"; and over the doorway of the New Testament into the Christian world stand the words of Jesus: "When he, the Spirit of truth is come, he shall guide you into all truth." That is to say, finality in the Koran is behind; finality in the Bible is ahead. We have not reached it. We cannot yet compass all of it. God is leading us out toward it. There are multitudes of Christians, then, who think, and rejoice as they think, of the Bible as the record of the progressive unfolding of the character of God to his people from early primitive days until the great unveiling in Christ; to them the Book is more inspired and more inspiring than ever it was before; and to go back to a mechanical and static theory of inspiration would mean to them the loss of some of the most vital elements in their spiritual experience and in their appreciation of the Book.

Here in the Christian church to-day are these two groups, and the question the Fundamentalists have raised is this: shall one of them drive the other out? Do we think the cause of Jesus Christ will be furthered by that? If he should walk through the ranks of this congregation this morning, can we imagine him claiming as his own those who hold one idea of inspiration and sending from him into outer darkness those who hold another? You cannot fit the Lord Christ into that Fundamentalist mold. The church would better judge his judgment. For in the Middle West the Fundamentalists have had their way in some communities and a Christian minister tells us the consequence. He says that the educated people are looking for their religion outside the churches.

Consider another matter upon which there is a serious and sincere difference of opinion between evangelical Christians: the second coming of our Lord. The second coming was the early Christian phrasing of hope. No one in the ancient world had ever thought, as we do, of development, progress, gradual change, as God's way of working out his will in human life and institutions. They thought of human history as a series of ages succeeding one another with abrupt suddenness. The Græco-Roman world gave the names of metals to the ages—gold, silver, bronze, iron. The Hebrews had their ages too—the original Paradise in which man began, the cursed world in which man now lives, the blessed Messianic Kingdom some day suddenly to appear on the clouds of heaven. It was the Hebrew way of expressing hope for the victory of God and righteousness. When the Christians came they took over that phrasing of expectancy and the New Testament is aglow with it. The preaching of the apostles thrills with the glad announcement, "Christ is coming!"

In the evangelical churches to-day there are differing views of this matter. One view is that Christ is literally coming, externally on the clouds of heaven, to set up his kingdom here. I never heard that teaching in my youth at all. It has always had a new resurrection when desperate circumstances came and man's only hope seemed to lie in divine intervention. It is not strange, then, that during these chaotic, catastrophic years there has been a fresh rebirth of this old phrasing of expectancy. "Christ is coming!" seems to many Christians the central message of the Gospel. In the strength of it some of them are doing great service for the world. But unhappily, many so overemphasize it that they outdo anything the ancient Hebrews or the ancient Christians ever did. They sit still and do nothing and expect the world to grow worse and worse until he comes.

Side by side with these to whom the second coming is a literal expectation, another group exists in the evangelical churches. They, too, say, "Christ is coming!" They say it with all their hearts; but they are not thinking of an external arrival on the clouds. They have assimilated as part of the divine revelation the exhilarating insight which these recent generations have given to us, that development is God's way of working out his will. They see that the most desirable elements in human life have come through the method of development. Man's music has developed from the rhythmic noise of beaten sticks until we have in melody and harmony possibilities once undreamed. Man's painting has developed from the crude outlines of the cavemen until in line and color we have achieved unforeseen results and possess latent beauties yet unfolded. Man's architecture has developed from the crude huts of primitive men until our cathedrals and business buildings reveal alike an incalculable advance and an unimaginable future. Development does seem to be the way in which God works. And these Christians, when they say that Christ is coming, mean that, slowly it may be, but surely, his will and principles will be worked out by God's grace in human life and institutions, until "he shall see of the travail of his soul, and shall be satisfied."

These two groups exist in the Christian churches, and the question raised by the Fundamentalists is: shall one of them drive the other out? Will that get us anywhere? Multitudes of young men and women at this season of the year are graduating from our schools of learning, thousands of them Christians who may make us older ones ashamed by the sincerity of their devotion to God's will on earth. They are not thinking in ancient terms that leave ideas of progress out. They cannot think in those terms. There could be no greater tragedy than that the Fundamentalists should shut the door of the Christian fellowship against such.

I do not believe for one moment that the Fundamentalists are going to succeed. Nobody's intolerance can contribute anything to the solution of the situation we have described. If, then, the Fundamentalists have no solution of the problem, where may we expect to find it? In two concluding comments let us consider our reply to that inquiry.

The first element that is necessary is a spirit of tolerance and Christian liberty. When will the world learn that intolerance solves no problems? This is not a lesson which the

Fundamentalists alone need to learn; the liberals also need to learn it. Speaking, as I do, from the viewpoint of liberal opinions, let me say that if some young, fresh mind here this morning is holding new ideas, has fought his way through, it may be by intellectual and spiritual struggle, to novel positions, and is tempted to be intolerant about old opinions, offensively to condescend to those who hold them and to be harsh in judgment on them, he may well remember that people who held those old opinions have given the world some of the noblest character and the most rememberable service that it ever has been blessed with, and that we of the younger generation will prove our case best, not by controversial intolerance, but by producing, with our new opinions, something of the depth and strength, nobility and beauty of character that in other times were associated with other thoughts. It was a wise liberal, the most adventurous man of his day— Paul the Apostle—who said, "Knowledge puffeth up, but love buildeth up."

Nevertheless, it is true that just now the Fundamentalists are giving us one of the worst exhibitions of bitter intolerance that the churches of this country have ever seen. As one watches them and listens to them, he remembers the remark of General Armstrong of Hampton Institute: "Cantankerousness is worse than heterodoxy." There are many opinions in the field of modern controversy concerning which I am not sure whether they are right or wrong, but there is one thing I am sure of: courtesy and kindliness and tolerance and humility and fairness are right. Opinions may be mistaken; love never is.

As I plead thus for an intellectually hospitable, tolerant, liberty-loving church, I am of course thinking primarily about this new generation. We have boys and girls growing up in our homes and schools, and because we love them we may well wonder about the church that will be waiting to receive them. Now, the worst kind of church that can possibly be offered to the allegiance of the new generation is an intolerant church. Ministers often bewail the fact that young people turn from religion to science for the regulative ideas of their lives. But this is easily explicable. Science treats a young man's mind as though it were really important. A scientist says to a

young man: "Here is the universe challenging our investigation. Here are the truths we have seen, so far. Come, study
with us! See what we already have seen and then look further
to see more, for science is an intellectual adventure for the
truth." Can you imagine any man who is worth while, turning from that call to the church, if the church seems to him
to say, "Come, and we will feed you opinions from a spoon.
No thinking is allowed here except such as brings you to certain specified, predetermined conclusions. These prescribed
opinions we will give you in advance of your thinking; now
think, but only so as to reach these results." My friends, nothing in all the world is so much worth thinking of as God,
Christ, the Bible, sin and salvation, the divine purposes for
humankind, life everlasting. But you cannot challenge the
dedicated thinking of this generation to these sublime themes
upon any such terms as are laid down by an intolerant church.

The second element which is needed, if we are to reach a
happy solution of this problem is a clear insight into the main
issues of modern Christianity and a sense of penitent shame
that the Christian church should be quarreling over little matters when the world is dying of great needs. If, during the
war, when the nations were wrestling upon the very brink of
hell and at times all seemed lost, you chanced to hear two
men in an altercation about some minor matter of sectarian
denominationalism, could you restrain your indignation? You
said, "What can you do with folks like this who, in the face of
colossal issues, play with the tiddledywinks and peccadillos of
religion?" So, now, when from the terrific questions of this
generation one is called away by the noise of this Fundamentalist controversy, he thinks it almost unforgivable that
men should tithe mint and anise and cummin, and quarrel
over them, when the world is perishing for the lack of the
weightier matters of the law, justice, and mercy, and faith.
These last weeks, in the minister's confessional, I have heard
stories from the depths of human lives where men and
women were wrestling with the elemental problems of misery
and sin—stories that put upon a man's heart a burden of vicarious sorrow, even though he does but listen to them. Here
was real human need crying out after the living God revealed
in Christ. Consider all the multitudes of men who so need

God, and then think of Christian churches making of themselves a cockpit of controversy when there is not a single thing at stake in the controversy on which depends the salvation of human souls. That is the trouble with this whole business. So much of it does not matter! And there is one thing that does matter—more than anything else in all the world—that men in their personal lives and in their social relationships should know Jesus Christ.

Just a week ago I received a letter from a friend in Asia Minor. He says that they are killing the Armenians yet; that the Turkish deportations still are going on; that lately they crowded Christian men, women and children into a conventicle of worship and burned them together in the house where they had prayed to their Father and to ours. During the war, when it was good propaganda to stir up our bitter hatred against the enemy we heard of such atrocities, but not now! Two weeks ago Great Britain, shocked and stirred by what is going on in Armenia, did ask the government of the United States to join her in investigating the atrocities and trying to help. Our government said that it was not any of our business at all. The present world situation smells to heaven! And now in the presence of colossal problems, which must be solved in Christ's name and for Christ's sake, the Fundamentalists propose to drive out from the Christian churches all the consecrated souls who do not agree with their theory of inspiration. What immeasurable folly!

Well, they are not going to do it; certainly not in this vicinity. I do not even know in this congregation whether anybody has been tempted to be a Fundamentalist. Never in this church have I caught one accent of intolerance. God keep us always so and ever increasing areas of the Christian fellowship: intellectually hospitable, open-minded, liberty-loving, fair, tolerant, not with the tolerance of indifference as though we did not care about the faith, but because always our major emphasis is upon the weightier matters of the law.

BILLY SUNDAY

Food for a Hungry World

"They need not depart; give ye them to eat."
—MATTHEW xiv, 16.

SOME FOLKS do not believe in miracles. I do. A denial of miracles is a denial of the virgin birth of Jesus. The Christian religion stands or falls on the virgin birth of Christ. God created Adam and Eve without human agencies. He could and did create Jesus supernaturally. I place no limit on what God can do. If you begin to limit God, then there is no God.

I read of a preacher who said that the miracles of the Bible were more of a hindrance than a help. Then he proceeded to spout his insane blasphemy. He imagined Jesus talking to the five thousand and like many speakers overrunning his time limit. The disciples, seeing night coming, said: "Master, you have talked this crowd out of their supper and there is nothing to eat in this desert place; dismiss them so they can go into the towns and country and get food."

He imagined Jesus saying: "We have some lunch, haven't we?"

"Yes, but not enough to feed this crowd."

"Well, let's divide it up and see." So, Jesus proceeds to divide his lunch with the hungry crowd.

An old Jew, seeing Jesus busy, asked, "What's he doing?" "Dividing his lunch." "Huh," grunts this old knocker, "he is the first preacher I've ever seen who practices what he preaches." Shamed by the example of Jesus, this old tightwad brought out his lunch basket and began to divide. Others caught the spirit and followed suit and in this way the five thousand were fed. This heretic of a so-called preacher thought such an occurrence more reasonable than the Bible account. Every attempt to explain the miracles by natural laws gets the explainer into great difficulty and shows him up as ridiculous.

I wish to draw some practical lessons from this miracle of Jesus feeding the five thousand. The world is hungry. Jesus stood face to face with the problem of physical hunger just as we in our day face the problem of hunger, not only physical but spiritual. If one were to believe all the magnificent articles in current and religious literature, one would think the world is disgusted and indifferent to the religion of Jesus Christ. I believe exactly the opposite is true. In no century since the morning stars sang together has there been more real hunger for genuine religion than this. And yet, many a preacher, instead of trying to feed this spiritual hunger, is giving some book review, staking a claim out on Jupiter or talking evolution, trying to prove we came from a monkey with his prehensile tail wrapped around a limb shying cocoanuts at his neighbor across the alley. The world is not disgusted with religion, but is disgusted with the worldliness, rituals, ceremonies and non-essentials in which we have lost religion.

There are some kinds of religion the world is not hungry for:

A religion of formal observances. In Isaiah, first chapter, the Lord says: "To what purpose is the multitude of your sacrifices? I am full of the burnt offerings of rams and the fat of fed beasts. Incense is an abomination unto me; your new moons and your appointed feasts my soul hateth. When you make prayers, I will not hear them. Your hands are full of blood. Put away the evil of your doings; cease to do evil, learn to do well."

Their formalism didn't make a hit with the Lord. He saw through their smoke screen. Religion does not consist in doing a lot of special things, even if branded as religious, but in doing everything in a special way as the Lord directs. Whenever the church makes its observances and forms the end instead of the means to the end, the world will turn its back on it.

Praying is not an act of devotion—reading the Bible is not an act of devotion—going to church is not an act of devotion—partaking of the communion is not an act of devotion; these are aids to devotion. The actual religion lies not in prayer, reading the Bible, church attendance but in the quality of life which these observances create in you. If the doing of these things does not change your life, then it profits you nothing to have them done. Thousands forget religion and allow the forms of religion to take the place of religion. They are substituting religiousness for righteousness. Jesus alone can save the world, but Jesus can't save the world alone. He needs our help.

The world is not hungry for a religion of theory. There was a time when people were interested intensely in fine-spun theological theories. You could announce a debate on the forms of baptism and pack the house with the S.R.O. sign hanging out. That day has passed; a debate on baptism or predestination would not draw a corporal's guard. The average man has not lost interest in the vital truths connected with these topics, but he has lost interest in the type of religion that spends its energy in argument, word battles, and wind jamming. Religion should relate to life and conduct as well as theory.

There has never been a time in my memory when religion has been so reduced to forms and ritual as today. In the mind of Jesus religion was not to build up the church, but the church was to build up religion. Religion was not the end but the means to the end. Jesus was so far removed from the formalism and traditions taught by the priests instead of teaching the commands of God that he was constantly at cross-purposes with them. A church of make-believers will soon beget a generation of non-believers.

The church in endeavoring to serve God and Mammon is growing cross-eyed, losing her power to know good from evil. Jesus dealt with fundamentals; his quietest talk had a torpedo effect on his hearers. Some sermons instead of being a bugle call to service are showers of spiritual cocaine. I am satisfied that there has never been a time when it is harder to live a consistent Christian life than now. I believe the conflict between God and the Devil, right and wrong, was never hotter. The allurements of sin have never been more fascinating. I do not believe there ever was a time since Adam and Eve were turned out of Eden when traps and pitfalls were more numerous and dangerous than today.

The world is not hungry for a religion of social service without Christ. I will go with you in any and all movements for the good of humanity providing you give Jesus Christ his rightful place. You cannot bathe anybody into the kingdom of God. You cannot change their hearts by changing their sanitation. It is an entirely good and Christian act to give a down-and-outer a bath, bed and a job. It is a Christian act to maintain schools and universities, but the road into the kingdom of God is not by the bath tub, the university, social service, or gymnasium, but by the blood-red road of the cross of Jesus Christ.

The Bible declares that human nature is radically bad and the power to uplift and change is external; that power is not in any man, woman or system, but by repentance and faith in the sacrificial death of Jesus Christ. The church is the one institution divinely authorized to feed the spiritual hunger of this old sin-cursed world.

You will notice that Jesus did not feed the multitude. He created the food and asked his disciples to distribute it. Jesus was the chef, not the waiter at this banquet. Jesus created salvation, the only food that will feed the spiritual hunger of the world; the task of distributing the food is in the hands of his human followers.

For every two nominal Christians, there are three who are not even nominal. Out of every two church members, one is a spiritual liability; four out of five with their names on our church records are doing nothing to bring the world to Jesus. There are twenty million young men in this country between the ages of sixteen and thirty. Nineteen million are not members of any church; nine million attend church occasionally; ten million never darken a church door. Seventy-four per cent of our criminals are young men under twenty-one years of age. In the past twenty-five years the age of prostitutes has fallen from twenty-six years of age to seventeen years of age. Five hundred girls fifteen years old and under were divorced or widowed last year. Juvenile crime increased in one year from thirty-two per cent to a hundred and thirty-eight per cent.

There are many institutions that enter into competition with the church in preaching certain phases of religion, but not in preaching religion itself. Associate charities preach charity sometimes with stronger emphasis than the church. Some organizations talk about justice and square dealing with more vehemence than the church. Some individuals thunder against vice and crime more than the pulpit. Many institutions and organizations preach one or more phases of religion, but it is to the church humanity must ever turn for the last word on salvation and eternal destiny.

People are dissatisfied with philosophy, science, new thought—all these amount to nothing when you have a dead child in the house. These do not solace the troubles and woes of the world. They will tell you that when they were sick and the door of the future was opening in their face, the only comfort they could find was in the gospel of Jesus Christ. Christianity is the only sympathetic religion that ever came into the world, for it is the only religion that ever came from God.

Take your scientific consolation into a room where a mother has lost her child. Try your doctrine of the survival of the fittest with that broken-hearted woman. Tell her that the child that died was not as fit to live as the one left alive. Where does that scientific junk lift the burden from her heart? Go to some dying man and tell him to pluck up courage for the future. Try your philosophy on him; tell him to be confident in the great to be and the everlasting what is it. Go to that widow and tell her it was a geological necessity for her husband to croak. Tell her that in fifty million years we will all be scientific mummies on a shelf—petrified specimens of an extinct race. What does all this stuff get her? After you have gotten through with your science, philosophy, psychology, eugenics, social service, sociology, evolution, protoplasms, and fortuitous concurrence of atoms, if she isn't bug-house, I will take the Bible and read God's promise, and pray—and her tears will be dried and her soul flooded with calmness like a California sunset.

Is the church drawing the hungry world to its tables? There is no dodging or blinking or pussy-footing the fact that in drawing the hungry world to her tables, the church is facing a crisis. That there is a chasm between the church and the masses no one denies. If the gain of the church on the population is represented by eighty during the past thirty years, during the last twenty years it is represented by four, and during the past ten years it is represented by zero. The birth rate is going on a limited express while the new birth rate is going by way of freight.

Need the world turn to other tables than those of the church for spiritual food? Jesus said, "They need not depart; give ye them to eat." The church has the power and the food with which to feed the hungry world. It can feed the spiritual hunger of the world by doing what Jesus did when he fed the five thousand. By a wise use of what it has on hand with the blessing of God upon it, what has the church on hand with which to feed the hungry world! It has two things:

A set of principles which if put into practice in the life of the individual and society and business and politics will solve every difficulty and problem of city, state, nation, and the world. There is no safer or saner method to settle all the world's problems than by the sermon on the mount. These principles are truth, justice, and purity. It has a person who has the power to create and make powerful these principles in the lives of men and women and that person is Jesus Christ, the Son of God.

Many skeptics have said, "Bill, if you will only preach the principles of Christianity instead of the Person, we will find no fault with you." Nothing doing, old top! Wherever a preacher or a church preaches a set of principles without the person Jesus Christ, that ministry, that church, becomes sterile and powerless. Truth is never powerful unless wrapped up in a person. I take truth and wrap it up in Christ and say, "Take it!" You say, "Give me truth but no Christ." Then you will be lost. You are not saved by truth but by the person Jesus Christ. Why take truth and reject Christ when it's Christ that inspires truth?

I take justice and wrap Christ up with it and say, "Here, take it." You say, "I will take justice. I deal squarely in business, pay my debts, give labor a square deal; I take justice but not your Christ." You are lost. Why take justice and cast Christ away when it is Christ that inspires justice.

I take purity and wrap it up with Jesus and say, "Here, take this." You say, "I will take the principle purity but not the person Jesus Christ." Then you are lost, for it is Christ that saves, not the principle of purity. "One thing thou lackest," the person Jesus.

Other religions have preached good things, but they have no Savior who can take these things and implant them in the human heart and make them grow. All other religions are built around principles, but the Christian religion is built around a person Jesus Christ, the Son of God, our Savior. Every other religion on earth is a religion you must keep, but the Christian religion saves you, keeps you, and presents you faultless before his throne. Oh, Christians! Have you any scars to show that you have fought in this conflict with the devil? When a war is over, heroes have scars to show; one rolls back his sleeve and shows a gunshot wound; another pulls down his collar and shows a wound on the neck; another says, "I never had use of that leg since Gettysburg"; another says, "I was wounded and gassed at the Marne in France." Christ has scars to show—scars on his brow, on his hands, on his feet, and when he pulls aside his robes of royalty, there will be seen the scar on his side.

When the Scottish chieftains wanted to raise an army, they would make a wooden cross, set it on fire and carry it through the mountains and the highlands among the people and wave the cross of flame and the people would gather beneath the standard and fight for Scotland. I come out with the cross of the son of God—it is a flaming cross, flaming with suffering, flaming with triumph, flaming with victory, flaming with glory, flaming with salvation for a lost world!

ABBA HILLEL SILVER

The Vision Splendid

Choose you this day whom you will serve.
JOSHUA 24:15.

WE ARE TOLD in sacred lore, that when their hours of study were over, and the wise men left the halls of the Academy, they departed from one another with the following quaint and beautiful blessing: "Mayest thou behold thy world during thy lifetime, but may thine end be in Life Eternal, and thy hopes, may they endure throughout all generations." On New Year's Day, we too take leave, not from one another, but from the old year, and from all that it held for us of good and evil, of gain and loss; and I know of no more seemly benediction which we can bestow upon one another at this hour, than this selfsame prayer of the Rabbis.

If I were to bless you this day, between the dark and the dawn of the New Year, with the choicest gift in the treasure-house of God, I could think of none more rare and precious than this. It is threefold benison, each part segment of a perfect whole: "Mayest thou behold thy world during thy lifetime." Is there anything more complete than this? To see our whole world while we live! The world of our desires and the world of our hopes! To win every goal, to taste every fruit, to slake every thirst at the fountain of success. What a generous benediction this is! Surely this is what we pray for on this, our Holy Day. "Grant us life, long life; grant us health, happiness, prosperity, peace. Let us not die ere the last mile of our journey is covered and the last beautiful scene glimpsed. Permit us to see our whole world while we live."

And how thoroughly human a prayer it is! What man is there who would wish to close the fascinating book of life before the last chapter is read and the last page is turned and the story is fully told! Unless he be of those who have suffered much, whose eyes have been darkened by unutterable sorrow, and from whose hearts anguish has drained all love of life. We all wish to live, to see all, to know all, to taste all, to have all. The world is so resplendent with the works of God and the works of man, with the beauty that dwells in the earth and in the habitations of the children of earth. Our souls are hungry for this earth beauty and this life beauty, for all the wonder and grace which are in existence. How very human then is this prayer, and how truly it voices our deep-most longings. And yet, somehow, the wise men of old, who uttered this valediction, keenly felt its incompleteness, for they hastened to supplement it: "But may thine end be in Life Eternal, and thy hopes, may they endure throughout all generations." On the face of it, a paradox! If one could see his whole world in his lifetime, why should his end be in life eternal? If one could realize all his cherished hopes here and now, why should they be extended throughout all subsequent generations?

But the Rabbis, who saw life steadily, felt this wish to be inadequate, because unattainable. They knew that no man can see his whole world in his lifetime, nor realize his high hopes in his generation. But they also knew of a world which every man could realize in his lifetime, and of a hope which every man could see fulfilled. In the eyes of the Rabbis there were two worlds; the world of our wishes and desires, and the world which these same wishes and desires create for us and in us. The world of our dreams and hopes, and the world which these dreams and hopes surround us with. In a sense every man builds his own world. Every man constructs his own world, his universe of wish and desire, the far-flung constellation of passionate cravings and longings, whose fiery center is self. The worlds of no two men are alike. Some build their world of clay, of carnal wishes and coarse desires. It is narrow, never extending beyond the reach of the senses. Others fashion their dream-empires of finer stuff, of the needs of the mind and soul as well as of the body. Theirs is a larger estate, reaching out through spiritual roads into distant worlds. Still others, who are caught up by some vision and touched by some inspiration, shape their worlds out of ineffable beauties, transcendent and measureless to man.

And each builder would like to see his dream-world come true in his lifetime. But God, the Master Builder, who has his

own plan and his own architectural design, has so ordered his
Universe, that none shall see his world fully realized in his
lifetime, and that the finer and subtler the stuff the dream-
world is made of, the more difficult shall it be of attainment.
Even the clay-world is hard to attain. Low desires and earthly
cupidity, even when satisfied, leave ashes in the mouth. Each
fulfilled desire incites to others, stronger and more impetuous. "The sea hath bounds, but deep desire hath none." Passion means suffering. Until our hankerings are appeased, we
suffer, and after they are appeased we soon weary of them.
When we are in want, we strive for the necessities of life;
when we have the necessities of life, we crave for comforts;
when we have comforts, we crave for luxury. When we have
luxury, we cry for the moon—a mounting fever of discontent,
an endless cycle of futility. The Greeks called it "The Torments of Tantulus."

Difficult as the clay-world is of attainment, even more difficult is the dream-world which some men wish to see fulfilled
in their lifetime—the world which is not circumscribed by the
ordinary wants of life, the world fashioned out of the silver
sheen of ideals and the gold of aspiration, the world patterned
after the similitude of God's own perfection. The man who,
conscious of his high estate, fashions such a world, and who,
by his dreams, would lengthen the road between himself and
the beast, and shorten the road between himself and God, the
man who projects a wish-world of justice and peace, an empire of knowledge and love, of truth and beauty, that man will
never see his world fulfilled in his lifetime. Such wish-worlds
are eternities in the making. No single hand can effect them,
no single generation can encompass them. Such dreams lead
the dreamer, not to the goal of consummation, but to the pit
and the dungeon, the rack and the cross, and all the miserable
artifices of a world afraid of his dreams. Such dreams lead the
dreamer along the dolorous road of frustration and loneliness,
to death.

Many illustrations come to our mind when we think of this.
Let us but choose two—an ancient and a modern one. Moses,
a leader of men, built for himself a dream-world of heroic design—to liberate a people from the yoke of bondage—to give
it a law and a land—to fashion it into a priest-people and to

send it forth a messenger of a new revelation and a new covenant. Did he see his world come true? On the top of Mount Nebo, he died a lonely and a world-wearied man, his tired eyes straining to catch a glimpse of the land of his unfulfilled promise. He freed the people. He broke the chains of their body. He could not break the chains of their soul. He gave them freedom, they enslaved themselves. He gave them a law, they flouted it. He gave them a hope, they destroyed it. Where was his world?

And what became of the dream-world of that modern dreamer—Woodrow Wilson? Somewhere in the Capital of our land, there lived for two years a broken old man, alone with his memories, ruminating among the ruins of his shattered dream-world. He had visioned mankind healed and redeemed, made one in peace and freedom. He failed. During the early years of the great world struggle he sought to maintain neutrality. He failed. He gave his life blood to establish a covenant of peoples to enforce peace. He failed. He hoped for peace without victory, and failed. He hoped for peace with victory, and failed. He hoped that justice and comity would follow the Pentecost of calamity, and behold, violence and hatred everywhere. Did he see his world in his lifetime? He died even as his dreams died.

Our ancient sages knew the sorry plight of such world builders. They therefore added to their benediction this phrase: "But may thine end be in Life Eternal, and thy hopes, may they endure throughout all generations." The end is not here—cannot, should not, be here. A world which a man can achieve in his lifetime is unworthy of him—unworthy of the reach of his imagination, the chivalry of his spirit, the hardihood of his faith. Only such tasks and ambitions are worthy of us as lay bare the finitude of our bodies and the infinitude of our souls, the impotence of flesh and the omnipotence of spirit, the brevity of our days and the eternity of our dreams. Blessed is the man whose dream outlives him! Blessed is the man who is strong enough to see himself grow old and powerless while his ideal remains young and green. For then, old age assumes a dignity which compensates for our infirmities. The flame of life may burn low, but the holy incense of our visions will rise inextinguishable from the undefiled altars of our ageless souls.

In his picture of *Dorian Gray*, Oscar Wilde tells us of a young man, radiant and beautiful as a god, whom a great artist painted in the full splendor of his youth. When the man beheld the finished masterpiece, he burst into tears. "How sad it is," he cried, "that I must grow old. My face shall become wrinkled and wizened, my eyes shall grow dim and colorless, but this picture shall remain always young. Oh, if it were only the other way! If the picture could change and I could remain always what I am now!" His wish was granted. Throughout the succeeding years his picture—his dream-world—changed with the changes that came over him, while he remained unalterably the same. Through successive stages of degradation and shame, through sin and cruelty and vice, he remained the same, young and beautiful—but his picture—the mirror and reflex of his soul—took on all the ugliness, all the viciousness, and all the spiritual disfigurement which were his. At last the horror of the picture, the ghastly deformity of his dream-world, drove him to madness and to self-destruction.

This is the tragedy of one who wishes to outlive his dream, whose life-picture is tied up with that which is physical and transitory. When such a man grows old, he will have memories which will embitter his days; for all his glory will be of yesterday, and all his hopes as if they had never been. In the midst of life he is in death. Israel Zangwill, in his *Italian Fantasies*, brilliantly sums up this truth. "He that dies in the full tilt of his ambitions is buried alive, and he that survives his hopes and fears is dead, unburied." And the ancestors of this brilliant writer, in their equally incisive way, declared: "The righteous are alive in death, the wicked are dead in life."

The world, then, of dreams and ideals which man creates for himself, cannot be, should not be, achieved in his lifetime. But the Rabbis knew of another world which they believed every man *could* and *should* achieve in his lifetime. It is the world created for man by his own ideals. It is built up of mental and spiritual reactions to those ideals, out of enthusiasms and exaltations which these very ideals and loyalties create within him. For the ideals of man give to his life a definite content and a definite scope which are his real world. This, then, was the meaning of the Rabbis: "May your life be blessed with the vision of a world so beautiful that it will crowd your life with beauty, even though the vision cannot be fulfilled in your lifetime. Life may deny you the world of achievement, it cannot deny you the world of poetry and romance and the rich savor of living which the very presence of the vision within you will create for you." Therein does the spiritual differ from the physical. The physical must be owned or consumed to be enjoyed, but we need not own or consume or realize our ideals in order to enjoy them. We enjoy them in the quest, and struggle for them, in our devotion to them.

An ethical book written by a Jewish mystic of the eighteenth century tells a naïve and charming folktale. There lived somewhere a lonely and pious Jew, poor and forgotten of men, whose entire possession in life was one single tract of the Talmud. He had no other books. The pious man spent all his days reading and re-reading this one sacred tract. It filled his entire life, it became his world. He guarded it, he loved it, he treasured it. When he died, so runs the tale, this precious tome of sacred lore was transformed into a radiant maiden of surpassing loveliness, who led this faithful devotee to the Gates of Paradise. Quaint, is it not? But how profoundly true! In similarwise did Beatrice lead Dante along the terraces of heaven. For every high devotion, for every transfiguring wish, or hope, or prayer, an angel is born unto us to be our ministrant and guardian.

Such is the potency of ideals. They give us a whole realm of celestial beauty in which to live, even while these ideals are passing through the tragic stages of denial and frustration which lead to their ultimate transfiguration. And such ideals are within the reach of all men. One need not to be learned, or highborn, or opulent, to have them. They are more precious than gold—and yet the pauper may have them for the asking. Some men have vast estates, but they are lost in waste and weeds. Others have a few square feet in front of their little homes, but love plants a flower-bed there and a tree, and behold, there is beauty and the dream of perfection.

The cobbler at his lathe may have an ideal of high artisanship. He will see the charm of his work during his lifetime. The day-laborer who is conscious of the indispensable character of his work, the merchant who is faithful to his standards of service, the employer who finds in his office a challenge to unselfishness, the professional man who regards his calling as a consecration, all of them have a dream-world which will outlive them, but one which will abundantly bless them throughout their lifetime.

These ideals are near at hand. You need not ascend mountains to find them. They have no habitation. They are everywhere. They are not only near, they are seeking us. Halevi, the mystic poet of the Middle Ages, exclaimed: "I have sought thy nearness, with my whole heart have I called upon thee, but when I went forth to find thee, I found that thou hadst been seeking me." Our ideal is seeking us. Open your eyes, it is here, in your home, in the multitudinous acts of mutual love and sacrifice, in the exalted experience of friendship, in shop, store and office, in your community, in social work, in civic work, in religious work, in the humblest and highest task it is there.

"Behold, I have set before thee this day, Life and the Good, Death and the Evil. Choose thou Life!" Amen.

C. C. LOVELACE

The Sermon

as heard by Zora Neale Hurston, at Eau Gallie in Florida, May 3, 1929

INTRODUCTION (*spoken*)

"OUR THEME this morning is the wounds of Jesus. When the Father shall ast, 'What are these wounds in thine hand?' He shall answer, 'Those are they with which I was wounded in the house of my friends.' (Zach. xiii. 6.)

"We read in the 53rd Chapter of Isaiah where He was wounded for our transgressions and bruised for our iniquities; and the apostle Peter affirms that His blood was spilt from before the foundation of the world.

"I have seen gamblers wounded. I have seen desperadoes wounded; thieves and robbers and every other kind of characters, law-breakers, and each one had a reason for his wounds. Some of them was unthoughtful, and some for being overbearing, some by the doctor's knife. But all wounds disfigures a person.

"Jesus was not unthoughtful. He was not overbearing. He was never a bully. He was never sick. He was never a criminal before the law and yet He was wounded. Now a man usually gets wounded in the midst of his enemies; but this man was wounded, says the text, in the house of His friends. It is not your enemies that harm you all the time. Watch that close friend. Every believer in Christ is considered His friend, and every sin we commit is a wound to Jesus. The blues we play in our homes is a club to beat up Jesus; and these social card parties . . ."

THE SERMON

Jesus have always loved us from the foundation of the world.
When God
Stood out on the apex of His power

Before the hammers of creation
Fell upon the anvils of Time and hammered out the ribs of
    the earth
Before He made ropes
By the breath of fire
And set the bounderies of the ocean by gravity of His
    power
When God said, ha!
Let us make man
And the elders upon the altar cried, ha!
If you make man, ha!
He will sin.
God my master, ha!
Christ, yo' friend said
Father!! Ha-aa!
I am the teeth of Time
That comprehended de dust of de earth
And weighed de hills in scales
Painted de rainbow dat marks de end of de departing
    storm
Measured de seas in de holler of my hand
Held de elements in a unbroken chain of controllment.
Make man, ha!
If he sin, I will redeem him
I'll break de chasm of hell
Where de fire's never quenched
I'll go into de grave
Where de worm never dies, Ah!
So God A'mighty, ha!
Got His stuff together
He dipped some water out of de mighty deep
He got Him a handful of dirt, ha!
From de foundation sills of de earth
He seized a thimble full of breath, ha!
From de drums of de wind, ha!
God my master!
Now I'm ready to make man
Aa-aah!
Who shall I make him after? Ha!
Worlds within worlds begin to wheel and roll

De Sun, Ah!
Gethered up de fiery skirts of her garments
And wheeled around de throne, Ah!
Saying, Ah, make man after me, Ah!
God gazed upon the sun
And sent her back to her blood-red socket
And shook His head, ha!
De Moon, Ha!
Grabbed up de reins of de tides
And dragged a thousand seas behind her
As she walked around de throne—
Ah-h, please make man after me
But God said, No.
De stars bust out from their diamond sockets
And circled de glitterin throne cryin
A-aah! Make man after me
God said, No!
I'll make man in my own image, ha!
I'll put him in de garden
And Jesus said, ha!
And if he sin,
I'll go his bond before yo mighty throne
Ah, He was yo friend
He made us all, ha!
Delegates to de judgement convention
Ah!
Faith hasnt got no eyes, but she's long-legged
But take de spy-glass of Faith
And look into dat upper room
When you are alone to yourself
When yo' heart is burnt with fire, ha!
When de blood is lopin thru yo veins
Like de iron monasters (monsters) on de rail
Look into dat upper chamber, ha!
We notice at de supper table
As He gazed upon His friends, ha!
His eyes flowin wid tears, ha!
"My soul is exceedingly sorrowful unto death, ha!
For this night, ha!
One of you shall betray me, ha!

It were not a Roman officer, ha!
It were not a centurion soldier
But one of you
Who I have choosen my bosom friend
That sops in the dish with me shall betray me."
I want to draw a parable.
I see Jesus
Leaving heben with all of His grandeur
Disrobin Hisself of His matchless honor
Yieldin up de sceptre of revolvin worlds
Clothing Hisself in de garment of humanity
Coming into de world to rescue His friends.
Two thousand years have went by on their rusty ankles
But with the eye of faith I can see Him
Look down from His high towers of elevation
I can hear Him when He walks about the golden streets
I can hear 'em ring under his footsteps
Sol me-e-e, Sol do
Sol me-e-e, Sol do
I can see Him step out upon the rim bones of nothing
Crying I am de way
De truth and de light
Ah!
God A'mighty!
I see Him grab de throttle
Of de well ordered train of mercy
I see kingdoms crush and crumble
Whilst de arc angels held de winds in de corner chambers
I see Him arrive on dis earth
And walk de streets thirty and three years
Oh-h-hhh!
I see Him walking beside de sea of Galilee wid His disciples
This declaration gendered on His lips
"Let us go on the other side"
God A'mighty!
Dey entered de boat
Wid their oarus (oars) stuck in de back
Sails unfurled to de evenin breeze
And de ship was now sailin
As she reached de center of de lake

Jesus was 'sleep on a pillow in de rear of de boat
And de dynamic powers of nature become disturbed
And de mad winds broke de heads of de western drums
And fell down on de Lake of Galilee
And buried themselves behind de gallopin waves
And de white-caps marbilized themselves like an army
And walked out like soldiers goin to battle
And de ziz-zag lightning
Licked out her fiery tongue
And de flying clouds
Threw their wings in the channels of the deep
And bedded de waters like a road-plow
And faced de current of de chargin billows
And de terrific bolts of thunder—they bust in de clouds
And de ship begin to reel and rock
God A'mighty!
And one of de disciples called Jesus
"Master!! Carest thou not that we perish?"
And He arose
And de storm was in its pitch
And de lightnin played on His raiments as He stood on the
    prow of the boat
And placed His foot upon the neck of the storm
And spoke to the howlin winds
And de sea fell at His feet like a marble floor
And de thunders went back in their vault
Then He set down on de rim of de ship
And took de hooks of his power
And lifted de billows in His lap
And rocked de winds to sleep on His arm
And said, "Peace be still."
And de Bible says there was a calm.
I can see Him wid de eye of faith
When He went from Pilate's house
Wid the crown of 72 wounds upon His head
I can see Him as He mounted Calvary and hung upon de
    cross for our sins.
I can see-eee-ee
De mountains fall to their rocky knees when He cried
"My God, my God! Why hast thou forsaken me?"

The mountains fell to their rocky knees and trembled
    like a beast
From the stroke of the master's axe
One angel took the flinches of God's eternal power
And bled the veins of the earth
One angel that stood at the gate with a flaming sword
Was so well pleased with his power
Until he pierced the moon with his sword
And she ran down in blood
And de sun
Batted her fiery eyes and put on her judgement robe
And laid down in de cradle of eternity
And rocked herself into sleep and slumber.
He died until the great belt in the wheel of time
And de geological strata fell aloose
And a thousand angels rushed to de canopy of heben
With flamin swords in their hands
And placed their feet upon blue ether's bosom and looked
    back at de dazzlin throne
And de arc angels had veiled their faces
And de throne was draped in mournin
And de orchestra had struck silence for the space of half an
    hour
Angels had lifted their harps to de weepin willows
And God had looked off to-wards immensity
And blazin worlds fell off His teeth
And about that time Jesus groaned on de cross and said, "It is
    finished"
And then de chambers of hell explode
And de damnable spirits
Come up from de Sodomistic world and rushed into de
    smoky camps of eternal night
And cried "Woe! Woe! Woe!"
And then de Centurion cried out
"Surely this is the Son of God."
And about dat time
De angel of Justice unsheathed his flamin sword and ripped
    de veil of de temple
And de High Priest vacated his office
And then de sacrificial energy penetrated de mighty strata

And quickened de bones of de prophets
And they arose from their graves and walked about in de
    streets of Jerusalem.
I heard de whistle of de damnation train
Dat pulled out from Garden of Eden loaded wid cargo goin
    to hell
Ran at break-neck speed all de way thru de law
All de way thru de prophetic age
All de way thru de reign of kings and judges—
Plowed her way thru de Jurdan
And on her way to Calvary when she blew for de switch
Jesus stood out on her track like a rough-backed mountain
And she threw her cow-catcher in His side and His blood
    ditched de train,
He died for our sins.
Wounded in the house of His friends.
Thats where I got off de damnation train
And dats where you must get off, ha!
For in dat mor-ornin', ha!
When we shall all be delegates, ha!
To dat judgement convention, ha!
When de two trains of Time shall meet on de trestle
And wreck de burning axles of de unformed ether
And de mountains shall skip like lambs
When Jesus shall place one foot on de neck of de sea, ha!
One foot on dry land
When His chariot wheels shall be running hub-deep in fire
He shall take His friends thru the open bosom of a
    unclouded sky
And place in their hands de hosanna fan
And they shall stand round and round His beatific throne
And praise His name forever.
                    Amen.

PAUL TILLICH

You Are Accepted

Moreover the law entered, that the offence might abound. But where sin abounded, grace did much more abound. ROMANS 5:20.

THESE WORDS of Paul summarize his apostolic experience, his religious message as a whole, and the Christian understanding of life. To discuss these words, or to make them the text of even several sermons, has always seemed impossible to me. I have never dared to use them before. But something has driven me to consider them during the past few months, a desire to give witness to the two facts which appeared to me, in hours of retrospection, as the all-determining facts of our life: the abounding of sin and the greater abounding of grace.

There are few words more strange to most of us than "sin" and "grace." They are strange, just because they are so well-known. During the centuries they have received distorting connotations, and have lost so much of their genuine power that we must seriously ask ourselves whether we should use them at all, or whether we should discard them as useless tools. But there is a mysterious fact about the great words of our religious tradition: they cannot be replaced. All attempts to make substitutions, including those I have tried myself, have failed to convey the reality that was to be expressed; they have led to shallow and impotent talk. There are no substitutes for words like "sin" and "grace". But there *is* a way of rediscovering their meaning, the same way that leads us down into the depth of our human existence. In that depth these words were conceived; and *there* they gained power for all ages; *there* they must be found again by each generation, and by each of us for himself. Let us therefore try to penetrate the deeper levels of our life, in order to see whether we can discover in them the realities of which our text speaks.

Have the men of our time still a feeling of the meaning of sin? Do they, and do we, still realize that sin does *not* mean an immoral act, that "sin" should never be used in the plural, and that not our sins, but rather our *sin* is the great, all-pervading problem of our life? Do we still know that it is arrogant and erroneous to divide men by calling some "sinners" and others "righteous"? For by way of such a division, we can usually discover that we ourselves do not *quite* belong to the "sinners", since we have avoided heavy sins, have made some progress in the control of this or that sin, and have been even humble enough not to call ourselves "righteous". Are we still able to realize that this kind of thinking and feeling about sin is far removed from what the great religious tradition, both within and outside the Bible, has meant when it speaks of sin?

I should like to suggest another word to you, not as a substitute for the word "sin", but as a useful clue in the interpretation of the word "sin": "separation". Separation is an aspect of the experience of everyone. Perhaps the word "sin" has the same root as the word "asunder". In any case, *sin is separation.* To be in the state of sin is to be in the state of separation. And separation is threefold: there is separation among individual lives, separation of a man from himself, and separation of all men from the Ground of Being. This three-fold separation constitutes the state of everything that exists; it is a universal fact; it is the fate of every life. And it is our human fate in a very special sense. For *we* as men know that we are separated. We not only suffer with all other creatures because of the self-destructive consequences of our separation, but also know *why* we suffer. We know that we are estranged from something to which we really belong, and with which we *should* be united. We know that the fate of separation is not merely a natural event like a flash of sudden lightning, but that it is an experience in which we actively participate, in which our whole personality is involved, and that, as fate, it is also *guilt.* Separation which is fate *and* guilt constitutes the meaning of the word "sin". It is *this* which is the state of our entire existence, from its very beginning to its very end. Such separation is prepared in the mother's womb, and before that time, in every preceding generation. It is manifest in the special actions of our conscious life. It reaches beyond our graves into all the succeeding generations. It is our existence itself. *Existence is separation!* Before sin is an act, it is a state.

We can say the same things about grace. For sin and grace are bound to each other. We do not even have a knowledge of sin unless we have already experienced the unity of life, which is grace. And conversely, we could not grasp the meaning of grace without having experienced the separation of life, which is sin. Grace is just as difficult to describe as sin. For some people, grace is the willingness of a divine king and father to forgive over and again the foolishness and weakness of his subjects and children. We must reject such a concept of grace; for it is a merely childish destruction of a human dignity. For others, grace is a magic power in the dark places of the soul, but a power without any significance for practical life, a quickly vanishing and useless idea. For others, grace is the benevolence that we may find beside the cruelty and destructiveness in life. But then, it does not matter whether we say "life goes on", or whether we say "there is grace in life"; if grace means no more than this, the word should, and will, disappear. For other people, grace indicates the gifts that one has received from nature or society, and the power to do good things with the help of those gifts. But grace is more than gifts. In grace something is overcome; grace occurs "in spite of" something; grace occurs in spite of separation and estrangement. Grace is the *re*union of life with life, the *re*conciliation of the self with itself. Grace is the acceptance of that which is rejected. Grace transforms fate into a meaningful destiny; it changes guilt into confidence and courage. There is something triumphant in the word "grace": in spite of the abounding of sin grace abounds much more.

And now let us look down into ourselves to discover there the struggle between separation and reunion, between sin and grace, in our relation to others, in our relation to ourselves, and in our relation to the Ground and aim of our being. If our souls respond to the description that I intend to give, words like "sin" and "separation", "grace" and "reunion", may have a new meaning for us. But the words themselves are not important. It is the response of the deepest levels of our being that is important. If such a response were to occur among us this moment, we could say that we have known grace.

Who has not, at some time, been lonely in the midst of a social event? The feeling of our separation from the rest of life is most acute when we are surrounded by it in noise and talk. We realize then much more than in moments of solitude how strange we are to each other, how estranged life is from life. Each one of us draws back into himself. We cannot penetrate the hidden centre of another individual; nor can that individual pass beyond the shroud that covers our own being. Even the greatest love cannot break through the walls of the self. Who has not experienced that disillusionment of all great love? If one were to hurl away his self in complete self-surrender, he would become a nothing, without form or strength, a self without self, merely an object of contempt and abuse. Our generation knows more than the generation of our fathers about the hidden hostility in the ground of our souls. Today we know much about the profusive aggressiveness in every being. Today we can confirm what Immanuel Kant, the prophet of human reason and dignity, was honest enough to say: there is something in the misfortune of our best friends which does not displease us. Who amongst us is dishonest enough to deny that this is true also of him? Are we not almost always ready to abuse everybody and everything, although often in a very refined way, for the pleasure of self-elevation, for an occasion for boasting, for a moment of lust? To know that we are ready is to know the meaning of the separation of life from life, and of "sin abounding".

The most irrevocable expression of the separation of life from life today is the attitude of social groups within nations towards each other, and the attitude of nations themselves towards other nations. The walls of distance, in time and space, have been removed by technical progress; but the walls of estrangement between heart and heart have been incredibly strengthened. The madness of the German Nazis and the cruelty of the lynching mobs in the South provide too easy an excuse for us to turn our thoughts from our own selves. But let us just consider ourselves and what we feel, when we read, this morning and tonight, that in some sections of Europe all children under the age of three are sick and dying, or that in some sections of Asia millions without homes are freezing and starving to death. The strangeness of life to life is evident in the strange fact that we can know all this, and yet can live to-day, this morning, tonight, as though we were completely ignorant. And I refer to the most sensitive people amongst us. In both mankind and nature, life is separated from life. Estrangement prevails among all things that live. Sin abounds.

It is important to remember that we are not merely separated from each other. For we are also separated from ourselves. *Man Against Himself* is not merely the title of a book, but rather also indicates the rediscovery of an age-old insight. Man is split within himself. Life moves against itself through aggression, hate, and despair. We are wont to condemn self-love; but what we really mean to condemn is contrary to self-love. It is that mixture of selfishness and self-hate that permanently pursues us, that prevents us from loving others, and that prohibits us from losing ourselves in the love with which we are loved eternally. He who is able to love himself is able to love others also; he who has learned to overcome self-contempt has overcome his contempt for others. But the depth of our separation lies in just the fact that we are not capable of a great and merciful divine love towards ourselves. On the contrary, in each of us there is an instinct of self-destruction, which is as strong as our instinct of self-preservation. In our tendency to abuse and destroy others, there is an open or hidden tendency to abuse and to destroy ourselves. Cruelty towards others is always also cruelty towards ourselves. Nothing is more obvious than the split in both our unconscious life and conscious personality. Without the help of modern psychology, Paul expressed the fact in his famous words, "For I do not do the good I desire, but rather the evil that I do not desire." And then he continued in words that might well be the motto of all depth psychology: "Now if I should do what I do not wish to do, it is not I that do it, but rather sin which dwells within me." The apostle sensed a split between his conscious will and his real will, between himself and something strange within and alien to him. He was estranged from himself; and that estrangement he called "sin". He also called it a strange "law in his limbs", an irresistible compulsion. How often we commit certain acts in perfect consciousness, yet with the shocking sense that we are being controlled by an alien power! That is the experience of the separation of ourselves from ourselves, which is to say "sin," whether or not we like to use that word.

Thus, the state of our whole life is estrangement from others and ourselves, because we are estranged from the Ground of our being, because we are estranged from the origin and aim of our life. And we do not know where we have come from, or where we are going. We are separated from the mystery, the depth, and the greatness of our existence. We hear the voice of that depth; but our ears are closed. We feel that something radical, total, and unconditioned is demanded of us; but we rebel against it, try to escape its urgency, and will not accept its promise.

We cannot escape, however. If that something is the Ground of our being, we are bound to it for all eternity, just as we are bound to ourselves and to all other life. We always remain in the power of that from which we are estranged. That fact brings us to the ultimate depth of sin: separated and yet bound, estranged and yet belonging, destroyed and yet preserved, the state which is called despair. Despair means that there is no escape. Despair is "the sickness unto death." But the terrible thing about the sickness of despair is that we cannot be released, not even through open or hidden suicide. For we all know that we are bound eternally and inescapably to the Ground of our being. The abyss of separation is not always visible. But it has become more visible to our generation than to the preceding generations, because of our feeling of meaninglessness, emptiness, doubt, and cynicism—all expressions of despair, of our separation from the roots and the meaning of our life. Sin in its most profound sense, sin, as despair, abounds amongst us.

"Where sin abounded, grace did much more abound", says Paul in the same letter in which he describes the unimaginable power of separation and self-destruction within society and the individual soul. He does not say these words because sentimental interests demand a happy ending for everything tragic. He says them because they describe the most overwhelming and determining experience of his life. In the picture of Jesus as the Christ, which appeared to him at the moment of his greatest separation from other men, from himself and God, he found himself accepted in spite of his being rejected. And when he found that he was accepted, he was able to accept himself and to be reconciled to others. The moment in which grace struck him and overwhelmed him, he was reunited with that to which he belonged, and from which he was estranged in utter strangeness. Do we know what it means to be struck by grace? It does *not* mean that we suddenly believe that God exists, or that Jesus is the Saviour, or that the Bible contains the truth. To believe that something *is*, is almost contrary to the meaning of grace. Furthermore, grace does not mean simply that we are making progress in our moral self-control, in our fight against special faults, and in our relationships to men and to society. Moral progress may be a fruit of grace; but it is not grace itself, and it can even prevent us from receiving grace. For there is too often a graceless acceptance of Christian doctrines and a graceless battle against the structures of evil in our personalities. Such a graceless relation to God may lead us by necessity either to arrogance or to despair. It would be better to refuse God and the Christ and the Bible than to accept Them without grace. For if we accept without grace, we do so in the state of separation, and can only succeed in deepening the separation. We cannot transform our lives, unless we allow them to be transformed by that stroke of grace. It happens; or it does not happen. And certainly it does *not* happen if we try to force it upon ourselves, just as it shall not happen so long as we think, in our self-complacency, that we have no need of it. Grace strikes us when we are in great pain and restlessness. It strikes us when we walk through the dark valley of a meaningless and empty life. It strikes us when we feel that our separation is deeper than usual, because we have violated another life, a life which we loved, or from which we were estranged. It strikes us when our disgust for our own being, our indifference, our weakness, our hostility, and our lack of direction and composure have become intolerable to us. It strikes us when year after year, the longed-for perfection of life does not appear, when the old compulsions reign within us as they have for decades, when despair destroys all joy and courage. Sometimes at that moment a wave of light breaks into our darkness, and it is as though a voice were saying: "You are accepted. *You are accepted*, accepted by that which is greater

than you, and the name of which you do not know. Do not
ask for the name now; perhaps you will find it later. Do not
try to do anything now; perhaps later you will do much. Do
not seek for anything; do not perform anything; do not intend anything. *Simply accept the fact that you are accepted!*" If
that happens to us, we experience grace. After such an experience we may not be better than before, and we may not believe more than before. But everything is transformed. In that
moment, grace conquers sin, and reconciliation bridges the
gulf of estrangement. And nothing is demanded of this experience, no religious or moral or intellectual presupposition,
nothing but *acceptance.*

In the light of this grace we perceive the power of grace in
our relation to others and to ourselves. We experience the
grace of being able to look frankly into the eyes of another,
the miraculous grace of reunion of life with life. We experience the grace of understanding each other's words. We understand not merely the literal meaning of the words, but also
that which lies behind them, even when they are harsh or angry. For even then there is a longing to break through the
walls of separation. We experience the grace of being able to
accept the life of another, even if it be hostile and harmful to
us, for, through grace, we know that it belongs to the same
Ground to which we belong, and by which we have been accepted. We experience the grace which is able to overcome
the tragic separation of the sexes, of the generations, of the
nations, of the races, and even the utter strangeness between
man and nature. Sometimes grace appears in all these separations to reunite us with those to whom we belong. For life
belongs to life.

And in the light of this grace we perceive the power of
grace in our relation to ourselves. We experience moments in
which we accept ourselves, because we feel that we have been
accepted by that which is greater than we. If only more such
moments were given to us! For it is such moments that make
us love our life, that make us accept ourselves, not in our
goodness and self-complacency, but in our certainty of the
eternal meaning of our life. We cannot force ourselves to accept ourselves. We cannot compel anyone to accept himself.
But sometimes it happens that we receive the power to say

"yes" to ourselves, that peace enters into us and makes us whole, that self-hate and self-contempt disappear, and that our self is reunited with itself. Then we can say that grace has come upon us.

"Sin" and "grace" are strange words; but they are not strange things. We find them whenever we look into ourselves with searching eyes and longing hearts. They determine our life. They abound within us and in all of life. May grace more abound within us!

REINHOLD NIEBUHR

The Providence of God

> *"You have heard that it was said, 'You shall love your neighbor and hate your enemy.' But I say to you, Love your enemies and pray for those who persecute you, so that you may be sons of your Father who is in heaven; for he makes his sun rise on the evil and on the good, and sends rain on the just and on the unjust. For if you love those who love you, what reward have you? Do not even the tax collectors do the same? And if you salute only your brethren, what more are you doing than others? Do not even the Gentiles do the same? You, therefore, must be perfect, as your heavenly Father is perfect."*
>
> MATTHEW 5:43–48, RSV

My TEXT is taken from the New Testament lesson: "But I say to you, Love your enemies and pray for those who persecute you, so that you may be sons of your Father who is in heaven; for he makes his sun rise on the evil and on the good, and sends rain on the just and on the unjust."

This text has been preached upon many times in the memory of all of us. Usually, however, the emphasis has been upon the moral admonition that we should love our enemies, and not much attention has been paid to the justification of the love of the enemy that Jesus gives by reference to the impartial character of God's love. It is on the second theme that I want to speak this morning.

There are many things to say about the first theme, for Jesus is suggesting in his Sermon on the Mount that you cannot be moral if you are too strictly moral. The highest morality of forgiveness is, as Berdyaev says, "the morality beyond morality." Nobody who is strictly moral can forgive, because forgiveness is at once the fulfillment of every concept of justice, and its annulment. Jesus justifies this "morality beyond all morality" by saying God is like that. The love of God is an impartial goodness beyond good and evil. The providence of God is an impartial concern for all men without any special privileges in it.

Thus, the structure of meaning for the Christian faith is completed against all the contradictions in history, where there are no simple correlations of reward for good and punishment for evil. God is like nature, says Jesus, like the impartial nature which you could accuse of not being moral at all, because the sun shines upon both the evil and the good, and the rain descends upon the just and the unjust. A nonmoral nature is made into the symbol of the transmoral mercy. Here is a very radical concept, and one of those words of Scripture that we never quite take in. It is a word of Scripture that has particular significance because it is set squarely against most of our religion, inside the Christian Church as well as anywhere else.

When we say that we believe in God, we are inclined to mean that we have found a way to the ultimate source and end of life, and this gives us, against all the chances and changes of life, some special security and some special favor. And if we do not mean that—which is religion on a fairly adolescent and immature level—at least we mean that we have discovered amidst the vast confusions of life what is usually called the moral order, according to which evil is punished and good rewarded, and we could hardly feel that life had any meaning if we were not certain of that.

The Bible is full of this debate between what might be called the instinct of religion and the gospel of Christ. The natural instincts of religion demand that my life be given meaning by a special security against all of the insecurities of life. If it should seem as if goodness and evil—punishment for evil and reward for good—were not being properly correlated in life, then God will guarantee finally that they will be properly correlated.

Thus, in the Scriptures the words of the Psalms, "A thousand may fall at your side, ten thousand at your right hand, but it will not come near you." Or the many intercessory prayers, the intent of which is "A thousand at your side, ten thousand at your right hand," let it not come to my loved one. What a natural prayer that is and finally how impossible! "For in the time of trouble He shall hide me, and he shall set me upon a rock." In a word, plead my cause, O Lord, against them that strive with me, fight against them that fight against me.

Examples can be multiplied and it must also be realized how very natural are these kinds of prayers. Has there ever been a conflict in the human community where we have not felt we could not fight the battle were not the Lord on our side? Perhaps, as Abraham Lincoln said, we did not as frequently ask the question of whether we were on the Lord's side. These are natural religious instincts, the natural efforts to close prematurely the great structure of life's meaning. Much more justified is the other aspect of this sense of special providence—not that God would give me special privileges, special securities against the other man—but that in a very hazardous world where it is not certain that good will be rewarded and evil punished, at least God should set that right.

"Blessed is he who considers the poor!" to use another word of the Psalm, "The Lord delivers him in the day of trouble." Many years ago, tithing was popular in some of the churches. A member of my congregation had started tithing as a twelve-year-old boy and had become a millionaire. He was quite convinced that the millions were the reward of his tithing.

"Blessed is he who considers the poor! The Lord delivers him in the day of trouble." I was never much convinced by this millionaire businessman because of my first pastoral experience when I took the church of my deceased father for six months. The first pastoral problem I had was dealing with an old man whom I greatly respected, who really had the grace of God in him. He had considered the poor to the degree of giving striking miners so much credit at his grocery store that he lost his business. In the seventy-eighth year of his life, he had to face the problem of bankruptcy, and the fact that there was no simple correlation between his goodness and the fortunes of his life.

Both kinds of faith were wrong. First, that if we pray to God fervently enough he will establish some special security for us against the security of the other person. Or secondly, the belief that there are simple moral correlations between the vast processes either of nature or of history and human virtue. The history of our Puritan fathers in New England illustrates how wrong are both of these propositions. There were some very great virtues and graces in their lives. But the doctrine of special providence represents the real defect in our Puritan inheritance. These Puritan forefathers of ours were sure that every rain and every drought was connected with the virtue and vice of their enterprise—that God always had his hand upon them to reward them for their goodness, and to punish them for their evil.

Their belief in special providence was unfortunate, particularly so when a religious community developed in the vast possibilities of America, where inevitably the proofs of God's favor turned out to be greater than the proofs of God's wrath. It may be the reason why we Americans are so self-righteous. It may be also the reason why we still have not come to terms, in an ultimate religious sense, with our responsibilities; with the problems of the special favors that our nation enjoys compared with other nations. But first of all we have to realize that this picture of God's love is not true. The Scriptures also are full of testimony that it is not true. Certainly it is the point of the Book of Job. Job first hopes that God is a God of simple justice, but it is proved to him that this cannot be the case. Then Job protests against the fact that if he does wrong he is convicted as a sinner, but if he does right, he is no better off: "I cannot lift up my head." Ours is a confused kind of world, says Job, in which there is no guarantee that the righteous man will prosper. Is there a God in this kind of world?

These are the protests that run through the Scriptures as they run through life. "My feet had almost stumbled," says the great seventy-third Psalm. "My steps had well nigh slipped . . . when I saw the prosperity of the wicked. . . . Their eyes swell out with fatness, . . . and they say, 'How can God know?' "

"When I saw the prosperity of the wicked"—here is man in history involved in the web of relationships and meanings, but not of simple ones. There must be some moral meaning here. Is there not some punishment of wickedness in life? And

I do not mean any of the arbitrary punishment which we inflict by our courts. For life is not completely at variance with itself. There *is* reward for goodness in life, and there *is* punishment for evil, but not absolutely. The same law which punishes the criminal punishes the Savior. And there are three crosses: two for criminals who cannot meet the moral mediocrities of life, and one for the Savior who rises above it. This is life.

Martin Buber, some years ago, made a remark about the special spiritual problems that we face in our world, where we cannot bring to any simple end the structure of moral meaning in which we stand. "When the Nazis ruled," he said, "even when they were at the height of their rule, I knew in my heart that they would fall, that they would be punished."

But now we face a future with greater threats of destruction than during the Nazi period. And this will continue partly because it is a problem that involves all the confusions of modern history against which our own goodness is not adequate. There is no simple moral resolution of the nuclear dilemma. These are the facts of our historic existence; life cannot be correlated easily into simple moral meanings; nor can the Christian faith be validated by proving special acts of providence in your own or somebody else's favor.

I have a certain embarrassment about this issue in the great debate between Christianity and secularism. I am convinced of the Christian faith in the God revealed in Christ and whom Christ says is partially revealed in the impartialities of nature. Yet it seems to me also true that a certain type of secularism has advantages over us on any point where, to quote William James, Christianity becomes "an effort to lobby in the courts of the Almighty for special favors."

Against this lobbying for special favors, one must admit that there is an element of nobility either in modern or ancient Stoicism. Marcus Aurelius said: "If so be the gods deliberated in particular on those things that should happen to me, I must stand to their deliberation, but if so be that they have not deliberated for me in particular, certainly they have on the whole and in general deliberated on those things which happen to me. In consequence and coherence of this general deliberation, I am bound to embrace and to accept them." There is a certain nobility in Stoic courage. It has no sense of an ultimate relationship to God as a final expression of the Christian faith, but as far as it goes, is it not true?

Modern man, under the influence of natural science, sees the problem more critically than it was seen before. We see that nature, whatever may be God's ultimate sovereignty over it, moves by its own laws. Even so good a theologian as the late William Temple did not understand this. He tried to solve it by saying the laws of nature are merely God's habitual way of doing things. If he does not want to act in the habitual way, he will choose another way. Surely this is too voluntaristic a conception of how the forces of nature work.

An analogous proposition would be that my heart beats in a habitual way, but if I choose, I could have it do something else. No, my heart has its own automatic processes as do the forces of nature. Many in our modern world have come to despair about this vast realm of seeming meaninglessness.

Though we have some sympathy from a modern scientific culture which says such special providence is not true, what concerns us more as Christians is the protest of Jesus against the underlying assumptions. It is not true that God gives special favors, and it is not true that there are simple moral meanings in the processes of history. We cannot speak simply of a moral order which if defied, would destroy us. Though Jesus is concerned about the whole dimension of the gospel, it is not so much whether these things are true or not upon their own levels, but whether they would be right. God's love would not be right if it were this kind of a love. This is the point that Christ makes in the Sermon on the Mount, that God's love would not be right. The Christian faith believes that within and beyond the tragedies and the contradictions of history we have laid hold upon a loving heart, the proof of whose love is first impartiality toward all of his children, and secondly a mercy which transcends good and evil.

How shall we appropriate this insistence of Christ in our life? All of us, including some who are not conventionally religious, have a desire for an ultimate security. Even people who are not conventionally religious often pray in the hour of crisis. In that sense, all men are religious. Yet under the discipline of the gospel, we should bring each one of these prayers under scrutiny.

This does not change radically the problem of intercessory prayer. Perhaps we have to consider life in three different dimensions. First, there is the vast dimension of nature where we cannot expect that God will put up a special umbrella for us against this or that possible disaster. In the realm of nature, we face the problem of natural evil. Jesus was asked, "Master, who sinned, this man or his parents, that he was born blind?" Jesus' answer repudiated the idea of special providence: "It was not that this man sinned or his parents have sinned but that the works of God might be made manifest in him." There is no meaning to this blindness except the ultimate possible meaning of how the blindness might become a source of grace. It is a most terrible thing to correlate natural evil immediately to any moral and spiritual meaning, and yet it is a wonderful thing to correlate it ultimately. Likewise Jesus replied, when asked about those killed by the fall of the tower in Siloam, "Were they worse offenders than all the others who dwell in Jerusalem? I tell you, no!" Do not try to relate natural catastrophes to moral meanings. Do not ask the question whether people killed in an earthquake are more guilty, more sinful, than others. "I tell you, no!" Ask the question, rather, what ultimate use, what final point for the grace of God is there in this calamity? But do not correlate it in such a way that it ceases to be a calamity, for this belongs to the realm of nature.

In the realm of history we have another problem, of course, because history is a realm of human freedom and human agency, and if it did not have any moral meaning at all, it would be intolerable. If there were not some reward for goodness, life would be absolutely askew. If there were no likelihood that forgiveness would produce the spirit of forgiveness, and mutuality the spirit of mutuality and reciprocity, it would be hard to love and trust each other. Yet in the processes of history these things are not simply correlated. The suffering of the innocent is one of the most terrible things in the collective enterprise of man. When, towards the end of the Second World War, we started to bomb the Germans into submission, we bombed Hamburg first, the city that had more anti-Nazi votes than any other German city. These anguishes are the facts of life as we find them in history.

There are no simple correlations. This does not mean that we will not pray for our loved ones in the hazards and tumults of history, when so frequently their destiny is a curious combination of the physical and the spiritual. We certainly will not stop praying for their health, particularly in view of what we know about psychosomatic characteristics in the human personality today. We will pray for the health of other people and pray for their healing.

This is the realm of history which is a vast middle ground between the realm of grace and the realm of nature. But ultimately, of course, our Christian faith lives in the realm of grace, in the realm of freedom. This is God's freedom and my freedom, beyond the structures of my body; the realm of grace where I know God and am persuaded, as St. Paul says, that he knows me.

In that realm, finally, all concern for immediate correlations and coherences and meanings falls away. The Christian faith stands in the sense of an ultimate meaning. We may be persuaded that God is on our side—not against somebody else—but on our side in this ultimate sense. We are "sure that neither death nor life, nor angels, nor principalities, nor things present, nor things to come, . . . will be able to separate us from the love of God in Christ Jesus our Lord."

It is on that level of meaning that the Christian faith makes sense. The lower levels are a threat, not only to the sense of the meaning of life, but finally to the morals of life. We must not deny that there is a kind of religion that enhances the ego and gives it an undue place in the world. But from the standpoint of our faith we should take our humble and contrite place in God's plan of the whole, and leave it to him to complete the fragmentation of our life.

O God, who has promised that all things will work together for good to those that love you, grant us patience amidst the tumults, pains and afflictions of life, and faith to discern your love, within, above, and beyond the impartial destinies of this great drama of life. Save us from every vainglorious pretension by which we demand favors which violate your love for all your children, and grant us grace to appropriate every fortune, both good and evil, for the triumph of the suffering, crucified, and risen Lord in our souls and life. In whose name we ask it.

C. L. FRANKLIN

The Eagle Stirreth Her Nest

THE EAGLE here is used to symbolize God's care and God's concern for his people. Many things have been used as symbolic expressions to give us a picture of God or some characteristic of one of his attributes: the ocean, with her turbulent majesty; the mountains, the lions. Many things have been employed as pictures of either God's strength or God's power or God's love or God's mercy. And the psalmist has said that The heavens declare the glory of God and the firmament shows forth his handiworks.

So the eagle here is used as a symbol of God. Now in picturing God as an eagle stirring her nest, I believe history has been one big nest that God has been eternally stirring to make man better and to help us achieve world brotherhood. Some of the things that have gone on in your own experiences have merely been God stirring the nest of your circumstances. Now the Civil War, for example, and the struggle in connection with it, was merely the promptings of Providence to lash man to a point of being brotherly to all men. In fact, all of the wars that we have gone through, we have come out with new outlooks and new views and better people. So that throughout history, God has been stirring the various nests of circumstances surrounding us, so that he could discipline us, help us to know ourselves, and help us to love another, and to help us hasten on the realization of the kingdom of God.

The eagle symbolizes God because there is something about an eagle that is a fit symbol of things about God. In the first place, the eagle is the king of fowls. And if he is a regal or kingly bird, in that majesty he represents the kingship of God or symbolizes the kingship of God. (Listen if you please.) For God is not merely a king, he is *the* king. Somebody has said that he is the king of kings. For you see, these little kings that we know, they've got to have a king over them. They've got to account to somebody for the deeds

826

done in their bodies. For God is *the* king. And if the eagle is a kingly bird, in that way he symbolizes the regalness and kingliness of our God.

In the second place, the eagle is strong. Somebody has said that as the eagle goes winging his way through the air he can look down on a young lamb grazing by a mountainside, and can fly down and just with the strength of his claws, pick up this young lamb and fly away to yonder's cleft and devour it—because he's strong. If the eagle is strong, then, in that he is a symbol of God, for our God is strong. Our God is strong. Somebody has called him a fortress. So that when the enemy is pursuing me I can run behind him. Somebody has called him a citadel of protection and redemption. Somebody else has said that he's so strong until they call him a leaning-post that thousands can lean on him, and he'll never get away. (I don't believe you're praying with me.) People have been leaning on him ever since time immemorial. Abraham leaned on him. Isaac and Jacob leaned on him. Moses and the prophets leaned on him. All the Christians leaned on him. People are leaning on him all over the world today. He's never given way. He's strong. That's strong. Isn't it so?

In the second place, he's swift. The eagle is swift. And it is said that he could fly with such terrific speed that his wings can be heard rowing in the air. He's swift. And if he's swift in that way, he's a symbol of our God. For our God is swift. I said he's swift. Sometimes, sometimes he'll answer you while you're calling him. He's swift. Daniel was thrown in a lions' den. And Daniel rung him on the way to the lions' den. And having rung him, why, God had dispatched the angel from heaven. And by the time that Daniel got to the lions' den, the angel had changed the nature of lions and made them lay down and act like lambs. He's swift. Swift. One night Peter was put in jail and the church went down on its knees to pray for him. And while the church was praying, Peter knocked on the door. God was so swift in answering prayer. So that if the eagle is a swift bird, in that way he represents or symbolizes the fact that God is swift. He's swift. If you get in earnest tonight and tell him about your troubles, he's swift to hear you. All you do is need a little faith, and ask him in grace.

Another thing about the eagle is that he has extraordinary

sight. Extraordinary sight. Somewhere it is said that he can rise to a lofty height in the air and look in the distance and see a storm hours away. That's extraordinary sight. And sometimes he can stand and gaze right in the sun because he has extraordinary sight. I want to tell you my God has extraordinary sight. He can see every ditch that you have dug for me and guide me around them. God has extraordinary sight. He can look behind that smile on your face and see that frown in your heart. God has extraordinary sight.

Then it is said that an eagle builds a nest unusual. It is said that the eagle selects rough material, basically, for the construction of his nest. And then as the nest graduates toward a close or a finish, the material becomes finer and softer right down at the end. And then he goes about to set up residence in that nest. And when the little eaglets are born, she goes out and brings in food to feed them. But when they get to the point where they're old enough to be out on their own, why, the eagle will begin to pull out some of that down and let some of those thorns come through so that the nest won't be, you know, so comfortable. So when they get to lounging around and rolling around, the thorns prick 'em here and there. (Pray with me if you please.)

I believe that God has to do that for us sometimes. Things are going so well and we are so satisfied that we just lounge around and forget to pray. You'll walk around all day and enjoy God's life, God's health and God's strength, and go climb into bed without saying, "Thank you, Lord, for another day's journey." We'll do that. God has to pull out a little of the plush around us, a little of the comfort around us, and let a few thorns of trial and tribulation stick through the nest to make us pray sometime. Isn't it so? For most of us forget God when things are going well with us. Most of us forget him.

It is said that there was a man who had a poultry farm. And that he raised chickens for the market. And one day in one of his broods he discovered a strange looking bird that was very much unlike the other chickens on the yard. [Whooping:]

And
       the man
             didn't pay too much attention.
       But he noticed
             as time went on
that
       this strange looking bird
             was unusual.
       He outgrew
             the other little chickens,
       his habits were stranger
             and different.
O Lord.
       But he let him grow on,
       and let him mingle
             with the other chickens.
O Lord.
       And then one day a man
       who knew eagles
             when he saw them,
       came along
             and saw that little eagle
             walking in the yard.
And
       he said to his friend,
       "Do you know
             that you have an eagle here?"
       The man said, "Well,
             I didn't really know it.
       But I knew he was different
             from the other chickens.
And
       I knew that his ways
             were different.
And
       I knew that his habits
             were different.
And
       he didn't act like
             the other chickens.

But I didn't know
        that he was an eagle."
But the man said, "Yes,
        you have an eagle here on your yard.
And what you ought to do
        is build a cage.
After while
when he's a little older
        he's going to get tired
        of the ground.
Yes he will.
        He's going to rise up
            on the pinion of his wings.
Yes,
and
        as he grows,
why,
        you can change the cage,
and
        make it a little larger
            as he grows older
            and grows larger."
The man went out
        and built a cage.
And
        every day he'd go in
            and feed the eagle.
But
        he grew
            a little older
            and a little older.
Yes he did.
        His wings
            began
      to scrape on the sides
            of the cage.
And
        he had to build
            another cage

and open the door of the old cage
and let him into
a larger cage.
Yes he did.
O Lord.
And

after a while
he outgrew that one day
and then he had to build
another cage.
So one day
when the eagle had gotten grown,
Lord God,
and his wings
were twelve feet
from tip to tip,
o Lord,
he began to get restless
in the cage.
Yes he did.
He began to walk around
and be uneasy.
Why,
he heard
noises
in the air.
A flock of eagles flew over
and he heard
their voices.

And

though he'd never been around eagles,
there was something about that voice
that he heard
that moved
down in him,
and made him
dissatisfied.
O Lord.
And

        the man watched him
                as he walked around
                uneasy.
O Lord.
        He said, "Lord,
                my heart goes out to him.
        I believe I'll go
                and open the door
                and set the eagle free."
O Lord.
        He went there
                and opened the door.
Yes.
        The eagle walked out,
                yes,
        spreaded his wings,
                then took 'em down.
Yes.
        The eagle walked around
                a little longer,
and
        he flew up a little higher
                and went to the barnyard.
And,
yes,
        he set there for awhile.
        He wiggled up a little higher
        and flew in yonder's tree.
Yes.
        And then he wiggled up a little higher
        and flew to yonder's mountain.
Yes.
Yes!
Yes.
        One of these days,
                one of these days.
        My soul
                is an eagle
        in the cage that the Lord
                has made for me.

My soul,

       my soul,

my soul

       is caged in,

       in this old body,

       yes it is,

and one of these days

the man who made the cage

will open the door

and let my soul

       go.

Yes he will.

You ought to

       be able to see me

       take the wings of my soul.

Yes, yes,

yes,

yes!

Yes, one of these days.

One of these old days.

One of these old days.

Did you hear me say it?

I'll fly away

       and be at rest.

Yes.

Yes!

Yes!

Yes!

Yes!

Yes.

One of these old days.

One of these old days.

And

when troubles

       and trials are over,

when toil

       and tears are ended,

when burdens

       are through burdening,

ohh!

Ohh.
Ohh!
Ohh one of these days.
Ohh one of these days.
One of these days.
One of these days,
my soul will take wings,
my soul will take wings.
Ohh!
Ohh, a few more days.
Ohh, a few more days.
A few more days.
O Lord.

FULTON J. SHEEN

How to Have a Good Time

It is to be noted that almost everyone associates happiness or pleasure with time. Hence we speak of depressions, plagues, hot and cold wars as "bad times," while pleasant companionship, good dinners and evenings out are identified with having a "good time." Seneca has said "Time hath often cured the wound which reason failed to heal"; on the other hand, Doctor Johnson observes: "You cannot give an instance of any man who is permitted to lay out his own time, contriving not to have tedious hours."

A "good" time is one of those catchwords which actually belies the true nature of happiness. The truth of the matter is that the greatest pleasures and joys come when we are unconscious of time.

The more conscious we are of the passing of time, the less we enjoy ourselves. The clock watcher never enjoys his work. "Serving time," a description of imprisonment, is synonymous with unhappiness and confinement. One prisoner who was sentenced to five years said to the judge: "I'll not live that long." The judge said: "At least, you can try." Boredom is in part due to the inability to fill up time. People who overstay their time in visiting make one appreciate the reflection of Benjamin Franklin: "Fish and visitors smell after three days." Once a visitor who had been standing on the doorstep for an hour, relating new items of gossip, finally said to her hostess: "I know there is something I forgot to say." The hostess retorted: "Maybe it was 'good-by.'" The very phrase "killing time" signifies that existence in time can be depressing. A number of very obvious pleasures, and sometimes highly intellectual pursuits, are nothing else than "pass-times" by which man seeks to forget his temporality. The less conscious we are of the passing of time, the more we enjoy ourselves. In moments of sheer delight, we say: "The time simply flew."

Romantic love gets beyond time by eternalizing the present second; it makes time stand still, and tries to get beyond its succession by obliterating the past or future. The present moment of ecstasy, the dance, the music, the moonlight and a drive through the park, the joys surrounding graduation, all are rendered static; what is now will always be, without change or alteration. Movies, novels, short stories, and particularly narratives with passion as the theme, take a segment of life or time and, by an intense description of that moment, make it stand for life itself.

A young woman once brought a young man to see her father. Her father objected, saying: "He earns only $25 a week." "I know, Daddy," she answered "but when you're in love, time passes so quickly."

Another evidence of the connection between timelessness and happiness is found in the fact that the "old men dream dreams, the young men see visions." Both old and young seek to escape the moment in which they live; the young look forward in hope to better days, the old look back in retrospect and memory to the "good old days." The old man becomes, in the language of Horace, "laudator temporis acti." Youth wishes to hurry time; old age tries to slow it down.

Time makes it impossible to combine our pleasures. It prevents us from making a club sandwich out of the various enjoyments of life. The mere fact that I exist in time makes it impossible for me to march in the army of Alexander and in the army of Caesar at the same time; it forbids the simultaneous thrill of Alpine ascents and Riviera pastimes; I cannot sit down to tea with both Homer and Vergil, or enjoy simultaneously listening to Aquinas on philosophy and Da Vinci on painting. We often see signs by the roadway which say: "Dine and dance," but no one can do both at the same time.

Temporal goods cannot be enjoyed all at once. The characteristic of the temporal enjoyment of various goods and objects is that they must be enjoyed in succession. Some begin where others leave off. When something new comes, something that we had before is taken away. We cannot have the ripe wisdom and the reflective serenity of maturity together with the impetuousness and the adventurousness of youth. All are good; yet none can be enjoyed except in the season of life appropriate to it. What is true individually is true socially. However much we may gain by what we call the advance in civilization, something has to be surrendered. For instance, our life is being made more secure, but with greater security there is a loss of adventure.

Real happiness brings together all the joys we have ever had, concentrating them in one focal point, bringing together the thrill of living at every second of existence from infancy to maturity; the joys of discovering truth, such as the scientist, the philosopher may have; the ecstasy of love, whether it be a patriot's for his country, a priest's for his Lord, a spouse's for his spouse. To intensify all this happiness in one focal point we would have to be outside time.

Happiness then has something to do with escape from time. But there can be a true and a false escape from time. First, we shall concern ourselves with the false, or the neurotic, escape from time. Time necessarily implies consciousness, and consciousness implies responsibility. One of the joys of sleep is its delightful irresponsibility. False escapes from time have something to do with flight from the burden of self-existence and responsibility.

Doctor Adler, the psychiatrist, has said: "Time is the neurotic's worst enemy and the degree of precision with which a man succeeds in solving the problem of time is one of the measures of his normality." A German philosopher, Franz von Baader, has written on *The Sufferings of Temporized Man*. Marcel Proust believes that time has a corrosive effect on us like "water of mineral springs on the objects immersed in it." A Spanish philosopher, Diego Ruiz, says: *Tempus est dolor*. There are various neurotic ways of escaping time; one is by opiates, which here stand for all forms of inducing unconsciousness to the passing of time. The empty soul which feels its emptiness seeks to put itself in a state of irresponsibility. The futility, the sterility, the gnawing of conscience, all of which are incidental to existence in time, cannot be endured. The self can be forgotten only by getting outside of time or consciousness. The narcotic which dopes the hunger of the soul enables a man to escape both his own misery, which he knows, and his possible salvation, which he knows not. The overemphasis on the unconscious represents also a flight from self, not only because too much self-analysis tends to break up into tiny fragments the unity and autonomy of personality, but also because the unconscious is identified with that for which we are not responsible.

Another neurotic way of killing time is by surrounding one-self with noise. Noise drowns out the consciousness of self and its passage through time. Silence becomes unbearable, because it makes the self reflective; noise, however, keeps one externalized. The neurotic regards stillness as a privation of movement, and silence as a structural flaw in the everlasting flow of noise. Silence becomes identified with emptiness. The Greek word for school was *schola*, which means "leisure." Education was inseparable from a certain amount of silence and freedom from pressure.

As Aldous Huxley wrote: "The twentieth century is among other things the age of noise . . . that most popular and in-fluential of all recent inventions, the radio, is nothing but a conduit through which pre-fabricated din can flow into our homes. And this din goes far deeper of course than the eardrums, it penetrates the mind, filling it with a babel of dis-tractions—news items, mutually irrelevant bits of information, blasts of corybantic or sentimental music, continually re-peated doses of drama that bring no catharsis, but merely cre-ate a craving for daily or even hourly emotional enemas. . . . Spoken or printed, broadcast over the ether or on wood pulp, all advertising copy has but one purpose—to prevent the will from ever achieving silence."

Another neurotic escape from time is flight and speed.

The opposite of flight is leisure, which implies a quiet mind, in a comparatively stationary body. Almost all the pro-ducers of great art and thought have been stationary. Socrates never left Greece, and rarely Athens. Kant never left Koenigs-berg. Leonardo da Vinci restricted himself to northern Italy, and Bach stayed permanently in Leipzig. Schubert spent most of his life around Vienna. Wordsworth, except for three years, remained in Westmoreland. Doctor Johnson stayed in Lon-don most of the time. Today, in contrast, many writers are ex-patriates: they have uprooted themselves from their countries as they have uprooted themselves from tradition. Their rest-lessness of soul translates itself into a restlessness of body. Incessant movement keeps them from making the greatest voyage of all—the discovery of self.

Max Picard says that our love of speed is a flight from God, a way of escaping the Great Pursuer, or what Francis Thompson has called "the Hound of Heaven." The man of faith, when he takes to flight, enters into himself. Today, flight is purely external. Hence we try to speed through time in order to fly from our origins and to escape the dread of being driven back within ourselves and being confronted with the spirit. Thanks to speed, man has gained the illusion that all things are subject to him. Like a mighty conqueror, he mounts his chariot, and all things pass by. In a world of faith man knows that God is everywhere. As the Psalmist put it: "If I go to hell, even there His power is present. . . . If I go to Heaven, there He reigns." In darkness, in flight, and in repose, God sees and knows me. By flight and speed, man hopes to escape this ubiquity of God. God is permanence and man tries to escape Him by constant change and movement. Speed, for the neurotic, is not something physical, it is something mental. This is not just a love of objective speed, but of subjective speed. It is a way of affirming his egotism through an identification of the ego with the power of the machine. It seems to annihilate time, but wholly in a neurotic way.

If time is an obstacle to true happiness, because it makes it impossible for us to combine our pleasures, it follows that the only way we can be really happy is by completely getting outside time, so that there is no "before" or "after," but, in the descriptive Latin words, *tota simul. Tota:* all enjoyments of which our personality is capable. *Simul:* simultaneously, that is, without any succession.

If happiness consists in transcending time, it follows that no complete happiness can be found until eternity, when there will be a total fulfillment of the deepest aspirations of the soul. But what are these? Suppose each of us could take out his heart and put it into his hand as a kind of crucible, to distill out of it its inmost yearnings and aspirations; what would he find them to be?

The first condition of happiness is life, for what good would riches and power be without the life to enjoy them? And the life we want is not for five more minutes or five more years, but always—an endless, ageless, timeless life.

The second requisite for happiness is the possession of truth.

We were made to know. But it is not so much truths we want to know, not isolated bits of information, but all truth—not, for instance, the truths of science alone, to the exclusion of the truths of theology, or literature, or music, but total truth. To be happy, our mind must be bathed in light and knowledge and for this we must perceive truth, not in fragments, but altogether in some complete and timeless perception.

The third requisite for happiness is love. It is not good for man to be alone. But this love must be timeless; therefore it must not age, or decay, or lose its ecstasy.

Though these are the conditions of happiness, we find that all of them are made impossible by the mere fact that we are in time. Life in its fullness is not to be found here, because here in time life is mingled with death. Neither is truth found here. Consider how often the prejudices of youth are corrected by study; how often those who come to mock remain to pray; how often, too, the more we study the less we feel we know, because we see the new avenues of knowledge down which we might travel for a lifetime. Neither is love in its fullness here, for while we are in time, love has its moments of satiety; even when love does remain fine and noble, a day must come when the laborer's shoulders are unburdened, the last embrace is passed from friend to friend. Nothing that ends can be perfect.

None of these conditions of happiness is to be found totally and completely here. But we are not to be cynics and say that happiness does not exist at all, for if there is a part there must be a whole, if we have a shadow there must be a light. It is like looking for the source of light in a television studio. It is not to be found under the cameras or the desk, for in those places, light is mingled with shadow. So, too, our reason tells us that we, if we are to find Life and Truth and Love, must go to a Life that is not mingled with its shadow, death; to a Truth that is not mingled with its shadow, error; and to a Love that is not mingled with its shadow, hate. We must go out to something that is Pure Life, Pure Truth, and Pure Love; that is the definition of God, and the possession of God is happiness.

MARTIN LUTHER KING JR.

Transformed Nonconformist

*Be not conformed to this world: but be ye trans-
formed by the renewing of your mind.*
ROMANS 12:2

"DO NOT CONFORM" is difficult advice in a generation when
crowd pressures have unconsciously conditioned our minds
and feet to move to the rhythmic drumbeat of the status quo.
Many voices and forces urge us to choose the path of least resistance, and bid us never to fight for an unpopular cause and
never to be found in a pathetic minority of two or three.

Even certain of our intellectual disciplines persuade us of
the need to conform. Some philosophical sociologists suggest
that morality is merely group consensus and that the folkways
are the right ways. Some psychologists say that mental and
emotional adjustment is the reward of thinking and acting
like other people.

Success, recognition, and conformity are the bywords of
the modern world where everyone seems to crave the anes-
thetizing security of being identified with the majority.

I

In spite of this prevailing tendency to conform, we as
Christians have a mandate to be nonconformists. The Apostle
Paul, who knew the inner realities of the Christian faith,
counseled, "Be not conformed to this world: but be ye transformed by the renewing of your mind." We are called to be
people of conviction, not conformity; of moral nobility, not
social respectability. We are commanded to live differently and
according to a higher loyalty.

Every true Christian is a citizen of two worlds, the world of
time and the world of eternity. We are, paradoxically, in the
world and yet not of the world. To the Philippian Christians,
Paul wrote, "We are a colony of heaven." They understood

what he meant, for their city of Philippi was a Roman colony. When Rome wished to Romanize a province, she established a small colony of people who lived by Roman law and Roman customs and who, though in another country, held fast to their Roman allegiance. This powerful, creative minority spread the gospel of Roman culture. Although the analogy is imperfect—the Roman settlers lived within a framework of injustice and exploitation, that is, colonialism—the Apostle does point to the responsibility of Christians to imbue an unchristian world with the ideals of a higher and more noble order. Living in the colony of time, we are ultimately responsible to the empire of eternity. As Christians we must never surrender our supreme loyalty to any time-bound custom or earthbound idea, for at the heart of our universe is a higher reality—God and his kingdom of love—to which we must be conformed.

This command not to conform comes, not only from Paul, but also from our Lord and Master, Jesus Christ, the world's most dedicated nonconformist, whose ethical nonconformity still challenges the conscience of mankind.

When an affluent society would coax us to believe that happiness consists in the size of our automobiles, the impressiveness of our houses, and the expensiveness of our clothes, Jesus reminds us, "A man's life consisteth not in the abundance of the things which he possesseth."

When we would yield to the temptation of a world rife with sexual promiscuity and gone wild with a philosophy of self-expression, Jesus tells us that "whosoever looketh on a woman to lust after her hath committed adultery with her already in his heart."

When we refuse to suffer for righteousness and choose to follow the path of comfort rather than conviction, we hear Jesus say, "Blessed are they which are persecuted for righteousness' sake: for theirs is the kingdom of heaven."

When in our spiritual pride we boast of having reached the peak of moral excellence, Jesus warns, "The publicans and the harlots go into the kingdom of God before you."

When we, through compassionless detachment and arrogant individualism, fail to respond to the needs of the underprivileged, the Master says, "Inasmuch as ye have done it unto one of the least of these my brethren, ye have done it unto me."

When we allow the spark of revenge in our souls to flame up in hate toward our enemies, Jesus teaches, "Love your enemies, bless them that curse you, do good to them that hate you, and pray for them which despitefully use you, and persecute you."

Everywhere and at all times, the love ethic of Jesus is a radiant light revealing the ugliness of our stale conformity.

In spite of this imperative demand to live differently, we have cultivated a mass mind and have moved from the extreme of rugged individualism to the even greater extreme of rugged collectivism. We are not makers of history; we are made by history. Longfellow said, "In this world a man must either be anvil or hammer," meaning that he is either a molder of society or is molded by society. Who doubts that today most men are anvils and are shaped by the patterns of the majority? Or to change the figure, most people, and Christians in particular, are thermometers that record or register the temperature of majority opinion, not thermostats that transform and regulate the temperature of society.

Many people fear nothing more terribly than to take a position which stands out sharply and clearly from the prevailing opinion. The tendency of most is to adopt a view that is so ambiguous that it will include everything and so popular that it will include everybody. Along with this has grown an inordinate worship of bigness. We live in an age of "jumboism" where men find security in that which is large and extensive— big cities, big buildings, big corporations. This worship of size has caused many to fear being identified with a minority idea. Not a few men, who cherish lofty and noble ideals, hide them under a bushel for fear of being called different. Many sincere white people in the South privately oppose segregation and discrimination, but they are apprehensive lest they be publicly condemned. Millions of citizens are deeply disturbed that the military-industrial complex too often shapes national policy, but they do not want to be considered unpatriotic. Countless loyal Americans honestly feel that a world body such as the United Nations should include even Red China, but they fear being called Communist sympathizers. A legion of thoughtful persons recognizes that traditional capitalism must continually undergo change if our great national wealth is to be more equitably distributed, but they are afraid their criticisms will make them seem un-American. Numerous decent, wholesome young persons permit themselves to become involved in unwholesome pursuits which they do not personally condone or even enjoy, because they are ashamed to say no when the gang says yes. How *few* people have the audacity to express publicly their convictions, and how *many* have allowed themselves to be "astronomically intimidated"!

Blind conformity makes us so suspicious of an individual who insists on saying what he really believes that we recklessly threaten his civil liberties. If a man, who believes vigorously in peace, is foolish enough to carry a sign in a public demonstration, or if a Southern white person, believing in the American dream of the dignity and worth of human personality, dares to invite a Negro into his home and join with him in his struggle for freedom, he is liable to be summoned before some legislative investigation body. He most certainly is a Communist if he espouses the cause of human brotherhood!

Thomas Jefferson wrote, "I have sworn upon the altar of God eternal hostility against every form of tyranny over the mind of man." To the conformist and the shapers of the conformist mentality, this must surely sound like a most dangerous and radical doctrine. Have we permitted the lamp of independent thought and individualism to become so dim that were Jefferson to write and live by these words today we would find cause to harass and investigate him? If Americans permit thought-control, business-control, and freedom-control to continue, we shall surely move within the shadows of fascism.

II

Nowhere is the tragic tendency to conform more evident than in the church, an institution which has often served to crystallize, conserve, and even bless the patterns of majority opinion. The erstwhile sanction by the church of slavery, racial segregation, war, and economic exploitation is testimony to the fact that the church has hearkened more to the authority of the world than to the authority of God. Called to be the moral guardian of the community, the church at times has preserved that which is immoral and unethical. Called to combat social evils, it has remained silent behind stained-glass windows. Called to lead men on the highway of brotherhood and to summon them to rise above the narrow confines of race and class, it has enunciated and practiced racial exclusiveness.

We preachers have also been tempted by the enticing cult of conformity. Seduced by the success symbols of the world, we have measured our achievements by the size of our parsonage. We have become showmen to please the whims and caprices of the people. We preach comforting sermons and avoid saying anything from our pulpits which might disturb the respectable views of the comfortable members of our congregations. Have we ministers of Jesus Christ sacrificed truth on the altar of self-interest and, like Pilate, yielded our convictions to the demands of the crowd?

We need to recapture the gospel glow of the early Christians, who were nonconformists in the truest sense of the word and refused to shape their witness according to the mundane patterns of the world. Willingly they sacrificed fame, fortune, and life itself in behalf of a cause they knew to be right. Quantitatively small, they were qualitatively giants. Their powerful gospel put an end to such barbaric evils as infanticide and bloody gladiatorial contests. Finally, they captured the Roman Empire for Jesus Christ.

Gradually, however, the church became so entrenched in wealth and prestige that it began to dilute the strong demands of the gospel and to conform to the ways of the world. And ever since the church has been a weak and ineffectual trumpet making uncertain sounds. If the church of Jesus Christ is to regain once more its power, message, and authentic ring, it must conform only to the demands of the gospel.

The hope of a secure and livable world lies with disciplined nonconformists, who are dedicated to justice, peace, and brotherhood. The trailblazers in human, academic, scientific, and religious freedom have always been nonconformists. In any cause that concerns the progress of mankind, put your faith in the nonconformist!

In his essay "Self-Reliance" Emerson wrote, "Whoso would

be a man must be a nonconformist." The Apostle Paul reminds us that whoso would be a Christian must also be a
nonconformist. Any Christian who blindly accepts the opinions of the majority and in fear and timidity follows a path of
expediency and social approval is a mental and spiritual slave.
Mark well these words from the pen of James Russell Lowell:

> They are slaves who fear to speak
> For the fallen and the weak;
> They are slaves who will not choose
> Hatred, scoffing, and abuse,
> Rather than in silence shrink
> From the truth they needs must think;
> They are slaves who dare not be
> In the right with two or three.

III

Nonconformity in itself, however, may not necessarily be
good and may at times possess neither transforming nor redemptive power. Nonconformity per se contains no saving
value, and may represent in some circumstances little more
than a form of exhibitionism. Paul in the latter half of the text
offers a formula for constructive nonconformity: "Be ye transformed by the renewing of your mind." Nonconformity is
creative when it is controlled and directed by a transformed
life and is constructive when it embraces a new mental outlook. By opening our lives to God in Christ we become new
creatures. This experience, which Jesus spoke of as the new
birth, is essential if we are to be transformed nonconformists
and freed from the cold hardheartedness and self-righteousness so often characteristic of nonconformity. Someone has
said, "I love reforms but I hate reformers." A reformer may
be an untransformed nonconformist whose rebellion against
the evils of society has left him annoyingly rigid and unreasonably impatient.

Only through an inner spiritual transformation do we gain
the strength to fight vigorously the evils of the world in a
humble and loving spirit. The transformed nonconformist,
moreover, never yields to the passive sort of patience which is
an excuse to do nothing. And this very transformation saves

him from speaking irresponsible words which estrange with-out reconciling and from making hasty judgments which are blind to the necessity of social progress. He recognizes that social change will not come overnight, yet he works as though it is an imminent possibility.

This hour in history needs a dedicated circle of transformed nonconformists. Our planet teeters on the brink of atomic annihilation; dangerous passions of pride, hatred, and selfishness are enthroned in our lives; truth lies prostrate on the rugged hills of nameless calvaries; and men do reverence before false gods of nationalism and materialism. The saving of our world from pending doom will come, not through the complacent adjustment of the conforming majority, but through the creative maladjustment of a nonconforming minority.

Some years ago Professor Bixler reminded us of the danger of overstressing the well-adjusted life. Everybody passionately seeks to be well-adjusted. We must, of course, be well-adjusted if we are to avoid neurotic and schizophrenic personalities, but there are some things in our world to which men of goodwill must be maladjusted. I confess that I never intend to become adjusted to the evils of segregation and the crippling effects of discrimination, to the moral degeneracy of religious bigotry and the corroding effects of narrow sectarianism, to economic conditions that deprive men of work and food, and to the insanities of militarism and the self-defeating effects of physical violence.

Human salvation lies in the hands of the creatively maladjusted. We need today maladjusted men like Shadrach, Meshach, and Abednego, who, when ordered by King Nebuchadnezzar to bow before a golden image, said in unequivocal terms, "If it be so, our God whom we serve is able to deliver us. . . . But if not . . . we will not serve thy gods"; like Thomas Jefferson, who in an age adjusted to slavery wrote, "We hold these truths to be self-evident, that all men are created equal, that they are endowed by their Creator with certain unalienable Rights, that among these are life, Liberty and the pursuit of Happiness"; like Abraham Lincoln, who had the wisdom to discern that this nation could not survive half slave and half free; and supremely like our Lord, who, in the midst of the intricate and fascinating military machinery of the Roman Empire, reminded his disciples that "they that take the sword shall perish with the sword." Through such maladjustment an already decadent generation may be called to those things which make for peace.

Honesty impels me to admit that transformed nonconformity, which is always costly and never altogether comfortable, may mean walking through the valley of the shadow of suffering, losing a job, or having a six-year-old daughter ask, "Daddy, why do you have to go to jail so much?" But we are gravely mistaken to think that Christianity protects us from the pain and agony of mortal existence. Christianity has always insisted that the cross we bear precedes the crown we wear. To be a Christian, one must take up his cross, with all of its difficulties and agonizing and tragedy-packed content, and carry it until that very cross leaves its marks upon us and redeems us to that more excellent way which comes only through suffering.

In these days of worldwide confusion, there is a dire need for men and women who will courageously do battle for truth. We need Christians who will echo the words John Bunyan said to his jailer when, having spent twelve years in jail, he was promised freedom if he would agree to stop preaching:

> But if nothing will do, unless I make of my conscience a continual butchery and slaughter-shop, unless, putting out my own eyes, I commit me to the blind to lead me, as I doubt is desired by some, I have determined, the Almighty God being my help and shield, yet to suffer, if frail life might continue so long, even till the moss shall grow on mine eyebrows, rather than thus to violate my faith and principles.

We must make a choice. Will we continue to march to the drumbeat of conformity and respectability, or will we, listening to the beat of a more distant drum, move to its echoing sounds? Will we march only to the music of time, or will we, risking criticism and abuse, march to the soul-saving music of eternity? More than ever before we are today challenged by the words of yesterday, "Be not conformed to this world: but be ye transformed by the renewing of your mind."

JOHN COURTNEY MURRAY

The Unbelief of the Christian

I SHOULD LIKE to begin with a somewhat general remark
which is related to the theme of my discourse. There is one
thing that has to be said about the massive phenomenon of
contemporary unbelief, namely that the issue it presents to
the Christian is not to be resolved by argument in the academy or by the academy. The issue can only be resolved in the
order of action and history, by the whole people of God in dialogue and in cooperation with the whole people temporal.
What we are confronted with today is not classical atheism, by
which I mean a simple denial of the existence of God on the
ground that the whole concept of God is unintelligible. The
Marxist, for instance, is quite willing to admit that the notion
of God is conceivable and even intelligible. The whole contemporary problem rather arises from the fact that atheism
has now found a positive basis. It is now based on an affirmation, an affirmation of the human person, his dignity and his
freedom. And this affirmation is accomplished by a will to
achieve the dignity of the person by achieving his autonomy,
by liberating him from the indignity and misery to which he
is subjected throughout large areas of the world. There is to-
day a new confidence that man has within himself resources,
purely human and secular resources, which are sufficient to
organize the world in such wise that it will be a proper
habitation for the man who is conscious of his dignity and
freedom.

Therefore the Christian position today confronts a new
counter-position. This counter-position is fairly simply stated.
It says that there is only one history, the history that man
makes and the history that makes man. The only forces operative in history, the only energies that galvanize history, are
the energies immanent within man himself, his intelligence
and his will, along with the modern prolongation of these
energies which goes by the name of technology. And as for

salvation, if there must be talk of salvation, the only form that man can hope for is a salvation to be achieved within history, by history, and by man himself, unaided.

Against this counter-position the Christian has to reaffirm the position that there are two histories. There is human secular history of which man is the agent, whose events are empirically observable and whose meaning is accessible to intelligence. But there is also, the Christian says, salvation history, whose operative principle is theandric, and whose basic agent is the Spirit of God. This Spirit, the Holy Spirit, is the power of God most high, who in this history summons men to be His co-workers, as Paul says in 1 Cor. 3:9 and Col. 4:11. The events of this sacred history are not empirically observable and their sense, that is to say, their direction, is not accessible to human intelligence but only to faith. These two histories the Christian says are distinct but not separate or separable. They are as it were two currents that flow through time together. They are coterminous in time. They began at the same moment and they run together, but they are not homogeneous in kind. One of them will end with the consummation of this world, the other is destined for a consummation beyond this world. Moreover, while the two histories run together, they are related in such wise (and this I think is the crucial point today) that the salvation of man even within the finite horizons of human history is mysteriously dependent upon another mode of salvation of which the theandric history is the bearer. In a word, if I had to state the issue that confronts us today in its broadest terms, I think I would be inclined to say that it could be put in this question: Are there two histories or only one?

Now within this large issue of the theological intelligibility of contemporary unbelief there is a narrower issue, at once more immediate and more urgent. For the Christian cannot simply regard unbelief as a brute fact to be accepted, to be faced, then perhaps to be forgotten. No, this phenomenon demands to be understood in the light of faith, and the immediate theological question is whether or not it can be integrated into the Christian understanding of the Church in the world, that is to say, of the two histories in their relation. It is to this question that I now wish to address myself.

I shall state a basic theme, and I would hope that this basic theme, if elaborated in two different directions, might lead us toward an answer to our theological question. I am very aware that I must speak in a somewhat tentative fashion because we are confronted today with a new phenomenon on which only recently theological reflection has been bent. My basic theme is that the Church is the sacrament of Christ. This notion of the Church was in a sense a conciliar ideal at Vatican II rather than a theme consciously developed, but it has indeed become a post-conciliar theme. It was taken up rather importantly at the international meeting in Rome at the end of September, 1966, and was the subject of two major discourses, one by the Dominican theologian Edward Schillebeeckx, and the other by the Jesuit scholar, Juan Alfaro.

This theme of the Church as the sacrament of Christ has, of course, deep biblical roots in the Pauline epistles, in 1 Corinthians, Romans and especially in Colossians and Ephesians. The background of the idea is not, as many think, the medieval speculation on the nature of sacrament which led to the definition of the seven sacraments. The background is rather the biblical notion of *the* sacrament which is the "mystery" of Eph. 3:3–4, where the Greek word μυστήριον is translated by the Vulgate *sacramentum*. In the earlier Pauline epistles the accent was on the eschatological fulfillment of the mystery of Christ, the mystery of God. In the captivity epistles, Colossians and Ephesians, the emphasis is upon the present, here and now, history of what Paul in Col. 2:2 calls the mystery of God, which is identically the mystery of Christ to which he refers in Col. 4:3 and Eph. 3:5. This mystery is simply the divine plan of salvation as it unrolls in history from the first coming of Christ to the Parousia. It is identical with the power and the action of God as operative for this salvation of man. Hidden from eternity in God the Father, this mystery was uttered in the eternal utterance of the Son and the eternal breathing of the Spirit. Here in time, although still hidden by the veils that conceal from man the face of God, it is nonetheless manifested in a sign, in a sacrament. It is revealed, as Paul says in Eph. 3:10, through the Church which is the manifestation of the manifold wisdom of God and the epiphany of the salvific plan of God. The Church, therefore, as visible and as historically active, is the sign and sacrament of Christ who is here and now with us in the Spirit according to His promise. The Church is the progressive realization of the divine plan of salvation for mankind, that reconciliation of all things of which Paul speaks in Col. 1:20, and that fulfillment of all things of which he speaks in Eph. 1:10.

Now I think it is important to realize, certainly for the sake of this discourse, that the Church about which we are speaking here is the concrete, living Church, which is, as Vatican II made quite clear in Chap. 7 of *Lumen gentium*, an eschatological reality in which there is an indissoluble tension between the "even now" and the "not yet." Even now the Church is, and is one, and is holy, and yet the Church is not yet one and is not yet holy. The Church indeed has been sanctified, washed by the blood of Christ, sanctified by the immolation of Christ Himself on the Cross. But the sanctification of the Church still remains an historical process which is not yet fulfilled, because the Church, even now the one and holy, is still the pilgrim people of God, capable at any moment of those betrayals that the original people of God were guilty of after their rescue from Egypt. One must therefore distinguish two aspects of the Church, but not dichotomize them. One cannot divide the institutional Church from the people who make it up, or, in more scholastic terms, one cannot divide the formal from the material elements in the Church. And in this living, concrete, historical totality, the Church is the sacrament, the sign of Christ. It is the realization and manifestation of the mystery of salvation which is even now being wrought out, though it has not yet been fully wrought out.

This, then, very briefly is my basic theme. I suggest that this theme is capable of development in two directions both of which are pertinent to our present inquiry. It is the second direction which is more directly pertinent to the unbelief of the Christian, but I should like to go through the first development first.

The first development leads to a sort of dialectical tension which was completely unresolved by Vatican II. The Church, as we have said, is the sign of salvation for all men, the new humanity inaugurated by Christ, the existential realization of the deepest meaning of human history. On the other hand, the Church is simply the little flock. From a numerical point of view it is almost insignificant in comparison with the vast mass of men who do not know and do not recognize either the Church or the Christ of which the Church is sign and sacrament. This gives rise to the question of the relationship between this little flock which is already gathered and the literally innumerable multitude of men who are still scattered. Is the relationship simply extrinsic, between those who are inside and those who are outside? Or is there possibly an intrinsic relationship? In asking this question, I think we come to the heart of the theological intelligibility of contemporary atheism.

Here is the point, I think, at which to refer to the biblical problematic, because *prima facie* it would seem that the biblical problematic is stated in terms of those who are inside and those who are outside. On the one hand, there is the people of God, there is the people that God Himself knew, in the biblical sense, that is to say, the people whom He loved and chose and the people who in return loved Him and chose Him and entered into a covenant relationship with Him. And there are, on the other hand, what Paul in 1 Thess. 4:5 calls the peoples who do not know God but reject Him and ignore Him, in the biblical sense of ignorance. They have chosen against Him and have thus become captive to what Paul calls in 2 Thess. 2:7 the mystery of iniquity, that counter-action in the world which opposes the salvific action of God. These other peoples are thus under the power and rule of the kingdom of darkness. In the biblical problematic, moreover, it seems evident that the ignorance of these peoples is somehow culpable. They have somehow chosen to stand outside the kingdom of light. We can see this in the Old Testament indictment of the idolater, which is pitiless and even scornful. We can see it even more clearly in the first chapter of Romans, where we find Paul's indictment of the pagan idolaters which ends with the words: "Therefore they are themselves without excuse." Their ignorance was not simply ignorance; it was an ignorance that was culpable. The same problematic appears in St. John, in his classic statement of the contrast between light and darkness. The light came into the darkness, he says, and there were those who "loved the darkness better than the light."

Now while this biblical problematic is perennially valid and must not be dissolved, it was in fact the product of a polemic, or at best, if you will, an apologetic. The prophetic indictment of idolatry in the Old Testament and the passage in Romans were directed exclusively to the people of God. Neither Paul nor the prophets were talking to the idolater. This polemic has had in fact a rather long historical life. It was installed in ecclesiastical literature certainly after the Constantinian settlement, and it has been maintained in papal literature right through Leo XIII up to Pius XII. Only at Vatican II did the inadequacy of this problematic begin to be appreciated and understood. Then the Church became more aware of herself as situated in the interior of history and not above it, as situated in the world and not apart from it. There was the consequent awareness that the relationship between the Church and the world, the relationship between the two histories, must be a dialogic relationship which implies a certain give and take. The proclamation of the Word of God today, as Paul VI made very clear in his encyclical *Ecclesiam suam*, must take the form of what he called the dialogue of salvation.

Consequently we now feel the need to enlarge the biblical problematic without destroying or discarding it. To do so we have to take very seriously a traditional doctrine that the order of grace is not coterminous with the visible, historical, empirical Church. The frontier between the kingdom of light and the kingdom of darkness does not coincide with the boundary, as it were, between the visible Church and something we call the world. On the contrary, the order of grace is pervasive through all humanity and the action of the Holy Spirit which supports sacred history is also somehow supportive of all human history including secular history. There is therefore a distinction to be made. The distinction is between the Church as the public manifestation of the mystery of Christ and the operative action of the grace of the Holy Spirit. The Church represents the fullness of Christian faith; the Church represents humanity in its consciously realized newness, and as such the Church is the sacrament, the sign, the manifestation of Christ. On the other hand, grace, and very notably the grace of faith, is somehow operative in all men, even in those we think of in terms of the biblical problematic as "those outside."

In consequence of this new conciliar awareness of the Church and of this newly realized distinction, a number of new theological themes have been cast up. There is the theme of the belief of the unbeliever, and the theme of the anonymous Christian. There is the theme of implicit faith, Christian faith that is implicit in all men of good will, in all men whose will is to the good, in all men who are animated by the spirit of love. There is the theme of the distinction between the manifest and the latent presence of the sacred in history. All these themes, all these theological theories, are pertinent to the issue of contemporary atheism because they serve to establish an intrinsic relationship between the Church and the world, between the two histories. These themes have, moreover, considerable theological fertility. They serve to enlarge and to deepen our notion of faith and to bring us back to a more biblical notion as over against the more intellectualized version of faith which was prominent in the scholastic tradition. These themes have besides a great pastoral significance insofar as they illustrate the necessity and possibility of dialogue; dialogue between the Church, which is the fullness of belief, and the world, in which there is indeed belief but a belief which has not come to a conscious conceptualization or even perhaps to an integrity of commitment.

Nevertheless, there is, I think, a danger today that these themes, especially the anonymous Christian idea, might lead to some dissolution of the biblical problematic. If you push these themes to their logical absurdity, you might be inclined to say that there are today no atheists, neither in foxholes nor anywhere else. You might be inclined to say that culpable unbelief is not a possibility, is not a viable option for man today, that there is no such thing really as conscious refusal or rejection of God. You might, if you pushed these themes to absurdity beyond the bounds of logic, be inclined to repeal the condemnation of Paul: "So that they themselves are without excuse in their idolatry." This we cannot afford to do, for the biblical problematic must stand.

Thus far I have been pursuing the first development of my basic theme of the Church as the sacrament of Christ, namely the dialectical tension between the institutional Church and those who have no visible relation to it. There is another line of development, however, one more directly pertinent to the unbelief of the Christian. A hint of it is to be found in Section 19 of the *Pastoral Constitution on the Church in the Modern World*, where there is a discussion of the forms and roots of contemporary atheism, and where explicit mention is made of the responsibility of Christians themselves for this massive contemporary phenomenon. Christians, the text says, "To the extent that they . . . are deficient in their religious, moral or social life, must be said to conceal rather than reveal the authentic face of God and religion," that is to say, the presence of God here and now.

Likewise in Section 8 of the *Dogmatic Constitution on the Church* we read that the Church "faithfully reveals the mystery of its Lord to the world, but under shadows, until finally the manifestation will be complete in fullness of light." Now these are very interesting statements and upon them hangs in a sense a kind of conciliar tail. For in these texts there is explicit reference to the culpability of individuals in the Church. There was a great resistance among the conciliar Fathers against any notion that somehow or other guilt or sin or defect or deficiency could be predicated of the Church herself. There was great opposition to what finally got into the document on ecumenism, as to the fault of the Church. With regard to the document on religious freedom, I can testify here personally to great opposition on the part of the Fathers to any notion that the Church herself had been guilty of default, defect and sin against the proclamation of that Christian and human freedom which is inherent in the Gospel. It was I who finally devised the formulation in Section 12: "even though there were some people among the people of God who did not act up to the example of Christ in regard of Christian freedom." That is the best we could get from the Fathers, and you have no idea what a strain it was to get this much into the documents, namely that somehow or other, here and there, now and again, one or another person in the history of the

Church may not have lived up to the fullness of the Christian revelation.

I must say, with all due deference to the Fathers of the Council, that they were the victims of a defective ecclesiology, very Platonic in its implications, as if somehow the Church were some supernal entity hovering *above* history and not involved at all *in* history or in the people who make up the Church. They seem to have acquiesced too readily in some division between the formal and material components of the Church, between the Church as sacramental and institutional, and the Church as an historical and existential reality. They would have been well advised to return to a stream of patristic thought which as a matter of fact they themselves had found without fully knowing it. As you know, in Chapter 7 of the *Constitution on the Church* they picked up the great patristic theme of the eschatological character of the Church and as soon as you get into that you get into the tension that I spoke of a while ago between the "even now" and the "not yet." This tension is a vital tension—the "even now" and the "not yet" exist in unity and simultaneity in the concrete living reality of the Church that you and I belong to, the pilgrim Church making its way through history.

If you take this theme of the eschatological character of the Church seriously, as we in the post-conciliar age can do, then I think you are obliged to admit not merely that individuals in the Church can be sinners and sinful, but that the Church herself at any and all given moments of her earthly pilgrimage can also be a sinning and a sinful Church, even though at the same time the Church remains the one and the holy Church. While it is true that the Church incurs guilt only through her members, it is nonetheless also true that the guilt her members incur can rightly be predicated of the Church herself. In other words, you could apply to the Church in an orthodox sense the famous Lutheran dictum with regard to the individual: *simul justus et peccator*, at once just and a sinner. And this seems to me implicit in the explicit conciliar acceptance of the Lutheran dictum that the Church must always be reformed. In Chapter 8 of the *Constitution* there is mention of the Church as at the same time holy and always to be purified;

and the Church is, as the text goes on to say, in continual quest both of conversion and also of renewal. This is what the Council said, and we in the post-conciliar period are allowed to take it seriously.

It is at this point that I come back to my theme, namely that there is a certain ambivalence to the Church as the sacrament and sign of Christ. On the one hand, the Church is the explicit and visible manifestation of God's plan in history, of the divine salvific action, of the abiding presence of Christ in His spirit. On the other hand, the intelligibility of this sign and sacrament is darkened by the shadows that conceal rather than reveal the authentic face of Christ who is the image of the Father.

The first shadow that falls on the face of the Church and obscures its intelligibility as the sacrament of Christ is the disunity of the Church herself. In John 17:21 the Lord said it was by the unity of His followers that men were to know that He had been sent by the Father. The disunity among His followers therefore is an obstacle to belief in Him. This disunity blurs the message of the Church, confuses her mission and obscures the significance of herself as sacrament. Note that I am speaking of the disunity of the Church, because here again Vatican II dissolved an older problematic. It used to be that you had the one, holy, Roman, Catholic and apostolic Church over here, then rather lamentably you had a group of separated brethren over there. But this will no longer do. Obviously the Council here did not follow out its own thought. In the *Decree on Ecumenism*, the Council acknowledged that there are ecclesial realities outside the visible communion of the Roman Church. There is the reality of the Word, the reality of baptism, the reality of faith, to some extent the reality of the Lord's Supper. These realities are not merely realities that sanctify the individual as such; they are also ecclesial, that is to say, they contribute to create and build the Church. In their ecclesial realizations outside the Roman Church, these realities play a role in the history of salvation. It is not then simply a question of the true Church over here and those unfortunately divided from the Church over there. No, the Church herself is divided. She is not yet possessed of her full ecclesial reality; she is not yet the one and holy, although she is even now the one and holy. Here again we have the eschatological tension.

You will see, I think, that at this point I am once more touching the ecclesial dimensions of the unbelief of the Christian. The Church is sacrament of Christ, Christ is the sacrament of the Father. The Church is the sacrament of Christ in the concrete totality of her presence and action in history. On the other hand, the concrete reality of the Church in history obscures, dims, clouds the visibility and the intelligibility of the Church as sacrament and sign of the mystery of Christ. Christ is forever the *lumen gentium*, the light of the peoples. In the opening words of the *Constitution on the Church*: "Upon Christ as the light of the peoples, the Church herself, who is to be the sign of Christ, casts shadows." And it is in this ecclesial sense that I think I would first speak of the unbelief of the Christian. It is the unbelief *in* the Church and the unbelief *of* the Church. The basic notion here is the notion of the Church as at once believing and unbelieving. It is the notion of the Church as at once realizing and signifying in history the divine plan, and in some sense being a negative realization of this plan and an obscuring of it. It is in such terms that I would in the first instance establish an intrinsic relationship between the Church, the world of belief, and those outside of it, the world of unbelief.

In some such terms I think one could reach a unified theological understanding both of the Church and of the world in their mutual relationship. There are of course the other factors mentioned by the Council itself: the faults of Christians, the neglect of education in the faith, misleading exposition of doctrine and defects of individuals in the Church. But you might raise this question: are there not also ecclesial defects, defects of the Church herself? Are not these related to defective structures in the Church, or to defective functioning of her institutions, whether these institutions be of divine law or of human institution? Do we not find defects in the organization of her prophetic ministry and its prolongation in theological education, defects in her pastoral mission, organized less in terms of love than perhaps simply in terms of efficiency? The *Constitution on the Liturgy* notes defects even in the liturgical practice of the Church, in so far as the liturgy is a proclamation of the Gospel. The present funeral Mass, for example, is a complete misrepresentation of the fundamental Christian theology of death. Instead of proclaiming the ultimate meaning of death as the beginning of the fullness of life in Christ, what it proclaims is *dies irae* and all that kind of thing. This is somehow an ecclesial fault, for we cannot say it is the fault of the one who composed the Mass; we don't even know who he was. This liturgy is an instrument of the Church used kerygmatically to veil from the world the supreme message which the Church has to give to the world. Similarly the social practice as well as the social doctrine of the Church as such has as a matter of historical fact obscured her message of salvation. There is no need for me to develop this line of thought any further. The point is that the Church is a burden and a trial to the belief of the Christian as well as a help and a support to this belief.

The Church does indeed fulfill the great mandate of Matthew 28:18–20, her apostolic mission to teach. But the Church also forever falls short in fulfilling this mandate. The Church exists in the world as the sacrament of Christ, and does indeed reveal by her existence and her action the mystery of Christ; but she does this in a shadowed and darkened kind of way, *fideliter sed sub umbris*, as the Council says. By her own unbelief the Church bears an intrinsic relationship to the unbelief of the world, as well as a responsibility for this unbelief, insofar as she herself, destined to be the sign and sacrament of the mystery of Christ, conceals instead of reveals the face of Christ. Yet the dialectic still holds: because the Church is the revelation of the mystery of Christ, she imposes upon the unbeliever a responsibility for his own unbelief. Thus we rejoin the biblical problematic: "So that they are inexcusable" who fail to recognize and acknowledge Christ in the sign of Christ. This biblical problematic is at root an affirmation both of the accessibility and the obscurity of faith. It is an assent to mystery, an assent that is given not on evidence but on the Word of God. Faith therefore contains within itself the seeds of its own imperfection; belief itself contains the seeds of unbelief.

In my opening remarks I underlined what I feel to be the central issue in the contemporary phenomenon of unbelief, namely whether there is something else in human life besides the history that makes man. For the Christian affirmation is that there is indeed another history, the history which God makes, and which takes place in and through the events of human history. This history of salvation can be seen only with the eyes of faith and its external manifestation is a sign, the sacrament which is the Church. Yet this instrument of Christ's revelation has, in cold historical fact, obscured His face and failed to proclaim His message. This the Church has done not through malice but simply because she is human. Her members are therefore themselves in some sense unbelievers, and must share responsibility for the unbelief of the world around them. This world in turn cannot be absolved from its own guilt, for there will always be men who freely choose to live in darkness rather than in light. Yet what the Christian must guard against, when he and his Church present themselves to the world in which they live, is that this world should not encounter in them that portion of darkness which is theirs. This we all pray for, that the light which is Christ may break through our darkness, and that contemporary unbelief may find in the Church a sacrament of Christian faith.

ABRAHAM JOSHUA HESCHEL

What We Might Do Together

A FAMOUS four-volume work on the history of atheism in the West, published sixty years ago, begins with the statement: "God has died. The time has come to write His history." Today, no historian would regard such a project as urgent; our major anxiety today seems to be diametrically opposed. Man may be dying and there will be no one to write his history. This is the problem that shatters all complacency, "Is man obsolete?" A generation ago people maintained: technological civilization contradicts religion. Today, we are wondering does technological civilization contradict man? The striking feature of our age is not the presence of anxiety, but the inadequacy of anxiety, the insufficient awareness of what is at stake in the human situation. It is as if the nightmare of our fears surpassed our capacity for fear.

Men all over the world see the writing on the wall, but are too illiterate to understand what it says. We all have that sense of dread for what may be in store for us, it is a fear of absolute evil, a fear of total destruction. It is more than an emotion. An apocalyptic monster has descended upon the world, and there is nowhere to go, nowhere to hide. What is the nature of that monster? Is it a demon the power of which is ultimate; in the presence of which there is only despair?

This is a time in which it is considered unreasonable to believe in the presence of the Divine, but quite reasonable to believe in the presence of the demonic. And yet, as a Jew, I recoil from the belief in the demonic. Over and against the belief in the ultimate power of the demon stands the admonition of Moses: "Know, therefore, this day and believe in your heart, that the Lord is God in heaven above, on the earth beneath; there is no one else." There are no demonic forces.

The great act of redemption brought about by Moses and the Prophets of Israel, was the elimination of the demons, the gods, and demigods from the consciousness of man; the demons which populated the world of ancient man are dead in the Bible. And yet, even Moses knew that man is endowed with the power to make a god; he has an uncanny ability to create or to revive a demon. Indeed, man's worship of power has resurrected the demon of power.

It is not a coincidence that the three of us who participate in this evening's panel discussion also serve as co-chairmen of the National Committee of Clergy and Laymen concerned about Vietnam.

The meeting place of this evening's discussion should be not the Palmer House in Chicago but somewhere in the jungles of Vietnam. An ecumenical nightmare—Christians, Jews, Buddhists, dying together, killing one another. So soon after Auschwitz, so soon after Hitler.

The question about Auschwitz to be asked is not: "Where was God?" but rather: "Where was man?" The God of Abraham has never promised always to hold back Cain's hand from killing his brother. To equate God and history is idolatry. God is present when man's heart is alive. When the heart turns stone, when man is absent, God is banished, and history, disengaged, is distress.

What should have been humanity's answer to the Nazi atrocities? Repentance, a revival of the conscience, a sense of unceasing, burning shame, a persistent effort to be worthy of the name human, to prevent the justification of a death of man theology, to control the urge to cruelty.

Is it not a desecration of our commitment to act as if that agony never happened, to go on with religion as usual at a time when nuclear disaster is being made a serious possibility?

We should have learned at least one lesson: *Don't hate!*

Today is the anniversary of the death of President Kennedy. His assassination shook the world. Yet it made no impact on our laws and customs. No lesson was learned, no conclusion was drawn. Guns are still available c.o.d. Mass killing in Chicago, in Houston, in Arizona, and elsewhere, is becoming a favorite past-time of young boys.

The Pentagons of the world are Temples. Within their hallowed walls the great decisions come about: How many shall live, how many shall die.

> The envoys of peace weep bitterly.
> The highways lie waste . . .
> Covenants are broken,
> Witnesses are despised,
> There is no regard for man.—(Isaiah 33:8)

Jonah is running to Tarshish, while Nineveh is tottering on the brink. Are we not all guilty of Jonah's failure? We have been running to Tarshish when the call is to go to Ninevah.

"What is the use of running, when you are on the wrong road?" What are the traps and spiritual pitfalls that account for the outrage of the war in Vietnam? What is the use of social security when you have a surplus of nuclear weapons?

Religion cannot be the same after Auschwitz and Hiroshima. Its teachings must be pondered not only in the halls of learning but also in the presence of inmates in extermination camps, and in the sight of the mushroom of a nuclear explosion.

The new situation in the world has plunged every one of us into unknown regions of responsibility. Unprepared, perplexed, misguided, the world is a spiritual no man's land. Men all over the world are waiting for a way out of distress, for a new certainty of the meaning of being human. Will help come out of those who seek to keep alive the words of the prophets?

This is, indeed, a grave hour for those who are committed to honor the name of God.

The ultimate standards of living, according to Jewish teaching, are *Kiddush Ha-Shem* and *Hillul Ha-Shem*. The one means that everything within one's power should be done to glorify the name of God before the world, the other that everything should be avoided to reflect dishonor upon the religion and thereby desecrate the name of God.

According to the ancient rabbis, the Lord said to Israel: "I have brought you out of Egypt upon the condition that you sacrifice your very lives should the honor of My name require it." (Sifra, ed. Weiss, 99d).

"All sins may be atoned for by repentance, by means of the Day of Atonement, or through the chastening power of affliction, but acts which cause the desecration of the name of God will not be forgiven. 'Surely this iniquity will not be forgiven you till you die, says the Lord of hosts' " (Isaiah 23:14).

In the light of these principles, e.g. a slight act of injustice is regarded as a grave offense when committed by a person whose religious leadership is acknowledged and of whose conduct an example is expected.

God had trust in us and gave us His word, some of His wisdom and some of His power. But we have distorted His word, His wisdom, and abused His gift of power.

Those who pray tremble when they realize how staggering are the debts of the religions of the West. We have mortgaged our souls and borrowed so much grace, patience and forgiveness. We have promised charity, love, guidance and a way of redemption, and now we are challenged to keep the promise, to honor the pledge. How shall we prevent bankruptcy in the presence of God and man?

God has moved out of the fortress of pedestrian certainties and is dwelling in perplexities. He has abandoned our complacencies and has entered our spiritual agony, upsetting dogmas, discrediting articulations. Beyond all doctrines and greater than human faith stands God, God's question of man, God's waiting for man, for every man, God in search of man. Deeper than all our understanding is our bold certainty that God is with us in distress, hiding in the scandal of our ambiguities. And now God may send those whom we have expected least "to do His deed—strange is His deed; to carry out his work—alien is His work." (Isaiah 28:21)

What is the use of running to Tarshish when the call is to go to Ninevah?

We must learn how to labor in the affairs of the world with fear and trembling. While involved in public affairs, we must not cease to cultivate the secrets of religious privacy.

Abraham who despised the spirit of Sodom and Gomorrah as much as Washington despises the ideology of Red China was nevertheless horrified by the Lord's design to rain napalm, brimstone and fire upon the sinful cities. But why? Destruction of Sodom and Gomorrah would be a spectacular manifestation of God's power in the world! So why did Abraham oppose an action which would have been a great triumph for "religion"? It is said in that story: "Abraham is still standing before the Lord" (18:22). To this very day Abraham is still pleading, still standing before the Lord "in fear and trembling."

It is necessary to go to Ninevah; it is also vital to learn how to stand before God. For many of us the march from Selma to Montgomery was both protest and prayer. Legs are not lips, and walking is not kneeling. And yet our legs uttered songs. Even without words, our march was worship.

Unlike Jonah, Jeremiah did not go into the desert of loneliness. He remained a solitary dissenter in the midst of his people. Defied by his contemporaries, bewildered by the ways of the Lord, he would rather be defeated with God than victorious without him.

The cardinal problem is not the survival of religion, but the survival of man. What is required is a continuous effort to overcome hardness of heart, callousness, and above all to inspire the world with the biblical image of man, not to forget that man without God is a torso, to prevent the dehumanization of man. For the opposite of human is not the animal. *The opposite of the human is the demonic.*

Contemporary man is a being afflicted with contradictions and perplexities, living in anguish in an affluent society. His anxiety makes a mockery of his boasts. Passing through several revolutions simultaneously, his thinking is behind the times. High standards of living, vulgar standards of thinking, too feeble to stop the process of the spiritual liquidation of man. Man is becoming obsolete, computers are taking over.

The issue we face is not secularization but total *mechanization, militarization. The issue is not empty pews, but empty hearts.*

If the ultimate goal is power, then modern man has come of age. However, if the ultimate goal is meaning of existence, then man has already descended into a new infancy.

At times it is as if our normal consciousness were a state of partly suspended animation. Our perceptivity limited, our categories onesided.

Things that matter most are of no relevance to many of us. Pedestrian categories will not lead us to the summit; to attain understanding for realness of God we have to rise to a higher level of thinking and experience.

This is an age in which even our common sense is tainted with commercialism and expediency. To recover sensitivity to the divine, we must develop in uncommon sense, rebel against seemingly relevant, against conventional validity; to unthink many thoughts, to abandon many habits, to sacrifice many pretensions.

The temple in Jerusalem has been destroyed. All that is left is a wailing wall. A stone wall stands between God and man. Is there a way of piercing the wall?

Is there a way of surmounting the wall?

What is the substance, of which that wall is made? Is it, as the prophets maintain, man's heart of stone? Or is it, as Isaiah also claims, the hiding of God? The darkening of his presence?

Perhaps this is the chief vocation of man: to scale the wall, to sense what is revealed wherever he is concealed, to realize that even a wall cannot separate man from God, that the darkness is but a challenge and a passageway.

We have pulled down the shutters and locked the doors. No light should enter, no echo should disturb our complacency. Man is the master, all else is a void. Religion came to be understood in commercial terms. We will pay our dues, and He will offer protection.

God has not complied with our expectations. So we sulk, and call it quits. Who is to blame? Is God simply wicked—has He failed to keep the deal?

The hour calls for a breakthrough through the splendid platitudes that dominate our thinking, for efforts to counteract the systematic deflation of man, for a commitment to recall the dimension of depth within which the central issues of human existence can be seen in a way compatible with the dangerous grandeur of the human condition.

Characteristic of our own religious situation is an awareness that theology is out of context, irrelevant to the emergencies engulfing us, pitifully incongruous with the energies technology has released, and unrelated to our anguish.

The word heaven is a problem, and so is the living, loving

God, and so is the humanity in man a grave problem. There are two ways of dealing with a problem: one is an effort to solve it, the other is an effort to dissolve it, to kill it . . .

Let us not make a virtue of spiritual obtuseness. Why canonize deficiencies? Why glorify failure?

The crisis is wider, the anguish is deeper. What is at stake is not only articles of the creeds, paragraphs of the law; what is at stake is the humanity of man, the nearness of God.

What do we claim? *That religious commitment is not just an ingredient of the social order, an adjunct or reinforcement of existence, but rather the heart and core of being human.*

We have been preoccupied with issues, some marginal, some obsolete, evading urgent problems, offering answers to questions no longer asked, adjusting to demands of intellectual comfort, cherishing solutions that disregard emergencies.

We suffer from the fact that our understanding of religion today has been reduced to ritual, doctrine, institution, symbol, theology, detached from the *pretheological* situation, the presymbolic depth of existence. To redirect the trend, we must lay bare what is involved in religious existence; we must recover the situations which both precede and correspond to the theological formulations; we must recall the questions which religious doctrines are trying to answer, the antecedents of religious commitment, the presuppositions of faith. What are the prerequisites, conditions, qualifications for being sensitive to God? Are we always ready to talk about Him?

There are levels of thinking where God is irrelevant, categories that stifle all intimations of the holy.

We are inclined to quantify quality as we are to canonize prejudice. Just as the primitive man sought to personalize the impersonal, the contemporary man seeks to depersonalize the personal, to think in average ways, yet every thought pertaining to God can only be conceived in uncommon ways.

God is *not a word but a name. It can only be uttered in astonishment.* Astonishment is the result of openness to the true mystery, of sensing the ineffable. It is through openness to the mystery that we are present to the presence of God, open to the ineffable Name.

The urgent problem is not only the truth of religion, but *man's capacity to sense the truth of religion, the authenticity of religious concern.* Religious truth does not shine in a vacuum. It is certainly not comprehensible when the antecedents of religious insight and commitment are wasted away; when the mind is dazzled by ideologies which either obscure or misrepresent man's ultimate questions; when life is lived in a way which tends to abuse and to squander the gold mines, the challenging resources of human existence. The primary issue of theology is *pretheological;* it is the total situation of man and his attitudes toward life and the world.

What is necessary is a recall to those ultimate sources of the spirit's life which commonplace thinking never touches. Theology must begin in *depth-theology.* Knowing must be preceded by listening to the call: "Do not come closer. Remove your sandals from your feet, for the place on which you stand is holy ground."

No one attains faith without first achieving the prerequisites of faith. First we praise, then we believe. We begin with a sense of wonder and arrive at radical amazement. The first response is reverence and awe, openness to the mystery that surrounds, and we are led to be overwhelmed by the glory.

God is not a concept produced by deliberation. God is an outcry wrung from heart and mind; God is never an explanation, it is always a challenge. It can only be uttered in astonishment.

Religious existence is a pilgrimage rather than an arrival. Its teaching—a challenge rather than an intellectual establishment, an encyclopedia of ready-made answers.

Perhaps the grave error in theology is the *claim to finality,* to absolute truth, as if all of God's wisdom were revealed to us completely and once and for all, as if God had nothing more to say.

God is a problem alive when the mind is in communion with the conscience, when realizing that in depth we are receivers rather than manipulators. The word God is an assault, a thunder in the soul, not a notion to play with. Prayer is the premise, moments of devotion are prerequisites of reflection. A word about God must not be born out of wedlock of heart and mind. It must not be uttered unless it has the stamp of one's own soul.

Detachment of doctrine from devotion, detachment of

reason from reverence, of scrutiny from the sense of the ineffable reduces God as a challenge to a logical hypothesis, theoretically important, but not overwhelmingly urgent. God is only relevant when overwhelmingly urgent.

It is a fatal mistake to think that believing in God is gained with ease or sustained without strain.

Faith is steadfastness in spite of failure. It is defiance and persistence in the face of frustration.

The most fruitful level for interreligious discussion is not that of dogmatic theology but that of *depth-theology.*

There are four dimensions of religious existence, four necessary components of man's relationships to God: (a) *the teaching,* the essentials of which are summarized in the form of a creed, which serve as guiding principles in our thinking about matters temporal or eternal, the dimension of the doctrine; (b) *faith,* inwardness, the direction of one's heart, the intimacy of religion, the dimension of privacy; (c) *the law,* or the sacred act to be carried out in the sanctuary in society or at home, the dimension of the deed; (d) *the context* in which creed, faith and ritual come to pass, such as the community or the covenant, history, tradition, the dimension of transcendence.

In the dimension of the deed there are obviously vast areas for cooperation among men of different commitments in terms of intellectual communication, of sharing concern and knowledge in applied religion, particularly as they relate to social action.

In the dimension of faith, the encounter proceeds in terms of personal witness and example, sharing insights, confessing inadequacy. On the level of doctrine we seek to convey the content of what we believe in, on the level of faith we experience in one another the presence of a person radiant with reflections of a greater presence.

I suggest that the most significant basis for meeting of men of different religious traditions is the level of fear and trembling, of humility and contrition, where our individual moments of faith are mere waves in the endless ocean of mankind's reaching out for God, where all formulations and articulations appear as understatements, where our souls are swept away by the awareness of the urgency of answering God's commandment, while stripped of pretension and conceit we sense the tragic insufficiency of human faith.

What divides us? What unites us? We disagree in law and creed, in commitments which lie at the very heart of our religious existence. We say "No" to one another in some doctrines essential and sacred to us. What unites us? Our being accountable to God, our being objects of God's concern, precious in His eyes. Our conceptions of what ails us may be different; but the anxiety is the same. The language, the imagination, the concretization of our hopes are different, but the embarrassment is the same, and so is the sigh, the sorrow, and the necessity to obey.

We may disagree about the ways of achieving fear and trembling, but the fear and trembling are the same. The demands are different, but the conscience is the same, and so is arrogance, iniquity. The proclamations are different, the callousness is the same, and so is the challenge we face in many moments of spiritual agony.

Above all, while dogmas and forms of worship are divergent, God is the same. What unites us? A commitment to the Hebrew Bible as Holy Scripture. Faith in the Creator, the God of Abraham, commitment to many of His commandments, to justice and mercy, a sense of contrition, sensitivity to the sanctity of life and to the involvement of God in history, the conviction that without the holy the good will be defeated, prayer that history may not end before the end of days, and so much more.

There are moments when we all stand together and see our faces in the mirror: the anguish of humanity and its helplessness; the perplexity of the individual and the need of divine guidance; being called to praise and to do what is required.

Many of our people still think in terms of an age in which Judaism *wrapped* itself in spiritual *isolation.* In our days, however, for the majority of our people *involvement* has replaced *isolation.*

The emancipation has brought us *to the very heart* of the total society. It has not only given us *rights,* but also imposed *obligations.* It has expanded the scope of our responsibility and concern. Whether we like it or not, the words we utter and the actions in which we are engaged affect the life of the total community.

We *affirm* the principle of separation of church and state, we *reject* the separation of religion and the human situation. We abhor the equation of state and society, of power and conscience, and perceive society in the image of human beings comprising it. The human individual is beset with needs and is called upon to serve ends.

To what religious ends must my fellowmen be guided?

The world we live in has become a single neighborhood, and the role of religious commitment, of reverence and compassion, in the thinking of our fellowmen is becoming a domestic issue. What goes on in the Christian world affects us deeply. Unless we learn how to help one another, we may only hurt each other.

Our society is in crisis not because we intensely disagree but because we feebly agree. "The clash of doctrines is not a disaster, it is an opportunity" (Alfred Whitehead).

The survival of mankind is in balance. One wave of hatred, callousness, or contempt may bring in its wake the destruction of all mankind. Vicious deeds are but an aftermath of what is conceived in the hearts and minds of man. It is from the inner life of man and from the articulation of evil thoughts that evil actions take their rise. It is therefore of extreme importance that the sinfulness of thoughts of suspicion and hatred and particularly the sinfulness of any contemptuous utterance, however flippantly it is meant, be made clear to all mankind. This applies in particular to thoughts and utterances about individuals or groups of other religions, races and nations. Speech has power and few men realize that words do not fade. What starts out as a sound ends in a deed.

In an age in which the spiritual premises of our existence are both questioned and even militantly removed, the urgent problem is not the competition among some religions but the condition of all religions, the condition of man, crassness, chaos, darkness, despair.

There is much we can do together in matters of supreme concern and relevance to both Judaism and Christianity.

The world is too small for anything but mutual care and deep respect; the world is too great for anything but responsibility for one another.

A full awareness and appreciation of our fellowmen's spiritual commitments becomes a moral obligation for all of us.

A Jew who hears what he prays cannot be indifferent to whether God's way is known in the world, to whether the gentiles know how to praise. In our liturgy we proclaim every day:

> Give thanks to the Lord,
> Call upon Him,
> Make known His deeds among the peoples!
> —(Psalms 105:1)

In the Omer liturgy it is customary to recite Psalm 67:

> May God be gracious to us and bless us and
> make His face to shine upon us, that Thy way
> may be known upon earth, Thy saving power
> among all nations.
> Let the peoples praise Thee, O God;
> let all the peoples praise Thee!

What is our task as Jews in relation to Gentiles? I rely upon the words of an inspired Hassidic sage in expounding Deuteronomy 28:9f. "The Lord shall establish you as His holy people . . . if you keep the commandments . . . and walk in His ways. And all the peoples of the earth shall see that the Lord's name is proclaimed upon you, and they will acquire reverence through you."

The real bond between people of different creeds is the awe and fear of God they have in common. It is easy to speak about the different dogmas we are committed to; it is hard to communicate the fear and reverence. It is easy to communicate the learning we have inherited, it is hard to communicate the praise, contrition and the sense of the ineffable. But souls which are in accord with what is precious in the eyes of God, souls to whom God's love for them is more precious than their own lives, will always meet in the presence of Him whose glory fills the hearts and transcends the minds.

What, then, is the purpose of interreligious cooperation?

It is neither to flatter nor to refute one another, but to help one another; to share insight and learning, to cooperate in academic ventures on the highest scholarly level, and what is even more important to search in the wilderness for well-springs of devotion, for treasures of stillness, for the power of love and care for man. What is urgently needed are ways of helping one another in the terrible predicament of here and now by the courage to believe that the word of the Lord endures for ever as well as here and now; to work for peace in Vietnam, for racial justice in our own land, to purify the minds from contempt, suspicion and hatred; to cooperate in trying to bring about a resurrection of sensitivity, a revival of conscience; to keep alive the divine sparks in our souls, to nurture openness to the spirit of the Psalms, reverence for the words of the prophets, and faithfulness to the Living God.

There ought to be standards and rules for interreligious dialogue. An example of such a rule for Catholics and Protestants would be not to discuss the supremacy of the bishop of Rome or Papacy; an example of such a rule for Christians and Jews would be not to discuss Christology.

The God of Abraham, the Creator of heaven and earth, deemed it wise to conceal His presence in the world in which we live. He did not make it easy for us to have faith in Him, to remain faithful to Him.

This is our tragedy; the insecurity of faith, the unbearable burden of our commitment. The facts that deny the divine are mighty, indeed; the arguments of agnosticism are eloquent, the events that defy Him are spectacular. Our Faith is too often tinged with arrogance, self-righteousness. It is even capable of becoming demonic . . . Even the creeds we proclaim are in danger of becoming idolatry. Our faith is fragile, never immune to error, distortion or deception.

There are no final proofs for the existence of God, Father and Creator of all. There are only witnesses. Supreme among them are the prophets of Israel.

Humanity is an unfinished task, and so is religion. The law, the creed, the teaching and the wisdom are here, yet without the outburst of prophetic demands coming upon us again and again, religion may become fossilized.

Here is the experience of a child of seven who was reading

in school the chapter which tells of the sacrifice of Isaac. "Isaac was on the way to Mount Moriah with his father; then he lay on the altar, bound, waiting to be sacrificed." My heart began to beat even faster; it actually sobbed with pity for Isaac. Behold, Abraham now lifted the knife. And now my heart froze within me with fright. Suddenly, the voice of the angel was heard: "Abraham, lay not thine hand upon the lad, for now I know that thou fearest God." And here I broke out in tears and wept aloud. "Why are you crying?" asked the Rabbi. "You know that Isaac was not killed." And I said to him, still weeping, "But, Rabbi, supposing the angel had come a second too late?"

The Rabbi comforted me and calmed me by telling me that "an angel cannot come late."

An angel cannot be late, but man, made of flesh and blood, may be late.

MARTIN LUTHER KING JR.

Sermon Delivered April 3, 1968

THANK YOU very kindly, my friends. As I listened to Ralph Abernathy in his eloquent and generous introduction and then thought about myself, I wondered who he was talking about. It's always good to have your closest friend and associate say something good about you. And Ralph is the best friend that I have in the world.

I'm delighted to see each of you here tonight in spite of a storm warning. You reveal that you are determined to go on anyhow. Something is happening in Memphis, something is happening in our world.

As you know, if I were standing at the beginning of time, with the possibility of general and panoramic view of the whole human history up to now, and the Almighty said to me, "Martin Luther King, which age would you like to live in?"—I would take my mental flight by Egypt through, or rather across the Red Sea, through the wilderness on toward the promised land. And in spite of its magnificence, I wouldn't stop there. I would move on by Greece, and take my mind to Mount Olympus. And I would see Plato, Aristotle, Socrates, Euripides and Aristophanes assembled around the Parthenon as they discussed the great and eternal issues of reality.

But I wouldn't stop there. I would go on, even to the great heyday of the Roman Empire. And I would see developments around there, through various emperors and leaders. But I wouldn't stop there. I would even come up to the day of the Renaissance, and get a quick picture of all that the Renaissance did for the cultural and esthetic life of man. But I wouldn't stop there. I would even go by the way that the man for whom I'm named had his habitat. And I would watch Martin Luther as he tacked his ninety-five theses on the door at the church in Wittenberg.

But I wouldn't stop there. I would come on up even to 1863, and watch a vacillating president by the name of

Abraham Lincoln finally come to the conclusion that he had to sign the Emancipation Proclamation. But I wouldn't stop there. I would even come up to the early thirties, and see a man grappling with the problems of the bankruptcy of his nation. And come with an eloquent cry that we have nothing to fear but fear itself.

But I wouldn't stop there. Strangely enough, I would turn to the Almighty, and say, "If you allow me to live just a few years in the second half of the twentieth century, I will be happy." Now that's a strange statement to make, because the world is all messed up. The nation is sick. Trouble is in the land. Confusion all around. That's a strange statement. But I know, somehow, that only when it is dark enough, can you see the stars. And I see God working in this period of the twentieth century in a way that men, in some strange way, are responding—something is happening in our world. The masses of people are rising up. And wherever they are assembled today, whether they are in Johannesburg, South Africa; Nairobi, Kenya; Accra, Ghana; New York City; Atlanta, Georgia; Jackson, Mississippi; or Memphis, Tennessee—the cry is always the same—"We want to be free."

And another reason that I'm happy to live in this period is that we have been forced to a point where we're going to have to grapple with the problems that men have been trying to grapple with through history, but the demands didn't force them to do it. Survival demands that we grapple with them. Men, for years now, have been talking about war and peace. But now, no longer can they just talk about it. It is no longer a choice between violence and nonviolence in this world; it's nonviolence or nonexistence.

That is where we are today. And also in the human rights revolution, if something isn't done, and in a hurry, to bring the colored peoples of the world out of their long years of poverty, their long years of hurt and neglect, the whole world is doomed. Now, I'm just happy that God has allowed me to live in this period, to see what is unfolding. And I'm happy that he's allowed me to be in Memphis.

I can remember, I can remember when Negroes were just going around as Ralph has said, so often, scratching where they didn't itch, and laughing when they were not tickled.

But that day is all over. We mean business now, and we are determined to gain our rightful place in God's world.

And that's all this whole thing is about. We aren't engaged in any negative protest and in any negative arguments with anybody. We are saying that we are determined to be men. We are determined to be people. We are saying that we are God's children. And that we don't have to live like we are forced to live.

Now, what does all of this mean in this great period of history? It means that we've got to stay together. We've got to stay together and maintain unity. You know, whenever Pharaoh wanted to prolong the period of slavery in Egypt, he had a favorite, favorite formula for doing it. What was that? He kept the slaves fighting among themselves. But whenever the slaves get together, something happens in Pharaoh's court, and he cannot hold the slaves in slavery. When the slaves get together, that's the beginning of getting out of slavery. Now let us maintain unity.

Secondly, let us keep the issues where they are. The issue is injustice. The issue is the refusal of Memphis to be fair and honest in its dealings with its public servants, who happen to be sanitation workers. Now, we've got to keep attention on that. That's always the problem with a little violence. You know what happened the other day, and the press dealt only with the window-breaking. I read the articles. They very seldom got around to mentioning the fact that one thousand, three hundred sanitation workers were on strike, and that Memphis is not being fair to them, and that Mayor Loeb is in dire need of a doctor. They didn't get around to that.

Now we're going to march again, and we've got to march again, in order to put the issue where it is supposed to be. And force everybody to see that there are thirteen hundred of God's children here suffering, sometimes going hungry, going through dark and dreary nights wondering how this thing is going to come out. That's the issue. And we've got to say to the nation: we know it's coming out. For when people get caught up with that which is right and they are willing to sacrifice for it, there is no stopping point short of victory.

We aren't going to let any mace stop us. We are masters in our nonviolent movement in disarming police forces; they don't know what to do. I've seen them so often. I remember in Birmingham, Alabama, when we were in that majestic struggle there we would move out of the 16th Street Baptist Church day after day; by the hundreds we would move out. And Bull Connor would tell them to send the dogs forth and they did come; but we just went before the dogs singing, "Ain't gonna let nobody turn me round." Bull Connor next would say, "Turn the fire hoses on." And as I said to you the other night, Bull Connor didn't know history. He knew a kind of physics that somehow didn't relate to the transphysics that we knew about. And that was the fact that there was a certain kind of fire that no water could put out. And we went before the fire hoses; we had known water. If we were Baptist or some other denomination, we had been immersed. If we were Methodist, and some others, we had been sprinkled, but we knew water.

That couldn't stop us. And we just went on before the dogs and we would look at them; and we'd go on before the water hoses and we would look at it, and we'd just go on singing "Over my head I see freedom in the air." And then we would be thrown in the paddy wagons, and sometimes we were stacked in there like sardines in a can. And they would throw us in, and old Bull would say, "Take them off," and they did; and we would just go in the paddy wagon singing, "We Shall Overcome." And every now and then we'd get in the jail, and we'd see the jailers looking through the windows being moved by our prayers, and being moved by our words and our songs. And there was a power there which Bull Connor couldn't adjust to; and so we ended up transforming Bull into a steer, and we won our struggle in Birmingham.

Now we've got to go on to Memphis just like that. I call upon you to be with us Monday. Now about injunctions: We have an injunction and we're going into court tomorrow morning to fight this illegal, unconstitutional injunction. All we say to America is, "Be true to what you said on paper." If I lived in China or even Russia, or any totalitarian country, maybe I could understand the denial of certain basic First Amendment privileges, because they hadn't committed themselves to that over there. But somewhere I read of the freedom of assembly. Somewhere I read of the freedom of speech.

Somewhere I read of the freedom of the press. Somewhere I read that the greatness of America is the right to protest for right. And so just as I say, we aren't going to let any injunction turn us around. We are going on.

We need all of you. And you know what's beautiful to me, is to see all of these ministers of the Gospel. It's a marvelous picture. Who is it that is supposed to articulate the longings and aspirations of the people more than the preacher? Somehow the preacher must be an Amos, and say, "Let justice roll down like waters and righteousness like a mighty stream." Somehow, the preacher must say with Jesus, "The spirit of the Lord is upon me, because he hath anointed me to deal with the problems of the poor."

And I want to commend the preachers, under the leadership of these noble men: James Lawson, one who has been in this struggle for many years; he's been to jail for struggling; but he's still going on, fighting for the rights of his people. Rev. Ralph Jackson, Billy Kiles; I could just go right on down the list, but time will not permit. But I want to thank them all. And I want you to thank them, because so often, preachers aren't concerned about anything but themselves. And I'm always happy to see a relevant ministry.

It's alright to talk about "long white robes over yonder," in all of its symbolism. But ultimately people want some suits and dresses and shoes to wear down here. It's alright to talk about "streets flowing with milk and honey," but God has commanded us to be concerned about the slums down here, and his children who can't eat three square meals a day. It's alright to talk about the new Jerusalem, but one day, God's preacher must talk about the New York, the new Atlanta, the new Philadelphia, the new Los Angeles, the new Memphis, Tennessee. This is what we have to do.

Now the other thing we'll have to do is this: Always anchor our external direct action with the power of economic withdrawal. Now, we are poor people, individually, we are poor when you compare us with white society in America. We are poor. Never stop and forget that collectively, that means all of us together, collectively we are richer than all the nations in the world, with the exception of nine. Did you ever think about that? After you leave the United States, Soviet Russia,

Great Britain, West Germany, France, and I could name the others, the Negro collectively is richer than most nations of the world. We have an annual income of more than thirty billion dollars a year, which is more than all of the exports of the United States, and more than the national budget of Canada. Did you know that? That's power right there, if we know how to pool it.

We don't have to argue with anybody. We don't have to curse and go around acting bad with our words. We don't need any bricks and bottles, we don't need any Molotov cocktails, we just need to go around to these stores, and to these massive industries in our country, and say, "God sent us by here, to say to you that you're not treating his children right. And we've come by here to ask you to make the first item on your agenda—fair treatment, where God's children are concerned. Now, if you are not prepared to do that, we do have an agenda that we must follow. And our agenda calls for withdrawing economic support from you."

And so, as a result of this, we are asking you tonight, to go out and tell your neighbors not to buy Coca-Cola in Memphis. Go by and tell them not to buy Sealtest milk. Tell them not to buy—what is the other bread?—Wonder Bread. And what is the other bread company, Jesse? Tell them not to buy Hart's bread. As Jesse Jackson has said, up to now, only the garbage men have been feeling pain; now we must kind of redistribute the pain. We are choosing these companies because they haven't been fair in their hiring policies; and we are choosing them because they can begin the process of saying, they are going to support the needs and the rights of these men who are on strike. And then they can move on downtown and tell Mayor Loeb to do what is right.

But not only that, we've got to strengthen black institutions. I call upon you to take your money out of the banks downtown and deposit your money in Tri-State Bank—we want a "bank-in" movement in Memphis. So go by the savings and loan association. I'm not asking you something that we don't do ourselves at SCLC. Judge Hooks and others will tell you that we have an account here in the savings and loan association from the Southern Christian Leadership Conference. We're just telling you to follow what we're doing. Put your money there. You have six or seven black insurance companies in Memphis. Take out your insurance there. We want to have an "insurance-in."

Now these are some practical things we can do. We begin the process of building a greater economic base. And at the same time, we are putting pressure where it really hurts. I ask you to follow through here.

Now, let me say as I move to my conclusion that we've got to give ourselves to this struggle until the end. Nothing would be more tragic than to stop at this point, in Memphis. We've got to see it through. And when we have our march, you need to be there. Be concerned about your brother. You may not be on strike. But either we go up together, or we go down together.

Let us develop a kind of dangerous unselfishness. One day a man came to Jesus; and he wanted to raise some questions about some vital matters in life. At points, he wanted to trick Jesus, and show him that he knew a little more than Jesus knew, and through this, throw him off base. Now that question could have easily ended up in a philosophical and theological debate. But Jesus immediately pulled that question from mid-air, and placed it on a dangerous curve between Jerusalem and Jericho. And he talked about a certain man, who fell among thieves. You remember that a Levite and a priest passed by on the other side. They didn't stop to help him. And finally a man of another race came by. He got down from his beast, decided not to be compassionate by proxy. But with him, administered first aid, and helped the man in need. Jesus ended up saying, this was the good man, this was the great man, because he had the capacity to project the "I" into the "thou," and to be concerned about his brother. Now you know, we use our imagination a great deal to try to determine why the priest and the Levite didn't stop. At times we say they were busy going to church meetings—an ecclesiastical gathering—and they had to get on down to Jerusalem so they wouldn't be late for their meeting. At other times we would speculate that there was a religious law that "One who was engaged in religious ceremonials was not to touch a human body twenty-four hours before the ceremony." And every now and then we begin to wonder whether maybe they were not going down to Jerusalem, or down to Jericho, rather to organize a "Jericho Road Improvement Association." That's a possibility. Maybe they felt that it was better to deal with the problem from the causal root, rather than to get bogged down with an individual effort.

But I'm going to tell you what my imagination tells me. It's possible that these men were afraid. You see, the Jericho road is a dangerous road. I remember when Mrs. King and I were first in Jerusalem. We rented a car and drove from Jerusalem down to Jericho. And as soon as we got on that road, I said to my wife, "I can see why Jesus used this as a setting for his parable." It's a winding, meandering road. It's really conducive for ambushing. You start out in Jerusalem, which is about 1200 miles, or rather 1200 feet above sea level. And by the time you get down to Jericho, fifteen or twenty minutes later, you're about 2200 feet below sea level. That's a dangerous road. In the days of Jesus it came to be known as the "Bloody Pass." And you know, it's possible that the priest and the Levite looked over that man on the ground and wondered if the robbers were still around. Or it's possible that they felt that the man on the ground was merely faking. And he was acting like he had been robbed and hurt, in order to seize them over there, lure them there for quick and easy seizure. And so the first question that the Levite asked was, "If I stop to help this man, what will happen to me?" But then the Good Samaritan came by. And he reversed the question: "If I do not stop to help this man, what will happen to him?"

That's the question before you tonight. Not, "If I stop to help the sanitation workers, what will happen to all of the hours that I usually spend in my office every day and every week as a pastor?" The question is not, "If I stop to help this man in need, what will happen to me?" "If I do not stop to help the sanitation workers, what will happen to them?" That's the question.

Let us rise up tonight with a greater readiness. Let us stand with a greater determination. And let us move on in these powerful days, these days of challenge to make America what it ought to be. We have an opportunity to make America a better nation. And I want to thank God, once more, for allowing me to be here with you.

You know, several years ago, I was in New York City autographing the first book that I had written. And while sitting there autographing books, a demented black woman came up. The only question I heard from her was, "Are you Martin Luther King?"

And I was looking down writing, and I said yes. And the next minute I felt something beating on my chest. Before I knew it I had been stabbed by this demented woman. I was rushed to Harlem Hospital. It was a dark Saturday afternoon. And that blade had gone through, and the X-rays revealed that the tip of the blade was on the edge of my aorta, the main artery. And once that's punctured, you drown in your own blood—that's the end of you.

It came out in the *New York Times* the next morning, that if I had sneezed, I would have died. Well, about four days later, they allowed me, after the operation, after my chest had been opened, and the blade had been taken out, to move around in the wheel chair in the hospital. They allowed me to read some of the mail that came in, and from all over the states, and the world, kind letters came in. I read a few, but one of them I will never forget. I had received one from the President and the Vice-President. I've forgotten what those telegrams said. I'd received a visit and a letter from the Governor of New York, but I've forgotten what the letter said. But there was another letter that came from a little girl, a young girl who was a student at the White Plains High School. And I looked at that letter, and I'll never forget it. It said simply, "Dear Dr. King: I am a ninth-grade student at the White Plains High School." She said, "While it should not matter, I would like to mention that I am a white girl. I read in the paper of your misfortune, and of your suffering. And I read that if you had sneezed, you would have died. And I'm simply writing you to say that I'm so happy that you didn't sneeze."

And I want to say tonight, I want to say that I am happy that I didn't sneeze. Because if I had sneezed, I wouldn't have been around here in 1960, when students all over the South started sitting-in at lunch counters. And I knew that as they were sitting in, they were really standing up for the best in the American dream. And taking the whole nation back to those great walls of democracy which were dug deep by the

Founding Fathers in the Declaration of Independence and the Constitution. If I had sneezed, I wouldn't have been around in 1962, when Negroes in Albany, Georgia, decided to straighten their backs up. And whenever men and women straighten their backs up, they are going somewhere, because a man can't ride your back unless it is bent. If I had sneezed, I wouldn't have been here in 1963, when the black people of Birmingham, Alabama, aroused the conscience of this nation, and brought into being the Civil Rights Bill. If I had sneezed, I wouldn't have had a chance later that year, in August, to try to tell America about a dream that I had had. If I had sneezed, I wouldn't have been down in Selma, Alabama, to see the great movement there. If I had sneezed, I wouldn't have been in Memphis to see a community rally around those brothers and sisters who are suffering. I'm so happy that I didn't sneeze.

And they were telling me, now it doesn't matter now. It really doesn't matter what happens now. I left Atlanta this morning, and as we got started on the plane, there were six of us, the pilot said over the public address system, "We are sorry for the delay, but we have Dr. Martin Luther King on the plane. And to be sure that all of the bags were checked, and to be sure that nothing would be wrong with the plane, we had to check out everything carefully. And we've had the plane protected and guarded all night."

And then I got into Memphis. And some began to say the threats, or talk about the threats that were out. What would happen to me from some of our sick white brothers?

Well, I don't know what will happen now. We've got some difficult days ahead. But it doesn't matter with me now. Because I've been to the mountaintop. And I don't mind. Like anybody, I would like to live a long life. Longevity has its place. But I'm not concerned about that now. I just want to do God's will. And He's allowed me to go up to the mountain. And I've looked over. And I've seen the promised land. I may not get there with you. But I want you to know tonight, that we, as a people will get to the promised land. And I'm happy, tonight. I'm not worried about anything. I'm not fearing any man. Mine eyes have seen the glory of the coming of the Lord.

Note on the Sermon Form

Most of the sermons printed in the first half of this volume are by Puritans, and follow a form and style that was particularly developed in the American colonies. The term "Puritan" was first applied in the 16th century to critics of the Church of England by its defenders. It had the connotation of purist, and was applied to those who protested that the Reformation had not gone far enough in England. A central demand of these "Puritans" was that the church reduce ritual and instead foster the preaching of sermons to educate hearers about Scripture. They developed an avid culture of sermon attendance, often meeting illicitly to hear preachers, while the canons of the Church of England prescribed only four sermons a year. Elizabeth I, as head of the Church of England, tried to restrict preaching to brief homilies, and under Charles I, Archbishop William Laud tried to limit preaching to catechizing.

In 1592 William Perkins wrote in *The Art of Prophecying*, a manual that long remained the basic textbook for Puritan clergy in America, that the preacher was required to do four things:

"1. To read the Text distinctly out of the Canonicall Scriptures.
2. To give the sense and understanding of it being read, by the Scripture itself.
3. To collect a few and profitable points of doctrine out of the naturall sense.
4. To apply (if he have the gift) the doctrines rightly collected, to the life and manners of men in a simple and plaine speech."

These rules were systematically applied by Puritan preachers. Most of the 17th- and 18th-century sermons in this volume are marked into distinct sections, following Perkins' standard form. The text itself comes first, and was often read from the annotated Geneva Bible, since the Authorized Version of 1611 was associated with King James and the Church of England. It was followed by the three parts of the sermon proper: a brief explication, often headed "Text"; a more substantial section, usually headed "Doctrine"; and a final section on the practical consequences of the doctrine for the hearers' lives, headed "Use." (These sections were also known as "Explication," "Confirmation," and "Application.") This structure was sometimes extended to sermon cycles, stretching to as many as 30 sermons; in

889

such cases the "Use" section alone could occupy several pulpit sessions. The "Doctrine" and "Use" sections of the Puritan sermon frequently have numbered subheadings, expressing the Puritan concern with systems of logic and rhetoric, but also allowing for easier note-taking. Until the late 18th century, extemporaneous preaching was extremely rare. Reading sermons aloud, however, was disdained. Puritan preachers typically wrote their sermons out, memorized them, and then preached either from memory or from numbered outline notes (hence the occasional inaccuracy of Scriptural citations). Many members of colonial congregations took down whole sermons in shorthand or made notes of the numbered points. "Doctrine" sections are especially concerned with logical ordering, and often contain paired headings such as "Question" and "Answer," or "Objection" and "Reply."

The plain style—Perkins' "simple and plaine speech"—emphasized clarity, but did not forgo figures of speech or erudition. Perkins wrote: "If any man thinke that by this means barbarism should be brought into pulpits; hee must understand that the Minister may, yea and must privately use at his libertie the arts, Philosophy, and variety of reading, whilest he is in framing his sermon: but he ought in publike to conceale all these from the people, and not make the least ostentation."

Most colonial Puritans heard sermons on Sunday morning and again on Sunday afternoon, as well as a "lecture" sermon, usually given on Thursday. Sermons commonly lasted an hour or longer, and were also preached on special occasions such as annual elections, fast days, funerals, ordinations, militia elections, and public executions. These occasional sermons were more likely to be published than were regular sermons, and many of the sermons in this volume derive from such occasions. Sermons were almost always revised before being printed. In the case of posthumously published sermons, or sermons by famous preachers, printers sometimes used notes made by members of the audience. John Cotton's "The Pouring out of the Seven Vials" was printed in this way in 1642.

Many of the most prominent English Puritan preachers immigrated to New England, where they developed both a culture of preaching and a distinctive form of Puritan religion that came to be known as Congregationalism, the Independent churches, or simply the New England Way. Its principal feature—besides a strongly Calvinist emphasis on the sovereignty of God rather than on free will, which it shared with Presbyterianism—was a vision of the church as a special community of the elect, formed in a covenant with one another and with God. Each church was independent, subject to no central authority; each church limited full membership and communion to those whom it deemed to be truly saved. The colonial churches required an examination of each candidate for membership, usually with a narrative of the candidate's conversion experience. This system was adjusted over time: in 1662, the New England Congregational churches admitted children of church members to some privileges of membership, but not full communion—a compromise known as the Half-Way Covenant. With such modifications, the Congregational model dominated New England until the 19th century.

Congregational preachers also dominate the published record of American sermons until the middle of the 18th century. Anglican ministers preached in Jamestown at least as early as 1607, but only one sermon is known to survive from the 17th century south of New England. Over time, other kinds of sermons came into prominence, and the Congregational tradition itself became more diverse. Especially significant was the rise in the latter half of the 18th century of extemporaneous preaching, particularly among Methodist and African-American exhorters. The second half of this volume contains several examples of extempore sermons recorded by hearers, as well as published sermons whose style and form were influenced by extempore preaching.

Biographical Notes

ROBERT CUSHMAN (c. 1579–1625) Cushman, a wool-carder and Separatist lay preacher, delivered this sermon on December 12, 1621, near the end of his only visit (November 11–December 13) to the Plymouth Colony. Born in Canterbury, Cushman had immigrated to the Netherlands in 1609 and joined the English Separatist exiles living in Leiden. On their behalf, he negotiated an agreement in 1620 with a group of London merchant adventurers for financing a settlement in North America. Under its terms, all of the land and livestock of the colony, along with all profits from fishing and fur trading, would be commonly owned by a partnership between the colonists and the merchants; the partnership would be dissolved and its assets divided among the shareholders after seven years. Cushman failed to gain the colonists' formal consent to the agreement before they set sail on the *Speedwell* and the *Mayflower* in August 1620, and after the *Speedwell* proved unseaworthy and was forced to return to port, Cushman stayed behind in England. The *Mayflower* landed 102 passengers at Plymouth in December 1620; only half of them survived their first winter in New England. They were joined in November 1621 by another 35 colonists who arrived on the *Fortune* with Cushman. During his visit Cushman succeeded in obtaining the colonists' consent to the agreement he had negotiated the previous year. In 1622 Cushman published in London a tract, *Reasons and Considerations Touching the Lawfulnesse of Removing Out of England*, and the text of his Plymouth sermon; it is the earliest sermon text from the English settlements in America known to be extant, and the first to be printed.

JOHN WINTHROP (1588–1649) Winthrop preached this lay sermon aboard the *Arbella*, flagship of the fleet carrying settlers to the Massachusetts Bay Colony, probably as the ship lay at anchor off the coast of England in the spring of 1630. Although "A Modell of Christian Charity" was not published until 1838, it circulated in manuscript from an early date, and its famous conclusion ("wee shall be as a Citty upon a Hill") is alluded to in mid-17th-century writings by Puritan leaders Peter Bulkeley, William Bradford, and Urian Oakes.

Winthrop was a Cambridge-educated lawyer with an extensive practice in London. When a group of Puritans obtained a grant of land in 1628 in what is now Massachusetts, Winthrop became interested in the venture. He agreed to head the migration on the condition that the Massachusetts Bay Company's charter be brought across the Atlantic, thereby allowing company meetings to be held in the colony. Winthrop was elected governor each year from 1630 to 1634, 1637 to 1640, 1642 to 1644, and from 1645 until his death. He led the prosecution of Anne Hutchinson for heresy (see note on John Cotton) and defended the authority of the governor and magistrates within the General Court that governed the colony. His *Journal* is a key source on colonial history.

JOHN COTTON (1584–1652)   After distinguishing himself as a scholar at Cambridge, John Cotton suffered a crisis of faith in 1609. Abandoning the polished style of the Anglican sermon in favor of the Puritan plain style, he became famous as a preacher. Ordained in the Church of England in 1610, he assumed the pulpit in Boston, Lincolnshire, where he preached for over 20 years. Many of the first settlers of Massachusetts were among his congregation, and he preached the farewell sermon to Winthrop's fleet, published as *God's Promise to his Plantation* (1630). Finally forced to resign for nonconformity, Cotton emigrated in 1633 and became minister of the church in Boston, Massachusetts.

The sermon printed here was one of a series published as *The Way of Life* (1641), and was first preached shortly before his emigration. Among Cotton's parishioners at the time was Anne Hutchinson, who followed him to America in 1634. In a series of popular discussion meetings she conducted after her arrival, she extended the doctrine of inner sanctification through the covenant of grace and the indwelling of the Holy Spirit. She was accused of heresy and tried in 1637. Cotton was at first sympathetic to Hutchinson, but under strong pressure from other ministers and Governor Winthrop, he repudiated her and agreed to her excommunication and banishment in 1638.

Cotton published numerous treatises, many of them based on his sermons, and was one of the principal authors of *The Whole Book of Psalms* (1640), commonly known as the *Bay Psalm Book*, the first book published in the English colonies. He also engaged in a long dispute with Roger Williams, after Williams' banishment from Massachusetts, in which Cotton defended Massachusetts orthodoxy against the principle of toleration.

THOMAS HOOKER (1586–1647)   Hooker entered Cambridge in 1603 and was a fellow and lecturer at Emmanuel College from 1609 until 1618, when he left to serve as a minister. A leading voice of nonconforming Puritanism, he fled to Holland in 1630 to avoid trial by the High Commission of the Church of England. In 1633 he sailed for New England on the same ship with John Cotton. He organized a church at New Towne (now Cambridge), but after a series of controversies he settled in 1636 with a large part of his congregation in Hartford and became a dominant figure in early Connecticut politics.

Hooker was an advocate of preparationism, holding—notably against Cotton, who stressed the absoluteness of God's indwelling grace—that the soul can prepare itself for conversion. He published many volumes of sermons dealing with the inner process of salvation, including *The Soules Preparation* (1632), *The Soules Humiliation, The Soules Implantation* (both 1637), *The Soules Vocation, The Soules Ingrafting,* and *The Soules Exaltation* (all 1638). "Of Gods Image in the Affections" comes from a series of sermons on Genesis 1:26, published in 1640 as *The Paterne of Perfection.* Hooker reviewed the process of conversion in a series of sermons called *The Application of Redemption* that were published between 1656 and 1659. His treatise on the Congregational doctrine and practice, *A Survey of the Summe of Church Discipline* was published posthumously in 1648.

THOMAS SHEPARD (1605–1649) Orphaned at the age of ten, Shepard attended Emmanuel College at Cambridge. He was ordained in 1627, but was silenced by Bishop William Laud in 1630. Shepard sailed for New England in 1634, was driven back by storm, went into hiding, and finally reached Massachusetts in October 1635, where he became minister at New Towne (Cambridge). After his first wife's death the following year, he married a daughter of Thomas Hooker. He participated in the founding of Harvard College, serving as its unofficial chaplain until his death.

Shepard promoted missionary work in *The Clear Sun Shine of the Gospel Breaking Forth upon the Indians of New England* (1648), and published a number of works on salvation, including *The Sincere Convert* (1641) and *The Sound Believer* (1645). Many of his works addressed whether, given the absolute nature of divine grace and predestination, one can know one's own salvation with any assurance. Shepard was an early exponent of using spiritual autobiography as evidence of conversion and condition of church membership, gathering narratives from his own congregation, keeping a spiritual journal, and writing his own autobiography not long before his death. He spent three days each week preparing his Sabbath sermons, and was described by Edward Johnson in *The Wonder-Working Providence of Sions Saviour* (1654) as a "soul-ravishing Minister."

The first text included here comes from a series of sermons, preached weekly from June 1636 to May 1640, that were taken down in shorthand and later published as *The Parable of the Ten Virgins*. "Of Ineffectual Hearing," a sermon on listening to sermons, was preached in 1641 and published in *Subjection to Christ* (1652).

JONATHAN MITCHEL (1624–1668) Born to a wealthy family in Yorkshire in 1624, Mitchel suffered an illness when he was ten that stiffened one of his arms for the rest of his life. In 1635 he immigrated with his family to New Towne (Cambridge), Massachusetts, where he became a student of Thomas Shepard. Mitchel graduated from Harvard in 1647 and succeeded Shepard as minister of the Cambridge church in 1650; he married Shepard's widow, Margaret, later that year.

In 1662 he played an influential role in the synod that adopted the compromise known as the Half-Way Covenant. It attempted to solve the problem of the status of church members' children that resulted from the Congregational churches' restriction of membership to those who could show evidence of their salvation. The Half-Way Covenant allowed such children some church privileges, but not full communion.

Increase Mather recorded that Mitchel wrote his sermons out in full and would then "commit all to his Memory without once looking into his Bible after he had named his Text." "Nehemiah on the Wall in Troublesom Times" was an election sermon preached in 1667 and published posthumously in 1671. Beginning with John Cotton in 1634, and then annually from 1640, sermons were delivered on election day in May to the assembled freemen, magistrates, and ministers, by specially appointed preachers. Generally laying out a vision of politics and the collective history of the colony, they were commonly longer than regular weekly sermons, and were usually printed at public expense.

SAMUEL DANFORTH (1626–1674) Danforth was born to a prominent family in Suffolk, England, in 1626. He immigrated with his widowed father in 1634, and was raised in Thomas Shepard's congregation after his father's death in 1638. After graduating from Harvard in 1643 in a class of four, he served as a tutor until his ordination in 1650 as the associate of John Eliot, "the Apostle to the Indians," in Eliot's Roxbury church; he also assisted Eliot in his mission to the Indians. Danforth also compiled almanacs for several years in the late 1640s, and wrote a treatise on astrological omens, *An Astronomical Description of the Late Comet or Blazing Star* (1665). His other published sermon, *The Cry of Sodom Inquired Into*, appeared in 1674. He was said to be "a Notable Text-Man," quoting 40 or 50 scriptures in each sermon, yet with such passion that, according to Cotton Mather, "he rarely, if ever ended a Sermon without Weeping."

"A Brief Recognition" was preached on election day in 1670 and published the following year. It is a prominent example of the jeremiad, a form that became popular among New England clergy following the deaths of Winthrop, Cotton, Hooker, and Shepard, the end of the Puritan Commonwealth in England at the Restoration of Charles II (1660), and the adoption of the Half-Way Covenant in Massachusetts (1662).

INCREASE MATHER (1639–1723)　The son of the minister Richard Mather, Increase was born in Dorchester, Massachusetts, and named for "the never-to-be-forgotten *Increase*, of every sort, wherewith God favoured the Country, about the time of his Nativity." After graduating from Harvard in 1657, he sailed to Dublin where he lived with his older brother Samuel (also a minister) and studied at Trinity College. He traveled and preached in England, but, refusing to conform to the Church of England after the Restoration of Charles II in 1660, returned to Boston in 1661. In 1662 he married his stepsister, a daughter of John Cotton. From 1664 until his death he presided over the Second Church of Boston (called the Old North Church). For half a century one of the most prominent political and ministerial figures of New England, Mather preached against the Indians during King Philip's War (1676); represented Massachusetts at court after James II revoked the original charter of the colony; and remained after the Glorious Revolution to negotiate a new charter with William and Mary. In 1692 he counseled moderation in the witchcraft trials, but did not end them.

Mather is reported to have spent an average of 16 hours a day in his study. He committed sermons to memory, keeping "a Page or two" of notes to consult while preaching. In 1683 Mather founded the Philosophical Society of Boston in imitation of the Royal Society of London, and in 1685 became the first American-born president of Harvard, serving until 1701. While in his 80s, he joined his son Cotton in advocating the then-dangerous practice of inoculation against smallpox.

Increase Mather published over a hundred books, sermons, and scientific treatises including *A Brief History of the Warr with the Indians in New England* (1676), *An Essay for the Recording of Illustrious Providences* (1684), *The Doctrine of Divine Providence* (1684), and such jeremiads as his 1677 election sermon, *A Discourse Concerning the Danger of Apostasy*, and two fast-day sermons that were published as *Ichabod* (1702).

COTTON MATHER (1663–1728) The son of Increase Mather and a grandson of John Cotton, Cotton Mather was born in Boston in 1663. He took his M.A. at Harvard in 1685, and was ordained that year as minister under his father at the Second Church. While Increase Mather was in England in 1689, Cotton was active in the overthrow of the royal governor Edmund Andros, as the Glorious Revolution against James II reached Massachusetts.

In February 1692, the first allegations of witchcraft surfaced at Salem, and in June, Cotton Mather, who had already published accounts of witchcraft, wrote the report of a group of ministers who, though counseling caution, endorsed the proceedings of the court charged with trying the accused. By the time royal governor William Phips ordered a suspension of the trials in October, 19 men and women had been convicted and hanged, and one man pressed to death under heavy stones for refusing to enter a plea. "An Hortatory and Necessary Address" is a special fast-day sermon preached amid the controversy, and published in *Wonders of the Invisible World* (1693), Mather's account of the proceedings. Although Mather continued to preach and write about witchcraft and devils, he confessed in a diary entry of January 15, 1697, his fear that God would punish him "for my not appearing with *Vigor* enough to stop the proceedings of the Judges, when the Inextricable Storm from the *Invisible World* assaulted the Country."

Cotton Mather published at least 445 works; chief among these was the *Magnalia Christi Americana* (1702), a massive history and biographical compendium of Puritan New England. In 1713 he was elected to the Royal Society of London; among his many scientific works are a medical treatise, *The Angel of Bethesda* (1722), and *The Christian Philosopher: A Collection of the Best Discoveries in Nature, with Religious Improvements* (1721). He also wrote poetry and literary criticism, kept a diary, and in 1710 published a popular book on ethics called *Bonifacius: Essays upon the Good*, which influenced Benjamin Franklin. "A Man of Reason" was preached in the previous year (1709) and first published in 1718.

SOLOMON STODDARD (1643–1729) Born in 1643, the son of "the ancientest shop-keeper" in Boston, Solomon Stoddard graduated from Harvard in 1662. After a two-year sojourn in Barbados, he assumed the pulpit in Northampton on the western frontier of Massachusetts, where he remained from 1669 until his death.

Stoddard became the most prominent challenger to the orthodoxy of Increase and Cotton Mather. In 1677 he moved beyond the still-controversial Half-Way Covenant and offered full communion to all members of the church—an innovation that Stoddard debated with Increase Mather at the Synod of 1679. By 1690 he was offering communion to all who sought it and were not scandalous in behavior, and in *The Doctrine of the Instituted Churches* (1700) Stoddard challenged the fundamental premise of New England Congregationalism: the notion that a church was limited to believers covenanting together and certifying one another's conversion. Stoddard promoted his views in numerous works, especially *A Guide to Christ* (1714), *A Treatise Concerning Conversion* (1719), and *The Defects of Preachers Reproved* (1724).

New Englanders heard sermons not only on Sundays and special occasions, but also on Thursdays, which were called "lecture days." Stoddard preached every Sunday and lecture day, until the age of 86, without notes. He wrote his sermons in such a minute hand that 150 of them are contained in a single small notebook. He also customarily gave an annual lecture in Boston, where "The Tryal of Assurance" was preached on July 7, 1698.

BENJAMIN COLMAN (1673–1747) Upon receiving his degree from Harvard in 1692, Benjamin Colman preached briefly in Medford and then returned for an M.A. He then preached in England, including two years in Bath, and courted the poet Elizabeth Singer (later Rowe) before returning to Boston in 1699. There, he established the Brattle-Street Church on relatively inclusive principles—including a willingness to extend communion to Anglicans—that were strongly criticized by Increase and Cotton Mather. Colman was distinguished by his interest in polite letters, which he promoted in such sermons as *The Government and Improvement of Mirth* (1707) and *God Deals with Us as Rational Creatures* (1723). Colman himself wrote and published poetry, introducing the Augustan style in New England, and admired Pope; his eldest daughter, Jane Turell, also became known as a poet before her early death. He served as a trustee of Harvard, publicized the revivals of Jonathan Edwards, and was the first Boston pastor to open his pulpit to George Whitefield.

"The Case of Satan's Fiery Darts" was first preached in May 1711, in Boston, and repeated in 1743; it was published in 1744. The title was proverbial; when Cotton Mather wrote that his father in early years suffered "Temptations unto Atheism," he added that the thoughts "were shot at him as "Fiery Darts from the Wicked One.""

CHARLES CHAUNCY (1705–1787) Chauncy was born in Boston in 1705, the great-grandson of Charles Chauncy, the second president of Harvard, where the younger Chauncy took his bachelor's degree in 1721 and an M.A. in 1724. In 1727 he became minister at the First

Church in Boston, remaining there until his death. New England's most prominent challenger to Calvinist orthodoxy, he attacked George Whitefield's revivals in *Enthusiasm Described* (1742), and criticized Jonathan Edwards in the lengthy *Seasonable Thoughts on the State of Religion in New England* (1743). A vocal foe of the Church of England, in the 1760s and 1770s he became a leading Whig preacher. In his later years, especially in the anonymously published work *The Mystery Hid from Ages, or The Salvation of All Men* (1784), he repudiated such Calvinist doctrines as predestination and damnation and extolled the idea of a benevolent deity.

Funeral sermons were often published if the deceased belonged to a prominent family. Sarah Byfield was the wife of Nathanael Byfield (1653–1733), a Boston merchant who helped found Bristol, Rhode Island, and had served as a judge and as the speaker of the Rhode Island house of representatives.

MATHER BYLES (1707–1788)   Byles was a year old when his father died; his education was directed by his uncle, Cotton Mather, and his grandfather, Increase. He received a bachelor's degree from Harvard in 1725, and wrote his master's thesis in 1728 on the proposition that "polite literature is an ornament to a theologian." By this time he had published numerous poems and essays in Boston newspapers, including *Proteus Echo*, an essay serial in imitation of *The Spectator* that ran in the *New England Weekly Journal* in 1727–28. In 1733 he became minister at the Hollis Street Church, and in the same year married the niece of Governor Jonathan Belcher.

Byles corresponded with Isaac Watts and Alexander Pope, and published his *Poems on Several Occasions* in 1744. A celebrated wit in Boston, he was the center of a literary coterie that included the poet Joseph Green, who parodied him in the *London Magazine* in 1733. His sermons were highly regarded, and two were reprinted by Benjamin Franklin in his *General Magazine* in 1741. He opposed the Calvinist revivalism of the Great Awakening, and was in turn attacked by its "New Light" preachers. Byles was a Loyalist during the Revolution. "Which is better," he asked the young Nathanael Emmons, "to be ruled by one tyrant three thousand miles away, or by three thousand tyrants not a mile away?" When the British evacuated Boston in 1776, Byles was found guilty of being "an enemy to the United States" for having entertained British officials in his home and was placed under house arrest for two years. Supported by friends, he lived quietly in Boston until his death.

JONATHAN EDWARDS (1703–1758)   Born in East Windsor, Connecticut, Edwards was the son, grandson, and great-grandson of ministers. In 1716 he entered Yale College, where he read Locke and Newton before graduating in 1720. He continued his studies at Yale for two years before serving in the pulpit of a Presbyterian church in New York City from 1722 until 1723, when he returned to New Haven and received his M.A. degree. Edwards served as a tutor at Yale from 1724 until 1726, then went to Northampton, Massachusetts, where he was ordained as a minister in the Congregational church of his grandfather Solomon Stoddard. In July 1727 he married Sarah Pierpont, the daughter of a New Haven minister, and in 1729 he became the sole minister of the Northampton church after Stoddard's death.

"A Divine and Supernatural Light" was preached in Northampton and published in 1734, the year in which Edwards' church became the center of a religious revival that spread through the Connecticut Valley. Edwards described the conversions among his congregation in his *Faithful Narrative of the Surprising Work of God* (1737), and in a series of sermons delivered in 1739 (posthumously printed as *A History of the Work of Redemption* in 1774). The revivals intensified in 1740 with the first American visit of the English Anglican evangelist George Whitefield and eventually extended throughout the 13 colonies, becoming known as the "Great Awakening." "Sinners in the Hands of an Angry God" was preached during this period at Enfield, Connecticut, on July 8, 1741; an eyewitness recorded that there was "such a breathing of distress and weeping" in the assembly that Edwards had to pause and ask for silence. Edwards continued to defend the revivals against opponents such as Charles Chauncy, who criticized their unrestrained emotionalism; in *Some Thoughts Concerning the present Revival of Religion in New-England* (1742) he wrote, "Our people do not so much need to have their heads stored, as to have their hearts touched; and they stand in the greatest need of that sort of preaching that has the greatest tendency to do this." In his *Treatise Concerning Religious Affections* (1746), he argued that emotion could be a valuable part of conversion and evidence of salvation.

In 1744 Edwards encountered resistance within his congregation to his assertion of ministerial authority when he publicly rebuked and disciplined a group of boys who reportedly were reading sexually explicit books on midwifery. He began repealing the reforms of his grandfather concerning church membership, and in 1748 aroused controversy when he refused to admit members to communion without "a profession of the things wherein godliness consists." In June 1750 a council of ministers from nine churches recommended that he be dismissed, and after a bitter dispute, the congregation agreed. Edwards preached his "Farewel-Sermon" on July 1, 1750, and published it the following year.

In 1751 he became a missionary to the Indians in the frontier town of Stockbridge, Massachusetts, where he composed a series of major theological treatises. *Freedom of the Will*, his defense of Calvinist doctrines of predestination and the absolute sovereignty of God against Arminian concepts of free will, was published in 1754; *The Great Christian Doctrine of Original Sin* (1758) and *The Nature of True Virtue* (1765) appeared posthumously. In 1757 Edwards was offered the presidency of the College of New Jersey (now Princeton), but three months after assuming the position he died of a smallpox inoculation.

SAMUEL JOHNSON (1696–1772) Born in Guilford, Connecticut, Johnson was educated at the Collegiate School (later Yale College) and served as a tutor at Yale, where he read Locke, Newton, and other writers of the "New Learning." Ordained as minister of the Congregational church in West Haven in 1720, Johnson created a sensation at the Yale commencement of 1722 when, along with several tutors at the college, he publicly adhered to the Anglican church. Later that year Johnson sailed to England, where he was ordained a priest in the Church of England. He returned in 1723 and founded the first Anglican congregation in Connecticut at Stratford. Johnson became a correspondent of Bishop George Berkeley and a leading American exponent of Berkeleyan idealism. "A Sermon Concerning the Intellectual World" was first preached during Advent in 1747; Johnson repeated it several times over the following years. From 1754 to 1763, he served as the first president of King's College (later Columbia) in New York, then returned to Stratford, where he remained until his death.

JONATHAN MAYHEW (1720–1766) Mayhew was born on Martha's Vineyard, Massachusetts, the son of Experience Mayhew, the island's minister and missionary to its Indian population. He was sent in 1740 to Harvard, where his reading included Puritan literature, the sermons of the late 17th-century Archbishop of Canterbury John Tillotson, and Pascal's *Pensées*. Mayhew graduated in 1744, and was ordained in 1747 at the West Church in Boston. In 1749 he published *Seven Sermons*, in which he adopted an Arminian view of salvation and a rationalistic religion, declaring Christianity to be "principally an institution of life and manners." *Seven Sermons* was warmly praised by Benjamin Hoadly, Bishop of Winchester, and attracted favorable attention in England and Scotland; in 1750 Mayhew received an honorary doctorate from Aberdeen University.

In January 1750 Mayhew created a furor in Boston with "A Discourse Concerning Unlimited Submission and Non-Resistance to the

Higher Powers." Before the printed text of the sermon reached book-sellers, Mayhew was attacked by a Boston newspaper as a "wrangling preacher" who had "belched out a flood of obloquy upon the pious memory of King Charles the first." For the next six months, the "Discourse" was the subject of intense public controversy. According to John Adams, it was "read by everybody, celebrated by friends, and abused by enemies," and continued to be circulated and reprinted in the colonies in the years preceding the Revolution.

Mayhew engaged in other controversies, criticizing both the New England orthodoxy and the Great Awakening revivalists. He defended the principle of free will in *Two Sermons on the Nature, Extent and Perfection of Divine Goodness* (1763) and was an outspoken opponent of the American activities of the Church of England's Society for the Propagation of the Gospel in Foreign Parts. In 1765 he spoke against the Stamp Act, and published an influential Thanksgiving sermon, "The Snare Broken," following its repeal in 1766.

SAMUEL DAVIES (1723–1761)   Born to a Welsh family in Delaware, Davies spent most of his career in Virginia. He was educated in Pennsylvania, at the academy of Samuel Blair, a "New Light" revivalist, and ordained in the Presbyterian ministry as an evangelist in Hanover County, Virginia. In 1753 he went to England along with the "New Light" Presbyterian evangelist Gilbert Tennent to raise funds for the College of New Jersey (now Princeton) and to secure legal rights for Dissenters in Virginia. Davies returned to Virginia in 1755 and wrote *The Crisis* (1757) and *The Curse of Cowardice* (1758) to encourage colonists to serve in the French and Indian War. In 1758 he succeeded Jonathan Edwards as president of the College of New Jersey and held the position until his death. The posthumous *Sermons on the most Useful and Important Subjects*, a three-volume edition edited by the English preacher Thomas Gibbons, went through many editions in the late 18th century; the sermon printed here was included in that collection. Davies was also a poet and a hymn writer, publishing many works in the *Virginia Gazette* and a collection, *Miscellaneous Poems*, in 1752. His hymn "Lord I am Thine, Entirely Thine" was included in many Methodist and Baptist hymnals.

SAMUEL FINLEY (1715–1766)   Born in Ireland, Finley immigrated to Philadelphia in 1734, and spent two years as an itinerant preacher in West Jersey before his ordination as a Presbyterian minister in 1742. Often at odds with orthodox ministers and authorities, he was arrested and expelled from New Haven, Connecticut, when he tried to preach to a Separatist church there in 1743. Finley settled as a pastor in Nottingham, Pennsylvania, in 1744 and remained there for 17 years. He wrote a Latin grammar, ran an academy for evangelical ministers, and in 1761 succeeded Samuel Davies as president of the College of New Jersey. In 1763 he received an honorary doctorate from the University of Glasgow.

Finley first gained widespread attention with his 1741 sermon "Christ Triumphing, and Satan Raging," which endorsed the efficacy of emotional preaching in bringing about conversion, and later published attacks on the doctrines of the Moravians in 1743, the Baptists in 1746 and 1748, and the Quakers in 1757. "The Madness of Mankind" was preached in Philadelphia in June 1754.

A SERMON IN PRAISE OF SWEARING The author of this anonymously published sermon, which appears to have been composed for the press rather than the pulpit, is not known.

SAMUEL COOKE (1709–1783) Born in Hadley, Massachusetts, Cooke graduated from Harvard in 1735 and took a pulpit in Cambridge in 1739. An opponent of George Whitefield, he expressed his sympathies for the natural rights of men, natural religion, and universal salvation in a series of published sermons. On May 30, 1770, Cooke gave the annual election sermon in Massachusetts, less than three months after the "Boston Massacre" of March 5, when British regulars fired into a crowd and killed five persons. Thomas Hutchinson, the royal governor, sat in the audience and is indirectly addressed as "His Honor" in the sermon.

As the Revolution approached Cooke became more outspoken in his opposition to British rule, and in April 1775 British troops looted his house during their retreat from Concord, stealing his wig and gown. Later in the war Cooke's parsonage became a hospital where he helped care for the wounded. His only subsequent publication was *The Violent Destroyed* (1777), a sermon commemorating those killed at Lexington in 1775 that identified the British with the Amalekites who waged war on Israel and called for armed resistance by the Americans.

NATHANAEL EMMONS (1745–1840) The youngest of 12 children, Emmons was born in East Haddam, Connecticut, received his degree from Yale in 1767, and served as an itinerant preacher in New York and New Hampshire before becoming pastor in 1773 of the Congregational church in Wrentham, Massachusetts (this part of the town was later renamed Franklin). He remained there until his retirement in 1827 at the age of 82. Throughout his career, Emmons was a faithful Calvinist, a leading voice in the "New Divinity" in the tradition of Jonathan Edwards, and a highly regarded preacher who

once declared his rule for speaking from the pulpit: "Have something to say; say it." He became a staunch Federalist, preaching a
fast-day sermon in 1801 on the election of Thomas Jefferson in which
he compared the new president to Jeroboam, the apostate king
"who made Israel sin."

Emmons first preached "The Dignity of Man" in 1787, delivered it
again in 1790 and 1796, and had it reprinted in 1798.

DEVEREUX JARRATT (1733–1801)   Born to a poor family in Virginia,
Jarratt was orphaned by the age of 13 and became a field worker. At
the age of 19, he was "called from the ax to the quill" when he was
asked to be a schoolteacher in Albemarle County; there, he was converted to the "New Light" faith of the local plantation mistress.
With the patronage of neighboring gentry, he went back to school
to learn Latin and Greek, and then sailed to England to be ordained
in the Church of England. In 1763 he returned to become the rector
at Bath Parish in Virginia. Jarratt often preached extemporaneously,
drawing large crowds on his many evangelical tours through Virginia
and North Carolina between 1763 and 1772. He emphasized the
emotional life of conversion, and often wrote of the necessity of
being "born again." Jarratt corresponded with John Wesley and
upon his death was eulogized by the Methodist Francis Asbury.

"The Nature of Love to Christ" was published in 1792 and was
followed by a three-volume collection, *Sermons on Various and Important Subjects*, in 1793–94. *The Life of the Reverend Devereux Jarratt*, an autobiography in the form of letters to a friend, was
published posthumously in 1806.

LEMUEL HAYNES (1753–1833)   Haynes was born in West Hartford,
Connecticut, the son of a white mother who disowned him and a
black father he never knew. At the age of five months he was inden-
tured to a pious family in Granville, Massachusetts, and began
preaching in his teens. When his indenture ended in 1774, he enlisted
in the Massachusetts militia and served in the siege of Boston and at
Fort Ticonderoga. Haynes began studying Latin and Greek in 1779
while he was teaching school; in 1783 he married Elizabeth Babbitt,
a white schoolteacher, with whom he would have ten children. He
was ordained a Congregationalist minister in 1785 and served white
congregations in Connecticut before becoming pastor in Rutland,
Vermont, in 1788. Haynes criticized slavery in his Fourth of July sermon "The Nature and Importance of True Republicanism" (1801)
and was eventually forced to leave Rutland in 1818 because of political controversies arising from his Federalist views. He then served as

a minister in Manchester, Vermont, from 1818 until 1822, when he moved to Granville, New York.

Strongly influenced by Jonathan Edwards, Haynes was a defender of Calvinist orthodoxy. He first preached "Universal Salvation" in 1805 in response to the Universalist leader Hosea Ballou (1771–1852), who had been preaching in New England since 1796 that the punishment of souls after death was only temporary, and that all souls would eventually be with God. "Universal Salvation" achieved wide recognition when it was published in 1806 and continued to be printed until the Civil War. Haynes also wrote "Mystery Developed" (1820), a popular sermon criticizing prison conditions and examining a case in which two men were almost hanged for a murder that had never been committed.

ABSALOM JONES (1746–1818) Born a slave in Sussex, Delaware, Jones taught himself to read, and was sent to Philadelphia at age 16 to work in his master's shop. In 1770 he married a fellow slave, whose freedom he was able to buy with help from his father-in-law and local Quakers; he bought his own freedom in 1784. Jones and his friend Richard Allen became lay preachers at St. George's Methodist Episcopal Church in 1786 and rapidly increased black attendance at services; when the church imposed segregated seating in November of that year, they left the congregation. Jones and Allen became leaders of the Philadelphia black community, forming the first Free African Society, a nondenominational mutual aid organization, in 1787 and the African Church in Philadelphia in 1791; they also wrote the *Narrative of the Proceedings of the Black People, During the Late Awful Calamity in Philadelphia* after the 1793 yellow fever epidemic. In 1794 Jones agreed to bring the African Church into the Episcopal Diocese of Pennsylvania, while Allen and other members joined the Methodists. Jones was ordained in 1804 as the first African-American Episcopalian priest.

In February 1807 Congress passed a law prohibiting the importation of slaves into the United States after January 1, 1808, the earliest date permitted under article I, section 9 of the Constitution (the law did not affect the internal slave trade among the states). Jones continued to oppose slavery, and in 1817 he and Allen helped to organize a large convention of African Americans to denounce the newly formed American Colonization Society, which sought to send freed slaves back to Africa.

JOHN COMLY (1774–1850) Born on a farm in Byberry, Pennsylvania, Comly attended the local Friends School and then a boarding school run by a Baptist minister, where he learned Latin and Greek. He taught at the Byberry and Westtown Friends Schools in Pennsylvania before founding the Pleasant Hill Boarding School for girls in 1804 with his wife, Rebecca. Comly was acknowledged by the Friends as a minister in 1813. He gave up teaching in 1815 to devote himself to farming and to traveling in his ministry in New England, New York, and the South. A quietist who believed in the indwelling Christ and distrusted the doctrines of vicarious atonement and original sin, Comly was influenced by John Woolman, whose writings he edited, and Elias Hicks. After the separation in 1827 between the "Hicksite" and "Orthodox" factions of the Society of Friends, Comly and his wife became members of Hicksite meetings. His writings include *English Grammar Made Easy to the Teacher and Pupil* (1803), *Comlys Spelling and Reading Book* (1842), and the posthumously published *Journal of the Life and Religious Labors of John Comly* (1853). The sermon included here was extemporized during a worship meeting.

WILLIAM ELLERY CHANNING (1780–1842) Born in Newport, Rhode Island, Channing graduated from Harvard in 1798, after which he spent a year and a half as tutor to the family of David Meade Randolph in Richmond, Virginia. He returned to Newport, studied theology, and in 1802 began serving as a proctor at Harvard College. In 1803 he was ordained as minister of the Federal Street Congregational Church in Boston, where he continued to serve until his death.

Channing began taking increasingly liberal positions in his sermons, abandoning the Calvinist insistence on the depravity of man, the absoluteness of divine will, and eternal damnation. He made a declaration of his principles in the sermon "Unitarian Christianity," preached in 1819, in which he proclaimed a Christianity that would promote the progressive improvement of mankind. Channing's fullest assault on Congregationalist orthodoxy was the 1820 essay "The Moral Argument against Calvinism": "Calvinism owes its perpetuity to the influence of fear in palsying the moral nature." A conference of liberal ministers organized by Channing in 1820 resulted in the founding in May 1825 of the American Unitarian Association.

Health problems caused Channing to turn over many of his pulpit duties to an associate in 1822; thereafter he devoted much of his energy to writing. An opponent of the War of 1812, Channing was a founder of the Massachusetts Peace Society, wrote an antimilitarist essay on Napoleon, and delivered a pacifist lecture on war in 1838. Strongly opposed to slavery since his stay in Virginia, he wrote *Slavery* (1835), *The Abolitionist* (1836), and *The Duty of the Free States* (1842). An important influence on Emerson and other Transcendentalist writers, Channing also wrote literary criticism, including an essay on Milton and *Remarks on National Literature* (1830).

"Likeness to God" was preached in 1828 at the ordination of F. A. Farley in Providence, Rhode Island. Orestes Brownson, who became a noted reformer, is said to have converted to Unitarianism upon hearing a friend read it aloud.

RALPH WALDO EMERSON (1803–1882) The son of William Emerson, minister of the First Church in Boston, Emerson graduated from Harvard in 1821 and worked as a schoolteacher. He resolved to become a minister, but confessed to his journal in 1824 that he was torn between "a passionate love for the strains of eloquence," which he attributed to his father and grandfather (also a minister), and his unfittedness for the pastoral role: "What is called a warm heart, I have not." Emerson was licensed to preach as a Unitarian minister in 1826 and was ordained as pastor of the Second Church of Boston in March 1829, serving under Henry Ware, Jr.

In June 1832, noting in his journal that "in an altered age, we worship in the dead forms of our forefathers," Emerson told a church committee of his concern that the Lord's Supper had become an empty ritual and asked them to consider alternatives closer to its purpose and spirit; they responded that they wanted the ritual maintained. In July, Emerson went to the mountains of New Hampshire. "What is the message that is given me to communicate next Sunday?" he asked in his journal, replying, "Religion in the mind is not credulity & in the practice is not form. It is a life." He fell ill upon his return to Boston, but finally preached the sermon included here to a crowded assembly on September 9, 1832, and submitted his resignation two days later. The church accepted his resignation in October and in December Emerson embarked on a long tour of Europe.

After his return to Boston he continued to preach as an itinerant and became a popular lecturer. Emerson settled in Concord in 1834, published *Nature* in 1836, delivered "The American Scholar" at Harvard in 1837, and in July of 1838 created a sensation with his address to the Harvard Divinity School, which extended many of the themes of his 1832 sermon on the Lord's Supper. His later writings include *Essays* (1841); *Essays: Second Series* (1844); *Poems* (1847); *Nature; Addresses, and Lectures* (1849); *Representative Men* (1850), *English Traits* (1856); *The Conduct of Life* (1860); *Society and Solitude* (1870), and *Selected Poems* (1876).

JOSEPH SMITH (1805–1844)   Born in Vermont, Smith settled with his family in 1816 on a farm near Palmyra, New York, in a region known as "the burned-over district" because of its frequent religious revivals. By his own account, Smith experienced the first of a series of prophetic visions in the spring of 1820, and on September 21, 1823, he received a vision of the Angel Moroni, who told him of a set of gold plates bearing ancient scripture. In 1827 he reported that a new vision had allowed him to retrieve the plates, along with an instrument that could be used to translate them. Smith published *The Book of Mormon* in 1830 and founded the Church of Christ (later the Church of Jesus Christ of Latter-day Saints) the same year. He moved with his followers in 1831 to Ohio, where his revelations were collected in 1833 as *A Book of Commandments for the Government of the Church of Christ* and expanded in 1835 as *The Doctrine and Covenants of the Church of the Latter-Day Saints.* Legal charges arising from a bank failure caused Smith to flee in 1838 to Missouri, where the Mormons encountered official hostility and mob violence; Smith narrowly escaped being summarily shot by Missouri militia and was imprisoned for several months on charges of treason against the state. In 1839 he fled to Illinois, where he founded the Mormon settlement of Nauvoo and received a revelation in 1843 sanctioning the practice of polygamy.

    The sermon included here was occasioned by the death of King Follett, a Mormon who died accidentally while digging a well in March 1844. It was given at a Church conference in April 1844 and recorded by three Church scribes and a member of the Quorum of the Twelve Apostles. Shortly afterward a schism occurred among the Mormons. On June 7 a group of dissenters printed a newspaper, the *Nauvoo Expositor,* in which they denounced "the vicious principles" of Joseph Smith, including polygamy and the doctrine that God is an "exalted man," which the dissenters denounced as "blasphemy." Smith ordered the press destroyed and was subsequently jailed in Carthage, Illinois, where an anti-Mormon mob of nearly 200 persons murdered him and his brother Hyrum on June 27.

THEODORE PARKER (1810–1860)   Born in Lexington, Massachusetts, Parker was the youngest of 11 children. He passed the entrance examination to Harvard, but was too poor to attend regular classes. By 1834 he had earned enough money to enter the Divinity School; the journal he kept there shows familiarity with 20 languages. In 1836 he began translating De Wette's *Einleitung in das Alte Testament,* a key work in the German "higher criticism" that used philological methods to treat the Bible as a historical text. Parker was ordained pastor at West Roxbury in 1837. After hearing Emerson's address to the Divinity School the following year, he began questioning miracles and revelation. His ordination sermon, "A Discourse of the Transient and Permanent in Christianity," created a sensation in 1841 by demanding that "we worship, as Jesus did, with no mediator, with nothing between us and the father of all." Parker was denounced by orthodox Congregationalists and even by liberal Unitarians, and after spending a year in Europe in 1843–44, he found that many Boston ministers refused to let their congregations hear him preach. A group of supporters then created the Twenty-Eighth Congregational Society, which met at the Boston Melodeon, where Parker drew large audiences; in 1852 the new church moved to the larger Music Hall. Parker commonly preached and lectured on war, temperance, slavery, education, prisons, divorce, and labor; he believed that true religion would be expressed in the progress of justice and the perfection of society. He became a radical antislavery leader and was indicted for his role in the attempted rescue of Anthony Burns, a fugitive slave, from the Boston federal courthouse in 1854 (the charges were later dismissed).

"A Sermon of War" was preached on June 7, 1846, during the first weeks of the Mexican War. After Texas joined the Union on December 29, 1845, President James Polk ordered U.S. troops to advance into the disputed border region between the Nueces and Rio Grande rivers. When news of a skirmish fought north of the Rio Grande on April 25, 1846, reached Washington, Polk sent a war message to Congress, which then declared on May 12 that "a state of war" existed between the U.S. and Mexico. In the spring of 1846 Polk also obtained authorization from Congress to terminate the joint Anglo-American occupation of Oregon established in 1818, but the northwestern border dispute was peaceably resolved by a treaty signed on June 18, 1846.

Parker developed tuberculosis in 1857 and in 1859 a hemorrhage ended his public career. He died in Florence, Italy, in 1860, and was buried in the Protestant cemetery there.

LUCRETIA COFFIN MOTT (1793–1880)   Born on Nantucket Island, Massachusetts, Coffin was educated in Boston. In 1813 she married James Mott, a schoolteacher; they had six children. Around 1818 she began speaking frequently in Quaker meetings. She traveled widely in the 1820s giving lectures on religion and social reform, influenced by her reading of William Ellery Channing. When the Quaker movement divided in the Great Separation of 1827, she became a member of the "Hicksite" wing that emphasized the "inner light." After meeting William Lloyd Garrison, she helped found the American Anti-Slavery Society in 1833, and in the 1850s she and her husband made their home a station on the Underground Railroad for fugitive slaves. In 1848 Mott joined Elizabeth Cady Stanton in organizing the Seneca Falls convention that founded the woman's rights movement.

Mott's sermons were extemporaneous, and all that survive were taken down stenographically. Henry Thoreau described her speaking in 1843: "At length, after a long silence, waiting for the spirit, Mrs. Mott rose, took off her bonnet, and began to utter very deliberately what the spirit suggested. Her self-possession was something to say, if all else failed—but it did not. Her subject was the abuse of the Bible—and thence she straightway digressed to slavery and the degradation of woman."

BROTHER CARPER (d. ca. 1850)   Carper is known through the work of the Methodist missionary James V. Watson, who wrote in *Tales and Takings, Sketches and Incidents, from the Itinerant and Editorial Budget of Rev. J. V. Watson, editor of the Northwestern Christian Advocate* (1856) that while traveling in northwestern Missouri, he was invited to a camp meeting held by Free-Will Baptists to hear "a mighty great preacher." Watson described Carper as "a light-colored mulatto, age about fifty, a little corpulent . . . he read with hesitancy and inaccuracy; seeming to depend less upon the text to guide him, than his memory" and wrote that he preached with "the genius of an Apollos and the force of an apostle."

After the sermon, Watson interviewed Carper, who said that he was born in Kentucky to a slave mother; only after the death of his master did Carper learn that the master was his father. Taken to Tennessee, he joined the Baptist church and began preaching to both black and white audiences. After he purchased his freedom, Carper followed his still-enslaved wife and children west to the headwaters of the Arkansas in Kansas, where his family and their master died in a cholera outbreak. Carper remained in the West until his death a few years after Watson heard him.

The text of the sermon, one of two printed by Watson, is his reconstruction from memory "of some its most eloquent passages." Watson wrote: "Of the length of the sermon, I have no recollection. Of the sermon itself I have the most distinct recollection."

HENRY WARD BEECHER (1813–1887)   Born in Litchfield, Connecticut, Beecher was the son of Lyman Beecher and the brother of Catharine Beecher and Harriet Beecher Stowe. His father was a leading Congregationalist preacher who opposed the liberal Christianity of William Ellery Channing and advocated temperance and other moral reforms. Beecher graduated from Amherst College in 1834, attended Lane Theological Seminary in Cincinnati, then headed by his father, and moved to Indianapolis in 1839, where he served as minister to the Second Presbyterian Church.

In 1847 he accepted the pulpit of the Plymouth Church (Congregational) in Brooklyn, where he became one of the most popular preachers in America. After a special semi-circular auditorium was built for him in 1849, he attracted crowds averaging 2,500 people a week, and special Sunday ferries brought tourists across the river from Manhattan to hear him. He preached extemporaneously, with stenographers recording most of his sermons, and wrote extensively, edited the *Christian Union* from 1870 to 1881, and became a nationally known advocate for reform issues. Beecher was noted for adapting the Calvinism of his father to a theology of a benevolent God, a personal and loving Jesus, and a religion of sentiment.

In 1870 Theodore Tilton, a former protegé, accused Beecher of having an affair with his wife, and in August 1874 sued him for adultery, resulting in a sensational trial that ended in a hung jury. Beecher's church absolved him, but the scandal shadowed his reputation until his death. Among his many books are *Norwood*, a novel, a biography of Christ, and the *Yale Lectures on Preaching* (1872–74).

"Peace, Be Still" was preached on a national fast-day, January 4, 1861, two weeks after the secession of South Carolina and two months before the inauguration of Abraham Lincoln. It appeared in *Fast-Day Sermons* (1861), which collected preaching from both northern and southern ministers, including the proslavery James Thornwell, author of *The Rights and Duties of Masters* (1850).

DAVID EINHORN (1809–1879) A native of Bavaria, Einhorn attended universities in Erlangen, Würzburg, and Munich, but his religious views were so radical that for ten years he was unable to find an appointment as a rabbi. When he did so in 1842, he had frequent clashes with his orthodox congregation. In 1851 he moved to Hungary, but within two months was silenced by the government. His theological treatise, *Das Prinzip des Mosaismus und dessen Verhaeltnis zum Heidenthum und Rabbinischen Judenthum* was published in 1854. Einhorn immigrated in 1855 to the United States, where he became a leader of the Reform movement and served as the rabbi of the Har Sinai Synagogue in Baltimore. Following an anti-Union riot in Baltimore in April 1861, Einhorn was forced to flee the city because of his antislavery preaching. He was elected rabbi of Keneseth Israel Congregation in Philadelphia, where "War with Amalek!" was preached in March 1864. In 1866 he moved to New York, where he served until 1879. Like many Reform rabbis in 19th-century America, Einhorn often preached and wrote in German. A collection of his sermons was posthumously published in 1880.

DWIGHT LYMAN MOODY (1837–1899)   Born in Massachusetts, Moody moved to Boston at age 17 to work in his uncle's shoe store. In 1856 he converted from Unitarianism to Congregationalism; later that year, he moved to Chicago, where he worked as a shoe sales-man. He formed a church school in a city slum in 1858 and in 1860 became an evangelist. Moody toured Britain and Ireland from 1873 until 1875, then made Northfield, Massachusetts, the headquarters for his organization, which used business and sales methods to arrange and promote evangelical tours designed to draw mass, non-denominational audiences throughout the U.S. He preached in an informal, anecdotal style, emphasizing a personal religion that con-trasted with the Social Gospel of the period. "On Being Born Again" dates from his tours of the late 1870s. Although he was never or-dained, Moody did involve local clergymen in his revivals. He pro-moted the rapid expansion of the YMCA and founded several schools, including the Chicago Bible Institute (now Moody Bible Institute) in 1889. Moody often toured with the composer Ira D. Sankey and collaborated with him on the popular hymn collections *Sacred Songs and Solos* (1873) and *Gospel Hymns* (1875).

OCTAVIUS BROOKS FROTHINGHAM (1822–1895)   Born in Boston, Frothingham graduated from Harvard in 1843, and after studying at the Divinity School was ordained in the North Church of Salem. His antislavery advocacy led to conflict with his church, and after eight years he moved to a Unitarian congregation in Jersey City. His pop-ularity led his followers to organize a church in New York City, later the Independent Liberal Church, specifically for him. Frothingham eventually left the Unitarian ministry and in 1867 returned to Boston, where he was a founder of the Free Religious Association. He retired from the pulpit in 1879 and lived in Boston until his death. His books include *The Religion of Humanity* (1872), a biogra-phy of Theodore Parker (1874), *Transcendentalism in New England* (1876), studies of Gerrit Smith (1877), George Ripley (1882), and William Henry Channing (1886), several collections of sermons, and an autobiography, *Recollections and Impressions* (1891). "The Dogma of Hell" appeared in his 1878 collection *The Rising and the Setting Faith*.

THOMAS DE WITT TALMAGE (1832–1902)   Born in New Jersey, Tal-mage attended the University of the City of New York and the New Brunswick Theological Seminary. He was ordained in the Dutch Re-formed Church in 1856 and held pulpits in Belleville, New Jersey, 1856–59; Syracuse, New York, 1859–62; and Philadelphia, 1862–69. In

1869 he was called to the Central Presbyterian Church in Brooklyn, N.Y., a post he retained until 1894, when he moved to the First Presbyterian Church in Washington, D.C.

Talmage's preaching style—gesticulatory and vivid, by turns sentimental, denunciatory, anecdotal, and humorous—drew both criticism and crowds. His Brooklyn church built him a large hall called the Tabernacle, with a semi-circular auditorium modeled on Henry Ward Beecher's. When this building burned in 1872, it was replaced with the largest church in America, holding 5,000 seats; the new building burned in 1889, its successor in 1894. Talmage's sermons were at one time carried in 3,500 newspapers weekly, and were collected in several volumes, including *The Abominations of Modern Society* (1872) and *Social Dynamite* (1887); he frequently attacked alcohol and Mormonism in his preaching. In 1879, the Brooklyn Presbytery examined him on charges of falsehood and "improper methods of preaching, which bring religion into contempt," but after a close vote, he was cleared.

"The Ministry of Tears" was delivered in London as the first sermon in his tour of England in 1879. So great was the crush of people in the church that Talmage left afterwards through the basement and the back door. As he stepped into his carriage, the crowd lifted it off the ground until police arrived to clear the way.

SAMUEL PORTER JONES (1847–1906) Born in Alabama, Jones moved with his family in 1856 to Georgia, where he began to drink heavily after his mother died. During the Civil War he became separated from his family while fleeing the Union army and moved in succession to Kentucky, Texas, and Alabama before he returned to Georgia. Promising his dying father that he would reform and give up drinking, he became an itinerant Methodist preacher in 1872. Jones often spoke to crowds of 10,000 or more on his tours. He was an ardent prohibitionist, and advocated a broad political program rooted in moral reform: "When you allow Sabbath-breaking, you let in a wedge that will open the way for communism and anarchy." He relished public dispute, and once described himself as "a sort of mixture between a mule and a billy goat" that can "kick with one end and butt with the other." After 1900 he confined his activities to the South; he died in Georgia.

The sermon included here was preached August 2, 1885, at a camp meeting near Cincinnati. Jones delivered it from "the top of an old piano box," to a crowd estimated at 12,000. It was printed in *Sermons Wise and Witty*, published in 1885 by the Cheap Publishing House.

PHILLIPS BROOKS (1835–1893)   A descendant of John Cotton and a cousin of Henry Adams, Brooks became an Episcopalian at age four when his family joined the church. He graduated from Harvard in 1855, taught at the Boston Latin School for six months, and then entered the Virginia Theological Seminary. He began his ministry in Philadelphia, becoming rector of Holy Trinity parish in 1862. His sermon "The Character, Life and Death of Mr. Lincoln," preached in 1865 as the President's body lay in state in Independence Hall, brought him to national attention. While traveling in Palestine in 1868, Brooks wrote the words of "O Little Town of Bethlehem." He moved to Boston in 1869 to become rector of Trinity Church; when fire destroyed the church in 1872, he built a new structure, designed by H. H. Richardson, in Copley Square. Brooks preached to Queen Victoria at Windsor Castle during a tour of England in 1880, and in 1891 he was chosen to become the Bishop of Boston, an office he filled until his death. Ten thousand people attended his funeral.

Brooks was a rapid speaker; his delivery was calculated by stenographers at 213 words a minute. James Bryce, author of *The American Commonwealth*, ranked him as the best of all preachers, writing, "He spoke to his audience as a man might speak to a friend." Justice John Marshall Harlan of the U.S. Supreme Court described him as "the most beautiful man I ever saw." In 1877 Brooks delivered the talks at the Yale Divinity School that were published as *Lectures on Preaching*. "The Seriousness of Life" is from *The Light of the World* (1890), the fifth volume of sermons published by him.

FRANCIS J. GRIMKÉ (1850–1937)   Grimké was the son of Nancy Weston, a slave, and Charles Grimké, the slaveholding owner of a plantation near Charleston, South Carolina. He graduated from Lincoln University in 1870 with financial help from his aunts Sarah Grimké and Angelina Grimké Weld, both of whom were active in the antislavery and woman's rights movements. After studying law at Lincoln and at Howard University, Grimké earned a divinity degree from Princeton Theological Seminary in 1878, the year he married Charlotte Forten, and was ordained at the Fifteenth Street Presbyterian Church in Washington, D.C. Grimké moved to the Laura Street Church in Jacksonville, Florida, in 1885, but returned to the Fifteenth Street Church in 1889 and served as its pastor until his retirement in 1928. He founded the Afro-Presbyterian Council in 1893 and, with Alexander Crummell, the American Negro Academy in 1897.

The sermon included here was delivered in 1902 while the Grand Army of the Republic, the organization of Union Civil War veterans, was meeting in Washington, D.C. An ally of W.E.B. Du Bois,

Grimké signed the appeal in 1909 calling for a national civil rights conference that resulted in the founding of the NAACP. In his sermons on racial discrimination and American religion, Grimké criticized Dwight L. Moody, Billy Sunday, the Princeton Theological Seminary, the American Bible Society, and his own denomination, the Presbyterian Church in the U.S.A.

JOHN GRESHAM MACHEN (1881–1937) Born in Baltimore, Maryland, Machen graduated from Johns Hopkins in 1901, received an M.A. from Princeton in 1904 and a B.D. from Princeton Theological Seminary in 1905, then studied at Marburg and Göttingen universities in Germany. He returned to Princeton Theological Seminary in 1906 as an instructor in New Testament studies and was ordained to the ministry of the Presbyterian Church in the U.S.A. in 1914. Machen delivered "History and Faith" during his inauguration as assistant professor of New Testament Literature and Exegesis at the seminary on May 3, 1915. During World War I, he also did YMCA work with French and American troops in Europe. A scholar loyal to the Westminster Confession of Faith, Machen avoided the term "fundamentalist" and the emotionalism of revivals, opposed church involvement in politics, and did not participate in the "anti-evolutionist" crusade. He became known as a spokesman for the fundamentalist coalition in his church when he published *Christianity and Liberalism* (1923), which argued that modernist theologians were undermining Christianity. Machen resigned under pressure when Princeton Theological Seminary was reorganized in 1929, then helped found Westminster Seminary, where he continued to teach New Testament studies. He was suspended from the ministry of the Presbyterian Church in the U.S.A. in 1935 for opposing its board of foreign missions, which he believed was abandoning the doctrine of salvation through the atoning work of Christ alone, and organizing an independent board. Machen withdrew from the church along with other conservatives and helped found the Presbyterian Church in America (later called the Orthodox Presbyterian church). Among Machen's other works are *The Origin of Paul's Religion* (1921) and *The Virgin Birth of Christ* (1930; 2d ed., 1932).

AIMEE SEMPLE MCPHERSON (1890–1944) Born Aimee Elizabeth Kennedy near Ingersoll, Ontario, Kennedy was converted to Pentecostalism in her youth and was influenced by her mother, Minnie Kennedy, who worked with the Salvation Army. She married evangelist Robert Semple in 1908 and served with him as a missionary in China until his death in 1910. After her return to the United States she married Harold S. McPherson in 1912, but soon began traveling alone as an itinerant preacher, holding revivals along the Atlantic coast.

"Sister Aimee," as she was called, preached "The Baptism of the Holy Spirit" in 1919, a year after settling in Los Angeles with her mother, who served as her business manager; she was divorced in 1921. McPherson became known for her healing services, founded the Echo Evangelistic Association, and built the Angelus Temple, broadcasting sermons she gave there over her own radio station. McPherson was involved in controversies and legal actions stemming from her business activities on behalf of the Temple, and after claiming in 1926 that she had been kidnapped, she was tried for fraud but was not convicted. In 1927 she organized the International Church of the Foursquare Gospel, which stressed the fourfold teaching of Christ as savior, healer, baptizer, and coming king. Her books include the sermon collections *This Is That* (1919) and *Divine Healing Sermons* (1920), as well as *In the Service of the King* (1927), and *Give Me My Own God* (1938). She died of an apparently accidental overdose of sleeping pills.

REUBEN ARCHER TORREY (1856–1928) Born in Hoboken, New Jersey, Torrey graduated from Yale University, earning a B.A. in 1875 and a B.D. in 1878, and after his ordination into the Congregational ministry studied at Leipzig and Erlangen in Germany from 1882 to 1883. He served for several years as superintendent of city missions in Minneapolis, Minnesota, then began working with revivalist Dwight L. Moody and from 1889 to 1908 was superintendent of Moody's Bible Institute in Chicago. Throughout this period Torrey continued to preach and made tours of the United States, Europe, Great Britain and Ireland, Australia, New Zealand, China, Japan, India, and Canada. In 1912 he went to Los Angeles to serve as dean of the Bible Institute there and in 1915 became pastor of the Church of the Open Door, where the sermon included here was delivered. Torrey published numerous books on the Bible, revivals, and Christian teachings.

HARRY EMERSON FOSDICK (1878–1969) The son of a teacher of Greek and Latin, Fosdick was born in Buffalo, New York. He earned a B.A. at Colgate University in 1900, was ordained into the Baptist ministry in 1903, and the following year received his B.D. from Union Theological Seminary and became pastor of First Baptist Church in Montclair, New Jersey. Fosdick continued his studies at Columbia University, earning an M.A. in 1908, then taught homiletics at Union; he left his New Jersey pastorate when he was made professor of practical theology in 1915, and continued teaching at Union until his retirement in 1946.

"Shall the Fundamentalists Win?" was delivered on May 21, 1922, at First Presbyterian Church in New York City, where, in an experiment in ecumenical ministry, Fosdick had been assistant pastor since 1919. The sermon was published as a pamphlet by the church, but began to raise controversy only after a condensed version, titled "The New Knowledge and the Christian Faith," was printed and widely circulated by a parishioner. Among those who attacked the sermon were well-known Presbyterians including William Jennings Bryan, J. Gresham Machen, and Clarence E. Macartney. After intense debate and a close vote, the Presbyterian General Assembly required that Fosdick either accept traditional Presbyterian doctrine or resign from First Church. Fosdick chose to resign, but in 1931, with financial assistance from John D. Rockefeller Jr., founded The Riverside Church in New York, a nonsectarian Protestant church devoted to promoting "interracial and international ideals." Fosdick preached more than 650 sermons at Riverside, including in late 1935 "The Church Must Go Beyond Modernism," which challenged Christians to rediscover the meaning of faith and to "stand out from," rather than accommodate themselves to, secular society. Many of his sermons were broadcast on radio. He retired from the church in 1946. A prolific writer, Fosdick published more than 40 books, including an autobiography, *The Living of These Days* (1956).

BILLY SUNDAY (1862–1935) The son of a Union Army soldier who died in 1862, William Ashley Sunday was born in Ames, Iowa, spent several years in an orphanage, and then was reared on a farm. After graduating from high school, he worked at several jobs before becoming a professional baseball player in 1883. Sunday played for National League teams in Chicago, Pittsburgh, and Philadelphia until 1890. He underwent a conversion experience in 1887 and after leaving baseball, worked for the YMCA in Chicago, then served as an assistant to evangelist J. Wilbur Chapman. By 1897 Sunday was holding his own revival meetings, and he was ordained to the Presbyterian ministry in 1903. Known for his dramatic style and use of modern slang in preaching, his championing of prohibition, opposition to political "liberalism," and his fundamentalist faith, Sunday is estimated to have held more than 300 revivals.

Sunday sometimes delivered the same sermon under different titles and with extemporaneous variations, and he freely admitted that he often had assistance in their preparation. "Food for a Hungry World" was published in *The American Pulpit* (1925), an anthology of preachers chosen by a poll of Protestant ministers throughout the United States.

ABBA HILLEL SILVER (1893–1963) Silver came to the United States from Lithuania with his family in 1902, grew up in New York, and was educated at the University of Cincinnati and Hebrew Union College. Ordained as a rabbi in 1915, he served Congregation L'Shem Shamayin in Wheeling, West Virginia, until accepting a call in 1917 from a Reform temple in Cleveland, Ohio, where he served until his death. "The Vision Splendid" was included in the 1927 edition of the *Best Sermons* series edited by Joseph F. Newton.

Silver was a leader of numerous organizations, including the Zionist Organization of America, the American Zionist Emergency Council, the United Jewish Appeal, United Palestine Appeal, and the Central Conference of American Rabbis, and was a prominent American advocate of the Zionist cause. Among his writings are *Democratic Impulse and Jewish History* (1928), *The World Crisis and Jewish Survival* (1941), *Where Judaism Differed* (1946), *Vision and Victory* (1949), and *A History of Messianic Speculation in Israel* (1959).

C. C. LOVELACE (fl. 1929) Zora Neale Hurston (1891–1960) heard this sermon by C. C. Lovelace on May 3, 1929, while living in the coastal town of Eau Gallie, where she was reviewing her anthropological fieldwork on the religion and culture of rural black Florida. She later wrote a friend that the sermon confirmed her belief that "the preacher is a true poet," but she is not known to have recorded any information about Lovelace. Hurston included the sermon in an article she wrote for the anthology *Negro* (1934), edited by Nancy Cunard, and used a version of it in her first novel, *Jonah's Gourd Vine* (1934); it was posthumously collected in Hurston's *The Sanctified Church* (1981).

PAUL TILLICH (1886–1965) The son of a pastor and superintendent of the Evangelical Lutheran Church in Prussia, Tillich was born in Starzeddel, Germany (now Starosiedle, Poland). He studied at several German universities, where he was influenced by the work of Jakob Böhme and Friedrich von Schelling, and received a Ph.D. in 1911 from Breslau; in 1912, he was ordained in the Evangelical Lutheran Church.

Tillich served as a chaplain in the German army during World War I, then taught theology and philosophy at German universities and in 1929 became professor of philosophy at the University of Frankfurt am Main. He was also active in the religious Socialist movement and published two books analyzing the religious and cultural dilemmas of the times (later translated as *Religious Realization* and *The Religious Situation*). Barred from teaching in 1933 because of his opposition to the Nazi regime, Tillich came to the United States at the invitation of Reinhold Niebuhr. He became a naturalized citizen in 1940 and was professor of philosophical theology at Union Theological Seminary, 1933–55, University Professor at Harvard, 1955–62, and Nuveen Professor of Theology at the University of Chicago Divinity School, 1962–65. "You Are Accepted" was first delivered at Union Theological Seminary and published in *The Shaking of the Foundations* (1948); Tillich's other sermon collections are *The New Being* (1955) and *The Eternal Now* (1963).

In his theological writings, Tillich developed a method of correlating traditional Christian teaching with questions that arise from the human cultural situation, and considered existentialist philosophy, depth psychology, and art as keys to the search for religious meaning. He also employed a new vocabulary to explore Christian belief, with "New Being" rather than "salvation" as the ultimate human goal; "ultimate concern" approximating "faith"; and "Being as Being" or "the Ground (and Power) of Being," God. Tillich's writings also include *The Interpretation of History* (1936), *The Protestant Era* (1948), *Systematic Theology* (3 volumes, 1951–63), *The Courage to Be* (1952), *Love, Power, and Justice* (1954), *Biblical Religion and the Search for Ultimate Reality* (1955), *The Dynamics of Faith* (1957), *Christianity and the Encounter of the World Religions* (1963), *My Search for Absolutes* (1967).

REINHOLD NIEBUHR (1892–1971) The son of an immigrant German Evangelical minister, Niebuhr was born in Wright City, Missouri, and in 1902 moved with his family to Lincoln, Illinois. He studied at Elmhurst College, Eden Theological Seminary, and Yale Divinity School, where he received a B.D. in 1914 and an M.A. in 1915. Ordained in the Evangelical Synod of North America, he was pastor of Bethel Evangelical Church in Detroit from 1915 until 1928, and wrote about his Detroit experience in *Leaves from the Notebook of a Tamed Cynic* (1929). In 1928, Niebuhr went to Union Theological Seminary in New York City as assistant professor of the philosophy of religion and in 1930 was made professor of applied Christianity; he taught at Union until his retirement in 1960.

Niebuhr delivered his sermons extemporaneously. Referring to himself as "one who loves preaching more than teaching," he gave sermons at Harvard, Princeton, and Yale, as well as at Union, and was frequently a guest preacher at Protestant churches. "The Providence of God," delivered at Union on February 3, 1952, was

posthumously transcribed from a tape recording and published in
Justice and Mercy (1974), a collection of sermons and prayers edited
by his widow, Ursula M. Niebuhr. Some of Niebuhr's other books
include *Does Civilization Need Religion?* (1927), *Moral Man and
Immoral Society* (1932), *An Interpretation of Christian Ethics* (1935),
Beyond Tragedy (1937), *Christianity and Power Politics* (1940), *The
Nature and Destiny of Man* (2 vols., 1941–43), *Faith and History*
(1949), *The Irony of American History* (1952), *The Self and the Dra-
mas of History* (1955), *The Structure of Nations and Empires* (1959),
and *Man's Nature and his Communities* (1965). Niebuhr helped to
plan his own memorial service, which was held at the First Congregational Church of Stockbridge, Massachusetts, where Jonathan Edwards had been a pastor. At Niebuhr's request, Rabbi Abraham
Heschel participated in the service and delivered a eulogy.

C. L. FRANKLIN (1915–1984) Clarence LaVaughn Franklin was
born near Indianola, Mississippi, and raised by his mother and step-
father, a sharecropper, in rural Doddsville, Boyle, and Cleveland,
Mississippi, where he attended local schools, helped with farming,
and was a soloist in his Baptist church choir. He preached his first
sermon as a teenager and, after doing migrant farm work for several
years, was ordained around 1922 as associate minister of St. Peter's
Rock in Cleveland. Franklin preached at a number of churches in the
area, then studied religion at Greenville Industrial College while
ministering to a church in Greenville, Mississippi, and later at
LeMoyne College while ministering to churches in Memphis. In
Memphis, Franklin also began preaching on the radio.

Franklin quit LeMoyne after his junior year to become pastor of
Friendship Baptist Church, a large congregation in Buffalo, New
York, where he continued studying literature as a special student at
the University of Buffalo. In 1946 he accepted a call to serve Detroit's New Bethel Baptist Church, a small congregation that met in
a renovated bowling alley. Franklin gained a wide audience when he
began preaching on WJLB radio in 1952, and soon recordings of his
sermons were being sold nationwide. He also made regular preaching tours with gospel groups, including the Ward Singers (sometimes his daughter, Aretha Franklin, was featured as a soloist on
these tours). Through his popularity as a preacher, Franklin raised
enough money to liquidate his church's debts and erect a new building, and he increased church membership to more than 2,000. "The
Eagle Stirreth Her Nest," one of his most famous sermons, was
recorded around 1953; a transcription was posthumously published in
Give Me This Mountain: Life History and Selected Sermons (1989),
edited by Jeff Todd Titon.

Franklin continued his preaching tours through the early 1960s. Active in the civil rights movement, he was a member of the Southern Christian Leadership Conference and of Jesse Jackson's PUSH, led a major march in Detroit in 1963, and preached at the Poor People's March on Washington in 1968. Franklin was shot in his home in Detroit by intruders in June 1979 and was in a coma for the remainder of his life.

FULTON J. SHEEN (1895–1979) Born on a farm in El Paso, Illinois, Sheen was ordained a Roman Catholic priest in 1919, received his Ph.D. from the University of Louvain, Belgium, in 1923, and taught theology and philosophy at Catholic University in Washington, D.C., from 1926 to 1950. A pioneer of the "electronic church," he was featured from 1930 to 1952 on the popular radio program *The Catholic Hour* and from 1951 to 1957 preached on his own weekly television show, *Life Is Worth Living*, which had an estimated 30 million viewers. "How to Have a Good Time" was delivered on the program and published in the last of a series of books of sermons titled *Life Is Worth Living* (1953–57). Sheen opposed communism as well as monopolistic capitalism, was a critic of Freudian psychoanalysis, and converted a number of famous people, including Clare Boothe Luce and Henry Ford II, to the Catholic faith. He was appointed national director of the Society for the Propagation of the Faith in 1950, became auxiliary bishop of New York in 1951, and served as bishop of Rochester from 1966 to 1969. Sheen was the author of more than 50 books.

MARTIN LUTHER KING JR. (1929–1968) Born in Atlanta, Georgia, the son and grandson of ministers, King was ordained to the Baptist ministry in 1948, the year he graduated from Morehouse College with a B.A. in sociology. He received a B.D. from Crozer Theological Seminary in 1951 and a Ph.D. in theology from Boston University in 1955, writing his dissertation on Paul Tillich. King married Coretta Scott in 1953 and the following year assumed the pulpit of the Dexter Avenue Baptist Church in Montgomery, Alabama. During the 1955–56 boycott of city buses in Montgomery, King became nationally known as a civil rights leader and began delivering sermons and speeches against segregation throughout the U.S. (over the next 12 years, he gave more than 2,000 such talks). Along with the Rev. Ralph Abernathy and other civil rights leaders, King formed the Southern Christian Leadership Conference in 1957 and became its president. In his book *Stride Toward Freedom: The Montgomery Story* (1958), he outlined a strategy, influenced by the work of Mahatma Gandhi, for nonviolent opposition to racial injustice. King moved in 1960 to Atlanta, where the SCLC had its headquarters, and became co-pastor of Ebenezer Church with his father. "Transformed Nonconformist" was first preached at Ebenezer Church around 1961 as King continued to lead protests against segregation, and it was revised by him for inclusion in a 1963 collection of sermons, *Strength to Love*. In 1963 King led major demonstrations in Birmingham, Alabama, during the spring, then delivered his "I Have a Dream" address at the March on Washington on August 28, 1963. He was awarded the Nobel Peace Prize in 1964, led a march from Selma to Montgomery, Alabama, in 1965 that helped win passage of the Voting Rights Act, and in 1966 began to speak out against American military intervention in Vietnam and housing discrimination in northern cities. King delivered his "I've Been to the Mountaintop" sermon on April 3, 1968, at the Masonic Temple in Memphis, Tennessee, where he had gone to support striking sanitation workers. The following day he was shot to death while standing on the balcony of his motel.

JOHN COURTNEY MURRAY (1904–1967) A native of New York City, Murray entered the Society of Jesus (the Jesuits) in 1920 after graduating from St. Francis Xavier High School. He received a B.A. from Weston College in 1925 and an M.A. from Boston College in 1927, then taught school in the Philippines for three years. Ordained to the Catholic priesthood in 1933, he earned an S.T.L. degree from Woodstock College, Maryland, in 1934, and a Th.D. from the Gregorian University in Rome in 1937, then taught theology at Woodstock for the next 30 years. In articles for lay and religious journals, including *Theological Studies*, which he edited, Murray explored the need for ecumenical and interfaith cooperation, and in the late 1940s he began exploring church-state relations and questions of constitutionally protected religious freedom. When conservative criticism from within the Church hierarchy resulted in his being silenced by his superiors on church-state relations in the 1950s, Murray wrote on a wide range of social issues. He often lectured at other schools, was visiting professor at Yale from 1951 to 1952, and participated in dialogues at the Center for the Study of Democratic Institutions, Santa Barbara, California. Despite conservative opposition, Murray was invited to act as an expert (*peritus*) at the Second Vatican Council, 1962–65, and he was primarily responsible for preparing the council's Declaration on Religious Freedom. In his last years, as director of the John La Farge Institute in Manhattan, he promoted dialogue between the races, religious denominations, and Marxists and Christians, and he also began exploring the concept of religious freedom with regard to the Church itself. Murray delivered "The Unbelief of the Christian" in the early spring of 1967 during Fordham University's Cardinal Bea Institute program on atheism. Among his books are *We Hold These Truths: Catholic Reflections on the American Proposition* (1960) and the posthumous collection *Bridging the Sacred and the Secular: Selected Writings of John Courtney Murray* (1994).

ABRAHAM JOSHUA HESCHEL (1907–1972)   Born in Warsaw, Poland, Heschel was descended from a long line of Hasidic rabbis. He studied in Vilna, where he was also part of a Yiddish poetry group (a volume of his poems was published in Warsaw in 1933), and then in Germany, earning a Ph.D. from the University of Berlin in 1935 and a rabbinical degree from the Hochschule in 1934. Heschel remained in Germany lecturing and teaching, and in 1937 he succeeded Martin Buber as director of the Mittelstelle für Jüdische Erwachsenen Bildung, serving until 1938, when he was deported along with thousands of other Polish Jews. He taught briefly in Warsaw and then in London before coming to the United States in 1940 to lecture on philosophy and rabbinical studies at Hebrew Union College, a Reform school in Cincinnati, Ohio. In 1945 Heschel became professor of Jewish ethics and mysticism at the Jewish Theological Seminary of America, a Conservative school in New York City, holding that position for the remainder of his life. A theologian and an activist in religious and civic affairs, Heschel was involved in Jewish-Christian dialogue and the civil rights movement, marched with Martin Luther King Jr. in Selma, Alabama, and opposed American involvement in Vietnam. He delivered "What We Might Do Together" during a panel discussion on ecumenical religious education; it was published in *Religious Education* (March–April 1967). Among Heschel's writings are *Man Is Not Alone: A Philosophy of Religion* (1951), *Man's Quest for God* (1954), *God in Search of Man: A Philosophy of Judaism* (1955), *The Prophets* (1962), *Who Is Man?* (1965), *Israel: An Echo of Eternity* (1969), and the posthumous collection *Moral Grandeur and Spiritual Audacity* (1996), edited by his daughter Susannah Heschel.

Note on the Texts

This volume collects the texts of 58 sermons preached between 1621 and 1968 and presents them in the approximate chronological order of their delivery. The preferred choice of texts for this volume is the first book or pamphlet publication during the lifetime of the preacher; when such a text is not known to be extant, the best available posthumously published text is used. Of the 58 sermons presented here, the texts of 43 are taken from versions published during the lifetime of the preacher; 23 of these are taken from pamphlet printings, 12 from books that collect the preacher's work, six from books that collect sermons or other writings by several authors, and two from periodical publications. The texts of the remaining 15 sermons are taken from posthumously published books, 11 from collections of the preacher's work, and four from books that collect the sermons of several preachers.

Texts are printed here as they appeared in the sources from which they were taken, with a few alterations. Errata that were listed in the original sources have now been incorporated into the texts. Marginalia in the source texts are either run into the body of the text, printed in "windows" (indented spaces within the texts), or, in the case of Biblical citations, listed in the "Notes" section of this volume. The text of "A Modell of Christian Charity" presented here is taken from volume 2 of *The Winthrop Papers* (Boston, 1931) and is based on a 17th-century manuscript transcription derived from John Winthrop's original holograph manuscript, which is not known to be extant. Bracketed editorial conjectural readings in the *Winthrop Papers* text in cases where the source manuscript was damaged or difficult to read are accepted in this volume without brackets. Where the *Winthrop Papers* text used the word *blank* in italics and within brackets to indicate a blank space in the manuscript, this volume uses a blank two-em space without brackets. Bracketed editorial insertions used in the *Winthrop Papers* to indicate cancellations in the manuscripts have been deleted in this volume. The text of "Abuses and Uses of the Bible" presented here is taken from *Lucretia Mott: Her Complete Speeches and Sermons* (New York, 1980) and is based on a stenographic transcript of the sermon. Missing words and punctuation that were editorially inserted within brackets in the source text are printed in this volume without brackets. The text of the sermon delivered by Joseph Smith on April 7, 1844, is taken from *Joseph Smith: Selected Sermons & Writings* (New York, 1989), but the bracketed editorial insertions used to clarify passages in the source text have been deleted here.

The following is a list of the sermons included in this volume, giving the source of each text and, for 17th- and 18th-century editions, the specific copy. (Titles that have been supplied in this volume are indicated by asterisks.)

Robert Cushman, *A Sermon Preached at Plimmoth in New-England December 9. 1621.* (London, 1622); Huntington Library copy.

John Winthrop, A Modell of Christian Charity. *The Winthrop Papers: Volume 2, 1623–1630* (Boston: Massachusetts Historical Society, 1931), 282–95.

John Cotton, Gal 2.20, Yet not I, but Christ liveth in me. *The Way of Life, Or, Gods Way and Course, in Bringing the Soule into, keeping it in, and carrying it on, in the wayes of life and peace. Laide downe in foure severall Treatises on foure Texts of Scripture* (London, 1641), 268–82; Huntington Library copy.

Thomas Hooker, Of Gods Image in the Affections. *The Paterne of Perfection. Exhibited in Gods Image on Adam: And Gods Covenant made with him* (London, 1640), 149–79; Princeton Theological Seminary Library copy.

Thomas Hooker, Book X, Doctrine 3: Application of special sins by the Ministry, is a means to bring men to sight of, and sorrow for them. *The Application of Redemption by the Effectual Work of the Word, and Spirt of Christ, for the bringing home of lost Sinners to God, the Ninth and Tenth Books* (London, 1657), 193–207; British Museum copy.

Thomas Shepard, Of Carnal Security in Virgin Churches. *The Parable of the Ten Virgins Opened* & *Applied: Being the Substance of divers Sermons on Math. 25.1–13. Wherein, the Difference between the Sincere Christian and the most Refined Hypocrite, the Nature and Characters of Saving and Common Grace, the Dangers and Diseases incident to most flourishing Churches or Christians, and other Spiritual Truths of greatest importance are clearly discovered and practically improved* (London, 1660), 1–11; Bodleian Library copy.

Thomas Shepard, Of Ineffectual Hearing the Word. *Subjection to Christ in all his ordinances, and appointments, the best means to preserve our liberty. Together with a treatise of ineffectual hearing the Word, How we may know whether we have heard the same effectually: And by what means it may be come effectual unto us* (London, 1652), 153–95; British Library copy.

Jonathan Mitchel, *Nehemiah on the Wall in Troublesom Times, Or, A Serious and Seasonable Improvement of that great Example of Magistratical Piety and Prudence, Self-denial and Tenderness, Fearlesness and Fidelity, unto Instruction and Encouragement of present and succeeding Rulers of Israel.* (Cambridge, Massachusetts, 1671); American Antiquarian Society copy.

Samuel Danforth, *A Brief Recognition of New-Englands Errand into the Wilderness.* (Cambridge, Massachusetts, 1671); American Antiquarian Society copy.

Increase Mather, *Sermon Occasioned by the Execution of a Man found Guilty of Murder.* (Boston, 1686); American Antiquarian Society copy.

Cotton Mather, An Hortatory and Necessary Address, To a Country now Extraordinarily Alarum'd by the Wrath of the Devil. *The Wonders of the Invisible World, Observations as well Historical as Theological, upon the Nature, the Number, and the Operations of the Devils* (Boston, 1693), 48–78; American Antiquarian Society copy.

Solomon Stoddard, *The Tryal of Assurance.* (Boston, 1698); American Antiquarian Society copy.

Cotton Mather, *A Man of Reason.* (Boston, 1718); Library of Congress copy.

Benjamin Colman, Job II: 9,10. "Then said his wife unto him, Dost thou still retain thy integrity?" *The Case of Satan's fiery Darts in Blasphemous Suggestions and Hellish Annoyances* (Boston, 1744), 5–46; American Antiquarian Society copy.

Charles Chauncy, *Man's Life considered under the Similitude of a Vapour, that appeareth for a little Time, and then vanisheth away.* (Boston, 1731); American Antiquarian Society copy.

Mather Byles, *A Discourse On the Present Vileness of the Body And Its Future Glorious Change by Christ.* (Boston, 1732); American Antiquarian Society copy.

Jonathan Edwards, *A Divine and Supernatural Light.* (Boston, 1734); American Antiquarian Society copy.

Jonathan Edwards, *Sinners in the Hands of an Angry God.* (Boston, 1741); American Antiquarian Society copy.

Samuel Johnson, A Sermon Concerning the Intellectual World. *Samuel Johnson, President of King's College: His Career and Writings, Volume 3: The Churchman,* edited by Herbert and Carol Schneider (New York: Columbia University Press, 1929), 501–14. © 1929 Columbia University Press. Reprinted with permission of the publisher.

Jonathan Mayhew, *A Discourse Concerning Unlimited Submission and Non-Resistance to the Higher Powers.* (Boston, 1750); American Antiquarian Society copy.

Samuel Davies, The Nature and Universality of spiritual Death. *Sermons on the most useful and important subjects, adapted to the family and closet in 3 volumes,* I (London, 1766), 123–57; Library Company of Philadelphia copy.

Samuel Finley, *The Madness of Mankind.* (Philadelphia, 1754); American Antiquarian Society copy.

Anon., *A Sermon In Praise of Swearing.* (Boston, 1767); American Antiquarian Society copy.

Samuel Cooke, *A Sermon preached at Cambridge, in the Audience of His Honor Thomas Hutchinson; Esq.* (Boston, 1770); American Antiquarian Society copy.

Nathanael Emmons, *The Dignity of Man.* (Providence, 1787); American Antiquarian Society copy.

Devereux Jarratt, *The Nature of Love to Christ, and the Danger of Not Loving*

Him, Opened and Explained. (Philadelphia, 1792); American Antiquarian Society copy.

Lemuel Haynes, *Universal Salvation: A Very Ancient Doctrine: With Some Account of the Life and Character of Its Author. A Sermon Delivered at Rutland, West-Parish in the Year 1805* (Rutland, Vermont, 1806).

Absalom Jones, *A Thanksgiving Sermon Preached January 1, 1808, In St. Thomas's, or the African Episcopal, Church, Philadelphia: On Account of The Abolition of the African Slave Trade On That Day, by the Congress of the United States.* (Philadelphia, 1808).

John Comly, Sermon Delivered at Darby, April 15, 1827.* *The Quaker, Being a series of sermons by members of the Society of Friends Taken in shorthand by Marcus T. C. Gould, stenographer,* volume 2 (Philadelphia, 1827), 37–42.

William Ellery Channing, *A Discourse Delivered at the Ordination of the Rev. Frederick A. Farley, as Pastor of the Westminster Congregational Society in Providence, Rhode Island, September 10, 1828* (Boston, 1828).

Ralph Waldo Emerson, Sermon Delivered September 9, 1832.* *The Complete Sermons of Ralph Waldo Emerson, Volume 4,* edited by Wesley T. Mott (Columbia: University of Missouri Press, 1992), 185–94; text copyright © 1992 by University of Missouri Press.

Joseph Smith, Sermon Delivered April 7, 1844.* *Joseph Smith: Selected Sermons & Writings,* edited by Robert L. Millet (New York: Paulist Press, 1989), 129–42. © 1989 by Dr. Robert L. Millet. Used by permission of Paulist Press.

Theodore Parker, *A Sermon of War.* (Boston, 1846).

Lucretia Mott, Abuses and Uses of the Bible. *Lucretia Mott: Her Complete Speeches and Sermons,* edited by Dana Greene (New York: Edwin Mellen Press, 1980), 123–34.

Brother Carper, The Shadow of a Great Rock in a Weary Land. *Tales and Takings, Sketches and Incidents, from the Itinerant and Editorial Budget of Rev. J.V. Watson, editor of the Northwestern Christian Advocate* (New York, 1856), 98–106.

Henry Ward Beecher, Peace, Be Still. *Fast-Day Sermons, or The Pulpit on the State of the Country* (New York: Rudd and Carleton, 1861), 265–92.

David Einhorn, *War with Amalek!* (Philadelphia: Stein & Jones, 1864).

Dwight Lyman Moody, On Being Born Again. *New Sermons, Addresses, and Prayers* (Chicago: Thompson & Wakefield, 1877), 121–26.

Octavius Brooks Frothingham, The Dogma of Hell. *The Rising and the Setting Faith and Other Discourses by O. B. Frothingham* (New York: G. P. Putnam's Sons, 1878), 139–61.

T. De Witt Talmage, The Ministry of Tears. *The Brooklyn Tabernacle: A Collection of 104 Sermons Preached by T. De Witt Talmage* (New York: George A. Sparks, 1886), 11–15

Sam P. Jones, Sermon Delivered August 2, 1885.* *Sermons Wise and Witty* (New York: Cheap Publishing House, 1885), 12–19.

Phillips Brooks, The Seriousness of Life. *The Light of the World And Other Sermons* (New York: E. P. Dutton & Co., 1890), 73–88.

Francis J. Grimké, *A Resemblance and a Contrast between the American Negro and the Children of Israel in Egypt, or the Duty of the Negro to Contend Earnestly for His Rights Guaranteed under the Constitution* (Washington D.C., 1902).

J. Gresham Machen, History and Faith. *The Princeton Theological Review* (July 1915).

Aimee Semple McPherson, The Baptism of the Holy Spirit. *This Is That: Personal Experiences, Sermons and Writings* (Los Angeles: Bridal Call Publishing House, 1919), 418–24. Reprinted by permission of Garland Publishing Inc.

Reuben Archer Torrey, The Most Wonderful Sentence Ever Written. *Sermon Classics by Great Preachers*, compiled by Peter F. Gunther (Chicago: Moody Press, 1982), 43–61. Copyright 1982, Moody Institute of Chicago. Used by permission.

Harry Emerson Fosdick, *Shall the Fundamentalists Win?* (New York, 1922).

Billy Sunday, Food for a Hungry World. *The American Pulpit*, edited by Charles Clayton Morrison (New York: Macmillan Co., 1925), 331–39.

Abba Hillel Silver, The Vision Splendid. *Best Sermons: Book Four*, edited by Joseph Fort Newton (New York: Harcourt, Brace and Company, 1927), 207–16. Copyright 1927 by Harcourt Brace & Company, reprinted by permission of the publisher.

C. C. Lovelace, The Sermon as heard by Zora Neale Hurston from C. C. Lovelace, at Eau Gallie in Florida. *Negro*, edited by Nancy Cunard (London, Wishart & Company, 1934), 50–54.

Paul Tillich, You Are Accepted. *The Shaking of the Foundations* (New York: Charles Scribner's Sons, 1948), 153–63. Reprinted with permission of Scribner, a Division of Simon & Schuster. Copyright 1948 by Charles Scribner's Sons; copyright renewed © 1976 by Hannah Tillich.

Reinhold Niebuhr, The Providence of God. *Justice and Mercy*, edited by Ursula M. Niebuhr (New York: Harper & Row, 1974), 14–22. © 1974 by Ursula M. Niebuhr, reprinted by permission of Yale University Press.

C. L. Franklin, The Eagle Stirreth Her Nest. *Give Me This Mountain: Life History and Selected Sermons*, edited by Jeff Todd Titon (Urbana: University of Illinois Press, 1989), 47–54. Copyright 1989 by the Board of Trustees of the University of Illinois. Used by permission of the University of Illinois Press.

Fulton J. Sheen, How to Have a Good Time. *Life Is Worth Living: Fifth Series* (New York: McGraw-Hill, 1957), 130–37.

Martin Luther King Jr., Transformed Nonconformist. *Strength to Love* (New York: Harper & Row, 1963), 8–15. Reprinted by arrangement with The Heirs to the Estate of Martin Luther King, Jr., c/o Writers House, Inc. as agent for the proprietor.

John Courtney Murray, The Unbelief of the Christian. *The Presence and Absence of God* (New York: Fordham University Press, 1969), 69–83.

Abraham Joshua Heschel, What We Might Do Together: A Vision for Ecumenical Religious Education. *Religious Education* (March–April 1967).

Martin Luther King Jr., Sermon Delivered April 3, 1968.* *A Testament of Hope: The Essential Writings and Speeches of Martin Luther King*, edited by James M. Washington (New York: HarperCollins, 1986), 279–86. Reprinted by arrangement with The Heirs to the Estate of Martin Luther King, Jr., c/o Writers House, Inc. as agent for the proprietor.

This volume presents the texts of the sermons chosen for inclusion here without change (other than the few alterations cited above), except for the correction of typographical errors and the modernization of the use of quotation marks in 17th- and 18th-century texts (only beginning and ending quotation marks are provided here, instead of placing a quotation mark at the beginning of every line of a quoted passage). It does not attempt to reproduce features of 17th- and 18th-century typography such as the long "s" and the use of "u" for "v" (for example, "haue" for "have"), "v" for "u" (for example, "vnder" for "under"), or "j" for "i" (for example, "ioy" for "joy"). Spelling, punctuation, and capitalization are often expressive features, and they are not altered, even when inconsistent or irregular. The following is a list of typographical errors corrected, cited by page and line number: 4.4, and and; 9.7, to to; 35.19, "Christ; 46.4, are are; 48.32, the the; 65.39, dspense; 66.31, Min-/nister; 71.7, like; 78.29, *Secuirity*; 83.6, Wold; 103.13, Yon; 106.14, Lods; 109.31, a-/against; 116.28, woice; 167.17, *Philistims*; 172.4, 1686/5; 174.40, Trre; 202.28, *one one*; 204.2, Commissiion; 206.3, some some; 213.34, Possessiing; 214.32, shoul; 214.32, *till eurn they*; 216.25, *Spitit*; 247.35, such *sudden*; 250.19, *down down*; 250.24, "Surely; 258.26, iu; 266.24, *know Heart*; 266.38, basphemous; 286.17, were; 291.1, *Futurites*; 296.9, Will Heaven; 303.6, a a; 345.8, as as; 418.2, goodness!; 429.6, than than; 436.3, "Lord; 442.35, youselves; 452.5, esape; 458.12, lorldy; 459.23, diests; 461.23, and and; 461.37, boasts; 464.27, shoots; 481.12, "They; 483.21, tendeness; 547.3, it it; 587.10, its in; 605.39, war?; 606.23, eight-and forty; 624.24, and and; 667.37, decendants; 671.20, posessed; 671.24, carricatures; 680.32, demured; 688.12, darkness shut; 688.17, benefactors; 695.8, troubles; 695.14, somwhere; 700.6, make; 703.8, panics truck; 704.8, nineteeth; 705.20, Tha; 710.29, joins church; 710.32, "A; 731.24, invason; 733.30–31, prosperty; 736.27, hatng; 738.36, What; 739.26, "What; 739.32, dreaemed; 739.35, wake."; 763.19, beleive; 787.25, He; 791.29, bug-house.; 818.34, life;; 828.21, 'em; 832.17, 'em; 883.4, casual; 885.5, becxause; 885.11, American. Errors corrected second printing: 252.26, DIETY (*LOA*); 865.2, "Surely (*LOA*).

Notes

In the notes below, the reference numbers denote page and line of this volume (the line count includes titles and headings). No note is made for material included in standard desk-reference books such as Webster's *Collegiate, Biographical,* and *Geographical* dictionaries, *Pelouet's Bible Dictionary,* or for references that can be located through the use of a Biblical concordance. Footnotes in the texts were in the originals. For further background information on the sermons and preachers, see the "Note on the Sermon Form" and "Biographical Notes" in this volume.

1.17 Captaine *Smith* . . . Description] John Smith (d. 1631), *A Description of New-England* (1616); Smith explored the New England coast in 1614.

2.28 Sathan] A marginal note in the original printing reads: *Rev.* 12.14.15.

2.30–3.4 by the dispersion . . . *Abraham.*] Marginal notes in the original read: *Act.* 11.20.21 / *Luk.* 2.32. / *Math.* 21.43. / *Amos* 7.14. / *2 King.* 17.23. / *Math.* 3.5.

4.39–5.7 If any . . . know it.] Marginal notes in the original read: 1 *Cor.* 2.4. / *Chap.* 8.2.

5.19–38 worldly policie . . . other way.] Marginal notes in the original read: *Luk.* 16.8 / *Pro.* 3.9 / *Psal.* 42.1.

6.8 *Apollo*] Apollos, a preacher of the Gospel (1 Corinthians 3:6).

6.9–13 yet the sower . . . constancie.] Marginal notes in the original read: *Math.* 13.25. / *Jude* 4. / 1 *Cor.* 11.13.

6.24–27 nippeth them . . . or not] Marginal notes in the original read: 2 *Cor.* 6.13. / 2 *Cor.* 13.5.

6.33–7.13 have their mouthes . . . sorrowfull] Marginal notes in the original read: *Jude* 16. / 2 *Cor.* 10.10. / *Ver.* 18. / *Job* 1.9. / *Rom.* 16.18. / *Math.* 19.21. / *Ver.* 22.

7.20–21 by Gods speciall . . . speake unto you] A marginal note in the original reads: *Act.* 10.33.

8.13–17 *Let a man . . . the Churches.*] Marginal notes in the original read: *Chap.* 4.1. / 1 *Cor.* 11.28. / 1 *Cor.* 14.34.

8.26–27 *That . . . Infidell.*] A marginal note in the original reads: 1 *Tim.* 5.8.

9.12–23 as *Absalon . . . their owne so inordinately.*] Marginal notes in the original read: 1 *Sam.* 15. 2.3.4. / 2. *King.* 12. 26. / *And* 21.2. / 1 *Sam.* 25.13 / 2 *Chron.* 16.10. / *And* 35.22 / *Isaiah* 39.2. / *Gal.* 2.11.12. / *Phil.* 2.21.

9.25–28 *looke . . . glory, &c.*] Marginal notes in the original read: *Philip.* 2.4. / 1 *Cor.* 13.6. / *Gal.* 5.26.

10.11–15 And where . . . men without] Marginal notes in the original read: *Psal.* 112.9. / *Eccle.* 11.1. / Luk. 6.35. / 2 *Cor.* 11.7.

10.22–26 sounding brasse . . . fire.] Marginal notes in the original read: 1 *Cor.* 13.1. / *Mat.* 25.41.42.

10.32–35 Many . . . and gaine] Marginal notes in the original read: *Act.* 24.26. / *Psal.* 4.7. *Amos* 8.5.

10.38–39 for gold . . . confidence] A marginal note in the original reads: *Job* 31.24.

11.4–6 like *Gehazi . . . Nehemiah*] Marginal notes in the original read: 2 *King.* 5.21. / *Neh.* 5.14.15.16

11.11–16 And *Paul . . . Corinth*] Marginal notes in the original read: *Act.* 20. / 2. *Thes.* 3.9. / *Ver.* 8. / 2 *Cor.* 11.12.

11.21 *Joseph . . . corne*] A marginal note in the original reads: *Gen.* 41.49.

11.25 like *Achan*] A marginal note in the original reads: *Josh.* 7.21.

11.33–38 *Scribes . . . weeds*] Marginal notes in the original read: *Luke* 11.46. / *Gen.* 2.15. / *Eccle.* 10.18. / *Pro.* 24.30.31.

12.7 of *Uriah*] A marginal note in the original reads: 2 *Sam.* 11.11.

12.14–18 new doctrines and devices . . . as *Jude*] Marginal notes in the original read: *Rom.* 16.16. / *Jud.* 12.

12.26 in *Nehemiah*] A marginal note in the original reads: *Neh.* 5.14.

12.33 A good man . . . alone] A marginal note in the original reads: *Job* 31.17.

13.5–8 as King *Saul . . . vaine glory*] Marginal notes in the original read: 1 *Sam.* 15.30. / *Gal.* 5.26.

13.20–22 *He needed . . . prayse*] Marginal notes in the original read: 2 *Cor.* 3.2. / 2 *Cor.* 10.12.

13.24–26 as *David . . . without it*] Marginal notes in the original read: 1 *Sam.* 18.[illegible] / 2 *King* 18.3.

13.32–33   wrong doers in *Corinth*]   A marginal note in the original reads:
1 *Cor.* 6.8.

14.2–4   *Samuel . . . King.*]   A marginal note in the original reads: 1 *Sam.*
8.19.

14.7–20   (like *Jezabell*) . . . conscience.]   Marginal notes in the original
read: 1 *King.* 19.2. / 2 *Sam.* 13.22. / *Gen.* 27.41. / 1 *Sam.* 15.34. / *Math.*
14.8.9.

14.29–32   this made *Absolon* . . . himselfe.]   Marginal notes in the original read: 2 *Sam.* 15.4. / *Hest.* 3.5. (Hester is a spelling for Esther).

15.3   as *Pharaohs* Butler]   A marginal note in the original reads: *Gen.*
40.23.

15.14–17   till she saw . . . before him;]   A marginal note in the original
reads: 1 *King.* 10. 7.8.

15.18–19   *Paul . . . God, &c.*]   A marginal note in the original reads:
Rom. 11.33.

15.34–37   with *David . . . him?*]   Marginal notes in the original read: 2
Sam. 7.18. / *Psal.* 8.3.

16.1   proannes]   Obselete form of proneness, i.e., inclination.

16.8–9   as *Peter . . . selfe*]   A marginal note in the original reads: *Matt.*
16.22.

16.9   *favour*]   Although this word is clearly spelled with an "f" rather
than a long "s" in the original printing, *favour* may be a printers error for
savour; cf. Matthew 16:23.

16.31–32   as *selfe-love . . . pleasure*]   Marginal notes in the original read:
Rom. 13.14. / 2 Tim. 3.4.

16.37–39   the greatest . . . clad?]   A marginal note in the original reads:
Psal. 73.5.7.

17.27–35   not buy . . . too much.]   Marginal notes in the original read:
1 *Cor.* 7.30.31. / *Job* 2.10. / *Phil.* 4.10. / *Eccl.* 7.6.

17.36–37   Againe . . . cheerfull]   A marginal note in the original reads:
Dan. 1.15.

18.3–5   I passe little . . . shame]   Marginal notes in the original read:
1 *Cor.* 4.3. / *Heb.* 12.2.

18.8–19   So for . . . ointment]   Marginal notes in the original read: 1
Sam. 25.34. / 1 *King.* 21.4. / *Eccle.* 10.1.

18.36–19.11   men may make . . . evils to come]   Marginal notes in the
original read: *Psal.* 78.5.7. / *Isa.* 57.1.

20.5–12   unjust Judge . . . enter in.]   Marginal notes in the original read: *Luk.* 18.5. / *Gen.*19.1.2. / *Judg.* 19.20.21. / *Job* 31.32.

20.19–28   *David* . . . goe naked.]   Marginal notes in the original read: 2 *Sam.* 9.1. / 1 *Cor.* 12.27.

21.22–23   as Christ . . . Samaritan woman]   A marginal note in the original reads: *John* 4.5.

22.9–25   the dayes . . . lovers of themselves]   Marginal notes in the original read: *Neh.* 5. / 1 *Sam.* 30.26.31. / 2 *Tim.* 3.2.

22.35–23.5   And even . . . to come.]   Marginal notes in the original read: *Ephes.* 5.1. / *Joh.* 1.16. / *Psal.* 113.6.7. / 2 *Tim.* 4.5. / *Joh.* 17.22. / *And* 15.13.

23.9–23   Even . . . crueltie.]   Marginal notes in the original read: *Judg.* 1.6.7. / *Mat.* 7.2. / *Mat.* 5.7. / *Prov.* 10. / 2 *Sam.* 21.7.8.9.

23.26–36   are given over . . . *another.*]   Marginal notes in the original read: *Rom.* 1.30. / *Psal.* 14.1. / *Math.* 25.33.

24.10–23   doe not the most . . . in againe.]   Marginal notes in the original read: *Luk.* 13.23.24. / *Mat.* 5.44.47. / *Psal.* 12.1. / *Rom.* 12.20.

24.36–38   Prodigall . . . my selfe;]   A marginal note in the original reads: *Luk.* 15.12.

25.5–11   Did not Sathan . . . one soule;]   Marginal notes in the original read: *Esay.* [Isaiah] 14.12.13. / *Jude* 6. / *Gen.* 13.5. / *Psal.* 133.1. / *Act.* 4.32.

25.23–27   for the hardnesse . . . lawes.]   Marginal notes in the original read: *Math.* 19.8. / 1 *Sam.* 8.5.

25.28–30   If others . . . in them]   A marginal note in the original reads: 2 *Thes.* 3.9.

25.33–38   Construe . . . both?]   Marginal notes in the original read: *Rom.* 1.29. / 1 *Sam.* 30. 10.24.

26.1–4   Apostle . . . deserts.]   Marginal notes in the original read: *Act.* 19.38. / 2 *Thes.* 3.10. / *Deut.* 19.15.

26.7–12   away with envie . . . before.]   Marginal notes in the original read: 1 *Sam.* 18.9. / *Rom.* 12.15. / *Pro.* 17.17.

26.13–27.9   Lay away . . . *Canaan.*]   Marginal notes in the original read: *Gen.* 42.1. / *Job* 2.8. / 1 *Sam.* 1.6.7. / *Gal.* 6.2. / 2 *Sam.* 15.33. / *Heb.* 10.29. / *Gen.* 13.7. / *Colos.* 4.5. / *Heb.* 13.2. / 2 *Pet.* 3.14. / *Heb.* 4.9.

37.21   or   ariseing]   The blank space appears in the document on which the *Winthrop Papers* text is based.

48.8   swoune]   Swoon.

54.28–29   *Bee not like . . . understanding*]   A marginal note in the original reads: Psal. 32.

56.30   Angell of light]   A marginal note in the original reads: 2 Cor. 11.14.

58.34–35   *The fruits . . . meeknesse*]   A marginal note in the original reads: Gal. 5.22.

59.29   the purples]   An eruption of purplish pustules.

60.16   *I shall perish . . . of Saul*]   A marginal note in the original reads: 1 Sā. 27.1.

60.40   *Samuel . . . mee.*]   A marginal note in the original reads: 1 Sam. 3.

61.4   *Blessed . . . counsell*]   A marginal note in the original reads: Chap. 25.

61.22–23   *The Word . . . good*]   A marginal note in the original reads: Esa. [Isaiah] 39.8.

70.33   *Cartwrights*]   Probably English Puritan theologian Thomas Cartwright (1536–1603), a professor of divinity at Cambridge whose writings include *A Body of Divinity* (posthumously published 1616), Biblical commentaries, and ecclesiastical works.

73.36   tickle]   Narrow, difficult, turbulent, often shallow.

83.8–9   *A little more . . . armed man*]   A marginal note in the original reads: Prov. 6.9, 10.

90.12–14   *Barnabas . . . unto him;*]   A marginal note in the original reads: Acts 11.23.

90.18   as *David*]   A marginal note in the original reads: 1 Sam. 17.16.

98.8–11   Happy . . . most.]   Marginal notes in the original read: *Rev.* 12.9. / *Rom.* 1.22.

114.31   *You . . . God*]   A marginal note in the original reads: 1 Thes. 2.3.

115.31–34   *My son, . . . soul.*]   Marginal notes in the original read: Prov. 3. / Vers.22.

121.37–38   *Alsted . . . Encyclop.*]   Johann Alsted (1588–1638), German writer in Latin of numerous works on theology and history.

125.3   *Mulier*]   Latin: Woman.

127.26   *Brightman*]   English Puritan clergyman Thomas Brightman (1557–1607); among his works are *Revelation Revealed, Predictions and Prophecies,* and studies of the Apocalypse, Book of Daniel, and the Canticles.

130.11   *Fiat . . . Cælum.*]   Latin saying: "Let justice be done though the heavens fall."

130.14–15 *Salus . . . Lex.*] Cicero, *De Legibus*, III.3: "The people's good is the highest law."

141.19–20 *Si tam . . . essemus*] If we should be so ready.

143.1 *Dulce . . . mori*] Horace, *Odes* 3.2.13: "It is sweet and right to die for one's country."

143.17 LXX.] The Septuagint (Latin: Seventy), a pre-Christian translation into Greek of the Hebrew Scriptures; according to tradition, it was translated by 72 persons in 72 days.

152.24 Θεάσασθω] To see.

178.3 (*c*)] No footnote is keyed to this reference in the original pamphlet.

199.3 *Ty-Dogs*] Tie-dogs, fierce dogs kept chained up.

210.7 *Hic Labor, Hoc Opus est!*] This is the labor, this is the work (to be done); in Virgil, *Aeneid*, 6:129, this reads *hoc opus, hic labor est.*

212.13–14 *Diaboli . . . Remedium*] The devil's whip; remedy for misery.

227.8–10 *Nam et . . . Turpia*] "For common intelligence makes this known to us, that which starts in our souls, such that honesty is placed in virtue, and shamefulness in vice."

240.5 *Festus* the Judge] Porcius Festus (d. c. A.D. 62), Roman administrator before whom St. Paul made his "appeal unto Caesar."

240.11 *Aristides*] Aristides (c. 530–c. 468 B.C.), called the Just, Athenian statesman who commanded Athenian forces at Plataea (479) and Byzantium (478).

240.13 *Fabritius*] Gaius Fabricius Luscinus (d. after 275 B.C.), Roman general and statesman who established a reputation for honesty when he rejected all attempts to bribe him.

240.14 *Regulus*] Marcus Atilius Regulus (d. c. 250 B.C.), Roman hero who defeated Carthaginian army (256), and, on his promise to return to Carthage, went back under hostile circumstances and was tortured to death.

256.15 Dr. *Tillotson*] John Tillotson (1630–94), an English prelate, preached against atheism, Puritanism, and Roman Catholicism.

267.3 *Maran-atha*] An Aramaic expression that may have been used in early Christian liturgies; it is variously translated "The Lord is coming!" or "The Lord is come!"

267.36–39 *Caveamus . . . Hoste*] "Let us beware that we not offer our ears to Satan when he solicits us against God with these little blasts; we are warned to refute blasphemies of this kind vigorously, as if they were the vomit of Satan. We ought to proffer vehemence; for a furious enemy is not to be played with."

271.15   *Janeway*]   James Janeway (1636–74), English nonconformist divine known for his preaching and for visiting the sick during the plague; his writings include Biblical commentaries and *The Saint's Encouragement to Diligence* (posthumously published 1675).

273.32–41   Sunt . . . molestissimam]   "There are temptations of Satan, with which he obtrudes thoughts even into the minds of the most pious against the majesty of God, the sufficiency of Christ etc.—that there is no God, nor any particle of providence—by which even the most egregiously pious are bothered, to the extent that they are troubled and assailed in the performance of the divine office. There are indeed in these suggestions horrendous crimes, but not in the tempted, who of course abhor these things, but in the tempter alone. The lot of the best, even of Christ himself, is a common one: to sustain insults of this kind from Satan, Matthew 4. That which he heroically shuns, and which he strongly resists, is not his sin; rather, indeed, it is the hardest cross, the most painful for him to bear."

308.5–7   *Hic . . . vitam.*]   "He rises, not from a conceived fetus, not from a seed. He forms out of a fertile death, and seeks a second life from as many funerals."

310.1   ταπεινώσεως]   Literally "lessening, humiliation."

382.37   Mr. *Leslie*]   Probably Charles Leslie, 1650–1722, an Anglican clergyman who refused to swear allegiance to William and Mary after the Glorious Revolution.

383.7–10   "To virtue . . . my sleep.]   Alexander Pope, *Imitations of Horace* (1733), Satire II.i.121–24.

397.38   marginal note, page 387]   The page numbers have been changed to conform to this volume.

398.11–12   *quantum meruit*]   As much as he deserved.

454.20   evanid]   Evanescent.

475.3   *Inter arma silent leges.*—]   "During war, the laws are silent." Cicero, *Pro Milone* (52 B.C.)

495.1–5   "Earth's disembowell'd, . . . spirit, pow'r!"]   From *Night Thoughts on Life, Death, and Immortality* (1745) by Edward Young (1683–1765), "Night," VI, part 1, 797–801.

508.21–25   the Poet's advice . . . again."]   Alexander Pope, "An Essay on Criticism" (1711), lines 215–18.

509.32   Dr. Doddridge]   Joseph Doddridge (1769–1826), a physician and Episcopalian minister who preached in the Ohio Territory.

513.6 *Maran-atha.*] See note 267.3.

532.11–15 "She pluck'd . . . MILTON] *Paradise Lost,* 9.781–84.

572.19 fourth Lateran Council] Council convened by Pope Innocent III in 1215 at the Lateran Palace, Rome, to define Eucharistic doctrine.

576.22 Sandemanians] Religious sect founded by Robert Sandeman (1718–71), Scottish theologian.

605.38 Dartmoor Prison] English prison where American prisoners were held during the War of 1812.

619.21–23 "Pious men . . . the dead,"] Sir Walter Scott's *Marmion, A Tale of Flodden Field,* Canto 6, Stanza 30.

620.14–16 "The earth . . . burial blent."] From Byron's *Childe Harold's Pilgrimage,* Canto 3, Stanza 28.

621.14–18 "The morn . . . glowing into day."] From Byron's *Childe Harold,* Canto 3, Stanza 98.

624.6 Penobscot or the Saco] Rivers in Maine. The boundary line dividing American territory in Maine and British territory in Canada was contested until the Webster-Ashburton Treaty settled the dispute in 1842.

644.36–39 'I shall bathe . . . peaceful breast.'] Fourth verse of the hymn, "The Saints' Delight," words by Isaac Watts.

670.40 Jehuda Hallevi] Usually transliterated Judah ha-Levi (or Yehuda ben Shemuel ha-Levi; c. 1075–1141), Spanish-born Hebrew poet, philosopher, and physician; he lived in Granada, then practiced medicine in Toledo until anti-Semitism forced him to return to Muslim Spain.

696.7 King Alphonso] Alfonso X of Castile and Leon (1221–84), known as Alfonso the Wise.

733.15–20 "Though . . . God."] James Russell Lowell, "On the Capture of Certain Fugitive Slaves near Washington" (1845), stanza 5.

738.6–11 "In a small . . . less."] James Russell Lowell, "William Lloyd Garrison," lines 1–6.

739.26–35 'What on . . . wake.'] Robert Browning, *Asolando: Epilogue,* lines 8–15.

741.23–26 "Be strong! . . . song."] From stanza 3 of "Be Strong! We Are Not Here To Play" (1901), a hymn by Maltbie Davenport Babcock.

812.8 *Man Against Himself*] Book (1938) by American psychologist Karl A. Menninger (1893–1990).

813.20 "the sickness . . . death."] A reference to Danish philosopher and theologian Sören Kierkegaard's study of despair in *The Sickness Unto Death* (1849).

826.2   *The Eagle . . . Nest*]   From Deuteronomy 32:11–12.

836.19   Horace . . . acti."]   "A praiser of times past," from *Ars Poetica*, line 173.

837.27   *Tempus est dolor*]   "Time is sorrow"; "time is anguish."

843.14–15   Longfellow . . . hammer,"]   In *Hyperion* (1839), book IV, chapter 7.

844.22–24   Jefferson . . . man."]   In a letter to Benjamin Rush, September 23, 1800.

846.7–14   They are . . . or three.]   From "Stanzas on Freedom," lines 25–32.

847.15   Professor Bixler]   Julius Seelye Bixler, professor at the Harvard Divinity School (1933–42) and president of Colby College (1942–60).

848.8   six-year-old daughter]   Yolande King, born on November 6, 1955.

850.9   theandric]   Relating to the union of the divine and the human.

852.11   *Lumen gentium*]   "Light of the peoples," the Dogmatic Constitution on the Church decreed by Vatican II on November 21, 1964. Its seventh chapter is titled "The Eschatological Nature of the Pilgrim Church and Its Union with the Church in Heaven."

854.21–22   *Ecclesiam suam*]   "His Church," issued on August 6, 1964.

856.7–8   *Pastoral . . . World*]   *Gaudiam et Spes* ("Joy and Hope"), approved by Vatican II on December 6, 1965.

856.16–17   *Dogmatic . . . Church*]   See note 852.11.

858.28   *Decree on Ecumenism*]   *Unitatis Redintegratio* ("The restoration of unity"), promulgated on November 21, 1964.

859.39   *Constitution . . . Liturgy*]   *Sacrosantum Concilium* ("This holy council"), issued on December 4, 1963.

860.23   *fideliter . . . umbris*]   Faithfully but under a shadow.

864.36   Sifra]   A midrash on Leviticus.

866.6–7   march . . . Montgomery]   Civil rights march through Alabama, March 21–25, 1965, led by Martin Luther King Jr.

879.5   Bull Connor]   Eugene "Bull" Connor was the public safety commissioner of Birmingham, Alabama, in 1963.

THE LIBRARY OF AMERICA SERIES

Library of Congress Cataloging-in-Publication Data

American sermons : the pilgrims to Martin Luther King, Jr.
     p. cm. — (The library of America ; 108)
  ISBN 1–883011–65–5 (alk. paper)
  1. Sermons, American.   I. Series.
BV4241.A514 1999
252—dc21   98–34295
                                                   CIP

Index of Preachers

*This book is set in 10 point Linotron Galliard,
a face designed for photocomposition by Matthew Carter
and based on the sixteenth-century face Granjon. The paper is
acid-free Ecusta Nyalite and meets the requirements for permanence
of the American National Standards Institute. The binding
material is Brillianta, a woven rayon cloth made by
Van Heek-Scholco Textielfabrieken, Holland.
The composition is by The Clarinda
Company. Printing and binding by
R.R.Donnelley & Sons Company.
Designed by Bruce Campbell.*